FAMOUS
FIRST FACTS™
ABOUT
SPORTS

Other H. W. Wilson titles by Irene M. Franck and David M. Brownstone

Facts About American Immigration (forthcoming)
The Wilson Chronology of Asia and the Pacific
The Wilson Chronology of Women's Achievements

Other titles in the Wilson Facts Series

Famous First Facts, Fifth Edition
Famous First Facts, International Edition
Famous First Facts About American Politics
Famous First Facts About the Environment (forthcoming)

Facts About the American Wars
Facts About the British Prime Ministers
Facts About Canada, Its Provinces and Territories
Facts About China (forthcoming)
Facts About the Cities, Second Edition
Facts About the Congress
Facts About the Presidents, Seventh Edition (forthcoming)
Facts About Retiring in the United States (forthcoming)
Facts About the Supreme Court of the United States
Facts About the Twentieth Century (forthcoming)
Facts About the World's Languages
Facts About the World's Nations

IRENE M. FRANCK & DAVID M. BROWNSTONE

FAMOUS FIRST FACTS™ ABOUT SPORTS

The H. W. Wilson Company
New York • Dublin
2001

Library of Congress Cataloging-in-Publication Data

Brownstone, David M.
    Famous first facts about sports / by David M. Brownstone and Irene M. Franck.
       p. cm.
    Includes bibliographical references and indexes.
    ISBN 0-8242-0973-7 (alk.paper)
     1. Sports—History 2. Sports records. I. Franck, Irene M. II. Title.
    GV571 .B76 2000
    796—dc21   00-43883

Printed in the United States of America

The H. W. Wilson Company
950 University Avenue
Bronx, NY 10452

Visit H.W. Wilson's Web site: www.hwwilson.com

Contents

Preface

Famous First Facts About Sports is a basic reference work for all those interested in sports firsts, sports facts, sports history, notable sports events, famous players and teams, awards and special occasions, major sports arenas, sports records, and remarkable bits of sports trivia. Fans will find this book a browser's delight, and libraries will find it an indispensable addition to their reference shelves. Beyond that, the book should be useful to broadcasters and journalists across the country and around the world. It is the kind of book that sportscasters turn to reflexively between innings or during time-outs, and that newspaper reporters and editors rely on for sports-page items such as "Did you know that the first three-point shot was made . . . ?"; "The first touchdown in the Houston Astrodome was . . ."; "The first figure skater to successfully complete a quadruple jump was . . ."; "The first no-hit game in the American League was pitched by . . ."; "The first modern Olympic Games were held in . . ."; "The first automobile race sponsored by the National Association for Stock Car Auto Racing (NASCAR) was . . ."; or "The first fighter to hold the world heavyweight championship three times was . . . ."

Famous First Facts About Sports contains more than 5,400 entries, covering more than 110 sports. All of the major and most of the minor sports played in the United States are included, as noted in the list on pages xi–xii. The most popular sports—baseball, football, basketball, tennis, golf, and hockey—receive the greatest attention, but the book covers the whole range of sports, from airplane racing to wrestling. Special emphasis is placed on American activities and interests, from the colonial period up until today. Sports primarily of interest outside the United States, such as cricket, are treated in less detail. However, some sports—such as tennis, golf, figure skating, track and field, and Olympic sports in general—are truly international in their appeal, and are covered accordingly.

Similarly, although the book includes interesting "firsts" from early and medieval times, most of the information concerns the modern world, during the two centuries when interest in sports has mushroomed. The book covers all sports through 1999, with highlights added for the year 2000, including notable events from the 2000 Olympic Games. Since the entries are organized chronologically under each sport, readers can easily get a sense of the sweep of a sport's development over the years. Readers can also see how developments in sports reflect, and sometimes even anticipate, changes in society at large.

To learn more about how the book is organized and how to find information most easily, see "How to Use This Book," on page ix.

Our thanks, as always, to the librarians of the northeastern library network, who provided us with many wide-ranging books through the Interlibrary Loan service, and especially to the staff of the Chappaqua Library, in particular director Mark Hasskarl; the expert reference staff, including Martha Alcott, Maryann Eaton, Carolyn Jones, Jane Peyraud, Paula Peyraud, Carolyn Reznick, and Michele Snyder; and the circulation staff, headed by Marilyn Coleman.

Our thanks also to vice president and director of general publications Michael Schulze and former senior editor Hilary Claggett of H. W. Wilson for their enthusiastic support for the book; to copy editor Michael Burke and indexer Mary F. Tomaselli for their expert attention to detail; and to Norris Smith, Gray Young, and the rest of the H. W. Wilson editorial and production staff for so capably seeing the work through from manuscript to published book.

Irene M. Franck
David M. Brownstone
March 2001

How to Use This Book

The main text of *Famous First Facts About Sports* is organized alphabetically by sport. (A list of the headings used is given at the end of this section.) Under the heading for each sport, entries are listed chronologically, starting with the earliest event. Readers interested in general information about a particular sport can simply browse through the entries under that heading.

For convenient browsing in sports with many entries, we have included subheads indicating time periods. The entries under **Golf**, for example, are grouped under these headings:

> **Golf (before 1700)**
> **Golf (1700-1799)**
> **Golf (1800-1849)**
> **Golf (1850-1899)**
> **Golf (1900-1909)**
> **Golf (1910-1919)**
> etc.

Each entry in the book has been given a unique identifying number. The entries are numbered sequentially from the beginning of the book, starting with 1001 and ending with 6415. In each entry, the key information about the sports "first" is given in bold type. For example, the following entry appears in the book in numerical order, listed under **Figure Skating (1900-1909)**:

> **2975. Figure skater to win the men's singles title in the Olympic Games** was world champion Ulrich Salchow of Sweden, on October 29, 1908, in London, England.

The entry number and key information are used in the book's five indexes, which are designed to help readers find material by subject, year, month and day, personal name, and place. For example, readers searching in these indexes will find references to the above entry (2975) in the following places:

> In the Subject Index: under **figure skating, men's**
>
> In the Index by Year: under **1908**
>
> In the Index by Month and Day: under **October 29**, subhead **1908**
>
> In the Personal Name Index: under **Salchow, Ulrich**
>
> In the Geographical Index: under **GREAT BRITAIN**, subhead **England**, subhead *London*; and under **SWEDEN**

Readers searching for information about a particular team, such as the Boston Celtics or the Dallas Cowboys, should turn first to the Subject Index. That is also the best place to go when seeking firsts about such general topics as African-Americans, women, bowl games, baseball stadiums and parks, and most valuable players, as well as specific events, arenas, institutions, or artifacts, such as the Ryder Cup, Harvard University, the Australian Open, Soldier Field, the Kentucky Derby, the Heisman Trophy, or the Zamboni ice-resurfacing machine. (Note that the names of people and places are not included in the Subject Index, but instead are listed separately in the Personal Name Index and the Geographical Index, as noted below.)

The Subject Index is also useful for finding general information in a sport with many entries. To find information about athletes named Most Valuable Player in the National Basketball Association, for example, you would look in the Subject Index under **National Basketball Association (NBA)** and then under the subhead "Most Valuable Player." Alternatively, you could look under **Most Valuable Player** and then under the subhead "basketball."

The Index by Year organizes entry references chronologically by year. To find out what notable sports "firsts" took place in 1958, for example, you simply turn to that year in the Index by Year. There you would find index references listed alphabetically, starting with "African-American athlete to be named *Sports Illustrated* Sportsman of the Year, *1152*" and ending with "World Biathlon Championships, *2430*."

The Index by Month and Day organizes entry references chronologically by month, and then by date. Entries that include only the month, but not a specific date, are listed first under each month. For example, under the month **January**, the first index entry is for the year 1897, "Intercollegiate golf association in the United States, *3620*." Under **January 1**, the first index entry is for 1902, "Rose Bowl football game, *3133*."

The Personal Name Index is designed to help readers find specific people mentioned in entries in the main text of the book. The index includes not only the athletes who achieved the "firsts" but also other individuals mentioned, so **Kelly, Grace** is in the Personal Name index because she is mentioned in an entry on her father, Olympic rower Jack Kelly.

Finally, the Geographical Index allows you to find what sports firsts are related to a particular location. The index includes not only the site of the event, but also the nationality of the athlete, as for the sample entry above (2975) about Ulrich Salchow.

Note that throughout the book, entries are alphabetized word by word, rather than letter by letter. That means that **Weight Throw**, which is two words, comes before **Weightlifting**. For the same reason, in the Personal Name Index, the first entry under **D** is **da Silva, Adhemar Ferreira**, followed by **Dafoe, Daggett, Dahlie**, and so on.

Below is a list of the headings used in the main text of the book. Note that some headings cover several related sports. If you do not find the specific sport you are looking for in this list, turn to the Subject Index. Note also that **Olym-**

pic Games and Track and Field (Athletics) are headings for general entries only, such as the first "Woman to win a gold medal in the Olympic Games" or "Track world record for which there was an official wind-speed reading." For more specific firsts, look under the individual event, such as Skiing or Marathon.

Airplane Racing
Archery
Automobile Racing
Awards, General
Badminton
Ballooning
Baseball
Basketball
Biathlon
Billiards
Bobsledding
Bowling and Bowls
Boxing
Canoe and Kayak Racing
Chole
Cricket
Croquet
Curling
Cycling
Darts
Decathlon
Disabilities, Athletes with
Discus Throw
Diving
Dog Racing
Duathlon
Equestrian Competitions
Extreme Sports
Fencing
Figure Skating
Football, American
Football, Australian Rules
Football, Canadian
Football, Gaelic
Frisbee
Gliding
Golf
Gymnastics

Hammer Throw
Handball
Heptathlon
High Jump
Hockey, Field
Hockey, Ice
Hockey, Roller (Rink)
Horse Racing
Horseshoe Competitions
Hurdles
Hurling
Ice Boating
Ice Skate Sailing
International Games
Jai Alai
Javelin Throw
Kolven
Lacrosse
Long Jump
Luge (Toboggan)
Marathon
Martial Arts
Motorboat (Powerboat) Racing
Motorcycle Racing
Netball
Olympic Games
Orienteering
Pentathlon
Pole Vault
Polo
Rackets
Racquetball
Rodeo
Roller Skating
Rowing
Rugby
Running
Sailboarding (Windsurfing)

Famous First Facts
About Sports

A

AIRPLANE RACING

1001. International airplane races were at the eight-day International Air Meet, held on August 22–29, 1909, near Rheims, France. Flying a Voisin biplane, Henry Farnam won the Grand Prix de Champagne for the longest flight; he covered almost 112 miles, remaining in the air for nearly 3 hours 5 minutes, setting both distance and air-time records. Hubert Letham of France won the altitude contest, flying up to 503 feet (153 meters). The other important race was on August 28 for the Bennett Cup, offered by James Gordon Bennett, publisher of New York City's *Herald*, who also offered a Bennett Cup for an annual hot-air balloon race. The inaugural winner was Glenn Curtis, the lone competitor from the United States, in his *Golden Flyer*, edging out France's Louis Bleriot with an average speed of 47.7 miles per hour.

1002. International air race in the United States was the second Bennett Cup race, held in 1910 at Belmont Park, Long Island, New York. Claude Grahame-White of Great Britain led the international field with an average speed of 66.2 miles per hour in his Bleriot plane. The Bennett Cup races would be held four more times.

1003. Woman pilot to fly across the English Channel was Harriet Quimby of the United States, who did so in 1912. Also a magazine journalist, she would be killed later that year in a flying exhibition in Boston, Massachusetts.

1004. Schneider Cup international seaplane (hydro-aeroplane) race was held in Monaco on April 6, 1913, sponsored by the Aero Club de France. Maurice Prevost of France won what became an annual race in his Deperdussin plane.

1005. Pulitzer Trophy airplane race was held on November 27, 1920, at Mitchel Field, Long Island, New York. Corliss Moseley, an Army captain from the United States, led a field of 37 starters and 25 finishers to win with an average speed of 156.5 miles per hour in his Verville-Packard airplane. The race would be held through 1925.

1006. National Air Races were held in September 1926 at Model Farms Field, in Philadelphia, Pennsylvania. Among 19 events, the featured race was for the Kansas City Rotary Club Trophy, won by Navy lieutenant George Cuddihy, flying a Boeing fighter, who set a speed record for his class at 180.5 miles per hour (290.4 kilometers per hour).

1007. Women's Air Derby was held on August 18, 1929. Twenty women pilots competed in the 2350-mile race from Santa Monica, California, to Cleveland, Ohio, which some derisively called the Powder Puff Derby. The winner of the heavy airplane division was Louise Thaden, who would be the first woman to win the Bendix Trophy airplane race, in 1936. Phoebe Fairgrave Omlie won the race for lighter planes.

1008. Thompson Trophy airplane race was held as part of the National Air Races in Chicago, Illinois, in 1930. The inaugural winner was Charles Holman, flying a Laird Solution plane at an average speed of 201.91 miles per hour.

1009. Bendix Trophy airplane race also called the Transcontinental Speed Classic, was held in 1931. Racing against the clock from Los Angeles, California, to Cleveland, Ohio, the first winner was Jimmy Doolittle, flying a Laird Super-Solution plane at an average speed of 223.038 miles per hour.

1010. Pilot to win both the Thompson Trophy and Bendix Trophy airplane races was Roscoe Turner. After winning the Bendix Trophy in a New York City–to–Los Angeles race in 1933, he won his first of three Thompson Trophy races in 1934, the others coming in 1938 and 1939, all in Cleveland, Ohio.

1011. Woman to fly in the Bendix Trophy airplane race was Jacqueline Cochran in 1935, when the 2043-mile race was from Burbank, California, to Cleveland, Ohio. She would win the event in 1938. During World War II, she headed the Women's Airforce Service Pilots (WASPs), and in 1953 became the first woman to break the sound barrier.

AIRPLANE RACING—*continued*

1012. Woman to win the Bendix Trophy airplane race was Louise Thaden, who won the 2450-mile New York City–Los Angeles race in 1936, flying a Beechcraft plane at an average speed of 165.346 miles per hour.

1013. Pilot to win the Thompson Trophy airplane race twice, and then three times was Roscoe Turner. After winning it first in 1934, he won it again in 1938 and 1939, both times in Cleveland, Ohio, flying a Laird-Turner plane at an average speed of 283.49 miles per hour in 1938 and 282.536 in 1939.

1014. Pilot to win the Bendix Trophy–Jet Division airplane race was Colonel Leon Grey, who won the 2048-mile race from Van Nuys, California, to Cleveland, Ohio, in 1946, flying a Lockheed jet at an average speed of 494.779 miles per hour.

1015. Pilot to win the Thompson Trophy–Jet Division airplane race was Lieutenant Gus Lundquist in Cleveland, Ohio, in 1946, flying a Lockheed jet at an average speed of 515.853 miles per hour.

1016. Pilot to win the Bendix Trophy race three times in a row was Paul Mantz. After earlier wins in 1947 and 1948, he won for the third time on September 4, 1948, after a 2080-mile race from Long Beach, California, to Cleveland, Ohio, flying a North American plane at an average speed of 447.980 miles per hour.

ARCHERY

1017. Law relating to archery on record dates from the 12th century in England, where archery was deemed so important that archers who accidentally killed someone while practicing were not subject to charges of murder or manslaughter. Literary references to archery are much older, dating back to Egypt, Greece, and Rome, while bows and arrows date back to at least 20,000 BC.

1018. Oyakazu archery contest was held in Kyoto, Japan, in 1606. It would be held until 1842.

1019. Scorton Arrow Contest was held in 1673 in Yorkshire, England. It would become the oldest continuing archery tournament on record.

1020. Organization for archery as a sport was the Toxophilite Society of London, founded in England in 1781, long after archery had ceased to have military uses.

1021. Archery organization to admit women as members was the Royal British Bowmen, founded in England in 1787, as the sport became widely popular in the upper classes.

1022. Archery club in the United States was the United Bowmen of Philadelphia, founded in 1828 in Pennsylvania.

1023. National organization for archery in the United States was the National Archery Association (NAA), founded in Crawfordsville, Indiana, on January 23, 1879, believed to be the oldest continuing amateur sports organization in the country.

1024. National archery tournament in the United States was on August 12–14, 1879, in Chicago, Illinois, sponsored by the National Archery Association, founded earlier that year. Of the 69 men and 20 women participating, Will Thompson emerged as victor in the men's division, the first of his six consecutive wins, and Mrs. S. Brown in the women's division.

1025. Archery events held in the Olympic Games all for men only, were in 1900 in Paris, France. Of the six events, all on May 28 and all now discontinued, four were won by archers from France: Henri Hérouin won the *au cordon doré*–50 meters event, Eugène Mougin the *au chapelet*–50 meters, Emmanual Foulon the *sur la perche à la herse*, and Emile Grumiaux the *sur la perche à la pyramide*. Hubert van Innis of Belgium won the other two: the *au chapelet*–33 meters and the *au cordon doré*–33 meters.

1026. Archer to win four Olympic gold medals in a single Olympic Games, and six overall was Hubert van Innis of Belgium. After winning the *au chapelet* and *au cordon doré* events, both at 33 meters, in 1900, he won four more in 1920 in Antwerp, Belgium: the individual and team moving bird target competitions, each at both 33 and 50 meters, all on August 5.

1027. Archery events for women held in the Olympic Games were two types of archery competitions at varying lengths held on September 19 and 20, 1904, in St. Louis, Missouri. Lida Howell, Emma Cooke, and Jessie Pollock, all of the United States, finished in that order in both events.

1028. Team archery event held in the Olympic Games was in 1904 in St. Louis, Missouri. The competition at 60 yards was won on September 21 by the Potomac Archers of Washington, D.C.: William Thompson, Robert Williams, Louis Maxson, and Galen Spencer.

1029. International governing body for archery was the Fédération Internationale de Tir à l'Arc (FITA), founded in 1931.

1030. World championships in target archery were held in Lvov, Poland, in 1931, under the auspices of the Fédération Internationale de Tir à l'Arc (FITA), the just-founded governing body in the sport. Polish archers won both individual events, Michal Sawicki the men's and Janina Kurkowska the women's. Archers from France won the men's team event. The first women's team event was not held until 1933, when the Polish team won. The championships would be held annually until 1959, then biennially.

1031. Archer to win two, and then up to seven, women's individual world championships was Janina Kurkowska of Poland. After winning the inaugural event in 1931, she would win again in 1932–1934, 1936, 1939, and 1947.

1032. Archer to win two, three, and four men's individual world championships was Hans Deutgen of Sweden, who won from 1947 through 1950.

1033. World championships in archery involving FITA rounds a format established by the sport's governing body, the Fédération Internationale de Tir à l'Arc (FITA), were in 1957.

1034. World field archery championships were held in 1959, originally for bare bow only, with recurve being added in 1969 and compound in 1990, when the competitions became biennial.

1035. Men's individual archery event in the modern format held in the Olympic Games was in 1972 in Munich, West Germany. John Williams of the United States broke his own world record with a total of 2528 points on September 10.

1036. Women's individual archery event in the modern format held in the Olympic Games was in 1972 in Munich, West Germany. The winner was Doreen Wilber of the United States, who had a world record total of 2424 points on September 10.

1037. Men's team archery event held in the Olympic Games was in 1988 in Seoul, South Korea. The South Korean team of Chun In-soo, Lee Han-sup, and Park Sung-soo won the inaugural event on October 1.

1038. Archer to win two titles in women's events in a single Olympic Games was Kim Soo-nyung of South Korea in 1988 in Seoul, South Korea. On September 30, she won the women's individual title, leading a South Korean medal sweep, and then on October 1 earned another championship in the team event. She would win another team gold in 1992.

1039. Archer from the United States to win the men's individual gold medal in the Olympic Games was Justin Huish, who won on August 1, 1996, in Atlanta, Georgia. He also helped win the first United States team title the next day.

1040. Archers from the United States to win a gold medal in the team event in the Olympic Games were Justin Huish, Richard Johnson, and Rod White on August 2, 1996, in Atlanta, Georgia. Huish had taken the individual gold medal the day before.

AUTOMOBILE RACING (BEFORE 1900)
1041. Automobile race on record was held in 1878 on a route between Green Bay and Madison, Wisconsin. The winning car was an Oshkosh steamer.

1042. Automobile race on record in Europe was probably the La Vélocipède race held in Paris, France, on April 20, 1887. Covering a distance of 19.3 miles (31 kilometers), it was won by Count Jules Felix Philippe Albert de Dion de Malfiance of France, who drove a de Dion steam quadricycle.

1043. Organized automobile race in the United States was held in November 1893 on a route between Chicago and Evanston, Illinois, sponsored by Chicago's *Times Herald*.

1044. Automobile track race on record was run at the Rhode Island State Fair in 1894.

1045. Organized long-distance automobile race was held on June 11–14, 1895, on a round-trip course between Paris and Bordeaux, France, a distance of 732 miles (1178 kilometers).

1046. Woman automobile racer was Madame Laumaille (her first name is unrecorded), who drove in a two-day race between Marseilles and Nice, France, in 1898. She finished fourth and her husband sixth.

AUTOMOBILE RACING (1900-1919)
1047. Woman driver to win an automobile race was Dorothy Levitt, who had her first win in 1903 in Cowes, England. Her 1906 book, *The Woman and the Car*, would help popularize driving among women.

AUTOMOBILE RACING—(1900-1919)—
continued

1048. International automobile racing organization was the Association Internationale des Automobiles Clubs Reconnus, founded in 1904. In 1946, it would become the Fédération Internationale de l'Automobile (FIA).

1049. Grand Prix automobile race was the French Grand Prix, first held in Le Mans in 1906. It would be one of the inaugural races in the Formula One Grand Prix circuit, beginning in 1950.

1050. International and transcontinental automobile race was held in 1907. Leaving Peking (now Beijing), China, on June 10 and arriving in Paris, France, on August 10, the winner was Prince Scipione Borghese of Italy.

1051. National championship in Indy Car racing then called the American Automobile Association National Championship, was held in 1909, when the winner was George Robertson. It became the United States Auto Club National Championship in 1955 and the CART (Championship Auto Racing Teams) World Series in 1998.

1052. Paved automobile racing track was the Indianapolis Motor Speedway, in Indianapolis, Indiana. It was built in 1909 of several million bricks, and so was nicknamed "the brickyard."

1053. Monte Carlo Rally was held in 1911, when the long-distance event centered on Monaco was won by Henri Rougier of France, driving a Turcat-Mery.

1054. Indianapolis 500 was held on May 30, 1911, at the Indianapolis Motor Speedway, in Indianapolis, Indiana, and would be held on Memorial Day weekend annually from then. The first winner was Ray Harroun, driving a Marmon Wasp, with an average speed of 74.590 miles per hour.

AUTOMOBILE RACING (1920-1929)
1055. Italian Grand Prix automobile race was held in Brescia in 1921, thereafter being run at Monza. It would be one of the initial races in the Formula One Grand Prix circuit, starting in 1950.

1056. Automobile racer to win the Indianapolis 500 twice was Tommy Milton. Racing at the Indianapolis Motor Speedway in Indianapolis, Indiana, he won it first in 1921 and then again in 1923, when he averaged 90.950 miles per hour in his H. C. S. Special.

1057. Le Mans 24-hours sports car race was held on May 26–27, 1923, at Sarthe, France, following a circuit of 10.73 miles (17.26 kilometers). The winners were André Lagache and René Leonard of France, driving a Chenard & Walcker automobile.

1058. Automobile race at the Circuit Pescara in Italy was in 1924. It would become a popular test track for new models, and would be part of the Formula One Grand Prix circuit in 1957.

1059. Pescara Grand Prix automobile race was held in Italy in 1924. It would become part of the Formula One Grand Prix circuit in 1957.

1060. Automobile racer to win the Indianapolis 500 with an average speed of more than 100 miles per hour was Peter DePaolo in 1925, who averaged 101.130 in his Duesenberg Special.

1061. Belgian Grand Prix automobile race was held in 1925. It would become one of the original races in the Formula One Grand Prix, starting in 1950.

1062. British Grand Prix automobile race called the RAC Grand Prix until 1948, was held at Brooklands, near Weybridge, Surrey, England, in 1926. It would be one of the inaugural races on the Formula One Grand Prix circuit in 1950.

1063. German Grand Prix automobile race was held in Avus in 1926. It would become part of the Formula One Grand Prix circuit in 1951.

1064. Monaco Grand Prix automobile race was held in Monte Carlo in 1929 and was won by a driver named Williams (first name unknown) in a Bugatti. It would be one of the first races included in the Formula One Grand Prix circuit, starting in 1950.

AUTOMOBILE RACING (1930-1949)
1065. Swiss Grand Prix automobile race was held in 1934 at Bremgarten, in Berne. It would be one of the races in the first Formula One Grand Prix circuit in 1950.

1066. Automobile racer to win the Indianapolis 500 with an average speed of more than 110 miles per hour was Wilbur Shaw in 1937, when he averaged 113.580 mph in his Shaw-Gilmore Special, for the first of his three Indy wins.

1067. Officially timed drag races were held in California in 1937, under the auspices of the Southern California Timing Association (SCTA). These drag races were often held on dry lake beds in desert country or on airstrips, as an alternative to illegal drag racing on streets and highways.

1068. Automobile racer to win the Indianapolis 500 three times, and to win it twice in a row was Wilbur Shaw. Racing at the Indianapolis Motor Speedway in Indianapolis, Indiana, he won it in 1937 and 1939 before notching his third win in 1940, when he averaged 114.277 miles per hour in his Boyle Special.

1069. Formula Two automobile racing circuit was established in 1947 in Europe, for younger drivers. It would be replaced in 1985 by the European Formula 3000 Championship.

1070. Automobile race sponsored by the National Association for Stock Car Auto Racing (NASCAR) was held in Daytona Beach, Florida, on February 15, 1948. The winner was Red Byron of the United States, driving a Ford Modified.

1071. National Association for Stock Car Auto Racing (NASCAR) was established in Daytona Beach, Florida, on February 15, 1948, after a preliminary organizational meeting in December 1947, sparked by Bill France, Sr.

1072. Automobile racer to win the Indianapolis 500 with an average speed of more than 120 miles per hour was Bill Holland, who averaged 121.327 mph in his Blue Crown Spark Plug Special in 1949.

1073. National Association for Stock Car Auto Racing (NASCAR) Winston Cup (Grand National) Series was in 1949. The first winner of an official Winston Cup event was Jim Roper at Charlotte, North Carolina, and the season's first champion was Red Byron.

AUTOMOBILE RACING (1950-1959)

1074. Governing body for drag racing was the National Hot Rod Association (NHRA), founded in 1950 in the United States, where the sport had been developed in the 1930s.

1075. Southern 500 automobile race was held at Darlington, South Carolina, in 1950, the first asphalt superspeedway in the United States. The inaugural winner was Johnny Mantz, who averaged 76.260 miles per hour in his Plymouth.

1076. World championship for automobile racers was established in 1950, by the Fédération Internationale de l'Automobile (FIA), with drivers gaining points toward the championship from a series of Formula One Grand Prix races held around the world. The first world champion was Nino (Giuseppe) Farina of Italy, who that year won the British, Italian, and Swiss Grand Prix races.

1077. British Grand Prix automobile race to be part of the Formula One Grand Prix circuit was held on May 13, 1950, at Silverstone, near Brackley, England. The inaugural winner was Nino (Giuseppe) Farina of Italy, driving an Alfa Romeo.

1078. Monaco Grand Prix automobile race to be part of the Formula One Grand Prix circuit was held on May 21, 1950, at Monte Carlo. The winner was Juan Manuel Fangio of Argentina, driving an Alfa Romeo.

1079. Indianapolis 500 automobile race to be part of the Formula One Grand Prix circuit was on May 30, 1950, in the circuit's inaugural year. The winner was Johnnie Parsons of the United States, driving a Kurtis Kraft that carried him to victory despite having a cracked block.

1080. Swiss Grand Prix automobile race to be part of the Formula One Grand Prix circuit was held on June 4, 1950, at Bremgarten, in Berne. Nino (Giuseppe) Farina of Italy won, driving an Alfa Romeo.

1081. Belgian Grand Prix automobile race to be part of the Formula One Grand Prix circuit was held on June 18, 1950, in Spa-Francorchamps. The winner was Juan Manuel Fangio of Argentina, driving an Alfa Romeo.

1082. French Grand Prix automobile race to be part of the Formula One Grand Prix circuit was held on July 2, 1950, at Rheims. The first winner was Juan Manuel Fangio of Argentina, driving an Alfa Romeo. He would win again in 1951 (sharing the title with Luigi Fagioli of Italy), 1954, and 1957.

1083. Italian Grand Prix automobile race to be part of the Formula One Grand Prix circuit was held on September 3, 1950, at Monza. The winner was Nino (Giuseppe) Farina of Italy, driving an Alfa Romeo.

1084. German Grand Prix automobile race to be part of the Formula One Grand Prix circuit was held on July 29, 1951, in Nürburgring. The first winner was Alberto Ascari of Italy, driving a Ferrari; he would win again in 1952.

AUTOMOBILE RACING—(1950-1959)—
continued

1085. Spanish Grand Prix automobile race to be part of the Formula One Grand Prix circuit was held on October 28, 1951, in Pedralbes. The winner was Juan Manuel Fangio of Argentina, driving an Alfa Romeo, en route to his first world championship.

1086. Automobile racer to be named Rookie of the Year in the Indianapolis 500 was Art Cross in 1952.

1087. Automobile racer to have six wins in a single season on the Formula One Grand Prix circuit was Alberto Ascari of Italy in 1952, when he won the first of two consecutive world championships.

1088. Dutch Grand Prix automobile race to be part of the Formula One Grand Prix circuit was held on August 17, 1952, in Zandvoort. The inaugural winner was Alberto Ascari of Italy, driving a Ferrari; he would win again in 1953.

1089. Automobile racer to have nine consecutive wins over two seasons on the Formula One Grand Prix circuit was Alberto Ascari of Italy in 1952 and 1953. He was world champion both years, after being runner-up in 1951.

1090. Automobile racer to win more than 10 races in a single season in the National Association for Stock Car Auto Racing (NASCAR) Winston Cup series was Herb Thomas in 1953, when he won 11 races driving his Hudson.

1091. Argentine Grand Prix automobile race was held on January 18, 1953, as part of the Formula One Grand Prix circuit. The inaugural winner was Alberto Ascari of Italy, driving a Ferrari. The Buenos Aires Grand Prix had been held at the site from 1947.

1092. Automobile racer to be world champion on the Formula One Grand Prix circuit two, three, four, and five times; the first to win the title three and four times consecutively; and the first from Argentina to be world champion was Juan Manuel Fangio. Runner-up for the first world championship in 1950, he won the title in 1951 and then again four times in a row, 1954–1957.

1093. Automobile racer to win the Indianapolis 500 with an average speed of more than 130 miles per hour was Bill Vukovich of the United States in 1954, when he averaged 130.840 mph in his second consecutive win, driving a Kurtis Kraft–Offenhauser.

1094. Automobile racer to win two consecutive championships on the National Association for Stock Car Auto Racing (NASCAR) Winston Cup circuit was Buck Baker of the United States, who won in 1956 and 1957.

1095. Automobile racer to win two, three, and four Argentine Grand Prix races was Juan Manuel Fangio of Argentina, who won four times in a row, 1954–1957, in 1956 having shared the drive with Luigi Musso.

1096. Automobile racer to have more than 20 wins on the Formula One Grand Prix circuit was Juan Manuel Fangio of Argentina, with 24 wins between 1950 and 1958. During that period, he was five times world champion (1951 and 1954–1957) and twice runner-up (1950 and 1953).

1097. Woman automobile racer to compete in a Grand Prix race eligible for world-championship points was Maria Teresa de Filippis of Italy. Driving a Maserati in the Belgian Grand Prix at Spa-Francorchamps on June 15, 1958, she placed tenth.

1098. Daytona 500 automobile race was held in 1959 in Daytona Beach, Florida. After a photo finish between Lee Petty and Johnny Beauchamp, officials took three days of examination before declaring Petty the winner, with an average speed of 135.520 miles per hour in his Oldsmobile. The Daytona 500 would become the traditional opening race of the National Association for Stock Car Auto Racing (NASCAR) season.

1099. United States Grand Prix automobile race to be part of the Formula One Grand Prix circuit was held on December 12, 1959, at Sebring, Florida. Driving a Cooper, Bruce McLaren of New Zealand won the event. Other United States Grand Prix races would be established later.

AUTOMOBILE RACING (1960-1969)
1100. Automobile racer to have five consecutive wins in a single season on the Formula One Grand Prix circuit was Jack Brabham of Australia in 1960, when he won the second of his three world championships, the others being in 1959 and 1966.

1101. World 600 automobile race was held in 1960 in Charlotte, North Carolina. Joe Lee Johnson won with an average speed of 107.752 miles per hour in his Chevrolet, in what became one of the top National Association for Stock Car Auto Racing (NASCAR) races.

1102. National Association for Stock Car Auto Racing (NASCAR) race to be televised was the 1961 Firecracker 400 in Daytona Beach, Florida, won by David Pearson driving a Pontiac, which was shown on the ABC television network.

1103. 24 Hours of Daytona automobile race was held in 1962, in Daytona Beach, Florida. The inaugural winner was Dan Gurney, who averaged 104.101 miles per hour in his Lotus.

1104. Automobile racer to win the Indianapolis 500 with an average speed of more than 140 miles per hour was Rodger Ward in 1962, when he averaged 140.293 mph in his Leader Card Roadster, for his second Indy win.

1105. Automobile racer to have seven wins in a single season on the Formula One Grand Prix circuit was Jim Clark of Scotland in 1963, when he won the first of his two world championships, the other being in 1965. He would be killed in a racing accident in 1968.

1106. Mexican Grand Prix automobile race to be part of the Formula One Grand Prix circuit was held on October 27, 1963, at the Hermanos Rodriguez circuit near Mexico City. Jim Clark of Scotland won the event, driving a Lotus. The race had been held for the first time in 1962.

1107. Austrian Grand Prix automobile race to be part of the Formula One Grand Prix circuit was held on August 23, 1964, at the Zeltweg circuit. Driving a Ferrari, Lorenzo Bandini of Italy won the inaugural event.

1108. Drag racer to reach a speed of over 200, and then 250, miles per hour was Don Garlits. He hit 201.34 on August 1, 1964, in Great Meadows, New Jersey, and 250.69 on October 11, 1975, in Ontario, Canada. By 1986 he would top 270 miles per hour.

1109. Automobile racer to win the Indianapolis 500 with an average speed of over 150 miles per hour was Jim Clark of Scotland, who averaged 150.686 when he won with a Lotus-Ford on Memorial Day weekend in 1965.

1110. Automobile racer to earn more than $100,000 in a single season in the National Association for Stock Car Auto Racing (NASCAR) Winston Cup series was Richard Petty of the United States, who won $130,275 for 27 wins in 1967.

1111. Automobile racer to win more than 20 races in a single season in the National Association for Stock Car Auto Racing (NASCAR) Winston Cup series was Richard Petty of the United States in 1967, when he won an astonishing 27 races. He would have 21 wins in 1971, but no one else in the century would top 20 wins in a season.

1112. Canadian Grand Prix automobile race part of the Formula One Grand Prix circuit, was held on August 27, 1967, at Mosport, near Bowmanville, Ontario. The inaugural winner was Jack Brabham of Australia, driving a Brabham car of his own construction.

1113. Automobile racer to have 25 wins on the Formula One Grand Prix circuit was Jim Clark of Scotland, who had 25 wins between 1960 and 1968, when he died in a racing accident.

1114. Automobile racer to win the Winston $1 million bonus for winning three of the top four National Association for Stock Car Auto Racing (NASCAR) races in a single season was LeeRoy Yarbrough of the United States in 1969, when he won the Daytona 500 at Daytona Beach, Florida; the World 600 at Charlotte, North Carolina; and the Southern 500 at Darlington, South Carolina.

1115. Talladega 500 automobile race was held in 1969 in Talladega, Alabama. The inaugural race was won by Richard Brickhouse, who averaged 153.778 miles per hour in his Dodge.

AUTOMOBILE RACING (1970-1979)
1116. Automobile racer to win three, four, five, six, and seven championships on the National Association for Stock Car Auto Racing (NASCAR) Winston Cup circuit was Richard Petty of the United States. Known as "the King," he won the titles in 1964, 1967, 1971, 1972, 1974, 1975, and 1979, ending his career in 1992 with 200 wins (95 more than his closest challenger) on the NASCAR circuit.

1117. Automobile racer to win the Indianapolis 500 with an average speed of more than 160 miles per hour was Mark Donohue of the United States in 1972, when he averaged 162.962 mph driving a McLaren-Offenhauser. He had been Indianapolis 500 rookie of the year in 1969.

1118. Automobile racer to be named *Sports Illustrated* Sportsman of the Year was Jackie Stewart of Great Britain in 1973, the year he won six Formula One Grand Prix races and his second world championship.

AUTOMOBILE RACING—(1970-1979)—
continued

1119. Woman automobile racer to win world-championship points in a Grand Prix race was Lelia Lombardi of Italy in the Spanish Grand Prix at Barcelona in 1975. She was in sixth place when the race was halted because of an accident.

1120. Woman automobile racer to win a national tournament of the National Hot Rod Association (NHRA) was Shirley Muldowney of the United States, who won the spring nationals in 1976 and again in 1977, when she also set a women's speed record of 252.10 miles per hour on January 15, which she later upped even more.

1121. Woman automobile racer to compete in a major stock car race was Janet Guthrie of the United States in May 1976, when she placed 15th in the World 600 at Charlotte, North Carolina. Earlier that month she had been the first woman to qualify for the Indianapolis 500, but had had to withdraw because of mechanical problems with her car.

1122. Japanese Grand Prix automobile race part of the Formula One Grand Prix circuit, was held on October 24, 1976, at Mount Fuji. It was won by Mario Andretti of the United States, driving a Lotus 77.

1123. Automobile racer to win the Indianapolis 500 four times was A. J. Foyt. Racing at the Indianapolis Motor Speedway in Indianapolis, Indiana, he had his first wins in 1961, 1964, and 1967, and then came back a decade later to win again in 1977, when he averaged 161.331 miles per hour in his Gilmore Racing Team car.

1124. Woman automobile racer to race in the Indianapolis 500 was Janet Guthrie of the United States in May 1977, though she had to withdraw after nine laps due to mechanical problems with her car. She had been the first woman to qualify for the race in 1976, but had been unable to race because of car troubles. She would place ninth in 1978.

1125. World rally championship for drivers was established in 1977, when the inaugural winner was Sandro Munari of Italy. This became the World Drivers' Championship from 1979.

1126. Automobile racer to earn more than $500,000 in a single season in the National Association for Stock Car Auto Racing (NASCAR) Winston Cup series was Cale Yarborough, who earned $530,751 with 10 wins in 1978, in his third straight Winston Cup championship.

1127. Automobile racer to win two Austrian Grand Prix races was Alan Jones of Australia, who won in 1977 at Zeltweg and then again in 1979 at Österreichring.

1128. National Association for Stock Car Auto Racing (NASCAR) automobile race of 500 miles to be televised live from start to finish was the 1979 Daytona 500, from Daytona Beach, Florida, won by Richard Petty, who averaged 143.977 miles per hour in his Oldsmobile.

AUTOMOBILE RACING (1980-1989)

1129. Automobile racer to win more than $1 million in a single season in the National Association for Stock Car Auto Racing (NASCAR) Winston Cup series was Darrell Waltrip in 1985, when he earned $1,318,735 with three wins.

1130. Automobile racer to win the Brazilian Grand Prix three, four, five, and six times was Alain Prost of France. His wins were in 1982, 1984, 1985, 1987, and 1988 in Rio de Janeiro, and in 1990 in São Paulo.

1131. European Formula 3000 automobile racing circuit was established in 1985, replacing some earlier circuits for younger drivers. Christian Danner of West Germany was the first winner on the circuit.

1132. Australian Grand Prix automobile race was held on November 3, 1985, in Adelaide, Australia, where the inaugural winner was Keke Rosberg of Finland, driving a Williams car.

1133. Automobile racer to win the Indianapolis 500 with an average speed of more than 170 miles per hour was Bobby Rahal of the United States in 1986, when he averaged 170.722 mph in his March-Cosworth.

1134. Automobile racer to win three Austrian Grand Prix races was Alain Prost of France. His three wins all came at Österreichring, in Austria, in 1983, 1985, and 1986.

1135. Automobile racer to win more than $2 million, and then $3 million, in a single season in the National Association for Stock Car Auto Racing (NASCAR) Winston Cup series was Dale Earnhardt. In 1987, when he won the third of his seven Winston Cup titles, he earned $2,099,243 in 11 wins on the circuit. In 1990, he earned $3,083,056 with nine wins and his fourth title.

1136. Automobile racer to have eight wins in a single season on the Formula One Grand Prix circuit was Ayrton Senna of Brazil in 1988, when he won the first of his three world championships, the others being in 1990 and 1991. He would die in a car crash in 1994.

1137. Automobile racer to win two Australian Grand Prix races was Alain Prost of France. After winning in 1986, he returned to win again on November 13, 1988, both times driving a McLaren car at Adelaide.

AUTOMOBILE RACING (1990-1999)

1138. Drag racer to reach a speed over 290 miles per hour was Connie Kalitta, who hit 291.54 on February 11, 1989, in Pomona, California. She had broken the 180 mph barrier in 1962.

1139. Automobile racer to win the Indianapolis 500 with an average speed of more than 180 miles per hour was Arie Luyendyk of the Netherlands in 1990, when he averaged 185.981 in his Lola-Chevrolet.

1140. Automobile racer to win five Belgian Grand Prix races was Ayrton Senna of Brazil. After winning first in 1985, he came back to win four times in a row, 1988–1991, all at Spa-Francorchamps.

1141. Automobile racer to have nine wins in a single season on the Formula One Grand Prix circuit was Nigel Mansell of Great Britain in 1992, including five in a row. He would win only once more, in 1994, before retiring in 1995.

1142. Drag racer to reach a speed over 300 miles per hour was Kenny Bernstein, who notched 301.70 on March 20, 1992, in a qualifying round of a race at Gainesville, Florida.

1143. Automobile racer to have more than 50 wins on the Formula One Grand Prix circuit was Alain Prost of France, who won 51 times between 1980 and 1993, en route to four world championships: 1985, 1986, 1989, and 1993.

1144. Automobile racer to earn more than $4 million in a single season in the National Association for Stock Car Auto Racing (NASCAR) Winston Cup series was Jeff Gordon of the United States in 1995, in his first championship season, when he won $4,347,343 with seven wins.

1145. Drag racer to reach a speed over 320 miles per hour was Joe Amato. He hit 323.50 on May 17, 1998, in Englishtown, New Jersey. He had earlier broken the 280-mile barrier in 1987 and the 310 in March 1998.

AWARDS, GENERAL

1146. Silver trophy known to be awarded at a sporting event in North America was a silver bowl presented at a horse race in Hempstead (then Hansted Plains), Long Island, in the colony of New York, in 1668. The trophy was donated by British governor Richard Nicolls, who had established a race track there a few years earlier. The winner is unclear, but may have been horse owner Sylvester Salisbury, a British army captain.

1147. Athlete to be named an All-American in both basketball and football was Bennie Oosterbaan. Playing for the University of Michigan, he was named for football in 1925 and 1927, and for basketball in 1927 and 1928.

1148. Sullivan Award the James E. Sullivan Memorial Trophy honoring amateur athletes of the United States, was given in 1930. It was named after the longtime president of the Amateur Athletic Union (AAU), which gives the award. The inaugural winner was golfer Bobby Jones, who that year won the first (and so far only) grand slam in golf.

1149. Woman to win the Sullivan Award was swimmer Ann Curtis in 1944. Only 18, she had already won eight U.S. national titles, that year winning every women's freestyle event at the National Outdoor Swimming Championships and setting two world records.

1150. African-American athlete to win the Sullivan Award was Malvin G. Whitfield in 1954. A middle-distance runner, Whitfield had been gold medalist at the 1948 and 1952 Olympic Games.

1151. Athlete to be named *Sports Illustrated* Sportsman of the Year was runner Roger Bannister of Great Britain in 1954, the year he broke the four-minute barrier in the mile.

1152. African-American athlete to be named *Sports Illustrated* Sportsman of the Year was decathlon champion Rafer Johnson of the United States in 1958.

1153. African-American woman to win the Sullivan Award was Wilma Rudolph in 1961. At the 1960 Olympics in Rome, Italy, she had won three gold medals, in the 100- and 200-meter events and the 4 x 400-meter relay.

1154. Sports commissioner to be named *Sports Illustrated* Sportsman of the Year was Pete Rozelle of the United States, commissioner of the National Football League, in 1963.

AWARDS, GENERAL—*continued*

1155. *Sports Illustrated* **Sportsman of the Year award to be given to a woman and to be shared** was in 1972. Tennis star Billie Jean King shared the award with John Wooden, basketball coach at the University of California at Los Angeles.

1156. Team to be named *Sports Illustrated* **Sportsman of the Year** was the U.S. Olympic ice hockey team in 1980, which had been the upset winner over the Soviet team in the Olympic Games that year.

1157. Athlete to win the Jesse Owens International Award presented to international athletes in Olympic sports, was Olympic and world champion speed skater Eric Heiden of the United States in 1981.

1158. Woman to win the Jesse Owens International Award was champion long-distance runner Mary Decker Slaney of the United States in 1983.

1159. African-American to win the Jesse Owens International Award was hurdler Edwin Moses of the United States in 1984, in the midst of a winning streak of more than 100 races that would stretch from 1977 to 1987.

1160. African-American woman to win the Jesse Owens International Award was champion sprinter Florence Griffith-Joyner of the United States in 1989.

1161. Athlete of Asian or Native American descent to be named *Sports Illustrated* **Sportsman of the Year** was Tiger (Eldrick) Woods of the United States in 1996, the year that he made his remarkable debut as a professional golfer. Woods is of African-American, Native-American, and Chinese-Thai descent.

1162. Athlete to win two Jesse Owens International Awards was runner Michael Johnson of the United States, who won in 1995 and again in 1996, when he won both the men's 200- and 400-meter titles in the Olympic Games.

1163. Women's team to be named *Sports Illustrated* **Sportsman of the Year** was the United States soccer team whose 20 members won the women's soccer world cup on July 10, 1999.

B

BADMINTON

1164. Standardized rules for badminton were written in the 1870s in India, where British army officers played the game. It was derived from the children's game battledore shuttlecock, which had neither nets nor boundaries, but similar games were played perhaps 2000 years ago in China. It was named for Badminton House, the home of the Beaufort family, in Gloucestershire, England, where the game was popular in the 19th century.

1165. National governing body for badminton was the Badminton Association founded in 1893 in England.

1166. All-England Championships in badminton were held in 1899, for doubles only. D. Oakes and Stewart Massey won the men's title, Meriel Lucas and Miss Graeme (first name unknown) the women's, and D. Oakes and Miss St. John (first name unknown) the mixed doubles. The inaugural winners were all from England, but this would become the main international badminton tournament until the foundation of the world championships.

1167. All-England Championships in badminton to include individual competitions were in 1900. Sydney Smith won the inaugural men's individual title and Ethel Thomson (later Larcombe) the women's. Both were noted tennis players who took titles at Wimbledon.

1168. International governing body for badminton was the International Badminton Federation (IBF), founded in 1934, and headquartered in Cheltenham, Gloucestershire, England.

1169. World team Thomas Cup badminton championships for men involving both singles and doubles play, were held in 1949. The team from Malaya won the event and received the Thomas Cup, donated by England's Sir George Thomas. At first held triennially, the competition would become biennial from 1982.

1170. World team Uber Cup badminton championships for women modeled after the men's competition, were held in 1957. The United States team won the inaugural event and the Uber Cup, donated by Betty Uber, a longtime badminton player from England. Initially held triennially, it became biennial from 1984.

1171. World championships in badminton were held in 1977, at first triennially, then from 1983 biennially. Danish players dominated the inaugural event: Flemming Delfs won the men's singles title, Lene Köppen the women's singles, and Steen Stovgarrd and Köppen won the mixed doubles. The men's doubles title was won by Johan Wahjudi and Tjun Tjun of Indonesia. The women's doubles title went to Etsuko Tuganoo and Emiko Vero of Japan.

1172. Sudirman Trophy awarded at the badminton world championships to the best mixed team was in 1989, when it was won by the team from Indonesia.

1173. World cup/grand prix competition in badminton was held in 1991. Andy B. Wiranata of Indonesia won the inaugural men's title and Huang Hwa of China the women's.

1174. Badminton events held in the Olympic Games as medal sports were on August 4, 1992, in Barcelona, Spain. Susi Susanti of Indonesia won the women's singles title, becoming Indonesia's first Olympic gold medalist. Later that day, the men's singles titles was taken by her boyfriend and Indonesian teammate Allan Budi Kusuma. The doubles titles were both won by South Korean pairs: Kim Moon-soo and Park Joo-bong on the men's side and Hwang Hye-young and Chung So-young on the women's.

1175. Badminton event for mixed doubles in the Olympic Games was held on August 1, 1996, in Atlanta, Georgia, where the winners were Kim Dong-moon and Gil Young-ah of South Korea.

BALLOONING

1176. People to fly in a balloon were Jean-François Pilâtre de Rozier and the Marquis d'Arlandes, who flew from the Bois de Boulogne, in France, on November 21, 1783. Their craft was a hot-air balloon invented and built by Joseph Montgolfier and his brother Jacques Etienne Montgolfier, who had sent the first modern balloon aloft on September 18, 1783, bearing three animals.

1177. Woman to fly in a hot-air balloon was Elisabeth Thible, who flew as a passenger in 1784 over Lyons, France. The best-known early woman balloonist would be Marie Sophie Blanchard, who flew with her husband, Jean Pierre Blanchard, and, after his death, flew solo, until she died in 1819, when her balloon caught fire over Paris.

1178. Flyers to cross the English Channel in a balloon were Jean Pierre Blanchard and J. Jeffries, who flew from Dover, England, to Calais, France, on January 7, 1785.

1179. Balloon flight in the United States was on January 9, 1793, in Philadelphia, Pennsylvania. The flight was made by Jean Pierre Blanchard, who had made the first flight across the English Channel eight years earlier.

1180. Woman to fly solo in a hot-air balloon in the United States was Madame Johnson (first name unknown), who flew in an exhibition in New York City in 1825. A better-known woman balloonist would be Carlotta (Mary H.) Myers, who first flew solo in Little Falls, New York, in 1880, and later flew at many fairs and exhibitions.

1181. Balloon race in the United States was intended to be a flight from Dayton, Ohio, to Chicago, Illinois, in 1876. However, none of the more than 100 balloons reached Chicago, and most did not last for more than a mile.

1182. International balloon race was the Bennett Cup race held in France in 1906, the aim being to fly the farthest distance in the time allowed. The trophy was offered by James Gordon Bennett, publisher of New York City's *Herald*, who would also later offer a Bennett Cup for an airplane race.

1183. People to circle the globe in a balloon were Bertrand Piccard of Switzerland and Brian Jones of England, who landed in Geneva, Switzerland, on March 20, 1999, after they and many other balloonists had failed in previous circumnavigation attempts. They had taken off in their *Breitling Orbiter 3* from Château-d'Oex, Switzerland, on March 1.

BASEBALL (BEFORE 1850)

1184. Baseball team on record was organized in September 1845, in New York City, by the New York Knickerbockers Baseball Club, which sponsored Alexander Cartwright's game-shaping set of rules for baseball. These included the diamond-shaped playing field, four bases, and the set of nine positions that were basic to the game, as well as several other playing rules. Baseball, which had been developed largely from cricket and rounders, had been played in several earlier forms before 1845, most notably by the Massachusetts Rules, which more closely resembled cricket. It is now generally accepted that baseball was not invented by Abner Doubleday and played at Cooperstown, New York, for the first time in 1839, as had long been thought. Cartwright went west in 1849, joining the California Gold Rush, and settled in Hawaii in 1852.

BASEBALL—(BEFORE 1850)—*continued*

1185. Baseball game on record played under Cartwright's Rules was a three-inning intra-club New York Knickerbockers game played on October 6, 1845, in New York City. Increasingly popular, baseball continued to be played under several sets of rules during the late 1840s.

1186. Baseball uniform was adopted by the New York Knickerbockers in April 1846. The Knicks uniforms included straw hats, blue pants, and white shirts.

1187. Inter-club baseball game on record under Cartwright's Rules was played at the Elysian Fields, Hoboken, New Jersey, on June 19, 1846. The New York Club defeated the New York Knickerbockers 23–1.

1188. Person to take the new sport of baseball west was Alexander Cartwright, who taught the new game while traveling west in 1849 during the California Gold Rush, and continued to introduce the game as played by Cartwright's Rules in California.

BASEBALL (1850-1859)

1189. Person to introduce baseball as played under Cartwright's Rules to Hawaii was Alexander Cartwright, who settled in Hawaii in 1852, after leaving California, and there became a substantial trader and financier.

1190. Baseball game on record to go into extra innings was a 16-inning game between the New York Knickerbockers and the Gotham Club, in New York City on June 30, 1854. The game was won by the Gothams 21–16.

1191. National Association of Base Ball Players convention was held at Smith's Hotel in New York City, on January 22, 1857, with representatives of 16 New York area baseball clubs attending. This founding convention was initiated by the New York Knickerbockers, and Dr. D. L. Adams of the Knicks became the first president.

1192. Baseball game on record at which admission was charged was an all-star game played at Long Island's Fashion Race Course on July 20, 1858, at which approximately 1,500 people paid 50 cents each. The opposing teams consisted of top players from New York City and Brooklyn.

1193. Intercollegiate baseball game on record was played on July 1, 1859, between Amherst and Williams colleges, at Pittsfield, Massachusetts. Amherst won 73–32, in a game played under the cricket-like Massachusetts Rules, rather than under the by-then-standard Cartwright's Rules.

BASEBALL (1860-1869)

1194. Baseball club tour was by the Brooklyn Excelsiors, who began their tour on June 30, 1860, and played at five cities in the next 10 days—Albany, Buffalo, Newburgh, Rochester, and Troy, all in New York.

1195. Shutout baseball game on record was won by the Brooklyn Excelsiors, who defeated the St. George Cricket Club 25–0, on November 8, 1860.

1196. Enclosed baseball field to which admission was charged was the Union Baseball Grounds, in Brooklyn, New York, which opened on May 15, 1862.

1197. Rule in baseball establishing the pitcher's box from which pitches must be delivered, was adopted by the 1866 annual convention of the National Association of Base Ball Players.

1198. Women's college baseball teams on record were organized at Vassar College, Poughkeepsie, New York, in 1866. They included the Laurels and the Abenakis.

1199. Baseball box score that was generally accepted was introduced by Henry Chadwick in 1867, in New York City. Chadwick was a leading early writer about baseball, who from the late 1850s covered the sport for many newspapers, published many guides to baseball, and was active in developing baseball's rules. He was the only writer to become a full member of baseball's Hall of Fame.

1200. Baseball game between Princeton and Yale was played on May 4, 1867, beginning what would become a traditional rivalry. Princeton won 58–52.

1201. Non-collegiate women's baseball team was organized at Peterborough, New Hampshire, in 1868. It was captained by Nannie Miller, who was also the team's catcher.

1202. Rule establishing that no baseball game can be completed until five innings have been played by both teams was adopted by the 1868 annual convention of the National Association of Base Ball Players meeting at Washington, D.C.

1203. Professional baseball team was the Cincinnati Red Stockings, which began its first season on March 15, 1869. The Cincinnati team had been organized as an amateur club in 1866, and had then played the game on an amateur basis, although like many baseball teams of the day it was, in fact, a mixed amateur-professional organization, with some of its players covertly receiving payments. The club turned openly professional in 1869 and traveled throughout the country. Annual salaries ranged from $800 to $1,200, depending on the position played. Cincinnati was undefeated during the 1869 season, winning 65 of its 66 games, with one tie. Its extraordinary popular success signaled the real beginning of professional baseball. Only two years later, in 1871, the fully professional National Association of Professional Baseball Players was founded.

BASEBALL (1870-1879)

1204. Cincinnati Red Stockings loss as a professional baseball team, and the end of the first winning streak in professional baseball occurred on June 14, 1870, when they were defeated by the Brooklyn Atlantics 8–7. That ended the Red Stockings' 84-game winning streak, one of the longest in professional baseball history.

1205. Cuban major league baseball player was Esteban Bellan, who played with the Troy Haymakers of Troy, New York, from 1871 to 1873.

1206. Professional baseball league was organized, at the founding convention of the National Association of Professional Baseball Players, more popularly known as the National Association (NA), in New York City on March 17, 1871. League members included the Boston Red Stockings, Brooklyn Atlantics, Brooklyn Eckfords, Chicago White Stockings, Cleveland's Forest City Club, Fort Wayne Kekiongas, New York Mutuals, Rockford's Forest City Club, Philadelphia Athletics, Troy Haymakers, Washington Olympics, and Washington (D.C.) Nationals. Cincinnati was not represented, because the Cincinnati Red Stockings had disbanded in 1870.

1207. All-professional baseball game on record was the first National Association game, between the Fort Wayne Kekiongas and the Forest City Club of Cleveland. The game was played at Fort Wayne, Indiana, on May 4, 1871, and was won by the Kekiongas, 2–0.

1208. Hit in an all-professional baseball game the first National Association game, was a double by Jim White of the Fort Wayne Kekiongas, in their 2–0 win over the Forest City Club of Cleveland in Fort Wayne, Indiana, on May 4, 1871.

1209. Shutout on record in professional baseball was in the first all-professional baseball game and the first National Association game, on May 4, 1871, at Fort Wayne, Indiana, when pitcher Bobby Matthews of the Fort Wayne Kekiongas had a 2–0 victory over the Forest City Club of Cleveland. Matthews was a leading pitcher in early baseball, who would win 42 games for the New York Mutuals in 1874.

1210. Professional baseball game played in Boston, Massachusetts was a 29–14 win by the Troy Haymakers over the Boston Red Stockings, both of the National Association, on May 16, 1871.

1211. Championship game in professional baseball was the National Association championship played on October 30, 1871. The Philadelphia Athletics had a 4–1 win over the Chicago White Stockings.

1212. Batter's box in baseball was established by the National Association of Professional Baseball Players, at their annual convention, held in Boston, Massachusetts, on March 2, 1874.

1213. Rules against professional baseball players betting on either their own or the opposing team were adopted by the National Association of Professional Baseball Players, at their annual convention, held in Boston, Massachusetts, on March 2, 1874.

1214. Baseball teams from the United States to tour England and Ireland were the Boston Red Stockings and Philadelphia Athletics, who played their first exhibition game at Lord's Cricket Grounds, in London, England, on August 3, 1874. Boston defeated Philadelphia 24–7. On a tour organized by American baseball great and then sports entrepreneur Albert Spalding, the two teams went on to play exhibition baseball and cricket matches elsewhere in England and in Ireland.

1215. Baseball glove on record was worn by first baseman Charles Waite of Boston, Massachusetts, in 1875. It covered the entire hand, except for a large hole in the back of the glove for ventilation.

1216. Professional baseball pitcher to win 200 games was pitcher Albert Spalding of the Boston Red Stockings, who ended the 1875 season with 207 career wins. Spalding went on to star with the National League's Chicago White Stockings and later became a major figure in the sporting goods industry.

13

BASEBALL—(1870-1879)—*continued*

1217. Baseball player to lead the National League in batting average was Ross Barnes of the Chicago White Stockings, who hit .429 in 1876. He had previously been a top hitter in the National Association of Professional Baseball Players as well, leading the league in 1873 and 1875.

1218. Jewish major league baseball player was Lipman Pike of the St. Louis Browns in 1876.

1219. National League was organized in New York City, on February 2, 1876. The new league, which became baseball's first enduring major league, was organized by William Hulbert, owner of the Chicago White Stockings of the National Association of Professional Baseball Players. Its first president was Morgan Bulkely, president of the Hartford team. It consisted of eight teams: Boston, Chicago, Cincinnati, Hartford, Louisville, New York, Philadelphia, and St. Louis. Hulbert became president of the National League in 1877, and remained in office until his death in 1882.

1220. Boston Red Stockings regular season baseball game played at South End Grounds in Boston, Massachusetts, was a 6–5 Boston win over Philadelphia on April 22, 1876. The Red Stockings would later be known by various names, including the Boston Nationals, Boston Doves, and Boston Rustlers; they finally became the Boston Braves in 1911. The South End Grounds would be their home until 1914.

1221. Hit made in baseball's National League was by Jim O'Rourke of the Boston Red Stockings in their 6–5 loss to the Philadelphia Athletics in Philadelphia, on April 22, 1876, during the first National League game ever played. O'Rourke, a leading hitter for more than two decades, later became a major league manager, minor league executive, and a member of baseball's Hall of Fame.

1222. National League baseball game was played in Philadelphia, Pennsylvania, on April 22, 1876, between the Boston Red Stockings and the Philadelphia Athletics, who won 6–5.

1223. Pitcher to pitch a shutout in baseball's National League was Chicago White Stockings pitcher and manager Albert Spalding, who defeated the Louisville Grays 4–0 at Louisville, Kentucky, on April 24, 1876. Spalding went on to pitch eight shutouts in that first National League season.

1224. Cincinnati Red Stockings regular season baseball game played at the Avenue Grounds in Cincinnati, Ohio, was a 2–1 Cincinnati win over St. Louis, on April 25, 1876. The Red Stockings who came to be known as the Cincinnati Reds, played at the Avenue Grounds from 1876 to 1879.

1225. Baseball player to hit a home run in the National League was Ross Barnes, star batter of the Chicago White Stockings, against the Cincinnati Red Stockings at Cincinnati, Ohio, on May 2, 1876.

1226. Chicago White Stockings regular season baseball game played at the State Street Grounds in Chicago, Illinois, was a 6–0 win over the Cincinnati Red Stockings, on May 10, 1876. The Chicago White Stockings team was later named the Chicago Colts, Chicago Orphans, and finally the Chicago Cubs. The team played at the State Street Grounds for only two years, moving to Lakefront Park in 1878.

1227. Triple play in baseball's National League was made on May 13, 1876, by the New York Mutuals against Hartford, which won 28–3. Dick Higham, who hit into the triple play, was later an umpire and in 1882 became the only umpire ever barred from baseball for dishonesty.

1228. Baseball player to have 6 hits in a 9-inning National League game was Dave Force of the Philadelphia Athletics, who hit 6-for-6 in Philadelphia's 14–13 victory over the Chicago White Stockings, on June 27, 1876.

1229. No-hitter pitched in baseball's National League was pitched by St. Louis pitcher George Bradley on July 15, 1876, in a 2–0 win over Hartford. In 1876, Bradley pitched in every one of his team's 64 games, won 45 games, and had 16 shutouts, setting a 19th-century major league shutout record.

1230. Doubleheader in baseball's National League was played on September 9, 1876, between Cincinnati and Hartford. With Candy Cummings pitching, Hartford won both games, 14–4 and 8–1.

1231. Pitcher in baseball's National League to pitch and win two games on the same day was Candy Cummings of Hartford. On September 9, 1876, Cummings pitched and won both games against Cincinnati. Cummings claimed to have invented the curveball, and is widely—though not universally—credited with having done so.

1232. National League championship was won by the Chicago White Stockings, who defeated Hartford on September 26, 1876. Chicago, managed by Albert Spalding, had a 52-14 record.

1233. Baseball chest protector was invented by William Gray of Hartford, Connecticut, in 1877 and introduced into the sport in 1878.

1234. Jewish major league baseball manager was Lipman Pike of the St. Louis Browns in 1877.

1235. Left-handed pitcher in the National League was Bobby Mitchell, who played for the Cincinnati Reds from 1877 to 1881.

1236. Major league baseball game played on Sunday was an exhibition game played between the Cincinnati Reds and the St. Louis Browns on June 10, 1877.

1237. Catcher's mask used in a National League game was worn by St. Louis Browns catcher Mike Dorgan on August 8, 1877, probably the first use of a catcher's mask in a major league baseball game. A catcher's mask was also patented by Frederick Thayer of the Harvard baseball club in 1878, after having been used by Louis Tyng at Lynn, Massachusetts, in 1877.

1238. African-American baseball player known to have played professionally with a previously all-white team was John W. Fowler (John Jackson), who was a pitcher for the Chelsea team in 1878. Fowler later played with the Lynn Live Oaks team. He is often credited with having played on an otherwise white team in New Castle, Pennsylvania, in 1872 and in some subsequent years.

1239. Baseball team to win two consecutive National League pennants was the Boston Braves, in 1877 and 1878.

1240. Cuban professional baseball league was founded in 1878. Cuban players soon began to move into professional baseball in the United States. Because they were dark-skinned, many Cuban and other Hispanic baseball players were classified as "African-American" and so were barred from all-white mainstream professional baseball.

1241. Pitcher to lead the National League in winning percentage for two consecutive years was Tommy Bond of the Boston Braves, in 1877 and 1878.

1242. Unassisted triple play in major league baseball has been credited by some to Providence centerfielder Paul Hines, in his team's 3–1 win over Boston on May 8, 1878. It was certainly a triple play; whether it was unassisted is a matter of conflicting opinion.

1243. Chicago White Stockings regular season baseball game played at Lakefront Park in Chicago, Illinois, was a 5–3 loss to Indianapolis on May 14, 1878. The White Stockings (later the Chicago Cubs) played at Lakefront Park from then until 1884.

1244. Major league baseball player born in Canada was Bill Phillips, born in St. John, New Brunswick, who played from 1879 to 1888.

1245. Reserve agreement among major league baseball club owners was made at a National League meeting on October 30, 1879. This first agreement, which was secret, provided that each club would be able to "reserve" five players with whom no other club could negotiate an interclub move. The "reserve clause" would be a major issue in baseball for almost a century.

BASEBALL (1880-1889)

1246. Cincinnati Reds regular season baseball game played at the Bank Street Grounds in Cincinnati, Ohio, was a 4–3 Chicago White Stockings win over Cincinnati on May 1, 1880. The Reds left the National League, did not play in 1881, and played in the American Association of Professionals from 1882 to 1890, then moving back to the National League.

1247. Sudden death rule to end games in major league baseball went into effect on the season's opening day, May 1, 1880. It provided that a game would end if the team batting last in the ninth inning was ahead when it came to bat or at any time it went ahead in the ninth inning. The Chicago White Stockings defeated the Cincinnati Reds 4–3 at Cincinnati, Ohio, playing under the new rules.

1248. "Rotating" pitchers in major league baseball were introduced on May 20, 1880, by Chicago team captain Cap Anson, who began to alternate using pitchers Fred Goldsmith and Larry Corcoran.

1249. Perfect game in professional baseball a complete game in which no opposing player reached first base, was pitched by Worcester pitcher John Lee Redmond as Worcester defeated Cleveland, 1–0, on June 10, 1880.

BASEBALL—(1880-1889)—*continued*

1250. Major league baseball team to win 21 games in a row was the Chicago White Stockings, which won its 21st game on July 8, 1880, defeating Providence 5–4.

1251. Night baseball game on record was played on September 2, 1880, at Nantasket Beach, Massachusetts, between amateur teams from two Boston department stores.

1252. Major league baseball player to hit four doubles in one game was John O'Rourke of the Boston Red Stockings, during Boston's 5–4 win over Providence on September 15, 1880.

1253. Professional baseball stadium in Manhattan was built at the Polo Grounds, literally a former polo field. The stadium was used by the newly organized Metropolitan baseball club, which rented the Polo Grounds in 1880. The Metropolitans defeated the Washington (D.C.) Nationals 4–2 in the first game played at the Polo Grounds, on September 29, 1880.

1254. Pitcher to lead the National League in wins and in losses in the same season was Boston's Jim Whitney, a rookie who won 31 games and lost 33 during the 1881 season.

1255. Major league baseball player to steal seven bases in a single game was Chicago's George Gore, on June 25, 1881, during a Chicago win over Providence. He led the league in runs scored during the 1881 and 1882 seasons.

1256. Grand slam home run in major league baseball was hit by Roger Connor of Troy, in an 8–7 win over Worcester, played at Albany, New York on September 10, 1881. Connor was one of the leading hitters in 19th-century baseball, with a career record of 136 home runs, which was surpassed only much later by Babe Ruth.

1257. American Association of Professionals a new professional baseball league, was founded on November 2, 1881. Generally called simply the American Association, it fielded five teams. It expanded to 12 teams in 1890 but did not survive, and was taken over by the National League in late 1891.

1258. Major league baseball professional umpire staff was authorized by the American Association in 1882, for the 1883 baseball season.

1259. National League player to lead the league in doubles in two consecutive years was King Kelly of Chicago, in 1881 and 1882.

1260. Umpire to be barred from major league baseball for dishonesty was former player Dick Higham, who in 1882 was banned for conspiring with gamblers to bring about losses for the Detroit baseball team.

1261. St. Louis Browns regular season baseball game played at a field called Sportsman's Park in St. Louis, Missouri, was a 9–7 win over Louisville on May 2, 1882. This Browns team would later be known as the St. Louis Cardinals.

1262. National League player to hit for the cycle (single, double, triple, and home run) in a single game was Curry Foley of Buffalo, on May 25, 1882.

1263. Major league pitcher to pitch left-handed and right-handed in the same game was Tony Mullane of Louisville in his team's 9–8 loss to Baltimore, on July 18, 1882. Mullane, who was also a switch-hitter, was one of baseball's most versatile players. He played many positions besides pitcher.

1264. National League team to score 35 runs in a single game was Chicago, in its 35–4 win over Cleveland, on July 24, 1882.

1265. Eighteen-inning shutout in major league baseball was the 1–0 Providence win over Detroit on August 17, 1882.

1266. Baseball player to lead the National League in batting average for two consecutive years was Dan Brouthers of Buffalo, who hit for .367 in 1882 and .371 in 1883.

1267. National League team to win three consecutive pennants was the Chicago White Stockings, from 1881 to 1883.

1268. New York Giants regular season baseball game played at Polo Grounds I in New York City was a 7–5 Giants win over Boston, Massachusetts, on May 1, 1883. Polo Grounds I was the original National League home of the Giants, where they would play until 1888. They played briefly at Oakland Park and St. George Grounds in 1889, and then moved into the second Polo Grounds, their home during 1889 and 1890.

1269. Philadelphia Phillies regular season baseball game played at Recreation Park in Philadelphia, Pennsylvania, was a 4–2 loss to Providence on May 1, 1883. The team moved to the Huntington Street Grounds in 1887.

1270. Major league pitcher to hit two home runs in a single game was John Mongomery Ward of Providence in his team's 10–9 win over the Boston Red Stockings on May 3, 1883.

1271. Baseball player to score 6 runs in a 9-inning National League game was Jim Whitney of the Boston Red Stockings on June 9, 1883, in a 30–9 Boston win over Detroit.

1272. Ladies' Day baseball game to which women were admitted free was hosted by the New York Giants on June 16, 1883.

1273. Union Association in baseball was established at a convention held in Pittsburgh, Pennsylvania, on September 12, 1883. This short-lived attempt to build a new major league in competition with the National League and American Association lasted for only one season, and did not draw enough well-known players and gate receipts to survive.

1274. African-American major league baseball player was Moses Fleetwood Walker, who was a catcher for the Toledo Mudhens in the American Association during the 1884 baseball season. His brother, Weldy Walker, also played for Toledo in 1884. Moses Walker played in 42 games in that season, and Weldy Walker in 5 games. Moses Walker had previously played for Oberlin College and had attended the University of Michigan law school, while Weldy Walker had also played for both schools.

1275. Major league baseball player to hit 27 home runs in a single season was Ned Williamson in 1884. His record would last until 1919, when Babe Ruth hit 29 home runs.

1276. Eastern League convention in baseball was held on January 4, 1884. This was not a new league, but rather a change of name from that of the Interstate League, formed in 1883. This minor league would later become the International League.

1277. Brooklyn Dodgers regular season baseball game played at Washington Park in Brooklyn, New York, was an 11–3 American Association win over Washington, D.C., on May 5, 1884. The team made its debut as the Brooklyn Bridegrooms of the American Association and would later become the Los Angeles Dodgers. Brooklyn played at Washington Park from 1884 to 1890, then moving to Eastern Park.

1278. Major league pitcher to strike out 19 batters in a single 9-inning game was Charlie Sweeney of Providence in a 2–1 Providence win over the Boston Red Stockings, on June 7, 1884. His record would stand until broken by Roger Clemens in 1986.

1279. African-American professional baseball team the Cuban Giants, was established at Babylon, Long Island, New York, in the summer of 1885. It was organized by Frank Thompson, headwaiter at the Argyle Hotel in Babylon, and initially consisted of Thompson and several of the African-American waiters at the hotel. It soon added players from other African-American teams and became the strongest African-American club of the 19th century. Weekly salaries paid by the team ranged from $12 to $18, depending on the position played.

1280. Batting and fielding cage in baseball was built in 1885, at Yale University, in New Haven, Connecticut, by Philip Batelle Stewart.

1281. St. Louis Browns American Association pennant came in 1885, when they led the league with a 79-33 winning record. The team would later be called the St. Louis Cardinals.

1282. Chicago White Stockings regular season baseball game played at West Side Park in Chicago, Illinois, was a 9–2 win over St. Louis, on June 6, 1885. The White Stockings played at West Side Park from 1885 to 1892. The team would later be known as the Chicago Cubs.

1283. Major league baseball player to get four triples, and five extra-base hits, in a single game was Philadelphia's George Strief, who hit four triples and a double in his team's 21–13 loss to Brooklyn, on June 25, 1885.

1284. Major league baseball players' union the Brotherhood of Ballplayers, was organized on October 22, 1885, led by New York shortstop John Montgomery Ward and several other New York players. Though kept secret at the start, the Brotherhood "went public" in 1886, and began negotiations with the club owners in 1887, though with little success.

1285. National League baseball game to be played in Kansas City Missouri, was a 6–5 Kansas City win over the Chicago White Stockings on April 30, 1886.

1286. American College Baseball Association was founded in 1887.

1287. Major league baseball team to score more than 1,000 runs in a single season was the St. Louis Browns, in the 1887 season.

1288. National Colored League organizing meeting was held in Baltimore, Maryland, on March 14, 1887. The six founding members of the new league were Baltimore, Boston, Louisville, New York, Philadelphia, and Pittsburgh.

BASEBALL—(1880-1889)—*continued*

1289. Philadelphia Phillies regular season baseball game played at Huntington Street Grounds in Philadelphia, Pennsylvania, was a 19–10 win over the New York Giants on April 30, 1887. The team moved to Shibe Park in 1927, back to the Huntington Street Grounds from 1928 to 1938, and then back to Shibe Park from 1938 to 1970.

1290. National Colored League baseball game was played in Pittsburgh, Pennsylvania, on May 6, 1887. Pittsburgh defeated the visiting New York team 11–8.

1291. Colored Championships of America tournament was held in New York City, in 1888. Participating were the Cuban Giants, who took first place; the Pittsburgh Keystones, second; the New York Gorhams, third; and the Norfolk Red Stockings, fourth.

1292. New York Giants National League pennant came in 1888, with an 84-47 winning record. The Giants would be one of the dominant teams in baseball during the next half century, winning 15 pennants between 1888 and 1937.

1293. Major league baseball player to pitch four consecutive shutouts was Ed Morris of the Pittsburgh Pirates, who pitched his fourth straight shutout, a 1–0 Pittsburgh win over the New York Giants, on September 15, 1888.

1294. United States baseball team to tour the world, and to visit Australia played its first exhibition in Sydney, Australia, in December 1888 and then went on to play in Ceylon, Egypt, Italy, France, and England before returning home in April 1889. The touring team was organized by Albert Spalding, who had led the first baseball tour of Britain in 1874.

1295. Major league baseball 26-game losing streak was set by the Louisville Colonels on June 22, 1889, with the loss of both games of a doubleheader to the St. Louis Browns.

1296. Players' League was organized by major league baseball players on July 4, 1889, after the Brotherhood of Ballplayers proved ineffective. The Players' League went into competition with the existing leagues, with many players joining the new organization. During the 1890 season, both the National League and the American Association were hard hit. The latter, which expanded in 1890, survived only a short while longer, merging into the National League in late 1891. The Players' League, however, quickly ran out of money and discontinued operations late in 1890.

1297. New York Giants regular season baseball game played at Polo Grounds II at 8th Avenue and 155th Street, in New York City, was a 7–5 Giants win over the Pittsburgh Pirates, on July 8, 1889. The Giants would move into their long-term home in the third Polo Grounds stadium in 1891. They would move to San Francisco in 1958.

1298. Baseball player to hit two home runs in his first major league game was Charles Reilly of Columbus, in a 10–6 Columbus victory over Philadelphia on October 9, 1889.

BASEBALL (1890-1899)

1299. African-American professional baseball team west of the Mississippi was organized in 1890. It was Nebraska's Lincoln Giants, a team that lasted for only a single season.

1300. Brooklyn Dodgers National League pennant came in 1890, with an 86-43 Brooklyn winning record.

1301. Major league baseball player to play in 577 consecutive games was George Pinckney, of the American Association's Brooklyn club. He played the final game of his record-breaking streak on May 1, 1890.

1302. Baseball player to lead the National League in stolen bases for two consecutive years was Billy Hamilton of Philadelphia, in 1890 and 1891.

1303. New York Giants regular season baseball game played at Polo Grounds III in New York City, was a 4–3 loss to the Boston Red Stockings on April 22, 1891. The Giants would make this final Polo Grounds their long-term home, from 1891 to 1957, leaving only when they moved to San Francisco, California, in 1958.

1304. Brooklyn Dodgers regular season baseball game played at Eastern Park in Brooklyn, New York, was a 6–5 loss to the New York Giants on April 27, 1891. Brooklyn played at Eastern Park from 1891 to 1897, then moving to Washington Park II.

1305. Two consecutive home runs by different players to open a major league baseball game were hit by Boston Red Stockings players Tom Brown and Bill Joyce, in a 13–5 victory over Baltimore on June 25, 1891.

1306. Scheduled Sunday games in the National League were authorized by the league in December 1891, after the American Association teams from Baltimore, Louisville, St. Louis, and Washington had survived the dissolution of that league and joined the National League.

1307. Scheduled Sunday game in the National League was played on April 17, 1892. The Cincinnati Reds defeated the visiting St. Louis Browns at Cincinnati, Ohio, 5–1.

1308. President of the United States to attend a major league baseball game was President Benjamin Harrison, at a 7–4 Cincinnati Reds win over Washington on June 6, 1892.

1309. Chicago White Stockings regular season baseball game played at the West Side Grounds in Chicago, Illinois, was a 13–12 loss to the Cincinnati Reds, on May 14, 1893. The White Stockings played at West Side Grounds from 1893 to 1915, and then settled down at Wrigley Field. From early in the 20th century, they would be known as the Chicago Cubs.

1310. Major league baseball player to hit a triple and a home run in the same inning was George Davis of the New York Giants, in an 11–10 Giants win over Chicago, on June 14, 1893.

1311. Major league baseball player to hit .440 in a single season was Hugh Duffy of the Boston Nationals, in 1894.

1312. National League player to hit 4 home runs in a 9-inning baseball game was Bobby Lowe of Boston, on May 30, 1894.

1313. Major league baseball player to hit five times in five at-bats during his first major league game was Fred Clarke of Louisville, in a 13–6 loss to Philadelphia on June 30, 1894.

1314. Major league baseball player to hit grand slam home runs in two consecutive games was Jimmy Bannon of Boston, on August 7, 1894.

1315. African-American college baseball league was organized in Atlanta, Georgia, in 1896. Founding members were Atlanta, Atlanta Baptist, Clark, and Morris Brown universities.

1316. National League player to hit 4 triples in a 9-inning baseball game was Bill Joyce of the New York Giants, against the Pittsburgh Pirates on May 18, 1897.

1317. Native American major league baseball player on record was Louis Sockalexis, a Penobscot who joined the Cleveland Spiders (later the Cleveland Indians) in 1897. During the first year of his brief career, Sockalexis emerged as a strong hitter, whose average was .338 early in 1897. However, he was injured early in July and played little thereafter.

1318. Brooklyn Dodgers regular season baseball game played at Washington Park II Brooklyn, New York, was a 6–4 loss to the Philadelphia Phillies on April 30, 1898. The team moved to Ebbets Field in 1913.

BASEBALL (1900-1909)
1319. Major league pitcher to have the best winning record in both the American League and the National League was Jack Chesbro, who led the American League with 28 wins and 6 losses for the Pittsburgh Pirates in 1902, and then led the National League with 41 wins and 12 losses for the New York Highlanders in 1904.

1320. Baseball pitcher to lead the American League in strikeouts was Cy Young, in 1901.

1321. Baseball player to lead the American League in batting average was hitting great Napoleon Lajoie of the Philadelphia Athletics, who led the new league in batting in 1901, its inaugural season. Lajoie's .422 would remain the league's top batting average.

1322. Baseball player to lead the American League in home runs was Napoleon Lajoie of the Philadelphia Athletics, with 14 home runs in 1901.

1323. Baseball player to lead the American League in runs scored was Napoleon Lajoie of the Philadelphia Athletics, with 105 runs in 1901.

1324. Baseball player to lead the American League in slugging average was Napoleon Lajoie of the Philadelphia Athletics, with a .635 slugging average in 1901.

1325. Baseball player to lead the American League in total bases was Napoleon Lajoie of the Philadelphia Athletics, with 345 total bases in 1901.

1326. Baseball team to win an American League pennant was the Chicago White Sox, in 1901, with a record of 83 wins and 53 losses.

1327. Pittsburgh Pirates National League pennant came in 1901, with a 90-49 winning record.

1328. Triple Crown hitter in the American League was Napoleon Lajoie of the Philadelphia Athletics, in 1901, with a .422 batting average, 14 home runs, and 145 runs batted in.

1329. American League convention on January 28, 1901, organized baseball's new major league into eight clubs: the Baltimore Orioles, Boston Puritans, Chicago White Sox, Cleveland Blues, Detroit Tigers, Milwaukee Brewers, Philadelphia Athletics, and Washington Sena-

BASEBALL—(1900-1909)—*continued*

tors. Ban Johnson was president of the new league. The American League offered highly competitive contracts and attracted many of the day's top players, quickly emerging as a very popular league, fully equal with the long-established National League.

1330. Baltimore Orioles regular season baseball game played at Oriole Park in Baltimore, Maryland, was a 10–0 win over the Boston Red Sox on April 6, 1901. The team played in Baltimore in 1901 and 1902, then moved to New York City as the New York Highlanders in 1903, later becoming the New York Yankees.

1331. American League baseball game saw the host team, the Chicago White Sox, defeat the visiting Cleveland Blues at Chicago, Illinois, 8–2, on April 24, 1901.

1332. Chicago White Sox regular season baseball game played at Southside Park which opened on April 24, 1901, was a 2–0 win over the Cleveland Blues. The game was the first to be played in the American League. The new stadium, with a capacity of 15,000, would be the home of the White Sox until they moved into Comiskey Park in 1910.

1333. Detroit Tigers regular season baseball game played at Bennett Park in Detroit, Michigan, was a 14–13 Detroit win over the Milwaukee Brewers, with an extraordinary 10-run rally in the bottom of the ninth inning, on April 24, 1901.

1334. Home run in the American League was hit by Cleveland Spiders second baseman Erve Beck on April 25, 1901, in the Detroit Tigers' 14–13 win over Cleveland.

1335. Philadelphia Athletics regular season baseball game played at Columbia Park in Philadelphia, Pennsylvania, was a 5–1 loss to the Washington Senators on April 26, 1901. The Athletics played at Columbia Park until 1908.

1336. Cleveland Indians regular season baseball game played at League Park I in Cleveland, Ohio, was a 4–3 win over the Milwaukee Brewers on April 29, 1901. The ball park would be the home of the team, then called the Cleveland Blues, from 1901 to 1909.

1337. Washington Senators regular season baseball game played in American League Park in Washington, D.C., was a 5–2 win over the Baltimore Orioles, on April 29, 1901. The Senators moved from American League Park into Griffith Stadium in 1903.

1338. Two home runs in a single American League game were hit by Dummy Hoy and Denny McFarland in the 19–9 Chicago White Sox win over the Detroit Tigers on May 1, 1901.

1339. Milwaukee Brewers regular season baseball game played at Lloyd Street Park in Milwaukee, Wisconsin, was an 11–3 Milwaukee loss to the Chicago White Sox, on May 4, 1901. The stadium was the home of the Brewers for only the 1901 season. In 1902, the team moved to St. Louis, Missouri, changing its name to the St. Louis Browns.

1340. Boston Red Sox regular season baseball game played at the Huntington Avenue Grounds in Boston, Massachusetts, was a 12–4 win over the Philadelphia Athletics, on May 8, 1901. The field would be the home of the Red Sox from 1901 to 1912, when Fenway Park opened. The team went by various names, including the Boston Puritans, Boston Pilgrims, Boston Somersets, and Plymouth Rocks, before adopting the name Red Sox in 1907.

1341. American League player to have 6 hits in a 9-inning baseball game was Mike Donlin of the Baltimore Orioles, who hit 6-for-6 on June 24, 1901.

1342. American League player to hit for the cycle (single, double, triple, and home run) in a single game was Harry Davis of the Philadelphia Athletics, on July 10, 1901.

1343. Baseball player to lead the American League in triples in two consecutive years was Jimmy Williams of the Baltimore Orioles, in 1901 and 1902.

1344. Colombian major league baseball player was Luis Castro, who played with the Philadelphia Athletics in 1902.

1345. Philadelphia Athletics American League pennant was won in 1902, with an 83-63 winning record, five games ahead of the runner-up St. Louis Browns. The World Series would not start until 1903. Connie Mack, who had begun his professional playing career in 1883, was in the second of his 50 years as the team's manager.

1346. Cincinnati Reds regular season baseball game played at The Palace of the Fans in Cincinnati, Ohio, was a 6–1 loss to the Chicago Cubs on April 17, 1902.

1347. St. Louis Browns regular season baseball game played at Sportsman's Park in St. Louis, Missouri, was a 5–2 Browns win over the Cleveland Broncos on April 23, 1902. This Browns team would later become the Baltimore Orioles.

1348. Three consecutive home runs in a single inning of an American League game were hit by Napoleon Lajoie, Charles "Piano Legs" Hickman, and Bill Bradley of the Cleveland Broncos on June 30, 1902, in Cleveland's win over the St. Louis Browns.

1349. Boston Red Sox World Series victory came in 1903, with a 5 games to 3 defeat of the Pittsburgh Pirates of the National League. The Red Sox, then called the Boston Pilgrims, had won the 1903 American League pennant with 91 wins and 47 losses. Boston went on to win the 1904 pennant too, but no World Series was held that year.

1350. Pitcher to pitch five complete games in a World Series was Deacon Phillippe of the Pittsburgh Pirates, in his team's 5 games to 3 loss to the Boston Pilgrims in the 1903 World Series. His five complete games became an enduring World Series record.

1351. Major league baseball game played by the New York Highlanders forerunners of the New York Yankees, was a 3–1 loss to the Washington Senators, on April 20, 1903. They had previously been the Baltimore Orioles.

1352. Washington Senators regular season baseball game played at Griffith Stadium in Washington, D.C., was a 3–1 win over the New York Giants, on April 22, 1903.

1353. New York Highlanders regular season baseball game played at Hilltop Park in New York City, was a 6–2 win over the Washington Senators, on May 1, 1903. The Highlanders had originated as the Baltimore Orioles and would become the New York Yankees. The team moved to the Polo Grounds in 1913, then to Yankee Stadium in 1923.

1354. Pitcher to win a World Series game was Deacon Phillippe of the Pittsburgh Pirates, who pitched a six-hitter on October 1, 1903, defeating Cy Young of the Boston Pilgrims in the first game of the 1903 World Series, at Boston, Massachusetts. Phillippe went on to pitch five complete games, of the eight that were played in the best-of-nine series.

1355. World Series was played in Boston, Massachusetts, and Pittsburgh, Pennsylvania, from October 1 to October 13, 1903, between the Pittsburgh Pirates of the National League and the Boston Pilgrims of the American League. Intended as a nine-game series, it was won by Boston, 5 games to 3.

1356. World Series game was played on October 1, 1903, between the American League's Boston Pilgrims and the National League's Pittsburgh Pirates, at Boston, Massachusetts. Pittsburgh defeated Boston 7–3, but Boston went on to win what was then a nine-game series, 5 games to 3.

1357. World Series home run was hit by Pittsburgh Pirates outfielder Jimmy Sebring, in the first World Series game, at Boston, Massachusetts, on October 1, 1903. Pittsburgh defeated the Boston Pilgrims, 7–3.

1358. Baseball pitcher to lead the American League in shutouts for two consecutive years was Cy Young of the Boston Red Sox, then called the Boston Pilgrims, in 1903 and 1904.

1359. Baseball player to lead the American League in batting average for two consecutive years was Napoleon Lajoie of the Cleveland Broncos, in 1903 and 1904.

1360. Baseball player to lead the American League in runs scored in two consecutive years was Patsy Dougherty of the Boston Red Sox, then called the Boston Pilgrims, in 1903 and 1904.

1361. Baseball player to lead the American League in slugging average for two consecutive years was Napoleon Lajoie of the Cleveland Broncos, in 1903 and 1904.

1362. Baseball player to lead the National League in hits in three consecutive years was Ginger Beaumont of the Pittsburgh Pirates, from 1902 to 1904.

1363. Baseball player to lead the National League in singles in three consecutive years was Ginger Beaumont of the Pittsburgh Pirates, from 1902 to 1904.

1364. Baseball team to win two consecutive American League pennants was the Boston Red Sox, then called the Boston Pilgrims, in 1903 and 1904.

1365. Major league baseball player of the 20th century to pitch for more than 40 wins in a single season was Jack Chesbro of the New York Highlanders, who had 41 wins in 1904, for an enduring major league record.

1366. Major league pitcher to pitch 30 consecutive complete games was Jack Chesbro of the New York Highlanders, during the 1904 season, also an enduring record.

1367. Baseball pitcher to lead the National League in strikeouts for three consecutive years was Christy Mathewson of the New York Giants, from 1903 to 1905.

BASEBALL—(1900-1909)—*continued*

1368. New York Giants World Series victory came in 1905, with a 4 games to 1 win over the Philadelphia Athletics. All five series games were shutouts, with Christy Mathewson pitching three of the Giants' four shutouts. The Giants had won the National League championship with a 105-48 winning record.

1369. Baseball player to lead the American League in singles in three consecutive years was Willy Keeler of the New York Highlanders, from 1904 to 1906.

1370. Major league pitcher of the 20th century to strike out four batters in a single inning was Hooks Wiltse of the New York Giants, on May 15, 1906, against the Cincinnati Reds. He struck out the next three batters he faced, as well, for a total of seven consecutive strikeouts in only two innings.

1371. Chicago White Sox World Series victory came in 1906, with a 4 games to 2 win by the American League champions over the Chicago Cubs of the National League. The series was played in Chicago, Illinois, from October 9 to October 14, 1906.

1372. World Series between two teams from the same city started on October 9, 1906, between the Chicago White Sox and the Chicago Cubs. The White Sox defeated the Cubs 4–2, for the team's first series win.

1373. Baseball pitcher to lead the American League in strikeouts for six consecutive years was Rube Waddell of the Philadelphia Athletics, from 1902 to 1907.

1374. Baseball player to lead the American League in home runs in four consecutive years was Harry Davis of the Philadelphia Athletics, from 1904 to 1907.

1375. Baseball player to lead the American League in triples in three consecutive years was Elmer Flick of the Cleveland Broncos, from 1905 to 1907.

1376. Chicago Cubs World Series victory came in 1907, with a 4 games to none victory (after a first-game tie) over the Detroit Tigers. The Cubs, one of the most powerful teams of the day, had won the National League pennant with a 107-45 record. They would again defeat Detroit in the World Series in 1908, and win another pennant in 1910.

1377. Detroit Tigers American League pennant was won in 1907, with a 90-63 record. The Tigers went on to lose the World Series to the Chicago Cubs, 4 games to none, after a first-game tie. The Tigers would repeat their pennant wins in 1908 and 1909, but lose the World Series to the Cubs again in 1908 and to the Pittsburgh Pirates in 1909.

1378. Baseball pitcher to lead the National League in winning percentage for three consecutive years was Ed Reulbach of the Chicago Cubs, from 1906 to 1908.

1379. Baseball team to win two consecutive World Series was the Chicago Cubs, in 1907 and 1908.

1380. Boys' baseball league was the Waynesburg Juvenile Baseball League, of Waynesburg, Pennsylvania, founded in 1908, composed of the Colts, North Side Cubs, and Times Pirates, the latter consisting of newpaper deliverers employed by the *Waynesburg Times*.

1381. Major league pitcher to throw two shutouts in one day was Ed Reulbach of the Chicago Cubs, who held the Brooklyn Dodgers scoreless, 5–0 and 3–0, on September 26, 1908.

1382. Baseball player to lead the American League in hits in three consecutive years was Ty Cobb of the Detroit Tigers, from 1907 to 1909.

1383. Baseball player to lead the American League in runs batted in for three consecutive years was Ty Cobb of the Detroit Tigers, from 1907 to 1909.

1384. Baseball player to lead the American League in total bases for three consecutive years was Ty Cobb of the Detroit Tigers, from 1907 to 1909.

1385. Baseball player to lead the National League in batting average for four consecutive years was Honus Wagner of the Pittsburgh Pirates, from 1906 to 1909.

1386. Baseball player to lead the National League in doubles in four consecutive years was Honus Wagner of the Pittsburgh Pirates, from 1906 to 1909.

1387. Baseball player to lead the National League in runs batted in for four consecutive years was Honus Wagner of the Pittsburgh Pirates, from 1906 to 1909.

1388. Baseball player to lead the National League in slugging average for three consecutive years was Honus Wagner of the Pittsburgh Pirates, from 1907 to 1909.

1389. Baseball player to lead the National League in total bases for four consecutive years was Honus Wagner of the Pittsburgh Pirates, from 1906 to 1909.

1390. Baseball team to win three consecutive American League pennants was the Detroit Tigers, from 1907 to 1909.

1391. Cork-centered baseball was introduced into major league baseball during the 1909 season. This livelier ball would become widely used in 1910, considerably affecting hitting records.

1392. Pittsburgh Pirates World Series victory came in 1909, with a 4 games to 3 win over the Detroit Tigers. The Pirates had won the National League pennant with a 110-42 winning record.

1393. Philadelphia Athletics regular season baseball game played at Shibe Park in Philadelphia, Pennsylvania, was an 8–1 win over the Boston Red Sox, on April 12, 1909. The Athletics would make Shibe Park their home until 1954, then moving to Kansas City, Missouri.

1394. Pittsburgh Pirates regular season baseball game played at Forbes Field Pittsburgh, Pennsylvania, was a 3–2 Pittsburgh loss to the Chicago Cubs on June 30, 1909. The Pirates played at Forbes Field from 1909 to 1970, then moving to Three Rivers Stadium.

1395. Unassisted triple play of the 20th century in major league baseball was made by shortstop Neal Ball of the Cleveland Broncos, in Cleveland's 6–1 win over the Boston Red Sox on July 19, 1909.

1396. Major league baseball pitcher to walk eight players in a single inning was William Gray of the Washington Senators, on August 28, 1909, against the Chicago White Sox; an enduring major league record.

BASEBALL (1910-1919)
1397. Baseball player to lead the National League in triples in two consecutive years was Mike Mitchell of the Cincinnati Reds, in 1909 and 1910.

1398. Philadelphia Athletics World Series victory came in 1910, with a 4 games to 1 victory over the Chicago Cubs. The Athletics had won their third American League pennant that year, with a 102-48 winning record.

1399. United States President to throw out the first ball in a major league baseball opening day game was William Howard Taft, in Washington, D.C., on April 14, 1910.

1400. Cleveland Indians regular season baseball game played at League Park II in Cleveland, Ohio, was a 5–0 loss to Detroit on April 21, 1910.

1401. Chicago White Sox regular season baseball game played at Comiskey Park in Chicago, Illinois, was a 2-0 Chicago loss to the St. Louis Browns on July 1, 1910. The stadium, with a capacity of 43,931, would be the team's home until replaced by the New Comiskey Park in 1991.

1402. African-American All-Star Team in professional baseball was selected by the *Indianapolis Freeman* in 1911. It included Harry Moore, Nate Harris, Pete Hill, Andrew Paine, Pete Booker, Rube Foster, Dan McClelland, and Charles Dougherty, all of the Leland Giants; John Henry Lloyd, Frank Duncan, and Bruce Petway of the Philadelphia Giants; and Felix Wallace of the St. Paul Gophers.

1403. Baseball pitcher to lead the American League in winning percentage for two consecutive years was Charles "Chief" Bender of the Philadelphia Phillies, in 1910 and 1911.

1404. Baseball player to lead the American League in runs scored in three consecutive years was Ty Cobb of the Detroit Tigers, from 1909 to 1911.

1405. Major league baseball players to be named Most Valuable Players of their leagues were Ty Cobb of the Detroit Tigers in the American League and Frank Schulte of the Chicago Cubs in the National League. The winners were announced on October 11, 1911.

1406. Baseball player to hit more than .400 in two consecutive years in the American League was Ty Cobb of the Detroit Tigers, with .420 in 1911, and .410 in 1912.

1407. Baseball player to lead the American League in slugging average for six consecutive years was Ty Cobb of the Detroit Tigers, from 1907 to 1912.

1408. Baseball player to lead the National League in bases on balls for two consecutive years was Jimmy Sheckard of the Chicago Cubs, in 1911 and 1912.

1409. Baseball player to lead the National League in stolen bases for four consecutive years was Bob Bescher of the Cincinnati Reds, from 1909 to 1912.

1410. Colored Intercollegiate Baseball Association (CIBA) was organized in 1912: Participating were Howard University, Virginia Union University, Hampton University, Shaw University, and Lincoln University of Pennsylvania.

BASEBALL—(1910-1919)—*continued*

1411. Triple Crown hitter in the National League was Heinie Zimmerman of the Chicago Cubs, who hit .372, with 14 home runs and 98 runs batted in, in 1912.

1412. Cincinnati Reds regular season baseball game played at Crosley Field in Cincinnati, Ohio, was a 10–6 Cincinnati win over the Chicago Cubs, on April 17, 1912. Cincinnati played at Crosley Field until 1970.

1413. Boston Red Sox regular season baseball game played at Fenway Park in Boston, Massachusetts, was an 11-inning, 7–6 Red Sox win over the New York Yankees on April 20, 1912. Guy Zinn of the Yankees was the first batter up and scored the first run. Charley Hall of the Red Sox was the winning pitcher. The new stadium, with a capacity of 38,871, became the permanent home of the Red Sox.

1414. Detroit Tigers regular season baseball game played at Tiger Stadium in Detroit, Michigan, was a 6–5, 11-inning win over the Cleveland Indians, on April 20, 1912. Napoleon Lajoie of the Indians was first up and made the first hit. In the same inning, Joe Jackson of the Indians scored the first run in the new ballpark. The stadium would become the permanent home of the Tigers.

1415. Brooklyn Dodgers regular season baseball game played at Ebbets Field in Brooklyn, New York, was a 1–0 loss to the Philadelphia Phillies on April 19, 1913.

1416. Boston Braves World Series victory came in 1914, when the Braves defeated the Philadelphia Athletics. The Braves, who finished the regular season with a 94-59 record, had been last in the league with less than two months of the season to go, but had won 68 of their last 87 games. They went on to sweep the Athletics in the Series, 4 games to none.

1417. Major league baseball pitcher of the 20th century to have an earned run average of less than 1.0 for a season was Dutch Leonard of the Boston Red Sox, who had an 0.96 earned run average in 1914.

1418. Baseball team to sweep the World Series was the Boston Braves, who won the fourth game of their 4-0 set of victories over the Philadelphia Athletics on October 13, 1914, by a score of 3–1.

1419. Baseball pitcher to lead the American League in shutouts for three consecutive years was Walter Johnson of the Washington Senators, from 1913 to 1915.

1420. Baseball player to lead the American League in batting average for nine consecutive years was Ty Cobb, from 1907 to 1915. Cobb also had the league's highest batting average from 1917 to 1919, and so led the league for 12 of 13 years.

1421. Baseball player to lead the National League in home runs in three consecutive years was Gavvy Cravath of the Philadelphia Phillies, from 1913 to 1915.

1422. Philadelphia Phillies National League pennant came in 1915, with a 90-62 winning record. The Phillies had entered the National League in 1883, and it took 32 years for them to win their first pennant. It would be 65 more years before they would win their first World Series, in 1980.

1423. Boston Braves regular season baseball game played at Braves Field in Boston, Massachusetts, was a 3–1 win over the St. Louis Cardinals on August 18, 1915. The Braves played at Braves Field until 1952, then moving to Milwaukee, Wisconsin.

1424. Major league baseball player of the 20th century to pitch 16 shutouts in a single season was Grover Cleveland Alexander of the Philadelphia Phillies, in 1916.

1425. Chicago Cubs regular season baseball game played at Wrigley Field in Chicago, Illinois, was an 11-inning, 7–6 win over the Cincinnati Reds on April 20, 1916. Red Killefer of the Reds was first up and hit a single, the first hit in the new ballpark. He also later scored the first run. Johnny Beall of the Reds hit the first home run in Wrigley Field.

1426. Baseball pitcher to lead the National League in earned run average for three consecutive years was Grover Cleveland Alexander of the Philadelphia Phillies, from 1915 to 1917.

1427. Baseball pitcher to lead the National League in shutouts for three consecutive years was Grover Cleveland Alexander of the Philadelphia Phillies, from 1915 to 1917.

1428. Baseball pitcher to lead the National League in strikeouts for four consecutive years was Grover Cleveland Alexander of the Philadelphia Phillies, from 1914 to 1917.

1429. Baseball player to lead the American League in stolen bases for three consecutive years was Ty Cobb of the Detroit Tigers, from 1915 to 1917.

1430. Baseball player to lead the National League in runs scored in two consecutive years was George Burns of the New York Giants, in 1916 and 1917.

1431. Major league baseball pitcher of the 20th century to pitch 19 straight wins was Rube Marquand of the New York Giants in 1917.

1432. Baseball pitcher to lead the American League in earned run average for two consecutive years was Walter Johnson of the Washington Senators, in 1918 and 1919.

1433. Baseball pitcher to lead the American League in strikeouts for eight consecutive years was Walter Johnson of the Washington Senators, from 1912 to 1919.

1434. Baseball player in the American League to hit four grand slam home runs in a single season was Babe Ruth of the Boston Red Sox, in 1919.

1435. Cuban, and first Hispanic-American, to play in a World Series game was Dolf (Adolfo) Luque, pitching in relief for the Cincinnati Reds in the third game of the 1919 World Series on October 3, 1919, against the Chicago White Sox, who won, 3–0. Luque's 27 wins in 1923 led the National League. He also pitched in the 1933 series.

1436. Cincinnati Reds World Series victory came on October 9, 1919, with a 5 games to 3 win over the Chicago White Sox, in the best-of-nine-games series. The Reds had won the National League pennant with a 96-44 record. This was the series that generated the "Black Sox" scandal, in which eight White Sox players were ultimately charged with having been bribed by gamblers to "throw" the series. None were convicted, but all were banned from baseball by the new commissioner, Kenesaw Mountain Landis.

BASEBALL (1920-1929)
1437. American League team to top 1 million paying customers at home in a single season was the New York Yankees, in 1920, with 1,289,422.

1438. Cleveland Indians World Series victory came in 1920, with a 7-game defeat of the Brooklyn Dodgers of the National League. Cleveland had won the 1920 American League pennant with 98 wins and 56 losses. It would be 28 years before Cleveland won another pennant, in 1948. They then also went on to win the World Series, defeating the Boston Braves.

1439. Major league baseball player to get 257 hits in a single season was Rogers Hornsby of the St. Louis Cardinals, in 1920.

1440. Unassisted triple play in the World Series was made by Cleveland Indians shortstop Bill Wambsganss, in the fifth game of the 1920 World Series, at Cleveland, Ohio, an 8–1 Cleveland win over the Brooklyn Dodgers.

1441. Convention of the Negro National League was held in Kansas City, Missouri, on February 13, 1920. The league's prime mover was Rube Foster, who had been a star pitcher for several baseball clubs and organized the Chicago American Giants in 1911. Foster became the chairman and undisputed leader of the Negro National League, which operated from 1920 to 1931, becoming the first substantial, relatively long-term African-American baseball league.

1442. Home run hit by Babe Ruth as a New York Yankees player was during a 6–0 win over his former team, the Boston Red Sox, at New York City on May 1, 1920.

1443. National League game to last 26 innings was the Brooklyn Dodgers' win over the Boston Braves, at Boston, Massachusetts, on May 1, 1920.

1444. Negro National League game was played on May 2, 1920. The Indianapolis ABCs defeated the Chicago American Giants, 4–2.

1445. St. Louis Cardinals regular season baseball game played at Sportsman's Park II in St. Louis, Missouri, was a 6–2 loss to the Pittsburgh Pirates on July 1, 1920. The park would be renamed Busch Stadium in 1953.

1446. Baseball player to die of injuries suffered during a major league baseball game was Cleveland Indians shortstop Raymond Chapman, who was hit in the head by a pitch thrown by New York Yankees pitcher Carl May at New York City's Polo Grounds on August 16, 1920. Chapman died the next day.

1447. Brothers to play on opposing teams in a World Series were Jimmy Johnston of the Brooklyn Dodgers and Wheeler Johnston of the Cleveland Indians, in the second game of the 1920 World Series, on October 6, 1920.

1448. Grand slam home run in World Series history was hit by Elmer Smith of the Cleveland Indians, in his team's 8–1 win over the Brooklyn Dodgers in the fifth game of the 1920 series, at Cleveland, Ohio, on October 10, 1920.

1449. Home run by a pitcher in a World Series was hit by Cleveland Indians pitcher Jim Bagby, in his team's 8–1 win over the Brooklyn Dodgers in the fifth game of the 1920 series, at Cleveland, Ohio, on October 10, 1920.

BASEBALL—(1920-1929)—*continued*

1450. Baseball player to have 100 extra-base hits in a single American League season was Babe Ruth of the New York Yankees, who hit 59 home runs, 44 doubles, and 16 triples for a total of 119 extra-base hits in 1921.

1451. Baseball player to lead the American League in bases on balls for two consecutive years was Babe Ruth of the New York Yankees, in 1920 and 1921.

1452. Baseball player to lead the National League in bases on balls for three consecutive years was George Burns of the New York Giants, from 1919 to 1921.

1453. Major league baseball player of the 20th century to score 177 runs in a single season was Babe Ruth of the New York Yankees, in 1921.

1454. New York Yankees American League pennant was won in 1921, with a 98-55 winning record. The Yankees lost the World Series to the New York Giants, 4 games to 2. The Yankees would win 35 pennants from 1921 to 1998, far more than any other team in major league baseball.

1455. World Series to be won by a team that lost the first two games of the Series occurred in 1921, when the New York Giants lost the first two games to the New York Yankees and came back to win the series 5 games to 3.

1456. Commissioner of Baseball was federal judge Kenesaw Mountain Landis, who became commissioner on January 21, 1921, following the 1920 Chicago White Sox ("Black Sox") scandal. Landis remained commissioner until his death in 1944.

1457. No-hitter on record in Negro League history was pitched by Bill Gatewood of the Detroit Stars, in a 4–0 victory over the Cuban Stars on June 6, 1921.

1458. Major league baseball game to be broadcast on radio was an 8–5 Pittsburgh Pirates win at Pittsburgh, Pennsylvania, over the visiting Philadelphia Phillies, carried by Pittsburgh station KDKA, on August 5, 1921, with Harold Arlin announcing.

1459. Major league baseball player to hit 59 home runs in a single season was Babe Ruth, who hit his 59th on October 2, 1921, in a 7–6 New York Yankees win over the Boston Red Sox.

1460. World Series game to be broadcast by radio was carried by Pittsburgh, Pennsylvania, station KDKA, with announcer Graham McNamee, on October 5, 1921. It was the first game of the 1921 World Series, between the New York Yankees and the New York Giants, played at the Polo Grounds in New York City. The Yankees won 3–0, and went on to win the series 5 games to 3.

1461. Baseball player to steal more than 30 bases and hit more than 30 home runs in a single season in the American League was Kenny Williams of the St. Louis Browns, who stole 37 bases and hit 39 home runs in 1922.

1462. Woman known to have played for a major league baseball team was Elizabeth Murphy, in an exhibition game between the Boston Red Sox and a team drawn from several American League clubs, played on August 14, 1922.

1463. Baseball player to lead the American League in doubles in four consecutive years was Tris Speaker of the Chicago White Sox, from 1920 to 1923.

1464. Major league baseball player to have 170 walks in a single season was Babe Ruth of the New York Yankees, in 1923.

1465. New York Yankees World Series victory came in 1923, with a 4 games to 2 win over the New York Giants. The Yankees had won the American League pennant with a 98-54 record. The Yankees would win 25 World Series between 1921 and 1999, far more than any other team in major league baseball.

1466. World Series to be broadcast nationally on radio was the 1923 series, between the New York Yankees and the New York Giants won the by Yankees 4 games to 2.

1467. New York Yankees regular season baseball game played at Yankee Stadium in New York City was a 4–1 win over the Boston Red Sox on April 18, 1923, attended by more than 74,000 people. Chick Fewster of the Red Sox was first up, and George Burns of the Red Sox had the first hit, but the first home run in the "house that Ruth built" was hit by Babe Ruth. Yankee Stadium became the permanent home of the Yankees.

1468. World Series to reach total receipts of more than $1 million was the six-game "subway series" between the New York Yankees and the New York Giants, played in New York City from October 10 to October 15, 1923.

1469. Baseball player to lead the American League in slugging average for seven consecutive years was Babe Ruth, playing for the Boston Red Sox in 1918 and 1919, and the New York Yankees from 1920 to 1924.

1470. Baseball team to win four consecutive National League pennants was the New York Giants, from 1921 to 1924.

1471. Washington Senators World Series victory came in 1924, with a 4 games to 3 win over the New York Giants. The Senators had won the American League pennant with a 92-62 record. The Senators won the pennant again in 1925 but lost the World Series to the Pittsburgh Pirates.

1472. Negro Leagues World Series was won by the Kansas City Monarchs, who defeated the Hillsdale team, of Philadelphia, Pennsylvania, 5 games to 4, in a series that began on October 3, 1924.

1473. Baseball player to lead the National League in batting average for six consecutive years was Rogers Hornsby of the St. Louis Cardinals, from 1920 to 1925.

1474. Baseball player to lead the National League in slugging average for six consecutive years was Rogers Hornsby of the St. Louis Cardinals, from 1920 to 1925.

1475. Triple Crown hitter in two seasons in the National League was Rogers Hornsby of the St. Louis Cardinals, in 1922 and 1925. In 1922, he hit .401 with 42 home runs and 152 runs batted in. In 1935 he hit .403 with 39 home runs and 143 runs batted in.

1476. St. Louis Cardinals World Series victory came in 1926, with a 4 games to 3 win over the New York Yankees. The Cardinals had won the National League pennant with an 89-65 winning record.

1477. Major league baseball player to score four runs in a single World Series game was Babe Ruth of the New York Yankees, on October 6, 1926.

1478. National League team to top 1 million paying customers at home in a single season was the Chicago Cubs, in 1927, with 1,159,168.

1479. New York Yankees baseball player to be named Most Valuable Player was first baseman Lou Gehrig, in 1927. Although overshadowed by Babe Ruth, as was so during most of his career, Gehrig had an extraordinary year in 1927. He hit .373, with 47 home runs, 52 doubles, and 175 runs batted in, and scored 149 runs. His slugging average was .765.

1480. Major league baseball player of the 20th century to reach 4,000 hits was Ty Cobb of the Philadelphia Athletics, against the Detroit Tigers, on July 18, 1927.

1481. Major league baseball player to hit 60 home runs in a single season was Babe Ruth of the New York Yankees, who hit his 60th on August 30, 1927. His record would stand until Roger Maris hit 61 home runs in 1961.

1482. Baseball pitcher to lead the National League in strikeouts for seven consecutive years was Dazzy Vance of the Brooklyn Dodgers, from 1922 to 1928.

1483. Baseball player to lead the American League in bases on balls for three consecutive years was Babe Ruth of the New York Yankees, from 1926 to 1928.

1484. Major league baseball player to hit for a World Series average of .625 was Babe Ruth, in the 1928 World Series, a 4–0 New York Yankees sweep of the St. Louis Cardinals.

1485. Major league baseball player to steal home 50 times in the course of his career was Ty Cobb, then of the Philadelphia Athletics, who stole home for the 50th time on June 15, 1928, in a 12–5 Philadelphia win over the Cleveland Indians.

1486. Baseball player to hit a home run the first time he came to bat in an American League game was Earl Averill of the Cleveland Indians in a 5–4 Cleveland win over Detroit Tigers on April 16, 1929.

1487. Major league baseball player to hit 500 home runs was Babe Ruth, who reached that milestone on August 11, 1929, in a New York Yankees win over the Cleveland Indians.

BASEBALL (1930-1939)

1488. Professional baseball team in Japan was Tokyo's Yomiuri Giants, which was organized in 1934, to play against a visiting United States touring team.

1489. Baseball player to have 100 extra-base hits in a season in the National League was Chuck Klein of the Philadelphia Phillies, who hit 40 home runs, 59 doubles, and 8 triples for a total of 107 extra-base hits in 1930.

1490. Major league baseball player to bat in 190 runs in a single season was Hack Wilson of the Chicago Cubs, in 1930.

1491. Major league baseball player to earn $80,000 per year was Babe Ruth, who signed with the New York Yankees for two years, at $80,000 per year, on March 8, 1930.

BASEBALL—(1930-1939)—*continued*

1492. Professional baseball game played at night under lights was played between Muskogee and Independence of the Western Association, on April 28, 1930.

1493. Negro League game played at Yankee Stadium was between the New York Lincoln Giants and the Baltimore Black Sox, in a game that drew an estimated 20,000 on July 9, 1930.

1494. Baseball pitcher to lead the American League in winning percentage for three consecutive years was Lefty Grove of the Philadelphia Athletics, from 1929 to 1931.

1495. Baseball player to be named Associated Press Athlete of the Year was Pepper Martin, in 1931.

1496. Baseball player to lead the American League in home runs for six consecutive years was Babe Ruth of the New York Yankees, from 1926 to 1931. Ruth had also led the league in home runs from 1919 to 1921, and in 1923 and 1924, for a total of 11 in 13 years.

1497. Philadelphia Athletics baseball player to be named Most Valuable Player was pitcher Lefty Grove, in 1931. The Athletics won their third consecutive American League pennant that year, with their best-ever 107-45 winning record. Grove led the way, with 31 wins and 4 losses, an .888 winning average, and a 2.06 earned run average, all league-leading figures. The team would become the Oakland Athletics in 1968.

1498. St. Louis Cardinals baseball player to be named Most Valuable Player was second baseman Frank Frisch, in 1931. Frisch hit .311, with 161 hits, and scored 96 runs. He led the Cardinals to a 101-53 regular season record and a National League pennant, and went on to lead the team in a 4 games to 3 World Series victory over the Philadelphia Athletics.

1499. Woman baseball team owner on record was Lucille Thomas, who bought the Topeka, Kansas, team of the Western League in January 1931.

1500. Woman to pitch against a major league baseball team was Jackie (Virne) Mitchell. She pitched for the Chattanooga team of the Southern Association against the New York Yankees in an exhibition game, on April 1, 1931, striking out both Babe Ruth and Lou Gehrig.

1501. Major league baseball player to reach a career total of 600 home runs was Babe Ruth of the New York Yankees, who reached that mark in an August 21, 1931, game against the Cleveland Indians.

1502. Major league baseball manager to win pennants in both the American and National Leagues was Joseph McCarthy of the New York Yankees. After winning his first pennant as manager of the National League's Chicago Cubs in 1929, he won the first of his eight pennants as Yankees manager in 1932. McCarthy's Yankee teams would win seven World Series, including four in a row, from 1936 to 1939.

1503. Philadelphia Phillies baseball player to be named Most Valuable Player was outfielder Chuck Klein, in 1932. One of the most notable power hitters of the era, Klein had hit .348, scored 152 runs, and had 226 hits, 38 of them home runs, all league-leading figures. He would win the Triple Crown in 1933 with a .368 batting average, 28 home runs, and 120 runs batted in.

1504. Baseball player to hit four home runs in a single regular season American League game was Lou Gehrig of the New York Yankees, on June 3, 1932.

1505. Mexican major league baseball player was Baldomero Almada, who played with the Boston Red Sox in 1933.

1506. New York Giants baseball player to be named Most Valuable Player was pitcher Carl Hubbell, in 1933. Hubbell won a league-leading 23 games, as well as leading the league with a 1.66 earned run average and 10 shutouts. He led the Giants to a pennant and a World Series win over the Washington Senators. He would win more than 20 games for five consecutive years, and repeat as Most Valuable Player in 1936.

1507. Revived Negro National League began operations in 1933. This league lasted until 1948, and then merged with the Negro American League, which operated until 1960.

1508. Baseball player to hit a home run in major league baseball's All-Star Game was Babe Ruth, on July 6, 1933, in a 4–2 American League win over the National League, at Comiskey Park in Chicago, Illinois.

1509. Major league baseball All-Star Game was played at Comiskey Park, in Chicago, Illinois, on July 6, 1933. The American League defeated the National League 4–2. The game was a feature of the Chicago World's Fair.

1510. Negro League East-West All-Star Game was played at Comiskey Park, in Chicago, Illinois, on September 10, 1933. The West defeated the East 11–7.

1511. Detroit Tigers baseball player to be named Most Valuable Player was catcher and player-manager Mickey Cochrane in 1934. Cochrane had also won the American League Most Valuable Player Award in 1928. In 1934, Cochrane led the Tigers to a pennant, but lost the World Series to the St. Louis Cardinals.

1512. Night baseball games authorized by the National League were in 1934, with a limit of seven night games per season, to begin in the 1935 season.

1513. Major league baseball player to hit 700 home runs was Babe Ruth, who reached that mark in Detroit, Michigan, on July 13, 1934.

1514. Major league baseball player to reach a total of 2,000 bases on balls was Babe Ruth, at Cleveland, Ohio, on July 17, 1934. Ruth's career total would be 2,056, an enduring record.

1515. Chicago Cubs baseball player to be named Most Valuable Player was catcher Gabby Hartnett, in 1935. He batted .344, with 142 hits, including 13 home runs, 32 doubles, and 6 triples; and his fielding average was .984.

1516. Detroit Tigers World Series victory came in 1935, with a 4 games to 2 win over the Chicago Cubs of the National League. The Tigers had won the 1935 American League pennant with a 93-58 record.

1517. Major league baseball night game was played on May 24, 1935, at Crosley Field, in Cincinnati, Ohio, between the Cincinnati Reds and the Philadelphia Phillies. The 2–1 Cincinnati win began after President Franklin D. Roosevelt, in Washington, D.C., pushed a button that switched on the massive set of lights on the eight light towers at Crosley Field.

1518. Major league baseball player to hit 714 home runs was Babe Ruth, who hit his final three career home runs at Pittsburgh, Pennsylvania, on May 25, 1935.

1519. Baseball player to hit a home run in a National League night game was Babe Herman of the Cincinnati Reds, on July 10, 1935.

1520. Major league baseball players to be named to the Baseball Hall of Fame were Ty Cobb, Babe Ruth, Honus Wagner, Christy Mathewson, and Walter Johnson, in 1936.

1521. Professional baseball league in Japan was organized in 1936. The first league game was an 8–5 win by Nagoya over Daitokyo.

1522. Baseball pitcher to have 17 strikeouts in a single American League game was 17-year-old Cleveland Indians rookie Bob Feller, in a 5–2 Cleveland win over the Philadelphia Athletics on September 13, 1936. Feller's 17 strikeouts also tied the major league single game strikeout record.

1523. Negro American League operations began in 1937. The new league lasted until 1960, taking over the Negro National League in 1948. Both leagues slowly failed after the color bar was broken in major league baseball.

1524. Night baseball games were authorized by the American League in 1937.

1525. Boston Red Sox baseball player to be named Most Valuable Player was first baseman Jimmie Foxx, in 1938. A perennial All-Star, Foxx was one of the top power hitters of his era, who batted in a league-leading 175 runs in 1938, won the Triple Crown in 1932, and led the American League in home runs four times.

1526. Cincinnati Reds baseball player to be named Most Valuable Player was catcher Ernie Lombardi, in 1938. Lombardi batted a league-leading .342, with 167 hits, including 19 home runs, 30 doubles, and a triple. His fielding average was .985.

1527. Puerto Rican Professional Baseball League began operations in 1938. Now the oldest "winter league," it has served as a staging ground for many Puerto Rican baseball players headed for the major leagues, as well as an off-season home for many major league players.

1528. Major league baseball player to hit 23 grand slam home runs was Lou Gehrig of the New York Yankees, reaching that milestone during an 11–3 Yankees win over the Philadelphia Athletics on August 20, 1938; an enduring record.

1529. Major league baseball team to win three consecutive World Series was the New York Yankees, who—after winning the series in 1936 and 1937—swept the 1938 World Series against the Chicago Cubs four games to none, winning the final game 8–3 on October 9, 1938.

1530. Major league baseball player to pitch two successive no-hitters was Johnny Vander Meer of the Cincinnati Reds. His first no-hitter, against the Boston Braves, was on June 11, 1938. His second came four days later, on June 15, against the Brooklyn Dodgers during the first night game at Ebbets Field in Brooklyn, New York.

BASEBALL—(1930-1939)—*continued*

1531. Baseball pitcher to lead the American League in earned run average for six consecutive years was Lefty Grove, from 1934 to 1939. From 1929 to 1932, he had become the first pitcher to lead the American League in earned runs for four consecutive years. Grove therefore led the league in earned run average for 10 of the 11 years from 1929 to 1939.

1532. Baseball team to win four consecutive American League pennants was the New York Yankees, from 1936 to 1939.

1533. Little League baseball league was founded by Carl Stotz, George Bebble, and Bert Bebble, as a three-team league in Williamsport, Pennsylvania, in 1939.

1534. Venezuelan major league baseball player was Alejandro Carrasquel, who played with the Washington Senators in 1939.

1535. Major league baseball player to play 2,130 consecutive games was New York Yankees great Lou Gehrig. Suffering from amyotrophic lateral sclerosis ("Lou Gehrig's disease"), he benched himself on May 2, 1939, ending his recordbreaking streak at 2,130 games and simultaneously ending his career.

1536. Baseball player to hit a home run in an American League night game was Frankie Hayes of the Philadelphia Athletics, on May 16, 1939.

1537. Baseball game to be televised was the intercollegiate Princeton-Columbia game, on May 17, 1939. The contest, announced by Bill Stern, was played at Columbia's Baker Field in New York City and broadcast over fledgling New York television station W2XBS.

1538. Major league baseball player whose uniform number was retired at the end of his career was Lou Gehrig, at a Yankee Stadium tribute on July 4, 1939. Gehrig died of amyotrophic lateral sclerosis ("Lou Gehrig's disease") on June 2, 1941.

1539. Major league baseball games to be televised were a doubleheader between the Brooklyn Dodgers and the Cincinnati Reds, played at Ebbets Field in Brooklyn, New York, on August 26, 1939, and broadcast over New York television station W2XBS. Dodgers announcer Red Barber called both games.

BASEBALL (1940-1949)

1540. Shutout in a major league baseball All-Star Game was a 4–0 win by the National League over the American League in the 1940 All-Star Game.

1541. Brooklyn Dodgers baseball player to be named Most Valuable Player was first baseman Dolph Camilli, in 1941. Camilli led the Dodgers to a National League pennant in 1941, with a 100-54 winning record, although the Dodgers lost the World Series to the New York Yankees. A leading power hitter, Camilli led the league in home runs, with 34, and in runs batted in, with 120. He had 151 hits, scored 92 runs, and hit .285.

1542. Major league baseball player to hit safely in 56 consecutive games was New York Yankees outfielder Joe DiMaggio, from May 15, 1941, to July 1, 1941, for an enduring record.

1543. Puerto Rican major league baseball player was Hiram Bithorn, who played with the Chicago Cubs in 1942.

1544. Batting helmet in professional baseball was introduced by Willie Wells, manager of the Newark Eagles in the Negro League, after he had been hit in the head during a July 4, 1942, game against the Baltimore Elite Giants.

1545. Baseball player to lead the American League in stolen bases for five consecutive years was George Case of the Washington Senators, from 1939 to 1943.

1546. Women's professional baseball league on record was the All-American Girls Professional Baseball League, founded in the United States Midwest in 1943, which continued in operation until 1954. The formation and wartime years of this women's league were the basis of the 1992 fiction film *A League of Their Own*, directed by Penny Marshall.

1547. St. Louis Browns American League pennant was won in 1944, with an 89-65 record. The 1944 World Series was an all–St. Louis series, with the Browns losing to the St. Louis Cardinals, 4 games to 2. The Browns would become the Baltimore Orioles in 1953.

1548. African-American baseball player of the 20th century to join the previously all-white mainstream baseball leagues was Jackie (John Roosevelt) Robinson, a former University of California at Los Angeles baseball, football, and basketball star, who had played one season with the Kansas City Monarchs of baseball's Negro League. On October 23, 1945, Branch Rickey, head of the Brooklyn Dodgers organization, announced that Jackie Robinson had signed with the Dodgers. On October 30, 1945, Robinson signed a contract for 1946 with the Montreal Royals of the International League, affiliated with the Dodgers organization.

1549. American League team to top 2 million paying customers at home in a single season was the New York Yankees, in 1946, with 2,265,512.

1550. African-American baseball player in the International League in the 20th century was Jackie Robinson, who played his first game with the Montreal Royals, against Jersey City, New Jersey, on April 18, 1946. Playing second base, Robinson led Montreal to the 1946 International League pennant, batting a league-leading .349.

1551. Baseball player to score 6 runs in a 9-inning American League game was Boston Red Sox shortstop Johnny Pesky, on May 8, 1946, in a 14–0 Boston win over the Chicago White Sox.

1552. Major league baseball playoff series was a best-2-of-3 series between the St. Louis Cardinals and the Brooklyn Dodgers, which had finished the regular season tied, each with 96 wins and 58 losses. St. Louis swept the series, played at Ebbets Field, Brooklyn, defeating the Dodgers 4–2 on October 1, 1946, and 8–4 on October 3.

1553. Boston Braves baseball player to be named Most Valuable Player was third baseman Bob Elliott, in 1947. A strong hitter and fielder, Elliott hit .317, with 176 hits, including 22 home runs, 35 doubles, and 5 triples, and batted in 113 runs, while scoring 93. He also had a league-leading .956 fielding average.

1554. College baseball team to win the National Collegiate World Championship was the University of California, which defeated Yale University 8–7, in 1947.

1555. Little League World Series was played at the Max M. Brown Memorial Park in Williamsport, Pennsylvania, the original home of the Little Leagues. The Maynard Midgets of Williamsport won the series on August 21, 1947, over the Lock Haven team.

1556. Major league baseball player to be named Rookie of the Year, and the first African-American to win the award was Jackie Robinson of the Brooklyn Dodgers, in 1947. Playing under extremely difficult personal conditions, because of the widespread racism he encountered, power hitter Robinson still hit .297, scored 125 runs, and had 175 hits, including 12 home runs, 31 doubles, and 5 triples. In the first two years, a single award was given for both leagues.

1557. Triple Crown hitter in 2 seasons in the American League was Ted Williams of the Boston Red Sox, in 1942 and 1947. In 1942, he had a .356 batting average, with 36 home runs and 137 runs batted in. In 1947, his batting average was .343, with 32 home runs and 114 runs batted in.

1558. African-American baseball player in the modern major leagues was Jackie Robinson, who joined the Brooklyn Dodgers of the National League in March 1947, and played his first game with the Dodgers on March 15, at first base, in a 5–3 Brooklyn win over the Boston Braves. His first major league hit came on March 17, also against the Braves.

1559. African-American baseball player to play for the St. Louis Browns was Henry "Hank" Thompson, who joined the club in July 1947, playing at second base. That month he was joined on the team by another African-American, center fielder Willard Brown.

1560. African-American baseball player in the American League was Larry Doby, who played his first game with the Cleveland Indians on July 5, 1947, with Cleveland losing to the Chicago White Sox 6–5. Doby, who had previously played in the Negro Leagues, became a perennial All-Star and later was a coach with several teams, becoming manager of the White Sox during the 1978 season.

1561. Two African-American major league baseball players to play for the same club in the same game were Henry "Hank" Thompson, at second base, and Willard Brown, in center field, who played together for the St. Louis Browns against the Boston Red Sox on July 20, 1947.

1562. African-American baseball player to hit a home run in the American League was Willard Brown of the St. Louis Browns, on August 13, 1947.

1563. African-American player to be a pitcher in major league baseball was Dan Bankhead of the Brooklyn Dodgers, who made his major league debut on August 26, 1947, pitching in relief against the Pittsburgh Pirates.

1564. World Series broadcast on television was the 1947, series, which began on September 30, 1947 with a 5–3 New York Yankees win over the Brooklyn Dodgers. The Yankees went on to win the series 4 games to 3.

1565. Major league baseball player to hit a home run as a pinch hitter in the World Series was Yogi Berra of the New York Yankees on October 2, 1947, during the third game of the World Series, a 9–8 Yankees win over the Brooklyn Dodgers.

BASEBALL—(1940-1949)—*continued*

1566. Boston Braves baseball player to be named Rookie of the Year was shortstop Alvin Dark, in 1948. He had a .322 batting average, and 176 hits, including 39 doubles, 6 triples, and 3 home runs. along with a .963 fielding average.

1567. Cleveland Indians baseball player to be named Most Valuable Player was shortstop and player-manager Lou Boudreau, in 1948. In that year, Boudreau hit .355 and 18 home runs, while batting in 106 runs and scoring 116. His team won the American League pennant and the World Series.

1568. African-American baseball player to be named Most Valuable Player in the National League was second baseman Jackie Robinson of the Brooklyn Dodgers, in 1949.

1569. African-American baseball player to lead one of the major leagues in batting average was Jackie Robinson, who led the National League in 1949 with a .342 batting average.

1570. African-American baseball player to play for the New York Giants was Henry "Hank" Thompson, who joined the Giants in 1949. In 1947 he had been the first African-American to play for the St. Louis Browns.

1571. Baltimore Orioles baseball player to be named Rookie of the Year was Roy Sievers in 1949. A slugging outfielder, Sievers batted in 75 runs in 1949, with 16 home runs and a .306 batting average. In 1957, he would lead the American League with 114 runs batted in and 42 home runs.

1572. Baseball player to lead the American League in bases on balls for four consecutive years was Ted Williams of the Boston Red Sox, from 1946 to 1949.

1573. College baseball player to win the Outstanding Player Award was Charles Teague of Wake Forest University, in 1949.

1574. African-American major league baseball players to appear in an All-Star Game were Jackie Robinson, Roy Campanella, and Don Newcombe for the National League, and Larry Doby for the American League, on July 12, 1949.

BASEBALL (1950-1959)

1575. Boston Red Sox baseball player to be named Rookie of the Year was first baseman Walt Dropo, in 1950. A leading power hitter, Dropo batted in a league-leading 141 runs, hit 34 home runs, and batted .322 in 1950.

1576. College baseball player to pitch 20 bases on balls in a College World Series was Rod Keogh of Washington State University, in 1950.

1577. College baseball team to win two consecutive National Collegiate World Championships was the University of Texas, which defeated Wake Forest University 10–3 in 1949 and Washington State University 3–0 in 1950.

1578. Perfect game in the Little League World Series was pitched by Fred Shapiro of the winning Delaware, New Jersey, team in 1950.

1579. African-American baseball player to play for the Boston Braves was Sam Jethroe, who played his first game for the Braves on April 18, 1950. Jethroe, who had starred with the Cleveland Buckeyes in the Negro League, became 1950 Rookie of the Year and led both leagues with 35 stolen bases. In 1951, he again led both leagues with 35 stolen bases.

1580. College baseball player to pitch a no-hitter was Jim Ehrler of the University of Texas, against Tufts University, on June 19, 1950.

1581. Major league baseball game in which 11 home runs were hit was the Detroit Tigers' 11–10 win over the New York Yankees on June 23, 1950.

1582. African-American baseball players to join the New York Yankees organization were Elston Howard and Frank Barnes, who joined the Yankees' Muskegon farm team in July 1950. Howard would move up to the Yankees in 1955.

1583. African-American baseball player to play for the Chicago White Sox was Sam Hairston, who played briefly for the White Sox during 1951.

1584. Hispanic-American major league baseball player to play in the All-Star Game was Chicago White Sox shortstop Alfonso "Chico" Carrasquel, in 1951. Carrasquel later became a very well known baseball broadcaster in Venezuela.

1585. Little League in Canada, and the first outside the United States was organized in 1951 in British Columbia.

1586. New York Giants baseball player to be named Rookie of the Year was outfielder Willie Mays, in 1951. Power hitter Mays, starting his extraordinary major league career, had 127 hits, including 20 home runs, 22 doubles, and 5 triples, and was a substantial factor in the Giants' 1951 pennant win. He would become a perennial All-Star, twice the league's Most Valuable Player.

1587. New York Yankees baseball player to be named Rookie of the Year was third baseman Gil McDougald, in 1951. McDougald hit .306, with 14 home runs, and 123 hits, scoring 72 runs.

1588. Major league baseball player widely recognized as black to play for the Chicago White Sox was Saturnino "Minnie" Minoso, a dark-skinned Cuban, who hit a home run in his first at-bat with the White Sox, on May 1, 1951. Minoso was named Rookie of the Year by *The Sporting News* for 1951. He was later a White Sox coach and held other positions in the White Sox organization.

1589. Rookie to hit a grand slam home run in the World Series was New York Yankees Rookie of the Year Gil McDougald, in the fifth game of the Yankees' 4-games-to-2 win over the New York Giants on October 9, 1951.

1590. College baseball player to score 11 runs in a College World Series was John Turco of Holy Cross College, in 1952.

1591. Philadelphia Athletics baseball player to be named Rookie of the Year was pitcher Harry Byrd, in 1952. Byrd won 15 games, with a 3.31 earned run average.

1592. Baseball team to win five consecutive American League pennants was the New York Yankees, from 1949 to 1953. The Yankees would win four more consecutive pennants from 1955 to 1958, and five more from 1960 to 1964, for a total of 14 pennants in 16 years.

1593. Detroit Tigers baseball player to be named Rookie of the Year was shortstop Harvey Kuenn, in 1953. Kuenn led the league with 209 hits and had a .308 batting average.

1594. Little League World Series to be televised was a 1–0 Birmingham, Alabama, win over the team from Schenectady, New York, in 1953.

1595. Native-American major league baseball player to be named to baseball's Hall of Fame was Ojibwa Charles "Chief" Bender, a leading pitcher with the Philadelphia Athletics from 1903 to 1913, who had pitched for several other clubs before he retired from play in 1917. He was later a college and minor league coach and manager. He was inducted into the Hall of Fame in 1953.

1596. Woman to play as a fully recognized regular on a men's major league baseball team was Toni Stone, as a reserve second basewoman on the Indianapolis Clowns of the Negro League in 1953. She also played on the Kansas City Monarchs in 1954.

1597. Milwaukee Braves regular season baseball game played at County Stadium in Milwaukee, Wisconsin, was a 10-inning 3–2 win over the St. Louis Cardinals on April 13, 1953. The Braves, who had just moved from Boston, Massachusetts, played at the County Stadium until 1965, then moving to Atlanta, Georgia.

1598. Twin major league baseball players to play in the same game on the same team were John O'Brien and Edward O'Brien of the Pittsburgh Pirates, on May 10, 1953.

1599. Major league baseball pitcher to strike out eight consecutive opposing batters was Max Surkont of the Boston Braves, against the Cincinnati Reds, on May 25, 1953.

1600. Major league baseball catcher to hit 38 home runs was Roy Campanella of the Brooklyn Dodgers, who hit his 38th on September 6, 1953. Campanella also won the second of his National League Most Valuable Player awards in 1953, the others being in 1951 and 1955.

1601. African-American baseball player to play for the Philadelphia Athletics was pitcher Bob Trice, who played in his first Athletics game on September 13, 1953. Trice had starred with Ottawa, in the International League, before moving up to Philadelphia.

1602. African-American baseball player to be named Associated Press Athlete of the Year was Willie Mays, in 1954.

1603. Mexican major league baseball player to win a batting title was Cleveland Indians second baseman Roberto "Bobby" Avila, who batted .341 in 1954, to lead the American League.

1604. National League team to top 2 million paying customers at home in a single season was the Milwaukee Braves, in 1954, with 2,131,388.

1605. African-American baseball player to play for the Pittsburgh Pirates was Curt Roberts, who played his first game with the Pirates, a 4–2 win against the Philadelphia Phillies, on April 13, 1954. Before joining the Pirates, Roberts had played with the Kansas City Monarchs of the Negro League and for Denver, in the Western League.

1606. African-American baseball player to play for the St. Louis Cardinals was Tom Alston, who played his first game with the Cardinals, a 13–4 loss to the Chicago Cubs, on April 13, 1954.

1607. Baltimore Orioles regular season baseball game played at Memorial Stadium in Baltimore was a 3–1 Baltimore win over over the Chicago White Sox on April 15, 1954.

BASEBALL—(1950-1959)—*continued*

1608. African-American baseball player to play for the Cincinnati Reds was Nino Escalera, who played his first game for Cincinnati against the Milwaukee Braves on April 17, 1954.

1609. Major league baseball player to hit five home runs in a doubleheader was Stan Musial of the St. Louis Cardinals, against the New York Giants at St. Louis, Missouri, on May 2, 1954.

1610. Major league baseball player widely recognized as black to play for the Washington Senators was Cuban outfielder Carlos Paula, who played in his first game for the Senators on September 6, 1954.

1611. Baseball player to be named *Sports Illustrated* **Sportsman of the Year** was Johnny Podres of the Brooklyn Dodgers in 1955.

1612. Brooklyn Dodgers World Series victory came in 1955, with a 4-games-to-3 win over the New York Yankees. The Dodgers had won the National League pennant with a 98-55 record. The Brooklyn win came after five World Series losses to the Yankees between 1941 and 1953. The Dodgers won five pennants in the 1950s.

1613. Cleveland Indians baseball player to be named Rookie of the Year was pitcher Herb Score in 1955. Score won 16 games that year and had 245 strikeouts.

1614. Kansas City Athletics regular season baseball game played at Muncipal Stadium in Kansas City, Missouri, was a 6–2 Athletics win over the Detroit Tigers on April 12, 1955. Formerly the Philadelphia Athletics, the team played at Municipal Stadium from 1955 to 1967, and then moved to California, becoming the Oakland Athletics.

1615. African-American baseball player to play for the New York Yankees was catcher Elston Howard, who played his first game for the Yankees, an 8–4 win over the Boston Red Sox, on April 14, 1955. Howard had starred for the Kansas City Monarchs of the Negro League before joining the Yankees organization in 1950.

1616. College baseball player to pitch 17 bases on balls in a single game was John Hoff of the University of Northern Colorado, against the University of Wyoming, on June 4, 1955.

1617. Baseball player to steal more than 30 bases and hit more than 30 home runs in a National League season was Willie Mays of the New York Giants, who stole 40 bases and hit 36 home runs in 1956.

1618. Chicago White Sox baseball player to be named Rookie of the Year was shortstop Luis Aparicio, in 1956. Aparicio, a perennial All-Star, was a top fielder and base stealer, who led the American League in steals that year.

1619. Cincinnati Reds baseball player to be named Rookie of the Year was outfielder Frank Robinson, in 1956. Just starting his extraordinary major league career, power hitter Robinson batted .290, scored a league-leading 122 runs, and had 161 hits, including 38 home runs, 30 doubles, and 6 triples.

1620. Dominican major league baseball player was Osvaldo "Ozzie" Virgil, who joined the New York Giants in 1956. After being traded to the Detroit Tigers in 1958, he was hailed as the first black player to play for the Tigers.

1621. Hispanic-American major league baseball player to be named Rookie of the Year was Venezuelan shortstop Luis Aparicio of the Chicago White Sox, in 1956.

1622. Major league baseball pitcher to win the Cy Young Award was African-American Don Newcombe, of the Brooklyn Dodgers, in 1956. Newcombe won 27 and lost 7, with a 3.06 earned run average. He also was named Most Valuable Player in 1956.

1623. Perfect game in the World Series was pitched by Don Larsen of the New York Yankees, who faced and retired all 27 Brooklyn Dodgers batters on October 8, 1956, in the fifth game of the 1956 World Series.

1624. Little League World Series won by a team from outside the United States was in 1957, when Monterrey, Mexico, defeated Portland, Oregon.

1625. Milwaukee Braves pitcher to win the Cy Young Award was Warren Spahn, in 1957. A perennial All-Star, Spahn won 21 and lost 10 in 1947, and had a league-leading 2.33 earned run average.

1626. Philadelphia Phillies baseball player to be named Rookie of the Year was Jack Sanford, in 1957. Sanford won 19 and lost 8, with a 3.08 earned run average and 188 strikeouts.

1627. African-American baseball player to play for the Philadelphia Phillies was John Kennedy, who played in his first Phillies game, a 5–1 loss to the Brooklyn Dodgers, on April 22, 1957.

1628. National League baseball player to play in 823 consecutive games was Stan Musial of the St. Louis Cardinals, who reached that mark on June 12, 1957.

1629. Baseball player to hit 13 grand slam home runs in the National League was Gil Hodges of the Brooklyn Dodgers, his 13th grand slam coming on August 1, 1957.

1630. New York Yankees pitcher to win the Cy Young Award was Bob Turley, in 1958. Turley won a league-leading 21 games, while losing 7, and also led the league with a .750 winning percentage and 19 complete games. His earned run average was 2.97. He went on to become the Most Valuable Player in the World Series, with a loss and two wins, the second of his wins coming in the decisive seventh game, against the losing Brooklyn Dodgers.

1631. Washington Senators Rookie of the Year was outfielder Albie Pearson, in 1958. Pearson had 146 hits, scored 63 runs, and hit .275. The Senators would become the Minnesota Twins two years later.

1632. San Francisco Giants regular season baseball game played at Seals Stadium in San Francisco, California, was an 8–0 win over the Los Angeles Dodgers, on April 15, 1958. This was the Giants' first regular season home game on the West Coast.

1633. Los Angeles Dodgers regular season baseball game played at Los Angeles Memorial Coliseum in Los Angeles, California, was a 6–5 Dodgers win over the San Francisco Giants on April 18, 1958. The Dodgers moved to Dodger Stadium in 1962.

1634. Major league baseball player widely recognized as black to play for the Detroit Tigers was Osvaldo "Ozzie" Virgil, who was a dark-skinned Dominican. His first Tigers game was an 11–2 win over the Washington Senators, on June 6, 1958. In 1956, when he joined the Giants, he had become the first Dominican to play in baseball's major leagues.

1635. Chicago White Sox baseball player to be named Most Valuable Player was second baseman Nellie Fox, in 1959. A top hitter, Fox was a major factor in the White Sox' 1959 pennant win with a 94-60 record, the team's first pennant win since 1919, four decades earlier.

1636. Chicago White Sox pitcher to win the Cy Young Award was Early Wynn, in 1959, which saw the team's first pennant win since 1919. Wynn led the American League in 1959, with 22 wins and 10 losses.

1637. Major league baseball player to be a unanimous All-Star Game selection was Hank (Henry) Aaron, in 1959.

1638. College baseball player to score five runs in a single game was Jerry White of Fresno State University, against Santa Clara University, on June 1, 1959.

1639. African-American baseball player to play for the Boston Red Sox was Elijah "Pumpsie" Green, who appeared in his first Red Sox game on July 21, 1959. The Red Sox were the last major league baseball team to become integrated.

BASEBALL (1960-1969)
1640. Baseball player to lead the American League in singles in seven consecutive years was Nellie Fox of the Chicago White Sox, from 1954 to 1960.

1641. Pittsburgh Pirates baseball player to be named Most Valuable Player was shortstop Dick Groat, in 1960. He led the Pirates to a 95-59 winning record and a National League pennant in 1960, followed by a 4 games to 3 World Series victory over the New York Yankees. Groat batted a league-leading .325, with 185 hits and 85 runs scored.

1642. Pittsburgh Pirates pitcher to win the Cy Young Award was Vernon Law, in 1960. Law made a major contribution to the Pirates' National League championship and World Series win over the New York Yankees in 1960, winning 20 and losing 9 during the regular season, while pitching 18 complete games. He went on to win two games in the World Series.

1643. San Francisco Giants regular season baseball game played at Candlestick Park (later 3Com Park) in San Francisco, California, was a 3–1 win over the St. Louis Cardinals, on April 12, 1960. Joe Cunningham of the Cardinals was the first batter. The Cardinals' only run came in the first inning, on a home run by Leon Wagner, although the first run to be scored in the new ballpark was by Don Blasingame of the Giants.

1644. Major league baseball player to bat in six runs in a single World Series game was Bobby Richardson of the New York Yankees, on October 8, 1960.

1645. Chicago Cubs baseball player to be named Rookie of the Year was Billy Williams, in 1961. Williams, who would be a perennial All-Star, hit 25 home runs and batted .278 in 1961.

35

BASEBALL—(1960-1969)—*continued*

1646. Washington Senators regular season baseball game played at Griffith Stadium in Washington, D.C., was a 4–3 loss to the Chicago Cubs, on April 10, 1961. This was the second Washington Senators team, replacing the original Washington Senators team, which had moved to Minnesota and become the Minnesota Twins. The new Washington Senators played at Griffith Stadium for only one year, then moving to Washington's RFK Stadium. They would become the Texas Rangers in 1971.

1647. Minnesota Twins regular season baseball game played at Metropolitan Stadium in Minneapolis, Minnesota, was a 5–3 loss by the Twins (formerly the Washington Senators) to the new Washington Senators team, on April 21, 1961. The Twins played at Metropolitan Stadium until 1981.

1648. Los Angeles Angels regular season baseball game played at Wrigley Field in Los Angeles, California, was a 4–2 loss to the Minnesota Twins on April 27, 1961. The Angels played at Wrigley Field, their temporary home during the 1961 season, before moving to Dodger Stadium in 1962. They would later become the California Angels and then the Anaheim Angels.

1649. Major league baseball player to hit 61 home runs in a single season was Roger Maris of the New York Yankees, breaking Babe Ruth's record of 60 home runs. Maris hit his 61st home run on October 1, 1961, in a 1–0 Yankee win over the Boston Red Sox. His record would stand until 1998.

1650. African-American player to be elected to baseball's Hall of Fame was Jackie Robinson, in 1962, the first year in which he was eligible.

1651. African-American to become a major league baseball coach was John "Buck" O'Neill of the Chicago Cubs, in 1962. O'Neill had previously been a star player and leading manager in the Negro National League, managing the Kansas City Monarchs from 1948 to 1955.

1652. College baseball player to pitch 38 strikeouts in a College World Series was Bob Garibaldi of Santa Clara University, in 1962.

1653. Senior Leagues for 13-year-old to 15-year-old players organized by Little League Baseball were established in 1962.

1654. Washington Senators regular season baseball game played at DC Stadium in Washington, D.C., was a 4–1 win over the Detroit Tigers on April 9, 1962. The Senators would play at the stadium from 1962 to 1971, then moving to Texas, to become the Texas Rangers. DC Stadium would be renamed RFK Memorial Stadium in June 1969.

1655. Los Angeles Dodgers regular season baseball game played at Dodger Stadium in Los Angeles, California, was a 6–3 loss to the Cincinnati Reds, on April 10, 1962. Eddie Kasko of the Reds who was the first batter, hit a double, and then scored, while Wally Post of the Reds was the first to hit a home run in the new ballpark.

1656. Baseball player to score 1,869 runs in the National League was Stan Musial of the St. Louis Cardinals, who reached that mark on April 13, 1962.

1657. New York Mets regular season baseball game played at the Polo Grounds in New York City was a 4–3 loss to the Pittsburgh Pirates on April 13, 1962. The Mets played at the Polo Grounds during 1962 and 1963, then moving to Shea Stadium.

1658. Los Angeles Angels regular season baseball game played at Dodger Stadium in Los Angeles, California, was a 5–3 loss to the Kansas City Royalsd then the Anaheim Angels.

1659. Baseball player to reach 3,431 hits in the National League was Stan Musial of the St. Louis Cardinals, who set the new record on May 19, 1962.

1660. Major league baseball player to reach 5,864 bases was Stan Musial of the St. Louis Cardinals, who reached that mark on June 22, 1962.

1661. Baseball player in the National League to reach 1,862 runs batted in was Stan Musial of the St. Louis Cardinals, who reached that mark on July 25, 1962.

1662. Major league baseball player to have 104 steals in one season was African-American shortstop Maury Wills of the Los Angeles Dodgers, who reached that mark on October 3, 1962. Ty Cobb's old record had been 96 stolen bases, set in 1915. Wills would be named the National League's Most Valuable Player of the 1962 season.

1663. African-American baseball player to be named Most Valuable Player in the American League was New York Yankees catcher Elston Howard, in 1963. In 1955, Howard had become the first African-American to play for the Yankees.

1664. College baseball player to hit four home runs in a College World Series was Bud Hollowell of the University of Southern California, in 1963.

1665. Dominican pitcher to pitch a no-hitter in the major leagues was Juan Marichal of the San Francisco Giants, who had a no-hitter against Houston on June 15, 1963.

1666. Baseball team to hit four successive home runs in an American League game was the Cleveland Indians, on July 31, 1963, against the California Angels.

1667. Hispanic-American All-Star Game in major league baseball was won by the National League team 5–2, on October 12, 1963. It was the only such game ever played.

1668. Los Angeles Angels pitcher to win the Cy Young Award was Dean Chance, in 1964. Chance pitched 11 shutouts that year, with a 22-9 winning record and a league-leading 1.64 earned run average.

1669. Baltimore Orioles baseball player to be named Most Valuable Player was third baseman Brooks Robinson in 1964. Robinson, a perennial All-Star, hit 28 homers that year, with 118 runs batted in and a .217 batting average.

1670. Baseball player to lead the American League in stolen bases for nine consecutive years was Luis Aparicio of the Chicago White Sox (1956–1962) and the Baltimore Orioles (1963 and 1964).

1671. New York Mets regular season baseball game played at Shea Stadium in New York City was a 4–3 loss to the Pittsburgh Pirates on April 17, 1964. Dick Schofield of the Pirates was the first batter, while Willie Stargell of the Pirates had the first hit in the new stadium, a second-inning home run.

1672. Major league baseball pitcher to pitch a losing 9-inning no-hitter was Ken Johnson of the Houston Astros on April 23, 1964, against the Cincinnati Reds. The Reds scored the game's only run on a Houston error.

1673. National League game to run 7 hours and 25 minutes over 23 innings was the San Francisco Giants' win over the New York Mets on May 31, 1964.

1674. Baseball player from Japan to play in United States major league baseball was pitcher Masanori Murakami, who made his first major league appearance as a relief pitcher for the San Francisco Giants on September 1, 1964.

1675. African-American to become a major league baseball broadcaster was Jackie Robinson, who made the breakthrough in 1965, with the ABC television network.

1676. Baseball player to be named Associated Press Athlete of the Year twice was pitcher Sandy Koufax of the Los Angeles Dodgers, in 1963 and 1965.

1677. Baseball player to lead the National League in stolen bases for six consecutive years was Maury Wills of the Los Angeles Dodgers, from 1960 to 1965.

1678. Baseball player to win batting titles in his first two major league years was Cuban outfielder Pedro "Tony" Oliva of the Minnesota Twins, who led the American League with .323 in 1964 and again with .321 in 1965. He was also 1964 Rookie of the Year.

1679. Minnesota Twins baseball player to be named Most Valuable Player was shortstop Xoilo Versalles in 1965. Versalles was a key factor in Minnesota's pennant-winning 102-60 record, scoring 127 runs, with 45 doubles and 12 triples. The Twins lost the World Series to the Los Angeles Dodgers.

1680. Houston Astros regular season baseball game played at the Houston Astrodome in Houston, Texas, was a 2–0 Astros loss to the Philadelphia Phillies on April 12, 1965. Tony Taylor of the Phillies was the first batter, while Bob Aspromonte of the Astros had the first hit. Dick Allen of the Phillies was the first to hit a home run.

1681. Major league baseball game played indoors and on an artificial surface (called AstroTurf) was on April 12, 1965, in the opening game of the Houston Astros' regular season, a 2–0 loss to the Philadelphia Phillies.

1682. Baseball player chosen in major league baseball's first free draft was Rick Monday, who was taken by the Philadelphia Athletics in the June 1965 draft.

1683. Major league baseball pitcher to reach 382 strikeouts in a single season was Sandy Koufax of the Los Angeles Dodgers, who reached that mark with a 13-strikeout, 2–1 win over the Boston Braves on October 2, 1965.

BASEBALL—(1960-1969)—*continued*

1684. Baltimore Orioles World Series victory came in 1966, with a 4 games to none sweep by the Orioles of the Los Angeles Dodgers of the National League, who were the defending champions. The Baltimore pitching staff turned in shutouts in the final three games of the series, setting a World Series record with 33 successive scoreless innings in all.

1685. Baseball pitcher to lead the National League in earned run average for five consecutive years was Sandy Koufax of the Los Angeles Dodgers, from 1962 to 1966.

1686. African-American to work as an umpire in major league baseball was Emmett Ashford, whose first major league game was the season opener between the Washington Senators and the Cleveland Indians, in Washington, D.C., on April 11, 1966.

1687. Atlanta Braves regular season baseball game played at Atlanta–Fulton County Stadium in Atlanta, Georgia, was a 13-inning, 3–2 loss to the Pittsburgh Pirates on April 12, 1966. The team had previously been the Milwaukee Braves, and before that the Boston Braves.

1688. California Angels regular season baseball game played at Anaheim Stadium in Anaheim, California, was a 3–1 Angels loss to the Chicago White Sox on April 19, 1966. Rich Reichardt of the Angels hit the field's first home run, the Angels' only run of the day. Earlier known as the Los Angeles Angels, they would later be called the Anaheim Angels. Anaheim Stadium would be renamed Edison International Field in 1997.

1689. St. Louis Cardinals regular season baseball game played at Busch Memorial Stadium in St. Louis, Missouri, was a 4–3, 12-inning win over the Atlanta Braves on May 12, 1966. First up was Felipe Alou of the Braves, and Gary Geiger of the Braves had the first hit. Later in the game, Alou hit the first home run in the new ballpark.

1690. Baseball player to be named Most Valuable Player in both major leagues was Frank Robinson. On November 8, 1966, he was named MVP of the American League, after leading the Baltimore Orioles in a World Series sweep over the Los Angeles Dodgers. He had previously been named MVP of the National League in 1961, when he was with the Cincinnati Reds.

1691. Boston Red Sox pitcher to win the Cy Young Award was Jim Lonborg, in 1967, who turned in a 22-9 winning record that year. Lonborg would win 157 and lose 137 during his 15-year career.

1692. Little League World Series won by an East Asian team was in 1967, when the team from West Tokyo, Japan, won the series.

1693. New York Mets baseball player to be named Rookie of the Year was Tom Seaver, in 1967. Seaver won 16 and lost 13, with a 2.20 earned run average and 205 strikeouts.

1694. San Francisco Giants pitcher to win the Cy Young Award was Mike McCormick, in 1967. McCormick won a league-leading 22 games and lost 10, and had a 2.85 earned run average and 150 strikeouts.

1695. Baseball team to hit three home runs in one inning of a World Series game was the Boston Red Sox, in the sixth game of the 1967 World Series, against the St. Louis Cardinals, on October 9, 1967. Two days later on October 11, St. Louis won the series, with a 7–2 seventh-game win.

1696. Baseball player to be named *The Sporting News* Sportsman of the Year was Denny McLain of the Detroit Tigers, in 1968.

1697. Big League Baseball leagues for 16-year-old to 18-year-old players were organized by Little League Baseball in 1968.

1698. Detroit Tigers pitcher to win the Cy Young Award was Denny McLain, who was elected unanimously in 1968. McLain won 31 games in 1968, losing only 6, and had a 1.96 earned run average, with 280 strikeouts. His 1969 record was 24 wins to 9 losses, and he tied for a second Cy Young Award with Mike Cuellar.

1699. St. Louis Cardinals pitcher to win the Cy Young Award was Bob Gibson, in 1968. Perennial All-Star Gibson won 22 and lost 9 that year, with a league-leading 1.12 earned run average, 13 shutouts, and 265 strikeouts.

1700. Oakland Athletics regular season baseball game played at the Oakland Alameda County Coliseum at Oakland, California, was a 4–1 loss to the Baltimore Orioles on April 17, 1968. Boog Powell had the first hit, a second-inning home run. Formerly the Philadelphia Athletics, then the Kansas City Athletics, the Oakland team made its permanent home at the County Coliseum, renamed the Network Associates Coliseum in 2000.

1701. Major league pitcher to pitch six successive shutouts was Don Drysdale of the Los Angeles Dodgers. His sixth shutout was the Dodgers' 5–0 defeat of the Pittsburgh Pirates on June 4, 1968.

1702. Major league pitcher to pitch 54 consecutive scoreless innings was Los Angeles Dodgers pitcher Don Drysdale, who ended his streak of scoreless innings during the Los Angeles defeat of the Pittsburgh Pirates on June 30, 1968.

1703. Baltimore Orioles pitcher to win the Cy Young Award was Cuban pitcher Mike Cuellar in 1969, in a tie with Denny McLain of the Detroit Tigers. Cuellar won 23 games and lost 11 in 1969, and had a 2.38 earned run average.

1704. Kansas City Royals baseball player to be named Rookie of the Year was outfielder Lou Piniella, in 1969. In that year, Piniella hit .282, and had 139 hits, including 11 home runs, 21 doubles, and 6 triples, as well as a .977 fielding average.

1705. Major league baseball team situated in Canada was the Montreal Expos, a National League expansion team in 1969.

1706. New York Mets pitcher to win the Cy Young Award was Tom Seaver, in 1969. Seaver won a league-leading 25 games and lost 7, for a league-leading .781 winning percentage. His earned run average was .221, and he struck out 206 batters. He went on to win two more Cy Young Awards, in 1973 and 1975.

1707. New York Mets World Series victory came in 1969, with a 4 games to 1 win over the Baltimore Orioles. The Mets had won their first National League pennant in 1969, with a 100-62 winning record.

1708. Kansas City Royals regular season baseball game played at Municipal Stadium in Kansas City, Missouri, was a 12-inning, 4–3 Royals win over the Minnesota Twins on April 8, 1969. Municipal Stadium was the temporary home of the Royals, from 1969 to 1972, before the team moved to Kauffman Stadium in 1973.

1709. San Diego Padres regular season baseball game played at San Diego Stadium in San Diego, California, was a 2–1 Padres win over the Houston Astros, on April 8, 1969. Jesus Alou of the Astros, the first batter, hit a single and scored the first run later in the first inning. Ed Spezio of the Padres hit the first home run in the new ballpark. The stadium would be renamed Jack Murphy Stadium in 1980 and Qualcomm Stadium at Jack Murphy Field in 1997.

1710. Montreal Expos regular season baseball game played at Jarry Park in Montreal, Quebec, Canada, was an 8–7 Expos win over the St. Louis Cardinals on April 14, 1969. The Expos played at Jarry Park from 1969 to 1976, then moving to Olympic Stadium.

1711. American League and National League championships were played in October 1969. The National League pennant was won by the New York Mets; the American League title by the Baltimore Orioles. The Mets went on to defeat Baltimore in a 5-game World Series.

BASEBALL (1970-1979)

1712. Minnesota Twins pitcher to win the Cy Young Award was Jim Perry, in 1970. Perry had a 20-12 winning record and a 3.03 earned run average, making a major contribution to the Twins' 96-64 record and Western Division championship. However, the Twins lost the American League pennant to the Baltimore Orioles.

1713. Montreal Expos baseball player to be named Rookie of the Year was pitcher Carl Morton, in 1970. Morton won 18 games and lost 11, with a 3.80 earned run average and 154 strikeouts.

1714. Successful set of actions against major league baseball's "reserve clause" began with a lawsuit by Curt Flood of the St. Louis Cardinals in January 1970. The ultimate success of Flood's lawsuit would decisively change baseball.

1715. Milwaukee Brewers regular season baseball game played at County Stadium in Milwaukee, Wisconsin, was a 12–0 loss to the California Angels on April 7, 1970. Sandy Alomar of the Angels was first up, but Alex Johnson of the Angels had the first hit, a second-inning triple, and then scored the first run. The Brewers had been the Seattle Pilots for one season, in 1969, and then moved to Milwaukee in 1970.

1716. Cincinnati Reds regular season baseball game played at Riverfront Stadium (later Cinergy Field) in Cincinnati, Ohio, was an 8–2 loss to the Atlanta Braves on June 30, 1970. First up was Sonny Jackson of the Braves, while Felix Millan of the Braves had the first hit and scored the first run. Hank Aaron of the Braves hit the first home run in the new ballpark.

1717. Pittsburgh Pirates regular season baseball game played at Three Rivers Stadium in Pittsburgh, Pennsylvania, was a 3–2 loss to the Cincinnati Reds on July 15, 1970. Ty Cline of the Reds was the first batter, and the first hit was Richie Hebner's first-inning single, on which he later scored. Tony Perez of the Reds hit the first home run in the park.

BASEBALL—(1970-1979)—*continued*

1718. African-American major league baseball player to win the American League's Cy Young Award was Vida Blue of the Oakland Athletics, who was also the league's Most Valuable Player in 1971.

1719. Chicago Cubs pitcher to win the Cy Young Award was Ferguson Jenkins, in 1971. He had a league-leading 24-13 record, with a 2.77 earned run average and 263 strikeouts. Jenkins also pitched 30 complete games.

1720. Oakland Athletics pitcher to win the Cy Young Award was Vida Blue, in 1971, with a 24-8 record and a league-leading .182 earned run average.

1721. Philadelphia Phillies regular season baseball game played at Veterans Stadium in Philadelphia, Pennsylvania, was a 4–1 win over the Montreal Expos on April 19, 1971. Boots Day of the Expos was first up, but Larry Bowa of the Phillies had the first hit. Don Money of the Phillies hit the first home run in the new ballpark.

1722. Major league baseball team consisting of nine black players took the field for the Pittsburgh Pirates against the Philadelphia Phillies on September 1, 1971. Some of the players regarded themselves primarily as Hispanics and Hispanic-Americans, rather than as African-Americans, but all were widely recognized as black.

1723. Cleveland Indians pitcher to win the Cy Young Award was Gaylord Perry in 1972. Perry won 24 and lost 16 games, with a 1.92 earned run average. A perennial All-Star, Perry led the American League in wins three times, and won a second Cy Young Award in 1978, this time in the National League, while playing for the San Diego Padres.

1724. Philadelphia Phillies pitcher to win the Cy Young Award was Steve Carlton, in 1972. Carlton led the league in wins, with 27, against 10 losses. His 1.97 earned run average also led the league, as did his 310 strikeouts and 30 complete games. He went on to win three more Cy Young Awards, in 1977, 1980, and 1982.

1725. Texas Rangers regular season baseball game played at Arlington Stadium in Arlington, Texas, was a 7–6 Rangers win over the California Angels on April 21, 1972. Previously the Washington Senators, the team changed its name to the Texas Rangers on the move to Texas. They played at Arlington Stadium from 1972 to 1993.

1726. College baseball player to steal five bases in a single game was Dave Nichols of Florida State University, against the University of Richmond on June 2, 1972.

1727. Major league baseball player to bat in 13 runs in a doubleheader was Nate Colbert of the San Diego Padres, defeating the Atlanta Braves in both games of a doubleheader on August 1, 1972.

1728. Major league baseball players' strike to stop the opening of a season lasted for 12 days, from its announcement on April 1, 1972, until it ended on April 13, 1972.

1729. Hispanic-born major league baseball player to become a member of baseball's Hall of Fame was Puerto Rican–born Pittsburgh Pirates star Roberto Clemente in 1973, a leading hitter who won four National League batting titles and a Most Valuable Player Award in 1966. Clemente's career was cut short when he died in the crash of a plane carrying relief supplies to Managua after the disastrous Nicaraguan earthquake, on December 31, 1972.

1730. Major league baseball player to come to bat as a designated hitter was Larry Hisle of the Pittsburgh Pirates, during an exhibition game on March 6, 1973. The American League had established the new designated hitter status on a trial basis in December 1972.

1731. Major league baseball player to appear as a designated hitter during a regular season game was Ron Blomberg of the New York Yankees, in a game against the Boston Red Sox on April 6, 1973.

1732. Kansas City Royals regular season baseball game at Kauffman Stadium in Kansas City, Missouri, was a 12–1 Royals win over the Texas Rangers on April 10, 1973. Dave Nelson of the Rangers was first up, but the first run was scored by Fred Patak of the Royals. John Mayberry of the Royals hit the first home run in the new ballpark.

1733. African-American to serve as a manager in baseball's major leagues was Ernie Banks, a coach of the Chicago Cubs, who functioned as Cubs manager in a game against the San Diego Padres on May 8, 1973.

1734. Little League baseball national agreement to fully admit girls came on September 7, 1973.

1735. College baseball team to win five consecutive National Collegiate World Championships was the University of Southern California, from 1970 to 1974.

1736. Texas Rangers baseball player to be named Most Valuable Player was outfielder Jeff Burroughs, in 1974. Burroughs, a leading power hitter, batted in a league-leading 118 runs, hit 25 home runs, and had a .301 batting average.

1737. Texas Rangers baseball player to be named Rookie of the Year was first baseman Mike Hargrove, in 1974. Hargrove hit .323, with 134 hits.

1738. Major league baseball player to hit 715 career home runs was Hank Aaron of the Atlanta Braves, who broke Babe Ruth's former record of 714 in an April 8, 1974, Braves win over the Los Angeles Dodgers. Aaron's career total of 755 home runs would set an enduring record.

1739. Major league baseball player to have 118 steals in a single season was African-American St. Louis Cardinals outfielder Lou Brock, who reached that mark on September 29, 1974, in a 7–3 Cardinals win over the Chicago Cubs.

1740. Free agents in major league baseball were Andy Messersmith of the Los Angeles Dodgers and Dave McNally of the Montreal Expos, who were declared free agents by a federal arbitration ruling on December 14, 1974. The ruling established the principle of free agency, in certain circumstances, greatly changing the economic balance between club owners and players in favor of the players.

1741. African-American to be named manager of a major league baseball team was perennial All-Star Frank Robinson, who was hired as player-manager by the Cleveland Indians in October 1975. Robinson had been a Rookie of the Year, and was twice the National League's Most Valuable Player.

1742. Nicaraguan major league baseball player was Dennis Martinez, who played with the Baltimore Orioles in 1976.

1743. San Diego Padres pitcher to win the Cy Young Award was Randy Jones, in 1976. Jones had a league-leading 22 wins, 14 losses, and a 2.74 earned run average.

1744. Seattle Mariners regular season baseball game played at the Seattle Kingdome in Seattle, Washington, was a 7–0 Mariners loss to the California Angels on April 6, 1977. Jerry Remy of the Angels was the first batter and scored the first run. Joe Rudi of the Angels hit the first home run in the new ballpark.

1745. Toronto Blue Jays regular season baseball game played at Exhibition Stadium in Toronto, Ontario, Canada, was a 9–5 Toronto win over the Chicago White Sox on April 7, 1977. The Blue Jays played at Exhibition Stadium until early in the 1989 season.

1746. Montreal Expos regular season baseball game played at Olympic Stadium in Montreal, Quebec, Canada, was a 7–2 loss to the Philadelphia Phillies, on April 15, 1977. Jay Johnstone of the Phillies was first up, but Dave Cash of the Expos had the first hit, while Greg Luzinski of the Phillies scored the first run. Ellis Valentine of the Expos hit the first home run.

1747. Baseball pitcher to win the Cy Young Award in both leagues was Gaylord Perry. He had won it first in the American League, when he was with the Cleveland Indians, in 1972. Then he won it again in 1978, this time in the National League, while playing for the San Diego Padres.

1748. College baseball coach to win 10 National Collegiate World Championships was Rod Dedeaux of the University of Southern California, between 1958 and 1978.

1749. National League team to top 3 million paying customers at home in a single season was the Los Angeles Dodgers, in 1978, with 3,347,845.

1750. Baseball player to lead the National League in triples in three consecutive years was Gary Templeton of the St. Louis Cardinals, from 1977 to 1979.

1751. California Angels baseball player to be named Most Valuable Player was outfielder Don Baylor in 1979. Baylor hit 36 home runs that season, with a .296 batting average and a league-leading 139 runs batted in. The team was later known as the Anaheim Angels.

1752. Junior League Baseball leagues organized by Little League Baseball for 13-year-olds were in 1979.

BASEBALL (1980-1989)
1753. Major league baseball player to earn $1 million a year was pitcher Nolan Ryan, who signed a three-year contract with the Houston Astros that paid him a million dollars a year for three years, starting in 1980.

1754. Kansas City Royals American League pennant was won in 1980, when they had a 97-65 record. The Royals went on to lose the World Series to the Philadelphia Phillies, 4 games to 2.

BASEBALL—(1980-1989)—*continued*

1755. Kansas City Royals baseball player to be named Most Valuable Player was third baseman George Brett, in 1980. A perennial All-Star, Brett hit a league-leading .390 that year, the highest batting average since 1941, when Ted Williams hit .401. Brett led the Royals to the American League pennant, but they lost to the Philadelphia Phillies in the World Series. In 1985, the Royals again won the pennant, and that time went on to win the World Series.

1756. Philadelphia Phillies World Series victory came in 1980, with a 4 games to 2 win over the Kansas City Royals. The Phillies had won the National League pennant with a 91-71 winning record. The Phillies had entered the National League in 1883, and it took 97 years for them to win their first World Series, although they had won their first pennant in 1915.

1757. Baseball team to win the Little League World Series in five consecutive years was the Chinese team from Taipei, Taiwan, which won from 1977 to 1981.

1758. College baseball player to bat in 17 runs in a College World Series was Stan Holmes of the University of Arizona, in 1981.

1759. Major league baseball rookie to win the Cy Young Award was Mexican pitcher Fernando Valenzuela of the Los Angeles Dodgers, in 1981.

1760. Milwaukee Brewers baseball player to be named Most Valuable Player, and to win the Cy Young Award was relief pitcher Rollie Fingers, in 1981. Fingers saved 35 games, with a 1.34 earned run average.

1761. Long-term baseball strike to completely shut down both major leagues occurred in 1981, when the players struck from June 12 to July 31 over the issue of free agency. The 50-day strike was the longest in the history of any U.S. sport. The 1981 baseball season, effectively cut in two, restarted on August 10; 708 games had been canceled.

1762. Major league baseball pitcher to win four Cy Young Awards was Steve Carlton, of the Philadelphia Phillies, who won the National League Cy Young Award in 1972, 1977, 1980, and 1982.

1763. Major league baseball player to earn $2 million a year was outfielder George Foster, who signed a five-year, $10 million contract with the New York Mets in 1982.

1764. Major league baseball player to reach 130 steals in a single season was African-American New York Yankees outfielder Rickey Henderson, who reached that mark in 1982.

1765. Milwaukee Brewers American League pennant came in 1982, when the Brewers turned in a 95–67 winning record. They were led by then-shortstop Robin Yount, who won the 1982 American League Most Valuable Player Award, and by pitcher Pete Vuckovich, who won the Cy Young Award. The Brewers moved to the National League in 1997.

1766. Minnesota Twins regular season baseball game played at the Hubert H. Humphrey Metrodome in Minneapolis, Minnesota, was an 11-7 loss to the Seattle Mariners, on April 6, 1982. The new stadium became the permanent home of the Twins. Julio Cruz of the Mariners was first up, but Dave Engle of the Twins had the first hit in the new stadium, a home run.

1767. Major league baseball player to get five hits in a single World Series game was Paul Molitor of the Milwaukee Brewers, on October 12, 1982.

1768. American League manager to be named Manager of the Year was Tony La Russa of the Chicago White Sox, in 1983. La Russa won the honor again in 1988 and 1992, both times while manager of the Oakland Athletics. He was the first American League coach to be named Manager of the Year three times.

1769. Dominican to be inducted into baseball's Hall of Fame was San Francisco Giants pitcher Juan Marichal, in 1983. A perennial All-Star, Marichal led the National League in wins twice, and played in eight All-Star Games.

1770. Major league baseball player to be named the American League Rookie of the Year and Most Valuable Player in consecutive years was Baltimore Orioles shortstop and perennial All-Star Cal Ripken, Jr., who—just beginning his phenomenal career—was named top rookie in 1982 and MVP in 1983.

1771. National League manager to be named Manager of the Year was Tommy Lasorda of the Los Angeles Dodgers, in 1983. He won the honor again in 1988, while still coaching the Dodgers, becoming the first National League coach to be named Manager of the Year twice.

1772. Detroit Tigers manager to be named Manager of the Year was Sparky Anderson, in 1984, the year he took the Tigers to a World Series win over the San Diego Padres. He repeated as Manager of the Year in 1987, when he took Detroit to a divisional title.

1773. Little League baseball teams in the new Challenger division were organized in 1984.

1774. Little League World Series won by a Korean team was in 1984, when the team from Seoul, South Korea, won the series.

1775. San Diego Padres National League pennant came in 1984, when the team amassed a 92-70 league-leading record. The Padres lost to the Detroit Tigers in the World Series.

1776. Seattle Mariners baseball player to be named Rookie of the Year was first baseman Alvin Davis, in 1984. Davis, who hit .284, had 161 hits, including 27 home runs, 34 doubles, and 3 triples, while batting in 116 runs.

1777. American League game to last more than 8 hours was a 25-inning, 7-6 Chicago White Sox win over the Milwaukee Brewers, which lasted 8 hours and 6 minutes. The game started on May 8, 1984, and ended the next day. Both parts of the game were played at Chicago.

1778. College baseball player to steal eight bases in a College World Series was Calvin James of the University of Miami, in 1985.

1779. Hispanic-born major league baseball star to appear on a U.S. postage stamp was Puerto Rican–born Hall-of-Famer Roberto Clemente, in 1985.

1780. Kansas City Royals pitcher to win the Cy Young Award was Brett Saberhagen in 1985. He was also the youngest player to win the Cy Young Award, and went on to become the Most Valuable Player in the World Series, won by the Royals.

1781. Kansas City Royals World Series win was a 4 games to 3 Royals victory over the St. Louis Cardinals, in 1985. The Royals had won the American League pennant with a 91-71 record. The Royals were an expansion team that had started play in 1969.

1782. Major league pitcher to reach 4,000 career strikeouts was Nolan Ryan of the Houston Astros, who hit that mark against the New York Mets, on July 11, 1985.

1783. Major league baseball player to reach 4,192 career hits was Pete Rose of the Cincinnati Reds, who hit that mark on September 11, 1985, against the San Diego Padres, breaking Ty Cobb's former record of 4,191 career hits. Rose retired with 4,256 hits.

1784. Boston Red Sox manager to be named Manager of the Year was John McNamara, in 1986. In that year, the Red Sox won the American League pennant, with 95 wins and 66 losses, but lost the World Series to the New York Mets 4 games to 3.

1785. College baseball player to bat in nine runs in a single game was Bill Reynolds of the University of Maine, against St. Johns University, in 1986.

1786. College baseball player to hit four home runs in a single game was Bill Reynolds of the University of Maine, against St. Johns University, in 1986.

1787. Houston Astros pitcher to win the Cy Young Award was Mike Scott, in 1986. Scott won 18 and lost 10, and led the league with a 2.22 earned run average and 306 strikeouts.

1788. Major league baseball player to hit a home run on the season's first pitch was Boston Red Sox player Dwight Evans, against the Detroit Tigers at Tiger Stadium on April 7, 1986.

1789. Major league pitcher to pitch 20 strikeouts in a single game was Roger Clemens of the Boston Red Sox, on April 29, 1986, against the Seattle Mariners.

1790. College baseball player to have six hits in a single game was Jimmy Barragon of Oklahoma State University, against the University of Richmond, on May 22, 1986.

1791. Major league baseball game to include three grand slam home runs was the 13–11 Texas Rangers win over the Baltimore Orioles on August 6, 1986.

1792. Honduran major league baseball player was Gerald Young, who played with the Houston Astros in 1987.

1793. Major league baseball rookie to hit 49 home runs in a single season was Mark McGwire of the Oakland Athletics, in 1987.

1794. Toronto Blue Jays baseball player to be named Most Valuable Player was outfielder George Bell, in 1987. A power hitter, Bell batted in a league-leading 134 runs and hit 47 home runs, with a .605 slugging average.

1795. Major league baseball player to hit six grand slam home runs in a single season was Don Mattingly of the New York Yankees, his sixth coming against the Boston Red Sox on September 29, 1987.

BASEBALL—(1980-1989)—*continued*

1796. World Series game to be played indoors was the first game of the 1987 Series, between the Minnesota Twins and the St. Louis Cardinals, played at the Hubert H. Humphrey Metrodome in Minneapolis, Minnesota, on October 17, 1987. Minnesota won 10–1.

1797. American League player to steal 40 bases and hit 40 home runs in a season was José Canseco of the Oakland Athletics, who stole 40 bases and hit 42 home runs in 1988.

1798. American League team to top 3 million paying customers at home in a single season was the Minnesota Twins, in 1988, with 3,030,672.

1799. College baseball team to have two consecutive Most Valuable Player Award winners was Stanford University, with Paul Carey winning the award in 1987 and Lee Plemel in 1988.

1800. Woman to play on a men's college baseball team was Julie Croteau, of St. Mary's College of Maryland, in 1988.

1801. Major league baseball club to hit a total of 10,000 home runs was the New York Yankees. The 10,000th was a Claudell Washington home run against the Minnesota Twins on April 20, 1988.

1802. Major league pitcher to pitch 59 consecutive regular season scoreless innings was Orel Hershiser of the Los Angeles Dodgers, who ended his streak with 10 scoreless innings pitched against the San Diego Padres on September 28, 1988. Hershiser went on to pitch eight more consecutive scoreless innings against the New York Mets in the first game of the league championship series.

1803. African-American to become president of a major baseball league was former perennial All-Star and broadcaster Bill White, who became president of the National League in 1989.

1804. Baltimore Orioles manager to be named Manager of the Year was Frank Robinson in 1989. A perennial All-Star during his long playing career, he became a member of baseball's Hall of Fame in 1982. In his second year as coach of the Orioles, he completely turned around that losing team, bringing it in second in the American League. In 1975, Robinson had become manager of the Cleveland Indians, the first African-American manager in major league baseball.

1805. Father and son to play at the same time in major league baseball were Ken Griffey, Sr., who in 1989 was playing for the Cincinnati Reds, and Ken Griffey, Jr., who that year was starting his major league career with the Seattle Mariners.

1806. Girl from the United States to appear in a Little League baseball World Series was Victoria Bruckner, who played for the winning San Pedro, California, team against Tampa, Florida, in the 1989 Little League Series.

1807. Toronto Blue Jays regular season baseball game played at the Skydome in Toronto, Ontario, Canada, was a 5–3 loss to the Milwaukee Brewers, on June 4, 1989. Paul Molitor of the Brewers was the first up, hit a double, and then scored. Fred McGriff of the Blue Jays hit the first home run in the new ballpark.

1808. Major league pitcher to reach 5,000 career strikeouts was Nolan Ryan, who reached that mark against the Oakland Athletics on August 22, 1989.

1809. World Series game to be canceled by an earthquake was the third game of the 1989 World Series, between the San Francisco Giants and the Oakland Athletics, on October 17, 1989. A few minutes before the Candlestick Park game was due to start, and with a worldwide television audience watching, a major earthquake occurred, causing substantial damage throughout the San Francisco Bay area, though little harm to the tens of thousands assembled at Candlestick Park to watch the game.

BASEBALL (1990-1999)

1810. Father and son to play as teammates in major league baseball were Ken Griffey, Sr., and Ken Griffey, Jr., who both played for the Seattle Mariners in 1990.

1811. Major league baseball player of the 20th century to pitch 57 saves in a single season was Bobby Thigpen of the Chicago White Sox, in 1990.

1812. American League team to top 4 million paying customers at home in a single season was the Toronto Blue Jays, in 1991, with 4,001,527.

1813. Houston Astros baseball player to be named Rookie of the Year was first baseman and power hitter Jeff Bagwell, who hit .273 and had 163 hits, including 15 home runs, 26 doubles, and 4 triples in 1991.

1814. Major league baseball player to earn $5 million a year was pitcher Roger Clemens, who signed a five-year contract with the Boston Red Sox in 1991 that paid him more than $5 million a year for 5 years.

1815. Minnesota Twins manager to be named Manager of the Year was Tom Kelly in 1991, who that year took the Twins to a 4 games to 3 World Series victory over the Atlanta Braves. His team had won the Western Division championship with a 95-67 record, and had gone on to defeat the Toronto Blue Jays for the American League pennant 4 games to 1.

1816. Chicago White Sox regular season baseball game played at New Comiskey Park in Chicago, Illinois, was a 16–0 White Sox loss to the Detroit Tigers on April 18, 1991. First up was Tony Phillips of the Tigers, though Alan Trammell of the Tigers had the first hit of the day. Cecil Fielder of the Tigers hit the first home run in the new ballpark.

1817. Milwaukee Brewers baseball player to be named Rookie of the Year was shortstop Pat Listach, in 1992. Listach hit .290, scored 93 runs, and had 168 hits.

1818. Toronto Blue Jays World Series victory came in 1992, with a 4 games to 2 defeat of the Atlanta Braves. It was 15 years after Toronto had entered the American League as an expansion team, in 1977. The Blue Jays had won their first American League pennant that year, with a 96-66 winning record. Toronto repeated its World Series victory in 1993, defeating the Philadelphia Phillies, 4 games to 2.

1819. Baltimore Orioles regular season baseball game played at Camden Yards in Baltimore, Maryland, was a 2–0 Baltimore win over the Cleveland Indians on April 6, 1992. Kenny Lofton of the Indians was the first batter, but Sam Horn of the Orioles scored the first run in the new ballpark.

1820. Baseball event held in the Olympic Games was in 1992 in Barcelona, Spain. The team from Cuba took the inaugural gold medal on August 5. Cuba would win again on August 2, 1996, becoming the first to win the gold medal twice.

1821. California Angels baseball player to be named Rookie of the Year was outfielder Tim Salmon, in 1993. Salmon, a leading power hitter, had 31 home runs, 35 doubles, and a triple, with 95 runs batted in, 146 hits, 93 runs scored, and a .283 batting average. The team would later be known as the Anaheim Angels.

1822. National League team to top 4 million paying customers at home in a single season was the Colorado Rockies, in 1993, with 4,483,350.

1823. Florida Marlins regular season baseball game played at Joe Robbie Stadium in Miami, Florida, was a 6–3 win over the Los Angeles Dodgers on April 5, 1993. José Offerman of the Dodgers was the first batter, and Bret Barbarie of the Marlins had the first hit. Tim Wallach of the Dodgers hit the first home run in the ballpark, which would be renamed the Pro Player Stadium in 1996.

1824. Colorado Rockies regular season baseball game played at Mile High Stadium in Denver, Colorado, was an 11–4 Rockies win over the Montreal Expos on April 9, 1993. An expansion team, the Rockies played at Mile High Stadium in 1993 and 1994.

1825. Houston Astros baseball player to be named Most Valuable Player was first baseman Jeff Bagwell, in 1994. During that strike-shortened season, power hitter Bagwell led the league with 116 runs batted in and scored a league-leading 104 runs. He batted .368, and had 147 hits, including 39 home runs, 32 doubles, and 2 triples.

1826. Major league baseball postseason playoffs to be canceled because of a players' strike were the 1994 World Series and the American League and National League pennant playoffs.

1827. Cleveland Indians regular season baseball game played at Jacobs Field in Cleveland, Ohio, was a 4–3 Cleveland win over the Seattle Mariners, on April 4, 1994. Rich Amaral of the Mariners was the first up, while Eric Anthony of the Mariners hit the first home run in the new ballpark.

1828. Texas Rangers regular season baseball game played at The Ballpark in Arlington, Texas, was a 4–3 loss to the Milwaukee Brewers on April 11, 1994. Pat Listach of the Brewers was first up, but David Hulse of the Rangers had the first hit, and Dave Nilsson of the Brewers scored the first run and hit the first home run in the new ballpark.

1829. Hispanic-born major league baseball manager to be named Manager of the Year was Dominican Felipe Alou of the Montreal Expos, in 1995. Alou had been a power-hitting three-time All-Star during his playing career.

1830. Seattle Mariners pitcher to win the Cy Young Award was Randy Johnson in 1995, when he won 18 and lost 2 games, for a league-leading .900 winning average. His earned run average was a league-leading 2.48. For the fourth straight year, he led league in strikeouts, with 294.

BASEBALL—(1990-1999)—*continued*

1831. Colorado Rockies regular season baseball game played at Coors Field in Denver, Colorado, was an 11–9 win over the New York Mets, on April 20, 1995. The first batter was Brett Butler of the Mets who singled, but Walt Weiss of the Rockies scored the first run. Rico Brogna of the Mets hit the first home run in the new ballpark.

1832. Major league baseball player to top Lou Gehrig's record of 2,130 consecutive games played was Cal Ripken, Jr., of the Baltimore Orioles, who on September 6, 1995, played his 2,131st game in a row, having started his recordbreaking streak on May 29, 1982. His record would extend to 2,632 games, ending on September 20, 1998.

1833. Baseball player to steal 40 bases and hit 40 home runs in a season in the National League was Barry Bonds of the San Francisco Giants, who stole 40 bases and hit 42 home runs in 1996.

1834. San Diego Padres baseball player to be named Most Valuable Player was third baseman Ken Caminiti, in 1996. Caminiti hit .326, batted in 130 runs, scored 109 runs, and had 178 hits, including 40 home runs, 37 doubles, and 3 triples.

1835. Toronto Blue Jays pitcher to win the Cy Young Award was Pat Hentgen, in 1996. Hentgen won 20 and lost 10, for a .667 winning average, and had a .322 earned run average and 160 strikeouts.

1836. Nine-inning American League baseball game to take as long as 4 hours and 20 minutes was the 16–15 Colorado Rockies win over the Los Angeles Dodgers, on June 3, 1996.

1837. Baseball player to lead the National League in bases on balls for four consecutive years was Barry Bonds of the San Francisco Giants, from 1994 to 1997.

1838. Colorado Rockies baseball player to be named Most Valuable Player was outfielder Larry Walker, in 1997. Power hitter Walker hit .363, scored 143 runs, batted in 130 runs, and had 208 hits, including 49 home runs, 46 doubles, and 4 triples.

1839. Florida Marlins World Series victory came in 1997, with a 4 games to 3 win over the Cleveland Indians. The Marlins had turned in a 92-70 regular season record, good enough to win a wild card berth in the playoffs, and had gone on to defeat the Atlanta Braves for the National League pennant.

1840. Major league baseball player from Canada to be named Most Valuable Player in either league was Larry Walker of the Colorado Rockies, who was named National League Most Valuable Player in 1997.

1841. Major league baseball player to earn $10 million a year was outfielder Albert Belle, who signed a $55 million, 5-year contract with the Chicago White Sox in 1997.

1842. Montreal Expos pitcher to win the Cy Young Award was Pedro Martinez, in 1997. Martinez won 19 and lost 7, with a 2.89 earned run average and 261 strikeouts.

1843. Seattle Mariners baseball player to be named Most Valuable Player was perennial All-Star outfielder Ken Griffey, Jr., in 1997. Griffey batted .304 and had 185 hits, including 56 home runs, 34 doubles, and 3 triples. He also scored 125 runs and batted in 147 runs.

1844. Atlanta Braves regular season baseball game played at Turner Field in Atlanta, Georgia, was a 5–4 Atlanta win over the Chicago Cubs on April 14, 1997. Brian McRae of the Cubs was the first batter, but Chipper Jones of the Braves had the first hit, while Michael Tucker of the Braves hit the first home run in the new ballpark.

1845. College baseball player to pitch 21 strikeouts in a single game was Jeff Weaver of Fresno State University, against Texas A&M University on May 22, 1997.

1846. College baseball player to have 15 hits in a College World Series was Jason Lane of the University of Southern California, in 1998.

1847. Major league baseball pitcher to pitch 1,071 games during his career was Dennis Eckersley of the Boston Red Sox, who had spent the first 13 years of his 24-year-long major league career (1975–1998) pitching in regular rotation and the final 11 as a relief pitcher.

1848. Major league baseball pitcher to win five Cy Young Awards was Roger Clemens, who won three of the awards while playing for the Boston Red Sox (1986, 1987, 1991) and two while playing for the Toronto Blue Jays (1997, 1998).

1849. Season in which both major league baseball Most Valuable Player Awards went to Hispanic players was in 1998. Juan Gonzalez of the Texas Rangers won in the American League and Sammy Sosa of the Chicago Cubs in the National League.

1850. Arizona Diamondbacks regular season baseball game played at the Bank One Ballpark in Phoenix, Arizona, was a 9–2 loss to the Colorado Rockies on March 31, 1998. Mike Lansing of the Rockies was first up and singled, but Vinny Castilla of the Rockies scored the first run and also hit the first home run in the new ballpark. Arizona was a National League expansion team in 1998, along with the Tampa Bay Devil Rays, in the American League.

1851. Tampa Bay Devil Rays regular season baseball game played at Tropicana Field at Tampa, Florida, was an 11–6 loss to the Detroit Tigers on March 31, 1998. Brian Hunter of the Tigers was the first batter, while Tony Clark of the Tigers had the first hit and scored the first run in the new ballpark. Luis Gonzalez of the Tigers hit the first home run. Tampa Bay, in the American League, was one of two new major league expansion teams in 1998. The other was the Arizona Diamondbacks, in the National League.

1852. Major league baseball player to play in 2,632 consecutive games was Cal Ripken, Jr., of the Baltimore Orioles. He started his recordbreaking streak on May 29, 1982, and ended it voluntarily on September 20, 1998.

1853. Major league baseball player to hit 70 home runs in a single season was Mark McGwire of the St. Louis Cardinals, who hit his 70th against Carl Pavano of the Montreal Expos on September 27, 1998, at Busch Memorial Stadium in St. Louis, Missouri. He had broken Roger Maris's record of 61 home runs with his 62nd, on September 8. Sammy Sosa of the Chicago Cubs also broke Maris's record in 1998, but his season total of 66 was lower than McGwire's.

1854. Major league baseball team to win 25 World Series was the New York Yankees, who swept the Atlanta Braves four games to none for their 25th World Series victory on October 27, 1999, at Yankee Stadium. The Yankees went on to win their 26th World Series the following year with a 4-games-to-1 victory over the New York Mets, on October 26, 2000. It was the Yankees' fourth series win in five years.

1855. Seattle Mariners regular season baseball game played at SAFECO Field in Seattle, Washington, was a 3–2 loss to the San Diego Padres, on July 15, 1999.

1856. Baseball team to hit nine home runs in a single National League game was the Cincinnati Reds, against the Philadelphia Phillies, on September 5, 1999.

1857. Major league baseball player to hit at least 60 home runs in two consecutive seasons was Sammy Sosa of the Chicago Cubs, in 1998 and 1999. His 60th home run of 1999 came against the Milwaukee Brewers on September 18, 1999. He had hit 66 home runs in 1998, breaking Roger Maris's record of 61.

BASEBALL (2000-)
1858. Detroit Tigers regular season baseball game played at Comerica Park in Detroit, Michigan, was a 5–2 win over the Seattle Mariners on April 11, 2000.

1859. Houston Astros regular season baseball game played at Enron Field in Houston, Texas, was a 4–1 loss to the Philadelphia Phillies on April 7, 2000.

1860. San Francisco Giants regular season baseball game played at Pacific Bell Park in San Francisco, California, was a 6–5 loss to the Los Angeles Dodgers on April 11, 2000.

1861. United States team to win the men's baseball title in the Olympic Games achieved this on September 27, 2000, at Sydney, Australia. Upsetting Cuba 4–0 in the final game, the team, composed of minor-leaguers, was led to victory by the Los Angeles Dodgers' former manager Tommy Lasorda.

1862. World Series game to last 4 hours and 51 minutes was played between the New York Yankees and the New York Mets on October 21, 2000, at Yankee Stadium in New York City. The Yankees won the game 4–3, on a single in the twelfth inning.

1863. Baseball team to play 14 games in the World Series without suffering a defeat was the New York Yankees, whose winning streak began in the 1996 Series, when the team came from behind to beat the Atlanta Braves 4 games to 2. The Yankees did not even reach the Series in 1997 but swept the contests in 1998 and 1999. They won their thirteenth game on October 21, 2000, against the New York Mets, and their fourteenth on October 22, both at Yankee Stadium in New York City.

BASKETBALL (BEFORE 1900)
1864. Basketball game was invented and organized by physical education instructor James Naismith in December 1891, at the School for Christian Workers in Springfield, Massachusetts. The school was later the International Young Men's Christian Association (YMCA) Training School, and still later Springfield College, and basketball spread first through the

BASKETBALL—(BEFORE 1900)—*continued*
YMCA branches. The game was improvised on the spot, using a soccer ball, with two peach baskets for goals. On the same day, Naismith invented and wrote down the first rules of the game.

1865. Basketball team was organized at the School for Christian Workers in Springfield, Massachusetts in 1892, and was composed of nine of James Naismith's physical education students.

1866. Women's basketball program was introduced by Senda Berenson Abbot at Smith College, Northampton, Massachusetts, in 1892.

1867. Article reporting on basketball's first game was written by James Naismith. Titled "Basket Ball," it was published in the national Young Men's Christian Association (YMCA) publication *The Triangle* on January 15, 1892. It also included Naismith's rules of the game.

1868. College women's basketball game was between the University of California at Berkeley and Miss Head's School, on November 18, 1892.

1869. Intercollegiate men's basketball game was played between the University of Iowa and Geneva College at the latter's home in Beaver Falls, Pennsylvania, in 1893.

1870. Women's college basketball team in the South was established at Sophie Newcomb College in New Orleans, Louisiana, in 1893, by Clara Gregory Baer.

1871. Women's basketball game in the South that was open to the public was played by Sophie Newcomb College students, according to Clara Gregory Baer's rules, at the Southern Athletic Club in New Orleans, Louisiana, in 1895.

1872. Women's basketball published set of rules was developed by Clara Gregory Baer at Sophie Newcomb College in New Orleans, Louisiana, in 1895. Baer's rules, published under the name "Basquette," were largely aimed at slowing down women's basketball, to prevent "fatigue" among the players.

1873. Professional basketball team was the Trenton Basketball Team, in Trenton, New Jersey, in 1896. It had been a Young Men's Christian Association (YMCA) amateur team since 1892.

1874. Professional basketball game was the 1896–1897 season-opener of the Trenton Basketball Team, a 16–1 win over the Brooklyn Young Men's Christian Association (YMCA) team, played at the Masonic Temple in Trenton, New Jersey, on November 7, 1896.

1875. Basketball rules setting the number of players on each team at five were generally adopted in Young Men's Christian Association (YMCA) games in 1897.

1876. National Amateur Athletic Union (AAU) basketball tournament was held in New York City in 1897. It was won by the 23rd Street Young Men's Christian Association (YMCA) team of New York City, which on winning turned professional. The AAU then banned the team from using YMCA gymnasiums, so it became the first touring professional basketball team, named the New York Wanderers for its lack of a home court.

1877. Professional basketball league was the National Basketball League, founded in 1898. It was largely a local league, centered in Philadelphia, which started with three teams in Pennsylvania (one in Germantown, now part of Philadelphia, and two in Philadelphia itself) and three in New Jersey (Trenton, Camden, and Millville). The league dissolved in 1903, after six seasons of play.

BASKETBALL (1900-1909)
1878. African-American basketball club in the New York City area was the Smart Set Club, founded in Brooklyn, New York, in 1905.

1879. World Professional Basketball Championship an African-American tournament, was between the Kansas City Blue Diamonds and the Company E Club, of Schenectady, New York, in 1905.

1880. African-American basketball league in the New York City area was the Olympian Athletic League (OAL), established in 1906. Original members were the Smart Set Club, St. Christopher Athletic Club, and Marathone Athletic Club.

1881. Olympian Athletic League (OAL) title was won by Brooklyn's Smart Set Club, in 1907.

BASKETBALL (1910-1919)
1882. African-American basketball team at Howard University began play in 1911. Most of its members had been part of the 12th Street Branch Young Men's Christian Association (YMCA) team in Washington, D.C.

1883. Leondi Big Five African-American basketball team was organized in Pittsburgh, Pennsylvania, in 1913 by Cumberland Posey, playing its home games at Pittsburgh's Labor Temple. Leondi was African-American basketball's top team into the early 1920s.

1884. New York Celtics semiprofessional basketball team began play in 1916, using the Amsterdam Opera House on West 44th Street in Manhattan as its home court.

1885. New York Celtics fully professional basketball team sometimes called the Original Celtics, began play in New York City in 1918, adding several established professional players to its formerly semiprofessional ranks. The team would ultimately become the Boston Celtics.

BASKETBALL (1920-1929)
1886. African-American professional basketball team was the Renaissance Big Five, founded in New York City in 1923 by Robert J. Forbes. Their first game was a 28–22 win over the Collegiate Big Five, in New York on November 2, 1923.

1887. Harlem Globetrotters professional basketball game was played at Hinckley, Illinois, on January 7, 1925.

1888. Professional basketball major league the American Basketball League, was organized in 1926. The new league opened with eight teams: the Chicago Bruins, Cleveland Rosenblums, Palace Five of Washington, D.C., Brooklyn Arcadians, Boston Whirlwinds, Fort Wayne Caseys, Buffalo Bisons, and Detroit Pulaskis.

1889. Women's basketball national championship played largely by men's rules was sponsored by the Amateur Athletic Union (AAU) in 1926.

1890. National Collegiate Athletic Association (NCAA) consensus Division I All-American college basketball team was named in 1929. It consisted of Charley Hyatt, Joe School, Charles Murphy, Vern Corbin, Thomas Mitchell, and John Thompson.

BASKETBALL (1930-1939)
1891. African-American women's basketball team began play in 1931, in Philadelphia, Pennsylvania, sponsored by the *Philadelphia Tribune*. This was one of the leading women's basketball teams in the United States until it broke up in 1940. The team included Ora Washington, better known as a star tennis player of the period.

1892. African-American professional basketball team to win a world championship was the Renaissance Big Five, with a win over the New York Celtics in New York City, on March 30, 1932.

1893. Nationally known women's professional basketball team was the All American Red Heads, founded in 1936. The team toured widely, playing by men's basketball rules and against men's basketball teams.

1894. Basketball event held in the Olympic Games was in 1936 in Berlin, Germany. For men only, it was won on August 14 by the undefeated team from Universal Studios, representing the United States. The competition was held outdoors on clay and sand tennis courts, at the end made sodden by rain. The United States would win every Olympic basketball competition until 1972.

1895. Basketball team to win college basketball's National Invitation Tournament was Temple University, which defeated the University of Colorado 60–36 in 1938.

1896. World Tournament of professional basketball was held in Chicago, Illinois, in 1939. It was sponsored by the Chicago *Herald-American* from 1939 to 1948. The first tournament was won by the Renaissance Big Five team, which defeated the National Basketball League champion Oshkosh All-Stars in the championship game, 39–25.

1897. National Collegiate Athletic Association (NCAA) Division I tournament basketball game was a 42–30 Villanova University win over Brown University, in Philadelphia, Pennsylvania, on March 17, 1939.

1898. National Collegiate Athletic Association (NCAA) Division I tournament basketball championship game was a 46–33 University of Oregon win over Ohio State University in Evanston, Illinois, on March 27, 1939.

BASKETBALL (1940-1949)
1899. Basketball player to be named Most Valuable Player of the Division I National Collegiate Athletic Association (NCAA) Final Four was Marv Huffman of Indiana University of Indiana in 1940.

1900. Indiana University championship in the National Collegiate Athletic Association (NCAA) Men's Basketball National Tournament came in 1940, with a 60–42 win over the University of Kansas.

1901. College basketball games to be televised were a doubleheader, from Madison Square Garden in New York City, on February 28, 1940. The University of Pittsburgh defeated Fordham University in the opener, 50–37. In the second game, New York University defeated Georgetown University, 50–27.

BASKETBALL—(1940-1949)—*continued*

1902. University of Wisconsin championship in the National Collegiate Athletic Association (NCAA) Men's Basketball National Tournament came in 1941, with a 39–34 win over Washington State University.

1903. Stanford University championship in the National Collegiate Athletic Association (NCAA) Men's Basketball National Tournament came in 1942, with a 53–38 win over Dartmouth College.

1904. University of Wyoming championship in the National Collegiate Athletic Association (NCAA) Men's Basketball National Tournament came in 1943, with a 46–34 win over Georgetown University.

1905. College basketball team to win two consecutive college basketball National Invitation Tournaments was St. John's University, in 1943 and 1944.

1906. University of Utah championship in the National Collegiate Athletic Association (NCAA) Men's Basketball National Tournament came in 1944, with a 42–40 win over Dartmouth College.

1907. Oklahoma State University championship in the National Collegiate Athletic Association (NCAA) Men's Basketball National Tournament came in 1945, with a 49–45 win over New York University.

1908. Basketball player to be named Most Valuable Player of the Division I National Collegiate Athletic Association (NCAA) Final Four twice in a row was Bob Kurland of Oklahoma State University in 1945 and 1946.

1909. National Collegiate Athletic Association (NCAA) Division I tournament championship basketball game to be televised was a 43–40 Oklahoma State University win over the University of North Carolina, seen in the New York City area, in 1946.

1910. National Collegiate Athletic Association (NCAA) team to win two consecutive Division I basketball championships was Oklahoma State University, which defeated New York University 49–45 in 1945 and the University of North Carolina 43–40 in 1946.

1911. Basketball Association of America (BAA) founding meeting was held in New York City on June 6, 1946. Maurice Podoloff became first president of the new league, which would become the National Basketball Association (NBA) in 1949.

1912. Basketball Association of America (BAA) season began on November 1, 1946. The new league consisted of eleven teams: the Boston Celtics, Chicago Stags, Cleveland Rebels, Detroit Falcons, New York Knickerbockers (Knicks), Philadelphia Warriors, Pittsburgh Ironmen, Providence Steamrollers, St. Louis Bombers, Toronto Huskies, and Washington Capitols. The league would be renamed the National Basketball Association (NBA) in 1949.

1913. Boston Celtics regular season basketball game played at Boston Garden was a 55–49 win over the Toronto Huskies, on November 16, 1946.

1914. All–National Basketball Association (NBA) First Team in the league then still known as the Basketball Association of America (BAA), consisted of Bob Feerick and Bones McKinney of the Washington Capitols, Joe Fulks of the Philadelphia Warriors, Stan Miasek of the Detroit Falcons, and Max Zaslofsky of the Chicago Stags, in 1947.

1915. Basketball player to lead the National Basketball Association (NBA) in single season scoring was Joe Fulks of the Philadelphia Warriors, who scored 1,389 points in the 1946–1947 season of the league still known as the Basketball Association of American (BAA).

1916. Basketball team to win the championship of the National Basketball Association (NBA) then still known as the Basketball Association of America (BAA), was the Philadelphia Warriors, who defeated the Chicago Stags in the championship finals 4 games to 1, in 1947.

1917. Holy Cross College championship in the National Collegiate Athletic Association (NCAA) Men's Basketball National Tournament came in 1947, with a 58–47 win over the University of Oklahoma.

1918. National Basketball Association (NBA) draft took place on July 1, 1947, by telephone. It included both national picks and regional picks of college players. In later years, it would be heavily promoted by the league, and become a major media event.

1919. African-American basketball player on an Olympic team was Don Barksdale of the University of California at Los Angeles, in 1948.

1920. Baltimore Bullets National Basketball Association (NBA) championship came in 1948, with a 4 games to 2 win over the Philadelphia Warriors, in the league then known as the Basketball Association of America (BAA).

1921. African-American basketball player to win an Olympic gold medal was Don Barksdale of the University of California at Los Angeles, who was on the undefeated United States team that won the basketball gold medal on August 13, 1948, in London, England.

1922. Basketball team to win two consecutive National Collegiate Athletic Association (NCAA) national college basketball tournaments was the University of Kentucky, which defeated Oklahoma State University 46–36 in 1949, after a previous win in 1948.

BASKETBALL (1950-1959)
1923. African-American basketball player to be drafted into the National Basketball Association (NBA) was Harold Hunter of North Carolina College, who was drafted by the Baltimore Bullets in 1950.

1924. African-American basketball player to join the Boston Celtics of the National Basketball Association (NBA) was Chuck Cooper of Duquesne University, in 1950.

1925. African-American basketball player to join the New York Knickerbockers of the National Basketball Association (NBA) was Nat "Sweetwater" Clifton of Xavier University, in 1950.

1926. African-American basketball player to join the Washington Capitols of the National Basketball Association (NBA) was Earl Lloyd, of West Virginia State College, in 1950.

1927. Basketball team to win two consecutive National Basketball Association (NBA) championships was the Minneapolis Lakers, in 1949 and 1950.

1928. City College of New York championship in the National Collegiate Athletic Association (NCAA) Men's Basketball National Tournament came in 1950, with a 71–68 win over Bradley University.

1929. National Basketball Association (NBA) game in which a total of only 37 points was scored was a 19–18 Fort Wayne Pistons win over the Minneapolis Lakers at Minneapolis, Minnesota, on November 22, 1950.

1930. Basketball player to be named Most Valuable Player of the National Basketball Association (NBA) All-Star Game was Ed McCauley of the Boston Celtics in 1951.

1931. Basketball player to lead the National Basketball Association (NBA) in scoring in three consecutive years was George Mikan of the Minneapolis Lakers, from 1949 to 1951.

1932. Rochester Royals National Basketball Association (NBA) championship came in 1951, with a 4 games to 3 win over the New York Knicks.

1933. College basketball national scandal erupted in January 1951, with players at Manhattan College, City College, and Long Island University quickly implicated. Players at several other colleges were later involved, including some at the University of Kentucky and Bradley University.

1934. National Basketball Association (NBA) All-Star Game was a 111–94 win by the East over the West, on March 2, 1951, at Boston, Massachusetts.

1935. University of Kansas championship in the National Collegiate Athletic Association (NCAA) Men's Basketball National Tournament came in 1952, with an 80–63 win over St. John's University.

1936. Basketball player to have 734 rebounds during a single Division I National Collegiate Athletic Association (NCAA) season was Walt Dukes of Seton Hall University, in 1953.

1937. National Basketball Association (NBA) player to be named Rookie of the Year was Don Meineke of the Fort Wayne Pistons, in 1953.

1938. Basketball player to have 51 rebounds during a single Division I National Collegiate Athletic Association (NCAA) game was Bill Chambers of the College of William and Mary, against the University of Virginia on February 14, 1953.

1939. Basketball team to have 57 free throws in a single National Basketball Association (NBA) playoff game was the Boston Celtics, against the Syracuse Nationals on March 21, 1953.

1940. Adoption of the "24-second" rule by the National Basketball Association (NBA) was in 1954, providing a 24-second limit on possession of the ball by the in-bounding team. This was a major change, greatly speeding up the game, and began a new stage in basketball history.

1941. African-American college basketball team to win a national title was Tennessee State University, which won the National Association of Intercollegiate Athletics (NAIA) championship in 1954, with a 92–73 win over Southeast Oklahoma State at Kansas City, Missouri. The team was coached by Johnny B.

51

BASKETBALL—(1950-1959)—*continued*
McLendon, who would become the first African-American professional basketball coach in 1961, when he resigned from Tennessee State University to coach the Cleveland Pipers of the American Basketball League.

1942. Baltimore Bullets player to be named National Basketball Association (NBA) Rookie of the Year was Ray Felix, in 1954.

1943. Basketball player to score 23 free throws in a Division I National Collegiate Athletic Association (NCAA) game was Bob Carney of Bradley University, against the University of Colorado, in 1954.

1944. Basketball player to score 55 free throws in a Division I National Collegiate Athletic Association (NCAA) championship series was Bob Carney of Bradley University, in 1954.

1945. Basketball player to shoot 355 free throws during a single Division I National Collegiate Athletic Association (NCAA) season was Frank Selvy of Furman University, in 1954.

1946. Basketball team to win three consecutive National Basketball Association (NBA) championships was the Minneapolis Lakers, from 1952 to 1954.

1947. Limit on the number of fouls per period in the National Basketball Association (NBA) was adopted in 1954, limiting each team to 6 fouls in a quarter, with penalty shots for all subsequent fouls in that quarter.

1948. La Salle University championship in the National Collegiate Athletic Association (NCAA) Men's Basketball National Tournament came in 1954, with a 92–76 win over Bradley University.

1949. Basketball player to score 100 points in a single Division I National Collegiate Athletic Association (NCAA) game was Frank Selvy of Furman University, against Newberry College, on February 13, 1954.

1950. Adoption of a lane-widening rule by the National Basketball Association (NBA) was in 1955, providing a 12-foot foul lane, rather than the previous 6-foot lane.

1951. African-American woman college basketball player to be named an All-American was Missouri Arledge of Philander-Smith College, Arkansas, in 1955.

1952. Basketball player to be named Division I National Collegiate Athletic Association (NCAA) United Press International (UPI) Player of the Year was Tom Gola of La Salle University, in 1955. A perennial All-American guard, Gola went on to a long career as a top player in the National Basketball Association (NBA), largely with the Philadelphia Warriors.

1953. Basketball player to have 1,751 rebounds during his Division I National Collegiate Athletic Association (NCAA) career was Tom Gola of La Salle University, from 1952 to 1955.

1954. Basketball player to have an average of 25.6 rebounds per game during a single Division I National Collegiate Athletic Association (NCAA) season was Charlie Slack of Marshall University, in 1955.

1955. Milwaukee Hawks player to be named National Basketball Association (NBA) Rookie of the Year was Bob Pettit, in 1955.

1956. Syracuse Nationals National Basketball Association (NBA) championship came in 1955, with a 4 games to 3 win over the Fort Wayne Pistons.

1957. United States women's basketball team to play in the Pan American Games was in 1955.

1958. University of San Francisco championship in the National Collegiate Athletic Association (NCAA) Men's Basketball National Tournament came in 1955, with a 77–63 win over La Salle University.

1959. African-American to be elected to an All-National Basketball Association (NBA) team was Maurice Stokes of the Rochester Royals, who was elected to the All-National Basketball Association second team in his rookie year in 1956.

1960. Basketball player to have 27 rebounds in a single Division I National Collegiate Athletic Association (NCAA) Final Four championship series game was Bill Russell of the University of San Francisco, against the University of Iowa, in 1956.

1961. Basketball player to have 34 rebounds in a Division I National Collegiate Athletic Association (NCAA) game was Fred Cohen of Temple University, against the University of Connecticut, in 1956.

1962. Basketball player to win the National Basketball Association (NBA) Most Valuable Player Award the Maurice Podoloff Trophy, was Bob Pettit of the St. Louis Hawks, in 1956.

1963. Rochester Royals player to be named National Basketball Association (NBA) Rookie of the Year was Maurice Stokes, in 1956.

1964. Basketball player to lead the National Basketball Association (NBA) in free throw percentage for five consecutive years was Bill Sharman of the Boston Celtics, from 1953 to 1957.

1965. Basketball team to have 487 rebounds in one National Basketball Association (NBA) Finals series was the Boston Celtics, against the St. Louis Hawks, in 1957.

1966. Basketball team to make 244 free throws in one set of National Basketball Association (NBA) playoffs was the St. Louis Hawks, against the Boston Celtics, in 1957.

1967. Basketball team to score 827 points in a National Basketball Association (NBA) Finals series was the St. Louis Hawks, against the Boston Celtics, in 1957.

1968. Boston Celtics National Basketball Association (NBA) championship came in 1957, with a 4 games to 3 win over the St. Louis Hawks. The Celtics went on to become professional basketball's greatest dynasty, winning 11 championships between 1957 and 1969.

1969. Boston Celtics player to be named National Basketball Association (NBA) Most Valuable Player of the Year was Bob Cousy, in 1957.

1970. Boston Celtics player to be named National Basketball Association (NBA) Rookie of the Year was Tom Heinsohn, in 1957.

1971. University of North Carolina championship in the National Collegiate Athletic Association (NCAA) Men's Basketball National Tournament came in 1957, with a 54–53 overtime win over the University of Kansas.

1972. Basketball team to make 45 free throws in a single National Basketball Association (NBA) Finals game was the St. Louis Hawks, against the Boston Celtics, on April 13, 1957.

1973. Basketball player to grab 32 rebounds in a single half of a National Basketball Association (NBA) game was Bill Russell of the Boston Celtics, against the Philadelphia Warriors, on November 16, 1957.

1974. African-American to become a member of the Collegiate Basketball Officials Association was William "Dolly" King in 1958. He had formerly been a star basketball player at Long Island University, Brooklyn, New York.

1975. Basketball Hall of Fame was founded in 1958 at Springfield, Massachusetts, the birthplace of basketball. The first group of inductees, named in 1959, included the game's inventor James Naismith, Forrest "Phog" Allen, Angelo "Hank" Luisetti, George Mikan, Amos Alonso Stagg, and the entire first team of the Original Celtics, the popular name for the New York Celtics before they moved to Boston.

1976. Basketball player to score more than 2,000 points in a single National Basketball Association (NBA) season was George Yardley of the Detroit Pistons, who scored 2,001 points in the 1957–1958 season.

1977. Basketball team to average 31.9 free throws per game in a single National Basketball Association (NBA) season was the New York Knicks, in 1958.

1978. Philadelphia Warriors player to be named National Basketball Association (NBA) Rookie of the Year was Woody Sauldsberry, in 1958.

1979. St. Louis Hawks National Basketball Association (NBA) championship came in 1958, with a 4-games-to-2 win over the Boston Celtics.

1980. Basketball player to make 19 free throws in a National Basketball Association (NBA) Finals game was Bob Pettit of the St. Louis Hawks, against the Boston Celtics, on April 9, 1958.

1981. African-American basketball players to be named to an All–National Basketball Association (NBA) first team were Bill Russell of the Boston Celtics and rookie Elgin Baylor of the Minneapolis Lakers, both in 1959.

1982. Basketball player to average 29.5 rebounds per game in an National Basketball Association (NBA) Finals series was Bill Russell of the Boston Celtics, against the Minneapolis Lakers, in 1959.

1983. Basketball team to have 525 rebounds in one set of National Basketball Association (NBA) playoffs was the Boston Celtics, against the Syracuse Nationals, in 1959.

1984. Basketball team to score 869 points in one set of National Basketball Association (NBA) playoffs was the Boston Celtics, against the Syracuse Nationals, in 1959.

1985. Minneapolis Lakers player to be named National Basketball Association (NBA) Rookie of the Year was Elgin Baylor, in 1959.

BASKETBALL—(1950-1959)—*continued*
1986. Basketball player to have 19 assists in a single half of a National Basketball Association (NBA) game was Bob Cousy of the Boston Celtics, against the Minneapolis Lakers, at Minneapolis, Minnesota, on February 27, 1959.

1987. Basketball player to shoot 24 consecutive free throws, and to shoot 100 percent in free throws, during a single Division I National Collegiate Athletic Association (NCAA) game was Arlen Clark of Oklahoma State University, who made 24 of 24 free throws against the University of Colorado, on March 7, 1959.

BASKETBALL (1960-1969)
1988. African-American assistant coach in the National Basketball Association (NBA) was Earl Lloyd of the Detroit Pistons, in 1960.

1989. Basketball player to be named Division I National Collegiate Athletic Association (NCAA) United Press International (UPI) Player of the Year three consecutive times was Oscar Robertson of the University of Cincinnati, from 1958 to 1960. In 1960, Robertson also became the first college basketball player to be named United States Basketball Writers Association Player of the Year in two consecutive years, 1959 and 1960.

1990. Basketball player to score more than 2,700 points in his rookie season in the National Basketball Association (NBA) was Wilt Chamberlain of the Philadelphia Warriors, who scored 2,707 points in the 1959–1960 season. His 37.6 average points per game was also a new rookie high.

1991. Basketball team to lead the National Basketball Association (NBA) with an average of 71.5 rebounds per game was the Boston Celtics, in 1960.

1992. Ohio State University championship in the National Collegiate Athletic Association (NCAA) Men's Basketball National Tournament came in 1960, with a 75–55 win over the University of California.

1993. Philadelphia Warriors player to be named National Basketball Association (NBA) Most Valuable Player of the Year was Wilt Chamberlain, in 1960. His extraordinary career would yield three more league MVP awards (1966–1968).

1994. Basketball player to score 58 points in a single National Basketball Association (NBA) game was Wilt Chamberlain of the Philadelphia Warriors, against the Detroit Pistons at Bethlehem, Pennsylvania, on January 25, 1960.

1995. Basketball team to have 97 rebounds in a single National Basketball Association (NBA) playoff game was the Boston Celtics, against the Philadelphia Warriors, on March 19, 1960.

1996. Basketball player to collect 40 rebounds in a single National Basketball Association (NBA) Finals game was Bill Russell of the Boston Celtics, against the St. Louis Hawks, on March 29, 1960.

1997. Basketball team to have a rebound percentage of .667 in a single National Basketball Association (NBA) Finals game was the Boston Celtics, against the St. Louis Hawks, on April 9, 1960.

1998. Basketball player to get 55 rebounds in a single National Basketball Association (NBA) game was Wilt Chamberlain of the Philadelphia Warriors, against the Boston Celtics at Boston, Massachusetts, on November 24, 1960.

1999. Basketball teams to have a combined total of 188 rebounds in a single National Basketball Association (NBA) game were the Boston Celtics and the Detroit Pistons, on December 24, 1960.

2000. African-American professional basketball coach was Johnny B. McLendon of the Cleveland Pipers of the American Basketball League, in 1961. McLendon, one of the leading coaches in college basketball, resigned as coach of the Tennessee State University team to coach the Pipers.

2001. Basketball player to be named Division I National Collegiate Athletic Association (NCAA) Associated Press (AP) Player of the Year was Jerry Lucas of Ohio State University, in 1961. Lucas was also named United Press International (UPI) and United States Basketball Writers Association Player of the Year, as well as *Sports Illustrated* Sportsman of the Year. Lucas went on to a long and highly successful career in professional basketball.

2002. Basketball player to be named *Sports Illustrated* Sportsman of the Year was Jerry Lucas of Ohio State University, in 1961.

2003. Basketball player to grab 2,149 rebounds in a single National Basketball Association (NBA) season was Wilt Chamberlain of the Philadelphia Warriors, in 1961.

2004. Basketball player to lead the National Basketball Association (NBA) in free throw percentage for seven years was Bill Sharman of the Boston Celtics, between 1953 and 1961.

2005. Basketball player to score more than 3,000 points in a single National Basketball Association (NBA) season was Wilt Chamberlain, of the Philadelphia Warriors, who scored 3,033 points in the 1960–1961 season.

2006. Cincinnati Royals player to be named National Basketball Association (NBA) Rookie of the Year was Oscar Robertson, in 1961.

2007. University of Cincinnati championship in the National Collegiate Athletic Association (NCAA) Men's Basketball National Tournament came in 1961, with a 70–65 win over Ohio State University.

2008. Basketball player to score 50 or more points in seven consecutive National Basketball Association (NBA) games was Wilt Chamberlain of the Philadelphia Warriors, from December 16 to December 29, 1961.

2009. Basketball player to average more than 50 points per game in a single season in the National Basketball Association (NBA) was Wilt Chamberlain of the Philadelphia Warriors, who averaged 50.4 points per game during the 1961–1962 season.

2010. Basketball player to be named Division I National Collegiate Athletic Association (NCAA) Associated Press (AP) Player of the Year in two consecutive years was Jerry Lucas of Ohio State University, in 1961 and 1962. He also won the United Press International (UPI) and United States Basketball Writers Association Player of the Year awards in both years.

2011. Basketball player to collect 189 rebounds in a National Basketball Association (NBA) Finals series was Bill Russell of the Boston Celtics, in 1962.

2012. Basketball player to score 284 points in a National Basketball Association (NBA) Finals series was Elgin Baylor of the Los Angeles Lakers, in 1962. Baylor's 284 points included 101 field goals and 82 free throws, all figures setting enduring records. Despite his extraordinary performance, the Boston Celtics won the championship, four games to three.

2013. Basketball player to score 30 points or more in 11 consecutive National Basketball Association (NBA) playoff games was Elgin Baylor of the Los Angeles Lakers, in 1962.

2014. Basketball player to score 50 or more points in 45 games during a single National Basketball Association (NBA) season was Wilt Chamberlain of the Philadelphia Warriors, in the 1961–1962 season.

2015. Basketball player to score more than 4,000 points in a single National Basketball Association (NBA) season was Wilt Chamberlain, of the Philadelphia Warriors, who scored 4,029 points in the 1961–1962 season.

2016. Chicago Bulls player to be named National Basketball Association (NBA) Rookie of the Year was Walt Bellamy in 1962.

2017. Basketball player to score 100 points in a single National Basketball Association (NBA) game was Wilt Chamberlain of the Philadelphia Warriors, on March 2, 1962, in a 169–147 Warriors win over the New York Knicks at Hershey, Pennsylvania.

2018. Basketball player to score 61 points in a National Basketball Association (NBA) Finals game was Elgin Baylor of the Los Angeles Lakers, against the Boston Celtics, on April 14, 1962.

2019. All–National Basketball Association (NBA) Rookie Team consisted of Terry Dischinger of the Chicago Bulls, Chet Walker of the Syracuse Nationals, Zelmo Beaty of the St. Louis Hawks, John Havlicek of the Boston Celtics, and Dave DeBusschere of the Detroit Pistons, in 1963.

2020. Basketball player to average 23.3 rebounds in a Division I National Collegiate Athletic Association (NCAA) championship series was Nate Thurmond of Bowling Green University, in 1963.

2021. Basketball player to win three consecutive National Basketball Association (NBA) Most Valuable Player Awards was Bill Russell of the Boston Celtics, from 1961 to 1963.

2022. Basketball team to make 333 field goals in one set of National Basketball Association (NBA) playoffs was the Boston Celtics, against the Cincinnati Royals, in 1963.

2023. Coach to be named National Basketball Association (NBA) Coach of the Year winning the Arnold "Red" Auerbach Trophy, was Harry Gallatin of the St. Louis Hawks, in 1963. The award was named for the longtime coach of the Boston Celtics.

2024. Basketball player to make 113 field goals in one set of National Basketball Association (NBA) playoffs was Wilt Chamberlain of the San Francisco Warriors, against the St. Louis Hawks, in 1964.

2025. Cincinnati Royals player to be named National Basketball Association (NBA) Most Valuable Player was Oscar Robertson, in 1964.

BASKETBALL—(1960-1969)—*continued*

2026. University of California at Los Angeles championship in the National Collegiate Athletic Association (NCAA) Men's Basketball National Tournament came in 1964, with a 98–83 University of California at Los Angeles win over Duke University.

2027. Basketball player to get 220 rebounds in one set of National Basketball Association (NBA) playoffs was Wilt Chamberlain of the Philadelphia Warriors, in 1965.

2028. Basketball player to make 18 free throws in a single Division I National Collegiate Athletic Association (NCAA) Final Four championship series game was Gail Goodrich of the University of California at Los Angeles, against the University of Michigan, in 1965.

2029. Basketball player to make 86 free throws in one set of National Basketball Association (NBA) playoffs was Jerry West of the Los Angeles Lakers, against the Baltimore Bullets, in 1965.

2030. Basketball player to score 58 points in a single Division I National Collegiate Athletic Association (NCAA) Final Four championship series game was Bill Bradley of Princeton University, against Wichita State University, in 1965.

2031. Basketball player to score an average of 46.5 points in one set of National Basketball Association (NBA) playoffs was Jerry West of the Los Angeles Lakers, against the Baltimore Bullets, in 1965.

2032. Basketball player to win the National Basketball Association (NBA) Most Valuable Player Award five times was Bill Russell of the Boston Celtics, in 1960–1963 and 1965.

2033. College basketball player to receive the James E. Sullivan Memorial Award was perennial All-American Bill Bradley of Princeton University, in 1965. He went on to become a top professional basketball player with the New York Knicks, and later a U.S. senator from New Jersey and a presidential candidate.

2034. New York Knicks player to be named National Basketball Association (NBA) Rookie of the Year was Willis Reed, in 1965.

2035. Basketball player to have 18 rebounds in a single quarter of a National Basketball Association (NBA) game was Nate Thurmond of the San Francisco Warriors, against the Baltimore Bullets, at Baltimore, Maryland, on February 28, 1965.

2036. African-American National Basketball Association (NBA) head coach was Bill Russell of the Boston Celtics, who became player/coach of the Celtics in 1966.

2037. Basketball player to lead the National Basketball Association (NBA) in scoring for seven consecutive years was Wilt Chamberlain, from 1960 to 1966, topping 2,000 points in all seven years.

2038. Basketball player to make 840 free throws in a single National Basketball Association (NBA) season was Jerry West of the Los Angeles Lakers, in 1966.

2039. Basketball team to score 827 points in a National Basketball Association (NBA) Finals series was the Boston Celtics, against the Los Angeles Lakers, in 1966.

2040. Basketball team to win eight consecutive National Basketball Association (NBA) titles was the Boston Celtics, from 1959 to 1966.

2041. San Francisco Warriors player to be named National Basketball Association (NBA) Rookie of the Year was Rick Barry, in 1966.

2042. Texas Western championship in the National Collegiate Athletic Association (NCAA) Men's Basketball National Tournament came in 1966, with a 72–65 win over the University of Kentucky.

2043. Championship win by a team with an all-African-American starting lineup in the final game, and the first championship for Texas Western, in the National Collegiate Athletic Association (NCAA) Men's Basketball National Tournament was Texas Western's 72–65 win over the all-white University of Kentucky team, on March 19, 1966.

2044. San Francisco Warriors regular season basketball game played at the Oakland Coliseum in Oakland, California, was a 108–101 win over the Chicago Bulls, on November 29, 1966. The team would become the Golden State Warriors in 1971. The arena would be renovated and renamed the New Arena in Oakland in 1997.

2045. Basketball player to make 14 free throws in a single quarter of a National Basketball Association (NBA) game was Rick Barry of the San Francisco Warriors, against the New York Knicks, on December 6, 1966, at New York City.

2046. Basketball player to get an average of 32 rebounds in a National Basketball Association (NBA) playoff series was Wilt Chamberlain of the Philadelphia 76ers, against the Boston Celtics, in 1967.

2047. Detroit Pistons player to be named National Basketball Association (NBA) Rookie of the Year was Dave Bing, in 1967.

2048. Basketball player to make 18 consecutive field goals in a single National Basketball Association (NBA) game was Wilt Chamberlain, in a Philadelphia 76ers win over the Baltimore Bullets at Pittsburgh, Pennsylvania, on February 24, 1967.

2049. Basketball player to grab 41 rebounds in a single National Basketball Association (NBA) playoff game was Wilt Chamberlain of the Philadelphia 76ers, against the Boston Celtics, on April 5, 1967.

2050. Basketball team to get 93 rebounds in a single National Basketball Association (NBA) Finals game was the Philadelphia 76ers, against the San Francisco Warriors, on April 16, 1967.

2051. American Basketball Association season began in October 1967. The new league had been announced on February 1, 1967, with former National Basketball Association (NBA) star George Mikan as its first commissioner.

2052. Philadelphia 76ers regular season basketball game played at The Spectrum in Philadelphia, Pennsylvania, was a 103–87 win over the Los Angeles Lakers, on October 18, 1967.

2053. Basketball player to score 16 consecutive field goals in a single Division I National Collegiate Athletic Association (NCAA) game was Doug Grayson of Kent State University, against the University of North Carolina, on December 6, 1967.

2054. Los Angeles Lakers regular season basketball game played at the Forum (later called the Great Western Forum) in Inglewood, California, was a 147–118 win over the San Diego Rockets, on December 31, 1967.

2055. Basketball player to win the American Basketball Association Most Valuable Player Award was Connie Hawkins of the Pittsburgh Condors, in 1968.

2056. Basketball player to win the American Basketball Association Rookie of the Year Award was Mel Daniels of the Minnesota Pipers, in 1968.

2057. Coach to win the American Basketball Association Coach of the Year Award was Vince Cazzeta of the Pittsburgh Condors, in 1968.

2058. Professional basketball player to be named *Sports Illustrated* Sportsman of the Year was perennial Boston Celtics All-Star Bill Russell, in 1968.

2059. New York Knicks regular season basketball game played at Madison Square Garden the fourth arena known by that name, was a 114–102 win over the San Diego Rockets, on April 14, 1968.

2060. Baltimore Bullets player to be named National Basketball Association (NBA) Most Valuable Player of the Year was Wes Unseld, in 1969.

2061. Basketball player to be named Most Valuable Player of the Division I National Collegiate Athletic Association (NCAA) Final Four three times in a row was Lew Alcindor, later known as Kareem Abdul-Jabbar, of the University of California at Los Angeles in 1967, 1968, and 1969.

2062. Basketball player to be named Most Valuable Player of the National Basketball Association (NBA) Finals was Jerry West of the Los Angeles Lakers, in 1969.

2063. Basketball player to lead the National Basketball Association (NBA) in field goal percentage for five successive years was Wilt Chamberlain, from 1965 to 1969.

2064. College women's basketball National Invitation Tournament was held at West Chester State College in Pennsylvania, in 1969. It was won by the West Chester State team, defeating Western Carolina University.

2065. Basketball player to make 30 free throws during a single Division I National Collegiate Athletic Association (NCAA) game was Pete Maravich of Louisiana State University, against Oregon State University, on December 22, 1969.

BASKETBALL (1970-1979)

2066. Basketball player to average 44.5 points per game in a single Division I National Collegiate Athletic Association (NCAA) season was Pete Maravich of Louisiana State University, in 1970.

2067. Basketball player to average 52.7 points per game in a Division I National Collegiate Athletic Association (NCAA) championship series was Austin Carr of the University of Notre Dame, in 1970.

BASKETBALL—(1970-1979)—*continued*

2068. Basketball player to score 1,381 points in a single Division I National Collegiate Athletic Association (NCAA) season was Pete Maravich of Louisiana State University, in 1970.

2069. Basketball player to score 61 points in a single Division I National Collegiate Athletic Association (NCAA) championship series game was Austin Carr of the University of Notre Dame, against the University of Ohio, in 1970.

2070. Basketball player to score a total of 3,667 points during his college career was Pete Maravich of Louisiana State University, in 1970.

2071. Basketball team to score 332 field goals in a National Basketball Association (NBA) Finals series was the New York Knicks, against the Los Angeles Lakers, in 1970.

2072. Milwaukee Bucks player to be named National Basketball Association (NBA) Rookie of the Year was Kareem Abdul-Jabbar, in 1970.

2073. New York Knicks National Basketball Association (NBA) championship came in 1970, with a 4 games to 3 win over the Los Angeles Lakers.

2074. New York Knicks player to be named National Basketball Association (NBA) Most Valuable Player of the Year was Willis Reed, in 1970.

2075. Basketball team to have 44 assists in a single National Basketball Association (NBA) Finals game was the Los Angeles Lakers, against the New York Knicks, on May 6, 1970.

2076. Portland Trail Blazers regular season basketball game played at the Memorial Coliseum in Portland, Oregon, was a 115–112 win over the Cleveland Cavaliers on October 16, 1970.

2077. Basketball player to have 1,224 rebounds during his Division I National Collegiate Athletic Association (NCAA) college career was Artis Gilmore of Jacksonville University, in 1970 and 1971.

2078. Milwaukee Bucks National Basketball Association (NBA) championship came in 1971, with a four games to none win over the Baltimore Bullets.

2079. Milwaukee Bucks player to be named National Basketball Association (NBA) Most Valuable Player of the Year was Kareem Abdul-Jabbar, in 1971.

2080. Portland Trail Blazers player to be named National Basketball Association (NBA) Rookie of the Year was Geoff Petrie, in 1971. He shared the honor with Dave Cowens of the Boston Celtics.

2081. African-American to become the general manager of a team in a major professional sport was Wayne Embry, who became general manager of the Milwaukee Bucks in 1972, after his career as a basketball player ended. The Hall-of-Famer would later be the longtime general manager of the Cleveland Cavaliers.

2082. Los Angeles Lakers National Basketball Association (NBA) championship came in 1972, with a 4 games to 1 win over the New York Knicks.

2083. Basketball team to have a road game winning percentage of .816 in a single National Basketball Association (NBA) season was the Los Angeles Lakers, in 1972.

2084. College basketball coach to be named *Sports Illustrated* Sportsman of the Year was John Wooden, coach at the University of California at Los Angeles, in 1972. His men's team was a dominant force in college basketball.

2085. College women's basketball United States National Tournament sponsored by the Association for Intercollegiate Athletics for Women (AIAW), was held at Illinois State Unversity in 1972, and was won by Immaculata College.

2086. Basketball team to win 16 consecutive road games in the National Basketball Association (NBA) was the Los Angeles Lakers, in a streak stretching from November 8, 1971, to January 7, 1972.

2087. Basketball team to win 33 consecutive games in the National Basketball Association (NBA) was the Los Angeles Lakers, with a winning streak that ran from November 5, 1971, to January 7, 1972.

2088. Basketball team from the Soviet Union to win the men's title in the Olympic Games won on September 10, 1972, in Munich, West Germany. A controversial ruling in the final seconds left the Soviet team undefeated in the competition at 9-0, giving the United States team its first loss since Olympic basketball competition had begun in 1936.

2089. Atlanta Hawks regular season basketball game played at The Omni in Atlanta, Georgia, was a 109–101 win over the New York Knicks, on October 15, 1972.

2090. Basketball player to be named Most Valuable Player of the National Basketball Association (NBA) Finals twice was Willis Reed of the New York Knickerbockers (Knicks), in 1970 and 1973.

2091. Basketball player to get 23,924 career rebounds, and to average 22.9 rebounds per game, in his National Basketball Association (NBA) career was Wilt Chamberlain, from 1959 to 1973. Both were enduring records.

2092. Basketball player to have a field goal average of 95.5 percent in a single Division I National Collegiate Athletic Association (NCAA) Final Four championship series game was Bill Walton of the University of California at Los Angeles, against Memphis State University, in 1973.

2093. Basketball player to have an average field-goal percentage of .727 in a single National Basketball Association (NBA) season one of his record nine seasons leading in that category, was Wilt Chamberlain, in 1973.

2094. Basketball player to lead the National Basketball Association (NBA) in rebounds for 11 seasons, and in field-goal percentage nine times was Wilt Chamberlain, between 1960 and 1973. Both were enduring records.

2095. Basketball player to score 50 points or more in 118 games during his National Basketball Association (NBA) career was Wilt Chamberlain, from 1959 to 1973.

2096. Basketball team to win seven consecutive Division I National Collegiate Athletic Association (NCAA) championships was the University of California at Los Angeles, from 1967 to 1973. UCLA also won Division I championships in 1964, 1965, and 1975, for a total of ten championships in 12 seasons under coach John Wooden.

2097. Women's Amateur Basketball Association was founded in 1973, replacing the Amateur Athletic Association as the national organization of U.S. women's basketball.

2098. Basketball team to get 39 offensive rebounds in a single National Basketball Association (NBA) game was the Boston Celtics, against the Capital Bullets, on October 20, 1973.

2099. Basketball player to have 17 blocked shots in a single National Basketball Association (NBA) game was Elmore Smith of the Los Angeles Lakers, against the Portland Trail Blazers, on October 28, 1973.

2100. Washington Bullets regular season game played at the US Air Arena in Landover, Maryland, was a 98–96 win over the Seattle SuperSonics, on December 2, 1973.

2101. Basketball player to be named Division I National Collegiate Athletic Association (NCAA) United States Basketball Writers Association Player of the Year in three consecutive years was Bill Walton of the University of California at Los Angeles, from 1972 to 1974. Walton also won the United Press International (UPI) Player of the Year and Naismith Awards all three years and the Associated Press (AP) Player of the Year Award in 1973 and 1974. He went on to become a major figure in professional basketball, although hampered by injuries during much of his career.

2102. Basketball player to go from high school into the American Basketball Association (ABA) without attending college was Moses Malone, in 1974.

2103. Basketball player to play 345 minutes in a single set of National Basketball Association (NBA) playoffs was Kareem Abdul-Jabbar of the Milwaukee Bucks, against the Boston Celtics, in 1974.

2104. Basketball team to average 37.5 rebounds per game in a single National Basketball Association (NBA) season was the Boston Celtics, in 1974.

2105. North Carolina State University championship in the National Collegiate Athletic Association (NCAA) Men's Basketball National Tournament came in 1974, with a 76–64 win over Marquette University.

2106. Basketball team to get 61 defensive rebounds in a single National Basketball Association (NBA) game was the Boston Celtics, against the Washington Bullets, on March 17, 1974.

2107. Indiana Pacers regular season game played at Market Square Arena in Indianapolis, Indiana, was a 129-101 loss to the San Antonio Spurs, on October 18, 1974. They would play there until November 1999, when they moved to the Conseco Fieldhouse.

2108. Basketball player to have a .739 field goal percentage in a National Basketball Association (NBA) Finals series was Derrek Dickey of the Golden State Warriors, in 1975.

2109. Buffalo Braves player to be named National Basketball Association (NBA) Most Valuable Player of the Year was Bob McAdoo, in 1975.

BASKETBALL—(1970-1979)—*continued*

2110. College women's basketball All-America team was selected by the Women's Basketball Coaches Association in 1975. The team consisted of Carolyn Bush, Marjorie Crawford, Nancy Dunkle, Lusia Harris, Jan Irby, Ann Meyers, Brenda Moeller, Debbie Oing, Sue Rojcewicz, and Susan Yaw.

2111. Golden State Warriors National Basketball Association (NBA) championship came in 1975, with a four-game sweep over the Washington Bullets.

2112. Professional basketball player to win the Pro Basketball Writers Association J. Walter Kennedy Citizenship Award was Wes Unseld of the Washington Bullets, in 1975.

2113. Women's basketball small college National Invitation Tournament was held at Southern Colorado College in 1975. The final game, for the women's small college championship, was a 60–49 win by Phillips University of Oklahoma over Talladega College of Alabama.

2114. Women's basketball game played in Madison Square Garden in New York City, was on February 22, 1975, between Queens College and Immaculata College.

2115. Basketball team to make 22 steals in a single National Basketball Association (NBA) playoff game was the Golden State Warriors against the Seattle SuperSonics, on April 14, 1975.

2116. Basketball team to have a defensive rebound percentage of .952 in a single National Basketball Association (NBA) playoff game was the Chicago Bulls, against the Golden State Warriors, on April 30, 1975.

2117. Denver Nuggets regular season game played at McNichols Sports Arena in Denver, Colorado, was a 118–101 win over the Spirits of St. Louis, on October 25, 1975, when both teams were in the American Basketball Association (ABA).

2118. Houston Rockets regular season game played at The Summit in Houston, Texas, was a 107–103 loss to the Milwaukee Bucks, on November 2, 1975. The arena would be renamed the Compaq Center in 1997.

2119. Basketball player to have 11 steals in a single National Basketball Association (NBA) game was Larry Kanon of the San Antonio Spurs, against the Kansas City–Omaha Kings, at Kansas City, Missouri, on December 26, 1975.

2120. Los Angeles Lakers player to be named National Basketball Association (NBA) Most Valuable Player of the Year was Kareem Abdul-Jabbar, in 1976.

2121. Basketball player to win the American Basketball Association Most Valuable Player Award in three consecutive years was Julius Erving of the New York Nets, from 1974 to 1976.

2122. Basketball team to have 240 defensive rebounds in a National Basketball Association (NBA) Finals series was the Boston Celtics, against the Phoenix Suns, in 1976.

2123. Basketball team to have 94 steals in a single set of National Basketball Association (NBA) playoffs was the Golden State Warriors, against the Phoenix Suns, in 1976.

2124. Phoenix Suns player to be named National Basketball Association (NBA) Rookie of the Year was Alvan Adams, in 1976.

2125. Women's basketball event held in the Olympic Games was in 1976 in Montreal, Quebec, Canada. The gold medal, awarded on July 27, went to the Soviet team.

2126. Basketball player in Division I of the National Collegiate Athletic Association (NCAA) to receive the Wooden Award as Player of the Year was Marques Johnson of the University of California at Los Angeles, in 1977. That same year, he also received the United Press International (UPI), Associated Press (AP), United States Basketball Writers Association, National Association of Basketball Coaches, and Naismith Player of the Year awards. The Wooden Award is named after longtime UCLA coach John Wooden.

2127. Basketball player to have 1,111 defensive rebounds in a single National Basketball Association (NBA) season was Kareem Abdul-Jabbar of the Los Angeles Lakers, in 1977.

2128. Basketball player to have 91 defensive rebounds in a National Basketball Association (NBA) Finals series was Bill Walton of the Portland Trail Blazers, in 1977.

2129. Basketball player to have 95 defensive rebounds in a single set of National Basketball Association (NBA) playoffs was Kareem Abdul-Jabbar of the Los Angeles Lakers, against the Golden State Warriors, in 1977.

2130. Basketball player to win the Broderick Cup as top college woman athlete of the year was Lusia Harris of Delta State College, in 1977.

2131. Marquette University championship in the National Collegiate Athletic Association (NCAA) Men's Basketball National Tournament came in 1977, with a 67–59 win over the University of North Carolina.

2132. Portland Trail Blazers National Basketball Association (NBA) championship came in 1977, with a 4 games to 2 win over the Philadelphia 76ers.

2133. Basketball team to have 46 defensive rebounds in a single National Basketball Association (NBA) Finals game was the Portland Trail Blazers, against the Philadelphia 76ers, on June 3, 1977.

2134. Basketball player to have 8 blocked shots in a National Basketball Association (NBA) Finals game was Bill Walton of the Portland Trail Blazers, against the Philadelphia 76ers, on June 5, 1977.

2135. All-Star Classic (All-American Classic) in women's college basketball was played in 1978, at the Greensboro Coliseum, in Greensboro, North Carolina, between teams of Eastern and Western women's intercollegiate basketball all-stars.

2136. Basketball player to win the Margaret Wade Trophy, awarded to the women's college basketball Player of the Year was Carol Blazejowski of Montclair State University, in 1978.

2137. Basketball team to average 12.9 steals per game in a single National Basketball Association (NBA) season was the Phoenix Suns, in 1978.

2138. Basketball team to have 233 assists in a single set of National Basketball Association (NBA) playoffs was the Milwaukee Bucks, against the Denver Nuggets, in 1978.

2139. Major college women's basketball player to score more than 3,000 points during her college career was Carol Blazejowski of Montclair State College, from 1975 to 1978. She finished her college career with 3,199 points.

2140. Portland Trail Blazers player to be named National Basketball Association (NBA) Most Valuable Player of the Year was Bill Walton, in 1978.

2141. Basketball player to score 13 field goals in a single quarter of a National Basketball Association (NBA) game was David Thompson of the Denver Nuggets, at Detroit, Michigan, on April 9, 1978.

2142. Basketball player to score 33 points in a single quarter of a National Basketball Association (NBA) game was George Gervin of the San Antonio Spurs, against the New Orleans Jazz, on April 9, 1978, at New Orleans, Louisiana.

2143. Basketball team to have 30 offensive rebounds in a single National Basketball Association (NBA) playoff game was the Seattle SuperSonics, against the Portland Trail Blazers, on April 23, 1978.

2144. Women's Professional Basketball League game was played on December 9, 1978, a 92–87 Chicago Hustle victory over the Milwaukee Does at the Milwaukee Arena, in Milwaukee, Wisconsin. The league lasted for three years, ending after the 1980–1981 season.

2145. Basketball team to have 53 assists in a single National Basketball Association (NBA) game was the Milwaukee Bucks, against the Detroit Pistons, on December 26, 1978.

2146. Basketball player to capture 587 offensive rebounds in a single National Basketball Association (NBA) season was Moses Malone, in 1979.

2147. Basketball team to have 142 offensive rebounds in a single set of National Basketball Association (NBA) playoffs was the Washington Bullets, against the San Antonio Spurs, in 1979.

2148. Houston Rockets player to be named National Basketball Association (NBA) Most Valuable Player of the Year was Moses Malone, in 1979.

2149. Kansas City Kings player to be named National Basketball Association (NBA) Rookie of the Year was Phil Ford, in 1979.

2150. Michigan State University championship in the National Collegiate Athletic Association (NCAA) Men's Basketball National Tournament came in 1979, with a 75–64 win over Indiana State University.

2151. Seattle SuperSonics National Basketball Association (NBA) championship came in 1979, with a 4 games to 1 win over the Washington Bullets.

2152. Woman basketball player to sign with a National Basketball Association (NBA) team was Ann Meyers, who signed a guaranteed $50,000 one-year contract with the Indiana Pacers in 1979. An All-American college basketball star at the University of California at Los Angeles, Meyers did not play for the Pacers, being cut from the squad before the season opened, although she was paid for the season.

BASKETBALL—(1970-1979)—*continued*

2153. Three-point goal scored in a National Basketball Association (NBA) game was shot by Chris Ford of the Boston Celtics, playing against the Houston Rockets at Boston, Massachusetts, on October 12, 1979.

BASKETBALL (1980-1989)
2154. Basketball player to win the National Basketball Association (NBA) Most Valuable Player Award six times was Kareem Abdul-Jabbar, with the Milwaukee Bucks in 1971 and 1972, and with the Los Angeles Lakers in 1974, 1976, 1977, and 1980.

2155. Basketball team to have 80 blocked shots in a National Basketball Association (NBA) Finals series was the Philadelphia 76ers, against the Los Angeles Lakers, in 1980.

2156. Basketball team to have a .580 rebound percentage in a National Basketball Association (NBA) Finals series was the Los Angeles Lakers, against the Philadelphia 76ers, in 1980.

2157. Basketball team to have a .782 defensive rebound percentage in a National Basketball Association (NBA) Finals series was the Los Angeles Lakers, against the Philadelphia 76ers, in 1980.

2158. Coach to be named National Basketball Association (NBA) Coach of the Year twice was Bill Fitch of the Boston Celtics, in 1980. He had been also been named Coach of the Year in 1976, while coaching the Cleveland Cavaliers.

2159. College women's basketball player to receive the Margaret Wade Trophy in two consecutive years was Nancy Lieberman (later Lieberman-Cline) of Old Dominion University, in 1979 and 1980.

2160. College women's basketball player to win the Broderick Cup in two consecutive years was Nancy Lieberman (later Lieberman-Cline) of Old Dominion University, in 1979 and 1980.

2161. University of Louisville championship in the National Collegiate Athletic Association (NCAA) Men's Basketball National Tournament came in 1980, with a 59–54 win over the University of California at Los Angeles.

2162. Basketball player to score 42 points in a National Basketball Association (NBA) Finals game in his rookie year was Earvin "Magic" Johnson of the Los Angeles Lakers, against the Philadelphia 76ers, on May 16, 1980.

2163. Basketball team from Yugoslavia to win the men's title in the Olympic Games was in 1980 in Moscow, the Soviet Union, in the United States–boycotted Olympics. Led by Drazen Dalipagic and Dragan Kicanovic, they defeated Italy in the final on July 30.

2164. Dallas Mavericks regular season game played at Reunion Arena in Dallas, Texas, was a 103–92 win over the San Antonio Spurs, on October 11, 1980.

2165. Basketball player to have 46 offensive rebounds in the National Basketball Association (NBA) Finals was Moses Malone of the Houston Rockets, against the Boston Celtics, in 1981.

2166. Basketball player to have a .958 free throw average in a single National Basketball Association (NBA) season was Calvin Murphy, in 1981.

2167. Basketball team to have a .410 offensive rebound average in a National Basketball Association (NBA) Finals series was the Boston Celtics, against the Houston Rockets, in 1981.

2168. Major college women's basketball player to score more than 3,500 points during her college career was Lynette Woodard of the University of Kansas, from 1978 to 1981. She finished her college career with 3,649 points.

2169. Utah Jazz player to be named National Basketball Association (NBA) Rookie of the Year was Darrell Griffith, in 1981.

2170. Basketball team to have 20 blocked shots in a single National Basketball Association (NBA) playoff game was the Philadelphia 76ers, against the Milwaukee Bucks, on April 5, 1981.

2171. Basketball team to have 28 offensive rebounds in a single National Basketball Association (NBA) Finals game was the Houston Rockets, against the Boston Celtics, on May 10, 1981.

2172. Women's National Basketball Championship was held at the Kemper Arena, Kansas City, Missouri, from August 12 to August 14, 1981. It was sponsored by the National Association for Intercollegiate Athletics (NAIA).

2173. New Jersey Nets regular season basketball game played at the Brendan Byrne Arena in East Rutherford, New Jersey, was a 103–99 loss to the New York Knicks, on October 30, 1981. The facility would later be renamed the Continental Airlines Arena.

2174. Basketball team to score an average of 126.5 points per game in a single National Basketball Association (NBA) season was the Denver Nuggets, in 1982.

2175. College women's basketball player to score 275 free throws in a single Division I National Collegiate Athletic Association (NCAA) season was Lorri Bauman of Drake University, in 1982.

2176. College women's basketball player to score 392 points in a single Division I National Collegiate Athletic Association (NCAA) season was Barbara Kennedy of Clemson University, in 1982.

2177. New Jersey Nets player to be named National Basketball Association (NBA) Rookie of the Year was Buck Williams, in 1982.

2178. Women's Basketball Coaches Association convention was held at Virginia Beach, Virginia, during the 1982 National Collegiate Athletic Association (NCAA) women's basketball national tournament. The organization had been founded in 1981.

2179. Women's basketball team to win the the National Collegiate Athletic Association (NCAA) national tournament was Louisiana Tech University, which defeated Cheyney State University 76–62, in 1982.

2180. College women's basketball team to have a 54-game winning streak was Louisiana Tech University, lasting from December 1, 1980, to January 27, 1982.

2181. Basketball player to have 21 offensive rebounds in a single National Basketball Association (NBA) game was Moses Malone of the Houston Rockets, against the Seattle Super-Sonics, on February 11, 1982.

2182. Basketball team to make 39 consecutive free throws in a single National Basketball Association (NBA) game was the Utah Jazz, against the Portland Trail Blazers, at Portland, Oregon, on December 7, 1982.

2183. Basketball player to be named Division I National Collegiate Athletic Association (NCAA) Associated Press (AP) Player of the Year in three consecutive years was Ralph Sampson of the University of Virginia, from 1981 to 1983. Sampson, who was by far the leading college center of his day, also won the United Press International (UPI), United States Basketball Writers Association, and Naismith Player of the Year awards from 1981 to 1983. In addition, he won the Wooden and National Association of Basketball Coaches awards in 1982 and 1983.

2184. Basketball player to be named National Basketball Association (NBA) Defensive Player of the Year was Sidney Moncrief of the Milwaukee Bucks, in 1983. Moncrief also won that honor in 1984, becoming the first to win it twice, and twice in a row.

2185. Basketball player to have a career average of 9.8 defensive rebounds per game in the National Basketball Association (NBA) was Dave Cowens, from 1970 to 1983.

2186. Basketball player to lead the National Basketball Association (NBA) in offensive rebounds for seven consecutive years was Moses Malone, between 1977 and 1983.

2187. Basketball player to win the National Basketball Association (NBA) Sixth Man Award was Bobby Jones of the Philadelphia 76ers, in 1983.

2188. College women's basketball player to have 40 rebounds in a single Division I National Collegiate Athletic Association (NCAA) game was Deborah Temple of Delta State College, in 1983.

2189. College women's basketball player to receive the Naismith Award was Ann Donovan, of Old Dominion University, in 1983. She also won the Women's Basketball Coaches Association Player of the Year Award.

2190. San Diego Clippers player to be named National Basketball Association (NBA) Rookie of the Year was Terry Cummings, in 1983.

2191. Basketball team to have a .707 field goal percentage in a single National Basketball Association (NBA) game was the San Antonio Spurs, against the Dallas Mavericks, at Dallas, Texas, on April 16, 1983.

2192. Basketball team to have 51 assists, and 56 defensive rebounds, in a single National Basketball Association (NBA) playoff game was the San Antonio Spurs, against the Denver Nuggets, on May 4, 1983.

2193. Basketball team to score 186 points, and 74 field goals, in a single National Basketball Association (NBA) game was the Detroit Pistons, against the Denver Nuggets, at Denver, Colorado, on December 13, 1983.

2194. National Basketball Association (NBA) game in which a total of 370 points was scored was the 186–184 Detroit Pistons win over the Denver Nuggets, at Denver, Colorado, on December 13, 1983, the highest scoring game in NBA history.

BASKETBALL—(1980-1989)—*continued*

2195. Basketball player to have 95 assists in a National Basketball Association (NBA) Finals series was Earvin "Magic" Johnson of the Los Angeles Lakers, against the Boston Celtics, in 1984.

2196. Basketball player to win the National Basketball Association (NBA) Defensive Player of the Year Award twice was Sidney Moncrief of the Milwaukee Bucks, in 1983 and 1984.

2197. Basketball team to have 131 offensive rebounds in a National Basketball Association (NBA) Finals series was the Boston Celtics, against the Los Angeles Lakers, in 1984.

2198. Basketball team to have 196 assists in a National Basketball Association (NBA) Finals series was the Los Angeles Lakers, against the Boston Celtics, in 1984.

2199. Basketball team to have 65 steals in a National Basketball Association (NBA) Finals series was the Boston Celtics, against the Los Angeles Lakers, in 1984.

2200. Basketball team to have an .894 free throw percentage in a single set of National Basketball Association (NBA) playoffs was the Dallas Mavericks, against the Seattle SuperSonics, in 1984.

2201. College women's basketball team to win the National Collegiate Athletic Association (NCAA) national championship in two consecutive years was the University of Southern California, in 1983 and 1984.

2202. Georgetown University championship in the National Collegiate Athletic Association (NCAA) Men's Basketball National Tournament came in 1984, with an 84–75 win over the University of Houston.

2203. National Basketball Association (NBA) draft lottery was held in 1984. The New York Knicks won the first pick, choosing star center Patrick Ewing, who would be their franchise player throughout his career.

2204. College women's basketball player to score 27 field goals in a single Division I National Collegiate Athletic Association (NCAA) game was Lorri Bauman of Drake University, against Southwest Missouri State College, on January 6, 1984.

2205. Basketball player to score 14 points in an overtime period in the National Basketball Association (NBA) was Butch Carter of the Indiana Pacers, against the Boston Celtics, on March 20, 1984.

2206. Basketball player to have 14 assists in a single quarter of a National Basketball Association (NBA) game was John Lucas of the San Antonio Spurs, against the Denver Nuggets, at Denver, on April 15, 1984.

2207. Basketball player to have 21 assists in a National Basketball Association (NBA) Finals game was Earvin "Magic" Johnson of the Los Angeles Lakers, against the Boston Celtics, on June 3, 1984.

2208. Basketball team from the United States to win the women's title in the Olympic Games was in 1984 in Los Angeles, California. Led by players such as Cheryl Miller, Teresa Edwards, and Lynette Woodard, the U.S. team won on August 7, in the absence of the Soviet team, which boycotted the Olympics.

2209. Los Angeles Clippers regular season basketball game played at the Memorial Sports Arena in Los Angeles, California, was a 107–105 win over the New York Knicks, on November 1, 1984.

2210. Basketball player to have 456 blocked shots, and an average of 5.56 blocked shots, in a single National Basketball Association (NBA) season was Mark Eaton of the Utah Jazz, in 1985.

2211. Basketball player to have an average of 14 assists per game in a National Basketball Association (NBA) Finals series was Earvin "Magic" Johnson of the Los Angeles Lakers, against the Boston Celtics, in 1985.

2212. Basketball player to have an average of 17.6 assists per game in a National Basketball Association (NBA) playoff series was Earvin "Magic" Johnson of the Los Angeles Lakers, against the Portland Trail Blazers, in 1985.

2213. Basketball player to lead the National Basketball Association (NBA) for three years in steals was Micheal Ray Richardson, in 1980, 1983, and 1985.

2214. Basketball player to win the National Basketball Association (NBA) Sixth Man Award twice in a row was Kevin McHale of the Boston Celtics, in 1984 and 1985.

2215. Basketball team to have a .545 field goal percentage in a single National Basketball Association (NBA) season was the Los Angeles Lakers, in 1985.

2216. Basketball team to have a .600 field goal percentage in the National Basketball Association (NBA) playoffs was the Los Angeles Lakers, against the Phoenix Suns, in 1985.

2217. Basketball team to have an average of 31.4 assists per game in a single National Basketball Association (NBA) season was the Los Angeles Lakers, in 1985.

2218. College women's basketball player to have 534 rebounds in a single Division I National Collegiate Athletic Association (NCAA) season was Wanda Ford of Drake University, in 1985.

2219. College women's basketball player to have an average of 18.5 rebounds per game in a single Division I National Collegiate Athletic Association (NCAA) season was Rosina Pearson, of Bethune-Cookman College, in 1985.

2220. Old Dominion University championship in the National Collegiate Athletic Association (NCAA) Women's Basketball National Tournament came in 1985, with a 70–65 win over the University of Georgia.

2221. Utah Jazz player to be named National Basketball Association (NBA) Defensive Player of the Year was Mark Eaton of the Utah Jazz, in 1985. He won the award again in 1989.

2222. Villanova University championship in the National Collegiate Athletic Association (NCAA) Men's Basketball National Tournament came in 1985, with a 66–64 win over Georgetown University.

2223. Woman basketball player to sign with the Harlem Globetrotters was African-American Lynette Woodard, in 1985.

2224. Basketball player to have ten blocked shots in a single National Basketball Association (NBA) playoff game was Mark Eaton of the Utah Jazz, against the Houston Rockets, on April 26, 1985.

2225. Basketball player to make all his field goal attempts in a National Basketball Association (NBA) Finals game was Scott Wedman of the Boston Celtics, who scored all 11 of 11 field goals in a Celtics win over the Los Angeles Lakers, on May 27, 1985.

2226. Basketball team to score 148 points, and 62 field goals, in a single National Basketball Association (NBA) Finals game was the Boston Celtics, against the Los Angeles Lakers, on May 27, 1985.

2227. Basketball team to have a defensive rebound percentage of .921 in a single National Basketball Association (NBA) Finals game was the Los Angeles Lakers, against the Boston Celtics, on May 30, 1985.

2228. Basketball player to average 5.0 steals per game during a single Division I National Collegiate Athletic Association (NCAA) season was Darron Brittman of Chicago State University, in 1986.

2229. Basketball player to be named National Basketball Association (NBA) Most Improved Player of the Year was Alvin Robertson of the San Antonio Spurs, in 1986.

2230. Basketball player to have 207 rebounds during a single Division I National Collegiate Athletic Association (NCAA) season was David Robinson of Navy, in 1986.

2231. Basketball player to have 23 blocked shots in a Division I National Collegiate Athletic Association (NCAA) championship series was David Robinson of Navy, in 1986.

2232. Basketball player to have 301 steals in a single National Basketball Association (NBA) season was Alvin Robertson, in 1986.

2233. Basketball team to have a .652 rebound percentage in the National Basketball Association (NBA) playoffs was the Los Angeles Lakers, against the San Antonio Spurs, in 1986.

2234. Basketball team to have a .976 home game winning percentage for a single National Basketball Association (NBA) season was the Boston Celtics, who won 40 and lost 1 at home in 1986.

2235. Basketball team to have an average of 8.7 blocked shots per game in a single National Basketball Association (NBA) season was the Washington Bullets, in 1986.

2236. College women's basketball player to have 1,887 rebounds in a single Division I National Collegiate Athletic Association (NCAA) career was Wanda Ford of Drake University, from 1983 to 1986.

2237. College women's basketball player to receive the Broderick Cup in three consecutive years was Cheryl Miller, of the University of Southern California, from 1984 to 1986.

2238. College women's basketball player to receive the Naismith Award in three consecutive years was Cheryl Miller, of the University of Southern California, from 1984 to 1986.

2239. San Antonio Spurs player to be named National Basketball Association (NBA) Defensive Player of the Year was Alvin Robertson, in 1986.

BASKETBALL—(1980-1989)—*continued*

2240. University of Texas championship in the National Collegiate Athletic Association (NCAA) Women's Basketball National Tournament came in 1986, with a 97–81 win over the University of Southern California.

2241. Basketball player to have 14 rebounds during a single Division I National Collegiate Athletic Association (NCAA) game was David Robinson of Navy, against the University of North Carolina at Wilmington, on January 4, 1986.

2242. Basketball team to have a .723 rebound percentage in a single National Basketball Association (NBA) playoff game was the Los Angeles Lakers, against the San Antonio Spurs, on April 17, 1986.

2243. Basketball player to score 63 points in a single National Basketball Association (NBA) playoff game was Michael Jordan of the Chicago Bulls, against the Boston Celtics, at Boston, Massachusetts, on April 20, 1986.

2244. College women's basketball player to score 17 consecutive field goals in a single Division I National Collegiate Athletic Association (NCAA) game was Dorinda Lindstrom of Santa Clara College, California, against Fresno State College, California, on November 30, 1986.

2245. Los Angeles Lakers player to be named National Basketball Association (NBA) Defensive Player of the Year was Michael Cooper, in 1987.

2246. Basketball player to be named Most Valuable Player of the National Basketball Association (NBA) Finals three times was Earvin "Magic" Johnson of the Los Angeles Lakers, in 1980, 1982, and 1987.

2247. Basketball player to have 406 assists during a single Division I National Collegiate Athletic Association (NCAA) season was Mark Wade, of the University of Nevada at Las Vegas, in 1987.

2248. Basketball player to make 35 consecutive field goals in the National Basketball Association (NBA) playoffs was Jack Sikma of the Milwaukee Bucks, against the Boston Celtics, in 1987.

2249. Basketball player to score ten 3-point field goals in a single Division I National Collegiate Athletic Association (NCAA) championship series game was Freddie Banks of the University of Nevada at Las Vegas, in 1987.

2250. Basketball player to shoot 158 3-point field goals during a single Division I National Collegiate Athletic Association (NCAA) season was Darren Fitzgerald of Butler University, in 1987.

2251. Basketball player to shoot 413 field goals during a single Division I National Collegiate Athletic Association (NCAA) season was Curtis Staples of the University of Virginia, in 1987. He also averaged 5.6 points from 3-point field goals per game, another enduring record.

2252. College women's basketball Naismith Coach of the Year Award was received by Pat Summitt, of the University of Tennessee, in 1987.

2253. College women's basketball player to have 355 assists in a single Division I National Collegiate Athletic Association (NCAA) season was Suzie McConnell of Pennsylvania State University, in 1987.

2254. College women's basketball player to score 974 points in a single Division I National Collegiate Athletic Association (NCAA) season was Cindy Brown of Long Beach State College, California, in 1987.

2255. Indiana Pacers player to be named National Basketball Association (NBA) Rookie of the Year was Chuck Person, in 1987.

2256. University of Tennessee championship in the National Collegiate Athletic Association (NCAA) Women's Basketball National Tournament came in 1987, with a 67–44 win over Louisiana Tech University.

2257. Basketball player to shoot 11 consecutive 3-point field goals during a single Division I National Collegiate Athletic Association (NCAA) game was Gary Bossert of Niagara University, against Siena College, on January 7, 1987.

2258. Basketball player to have 22 assists during a single Division I National Collegiate Athletic Association (NCAA) game was Tony Fairley of the University of Charleston, against Armstrong Atlantic College, on February 9, 1987.

2259. College women's basketball player to score 60 points in a single Division I National Collegiate Athletic Association (NCAA) game was Cindy Brown of Long Beach State College, California, against San Jose State College, of California, on February 16, 1987.

2260. College women's basketball team to score 149 points in a single Division I National Collegiate Athletic Association (NCAA) game was Long Beach State College, California, against San Jose State College, which scored 69 points, on February 16, 1987.

2261. Basketball player to have 13 steals during a single Division I National Collegiate Athletic Association (NCAA) game was Mookie Blaylock of the University of Oklahoma against Centenary College, on December 12, 1987.

2262. Basketball player to average 13.3 assists per game during a single Division I National Collegiate Athletic Association (NCAA) season was Avery Johnson of Southern University, in 1988.

2263. Basketball player to have 115 assists in the National Basketball Association (NBA) playoffs was John Stockton of the Utah Jazz, against the Los Angeles Lakers, in 1988. He also had a record-breaking 38 steals in the same series.

2264. Basketball player to have 150 steals during a single Division I National Collegiate Athletic Association (NCAA) season was Mookie Blaylock of the University of Oklahoma, in 1988.

2265. Basketball player to have 23 steals in a Division I National Collegiate Athletic Association (NCAA) championship series was Mookie Blaylock of the University of Oklahoma, in 1988.

2266. Basketball player to have 868 assists in his rookie year in the National Basketball Association (NBA) was Mark Jackson of the New York Knicks, in 1988.

2267. Basketball player to have a field goal average of .599 over his National Basketball Association (NBA) career was Artis Gilmore, from 1977 to 1988.

2268. Basketball player to have six blocked shots in a single Division I National Collegiate Athletic Association (NCAA) Final Four championship series game was Danny Manning of the University of Kansas, against Duke University, in 1988.

2269. Chicago Bulls player to be named National Basketball Association (NBA) Defensive Player of the Year was Michael Jordan, in 1988.

2270. Chicago Bulls player to be named National Basketball Association (NBA) Most Valuable Player of the Year was Michael Jordan, in 1988. He would win the award again in 1991, 1992, 1996, and 1998.

2271. College women's basketball United States Basketball Writers Association All-American first team consisted of Suzie McConnell, Michelle Edwards, Vickie Orr, Sue Wicks, and Bridgette Gordon, in 1988.

2272. Louisiana Tech University championship in the National Collegiate Athletic Association (NCAA) Women's Basketball National Tournament came in 1988, with a 56–54 win over Auburn University.

2273. College women's basketball player to score nine consecutive 3-point goals in a single Division I National Collegiate Athletic Association (NCAA) game was Susan Smith of Eastern Washington University, against Weber State College, on February 13, 1988.

2274. Basketball team to have an offensive rebound average of .556 in a single National Basketball Association (NBA) Finals game was the Detroit Pistons, against the Los Angeles Lakers, on June 16, 1988.

2275. Basketball team from the United States to win the women's title in a non-boycotted Olympic Games was in 1988 in Seoul, South Korea. Led by Teresa Edwards, Teresa Weatherspoon, and Cynthia Cooper, the U.S. team won on September 29, to achieve its first victory over the Soviet team.

2276. Charlotte Hornets regular season game played at the Charlotte Coliseum in Charlotte, North Carolina, was a 133–93 loss to the Cleveland Cavaliers, on November 4, 1988.

2277. Detroit Pistons regular season game played at The Palace of Auburn Hills in Auburn Hills, Michigan, was a 94–85 win over the Charlotte Hornets, on November 5, 1988.

2278. Miami Heat regular season basketball game played at the Miami Arena in Miami, Florida, was a 111–91 Miami loss to the Los Angeles Clippers, on November 5, 1988. The team would play there through 1999, moving into the new American Airlines Arena on January 2, 2000.

2279. Milwaukee Bucks regular season basketball game played at the Bradley Center in Milwaukee, Wisconsin, was 107–94 loss to the Atlanta Hawks, on November 5, 1988.

2280. Sacramento Kings regular season basketball game played at the ARCO Arena in Sacramento, California, was a 97–75 loss to the Seattle SuperSonics, on November 8, 1988.

2281. Basketball player to score 184 points in a Division I National Collegiate Athletic Association (NCAA) championship series was Glen Rice of the University of Michigan, in 1989.

BASKETBALL—(1980-1989)—*continued*

2282. Basketball player to score 75 field goals in a Division I National Collegiate Athletic Association (NCAA) championship series was Glen Rice of the University of Michigan, in 1989.

2283. Basketball player to score more than 38,000 points in his National Basketball Association (NBA) career was Kareem Abdul-Jabbar, who scored 38,387 points from 1969 to 1989.

2284. College women's basketball player to have 151 blocked shots, and 5.6 rebounds per game, in a single Division I National Collegiate Athletic Association (NCAA) season was Michelle Wilson of Texas Southern University, in 1989.

2285. College women's basketball player to score 3,122 points during her National Collegiate Athletic Association (NCAA) Division I career was Patricia Hoskins of Mississippi Valley College, from 1985 to 1989.

2286. College women's basketball player to score an average of 28.4 points per game during her Division I National Collegiate Athletic Association (NCAA) career was Patricia Hoskins of Mississippi Valley College, from 1985 to 1989.

2287. Detroit Pistons National Basketball Association (NBA) championship came in 1989, with a 4 games to none win over the Los Angeles Lakers.

2288. Orlando Magic regular season basketball game played at the Orlando Arena in Orlando, Florida, was a 111–106 loss to the New Jersey Nets, on November 4, 1989.

BASKETBALL (1990-1999)
2289. Basketball player to have an average of 14.5 assists per game in a single National Basketball Association (NBA) season was John Stockton of the Utah Jazz, in 1990.

2290. Basketball player to lead the National Basketball Association (NBA) in offensive rebounds for eight years was Moses Malone, between 1977 and 1990.

2291. Basketball player to score eleven 3-point field goals in a single Division I National Collegiate Athletic Association (NCAA) championship series game was Jeff Fryer of Loyola Marymount College, against Western Michigan University, in 1990.

2292. Detroit Pistons player to be named National Basketball Association (NBA) Defensive Player of the Year was Dennis Rodman, in 1990. Rodman won the honor again in 1991.

2293. Stanford University championship in the National Collegiate Athletic Association (NCAA) Women's Basketball National Tournament came in 1990, with an 88–81 win over the University of Tennessee.

2294. University of Nevada at Las Vegas championship in the National Collegiate Athletic Association (NCAA) Men's Basketball National Tournament came in 1990, with a 103–73 win over Duke University.

2295. Basketball team to make 61 free throws in a single National Basketball Association (NBA) game was the Phoenix Suns, against the Utah Jazz, at Salt Lake City, Utah, on April 9, 1990.

2296. Basketball team to score 157 points in a single National Basketball Association (NBA) playoff game was the Boston Celtics, against the New York Knicks, on April 28, 1990.

2297. Basketball player to make 15 consecutive free throws in a National Basketball Association (NBA) Finals game was Terry Porter of the Portland Trail Blazers, against the Detroit Pistons, on June 7, 1990.

2298. Minnesota Timberwolves regular season basketball game played at the Target Center in Minneapolis, Minnesota, was a 98–85 win over the Dallas Mavericks, on November 2, 1990.

2299. Basketball player to have 30 assists in a single National Basketball Association (NBA) game was Scott Skiles of the Orlando Magic, against the Denver Nuggets, at Denver, Colorado, on December 30, 1990.

2300. Basketball player to have 1,164 assists in a single National Basketball Association (NBA) season was John Stockton of the Utah Jazz, in 1991.

2301. Basketball player to have 376 steals during his Division I National Collegiate Athletic Association (NCAA) college career was Eric Murdoch of the University of Providence, from 1988 to 1991.

2302. Basketball player to receive the Associated Press (AP) Athlete of the Year Award was Michael Jordan of the Chicago Bulls on 1991. One of the greatest players in the history of the game, Jordan also won the Associated Press award in 1992 and 1993, becoming the first athlete of any kind to win the award three times.

2303. Basketball team to have an average of 18.54 offensive rebounds per game in a single National Basketball Association (NBA) season was the Denver Nuggets, in 1991.

2304. Chicago Bulls National Basketball Association (NBA) championship came in 1991, with a 4 games to 1 win over the Los Angeles Lakers. Led by Michael Jordan, Chicago would become by far the leading team of the 1990s, winning six NBA championships between 1991 and 1998.

2305. College women's basketball player to score 126 3-point goals in a single Division I National Collegiate Athletic Association (NCAA) season was Lisa McMullen, of Alabama State University, in 1991.

2306. Duke University championship in the National Collegiate Athletic Association (NCAA) Men's Basketball National Tournament came in 1991, with a 71–51 win over the University of Michigan.

2307. College women's basketball player to have 23 assists in a single Division I National Collegiate Athletic Association (NCAA) game was Michelle Burden of Kent State University, against Ball State University, on February 6, 1991.

2308. Basketball team to have a field goal percentage of .617 in a single National Basketball Association (NBA) Finals game was the Chicago Bulls, against the Los Angeles Lakers, on June 5, 1991.

2309. Utah Jazz regular season basketball game played at the Delta Center in Salt Lake City, Utah, was a 103–95 loss to the Seattle SuperSonics, on November 7, 1991.

2310. College women's basketball player to score 23 free throws in a single Division I National Collegiate Athletic Association (NCAA) game was Shaunda Greene of the University of Washington, against Northern Illinois University, on November 30, 1991.

2311. Basketball team to have 22 blocked shots in a single National Basketball Association (NBA) game was the New Jersey Nets, against the Denver Nuggets, on December 12, 1991.

2312. Basketball player to miss on 17 consecutive field goal attempts in a single National Basketball Association (NBA) game was Tim Hardaway of the Golden State Warriors, at Minneapolis, Minnesota, on December 27, 1991.

2313. Basketball player to block 11 shots in a single Division I National Collegiate Athletic Association (NCAA) championship series game was Shaquille O'Neal of Louisiana State University, against Brigham Young University, in 1992.

2314. Charlotte Hornets player to be named National Basketball Association (NBA) Rookie of the Year was Larry Johnson, in 1992.

2315. Coach to be named National Basketball Association (NBA) Coach of the Year three times was Don Nelson, who won for the third time as coach of the Golden State Warriors, in 1992. He had also been named Coach of the Year in 1983 and 1985, while coaching the Milwaukee Bucks.

2316. Olympic basketball competition to include openly professional athletes was in 1992 in Barcelona, Spain. The result was the "Dream Team"—including stars such as Earvin "Magic" Johnson, Larry Bird, Michael Jordan, Charles Barkley, Karl Malone, and David Robinson—which dominated the competition, as expected.

2317. Basketball team to have a perfect free throw record in a National Basketball Association (NBA) Finals game was the Portland Trail Blazers, who made all 21 of 21 free throw attempts against the Chicago Bulls on June 14, 1992.

2318. Phoenix Suns regular season basketball game played at the America West Arena in Phoenix, Arizona, was a 111–105 win over the Los Angeles Lakers, on November 7, 1992.

2319. College women's basketball player to block 15 shots in a single Division I National Collegiate Athletic Association (NCAA) game was Amy Lundquist of Loyola Marymount College, against Western Illinois University, on December 20, 1992.

2320. Basketball player to make 20 free throws in a single half of a National Basketball Association (NBA) game was Michael Jordan of the Chicago Bulls, against the Miami Heat, on December 30, 1992, at Miami, Florida.

2321. Basketball player to have 1,076 assists during his Division I National Collegiate Athletic Association (NCAA) career was Bobby Hurley of Duke University, from 1990 to 1993.

2322. Basketball player to have 17 3-point field goals in a National Basketball Association (NBA) Finals series was Dan Majerle of the Phoenix Suns, in 1993.

2323. Basketball player to have an average of 41 points per game in a National Basketball Association (NBA) Finals series was Michael Jordan of the Chicago Bulls, against the Phoenix Suns, in 1993.

BASKETBALL—(1990-1999)—*continued*

2324. Basketball player to have eight steals in a Division I National Collegiate Athletic Association (NCAA) championship series game was Darrell Hawkins of the University of Arkansas, against Holy Cross College, in 1993.

2325. Houston Rockets player to be named National Basketball Association (NBA) Defensive Player of the Year was Hakeem Olajuwon, in 1993. He won the honor again in 1994.

2326. Orlando Magic player to be named National Basketball Association (NBA) Rookie of the Year was Shaquille O'Neal, in 1993.

2327. Phoenix Suns player to be named National Basketball Association (NBA) Most Valuable Player of the Year was Charles Barkley, in 1993.

2328. Texas Tech University championship in the National Collegiate Athletic Association (NCAA) Women's Basketball National Tournament came in 1993, with an 84–82 win over Ohio State University.

2329. San Antonio Spurs regular season basketball game played at the Alamodome in San Antonio, Texas, was a 91--85 win over the Golden State Warriors, on November 5, 1993.

2330. Basketball player to make 97 consecutive free throws in the National Basketball Association (NBA) was Michael Williams of the Minnesota Timberwolves, in a streak running from March 24, 1993, to November 9, 1993.

2331. Basketball player to have a perfect field goal percentage in a Division I National Collegiate Athletic Association (NCAA) game was Clifford Rozier of University of Louisville, who shot 15 for 15 against Eastern Kentucky University on December 11, 1993.

2332. Basketball player to have 38 blocked shots in a single set of National Basketball Association (NBA) playoffs was Dikembe Mutombo of the Denver Nuggets, against the Utah Jazz, in 1994.

2333. Basketball team to get 246 defensive rebounds in a single set of National Basketball Association (NBA) playoffs was the Houston Rockets, against the Phoenix Suns, in 1994.

2334. Basketball team to have 71 blocked shots in a single set of National Basketball Association (NBA) playoffs was the Denver Nuggets, against the Utah Jazz, in 1994.

2335. College women's basketball United States Basketball Writers Association Coach of the Year Award was received by Ceal Barty, of the University of Colorado, in 1994.

2336. College women's basketball United States Basketball Writers Association Player of the Year was Lisa Leslie, of the University of Southern California, in 1994.

2337. Houston Rockets National Basketball Association (NBA) championship came in 1994, with a 4-games-to-3 win over the New York Knicks.

2338. University of Arkansas championship in the National Collegiate Athletic Association (NCAA) Men's Basketball National Tournament came in 1994, with a 77–72 win over Duke University.

2339. University of North Carolina championship in the National Collegiate Athletic Association (NCAA) Women's Basketball National Tournament came in 1994, with a 60–59 win over Louisiana Tech University.

2340. Basketball team to have an offensive rebounding percentage of .609 in a single National Basketball Association (NBA) playoff game was the New York Knicks, against the Indiana Pacers, on June 5, 1994.

2341. Chicago Bulls regular season game played in the United Center in Chicago, Illinois, was a 89–83 loss to the Charlotte Hornets, on November 4, 1994. The Bulls were sharing the new center with the Chicago Blackhawks hockey team.

2342. Cleveland Cavaliers regular season game played in the Gund Arena in Cleveland, Ohio, was a 100–98 loss to the Houston Rockets, on November 8, 1994.

2343. Basketball player to make eight consecutive 3-point field goals in the National Basketball Association (NBA) in a single game was Jeff Hornacek of the Utah Jazz, on November 23, 1994, against the Seattle SuperSonics.

2344. Basketball player to have 6,371 offensive rebounds in his National Basketball Association (NBA) career was Moses Malone, between 1977 and 1995.

2345. Basketball player to have 8,551 free throws in his National Basketball Association (NBA) career was Moses Malone, from 1976 to 1995.

2346. Basketball player to score 28 3-point goals in a single set of National Basketball Association (NBA) playoffs was Dennis Scott of the Orlando Magic, against the Indiana Pacers, in 1995.

2347. Basketball team to score 41 3-point field goals in a National Basketball Association (NBA) Finals series was the Orlando Magic, against the Houston Rockets, in 1995.

2348. College women's basketball Associated Press (AP) All-American first team was named in 1995: Rebecca Lobo, Shelley Sheetz, Nikki McCray, Charlotte Smith, and Niesa Johnson.

2349. College women's basketball Associated Press (AP) Coach of the Year Award was given to Geno Auriemma, of the University of Connecticut, in 1995.

2350. College women's basketball Associated Press (AP) Player of the Year was Rebecca Lobo, of the University of Connecticut, in 1995.

2351. College women's basketball player to have 191 steals, and an average of 6.4 steals per game, in a single Division I National Collegiate Athletic Association (NCAA) season was Natalie White, of Florida A&M University, in 1995.

2352. Dallas Mavericks player to be named National Basketball Association (NBA) Rookie of the Year was Jason Kidd in 1995. He shared the honor with Grant Hill, of the Detroit Pistons.

2353. Denver Nuggets player to be named National Basketball Association (NBA) Defensive Player of the Year was Dikembe Mutombo, in 1995. Mutombo would win the honor again in 1996 and 1998, becoming the first to win it three times.

2354. San Antonio Spurs player to be named National Basketball Association (NBA) Most Valuable Player of the Year was David Robinson, in 1995.

2355. University of Connecticut championship in the National Collegiate Athletic Association (NCAA) Women's Basketball National Tournament came in 1995, with a 70–64 win over the University of Tennessee.

2356. College women's basketball player to score 12 3-point goals in a single Division I National Collegiate Athletic Association (NCAA) game was Cornelia Gayden of Louisiana State University, against Jackson State College, on February 9, 1995.

2357. Basketball team to score 14 3-point goals in a single National Basketball Association (NBA) Finals game was the Houston Rockets, against the Orlando Magic, on June 7, 1995.

2358. Basketball player to have seven steals in a single National Basketball Association (NBA) Finals game was Robert Horry of the Houston Rockets, against the Orlando Magic, on June 9, 1995.

2359. Boston Celtics regular season basketball game played at the FleetCenter in Boston, Massachusetts, was a 101–100 loss to the Milwaukee Bucks, on November 3, 1995.

2360. Portland Trail Blazers regular season basketball game played at The Rose Garden in Portland, Oregon, was a 92–80 loss to the Vancouver Grizzlies, on November 3, 1995.

2361. Seattle SuperSonics regular season game played in the Key Arena in Seattle, Washington, was a 103–89 victory over the Los Angeles Lakers, on November 4, 1995.

2362. Vancouver Grizzlies regular season basketball game played at Bear Country at General Motors Place in Vancouver, British Columbia, Canada, was a 105–103 victory over the Minnesota Timberwolves, on November 5, 1995.

2363. Basketball player to average 2.71 steals per game in his National Basketball Association (NBA) career was Alvin Robertson, between 1985 and 1996.

2364. Basketball player to lead the National Basketball Association (NBA) for three consecutive years in blocked shots was Dikembe Mutombo of the Denver Nuggets, from 1994 to 1996.

2365. Basketball player to lead the National Basketball Association (NBA) in assists for nine consecutive years was John Stockton of the Utah Jazz, from 1988 to 1996.

2366. Basketball player to make 267 3-point field goals in a single National Basketball Association (NBA) season was Dennis Scott of the Orlando Magic, during the 1995–1996 season.

2367. Basketball team to average 8.96 3-point goals per game in a single National Basketball Association (NBA) season was the Dallas Mavericks, in 1996.

2368. Basketball team to have an .851 field goal percentage in a National Basketball Association (NBA) Finals series was the Seattle SuperSonics, against the Chicago Bulls, in 1996.

2369. Basketball team to have an .878 winning percentage for a National Basketball Association (NBA) season was the Chicago Bulls, in 1996.

BASKETBALL—(1990-1999)—*continued*

2370. Basketball team to win 44 straight National Basketball Association (NBA) home games was the Chicago Bulls, with a winning streak that included the final seven games of the 1994–1995 season and the first 37 games of the 1995–1996 season.

2371. Toronto Raptors player to be named National Basketball Association (NBA) Rookie of the Year was Damon Stoudamire, in 1996.

2372. Women's National Basketball Association (WNBA) was founded in 1996. The new league's eight charter teams were the Charlotte Sting, Cleveland Rockers, Houston Comets, Los Angeles Sparks, New York Liberty, Phoenix Mercury, Sacramento Monarchs, and Utah Starzz. The first president of the WNBA was Val Ackerman.

2373. Basketball player to make 11 3-point field goals in a single National Basketball Association (NBA) game was Dennis Scott of the Orlando Magic, against the Atlanta Hawks, on April 18, 1996.

2374. Basketball team to have 20 3-point field goals in a single National Basketball Association (NBA) playoff game was the Seattle SuperSonics, against the Houston Rockets, on May 6, 1996.

2375. Philadelphia 76ers regular season basketball game played at the First Union Center in Philadelphia, Pennsylvania, was a 111–103 loss to the Milwaukee Bucks, on November 1, 1996.

2376. Basketball team to score 25 points in a single overtime period of a National Basketball Association (NBA) game was the New Jersey Nets, against the Los Angeles Clippers, at Los Angeles, California, on November 30, 1996.

2377. Basketball player to shoot 15 3-point field goals in a single Division I National Collegiate Athletic Association (NCAA) game was Keith Veney of Marshall University, against Morehead State University, on December 14, 1996.

2378. Basketball team to have 19 3-point goals in a single National Basketball Association (NBA) game was the Atlanta Hawks, against the Dallas Mavericks, at Dallas, Texas, on December 16, 1996.

2379. College women's basketball player to score 20 consecutive free throws in a single Division I National Collegiate Athletic Association (NCAA) game was Kristeena Alexander of George Mason University, against Central Florida College, on December 29, 1996.

2380. Basketball player to win three, and then four, gold medals in the Olympic Games was Teresa Edwards of the United States. Member of the gold-medal-winning U.S. women's basketball teams in 1984 and 1988, she won her third Olympic women's basketball championship in Atlanta, Georgia, on August 4, 1996. She then added a fourth gold medal on September 30, 2000, at Sydney, Australia. In 1984 she had been the youngest player ever to win a gold medal in basketball; by 2000 she had become the oldest. She had also been co-captain of the 1992 U.S. women's team, which won the bronze medal, giving her five medals in all.

2381. Basketball player to have 10,117 defensive rebounds in his National Basketball Association (NBA) career was Robert Parish, between 1977 and 1997.

2382. Basketball player to play 21 seasons in the National Basketball Association (NBA) was Robert Parish, from 1977 to 1997.

2383. Basketball team to have a .428 field goal percentage for a single National Basketball Association (NBA) season was the Charlotte Hornets, in 1997.

2384. University of Arizona championship in the National Collegiate Athletic Association (NCAA) Men's Basketball National Tournament came in 1997, with an 84–79 win over the University of Kentucky.

2385. Utah Jazz player to be named National Basketball Association (NBA) Most Valuable Player of the Year was Karl Malone, in 1997.

2386. Women referees in the National Basketball Association (NBA) were Violet Palmer and Dee Kantner, hired by the league in 1997.

2387. Women's National Basketball Association (WNBA) All-WNBA First Team was named in 1997. It included Tina Thompson of the Houston Comets, Eva Nemcova of the Cleveland Rockers, Lisa Leslie of the Los Angeles Sparks, Cynthia Cooper of the Houston Comets, and Ruthie Bolton-Holifield of the Sacramento Monarchs.

2388. Women's National Basketball Association (WNBA) Coach of the Year was Van Chancellor of the Houston Comets, in 1997.

2389. Women's National Basketball Association (WNBA) Defensive Player of the Year was Teresa Weatherspoon of the New York Liberty, in 1997.

2390. Women's National Basketball Association (WNBA) Most Valuable Player of 1997 was Cynthia Cooper of the Houston Comets. She would win again in 1998, becoming the first to win it twice.

2391. Women's National Basketball Association (WNBA) player to win the league's Sportsmanship Award was Haizia Zheng of the Los Angeles Sparks, in 1997.

2392. Basketball team to have 27 steals in a single National Basketball Association (NBA) game was the Seattle SuperSonics, against the Toronto Raptors, on January 15, 1997.

2393. Basketball player to make nine 3-point field goals in a single National Basketball Association (NBA) playoff game was Rex Chapman of the Phoenix Suns, against the Seattle SuperSonics, on April 25, 1997.

2394. Basketball player to make seven consecutive 3-point field goals in a single National Basketball Association (NBA) playoff game was Robert Horry of the Los Angeles Lakers against the Utah Jazz, on May 6, 1997.

2395. Women's National Basketball Association (WNBA) began its first season of play on June 21, 1997.

2396. Women's National Basketball Association (WNBA) championship was won by the Houston Comets, who defeated the New York Liberty 65–51, at Houston, Texas, on August 30, 1997. Cynthia Cooper of the Comets was named Most Valuable Player in the championship game.

2397. Basketball player to play more than 900 consecutive games in the National Basketball Association (NBA) was A. C. Green of the Dallas Mavericks, who reached 907 games on November 20, 1997, in Dallas, Texas, passing the mark of 906 games reached by Randy Smith in 1983. By late in the 1998–1999 season, by then with the Los Angeles Lakers, Green had played more than 1,000 consecutive games.

2398. Washington Wizards regular season basketball game played at the MCI Center in Washington, D.C., was a 95–78 win over the Seattle SuperSonics, on December 2, 1997.

2399. College women's basketball team to score 18 3-point goals in a single Division I National Collegiate Athletic Association (NCAA) game was Villanova University, against the University of Pennsylvania, on December 20, 1997.

2400. Basketball player to be named Most Valuable Player of the National Basketball Association (NBA) Finals six times was Michael Jordan of the Chicago Bulls, in 1991, 1992, 1993, 1996, 1997, and 1998.

2401. Basketball player to be named National Basketball Association (NBA) Defensive Player of the Year three times was Dikembe Mutombo of the Atlanta Hawks, who won his third such honor in 1998. He had won it previously in 1995 and 1996, when he was with the Denver Nuggets.

2402. Basketball player to be named Women's National Basketball Association (WNBA) Most Valuable Player twice in a row was Cynthia Cooper of the Houston Comets, in 1997 and 1998.

2403. Basketball player to have a .904 free throw average in his National Basketball Association (NBA) career was Mark Price, from 1987 to 1998.

2404. Basketball player to have a field goal percentage of .783 in a single set of National Basketball Association (NBA) playoffs was Dale Davis of the Indiana Pacers, against the Cleveland Cavaliers, in 1998.

2405. Basketball player to lead the National Basketball Association (NBA) in rebounds for seven consecutive seasons was Dennis Rodman, from 1992 to 1998.

2406. Basketball player to lead the National Basketball Association (NBA) in scoring ten times was Michael Jordan of the Chicago Bulls, between 1987 and 1998.

2407. Basketball player to score more than 2,000 points in 11 consecutive National Basketball Association (NBA) seasons was Karl Malone of the Utah Jazz, from 1988 to 1998.

2408. College women's basketball coach to receive the Naismith Coach of the Year Award four times was Pat Summitt, of the University of Tennessee, in 1987, 1989, 1994 and 1998.

2409. College women's basketball player to win *The Sporting News* Player of the Year Award was Chamique Holdsclaw of the University of Tennessee, in 1998. In the same year, she won the Naismith Trophy, and the Associated Press (AP) and United States Basketball Writers Association Player of the Year awards.

BASKETBALL—(1990-1999)—*continued*

2410. College women's basketball team to have 39 wins in a single National Collegiate Athletic Association (NCAA) season was the University of Tennessee, in 1998.

2411. Basketball team to win the Women's National Basketball Association (WNBA) championship twice in a row was the Houston Comets, who defeated the Phoenix Mercury 2 games to 1. In the third and deciding game of the championship series, Houston defeated Phoenix 80–71, at Houston, Texas, on September 1, 1998. For the second time, Cynthia Cooper of the Comets was named Most Valuable Player in the championship series.

2412. Basketball player to have 3,582 blocked shots in his National Basketball Association (NBA) career was Hakeem Olajuwon of the Houston Rockets, who reached that mark in 1999, while his career continued.

2413. Basketball player to have more than 2,700 steals in his National Basketball Association (NBA) career was John Stockton of the Utah Jazz, who reached 2,701 career steals in 1999, while his career continued.

2414. Basketball player to make more than 13,000 assists in his National Basketball Association (NBA) career was John Stockton of the Utah Jazz, who reached 13,087 career assists in 1999, in a continuing career.

2415. Basketball player to make more than 1,700 3-point field goals in his National Basketball Association (NBA) career was Reggie Miller of the Indiana Pacers, who reached 1,702 field goals in 1999, in a continuing career.

2416. Purdue University championship in the National Collegiate Athletic Association (NCAA) Women's Basketball National Tournament came in 1999, with a 62–45 win over Duke University.

2417. San Antonio Spurs National Basketball Association (NBA) championship came in 1999, with a 4 games to 1 win over the New York Knicks.

2418. Women's National Basketball Association (WNBA) players union league contract was in 1999. It was the first women's professional team sports labor contract to be successfully negotiated in the United States.

2419. Toronto Raptors regular season basketball game played at the Air Canada Centre in Toronto, Ontario, Canada, was a 102–87 victory over the Vancouver Grizzlies, on February 21, 1999.

2420. Basketball player to have 10 steals in a single National Basketball Association (NBA) playoff game was Allen Iverson of the Philadelphia 76ers, against the Orlando Magic, on May 13, 1999.

2421. Women's National Basketball Association (WNBA) All-Star Game was won by the Western Conference, which defeated the Eastern Conference 79–61, on July 14, 1999, at Madison Square Garden in New York City.

2422. Women's National Basketball Association (WNBA) team to win the league championship three times, and in three consecutive years was the Houston Comets, who defeated the New York Liberty two games to one. In the third and deciding game of the championship series, Houston defeated New York 59–47, at Houston, Texas, on September 5, 1999. For the third time, Cynthia Cooper of the Comets was named Most Valuable Player in the championship series.

2423. Los Angeles Clippers regular season game played in the Staples Center in Los Angeles, California, was a 104–92 loss to the Seattle SuperSonics, on November 2, 1999. The new center was being shared by the Clippers, the Los Angeles Lakers basketball team, and the Los Angeles Kings hockey team.

2424. Los Angeles Lakers regular season game played in the Staples Center in Los Angeles, California, was a 103–88 victory over the Vancouver Grizzlies, on November 3, 1999. The new center was being shared by the Lakers, the Los Angeles Clippers basketball team, and the Los Angeles Kings hockey team.

2425. Atlanta Hawks regular season basketball game played at the Philips Arena in Atlanta, Georgia, was a 119–109 loss to the Milwaukee Bucks, on November 4, 1999.

2426. Indiana Pacers regular season basketball game played at the Conseco Fieldhouse in Indianapolis, Indiana, was a 115–108 victory over the Boston Celtics, on November 6, 1999.

BIATHLON

2427. Skiing and shooting competition (later known as biathlon) on record was held in Norway in 1767, between two groups of guards who patrolled the border between Norway and Sweden.

2428. Ski and shooting club was the Trysil Rifle and Ski Club founded in Trysil, Norway, in 1861. The members' aim was to beef up border defense with local units, but they gave rise to the sport now known as biathlon.

2429. Individual skiing-and-shooting competition later known as biathlon, was sponsored by the Norwegian military in 1912. Previous competitions had been between teams.

2430. World Biathlon Championships were held at Saalfelden, Austria, in 1958. The 20-kilometer race involved 25 athletes from seven countries. Competitions were for men only until 1984, when separate competitions were established for women.

2431. Men's 20-kilometer biathlon competition at the Olympic Winter Games was in 1960 at Squaw Valley, California. Klas Lestander of Sweden won the inaugural event on February 21.

2432. Men's 4 x 7.5-kilometer relay biathlon team event held at the Olympic Winter Games was in 1968 at Grenoble, France. The team from the Soviet Union—Aleksandr Tikhonov, Nikolai Pusanov, Victor Mamatov, and Vladimir Gundartsev—won the event on February 15. Soviet teams would win the event through 1988.

2433. Athlete to win two consecutive gold medals in the biathlon in the Olympic Winter Games was Magnar Solberg of Norway. He won his second men's 20-kilometer title on February 9, 1972, at Sapporo, Japan, after winning his first in 1968.

2434. Year when the small-bore .22 rifle became standard in biathlon was 1978. Before that, contestants used larger rifles, from 1958 various NATO-caliber models.

2435. Men's 10-kilometer biathlon competition at the Olympic Winter Games was in 1980 at Lake Placid, New York. Frank Ullrich of East Germany won the event on February 19.

2436. World Biathlon Championships to include women's competitions were in 1984, at Chamonix, France. Venera Chernyshova of the Soviet Union won the two inaugural 5- and 10-kilometer events, and the Soviet team won their first of eight team championships (1984–1991).

2437. Introduction of the "skating" technique to biathlon was in 1985. The innovation involved using longer poles and shorter skis to maximize propulsion with the legs and arms.

2438. Athlete to win two biathlon gold medals at a single Olympic Winter Games was Frank-Peter Roetsch of East Germany, who won the men's 20-kilometer event on February 20, 1988, and then the men's 10-kilometer event on February 23, at Calgary, Alberta, Canada.

2439. Women's 7.5-kilometer biathlon competition held in the Olympic Winter Games was in 1992. Anfisa Reztsova of the Soviet Union won the inaugural event on February 11 at Albertville, France, becoming the first woman to win gold medals in different sports at the Winter Olympics, after her 1988 Olympic gold medal in cross-country skiing.

2440. Women's 4 x 7.5-kilometer biathlon relay competition held in the Olympic Winter Games was in 1992 at Albertville, France. The French team—Corinne Niogret, Véronique Claudel, and Anne Briand—won the inaugural event on February 14.

2441. Women's 15-kilometer biathlon competition held in the Olympic Winter Games was in 1992 at Albertville, France. It was won by Antje Misersky of Germany on February 19.

2442. Woman to win gold medals in two biathlon events in the same Olympic Winter Games was Myriam Bédard of Canada in 1994 at Lillehammer, Norway. She first won the women's 15-kilometer event on February 18, then the 7.5-kilometer competition on February 23.

BILLIARDS

2443. Written reference to billiards dates to 1429 in France.

2444. World professional championships in billiards were held in 1870 in England. Originally a challenge event, it was first won by William Cook of England.

2445. Snooker game on record was played in 1875 in Jubbulpore, India. Neville Chamberlain, a British Army colonel (not the future prime minister), is credited with developing and naming the game.

2446. Three-cushion billiards using a pocketless table, was played in 1878 or earlier, becoming popular in both the United States and in Europe, where it is called *carom*.

2447. World championship in billiards was held in 1884, when George Slosson of the United States won the 14.2 balkline billiards title in 1884. He would also win the 18.1 balkline title in 1897.

2448. National governing body for billiards and snooker was the Billiards Association, founded in 1885.

2449. Official code of rules for billiards was drawn up in Britain in 1885, by the newly formed Billiards Association.

BILLIARDS—*continued*

2450. World championships in 18.1 balkline billiards were in 1897. The first champion was George Slosson of the United States, who had also won the first 14.2 billiards title in 1884.

2451. Official code of rules for snooker was written in 1900 and approved by the Billiards Association.

2452. World amateur championships in billiards were held in 1926, with the inaugural winner being Joe Earlham of England.

2453. World professional championships in snooker were held in 1926, becoming an annual event except during World War II. The first champion was Joe Davis of England. He would remain champion through 1940, and then would win the first postwar championship in 1946.

2454. World championships for three-cushion billiards (carom) were held in 1928, under the auspices of the newly founded Union Mondiale de Billard (UMB).

2455. Women's world amateur championships in billiards were held in 1931, sponsored by the newly founded Women's Billiards Association, later the Billiards and Snooker Association.

2456. Women's world amateur championships in snooker were held in 1933, sponsored by the Women's Billiards Association, later the Billiards and Snooker Association.

2457. World amateur snooker championships were held in 1963 in Calcutta, India, sponsored by the International Billiards and Snooker Federation (IBSF), the main governing body for the amateur sport. The first winner was Gary Owen of England, who would win again in 1966. The championships were held biennially from 1966, then annually from 1984.

2458. African-American to win a world title in billiards was Cicero Murphy, who won the pocket billiards title in 1965, after a 36-day world tournament in Burbank, California.

2459. Masters Tournament in snooker was held in 1975, originally sponsored by Benson & Hedges. An invitation-only competition for the sport's top 16 players, it was first won by John Spencer of England.

2460. Women's world open championships in snooker were held in 1976. The winner was Vera Selby of England, who would win again in 1981.

2461. World rankings for snooker were developed by the World Professional Billiards and Snooker Association in 1976. The first player to be ranked number one was Ray Reardon of Wales, who would hold the top spot through 1980.

2462. Grand Prix in snooker was held in 1982, when Ray Reardon of Wales was the first champion. Originally known as the Professional Players Tournament, it would go under several names before becoming the Grand Prix.

2463. World matchplay championships in snooker were held in 1988, when the invitation-only tournament was won by Steve Davis of England, who won the sport's first £100,000 prize.

2464. World championships for nine-ball pool were held in 1990, sponsored by the World Pool-Billiard Association (WPA). The inaugural winners, both from the United States, were Earl Strickland in the men's competition and Robin Bell on the women's side.

BOBSLEDDING

2465. Runs specially built for bobsleds were constructed in 1902 in St. Moritz, Switzerland. Bobsleds had been created in the 1880s, originally by tying together two toboggans (luges).

2466. Governing body for bobsled events was the Fédération Internationale de Bobsleigh et de Tobogganing (FIBT), founded in 1923.

2467. Bobsled event held at the Olympic Winter Games was the four-man bobsled competition held at Chamonix, France, in 1924. The inaugural competition was won on February 3 by the team from Switzerland: Eduard Scherrer, Alfred Neveu, Alfred Schläppi, and Heinrich Schläppi.

2468. Bobsledders from the United States to win the five-man bobsled title at the Olympic Winter Games were William Fiske, Nion Tucker, Geoffrey Mason, Clifford Gray, and Richard Parke, who won on February 18, 1928, at St. Moritz, Switzerland. For the first and last time, the teams had five members, instead of the usual four.

2469. World championships in bobsledding for men only, were held in 1930 and annually thereafter, except during Winter Olympic years. The inaugural competition, for the four-man bobsled, was won by a team from Italy. The two-man competition began in 1931.

2470. Bobsled run in the United States was built in 1931 at Lake Placid, New York, in preparation for the 1932 Olympic Winter Games.

2471. Two-man bobsled competition held in the Olympic Games was held in 1932 at Lake Placid, New York. Two local residents, brothers J. Hubert Stevens and Curtis Stevens, won the inaugural event on February 10.

2472. Bobsledders to win two straight titles in the four-man bobsled at the Olympic Winter Games were William Fiske and Clifford Gray. On February 15, 1932, Fiske, Gray, Edward Eagan, and Jay O'Brien of the United States won the competition at Lake Placid, New York. Fiske and Gray had been on the gold medal–winning five-man bobsled team in 1928. Gray was also a songwriter, whose works included "If You Were the Only Girl in the World." Eagan became the first person to win medals in both the Winter and Summer Olympics, because he had also won the 1920 Olympic light heavyweight boxing title.

2473. Woman bobsledder to win the U.S. national bobsled championship was Katherine Dewey in 1938. Women would not be allowed to compete in bobsled events in the Olympics through the 20th century, however.

2474. Olympic Winter Games host city to refuse to build a bobsled run was Squaw Valley, California, in 1960, on the grounds that not enough countries were sending bobsled teams to the Olympics.

2475. World cup in bobsledding was held as a series of events in 1984 and 1985. Bobsledders from West Germany won the two-man and combined titles, and the four-man was won by United States competitors.

2476. Caribbean Cup an unofficial competition for Olympic two-man bobsled teams from countries with little or no snow, was held at the 1988 Olympic Winter Games. It was won by Alexander Peterson and Peter Henry of New Zealand, though the four-man bobsled team from Jamaica—led by driver Dudley Stokes—got the most publicity.

2477. Bobsledders to win two consecutive two-man bobsled titles at the Olympic Winter Games were Gustav Weder and Donat Acklin of Switzerland. Their second win came on February 20, 1994, at Lillehammer, Norway, where Acklin's younger brother, Guido Acklin, was a silver medalist in the same event. Weder and Acklin's first win had come in Albertville, France, in 1992.

BOWLING AND BOWLS

2478. Code of rules for bowls was written in 1849 by William Mitchell of Glasgow, Scotland. However, the game dates back to before 1300 in England and elsewhere in northern Europe, while bowling at pins dates back several millennia to early Egypt.

2479. National governing body for bowling in the United States was the National Bowling Association, founded in 1875 in New York City. It would be replaced in 1895 by the American Bowling Congress (ABC).

2480. Code of rules for modern bowling was developed by the American Bowling Congress, founded in 1895.

2481. Establishment of the American Bowling Congress (ABC) was on September 8, 1895, in New York City. Replacing the earlier National Bowling Association, it became the main governing body in the game, sponsoring national championships from 1901.

2482. National bowling championships in the United States were held in 1901 in Chicago and sponsored by the American Bowling Congress (ABC). Frank Brill won both the singles and all-events titles, while the Standards, from Chicago, won the team title.

2483. International governing body for bowls was the International (later Imperial) Bowling Association, founded in 1899. It was short-lived, however, and was replaced by the International Bowling Board, now the World Bowls Board, in 1905.

2484. Bowling league for women in the United States was established in St. Louis, Missouri, in 1907, by Dennis J. Sweeney, a local sportswriter and owner of a bowling alley.

2485. Bowler to win four titles in the American Bowling Congress (ABC) national championships was John Koster. After winning two team titles (1902 and 1912), and an all-events title (1902), he won the doubles title in 1913. His four-title record would stand for almost five decades.

2486. National bowling championships for women in the United States were held in 1916 in St. Louis, Missouri. They were organized by women bowlers, many of whom had accompanied their husbands to the American Bowling Congress (ABC) tournament in St. Louis. Mrs. A. J. Koester won the singles and all-events titles, while Mrs. Roy Acker and Mrs. Jack Riley won the doubles title. (Their own first names were not given, following the style of the day.) The team title was won by the Progress of St. Louis.

BOWLING AND BOWLS—*continued*

2487. National bowling organization for women in the United States was the Women's National Bowling Association, founded in 1916 in St. Louis, Missouri, in the Washington Recreation Parlor, owned by Dennis J. Sweeney, who in 1907 had founded the first women's bowling league. Sponsoring annual championships from its first year, the organization would become today's Women's International Bowling Congress.

2488. Bowler to win two all-events titles in the American Bowling Congress (ABC) championships was James Smith, who won in 1911 and again in 1920.

2489. World championships in bowling were held in 1923, sponsored by the International Bowling Association (IBA). The inaugural singles competition, for men only, was won by Thure Sandström of Sweden. The Swedish team also won the doubles and five-member team competitions.

2490. Bowler to bowl two consecutive 300 games was Frank Carauna, who did so on March 5, 1924, in Buffalo, New York.

2491. National governing body for duck pin bowling was the National Duck Pin Bowling Congress, founded in 1927 in the United States.

2492. National Award tournament in duck pin bowling was held in Baltimore, Maryland, in 1928. Howard Campbell won the men's all-events title and Irene Mischou the women's.

2493. Woman bowler to bowl a 300 game was Rose Jacobs in Schenectady, New York, in 1929.

2494. African-American bowler to bowl a 300 game in an American Bowling Congress (ABC) tournament was Kirk Ramsey at the Garfield Bowl Lanes in Chicago, Illinois, in 1952.

2495. Automatic pin-setter to be used in a bowling alley was in August 1952 in Brooklyn, New York.

2496. Bowler to bowl a 300 game in a televised match was Steven Nagy in 1954.

2497. Tournament of Champions in bowling sponsored by the Professional Bowlers' Association, was held in 1962, and annually thereafter. The inaugural winner was Joe Joseph.

2498. World championships in bowling to include women were in 1963. The inaugural women's winner in the quadrennial competition was Helen Shablis of the United States. The United States also won the first women's doubles competition that year.

2499. World outdoor championships in bowls were held in 1966, originally for men only. The inaugural winners were David Bryant of England, in men's singles, and Geoff Kelly and Bert Palm of Australia in men's pairs, with New Zealanders winning the men's fours, and Australians taking the men's triples and the overall Leonard Trophy.

2500. International organization for women's bowls was the Women's International Bowling Board, established in 1969.

2501. World outdoor championships in bowls to include women players were in 1969. Gladys Doyle of Papua New Guinea won the women's singles title, and Elsie McDonald and May Cridlan of South Africa the women's doubles. South Africans also won the women's triples, women's fours, and team titles.

2502. World indoor championships in bowls were held in 1979. David Bryant of England won the inaugural championship, originally for men's singles only. Men's pairs were added in 1986.

2503. Women's world indoor championships in bowls were held in 1988, when the inaugural winner was Margaret Johnston of Ireland.

BOXING (BEFORE 1800)

2504. Boxing event in the Olympic Games was in 688 BC, when the sport was reportedly added to the competition in Olympia, Greece.

2505. Boxing school the School of Arms and Self-Defense, was established in London, England, in 1719 by James Figg, sometimes considered the first boxing champion and the father of boxing as a competitive sport.

2506. Boxing code of rules was written in 1743 in England by champion fighter Jack Broughton, for what was then a bare-knuckle sport.

BOXING (1800-1849)

2507. African-American boxer to fight in a title bout was Tom Molineaux, a former slave from the United States, who lost to English champion Tom Cribb in a contest in Copthall Common, England, on December 18, 1810. Some grant that honor to Molineaux's mentor, William Richmond, a free African-American, who had fought and lost to Cribb on October 8, 1805. Molineaux had won his freedom by winning a boxing match between slaves, arranged by plantation owners.

2508. Boxing match under English rules held in the United States was between Jacob Hyer and Tom Beasley in New York City in 1816.

2509. Boxer to be barred by a boxing authority for throwing a fight was Jem Ward, who was disciplined by England's Pugilistic Society for deliberately losing to Bill Abbott in 1822. Undefeated until then, Ward later admitted that he had been paid £100 to lose. Reinstated in 1823, he became the English champion (1825–1831).

2510. London Prize Ring Rules for boxing were introduced in England in 1838, replacing Jack Broughton's 1743 code.

2511. Boxing title fight under the London Prize Ring Rules was on February 12, 1839, in Heather, England, when James (Deaf) Burke fought William (Bendigo) Thompson, who lost by disqualification.

BOXING (1850-1899)
2512. Queensberry rules for boxing were written in 1867 in England by John Graham Chambers for the 8th Marquess of Queensberry. The widely adopted rules called for boxers to wear gloves, rather than fight bare-knuckled, and established three-minute rounds, with one-minute breaks between them.

2513. Boxing match between women on record in the United States was on March 16, 1876, when Nell Saunders defeated Rose Harland.

2514. National boxing organization was the Amateur Boxing Association (ABA), founded in England in 1880. It offered its first championships starting in 1881, in four classes: heavyweight, middleweight, lightweight, and featherweight.

2515. Boxer to be undisputed world heavyweight champion was John L. Sullivan of the United States, the "Boston Strong Boy," who became bare-knuckle champion on February 7, 1882, when he defeated Paddy Ryan with a knockout in Mississippi City, Mississippi.

2516. Boxer to be world middleweight champion was Irish-born Jack Dempsey, the original fighter of that name, nicknamed the Nonpareil, who defeated George Fulljames by a knockout on July 30, 1884, in Great Kills, New York.

2517. Boxer to be world heavyweight champion under the Queensberry rules was John L. Sullivan of the United States. Already bare-knuckle champion, he defeated Paddy Ryan under the Queensberry rules with a technical knockout in the first round on January 19, 1885, in New York City.

2518. Boxer to be undisputed world lightweight champion was Jack McAuliffe of Ireland, who won the title on October 29, 1886, by a knockout in a 21-round Boston match, and retired undefeated in 1894. He came back twice, in 1896 and 1897, winning both matches.

2519. Boxer of African descent to win a national boxing title was George Dixon of Canada. Fighting on June 27, 1890, in London, England, he became British bantamweight champion with a knockout of Nunc Wallace in the 18th round. He was later longtime featherweight champion (1892–1897; 1898–1900).

2520. Boxer to be world featherweight champion was "Young Griffo," born Albert Griffiths, of Australia. Fighting on September 2, 1890, in Sydney, Australia, he won the title with a technical knockout of "Torpedo" Billy Murphy, whom some consider to have held the title first, starting earlier in 1890.

2521. Boxer of African descent to win a United States boxing title, and probably the first athlete of African descent to hold a U.S. title in any sport was George Dixon of Canada. On March 31, 1891, in Troy, New York, he defeated Cal McCarthy for the U.S. bantamweight crown with a knockout in the 22nd round. They had fought for 70 rounds in a no-contest decision on February 7, 1890. Dixon had subsequently won the world bantamweight title on June 27, 1890.

2522. Boxer to be undisputed world welterweight champion was "Mysterious" Billy Smith of the United States, who won the title in 1892 and held it until 1894. However, some credit Paddy Duffy with holding the title first (1888–1890).

2523. Boxer of African descent to win a world boxing title was George Dixon of Canada. He became world featherweight champion on June 27, 1892, when he knocked out Fred Johnson in the 14th round in Coney Island, New York.

BOXING (1900-1919)
2524. African-American boxer born in the United States to win a world boxing title was Joe Gans (Joseph Gaines). He won the title on May 12, 1902, by knocking out Frank Erne in the first round at Fort Erie, Ontario, Canada, for the world lightweight championship. He had lost to Erne when they first met, in 1900.

2525. Boxer to hold the undisputed world light heavyweight title was Jack Root (Janos Ruthaly) of Austria. He won it in 1903, but quickly lost it to George Gardner of Ireland.

BOXING—(1900-1919)—*continued*

2526. Boxer to hold world titles in three different weight classes was Bob Fitzsimmons of Great Britain, who won the middleweight title in 1891, the heavyweight in 1897, and the light-heavyweight in 1903.

2527. Bantamweight and featherweight boxing events held in the Olympic Games, and the first boxer to win two gold medals in a single Olympic Games were in 1904 in St. Louis, Missouri. Oliver Kirk won both titles on September 22: the bantamweight over George Finnegan, after the referee stopped the fight in the third round, and the featherweight by a decision over Frank Haller. All three boxers were from the United States. Finnegan won the flyweight title that same day.

2528. Flyweight boxing event in the Olympic Games was in 1904 in St. Louis, Missouri. George Finnegan won over Miles Burke, both of the United States, on September 22, after the referee stopped the match in the first round. Finnegan was also silver-medalist in the bantamweight class that same day.

2529. Heavyweight boxing event held in the Olympic Games was in 1904 in St. Louis, Missouri. The inaugural winner was Samuel Berger of the United States, with a decision on September 22. His opponent was Charles Mayer, who won the middleweight title that same day. From 1984, this unlimited weight class in the Olympics would be called super heavyweight, with the heavyweight class being limited to fighters not over 200.5 pounds (91 kilograms).

2530. Lightweight boxing event held in the Olympic Games was in 1904 in St. Louis, Missouri. The winner was Harry Spanger in a decision over teammate James Eagan on September 22. That same day he was silver-medalist in the welterweight event.

2531. Middleweight boxing event held in the Olympic Games was in 1904 in St. Louis, Missouri. Charles Mayer of the United States won over teammate Benjamin Spradley on September 22, after the referee stopped the match in the third round. That same day Mayer was silver-medalist in the heavyweight match.

2532. Welterweight boxing event held in the Olympic Games was in 1904 in St. Louis, Missouri. On September 22, Albert Young of the United States won by a decision over teammate Harry Spanger, who won the lightweight title that same day.

2533. Boxer to retire undefeated as world heavyweight champion was James J. Jeffries of the United States. He won the title by defeating Bob Fitzsimmons on June 9, 1899, and held it until 1905, when he retired undefeated. He returned in 1910, but was unable to beat then-champion Jack Johnson.

2534. Boxer of African descent to become world heavyweight champion was Jack (John Arthur) Johnson of the United States, who won the title from Tommy Burns on December 26, 1908, in Sydney, Australia. Johnson received $5000 of the total $40,000 purse. Before then, top white fighters had refused to fight Johnson. Though subjected to powerful attacks because of his race, as told in the play and movie *Great White Hope*, he held the title until 1915.

2535. International governing body for boxing was the International Boxing Union (IBU), founded in 1911 in Paris, France. It was replaced by the European Boxing Union (EBU) from 1946.

2536. Boxer to be undisputed world flyweight champion was Sid Smith of Great Britain, who won the title in 1913, but lost it later that year.

BOXING (1920-1939)

2537. Governing body for boxing in the United States was the New York State Athletic Commission (NYSAC), established under the 1920 Walker Law that legalized boxing in the state, making it a center for the sport.

2538. Light heavyweight boxing event held in the Olympic Games was in 1920 in Antwerp, Belgium. Edward Eagan of the United States won in a decision over Sverre Sörsdal of Norway on August 24. Eagan would win another gold medal as part of the four-man bobsled team in 1932, making him the first person ever to win gold medals in both the Summer and Winter Olympics.

2539. National governing body for boxing in the United States was the National Boxing Association (NBA), founded in New York City in 1921 by the athletic commissions of 15 states, though New York was not among them. In many other states, boxing was still illegal. The NBA would become the World Boxing Association (WBA) in 1962. Other boxing authorities proliferated, resulting in multiple "world champions."

2540. Boxing match to be broadcast on radio was a ten-round featherweight fight between Johnny Ray and Johnny Dundee on April 11, 1921, at the Pittsburgh Motor Garden, in Pittsburgh, Pennsylvania. Florent Gibson, sports editor of Pittsburgh's *Post*, called the bout, won by Ray.

2541. Boxing match to have a $1 million gate, and the first heavyweight bout to be broadcast on radio was on July 2, 1921, when Jack Dempsey of the United States defeated Georges Carpentier of France by a knockout in Jersey City, New Jersey. The gate was $1.8 million, and J. Andrew White called the bout. Born William Harrison Dempsey, the winner had adopted the name Jack in honor of the great early fighter Jack Dempsey (the Nonpareil).

2542. Boxer to hold the super-featherweight (junior lightweight) title was Johnny Dundee of the United States, born Giuseppe Carrora in Italy. He won the title on November 18, 1921, in New York City.

2543. Boxer to be undisputed world super-bantamweight (junior featherweight) champion was Jack "Kid" Wolfe, who won the title in 1922.

2544. Boxer to hold the world super-lightweight (junior welterweight) title was Pinkey Mitchell of the United States, who won the title in 1922.

2545. Boxer to win two consecutive middleweight titles in the Olympic Games was Henry Mallin of Great Britain. After winning first in 1920, he won again with a decision on July 20, 1924, in Paris, France. Earlier, in the quarterfinals, his opponent, Roger Brousse of France, was disqualified for biting Mallin in the chest, as he had also done to a previous opponent.

2546. Golden Gloves matches were held in 1927 in New York City. Originally local affairs sponsored by New York's *Daily News*, the bouts spread around the country, becoming national championships.

2547. Boxer to win both Olympic and professional world championships was Fidel LaBarba of the United States. After winning the Olympic flyweight title on July 20, 1924, he turned professional and won the world flyweight championship on January 21, 1927, over Elky Clark in New York City.

2548. Boxer named Fighter of the Year by *Ring* **magazine** was Gene (James Joseph) Tunney of the United States in 1928, when he defended his world heavyweight crown against challenger Tom Heeney, after which he retired.

2549. Boxer to be awarded the Val Barker Cup presented to the Olympic fighter with the best technique and style, was Louis Laurie of the United States, in 1936, the year he won the bronze medal in the flyweight competition at the Olympic Games in Berlin, Germany.

2550. Boxer to win three different world boxing titles within one year was Henry Armstrong. He first won the world featherweight title, by defeating Petey Sarron in New York City on October 29, 1937. Next came the world welterweight title, won from Barney Ross on May 31, 1938, in Long Island City, New York. Finally he won the world lightweight title, besting Lou Ambers on August 17, 1938, in New York City.

2551. Boxer named Fighter of the Year by *Ring* **magazine two, three, and four times** was Joe Louis of the United States, who was so honored in 1936, 1938, 1939, and 1941, the last three during his long and undefeated reign as world heavyweight champion (1937–1949).

2552. Boxing match to be broadcast on television in the United States was a heavyweight bout between Lou Nova and Max Baer at Yankee Stadium in New York City on June 1, 1939. It was seen on WNBT-TV, with Sam Taub calling the bout, won by Nova.

BOXING (1940-1959)

2553. Woman to be licensed as a boxing referee was Belle Martell, who received a license in California on April 30, 1940, and refereed her first match in San Bernardino on May 2, 1940.

2554. Heavyweight boxing match to be broadcast on television, and the first at which top-price tickets cost $100 was a fight between Joe Louis and Billy Conn at Yankee Stadium in New York City, on June 19, 1946. The eight-round fight, won with a knockout by Louis, appeared locally on WNBT-TV.

2555. Boxer to hold a world boxing title for more than 10 years, and to defend a world boxing title 25 times was Joe Louis of the United States. He originally won the world heavyweight title on June 22, 1937, in Chicago, Illinois, and then held it against all challengers until he retired in 1949. A 1950 comeback attempt failed.

2556. Heavyweight boxing match to be broadcast nationally on television was a title fight between Jersey Joe Walcott and Ezzard Charles, held at Municipal Stadium in Philadelphia, Pennsylvania, on June 5, 1952. Walcott kept his title on points.

BOXING—(1940-1959)—*continued*

2557. African-American boxers to win gold medals in the Olympic Games were Nathan Brooks in the flyweight class and Norvel Lee in the light heavyweight class, both of whom won unanimous decisions on August 2, 1952, in Helsinki, Finland. Four years earlier Lee had been arrested for sitting in the front section of a bus normally reserved for whites, in an action that presaged the coming civil rights movement.

2558. Light middleweight boxing event held in the Olympic Games was in 1952 in Helsinki, Finland. The winner was László Papp of Hungary in a unanimous decision over Theunis van Schalkwyk of South Africa on August 2. The 1948 middleweight champion would win the light middleweight title again in 1956, later turning professional.

2559. Light welterweight boxing event, and the first match between a Soviet and a United States boxer, in the Olympic Games was in 1952 in Helsinki, Finland, where Charles Adkins of the United States won in a 2–1 decision over Viktor Mednov of the Soviet Union on August 2.

2560. Boxer to win three gold medals, and two consecutive light middleweight titles, in the Olympic Games was László Papp of Hungary. After taking the middleweight title in 1948 and the light middleweight in 1952, he went to Melbourne, Australia, to win on December 1, 1956, in a decision over José Torres of the United States.

2561. Boxer from a Communist country to turn professional was László Papp of Hungary, who was able to do so only with permission from his government, in 1957. Three-time Olympic gold medalist as a light middleweight (1948) and middleweight (1952 and 1956), he became European middleweight champion, but was denied government permission to challenge for the world championship.

2562. Boxer to be named *Sports Illustrated* Sportsman of the Year was Ingemar Johansson of Sweden in 1959, the year he won the world heavyweight title from Floyd Patterson. Johansson would lose the title to Patterson the following year.

BOXING (1960-1979)

2563. Boxer from the United States to win the light middleweight title in the Olympic Games was Wilbert McClure, popularly known as Skeeter, who won a 4–1 decision over Carmelo Bossi of Italy on September 5, 1960, in Rome, Italy.

2564. Boxer to become world super-welterweight (junior middleweight) champion was Denny Moyer of the United States, who won the title in 1962. However, others awarded that title to Emile Griffith, who was European Boxing Union (EBU) champion.

2565. Olympic light heavyweight boxing champion to become world heavyweight champion was Cassius Clay, later known as Muhammad Ali, of the United States. After winning his Olympic title in 1960, he turned professional, winning his first world heavyweight title on February 25, 1964, over Sonny Liston in Miami, Florida.

2566. Boxer to win the world heavyweight championship three times was Muhammad Ali of the United States. As Cassius Clay, he had first won the title by defeating Sonny Liston on February 25, 1964, in Miami Beach, then changing his name to Muhammad Ali. In 1967, he was stripped of his title and barred from fighting, but returned to boxing in 1970. He regained the title on October 30, 1974, when he defeated champion George Foreman in Kinshasa, Zaire. He held the title until February 15, 1978, when he lost to Leon Spinks, but then defeated Spinks in a September 15, 1978, rematch to regain the title.

2567. Olympic heavyweight boxing champion to become world heavyweight champion was Joe Frazier of the United States. After winning his Olympic title in 1964, he won his first world professional crown on March 4, 1968, in a bout with Buster Mathis in New York City.

2568. Boxer to win two consecutive light middleweight titles in the Olympic Games was Boris Lagutin of the Soviet Union. After winning his first in 1964, he came to Mexico City for his second, winning in a unanimous decision on October 26, 1968.

2569. Boxer to win two consecutive light welterweight titles in the Olympic Games was Jerzy Kulej of Poland. After winning in 1964, he returned to win in a 3–2 decision on October 26, 1968, in Mexico City.

2570. Light flyweight boxing event held in the Olympic Games was in 1968 in Mexico City. The winner by a 3–2 decision on October 26 was Francisco Rodriguez of Venezuela, his country's first gold medalist.

2571. World amateur boxing championships were held in 1974 in Havana, Cuba. They would become biennial from 1989.

2572. Boxer to be world junior flyweight (light-flyweight) champion was Franco Udella of Italy. He won the title in 1975, when the weight class was introduced, but lost it later that year. Some consider him the first world strawweight (mini-flyweight) champion as well, also in 1975.

2573. Woman to become a boxing judge was Carol Polis, who received her license in March 1975.

2574. Brothers to win Olympic boxing titles on the same day were Michael Spinks and Leon Spinks of the United States on July 31, 1976, in Montreal. First Michael won the middleweight title over Rufat Riskiyev of the Soviet Union, then immediately afterward Leon won the light heavyweight crown over Sixto Soria of Cuba. In both matches, the referee stopped action in the third round. The brothers would go on to become world champions, Michael as a light heavyweight, Leon as a heavyweight.

2575. Boxer to win two, and then three, consecutive heavyweight titles, and three boxing titles in a single class, in the Olympic Games was Jamaican-born Teófilo Stevenson Lorenzo of Cuba. After winning first in 1972, he returned to win again over Mircea Simion of Romania with a knockout in the third round on July 31, 1976, in Montreal, Quebec, Canada, and then again in a 4–1 decision over Pyotr Zayev of the Soviet Union on August 2, 1980, in Moscow.

2576. Woman boxing judge to officiate at a world championship bout was Eva Shain, who worked the match between Muhammad Ali and Earnie Shavers for the heavyweight title on September 29, 1977, at Madison Square Garden in New York City.

2577. Boxer to hold the world cruiserweight title was Marvin Camel of the United States, who won it in 1979 after the new weight class was introduced by the World Boxing Council (WBC). He was not recognized by other boxing organizations, however, some of which called this the junior heavyweight class.

BOXING (1980–1999)
2578. Boxer to be world super-flyweight (junior bantamweight) champion was Rafael Orono of Venezuela, who won the title in 1980 when the weight class was first introduced by the World Boxing Council (WBC).

2579. Boxer to compete in four Olympic Games was György Gedó of Hungary, who competed in the first four light flyweight events (1968–1980), winning the gold medal in 1972.

2580. Boxer to hold the world super middleweight title was Murray Sutherland of Canada, who won the International Boxing Federation (IBF) title when the class was introduced in 1984.

2581. Heavyweight boxing event with a limited weight held in the Olympic Games was in 1984 in Los Angeles, California, when the weight was limited to 200.5 pounds (91 kilograms). The winner, by a unanimous decision over William deWit of Canada on August 11, was Henry Tillman of the United States, who had learned to box while in prison for armed robbery.

2582. Superheavyweight boxing event in the Olympic Games was held in 1984 in Los Angeles. This was a new unlimited weight class, after the heavyweight class became limited to 200.5 pounds (91 kilograms). The winner was Tyrell Biggs of the United States, with a 4–1 decision over Francesco Damiani of Italy on August 11 in Los Angeles, California.

2583. Boxer to hold the undisputed world cruiserweight (junior heavyweight) title was Evander Holyfield of the United States in 1988. The new weight class had been introduced in 1979, with various fighters had been recognized by different organizations; Holyfield won his first cruiserweight title in 1986, gradually unifying them.

2584. Boxer to hold world titles in five different weight classes was "Sugar" Ray Leonard of the United States, who won successively the World Boxing Council (WBC) welterweight title in 1979, the World Boxing Association (WBA) junior middleweight in 1981, the WBC middleweight in 1987, and then the WBC light-heavyweight and super-middleweight, both in 1988.

2585. Black African-born boxer to win a boxing title in the Olympic Games was Robert Wangila of Kenya, who won the welterweight title with a knockout in the second round on October 1, 1988, in Seoul, South Korea. Later turning professional, he fell into a coma after a 1994 match and died two days later.

2586. Boxer to hold the undisputed world heavyweight title after 1980 was Mike Tyson of the United States. In a period of disputing organizations and divided titles, he won the World Boxing Council (WBC) title in 1986, then defeated champions of two other organizations and several other fighters to become, by 1989, the acknowledged world champion, until he lost to James (Buster) Douglas on February 10, 1990, in Tokyo.

BOXING—(1980-1999)—*continued*

2587. Boxer to hold world titles in six different weight classes was Thomas Hearns of the United States, who won successively the World Boxing Association (WBA) welterweight title in 1980, the World Boxing Council (WBC) junior middleweight in 1982, the WBC light-heavyweight and middleweight in 1987, the World Boxing Organization (WBO) super-middleweight in 1988, and the WBA light-heavyweight in 1991.

2588. Boxing competitions in the Olympic Games to use computer scoring were in 1992 in Barcelona, Spain, under the auspices of the International Amateur Boxing Association (AIBA). Judges pushed buttons on a computer console whenever a fighter connected with a punch. In previous Olympics, the judges scored each round at the end, leaving more room for subjectivity and favoritism.

2589. Mexican-American boxer to win the lightweight title in the Olympic Games was Oscar De La Hoya, who won 7–2 over Marco Rudolph of Germany on points on August 8, 1992, in Barcelona, Spain, then going on to a notable professional career.

2590. Women's amateur boxing match sponsored by USA Boxing was held in February 1994. Tracy Desmond won the match in a technical knockout over Jacqueline Ta.

2591. Boxer to win two consecutive light welterweight titles in the Olympic Games was Héctor Vinent Charon of Cuba. After winning first in 1992, he returned on August 4, 1996, to win again in Atlanta, Georgia.

2592. Match between women boxers to be televised live was in February 1996, when Christy Martin won a bout against Sue Chase with a technical knockout.

2593. Women's boxing match to be watched by more than 1 million television viewers was on March 16, 1996, when Christy Martin of the United States won a unanimous decision over Deirdre Gogarty of Ireland in the six-round match, the "undercard" for the Mike Tyson–Frank Bruno match with which it was paired on a pay-per-view arrangement.

2594. Women's national championships in boxing sponsored by USA Boxing, were held on July 19, 1997, in Augusta, Georgia. Patricia Martinez won in the 106-pound class, Elizabeth McGonigal in the 112, Patricia Alcivar in the 119, Alicia Ashley in the 125, Melissa Salamone in the 132, Denise Lutrick in the 139, Sky Hosoya in the 147, Evelyn Rodriquez in the 156, LaKiea Coffen in the 165, Veronica Simms in the 178, and Tiffany Logan in the 201.

C

CANOE AND KAYAK RACING

2595. International governing body for canoeing was the Champst für Kanusport, founded in 1924. From 1946 it would be known as the International Canoe Federation (FIC), based in Budapest, Hungary.

2596. Men's Canadian pairs 1000-meter canoeing event held in the Olympic Games was in 1936 in Berlin, Germany. Winning on August 8 were Vladimir Syrovatka and Jan Brzak-Felix of Czechoslovakia, with a time of 4:50.1 minutes.

2597. Men's Canadian singles 1000-meter canoeing event held in the Olympic Games was in 1936 in Berlin, Germany. The inaugural winner, Francis Amyot of Canada, posted a time of 5:32.1 minutes on August 8.

2598. Men's pairs 1000-meter kayaking event held in the Olympic Games was in 1936 in Berlin, Germany. The inaugural race was won on August 8 by Adolf Kainz and Alfons Dorfner of Austria, with a time of 4:03.8 minutes.

2599. Men's singles 100-meter kayak event held in the Olympic Games was in 1936 in Berlin, Germany. The inaugural winner was Gregor Hradetzky of Austria, with a time of 4:22.9 minutes on August 8.

2600. Canoe racing world championships were held in 1938. They were not held again until 1948, and from 1970 became annual, except during Olympic years.

2601. Canoe sailing world championships were held in 1938 and then irregularly from 1961.

2602. Canoer to win two men's Canadian pairs 1000-meter titles in the Olympic Games was Jan Brzak-Felix of Czechoslovakia. He had won his first in 1936, paired with Vladimir Syrovatka. Twelve years later, in the next Olympics, he won again, this time paired with Bohumil Kudma, with a time of 5:07.1 minutes on August 12, 1948, in London, England.

2603. Women's 500-meter singles kayaking event held in the Olympic Games was in 1948 in London, England. Karen Hoff of Denmark won the inaugural event on August 12 with a time of 2:31.9 minutes.

2604. Canoe slalom world championships were held in 1949, and biennially since then. The inaugural winners were Pierre d'Alençon of France in the men's C1 slalom, Othmar Eiterer of Austria in the men's K1 slalom, and Hedi Pillwein of Austria in the women's K1 slalom.

2605. Canoe racer to win two consecutive men's Canadian singles 1000-meter titles in the Olympic Games was Josef Holecek of Czechoslovakia. After winning his first in 1948, he took his second with a time of 4:56.3 minutes on July 28, 1952, in Helsinki, Finland.

2606. Canoe racers to win both the men's 1000- and 10,000-meter pairs kayak events in the Olympic Games were Kurt Wires and Yrjö Hietanen of Finland. Competing in Helsinki, Finland, they won the 10,000 on July 27, 1952, with a time of 44.21.3 minutes, and then the 1000 on July 28, with a time of 3:51.1 in a photo finish.

2607. Canoe racer to win two, and then three, consecutive titles in the men's singles 1000-meter kayak event in the Olympic Games was Gert Fredriksson of Sweden. After winning his first title in 1948, he came back for another on July 28, 1952, in Helsinki, Finland, and a third on December 1, 1956, in Melbourne, Australia.

2608. Wild-water world championships were held in 1959, and biennially from then on.

2609. Canoe racer to win six gold medals, and eight medals overall, in the Olympic Games was Gert Fredriksson of Sweden. He won three consecutive titles in the men's 100-meter kayak singles, in 1948, 1952, and 1956. He also won two titles in the men's 10,000-meter kayak singles (1948 and 1956). His sixth medal came in the men's 1000-meter pairs on August 29, 1960, when he and Sven-Olov Sjödelius posted a time of 3:34.73 minutes.

2610. Women's 500-meter pairs kayaking event held in the Olympic Games was in 1960 in Rome, Italy. The winners were Maria Chubina and Antonina Seredina of the Soviet Union, with a time of 1:54.76 minutes on August 29.

2611. Men's fours 1000-meter kayaking event held in the Olympic Games was in 1964 in Tokyo. Winning on October 22 with a time of 3:14.67 minutes was the team from the Soviet Union: Mykola Chuzhykov, Anatoly Grishin, Vyacheslav Ionov, and Volodymyr Morozov.

2612. Canoe racer to win two consecutive titles in the women's 500-meter singles kayak event was Lyudmila Khvedosyuk Pinayeva of the Soviet Union. After winning her first in 1964 as Khvedosyuk, she came back to win again on October 25, 1968, in Mexico City with a time of 2:11.09 minutes.

2613. Canoe racers to win two consecutive women's 500-meter kayak pairs event in the Olympic Games were Roswitha Esser and Annemarie Zimmermann of Germany. After winning first in 1964, they went to Mexico City in 1968 to win a second with a time of 1:56.44 minutes on October 25.

2614. Women's slalom singles kayaking event held in the Olympic Games was in 1972 in Munich, West Germany. The inaugural winner, on August 30, was Angelika Behmann of East Germany.

2615. Men's kayak slalom white-water canoeing events held in the Olympic Games were in 1972 in Munich, West Germany. The inaugural winners were all from East Germany, which practiced on a course identical to that used in the Olympics. Siegbert Horn won the kayak slalom singles event and Reinhard Eiben the Canadian slalom singles, both on August 28, and Walter Hofmann and Rolf-Dieter Amend the Canadian slalom pairs on August 30.

2616. Men's Canadian singles 500-meter canoeing event held in the Olympic Games was in 1976 in Montreal, Quebec, Canada, where the inaugural winner was Aleksandr Rogov of the Soviet Union, with a time of 1:59.23 minutes.

2617. Men's pairs 500-meter kayaking event held in the Olympic Games was in 1976 in Montreal, Quebec, Canada. The winners were Joachim Mattern and Bernd Olbricht of East Germany with a time of 1:35.87 minutes on July 28.

CANOE AND KAYAK RACING—*continued*

2618. Men's Canadian pairs 500-meter canoeing event held in the Olympic Games was in 1976 in Montreal, Quebec, Canada. The winners were Serhei Petrenko and Aleksandr Vinogradov of the Soviet Union, with a time of 1:45.81 minutes on July 30.

2619. Men's singles 500-meter kayak event held in the Olympic Games was in 1976 in Montreal, Quebec, Canada. Vasile Diba of Romania was the first winner, with a time of 1:46.41 minutes on July 30.

2620. Canoe racer to win a gold medal in both the singles and pairs in the women's 500 meters in the Olympic Games was Agneta Andersson of Sweden in 1980, in Moscow, the Soviet Union. She won the singles with a time of 1:57.96 minutes, then won the pairs with Anna Olsson in 1:45.25 minutes, both on August 10.

2621. Canoe racer to win three gold medals in a single Olympic Games was Vladimir Parfenovich of the Soviet Union in 1980. Competing in his homeland in Moscow, he won the men's 500-meter kayak singles title on August 1, and joined with Serhei Chukhray to take the 500-meter kayak pairs title on July 28 and the 1000-meter kayak pairs on August 2.

2622. Canoer to win three titles in the men's Canadian pairs 1000-meter event in the Olympic Games was Ivan Patzaichin of Romania. After taking gold in 1968 and silver in 1972, both with Serghei Covaliov, he paired with Toma Simionov to win two more gold medals in 1980 and 1984, the latter on August 11, in Los Angeles, California. He also won a gold medal in the Canadian singles 1000-meters in 1972.

2623. Women's 500-meter fours kayaking event held in the Olympic Games was in 1984 in Los Angeles, California. Winning on August 11 with a time of 1:38.34 minutes were Agafia Buhaev Constantin, Nastasia Ionescu, Tecia Marinescu, and Maria Mihoreanu Stefan of Romania.

2624. Canoe marathon world championships were held at Holme Pierrepont, Nottingham, England, in 1988, and then biennially. The inaugural winners were John Jacoby of Australia in the men's K1; Thor Nielsen and Lars Koch of Denmark in the men's K2; Pál Pétervári of Hungary in the men's C1; Stephen Train and Andrew Train from Great Britain in the men's C2; Jane Hall of Australia in the women's K1; and Gayl Mayes and Denise Cooper of Australia in the women's K2.

2625. Canoe racers to win two consecutive titles in the men's pairs 500-meter kayak event in the Olympic Games were Ian Ferguson and Paul MacDonald of New Zealand. After winning their first championship in 1984, they returned for a second with a time of 1:33.98 minutes on September 30, 1988, in Seoul, South Korea.

2626. Canoe racer from the United States to win the men's singles 1000-meter kayak event, and to win a gold medal in any kayaking event, in the Olympic Games was Gregory Barton, who won on October 1, 1988, in Seoul, South Korea, with a time of 3:55.27 minutes. Barton and Norman Bellingham also won the 1000-meter pairs event at Seoul on the same day.

2627. Canoe polo world championships were held in 1994, when teams from Australia won both the men's and women's events.

2628. Canoe racer to win five gold medals, and eight medals overall, in women's events in the Olympic Games was Birgit Fischer Schmidt of East Germany. Her fifth gold medal came on August 3, 1996, in Atlanta, Georgia, where she won the gold medal in the women's 500-meter kayak fours, in which she had won gold in 1988 and silver in 1992. Her eighth medal overall came on August 4, when she was on the second-place team in the 500-meter kayak pairs, which she had won in 1988. Her other medals came in the women's 500-meter kayak singles (gold 1980, as Fischer, and 1992; silver 1988).

CHOLE

2629. Written reference to *chole* was in 1353 in Flanders (now Belgium), though some evidence suggests that the sport was played in France and Belgium at least as early as the 1100s. The game involved using a club to hit a ball at a distant target and may be related to several later games, including golf, hockey, and shinty.

2630. Introduction of *chole* to the British Isles was in 1421. Three Scottish soldiers— Hugh Kennedy, Robert Stewart, and John Smale—are generally given credit for bringing the game back to Scotland, where it is believed to have given rise to the game of golf. They were part of a Scottish regiment fighting with the French against the English at the siege of Baugé, France, during the Hundred Years' War.

CRICKET

2631. Cricket reference on record is in a book dated 1598 in Guildford, Surrey, England, which discussed the game as being played in the late 1550s.

2632. Cricket game on record played outside the British Isles was in 1676, when it was among the games listed as being played by English people living in Aleppo, Syria.

2633. Cricket reference in North America was on April 25, 1709, when William Byrd the Younger of Westover, Virginia, noted in his diary that he had played cricket with friends.

2634. Cricket ground set aside for play was on Kennington Common in England, as described in the announcement of a match between teams from London and Sevenoaks, played on July 12, 1731.

2635. Code of rules for cricket that has survived was written in 1744 in England.

2636. Cricket match at which admission was charged, and the first cricket game to be fully documented was played at the Artillery Ground in London, England, in 1744.

2637. Women's cricket match on record was played on Gosden Common near Guildford, Surrey, England, in 1745.

2638. Governing body in cricket was the Marylebone Cricket Club (MCC), founded in 1787 at Lord's Cricket Ground in London, England. Though supplanted on the international scene by the International Cricket Council in 1968, it remained the authority on cricket rules.

2639. Cricket match on record at Lord's Cricket Ground was played at its old location in London, England, on May 21, 1787, between members of the White Conduit Club and players from the County of Middlesex.

2640. Cricket club in India was the Calcutta Cricket Club, established in 1792, though the game had been played there since at least 1721.

2641. Record of cricket being played in the West Indies was on May 12, 1806, when a newspaper mentioned the St. Anne's Cricket Club in Barbados, suggesting that the game had been played for some years by then.

2642. Cricket match on record at the current location of Lord's Cricket Ground in London, England, was on June 22, 1814, when players from the Marylebone Cricket Club, based at Lord's, defeated a team from Hertfordshire.

2643. Protective gear worn by cricket players was padded gloves, introduced in approximately 1818 in England.

2644. Cricket club in Australia was the Military Cricket Club, founded in Sydney in 1826 for British soldiers serving there.

2645. Cricket match on record between teams from Oxford and Cambridge universities was played on June 4, 1827, at Lord's Cricket Ground in London, England. The match ended in a draw when it was stopped by rain.

2646. Cricket team from outside England to play in England was the Phoenix Park Club of Dublin, Ireland, which lost to the Liverpool Club in Liverpool on July 29, 1839.

2647. International cricket match outside Great Britain was played on September 24–26, 1844, in New York City. Members of the city's St. George's Club, representing the United States, defeated a team from Canada.

2648. Professional touring cricket team was the All England XI, captained by William Clarke of Nottinghamshire. They played their first match against a Sheffield team at Sheffield, England, on August 31, 1846.

2649. Cricket team from outside the British Isles to tour England was a team of Native Australians (Aborigines) in 1868. They had been organized by Charles Lawrence, an English player who became a cricket coach after emigrating to Australia.

2650. Test match in cricket between all-stars representing different countries was played on March 15–19, 1877, at Melbourne, Australia, between a touring English team, led by James Lillywhite, and an Australian team. However, some regard the first test matches as those played in Australia by a touring English team in 1861–1862.

2651. Women's cricket club was the White Heather Club, founded in 1887 at Nun Appleton, Yorkshire, England. Their first match was played the following year.

2652. Women's touring cricket team was the Original English Lady Cricketers, actually two teams that toured England in 1890. They played their inaugural match in Liverpool before 15,000 spectators.

2653. Cricket event at the Olympic Games was in Paris, France, in 1900, the only time the sport was included. The team from Great Britain, from the Devon and Somerset Wanderers Cricket Club, won on August 20.

2654. International cricket organization was the Imperial Cricket Conference, founded in 1909, by cricketers from England, Australia, and South Africa. Other countries later joined the organization, called "International" instead of "Imperial" from 1965.

CRICKET—*continued*

2655. Radio broadcast of a cricket game was in November 1922, with Lionel Watt announcing a match played by New South Wales cricketers at Sydney Cricket Ground in Australia.

2656. National cricket organization for women was the Women's Cricket Association (WCA), founded in England in 1926. It would later merge with the England and Wales Cricket Board.

2657. Women's test match in cricket was played in Brisbane, Australia, on December 28–31, 1934, where the team from England defeated one from Australia.

2658. Cricket game to be broadcast on television was on June 24, 1938, when the British Broadcasting Corporation (BBC) covered a test match between England and Australia at Lord's Cricket Ground in London, England, with announcer Teddy Wakelam.

2659. International cricket organization for women was the International Women's Cricket Council (IWCC), founded on February 19, 1958, in Australia.

2660. World cup in women's cricket was held in England in June and July 1973, won by the team from England.

2661. World cup in men's cricket was held at Lord's Cricket Ground in London, England, starting on June 7, 1975. In the final on June 21, the team from the West Indies defeated one from Australia.

2662. International Cricket Conference (ICC) competition was held in 1979 at Worcester, England, with 14 nations contesting. Winning the ICC trophy was the team from Sri Lanka, which defeated Canada on June 21. Sri Lankan cricketer Duleep Mendis was named Man-of-the-Match.

CROQUET

2663. Croquet sets were manufactured in the 1850s in England by manufacturer Jean Jaques, who published an 1857 book on the sport. The game was probably descended from a French game, *paille-maille* (*pall-mall*), which dates back to at least the 13th century.

2664. Croquet club in the United States was the Park Place Croquet Club founded in Brooklyn, New York, in 1864.

2665. Open championship in croquet was held in 1867 at Moreton-on-Marsh in England. The first champion was Walter James Whitmore, who helped popularize the sport in Great Britain, writing an 1868 book, *Croquet Tactics*.

2666. All England Croquet Club was established in 1869, in Wimbledon, England. The lawn courts there would come to be used also for tennis, which later overwhelmed croquet. The club itself would become the All England Croquet and Lawn Tennis Club in 1875 and then just the All England Lawn Tennis Club by 1880.

2667. Governing body for croquet in the United States was the National Croquet Association, founded in 1882.

2668. Rules for roque (a variation on croquet) were developed in New York in 1889 by members of the National Croquet Association.

2669. Organization for croquet in Britain was the Croquet Association, founded in 1896. It became the governing body for the British version of the sport, called *association croquet*.

2670. Croquet events at the Olympic Games were in Paris, France, in July 1900, the first and last time the sport was included. French contestants won all three croquet events.

2671. Roque event (a type of croquet) at the Olympic Games was in St. Louis, Missouri, in 1904, the only time it was included. United States players took all the top spots, with Charles Jacobus becoming champion on August 13.

CURLING

2672. Curling games in the Americas were played in Quebec City in around 1760. The game was introduced by soldiers from Scotland, where the game had originated more than two centuries earlier.

2673. Curling organization in the United States was the Orchard Lake Club, founded in Michigan in 1832.

2674. Governing organization for curling was the Grand Caledonian Curling Club, founded in Edinburgh, Scotland, in 1838, which became the "Royal Caledonian" in 1843. A kind of bowls played on ice, closely associated with Scotland, curling may have originated in the Netherlands before the 16th century.

2675. International curling competition between Canada and the United States was established in 1884. It would lead to the annual Gordon International Medal competitions.

2676. Strathcona Cup curling competition between teams from Canada and Scotland was established in 1903.

2677. World championships in curling were held in 1959. They were won by a team from Canada, with Ernie Richardson being winning skip. Women's competitions would not begin until 1979.

2678. International governing organization for curling was the World Curling Federation, founded in 1966, in Edinburgh, Scotland.

2679. Women's world championships in curling were held in 1979. The winning team was from Switzerland, with Gaby Casanova being named the winning skip.

2680. Curling event held in the Olympic Games was in 1998 in Nagano, Japan. The men's title was won by Switzerland and the women's by Canada, both on February 15.

CYCLING (BEFORE 1900)

2681. Cycling club was the Liverpool Velocipede Club, established in 1867. The first practical bicycle, the *vélocipède*, had been developed in March 1861 in Paris, France, by a father and son, Pierre and Ernest Michaux.

2682. Cycling race on record was held in 1868 in Paris, France, in a 1200-meter course in the Parc St. Cloud. The winner was James Moore of England.

2683. International cycling organization was the International Cyclist Association (ICA), founded in 1892. The main governing body in the sport would be the Union Cycliste International, founded in 1900.

2684. World championships in cycling were held in Chicago, Illinois, in 1893, and sponsored by the International Cyclist Association (ICA). For men only, the competition involved a 2000-meter sprint and a 1000-meter trial. The first champion was Arthur Zimmerman. Road race events would not be included until 1921.

2685. Men's 1000-meter match sprint cycling race held in the Olympic Games was on April 11, 1896, in Athens, Greece, where the inaugural winner was Paul Masson of France, with a time of 4:58.2 minutes.

2686. Men's road race cycling event held in the Olympic Games was on April 12, 1896, in Athens, Greece, on a round-trip course from Athens to Marathon and back. The winner was Aristidis Konstantinidis of Greece, with a time of 3:21:10 hours.

2687. Cyclist to win the men's 12-hour cycling race in the Olympic Games was Adolf Schmal of Austria, who won the event the only time it was held, on April 13, 1896, in Athens Greece.

2688. Cyclist to win two, and then three, cycling gold medals in the Olympic Games was Paul Masson of France in 1896 in Athens, Greece. On April 11 he won two soon-discontinued events: the men's one-lap race and the 10-kilometer track race. On the following day he won the inaugural men's 1000-meter match sprint race.

CYCLING (1900-1949)

2689. Tour de France cycling race was held in 1903, with the first winner being Maurice Garin of France. Following a different route each time, the event would be held annually except in wartime.

2690. Primavera cycling race from Milan to San Remo, Italy, was held in 1907, becoming one of the "Continental Classics" of cycling.

2691. Cyclist to win the Tour de France twice consecutively was Lucien Petit-Breton of France, who won in both 1907 and 1908.

2692. Men's 4000-meter team pursuit cycling event held in the Olympic Games was in 1908 in London, England. Winning the event with a time of 2:18.6 minutes on July 17 was the team from Great Britain: Leonard Meredith, Benjamin Jones, Ernest Payne, and Clarence Kingsbury.

2693. Tour of Italy (Giro d'Italia) cycling race was held in 1909, when the winner was Luigi Ganna of Italy.

2694. Cyclist to win the Tour de France three times was Philippe Thys of Belgium. After winning twice in a row (1913–1914), he came back after World War I to win again in 1920.

2695. Cyclo-cross races involving cycling over a cross-country course, were held in Europe in the 1920s, probably having been developed in the first decade of the 20th century in France.

2696. Men's 1000-meter time trial cycling event held in the Olympic Games was on August 7, 1928, in Amsterdam, the Netherlands. The inaugural winner was Villy Falck Hansen of Denmark, with a time of 1:14.4 minutes.

2697. Tour of Spain (Vuelta a España) cycling race was held in 1935, with the winner being Gustave Delour of Belgium.

CYCLING (1950-1979)

2698. World championships in cyclo-cross were held in 1950, with the winner being Jean Robic of France.

2699. Cyclist to win the Tour de France three consecutive times was Louison Bobet of France, who won in 1953, 1954, and 1955.

CYCLING—(1950-1979)—*continued*

2700. World championships in cycling to include women racers were in 1959.

2701. Cyclist to win the Tour de France five times, and four times consecutively was Jacques Anquetil of France, who won first in 1957 and then four times in a row: 1961–1964.

2702. Men's 4000-meter individual pursuit cycling event held in the Olympic Games was on October 17, 1964, in Tokyo. The inaugural winner was Jiri Daler of Czechoslovakia, with a time of 5:04.75 minutes.

2703. Cyclist to win two consecutive men's titles in the 1000-meter match sprint in the Olympic Games was Daniel Morelon of France. After winning first in 1968, he won again in Munich, West Germany, on September 2, 1972.

2704. Cyclist to win two consecutive titles in the men's 4000-meter team pursuit in the Olympic Games was Günther Schumacher of Germany. After winning in 1972, he joined three new teammates to win again on July 24, 1976, with a time of 4:21.06 minutes in Montreal, Quebec, Canada.

CYCLING (1980-1999)

2705. Race Across America (RAAM) bicycle marathon originally called the Great American Bike Race, was held in 1982. The founder, John Marino, was one of four contestants in the first race, from Santa Monica, California, to New York City. The others were John Howard, Michael Shermer, and the winner Lon Haldeman.

2706. Women's Tour de France cycling race a 616-mile road race, was held in 1984, when Marianne Martin of the United States won the inaugural championship.

2707. Cyclist from the United States to win the men's road race in the Olympic Games was Alexi Grewal, a naturalized U.S. citizen of Anglo-German–East Indian descent, who won the event on July 29, 1984, in Los Angeles, California.

2708. Women's road race cycling event held in the Olympic Games was on July 29, 1984, in Los Angeles, California. The winner, with a time of 2:11:14 hours over the 79.2-kilometer course, was Connie Carpenter-Phinney of the United States.

2709. Cyclist from the United States to win the men's 4000-meter individual pursuit in the Olympic Games was Steve Hegg in 1984 in Los Angeles, California. Also a U.S. champion downhill skier, he won the event on August 1 with a time of 4:39.35 minutes.

2710. Cyclist from the United States to win the men's 1000-meter match sprint in the Olympic Games was Mark Gorski, who won the event on August 3, 1984, in Los Angeles, California.

2711. Men's points cycling race held in the Olympic Games was on August 3, 1984, in Los Angeles, California, where the inaugural winner was Roger Ilegems of Belgium.

2712. Cyclist from the United States to win the Tour de France was Greg LeMond, who won first in 1986. He would win twice more, in 1989 and 1990.

2713. Women's 1000-meter match sprint cycling event held in the Olympic Games was on September 24, 1988, in Seoul, South Korea. The inaugural winner was Erika Salumäe, an Estonian cyclist from the Soviet Union.

2714. Cyclist to be named *Sports Illustrated* Sportsman of the Year was Greg LeMond of the United States in 1989, the year he had his second of three Tour de France wins.

2715. World cup in cycling was established in 1989. The inaugural winner of the series of races was Sean Kelly of Ireland.

2716. World championships in mountain biking were held in 1990. The winners on the men's side were Ted Overend in the cross-country and Greg Herbold in the downhill, both from the United States. On the women's side, Julie Furtado of the United States was the inaugural winner in the cross-country and Cindy Devine of Canada in the downhill.

2717. Cyclist to win the Jesse Owens International Award was Greg LeMond of the United States in 1991. He had won three Tour de France titles, in 1986, 1989, and 1990.

2718. Cyclist to win two consecutive women's titles in the 1000-meter match sprint in the Olympic Games was Erika Salumäe. She had won first in 1988, competing for the Soviet Union, then returned to win again for Estonia on July 31, 1992, in Barcelona, Spain.

2719. Women's 3000-meter individual pursuit cycling event in the Olympic Games was on July 31, 1992, in Barcelona, Spain. The inaugural winner was Petra Rossner of Germany, with a time of 3:41.753 minutes.

2720. Cycling races to include both amateurs and professionals were in 1993, when the distinction between the two was effectively erased.

2721. Cyclist to win the Tour de France five consecutive times was Miguel Induráin of Spain, who won from 1991 through 1995.

2722. Women's points race cycling event held in the Olympic Games was in 1996 in Atlanta, Georgia. Winning on July 28 was Nathalie Lancien of France.

2723. Men's cross-country (mountain bike) race held in the Olympic Games was in 1996 in Atlanta, Georgia. Bart Jan Brentjens of the Netherlands won the men's event on July 30.

2724. Women's cross-country cycling race held in the Olympic Games was in Atlanta, Georgia, in 1996. Paola Pezzo of Italy won the first women's title on July 30.

2725. Men's road time trial cycling event held in the Olympic Games was on August 3, 1996 in Atlanta, Georgia. The inaugural winner, in the first Olympics to allow professional cyclists, was Miguel Induráin, five-time winner of the Tour de France.

2726. Women's road time trial cycling event held in the Olympic Games was on August 3, 1996, in Atlanta, Georgia, where the winner was Zulfiya Zabirova of Russia.

2727. Cyclist to win the Tour de France after recovering from cancer was Lance Armstrong of the United States, who won in 1999, after undergoing surgery and radiation treatment for testicular cancer, first diagnosed in 1996, and returning to competition only in 1998.

CYCLING (2000-)
2728. Women's 500-meter time trial cycling event held in the Olympic Games was in 2000 in Sydney, Australia. Felicia Ballanger of France won the event on September 16, with a time of 34.140 seconds.

2729. Men's Olympic sprint cycling event held in the Olympic Games occurred in 2000 in Sydney, Australia. Olympic sprint cycling involves a three-lap race by three-man teams. The winners were Laurent Gane, Florian Rousseau and Arnaut Tournant of France, who had a time of 44.233 seconds on September 17.

2730. Cycling team to break the 4-minute mark in the men's 4000-meter team pursuit race in the Olympic Games was from Germany. On September 19, 2000, at Sydney, Australia, Guido Fulst, Robert Bartko, Daniel Becke, and Jens Lehmann posted a time of 3.59.710 minutes. That broke the previous world record of 4:00:830 minutes set just an hour earlier by a Ukrainian team.

2731. Men's Keirin cycling event held in the Olympic Games took place in 2000 in Sydney, Australia. The event, an 8-lap race with motor-cycle pacing for the first 5 1/2 laps, was won with a time of 11.020 seconds on September 21 by Florian Rousseau of France, who also took gold in the inaugural Olympic sprint cycling event, as part of a three-man team.

2732. Men's Madison cycling event held in the Olympic Games took place in 2000 in Sydney, Australia. The Madison is a 60-kilometer race by two-man teams. The Australian duo of Brett Aitken and Scott McGrory won with a score of 26 points on September 21.

D

DARTS

2733. Playing of darts on record in North America was in 1620 by the Pilgrims, who played the game on the *Mayflower* en route to New England.

2734. Rules for modern darts were developed in 1896 by Brian Gamlin in Bury, Lancashire, England.

2735. World professional darts championships were held in 1978 at the Midlands Nightclub in Nottingham, England, sponsored by the British Darts Organization (BDO). The winner was Leighton Rees of Wales.

DECATHLON

2736. Decathlon championship on record was in 1900 in Denmark. The 10-event competition was largely developed in the Scandinavian countries in the late 19th century, with varying events. The original Olympic Games had only a pentathlon, composed of five events.

2737. Men's decathlon event held in the Olympic Games was on July 4, 1904, in St. Louis, Missouri. Then called the All-Around Championship, the ten events were all held on the same day. The winner was Thomas Kiely of Ireland.

DECATHLON—*continued*

2738. Athlete to win both the men's decathlon and pentathlon in the Olympic Games, and the first Native American to win an Olympic gold medal was Jim Thorpe of the United States. He was of Sac and Fox descent. Competing in Stockholm, Sweden, he won the 5-event pentathlon on July 7, 1912, and then the 3-day, 10-event decathlon on July 15. He had already won the high jump. In 1913, he was stripped of his medals when it was learned that he had previously played minor league baseball for $25 a week, and so was considered a professional, ineligible for the Olympics. In 1950, an Associated Press poll of sports writers and announcers named Thorpe the outstanding U.S. athlete of the first half of the 20th century. His name and medals were restored in 1983, three decades after his death.

2739. Decathlete to hold the officially accepted world record in the men's decathlon was Aleksandr Klumberg of Estonia, who won the competition on September 17, 1922, in Helsinki, Finland. The competition included the 100- and 400-meter races, long jump, shot put, and high jump on the first day, and the 110-meter hurdles, discus, pole vault, javelin, and 1500-meter race on the second. The allocation of points would be adjusted several times over the years, so point totals over the years are not fully comparable.

2740. Decathlete from the United States to hold the world record in the men's decathlon was Harold Osborn, who won the gold medal at the Olympic Games in Paris, France, on July 12, 1924.

2741. Athlete to win an Olympic gold medal, or to hold the world record, in both the men's decathlon and an individual track and field event was Harold Osborn of United States. He set a world record in the high jump, with a jump of 6 feet 8 inches on May 27, 1924, in Urbana, Illinois. Then at the Olympic Games in Paris, France, he won the high jump on July 7 with an Olympic-record jump of 6 feet 6 inches. Five days later, he won the decathlon with a world-record 6476 points.

2742. Decathlete to win two consecutive titles in the men's decathlon in the Olympic Games was Robert Mathias of the United States. After first winning in 1948, he returned to win again on July 26, 1952, in Helsinki, Finland, with a world-record point total.

2743. African-American decathlete to win the men's title in the Olympic Games was Milton Campbell, who won the event on November 30, 1956, in Melbourne, Australia. The silver-medalist was his African-American teammate, world-record-holder Rafer Johnson, who would win the title in 1960.

2744. Decathlete to score more than 8500 points in the men's decathlon was Bruce Jenner of the United States. At the Olympic Games at Montreal, Quebec, Canada, on July 30, 1976, Jenner scored 8618 points, the equivalent of 8634 points on the scoring tables that came into use in 1985.

2745. Decathlete to score 8,891 points in the men's decathlon was Dan O'Brien of the United States, who did so on September 5, 1992, in Talence, France. He had failed to qualify for the Olympics that year, after having problems with the pole vault, but would be the Olympic gold-medalist in 1996.

DISABILITIES, ATHLETES WITH

2746. International organization for athletes with disabilities was the Comité International des Sports des Sourds (Committee International on Silent Sports) (CISS), founded in connection with the World Games for the Deaf, held in Paris, France, in 1924. It would sponsor world games quadrennially from 1924 for summer sports and from 1949 for winter sports.

2747. International tournament for athletes with disabilities was the World Games for the Deaf, held in Paris, France, in 1924.

2748. Wheelchair sports tournaments were the Stoke Mandeville Games for the Paralyzed, first held in 1948, developed for war veterans in wheelchairs at the National Spinal Injuries Centre of the Stoke Mandeville Hospital in Aylesbury, England. It would become an international tournament when athletes from abroad participated starting in 1952, with the International Stoke Mandeville Games Federation (ISMGF) as its governing organization.

2749. National organization for basketball players in wheelchairs was the National Wheelchair Basketball Association, established in 1949.

2750. National tournament for athletes in wheelchairs held in the United States was the National Wheelchair Games held in 1958. Out of this would grow the National Wheelchair Association (later Wheelchair Sports, USA), which came to govern all wheelchair sports except basketball.

2751. Olympics-like tournament for athletes with disabilities was the First International Games for the Disabled, held in Rome, Italy, in 1960. As the Olympics for the Disabled, they would be held every four years. After 1980, at the request of the International Olympic Committee, it changed its name to Paralympics.

2752. Special Olympics were founded in 1968 by Eunice Kennedy Shriver for children and adults with mental retardation. It developed out of a private program begun at her home in Rockville, Maryland, in 1963.

2753. Olympics for the Physically Disabled to include athletes other than those with spinal injuries were held in Toronto, Ontario, Canada, in 1976, after the Montreal Olympic Games, for the first time including athletes who were blind or had had limb amputations. Ambulatory athletes with cerebral palsy were welcomed from 1980. In the United States, athletes with various kinds of disabilities were increasingly integrated into regular sports programs following the Amateur Sport Act of 1978.

DISCUS THROW

2754. Men's discus throw event held in the Olympic Games was in 1896 in Athens, Greece. Winning the inaugural competition on April 6 was Robert Garrett of the United States, with a throw of 95 feet 7½ inches (29.15 meters). The Princeton University student, who paid his own way to Athens, had begun throwing the discus just weeks earlier. He also won the shot put event.

2755. Discus throw event in the Olympic Games to be decided by a throw-off was on September 3, 1904, in St. Louis, Missouri. After tying each other with Olympic-record throws of 128 feet 10½ inches (39.28 meters), United States teammates Martin Sheridan and Ralph Rose participated in a throw-off, won by the Irish-born Sheridan.

2756. Men's Greek-style discus throw event held in the Olympic Games was in 1906, in the unofficial Olympics in Athens, Greece. The winner was Verner Järvinen of Finland, with a throw of 115 feet 4½ inches (35.17 meters) on May 1. His son, Matti Järvinen, would win the 1936 Olympic javelin throw.

2757. Discus-thrower to win two, and then three, consecutive men's titles in the Olympic Games was Irish-born Martin Sheridan of the United States. After winning the 1904 event in a throw-off, he won again in the unofficial Olympics, in Athens, Greece, with a throw of 136 feet 0 inches (41.46 meters) on April 25, 1906, and then again in the official Olympics in London, England, with an Olympic-record throw of 134 feet 2 inches (40.89 meters) on July 16, 1908.

2758. National team to sweep the top spots in the men's discus throw in the Olympic Games was from the United States, led by Irish-born three-time Olympic gold-medalist Martin Sheridan, who had a throw of 134 feet 2 inches (40.89 meters) on July 16, 1908, in London, England.

2759. Discus-thrower from the United States to win the men's Greek-style title in the Olympic Games was Irish-born Martin Sheridan. He had an Olympic-record throw of 124 feet 8 inches (38.00 meters) on July 18, 1908, in London, England, the second and last time the event was held.

2760. Discus-thrower to hold the officially accepted world record in the men's event was James Duncan of the United States, with a distance of 156 feet 1 inch (47.58 meters), set on May 27, 1912, in New York City. The record would stand until 1924.

2761. Men's discus throw event for both hands held in the Olympic Games was on July 13, 1912, in Stockholm, Sweden. The only time the event was held, it was won by Armas Taipale of Finland, whose total for the two throws was 271 feet 10 inches (82.86 meters).

2762. Women's discus throw event, and the first women's field event, held in the Olympic Games was on July 31, 1928, in Amsterdam, the Netherlands. The inaugural winner was Halina Konopacka of Poland, who had a world-record throw of 129 feet 11¾ inches (39.62 meters).

2763. Discus-thrower to break the 160-foot and 50-meter barriers was Eric Krenz of the United States. He broke the first with a distance of 163 feet 8 inches (49.90 meters) on March 9, 1929, and the second with 167 feet 5 inches (51.03 meters) on May 17, 1930, both in the men's event at Palo Alto, California.

2764. Discus-thrower from the United States to win the women's event in the Olympic Games was Lillian Copeland, with an Olympic-record throw of 133 feet 2 inches (40.58 meters) on August 2, 1932, in Los Angeles, California.

DISCUS THROW—*continued*

2765. Discus-thrower to break the 170-foot barrier was Harald Andersson of Sweden, with a throw of 172 feet 0 inches (52.42 meters) on August 25, 1934, in Oslo, Norway.

2766. Discus-thrower to hold the officially accepted world record in the women's event was Gisela Mauermayer of Germany. She set her world record of 158 feet 6 inches (48.31 meters) on July 11, 1936, in Berlin. Then on August 4, in the Berlin Olympics, she threw for an Olympic-record 156 feet 3 inches (47.63 meters).

2767. Discus-thrower to break the 180-foot barrier was Robert Fitch of the United States, with a throw of 180 feet 3 inches (54.93 meters) in the men's event on June 8, 1946, in Minneapolis, Minnesota.

2768. Discus-thrower to break the 50-meter and 160-, 170-, and 180-foot barriers in the women's event was Nina Dumbadze, with throws of 174 feet 8 inches (53.25 meters) on August 8, 1948, in Moscow, the Soviet Union, and 187 feet 2 inches (57.04 meters) on October 18, 1952, in Tbilisi, the Soviet Union. She was the first thrower from the Soviet Union to hold the world record in the event.

2769. Discus-thrower to break the 190-foot barrier was Fortune Gordien of the United States, who had a throw of 190 feet 7 inches (58.10 meters) in the men's event on July 11, 1953, in Pasadena, California, for the third of his four world records in the event. Less than a month earlier, his teammate Simeon Inness had had a throw of exactly 190 feet (57.93 meters) on June 20, 1953, in Lincoln, Nebraska.

2770. Discus-thrower to win two titles in the women's event in the Olympic Games was Nina Romaschkova Ponomaryeva of the Soviet Union. After taking her first gold medal in 1952 (as Romaschkova) and a silver in 1956, she gained another gold on September 5, 1960, with an Olympic-record throw of 180 feet 9 inches (55.10 meters) in Rome, Italy.

2771. Discus-thrower to break the 60-meter barrier was Jay Silvester of the United States, with a throw of 198 feet 8 inches (60.56 meters) in the men's event on August 11, 1961, in Frankfurt am Main, West Germany. It was the first of his four world records in the event.

2772. Discus-thrower to break the 190-foot barrier in the women's event was Tamara Press of the Soviet Union, with a throw of 190 feet 6 inches (58.06 meters) on September 1, 1961, in Sofia, Bulgaria, for the third of her six world records in the event.

2773. Discus-thrower to break the 200-foot barrier was Alfred Oerter of the United States, with a throw of 200 feet 5 inches (61.10 meters) in the men's event on May 18, 1962, in Los Angeles, California. A four-time Olympic gold-medalist in the event (1956, 1960, 1964, and 1968), he would set three more world records.

2774. Discus-thrower to break the 210-foot barrier was Ludvik Danek of Czechoslovakia, with a throw of 211 feet 9 inches (64.55 meters) in the men's event in Turnov, Czechoslovakia, on August 2, 1964. The first Czech to hold the world record in the event, he would up that to 213 feet 11 inches in 1965.

2775. Discus-thrower to break the 60-meter and 200-foot barriers in the women's event was Liesel Westermann of West Germany. Her throw of 201 feet 0 inches (61.26 meters) was made on November 5, 1967, in São Paulo, Brazil.

2776. Discus-thrower to break the 220-foot barrier was Jay Silvester of the United States, with his fourth and last world record, a throw of 224 feet 5 inches (68.40 meters) in the men's event on September 18, 1968, in Reno, Nevada.

2777. Discus-thrower to win four consecutive men's titles in the Olympic Games, and the first to win any Olympic event four consecutive times was Alfred Oerter of the United States, setting an Olympic record each time. His first three Olympic wins came in 1956, 1960, and 1964—despite being severely injured in a 1957 automobile accident—and his fourth on October 15, 1968, in Mexico City, with a throw of 212 feet 6 inches (64.78 meters).

2778. Discus-thrower to break the 210-foot barrier in the women's event was Faina Melnik of the Soviet Union, with a throw of 210 feet 8 inches (64.22 meters) on August 12, 1971, in Helsinki, Finland. It was the first of her 11 world records in the event.

2779. Discus-thrower to break the 220-foot barrier in the women's event was Argentina Menis of Romania, with a throw of 220 feet 10 inches (67.32 meters) on September 23, 1972, in Constanta, Romania.

2780. Discus-thrower to break the 230-foot and 70-meter barriers was Faina Melnik of the Soviet Union, with a throw of 230 feet 4 inches (70.20 meters) in the women's event on August 20, 1975, in Zürich, Switzerland.

2781. Discus-thrower to break the 230-feet and 70-meter barriers in the men's event was Mac Wilkins of the United States. For his second world record, he threw for 230 feet 5 inches (70.24 meters) on May 1, 1976, in San Jose, California, then upped it twice more on the same day to 232 feet 6 inches (70.86 meters).

2782. Discus-thrower to win two consecutive women's titles in the Olympic Games was Evelin Schlaak Jahl of East Germany. After winning in 1976 (as Schlaak), she won again on August 1, 1980, with an Olympic-record throw of 229 feet 6 inches (69.96 meters) in Moscow, the Soviet Union.

2783. Discus-thrower to break the 240-foot barrier was Balina Savinkova of the Soviet Union, with a throw of 240 feet 4 inches (73.26 meters) in the women's event on May 22, 1983, in Leselidze, the Soviet Union.

2784. Discus-thrower to break the 240-foot barrier in the men's event was Jurgen Schult of East Germany, with a throw of 243 feet 0 inches (74.08 meters) on June 6, 1986, in Neubrandenburg, East Germany.

2785. Discus-thrower to break the 250-foot barrier was Gabriele Reinsch of East Germany, with a throw of 252 feet 0 inches (76.80 meters) in the women's event on July 9, 1988, in Neubrandenburg, East Germany.

DIVING (BEFORE 1900)
2786. Book on diving was written by H. L. Kluge and published in Germany in 1843.

2787. Diving tournament on record was a plunge diving event held by the Amateur Swimming Association in Great Britain in 1883.

2788. Formally organized diving competition was held in Scotland in 1889.

2789. National diving competition was held in Scotland in 1895, sponsored by the Royal Life Saving Society.

DIVING (1900-1949)
2790. Governing body for diving was the Amateur Diving Association, founded in 1901 following exhibitions by several Swedish divers held in London, England.

2791. Men's platform diving event held in the Olympic Games was in 1904 in St. Louis, Missouri. George Sheldon of the United States took the first crown on September 7.

2792. Men's springboard diving event held in the Olympic Games was in 1908 in London, England. The inaugural winner was Albert Zürner of Germany on July 18.

2793. National team to sweep the top medals in men's platform diving in the Olympic Games was from Sweden in 1908. Hjalmar Johansson, Karl Malmström, and Arvid Spångberg finished in that order on July 24, followed by their teammate Robert Andersson.

2794. National team to sweep the top medals in men's springboard diving in the Olympic Games was from Germany in 1912. Winning on July 9 in Stockholm, Sweden, the top four divers were Paul Günther, Hans Luber, Kurt Behrens, and Albert Zürner, who had been the gold medalist in 1908.

2795. Men's plain high dive event held in the Olympic Games was on July 11, 1912, in Stockholm, Sweden. Erik Adlerz led a Swedish sweep of the medals. The event was discontinued in 1924.

2796. Diver from the United States to win the men's springboard diving event in the Olympic Games was Louis Kuehn, who won on August 27, 1920, in Antwerp, Belgium.

2797. Women's springboard diving event held in the Olympic Games was on August 29, 1920, in Antwerp, Belgium. In a day when women divers still wore short-sleeved, knee-length dresses as bathing suits, 14-year-old Aileen Riggin led a United States sweep of the medals. Silver-medalist in 1924, she later became one of the earliest women sportswriters.

2798. Athlete to win Olympic medals in both diving and swimming was Aileen Riggin of the United States. She won the springboard diving competition in 1920, coming in second in 1924 in Paris, France, where she also won a bronze medal in swimming, in the 100-meter backstroke competition on July 20.

2799. Diver to win both the men's springboard and platform diving titles in the same Olympic Games was Albert White of the United States in 1924 in Paris, France. After winning the springboard title on July 17, he came back on July 20 to win the platform championship, heading a U.S. medal sweep in both events.

2800. National team to sweep the top medals in the women's platform diving event in the Olympic Games was from the United States. Dorothy Poynton (later Poynton Hill), Georgia Coleman, and Marion Roper finished in that order on August 12, 1932, in Los Angeles, California.

DIVING—(1900-1949)—*continued*

2801. Diver to win two consecutive women's platform diving titles in the Olympic Games was Dorothy Poynton Hill of the United States. After winning her first in 1932 as Poynton, she returned to take her second crown on August 13, 1936, in Berlin.

2802. Diver to win both the women's springboard and platform diving titles in the same Olympic Games was Victoria Draves of the United States in 1948 in London, England, where she won the springboard title on August 3 and the platform on August 6.

DIVING (1950-1999)

2803. Diver to win two consecutive men's platform diving titles in the Olympic Games was Samuel Lee of the United States. A Korean-American army doctor, he won first in 1948 and then won his second title on August 1, 1952, in Helsinki, Finland.

2804. Diver to win two consecutive titles in both springboard and platform diving events, and the first to win four gold medals in diving, in the Olympic Games was Patricia McCormick of the United States. After winning the women's title in the two events in 1952, she went to Melbourne, Australia, in 1956 to win them both again, taking her second springboard title on December 4, and her second platform on December 7.

2805. Men's highboard platform diving event held at the world championships was in 1973 in Belgrade, Yugoslavia. Klaus Dibiasi of Italy won the title and defended it successfully in 1975.

2806. Men's springboard diving event held at the world championships was in 1973 in Belgrade, Yugoslavia. Phil Boggs of the United States won the first title and the next two. Separate one- and three-meter springboard competitions would be held from 1991.

2807. Women's highboard platform diving event held in the world championships was in 1973 in Belgrade, Yugoslavia, where the first champion was Ulrike Knape of Sweden.

2808. Women's springboard diving event held at the world championships was in 1973 in Belgrade, Yugoslavia, where the inaugural winner was Christine Kohler of East Germany. Separate one- and three-meter springboard competitions would be held from 1991.

2809. Diver to win two, and then three, consecutive men's springboard diving titles in the world championships was Phil Boggs of the United States, who won the title the first three times it was offered, in 1973 in Belgrade, Yugoslavia; in 1975 in Cali, Colombia; and in 1978 in West Berlin, West Germany.

2810. Diver to win two consecutive men's highboard platform diving titles at the world championships was Klaus Dibiasi of Italy, who won in 1973, the first time the competition was held, and again in 1975 in Cali, Colombia.

2811. Diver to win three consecutive men's platform diving titles in the Olympic Games was Klaus Dibiasi of Italy. After winning in 1968 and 1972, he went to Montreal to win his third straight crown on July 27, 1976. He had been silver-medalist in 1964. The first Italian to win an Olympic gold medal in swimming or diving, he was coached by his father, Carlo Dibiasi, a 1936 Olympic diver.

2812. Diver to hold women's world titles in both springboard and highboard platform diving at the same time was Irina Kalinina of the Soviet Union. She won both titles in 1978 in West Berlin, West Germany, after previously winning the springboard title in 1975.

2813. Diver to win two consecutive women's world titles in springboard diving was Irina Kalinina of the Soviet Union. After winning her first in 1975, she went to West Berlin, West Germany, to win her second in 1978.

2814. World cup in diving with national teams competing, was held in 1979, becoming a biennial event.

2815. Diver to hold the men's world titles in both springboard diving and highboard platform diving at the same time was Gregory Louganis of the United States. He won both titles first in 1982 in Guayaquil, Ecuador, and then again in 1986 in Madrid, Spain. He had previously won the platform title in 1978.

2816. Diver to win three consecutive men's highboard platform diving titles in the world championships was Gregory Louganis of the United States. His three titles came in in 1978 in West Berlin, West Germany; in 1982 in Guayaquil, Ecuador; and in 1986 in Madrid, Spain.

2817. Diver to win the Jesse Owens International Award was Gregory Louganis of the United States in 1987. In 1986, he won his third straight men's highboard platform diving world title; in 1988 he would win his second straight platform and springboard titles in the Olympic Games.

2818. Diver to win both the men's platform and springboard diving titles in two consecutive Olympic Games was Gregory Louganis of the United States. After winning the two titles in 1984, he won them both again in Seoul, South Korea, in 1988, the springboard on September 20 and the platform on September 27. Seven years later he would reveal that he was being treated for AIDS at the time.

2819. Diver to be awarded more than 100 points on a single dive was Mark Lenzi of the United States. Competing at the 1991 U.S. Indoor Championships, he received 101.85 points for a reverse 3½ somersault tuck dive. He would be the Olympic gold medalist in 1992.

2820. Diver to hold the women's world titles in both the one- and three-meter springboard diving at the same time was Gao Min of China. She won both in 1991 in Perth, Australia, the first time two separate springboard titles were offered, having won the single springboard title previously in 1986.

2821. Men's one-meter springboard diving event held at the world championships was in 1991 in Perth, Australia, where the winner was Edwin Jongejans of the Netherlands. This was the first year that separate one- and three-meter competitions were held.

2822. Women's one-meter springboard diving event held at the world championships was in 1991 in Perth, Australia. The winner was Gao Min of China. Separate one- and three-meter competitions were held for the first time that year.

2823. Diver to win two consecutive women's highboard platform diving titles at the world championships was Fu Mingxia of China. After winning her first in 1991, she went to Rome, Italy, in 1994 for her second.

2824. Women's synchronized platform diving event held at the world championships was in Perth, Australia, in 1998. Olena Zhupyna and Svilana Serbina of Ukraine were the winners.

2825. Women's synchronized three-meter springboard diving event held at the world championships was in 1998 in Perth, Australia, where the inaugural competition was won by Irina Lashko and Yuliya Pakhalina of Russia.

DIVING (2000-)

2826. Men's synchronized platform diving event held in the Olympic Games was in 2000 in Sydney, Australia. The Russian duo of Igor Loukachine and Dmitri Sautin won the gold medal on September 23 with a grand total of 365.04 points. Sautin also won bronze medals in the men's synchronized springboard diving event and the men's individual platform and springboard diving events. With his 1996 platform gold medal, that gave him five Olympic medals overall.

2827. Women's synchronized springboard diving event held in the Olympic Games was in 2000 in Sydney, Australia. Vera Ilina and Yuliya Pakhalina of Russia won the gold on September 23 with a grand total of 332.64 points.

2828. Men's synchronized springboard diving event held in the Olympic Games was in 2000 in Sydney, Australia. The winners were Xiao Hailiang and Xiong Ni of China, who scored a grand total of 365.58 points on September 28. Xiong also won the men's individual springboard title.

2829. Women's synchronized platform diving event held in the Olympic Games was in 2000 in Sydney, Australia. Li Na and Sang Xue, both of China, won the event with a grand total of 345.12 points on September 28. Four days earlier, Li had been the silver medalist in the women's individual platform event, with Sang coming in fourth.

DOG RACING

2830. Dog racing club was the Swaffham Club, organized in Norfolk, England, by Lord Orford in 1776. The sport of dog racing, or coursing, dates back thousands of years, with greyhounds becoming preferred because of their great speed.

2831. Waterloo Cup offered to the unofficial British national champion in dog racing, was offered in 1836.

2832. National governing body for dog racing in England was the National Coursing Club, founded in 1858.

2833. National organization for dog racing in the United States was the National Coursing Organization, founded in 1897.

2834. Mechanical rabbit used in dog racing was in 1919, when Owen P. Smith introduced the electrically operated lure at a dog racing track in Emeryville, California. Before that, racing dogs had chased live animals, often rabbits.

DUATHLON

2835. World championships in duathlon were held in 1990, involving running 10 kilometers, cycling 40 kilometers, and then running another 5 kilometers. Ken Souza of the United States took the inaugural men's title and Thea Sijbesma of the Netherlands the women's.

2836. World championships in long-distance duathlon were held in 1997. Athletes from Switzerland took both titles—Urs Dellsperger for the men and Natascha Badmann for the women—after running 8.5 kilometers, cycling 150 kilometers, and then running 30 kilometers.

E

EQUESTRIAN COMPETITIONS (BEFORE 1900)

2837. Equestrian show jumping competition was held on April 15, 1864, in the first Horse Show held by the Royal Dublin Society in Ireland.

2838. Equestrian show jumping competition held in France was the Concours Hippique held in 1866 in Paris, France, sponsored by the Société Hippique Française, founded the year before.

2839. Equestrian show jumping competition held in England was in 1869 at the Agricultural Hall in London, England.

2840. National Horse Show opened on October 22, 1883, in New York City, at Madison Square Garden, where it would remain an annual event.

EQUESTRIAN COMPETITIONS (1900-1919)

2841. Individual jumping equestrian event held in the Olympic Games was on May 29, 1900, in London, England. The inaugural winner was Aimé Haegeman of Belgium, riding Benton II.

2842. Royal International Horse Show was held in 1907, in London, England. It would become the site of annual Nations Cup competition.

2843. Nations Cup equestrian team event was held in 1909 at the Royal International Horse Show, in London, England.

2844. King George V Gold Cup was presented in 1911 to the top male show jumper at the Royal International Horse Show in London, England.

2845. Individual dressage equestrian competition held in the Olympic Games was on July 15, 1912, in Stockholm, Sweden. Riding his horse Emperor, Carl Bonde led a Swedish sweep of the top medals, with Swedish riders taking six of the eight top places. The competition was limited to commissioned military officers and to men only until 1952.

2846. Equestrian to win both individual and team gold medals in the three-day event competitions in the Olympic Games was Axel Nordlander of Sweden. Riding Lady Artist, he took individual honors and also led his team to a gold medal on July 17, 1912.

2847. Team jumping (Prix des Nations) equestrian event held in the Olympic Games was on July 17, 1912, in Stockholm, Sweden. The winning team, from Sweden, included Carl-Gustaf Lewenhaupt riding Medusa, Gustaf Kilman on Gatan, and Hans von Rosen on Lord Iron.

2848. Three-day event individual equestrian competition held in the Olympic Games was in 1912 in Stockholm, Sweden. Winning the inaugural event on July 17 was Axel Nordlander of Sweden, riding Lady Artist.

2849. Three-day event team equestrian competition held in the Olympic Games was in 1912 in Stockholm, Sweden. On July 17, the winning team was from Sweden: Axel Nordlander (also the individual gold-medalist) riding Lady Artist, Nils Adlercreutz on Atout, and Ernst Casparsson on Irmelin.

EQUESTRIAN COMPETITIONS (1920-1939)

2850. Figure riding individual and team events held in the Olympic Games were on September 11, 1920, in Antwerp, Belgium. Belgian riders took the top honors; the individual gold medalist was named Bouckaert, who led his teammates, named Finet and van Ranst, to the team title (first names unknown). For army officers only, the competitions were held just this once in the Olympics.

2851. Equestrian to win two consecutive medals in the team jumping (Prix des Nations) event in the Olympic Games was Hans von Rosen of Sweden. He had been on the winning team in 1912. Then in the first post–World War I Olympics he was on a second winning team, riding his horse Poor Boy on September 12, 1920, in Antwerp, Belgium.

2852. International governing body for equestrian competitions was the Fédération Equestre Internationale (FEI), founded in Brussels, Belgium, in 1921.

2853. Equestrian to win both an individual and a team medal in dressage in the Olympic Games was Carl Friedrich Freiherr von Langen-Parow of Germany. Riding his horse Draufgänger, he took the individual title and led the way to the team title, both on August 11, 1928.

2854. Equestrians to win two consecutive three-day event team titles were from the Netherlands: Adolph van der Voort van Ziip riding Silver Piece, Charles Pahud de Mortanges (the individual gold-medalist in 1928 and 1932) on Marcroix, and Gerard de Kruyuff on Va-t-en. After winning their first title in 1924, they won their second on August 11, 1928, in Amsterdam, the Netherlands.

2855. Team dressage equestrian event held in the Olympic Games was on August 11, 1928, in Amsterdam, the Netherlands. The inaugural winning team was from Germany: Carl Friedrich Freiherr von Langen-Parow riding Draufgänger, Hermann Lindenbach on Simpel, and Eugen Freiherr von Lotzbeck on Caracalla. The competition would be limited to commissioned officers and men until 1952.

2856. Equestrian to win the individual jumping event in the Olympic Games without a single fault was Frantisek Ventura of Czechoslovakia, who rode his horse Eliot to a fault-free win on August 12, 1928, in Amsterdam, the Netherlands.

2857. Equestrian to win two consecutive three-day event individual titles was Charles Pahud de Mortanges of the Netherlands. After winning in 1928, he won again in Los Angeles, California, on August 13, 1932, both times riding Marcroix. He was also on the gold-medal-winning teams in 1924 and 1928.

2858. Equestrian to win two consecutive titles in team dressage in the Olympic Games was André Jousseaume of France. After winning first in 1932, he won again in Berlin, Germany, on August 13, 1936, with a new horse, Favorite, and two new teammates.

2859. Equestrian to win gold medals in both individual and team jumping in the same Olympic Games was Kurt Hasse of Germany in 1936, in Berlin, Germany. Riding his horse Tora, he won the individual title on August 16, on the same day joining Marten von Barnekow on Nordland and Heinz Brandt on Alchimist in the team championship.

EQUESTRIAN COMPETITIONS (1940-1959)

2860. Equestrian to be stripped of his dressage title because he was not a commissioned officer was Gehnäll Persson, part of Sweden's winning team in 1948 in London, England. Though they won the event, Persson and his teammates, Gustav-Adolf Boltenstern, Jr., and Henri Saint Cyr, were disqualified some months later because Persson was "only" a sergeant, and their medals awarded instead to the French team. From 1952 on, dressage events would be open to all.

2861. Queen Elizabeth II Cup awarded to the top female show jumper at the Royal International Horse Show, in London, England, was in 1949. The inaugural winner was Iris Killett of Ireland, riding Rusty.

2862. Individual and team dressage equestrian competitions open to women, and to men other than commissioned military officers, in the Olympic Games were in 1952 in Helsinki, Finland.

2863. Woman equestrian to win a team dressage medal in the Olympic Games was Ida von Nagel of Germany. Riding her horse Afrika, she won the silver medal on July 29, 1952, in Helsinki, Finland, in the first competition open to women. Her teammates were Heinz Rollay and Fritz Thiedemann.

2864. Woman equestrian to win an individual dressage medal in the Olympic Games was Lis Hartel of Denmark, in the first competition to include women. She won the silver medal on July 29, 1952, in Helsinki, Finland, though she was paralyzed below the knees from polio contracted in 1944 and had to be helped on and off her horse, Jubilee. She was silver-medalist again in 1956.

2865. World championships in show jumping were held in 1953. The inaugural winner was Francisco Goyoago of Spain, riding Quorum. Competition was limited to men until 1965.

2866. Equestrian to win two consecutive individual and team dressage titles in the Olympic Games was Henri Saint Cyr of Sweden. After winning the individual and team titles in 1952 on Master Rufus, he won both titles again on June 16, 1956, in Stockholm, Sweden, on a new horse, Juli. He had won the team dressage competition first in 1948, but was stripped of his gold medal because one member of the team was not a commissioned officer.

EQUESTRIAN COMPETITIONS (1960-1979)

2867. Equestrians to win two consecutive titles in team jumping in the Olympic Games were Hans-Günter Winkler and Fritz Thiedemann of Germany. After winning in 1956, they won again on September 11, 1960, in Rome, Italy, with Winkler riding Halla, Thiedemann on Meteor, and teammate Alwin Schockenmöhle on Ferdl. Winkler would be on the winning teams again in 1964 and 1972.

2868. Woman to compete in the three-day event individual equestrian competition in the Olympic Games held since 1912, was Helen Dupont of the United States, who finished in 33rd place on October 19, 1964, in Tokyo.

2869. Equestrian to win three consecutive titles in team jumping in the Olympic Games was Hans-Günter Winkler of Germany. After winning in 1956 and 1960, Winkler returned with a new horse, Fidelitas, and two new teammates—Hermann Schridde on Dozent and Kurt Jarasinski on Torro—to win his third team title on October 24, 1964, in Tokyo. He would win a fourth in 1972.

2870. World championships in show jumping to include women riders were in 1965, when separate women's competitions were included. The inaugural winner was Marion Coakes (later Mould) of Great Britain. After 1974, men and women competed in the same events.

2871. World championships in dressage an equestrian competition with men and women competing equally, were held in 1966. The first winner was Josef Neckermann of West Germany, riding Mariano.

2872. World championships in three-day event equestrian competition were held in 1966, with men and women competing equally from the start. The inaugural winner was Carlos Moratorio of Argentina, riding Chalon.

2873. Equestrian from the United States to win the individual jumping title in the Olympic Games was William Steinkraus, who won it riding Snowbound on October 23, 1968, in Mexico City.

2874. Woman equestrian to win an individual jumping medal in the Olympic Games was Marion Coakes (later Mould) of Great Britain, who was the silver-medalist on October 23, 1968, in Mexico City.

2875. Woman equestrian to win a gold medal in team dressage in the Olympic Games was Liselott Linsenhoff of Germany. Riding her horse Piaff, she won the event on October 24, 1968, in Mexico City, along with Josef Neckermann on Mariano and Reiner Klimki on Dux. She would win the individual dressage title in 1972.

2876. Woman rider to win the world championships in dressage was Yelena Petuchkova of the Soviet Union, riding Pepel, in 1970, the second time the competition was held.

2877. Woman to win the world championships in the three-day event equestrian competition was Mary Gordon-Watson of Britain in 1970, riding Cornishman V.

2878. World championships in carriage driving sponsored by the Fédération Equestre Internationale (FEI), was held in 1972, and biennially from then. August Dubey of Switzerland was the first individual winner, while Great Britain took the team title.

2879. Woman equestrian to win the individual dressage title in the Olympic Games was Liselott Linsenhoff of Germany, who won on September 7, 1972, in Munich, West Germany, riding her horse Piaff. She had also won a team gold medal in 1968.

2880. Equestrian to win four titles in team jumping in the Olympic Games was Hans-Günter Winkler of Germany. On the winning team in 1956, 1960, and 1964, he had had to settle for bronze in 1968, but returned to win again, with three other teammates, on September 11, 1972, in Munich, West Germany, this time riding his horse Torphy. He would also be silver-medalist in 1976.

2881. Equestrians from the United States to win the three-day event individual competition, and team competition, in the Olympic Games were Edmund Coffin, J. Michael Plumb, and Bruce Davidson. In the individual event, Coffin rode Bally-Cor to victory on July 25, 1976, in Montreal, Quebec, Canada, just ahead of Plumb on Better & Better. With Davidson riding Irish-Cap, they also took the team title on the same day.

2882. World Cup in show jumping was held in 1979, sponsored by the Fédération Equestre Internationale (FEI). The inaugural winner was Hugo Simon of Austria, riding Gladstone. Simon would win again in 1996 and 1997.

EQUESTRIAN COMPETITIONS (1980-1999)

2883. Woman show jumper to win the World Cup in which men and women competed equally, was Melanie Smith of the United States, who won riding Calypso in 1982.

2884. Woman to win a medal in the three-day event team equestrian competition in the Olympic Games, and to lead her team to a gold medal was Karen Stives of the United States. Her performance led the U.S. team to the gold medal on August 2, 1984, in Los Angeles, California, and also brought her an individual silver medal.

2885. Women to win medals in the three-day individual equestrian event in the Olympic Games were Karen Stives of the United States riding Ben Arthur and Virginia Holgate of Great Britain riding Priceless, who won the silver and gold medals respectively on August 3, 1984, in Los Angeles, California. Though just short of an individual gold medal, Stives's performance also secured first place for the United States in the team competition.

2886. Woman equestrian to win a medal in team jumping in the Olympic Games was Melanie Smith riding Calypso on August 7, 1984, in Los Angeles, California, where she and three other teammates were the first United States team to take the team jumping title.

2887. World championships in endurance riding an equestrian competition in which men and women compete equally, was held in 1986 and biennially from then. The first individual winner was Cassandra Schuler of the United States, riding Skiko's Omar, with Great Britain taking the team title.

2888. World championships in vaulting an equestrian event, were held in 1986 and biennially after that. Dietmar Ott and Silke Bernhard, both of West Germany, took the men's and women's individual titles, respectively, and West Germany also took the team title.

2889. World cup in dressage an equestrian competition with men and women competing equally, was held in 1986. The inaugural winner was Anne Grethe Jensen of Denmark, riding Marzog.

2890. Individual dressage equestrian competition in the Olympic Games in which women riders swept the top medals was on September 27, 1988, in Seoul, South Korea. Winning in this order were Nicole Uphoff of Germany riding Rembrandt, Margit Otto-Crépin of France on Corlandus, and Christine Stückelberger of Switzerland on Gauguin De Lully. Women also held four of the next five places in the competition.

2891. Male rider to win the world cup in dressage was Sven Rothenberger of West Germany, riding Andiamo, in 1990, the fifth time the competition was held.

2892. World Equestrian Games were held in 1990, in Stockholm, Sweden.

2893. Woman rider, and the first horse, to win two consecutive gold medals in the individual dressage competition, and in team dressage, in the Olympic Games were Nicole Uphoff of Germany and her horse Rembrandt. After their individual and team wins in 1988, the pair returned to win their second championship in each, the team on August 2, 1992, and the individual on August 5, in Barcelona, Spain.

2894. Freestyle dressage equestrian event held in the Olympic Games was in 1996 in Atlanta, Georgia. Open to both women and men, the inaugural competition was won by Isabell Werth of Germany on August 3.

EXTREME SPORTS

2895. Eco-Challenge extreme sports race was held in 1994. The "adventure race" pits teams of athletes performing five types of activities—horse riding, canoeing, kayaking, fixed-rope climbing, and orienteering—over harsh terrain.

2896. Extreme Games were held in June 1995 in Newport, Rhode Island. "Extreme sports" involve far more endurance or danger than most traditional sports, although there are "extreme" versions of such mainstream sports as cycling and diving. So-called "outlaw sports," like "street luge," which is luge on paved roads, are banned in some places.

F

FENCING (BEFORE 1900)

2897. Men's individual foil fencing competition held in the Olympic Games was on April 7, 1896, in Athens, Greece. The inaugural winner was Eugène-Henri Gravelotte of France.

FENCING—(BEFORE 1900)—*continued*

2898. Men's masters foil fencing competition held in the Olympic Games was on April 7, 1896, in Athens, Greece. Open to professional fencing teachers, it was won by Leon Pyrgos of Greece. The event would be held only once more, in 1900.

2899. Men's individual sabre fencing competition held in the Olympic Games was on April 9, 1896, in Athens, Greece. The winner was a Greek fencer, Ioannis Georgiadis, who would win the title again in 1906.

FENCING (1900-1949)

2900. National team to sweep the medals in the men's individual foil fencing competition in the Olympic Games was from France. Competing on May 21, 1900, in Paris, France, Emile Coste, Henri Masson, and Marcel Jacques Boulenger took the top three places, with four other French fencers following them.

2901. National team to sweep the medals in the men's masters foil fencing event in the Olympic Games was from France. On May 22, 1900, Lucien Mérignac, Alphonse Kirchhoffer, and Jean-Baptiste Mimiague placed in that order in the event, open to professionals, the second and last time it was held.

2902. Men's individual épée fencing competition held in the Olympic Games was on June 14, 1900, in Paris, France. The inaugural winner was 16-year-old Ramón Fonst of Cuba, who would win again in 1904. A separate masters épée competition was won by Fonst's teacher, Albert Ayat of France.

2903. Men's masters épée fencing competition held in the Olympic Games was on June 14, 1900, in Paris, France. Open to professional fencing masters, it was won by Albert Ayat of France, whose pupil, Ramón Fonst of Cuba, won the men's individual épée event limited to amateurs. The event would be held only once more, in 1906.

2904. Men's amateurs and masters épée fencing competition held in the Olympic Games was on June 15, 1900, in Paris, France, the only time that amateurs and professionals—the top four from each category—competed directly against each other. The winner was Albert Ayat of France, with the runner-up being his amateur pupil Ramón Fonst of Cuba.

2905. Masters sabre fencing competition held in the Olympic Games was on June 27, 1900, in Paris, France. In the competition for fencing professionals, the inaugural winner was Antonio Conte of Italy. The event would be held only once more, in 1906.

2906. Men's team foil fencing competition held in the Olympic Games was on September 8, 1904, in St. Louis, Missouri. The winning team was an international one, with Ramón Fonst and Manuel Diaz from Cuba and Albertson Van Zo Post from the United States. Fonst also won his second straight individual épée title.

2907. Fencer to win both the men's masters épée and masters sabre competitions in the Olympic Games was Cyril Verbrugge of Belgium. He won both competitions for fencing professionals on April 28, 1906, in Athens, Greece, the last time the events were held.

2908. Fencer to win men's individual and team épée titles in the same Olympic Games was Georges de la Falaise of France. Competing on April 28, 1906, in Athens, Greece, he won the individual title and joined two others in taking the team title.

2909. Fencer to win two men's individual sabre titles in the Olympic Games was Ioannis Georgiadis of Greece. After winning the event in 1896 at the first modern Olympics in Athens, Greece, he won again when the Games returned to Athens, on April 28, 1906.

2910. Men's team épée fencing competition held in the Olympic Games was on April 28, 1906, in Athens, Greece. The team from France won: Pierre d'Hugues, Georges Dillon-Kavanagh Mohr, and Georges de la Falaise.

2911. Men's team sabre fencing competition held in the Olympic Games was in 1906 in Athens, Greece. Competing on April 28, the winning team was from Germany: Gustav Casmir, Jacob Erckrath de Bary, August Petri, and Emil Schön.

2912. Fencer to win both the men's individual sabre and épée titles in the Olympic Games was Georges de la Falaise of France. After winning the sabre title in 1900, in Paris, France, he won the épée title on April 28, 1906, in Athens, Greece.

2913. National team to sweep the top honors in the men's individual épée competition in the Olympic Games was France, on July 24, 1908, in London, England, where Gaston Alibert, Alexandre Lippmann, and Eugène Olivier finished in that order.

2914. Fencer to win two consecutive men's individual sabre titles, and men's team sabre titles, in the Olympic Games was Jenö Fuchs of Hungary. After winning both events in 1908 in London, England, he won the team event again on July 15, 1912, in Stockholm, Sweden. Then on August 23, he won the individual event again, leading a Hungarian sweep of the top four places in the event. The title would be won by Hungarian fencers from 1908 through 1964, except for 1920, when Hungary was barred from competition because of its alliance with Germany in World War I.

2915. International governing body for fencing was the Fédération Internationale d'Escrime (FIE), founded in Paris, France, in 1913.

2916. Fencer to win five gold medals in a single Olympic Games, and to win two consecutive men's individual foil titles in the Olympic Games was Nedo Nadi of Italy. After winning the individual foil title in 1912, when he was just 18, he won his second in the first post–World War I Olympics at Antwerp, Belgium, on August 18, 1920. He also won the individual sabre title on August 26, while leading his Italian team to championships in the foil (August 17), épée (August 21), and sabre (August 26).

2917. World championships in fencing were held in 1921 and annually from then on, except in Olympic years. Called the European championships until 1935, the first competition was épée for men only, won by Lucien Gaudin of France. Other events were added later, and women competed from 1929.

2918. Men's sabre competition held in the world championships of fencing was in 1922, when the winner was Adrianus de Jong of the Netherlands.

2919. Fencer to win two consecutive men's sabre titles in the world championships was Adrianus de Jong of the Netherlands, who won in 1923, after winning the inaugural event in 1922.

2920. Women's individual foil fencing competition held in the Olympic Games was in 1924 in Paris, France. Competing on July 4, Ellen Osiier of Denmark became the first woman Olympic fencing champion. Her husband, Ivan Osiier, competed in the men's épée seven times over 40 years (1908–1948), winning the silver medal in 1912.

2921. Men's foil competition held in the world championships of fencing was in 1926, the fifth annual championships. The inaugural winner was Giorgio Chiavacci of Italy.

2922. Fencer to win two consecutive men's foil titles in the world championships was Oreste Puliti of Italy, who won in 1929, after first winning in 1927.

2923. World championships in fencing to include women were in 1929. The inaugural winner was Helene Mayer of Germany, who would win again in 1931 and 1937.

2924. Fencer to win two consecutive men's épée titles in the world championships was Philippe Cattiau of France, who won in both 1929 and 1930.

2925. Fencer to win two, and then three, women's foil titles in the world championships was Helene Mayer of Germany, who won her second in 1931 and her third in 1937, after taking the inaugural event in 1929.

2926. Fencer to win two men's team foil titles in the Olympic Games was Philippe Cattiau of France. Part of the winning team in 1924, he won gold again on August 1, 1932, in Los Angeles, California.

2927. Fencer to win three men's épée titles in the world championships was Georges Buchard of France, who won in 1927, and then twice more in 1931 and 1933.

2928. Fencer to win two consecutive women's foil titles in the world championships was Ilona Elek of Hungary, who won in 1934 and 1935. She would win a third time in 1951.

2929. Fencer to win two consecutive women's individual foil titles in the Olympic Games was Ilona Elek of Hungary. After first winning in 1936, she won again after World War II in London, England, on August 2, 1948.

FENCING (1950-1999)
2930. Fencer to win three consecutive women's foil titles in the world championships was Ellen Müller-Preiss of Austria, who won in 1947, 1949, and 1950, the last time sharing the title with Renée Garilhe of France.

2931. Fencer to win two, three, and four men's team épée titles in the Olympic Games was Edoardo Mangiarotti of Italy. On the winning team in 1936 and the second-place team after World War II in 1948, he then won three team titles in a row: on July 26, 1952, in Helsinki, Finland; on November 28, 1956, in Melbourne, Australia; and on September 9, 1960, in Rome, Italy. Over 40 years, he would win 13 Olympic fencing medals.

2932. Fencer to win three, and then four, men's foil titles in the world championships was Christian d'Oriola of France. After winning in the first post–World War II competition in 1947, he won again in 1949, 1953, and 1954.

2933. Fencer to win two consecutive men's individual foil titles in the Olympic Games was Christian d'Oriola of France. After winning first in 1952, he won his second in Melbourne, Australia, on November 26, 1956. He had also won two gold medals (1948 and 1952) in the team foil competition.

FENCING—(1950-1999)—*continued*

2934. Fencer to win 13 medals in the Olympic Games was Edoardo Mangiarotti of Italy. His strongest event was the épée, in which he took one individual gold medal (1952) and two individual bronze (1948 and 1952), along with four team gold (1936, 1952, 1956, and 1960) and one silver (1948). In the foil, he also won an individual silver medal (1952) plus one team gold medal (1956) and three silver (1948, 1952, and 1960). His older brother, Dario Mangiarotti, would also win three Olympic medals, all in the épée: an individual silver (1952, behind his brother), and two team (silver, 1948; gold, 1952).

2935. Women's team foil fencing competition held in the Olympic Games was on September 3, 1960, in Rome, Italy. The winning team was from the Soviet Union: Tatyana Petrenko (later Samusenko), Valentina Rastvorova, Lyudmila Shishova, Valentina Prudskova, Aleksandra Zabelina, and Galina Gorokhova.

2936. Fencer to win three men's sabre titles in the world championships was Jerzy Pawlowski of Poland. After winning in 1957 and 1965, he captured his third title in 1966.

2937. Fencers to win two gold medals in the women's team foil competition in the Olympic Games were Aleksandra Zabelina, Galina Gorokhova, and Tatyana Petrenko Samusenko of the Soviet Union. They had been on the winning team in 1960, and repeated their win with two other teammates on October 24, 1968, in Mexico City.

2938. Fencers to win three gold medals in the women's team foil competition in the Olympic Games were Aleksandra Zabelina, Galina Gorokhova, and Tatyana Petrenko Samusenko of the Soviet Union. On the winning teams in 1960 and 1968, they won their third title with other teammates on September 8, 1972, in Munich, West Germany.

2939. Fencer to win five men's foil titles in the world championships was Aleksandr Romankov of the Soviet Union, who won in 1974, 1977, 1981, 1982, and 1983.

2940. National team to sweep the medals in the women's individual foil fencing competition in the Olympic Games was from Germany. Anja Fichjtel, Sabine Bau, and Zita-Eva Funkenhauser finished in that order on September 22, 1988, in Seoul, South Korea.

2941. Women's épée competition held in the world championships of fencing was in 1989, when the winner was Anja Straub of Switzerland.

2942. Fencer to win two consecutive women's épée titles in the world championships was Marianne Horváth of Hungary, who won in 1991 and 1992.

2943. Fencer to win four men's sabre titles in the world championships was Grigoriy Kirienko. He won in 1989 and 1991 competing for the Soviet Union, then again in 1993 and 1995 for Russia.

2944. Women's individual and team épée competitions held in the Olympic Games were in 1996 in Atlanta, Georgia. Laura Flessel of France won the individual title on July 21, then captured the team title on July 24 with teammates Sophie Moresee-Pichot and Valerie Barlois.

FIGURE SKATING (BEFORE 1800)
2945. Literary reference to skating is in the Eddas of Scandinavia, dating back to at least 156, which include numerous references to skating, including one to Uller, the god of winter, who "runs on the bones of animals."

2946. Ice skating accident on record was that of Lydwina, who fell in 1396, breaking a rib. An engraving of the fallen skater dates back to 1498. She later became Saint Lydwina of Schiedam, the Netherlands, named the patron saint of skating by the Catholic Church in 1944.

2947. Iron skates on record were developed in 1572, though some may have been developed before then. Earlier skates had been made of wood with waxed runners or bone.

2948. Iron skates in England were imported by the ruling Stuart family in 1660, when they returned from exile in the Netherlands. They also brought with them the semicircular skating pattern called the Dutch roll.

2949. Ice skating club was the Edinburgh Skating Club, founded in Scotland in 1742. Members had to pass tests of their skating skills before being accepted into the club, limited to men only for a century.

2950. Book on ice skating techniques was *Treatise on Skating*, published in Great Britain in 1772, written by Robert Jones. He expressed regret that so few women skated.

FIGURE SKATING (1800-1899)
2951. Ice skating club in the United States was the Skaters' Club of the City and County of Philadelphia, founded on December 21, 1849, in Philadelphia, Pennsylvania, with James Page as the first president.

2952. Ice skates with steel blades which were clipped onto boots, were developed in 1850, by E. W. Bushnell of the United States. That invention laid the basis for the spread of ice skating.

2953. Ice skating club in mainland Europe was the Vienna Ice Club, in Austria, established in 1867. It was a center for the balletic skating approach of the American skating master Jackson Haines, who had settled in Vienna in the mid-1860s. With his figure skating tours, Haines helped make the sport widely popular in Europe. He is also credited with being the first to use blades screwed to the soles of his boots and to develop the sit spin.

2954. Ice skating rink using artificial ice was built in 1870 in New York City. It used underfloor tubes of ammonia and other gases to freeze a flooded surface.

2955. Ice skating rink in Great Britain to use artificial ice was the Glaciarium, which opened in London, England, in 1876.

2956. Ice skating rink in Switzerland was opened in Davos in 1877. It would be the site of many figure skating championships.

2957. National ice skating organization in North America was the Amateur Skating Association, founded in Canada in 1878 at the inspiration of Louis Rubinstein, who brought back from Europe the new style of skating pioneered by Jackson Haines.

2958. Indoor ice skating rink was built at Madison Square Garden, in New York City, by Thomas L. Rankin in 1879.

2959. National ice skating organization in Great Britain was the National Skating Association of Britain founded in 1879 in Cambridge.

2960. International figure skating competition was held in Vienna, Austria, in 1882.

2961. National ice skating organization in the United States was the U.S. Figure Skating Association founded in 1886.

2962. International governing body for ice skating was the Internationale Eislauf Vereinigung, later the International Skating Union (ISU), founded at a meeting in the Netherlands in 1892 by representatives from Austria, Great Britain, Germany, Sweden, Hungary, and the Netherlands. It would sponsor world championships from 1896 and set international rules for both figure skating and speed skating.

2963. Figure skater to win the men's singles title at the world championships was Gilbert Fuchs of Germany at St. Petersburg, Russia, in 1896. He would win again in 1906. Busy with his medical practice, he competed only twice in between, placing third in 1898 and second in 1901.

2964. World championships in figure skating were held in 1896 in St. Petersburg, Russia. Then called the International Skating Union Championship, and tacitly intended for men only, it was won by Gilbert Fuchs of Germany. Tracing of set designs, called school figures, accounted for much of the score, and would do so until 1989.

2965. Figure skater to win two, and then three, men's singles titles at the world championships was Gustav Hugel of Austria. His second title came in 1899 and his third in 1900, both at Davos, Switzerland. He had earlier won in 1897 and was runner-up at the first world championships in 1896 and again in 1898.

FIGURE SKATING (1900-1909)

2966. Woman figure skater to compete in a world championship, and to win a world figure skating medal was Madge (Florence) Syers of Great Britain in 1902. The annual competition was tacitly intended for men only, but Syers was allowed to enter in 1902, where she won the silver medal. After the competition, the International Skating Union (ISU) barred women from the world championships, arguing that their below-the-ankle skirts prevented judges from seeing their footwork. Syers countered by introducing a mid-calf-length skirt for figure skating.

2967. Figure skater to win five consecutive men's singles titles at the world championships was Ulrich Salchow of Sweden, whose first string of five consecutive victories began and ended in Stockholm, Sweden (1901–1905). After a year's break from competition, he would return to win five more (1907–1911).

2968. Figure skater to win the women's singles title in the world championships was Madge (Florence) Syers of Great Britain at Davos, Switzerland, in 1906. The establishment of this separate women's competition was largely due to Syers' silver-medal-winning performance at the 1902 world championships, before women were formally excluded from them, and her later performances against men in open competition.

FIGURE SKATING—(1900-1909)—*continued*

2969. Woman figure skater to perform the sit spin was Jenny Herz of Austria, in Davos, Switzerland, in 1906, at the first world championship to have a separate competition for women.

2970. Figure skater to perform the salchow jump in competition was Ulrich Salchow of Sweden, who introduced the jump in 1907, the year he won the sixth of his 10 world championship titles (1901–1905 and 1907–1911).

2971. Figure skater to win two consecutive women's singles titles in the world championships was Madge (Florence) Syers of Great Britain, who won in Vienna, Austria, in 1907, after winning the inaugural competition in 1906.

2972. Figure skater from Hungary to win the women's singles title in the world championships was Lily Kronberger, who won the first of her four straight titles (1908–1911) in Troppau, Czechoslovakia.

2973. Figure skaters to win the pairs title in the world championships, and the first to win two titles were Anna Hubler and Heinrich Burger of Germany, who won in 1908, at St. Petersburg, Russia. They would win a second world title in 1910, after sitting out 1909.

2974. Figure skating competition at the Olympic Games was in October 1908, in London, England. Winter sports were not then part of the Olympics, but figure skating was held that year because London had a suitable indoor rink, Prince's Skating Rink. Figure skating competition would not be held in the Olympics again until 1920.

2975. Figure skater to win the men's singles title in the Olympic Games was world champion Ulrich Salchow of Sweden, on October 29, 1908, in London, England.

2976. Figure skater to win the title for special figures in the Olympic Games was Nikolai Kolomenkin of Russia, competing under the pseudonym Nikolai Panin, on October 29, 1908, in London, England. A separate special figures medal was never again awarded, but school figures, with skaters tracing set patterns on the ice, would be part of figure skating competitions until 1989. Kolomenkin founded a school that laid the basis for the Russian (later Soviet) figure skating program.

2977. Figure skater to win the women's singles title at the Olympic Games was Madge (Florence) Syers of Great Britain, on October 29, 1908, in London, England. She and her husband, Edgar Syers, also won the bronze medal in the pairs competition. She then retired from competition.

2978. Figure skaters to win the pairs title at the Olympic Games were Anna Hubler and Heinrich Burger of Germany, who won the inaugural event on October 29, 1908, in London, England.

2979. National team to sweep the men's singles figure skating medals at the Olympic Winter Games was from Sweden in 1908, led by Ulrich Salchow on October 29 in London, England.

2980. Figure skaters from Great Britain, and the first married couple, to win the pairs title in the world championships were Phyllis Squire Johnson and James Johnson, who won the title in 1909, at Stockholm, Sweden. They would win again in 1912.

2981. Open-air rink featuring artificial ice was built in 1909 in Vienna, Austria. It was designed by European skater and engineer Edward Engelmann.

FIGURE SKATING (1910-1919)

2982. Figure skater to win three and then four consecutive women's singles titles in the world championships was Lily Kronberger of Hungary. Her third title came in 1910 in Berlin, and her fourth in Vienna, Austria, in 1911, after her first two in 1908 and 1909. Unhappy with the poor quality of musicians provided at competitions, Kronberger brought her own brass band in 1911.

2983. Figure skater to win 10 men's singles titles at the world championships was Ulrich Salchow of Sweden, who won all 10 of the championships in which he competed between 1901 and 1911. He did not compete in 1906. Salchow was later president of the International Skating Union.

2984. Figure skaters from Finland to win the pairs title in the world championships were Ludovika Eilers (later Jakobsson) and Walter Jakobsson, who won the 1911 competition in Vienna, Austria. Married the following year, they would win twice more, in 1914 and 1923.

2985. Woman figure skater to perform an axel in competition was Dorothy Greenough-Smith of Great Britain at the world championships in Davos, Switzerland, in 1912. Developed in the 1880s by Axel Paulsen of Norway, the jump called for one-and-a-half revolutions in the air and may have cost her the gold medal (she took silver), for it was criticized as "unfeminine."

2986. Figure skaters from Austria to win the pairs title in the world championships were Helene Engelmann and Karl Meistrik, who won in 1913 at Stockholm, Sweden. Engelmann won two more gold medals, in 1922 and 1924, with a different partner, Alfred Berger.

2987. Figure skater to win the men's singles title in the U.S. national championships was Norman Scott of Canada, in 1914 in New Haven, Connecticut. All three men's singles medalists also competed in the pairs event, which Scott also won, in his only national championship appearance.

2988. Figure skater to win the women's singles title at the U.S. national championships was Theresa Weld (later Blanchard) in 1914, in New Haven, Connecticut. She would win five more titles (1920–1924), as well as nine straight pairs titles, skating with Nathaniel Niles (1918–1927).

2989. Figure skaters to win a gold medal in ice dancing in the U.S. national championships were Theresa Weld (later Blanchard) and Nathaniel Niles, who won the single waltz competition in 1914 in New Haven, Connecticut. Other dances would be added in later years, but a national ice dancing title would not be awarded until 1936.

2990. Figure skaters to win the pairs title in the U.S. national championships were Jeanne Chevalier and Norman Scott of Canada in 1914 in New Haven, Connecticut, where Scott also won the men's singles title. Runners-up were Theresa Weld and Nathaniel Niles, who would win the next nine U.S. national titles.

2991. National figure skating championships in the United States were held at the Arena Skating Rink in New Haven, Connecticut, in 1914. Competitions included men's singles, women's singles, pairs, and a single ice dance, the waltz.

FIGURE SKATING (1920-1929)

2992. Figure skater from Austria to win the women's singles title in the world championships was Herma Planck-Szabo (later Jaross-Szabo), who won in Stockholm, Sweden, in 1922. She would win four more consecutive titles (1923–1926) before falling to Sonja Henie in 1927.

2993. Figure skater to win two consecutive men's singles titles in the U.S. national championships was Sherwin Badger, who won his second title in 1921 in Philadelphia, Pennsylvania, after his first in 1920. He would extend his string of consecutive wins to five (1920–1924). Also a noted pairs skater, he would later win three straight U.S. pairs titles with Beatrix Loughran (1930–1932).

2994. Figure skater to win two straight women's singles titles at the U.S. national championships was Theresa Weld Blanchard, who won her second in 1921 in Philadelphia, Pennsylvania, after winning the previous year. She would gather five straight singles titles (1920–1924), to add to her first in 1914. Her string of pairs titles extended to nine (1918–1927), all with Nathaniel Niles.

2995. Figure skaters to win three pairs titles in the world championships were Ludovika Eilers Jakobsson and Walter Jakobsson of Finland, who had their third win in 1923 in Oslo, Norway. Their first title had come in 1911, and their second in 1914, just before the World War I hiatus (1915-1921). They were also runners-up in 1912, 1913, and 1922.

2996. International figure skating competition at which recorded music was standard was the Olympic Games held in 1920 at Antwerp, Belgium. From then on, skaters were no longer at the mercy of unfamiliar and often under-rehearsed musicians.

2997. Figure skater from Sweden to win the women's singles title in the Olympic Games was Magda Julin-Mauroy, on April 25, 1920, in Antwerp, Belgium. It was her first and only international competition.

2998. Woman figure skater to perform a full-revolution jump, the salchow, in competition was Theresa Weld (later Blanchard) of the United States on April 25, 1920, at the Olympic Games in Antwerp, Belgium. Criticized as not ladylike, because her skirts flew up to her knees, she was penalized by the judges and earned only the bronze medal.

FIGURE SKATING—(1920-1929)—*continued*

2999. Figure skaters from Finland to win the pairs title in the Olympic Games were Ludovika Eilers Jakobsson and Walter Jakobsson, who won on April 26, 1920, in Antwerp, Belgium.

3000. Figure skater from Austria to win the women's singles title at the Olympic Games was Herma Planck-Szabo (later Jaross-Szabo) on January 29, 1924, at Chamonix, France, in the first separate Olympic Winter Games.

3001. Figure skater to win two, and then three, consecutive men's singles titles in the Olympic Games was Gillis Grafstrom of Sweden. After triumphing in 1920, he won his second title on January 30, 1924, at Chamonix, France, and his third on February 17, 1928, at St. Moritz, Switzerland. Also a three-time world champion (1922, 1924, and 1929), Grafstrom introduced such moves as the spiral, the change sit spin, the flying sit spin, and the Grafstrom spin.

3002. Figure skaters from Austria to win the pairs title at the Olympic Winter Games were Helene Engelmann and Alfred Berger, who won on January 31, 1924, at Chamonix, France, defeating the defending champions Ludovika Eilers Jakobsson and Walter Jakobsson.

3003. Figure skater to win both the singles and pairs title at the same world championships was Herma Jaross-Szabo (formerly Planck-Szabo) of Austria in 1925 in Vienna, Austria. The singles title was her fourth of five (1922–1926). Her pairs partner was Ludwig Wrede.

3004. Figure skater to win five consecutive women's singles championships was Herma Jaross-Szabo (formerly Planck-Szabo) of Austria, whose fifth title came in 1926 in Stockholm, Sweden, where she had won her first in 1922. With Ludwig Wrede, she also won two pairs world titles (1925 and 1927).

3005. Figure skaters from France to win the pairs title in the world championships were Andrée Joly Brunet and Pierre Brunet at Berlin in 1926. They would win three more titles (1928, 1930, and 1932).

3006. Figure skater from Norway to win the women's singles title in the world championships was Sonja Henie, who won the first of her 10 straight world titles (1927–1936) in Oslo, Norway. Noted for her spinning, Henie pioneered in wearing skirts well above the knee.

3007. Figure skater from Norway to win the women's singles title at the Olympic Winter Games was Sonja Henie on February 18, 1928, at St. Moritz, Switzerland. She would win two more Olympic titles (1932 and 1936) and ten straight world crowns (1927–1936), before turning professional.

3008. Figure skaters from France to win the pairs title in the Olympic Winter Games were Andrée Joly Brunet and Pierre Brunet, who won on February 19, 1928, at St. Moritz, Switzerland. The married duo would return to win their second Olympic crown in 1932.

FIGURE SKATING (1930-1939)

3009. Figure skaters from Hungary to win the pairs title in the world championships were Emilie Rotter and Laszlo Szollas, who won in Berlin in 1931. They dropped to silver in 1932, but then returned to win three more titles (1933–1935).

3010. Figure skaters to complete a grand slam, winning the European, world, and Olympic titles in the same year were Sonja Henie of Norway and Karl Schafer of Austria in 1932. Both would repeat their grand slams in 1936.

3011. Figure skaters to win four pairs titles in the world championships were Andrée Joly Brunet and Pierre Brunet of France, who had their fourth win at Montreal, in 1932. Noted for their daring lifts and side-by-side jumps, the Brunets had earlier won in 1926, 1928, and 1930. They did not compete in 1929 and 1931.

3012. Figure skater from Austria to win the men's singles titles in the Olympic Winter Games was Karl Schafer, who won on February 9, 1932, at Lake Placid, New York, defeating three-time Olympic champion Gillis Grafstrom of Sweden. Seven-time world champion (1930–1936), Schafer won again in 1936, the last Olympic Winter Games until 1948.

3013. Figure skaters to win two consecutive pairs titles at the Olympic Winter Games were Andrée Joly Brunet and Pierre Brunet of France. The four-time world champions won their second gold medal on February 12, 1932, at Lake Placid, New York, after winning their first in 1928. Pierre Brunet later became a noted skating coach in the United States.

3014. Figure skater to win two, and then three, consecutive women's singles titles at the Olympic Winter Games was Sonja Henie of Norway. After her first title in 1928, she won her second on October 9, 1932, in Lake Placid, New York, and her third on February 15, 1936, at Garmisch-Partenkirchen, Germany.

3015. Figure skater to win six, and then seven, consecutive men's singles titles in the U.S. national championships was Roger Turner. His record-breaking sixth consecutive title came in 1933 at New Haven, Connecticut, after his five earlier wins (1928–1932). He would extend his winning streak to seven in Philadelphia, Pennsylvania, in 1934.

3016. Figure skater to win six consecutive women's singles titles, and nine overall, at the U.S. national championships was Maribel Vinson (later Owen), who won her sixth title in 1933 at New Haven, Connecticut, after five straight earlier titles (1928–1932). After a break from competition in 1934, she won three more singles titles (1935–1937), extending her total to nine before retiring. Also a six-time pairs champion (1928–1929 with Thornton Coolidge; 1933 and 1935–1937 with George Hill), Maribel Vinson Owen became a noted figure-skating teacher; she and her daughters, also skaters, died in the 1961 plane crash in Brussels, Belgium, that killed the entire U.S. figure skating team en route to the world championships.

3017. Brother-and-sister figure skaters to win the pairs title at the U.S. national championships were Grace Madden and J. Lester Madden, who won the pairs competition in 1934 at Philadelphia, Pennsylvania.

3018. Figure skaters to win two, and then three, consecutive pairs titles in the world championships were Emilie Rotter and Laszlo Szollas of Hungary. Their second straight title came in 1934 in Helsinki, Finland, and their third in 1935 in Budapest, Hungary. Their first title in the string had come in 1933. They had also won in 1931, but had fallen to silver in 1932.

3019. Figure skater to win 10 consecutive women's singles titles in the world championships was Sonja Henie of Norway. Her string of victories had extended from 1927 in Oslo, Norway, to 1936 in Paris, France. She then retired to become a professional, starring in several movies.

3020. Figure skater to win seven consecutive men's singles titles in the world championships was Karl Schafer of Austria. His seventh win and his final before retirement came at Paris, France, in 1936, after six previous titles (1930–1935). Ulrich Salchow had earlier won ten titles (1901–1905 and 1907–1911), but did not compete in 1906.

3021. Figure skaters to win the ice dancing title at the U.S. national championships were Marjorie Parker (later Smith) and Joseph Savage at Boston, Massachusetts, in 1936. Titles had previously been awarded for individual dances, but this was the first time a national ice dancing title was awarded.

3022. Woman figure skater to complete a double jump in competition was Cecilia Colledge of Great Britain, who performed a double salchow at the European championships in 1936.

3023. Figure skaters to win two consecutive ice dancing titles at the U.S. national championships were Nettie Prantell and Harold Hartshorne. They won their second straight title in Philadelphia, Pennsylvania, in 1938, after their first in 1937. Both skated with other partners; Hartshorne would win three more titles with Sandy MacDonald (1939–1941).

3024. Figure skater from Great Britain to win the men's singles title at the world championships was Graham Sharp at Budapest, Hungary, in 1939. Sharp could not defend his title, because the world championships would be suspended (1940–1946) because of World War II.

3025. Figure skaters to win four consecutive pairs titles in the world championships were Maxi Herber and Ernst Baier of Germany. Their fourth straight win came at Budapest, Hungary, in 1939, following their three earlier titles (1936–1938). They pioneered the overhead lift and were noted for their side-by-side "shadow skating."

FIGURE SKATING (1940-1949)

3026. Season for the Ice Capades was in 1940, when the figure skating exhibition began touring the United States. Belita (Gladys Lynne Jepson-Turner) of Great Britain was among the stars in that first season, with notables such as Bobby Specht and Donna Atwood of the United States joining in 1941.

3027. Figure skater to win five consecutive ice dancing titles at the U.S. national championships was Harold Hartshorne. His fifth straight title came in Boston, Massachusetts, in 1941, with Sandy MacDonald. He had two other titles with MacDonald (1939 and 1940) and two with Nettie Prantell (1937 and 1938).

3028. Figure skater from Canada and from the Americas to win the women's singles title in the world championships was Barbara Ann Scott at Stockholm, Sweden, in 1947. Scott would successfully defend her title in 1948, when she also won the Olympic gold medal.

FIGURE SKATING—(1940-1949)—*continued*

3029. Figure skater from Switzerland to win the men's singles title at the world championships was Hans Gerschwiler at Stockholm, Sweden, in 1947, the first post–World War II world competition.

3030. Figure skater to perform the flying camel spin was Dick Button of the United States, who introduced the move in 1947 at the world championships in Stockholm, Sweden, where he won the silver medal.

3031. Figure skaters from Belgium to win the pairs title in the world championships were Micheline Lannoy and Pierre Baugniet, who won in 1947 at Stockholm, Sweden. They successfully defended their title in 1948.

3032. Figure skater from Canada or from the Americas to win the women's singles title at the Olympic Winter Games was Barbara Ann Scott on February 6, 1948, at St. Moritz, Switzerland. She was threatened with disqualification for accepting a car from her home city of Ottawa, Ontario; she returned it, but accepted it back after winning.

3033. Figure skater from the United States to win the men's singles title at the world championships was Dick Button in 1948 at Davos, Switzerland. Button went on to win four more consecutive world titles, for a total of five (1948–1952), before turning professional.

3034. Figure skater to win the men's singles U.S., world, and Olympic championships in the same year, and then twice in a row was Dick Button of the United States in 1948 and 1952. His 1948 and 1952 U.S. titles, both won at Colorado Springs, Colorado, were two of his seven straight national titles. His 1948 and 1952 world titles (won at Davos, Switzerland, and Paris, France, respectively) were the first and last of his five straight world championships. His Olympic wins came in St. Moritz, Switzerland, in 1948 and Oslo, Norway, in 1952. After that he turned professional and entered Harvard Law School.

3035. Figure skater from the United States to win the men's singles titles in the Olympic Games was Dick Button, who won on February 5, 1948, at St. Moritz, Switzerland, in the first Winter Games held after the World War II hiatus. Button would win again in 1952, meanwhile also winning five world titles (1948–1952) and seven U.S. titles (1946–1952).

3036. Figure skaters from Belgium to win the pairs title at the Olympic Winter Games were Micheline Lannoy and Pierre Baugniet, who won on February 7, 1948, at St. Moritz, Switzerland.

3037. Figure skater from Czechoslovakia to win the women's singles title in the world championships was Alena Vrzanova at Paris, France, in 1949. She returned in 1950 to win her second title, but then retired.

3038. Figure skater to perform the double loop–double loop combination jump in competition was Dick Button of the United States in 1949. The now-standard jump involves two in-air revolutions, a clean landing, and an immediate takeoff for another two revolutions. He would extend that to a triple combination, with three double loops in a row, in 1950.

3039. Figure skater to win the James E. Sullivan Award presented to the year's top amateur athlete, was Dick Button of the United States, who was so honored in 1949. In that year he won his second of five world titles (1948–1952) and his fourth of seven U.S. titles (1946–1952), following his first of two Olympic titles (1948 and 1952).

FIGURE SKATING (1950-1959)
3040. Figure skaters from the United States to win the pairs title in the world championships were Karol Kennedy and Peter Kennedy, a sister-and-brother duo, who won in 1950. Noted for their speed and liveliness, they were five-time U.S. champions (1948–1952).

3041. International pairs figure skating competition in which all the medalists were brother-and-sister pairs was the 1950 world championships at London, England, where the medalist pairs were Karol Kennedy and Peter Kennedy of the United States, Jennifer Nicks and John Nicks of Great Britain, and Marianne Nagy and Laszlo Nagy of Hungary, in that order.

3042. Figure skater to perform a double axel in competition was Dick Button of the United States, who introduced the now-standard jump at the 1951 world championships, held at Milan, Italy. The double axel requires the skater to complete two-and-a-half revolutions in the air. The axel had originally been developed in the 1880s by Axel Paulsen of Norway.

3043. Figure skater from France to win the women's singles title in the world championships was Jacqueline du Bief in Paris, France, in 1952. Noted for her dazzling and often revealing costumes, she then turned professional.

3044. Figure skater to perform a triple loop–triple loop combination jump in competition was Dick Button of the United States, who performed a triple-loop combination jump at the 1952 world championships in Milan, Italy. The now-standard move involves three in-air revolutions, a clean landing, and an immediate takeoff for another three revolutions.

3045. Figure skaters from the United States to sweep the men's singles medals in the world championships were Dick Button, James Grogan, and Hayes Allen Jenkins, who emerged in that order at the 1952 world competition in Paris, France. Five-time world champion Button then retired; Jenkins would succeed him as world champion for the next four years.

3046. Figure skaters to win the ice dancing title in the world championships, and the first to win it two, three, and four times were Jean Westwood and Laurence Demmy of Great Britain. After winning the inaugural competition in 1952 in Paris, France, they would win again in 1953, 1954, and 1955. Both remained key figures in the sport, Westwood as a coach and Demmy as head of the ice dancing committee of the International Skating Union. British skaters would hold the world ice dancing title through 1960.

3047. Figure skater to perform a triple jump in competition requiring three full revolutions in the air, was Dick Button of the United States. He introduced the triple loop in 1952, at a skating exhibition in Vienna, Austria, then performed it for the first time in competition shortly afterward in the Winter Olympics at Oslo, Norway, where he won his second consecutive Olympic gold medal on February 21.

3048. Figure skater from the United States to win the women's singles title in the world championships was Tenley Albright in Davos, Switzerland, on February 15, 1953. She would win again in 1955, after placing second in 1954. In the same period, she won five straight U.S. titles (1952–1956).

3049. Figure skater from Germany to win the women's singles title in the world championships was Gundi Busch of West Germany, who won at Oslo, Norway, in 1954, after being runner-up in 1953.

3050. Figure skaters from Canada to win the pairs title in the world championships were Frances Dafoe and Norris Bowden, who won in Oslo, Norway, in 1954, successfully defending their title in 1955.

3051. Figure skaters to take all three medals in the same order in the U.S., world, and Olympic men's singles competitions were Hayes Allen Jenkins, Ronald Robertson, and David Jenkins, in that order. This remarkable triple sweep was accomplished in 1956, at the U.S. competition in Philadelphia, Pennsylvania; at the world competition in Garmisch, Germany; and at the Olympic Games in Cortina d'Ampezzo, Italy. Hayes Jenkins won his fourth consecutive U.S. and world titles; he would be succeeded by his younger brother, David, who became U.S. (1957–1960), world (1957–1959) and Olympic (1960) champion.

3052. Precision team figure skating event was organized in 1956 in Ann Arbor, Michigan, beginning with a marching drill team at a local skating club.

3053. Figure skater from the United States to win the women's singles title at the Olympic Winter Games was Tenley Albright on February 2, 1956, at Cortina d'Ampezzo, Italy, the last time the Olympic figure skating competition was held outdoors. Albright won despite cutting her ankle severely just before the competition. She later became a surgeon.

3054. Married figure skaters to win the pairs title at the U.S. national championships were Nancy Rouillard Luddington and Ronald Luddington at Minneapolis, Minnesota, in 1958. They had also won the previous year, before their marriage, and would win again in 1959 and 1960, then turning professional. He was later a noted pairs teacher.

FIGURE SKATING (1960-1969)

3055. Figure skaters from Canada to win the pairs title at the Olympic Winter Games were Barbara Wagner and Robert Paul, who won on February 19, 1960, at Squaw Valley, California. They then turned professional, joining the Ice Capades; he later became a noted choreographer for skaters such as Peggy Fleming and Dorothy Hamill.

3056. Figure skater to win the women's singles U.S., world, and Olympic championships in the same year was Carol Heiss (later Jenkins), who won her fourth straight U.S. title on January 29, 1960, at Seattle, Washington; her fifth straight world title that same year in Vancouver, British Columbia, Canada; and her Olympics title on February 23 at Squaw Valley, California. She later became a noted figure-skating teacher.

FIGURE SKATING—(1960-1969)—*continued*

3057. World figure skating championship to be canceled other than because of war was in 1961, when the entire U.S. figure skating team was killed in a plane crash at Brussels, Belgium, en route to the competition scheduled for Prague, Czechoslovakia. Among the skaters, coaches, and trainers who died were nine-time U.S. champion Maribel Vinson Owen and her two daughters, Maribel Y. Owen and Laurence Owen, also skaters.

3058. Figure skater from Canada to win the men's singles title at the world championships was Donald Jackson, who took the gold medal at Prague, Czechoslovakia, in 1962. His free-skate performance included the first triple lutz jump landed in competition, and earned him a record seven (out of nine) perfect 6.0 scores from the judges. He turned professional after 1962.

3059. Figure skater from the Netherlands to win the women's singles title in the world championships was Sjoukje Dijkstra at Prague, Czechoslovakia, in 1962, for the first of her three straight world titles (1962–1964). Dijkstra had been silver-medalist in 1960; no competition had been held in 1961, following the airplane crash that killed the entire U.S. figure skating team.

3060. Figure skater to land a triple lutz jump in competition was Donald Jackson of Canada, at the 1962 world championships at Prague, Czechoslovakia, en route to the men's singles gold medal. The lutz, a jump involving a clockwise rotation in the air, was developed in the 1930s by Tomas Lutz of Italy, and double lutzes had been performed from the mid-1930s.

3061. Figure skaters from Czechoslovakia to win the ice dancing title in the world championships were Eva Romanova and Pavel Roman, the brother-and-sister team who won in 1962 in their hometown of Prague, Czechoslovakia. The only non-British team to hold the world title between its start in 1952 and 1969, they won three more times (1963–1965).

3062. Figure skaters from the Soviet Union to win the pairs title in the world championships were Ludmila Belousova and Oleg Protopopov in 1962 at Prague, Czechoslovakia. Runners-up in 1963 and 1964, they came back to win four straight titles (1965–1968). Married in 1957, they were noted for their elegant, balletic skating, all the more astonishing because they had both come to skating late and had no coach. They defected to the West in 1979 and skated professionally until 1992, when he was nearly 60.

3063. Figure skater from Germany to win the men's singles title at the Olympic Winter Games was Manfred Schnelldorfer of West Germany, who won at Innsbruck, Austria, in 1964. Noted for his elegance, Schnelldorfer also won the world title that same year, then turned professional.

3064. Figure skaters from the Soviet Union to win the pairs title at the Olympic Winter Games were Ludmila Belousova and Oleg Protopopov, who won their first title on January 29, 1964, at Innsbruck, Austria. The married duo would win again in 1968, helping to establish the Soviet/Russian domination of the Olympic pairs competition that lasted through the end of the century.

3065. Figure skater from the Netherlands to win the women's singles title at the Olympic Winter Games was Sjoukje Dijkstra on February 2, 1964, at Innsbruck, Austria.

FIGURE SKATING (1970-1979)

3066. Figure skaters from the Soviet Union to win the ice dancing title in the world championships were Ludmila Pakhomova and Aleksandr Gorshkov, who won in 1970 in Ljubljana, Yugoslavia. They would win five more times (1971–1974 and 1976), helping to establish the Soviet and later Russian domination of ice dancing from 1970 through 1999, except for the four years when Jayne Torvill and Christopher Dean of Great Britain held the title (1981–1984).

3067. Figure skater from Czechoslovakia to win the men's singles title at the world championships was Ondrej Nepala at Lyon, France, in 1971. He would return for two more world titles, in 1972 and 1973, plus an Olympic gold medal in 1972.

3068. Figure skaters to win five consecutive ice dancing titles with the same partner at the U.S. national championships were Judy Schwomeyer and James Sladky, who won their fifth straight title in 1972 at Long Beach, California. Their highest medal in the world arena was a silver at the 1970 world championships.

3069. Woman figure skater to perform a triple salchow in competition was Sonya Morgenstern of East Germany, who performed the triple jump at the 1972 world championships in Long Beach, California. She never won a world medal, however, because of her weakness in *school figures*, then-compulsory skating variations.

3070. Figure skater from Czechoslovakia to win the men's singles title at the Olympic Winter Games was Ondrej Nepala, who won the gold medal at Sapporo, Japan, on February 11, 1972. He was also a three-time world champion (1971–1973).

3071. Figure skater from the Soviet Union to win the men's singles title at the world championships was Sergei Volkov at Colorado Springs, Colorado, in 1975, after winning the silver medal the year before.

3072. Figure skater, and the first female athlete, to sign a contract for $1 million a year was Dorothy Hamill of the United States in 1976. She signed with the Ice Capades (which she would buy in 1993) after winning both the Olympic and world gold medals that year, to go along with her three U.S. titles (1974–1976).

3073. Figure skater to perform a back flip in competition was Terry Kubicka, the U.S. men's singles champion, at the 1976 world championships in Gothenberg, Sweden. The backward somersault on the ice was immediately banned by the International Skating Union (ISU) as too dangerous, though it is often performed in exhibitions.

3074. Figure skaters from the United States to win an Olympic medal in ice dancing were Colleen O'Connor and Jim Millns, at Innsbruck, Austria, in 1976, when ice dancing was first officially offered as an Olympic sport. O'Connor and Millns won the bronze medal, behind two Soviet teams: Ludmila Pakhomova and Aleksandr Gorshkov, and Irina Moiseeva and Andrei Minenkov.

3075. Figure skater to win a pairs title in the Olympic Winter Games with two different partners was Irina Rodnina of the Soviet Union. She won her second pairs crown on February 7, 1976, at Innsbruck, Austria, with Aleksandr Zaitsev, with whom she would win again in 1980. Her first Oympic pairs title had been won with Alexsei Ulanov in 1972.

3076. Figure skaters to win the ice dancing title in the Olympic Winter Games were Ludmila Pakhomova and Aleksandr Gorshkov of the Soviet Union, who won on February 9, 1976, at Innsbruck, Austria, the first time ice dancing was offered officially. Five-time world champions, they had been out of competition for a year because Gorshkov had a long illness.

3077. Figure skater from Great Britain to win the men's singles title at the Olympic Winter Games was John Curry, who won at Innsbruck, Austria, on February 11, 1976, when he also won the world title. As a professional, Curry then used his artistry to develop a figure-skating ensemble using dance principles, as in his famous interpretation of Debussy's *Afternoon of a Faun*. He died of AIDS-related complications in 1994.

3078. Figure skaters to perform a quadruple twist lift in competition were Marina Tcherkasova and Sergei Shakrai of the Soviet Union, who completed the difficult maneuver on January 26, 1977, in Helsinki, Finland.

3079. Figure skater to perform a triple axel in competition was Vern Taylor of Canada, who introduced the jump at the 1978 world championships at Ottawa, Ontario, Canada. The move requires the skater to complete three-and-a-half revolutions in the air.

3080. Figure skater to win 10 consecutive pairs titles in the world championships was Irina Rodnina of the Soviet Union. She completed this remarkable feat in 1978, when she and Aleksandr Zaitsev won the world title in Ottawa, Ontario, Canada. It was their sixth title in a row (1973–1978). However, Rodnina had also won the four previous titles (1969–1972) with another partner, Alexsei Ulanov. Rodnina also won three Olympic gold medals, one with Ulanov and two with Zaitsev. She later became a skating teacher in the United States.

3081. Woman figure skater to perform a triple lutz in competition was Denise Biellmann of Switzerland, who performed the jump in 1978.

3082. Figure skaters to perform simultaneous triple jumps in competition were Marina Tcherkasova and Sergei Shakrai of the Soviet Union on February 1, 1978, in Strasbourg, France.

FIGURE SKATING (1980-1989)

3083. Figure skaters from Hungary to win the ice dancing title in the world championships were Kristina Regoczy and Andras Sallay, who won in Dortmund, West Germany, in 1980. The first pair outside Great Britain or the Soviet Union ever to win the world ice dancing title, they were runners-up in the 1980 Olympics, retiring after that year.

3084. Figure skater to win three consecutive medals in pairs competition at the Olympic Winter Games was Irina Rodnina of the Soviet Union, who won her third title on February 17, 1980, at Lake Placid, New York. Her partner, then and in 1976, was Aleksandr Zaitsev; in 1972 she had won with Alexsei Ulanov. She also won a record 10 world titles with the two partners (1969–1978).

3085. Figure skater from Germany to win the women's singles title at the Olympic Winter Games was Anett Poetzsch of East Germany on February 23, 1980, at Lake Placid, New York. She retired that year, later marrying the brother of Katarina Witt, her teammate and successor as world and Olympic champion.

3086. Figure skater from Switzerland to win the women's singles title in the world championships was Denise Biellmann at Hartford, Connecticut, in 1981. It was her only world gold medal, but her influence remained in the Biellmann spin she originated, which involved pulling one leg over her head while spinning on the ice.

3087. Figure skaters to win unanimous top scores for artistic impression, and the first from Great Britain to win the ice dancing title, at the Olympic Winter Games were Jayne Torvill and Christopher Dean at Sarajevo, Yugoslavia, in 1984. Their performance of *Bolero* in the free-dance portion of the competition brought them their unprecedented nine 6.0's for artistic impression, while their innovative choreography helped change the face of ice dancing.

3088. Asian-American figure skater to win the women's singles title at the U.S. national championships was Tiffany Chin in 1985 at Kansas City, Missouri. Her later career was hindered by injuries.

3089. African-American figure skater to win the women's singles title at the U.S. national championships was Debi Thomas, who won in 1986 at Hicksville, New York. She became world champion that same year and U.S. champion again in 1988, when she was bronze-medalist at the Olympics, before turning professional and pursuing medical studies.

3090. African-American figure skater to win the women's singles title in the world championships was Debi Thomas at Geneva, Switzerland, in 1986. At that competition, she defeated Katarina Witt of East Germany, but she would fall behind Witt the next two years, taking silver in 1987 and bronze in 1988 at both the world championships and the Olympics.

3091. Figure skater to perform a quadruple jump in competition was Kurt Browning of Canada in 1988. He first successfully completed a quadruple toe loop, a jump requiring four revolutions in the air, at the world championships at Budapest, Hungary. Though out of medal contention that year, he would become three-time world champion (1989–1991).

3092. Figure skater to perform the tano lutz jump in competition was Brian Boitano, who introduced it in 1988, the year he won the men's singles Olympic gold medal. In this version of the triple-rotation jump, named for Boitano, the arm is raised overhead, making the jump more balletic but more difficult.

3093. Figure skaters from Canada to win a medal in ice dancing at the Olympic Winter Games were Tracy Wilson and Robert McCall, who won a bronze medal on February 23, 1988, at Calgary, Alberta, Canada.

3094. Figure skater from Japan to win the women's singles title in the world championships was Midori Ito in Paris, France, in 1989, the high point of her career. She later became an announcer in Japan.

3095. Figure skaters to win Emmy awards for a television special were Katarina Witt of East Germany, Brian Boitano of the United States, and Brian Orser of Canada, who won in the classical music/dance category for their roles as Carmen, Don José, and the bullfighter Escamillo respectively in a 1989 television film *Carmen on Ice*. It was one of a series of specials staged by Boitano, several of them also starring Witt.

FIGURE SKATING (1990-1999)

3096. Figure skaters for France to win the ice dancing title in the world championships were Isabelle Duchesnay and Paul Duchesnay, who won in Munich, Germany, in 1991. Though born in Canada, they chose to skate for France and would later turn professional.

3097. Figure skaters from the United States to sweep the women's singles medals in the world championships were Kristi Yamaguchi, Tonya Harding, and Nancy Kerrigan, in that order, at the 1991 world competition in Munich, Germany. Yamaguchi would win again in 1992, and also take the Olympic gold medal.

3098. Figure skater from Ukraine to win the men's singles title at the world championships was Viktor Petrenko at Oakland, California, in 1992. With the Soviet Union just in the process of breaking up, Petrenko competed as part of a combined team for the Commonwealth of Independent States. He also took the Olympic gold medal that year.

3099. Japanese-American figure skater to win the women's singles title at the U.S. national championships was Kristi Yamaguchi, who won at Orlando, Florida, in 1992, after three straight years as runner-up. That same year, she won the gold medal at the Olympics and also gained her second world championship (1991–1992), then turning professional. Yamaguchi was also a two-time U.S. pairs champion (1989–1990), partnered by Rudy Galindo.

3100. Figure skater from Ukraine to win the men's singles title at the Olympic Winter Games was Viktor Petrenko in Albertville, France, on February 15, 1992. He competed as part of a combined team from the Commonwealth of Independent States, after the break-up of the Soviet Union. After also winning the world title that year, Petrenko then turned professional.

3101. Figure skater to perform a quadruple jump in the Olympic Games was Petr Barna of Czechoslovakia, who performed the feat en route to a bronze medal on February 15, 1992, in Albertville, France.

3102. Japanese-American figure skater to win the women's singles title at the Olympic Winter Games was Kristi Yamaguchi, who won the crown on February 21, 1992, at Albertville, France.

3103. Figure skater from Ukraine to win the women's singles title in the world championships was Oksana Baiul at Prague, Czech Republic, in 1993, when she was only 15. Effectively orphaned, she had been helped by her countryman Viktor Petrenko, whose coach took her in. She would go on to win the Olympics the following year.

3104. Figure skater to be stripped of the U.S. national women's singles title was Tonya Harding in 1994. She had won it earlier that year in Detroit, Michigan, following the withdrawal of the 1993 champion Nancy Kerrigan, whose legs had been hurt in an attack. It transpired that the attack was organized by Harding's ex-husband, still her companion; when Harding admitted to knowing about it, the U.S. Figure Skating Association voided her title and banned her for life.

3105. International precision team figure skating competition officially recognized by the International Skating Union (ISU) was in 1994.

3106. Professional figure skaters to win a gold medal in the Olympic Winter Games after being reinstated to amateur competition were Ekaterina Gordeeva and Sergei Grinkov of Russia, who returned to win their second title on February 15, 1994, at Lillehammer, Norway. The married duo had won their first gold medal in 1988, skating for the Soviet Union, and turned professional in 1990. Grinkov died suddenly of a heart attack on November 20, 1995; Gordeeva became a solo skater.

3107. Figure skater from Russia to win the men's singles title at the Olympic Winter Games was Aleksei Urmanov, who was an upset winner in Lillehammer, Norway, on February 19, 1994.

3108. Figure skater from Ukraine to win the women's singles title at the Olympic Winter Games was Oksana Baiul, who won the title on February 25, 1994, at Lillehammer, Norway. She was the surprise winner in an event originally expected to be a battle between United States skaters Nancy Kerrigan and Tonya Harding. The latter would later be banned from figure skating because of her connection with an attack on Kerrigan.

3109. Figure skater from China to win the women's singles title in the world championships was Chen Lu at Birmingham, Great Britain, in 1995. A year earlier, in 1994, she had been the first figure skater from China to win an Olympic medal, when she won the bronze medal, as she would in 1998, then turning professional.

3110. Figure skaters from the Czech Republic to win the pairs title in the world championships were Radka Kovarikova and Rene Novotny, who won in 1995 at Birmingham, Great Britain, then turned professional.

3111. Figure skaters to receive six perfect scores (6.0) for artistic impression in the U.S. national pairs competition were Jenni Meno and Todd Sand of the United States, en route to their second of three national titles (1994–1996) in 1995 in Providence, Rhode Island.

FIGURE SKATING—(1990-1999)—*continued*

3112. Champions Series in figure skating a World Cup–style set of five competitions, was held in 1996. The winners in that inaugural year were Aleksei Urmanov of Russia in the men's singles, Michelle Kwan of the United States in the women's singles, Yevgeniya Shishkova and Vadim Naumov of Russia in the pairs, and Oksana (later Pasha) Gritschuk and Evgeny Platov of Russia in ice dancing.

3113. International Skating Union (ISU) events to offer cash prizes to amateur figure skaters were the world and European championships and newly established Champions Series, all in 1996.

3114. Figure skaters to win two consecutive ice dancing titles at the Olympic Winter Games were Pasha (Oksana) Gritschuk and Evgeny Platov of Russia, who took their second straight title on February 16, 1998, at Nagano, Japan, after their first in 1994. Runner-ups both times were teammates Maia Usova and Aleksandr Zhulin. The two pairs would switch partners in 1999.

3115. Male figure skater to win the pairs title at the Olympic Winter Games with two different partners was Artur Dmitriev of Russia. His second title was won on February 10, 1998, in Nagano, Japan, with Oksana Kazakova. His first had been won skating with Natalia Mishkutenok on the combined team from the Commonwealth of Independent States on February 11, 1992, at Albertville, France.

3116. Figure skater to land three quadruple jumps, and two different ones, in a single international competition was Timothy Goebel of the United States. Competing at Skate America, in Colorado Springs, Colorado, on October 31, 1999, he completed a quadruple salchow-triple toe loop combination, a quadruple toe loop, and a quadruple salchow. He had earlier that year been the first to land the latter jump in competition.

FOOTBALL, AMERICAN (BEFORE 1900)
3117. Intercollegiate football game in the United States was a match between Princeton and Rutgers universities, on November 6, 1869, at New Brunswick, New Jersey. The teams consisted of 25 players on each side, with goal posts 25 feet apart. Handling the ball was prohibited; as in soccer, the ball was either kicked or struck with the head. Rutgers scored the required six points first, winning the game 6–4.

3118. International game of American-style football, and the first to use football goal posts was played on May 14, 1874, between teams from Harvard University and McGill University of Montreal, Quebec, Canada, on Harvard's grounds in Cambridge, Massachusetts. Harvard won 3–0, in the first of three games between the teams.

3119. Line of scrimmage system in American-style football was developed by Walter Camp, a former Yale University football star and a key figure in the development of the American game. It was adopted for intercollegiate play in 1882, as were the system of downs in the following year and the offsides penalty (the first penalty rule) in 1885.

3120. African-American college football player on an otherwise largely white team was William Henry Lewis, in 1889 at Amherst College. His only African-American teammate was William Tecumseh Sherman Jackson, of Alexandria, Virginia, who later became a leading figure in American education. Lewis had graduated from Virginia State University (then Virginia Normal and Industrial) before entering Amherst.

3121. All-America college football team named by Walter Camp was in 1889, and consisted of end Arthur Cummock, guard John Cranston, and halfback James T. Lee, all of Harvard University; tackle Hector Cowan, center William George, quarterback Edgar Allen Poe, halfback R. H. Channing, and fullback Knowlton Ames, all of Princeton University; and guard William "Pudge" Heffelfinger, tackle Charles O. Gill, and end Alonzo Stagg, of Yale University.

3122. African-American football player to captain an otherwise largely white college team was William Henry Lewis of Amherst College, in 1890. Lewis entered Harvard Law School in 1892. In 1911, he would become the first African-American assistant attorney-general of the United States.

3123. Army-Navy football game was on November 29, 1890, when Navy defeated Army 24–0.

3124. African-American college football player named to Walter Camp's All-America team was William Henry Lewis of Harvard Law School, in 1892, whom Camp named All-American at center-rush. Lewis had been the first African-American player on an otherwise largely white team in 1889, at Amherst College.

3125. Professional football player was William "Pudge" Heffelfinger, a star guard for Yale University in the late 1880s and a member of the first All-America team, who took a subsequently denied $500 fee and $25 in expenses to play for the Allegheny Athletic Association against Pittsburgh's East End Gymnasium Club, on November 12, 1892.

3126. College football game between two African-American colleges was between Livingstone College and Biddle University (later Johnson C. Smith University), on December 27, 1892, at Salisbury, North Carolina. Biddle won, 4–0.

3127. Professional football player who acknowledged being a professional was quarterback John Brallier of the Latrobe, Pennsylvania, Young Men's Christian Association (YMCA) football team, who was paid $10 in expenses for a game in 1895, and went on to a career as a professional player and coach.

3128. Fully professional football team was the Allegheny Athletic Association, of Allegheny, Pennsylvania, near Pittsburgh, which paid all of its players in 1896.

FOOTBALL, AMERICAN (1900-1909)

3129. African-American professional football player was Charles W. Follis of Wooster, Ohio, who played with Ohio's Shelby Athletic Association team from 1902 to 1906.

3130. College football player to score five rushing touchdowns in a major bowl game was Neil Snow of the University of Michigan, against Stanford University in the first Rose Bowl, in 1902.

3131. Professional football game played at night was between the Philadelphia Athletics and the Kanaweola Athletic Club, played in Elmira, New York, in 1902, with Philadelphia winning 39–0.

3132. Professional football league organized in 1902, was the American Football League, consisting of the Philadelphia Phillies, the Philadelphia Athletics, and the team from Latrobe, Pennsylvania.

3133. Rose Bowl football game the oldest of all the college football "bowls," was played at Pasadena, California, on January 1, 1902, between the University of Michigan and Stanford University. Michigan won, 49–0. The second Rose Bowl game would be played fourteen years later, in 1916, then becoming an annual event.

3134. Football stadium, built specifically for the sport was the Harvard University stadium, which opened on November 14, 1903.

3135. Use of the forward pass in American-style football was in 1906, when the move was made legal in college football. However, it was not widely used until 1913, when Notre Dame University—featuring quarterback Gus Dorais and end Knute Rockne—used the forward pass to upset Army 35–13.

3136. Use of numbers on college football uniforms was briefly in 1908 by Washington and Jefferson College, of Washington, Pennsylvania. The practice was picked up by the University of Chicago in November 1913 but did not become widespread until the 1920s.

FOOTBALL, AMERICAN (1910-1919)

3137. African-American All-America team was selected in 1911, including players from Howard University, Hampton Institute, Shaw College, and Lincoln University.

3138. Use of the double-wing formation in football was on November 9, 1912, when it was introduced by Pop Warner, coach of the Carlisle Indian School, in a game against Army. Among the notables playing in this 27–6 Carlisle win were future Olympian James Thorpe for Carlisle and future general and president Dwight D. Eisenhower as halfback for Army.

3139. African-American college football running back to be named to Walter Camp's All-America team was Fritz (Frederick Douglass) Pollard, of Brown University, on December 30, 1915.

3140. African-American college football player to play in the Rose Bowl was running back Fritz (Frederick Douglass) Pollard of Brown University, on January 1, 1916, in Pasadena, California.

3141. Washington State University win in college football's Rose Bowl was a 14–0 defeat of Brown University, in Pasadena, California, on January 1, 1916.

3142. University of Oregon win in college football's Rose Bowl was a 14–0 defeat of the University of Pennsylvania, in Pasadena, California, on January 1, 1917.

3143. African-American lineman to be named to Walter Camp's All-America football team was end Paul Bustil Robeson of New Jersey's Rutgers University, in 1918. Robeson also starred in baseball, basketball, and track and field at Rutgers. He later played professional football with Akron and Milwaukee, while attending Columbia Law School. Robeson later became one of the leading singers and actors of his time, as well as a major political figure.

FOOTBALL, AMERICAN—(1910-1919)—
continued

3144. African-American professional football coach was Fritz (Frederick Douglass) Pollard, who became player/coach of the Akron Indians in 1919. An All-American running back, Pollard had formerly starred for Brown University.

FOOTBALL, AMERICAN (1920-1929)
3145. Harvard University win in college football's Rose Bowl was a 7–6 defeat of the University of Oregon, in Pasadena, California, on January 1, 1920.

3146. American Professional Football League convention on September 17, 1920, established a league that consisted of the Akron Pros, Buffalo All-Americans, Canton Bulldogs, Chicago Tigers, Cleveland Tigers, Columbus Panhandlers, Dayton Triangles, Decatur Staleys, Detroit Heralds, Hammond Pros, Muncie Flyers, Racine Cardinals, Rock Island Independents, and Rochester Jeffersons. The league changed its name to the National Football League in 1921.

3147. American Professional Football League game was a 14–0 Dayton Triangles win over the Columbus Panhandlers, on October 3, 1920, at Dayton, Ohio.

3148. College football game to be broadcast on radio was a 7–3 Texas A & M University loss to the University of Texas on November 15, 1920. It was broadcast locally on WTAW in A & M's hometown of College Station, Texas.

3149. University of California win in college football's Rose Bowl was a 28–0 defeat of Ohio State University, in Pasadena, California, on January 1, 1921.

3150. American Professional Football League champions were the Akron Pros, declared champions by the league's owners on April 30, 1921.

3151. College football game to be broadcast nationally on radio was a Princeton University win, 21–18, over the University of Chicago, played at Chicago, Illinois, on October 28, 1922. The game was broadcast by New York City station WEAF and picked up by other stations across the country.

3152. University of Southern California win in college football's Rose Bowl was a 14–3 defeat of Pennsylvania State University, in Pasadena, California, on January 1, 1923.

3153. College football All-America team named by Grantland Rice was in 1925, and consisted of University of Michigan end Bennie Oosterbaan; University of Nebraska tackle Ed Weir; guard Carl Diehl and halfback Andy Oberlander, both of Dartmouth University; Princeton University center Edward McMillan; Ohio State University guard Edwin Hess; University of Pittsburgh tackle Ralph Chase; University of Pennsylvania end George Thayer; University of Illinois quarterback Harold (Red) Grange; University of Washington halfback George Wilson; and Stanford University fullback Ernie Nevers.

3154. Notre Dame University win in college football's Rose Bowl was a 29–10 defeat of Stanford University, in Pasadena, California, on January 1, 1925.

3155. American Football League season was played in 1926, but the new league, founded in competition with the National Football League, lasted only one season.

3156. University of Alabama win in college football's Rose Bowl was a 20–19 defeat of the University of Washington, in Pasadena, California, on January 1, 1926.

3157. Stanford University win in college football's Rose Bowl was a 7–6 defeat of the University of Pittsburgh, in Pasadena, California, on January 2, 1928.

3158. African-American college football bowl game was the Prairie View Bowl, played at Houston, Texas, on January 1, 1929.

3159. Georgia Tech win in college football's Rose Bowl was an 8–7 defeat of the University of California, in Pasadena, California, on January 1, 1929.

3160. Professional football player to score all 40 of his team's points was Ernie Nevers, who on November 28, 1929, ran for six touchdowns and kicked four extra points for the Chicago Cardinals, in a 40–6 victory over the Chicago Bears, for an enduring record.

FOOTBALL, AMERICAN (1930-1939)
3161. National Collegiate Athletic Association major college football team to have 44 consecutive winning seasons was Notre Dame University, from 1889 to 1932.

3162. National Football League game played indoors was a playoff for the league title, to break a tie between the Portsmouth Spartans (later the Detroit Lions) and the Chicago Bears. It was played inside Chicago Stadium, because of inclement weather, on December 18, 1932. Led by fullback Bronko Nagurski and receiver Harold (Red) Grange, Chicago won 9–0.

3163. Orange Blossom Classic an African-American college football bowl game sponsored by Florida A&M University, was held in Jacksonville, Florida, in 1933. Florida A&M defeated Howard University, 9–6.

3164. National Football League championship was won by the Chicago Bears, with a 23–21 defeat of the New York Giants at Chicago, Illinois, on December 17, 1933.

3165. College football All-Star Game was sponsored by the *Chicago Tribune* and played at Soldier Field, Chicago, Illinois, in 1934. It pitted a college all-star team against the Chicago Bears.

3166. Columbia University win in college football's Rose Bowl was a 7–0 defeat of Stanford University, in Pasadena, California, on January 1, 1934.

3167. New York Giants National Football League championship came with a 30–13 defeat of the Chicago Bears at New York City on December 9, 1934.

3168. College football coach to be named Coach of the Year by the American Football Coaches Association was Northwestern University coach Lynn Waldorf, in 1935.

3169. Orange Bowl football game was played at Miami Field Stadium, in Miami, Florida, on January 1, 1935, between Bucknell University and the University of Miami. Bucknell won 26–10. The game then became an annual year-end college football event.

3170. Sugar Bowl football game was played on January 1, 1935, at Tulane Stadium, in New Orleans, Louisiana, between Tulane University and Temple University. Tulane won 20–14.

3171. College football player to be awarded the Heisman Trophy as the outstanding college football player of the year was All-American University of Chicago halfback Jay Berwanger, on December 9, 1935. The award was originally called the Downtown Athletic Club Trophy, being awarded by that New York City club. It was renamed in 1936 in honor of the recently deceased John William Heisman, a leading college football coach, most notably at Georgia Tech, and later the club's first athletic director.

3172. Detroit Lions National Football League championship came with a 26–7 defeat of the New York Giants at Detroit, Michigan, on December 15, 1935.

3173. African-American coach of a Big Ten college football team was Homer Harris at the University of Iowa, in 1936.

3174. College football team to be named national champions by the Associated Press (AP) Sportswriters Poll was from the University of Minnesota, in 1936.

3175. Sun Bowl football game was played on January 1, 1936, at Kidd Field, in El Paso, Texas, between Hardin-Simmons College and the University of New Mexico. It was a 14–14 tie.

3176. National Football League college draft was held at the Ritz-Carlton Hotel, in Philadelphia, Pennsylvania, on February 8, 1936.

3177. Green Bay Packers National Football League championship came with a 21–6 defeat of the Boston Redskins at New York City, on December 13, 1936.

3178. College football player to receive the Maxwell Award (the Player of the Year award of the Maxwell Memorial Football Club of Philadelphia, Pennsylvania) was Yale University halfback Clint Frank, in 1937.

3179. College football player to rush for 1,000 yards or more in a single season was Byron "Whizzer" White of the University of Colorado, in 1937. White later became an associate justice of the U.S. Supreme Court.

3180. Cotton Bowl football game was played on January 1, 1937, at Fair Park Stadium, in Dallas, Texas, between Texas Christian University and Marquette University. Texas Christian won 16–6.

3181. University of Pittsburgh win in college football's Rose Bowl was a 21–0 defeat of the University of Washington, in Pasadena, California, on January 1, 1937.

3182. Washington Redskins National Football League championship came with a 28–21 defeat of the Chicago Bears at Chicago, Illinois, on December 12, 1937.

3183. National Football League player to be named the league's Most Valuable Player was New York Giants center Mel Hein, in 1938. Perennial All-Pro Hein was also the first interior lineman to be awarded this National Football League award. He later became a coach and ended his career as NFL supervisor of officials.

3184. College football team to win the Sugar Bowl in two consecutive years was Santa Clara University, which defeated Louisiana State University 6–0 on January 1, 1938, after their previous win in 1937.

FOOTBALL, AMERICAN—(1930-1939)—
continued

3185. College football player to win the Associated Press (AP) Athlete of the Year Award was Niles Kinnick of the University of Iowa, in 1939. An All-American runner, passer, and kicker, Kinnick also won several other awards in 1939, including the Heisman Trophy, Walter Camp Memorial Trophy, and Maxwell Award. A naval aviator during World War II, he died in a 1943 plane crash.

3186. National Football League Pro Bowl was played at Wrigley Field, Los Angeles, California, on January 15, 1939, between the New York Giants and a team of Pro All-Stars. The Giants won, 13–10. It was the first of five such games, pitting a National Football League team against an All-Star team.

3187. College football game to be televised was a 34–7 win by Fordham University over Waynesburg College, at Triboro Stadium on Randall's Island, New York City, on September 30, 1939. It was broadcast on station W2XBS, New York City, with the call by Bill Stern.

3188. Professional football game to be televised was a Brooklyn Dodgers 23–14 defeat of the Philadelphia Eagles, played at Ebbets Field in Brooklyn, New York, on October 22, 1939, with Allen "Skip" Walz announcing.

FOOTBALL, AMERICAN (1940-1949)

3189. National Football League team to win two consecutive league championships was the Chicago Bears, who defeated the Washington Redskins by the recordbreaking score of 73–0 in Washington, D.C., on December 8, 1940, and then the New York Giants 37–9 in Chicago, Illinois, on December 21, 1941.

3190. National Football League player to win two consecutive Most Valuable Player Awards was end Don Hutson of the Green Bay Packers, in 1941 and 1942. A perennial All-Pro selection, Hutson was the top receiver in the league in the late 1930s and early 1940s.

3191. Oregon State University win in college football's Rose Bowl, and the only Rose Bowl not played in Pasadena, California was a 20–16 defeat of Duke University, at Durham, North Carolina, on January 1, 1942.

3192. University of Georgia win in college football's Rose Bowl was a 9–0 defeat of the University of California at Los Angeles, in Pasadena, California, on January 1, 1943.

3193. National Football League player to pass for seven touchdowns in a single game was Sid Luckman of the Chicago Bears, against the New York Giants, on November 14, 1943.

3194. College football player to win the James E. Sullivan Memorial Award was perennial All-American Doc (Felix) Blanchard, fullback for the Army team, at West Point, New York, in 1945.

3195. National Football League player to lead the league eight times in pass receptions was Don Hutson of the Green Bay Packers, between 1936 and 1945.

3196. Cleveland Rams National Football League championship came with a 15–14 defeat of the Washington Redskins at Cleveland, Ohio, on December 16, 1945.

3197. African-American professional football player to join the Cleveland Browns of the All America Football Conference, was running back Marion Motley, in 1946.

3198. African-American professional football players to play in the National Football League in the modern period, and the first to play with the Los Angeles Rams were running back Kenny Washington and end Woody (Woodrow Wilson) Strode, in 1946. Their entry into the NFL ended the covert "gentlemen's agreement" among NFL club owners that had barred African-Americans from the league from 1934 to 1946. Strode was later a distinguished American film actor.

3199. All America Football Conference (AAFC) championship was won by the Cleveland Browns, with a 14–9 defeat of the New York Yankees at Cleveland, Ohio, in 1946. Cleveland went on to win all four AAFC championships (1946–1949). When the league dissolved, in 1949, Cleveland joined the National Football League.

3200. All America Football Conference (AAFC) season was played in 1946. The league consisted of two divisions: the New York Yankees, Buffalo Bills, Brooklyn Dodgers, and Baltimore Colts in the East; and the Cleveland Browns, San Francisco 49ers, Los Angeles Rams, and Chicago Rockets in the West. The new league lasted only four years, before merging with the National Football League in 1949.

3201. College football player to be awarded the Outland Trophy as the nation's outstanding interior lineman, was Notre Dame University tackle and linebacker George Connor, in 1946. Connor went on to become a professional football star, with the Chicago Bears.

3202. Football player to be named Most Valuable Player of the All America Football Conference (AAFC) was Brooklyn Dodgers halfback Glenn Dobbs, in 1946.

3203. College football player to pass for or himself score a total of six touchdowns in a major bowl game was Bobby Layne of the University of Texas, against the University of Missouri on January 1, 1946, in the Cotton Bowl.

3204. Gator Bowl football game was played on January 1, 1946, at Florida Field, in Gainesville, Florida, between Wake Forest University and the University of South Carolina. Wake Forest won, 26–14.

3205. Cleveland Browns regular season football game played at Municipal Stadium in Cleveland, Ohio, was a 44–0 win over the Miami Seahawks, on September 6, 1946. The first score was a Browns touchdown, on a pass from Cliff Lewis to Mac Speedie.

3206. African-American professional football player to join the Brooklyn Dodgers of the All America Football Conference (AAFC) was running back Elmore Harris, in 1947.

3207. African-American professional football player to join the Chicago Rockets of the All America Football Conference (AAFC) was running back Bill Bass, in 1947.

3208. African-American professional football player to join the Los Angeles Rams of the All America Football Conference (AAFC) was running back Bert Piggott, in 1947.

3209. African-American professional football player to join the New York Giants in the modern period was Emlen Tunnel, in 1947. Tunnel became a perennial pick for the Pro Bowl and the All-Pro team.

3210. African-American professional football player to join the New York Yankees of the All America Football Conference (AAFC) was running back Buddy Young, in 1947.

3211. National Football League Coach of the Year was Jimmy Conzelman of the Chicago Cardinals, in 1947. He took his team to its only National Football League title that year.

3212. African-American college football player to score a touchdown in the Rose Bowl was Buddy Young of the University of Illinois, against the University of Southern California, on January 1, 1947.

3213. Tangerine Bowl football game was played on January 1, 1947, at the Tangerine Bowl Stadium, in Orlando, Florida, between Catawba College and Maryville College. Catawba won, 31–6. The annual game was later renamed the Florida Citrus Bowl.

3214. University of Illinois win in college football's Rose Bowl was a 45–14 defeat of the University of California at Los Angeles, in Pasadena, California, on January 1, 1947.

3215. Chicago Cardinals National Football League championship came with a 28–21 defeat of the Philadelphia Eagles at Chicago, Illinois, on December 28, 1947.

3216. African-American player to be captain of the football team at Yale University was Levi Jackson, in 1948.

3217. African-American professional football player to join the San Francisco 49ers of the All America Football Conference (AAFC) was running back Joe Perry, in 1948.

3218. African-American professional football players to join the Detroit Lions in the modern period were Bob Mann of the University of Michigan and Mel Groomes of the University of Indiana, both in 1948.

3219. College football team to win two consecutive Tangerine Bowl games was Catawba College, which won on January 1, 1948, after winning the inaugural bowl game in 1947.

3220. University of Michigan win in college football's Rose Bowl was a 49–0 defeat of the University of Southern California, in Pasadena, California, on January 1, 1948.

3221. Philadelphia Eagles National Football League championship came with a 7–0 defeat of the Chicago Cardinals at Philadelphia, Pennsylvania, on December 28, 1948.

3222. African-American football player from an African-American college to join a major professional football team was Paul Younger of Grambling University, who joined the Los Angeles Rams of the All America Football Conference (AAFC) in 1949.

3223. Northwestern University win in college football's Rose Bowl was a 20–14 defeat of the University of California, in Pasadena, California, on January 1, 1949.

FOOTBALL, AMERICAN (1950-1959)
3224. College football team to be named national champions by the United Press International (UPI) Sportwriters Poll was the University of Oklahoma, in 1950.

3225. National Football League player to receive 18 completed passes in a single game was Tom Fears of the Los Angeles Rams, against the Green Bay Packers, on December 3, 1950.

FOOTBALL, AMERICAN—(1950-1959)—
continued

3226. Cleveland Browns National Football League championship came with a 30–28 defeat of the Los Angeles Rams at Cleveland, Ohio, on December 24, 1950.

3227. National Football League player to be named the league's Most Valuable Player by United Press International (UPI) was Cleveland Browns quarterback Otto Graham, in 1951. Graham led Paul Brown's Cleveland Browns to four consecutive All America Football Conference (AAFC) championships, and then to three National Football League championships. In college he had been the first player to become an All-American in both football and basketball.

3228. National Football League player to be named Most Valuable Player at the season-ending Pro Bowl was quarterback Otto Graham, of the Cleveland Browns, on January 14, 1951.

3229. National Football League Pro Bowl game between two All-Star teams was a 28–27 National Conference win over the American Conference, at the Los Angeles Memorial Coliseum, on January 14, 1951.

3230. National Football League player to pass for 554 yards in a single game was Norm Van Brocklin of the Los Angeles Rams, against the New York Yankees, on September 28, 1951.

3231. Los Angeles Rams National Football League championship came with a 24–17 defeat of the Cleveland Browns at Los Angeles, California, on December 23, 1951.

3232. National Collegiate Athletic Association major college football player to intercept 29 passes during his college career was Al Brosky of the University of Illinois, from 1950 to 1952.

3233. Detroit Lions National Football League championship in the modern era came with a defeat of the Cleveland Browns at Cleveland, Ohio, on December 28, 1952.

3234. African-American football player from an African-American college to be named to the Associated Press (AP) Little All-America Team was Leo Lewis of Lincoln University, Missouri, in 1953.

3235. College football player to win the Maxwell Award twice was Notre Dame University halfback John Lattner, in 1952 and 1953. A consensus All-American, Lattner also won the Heisman Trophy in 1953, as well as the Walter Camp Memorial Trophy and several other honors.

3236. National Football League player to win *The Sporting News* **Most Valuable Player Award** was Lou Groza, a perennial All-Pro and star field goal kicker for the Cleveland Browns, in 1954.

3237. African-American college football player to win the Outland Trophy was guard Calvin Jones of the University of Iowa, in 1955.

3238. National Football League player to be named Rookie of the Year was Baltimore Colts fullback Alan Ameche, in 1955. He had previously been a consensus All-American at the University of Wisconsin.

3239. African-American football players to appear in the Orange Bowl in Miami, Florida, were Jon McWilliams and Charles Bryant, both of the University of Nebraska, on January 1, 1955.

3240. African-American professional football player to be named National Football League Rookie of the Year was halfback Lenny Moore of the Baltimore Colts, in 1956.

3241. College football coach to be named Coach of the Year by the Football Writers Association of America was Ohio State University coach Woody Hayes, in 1957. He was also named Coach of the Year by the American Football Coaches Association that year.

3242. National Collegiate Athletic Association major college football team to win 47 consecutive games was the University of Oklahoma, from 1953 to 1957.

3243. National Football League player, and the first African-American football player, to win the Associated Press (AP) Most Valuable Player Award was fullback Jim Brown of the Cleveland Browns, in 1957. One of the greatest players in the history of the game, Brown was also the 1957 Rookie of the Year.

3244. University of Iowa win in college football's Rose Bowl was a 35–19 defeat of Oregon State University, at Pasadena, California, on January 1, 1957.

3245. Green Bay Packers regular season football game played at Lambeau Field in Green Bay, Wisconsin, was a 21–17 Packers win over the Chicago Bears, on September 29, 1957. The first score was a Bears touchdown, on a run by Ed Brown.

3246. Baltimore Colts National Football League championship came with a 23–17 Baltimore defeat of the New York Giants at New York City, on December 28, 1958. It was also the first NFL championship game to be nationally televised and the first sudden death overtime game in the NFL.

3247. National Football League game to be nationally televised was the NFL championship between the Baltimore Colts and the New York Giants, won by Baltimore 23–17 in a sudden death overtime game in New York City on December 28, 1958.

3248. Sudden death overtime game in the National Football League was an NFL championship game in New York City between the Baltimore Colts and the New York Giants, won by the Colts 23–17, on December 28, 1958.

3249. College football team to win two consecutive Orange Bowl games was the University of Oklahoma, which defeated Syracuse University 21–6 on January 1, 1959, after defeating Duke University 48–21 in 1958.

3250. Liberty Bowl football game was played on December 19, 1959, at Municipal Stadium, in Philadelphia, Pennsylvania, between Pennsylvania State University and the University of Alabama. Penn State won, 7–0.

FOOTBALL, AMERICAN (1960-1969)
3251. African-American professional football player to be named American Football Conference Player of the Year was halfback Abner Haynes of the Dallas Texans, in 1960, when he was also named conference Rookie of the Year.

3252. African-American professional football player to play in a National Football League championship game was Marion Motley of the Cleveland Browns, in 1960.

3253. National Football League player to lead the league in passing touchdowns for four consecutive years was Johnny Unitas of the Baltimore Colts, from 1957 to 1960.

3254. National Football League player to score a total of 176 points in a single season was halfback Paul Hornung of the Green Bay Packers, in 1960.

3255. Denver Broncos regular season football game played at Mile High Stadium in Denver, Colorado, was a 31–14 win over the Oakland Raiders, on October 2, 1960. The first score was a Broncos field goal, kicked by Eugene Mingo.

3256. College football team to win two consecutive Liberty Bowl games was Pennsylvania State University, which defeated the University of Oregon, 41–12, on December 17, 1960, after winning the inaugural bowl game in 1959.

3257. African-American college football player to win the Heisman Trophy was halfback Ernest Davis of Syracuse University, in 1961.

3258. National Football League player to be named Most Valuable Player in the Pro Bowl for two consecutive years was Baltimore Colts quarterback Johnny Unitas, in 1960 and 1961.

3259. American Football Conference championship was won by the Houston Oilers, with a 24–16 win over the Los Angeles Chargers at Houston, Texas, on January 1, 1961, ending the 1960 season.

3260. African-American quarterback to appear in the Rose Bowl college football game was Sandy Stephens of the University of Minnesota, on January 2, 1961, in Pasadena, California. He also appeared for Minnesota in the Rose Bowl in 1962.

3261. Washington Redskins regular season football game played at DC Stadium in Washington, D.C., was a 24–21 loss to the New York Giants, on October 1, 1961. The stadium would be renamed RFK Memorial Stadium in June 1969. The Redskins would play there through 1996, then moving to FedEx Field.

3262. American Football League team to win two consecutive conference championships was the Houston Oilers. Having defeated the then–Los Angeles Chargers in the 1960 season, the Oilers went on to defeat the San Diego Chargers in San Diego, California, on December 24, 1961.

3263. African-American professional football player to join the Washington Redskins was Bobby Mitchell, in 1962. The Redskins were the last National Football League team to field an all-white team.

3264. College football player to receive the *Sports Illustrated* Sportsman of the Year Award was Oregon State University quarterback Terry Baker. An All-American, Baker also won the Heisman Trophy and the Maxwell Award in 1962.

FOOTBALL, AMERICAN—(1960-1969)—
continued

3265. National Football League player to win the *Pro Football Weekly* Most Valuable Player Award was Los Angeles Rams defensive end Andrew Robustelli, in 1962. He was a perennial All-Pro with the Rams and then with the New York Giants.

3266. University of Minnesota win in college football's Rose Bowl was a 21–3 defeat of the University of California at Los Angeles, at Pasadena, California, on January 1, 1962.

3267. Dallas Texans American Football League championship came with a 20–17 defeat of the Houston Oilers at Houston, Texas, on December 23, 1962.

3268. Pro Football Hall of Fame inductees were honored at the opening of the Hall of Fame at Canton, Ohio, on September 17, 1963. They were players Sammy Baugh, Dutch (Earl) Clark, Red (Harold) Grange, Mel Hein, Pete (Wilbur) Henry, Cal Hubbard, Don Hutson, Blood (Johnny) McNally, Bronko Nagurski, Ernie Nevers, and Jim Thorpe; and owners, coaches, and league officials Bert Bell, Joe Carr, George Halas, Curly (Earl) Lambeau, Tim Mara, and George Preston Marshall.

3269. Instant replay was shown on the CBS television network on December 7, 1963, during an Army-Navy game. It showed a faked handoff by Army quarterback Rollie Stichweh, who then ran the ball in for a touchdown.

3270. African-American college football player to become a quarterback at Harvard University was John McClusky, in 1964.

3271. San Diego Chargers American Football League championship came with a 51–10 defeat of the Boston Patriots at San Diego, California, on January 5, 1964, ending the 1963 season.

3272. Buffalo Bills American Football League championship came with a 20–7 defeat of the San Diego Chargers at Buffalo, New York, on December 26, 1964

3273. National Football League player to lead the league in rushing touchdowns five times was Jim Brown of the Cleveland Browns, in 1957, 1958, 1959, 1963, and 1965.

3274. National Football League player to lead the league in rushing yards eight times was Jim Brown of the Cleveland Browns, in 1957–1961 and 1963–1965.

3275. University of California at Los Angeles win in college football's Rose Bowl was a 14–12 defeat of Michigan State University, at Pasadena, California, on January 1, 1965.

3276. National Football League player to be named Defensive Player of the Year in 1966, was St. Louis Cardinals safety Larry Wilson, a perennial Pro Bowler who is credited with being the first to use the "safety blitz." He later became a scout and then front office executive for the Cardinals.

3277. Season in which the National Football League (NFL) and American Football League (AFL) were merged was in 1966. It resulted in a 34–27 Green Bay Packers victory over the Dallas Cowboys for the NFL championship and a 31–7 Kansas City Chiefs win over the Buffalo Bills for the AFL championship. The two winning teams then met in Super Bowl I. The two leagues had agreed to merge on June 8, 1966.

3278. African-American professional football player to be named to the Pro Football Hall of Fame was defensive back Emlen Tunnel in 1967. He had played for the University of Iowa, New York Giants, and Green Bay Packers.

3279. Team to win three consecutive National Football League championships was the Green Bay Packers, who defeated the Cleveland Browns in 1965 and the Dallas Cowboys in 1966 and 1967.

3280. Kansas City Chiefs American Football League championship came with a 31–7 defeat of the Buffalo Bills at Buffalo, New York, on January 1, 1967.

3281. Purdue University win in college football's Rose Bowl was a 14–13 defeat of the University of Southern California, at Pasadena, California, on January 2, 1967.

3282. Super Bowl was played on January 15, 1967, at Los Angeles, California. The Green Bay Packers of the National Football League defeated the Kansas City Chiefs of the American Football League 35–10 in Super Bowl I. Bart Starr of the Packers was named the game's Most Valuable Player.

3283. San Diego Chargers regular season football game played at San Diego Stadium in San Diego, California, was a 28–14 win over the Boston Patriots, on September 9, 1967. The first score was a Chargers touchdown, on a run by Paul Lowe. The stadium would be renamed Jack Murphy Stadium in 1980 and Qualcomm Stadium at Jack Murphy Field in 1997.

3284. National Football League player to kick seven field goals in a single game was Jim Bakken of the Los Angeles Rams, against the Pittsburgh Steelers, on September 24, 1967.

3285. Oakland Raiders American Football League championship came with a 40–7 defeat of the Houston Oilers at Oakland, California, on December 31, 1967.

3286. African-American college football player to receive the Maxwell Award was University of Southern California running O. J. (Orenthal James) Simpson, in 1968. In the same year, Simpson was the first African-American football player to be named Player of the Year by the Associated Press (AP) and United Press International (UPI).

3287. African-American quarterback to play regularly on a professional football team was Marlin Briscoe, who played for the Denver Broncos in the American Football League in 1968. Willie Thrower had played briefly with the Chicago Bears in the 1953 season.

3288. National Collegiate Athletic Association major college football player to intercept 14 passes in a single season was Al Worley of the University of Washington, in 1968.

3289. Professional football player to kick four field goals in a single Super Bowl game was Don Chandler of the Green Bay Packers, in the Packers' 33–14 Super Bowl II win over the Oakland Raiders, on January 14, 1968, at Miami, Florida.

3290. Professional football team to win two consecutive Super Bowl games was the Green Bay Packers, in 1967 and 1968. In Super Bowl II, the Packers defeated the Oakland Raiders 33–14, on January 14, 1968, at Miami, Florida. Bart Starr of the Packers was again named the game's Most Valuable Player, becoming the first player to be MVP in two consecutive years.

3291. Houston Oilers regular season football game played at the Houston Astrodome in Houston, Texas, was a 26–21 loss to the Kansas City Chiefs, on September 8, 1968. The first score was an Oilers touchdown, on a run by Hoyle Granger.

3292. College football player to receive 20 passes in a major bowl game was Walker Gillette of the University of Richmond, against University of Ohio, on December 27, 1968, in the Tangerine Bowl.

3293. New York Jets American Football League championship came on December 29, 1968, with a 27–12 win over the Oakland Raiders, in New York City.

3294. Peach Bowl football game was played on December 30, 1968, between Louisiana State University and Florida State University, at Grant Field, in Atlanta, Georgia. LSU won, 31–27.

3295. Professional football player to be named Most Valuable Player in the Super Bowl twice in a row was Bart Starr of the Green Bay Packers, who won that honor for the second straight time in Super Bowl II on January 14, 1968, in Miami, Florida.

3296. New York Jets win in the National Football League's Super Bowl was a 16–7 defeat of the Baltimore Colts in Super Bowl III, on January 12, 1969, at Miami, Florida. Joe Namath of the Jets was named the game's Most Valuable Player.

3297. National Collegiate Athletic Association major college football player to score six touchdowns on pass receptions in a single game was Tim Delaney of San Diego State College, against New Mexico State University, on November 5, 1969.

FOOTBALL, AMERICAN (1970-1979)
3298. African-American college football player to become a quarterback at Georgia Tech was Eddie McAshan, in 1970.

3299. College football player to win the Lombardi Award as the nation's outstanding lineman, was Ohio State University middle guard Jim Stillwagon, in 1970. Vince Lombardi was a leading professional coach, most notably of the Green Bay Packers.

3300. Monday Night Football televised National Football League games were introduced in 1970, drawing a huge national audience.

3301. National Football League player to be named Most Valuable Player of the American Football Conference was Oakland Raiders quarterback George Blanda, a durable, multitalented passer and kicker, in 1970.

3302. National Football League player to be named Most Valuable Player of the National Football Conference was San Francisco 49ers quarterback John Brodie, in 1970.

3303. College football team to win two consecutive Cotton Bowl games was the University of Texas, which defeated the University of Tennessee 35–13 in 1969 and then Notre Dame University 21–17 in 1970, both in January.

3304. Kansas City Chiefs American Football League championship came with a 17–7 defeat of the Oakland Raiders at Oakland, California, on January 4, 1970.

FOOTBALL, AMERICAN—(1970-1979)—
continued

3305. Minnesota Vikings National Football League championship came with a 27–7 defeat of the Cleveland Browns at Minneapolis, Minnesota, on January 4, 1970.

3306. Kansas City Chiefs win in professional football's Super Bowl was a 23-7 defeat of the Minnesota Vikings in Super Bowl IV, on January 11, 1970, at New Orleans, Louisiana. Len Dawson of the Chiefs was named the game's Most Valuable Player.

3307. Pittsburgh Steelers regular season football game played at Three Rivers Stadium in Pittsburgh, Pennsylvania, was a 19–7 loss to the Houston Oilers, on September 20, 1970. The first score was an Oilers touchdown, on a catch by Jerry LeVies.

3308. Cincinnati Bengals regular season football game played at Riverfront Stadium in Cincinnati, Ohio, was a 31–21 win over the Oakland Raiders, on September 21, 1970. The first score was a Bengals touchdown, on a run by Sam Wyche. The stadium would be called Cinergy Field from 1996. The Bengals played there until the 2000 season, when they move into the Paul Brown Stadium.

3309. National Football League player to kick a 63-yard field goal was Tom Dempsey of the New Orleans Saints, against the Detroit Lions on November 8, 1970.

3310. National Football League player to kick at least one field goal in 31 consecutive games was Fred Cox of the Minnesota Vikings, whose streak ran from November 17, 1968, to December 5, 1970.

3311. African-American professional football player to be named Most Valuable Player of the National Football Conference was defensive end Alan Page of the Minnesota Vikings, in 1971.

3312. Baltimore Colts American Football Conference championship came with a 27–17 defeat of the Oakland Raiders at Baltimore, Maryland, on January 3, 1971. The conference championship games were now the last step before the Super Bowl, which decided the league championship.

3313. Dallas Cowboys National Football Conference championship came with a 17–10 defeat of the San Francisco 49ers at San Francisco, California, on January 3, 1971.

3314. Baltimore Colts win in professional football's Super Bowl was a 16–13 defeat of the Dallas Cowboys in Super Bowl V, on January 17, 1971, at Miami, Florida. Chuck Howley of the Colts was named the game's Most Valuable Player.

3315. Chicago Bears regular season football game played at Soldier Field in Chicago, Illinois, was a 17–15 win over the Pittsburgh Steelers, on September 19, 1971. The first score was a Steelers touchdown, resulting from a Bears fumble in the end zone.

3316. New England Patriots regular season football game played at Foxboro Stadium in Foxboro, Massachusetts, was a 20–6 win over the Oakland Raiders, on September 19, 1971. The first score was a Raiders touchdown, on a run by Pete Banaszak.

3317. Philadelphia Eagles regular season football game played at Veterans Stadium in Philadelphia, Pennsylvania, was a 42–7 defeat by the Dallas Cowboys, on September 26, 1971. The first score was a Cowboys touchdown, on a run by Calvin Hill.

3318. San Francisco 49ers regular season football game played at Candlestick Park in San Francisco, California, was a 20–13 loss to the Los Angeles Rams, on October 10, 1971. The first score was a 49ers field goal, kicked by Bruce Gossett.

3319. Dallas Cowboys regular season football game played at Texas Stadium in Irving, Texas, was a 44–21 win over the New England Patriots, on October 24, 1971. The first score was a Cowboys touchdown, on a run by Duane Thomas.

3320. Fiesta Bowl football game was played on December 27, 1971, at Sun Devil Stadium, in Tempe, Arizona, between Arizona State University and Florida State University. Arizona State won, 45–38.

3321. African-American college football player to win the Lombardi Award as the country's top lineman was guard Rich Glover of the University of Nebraska, in 1972.

3322. National Football League team to win 14 consecutive games in a single season, and to have an undefeated season was the Miami Dolphins, in 1972. Their "perfect" season extended through to their win in Super Bowl VII on January 14, 1973.

3323. Miami Dolphins American Football Conference championship came with a 21–0 defeat of the Baltimore Colts at Baltimore, Maryland, on January 3, 1972.

3324. Dallas Cowboys win in professional football's Super Bowl was a 24–3 defeat of the Miami Dolphins in Super Bowl VI, on January 16, 1972, at New Orleans, Louisiana. Roger Staubach of Dallas was named the game's Most Valuable Player.

3325. Kansas City Chiefs regular season football game played at Arrowhead Stadium in Kansas City, Missouri, was a 20–10 loss to the Miami Dolphins, on September 17, 1972. The first score was a Dolphins touchdown, on a catch by Mark Briscoe.

3326. College football team in a major bowl game to gain a total of 718 yards was Arizona State University, against the University of Missouri, on December 23, 1972, in the Fiesta Bowl.

3327. Washington Redskins National Football Conference championship came with a 26–3 defeat of the Dallas Cowboys at Washington, D.C., on December 31, 1972.

3328. College football coach to be named Coach of the Year three times by the American Football Coaches Association was University of Alabama coach Bear (Paul W.) Bryant, in 1961, 1971, and 1973.

3329. Team to win three consecutive American Football Conference championships was the Miami Dolphins, from 1971 to 1973.

3330. College football team to win three consecutive Orange Bowl games was the University of Nebraska, which defeated Notre Dame University 40–6 on January 1, 1973, after defeating Louisiana State University 17–12 in 1971 and the University of Alabama 38–6 in 1972.

3331. Miami Dolphins win in professional football's Super Bowl was a 14–7 defeat of the Washington Redskins in Super Bowl VII, on January 14, 1973, at Los Angeles, California. Jake Scott of the Dolphins was named the game's Most Valuable Player.

3332. Buffalo Bills regular season football game played at Rich Stadium in Buffalo, New York, was a 9–7 win over the New York Jets, on September 30, 1973. The first score was a Bills field goal, kicked by John Leypoldt. The stadium was renamed Ralph Wilson Stadium in 1998.

3333. College football team to win three consecutive Fiesta Bowl games was Arizona State University, which won its third straight on December 21, 1973, over the University of Pittsburgh, 28–7, after winning the first two in 1971 and 1972.

3334. Minnesota Vikings National Football Conference championship came with a 27–10 defeat of the Dallas Cowboys at Dallas, Texas on December 30, 1973.

3335. Bayou Classic African-American college football game was between Grambling University and Southern University in 1974, at the Louisiana Superdome, in New Orleans, Louisiana, and was won by Grambling 21–0.

3336. Women's professional football league was the National Woman's Football League, established in 1974, which would survive into the mid-1980s. Half a century earlier, in 1926, a women's team had been used as "half-time entertainment" during some professional football games.

3337. World Football League championship was won by the Birmingham Americans, with a 22–21 win over the Florida Blazers at Birmingham, Alabama, in 1974. It was the only season played by the short-lived league.

3338. Pittsburgh Steelers American Football Conference championship came with a 24–13 defeat of the Oakland Raiders in Oakland, California, on December 29, 1974.

3339. African-American professional football player from an African-American college to be inducted into the Pro Football Hall of Fame was Roosevelt Brown of Morgan State University, in 1975, who had been a perennial All-Pro during his long career with the New York Giants.

3340. National Football League player to be named Most Valuable Player by the Professional Football Writers Association was Minnesota Vikings quarterback Francis "Fran" Tarkenton, a college All-American and perennial All-Pro, in 1975.

3341. Professional football player to play for 26 seasons in major league football was George Blanda, whose career extended from 1949 to 1975, except for 1959. Blanda, a quarterback and kicker who played college football at the University of Kentucky, started as a professional with the Chicago Bears in the National Football League, moved to the American Football League with the Houston Oilers in 1960, and was traded to the Oakland Raiders in 1967, retiring in 1975. He played in a record 340 professional games.

3342. Professional football player to score a career total of 2,002 points was George Blanda, between 1949 and 1975.

FOOTBALL, AMERICAN—(1970-1979)— *continued*

3343. African-American professional football player to be named Most Valuable Player in the Super Bowl was running back Franco Harris, in Super Bowl IX, on January 12, 1975.

3344. Pittsburgh Steelers win in professional football's Super Bowl was a 16–6 defeat of the Minnesota Vikings in Super Bowl IX, on January 12, 1975, at New Orleans, Louisiana. Franco Harris was named the game's Most Valuable Player. The Steelers would go on to win four Super Bowl games in six years, also winning in 1976, 1979, and 1980.

3345. New Orleans Saints regular season football game played at the Louisiana Superdome in New Orleans, Louisiana, was a 21–0 loss to the Cincinnati Bengals, on September 28, 1975. The first score was a Bengals touchdown, on a catch by Isaac Curtis.

3346. Detroit Lions regular season football game played at the Pontiac Silverdome in Pontiac, Michigan, was a 36–10 loss to the Dallas Cowboys, on October 6, 1975. The first score was a Cowboys field goal, kicked by Toni Frisch.

3347. Football player to win the Heisman Trophy twice was Ohio State University running back Archie Griffin, who won the award on December 2, 1975, after having been honored first in 1974.

3348. Seattle Seahawks regular season football game played at the Seattle Kingdome in Seattle, Washington, was a 30–24 loss to the St. Louis Cardinals on September 12, 1976. The first score was a Cardinals field goal, kicked by Jim Bakken. They would play at the Kingdome through 1999, then moving into temporary quarters at the University of Washington's Husky Stadium until 2002, when the Seattle Stadium was scheduled to open.

3349. Tampa Bay Buccaneers regular season football game played at Tampa Stadium in Tampa, Florida, was a 23–0 loss to the San Diego Chargers, on September 19, 1976.

3350. New York Giants regular season football game played at Giants Stadium in East Rutherford, New Jersey, was a 21–14 loss to the Dallas Cowboys, on October 10, 1976. The first score was a Cowboys touchdown, on a run by Robert Newhouse.

3351. Independence Bowl football game was played on December 13, 1976, at Independence Stadium, in Shreveport, Louisiana, between McNeese State College and the University of Tulsa. McNeese won, 20–16.

3352. Oakland Raiders American Football Conference championship came with a 24–7 victory over the Pittsburgh Steelers at Oakland, California, on December 26, 1976.

3353. African-American professional football player to be named National Football League Player of the Year by the Pro Football Writers Association was running back Walter Payton of the Chicago Bears, in 1977.

3354. Davey O'Brien Award then called the O'Brien Memorial Trophy, was given to running back Earl Campbell of the University of Texas, in 1977. Named after outstanding quarterback Davey O'Brien, the annual award is now given to the top collegiate quarterback in the Southwest.

3355. Oakland Raiders win in professional football's Super Bowl was a 32-14 defeat of the Minnesota Vikings in Super Bowl XI, on January 9, 1977, at Pasadena, California. Fred Biletnikoff of the Raiders was named the game's Most Valuable Player. It was the first Super Bowl attended by more than 100,000 spectators (103,428).

3356. National Collegiate Athletic Association major college football player to kick a 67-yard field goal was Russell Erxleben of the University of Texas, against Rice University, on October 1, 1977.

3357. National Football League rusher to gain 275 yards in a single game was Walter Payton of the Chicago Bears, against the Minnesota Vikings, on November 20, 1977.

3358. Denver Broncos American Football Conference championship came with a 20–17 defeat of the Oakland Raiders at Denver, Colorado on January 1, 1978.

3359. National Football League player to reach 81 career interceptions was Paul Krause of the Minnesota Vikings, from 1964 to 1979.

3360. National Football League player to rush for 200 or more yards in six different games during his career was O. J. Simpson, from 1969 to 1979.

3361. Professional football player to play 282 consecutive games was Jim Marshall of the Minnesota Vikings. Marshall's recordbreaking streak started on September 25, 1960, while he was playing for the Cleveland Browns, and ended 282 games later in 1979.

3362. Professional football coach to take his team to six Super Bowl games was Don Shula of the Miami Dolphins, who took the Baltimore Colts to the Super Bowl in 1969, and the Dolphins in the 1971, 1972, 1973, 1982, and 1984 seasons.

FOOTBALL, AMERICAN (1980-1989)

3363. National Football League coach to lead his team to four wins in the Super Bowl was Chuck Noll, whose Pittsburgh Steelers won a record of four Super Bowl games: 1975, 1976, 1979, and 1980.

3364. College football team to win three consecutive Sugar Bowl games was the University of Alabama, which defeated the University of Arkansas 24–9 on January 1, 1980, after earlier wins over Ohio State University, 35–6 in 1978, and Pennsylvania State University, 14–7 in 1979.

3365. Los Angeles Rams National Football Conference championship came with a 9–0 defeat of the Tampa Bay Buccaneers at Tampa, Florida, on January 6, 1980.

3366. National Football League Pro Bowl played at Aloha Stadium in Honolulu, Hawaii, was on January 27, 1980. The National Football Conference won, 37–27. Honolulu then became the permanent home of the Pro Bowl.

3367. Los Angeles Rams regular season football game played at Anaheim Stadium in Anaheim, California, was a 41–20 loss to the Detroit Lions, on September 7, 1980. The first score was a dramatic Rams touchdown, on a 98-yard kickoff return by Drew Hill.

3368. National Collegiate Athletic Association major college football player to rush 403 times in a single season was Marcus Allen, of the University of Southern California, in 1981.

3369. Philadelphia Eagles National Football Conference championship came with a 20–7 defeat of the Dallas Cowboys at Philadelphia, Pennsylvania, on January 11, 1981.

3370. National Football League players' strike cost the league nine of its scheduled regular season football games in 1982.

3371. Cincinnati Bengals American Football Conference championship came with a 27–7 defeat of the San Diego Chargers at Cincinnati, Ohio, on January 10, 1982.

3372. San Francisco 49ers National Football Conference championship came with a 28–27 victory over the Dallas Cowboys at San Francisco, California, on January 10, 1982.

3373. San Francisco 49ers win in professional football's Super Bowl was a 26–21 defeat of the Cincinnati Bengals in Super Bowl XVI, on January 24, 1982, at Pontiac, Michigan. Joe Montana of the 49ers was named the game's Most Valuable Player.

3374. Minnesota Vikings regular season football game played at the Hubert H. Humphrey Metrodome in Minneapolis, Minnesota, was a 17–10 win over the Tampa Bay Buccaneers, on September 12, 1982. The first score was a Buccaneers field goal, kicked by Bill Capece.

3375. Los Angeles Raiders regular season football game played at the Los Angeles Memorial Coliseum in Los Angeles, California, was a 28–24 win over the San Diego Chargers, on November 22, 1982. The first score was a Chargers field goal, kicked by Rolf Benirschke. The team had been, and would later again be, the Oakland Raiders.

3376. Aloha Bowl football game was played on December 25, 1982, at Aloha Stadium, in Honolulu, Hawaii, between the University of Washington and the University of Maryland. Washington won, 21–20.

3377. College football player to be awarded the Outland Trophy twice was University of Nebraska center Dave Rimington, in 1982 and 1983. He also won the Lombardi Award in 1982. Rimington went on to a career in professional football.

3378. National Collegiate Athletic Association major college team to score 624 points in a single season was the University of Nebraska, in 1983.

3379. National Collegiate Athletic Association major college team to score 89 touchdowns in a single season was the University of Nebraska, in 1983.

3380. National Collegiate Athletic Association major college team to score a total of 84 touchdowns rushing and passing in a single season was the University of Nebraska, in 1983.

3381. United States Football League championship was won by the Michigan Panthers, with a 24–22 win over the Philadelphia Stars at Denver, Colorado, in 1983.

3382. National Football League player to rush for 99 yards from the line of scrimmage was Tony Dorsett of the Dallas Cowboys, against the Minnesota Vikings, on January 3, 1983.

FOOTBALL, AMERICAN—(1980-1989)—
continued

3383. Washington Redskins win in professional football's Super Bowl was a 27–17 defeat of the Miami Dolphins in Super Bowl XVII, on January 30, 1983, at Pasadena, California. John Riggins of the Redskins was named the game's Most Valuable Player.

3384. National Football League player to score at least one touchdown in 13 consecutive games was John Riggins of the Washington Redskins, his streak running from December 26, 1982, to November 27, 1983.

3385. College football player to kick five field goals in a major bowl game was Jess Atkinson of the University of Maryland, against the University of Tennessee, on December 17, 1983, in the Florida Citrus Bowl.

3386. Circle City Classic African-American college football game was between Mississippi Valley State College and Grambling University, at the Indianapolis Hoosierdome at Indianapolis, Indiana, in 1984. It was won by Mississippi, 48–36.

3387. National Collegiate Athletic Association major college football player to kick 29 field goals in a single season was John Lee of the University of California at Los Angeles, in 1984.

3388. National Football League defensive player to reach 22 sacks in a single season was Mark Gastineau of the New York Jets, in 1984.

3389. National Football League player to complete passes totaling 5,084 yards in a single season was Dan Marino of the Miami Dolphins, in 1984.

3390. National Football League player to pass for 48 touchdowns in a single season was Dan Marino of the Miami Dolphins, in 1984.

3391. National Football League player to rush for 2,105 yards in a single season was Eric Dickerson of the Los Angeles Rams, in 1984.

3392. National Football League team to win 15 games in a single season was the San Francisco 49ers, in 1984.

3393. Los Angeles Raiders American Football Conference championship came with a 30–14 defeat of the Seattle Seahawks at Los Angeles, California, on January 8, 1984.

3394. Los Angeles Raiders win in professional football's Super Bowl was a 38–9 defeat of the Washington Redskins in Super Bowl XVIII, on January 22, 1984, at Tampa, Florida. Marcus Allen of the Raiders was named the game's Most Valuable Player.

3395. Indianapolis Colts regular season football game played at the RCA Dome in Indianapolis, Indiana, was a 23–14 loss to the New York Jets, on May 3, 1984. The first score was a Colts touchdown, on a run by Curtis Dickey.

3396. New York Jets regular season football game played at Giants Stadium in East Rutherford, New Jersey, was a 23–17 loss to the Pittsburgh Steelers, on September 6, 1984. The Steelers scored first, on a 6-yard touchdown pass to Louis Lipps.

3397. College football player to pass for six touchdowns in a major bowl game was Chuck Long of the University of Iowa, against the University of Texas, on December 16, 1984, in the inaugural Freedom Bowl, in Anaheim Stadium, in Anaheim, California.

3398. Butkus Award was presented to University of Oklahoma linebacker Brian Bosworth, in 1985. Named for top college and Chicago Bears linebacker Dick Butkus, the award is given to the top collegiate linebacker of the year. Bosworth won the award again in 1986, becoming the first player to receive the award in two consecutive years.

3399. National Football League player to gain a total of 2,535 yards running in a single season was Lionel James of the San Diego Chargers, in 1985.

3400. Professional football player to score 18 points in a single Super Bowl game was Roger Craig of the San Francisco 49ers, who scored three touchdowns in the 49ers' 38–16 Super Bowl XIX win over the Miami Dolphins, on January 20, 1985, at Palo Alto, California.

3401. Jim Thorpe Award was presented to Thomas Everett of Baylor University in 1986. Named for champion runner, All-American college football player, and professional football player Jim Thorpe, the award is given to the top defensive back of the year.

3402. National Collegiate Athletic Association major college football player to kick 80 field goals during his college career was Jeff Jaeger of the University of Washington, from 1983 to 1986.

3403. Chicago Bears National Football Conference championship came with a 24–0 defeat of the Los Angeles Rams at Chicago, Illinois, on January 12, 1986.

3404. New England Patriots American Football Conference championship came with a 31–14 victory over the Miami Dolphins at Miami, Florida, on January 12, 1986.

3405. Chicago Bears win in professional football's Super Bowl was a 46–10 defeat of the New England Patriots in Super Bowl XX, on January 26, 1986, at New Orleans, Louisiana. Richard Dent of the Bears was named the game's Most Valuable Player.

3406. Hall of Fame Bowl football game was played on December 23, 1986, at Tampa Stadium, in Tampa, Florida, between Boston College and the University of Georgia. Boston College won, 27–24. In 1996, the game would be renamed the Outback Bowl.

3407. Johnny Unitas Golden Arm Award was presented to Syracuse University quarterback Dan McPherson, in 1987. Named for quarterback Johnny Unitas, a member of the National Football League Hall of Fame, the award is given to the top senior college quarterback of the year.

3408. National Football League player to gain a career total of 16,726 yards rushing was Walter Payton of the Chicago Bears, who amassed that all-time career record from 1975 to 1987.

3409. National Football League player to gain a career total of 21,803 yards running was Walter Payton of the Chicago Bears, from 1975 to 1987. This record included running in all of its forms, including rushing, pass receptions, and kick returns.

3410. National Football League player to receive for 22 touchdowns in a single season was Jerry Rice of the San Francisco 49ers, in 1987.

3411. National Football League player to rush for 100 yards or more in 77 games was Walter Payton of the Chicago Bears, from 1975 to 1987.

3412. Walter Payton Player of the Year Award was given to Kenny Gamble of Colgate University in 1987. Named after Walter Payton, the National Football League's all-time top runner, the award is given to the National Collegiate Athletic Association Division 1-A player of the year.

3413. New York Giants National Football Conference championship came with a 17–0 defeat of the Washington Redskins at New York City on January 11, 1987.

3414. New York Giants win in professional football's Super Bowl was a 39–20 defeat of the Denver Broncos in Super Bowl XXI, on January 25, 1987, at Pasadena, California. Phil Simms of the Giants was named the game's Most Valuable Player.

3415. Miami Dolphins regular season football game played at Joe Robbie Stadium in Miami, Florida, was a 42–0 win over the Kansas City Chiefs, on October 11, 1987. The first score was a Dolphins touchdown, on a run by Ricky Isam. The stadium would be renamed the Pro Player Stadium in 1996.

3416. National Football League player to receive at least one touchdown pass in 13 consecutive games was Jerry Rice of the San Francisco 49ers, in a streak running from December 19, 1986, to December 27, 1987.

3417. African-American college football player to win the Butkus Award as the country's best linebacker was Derrick Thomas of the University of Alabama, in 1988.

3418. National Collegiate Athletic Association major college football player to gain 2,628 yards in a single season was Barry Sanders of Oklahoma State University, in 1988. Sanders also scored a record total of 234 points passing and rushing, averaged a record 39 points per game, gained a recordbreaking 300 yards or more rushing in four games, and scored a recordbreaking 37 touchdowns. After the regular season ended, he became the first college football player in a major bowl game to score 30 points, against the University of Wyoming, in the 1988 Holiday Bowl.

3419. African-American quarterback to play in and to win football's Super Bowl was Doug Williams, who led the Washington Redskins to a 42–10 victory over the Denver Broncos, in Super Bowl XXII, on January 31, 1988, in San Diego, California. Williams was named the game's Most Valuable Player.

3420. Professional football player to rush for 204 yards in a single Super Bowl game was Timmy Smith of the Washington Redskins, in the Redskins' 42–10 Super Bowl XXII win over the Denver Broncos, on January 31, 1988, at San Diego, California.

FOOTBALL, AMERICAN—(1980-1989)—
continued

3421. Phoenix Cardinals regular season football game played at Sun Devil Stadium in Tempe, Arizona, was a 17–14 loss to the Dallas Cowboys, on September 12, 1988. The first score was a Cowboys field goal, kicked by Luis Zendejas. The team would be called the Arizona Cardinals starting in 1994.

3422. National Collegiate Athletic Association major college team to gain 768 yards rushing in a single game was the University of Oklahoma, against Kansas State University, on October 15, 1988.

3423. College football player to score 30 points in a major bowl game was Barry Sanders, of Oklahoma State University, against the University of Wyoming, on December 30, 1988, in the Holiday Bowl.

3424. National Collegiate Athletic Association major college football player to gain 510 yards in a single half of a game was Andre Ware of the University of Houston, against Southern Methodist University, in 1989.

3425. National Collegiate Athletic Association major college football player to receive 141 passes in a single season was Manny Hazard of the University of Houston, in 1989.

3426. National Collegiate Athletic Association major college team to gain 6,874 all-purpose yards in a single season was the University of Houston, in 1989.

3427. College football player to receive for 252 yards in a major bowl game was Andre Rison of Michigan State University, against the University of Georgia, on January 1, 1989, in the Gator Bowl.

3428. Professional football player to gain 215 yards receiving in a single Super Bowl game was Jerry Rice of the San Francisco 49ers, in the 49ers' 20–18 Super Bowl XXIII win over the Cincinnati Bengals, on January 22, 1989, at Miami, Florida. Rice was named the game's Most Valuable Player.

3429. Professional football player to gain 357 yards passing in a single Super Bowl game was Joe Montana of the San Francisco 49ers, in the 49ers' 20–18 Super Bowl XXIII win over the Cincinnati Bengals, on January 22, 1989, at Miami, Florida.

3430. National Collegiate Athletic Association major college team to gain 1,021 all-purpose yards in a single game was the University of Houston, against Southern Methodist University, on October 21, 1989.

3431. National Football League player to receive for 336 yards in a single game was Willie Anderson of the Los Angeles Rams, against the New Orleans Saints, on November 26, 1989.

3432. College football player to gain 280 yards rushing in a major bowl game was James Gray of Texas Tech University, against Duke University, on December 28, 1989, in the All-American Bowl.

3433. College football player to gain 594 all-purpose yards in a major bowl game was Ty Detmer of Brigham Young University, against Pennsylvania State University on December 29, 1989, in the Holiday Bowl.

3434. College football team to gain 576 yards passing in a major bowl game was Brigham Young University, against Pennsylvania State University, on December 29, 1989, in the Holiday Bowl.

3435. Copper Bowl football game was played on December 31, 1989, at Arizona Stadium, in Tucson, Arizona, between the University of Arizona and North Carolina State University. Arizona won, 17–10.

FOOTBALL, AMERICAN (1990-1999)

3436. Doak Walker National Running Back Award was given to Greg Lewis of the University of Washington, in 1990. Named after Heisman Trophy winner Doak Walker, the award is given to the top major college junior or senior running back of the year.

3437. National Collegiate Athletic Association major college football player to complete 54 touchdown passes in a single season was David Klingler of the University of Houston, in 1990.

3438. National Collegiate Athletic Association major college football player to gain more than 400 yards per game in five consecutive games was Ty Detmer of Brigham Young University, in 1990.

3439. Professional football player to kick seven points after touchdown in a single Super Bowl game was Mike Cofer of the San Francisco 49ers, in the 49ers' 55–10 Super Bowl XXIV win over the Denver Broncos, on January 28, 1990, at New Orleans, Louisiana.

3440. Professional football player to complete 13 consecutive passes in a single Super Bowl game was Joe Montana of the San Francisco 49ers, in the 49ers' 55–10 Super Bowl XXIV win over the Denver Broncos, on January 29, 1990, at New Orleans, Louisiana. He was named the game's Most Valuable Player.

3441. National Collegiate Athletic Association major college football player to score eight rushing touchdowns in a single game was Howard Griffith of the University of Illinois, against Southern Illinois University, on September 22, 1990.

3442. National Football League player to make seven sacks in a single game was Derrick Thomas of the Kansas City Chiefs, against the Seattle Seahawks, on November 11, 1990.

3443. National Collegiate Athletic Association major college team to score 11 passing touchdowns in a single game was the University of Houston, against Eastern Washington University, on November 17, 1990.

3444. National Collegiate Athletic Association major college football player to gain 5,221 yards in a single year was David Klingler of the University of Houston, in 1990. Klingler also gained 732 yards in a single game against Arizona State University, on December 2, 1990.

3445. Carquest Bowl football game was played on December 28, 1990, at Joe Robbie Stadium, in Miami Florida, between Florida State University and Pennsylvania State University. Florida State won, 24–17. The game was later renamed the Micron PC Bowl.

3446. Heritage Bowl African-American college football game was between Alabama State College and North Carolina A&T, in Atlanta, Georgia, in 1991. It was won by Alabama State, 36–13.

3447. National Collegiate Athletic Association major college football player to gain 15,397 college career yards was Ty Detmer of Brigham Young University, from 1988 to 1991. Detmer also set records with 958 passes and 121 touchdown passes during his college career.

3448. National Collegiate Athletic Association major college football player to gain more than 4,000 yards per season three times was Ty Detmer of Brigham Young University, from 1989 to 1991.

3449. National Football League player to complete 404 passes in a single season was Warren Moon of the Houston Oilers, in 1991.

3450. World Bowl championship of the World League of American Football was held in 1991, when the London Monarchs defeated the Barcelona Dragons 21–0.

3451. World League of American Football was founded in 1991 by the National Football League (NFL) as a spring league with teams in Europe and the Americas. It would last only until 1993, but then would be replaced in 1995 by a European league for American-style football.

3452. Buffalo Bills American Football Conference championship came with a 51–3 victory over the Los Angeles Raiders at Buffalo, New York, on January 20, 1991.

3453. Lou Groza Collegiate Place Kicker Award was given to Joe Allison of the University of Memphis, in 1992. Named after top National Football League kicker Lou Groza, the award is given to the top college kicker of the year.

3454. Atlanta Falcons regular season football game played at the Georgia Dome in Atlanta, Georgia, was a 20–17 win over the New York Jets, on September 6, 1992. The first score was a Falcons field goal, kicked by Norm Johnson.

3455. Las Vegas Bowl football game was played on December 18, 1992, at Sam Boyd Stadium, in Las Vegas, Nevada, between Bowling Green University and the University of Nevada. Bowling Green won, 35–34.

3456. Bronko Nagurski Award was given to Rob Waldrop of the University of Arizona, in 1993. Named after National Football League Hall of Fame lineman Bronko Nagurski, the award is given to the top college defensive player of the year.

3457. Team to win four consecutive American Football Conference championships was the Buffalo Bills, for the seasons 1990 to 1993.

3458. Alamo Bowl football game was played on December 31, 1993, at the Alamodome, in San Antonio, Texas, between the University of California and the University of Iowa. California won, 37–3.

3459. Fred Biletnikoff Receiver Award was given to Bobb Engram of Pennsylvania State Unversity, in 1994. Named after top receiver Fred Biletnikoff, a college and professional Hall-of-Famer, the award is given to the top college receiver of the year.

3460. Professional football player to complete 31 passes in a single Super Bowl game was Jim Kelly of the Buffalo Bills, in the Bills' 30–13 Super Bowl XXVIII loss to the Dallas Cowboys on January 30, 1994, at Atlanta, Georgia.

FOOTBALL, AMERICAN—(1990-1999)—
continued

3461. National Collegiate Athletic Association major college football player to gain 347 yards in a single quarter was Jason Davis of the University of Nevada at Las Vegas, against the University of Idaho, on September 17, 1994.

3462. National Collegiate Athletic Association major college football player to receive 23 passes in a single game was Randy Gatewood of the University of Nevada at Las Vegas, against the University of Idaho, on September 17, 1994.

3463. National Football League player to complete 45 passes in a single game was Drew Bledsoe of the New England Patriots, against the Minnesota Vikings, on November 13, 1994.

3464. National Collegiate Athletic Association major college football player to kick 71 consecutive points after touchdown in a single season was Bart Edmiston of the University of Florida, in 1995.

3465. National Football League player to receive 123 passes in a single season was Herman Moore of the Detroit Lions, in 1995.

3466. National Football League player to receive for 1,848 yards in a single season was Jerry Rice of the San Francisco 49ers, in 1995.

3467. National Football League player to score 25 touchdowns rushing in a single season was Emmitt Smith of the Dallas Cowboys, in 1995.

3468. Professional football coach to win 328 games was Don Shula, who amassed his enduring winning record while head coach of the Baltimore Colts (1963–1969) and the Miami Dolphins (1970–1995).

3469. College football player to gain 359 all-purpose yards in a major bowl game was Sherman Williams of the University of Alabama, against Ohio State University, on January 2, 1995, in the Florida Citrus Bowl.

3470. Jacksonville Jaguars regular season football game played at the ALLTEL Stadium in Jacksonville, Florida, was a 10–3 loss to the Houston Oilers, on September 3, 1995.

3471. National Collegiate Athletic Association major college football player to complete 55 passes in a single game was Rusty LaRue of Wake Forest University, against Duke University, on October 28, 1995.

3472. St. Louis Rams regular season football game played at the Trans World Dome in St. Louis, Missouri, was a 28–17 win over the Carolina Panthers, on November 12, 1995. The first score was a one-yard St. Louis touchdown run by Jerome Bettis.

3473. National Football League player to gain a total of 404 yards running in a single game was Glyn Milburn of the Seattle Seahawks, against the Denver Broncos, on December 10, 1995.

3474. National Collegiate Athletic Association major college football player to gain 4,518 yards receiving during his college career was Marcus Harris of the University of Wyoming, from 1993 to 1996.

3475. National Football League player to kick 37 field goals in a single season was John Kasey of the Carolina Panthers, in 1996.

3476. College football team to gain 524 yards rushing in a major bowl game was the University of Nebraska, against the University of Florida, on January 2, 1996, in the Fiesta Bowl.

3477. Carolina Panthers regular season football game played at Ericsson Stadium in Charlotte, North Carolina, was a 29–6 win over the Atlanta Falcons, on September 1, 1996. The first score was a Panthers touchdown reception by Mark Carrier.

3478. National Collegiate Athletic Association major college football player to score touchdowns on pass receptions in 12 consecutive games was Randy Moss of Marshall College, in 1997.

3479. National Football League player to lead the league six times in completed passes was Dan Marino of the Miami Dolphins, between 1984 and 1997.

3480. Green Bay Packers National Football Conference championship came with a 30–13 victory over the Carolina Panthers at Green Bay, Wisconsin, on January 12, 1997.

3481. National Football League player to gain 99 yards with a single Super Bowl punt return was Desmond Howard of the Green Bay Packers, in the Packers' 35–21 Super Bowl XXXI win over the New England Patriots, on January 26, 1997, at New Orleans, Louisiana. He was named the game's Most Valuable Player.

3482. Washington Redskins regular season football game played at Jack Kent Cooke Stadium in Landover, Maryland, was a 19–13 sudden-death overtime victory over the Arizona Cardinals on September 14, 1997. It would later be renamed FedEx Field.

3483. National Football League player to rush for 100 or more yards in ten consecutive games was Barry Sanders of the Detroit Lions, from September 14, 1997 to December, 21, 1997.

3484. Motor City Bowl football game was played on December 26, 1997, at the Pontiac Silverdome, in Pontiac, Michigan, between the University of Mississippi and Marshall University. Mississippi won, 34–31.

3485. Humanitarian Bowl football game was played on December 29, 1997, at Bronco Stadium, in Boise, Idaho, between the University of Cincinnati and Utah State University. Cincinnati won, 35–19.

3486. National Collegiate Athletic Association major college football player to complete 400 passes in a single season was Tim Couch of the University of Kentucky, in 1998.

3487. National Collegiate Athletic Association major college football player to gain 1,996 yards receiving in a single season was Troy Edwards of Louisiana Tech University, in 1998.

3488. National Collegiate Athletic Association major college football player to receive 295 passes during his college career was Geoff Noisy of the University of Nevada, from 1995 to 1998.

3489. National Collegiate Athletic Association major college football player to rush for 6,279 college career yards was Ricky Williams of the University of Texas, from 1995 to 1998. Williams also gained a recordbreaking 7,206 all-purpose yards and scored a record 72 touchdowns during his college career.

3490. National Football League defensive player to reach 192.5 career sacks was Reggie White, from 1985 to 1998.

3491. National Football League kicker to have a perfect season was Gary Anderson of the Minnesota Vikings, in 1998. Anderson kicked all 35 of his 35 field goal attempts, and all 59 of his 59 point after touchdown attempts, scoring a total of 164 points, the largest number of points scored by any NFL kicker in a single season.

3492. National Football League kicker to reach 420 career field goals was Gary Anderson of the Minnesota Vikings, from 1982 to 1998. He added 19 more in 1999, in a continuing career.

3493. National Football League player to gain 1,000 or more yards rushing in ten consecutive years was Barry Sanders of the Detroit Lions, from 1989 to 1998.

3494. College football player to complete 19 consecutive passes in a major bowl game was Mike Bobo of the University of Georgia, against the University of Wisconsin, on January 1, 1998, in the Outback Bowl.

3495. College football team to win two consecutive Gator Bowl games was the University of North Carolina, which defeated Virginia Tech 42–3 on January 1, 1998, after besting the University of West Virginia 20–13 in 1997.

3496. Denver Broncos win in professional football's Super Bowl was a 31–24 defeat of the Green Bay Packers in Super Bowl XXXII, on January 25, 1998, at San Diego, California. Terrell Davis of the Broncos was named the game's Most Valuable Player.

3497. National Collegiate Athletic Association major college football player to gain 405 yards receiving in a single game was Troy Edwards of Louisiana Tech University, against the University of Nebraska, on August 29, 1998.

3498. Baltimore Ravens regular season game played in the PSINet Stadium in Baltimore, Maryland, was a 20–13 loss to the Pittsburgh Steelers, on September 6, 1998. The first score was a Pittsburgh field goal, kicked by Norm Johnson. Formerly the Cleveland Browns, the team had been moved to Maryland in 1996.

3499. Tampa Bay Buccaneers regular season football game played at Raymond James Stadium in Tampa Bay, Florida, was a 27–15 win over the Chicago Bears, on September 20, 1998. The first score was a Chicago field goal, kicked by Jeff Jaeger.

3500. National Collegiate Athletic Association major college football player to complete 23 consecutive passes in a single game was Tee Martin of the University of Tennessee, against the University of South Carolina, on October 31, 1998.

3501. National Football League player to receive a pass in 193 consecutive games was Jerry Rice of the San Francisco 49ers, from December 9, 1985, to December 27, 1998.

3502. Music City Bowl football game was played on December 29, 1998, at Vanderbilt Stadium, in Nashville, Tennessee, between Virginia Tech and the University of Alabama. Virginia Tech won, 38–7.

3503. National Collegiate Athletic Association (NCAA) major college football player to rush for 6,397 college career yards was Ron Dayne of the University of Wisconsin, from 1996 to 1999. Dayne also won the 1999 Heisman Trophy.

FOOTBALL, AMERICAN—(1990-1999)—
continued

3504. National Football League player to reach 18,442 career receiving yards was Jerry Rice of the San Francisco 49ers, from 1983 to 1999.

3505. National Football League player to reach a career total of 1,206 passes received was Jerry Rice of the San Francisco 49ers, from 1985 to 1999.

3506. National Football League player to receive 169 career touchdowns was Jerry Rice of the San Francisco 49ers, from 1985 to 1999.

3507. National Football League player to score 136 career touchdowns rushing was Emmitt Smith of the Dallas Cowboys, from 1990 to 1999.

3508. Atlanta Falcons National Football Conference championship came with a 30–27 defeat of the Minnesota Vikings at Minneapolis, Minnesota, on January 17, 1999.

3509. National Football League game played in Australia was the "American Bowl" exhibition game, played at the new Olympic Stadium at Sydney, Australia, on August 8, 1999. The Denver Broncos defeated the San Diego Chargers, 20–17.

3510. Cleveland Browns regular season game played in the Cleveland Browns Stadium in Cleveland, Ohio, was a 43–0 loss to the Pittsburgh Steelers, on September 12, 1999. The first score in the new stadium was a one-yard touchdown run by Pittsburgh quarterback Kordell Stewart. The new Browns team and the stadium were making a joint regular-season debut; the previous Browns had been moved to Maryland in 1996, to become the Baltimore Ravens.

3511. Tennessee Titans regular season football game played at the Adelphia Coliseum in Nashville, Tennessee, was a 36–35 win over the Cincinnati Bengals, on September 12, 1999. The first score was a Titans touchdown, on a one-yard touchdown run by quarterback Steve McNair.

3512. National Football League player to pass for 60,000 career yards was Dan Marino of the Miami Dolphins, who reached that mark during a 31–30 Miami win over the New England Patriots on October 17, 1999.

FOOTBALL, AMERICAN (2000-)

3513. St. Louis Rams Super Bowl win was a 23–16 victory over the Tennessee Titans in a game played on January 30, 2000, at the Georgia Dome in Atlanta, Georgia. Previously unheralded Rams quarterback Kurt Warner was named the game's Most Valuable Player, with a Super Bowl–record of 414 yards passing, to go with his regular season MVP award.

3514. Cincinnati Bengals regular season football game played at Paul Brown Stadium in Cincinnati, Ohio, was a 24–7 loss to the Cleveland Browns on September 10, 2000.

FOOTBALL, AUSTRALIAN RULES

3515. Australian rules football was developed as a distinct sport primarily at the Melbourne Football Club, founded in 1858, with the two key figures in its development being Henry Colden Harrison and Thomas Wills.

3516. State organization for Australian rules football was the Victorian Football Association, founded in 1877.

3517. Inter-state game in Australian rules football was in 1879, between Victoria and South Australia.

3518. Grand final for Australian rules football was played in 1897 at the Melbourne Cricket Ground, the traditional home of what became an annual event. The winning team was from Essendon.

3519. Inter-state carnival in Australian rules football effectively a national championship, was held in 1908, when the winner was from the state of Victoria.

FOOTBALL, CANADIAN

3520. Football game on record in Canada was played in 1861 between teams of students from the University of Toronto. Canadian-style football would be similar to American-style, but would have 12, rather than 11, members on a team.

3521. Professional league for Canadian-style football was the Canadian Football League (CFL), founded in 1958.

FOOTBALL, GAELIC

3522. Gaelic football match on record was in 1712 in Slane, Ireland, between teams from Meath and Louth. The 15-a-side game has affinities to soccer, Australian rules football, and rugby.

3523. Code of rules for Gaelic football was established in Ireland in 1884 by the newly formed Gaelic Athletic Association.

3524. All-Ireland championships in Gaelic football for the Sam Maguire Cup were held in 1887 in Croke Park in Dublin. They would be held annually after that on the third Sunday of September.

FRISBEE (FLYING DISC)

3525. Frisbee was marketed in 1958 in the United States. However, similar flying discs had been made and used under other names from at least the 1930s and perhaps earlier. The version that became the Frisbee had originally been developed by Fred Morrison in California in 1948.

3526. International Frisbee Tournament was held in Escanaba, Michigan, in 1958.

3527. Ultimate a game played with a Frisbee, was developed in 1968 at Columbia High School in Maplewood, New Jersey.

3528. Intercollegiate Ultimate match a team Frisbee game, was played on November 6, 1972, at New Brunswick, New Jersey, between teams from Rutgers and Princeton universities.

3529. World Flying Disc Conference was held in 1985 in Helsingborg, Sweden. Out of this came the World Flying Disc Federation.

G

GLIDING

3530. International governing body for gliding (soaring) competitions was the Fédération Aéronautique Internationale (FAI), founded in 1905. Gliders had been developed in Germany in the 1890s by Otto Lilienthal.

3531. World championships in gliding (soaring) were held in Wasserkuppe, Germany, in 1937. The men-only open competition was won by Heini Dittmar of Germany. Other events would be added later to the biennial championships.

3532. National championships for gliding (soaring) in the United States were held in Angeles National Forest near Sylmar, California, on October 25, 1973. The inaugural winner was Chris Wills, a pre-medical student.

3533. World championships in hang gliding were held in 1976 in Kössen, Austria, for men only. Christian Steinbach of Austria won the Class I Standard competition, Terry Dolore of New Zealand the Class II High Aspect Ratio, and Ken Battle of Australia the Class III Open. Austria won the team title. A separate women's championship would be held from 1987.

3534. World championships in hang gliding for women were held in 1987. The inaugural individual champion was Judy Leden of Great Britain, who would also win the next competition, in 1991.

GOLF (BEFORE 1700)

3535. Written reference to golf was in 1457 when King James II and the Parliament of Scotland banned the playing of golf (then called *gowf* or *goff*) and football (then called *fut bawe* or *futball*; in the United States later known as soccer) on the grounds that these sports diverted men from training for battle. The ban would be reaffirmed by Scots Parliaments under James III in 1470 and James IV in 1491, and would not be lifted until 1502. In practice, the playing of both golf and football seems to have continued.

3536. Purchase of golf equipment on record was a set of golf clubs and balls, bought in February 1502 by Scotland's King James IV from a bow-maker in Perth, Scotland.

3537. Golf reference on record in England was in 1513, when England's Queen Catherine of Aragon, wife of Henry VIII, commented on the sport's growing popularity in a letter to Cardinal Wolsey. The sport was believed to have been introduced to England by Scotland's King James IV, who married England's Princess Margaret Tudor in 1503.

3538. Confirmation of the public's right to play golf was in 1552. In the St. Andrews Charter, Bishop Hamilton of St. Andrews, Scotland, affirmed the right of the local people to play golf on the links at St. Andrews, now the most venerated site in golfdom.

3539. Woman golfer on record was Mary, Queen of Scots, who was reported to have played the game in 1567, just a few days after her husband, Lord Darnley, was murdered. Mary had young pages carry her bags; French-raised, she called them by the French term *cadets*, which probably gave rise to the term *caddie*.

3540. Confirmation of people's right to play golf and other sports on Sundays was in 1618 by edict of King James, VI of Scotland and I of England. His son, King Charles I of England, would affirm the proclamation in 1633. Charles would be playing golf in 1641 when he learned of the rebellion against him and would play golf while imprisoned, from at least 1646 until his execution in 1649.

GOLF—(BEFORE 1700)—continued

3541. Patent for a golf ball was granted in 1618 to William Berwick by King James, VI of Scotland and I of England. Called the "feathery" ball, it was made by stuffing boiled feathers into a soaked leather sphere, which shrank as it dried, while the feathers expanded. Requiring both time and skill, the balls were expensive, limiting the number of people who could afford to play the game. They did not fly as far as modern golf balls, the longest drive ever recorded with a feathery ball being 361 yards in 1836.

3542. Death in a golf accident on record was in 1632, when Thomas Clatto died after being hit in the head by a golf ball while watching a golf match in a churchyard in Kelso, Scotland.

3543. Golf book was written in 1636 by David Wedderburn, who wrote it in the form of a Latin Grammar for use in Scotland's Aberdeen Grammar School, where he was master.

3544. License for producing golf balls was granted to John Dickson of Aberdeen, Scotland, in 1642.

3545. International golf match was in 1682, when the Duke of York (later James VII of Scotland and James II of England) and shoemaker John Paterson, both of Scotland, defeated two English aristocrats on the links at Leith, Scotland.

GOLF (1700-1799)

3546. Golf course in the west of Scotland was Glasgow Green, first referred to in 1721. However, golf had been played in the region from at least the 1500s.

3547. Golf match reported in a newspaper was in 1724 between Captain John Porteous and Alexander Elphinstone, described in an English newspaper.

3548. Literary work about golf was *The Goff*, written in the form of a mock epic poem, by Thomas Mathison, in 1743.

3549. Golf club was founded in 1744 by the Company of Gentlemen Golfers in Edinburgh, Scotland. In 1800, Edinburgh would charter the group as the Honourable Company of Edinburgh Golfers. The Gentlemen Golfers played primarily at Leith, but also elsewhere, for they were always short of space. In 1836 they would forsake the badly deteriorated links of Leith for Musselburgh, and then in 1891 would create the course at Muirfield.

3550. Open competition in golf was played on the links at Leith in 1744, with the City of Edinburgh offering a Silver Club as the challenge trophy. The first winner of what would become an annual competition was John Rattray, an Edinburgh surgeon.

3551. Golf rules on record were written down on March 7, 1744, by the Company of Gentlemen Golfers at Edinburgh, Scotland. They would be the basis for the first published code of golf rules in 1754 by the Society of St. Andrews Golfers, in St. Andrews, Scotland.

3552. Golf rules to be published were produced by the Society of St. Andrews Golfers, in St. Andrews, Scotland, in 1754. They were based on the 1744 rules developed by the Company of Gentlemen Golfers at Edinburgh, Scotland. St. Andrews would later become the international authority on golf rules, except for the United States and Mexico.

3553. Open golf competition at St. Andrews, Scotland was held in 1754, with the prize being a Silver Club, modeled on that offered from 1744 by Edinburgh. Bailie William Landale, a St. Andrews merchant, won the first competition, played on the Old Course at St. Andrews, then called the Pilmor Links. From 1834, by command of King William IV, the society would be known as the Royal and Ancient Golf Club of St. Andrews.

3554. Stroke play game recorded in golf was in 1759, at St. Andrews, Scotland. Before that, all recorded golf games were match play.

3555. Golf course with 18 holes was established in 1764 at St. Andrews, Scotland; it would become the model for the sport. Before that the number of holes had varied; at St. Andrews, the course earlier had had 22 holes (11 out and 11 back), before the first four holes were combined into two, for a total of 18 (9 out and 9 back). Many other courses at that time had as few as 5 or 7 holes.

3556. Restriction of golf competition to club members was in 1764, when the Honourable Company of Edinburgh Golfers allowed only its members to compete in the annual tournament at Leith, Scotland, for the Silver Cup. Nine years later, the course at St. Andrews was restricted to members of the St. Andrews and Leith clubs.

3557. Golf club outside Scotland was the Blackheath Club, established in 1766 outside London, England.

3558. Golf clubhouse was built in 1768 at Leith, Scotland, called the Golf House. Before then, early golf clubs often met at taverns near their golf courses, or links.

3559. Golf course professional was hired by the Royal Burgess Golfing Society of Edinburgh, Scotland, in 1774. He worked part-time and doubled as greenskeeper at the course, established just a year earlier. Most early golf professionals would do double and triple duty, often making golf balls and serving as caddies.

3560. Golf game on record in North America was in 1779, when Scottish soldiers played the game while stationed in New York City during the Revolutionary War.

3561. Golf club in the Americas, and the first outside Great Britain was the South Carolina Golf Club, established in Charleston, South Carolina, in 1786.

GOLF (1800-1849)
3562. Golf competition for women on record was on January 9, 1811, when the golf club at Musselburgh, Scotland, held a competition for local women, many of them fisherwomen.

3563. Importation of North American hickory to Britain for golf clubs was in approximately 1825. Both tough and flexible, hickory would be the dominant material used in golf clubs until the introduction of steel shafts a century later.

3564. Golf club in Asia was the Calcutta Golf Club (later the Royal Calcutta), established in Calcutta, India, in 1829.

3565. Golf club to include women in its regular activities was the North Berwick Club in Scotland in 1832. However, women were not allowed to enter golfing competitions.

3566. Golf club to be awarded the title "Royal" was the Perth Golfing Society in 1833. Founded in Perth, Scotland, in 1824, it became the Royal Perth by command of King William IV. The following year, the St. Andrews club would receive the title of "Royal and Ancient."

3567. Golf ball made of gutta-percha was developed in 1848 at St. Andrews, Scotland, by golf enthusiast James Patterson, using a rubbery material that had served as the packing around a Hindu statue shipped from Malaya. Known as "gutties," such balls flew much farther than feathery balls; they also lasted longer and were less expensive, making golf even more widely popular.

GOLF (1850-1899)
3568. Course specifically designed for golf was established in Prestwick, Scotland, in 1851, designed by Tom Morris, Sr., popularly known as "Old Tom." The first twelve British Opens (1860–1870 and 1872) would be played at Prestwick. Morris would win four of those, and his son, Tom Jr. ("Young Tom"), born the year of the move to Prestwick, would win another four.

3569. Golf club in Ireland was the Royal Curragh Golf Club, founded in Kildare in 1856.

3570. Golf club on the European mainland was the Pau Golf Club, founded in Pau, a resort town in southwestern France, in 1856.

3571. Book about how to play golf was *The Golfer's Manual*, published in 1857 by H. B. Farnie, writing as "A Keen Hand."

3572. Championship Meeting in golf was held at St. Andrews, Scotland, in 1857. Sparked by the Prestwick Golf Club, founded just six years earlier, it was attended by ten other clubs. The winners of the interclub foursome competition were George Glennie and J. C. Stewart from Blackheath.

3573. Championship Meeting in golf employing the individual match play format was held at St. Andrews, Scotland, in 1858. The winner was Robert Chambers of Brunstfield.

3574. Golfer to score under 80 at the Old Course at St. Andrews, Scotland was Allan Robertson, who scored 79 in 1858. The first great professional golfer, he would die just a year later. Others before him were golf professionals, including his grandfather, Peter Robertson, who lived until 1803. The family's recorded connections to golf dated back to 1610, when the daughter of a St. Andrews golf ball maker, Thomas Buddo, married into the Robertson family, which came to include generations of golf professionals and makers of golf balls. Allan Robertson, a noted maker of feathery balls, tried to block production and acceptance of the gutta-percha balls introduced in 1848, for they undercut his livelihood.

3575. Amateur golf championship was held in Scotland in 1859. The tournament was won by George Condie of Perth.

3576. British Open golf tournament was held on a single day, October 17, 1860, when eight golfers played 36 holes on the links at Prestwick, Scotland, with the winner being Willie Park, Sr. Sponsored by the Prestwick Golf Club, which offered the first Open Championship Belt, the tournament was initially called

GOLF—(1850-1899)—*continued*

the Open Professional Golf Championship and limited to professionals. One-to-one match play had been the usual format in golf up to this point, but this first Open would set the pattern for the stroke play golf which would come to predominate.

3577. Golfer to win the British Open was Willie Park, Sr., of Musselburgh, Scotland, who led a field of eight golfers at Prestwick, Scotland, on October 17, 1860. Founder of a golf dynasty, he would later win the championship three more times (1863, 1866 and 1875), while his brother Mungo Park (not related to the explorer) would win in 1874 and his son, Willie Park, Jr., would win in 1887 and 1889.

3578. British Open golf championship open to amateurs was held at Prestwick, Scotland, in 1861. It was won by Tom Morris, Sr., who had been runner-up in 1860, when the tournament was limited to golf professionals, and who would win three of the next six Open tournaments. Originally an apprentice to Allan Robertson, considered the first great golf professional, he was popularly known as "Old Tom," because his son, "Young Tom," would also win four British Open titles.

3579. Golfer to win the British Open championship twice in a row was Tom Morris, Sr., in 1861 and 1862, both at Prestwick, Scotland. Widely known as "Old Tom," he would win the title twice more, in 1864 and 1867.

3580. Golf club for women was the Ladies' Golf Club founded at St. Andrews, Scotland, in 1867. In many golf clubs in those years, women played on the courses only on days when men were barred from the club. Wearing long full skirts with voluminous petticoats, women golfers often played shorter courses than men did.

3581. Golfer to win four British Open championships was Tom Morris, Sr., who won in 1867, after earlier wins in 1861, 1862, and 1864, all at Prestwick, Scotland. He was popularly called "Old Tom" Morris, to distinguish him from his equally noted son, "Young Tom," who would win the next four British Open titles (1868–1870 and 1872; no tournament was held in 1871).

3582. Golfer under the age of 20 to win the British Open championship was Tom Morris, Jr., in 1868, who was only 17 years, 5 months, and 8 days old when he won in Prestwick, Scotland, with a 36-hole score of 154. Popularly known as "Young Tom," he had been brought up on the Prestwick course, designed by his father, Tom Morris, Sr. ("Old Tom"), who was also a four-time winner of the British Open.

3583. Golf club in Australia was the Royal Adelaide Golf Club, established in Adelaide in 1870.

3584. Golfer to win the British Open championship three times in a row all at Prestwick, Scotland, was "Young Tom" Morris (1868, 1869, and 1870), so-called because his father, "Old Tom" Morris, had been a previous champion. Young Morris's three wins meant that he could keep the Open Championship Belt permanently. His 36-hole total of 149 in 1870 would not be bettered until the 20th century. His margin of victory was 12 strokes, astonishing in only 36 holes.

3585. Golfer to win the British Open championship four times in a row was Tom Morris, Jr., whose fourth title came in 1872, when he was the first to be presented with the now-famous Claret Jug. After three straight titles (1868–1870), he had been given the Open Championship Belt to keep permanently. No tournament was held in 1871, because no trophy was offered. The Claret Jug was the new trophy, offered by golf clubs at Prestwick, St. Andrews, and Edinburgh. All four of "Young Tom" Morris's titles were won at Prestwick, Scotland, on the course designed by his father, Tom Morris, Sr. ("Old Tom"), also a four-time British Open winner. One key to Young Morris's success was his specially designed irons, which he used for far wider purposes than earlier players, so that many consider him the first modern professional golfer.

3586. British Open golf championship held at the Old Course at St. Andrews, Scotland was in 1873. The 36-hole championship was won by Tom Kidd with a score of 179. All previous British Opens had been held at the Prestwick Golf Club, but starting in 1873 the Open would rotate between Prestwick, the Royal and Ancient Golf Club of St. Andrews, and the Honourable Company of Edinburgh Golfers, all in Scotland.

3587. Golf club in Canada was the Royal Montreal Golf Club, established in 1873. Its first president was Alexander Dennistoun of Scotland.

3588. British Open golf championship held at Musselburgh, Scotland was in 1874, under a rotating championship pattern established the year before, when the first British Open was held at St. Andrews, Scotland. All previous British Opens had been held at Prestwick, Scotland. Musselburgh was the home course for several notable golf clubs, including the Honourable Company of Edinburgh Golfers, the Royal Burgess Club, the Bruntsfield Links Club, and the Royal Musselburgh Club.

3589. University golf clubs were established at Oxford and Cambridge universities in England in 1875.

3590. Golfer to win the British Open after a default in a playoff was Robert Martin in 1876 at St. Andrews, Scotland. At the end of 36 holes, Martin was tied with David Strath; when Strath refused to participate in a playoff, Martin was declared the winner by default.

3591. University golf match was played on the London Scottish Golf Club course at Wimbledon, England, in 1878. It was won by Oxford University.

3592. Golf balls manufactured with "dimples" were made in 1880. Moulds were developed to simulate used balls, after golfers found that the gutta-percha balls flew better through the air after they had been hit a few times.

3593. Golfer to win the British Open in a playoff was Willie Fernie, who defeated Robert Ferguson to take the title in 1883 at Musselburgh, Scotland. Earlier, in 1876, Robert Martin had been declared the winner by default when David Strath, with whom he was tied, refused to participate in a playoff.

3594. British Amateur Championship was held in 1885, sponsored by the Royal Liverpool Club and played on their home course at Hoylake, England. The first winner was A. F. Macfie, a Scot who had moved south and become a member of the Liverpool Club.

3595. Golf club in Africa was the Royal Cape Golf Club, founded at Wynberg, South Africa, in 1885.

3596. Golf course in the United States opened at the St. Andrews Golf Club, in Yonkers, New York, on March 30, 1889. John T. Reid had created the six-hole course out of a former cow pasture.

3597. Amateur, and the first non-Scot, to win the British Open golf championship was John Ball, Jr., of England, who won at Prestwick, Scotland, in 1890, with a 36-hole score of 164.

3598. Bogey as a score in golf was invented by Hugh Rotherham in 1890. Originally it represented a hypothetically perfect score for each hole. In the 20th century, after the rubber-cored ball was developed, golfers' scores began to drop, so the bogey came to refer to a score that was one over par for a hole.

3599. British Open championship held at Muirfield, Scotland was in 1892. The champion was Harold Hilton. Previously the British Open had generally consisted of 36 holes, but from 1892 on it would be played in 72 holes.

3600. Golf clubhouse in the United States was established in 1892 at Shinnecock Hills Golf Club, which had been founded the previous year in Southampton, New York, on Long Island. The clubhouse was designed by the noted architect Stanford White.

3601. Golf match to charge fees for spectators was at Cambridge, England, in 1892, for a match between Douglas Rollard and Jack White. Gate receipts would gradually become a main source of prize money.

3602. International golf championship was the Amateur Golf Championship of India and the East, established in 1892.

3603. Golf course for women in the United States was opened at Shinnecock Hills Golf Club in 1893, just two years after the Long Island club's founding in Southampton, New York.

3604. British Ladies' Open Amateur golf championship was played in 1893, with the players going twice around a nine-hole course on the Old Links at Royal Lytham and St. Anne's, England. Sponsored by the just-founded Ladies' Golf Union, the tournament was won on June 13, 1893, by Lady Margaret Scott, who also won in 1894 and 1895. Participants included women from Ireland and France, as well as England, but none from Scotland would play in the championship until 1897.

3605. British Open golf tournament held in England was at Sandwich in 1894. It was won by English golf professional John Henry Taylor. All previous Opens had been held on Scottish courses.

3606. Golf clubs made in the United States were sold in 1894 by the A. G. Spalding & Bros. sporting goods company. Previously, players had used imported clubs, primarily from Scotland.

3607. Separate golf course for women in the United States was established in 1894 by women golfers in Morristown, New Jersey.

GOLF—(1850-1899)—*continued*

3608. National golf championship in the United States was held on September 3–4, 1894, at the Newport Golf Club, in Newport, Rhode Island. The winner was W. G. Lawrence. Another national championship was held that year at the St. Andrews Golf Club, in Yonkers, New York. Neither survived.

3609. National governing body for golf in the United States was the Amateur Golf Association of the United States founded, on December 22, 1894, by the Chicago Golf Club of Wheaton, Illinois; the Country Club of Brookline, Massachusetts; the Newport Golf Club of Newport, Rhode Island; the St. Andrews Golf Club of Yonkers, New York; and the Shinnecock Hills Golf Club, of Southampton, New York. Newport's Theodore A. Havemeyer was its first president. This would later become the United States Golf Association (USGA). With the Royal and Ancient Golf Club of St. Andrews, it would later help set and revise international rules for the game.

3610. Eighteen-hole golf course in the United States was opened by the Chicago Golf Club in Wheaton, Illinois, in 1895. It was designed by Charles Blair Macdonald.

3611. Golf book published in the United States was *Golf in America: A Practical Manual*, by James Lee, which appeared in 1895.

3612. Golf club on the West Coast of North America was the Tacoma Golf Club, founded in Washington in 1895.

3613. U.S. Amateur golf tournament was held on October 3, 1895, at the Newport Golf Club in Newport, Rhode Island. Charles B. Macdonald won the match play event; it would change to stroke play only in 1965.

3614. U.S. Open golf tournament was held on October 4, 1895, at the Newport Golf Club in Newport, Rhode Island. In a field of 12, Horace Rawlins was the first champion. He and other Scots golfers would dominate U.S. Open play in the early years. The tournament was sponsored by the Amateur Golf Association of the United States, the forerunner of the United States Golf Association (USGA).

3615. U.S. Women's Amateur golf tournament was held at the Meadow Brook Country Club in Westbury, New York, in November 1895. The winner of the 18-hole match-play event was Mrs. Charles Brown (her own first name was not recorded), over runner-up Nellie Sargent.

3616. Amateur golfer to win two British Open championships was Harold Hilton, who won his second at Hoylake, England, in 1897, after winning his first in 1892.

3617. Golfer to win the U.S. Amateur Championship twice in a row was H. J. Whigham. After his first win in 1896, he won his second straight title in the match play event in 1897 at the Chicago Golf Club in Wheaton, Illinois, defeating W. Rossiter Betts.

3618. Golfing magazine in North America was *Golf*, which began publication in 1897.

3619. Rules of Golf committee was established in 1897 by the Royal and Ancient Golf Club of St. Andrews, Scotland, representing leading golf clubs in Britain. St. Andrews would become recognized as the international authority for the game everywhere except in the United States and Mexico, where the final authority was the USGA (United States Golf Association).

3620. Intercollegiate golf association in the United States was founded in January 1897 by four universities: Columbia, Harvard, Princeton, and Yale.

3621. Intercollegiate golf tournament in the United States was held on May 13–14, 1897, at Ardsley Casino Golf Club in Ardsley, New York. The team title was won by Yale University and the individual champion was Louis Bayard, Jr., of Princeton University. It would be a match-play tournament through 1964.

3622. Golfer to win the U.S. Women's Amateur Championship twice, and then three times, in a row was Beatrix Hoyt, who won her second straight title on August 26, 1897, at the Essex Golf Club in Manchester, Massachusetts, after winning the event in 1896. Her third win would come on October 16, 1898, at the Ardsley Golf Club in Ardsley, New York.

3623. Rubber-cored golf ball, and the first golf ball manufactured in the United States was first sold in 1898. Designed by Coburn Haskell and sold by the A. G. Spalding & Bros sporting goods company, it had a solid rubber core, though some would later be made with a liquid core and would use various synthetic materials. Within a few years, they were widely adopted, especially after the ball was used by Walter J. Travis in winning his 1901 U.S. Amateur title and by Sandy Herd in winning the 1902 British Open.

3624. U.S. Open to use a 72-hole format was in 1898, at the Myopia Hunt Club in Hamilton, Massachusetts. The winner was Fred Herd, with a score of 328.

3625. Golf tee was patented in 1899 by George F. Grant, an African-American dentist, in Boston, Massachusetts. Before the tee was developed, players built small mounds of dirt to hold their golf balls.

3626. Western Open was played at Glen View Country Club in Golf, Illinois, in 1899. From this tournament would develop the Professional Golfers' Association (PGA) Tour, which would be founded in 1916.

3627. Golfer born in the United States to win a U.S. national championship was Herbert M. Harriman, who won the U.S. Amateur Golf Championship on July 8, 1899, at the Onwentsia Club, Lake Forest, Illinois, over defending champion Findlay S. Douglas.

GOLF (1900-1909)
3628. Golfer to win both the U.S. Open and British Open was Harry Vardon from Jersey, one of England's Channel Islands. He won the U.S. Open at the Chicago Golf Club in Wheaton, Illinois, in 1900. He had previously won British Open titles in 1896, 1898, and 1899, and would win three more, in 1903, 1911, and 1914. Vardon would also be noted for popularizing the overlapping grip named after him, most notably in his 1905 book *The Complete Golfer.*

3629. Men's golf event in the Olympic Games was in Paris, France, in 1900. The winner was Charles Sands of the United States on October 2. Golf would be played as an individual and team event in 1904, but then dropped from the Olympics.

3630. Women's golf event in the Olympic Games was in Paris, France, in 1900, the only time it was included. Margaret Abbott of the United States won the event on October 3, becoming the first American woman to win an Olympic gold medal, although she never realized that the tournament had been part of the Olympics.

3631. Association of professional golfers was the London and Counties Professional Golfers' Association, founded in Britain in 1901. The leader of the movement to organize Britain's professional golfers was John Henry Taylor, who had already won the British Open three times (1894, 1895, and 1900), and would win it twice more (1909 and 1913). As the Professional Golfers' Association, it would become the key association for British golf professionals.

3632. Golf course developed on cleared land, with grass grown entirely from seed was in Sunningdale, England, in 1901. Previously courses had generally been built in meadows or on coastal shores, and were often water-logged.

3633. Golfer to win a major tournament with a rubber-cored golf ball (the Haskell ball) was Walter J. Travis, who won the U.S. Amateur Championship at the Myopia Hunt Club in Hamilton, Massachusetts, in 1901. When golfers using the new ball won both the British Open (Sandy Herd) and the U.S. Open (Laurie Auchterlonie) in 1902, the Haskell ball's dominance was assured.

3634. Golfer to win the U.S. Open in a playoff was Willie Anderson of Scotland, who defeated Alex Smith 85–86 in a playoff on June 17, 1901, after they had tied at 331 for 72 holes at the Myopia Hunt Club in Hamilton, Massachusetts. Anderson would become the first golfer to win the U.S. Open four times, with later wins in 1903, 1904, and 1905.

3635. Golfer to shoot under 80 in all four rounds of the U.S. Open was Laurie Auchterlonie in 1902, who shot a total of 307 at the Garden City Golf Club in Garden City, New York. He used the new rubber-cored Haskell ball, helping to ensure its popularity.

3636. Golfer to win three men's U.S. Amateur titles was Walter J. Travis, who won his third in a match play event over Walter E. Egan in 1903 at the Nassau Country Club in Glen Cove, New York, after winning earlier titles in 1900 and 1901. Beatrix Hoyt had previously won three straight U.S. Women's Amateur titles (1896–1898).

3637. Golfer to win two U.S. Open championships was Willie Anderson of Scotland, who won his second title at Baltusrol Golf Club in Short Hills, New Jersey, in 1903. Anderson defeated David Brown 82–84 in a playoff, after they had tied at 307 in 72 holes. Anderson's first U.S. Open victory, in 1901, had also come in a playoff. He would win two more Open titles, in 1904 and 1905.

3638. Golfer from the United States to win the British Amateur Championship was Walter J. Travis in 1904, at Royal St. George's in Sandwich, England.

3639. Golfer to win the British Open golf championship in under 300 for 72 holes was Jack White in 1904. At Sandwich, England, he shot 80-75-72-69 for a total of 296.

143

GOLF—(1900-1909)—*continued*

3640. Golfer to win the U.S. Open championship four times, and two and three times consecutively was Willie Anderson of Scotland. His fourth title—and his third straight—came in 1905 at the Myopia Hunt Club in Hamilton, Massachusetts. His previous wins had come in 1901 at Myopia; in 1903 at the Baltusrol Golf Club, in Short Hills, New Jersey; and in 1904 at the Glen View Club in Golf, Illinois. Three other notable golfers—Bobby Jones, Ben Hogan, and Jack Nicklaus—would win four U.S. Open titles, but none would win three in a row.

3641. International match between female golfers was in 1905, when a group of women from Great Britain beat a group from the United States 6 matches to 1 at Cromer, England.

3642. Patent for dimple-patterned golf balls was granted in 1905 to William Taylor of England. Dimples helped the ball to fly through the air better; golfers had previously noticed that older balls—scuffed and pitted—often outperformed new ones.

3643. Golf ball with compressed air inside the rubber core was the Pneu-matic developed in 1906 by Goodrich. Lively in play, it had an unfortunate tendency to explode in warm weather, sometimes in the golfer's pocket. It was later discontinued and the rubber-cored Haskell ball became the accepted standard.

3644. Golfer to win the U.S. Open with a 72-hole score under 300 was Alex Smith, who posted a 295 in the 1906 tournament, played at the Onwentsia Club, in Lake Forest, Illinois.

3645. Golfer from outside Great Britain to win the British Open was Arnaud Massey of France, in 1907, playing at Hoylake, England. He was also the first golfer from France to win the Open.

3646. Woman golf professional was Mrs. Gordon Robertson (her own first name is unknown) of the Princes Ladies Golf Club in 1908.

3647. Golfer to win both the British Women's Amateur and the U.S. Women's Amateur titles was Dorothy Iona Campbell of Scotland, who won them both in 1909. She won the U.S. title again in 1910 and the British in 1911.

GOLF (1910-1919)

3648. Golf club with a steel shaft was patented in 1910 by Arthur F. Knight. Such clubs would not be formally accepted by golf's governing bodies until the late 1920s, but would then gradually replace hickory clubs by the late 1930s. The last major tournament won with hickory clubs was the 1936 U.S. Amateur, won by Johnny Fischer.

3649. Golfer to win five British Open championships was James Braid of Scotland, who won his fifth at St. Andrews in 1910. His earlier wins were in 1901, 1905, 1906, and 1908.

3650. Golfer born in the United States to win the U.S. Open was John McDermott in 1911, at the Chicago Golf Club in Wheaton, Illinois. Not yet 20 years old, McDermott triumphed in a three-way playoff with a score of 80, as against 82 for Mike Brady and 85 for George Simpson, after all three had tied at 307 after 72 holes. McDermott would win again in 1912.

3651. Golfer to win British Open titles in three decades was Harry Vardon, with wins in 1896, 1903, and 1911. His record six British Open titles also included championships in 1899, 1909, and 1914.

3652. Golfer to win eight British Amateur championships was John Ball, who won his eighth title in 1912, after earlier wins in 1888, 1890, 1892, 1894, 1899, 1907, and 1910. His record would endure.

3653. Amateur golfer to win the U.S. Open was 20-year-old Francis Ouimet of the United States at the Country Club in Brookline, Massachusetts, in 1913. He won in a three-way playoff with a score of 72, over the heavily favored Harry Vardon with 77 and Ted (Edward) Ray with 78, after they had all tied with 304 for 72 holes. The following year, Ouimet would win both the U.S. and French Amateur titles. In 1916 he was banned from amateur play because he was involved in a sporting goods business, but after widespread protests the ruling was overturned and he was reinstated as an amateur in 1918. He would win the U.S. Amateur title again in 1931.

3654. Golfer to win four U.S. Amateur titles was Jerome Travers, who won his fourth title in 1913 in a match play event at the Garden City Golf Club in Garden City, New York. His earlier wins had come in 1907, 1908, and 1912.

3655. Golf club in Japan was the Tokyo Club, built at Komozawa, Japan, in 1914. It would spark a golf boom in the country.

3656. Golfer to win six British Open golf championships was Harry Vardon, who won his last Open title at Prestwick, Scotland, in 1914. His others had come in 1896, 1898, 1899, 1903, and 1911. Vardon's record of six titles would endure. He might even have won more titles, but the British Open was not held from 1915 through 1919 because of World War I.

3657. Miniature golf course was opened in 1916, in Pinehurst, North Carolina.

3658. Professional Golfers' Association (PGA) Championship was held in 1916, established by the newly founded Professional Golfers' Association of America. Played at Siwanoy Country Club in Bronxville, New York, the first tournament was won on October 14 by James Barnes of England over Jock Hutchinson of Scotland. In the early years, up through 1957, the PGA championship was a match play tournament; it only became a stroke play tournament in 1958. Barnes would win again in 1919, after World War I, the next time the championship was held.

3659. Golfer to win both the U.S. Amateur and U.S. Open championships in the same year, and to win the U.S. Open in under 290 for 72 holes was Charles "Chick" Evans, Jr., who won the U.S. Open on June 30, 1916, with a 286 at the Minikahda Club in Minneapolis, Minnesota, and the amateur title on September 9, 1916, at the Merion Cricket Club in Ardmore, Pennsylvania. He would play in 50 straight U.S. Amateur tournaments, winning again in 1920. He founded the Evans Scholarship Foundation for caddies.

3660. Golf book to use high-speed sequential photographs was *Picture Analysis of Golf Strokes*, published in 1919 by James Barnes, winner of the first two Professional Golfers' Association (PGA) Championships (1916 and 1919; none was held in 1917 or 1918 due to World War I).

3661. Golfer to be a full-time tournament professional in the United States was Walter Hagen in 1919. He would win the Professional Golfers' Association (PGA) Championship five times (1921 and 1924–1927), the British Open four times (1922, 1924, 1928, and 1929) and the U.S. Open twice (1914 and 1919).

3662. Golfer to win two straight Professional Golfers' Association (PGA) Championships was James Barnes. Playing at the Engineers Country Club in Roslyn, New York, he defeated Fred McLeod in 1919, to win what was then a match play tournament. Barnes had also won the inaugural PGA championship in 1916. The PGA championship was not held in 1917 or 1918 because of World War I.

GOLF (1920-1929)

3663. African-American golfer to be a member of the Professional Golfers' Association (PGA) was Dewey Brown, a caddy and instructor who was listed as a PGA member in the 1920s, before membership was wholly restricted to whites.

3664. British Open golf championship to be administered by the Royal and Ancient Golf Club of St. Andrews Scotland, was in 1920, under a 1919 grant of authority. Played at Deal, England, the first year after suspension for World War I ended, the tournament was won by George Duncan of Scotland. The "R&A" also ran the British Amateur championship from then on.

3665. Golf practice range was established at Pinehurst, North Carolina, in 1920.

3666. Golfer born in the United States to win the Professional Golfers' Association (PGA) Championship was Walter Hagen, who won at the Inwood Country Club in Far Rockaway, New York, in 1921. It was his first of five PGA titles, the other four consecutive (1924–1927).

3667. Golfer who was a United States citizen to win the British Open was Jock Hutchinson in 1921. A naturalized citizen, Hutchinson had been born and raised in St. Andrews, Scotland, where the 1921 tournament was played. A native-born U.S. golfer would not win the trophy until the next year, when Walter Hagen took the prize, but Hutchinson's win signaled the beginning of a period of American domination of the British Open. Hutchinson used golf clubs with deep grooves, which were controversial and would later be banned.

3668. Ruling limiting the size and weight of a golf ball was issued in 1921 by the Royal and Ancient Golf Club of St. Andrews, which had become the main authority for the game in 1919 in most of the world. The exceptions were the United States and Mexico, where the United States Golf Association (USGA)—with whom the "R & A" would sometimes disagree—was the prime authority.

GOLF—(1920-1929)—*continued*

3669. Amateur Public Links Championship was held in 1922, sponsored by the United States Golf Association (USGA). The inaugural winner was Edmund R. Held.

3670. Golfer born in the United States to win the British Open was Walter Hagen at Sandwich, England, in 1922. It was the first of his four British Open titles, the others coming in 1924, 1928, and 1929. The 1921 winner, Jock Hutchinson, was a United States citizen, but had been born and raised in St. Andrews, Scotland.

3671. Professional golfer to found a company selling clubs under his own name was Walter Hagen in 1922, the same year he won the first of his four British Open titles.

3672. U.S. Open golf tournament to charge admission to spectators was held in 1922, at the Skokie Country Club in Glencoe, Illinois.

3673. Walker Cup golf match was held in 1922. Playing at the National Golf Links of America in Southampton, New York, the United States team defeated their counterparts from Great Britain and Ireland by a score of 8 to 4. The Walker Cup competition was established by George Herbert Walker, whose grandson—George Herbert Walker Bush—would become the 41st president of the United States. From 1947, the competition would be held biennially, in odd-numbered years.

3674. Golfer to win the U.S. Open and the Professional Golfers' Association (PGA) Championship in the same year was Gene Sarazen, who won the Open on July 15, 1922, at the Skokie Country Club in Glencoe, Illinois, and the PGA on August 18, 1922, at the Oakmont Country Club in Oakmont, Pennsylvania. He would win the PGA again in 1923.

3675. Texas Open golf tournament was played in 1923. It would be a key part of the winter circuit that developed for golf professionals.

3676. Walker Cup golf match played in Britain was in 1923. Playing at St. Andrews, Scotland, the United States team defeated the team from Great Britain and Ireland by a score of 6½ to 5½. The matches would be held biennially from 1924 to 1938; then, after a break during World War II, they resumed in odd-numbered years, starting in 1947.

3677. Golfer to win two straight individual titles at the U.S. intercollegiate golf championships was Dexter Cummings of Yale University, who was champion in both 1923 and 1924.

3678. Golfer to win three Professional Golfers' Association (PGA) Championships was Walter Hagen. His first three wins, in what was then a match play tournament, came in 1921, 1924, and 1925. He would win again in 1926 and 1927, stretching his career record to five PGA titles.

3679. Irrigation system for fairways on a golf course was established in 1925 in Dallas, Texas.

3680. Golf tournament to offer a $10,000 purse was the Los Angeles Open in 1926, the first year of its existence.

3681. Golfer born in the United States to win the British Amateur Championship was Jesse Sweetser in 1926, playing at Muirfield, Scotland.

3682. Golfer to win both the U.S. Open and the British Open in the same year was Bobby Jones of the United States in 1926. He won the U.S. Open at the Scioto Country Club in Columbus, Ohio, with a score of 293, and the British Open at Royal Lytham and St. Anne's, England, with a score of 291. One of the best golfers of all time, he would win a total of four U.S. Open titles, the others coming in 1923, 1929, and 1930, and three British Open titles, the others in 1927 and 1930, the year of his grand slam of golf.

3683. National golf organization founded by African-Americans was the United Golfers Association (UGA), founded in Stow, Massachusetts, in 1926. The founding members included several Washington, D.C., physicians, most notably George Adams and Albert Harris, who were barred from golf clubs in their home area, and were forced to travel to New England in the summer to play. The first president was Robert Hawkins of Boston. In the first UGA tournament, Harry Jackson of Washington, D.C., took the men's title and Marie Thompson of Chicago, Illinois, the women's.

3684. Golf club for African-American women was the Wake Robin Golf Club, founded in 1927 in Washington, D.C., an area where Black players were barred from playing at many courses.

3685. Golfer to win the British Open golf championship in under 290 for 72 holes was Bobby Jones of the United States in 1927, who shot 68-72-73-72 at St. Andrews, Scotland, for a total of 285. It was the second of Jones' three British Open titles, the others being in 1926 at Royal Lytham and St. Anne's, England, and in 1930 at Hoylake, England.

3686. Golfer to win the Professional Golfers' Association (PGA) Championship four times in a row, and five times overall was Walter Hagen, who won in 1927 in Dallas, Texas, over Joe Turnesa, in what was then a match play tournament, after winning in 1921, 1924, 1925, and 1926.

3687. Ryder Cup golf match was played on June 3–4, 1927, between a United States team and a British team, at the Worcester Country Club in Worcester, Massachusetts. The U.S. team won by a score of 9½ to 2½. Held biennially from then on, except during World War II, the British team would in 1979 be expanded to include members from throughout Europe. The Ryder Cup developed from an unofficial match played in 1926 between members of the United States and British golfers' associations.

3688. Golfer to win four, and then five and six, U.S. Women's Amateur Championships was Glenna Collett (later Vare). After wins in 1922, 1925, and 1928, she won her fourth title in 1929 at Oakland Hills Country Club in Birmingham, Michigan. Her fifth title came in 1930 at the Los Angeles Country Club in Beverly Hills, California. She would win a sixth in 1935.

3689. Golfer to win more than 10 titles in golf's four major tournaments was Walter Hagen, who won his 11th major championship in 1929, when he won his fourth British Open, at Muirfield, Scotland, with a score of 292. His previous British Open titles had come in 1922, 1924, and 1928. Added to these were his five Professional Golfers' Association (PGA) Championships (1921, 1924, 1925, 1926, and 1927) and his two U.S. Open titles (1914 and 1919). He might have won even more, except that during World War I the British Open was suspended from 1915 to 1919, and the U.S. Open and PGA Championship from 1917 to 1918. The fourth major tournament, the Masters, did not begin until 1934.

3690. Ryder Cup golf match played in Britain was the 1929 meeting at Moortown, near Leeds, England. There the British team defeated the U.S. team by a score of 7 to 5.

GOLF (1930-1939)

3691. Amateur golfer to win three British Open championships was Bobby Jones of the United States. His third win, in 1930, came at Hoylake, England, following earlier wins in 1926 and 1927.

3692. Golfer to win five U.S. Amateur titles was Bobby Jones of the United States, who won his fifth over Eugene V. Homans in a match play event at the Merion Cricket Club in Ardmore, Pennsylvania, in 1930, the year he won his grand slam: all four of golf's major tournaments. Jones' other U.S. Amateur titles had come in 1924, 1925, 1927, and 1928. He effectively retired from competitive play after 1930.

3693. Golfer to complete a grand slam was Bobby Jones of the United States, when he won the Open and Amateur tournaments in both the United States and Britain in the same calendar year, 1930. He won the British Amateur Championship on May 31 at St. Andrews, Scotland; the British Open on June 20; the U.S. Open at Minneapolis, Minnesota, on July 12; and the U.S. Amateur at Philadelphia, Pennsylvania, on September 27. Jones was, and remained, an amateur, so he received no financial reward for his feat. Between 1923 and 1930 he would win a total of 13 titles in these four tournaments.

3694. Golfer to win a major tournament using steel-shafted golf clubs was Billy Burke in 1931, who won the U.S. Open at the Inverness Club in Toledo, Ohio. He was tied with George Von Elm after regulation play and after a 36-hole playoff; he finally won after a 72-hole playoff, the longest ever recorded.

3695. Curtis Cup golf match was held in 1932, between teams of amateur women golfers from the United States and Britain. Playing at the Wentworth Golf Club in Wentworth, England, the U.S. team defeated the British team by a score of 5½ to 3½. The matches were established by two American sisters, who held four U.S. Women's Amateur titles between them: Margaret Curtis (1907, 1911, and 1912) and her sister Harriot Curtis (1906). From 1932 on, the matches were held biennially in even-numbered years, except during World War II.

3696. Corporate title sponsor for a professional golf tournament was the Hershey Chocolate Company, which sponsored the Hershey Open in 1933.

3697. Curtis Cup golf match played in the United States was in 1934. Playing at Chevy Chase, Maryland, amateur women golfers from the United States defeated their counterparts from Great Britain by a score of 6½ to 2½.

GOLF—(1930-1939)—*continued*

3698. Masters golf tournament was played in 1934, at the Augusta National Golf Club in Augusta, Georgia. The winner was Horton Smith, who shot a 284 for 72 holes. The course, designed by Alister Mackenzie with advice from celebrated amateur golfer Bobby Jones, would become the permanent home of the Masters tournament.

3699. Golfer to win 32 straight matches was W. Lawson Little in 1934 and 1935, among them the U.S. and British Amateur titles in both years.

3700. Golfer to win all four of golf's major tournaments was Gene Sarazen, who completed his career grand slam in 1935, when he won the Masters. He had previously won the U.S. Open (1922 and 1932), the Professional Golfers' Association (PGA) Championship (1922, 1923, and 1933), and the British Open (1932).

3701. Golfer to win six U.S. Women's Amateur championships was Glenna Collett Vare, whose sixth title came in 1935 at the Interlachen Country Club in Minneapolis, Minnesota. Her previous amateur titles (as Glenna Collett) had come in 1922, 1925, 1928, 1929, and 1930. The Vare Trophy, given annually to the woman golfer with the lowest average, was named after her.

3702. Golfer to win two Masters championships was Horton Smith. He won his second in 1936, with a score of 285, having won the inaugural Masters tournament in 1934, both at its permanent home at the Augusta National Golf Club in Augusta, Georgia.

3703. Golfer over 50 to win a Professional Golfers' Association (PGA) recognized tournament was James Barnes, who was 51 years, 3 months, and 7 days old when he won the 1937 Long Island Open.

3704. Golfer to win the Vardon Trophy awarded to the golfer with the lowest average in the Professional Golfers' Association (PGA), was Harry Cooper, in 1937. The trophy was named after six-time British Open winner Harry Vardon, who had died that year.

3705. Professional-amateur golf tournament was the Bing Crosby Pro-Am, first held in 1937 at Rancho Santa Fe in San Diego, California. It later moved to the Monterey Peninsula in northern California.

3706. Professional Golfers' Association (PGA) Seniors' Championship was held in 1937, at the Augusta National Golf Club in Augusta, Georgia. Jock Hutchinson, a Scottish American, won the event, which would in 1980 become part of the Senior Professional Golfers' Association (PGA) Tour.

3707. British win of the Walker Cup golf tournament came in 1938, when a team of British amateurs defeated United States amateurs in matches played at the Old Course at St. Andrews, Scotland.

3708. Intercollegiate golf tournament for African-American players was held in 1938. Sponsored by Tuskegee Institute (now University), in Tuskegee, Alabama, it included players from Alabama State University, Florida A & M University, Morehouse College, Morris Brown College, and Fort Valley State College, the latter sending women players only. Alfred Holmes and Maxwell Vails, both of Tuskegee, shared the men's title, and Cora Lee McClinick won the women's. In that period, a very few African-American golfers played in white colleges, most notably Hayden Golden at the University of Oregon.

3709. Golfer to win the Masters in under 280 for 72 holes was Ralph Guldahl, who shot a 279 in the 1939 tournament, played at its traditional course, the Augusta National Golf Club in Augusta, Georgia.

3710. Reigning monarch to play in a national golf championship was King Leopold of Belgium, who played in the Belgian Amateur Championships in 1939. He reached the final 16 in the tournament played at Zoute. After World War II, he would be the leading amateur in the Swiss Open Championship in 1946 and would be in the final eight in the French Amateur Championship in 1949.

GOLF (1940-1949)

3711. Hale America golf tournaments were held in 1942, to help raise money for the war effort during World War II. Used golf balls were collected at recycling points for their rubber content.

3712. Organization for women golf professionals in the United States was the Women's Professional Golf Association (WPGA), founded in 1944 by Hope Seignious, Betty Hicks, and Ellen Griffin. It lasted only five years, disbanding in 1949, but it would be succeeded later that year by the Ladies Professional Golf Association (LPGA).

3713. Golfer to score under 260 for 72 holes in a Professional Golfers' Association (PGA)–recognized event was Byron Nelson in 1945. Playing in the Seattle Open, at the Broadmoor Golf Club in Seattle, Washington, he shot 62-68-63-66 for a total of 259, which was 21 under par. His record would be broken 10 years later by Mike Souchak's 257. During 1945, Nelson also shot a record of 19 straight rounds under 70.

3714. Golfer to win more than 10 straight titles, and to win 18 titles overall during a single year, on the Professional Golfers' Association (PGA) Tour was Byron Nelson, who won 11 championships in a row in 1945, a record that would endure. His run started with his win at the Miami Four Ball (with Jug McSpaden) on March 11, 1945, at the Miami Springs Course in Miami, Florida, and ended with his capture of the Canadian Open title on August 4, 1945, at the Thornhill Country Club in Toronto, Ontario, Canada. Nelson's total winnings during that streak were $30,250. During that streak, he won the Professional Golfers' Association (PGA) Championship, as well as a 12th event not recognized by the PGA. He retired from regular competition the following year.

3715. U.S. Women's Open golf championship was held in 1946 at the Spokane Country Club in Spokane, Washington, sponsored by the Women's Professional Golf Association (WPGA). Winning the event on September 1 was Patty Berg, a founding member and first president (1949–1952) of the Ladies Professional Golf Association (LPGA), which picked up sponsorship of the event from 1950. It became the longest-running event in women's golf, sponsored by the United States Golf Association (USGA) from 1953.

3716. Golf tournament to be shown on television was the 1947 U.S. Open, which was televised by KSD-TV, a local station in St. Louis, Missouri. Played at the St. Louis Country Club in Clayton, Missouri, it was won by Lew Worsham in a playoff over Sam Snead.

3717. Golfer from the United States to win the British Women's Amateur Championship was Babe Didrikson Zaharias on June 12, 1947, at Gullane, Scotland, the year after she won the U.S. Women's Amateur. A noted all-around athlete, she became a professional the following year and would lead the money list for women golfers from 1948 through 1951.

3718. Golfer to win the U.S. Open in under 280 for 72 holes was Ben Hogan, who shot 276 at the Riviera Country Club in Los Angeles, California, in 1948.

3719. U.S. Junior Amateur golf championship was held in 1948. The winner was Dean Lind, over runner-up Ken Venturi.

3720. African-American golfers to play in a Professional Golfers' Association (PGA)–recognized event were Bill Spiller and Ted Rhodes, who finished 25th and 11th respectively at the Los Angeles Open in January 1948. At that time, most clubs barred black golfers. That would slowly begin to change, especially from the late 1950s, but not until 1990 did the PGA and the United States Golf Association (USGA) require that clubs on their tours meet open membership guidelines—and even then some clubs withdrew rather than comply.

3721. Golfer from the British Commonwealth to win the British Open was Bobby Locke of South Africa, who won at Sandwich, England, in 1949. It was the first of his four British Open titles, the others coming in 1950, 1952, and 1957.

3722. President of the Ladies Professional Golf Association (LPGA) was Patty Berg, one of the founding members of the organization for professional women golfers. She served from the LPGA's founding in 1949 until 1952, when she was succeeded by Louise Suggs. In its first season, the LPGA had 11 events, offering a total of approximately $50,000.

3723. Sudden-death playoff in golf that ran more than 10 holes was in 1949, when Cary Middlecoff and Lloyd Mangrum were still tied after 11 holes at the Motor City Open. With their agreement, they were declared co-winners of the tournament.

GOLF (1950-1959)

3724. Golfer to win the British Open golf championship in under 280 for 72 holes was Bobby Locke of South Africa in 1950, who shot 69-72-70-68 at Troon, Scotland, for a total of 279. It was the second of Locke's four British Open titles, the others being in 1949, 1952, and 1957, when he again shot a 279.

3725. Golfer to win three major tournaments, and six titles overall, on the Ladies Professional Golf Association (LPGA) Tour in a single season was Babe Didrikson Zaharias in 1950. Her sixth title and third major was the U.S. Women's Open, which she won on October 1 at the Rolling Hills Country Club in Wichita, Kansas. She also won two other tournaments then considered majors—the Titleholders Championship at the Augusta Country Club in Augusta, Georgia, on March 19, and the Western Open at Cherry Hills in Denver, Colorado, on June 24—and three other tour events.

GOLF—(1950-1959)—*continued*

3726. Golfer to win two U.S. Women's Open championships was Babe Didrikson Zaharias, who won her second title on October 1, 1950, at the Rolling Hills Country Club in Wichita, Kansas. Her first had come in 1948; she would win again in 1954.

3727. Golfer from the United States to become captain of the Royal and Ancient Golf Club of St. Andrews Scotland, was Francis Ouimet, in 1951.

3728. Golfer to win the Masters three times was Jimmy Demaret, who won his third in 1951 with a 283 at the tournament's permanent home, the Augusta National Golf Club in Augusta, Georgia. His two earlier wins had come in 1940 and 1947.

3729. Golfer to win her first tournament on the Ladies Professional Golf Association (LPGA) Tour was Beverly Hanson, when she won the Eastern Open at the Berkshire Country Club in Reading, Pennsylvania, in her debut on July 1, 1951.

3730. British win of the Curtis Cup golf match was in 1952, when the British women's team defeated their United States counterparts at Muirfield, Scotland.

3731. Ladies Professional Golf Association (LPGA) Tour season purse to top $100,000 was in 1952, when the total prize money available to women golfers was $150,000 for 21 events.

3732. Canada Cup golf tournament called the World Cup from 1967, was held in 1953, involving two-man national teams. Played at the Beaconsfield Golf Club in Montreal, Quebec, Canada, the inaugural event was won by the team from Argentina: Antonio Cerda and Roberto de Vicenzo. Cerda had the lowest individual score, to win the first International Trophy.

3733. Golf tournament to be televised nationally was the Tam O'Shanter World Championship, played at the Tam O'Shanter Club near Chicago, Illinois, in 1953. Lew Worsham won the title with a stunning wedge shot for an eagle at the last hole.

3734. Golfer to win the Tournament of Champions was Al Besselink, who won with a score of 280 in 1953 at the Desert Inn Country Club in Las Vegas, Nevada, the tournament's home site through 1966. Limited to tournament winners from the previous year, it was later called the Mercedes Championships.

3735. Golfer to win the U.S. Open, the Masters, and the British Open in the same year, and the first to score under 275 for 72 holes was Ben Hogan in 1953. His record-breaking 274 was scored at the Masters' traditional home at the Augusta National Golf Club in Augusta, Georgia. At the Masters, he was the first person to score under 275 for 72 holes. His U.S. Open win came at the Oakmont Country Club, in Oakmont, Pennsylvania, and his British Open win at Carnoustie, Scotland. Hogan's achievement was all the more remarkable because he had been in a near-fatal automobile accident in 1949. He did not compete in the Professional Golfers' Association (PGA) Championship that year, and so missed the possibility of completing a grand slam.

3736. Golfer to win the Vare Trophy for the lowest average score on the Ladies Professional Golf Association (LPGA) Tour was Patty Berg in 1953, with a scoring average of 75.00. The trophy was offered by LPGA charter member Betty Jameson, who named it after the noted amateur Glenna Collett Vare. Berg would win it again in 1955 and 1956.

3737. Professional Golfers' Association (PGA) Tour season purse to top $500,000 was in 1953.

3738. Golfer to win 10 major tournaments recognized by the Ladies Professional Golf Association (LPGA) Tour was Patty Berg, who crossed that threshold on March 15, 1953, when she won the Titleholders Championship (considered a major until 1967). She ended her career with a record total of 15 major titles, including three as an amateur, and 57 titles overall.

3739. Golfer to win the U.S. Women's Open in a playoff was Betsy Rawls, who defeated Jackie Pung in an 18-hole playoff on June 27, 1953, at the Country Club of Rochester in Rochester, New York.

3740. Golf tournament to offer a $100,000 purse was the Tam O'Shanter World Championship, played at the Tam O'Shanter Club near Chicago, Illinois, in 1954.

3741. Golfer to score under 190 for three consecutive 18-hole rounds in a Professional Golfers' Association (PGA) recognized event was Chandler Harper, who shot 63-63-63 for a 24-under-par 189 in the final three rounds of the 1954 Texas Open at Brackenridge Park Golf Course in San Antonio, Texas. His first round of 70 gave him a winning total of 259, which was 25 under par, tying a PGA Tour record set nine years earlier by Byron Nelson.

3742. Golfer to win the Masters tournament three times was Sam Snead, who won his third in 1954. His first two Masters titles had come in 1949 and 1952, all at the tournament's home at the Augusta National Golf Club in Augusta, Georgia.

3743. U.S. Open golf tournament to be televised nationally was in 1954, when Ed Furgol defeated Gene Littler at the Baltusrol Golf Club in Springfield, New Jersey.

3744. Golfer to win the U.S. Women's Open three times was Babe Didrikson Zaharias, who took her third title on July 3, 1954, at the Salem Country Club in Peabody, Massachusetts. She had earlier won the championship in 1948 and 1950.

3745. Golfer to score 257 for 72 holes in a Professional Golfers' Association (PGA) recognized event was Mike Souchak, who scored 60-68-64-65, in the Texas Open at Brackenridge Park Golf Course in San Antonio, Texas, on February 17–20, 1955. His 257, which was 27 under par, would be an enduring record.

3746. Ladies Professional Golf Association (LPGA) Championship was held in 1955 at the Orchard Ridge Country Club in Fort Wayne, Indiana. Winning the inaugural event on July 17 was Beverly Hanson, with a three-over-par 220, over runner-up Louise Suggs.

3747. Golfer to win the Tournament of Champions twice, and then three times, in a row was Gene Littler, who won his second in 1956 and his third in 1957, after his initial win in 1955. All three tournaments were played at the Desert Inn Country Club in Las Vegas, Nevada, then the home site for the tournament now called the Mercedes Championships.

3748. National golf team that won the Canada Cup twice was from the United States. Ben Hogan and Sam Snead won in 1956, with Hogan winning the International Trophy. The previous year, Ed Furgol had won the individual trophy, and formed a winning duo with Chick Harbert.

3749. Golfer to win the Ladies Professional Golf Association (LPGA) Championship in a sudden-death playoff was Marlene Bauer Hagge, who won over Patty Berg at the Forest Lake Country Club in Detroit, Michigan, on June 24, 1956.

3750. African-American golfer to win a title in a significant predominantly white tournament was Charles Sifford, who won the Long Beach Open in Long Beach, California, in 1957.

3751. Golfer on the Professional Golfers' Association (PGA) Tour to be named Rookie of the Year was Ken Venturi, who received that honor at its first presentation in 1957.

3752. Golfer to win 10 titles recognized by the Ladies Professional Golf Association (LPGA) Tour in a single season was Betsy Rawls in 1957, whose wins included the U.S. Women's Open. After she retired in 1975, she would become the LPGA's tournament director.

3753. Golfer to win the Professional Golfers' Association (PGA) Championship after it was converted into a stroke play tournament was Dow Finterswald in 1958, with a 72-hole score of 276 at Llanerch, Pennsylvania.

3754. Total purse on the Professional Golfers' Association (PGA) Tour to top $1 million was in 1958, when the total offered for 39 events was $1,005,800.

3755. African-American golfer to be classified as an "approved player" on the Professional Golfers' Association (PGA) Tour was Charles Sifford, who in 1959 was given a card putting him in this category, which usually applied to people from outside the United States.

3756. African-American golfer to win a national championship was Bill Wright, who won the U.S. Amateur Public Links Championship in 1959.

3757. Golfer to win two consecutive U.S. Women's Open titles was Mickey (Mary Kathryn) Wright, who won in 1959 at the Churchill Valley Country Club in Pittsburgh, Pennsylvania, after a previous win in 1958. She would win again in 1961 and 1964.

3758. Ladies Professional Golf Association (LPGA) Tour season purse to top $200,000 was in 1959, when the total prize money available to women golfers was $202,500 for 26 events.

3759. Lifting of the "no blacks allowed" clause from the constitution of the Professional Golfers' Association (PGA) was in 1959, largely in response to lawsuits like the one filed by African-American players Bill Spiller, Ted Rhodes, and Madison Gunter. However, many golf clubs continued to have "white only" policies. Not until 1990 would the PGA and the United States Golf Association (USGA) require that clubs on their tours meet open membership guidelines—and even then some clubs withdrew rather than comply.

GOLF (1960-1969)

3760. Golfer to be named *Sports Illustrated* **Sportsman of the Year** was Arnold Palmer of the United States in 1960, the year he won both the Masters and U.S. Open.

3761. JCPenney Classic golf tournament was held in 1960 at the Pinecrest Lake Club in Avon Park, Florida, and Harder Hall in Sebring, Florida. Originally called the Haig & Haig Scotch Foursome, the tournament paired top male and female golfers, with the first tournament won by Jim Turnesa and Gloria Armstrong.

3762. Golfer to win two, and then three, Ladies Professional Golf Association (LPGA) Championships was Mickey (Mary Kathryn) Wright. Her second win came on July 4, 1960, at the Sheraton Country Club in French Lick, Indiana, and her third on October 15, 1961, at the Stardust Golf Club, in Las Vegas, Nevada. Her first win had come in 1958.

3763. African-American golfer to play in a Professional Golfers' Association (PGA) Tour tournament in the South was Charles Sifford, who played at the Greater Greensboro Open in Greensboro, North Carolina, in 1961, the year that the PGA had eliminated the Caucasians-only clause from its constitution.

3764. Golfer to score eight consecutive birdies in a Professional Golfers' Association (PGA) recognized event was Bob Goalby as part of a 65-stroke fourth round in the St. Petersburg Open at the Pasadena Golf Club in St. Petersburg, Florida, in 1961.

3765. Golf package was offered in 1962 at Myrtle Beach, South Carolina. With the package, golfers received rooms, meals, and greens fees for a single price.

3766. Golfer named Rookie of the Year on the Ladies Professional Golf Association (LPGA) Tour was Mary Mills in 1962. Her earnings during that debut year totaled $8000. The following year she would win the U.S. Women's Open.

3767. World Series of Golf was held in 1962, in Akron, Ohio, where the winner was Jack Nicklaus. Originally, and for its first 14 years, the contestants included the winners of the Masters, the U.S. Open, the British Open, and the Professional Golfers' Association (PGA) Championship, with a two-round, 36-hole exhibition format and a $50,000 prize for the winner. In 1976 it would be expanded to a 72-hole format open to male golfers who had won at least one tournament in the previous year.

3768. Golfer on the Ladies Professional Golf Association (LPGA) Tour to win four consecutively scheduled tournaments was Mickey (Mary Kay) Wright, who won the Heart of America Invitational at the Hillcrest Country Club in Kansas City, Kansas, on August 12, 1962, followed by the Albuquerque Swing Parade in Albuquerque, New Mexico, on August 19; the Salt Lake City Open at the Willow Creek Country Club in Salt Lake City, Utah, on August 26; and the Spokane Open in Spokane, Washington, on September 3. She would have another run of four consecutive wins in 1963.

3769. Golfer to earn more than $100,000 in official prize money during a single year was Arnold Palmer, who did so in 1963, when his official winnings were $128,230, to which he added another $2,605 in unofficial tournaments, for a total of $130,835.

3770. Golfer to win the World Series of Golf twice in a row was Jack Nicklaus, who won the first two tournaments, held in Akron, Ohio, in 1962 and 1963. He would later win three times more, in 1967, 1970, and 1976.

3771. Total purse on the Professional Golfers' Association (PGA) Tour to top $2 million was in 1963, when the overall purse for 43 events was $2,044,900.

3772. Ladies Professional Golf Association (LPGA) tournament to be nationally televised was the final round of the U.S. Women's Open on July 20, 1963. The winner, Mary Mills, took home a prize of $9,000, more than she had earned in all of 1962, when she was LPGA Rookie of the Year.

3773. Golfer to win 13 titles recognized by the Ladies Professional Golf Association (LPGA) Tour in a single season was Mickey (Mary Kathryn) Wright in 1963, highlighted by the LPGA Championship. Wright's 13th title came in the Mixed Foursome International on December 8, paired with Dave Ragan, Jr.

3774. Golfer to win the Ladies Professional Golf Association (LPGA) Championship with a score under 280 was Mary Mills, who in 1964 posted a 6-under-par 278 at the Stardust Country Club in Las Vegas, Nevada.

3775. Golfer to win the Masters tournament four times was Arnold Palmer, who won his fourth in 1964 at the traditional Masters course, the Augusta National Golf Club in Augusta, Georgia. His earlier Masters wins had come in 1958, 1960, and 1962.

3776. National golf team to win five consecutive Canada Cup tournaments was from the United States (1960–1964). In their fourth and fifth consecutive wins, in 1963 and 1964, the United States was represented by Arnold Palmer and Jack Nicklaus, with Nicklaus winning the International Trophy both times. The first three wins had been led by Sam Snead, joined in 1960 and 1962 by Palmer and in 1961 by Jimmy Demaret. The event was later called the World Cup of Golf.

3777. Women's World Amateur Team Championship was held in 1964, with the team from France taking the first title. It was held biennially from then on, with three-woman teams playing for the Espirito Santo Trophy.

3778. Golfer to win the U.S. Women's Open four times was Mickey (Mary Kathryn) Wright, who notched her fourth win on July 11, 1964, at the San Diego Country Club in Chula Vista, California. Her previous U.S. Women's Open victories had come in 1958, 1959, and 1961.

3779. Golfer to have 15 consecutive seasons with a victory on the Ladies Professional Golf Association (LPGA) Tour was Betsy Rawls, starting with the U.S. Women's Open and the Sacramento Open in 1951 and ending with the Pensacola Invitational and the Waterloo Open in 1965. Winless in 1966 and 1967, she would come back to win five more tournaments, including the 1969 LPGA Championship, before retiring in 1975.

3780. Golfer to win more than 80 tournaments on the Professional Golfers' Association (PGA) Tour, and to win the same PGA event eight times was Sam Snead, who won his 81st PGA title at the Greater Greensboro Open, in Greensboro, North Carolina, in 1965. He had won the event seven times before, in 1938, 1946, 1949, 1950, 1955, 1956, and 1960. The 27-year stretch between first and last victories at the same event was also a record, as was his age at the time: 52.

3781. Qualifying School of the Professional Golfers' Association (PGA) Tour was established in 1965. Of the 49 attendees, 17 went on to win playing cards, allowing them to compete on the PGA Tour.

3782. Golfer to be named Ladies Professional Golf Association (LPGA) Player of the Year was Kathy Whitworth in 1966. She would win it six more times (1967–1969 and 1971–1973).

3783. Golfer to win the Masters tournament twice in a row was Jack Nicklaus. Playing at the traditional Masters course, the Augusta National Golf Club in Augusta, Georgia, he won in 1965 with a tournament-record 271 and then again in 1966 with a much higher but still sufficient 288. They were the second and third of his record six wins at the Masters, the others being in 1963, 1972, 1975, and 1986.

3784. Golfer to win the Tournament of Champions in a playoff was Arnold Palmer in 1966, when he defeated Gay Brewer at the Desert Inn Country Club in Las Vegas, Nevada. It was the last of Palmer's three wins in the tournament, limited to champions from the previous year, the others coming in 1962 and 1965.

3785. Ladies Professional Golf Association (LPGA) Tour season purse to top $500,000 was in 1966, when the total prize money available to women golfers was $509,500 for 37 events.

3786. African-American woman to play on the Ladies Professional Golf Association (LPGA) tour was Renee Powell, who broke the color barrier in women's golf in 1967. Three years earlier she had won the women's title of the United Golf Association (UGA), an organization for African-American golfers. Black tennis star Althea Gibson also briefly joined her on the tour in the late 1960s.

3787. Amateur golfer to win the U.S. Women's Open was Catherine Lacoste of France in 1967, playing at the Hot Springs Golf Club in Hot Springs, Virginia. The niece of tennis star René Lacoste, famed for his polo shirts, she was also the first golfer from France to win the tournament.

3788. Golfer to win more than $1 million in official prize money on the Professional Golfers' Association (PGA) Tour during his career was Arnold Palmer, who passed that milestone in 1968. Followed by fans known as "Arnie's Army," Palmer became the first golfer to fly his own plane to tournaments.

3789. Total purse on the Professional Golfers' Association (PGA) Tour to top $5 million was in 1968, when the total offered for 45 events was $5,077,600.

3790. African-American golfer to win a featured event on the Professional Golfers' Association (PGA) Tour was Charles Sifford in 1969, when he won the Los Angeles Open.

GOLF (1970-1979)

3791. African-American golfer to play in the South African Professional Golfers' Association (PGA) Open was Lee Elder in 1971.

3792. Golfer to win more than $200,000 in official prize money in a single season was Jack Nicklaus of the United States in 1971, the year he won the Professional Golfers' Association (PGA) Championship.

3793. Golfer to win the U.S., Canadian, and British Opens in the same year was Lee Trevino in 1971.

3794. Golfer to win two Professional Golfers' Association (PGA) Championships, after the tournament was converted to a stroke play format in 1958, was Jack Nicklaus, who won his second at the PGA National Golf Club in Palm Beach Gardens, Florida, in 1971, with a 72-hole score of 281. His first had come in 1963. Nicklaus would accumulate a record of five PGA titles, the others coming in 1973, 1975, and 1980.

3795. Golf shot taken on the moon was on February 5, 1971, by astronaut Alan Shepard of the United States.

3796. Golf tournaments held on the Professional Golfers' Association (PGA) European Tour were in 1972. The Tour had been founded the year before.

3797. Golfer to have a double, and then triple, grand slam, winning golf's four major tournaments twice, and then three times, each was Jack Nicklaus. He completed his first double career grand slam with his second title at the U.S. Open in 1972, after his first in 1967. He had previously won the Masters four times (1963, 1965, 1966, and 1972) and would win it twice more (1975 and 1986). He already had two Professional Golfers Association (PGA) Championships (1963 and 1971), winning three more (1973, 1975, and 1980). With his third British Open title (1966, 1970, and 1978), he completed his triple career grand slam.

3798. Golfer to win more than $300,000 in official prize money in a single season was Jack Nicklaus of the United States in 1972, the year he won his second U.S. Open and fourth Masters.

3799. Dinah Shore golf tournament was established in 1972, with Jane Blalock winning on April 16 at the Mission Hills Country Club in Rancho Mirage, California. The first tournament to offer substantial money to professional women golfers, it was designated one of the four major tournaments on the Ladies Professional Golf Association (LPGA) Tour in 1983.

3800. Golfer to be named Ladies Professional Golf Association (LPGA) Player of the Year seven times was Kathy Whitworth, who in 1973 was so honored for the seventh time in eight years (1966–1969 and 1971–1973).

3801. Golfer to win more than $2 million in official prize money during his career was Jack Nicklaus, who passed that milestone in 1973.

3802. Golfer to win the Tournament of Champions four and five times was Jack Nicklaus. His fourth win in 1973 and his fifth in 1977 were both at the La Costa Country Club in Carlsbad, California, as was his 1971 win. He had previously won in 1963 and 1964. Limited to champions from the previous year, the tournament is now called the Mercedes Championships.

3803. Golfer to win three straight individual titles at the U.S. intercollegiate golf championships was Ben Crenshaw of the University of Texas, who won the National Collegiate Athletic Association (NCAA) Division I championship in 1971, 1972 (tied with Texas teammate Tom Kite), and 1973. Joining the tour later in 1973, he won his first tournament as a professional on the Professional Golfers' Association (PGA) Tour, the San Antonio Open.

3804. Ladies Professional Golf Association (LPGA) Tour season purse to top $1 million was in 1973, when the total prize money available to women golfers was $1,471,000 for 36 events.

3805. Golfer to win $100,000 in a single tournament was Miller Barber, on November 17, 1973, when he won the World Open in Pinehurst, North Carolina.

3806. Tournament Players Championship was held in 1974 at the Atlanta Country Club in Atlanta, Georgia. Jack Nicklaus won the inaugural tournament with a score of 272; he would win again in 1976 and 1978. Limited to the tournament winners from the previous year, it was later called the Players Championship, regarded by many as a fifth "major."

3807. Golfer to win five Masters tournaments was Jack Nicklaus. He won his fifth title in 1975, with a score of 276 for 72 holes. He had previously won in 1963, 1965 (when he set a Masters record with 271), 1966, and 1972, and would win again in 1986, all at the traditional Masters course, the Augusta National Golf Club in Augusta, Georgia.

3808. African-American golfer to play in the Masters tournament was Lee Elder, who first teed off at the Augusta National Golf Club in Augusta, Georgia, on April 10, 1975.

3809. Golfer to win the World Series of Golf in its new 72-hole format was Jack Nicklaus in 1976. It was the last of his five wins in the Akron, Ohio, tournament, the others coming in 1962, 1963, 1967, and 1970. This was the first year that the Series was open to male golfers who had won a tournament in the previous year. Nicklaus had won four previous times, in 1962, 1963, 1967, and 1970, when the tournament was still a four-man, 36-hole exhibition.

3810. Woman golfer to earn more than $100,000 in official prize money in a season was Judy Rankin, who topped that figure in 1976, the year she won six tournaments, including the Dinah Shore.

3811. British Open golf championship in which the top ten golfers were all from the United States was in 1977 at Turnberry, Scotland. The winner was Tom Watson, in the second of his five British Open titles, the others coming in 1975, 1980, 1982, and 1983.

3812. Golfer to win more than $3 million in official prize money during his career was Jack Nicklaus, who passed that milestone in 1977.

3813. Golfer to win the British Open golf championship in under 270 for 72 holes was Tom Watson of the United States in 1977, who at Turnberry, Scotland, shot 68-70-65-65 for a total of 268. It was the second of Watson's five British Open titles, the others coming in 1975, 1980, 1982, and 1983.

3814. Sudden-death playoff in one of golf's major tournaments was in 1977 in the Professional Golfers' Association (PGA) Championship, at the Pebble Beach Golf Links in Pebble Beach, California, when Lanny Wadkins bested Gene Littler on the third extra hole.

3815. Golfer to score under 60 in an 18-hole round in a Professional Golfers' Association (PGA) recognized event was Al Geiberger, who shot a 13-under-par 59 on June 10, 1977, in the second round of the Memphis Classic at the Colonial Country Club in Memphis, Tennessee.

3816. Golfer to be named Rookie of the Year and Player of the Year, and to win the Vare Trophy for lowest scoring average in the same year was Nancy Lopez at the end of her stellar debut year in 1978, during which she won nine tournaments. She would win Player of the Year and Vare honors again in 1979.

3817. Legends of Golf tournament was played in 1978 at Onion Creek Country Club in Austin, Texas, won by the team of Sam Snead and Gardner Dickinson. It helped spark the establishment of the Professional Golfers' Association (PGA) Senior Tour in 1980.

3818. Total purse for the Professional Golfers' Association (PGA) Tour to top $10 million was in 1978, when the total prize money for 48 events was $10,337,332.

3819. World Series of Golf won in a playoff was in 1978, when Gil Morgan tied Hubert Green with a 278 at the Firestone Country Club in Akron, Ohio, and then won on the first extra hole.

3820. Golfer to win five straight tournaments in which she played was Nancy Lopez, who did so during her stunning rookie year in 1978. Her run began at the Greater Baltimore Open at the Pine Ridge Country Club in Timonium, Maryland, on May 14, and ran through the Bankers Trust Classic at the Locust Hill Country Club in Rochester, New York, on June 18. She did not play in the Peter Jackson Classic on June 1–4. She would end the season with a total of nine wins, and would win another eight in 1979.

3821. Ryder Cup to include players from the European mainland was in 1979, when European players joined those from the British Isles in competing against players from the United States, who won 17–11.

3822. Women's Professional Golfers' Association (WPGA) European Tour was established in 1979, when Alison Sheard of Great Britain topped the money list with earnings of £4,965.

3823. Du Maurier Classic was held at the Richelieu Valley Country Club in Montreal, Quebec, Canada, 1979. Amy Alcott won the inaugural event on July 29. As the Peter Jackson Classic, the event had been part of the Ladies Professional Golf Association (LPGA) Tour since 1973, but was designated a major only in 1979.

3824. African-American golfer to represent the United States in the Ryder Cup tournament was Lee Elder on September 13–15, 1979. Playing at the Greenbrier in White Sulphur Springs, West Virginia, he helped to lead his team to a 17–11 victory over the European team.

GOLF (1980-1989)

3825. Golfer to earn more than $500,000 in official prize money in a single season was Tom Watson of the United States in 1980, when he won four tournaments.

3826. Golfer to win five Professional Golfers' Association (PGA) Championships was Jack Nicklaus, who won his record fifth in 1980 at Oak Hill with a score of 274. His earlier PGA titles had come in 1963, 1971, 1973, and 1975.

3827. Golfer to win the U.S. Open in under 275, and to win the U.S. Open twice on the same course was Jack Nicklaus, who shot 272 at the Baltusrol Golf Club in Springfield, New Jersey, in 1980. He had won his first Open title at Baltusrol in 1967.

3828. Ladies Professional Golf Association (LPGA) Tour season purse to top $5 million was in 1980, when the total prize money available to women golfers was $5,150,000 for 40 events.

3829. World Championship of Women's Golf was held at the Country Club in Brookline, Massachusetts, in 1980. The winner was Beth Daniel, who posted a 6-under-par 282. She would win the event again in 1981 and in 1994.

3830. Senior Professional Golfers' Association (PGA) Tour was founded on January 16, 1980. Among those attending the founding meeting were Sam Snead, Don January, Bob Goalby, Julius Boros, Gardner Dickinson, and Dan Sikes. Its first season later that year included four official events: the Atlantic City Senior International, the U.S. Senior Open, the Suntree Classic, and the PGA Seniors' Championship.

3831. Women to be caddies at the U.S. Open golf tournament were Pamela Shuttleworth, caddying for Jim Dent, and Jane Betley, for her husband, Bob Betley, at the Baltusrol Golf Club in Springfield, New Jersey, in June 1980.

3832. Tournament on the Senior Professional Golfers' Association (PGA) Tour was the Atlantic City Senior Invitational, played at the Atlantic City Country Club in Northfield, New Jersey. It was won by Don January on June 22, 1980.

3833. U.S. Senior Open golf tournament the second event in the first Senior Professional Golfers' Association (PGA) Tour season, was played at Winged Foot Golf Club in Mamaroneck, New York, in 1980. Roberto de Vicenzo of Argentina won the event on June 29, 1980.

3834. African-American golfer to win a Senior Professional Golfers' Association (PGA) Tour event was Charles Sifford, on November 16, 1980. He won the Suntree Classic, the third event on the inaugural Senior PGA Tour, played at the Suntree Country Club, Melbourne, Florida.

3835. Woman golfer to earn more than $1 million in official prize money during her career was Kathy Whitworth of the United States, who passed that milestone in 1981, when she won one individual and one team title. By the end of her career in 1985, she had notched up a record of 88 wins, including three Ladies Professional Golf Association (LPGA) Championships, in 1967, 1971, and 1975, and had led the LPGA Tour money list for eight years (1965–1968 and 1970–1973).

3836. Golfer to win the World Championship of Women's Golf twice in a row and then three times, was Beth Daniel. After winning the inaugural event in 1980, she would win it again on August 23, 1981, at the Shaker Heights Country Club in Shaker Heights, Ohio. She would win the event a third time on October 17, 1994, at the Naples National Golf Club in Naples, Florida.

3837. Golfer on the Senior Professional Golfers' Association (PGA) Tour to win more than $100,000 in a season was Miller Barber, who won $106,890 in 1982, the third year of the Senior PGA Tour.

3838. Woman golfer to earn more than $300,000 in a single season was JoAnne Gunderson Carner of the United States, who reached $310,400 in 1982, when she won six titles. Carner had been a five-time winner of the U.S. Women's Amateur title (1957, 1960, 1962, 1966, and 1968) before turning professional.

3839. Ladies Professional Golf Association (LPGA) Tour tournament to be nationally televised for all four rounds was the Dinah Shore tournament on April 1–4, 1982. Sally Little won the event with a 10-under-par 278 at the Mission Hills Country Club in Rancho Mirage, California. The following year it would be designated as one of the four majors on the LPGA Tour.

3840. Golfer to win more than $4 million in official prize money during his career was Jack Nicklaus, who passed that milestone in 1983, although he won no tournaments that year.

3841. Skins Game was held in 1983 at the Desert Highlands Country Club in Scottsdale, Arizona. The winner, Gary Player of South Africa, took home $170,000.

3842. African-American golfer to win the Vardon Trophy for the lowest stroke average on the Professional Golfers' Association (PGA) Tour was Calvin Peete in 1984. He led the PGA in both money and events won between 1982 and 1985.

3843. Total purse on the Professional Golfers' Association (PGA) Tour to top $20 million was in 1984, when the prizes for 46 events totaled $21,251,382.

3844. Golfer to win two of golf's major tournaments in her rookie year on the Ladies Professional Golf Association (LPGA) Tour was Juli Inkster, who won the Dinah Shore on April 8, 1984, at the Mission Hills Country Club in Rancho Mirage, California, and the du Maurier Classic at St. George's Golf and Country Club in Toronto, Ontario, Canada, on July 29. Named Rookie of the Year for 1984, Inkster had actually turned professional late in 1983.

3845. African-American golfer to win the Tournament Players Championship was Calvin Peete in 1985, playing at the tournament's permanent home at the Sawgrass Country Club in Ponte Vedra Beach, Florida. Now called simply the Players Championship, it is sometimes considered a fifth "major."

3846. Woman golfer to earn more than $400,000 in official prize money in a single season was Nancy Lopez, who topped that figure in 1985, when she won five tournaments, including the Ladies Professional Golf Association (LPGA) Championship, and was named LPGA Player of the Year.

3847. Woman golfer to score 20 below par in 72 holes was Nancy Lopez in 1985, who posted a 66-67-69-66 for a total of 268 at the Henredon Classic at the Willow Creek Golf Club in High Point, North Carolina. That year she won her third Vare Trophy for the lowest scoring average on the Ladies Professional Golf Association (LPGA) Tour.

3848. African-American golfer to win the Tournament of Champions later called the Mercedes Championships, was Calvin Peete in 1986 at the La Costa Country Club in Carlsbad, California.

3849. Golf tournament to offer a purse of $1 million was the Panasonic Las Vegas Invitational in 1986.

3850. Golfer to win 18 titles in golf's four major tournaments, and six Masters championships was Jack Nicklaus, who won his 18th major championship and his sixth Masters with a score of 279 at Augusta National Golf Club in Augusta, Georgia, in 1986, more than two decades after his first Masters win in 1963. His other Masters titles had come in 1965, 1966, 1972, and 1975. Added to these were five Professional Golfers' Association (PGA) Championship titles (1963, 1971, 1973, 1975 and 1980), four U.S. Open titles (1962, 1967, 1972, and 1980), and three British Open crowns (1966, 1970, and 1978). His nearest rival in total major titles was Walter Hagen with 11, though Hagen played before the Masters tournament was inaugurated and when the other three major tournaments were suspended for several years during World War I.

3851. Ladies Professional Golf Association (LPGA) Tour season purse to top $10 million was in 1986, when the total prize money available to women golfers reached that mark for 36 events.

3852. Woman golfer to earn more than $2 million in official prize money during her career was Pat Bradley of the United States, who passed that milestone in 1986, when she won five tournaments, including the Dinah Shore, the Ladies Professional Golf Association (LPGA) Championship, and the du Maurier Classic. JoAnne Gunderson Carner of the United States also reached the $2 million mark that same year.

3853. Professional Golfers' Association (PGA) Tour event with a purse of $2 million was the Nabisco Championship of Golf, in its inaugural year, 1987. The event was won by Tom Watson.

3854. Total purse on the Professional Golfers' Association (PGA) Tour to top $30 million was in 1987, when the purses offered totaled $32,106,093.

3855. Tour Championship a season-ending tournament for the 30 highest-earning golfers on the Professional Golfers' Association (PGA) Tour, was held in 1987 at the Oak Hills Country Club in San Antonio, Texas. Initially called the Nabisco Championship of Golf, it was won by Tom Watson with a score of 268; Watson had not had a victory for three years before then.

GOLF—(1980-1989)—*continued*

3856. Woman to be elected to the executive committee of the United States Golf Association (USGA) was Judy Bell in 1987.

3857. Golf course in China was at the Zhongshan Hot Springs Resort in 1988, designed by Arnold Palmer.

3858. Golfer to earn more than $1 million in a single season in official prize money was Curtis Strange in 1988, the year he won his first U.S. Open. He vaulted over the million-dollar milestone when he earned $360,000 for winning the season-ending Nabisco Championship (later called the Tour Championship) for a final total of $1,147,644.

3859. Golfer to win more than $5 million in official prize money during his career was Jack Nicklaus, who passed that milestone in 1988, though he won no tournaments that year.

3860. Golfer to win the Tour Championship in a playoff was Curtis Strange in 1988 at the Pebble Beach Golf Links in Pebble Beach, California. Tied with Tom Kite for 279 at the end of 72 holes, in what was then called the Nabisco Golf Championship, Strange won the playoff with a birdie on the second extra hole.

3861. Woman golfer to earn more than $500,000 in official prize money in a season was Betsy King, who topped that figure in 1989, when she won six tournaments, including the U.S. Women's Open.

GOLF (1990-1999)

3862. African-American golfer to become a member of the Augusta National Golf Club home of the prestigious Masters golf tournament, was television executive Ron Townsend in 1990. The Augusta changed its previous whites-only policy after a highly public controversy involving another whites-only club, the Shoal Creek Country Club in Birmingham, Alabama. The scheduling of the 1990 Professional Golfers' Association (PGA) Championship at Shoal Creek had sparked withdrawal of millions of dollars of corporate sponsorship, in protest over the club's restrictions against African-Americans.

3863. Ben Hogan Tour essentially a minor league sponsored by the Professional Golfers' Association (PGA) Tour, was held in 1990.

3864. Golfer to be named Rookie of the Year and Player of the Year on the Senior Professional Golfers' Association (PGA) Tour was Lee Trevino in 1990, the first year both honors were offered.

3865. Golfer to win more than $1 million in a single season on the Senior Professional Golfers' Association (PGA) Tour was Lee Trevino in 1990, when he won $1,190,518.

3866. Golfer to win more than $6 million in official prize money during his career was Jack Nicklaus, who passed that milestone in 1990.

3867. Woman golfer to earn more than $3 million in official prize money during her career was Pat Bradley of the United States, who passed that milestone in 1990, when she won three tournaments.

3868. Woman golfer to earn more than $600,000 in official prize money in a single season was Beth Daniel, who topped that figure in 1990, when she won eight tournaments, including the Ladies Professional Golf Association (LPGA) Championship.

3869. Solheim Cup golf competition was held on November 16–18, 1990, at the Lake Nona Golf Club, in Orlando, Florida. Modeled after the Ryder Cup for male golfers, it featured United States–born golfers in the Ladies Professional Golf Association (LPGA) competing against European-born golfers in the European Ladies' Professional Golf Association. The U.S. team won the inaugural tournament 11½ to 4½.

3870. Oversized golf clubs were introduced in 1991. The most popular of these large metal "woods" was the Big Bertha, which would become one of the all-time best-selling golf clubs.

3871. African-American golfer to win the U.S. Junior Amateur title was Tiger (Eldrick) Woods, also of Native-American and Asian ancestry, who won the event in July 1991. At only 15 years and 7 months, he was also the youngest winner of the event, which he would win again in 1992.

3872. African-American golfers to become members of the executive committee of the United States Golf Association (USGA) were John Merchant and Leroy Richie in 1992, in the wake of widespread protests about tour events being played at whites-only clubs, which led the USGA and other major golf organizations to require a lifting of restrictions.

3873. Ladies Professional Golf Association (LPGA) Tour season purse to top $20 million was in 1992, when the total prize money available to women golfers was $21,325,000 for 39 events.

3874. Three-Tour Challenge was held in 1992, with representatives of the Ladies Professional Golf Association (LPGA) Tour, the Professional Golfers' Association (PGA), and the Senior Professional Golfers' Association (Senior PGA) Tour competing. The LPGA won the inaugural event on December 27, represented by Patty Sheehan, Nancy Lopez, and Dottie Mochrie (later Pepper), who posted a 4-under-par 212.

3875. Golfer to win the British Open in 267 for 72 holes was Greg Norman, who did so at Sandwich, England, in 1993, bettering Tom Watson's 268 set in 1977.

3876. Total purse on the Professional Golfers' Association (PGA) Tour to top $50 million was in 1993, when the purses for 43 events totaled $53,203,611.

3877. Golfer to win the Professional Golfers' Association (PGA) Championship in under 270 was Nick Price, who posted a score of 269 in 1994 at the Southern Hills Country Club in Tulsa, Oklahoma. That score would be bettered a year later when Steve Elkington and Colin Montgomerie tied at 267 in the 1995 PGA Championship, with Elkington winning in a playoff.

3878. Golfer to win the U.S. Open in a sudden-death playoff was Ernie Els in 1994, playing at the Oakmont Country Club in Oakmont, Pennsylvania. At the end of 72 holes, Els was tied at 279 with Loren Roberts and Colin Montgomerie. After an additional 18 holes, Els and Roberts were still tied with 74, and went into sudden-death, which Els won on the second hole.

3879. Golfer of African-American or Asian-American descent to win the U.S. Amateur Championship was Tiger (Eldrick) Woods, who first won the event on August 28, 1994, at the Sawgrass Country Club in Ponte Vedra Beach, Florida. With African-American, Chinese, and Thai ancestry, Woods was also the youngest winner of the title, at just 18. He would win again in 1995 and 1996, before turning professional.

3880. Presidents Cup Match in golf was played on September 16–18, 1994, at the Robert Trent Jones Golf Club in Lake Manassas, Virginia, pitting golfers from the United States in match play against an international team of non-European players. The U.S. team, captained by Hale Irwin, won the inaugural tournament 20–12 against the international team led by David Graham. The biennial event offers no

purses to individual golfers, all net profits going to charity. The course was designed by and named for golf course architect Robert Trent Jones, Jr. (no relation to noted amateur golfer Bobby Jones).

3881. Golf course to host the British Open championship 25 times was at St. Andrews, Scotland. Its 25th championship came in 1995, when John Daly of the United States won. Its first use for the British Open had come in 1873; before then all Open tournaments had been held at Prestwick, Scotland.

3882. Woman golfer to win more than $5 million, and then $6 million, in official prize money during her career was Betsy King. She crossed the $5 million threshold on May 7, 1995, when she was ranked fifth on the Ladies Professional Golf Association (LPGA) Tour and won the LPGA Classic. Three years later, on March 22, 1998, she would also be the first woman to pass the $6 million mark in professional golf winnings.

3883. Golfer to win 100 professional tournaments was Jack Nicklaus, who won his 100th, The Tradition, in 1996 on the Senior Professional Golfers' Association (PGA) Tour. His extraordinary record began in 1962 with his first tournament win as a professional, in a sudden-death playoff against Arnold Palmer at the U.S. Open, and included 18 wins in golf's four major tournaments: six at the Masters, five at the Professional Golfers' Association (PGA) Championship, four at the U.S. Open, and three at the British Open.

3884. Golfer to win more than $1 million in her rookie year on the Ladies Professional Golf Association (LPGA) Tour was Karrie Webb of Australia, who won $1,002,000 in 1996. After four victories in that debut year, including the LPGA Tour Championship, she was named Rookie of the Year and was also the LPGA's leading money-winner.

3885. Golfer to win more than $10 million in official prize money during a career was Greg Norman of Australia, who passed that landmark in 1996.

3886. Golfer to win more than $2 million in official prize money in a single season was Tiger (Eldrick) Woods in 1997, when he broke the barrier with earnings of $2,066,833, in only his first full year on the Professional Golfers' Association (PGA) Tour. He had turned professional late in 1996 and earned his first $1 million in just 9 events, also a record.

GOLF—(1990-1999)—*continued*

3887. Total purse on the Professional Golfers' Association (PGA) Tour to top $75 million was in 1997, when the prizes for 45 events totaled $77,680,800.

3888. Golfer of African-American or Asian-American descent to win one of golf's major tournaments was Tiger (Eldrick) Woods, when he won the Masters on April 13, 1997, with a tournament-record 18-under-par score of 270 at the championship's traditional home, the Augusta National Golf Club in Augusta, Georgia. Woods is of mixed African-American, Asian, and Native-American ancestry.

3889. Golfer to win more than $2.5 million in official prize money in a single season was David Duval of the United States, who won $2,591,031 in 1998. The previous record of $2,066,833, set by Tiger (Eldrick) Woods in 1997, was also broken in 1998 by another player: Vijay Singh of Fiji, with $2,238,998.

3890. Golfer to win more than $400,000 in the Skins Game was Mark O'Meara, who won $430,000 in 1998 at the Rancho La Quinta Golf Club in La Quinta, California.

3891. Woman golfer to have a season scoring average of under 70 was Annika Sorenstam of Sweden, who averaged 69.99 in 1998, her fifth year on the Ladies Professional Golf Association (LPGA) Tour. That record-setting average brought her the Vare Trophy for the third time in four years, the others being in 1995 and 1996. Sorenstam broke a scoring record of 70.00 set by Karrie Webb just one year earlier.

3892. U.S. Women's Open to be won in a sudden-death playoff was on July 5, 1998, at the Blackwolf Run Golf Resort in Kohler, Wisconsin. Se Ri Pak of South Korea and amateur Jenny Chuasiriporn were tied at 290 at the end of 72 holes and still tied at the end of an 18-hole playoff. Pak won on the second hole of sudden-death.

3893. Presidents Cup Match won by the international team was on December 13, 1998, at the Royal Melbourne Golf Club in Melbourne, Australia, the third time the biennial event was held. The international team, led by Peter Thomson of Australia, won 20½ to 11½ over the United States team captained by Jack Nicklaus. The charity event pits non-European international players against a U.S. team.

3894. Golfer to win more than $7 million in official prize money in a single season was Tiger (Eldrick) Woods, who won $7,681,626 in 1999, more than doubling the previous record of $2.59 million set in 1998 by David Duval. Woods had a total of eight victories during the year, including the last four tournaments in a row, culminating with a $1 million win at the season-ending World Golf Championships at the Valderrama Golf Club in Andalusia, Spain.

3895. Total purse on the Professional Golfers' Association (PGA) Tour to top $100 million was in 1999, when the purses offered for 47 events totaled $131,700,000, a jump of more than $35 million in the total purse in just one year.

3896. Father and son to win golf tournaments on the same day were Bob Duval, who won the Emerald Coast Classic, in Milton, Florida, on the Senior Professional Golfers' Association (PGA) Tour, on March 28, 1999, the same day his son, David Duval, won the Players Championship in Ponte Vedra Beach, Florida, on the Professional Golfers' Association (PGA) Tour.

3897. Golfer to come from 10 strokes behind to win a Professional Golfers' Association (PGA) recognized tournament was Paul Lawrie of Scotland, who on July 18, 1999, was 10 strokes down at the beginning of the fourth round of the British Open at Carnoustie, Scotland, but ended up being tied with Jean Van de Velde of France and Justin Leonard of the United States at a 6-over-par 290 at the end of 72 holes. He then won a four-hole playoff.

3898. Golf event to be broadcast live on network television in prime time was the made-for-TV match play competition between Tiger (Eldrick) Woods and David Duval, played at the Sherwood Country Club in Thousand Oaks, California, on August 2, 1999. In the exhibition for ABC Sports, Woods had a 2-and-1 victory, winning $1.1 million to Duval's $400,000. Each was donating $200,000 to charity.

GOLF (2000-)

3899. Golfer to hold the record low (under-par) scores in all four Professional Golfers Association (PGA) major tournaments was Tiger Woods. He had set a record at the Masters on April 13, 1997, with an 18-under-par score of 270 at the Augusta National Golf Club in Augusta, Georgia. On June 18, 2000, he had a 12-under-par 272, 15 strokes ahead of the field, at the U.S. Open at the Pebble Beach Golf Club in Pebble Beach, California, tying a record first set by Jack Nicklaus in 1980 and also tied by Lee Janzen in 1993. On July 23, 2000, Woods had a 19-under-par score of 269 at the British Open in St. Andrews, Scotland. Finally, on August 20, 2000, he had an 18-under-par Score of 270 at the PGA Championships at the Valhalla Golf Club in Louisville, Kentucky. At 24, he was also the youngest of the five players ever to win all four majors, for a career grand slam in golf.

GYMNASTICS (BEFORE 1900)

3900. Gymnastics school to teach the modern sport was Basedow's School in Dessau, Germany, where Johann Friedrich Simon introduced new approaches to gymnastics from 1776. Germans at home and as emigrants abroad were key to the development of modern gymnastics.

3901. International governing body for gymnastics was the Fédération Internationale de Gymnastique (FIG), founded in 1891.

3902. Men's horizontal bar gymnastics competitions held in the Olympic Games were on April 9, 1896, in Athens, Greece. The inaugural individual winner was Hermann Weingärtner of Germany, who was also on the winning German team, the only time that a gymnastics team competition was held.

3903. Men's long horse vault gymnastics competition held in the Olympic Games was on April 9, 1896, in Athens, Greece. The winner of the inaugural title was Carl Schuhmann of Germany.

3904. Men's rings gymnastics competition held in the Olympic Games was on April 9, 1896, in Athens, Greece. The winner was Ioannis Mitropoulous of Greece.

3905. Men's side (pommel) horse gymnastics competition held in the Olympic Games was on April 9, 1896, in Athens, Greece, where the initial winner was Louis Zutter of Switzerland.

3906. Men's parallel bars gymnastics competitions held in the Olympic Games were in 1896, in Athens, Greece. The winner of the individual event, on April 10, was Alfred Flatow of Germany, who would die 46 years later in the German concentration camp at Theresienstadt. The previous day, Flatow had won gold medals in the team events in both the parallel bars and horizontal bar, the only time they were held.

3907. Men's rope climbing gymnastics competition held in the Olympic Games was on April 10, 1896. in Athens, Greece. The inaugural winner was Nikolaos Andriakopoulous of Greece. The event would be discontinued after 1932.

3908. National championships in gymnastics held in the United States were sponsored by the Amateur Athletic Union (AAU) in 1897. Earl Linderman was crowned the first all-around champion.

GYMNASTICS (1900-1909)

3909. Men's all-around gymnastics competition held in the Olympic Games was in 1900 in Paris, France. Gustave Sandras led a French sweep of the top medals, on July 30.

3910. World championships in gymnastics were held in 1903 in Antwerp, Belgium. For men only until 1934, they were held at varying intervals thereafter except for Olympic years and war years. The 1903 team winner was France. Joseph Martinez, an Algerian competing for France, won the first all-around title. He also shared top honors with Pierre Payssé of France in the horizontal bar, with François Hentges of Luxembourg in the parallel bars, and with Jos Lux of France in the rings. The other competition in 1903 was the horse vault, for which Lux and G. De Jaeghere of France and N. Thysen of the Netherlands shared the title.

3911. Men's team combined exercises gymnastics competition in the Olympic Games was held on July 2, 1904, in St. Louis, Missouri. Of the various United States teams competing, the winners were the Turngemeinde Philadelphia team, from Pennsylvania.

3912. Gymnast with a wooden leg to win a medal in the Olympic Games was George Eyser of the United States at St. Louis, Missouri, in 1904. Wearing a wooden left leg, after an amputation following a train accident, he won an astonishing three gold medals (parallel bars, long horse vault, and rope climbing), two silver (pommel horse and four-event combined competition), and one bronze (horizontal bar), all on October 28.

3913. National team to sweep the top honors in the men's horizontal bar, long horse vault, side (pommel) horse, and rings gymnastics competitions in the Olympic Games was from the United States. Competing in St. Louis, Missouri, on October 28, 1904, Anton Heida, Edward Hennig, and George Eyser finished in that order in the parallel bars, although Eyser had a wooden left leg. That same day, Eyser, Heida, and William Merz of the United States led the field in the long horse vault and the four-event combined exercises; Heida, Eyser, and Merz took top honors in the side (pommel) horse; Hermann Glass, Merz, and Emil Voigt took the medals in the rings; and Eyser, Charles Krause, and Voigt were the top three in rope climbing.

GYMNASTICS—(1900-1909)—*continued*

3914. Gymnast to win two consecutive men's horse vault titles in the world championships was G. de Jaeghere of France, who shared the inaugural title with two others in 1903 and then won it solo in 1905.

3915. Gymnast to win two consecutive men's parallel bar titles in the world championships was Joseph Martinez of Algeria, competing for France. He shared the inaugural title in 1903 and then won it alone in 1905.

3916. Gymnast to win two men's horizontal bar titles in the world championships was Joseph Martinez of Algeria, competing for France. After sharing the inaugural title in 1903, he shared it again in 1909.

GYMNASTICS (1910-1919)
3917. Pommel horse competition held at the world championships in gymnastics was in 1911, when the inaugural winner was Osvaldo Palazzi of Italy.

3918. Gymnast to win two consecutive men's all-around titles in the Olympic Games was Alberto Braglia of Italy. After his first win in 1908, he came back for his second on July 12, 1912, in Stockholm, Sweden, where the events included the horizontal bar, parallel bars, rings, and side (pommel) horse.

3919. Floor exercise competition held at the world championships in gymnastics was in 1913, when the top honors were shared by Giorgio Zampori of Italy and V. Rabic of Bohemia (Czechoslovakia).

3920. Gymnast to win three consecutive men's horizontal bar titles in the world championships was Josef Cada of Bohemia (Czechoslovakia). He shared the title with two others in 1909 and then won it solo in 1911 and 1913.

3921. Gymnast to win two consecutive men's pommel horse titles in the world championships was Osvaldo Palazzi of Italy, who was the inaugural winner in 1911 and then shared the title with two others in 1913.

GYMNASTICS (1920-1929)
3922. Gymnasts to win two consecutive gold medals in the men's team combined exercises in the Olympic Games were Pietro Bianchi, Giuseppe Domenichelli, Carlo Fregosi, Francesco Loi, Paolo Salvi, Giorgio Zampori, and Angelo Zorzi of Italy. Members of the winning team in 1912, they returned with new teammates after World War I to win again on August 24, 1920, in Antwerp, Belgium.

3923. Gymnast to win two consecutive men's all-around titles in the world championships was Peter Sumi of Yugoslavia, who shared the championship in 1922 with Frantisek Pechacek of Bohemia (Czechoslovakia), but then won it outright in 1926.

3924. Gymnast to win three consecutive gold medals in the men's team combined exercises in the Olympic Games was Giorgio Zampori of Italy. He had been on the winning team in 1912 and, with six returning teammates, had won again in 1920. But only he won again with new teammates on July 20, 1924, in Paris, France.

3925. Gymnast to win two consecutive men's rings titles in the world championships was Leon Stukelj of Yugoslavia. He shared the title with three others in 1922, then won it outright in 1926.

3926. Women's team combined exercises gymnastics competition held in the Olympic Games was in 1928 in Amsterdam, the Netherlands, where the team from the Netherlands won on August 10. Four of the ten-member team were Jewish, and three of them would die in German concentration camps during World War II.

GYMNASTICS (1930-1939)
3927. National gymnastics competition in the United States to include women was in 1931, sponsored by the Amateur Athletic Union (AAU). The inaugural all-around champion was Roberta Ranck.

3928. Men's floor exercises gymnastics competition held in the Olympic Games was in 1932 in Los Angeles, California. Competing on August 8, the winner was István Pelle of Hungary.

3929. Men's tumbling gymnastics competition held in the Olympic Games was on August 10, 1932, in Los Angeles, California. Led by Rowland Wolfe, athletes from the United States swept the event, the only time it was held.

3930. World championships in gymnastics to include women was in 1934. Vlasta Dekanova of Czechoslovakia won the inaugural women's all-around title and led her national team to the team title. Titles were not awarded in individual events.

3931. Gymnast to win two consecutive women's all-around titles in the world championships was Vlasta Dekanova of Czechoslovakia, who won in 1938 after taking the inaugural title in 1934.

3932. World championships in gymnastics to award women's titles in specific events was in 1938. Vlasta Dekanova of Czechoslovakia, the women's all-around titlist, won the inaugural balance beam title, as well as the parallel bars title, an event not again offered for women. Matylda Palfyova of Czechoslovakia won the floor exercise title and shared the horse vault honors with Marta Majowska of Poland.

GYMNASTICS (1940-1959)
3933. Uneven (asymmetrical) bars competition held in the world championships for gymnastics was in 1950, for women only. The inaugural title was shared by Gertchen Kolar of Austria and Anna Pettersson of Sweden.

3934. Women's all-around gymnastics competition held in the Olympic Games was in 1952 in Helsinki, Finland. Competing on July 23, the inaugural winner was Maria Horokhovska of the Soviet Union.

3935. Women's balance beam gymnastics competition held in the Olympic Games was on July 23, 1952, in Helsinki, Finland. The inaugural winner was Nina Bocharova of the Soviet Union, edging out her teammate Maria Horokhovska.

3936. Women's floor exercises gymnastics competition held in the Olympic Games was on July 23, 1952, in Helsinki, Finland. The inaugural winner was Agnes Keleti of Hungary, who would win again in 1956.

3937. Women's side horse vault gymnastics competition held in the Olympic Games was on July 23, 1952, in Helsinki, Finland. Yekaterina Kalinchuk led a Soviet Union sweep of the top six places in the competition.

3938. Women's uneven (asymmetrical) bars gymnastics competition held in the Olympic Games was on July 23, 1952, in Helsinki, Finland. The inaugural winner was Margit Korondi of Hungary.

3939. Male gymnast to win more than 10 medals in the Olympic Games was Viktor Chukarin of the Soviet Union, who took home 11. Along with the men's individual all-around titles in both 1952 and 1956, his other medals came in the parallel bars (silver, 1952; gold, 1956); the long horse vault (gold, 1952); the side (pommel) horse (gold, 1952; bronze, 1956); the rings (silver, 1952); the floor exercise (tied for silver, 1956); and the team combined exercises (gold, 1952 and 1956).

3940. Woman gymnast to win 10 medals in the Olympic Games was Agnes Keleti of Hungary, in 1952 and 1956. The medals came in the uneven (asymmetrical) bars (bronze, 1952; gold, 1956); the balance beam (gold, 1956); the floor exercises (gold, 1952 and 1956); the all-around competition (silver, 1956); the team combined exercises (silver, 1952 and 1956); and the now-discontinued team exercise with portable apparatus (bronze, 1952; gold, 1956).

3941. Gymnast to win two consecutive women's floor exercise titles in the Olympic Games was Agnes Keleti of Hungary. After winning the inaugural event in 1952, she went to Melbourne, Australia, to win her second on December 5, 1956, where she also won gold medals in the uneven (asymmetrical) bars, the balance beam, and the team exercise with portable apparatus, a now-discontinued event.

3942. Gymnast to win two consecutive men's floor exercise titles in the world championships was Masao Takemoto of Japan, who shared the title with Valentin Muratov of the Soviet Union in 1954 and won it outright in 1958.

GYMNASTICS (1960-1969)
3943. National governing body specifically for gymnastics in the United States was the United States Gymnastics Federation (USGF), founded in 1963. It would become USA Gymnastics in 1994.

3944. Gymnast to win two consecutive women's all-around titles in the Olympic Games was Larisa Latynina of the Soviet Union. After winning first in 1956, she won her second on September 8, 1960, in Rome, Italy. She would end her career with 18 Olympic medals, including silver in the all-around in 1964.

3945. Gymnasts to win two consecutive gold medals in the women's team combined exercises were Larisa Latynina and Sofia Muratova of the Soviet Union. Part of the winning team in 1956, they led the team to victory again on September 8, 1960, in Rome, Italy.

3946. National team to sweep the top medals in the women's all-around gymnastics competition in the Olympic Games was from the Soviet Union. On September 8, 1960, in Rome, Italy, Larisa Latynina, Sofia Muratova, and Polina Astakhova took the top spots, followed by teammate Marharyta Nikolayeva.

3947. Gymnast to win two consecutive men's horizontal bar titles in the Olympic Games was Takashi Ono of Japan. After winning his first in 1956, he went to Rome, Italy, to take his second, on September 10, 1960.

GYMNASTICS—(1960-1969)—*continued*

3948. Gymnast to win two consecutive titles in the men's rings competition in the Olympic Games was Albert Azaryan of the Soviet Union. An Armenian, he won first in 1956, then went to Rome, Italy, for his second on September 10, 1960. In 1953, he had developed the move now known as the Olympic cross.

3949. World championships in rhythmic sportive gymnastics was held in 1963, a year after the Fédération Internationale de Gymnastique (FIG) recognized it as a sport. Lyudmila Savinkova of the Soviet Union led the field in the all-women competition, while Bulgaria took the all-around team title.

3950. Gymnast to win 9 gold medals and 18 medals overall in the Olympics Games was Larisa Latynina of the Soviet Union, between 1956 and 1964. The medals came in the individual all-around competition (gold, 1956 and 1960; silver, 1964), the side horse vault (gold, 1956; bronze, 1960; silver, 1964), the uneven (asymmetrical) bars (silver, 1956 and 1960; bronze, 1964), the balance beam (silver, 1960; bronze, 1964), the floor exercises (silver, 1956; gold, 1960 and 1964), the team combined exercises (gold, 1956, 1960, and 1964), and the now-discontinued team exercise with portable apparatus (tied for bronze, 1956).

3951. Gymnast to win three consecutive gold medals in the team combined exercises in the Olympic Games was Larisa Latynina of the Soviet Union. On the winning team in 1956 and 1960, she led her team to victory again on October 21, 1964, in Tokyo, Japan, the only gymnast to be part of all three teams.

3952. Gymnast to win two consecutive titles in the women's uneven (asymmetrical) bars in the Olympic Games was Polina Astakhova of the Soviet Union. Following her first win in 1960, she won again on October 22, 1964, in Tokyo, Japan.

3953. Gymnast to win two consecutive women's horse vault titles in the world championships was Vera Caslavska of Czechoslovakia. After winning her first in 1962, she won again in 1966, when she also captured the women's all-around title.

3954. Gymnast to win two consecutive women's side horse vault titles in the Olympic Games was Vera Caslavska of Czechoslovakia. After taking her first title in 1964, she won her second on October 25, 1968, in Mexico City. She also won the women's all-around titles in both years, the balance beam in 1964, and the floor exercises and the uneven (asymmetrical) bars title in 1968.

3955. Gymnast to win two consecutive men's side (pommel) horse titles in the Olympic Games was Miroslav Cerar of Yugoslavia. After his first in 1964, he won his second on October 26, 1968, in Mexico City.

GYMNASTICS (1970-1979)

3956. Gymnast to win three consecutive men's side (pommel) horse titles in the world championships was Miroslav Cerar of Yugoslavia, who won in 1962, 1966, and 1970.

3957. Gymnast to win the all-around title two, and then three, times in the world championships of rhythmic sportive gymnastics was Maria Gigova of Bulgaria, who won in 1969, 1971, and 1973, the last time sharing the title with Galina Shugarova of the Soviet Union.

3958. Gymnast to win two consecutive women's floor exercise titles in the world championships was Lyudmila Tourischeva of the Soviet Union, who won in 1970 and 1974, also winning the all-around title both times.

3959. World cup in gymnastics was held in 1975. The overall winners were both from the Soviet Union: Nikolai Andrianov for the men and Lyudmila Tourischeva for the women.

3960. Gymnast to receive a perfect score of 10 in the Olympic Games was Nadia Comaneci of Romania in 1976 in Montreal, laying the ground for Romanian dominance in gymnastics. She started with two perfect scores during the team competition on July 19, on the uneven (asymmetrical) bars and the balance beam, and would have a total of seven by the end of the gymnastics events, on the way to the women's all-around title and gold medals also in the uneven bars and the balance beam. Nelli Kim of the Soviet Union also received two perfect scores, in the vault and the floor exercises, at the Montreal Olympics.

3961. Male gymnast to win 8 gold medals, and 12 medals overall, in the Olympics Games was Sawao Kato of Japan between 1968 and 1976.

3962. Gymnast to win two consecutive men's floor exercises titles in the Olympic Games was Nikolai Andrianov of the Soviet Union. After winning first in 1972, he won again on July 23, 1976, in Montreal.

3963. Gymnast to win two consecutive men's parallel bars titles in the Olympic Games was Sawao Kato of Japan. After an initial win in 1972, he captured his second crown on July 23, 1976 in Montreal.

GYMNASTICS (1980-1989)

3964. Male gymnast to receive a perfect score of 10 in the Olympic Games was Aleksandr Dityatin of the Soviet Union. For his performance on the long horse vault in the men's all-around competition, he received a 10 on July 24, 1980, in his home country in Moscow, the Soviet Union. The title would be one of his record-breaking eight titles in a single Olympic Games.

3965. Gymnast to win two consecutive titles in the men's long horse vault in the Olympic Games was Nikolai Andrianov of the Soviet Union. After winning first in 1976, he won again in his home country in Moscow on July 25, 1980.

3966. Gymnast to win two consecutive titles in the women's balance beam competition in the Olympic Games was Nadia Comaneci of Romania. After winning first in 1976, she won for a second time on July 25, 1980, in the United States–boycotted Games in Moscow, the Soviet Union.

3967. Athlete to win eight medals in a single Olympic Games all in gymnastics, was Aleksandr Dityatin of the Soviet Union, in the United States–boycotted Games in 1980, in Moscow, the Soviet Union. They included three gold medals (in the men's team combined exercises on July 22, the all-around individual competition on July 24, and the rings on July 25); four silver (in the horizontal bar, parallel bars, pommel horse, and long horse vault); and a bronze in the floor exercises.

3968. Gymnast to win two, and then three, consecutive women's uneven (asymmetrical) bars titles in the world championships was Maxi Gnauck of East Germany. After sharing the title in 1979, she won it outright in 1981 and 1983.

3969. National championships in gymnastics sponsored by the National Collegiate Athletic Association (NCAA) were in 1982, when the team title was won by the University of Utah.

3970. World cup in rhythmic sportive gymnastics was held in 1983. The Soviet Union won the inaugural team honors, and Lilia Ignatova of Bulgaria took the individual title, as she would again in 1986.

3971. Gymnast to be named *Sports Illustrated* Sportsman of the Year was Mary Lou Retton of the United States in 1984, the year she won the women's all-around title in gymnastics in the Olympic Games. She shared the award with hurdler Edwin Moses.

3972. Gymnasts from the United States to win the men's combined exercises title in the Olympic Games were Peter Vidmar, Bart Conner, Mitchell Gaylord, Timothy Daggett, James Hartung, and Scott Johnson. In the Soviet-boycotted Olympics in Los Angeles, California, they emerged as winners over the strongly favored Chinese team on July 31, 1984.

3973. Gymnast from the United States to win the all-around women's title in the Olympic Games was Mary Lou Retton on August 3, 1984, in the Soviet-boycotted Games in Los Angeles, California. In an extremely close competition, she won the title with two perfect scores of 10, on her vault and floor exercise.

3974. Rhythmic gymnastics all-around individual competition held in the Olympic Games for women only, was in 1984 in Los Angeles, California. Competing on August 11, the winner was Lori Fung of Canada.

3975. Gymnast to win two women's balance beam titles in the world championships was Daniela Silivas of Romania, whose second win came in 1989, following her first in 1985.

GYMNASTICS (1990-1999)

3976. Gymnast to win six gold medals in a single Olympic Games was Vitaly Scherbo of Belarus in Barcelona, Spain, in 1992. The medals were for the team combined exercises on July 29, the individual all-around title on July 31, and the side (pommel) horse (a tie with Pae Gil-su of North Korea), the parallel bars, the long horse vault, and the rings on August 2.

3977. Gymnast to win three, and then four, men's rings titles in the world championships was Yuri Chechi of Italy, who won the event four times in a row (1993, 1994, 1995, and 1997), winning the Olympic title as well in 1996.

3978. Gymnasts from the United States to win the women's team title in the Olympic Games were Amanda Borden, Amy Chow, Dominique Dawes, Shannon Miller, Dominique Moceanu, Jaycie Phelps, and Kerri Strug. They won in dramatic fashion on July 23, 1996, in Atlanta, Georgia, Strug nailed the team victory with a final vault, despite having badly sprained an ankle on her previous attempt.

3979. Rhythmic gymnastics team competition held in the Olympic Games was on August 2, 1996, in Atlanta, Georgia. The team from Spain had an upset win over strongly favored Bulgaria.

GYMNASTICS (2000-)

3980. Gymnasts from China to win the men's team title at the Olympic Games were Huang Xu, Li Xiaopeng, Xiao Junfeng, Xing Aowei, Yang Wei, and Zheng Lihui in Sydney, Australia, on September 18, 2000. It was a vindication for Chinese gymnasts, who had won five recent world championships but previously only silver at the Olympics. Li also won the individual men's parallel bars title on September 25.

H

HAMMER THROW

3981. Hammer-throw event held at the Olympic Games was in 1900 in Paris, France. Irish-born John Flanagan of the United States won the event with a throw of 163 feet 1 inch (49.73 meters) on July 16. He would also win the event the next two times it was held, in 1904 and 1908.

3982. Hammer-thrower to hold the officially accepted world record in the men's event was Irish-born Patrick Ryan of the United States. His record distance was 189 feet 6 inches (57.77 meters), set on August 17, 1913, in New York. It would not be broken until 1938.

3983. Hammer-thrower born in the United States to win the men's event in the Olympic Games was Frederick Tootel, with a throw of 174 feet 10 inches (53.295 meters) on July 10, 1924, in Paris, France. United States throwers had won the five previous hammer-throw events, but all had been born in Ireland.

3984. Athlete from independent Ireland to win a gold medal in the Olympic Games was Patrick O'Callaghan, who won the hammer throw on July 30, 1928, in Amsterdam, the Netherlands. He would win again in 1932. Other Irish-born athletes had won earlier, competing for Great Britain or the United States.

3985. Hammer-thrower representing Ireland to win the men's event in the Olympic Games was Patrick O'Callaghan, with a throw of 168 feet 7 inches (51.39 meters) on July 30, 1928, in Amsterdam, the Netherlands. He would win again in 1932. The winners of the first five events (1900–1920) were Irish-born, but all competed for the United States.

3986. Hammer-thrower to break the 190-foot barrier was Erwin Blask of Germany, who broke a 25-year-old record with a throw of 193 feet 7 inches (59.00 meters) on August 27, 1938, in Stockholm, Sweden.

3987. Hammer-thrower to break the 60-meter barrier was József Csermák of Hungary, with a throw of 197 feet 11 inches (60.34 meters) in the men's event on July 24, 1952, in the Olympic Games at Helsinki, Finland.

3988. Hammer-thrower to break the 200-foot barrier was Sverre Strandli of Norway. On September 14, 1952, in Oslo, Norway, he threw for 200 feet 11 inches (61.25 meters), a distance he would better by almost 4 feet in 1953.

3989. Hammer-thrower to break the 210-foot barrier was Stanislav Nyenashev of the Soviet Union, with a throw of 210 feet 1 inch (64.05 meters) in the men's event on December 12, 1954, in Baku, the Soviet Union.

3990. Hammer-thrower to break the 220-foot barrier was Mikhail Krivonosov of the Soviet Union. His throw of 220 feet 10 inches (67.32 meters) in the men's event on October 22, 1956, in Tashkent, the Soviet Union, was the last of his six world records.

3991. Hammer-thrower to break the 70-meter and 230-foot barriers was Harold Connolly of the United States. In the third of his six world records in the men's event, he threw for 230 feet 9 inches (70.33 meters) on August 12, 1960, in Walnut, California. He had become famous in 1956 for his Olympics romance with Czech discus-thrower Olga Fikotová; they married despite Cold War tensions.

3992. Hammer-thrower to break the 240-foot barrier was Gyula Zsivótsky of Hungary, with a throw of 241 feet 11 inches (73.74 meters)—an astonishing 8 feet 2 inches better than the previous record—in the men's event on September 4, 1965, in Debrecen, Hungary. He would up that to 242 feet 0 inches (73.76 meters) in 1968, just before the Mexico City Olympics, where he won the hammer-throw event.

3993. Hammer-thrower to break the 250-foot and 260-foot barriers was Walter Schmidt of West Germany. He broke the first with a throw of 250 feet 8 inches (76.40 meters) in the men's event on September 4, 1971, in Lahr, West Germany, and the second with 260 feet 2 inches (79.30 meters) on August 14, 1975, in Frankfurt am Main, West Germany.

3994. Hammer-thrower to break the 80-meter barrier was Boris Zaychuk of the Soviet Union, with a throw of 262 feet 11 inches (80.14 meters) in the men's event on July 9, 1978, in Moscow, the Soviet Union.

3995. Hammer-thrower to break the 270-foot barrier was Sergey Litvinov of the Soviet Union, who did so decisively on June 4, 1982, with a throw of 275 feet 6 inches (83.98 meters) in the men's event, for the second of his three world records.

3996. Hammer-thrower to break the 280-foot barrier was Yuriy Sedykh of the Soviet Union, with a throw of 283 feet 3 inches (86.34 meters) in the men's event on July 3, 1984, in Cork, Ireland. It was the fourth of his six world records. He was unable to compete in the 1984 Olympics because of the Soviet boycott of the Games.

3997. Hammer-thrower to hold the officially accepted world record in the women's event was Olga Kuzenkova of Russia. Her benchmark throw of 219 feet 3 inches (66.84 meters) was set on February 23, 1994, in Adler, the Czech Republic. The hammer in the women's event weighs 4 kilograms, 3.26 kilograms less than the men's.

3998. Women's hammer-throw event held in the Olympic Games was in 2000 in Sydney, Australia. Kamila Skolimowska of Poland won with a throw of 71.16 meters on September 29.

HANDBALL

3999. International court (four-wall) handball competition was held in 1887, pitting two national champions. Phil Casey of the United States defeated Bernard McQuade of Ireland.

4000. Modern handball development was in Germany in approximately 1895.

4001. United States national four-wall handball championships were held in 1919.

4002. International team handball match was played on September 3, 1925 in Halle/Salle, Germany. The team from Austria beat the one from Germany 6–3.

4003. International government body in handball was the International Amateur Handball Federation (FIHA), founded in 1928. Its first president was Avery Brundage of the United States, later head of the International Olympic Committee. It was replaced in 1946 by the International Handball Federation (IHF).

4004. Men's team handball event held in the Olympic Games was in 1936 in Berlin, Germany. In the finals on August 14, the German team won.

4005. World championships in handball originally for men only, were held in 1938. Teams from Germany won both the 11-a-side outdoor and 7-a-side indoor competitions. Women's competitions would not be added until 1949.

4006. World championships in handball to include women were in 1949, when Hungary won the 11-a-side outdoor women's competition. A 7-a-side women's competition would be added in 1957, played indoors from 1965.

4007. Women's team handball event held in the Olympic Games was in 1976 in Montreal, Quebec, Canada. The finals, on July 28, were won by the team from the Soviet Union.

4008. Handball players to win two consecutive gold medals in women's team handball in the Olympic Games were Natalya Sherstyuk Tymoshkina, Larysa Karlova, Zinaida Turchyna, Tetyana Makarets Kocherhina, Lyudmila Bobrus Poradnyk, Aldona Cesaityte Neneniene, and Lyubov Berezhnaya Odynokova. They had all been on the Soviet Union's winning team in the inaugural event in 1976, then won a second title in their home country in Moscow on July 29, 1980.

4009. International Handball Federation (IHF) Cup team competition was held in 1982. The inaugural winners were the Vfl Gummersbach team of West Germany on the men's side and the IHK Tresnjevka, Zagreb team of Yugoslavia on the women's.

4010. World four-wall handball championships were held in 1984. For men only, the competition was won by Merv Deckert of Canada.

4011. Handball player to win two consecutive gold medals in men's team handball in the Olympic Games was Andrei Lavrov of the Soviet Union. After leading his team to victory in 1988, he did so again on August 8, 1992, in Barcelona, Spain.

HEPTATHLON

4012. Heptathlete to hold the world record in the women's heptathlon was Romana Neubert of East Germany. Competing in Kiev, the Soviet Union, she won the two-day event on June 28, 1981. It included the 100-meter hurdles, 200-meter race, shot put, and high jump on the first day, and the long jump, javelin, and 800-meter race on the second.

4013. Women's heptathlon event held in the Olympic Games was in 1984 in Los Angeles, California, replacing the women's pentathlon. The inaugural winner of the two-day, seven-event competition was Glynis Nunn of Australia on August 4.

HEPTATHLON—*continued*

4014. Heptathlete from the United States, and the first African-American, to hold the world record in the women's event was Jacqueline Joyner-Kersee, who set the first of her four world records in the two-day, seven-event competition on July 7, 1986, in Moscow, the Soviet Union.

4015. Heptathlete from the United States, and the first African-American, to win the women's heptathlon in the Olympic Games was Jacqueline Joyner-Kersee, when she had a world-record performance to win on September 24, 1988, in Seoul, South Korea. Coached by her husband, Bob Kersee, she would win again in 1992; she had been silver medalist in 1984.

4016. Heptathlete to win two consecutive women's heptathlon titles in the Olympic Games was Jacqueline Joyner-Kersee of the United States. After winning in 1988, she returned for another gold medal on August 2, 1992, in Barcelona, Spain. She returned to defend her title in 1996, but was forced to withdraw because of injury.

HIGH JUMP

4017. High-jumper to clear six feet was Marshall Jones Brooks, who jumped 6.20 feet (1.89 meters) on March 17, 1876, at Oxford University in Oxford, England, using the scissors style of jump.

4018. Organized women's high jump competitions were held at Vassar College, in Poughkeepsie, New York, in 1895.

4019. Men's high jump event held in the Olympic Games was on April 10, 1896, in Athens, Greece. Ellery Clark of the United States won the inaugural event with a jump of 5 feet 11¼ inches (1.81 meters), leading a United States sweep of the top three medals.

4020. Men's standing high jump event held in the Olympic Games was on July 16, 1900, in Paris, France. Winning with a jump of 5 feet 5 inches (1.65 meters) was Raymond Ewry of the United States, who would win it again in 1906 and 1908. The event would be discontinued after 1912.

4021. High-jumper to hold the officially accepted world record in the men's event was George Horine of the United States, who jumped 6 feet 7 inches (2.00 meters) on May 18, 1912, in Palo Alto, California.

4022. Women's high jump event held in the Olympic Games was on August 5, 1928, in Amsterdam, the Netherlands. Ethel Catherwood of Canada, popularly called the Saskatoon Lily, won that first event, clearing a height of 5 feet 2½ inches (1.59 meters).

4023. High-jumpers to hold the officially accepted world record in the women's event, and the first from the United States to win the women's event in the Olympic Games were Jean Shiley and Babe (Mildred) Didrikson (later Zaharias), on August 7, 1932, in Los Angeles, California. Both cleared 5 feet 5 inches (1.65 meters), sharing the world record. However, Shiley was given the gold medal and Didrikson the silver because the Olympic judges disapproved of Didrikson's unconventional jumping style, made legal soon afterward.

4024. African-American high-jumper to win the men's title in the Olympic Games was Cornelius Johnson of United States. Competing in Berlin, Germany, he won the event with an Olympic-record jump of 6 feet 8 inches (2.03 meters) on August 2, 1936. The silver-medalist was his African-American teammate David Albritton. German chancellor Adolf Hitler left the stadium before the award ceremony, presumably so he could avoid personally congratulating the winners, as he had done for previous events that day.

4025. High-jumper to clear seven feet was Charles Dumas of the United States. Using the straddle-style jump, he leaped 7 feet ½ inch (2.15 meters) in the men's event on June 29, 1956, at the United States Olympic trials in Los Angeles, California. He would win at the Olympics on November 23 in Melbourne, Australia, with a jump of 6 feet 11½ inches.

4026. High-jumper to clear six feet in the women's event was Iolanda Balas of Romania. Competing in her homeland, in Bucharest, on October 18, 1958, she leaped 6 feet 0 inches (1.83 meters), for the sixth of her 14 world records.

4027. High-jumper to set or equal four world records in the men's event in a single year was John Thomas of the United States, who jumped 7 feet 1½ inches (2.17 meters) on April 30, 1960, in Philadelphia, Pennsylvania. He equaled that on May 21 in Cambridge, Massachusetts; raised it by ½ inch on June 24 in Bakersfield, California, and then on July 1 reached 7 feet 3½ inches in Palo Alto, California.

4028. High-jumper to set more than 10 world records in the women's event was Iolanda Balas of Romania, who set 14. Her final record was 6 feet 3¼ inches (1.91 meters), set on July 16, 1961, in Sofia, Bulgaria. It would stand for more than 10 years.

4029. High-jumper to set six world records in the men's event was Valeriy Brumel of the Soviet Union. His first record was 7 feet 3¼ inches (2.23 meters), set on June 18, 1961, in Moscow, the Soviet Union. He raised that five more times, finally on July 21, 1963, to 7 feet 5¾ inches (2.28 meters), also in Moscow.

4030. High-jumper to win two consecutive women's titles in the Olympic Games was Iolanda Balas of Romania. After winning in 1960, she won again in Tokyo, Japan, with an Olympic-record jump of 6 feet 2¾ inches (1.90 meters) on October 15, 1964.

4031. High-jumper to use the "Fosbury flop" jumping method was Richard Fosbury of the United States, who introduced the backward-arching jump internationally at the Olympic Games in Mexico City, where he won the men's event with an Olympic-record leap of 7 feet 4¼ inches (2.24 meters) on October 20, 1968. The technique would become standard within a decade.

4032. High-jumper to reach, and then break, the 8-foot barrier was Javier Sotomayor Sanabria of Cuba. He had a jump of 8 feet 0 inches (2.44 meters) on July 29, 1989, in San Juan, Puerto Rico. Four years later, on July 27, 1993, he would leap 8 feet ¼ inch (2.45 meters) in Salamanca, Spain.

HOCKEY, FIELD

4033. National governing body for field hockey was the English Hockey Association, founded in London in 1875. The modern game developed in England in the 19th century, though stick-and-ball games date back thousands of years.

4034. Field hockey club established in India was founded in Calcutta in 1885.

4035. Introduction of field hockey into the United States was in 1901, when Constance Applebee of Great Britain taught the game to students at several eastern women's colleges, most notably Vassar College, Wellesley College, Smith College, Mount Holyoke College, and Bryn Mawr College. In the United States, it would remain a popular sport in women's schools and colleges, though the Olympic competitions would be for men only until 1980.

4036. Men's field hockey event held in the Olympic Games was in 1908 in London, England. Winning on October 31 was a team from England, which was undefeated, followed by teams from Ireland, Scotland, and Wales.

4037. National field hockey organization in the United States was the United States Field Hockey Association, founded in 1922. Though founded by women, the organization's first president was a man, Edward B. Krumbhaar.

4038. Field hockey players to win two gold medals in the Olympic Games were Richard Allen, Leslie Hammond, Broome Eric Pinniger, and Dhyan Chand of India, competing under the flag of Great Britain. After taking their first title in 1928, they won again with other teammates on August 11, 1932, in Los Angeles, California. Allen and Chand would win again in 1936.

4039. Field hockey players to win three gold medals in the Olympic Games were Richard Allen and Dhyan Chand of India, competing under the flag of Great Britain. After winning the event in 1928 and again in 1932, they joined new teammates to win again on August 15, 1936, in Berlin, Germany. Chand, who played barefoot, was later coach of India's national team, which would win the next three competitions (1948, 1952, and 1956), before losing to Pakistan in 1960.

4040. Women's field hockey event held in the Olympic Games was in 1980 in Moscow, the Soviet Union. After the United States and other teams pulled out because of the Olympic boycott, several other teams were hurriedly put together. One of them was from Zimbabwe, which won the event on July 31. It was the country's first Olympics following the takeover of the government by the black majority, but the team was all white.

HOCKEY, ICE (BEFORE 1900)

4041. Ice hockey game was played at the Victoria Skating Rink in Montreal, Quebec, Canada, on March 3, 1875, between two teams of nine men each. Nova Scotian James Creighton, who captained one of the teams, was a key figure in the very popular sport that then emerged, based on a variety of similar games played in Nova Scotia.

4042. Intercollegiate ice hockey game on record was between Oxford and Cambridge universities, both from Great Britain, playing in St. Moritz, Switzerland, in 1885.

HOCKEY, ICE—(BEFORE 1900)—*continued*

4043. Canadian ice hockey league was the Amateur Hockey Association of Canada, founded in the winter of 1886–1887. It consisted of three teams from Montreal, Quebec, plus a fourth from Montreal's McGill University and a fifth from Ottawa, Ontario.

4044. International ice hockey tournament was held at Burlington, Vermont, during the Burlington Winter Carnival, on Lake Champlain, Vermont, on February 22–26, 1886. It was won by the Montreal Hockey Club of the Montreal Amateur Athletic Association from Montreal, Quebec, Canada, which defeated Burlington's Van Ness House Club and the Montreal Crystals in a three-team tournament.

4045. Ice hockey team to win the Stanley Cup was the Montreal Amateur Athletic Association in 1893, from Montreal, Quebec, Canada. Donated by Lord Stanley of Preston, Governor General of Canada, the cup was initially given to the best amateur hockey team in Canada. Only later did professional clubs and clubs outside Canada also compete for the trophy. From 1926 the trophy would be restricted to National Hockey League teams.

4046. Ice hockey team to win the Stanley Cup twice in a row was the Montreal Amateur Athletic Association, from Montreal, Quebec, Canada, which took the trophy for a second time in 1894, after having won the inaugural offering in 1893.

4047. Ice hockey exhibition game in Great Britain took place in 1895, though informal games resembling ice hockey reportedly took place from at least the 1850s.

4048. United States ice hockey league was the American Amateur Hockey League, founded in the winter of 1898–1899.

4049. American Amateur Hockey League championship was won by the Brooklyn Skating Club in 1899 of Brooklyn, New York.

4050. Ice hockey game on record in Russia took place on the Neva River in St. Petersburg in 1899, between a Russian team named Sport and a team composed of Britons living in Russia.

4051. Professional ice hockey player of Black African ancestry on record was Hipple Galloway of Dunnville, Ontario, Canada, who played with the Woodstick team of the Central Ontario Hockey Association, in 1899.

HOCKEY, ICE (1900-1909)

4052. Ice hockey team to win the Stanley Cup three times was the Montreal Amateur Athletic Association, of Montreal, Quebec, Canada. The team had won the trophy the first two times it was offered, in 1893 and 1894, and then won it again in 1902. At that time, the trophy was offered to the best amateur hockey team in Canada, not to professionals or to clubs outside Canada.

4053. Professional ice hockey club in the United States was the Portage Lakes, Michigan, team, organized by J. L. Gibson, in 1903. Gibson went on to found the professional International Hockey League in 1904.

4054. International professional ice hockey league was founded by J. L. Gibson in 1904: the International Hockey League, composed of several Canadian and American teams.

4055. Ice hockey team to win the Stanley Cup three times in a row was the Ottawa Silver Seven, of Ottawa, Ontario, Canada, captained by A. T. Smith, which won it in 1903, 1904, and 1905. Only later, after 1926, would the Stanley Cup be restricted to National Hockey League team competition.

4056. Ice hockey game played in Australia was in 1907, between a Melbourne team and a team drawn from the crew of the United States warship *Baltimore*, then visiting Australia.

4057. Major international ice hockey organization was the International Ice Hockey Federation (IIHF), founded in 1908 by the national ice hockey federations of Great Britain, France, Belgium, and Switzerland.

HOCKEY, ICE (1910-1919)

4058. English Ice Hockey League Championship was held in 1910 and was won by the London Canadians, one of the five teams in the league, which also included Cambridge University, the Princes team, Argyll, and the Amateur Skating Club.

4059. Professional ice hockey league on North America's West Coast was the Pacific Coast Hockey Association, founded in 1911. Organized by Lester Patrick and Frank Patrick, the new league was headquartered in Vancouver, British Columbia, Canada.

4060. Pacific Coast Hockey Association championship was held in 1912 and was won by the New Westminster Royals, with a 9-6 won-lost record that topped the league.

4061. Four teams in the National Hockey League were the Montreal Canadiens, the Toronto Arenas, the Ottawa Senators, and the Montreal Wanderers, in the 1917–1918 season. The Quebec Bulldogs were also a franchise, but did not begin play until 1919.

4062. Hockey player from the United States to play in the National Hockey League was Jerry Geran, who joined the Montreal Wanderers in 1917 and played with them during the 1917–1918 season.

4063. Hockey team from outside Canada to win the Stanley Cup was the Seattle Metropolitans, of Seattle, Washington, in 1917. That was before National Hockey League clubs vied for the trophy, when it was still offered to the best amateur hockey team.

4064. National Hockey League game was a 10–9 Montreal Wanderers win over the Toronto Arenas, on December 19, 1917.

4065. National Hockey League goal was scored by Dave Ritchie of the Montreal Wanderers, against the Toronto Arenas, on December 19, 1917.

4066. Hockey player to lead the National Hockey League in scoring was Joe Malone of the Montreal Canadiens, with 44 points in the 1917–1918 season. The Leading Scorer Trophy would be renamed the Art Ross Trophy in 1947, after the former manager-coach of the Boston Bruins.

4067. National Hockey League team to win the Stanley Cup was the Toronto Arenas, in 1918. The Arenas and the Montreal Canadiens ended the NHL's first season tied, with a record of 13-9. Toronto won a two-game playoff to become NHL champion and then went on to defeat a non-NHL Vancouver team for the Stanley Cup. The Arenas would be renamed the Toronto St. Patricks in 1919 and then the Toronto Maple Leafs in 1926. The Stanley Cup had earlier been offered only to amateur hockey teams in Canada.

4068. National Hockey League shutout was a 9–0 Montreal Canadiens win over the Toronto Arenas on February 18, 1918, with Georges Vezina playing goaltender for the Canadiens.

4069. Stanley Cup hockey playoffs to be canceled was the series between the Montreal Canadiens and the Seattle Metropolitans in 1919. The competition was called off because of the flu pandemic that killed millions of people worldwide in 1918–1919.

HOCKEY, ICE (1920-1929)

4070. Men's world championships in ice hockey were held in 1920, when the first title was won by Canada. They would be held annually from 1930.

4071. Ottawa Senators National Hockey League Stanley Cup championship came in 1920, with a three games to two win over the Seattle Metropolitans.

4072. National Hockey League player to score seven goals in a single game was Joe Malone of the Quebec Bulldogs, against the Toronto St. Patricks, on January 31, 1920.

4073. Ice hockey event to be held in the Olympic Games was in 1920 in Antwerp, Belgium. The Winnipeg Falcons, who had just won the Canadian championship, represented Canada and emerged victorious on April 26. Olympic ice hockey events would be all male until 1998, when women's ice hockey was first introduced into the Olympics.

4074. National Hockey League team to win the Stanley Cup twice in a row was the Ottawa Senators, coached by Pete Green, who won it in 1920 and 1921. They had previously won the Stanley Cup as a non-NHL team in 1909.

4075. International hockey game played in Sweden was a 4–1 win by an Uppsala, Sweden, team over a Berlin, Germany, team, on January 31, 1921.

4076. Toronto St. Patricks National Hockey League Stanley Cup championship came in 1922, with a three games to two win over the Vancouver Millionaires.

4077. National Hockey League tie game was a 4–4 game between the Ottawa Senators and the Toronto St. Patricks, on February 11, 1922, at Ottawa, Ontario, Canada.

4078. National Hockey League goaltender to score at least one goal in 16 consecutive games was Harry Broadbent of the Montreal Canadiens, with the last game in his streak coming on February 15, 1922.

4079. National Hockey League game played without any penalties being assessed was a 5–4 Montreal Canadiens win over the Hamilton Tigers, on January 31, 1923.

4080. Montreal Canadiens National Hockey League Stanley Cup championship came in 1924 with a two-games-to-none win over the Calgary Tigers.

4081. National Hockey League player to win the Hart Memorial Trophy as the league's Most Valuable Player was Frank Nighbor of the Ottawa Senators in 1924.

HOCKEY, ICE—(1920-1929)—*continued*

4082. Team from the United States to join the National Hockey League was the Boston Bruins, in the 1924–1925 season, playing along with five Canadian teams.

4083. National team to win two consecutive ice hockey titles at the Olympic Winter Games was from Canada in 1924 at Chamonix, France. Representing Canada, the Toronto Granites won the championship on February 8. The Winnipeg Falcons had won for Canada in 1920.

4084. National Hockey League 0–0 tie was between the Hamilton Tigers and the Ottawa Senators, on December 24, 1924. The goalies were Alex Connell for Ottawa and Jake Forbes for Hamilton.

4085. National Hockey League player to win the Lady Byng Memorial Trophy as the most gentlemanly player was Frank Nighbor of the Ottawa Senators in 1925. He also won it again in 1926.

4086. Goalie to have 20 career shutouts in the National Hockey League was Clint Benedict of the Ottawa Senators, who reached that milestone on January 20, 1925.

4087. American Division was formed in the National Hockey League in the 1926–1927 season. It included the New York Rangers, Boston Bruins, Chicago Blackhawks, Pittsburgh Pirates, and Detroit Cougars. They played against the Canadian Division, which also included a United States team, the New York Americans (formerly the Quebec Bulldogs), along with four Canadian teams: the Ottawa Senators, the Montreal Canadiens, the Montreal Maroons, and the Toronto St. Patricks, which in that year became the Toronto Maple Leafs.

4088. Montreal Maroons National Hockey League Stanley Cup championship came in 1926, with a three games to one win over the Victoria Cougars.

4089. National Hockey League player to be named outstanding goaltender was George Hainsworth of the Montreal Canadiens in 1927, with a season goals-against average of 1.52.

4090. National Hockey League team to win 25 games in a single season was the Ottawa Senators, who reached that milestone with a 2–1 win over the Pittsburgh Pirates, on March 3, 1927.

4091. National Hockey League goaltender to be credited with four shutouts in a single set of Stanley Cup playoffs was Clint Benedict of the Montreal Maroons, in 1928.

4092. National Hockey League player to be named outstanding goaltender two, and then three, consecutive times was George Hainsworth of the Montreal Canadiens. He won the honor the first three times it was awarded, in 1927, 1928, and 1929, when his goals-against average dropped to 0.98.

4093. New York Rangers National Hockey League Stanley Cup championship came in 1928, with a three games to two win over the Montreal Maroons.

4094. International hockey game between Sweden and Finland was an 8–1 Swedish IK Gota defeat of the Helsinki Selects, at Helsinki, Finland, on January 29, 1928.

4095. National Hockey League goaltender to have six consecutive shutouts was Alex Connell of the Ottawa Senators, with a 1–0 win over the Montreal Canadiens, on February 18, 1928.

4096. National team to win three consecutive ice hockey titles at the Olympic Winter Games was Canada in 1928 at St. Moritz, Switzerland. The Toronto Graduates, formerly the 1926 Toronto University team, won for Canada on February 19. Teams representing Canada had also won the first two Olympic ice hockey titles in 1920 and 1924.

4097. National Hockey League goaltender to reach 50 career shutouts was Alex Connell of the Ottawa Senators, with a 5–0 win over the New York Americans, on March 22, 1928.

4098. Boston Bruins regular season hockey game played at Boston Garden in Boston, Massachusetts, was a 1–0 Bruins loss to the Montreal Canadiens, on November 20, 1928.

4099. Boston Bruins National Hockey League Stanley Cup championship came in 1929, with a two games to none win over the New York Rangers.

4100. National Hockey League goaltender to be credited with 22 shutouts in a single season was George Hainsworth of the Montreal Canadiens, in 1929.

HOCKEY, ICE (1930-1939)

4101. National Hockey League goaltender to wear a facemask in a scheduled game was Clint Benedict of the Montreal Maroons, who wore the mask while injured, in a game against the New York Americans, on February 20, 1930.

4102. All-Star National Hockey League Team selected by the Professional Hockey Writers' Association was in 1931. That first team included Aurel Joliet, left wing, and Howie Morenz, center, both of the Montreal Canadiens; right wing Bill Cook of the New York Rangers; defensemen Eddie Shore of the Boston Bruins and King Clancy of the Toronto Maple Leafs; and goaltender Charles Gardiner of the Chicago Blackhawks.

4103. National Hockey League game in which three assists were credited on a single goal was a 1–1 tie between the Toronto Maple Leafs and the Detroit Falcons, on February 14, 1931.

4104. Toronto Maple Leafs regular season hockey game played at Maple Leaf Gardens in Toronto, Ontario, Canada, was a 3–1 loss to the Chicago Blackhawks, on November 12, 1931. The team would play at Maple Leaf Gardens until 1999.

4105. National Hockey League player to be named the league's Most Valuable Player twice in a row was Howie Morenz of the Montreal Canadiens, who was so honored in 1931 and 1932. He had previously been named MVP in 1928.

4106. Toronto Maple Leafs National Hockey League Stanley Cup championship came in 1932, with a three games to none win over the New York Rangers.

4107. National team to win four consecutive ice hockey titles at the Olympic Winter Games was Canada in 1932 at Lake Placid, New York. Drawn from Winnipeg, the Canadian team won on February 13. Other teams representing Canada had won in 1920, 1924, and 1928.

4108. National Hockey League player to be named Rookie of the Year was Carl Voss of the Detroit Red Wings in 1933. The award was named the Calder Trophy in 1937, after NHL president Frank Calder, and from 1943 the Calder Memorial Trophy.

4109. National Hockey League player to reach 250 career goals was Howard Morenz of the Montreal Canadiens, who reached that milestone on December 28, 1933.

4110. Chicago Blackhawks National Hockey League Stanley Cup championship came in 1934, with a three games to one win over the Detroit Red Wings.

4111. National Hockey League All-Star Game was played on February 14, 1934, when the Toronto Maple Leafs defeated the NHL All-Stars 7–3. Played at Maple Leaf Gardens, in Toronto, Ontario, Canada, the game was a benefit for Toronto left wing Ace Bailey, who had been forced into retirement after a skull injury earlier in the season. Annual all-star games would not be held until 1947 and would be competitions between divisions or conferences only from 1969.

4112. National Hockey League player to lead the league in scoring twice in a row was Charlie Conacher of the Toronto Maple Leafs, who had 52 points in 1934 and 57 in 1935.

4113. National Hockey League player to win the Lady Byng Memorial Trophy as the most gentlemanly player seven times was Frank Boucher of the New York Rangers (1928–1931 and 1933–1935).

4114. Detroit Red Wings National Hockey League Stanley Cup championship came in 1936, with a three games to one win over the Toronto Maple Leafs.

4115. Ice hockey team from Great Britain to win the gold medal at the Olympic Winter Games won in 1936 at Garmisch-Partenkirchen, Germany. Winning on February 16, they were the first non-Canadian team to win the Olympic ice hockey championship.

4116. National Hockey League player to reach 250 career assists was Frank Boucher of the New York Rangers, who did so on March 9, 1937.

4117. National Hockey League European tour was a series of exhibition games played by the Detroit Red Wings and Montreal Canadiens in 1938.

HOCKEY, ICE (1940-1949)

4118. National Hockey League player to score five goals in a single Stanley Cup playoff game was Maurice Richard of the Montreal Canadiens, against the Toronto Maple Leafs, on March 23, 1944.

4119. National Hockey League player to score 50 goals in a single season was Maurice Richard of the Montreal Canadiens, who scored his 50th during the last game of the season, a 4–2 Canadiens win over the Boston Bruins, on March 18, 1945.

4120. National Hockey League player to be named outstanding goaltender four times in a row was Bill Durnan of the Montreal Canadiens (1944–1947).

HOCKEY, ICE—(1940-1949)—*continued*

4121. National Collegiate Athletic Association college hockey championship was won by the University of Michigan, with an 8–4 defeat of Dartmouth College at Colorado Springs, Colorado, in 1948.

4122. National team to win five ice hockey titles at the Olympic Winter Games was Canada. The fifth Canadian title came on February 8, 1948, at St. Moritz, Switzerland, in the first post–World War II Olympics. That gave Canada five of the first six Olympic ice hockey titles, with wins in 1920, 1924, 1928, and 1932, before a loss in 1936.

4123. National Hockey League team to win the Stanley Cup three times in a row was the Toronto Maple Leafs, who had their third consecutive win in 1949, following wins in 1947 and 1948. Previously known as the Toronto Arenas, then the Toronto St. Patricks, they were in this period coached by Hap Day.

HOCKEY, ICE (1950-1959)
4124. National Hockey League player to be named outstanding goaltender six times was Bill Burnan of the Montreal Canadiens (1944–1947 and 1949–1950).

4125. National Collegiate Athletic Association hockey player to score five goals in a single "Frozen Four" tournament game was Carl Lawrence of the University of Colorado, against Boston College, on March 16, 1950.

4126. National Hockey League All-Star Game to be televised was the 7–1 Detroit Red Wings win over an All-Star team, on October 8, 1950, at Olympia Stadium, in Detroit, Michigan.

4127. National Hockey League goaltender to reach 300 career wins was Turk Broda of the Toronto Maple Leafs, who reached that mark with a 6–1 win over the Montreal Canadiens, on December 20, 1950.

4128. National team to win six ice hockey titles at the Olympic Winter Games was Canada in 1952 in Oslo, Norway. The Canadian team took their sixth title in seven Olympic competitions on February 24, their other wins having come in 1920, 1924, 1928, 1932, and 1948.

4129. National Collegiate Athletic Association hockey team to win the "Frozen Four" tournament in three consecutive years was the University of Michigan, from 1951 to 1953.

4130. National Hockey League coach to reach 600 career wins was Dick Irvin of the Montreal Canadiens, who reached that milestone with a 3–2 win over the Chicago Blackhawks, on October 22, 1953.

4131. National Hockey League player to be named outstanding defenseman was Red Kelly of the Detroit Red Wings in 1954.

4132. National Hockey League player to lead the league in scoring four times in a row was Gordie Howe of the Detroit Red Wings. He won the Art Ross Trophy for scoring in four consecutive years (1951–1954), and then went on to win it twice more, in 1957 and 1963.

4133. National Collegiate Athletic Association hockey player to score seven points in a single "Frozen Four" tournament game was John Mayasich of the University of Minnesota, against Boston College, on March 11, 1954.

4134. National Hockey League player to reach 400 career goals was Maurice Richard of the Montreal Canadiens, during a 4–2 Montreal win over the Chicago Blackhawks, on December 18, 1954.

4135. Ice hockey team from the Soviet Union to win the gold medal at the Olympic Winter Games was on February 4, 1956, at Cortina d'Ampezzo, Italy.

4136. National Hockey League player to reach 500 career goals was Maurice Richard of the Montreal Canadiens, during a 3–1 win over the Chicago Blackhawks, on October 19, 1957.

4137. National Hockey League player to be named outstanding defenseman four times in a row was Doug Harvey of the Montreal Canadiens (1955–1958). He would win the award twice more with Montreal (1960 and 1961 seasons) and again with the New York Rangers (1962).

4138. African-American to play in the National Hockey League was Willie O'Rhee, who played with the Boston Bruins, starting on January 18, 1958.

HOCKEY, ICE (1960-1969)
4139. National Hockey League player to be named outstanding goaltender five times in a row was Jacques Plante of the Montreal Canadiens (1956–1960).

4140. National Hockey League team to win the Stanley Cup five times in a row was the Montreal Canadiens (1956–1960), coached by Toe Blake.

4141. Ice hockey team from the United States to win the title at the Olympic Winter Games was at Squaw Valley, California, on February 28, 1960. Led by goaltender Jack McCartan, it was the first U.S. team to defeat a Soviet Olympic ice hockey team.

4142. National Hockey League player to reach 1,000 career points was Gordie Howe of the Detroit Red Wings, during a 2-0 win over the Toronto Maple Leafs, on November 27, 1960.

4143. National Hockey League player to be named Most Valuable Player of the NHL All-Star Game was Eddie Shack of the Toronto Maple Leafs on October 6, 1962.

4144. National Hockey League player to be named the league's Most Valuable Player six times was Gordie Howe of the Detroit Red Wings (1952, 1953, 1957, 1958, 1960, and 1963).

4145. National Hockey League Amateur Draft was conducted on June 5, 1963, in Montreal, Quebec, Canada. The first pick in the draft went to the Montreal Canadiens, who selected Garry Monahan of the St. Michael's Juveniles team from Toronto, Ontario, Canada.

4146. National Collegiate Athletic Association college hockey team to win the "Frozen Four" tournament seven times was the University of Michigan, between 1948 and 1964.

4147. National Hockey League player to win the Conn Smythe Trophy as the Most Valuable Player of the playoffs was Jean Beliveau of the Montreal Canadiens in 1965.

4148. National Hockey League goaltender to reach 400 career wins was Terry Sawchuk of the Toronto Maple Leafs, with a 5–2 win over the Montreal Canadiens, on February 4, 1965.

4149. Pittsburgh Penguins regular season hockey game played at the Pittsburgh Civic Arena in Pittsburgh, Pennsylvania, was a 2–1 loss to the Montreal Canadiens, on October 11, 1967. Popularly called the Igloo, because of its shape, it was renamed the Mellon Arena in 1999.

4150. Philadelphia Flyers regular season hockey game played at The Spectrum in Philadelphia, Pennsylvania, was a 1–0 win over the Pittsburgh Penguins, on October 19, 1967.

4151. New York Rangers regular season hockey game played at Madison Square Garden in New York City was a 3–1 win over the Philadelphia Flyers, on February 18, 1968.

4152. National Hockey League player to score 100 points in a single season was Phil Esposito of the Boston Bruins, who scored his 99th and 100th points in a 4–0 Bruins win over the Pittsburgh Penguins, on March 2, 1969.

HOCKEY, ICE (1970-1979)

4153. Hockey player to be named *Sports Illustrated* Sportsman of the Year was Bobby Orr of Canada, a key scorer and defenseman for the Boston Bruins, in 1970.

4154. National Hockey League goaltender to reach a career total of 103 shutouts was Terry Sawchuk, in a 21-year-long career (1949–1970) that saw him play 971 games and post 447 wins.

4155. National Collegiate Athletic Association college hockey player to score five assists in a single "Frozen Four" tournament game was Bob Pollenroth of the University of Wisconsin, against Michigan Tech University, on March 21, 1970.

4156. Vancouver Canucks regular season hockey game played at the Pacific Coliseum at Vancouver, British Columbia, Canada, was a 3–1 loss to the Los Angeles Kings, on October 9, 1970. The Canucks would play at the Coliseum until 1995.

4157. Buffalo Sabres regular season hockey game played at Memorial Auditorium at Buffalo, New York, was a 3–0 loss to the Montreal Canadiens, on October 15, 1970. Memorial would be the Sabres' home field until 1996.

4158. National Hockey League player to reach 1,000 career assists was Gordie Howe of the Detroit Red Wings, during a 5–3 Detroit win over the Boston Bruins, on October 29, 1970.

4159. National Hockey League defenseman to have 102 assists in a single season was Bobby Orr of the Boston Bruins, in 1971.

4160. National Hockey League player to be named Most Valuable Player of the NHL All-Star Game twice in a row was Bobby Hull, of the Chicago Blackhawks, in 1970 and 1971.

4161. Ice hockey competition in the Olympic Winter Games to be boycotted was in 1972 at Sapporo, Japan. Six-time Olympic champions, the Canadians did not participate in the competition, in protest over having to play against government-supported professionals from the Soviet Union and other Communist countries. Canada would boycott again in 1976, joined by Sweden, but both countries would return to the Games in 1980.

HOCKEY, ICE—(1970-1979)—*continued*

4162. New York Islanders regular season hockey game played at the Nassau Veterans Memorial Coliseum in Uniondale, New York, was a 3–2 loss to the Atlanta Flames, on October 7, 1972.

4163. Quebec Nordiques regular season hockey game played at the Colisée de Québec in Quebec City, Quebec, Canada, was a 6–0 win over the Alberta Oilers (later the Edmonton Oilers), on October 13, 1972.

4164. National Hockey League coach to be named Coach of the Year was Fred Shero of the Philadelphia Flyers in 1974.

4165. Philadelphia Flyers National Hockey League Stanley Cup championship came in 1974, with a four games to two win over the Boston Bruins.

4166. Washington Capitals regular season hockey game played at the US Air Arena in Landover, Maryland, was a 1–1 tie with the Los Angeles Kings, on December 15, 1974. The Capitals would play at the Arena until 1997.

4167. National Hockey League player to be named outstanding defenseman eight times in a row was Bobby Orr of the Boston Bruins, who won the honor from 1968 through 1975.

4168. National Hockey League player to be named the Most Valuable Player of the playoffs twice in a row was Bernie Parent of the Philadelphia Flyers in 1974 and 1975.

4169. New England Whalers regular season hockey game played at the Hartford Civic Center Coliseum in Hartford, Connecticut, was a 4–3 win over the San Diego Mariners, on January 11, 1975.

4170. National Hockey League player to score 19 goals in a single set of Stanley Cup playoffs was Reggie Leach of the Philadelphia Flyers, in 1976.

4171. National Hockey League team to win 60 games in a single season was the Montreal Canadiens, in 1977.

4172. National Hockey League team to win the Stanley Cup more than 20 times was the Montreal Canadiens, who won their 20th Stanley Cup as an NHL team in 1978, building their total to 23 through 1999. The team had also won a Stanley Cup in 1916 as a non-NHL team.

4173. Canada Cup ice hockey competition was held in 1979, with the top six teams in the world competing. The team from Canada won the first tournament. Sponsored by the International Ice Hockey Federation (IIHF), it would be held irregularly until 1996, when it was replaced by the World Cup.

4174. Hockey player to play for more than 25 seasons in the National Hockey League was Gordie Howe, who spent 25 years with the Detroit Red Wings (1946–1971), then came back for a final season with the Hartford Whalers (1979–1980). Howe's very long career also included seven years with World Hockey Association teams, concluding with two seasons at the Hartford Whalers, which joined the NHL for Howe's last season.

4175. Edmonton Oilers regular season hockey game played at the Northlands Coliseum at Edmonton, Alberta, Canada, was a 3–3 tie with the Detroit Red Wings, on October 13, 1979. Northlands was later renamed the Edmonton Coliseum and, in 1998, theSkyreach Centre.

4176. Winnipeg Jets regular season hockey game played at the Winnipeg Arena, in Winnipeg, Manitoba, Canada, was a 4–2 win over the Colorado Rockies, on October 14, 1979.

4177. Detroit Red Wings regular season hockey game played at Joe Louis Arena in Detroit, Michigan, was a 3–2 loss to the St. Louis Blues, on December 27, 1979. Brian Sutter of the Blues scored the first goal.

HOCKEY, ICE (1980-1989)

4178. Hockey player to play more than 1,700 games in the National Hockey League was Gordie Howe, who played in 1,767 games over 26 years (1946–1971 and 1979–1980).

4179. New York Islanders National Hockey League Stanley Cup championship came in 1980, with a four games to two win over the Philadelphia Flyers.

4180. Father and son to be named Most Valuable Player of the National Hockey League All-Star Game were Bobby Hull of the Chicago Blackhawks, in 1970 and 1971, and his son Brett Hull of the St. Louis Blues, in 1982.

4181. Hockey player to win the Associated Press Athlete of the Year Award was perennial National Hockey League Most Valuable Player and top scorer Wayne Gretzky, then center for the Edmonton Oilers, in 1982.

4182. National Hockey League player to score 92 goals in a single season was Wayne Gretzky of the Edmonton Oilers, in 1982.

4183. National Hockey League player to score 200 points in a single season was Wayne Gretzky of the Edmonton Oilers, who reached that landmark during a 7–2 Oilers win over the Calgary Flames, on March 25, 1982.

4184. National Hockey League player to have six assists in a single Stanley Cup playoffs game was Mikko Lainonen of the New York Rangers, against the Philadelphia Flyers, on April 8, 1982.

4185. New Jersey Devils regular season hockey game played at Brendan Byrne Arena in East Rutherford, New Jersey, was a 3–3 tie with the Pittsburgh Penguins, on October 5, 1982. Don Lever of the Devils scored the first goal. The Byrne Arena would be renamed the Continental Airlines Arena in 1996.

4186. Calgary Flames regular season hockey game played at the Olympic Saddledome at Calgary, Alberta, Canada, was a 4–3 loss to the Edmonton Oilers, on October 15, 1983. The stadium was later renamed the Pengrowth Saddledome.

4187. Edmonton Oilers National Hockey League Stanley Cup championship came in 1984, with a four games to one win over the New York Islanders.

4188. United States collegiate women's hockey league was sponsored by the Eastern Collegiate Athletic Conference in 1984.

4189. National Hockey League defenseman to have 25 assists in a single set of Stanley Cup playoffs was Paul Coffey of the Edmonton Oilers, in 1985.

4190. National Hockey League defenseman to score 12 goals in a single set of Stanley Cup playoffs was Paul Coffey of the Edmonton Oilers, in 1985.

4191. National Hockey League defenseman to score 37 points in a single set of Stanley Cup playoffs was Paul Coffey of the Edmonton Oilers, in 1985.

4192. National Hockey League player to score 47 points in a single set of Stanley Cup playoffs was Wayne Gretzky of the Edmonton Oilers, in 1985.

4193. National Hockey League defenseman to score 48 goals in a single season was Paul Coffey of the Edmonton Oilers, in 1986.

4194. National Hockey League player to have 163 assists in a single season was Wayne Gretzky of the Edmonton Oilers, in 1986.

4195. Hockey player to be named the National Hockey League's Most Valuable Player eight consecutive times, and nine overall was Wayne Gretzky, who was eight-time MVP with the Edmonton Oilers (1980–1987) and then again with the Los Angeles Kings (1989).

4196. National Hockey League player to lead the league in scoring seven times in a row was Wayne Gretzky of the Edmonton Oilers (1981–1987).

4197. National Hockey League coach to be named Coach of the Year twice in a row was Jacques Demers of the Detroit Red Wings in 1987 and 1988.

4198. National Hockey League player to have 31 assists in a single set of Stanley Cup playoffs was Wayne Gretzky of the Edmonton Oilers, in 1988.

4199. National Hockey League player to score eight points in a single Stanley Cup playoffs game was Patrick Sundstrom of the New Jersey Devils, against the Washington Capitals, on April 25, 1988.

HOCKEY, ICE (1990-1999)
4200. Women's world championships in ice hockey were held at Ottawa, Canada, in 1990, sponsored by the International Ice Hockey Federation (IIHF). The team from Canada would win the gold medal the first four times the event was held, in 1990, 1992, 1994, and 1997.

4201. National Hockey League player to be named Most Valuable Player of the NHL All-Star Game three times was Mario Lemieux of the Pittsburgh Penguins. His third such honor, on January 21, 1990, followed two earlier namings in 1985 and 1988.

4202. Father and son to be named Most Valuable Player of the National Hockey League were Bobby Hull of the Chicago Blackhawks, who won that honor in 1965 and 1966, and his son Brett Hull of the St. Louis Blues, who was so named in 1991.

4203. Pittsburgh Penguins National Hockey League Stanley Cup championship came in 1991, with a four games to two win over the Minnesota North Stars.

4204. Woman to play in a professional hockey game was goaltender Manon Rheaume of Quebec, who played for the Tampa Bay Lightning against the St. Louis Blues in a National Hockey League exhibition game, in 1992.

HOCKEY, ICE—(1990-1999)—*continued*

4205. Ottawa Senators regular season hockey game played at the Ottawa Civic Center at Ottawa, Ontario, Canada, was a 5–3 win over the Montreal Canadiens, on October 4, 1992. Neal Brady of the Senators scored the first goal. The Senators wouldplay at the Center until 1998.

4206. Tampa Bay Lightning regular season hockey game played at the Thunderdome in Tampa, Florida, was a 7–3 win over the Chicago Blackhawks, on October 7, 1992. The Lightning would move to the Ice Palace in 1996.

4207. Dallas Stars regular season hockey game played at the Reunion Arena at Dallas, Texas, was a 6–4 win over the Detroit Red Wings on October 5, 1993. Neal Broten of the Stars scored the first goal.

4208. Mighty Ducks of Anaheim regular season hockey game played at The Pond of Anaheim at Anaheim, California, was a 7–2 loss to the Detroit Red Wings, on October 8, 1993. Aaron Ward of the Red Wings scored the first goal. The stadium was later renamed The Arrowhead Pondof Anaheim.

4209. Florida Panthers regular season hockey game played at Miami Arena in Miami, Florida, was a 2–1 loss to the Pittsburgh Penguins, on October 12, 1993. Martin Straka of the Penguins scored the first goal. The Panthers would play at theArena until 1998.

4210. San Jose Sharks regular season hockey game played at San Jose Arena in San Jose, California, was a 2-1 loss to the Calgary Flames, on October 13, 1993.

4211. Woman goaltender to be credited with a win in a professional hockey game was Erin Whitten of the Toledo Storm, in the East Coast Hockey League, on October 30, 1993.

4212. National Hockey League player to lead the league in scoring 10 times was Wayne Gretzky. That included seven times with the Edmonton Oilers (1981–1987) and three more times with the Los Angeles Kings (1990, 1991, and 1994).

4213. State to recognize women's high school ice hockey as a varsity sport was Minnesota, in 1994.

4214. Women's college hockey Player of the Year Award was given to Team USA goaltender Erin Whitten, in 1994.

4215. Ice hockey team from Sweden to win the title at the Olympic Winter Games was in 1994 in Lillehammer, Norway. The Swedish team won on February 27, defeating Canada.

4216. National Hockey League player to reach 802 career goals and so top Gordie Howe's historic record of 801 goals, was Wayne Gretzky of the Los Angeles Kings, during a 6–3 Kings loss to the Vancouver Canucks, on March 23, 1994. By his career's end in 1999, he had raised that to a total of 894 regular season career goals, to which he added 122 playoff goals, for a grand total of 1016.

4217. New Jersey Devils National Hockey League Stanley Cup championship came in 1995, with a four-game sweep over the Detroit Red Wings.

4218. Chicago Blackhawks regular season game played in the United Center in Chicago, Illinois, was a 5–1 victory over the Edmonton Oilers, on January 25, 1995. The first score was made by Blackhawks forward Joe Murphy. The Blackhawks were sharing the new center with the Chicago Bulls basketball team.

4219. Boston Bruins regular season hockey game played at the FleetCenter in Boston, Massachusetts, was a 4–4 tie with the New York Islanders on October 7, 1995.

4220. Vancouver Canucks regular season hockey game played at General Motors Place in Vancouver, British Columbia, Canada, was 5–3 loss to the Detroit Red Wings, on October 9, 1995.

4221. Colorado Avalanche National Hockey League Stanley Cup championship came in 1996, with a four-game sweep over the Florida Panthers.

4222. World Cup in ice hockey was held in 1996. The inaugural winner was the team from the United States. The competition replaced the Canada Cup.

4223. Ottawa Senators regular season hockey game played at the Palladium in Kanata, Ontario, Canada, was a 3–0 loss to the Montreal Canadiens on January 17, 1996. The Palladium was renamed the Corel Centre a month later.

4224. Montreal Canadiens regular season hockey game played at the Molson Center (La Centre Molson) in Montreal, Quebec, Canada, was a 4–2 win over the New York Rangers, on March 16, 1996.

4225. Philadelphia Flyers regular season hockey game played at the First Union Center in Philadelphia, Pennsylvania, was a 3–1 loss to the Florida Panthers, on October 5, 1996.

4226. Phoenix Coyotes regular season hockey game played at the America West Arena in Scottsdale, Arizona, was a 4–1 win over the San Jose Sharks on October 10, 1996. The Coyotes had previously been the Winnipeg Jets.

4227. Buffalo Sabres regular season hockey game played at Marine Midland Arena in Buffalo, New York was a 6–1 loss to the Detroit Red Wings on October 12, 1996. The Marine Midland Arena would be renamed the HSBC Arena in 2000.

4228. Tampa Bay Lightning regular season hockey game played at the Ice Palace in Tampa, Florida, was a 5–2 win over the New York Rangers, on October 21, 1996.

4229. Washington Capitals regular season hockey game played at the MCI Center in Washington, DC, was a 3–2 overtime win over the Florida Panthers, on December 5, 1997.

4230. Women's ice hockey event held in the Olympic Games was in 1998, in Nagano, Japan. The inaugural event was won by the team from the United States on February 17, with Canada coming in second.

4231. Florida Panthers regular season hockey game played at the National Car Rental Center in Sunrise, Florida, was a 4–1 win over the Tampa Bay Lightning on October 9, 1998.

4232. Nashville Predators regular season hockey game played at the Nashville Arena in Nashville, Tennessee, was a 1–0 loss to the Florida Panthers on October 13, 1998. The Arena was called the Gaylord Entertainment Center from August 1999.

4233. Atlanta Thrashers regular season hockey game played at the Philips Arena in Atlanta, Georgia, was a 1–4 loss to the New Jersey Devils, on October 2, 1999.

4234. Toronto Maple Leafs regular season hockey game played at Air Canada Centre in Toronto, Ontario, Canada, was a 4–0 win over the Boston Bruins, on October 4, 1999.

4235. Colorado Avalanche regular season hockey game played at the Pepsi Center in Denver, Colorado, was a 2–1 win over the Boston Bruins on October 13, 1999. The Colorado team had previously been the Quebec Nordiques.

4236. Los Angeles Kings regular season game played in the Staples Center in Los Angeles, California, was a 2–2 tie with the Boston Bruins, on October 20, 1999. The first score was made by Anson Carter of the Bruins. The Kings were sharing the new center with the Los Angeles Lakers and Los Angeles Clippers basketball teams.

4237. Carolina Hurricanes regular season hockey game played at the Raleigh Entertainment and Sports Arena in Raleigh, North Carolina, was a 4–2 loss to the New Jersey Devils on October 29, 1999.

HOCKEY, ICE (2000-)

4238. St. Louis Blues regular season hockey game played at the Kiel Center in St. Louis, Missouri, was a 3–1 win over the Los Angeles Kings, on January 26, 1995. The Kiel Center was renamed the Savvis Center in 2000.

HOCKEY, ROLLER (RINK)

4239. National organization for roller hockey (rink hockey) was founded in Great Britain in approximately 1898, becoming the Amateur Rink Hockey Association in 1908. A five-a-side team game played on roller skates, it was developed—primarily in Europe—from ice hockey.

4240. World championships in roller hockey (rink hockey) were held in Stuttgart, Germany, in 1936, and biennially from then. The inaugural competition, for men only, was won by the team from England.

4241. Women's world championships in roller hockey (rink hockey) were held in 1992, and biennially from then. The team from Canada won the first competition.

4242. World championships for roller hockey (rink hockey) played with in-line skates were held in 1995 and won by the team from the United States.

HORSE RACING (BEFORE 1700)

4243. Horse races held in the Olympic Games were four-horse chariot races introduced to the competition in approximately 680 BC in Olympia, Greece. Other chariot races would be added later. Chariot racing would remain popular for centuries, as power passed from Greek to Rome, and would be held in the city of Rome until 549 AD.

4244. Races for horses and riders held in the Olympic Games were introduced in 648 BC in Olympia, Greece. Various types of horse races would be added later, in addition to the earlier chariot races.

4245. Horse race in Britain was a race of Arabian horses imported by the Romans, held in approximately 210 in what is now Netherby, in northern Yorkshire.

4246. Public track for horse racing in Britain was the Smithfield Track, established in approximately 1174.

HORSE RACING—(BEFORE 1700)—_continued_

4247. Horse race for a purse on record was held on a three-mile course in England during the 1190s, with knights racing for a prize of £40.

4248. Palio horse race was held in Siena, Italy, in 1482, though the modern course around the city's Piazza del Campo would not be established until 1659. More fully called the _Corsa del Palio_ (Course of the Banner), the bareback horse race involves contestants representing the city's wards, each with its own distinctive banner. Similar races had been held in Siena and other Italian cities for at least several centuries.

4249. Documented horse race was held in 1651 in France, following a bet between two aristocrats. Horse racing would continue to be a popular sport among the aristocracy, and the world's first jockey club would be established in the last quarter of the 18th century under King Louis XVI.

4250. Rules for horse racing on record were written during the reign of England's King Charles II (1660–1685), originally for a series of races for prizes, called the King's Plates. In this period Newmarket became the center of English racing.

4251. Newmarket Town Four Mile Race was held in 1665. Started by racing enthusiast King Charles II, it would become the oldest continually run horse race in England.

4252. Organized horse races in colonial North America were held in approximately 1665 at Hempstead (then Hansted Plains), Long Island, in the colony of New York, on a track established by Britain's governor of New York, Richard Nicolls. In 1668, he offered a silver trophy to a winner there, the first sports trophy on record in North America.

HORSE RACING (1700-1899)

4253. Organized record of match race performances was kept by John Cheny of Newmarket, England, who began publishing _Cheny's Horse Matches_ in 1727.

4254. Jockey club in North America was the Charles Town Jockey Club, founded in the colony of Virginia (in what is now Charleston, West Virginia) in 1734.

4255. Jockey Club in England was founded in Newmarket, England, in 1750. Its rules replaced the rules earlier established for the King's Plates races and gradually spread beyond Newmarket, making it the governing authority for the sport in England.

4256. Steeplechase horse race on record was held in 1752 in County Cork, Ireland. The sport developed from foxhunting.

4257. Wearing of racing colors by jockeys began in 1762 in Newmarket, England, when horse owners agreed that distinctive colors would be reserved for each owner, to be worn by jockeys racing that owner's horses.

4258. _Racing Calendar_ was published in England in 1773 by James Weatherby. Following on from the earlier _Cheny's Horse Matches_, the annual publication became the standard source of information about the sport, though names of jockeys and trainers were not consistently recorded, except for the winners, until the mid-19th century.

4259. St. Leger horse race one of England's Classics and part of its Triple Crown, was run in Doncaster, England, in 1776.

4260. Oaks horse race one of England's Classics, was run in 1779 at Epsom Downs, in Epsom, England.

4261. Derby horse race one of England's Classics and part of its Triple Crown, was run at Epsom Downs, in Epsom, England, in 1780. The winner was Diomed, ridden by jockey Sam Arnull. He would win again in 1782, 1787, and 1798, becoming the first jockey to win four Derbys. Diomed would be one of many English horses imported to the United States.

4262. Jockey who won three Derbys at Epsom Downs was Charles Hundley, who won in 1781, 1783, and 1785, in Epsom, England.

4263. Stud book for horse racing was _An Introduction to a General Stud Book_, published in England by James Weatherby in 1791. It would later become an annual publication.

HORSE RACING (1800-1849)

4264. Woman jockey on record was Alicia Meynell, who raced against Captain William Flint on August 25, 1804, on a 4-mile race course in York, England. She was the mistress of the horse's owner.

4265. African-American jockey known by name was "Monkey" Simon, who was racing by 1806. In the American South, the majority of the jockeys and trainers in this period were slaves, often pitted against each other in match races, while most northern jockeys were white Americans or Englishmen.

4266. Jockey who won five Derbys at Epsom Downs in Epsom, England, was John Arnull, who won in 1784, 1790, 1796, 1799, and 1807.

4267. 2000 Guineas horse race one of England's Classics and part of its Triple Crown, was run in 1809 at Newmarket.

4268. 1000 Guineas horse race one of England's Classics, for fillies only, was run in 1814 at Newmarket.

4269. Jockey who won six Derbys at Epsom Downs in Epsom, England, was Jem Robinson, who won in 1817, 1824, 1825, 1827, 1828, and 1836.

4270. Prix du Jockey Club horse race one of France's Classics, was run in 1836, sponsored by La Société d'Encouragement pour l'Amélioration des Races de Chevaux en France founded three years earlier.

4271. Grand National Steeplechase horse race originally called the Grand Liverpool Steeple Chase, was held on the Aintree course, in Liverpool, England, in 1839, established by William Lynn. Jockey Jem Mason won riding Lottery. Earlier steeplechase races had been held at Aintree from at least 1836.

4272. Happy Valley horse race track was established in Hong Kong in 1846. Before then, European colonials had generally held horse races in nearby Macau.

HORSE RACING (1850-1899)
4273. Horse to win England's Triple Crown was West Australian, which won the 2000 Guineas, the Derby, and the St. Leger horse races in 1853.

4274. Melbourne Cup horse race was held in Melbourne, Australia, in 1861. One of the most popular contests in the Southern Hemisphere, the handicap race is traditionally held on the first Tuesday in November.

4275. Grand Prix du Paris horse race one of France's Classic races, was held in 1863.

4276. Belmont Stakes horse race one of the United States Classics and part of its Triple Crown, was held on June 19, 1867. Competing at Jerome Park, in the Bronx, New York, jockey J. Gilpatrick won by a head on Ruthless. Named after financier and sportsman August Belmont, the annual race would come to be held in Belmont Park near New York City.

4277. Grand Circuit series of harness horse races was held in 1873, sparked by Colonel Billy Edwards. Originally called the Quadrilateral Trotting Combination, the original series included races in Cleveland, Ohio; Utica and Buffalo, New York; and Springfield, Massachusetts.

4278. Preakness Stakes horse race one of the United States Classics and part of its Triple Crown, was held on May 27, 1873. Riding Survivor, jockey G. Barbee won by 10 lengths at Pimlico Race Track in Baltimore, Maryland.

4279. Kentucky Derby horse race one of the United States Classics and part of its Triple Crown, was held on May 17, 1875, at Churchill Downs in Louisville, Kentucky. Jockey Oliver Lewis won by a length on Aristides. Of the 15 jockeys, 14 were African-Americans, including Lewis.

4280. National organization for harness (trotting) horse owners in the United States was the National Association of Trotting Horse Breeders, founded in 1876.

4281. Horse bred and trained in the United States to win England's Derby at Epsom Downs, in Epsom, England, was Iroquois, the 1881 winner ridden by Fred Archer.

4282. Harness race held at night on record in the United States was at the Fort Miami track in Fostoria, Ohio, in 1888, where the track was lit by standing gas pipes. The same track would attempt to establish night racing in 1929.

4283. Jockey to win three Kentucky Derbys, and the first to win two in a row was African-American Isaac Murphy, who won first on Buchanan on May 16, 1884, then came back to win twice more, on May 14, 1890, on Riley and on May 13, 1891, on Kingman, all at Churchill Downs, in Louisville, Kentucky.

4284. Establishment of the North American Jockey Club later known simply as the Jockey Club, was in New York City in 1984. It became a key authority in the sport, publishing racing calendars and stud books, though in the United States the sport would legally be controlled by state commissions.

4285. Maryland Hunt Cup Race an amateur steeplechase horse race, was held in Glyndon, Maryland, in 1894.

4286. National organization for steeplechase racing in the United States was the National Steeplechase Association (NSA), founded in 1895.

4287. Stud book for horse racing published in North America was *The American Stud Book*, published in 1897, which included horses from the United States, Canada, Puerto Rico, and Mexico.

HORSE RACING (1900-1949)

4288. Horse to be named Horse of the Year in the United States was Granville, owned and bred by Belair Stud and trained by James Fitzsimmons. Honorees were selected by the *Daily Racing Form*, after 1970 in conjunction with the Thoroughbred Racing Association and the National Turf Writers Association.

4289. Horse to win America's Triple Crown was Sir Barton in 1919. Ridden by jockey John Loftus and owned by J. K. L. Ross, Sir Barton won the Kentucky Derby, Belmont Stakes, and the Preakness Stakes.

4290. Prix de l'Arc de Triomphe horse race one of France's and Europe's most important races, was held in 1920 at Longchamps. The winning jockey was Frank Bullock, riding Comrade.

4291. Cheltenham Gold Cup horse race was held in 1924 in Cheltenham, England, where the winning jockey was Dick Rees, riding Red Splash.

4292. Hambletonian Stakes harness race was held in Syracuse, New York, on August 26, 1926. The inaugural winner of the trotting race was Nat Ray, driving Guy McKinney. The race was named for the horse Hambletonian, who figured large in the bloodlines of American trotters.

4293. Champion Hurdle horse race was held in 1927 at Cheltenham, England. The winning jockey was George Duller, riding Blaris.

4294. Use of an electric-eye photo finish camera in horse racing was at the Hialeah Race Track in Hialeah, Florida, on January 16, 1936.

4295. Establishment of the United States Trotting Association was in 1939. It would become the national governing body for harness racing, replacing three earlier regional bodies.

4296. Horse to be named Horse of the Year twice consecutively in the United States was Challedon, winning that honor in 1939 and 1940. The horse was owned by William L. Brann, bred by Branncastle Farm, and trained by Louis J. Schaefer.

4297. Regularly held night harness racing began in 1940 at the Roosevelt Raceway in Westbury, New York.

4298. Iroquois Steeplechase horse race was held on May 10, 1941, in Nashville, Tennessee. The course was named after the first American bred and trained horse to win England's Derby, in 1881.

4299. Little Brown Jug harness race named after a noted 19th-century trotter, was held in Delaware, Ohio, in 1946. Wayne Smart won the inaugural race driving the trotter Ensign Hanover.

4300. Jockey to win America's Triple Crown twice was Eddie Arcaro. He won first in 1941 on Whirlaway, then came back to win again in 1948 on Citation.

HORSE RACING (1950-1999)

4301. Jockey to win the Kentucky Derby five times was Eddie Arcaro. At Churchill Downs, in Louisville, Kentucky, he stood in the winner's circle with Lawrin in 1938, Whirlaway in 1941, Hoop, Jr., in 1945, Citation in 1948, and Hill Gail in 1952. With Whirlaway and Citation, he won the Triple Crown.

4302. Whitbread Gold Cup horse race was run in 1957 at Sandown Park, near Esher, England, where jockey Henry East rode Much Obliged to the inaugural win. It was the first race to draw substantial commercial sponsorship.

4303. Horse to be named Horse of the Year three, four, and five times consecutively was Kelso, honored 1960–1964. The horse was owned by Bohemia Stable, bred by Mrs. R. C. duPont, and trained by C. Hanford.

4304. Woman to be licensed as a jockey in the United States was Kathy Kusner in 1968, though the first to race professionally was Diane Crump a year later.

4305. Woman jockey to race at a pari-mutuel track in the United States was Diane Crump on February 7, 1969, where she finished 10th of 12 at Hialeah, Florida.

4306. Woman jockey to win a professional horse race in the United States was Barbara Jo Rubin, who rode Cohesian to victory at Charleston, West Virginia, on February 22, 1969.

4307. Woman jockey to ride in the Kentucky Derby at Churchill Downs, in Louisville, Kentucky, was Diane Crump, on May 2, 1970. A year earlier she had become the first woman to ride as a professional jockey in the United States.

4308. Legal off-track betting operation in the United States was opened on April 7, 1971, in New York City.

4309. African-American woman to win a Thoroughbred horse race in the United States was Cheryl White, who won on Jetolara at Waterford Park in West Virginia, on September 2, 1971.

4310. Two-year-old horse to be unanimously named Horse of the Year was Secretariat in 1973, when he won the Triple Crown, including the Belmont Stakes by an astounding 31-length margin.

4311. Jockey who won seven, eight, and nine Derbys at Epsom Downs in Epsom, England, was Lester Piggott, who won in 1954, 1957, 1960, 1968, 1970, 1972, 1976, 1977, and 1983.

4312. Jockey to be named *Sports Illustrated* Sportsman of the Year was Steve Cauthen of the United States in 1977, when he had 487 wins and more than $6.1 million in winnings. The next year he would win the Triple Crown riding Affirmed.

4313. International Women's Driving Tournament was held in the autumn of 1978, sponsored by the United States Trotting Association and involving 16 harness races. The inaugural winner was Bea Farber of the United States, who that year also became the first woman to be among the top ten harness drivers, ranking second nationally.

4314. Japan Cup horse race was held in 1981. Jockey Cash Asmussen won on Mairzy Doates.

4315. Sport of Kings Challenge steeplechase horse race was held at the Iroquois Steeplechase in Nashville, Tennessee, in October 1987, sponsored by the International Steeplechase Group (ISG).

4316. Jockey to win nine races in a single day was Chris Antley of the United States on October 31, 1987. He won four races at the Aqueduct race track, in Jamaica, New York. He then traveled across the Hudson River to East Rutherford, New Jersey, where he won five more races at the Meadowlands.

4317. Woman jockey to win one of America's Triple Crown horse races was Julie Krone, who won the Belmont Stakes on Colonial Affair on June 5, 1993, in Belmont Park, near Elmont, New York.

4318. Dubai World Cup horse race was held in 1996. It was the richest race ever, offering a purse of $4 million, with $2.4 million for the winner. Jockey Jerry Bailey of the United States won on Cigar. Bailey would win again in 1997, this time on Singspiel.

4319. Jockey to win 8,834 horse races was Panama-born Laffit Pincay, Jr., who on December 10, 1999, won riding Irish Nip at Hollywood Park, in Inglewood, California, to break Bill Shoemaker's record of 8,833 wins, which had stood for 29 years. Pincay's career continued.

HORSESHOE COMPETITIONS

4320. Horseshoe club on record was founded in 1892 in Meadville, Pennsylvania.

4321. International horseshoe tournament was held in 1909 in Bronson, Kansas, drawing mostly players from the Midwest United States. The winner was Frank Jackson.

HURDLES

4322. Men's 110-meter hurdles event held in the Olympic Games was in 1896 in Athens, Greece. That first competition was won by Thomas Curtis of the United States, with a time of 17.6 seconds on April 10.

4323. National team to sweep the medals in the men's 110-meter hurdles in the Olympic Games was from the United States. Led by Alvin Kraenzlein, United States hurdlers took the top three spots on July 14, 1900, in Paris, France.

4324. Men's 400-meter hurdles event held in the Olympic Games was in Paris, France, in 1900. The winner was John Walter Tewksbury of the United States, who raced the event in 57.6 seconds on July 15.

4325. Men's 200-meter hurdles event held in the Olympic Games was in 1900 in Paris, France. Competing on July 16, the winner was Alvin Kraenzlein of the United States, for one of his four gold medals in Paris. The event would be discontinued after 1904.

4326. Hurdler to hold the officially accepted world record in the men's 400-meter hurdles, and to set a 400-meter hurdle record that would stand for more than 10 years was Charles Bacon of the United States, who set a record of 55.0 seconds on July 22, 1908, in London, England. It would stand until 1920.

4327. Hurdler to hold the officially accepted world record in the men's 110-meter hurdles, and to set a 110-meter hurdle record that would stand for more than 10 years was Forrest Smithson of the United States, who set a time of 15.0 seconds on July 25, 1908, in London, England. It would stand until August 18, 1920, when Earl Thomson of Canada raced the distance in 14.8 seconds.

4328. Hurdler to race the 400-meter hurdles in under 55 seconds was John Norton of the United States, who set a time of 54.2 seconds on June 26, 1920, in Pasadena, California.

4329. Hurdler to race the men's 400-meter hurdles in under 54 seconds was Sten Pettersson of Sweden, who set a time of 53.8 seconds in Paris, France, on October 4, 1925.

HURDLES—*continued*

4330. Hurdler to race the men's 400-meter hurdles in under 53 seconds was John Gibson of the United States, who had a time of 52.6 seconds in Lincoln, Nebraska, on July 2, 1927.

4331. Hurdler to hold the world record in both the men's 110- and 400-meter events was Sten Pettersson of Sweden. He had set a 400-meter record of 53.8 seconds on October 4, 1925, in Paris, France. His 110-meter record of 14.8 seconds came on September 18, 1927, at Stockholm, Sweden.

4332. Women's 80-meter hurdles event held in the Olympic Games was on August 4, 1932, in Los Angeles, California. The winner was Babe (Mildred) Didrikson (later Zaharias) of the United States, who had a world record time of 11.7 seconds. The event would become the 100-meter hurdles in 1972.

4333. Hurdler to hold the officially accepted world record in the women's 80-meter event was Ruth Engelhard of Germany, with a time of 11.6 seconds, set on August 11, 1934, in London, England.

4334. Hurdler to race the men's 400-meter hurdles in under 52 seconds was Glenn Hardin of the United States, who broke his own record of 52 seconds with a time of 51.8 seconds on June 30, 1934, in Los Angeles, California. He would lower that to 50.6 seconds on July 26, 1934, in Stockholm, Sweden, a record that would stand until 1953.

4335. Hurdler to race the men's 110-meter hurdles in under 14 seconds was Forrest Towns of the United States. Racing in Oslo, Norway, on August 27, 1936, he pared his own previous record of 14.1 to 13.7 seconds. It would not be bettered until 1950.

4336. African-American hurdler to win the men's 110-meter titles in the Olympic Games was Harrison Dillard, who won with an Olympic-record time of 13.7 seconds on July 24, 1952, in Helsinki, Finland.

4337. Hurdler to race the men's 400-meter hurdles in under 50 seconds was Glenn Davis of the United States, when he had a time of 49.5 seconds on June 29, 1956, in Los Angeles, California. He lowered that to 49.2 on August 6, 1958, in Budapest, Hungary.

4338. Hurdler to win two consecutive titles in the women's 80-meter hurdles in the Olympic Games was Shirley Strickland de la Hunty of Australia. After winning in 1952, she won again with an Olympic-record 10.7 seconds on November 28, 1956, in Melbourne, Australia.

4339. Hurdler to win two consecutive titles in the men's 400-meter hurdles in the Olympic Games was Glenn Davis of the United States. On September 2, 1960, in Rome, Italy, he set an Olympic record with 49.3 seconds, after winning his first title in 1956.

4340. Hurdler to win two consecutive titles in the men's 110-meter hurdles in the Olympic Games was Lee Calhoun of the United States. After winning first in 1956, he went to Rome, Italy, where he posted a winning time of 13.8 seconds on September 5, 1960.

4341. Hurdler to race the men's 400-meter hurdles in under 49 seconds was Geoffrey Vanderstock of the United States, who cut the record time to 48.8 seconds on September 11, 1968, in Echo Summit, California.

4342. Hurdler to hold the officially accepted world record in the women's 100-meter hurdles was Karin Balzer of East Germany. Competing on June 20, 1969, in Warsaw, Poland, she set a benchmark time of 13.3 seconds, tied 8 minutes later by Teresa Sukniewicz of Poland.

4343. Electronically timed world record in the men's 110-meter hurdles was the time of 13.24 seconds set by Rod Milburn of the United States on September 7, 1972, in the Olympic Games at Munich, West Germany. It had been manually timed at 13.2 seconds.

4344. Hurdler to hold the officially accepted world record in the women's 400-meter hurdles was Krystyna Kacperczyk of Poland. Her benchmark time of 56.51 seconds, the first of her two world records, was set on July 13, 1974, in Augsburg, West Germany.

4345. African-American hurdler to win the men's 400-meter title in the Olympic Games was Edwin Moses, who set a world record of 47.64 seconds on July 25, 1976, in Montreal, Quebec, Canada. It was the first of his four world records.

4346. Hurdler to race the men's 110-meter hurdles in under 13 seconds was Renaldo Nehemiah of the United States. His time of 12.93 seconds, set on August 19, 1981, in Zürich, Switzerland, was his third world record in the event.

4347. Hurdler to win the men's 110-meter event in the World Championships in Athletics was Greg Foster of the United States, who had a time of 13.42 seconds in 1983 in Helsinki, Finland. He would win again in 1987 and 1991, becoming the first to win it twice and three times.

4348. Hurdler to win the men's 400-meter hurdles held in the World Championships in Athletics was Edwin Moses of the United States, with a time of 47.50 seconds in 1983 in Helsinki, Finland. He would win it again in 1987.

4349. Hurdler to set four new world records in the men's 400-meter hurdles was Edwin Moses of the United States. His first world record was 47.64 seconds, set in the Montreal Olympics on July 25, 1976. He lowered that successively to his fourth record, 47.02, set on August 31, 1983, in Koblenz, West Germany. He was the first to take 13 steps between every hurdle, rather than the 15 that had earlier been standard.

4350. Women's 400-meter hurdles event held in the Olympic Games was in 1984 at Los Angeles, California. The event was won on August 8 by Nawal El Moutawakel of Morocco, with a time of 54.61 seconds. She was the first Olympic gold-medalist from her country and the first female medalist from an Islamic country.

4351. Hurdler to win two, and then three, consecutive titles in the men's 110-meter hurdles in the World Championships in Athletics was Greg Foster of the United States. After winning first in 1983, he had times of 13.21 seconds in Rome, Italy, in 1987, and 13.06 in Tokyo, Japan, in 1991.

4352. Hurdler to win two consecutive titles in the men's 400-meter hurdles in the World Championships in Athletics was Edwin Moses of the United States. After winning the inaugural event in 1983, he won again in 1987 in Rome, Italy, with a time of 47.46 seconds.

4353. Hurdler to race the men's 400-meter hurdles in under 47 seconds was Kevin Young of the United States. His new time of 46.78 seconds was set at the Olympic Games in Barcelona, Spain, on August 6, 1992.

4354. Hurdler from Great Britain to win the men's title in the 110-meter hurdles in the World Championships in Athletics was Colin Jackson, with a time of 12.91 seconds, on August 20, 1993, in Stuttgart, Germany.

HURLING

4355. Ban on hurling dates from 1367 in Kilkenny, Ireland. However, written references to the game date back many centuries. With similarities to field hockey, the 15-a-side team game played with stick and ball became a national sport in Ireland.

4356. National organization for hurling was the Irish Hurling Union, founded in 1879.

4357. Standardization of the rules of hurling was in 1884, with the foundation of the Gaelic Athletic Association in Thurles, in the County of Tipperary, Ireland. A women's version is called *camogie*.

4358. All-Ireland Championships in hurling were held in 1887 in Croke Park, Dublin, and annually since then. The winner of the inaugural competition was the team from Tipperary.

I

ICE BOATING

4359. Ice boating club in the United States was the Poughkeepsie Ice Yacht Club, established in 1865 in Poughkeepsie, New York. Using yachts on sled runners, the sport had been popular in the region since at least 1790, brought from Europe by immigrants from the Netherlands.

ICE SKATE SAILING

4360. Ice skate sailing competition with ice skaters carrying sails on their backs skimming along frozen lakes and rivers, was on Lilla Värtan Lake, near Stockholm, Sweden, in 1887.

4361. Icewing sail for ice skate sailing was developed in 1973 in Stockholm, Sweden, by Anders Ansar.

4362. World ice and snow sailing championships were held in 1980.

INTERNATIONAL GAMES; SEE ALSO OLYMPIC GAMES

4363. Establishment of the Tailteann Games traditional competitions in early Ireland, are believed to date back to 1829 BC. They would be held into the 12th century AD.

4364. Scottish Highland Gathering popularly called the Highland Games, is believed to have been held in 1044, sponsored by Celtic prince Malcolm Canmore, on the Braes of Mar, in Scotland. However, the first fully documented Gathering was one held in 1314.

4365. Nordic Games were held in 1901, and every four years thereafter.

4366. Inter-Empire Sports tournament was held in 1911 at the Crystal Palace in London, England, to celebrate George V's coronation, with athletes from Australia, Britain, Canada, and New Zealand participating. It was a predecessor to the British Empire Games, later the British Commonwealth Games.

INTERNATIONAL GAMES; SEE ALSO OLYMPIC GAMES—*continued*

4367. Far Eastern Games were held in Manila, Philippines, in 1913. Most participating athletes were from China and the Philippines, but two were from Japan. The Games would be held irregularly until 1934. After World War II, they would be succeeded by the Asian Games.

4368. International Universities Games were held in Warsaw, Poland, in 1924, sponsored by the Conféderation Internationale des Étudiants (CIE).

4369. British Empire Games (later the British Commonwealth Games) were held at Hamilton, Ontario, Canada, starting on August 16, 1930, with athletes from Australia, Bermuda, British Guiana, Canada, England, Ireland, Newfoundland, New Zealand, Scotland, South Africa, and Wales. Sports included athletic events, with a single women's event in swimming. Women would not compete in track-and-field events until 1934. The Games would be held every four years, except during World War II.

4370. Pan-American Games involving athletes from throughout the Americas, were held in 1951 in Buenos Aires, Argentina. Originally planned for 1942, they had been postponed because of World War II.

4371. World Youth Games sponsored by Communist countries to rival the International Universities Games, were held in Berlin, Germany, in 1951, adopting that name in 1954. They would be held annually through 1962, then merging with the Universiade or World Student Games.

4372. Asian Games were held on March 8–11, 1951, in New Delhi, India. They would be held again in 1954 and every four years from then on.

4373. Pan-Arab Games instituted by the Arab League, were held in 1953, and then every four years until 1965, resuming in 1985.

4374. South-East Asia Games were held in Bangkok, Thailand, in 1959. They would be held every two years, skipping 1963.

4375. Universiade (World Student Games) were held in 1962 in Porto Alegre, Brazil. They were a result of the merger of several earlier student games, including the International Universities Games and the Communist-sponsored World Youth Games.

4376. All-African Games were held on July 18–25, 1965, in Brazzaville, Congo, sponsored by the Organization for African Unity. They would be held irregularly, but every four years from 1987.

4377. World Games international championships for sports not included in the Olympic Games, were held in 1981 in Santa Clara, California, and every four years from then on.

4378. Gay Games international Olympics-like competitions for homosexual men and women, were held in 1982 in San Francisco, California. They would be held every four years, in the second year between the Summer Olympic Games.

4379. Goodwill Games were held in 1986 in Moscow, the Soviet Union. Sponsored primarily by the Turner Broadcasting System, they sought to bridge the distance between the United States, which had boycotted the 1980 Olympics in Moscow, and the Soviet Union, which had boycotted the 1984 Olympics in Los Angeles, California. They were held every four years.

J

JAI ALAI

4380. Jai alai game in the United States was played in 1904, when the game was introduced to the country at the World's Fair in St. Louis, Missouri. The homeland of jai alai is the Basque country of northern Spain and southern France, where it is one of a group of ball games, generically called *pelota*, that are related to early forms of tennis.

JAVELIN THROW

4381. Men's freestyle javelin event held in the Olympic Games was in 1906, in the unofficial Olympics in Athens, Greece. Erik Lemming of Sweden won the event the only two times it was held, with throws of 176 feet 10 inches (53.00 meters) on July 27, 1906, in Athens, and 178 feet 7½ inches (54.45 meters) on July 15, 1908, in London, England.

4382. Men's javelin-throw event held at the Olympic Games was in 1908 in London, England. The winner was Erik Lemming of Sweden, with a world-record throw of 179 feet 10 inches (54.825 meters) on July 17. He would win again in 1912.

4383. Men's javelin event for both hands held in the Olympic Games was in 1912 in Stockholm, Sweden. With a total distance for the two throws of 359 feet 0 inches (109.42 meters), Juho Julius Saaristo of Finland won on July 9, the only time the event was held.

4384. Javelin-thrower to hold the officially accepted world record in the men's event was Erik Lemming of Sweden, with a throw of 204 feet 5 inches (62.32 meters) in Stockholm, Sweden, on September 29, 1912. Winner of the Olympic title in 1908 and 1912, he also held 13 unofficial world records, set before 1912.

4385. Javelin-thrower to break the 210-foot barrier was Jonni Myyrä of Finland, with a throw of 216 feet 10 inches (66.10 meters)—more than 12 feet beyond the previous record—on August 25, 1919, in Stockholm, Sweden.

4386. Javelin-thrower to win two consecutive men's titles in the Olympic Games was Jonni Myyrä of Finland. After his initial win in 1920, he went to Paris, France, for his second gold medal, throwing for 206 feet 7 inches (62.96 meters) on August 15, 1924, more than 10 feet short of his own world record.

4387. Javelin-thrower to break the 220-foot barrier was Eino Penttilä of Finland, with a throw of 229 feet 3 inches (69.88 meters) in the men's event in Viipuri, Finland, on October 8, 1927.

4388. Javelin-thrower to break the 230-foot and 70-meter barriers was Erik Lundqvist of Sweden, with a throw of 232 feet 11 inches (71.01 meters) in the men's event on August 15, 1928, in Stockholm, Sweden.

4389. Javelin-thrower to hold the officially accepted world record in the women's event was Nan Gindele of the United States, who set a benchmark of 153 feet 4 inches (46.745 meters) on June 18, 1932, in Chicago, Illinois. However, she placed only fifth in the Olympics that August.

4390. Women's javelin-throw event held in the Olympic Games was on July 31, 1932, in Los Angeles, California. The winner, with a throw of 143 feet 4 inches (43.68 meters), was Babe (Mildred) Didrikson (later Zaharias) of the United States. It was the first of her two 1932 gold medals.

4391. Javelin-thrower to break the 240- and 250-foot barriers was Matti Järvinen of Finland. In the fifth of his 10 world records in the men's event, he threw for 242 feet 10 inches (74.02 meters) on June 27, 1932, in Turku, Finland. Then in his ninth, on September 7, 1934, in Turin, Italy, he threw for 251 feet 6 inches

(76.66 meters), extending that nearly 2 feet more in his final record in 1936. His father was Verner Järvinen, who had won Finland's first Olympic gold medal, in the Greek-style discus in the unofficial 1906 Athens Olympics.

4392. Javelin-thrower to break the 160- and 170-foot and 50-meter barriers in the women's event was Natalya Smirnitskaya of the Soviet Union. She set her first record of 162 feet 8 inches (49.59 meters) on July 25, 1949, then upped that to 175 feet 2 inches (53.41 meters) on August 5, both in Moscow, the Soviet Union.

4393. Javelin-thrower from the United States to win the men's event in the Olympic Games was Cyrus Young, with an Olympic-record throw of 242 feet 1 inch (73.78 meters) on July 23, 1952, in Helsinki, Finland. Ironically, Finnish throwers had dominated the event for years.

4394. Javelin-thrower to break the 260-foot and 80-meter barriers, and the first from the United States to hold the world record in the men's event was Bud Held. With a throw of 263 feet 10 inches (80.41 meters) on August 8, 1953, in Pasadena, California, he broke the nearly 15-year-old record. He would extend that to 268 feet 2 inches (81.75 meters) in 1955.

4395. Javelin-thrower to break the 180-foot barrier in the women's event was Nadezhda Konyayeva of the Soviet Union, with a throw of 180 feet 9 inches (55.11 meters) on May 22, 1954, in Kiev, the Soviet Union, for the second of her three world records.

4396. Javelin-thrower to break the 270-foot barrier was Soini Nikkinen of Finland, with a throw of 274 feet 1 inch in the men's event on June 24, 1956, in Kuhmoinen, Finland.

4397. Javelin-thrower to break the 280-foot barrier and to hold the world record in the men's event was Egil Danielsen of Norway, with a world record throw of 281 feet 2 inches (85.71 meters) on November 26, 1956, at the Olympic Games in Melbourne, Australia, using a steel javelin borrowed from Soviet competitor Viktor Tsybulenko, who placed third, but would win in 1960.

4398. Javelin-thrower to reach the 190-foot barrier in the women's event was Elvira Ozolina of the Soviet Union, with a throw of 190 feet 0 inches (57.92 meters) on May 3, 1960, in Leselidze, the Soviet Union. She would up that to 196 feet 1 inch (59.78 meters) by July 3, 1963.

187

JAVELIN THROW—*continued*

4399. Javelin-thrower to break the 300-foot and 90-meter barriers in the men's event was Terje Pederson of Norway, with a throw of 300 feet 11 inches (91.72 meters)—more than 15 feet beyond his own two-month-old world record—on September 2, 1964, in Oslo, Norway. However, at the Olympic Games in mid-October, he failed to make the finals.

4400. Javelin-thrower to break the 200-foot and 60-meter barriers in the women's event was Yelena Gorchakova of the Soviet Union. Competing at the Olympic Games in Tokyo, Japan, on October 16, 1964, she had a throw of 204 feet 9 inches (62.40 meters) in an early round. However, in the final, she placed only third.

4401. Javelin-thrower to break the 210- and 220-foot barriers in the women's event was Ruth Fuchs of East Germany. She broke the first with a throw of 213 feet 5 inches (65.06 meters) on June 11, 1972, in Potsdam, East Germany, and the second with 220 feet 6 inches (67.22 meters) on September 3, 1974, in Rome, Italy.

4402. Javelin-thrower to win two consecutive women's titles in the Olympic Games was Ruth Fuchs of East Germany. After winning first in 1972, she won again with an Olympic-record throw of 216 feet 4 inches (65.94 meters) on July 24, 1976, in Montreal, Quebec, Canada.

4403. Javelin-thrower to break the 310-foot barrier was Miklos Németh of Hungary, who threw for a world-record distance of 310 feet 4 inches (94.58 meters) on July 25, 1976, at the Olympic Games in Montreal, Quebec, Canada. His father, Imre Németh, had been the 1948 Olympic hammer-throw champion.

4404. Javelin-thrower to break the 70-meter barrier in the women's event was Tatyana Biryulina of the Soviet Union, who threw for 70.08 meters (229 feet 11 inches) on July 12, 1980, in Podolsk, the Soviet Union.

4405. Javelin-thrower to break the 230-foot barrier in the women's event was Antoaneta Todorova of Bulgaria, with a throw of 235 feet 10 inches (71.88 meters) on August 15, 1981, in Zagreb, Yugoslavia.

4406. Javelin-thrower to break the 240-foot barrier in the women's event was Sofia Sakorafa of Greece, whose mark of 243 feet 5 inches (74.20 meters) was set in Khania, on the Greek island of Crete, on September 26, 1982.

4407. Javelin-thrower to break the 330- and 340-foot and 100-meter barriers in the men's event was Uwe Hohn of East Germany, with a throw of 343 feet 10 inches (104.80 meters) on July 20, 1984, in Berlin. His was the last record with the "old javelin." From 1986, the sport used a new javelin, weighted differently to carry less far.

4408. Javelin-thrower to break the 250-foot barrier in the women's event was Fatima Whitbread of Great Britain, with a throw of 254 feet 1 inch (77.44 meters) on August 28, 1986, in Stuttgart, West Germany.

4409. Javelin-throw world record set using the new javelin in the men's event was in 1986, when the sport shifted to a differently weighted javelin, to go a shorter distance and to stick in the ground, to avoid injury to spectators. The first official record was 281 feet 3 inches (85.74 meters), set by Klaus Tafelmeier of West Germany in the men's event on September 21, 1986, in Como, Italy.

4410. Javelin-thrower to break the 260-foot barrier, and to reach the 80-meter barrier, in the women's event was Petra Felke of East Germany, with a throw of 262 feet 5 inches (80.00 meters) in Potsdam, East Germany, on September 9, 1988. It was the last of her four world records. On September 26, she also won the Olympics in Seoul, South Korea.

4411. Javelin-thrower to break the 290-foot barrier with the new javelin was Patrik Bodén of Sweden, with a throw of 292 feet 4 inches (89.10 meters) in the men's event on March 24, 1990, in Austin, Texas.

4412. Javelin-thrower to break the 300-foot and 90-meter barriers with the new javelin was Steve Backley of Great Britain with a throw of 300 feet 1 inch (91.46 meters) in the men's event on January 25, 1992, in Auckland, New Zealand.

4413. Javelin-thrower to break the 310- and 320-foot barriers with the new javelin was Ján Zelezny of Czechoslovakia. He broke the first on April 6, 1993, in Pietersburg, South Africa, with a throw of 313 feet 5 inches (95.54 meters) in the men's event, and the second on May 25, 1996, with 323 feet 1 inch (98.48 meters) in Jena, Germany.

K

KOLVEN

4414. Written reference to *kolven* was in about 1300 in the Netherlands. Possibly an ancestor of golf and hockey, the game involved using clubs similar to golf clubs to slide a large ball along ice.

4415. Written reference to *kolven* **in North America** was in 1659, when the people of Albany, New York, were banned from playing the game from the Netherlands in the streets. The game involved using clubs with heads to slide a large ball over ice; it may be related to both golf and hockey, among other games.

L

LACROSSE

4416. Lacrosse organization was the Olympic Club, founded in Montreal, Quebec, Canada, in 1842. Named in 1636 by French Jesuit missionary Jean de Brébeuf, the sport was derived from a game called *baggataway*, played by the Iroquois and other Native Americans.

4417. National organization for lacrosse was the National Lacrosse Association, founded in Canada in 1867. That year, touring lacrosse players introduced the game into Britain, and play quickly began in the United States as well.

4418. Collegiate lacrosse team in the United States was organized at New York University in 1877.

4419. Intercollegiate Lacrosse Association was founded in 1882 by representatives from Harvard, Columbia, and Princeton universities, with Harvard winning the first collegiate title.

4420. Lacrosse event held in the Olympic Games was in 1904 in St. Louis, Missouri. The final, on July 7, was won by a team from Canada, which would win again in 1908, the second and last time the sport was included in the Olympics.

4421. Women's lacrosse organization was the All-England Women's Lacrosse Association, founded in 1912.

4422. International governing organization for lacrosse was the International Federation of Amateur Lacrosse (IFAL), founded in 1928.

4423. Wilson Wingate Trophy presented to the top collegiate lacrosse team in the United States, was awarded in 1936. The first winner was the University of Maryland.

4424. World championships for men's lacrosse were held in 1967 in Toronto, Ontario, Canada. United States teams won in 1967 and in six of the quadrennial championships between 1974 and 1998, with Canada winning in 1978.

4425. World championships for women's lacrosse were held in 1969, with the winner being a team from Great Britain. From 1982 the competition would be called the World Cup.

LONG JUMP

4426. Men's long jump event held in the Olympic Games was on April 7, 1896, in Athens, Greece. Athletes from the United States took the top three spots, led by Ellery Clark, who had a jump of 20 feet 10 inches (6.35 meters).

4427. Men's standing long jump event held in the Olympic Games was on July 16, 1900, in Paris, France. It was won by Raymond Ewry of the United States, with a jump of 10 feet 6 1.4 inches (3.21 meters). He would win it again in 1904, 1906, and 1908. The event was discontinued after 1912.

4428. Long-jumper to hold the officially accepted world record in the men's event was Peter O'Connor of Ireland, competing for Great Britain, with a jump of 24 feet 11¾ inches (7.61 meters) on August 5, 1901, in Dublin, Ireland. His record would stand until 1921.

4429. Long-jumper to win two consecutive men's titles in the Olympic Games was Meyer Prinstein of the United States. His second win came in the unofficial games in Athens, Greece, where he won with a jump of 23 feet 7½ inches (7.20 meters) on April 27, 1906. His first, fully official, had come in 1904. He might also have won in 1900, when he was world record-holder, but officials had barred his Syracuse team from competing in the final because it was held on a Sunday, even though Prinstein was Jewish.

4430. Long-jumper to break the 25-foot barrier was Edward Gourdin, with a jump of 25 feet 3 inches (7.69 meters) on July 23, 1921, in Cambridge, Massachusetts. The first African-American, and the first from the United States, to hold the world record in the long jump, he would later become the first African-American on the Massachusetts Supreme Court.

LONG JUMP—*continued*

4431. Long-jumper to hold the officially accepted world record in the women's event, and the first female athlete from Asia to set a world track and field record was Kinue Hitomi of Japan. Competing at Osaka, Japan, on May 20, 1928, she jumped 19 feet 7½ inches (5.98 meters). Her record would stand until 1939.

4432. Long-jumper to break the 26-foot barrier was Silvio Cator of Haiti, who jumped 26 feet ¼ inch (7.93 meters) at Paris, France, on September 9, 1928, just six weeks after he had been silver medalist in the Olympic Games.

4433. Athlete to hold the world record in both the men's long jump and triple jump was Chuhei Nambu of Japan. He set a long-jump record of 26 feet 2¼ inches (7.98 meters) on October 27, 1931, in Tokyo, Japan, and then set a triple-jump record of 51 feet 7 inches (15.72 meters) on August 4, 1932, at the Olympic Games in Los Angeles, California.

4434. Long-jump record to stand for more than 25 years was set by Jesse (James Cleveland) Owens of the United States. His jump of 26 feet 8¼ inches (8.13 meters) on May 25, 1935, in Ann Arbor, Michigan, would not be bettered until August 12, 1960, when Ralph Boston of the United States jumped 3 inches farther.

4435. Long-jumper to break the 20-foot and 6-meter barriers in the women's event was Christel Schulz of Germany. Her jump of 20 feet 1 inch (6.12 meters) was made on July 30, 1939, in Berlin, Germany.

4436. Women's long jump event held in the Olympic Games was on August 4, 1948, in London, England. The winner was Olga Gyarmati of Hungary with a jump of 18 feet 8¼ inches (5.695 meters). That was far short of the world record of 20 feet 6 inches (6.25 meters) held by Fanny (Francina) Blankers-Koen, who won gold medals in four other events in London, but did not compete in this one.

4437. Men's long jump event in which the top four contestants jumped more than 26 feet was on September 2, 1960, in the Olympic Games in Rome, Italy. The gold medalist was Ralph Boston of the United States, with an Olympic-record 26 feet 7¾ inches (8.12 meters).

4438. Long-jumper to break the 27-foot barrier was Ralph Boston of the United States, with a jump of 27 feet ½ inch (8.24 meters) on May 27, 1961, in Modesto, California. It would be the second of his six world records, extending to 27 feet 5 inches (8.35 meters) on May 29, 1965.

4439. Long-jumper to break the 28- and 29-foot barriers was African-American Robert Beamon of the United States. His extraordinary record of 29 feet 2¼ inches (8.90 meters) was set on October 18, 1968, at the Olympic Games in Mexico City. The previous record had been 27 feet 5 inches (8.35 meters). Beamon's record would stand until August 30, 1991, when Mike Powell of the United States bettered it by 2 inches.

4440. Long-jumper to break the 7-meter barrier in the women's event was Vilma Bardauskiene of the Soviet Union. In Kishinev, the Soviet Union, on August 18, 1978, she leapt 7.07 meters (23 feet 2¼ inches), for the first of her two world records.

4441. Long-jumper from the United States to set or equal the world record in the women's event was Jacqueline Joyner-Kersee. On August 13, 1987, competing in Indianapolis, Indiana, she tied the record of 24 feet 5½ inches (7.45 meters), set the previous year by Heike Daute Drechsler of East Germany.

4442. Long-jumper from the United States to win the women's event in the Olympic Games was Jacqueline Joyner-Kersee, with an Olympic-record jump of 24 feet 3¾ inches (7.40 meters) on September 29, 1988, in Seoul, South Korea. She had already won the 1988 gold medal in the heptathlon. In the long jump, she would win the silver medal in 1992 and the bronze in 1996, despite an injury that caused her to withdraw from the heptathlon.

4443. Long-jumper to win three, and then four, consecutive men's titles in the Olympic Games was Carl Lewis of the United States. He had been undefeated in the long jump for more than 10 years, a winning streak that included gold medals in the 1984 and 1988 Olympics. He won his third in Barcelona, Spain, on August 6, 1992, with a jump of 28 feet 5½ inches (8.67 meters). The silver medalist was Mike Powell, who on August 30, 1991, had broken Lewis's winning streak, as well as Robert Beamon's 22-year-old record, with a jump of 29 feet 4¼ inches (8.95 meters). Lewis captured his fourth gold medal in Atlanta, Georgia, with a jump of 27 feet 10¾ inches (8.50 meters) on July 29, 1996.

4444. Athlete from Africa to win the long jump, or any field event, in the Olympic Games was Chioma Ajunwa of Nigeria, who won the women's event on August 2, 1996, in Atlanta, Georgia, with a jump of 23 feet 4½ inches (7.12 meters).

LUGE (TOBOGGAN)

4445. Written reference to tobogganing dates back to 1520, from writings by Hans Sachs.

4446. Specially built luge (toboggan) runs were made in 1879 in Davos, Switzerland, which became a favorite site for local and international competitions.

4447. International luge (toboggan) competition was held in March 1883 in Davos, Switzerland, where special luge runs had been built in 1879. The winner was Peter Minch, a local postman.

4448. Skeleton luge (toboggan) built on a simpler, skeleton-like frame, was developed in 1884 by W. H. Bulpetts of England. It was designed for use on a toboggan run in the Cresta Valley, in St. Moritz, Switzerland, and so is also called the Cresta Run luge.

4449. Grand National luge (toboggan) race held on the Cresta run in St. Moritz, Switzerland, was on February 18, 1885, with the team from St. Moritz losing to that from Davos.

4450. Slider to ride the skeleton (Cresta Run) luge (toboggan) face forward was a man named McCormick (first name unknown) in 1888 at the Cresta Run in St. Moritz, Switzerland.

4451. Sliding seat developed for the luge (toboggan) was in 1901 by a man named Bott (first name unknown), a five-time winner of the Grand National competition in St. Moritz, Switzerland.

4452. Men's skeleton luge event at the Olympic Winter Games was in 1928, in St. Moritz, Switzerland, at the Cresta Run, originally built in 1884. The inaugural title was won by Jennison Heaton of the United States on February 17; his brother, John Heaton, was the silver medalist. The event would be held again only in 1948, also at St. Moritz.

4453. World championships in luge (toboggan) were held in Oslo, Norway, in 1955, and annually from then on, except during Olympic years, becoming biennial from 1981. The inaugural winners were Anton Salvesen of Norway in the men's singles, Hans Krausner and Herbert Thaler of Austria in the men's doubles, and Karla Kienzl of Austria in the women's singles.

4454. International governing body specifically for luge events was the Fédération Internationale de Luge de Course (FIL), founded in 1957.

4455. Men's singles luge (toboggan) event held in the Olympic Winter Games was in the 1964 Olympic Winter Games at Innsbruck, Austria. The winner of the men's singles title was Thomas Köhler of Germany, on February 1. Many people thought luge was too dangerous to be an Olympic sport, even before the death of Polish-born slider Kazimierz Kay-Skrzypeski in practice just before the 1964 Olympics and the serious injury of two German sliders in another accident.

4456. Two-seater luge (toboggan) event at the Olympic Winter Games was held in 1964 at Innsbruck, Austria. Josef Feistmantl and Manfred Stengl of Austria won the inaugural event on February 1. The event would be for men only until 1994, when it became a coed event, though as of 1998 no women had entered.

4457. Women's singles luge (toboggan) event held in the Olympic Winter Games was in 1964 at Innsbruck, Austria. The winner of the inaugural women's singles event was Ortrun Enderlein of East Germany, on February 4.

4458. Two-seater luge (toboggan) event to have two pairs of gold medalists in a single Olympic Winter Games was in 1972 at Sapporo, Japan. Paul Hildgartner and Walter Plaikner of Italy and Horst Hörnlein and Reinhard Bredow of East Germany each received gold medals on Feburary 10. The first run, won by Hildgartner and Plaikner, was voided, because the starting gate had malfunctioned. That left the two teams tied.

4459. National team to sweep the medals in the men's singles luge (toboggan) event at the Olympic Winter Games was East Germany, which had the top four finishers in the event on February 7, 1972, at Sapporo, Japan, led by Wolfgang Scheidel.

4460. National team to sweep the medals in the women's singles luge (toboggan) event at the Olympic Winter Games was East Germany, topped by Anna-Maria Müller, on February 7, 1972, at Sapporo, Japan.

4461. World cup in luge (toboggan) was held during 1977 and 1978. The winners of that first world cup series were Anton Winkler of West Germany in the men's singles and Regina König of West Germany in the women's singles. Men's doubles were added in 1979.

LUGE (TOBOGGAN)—continued

4462. Sliders to win two consecutive luge (toboggan) titles at the Olympic Winter Games were Hans Rinn and Norbert Hahn of East Germany. They won their second title in the two-seater luge event on February 19, 1980, at Lake Placid, New York, after having won their first in 1976.

4463. Slider to win two consecutive women's singles luge (toboggan) titles at the Olympic Winter Games was Steffi Martin Walker of East Germany. Her second win came on February 16, 1988, at Calgary, Alberta, Canada, after her first (as Martin) in 1984.

4464. Coed luge (toboggan) event in the Olympic Winter Games was the two-seater competition held in 1994 at Lillehammer, Norway. However, it was coed in theory only, for no women were entered.

4465. Slider to win two, and then three, consecutive men's singles luge (toboggan) titles in the Olympic Winter Games was Georg Hackl of Germany. After winning his first title in 1992, he won his second in Lillehammer, Norway, on February 14, 1994, and his third in Nagano, Japan, on February 9, 1998.

M

MARATHON (BEFORE 1900)

4466. Meeting of the Boston Athletic Association was on March 15, 1887. With a clubhouse established that year, they provided a home for many sports, but would become most famous for sponsoring the Boston Marathon, from 1897.

4467. Marathon runner to be stripped of his medal was Spiridon Belokas of Greece. At the first modern Olympic Games in Athens, Greece, he originally appeared to finish third on April 10, 1896, but later was revealed to have traveled part of the route in a carriage.

4468. Men's marathon race held in the Olympic Games was on April 10, 1896, in Athens, Greece. The keynote event of the first modern Olympic Games, it was won by Spiridon Louis of Greece, with a time of 2:58:50 hours. Inspired by the story of Pheidippides, who is supposed to have run some 26 miles to Athens to report a Greek victory over the Persians at Marathon in 490 BC, the marathon was never an event in the ancient Games. The marathon distance was not standardized to 26 miles, 385 yards until 1924.

4469. Boston Marathon originally named the American Marathon, was held on April 19, 1897, in Boston, Massachusetts, as part of the 1897 Boston Athletic Association Games. The inaugural winner was John J. McDermott of the United States, with a time of 2:55:10 hours over the 24.5 mile distance. Women could not race in it officially until 1972, though some did so unofficially starting in 1966. The world's oldest annual race, the Boston Marathon is held on or about April 19, the date of the opening battles of the American Revolution.

MARATHON (1900-1949)

4470. Runner to win two consecutive Boston Marathons was John Caffery of Canada, who won in both 1900 and 1901, with a time of 2:29:23 hours on the latter occasion.

4471. Runner for the United States to win the men's marathon at the Olympic Games was English-born Thomas Hicks, who had a time of 3:28:53 hours to win on August 30, 1904, at St. Louis, Missouri. He was given various mixtures, some including strychnine, during the race to keep him going, a procedure that would later be banned.

4472. Runner to hold the officially accepted world record in the men's marathon, and the first United States runner to win the Olympic marathon was John Hayes, who had a time of 2:55:18.4 hours at the Olympic Games in London, England, on July 24, 1908. Dorando Pietri of Italy had entered the stadium first but collapsed and received assistance, and so was disqualified, a situation that caused enormous controversy. The two turned professional, often racing against each other.

4473. Runner to complete the men's marathon in under 2:55 hours was James Clark of the United States. His record of 2:46:52.2 hours was set in New York City on February 12, 1909.

4474. Boston Marathon to be canceled was in 1918, during World War I.

4475. Standardization of the marathon distance was in 1924. The distance settled on was 26 miles, 385 yards (42.195 kilometers), based on the 1908 Olympic course from Windsor to the White City Stadium in London, England.

4476. Runner to win three consecutive Boston Marathons was Clarence DeMar of the United States. After winning in 1922 and 1923, he returned to win again in 1924, with a time of 2:29:40 hours. He had also won in 1911, and would win three times more (1927, 1928, and 1930).

4477. Runner to complete the men's marathon in under 2:30 hours was Albert Michelsen of the United States, with a time of 2:29:01.8 hours, set on October 12, 1925, in Port Chester, New York.

4478. Runner to hold the officially accepted world record in the women's marathon was Violet Piercy of Great Britain. Racing in London, England, on October 3, 1926, she covered the distance in 3:40.2 hours. Her time would not be officially broken until 1963. It was, indeed, rarely challenged, because women's races longer than 200 meters would be banned internationally from 1928 for decades, in the Olympic Games until 1960.

4479. Runner to win seven Boston Marathons was Clarence DeMar of the United States. His seventh title came in 1930 with a time of 2:34:48 hours. His first had come in 1911, followed by wins in 1922–1924, 1927, and 1928.

4480. Record in the men's marathon to stand for more than 10 years was the time of 2:26:42.0 hours set by Sohn Kee Chung of South Korea (forced to race for Japan as Kitei Son) on November 3, 1935, in Tokyo, Japan. It would stand until April 19, 1947, when Yun Bok Suh of South Korea ran the Boston Marathon in 2:25:39.0 hours.

4481. Asahi Marathon was held in 1947 at Kumamoto, Japan. In 1951, it would be shifted to Fukuoka and called the Fukuoka Marathon.

4482. Runner officially representing South Korea to hold the world record in the men's marathon, and to win the Boston Marathon was Yun Bok Suh, who set a record of 2:25:39.0 hours in 1947, at the Boston Marathon. The previous world record had been set in 1935 by his countryman Sohn Kee Chung, forced to compete for Japan, which then occupied South Korea.

MARATHON (1950-1969)
4483. Runners from a single country outside the United States to take the top three spots in the Boston Marathon were Kee Yong Ham, Ki Yoon Song, and Yun Chi Choi of South Korea, who finished in that order in 1950.

4484. Fukuoka Marathon was run in Fukuoka, Japan, in 1951, the successor to the Asahi Marathon first held in 1947. It would be held annually in December from 1964, remaining a men-only race into the 21st century.

4485. Runner to complete the men's marathon in under 2:20 hours was Jim Peters of Great Britain. His time of 2:18:40.2 hours, set on June 13, 1953, in London, England, was his second of four world records in the event.

4486. Boston Marathon winner who was a member of the Boston Athletic Association the event's sponsor, was John J. Kelley, who won in 1957 with a time of 2:20:05 hours. He was the only runner from the United States to win from 1946 through 1967.

4487. Black African runner to win the men's marathon title at the Olympic Games, and to hold the world record in the event was Abebe Bikila of Ethiopia. Running barefoot, he posted a world-record time of 2:15:16.2 hours on September 10, 1960, in Rome, Italy, the first Olympic marathon run at night. Bikila had only run two marathons before then. He would win his second Olympic gold medal, lowering the world record to 2:12:11.2, on October 21, 1964, in Tokyo, Japan.

4488. Runner to break the 1926 record in the women's marathon, and the first from the United States to hold the world record in the event was Merry Lepper of the United States, who set a time of 3:37.07 hours on December 16, 1963, in Culver City, California. Violet Piercy's 37-year-old record had not been officially challenged because long races for women were prohibited internationally for decades from 1928.

4489. Runner to win two consecutive marathon titles in the Olympic Games was Abebe Bikila of Ethiopia. After winning his first men's marathon barefoot in 1960, he went to Tokyo, Japan, wearing shoes to win his second on October 21, 1964, with a time of 2:12:11.2 hours. Astonishingly, he had had an appendectomy less than six weeks earlier. He was paralyzed after a traffic accident in 1969 and died at just 41.

4490. Woman to race in the Boston Marathon was Roberta Gibb of the United States. Before women were allowed as official entrants, she ran unofficially in the event in 1966, finishing in 126th place with a time of 3:21:40 hours. She would lead the unofficial women entrants in 1967 and 1968.

4491. Woman to run in the Boston Marathon wearing an official number was Katherine Switzer in 1967. Women were not yet officially allowed into the race, but she received a number by registering as "K. Switzer." She would be women's champion of the New York Marathon in 1974.

MARATHON—(1950-1969)—*continued*

4492. Runner to race the men's marathon in under 2:12 hours, and the first representing Australia to hold the world record in the event was British-born Derek Clayton. His time of 2:9:36.4 hours was set in the Fukuoka Marathon, in Fukuoka, Japan, on December 3, 1967. He would lower that to 2:8:33.6 on May 30, 1969, in Antwerp, Belgium.

MARATHON (1970-1979)

4493. New York Marathon was run in 1970. It included both women and men from the start, but no women finished that first year. The men's champion was Gary Muhrcke of the United States. An annual event, the race was originally held in New York City's Central Park but from 1976 would be run through all five of the city's boroughs.

4494. Woman to be women's champion in the New York Marathon was Beth Bonner of the United States, who won the event the second year it was held, in 1971. No women finished in 1970.

4495. Woman to race the marathon in under 3:00 hours is in great dispute, because of uncertainties in distances and the lack of official monitors. The prime claimants are Adrienne Beames of Australia, in 2:46:30 hours on August 31, 1971, in Werribee, Australia, and three United States marathoners: Beth Bonner, in 2:55:22 hours on September 19, 1971, in New York City; Cheryl Bridges, in 2:46:36 hours on December 5, 1971, in Culver City, California; and Miki (Michiko) Gorman, in 2:46:36 hours, on December 2, 1973, also in Culver City.

4496. Boston Marathon to include women as official participants was in 1972. Nina Kuscsik of the United States led a seven-woman field with a time of 3:10:26 hours.

4497. Woman to complete the Boston Marathon in under 3:00 hours was Miki (Michiko) Gorman of the United States, who had a time of 2:47:11 hours in 1974.

4498. Wheelchair entrant in the Boston Marathon was Bob Hall, who was allowed to race on the condition that he complete the course in under three hours. He did so in 2:58:00 hours in 1975. From this the Wheelchair Division would develop.

4499. New York Marathon to traverse New York City's five boroughs was in 1976. The men's winner was Bill Rodgers of the United States, with a time of 2:10:10 hours. He would win the next three as well (1977-1979). The women's winner was Miki (Michiko) Gorman of the United States, with a time of 2:39:11 hours; she would repeat in 1977. Before 1976, the race was run in Central Park.

4500. Chicago Marathon originally called the Mayor Daley Marathon, was held in 1977 in Chicago, Illinois.

4501. Runner to win the women's title in both the Boston Marathon and the New York Marathon in the same year was Miki (Michiko) Gorman in 1977. It was her second win in each, her previous wins coming in 1974 in Boston and 1976 in New York City.

4502. Champion of the women's wheelchair division in the Boston Marathon was Sharon Rahn of the United States, who completed the course in 3:48:51 hours in 1977.

4503. Runner to win the men's title in both the Boston Marathon and the New York Marathon in the same year was Bill Rodgers of the United States in 1978. His win in Boston was his second of four titles there (1975 and 1978-1980). His October 22 win in New York City was his third of four (1976-1979).

4504. Runner to win four consecutive New York Marathons was Bill Rodgers of the United States, who won from 1976 through 1979.

4505. Runner to race the women's marathon in under 2:30 hours was Grete Andersen Waitz in 1979. In her second of four world women's marathon records and of nine New York Marathon wins, she had a time of 2:27:32.6 hours, on October 21.

MARATHON (1980-1989)

4506. Rotterdam Marathon was held in 1981, in Rotterdam, the Netherlands. The first winner of the event, until 1983 for men only, was John Graham of Great Britain with a time of 2:09:28 hours.

4507. London Marathon was held on March 29, 1981, in London, England. Including both women and men from the start, it was organized by 1956 British Olympic steeplechase gold-medalist Christopher Brasher. Dick Beardsley of the United States and Inge Simonsen of Norway shared the inaugural men's championship, with a time of 2:11:48 hours. Joyce Smith of Great Britain was the women's champion with 2:29:57 hours.

4508. Runner to win the men's marathon in the World Championships in Athletics was Robert de Castella of Australia, with a time of 2:10:03 hours in 1983 in Helsinki, Finland.

4509. Runner to win the women's championship in the Rotterdam Marathon was Rosa Mota of Portugal in 1983, with a time of 2:32:27 hours, in Rotterdam, the Netherlands.

4510. Women's World Road Race Championship sponsored by the International Amateur Athletic Federation (IAAF), was held in 1983. The winning team was from the United States, with Wendy Sly of Great Britain being the individual champion, with a time of 32.23 minutes over the 10-kilometer distance. From 1985 the distance would be 15 kilometers, with the annual event replaced after 1991 by the IAAF World Half Marathon Championship.

4511. Runner to win two official women's championships in the Boston Marathon was Joan Benoit (later Samuelson). She won in both 1979 and 1983, in the latter setting a women's marathon world record with a time of 2:22:43 hours.

4512. Women's marathon held in the Olympic Games was on August 5, 1984, in Los Angeles, California. World record-holder Joan Benoit (later Samuelson) won the inaugural race with a time of 2:24:52 hours.

4513. Runner to win both the women's title in the Boston Marathon and the women's marathon in the Olympic Games was Joan Benoit (later Samuelson). She won the Boston Marathon in 1979 and 1983. She then won the Olympic title on August 5, 1984, with a time of 2:24.52 hours, in Los Angeles, California.

4514. World Cup Marathon sponsored by the International Amateur Athletic Federation (IAAF), was held in 1985 in Hiroshima, Japan. The winning men's team was from Djibouti, home country of the leading individual male marathoner, Ahmed Salah, who had a time of 2:08.09 hours. Italy had the leading women's team, with Katrin Dörre of East Germany being the first women's individual winner, with a time of 2:33:30 hours. From 1997 the event would be incorporated into the World Championships in Athletics.

4515. Boston Marathon to offer prize money was in 1986. Men's champion Robert de Castella of Australia received $60,000, while women's champion Ingrid Kristiansen of Norway got $35,000. Each was also given a car.

4516. Runner from Africa to win the men's title in the New York Marathon was Ibrahim Hussein of Kenya, who won in 1987.

4517. Runner to race the men's marathon in under 2:7 hours was Belayneh Densimo of Ethiopia, who had a time of 2:6:50.0 hours on April 17, 1988, in Rotterdam, the Netherlands. He was unable to compete in the 1988 Olympics because Ethiopia boycotted them.

4518. Runner from Africa to win the men's title in the Boston Marathon was Ibrahim Hussein of Kenya, who first won in 1988. In the event's closest finish ever, his time of 2:08:43 hours won the event by 1 second, over Juma Ikangaa of Tanzania. Hussein would win twice more, in 1991 and 1992, beginning a Kenyan domination of the event through the 1990s.

4519. Runner to win two consecutive women's titles in the Boston Marathon, and three overall was Rosa Mota of Portugal. After winning in 1987, she returned with a time of 2:24:30 hours to lead in 1988, then won again in 1990 with 2:25:24.

MARATHON (1990-1999)

4520. Runner to race in more than 60 Boston Marathons was John A. Kelley. His first was in 1928 and his last in 1991, when he was 83. Overall he had 61 starts and 58 finishes, including two wins (1935 and 1945).

4521. World Half Marathon Championship sponsored by the International Amateur Athletic Federation (IAAF), was held in 1992, and annually from then on. On the men's side, Kenya had both the winning national team and the individual champion, Benson Masya, whose time was 60:24 minutes. For the women, the winning team was from Japan and the individual champion was Liz McColgan of Scotland. For women, the event replaced the earlier IAAF Women's World Road Race Championship (1983–1991).

4522. World Road Relay Championship sponsored by the International Amateur Athletic Federation (IAAF), was held in 1992, biennially pitting national relay teams over a marathon distance. At the inaugural event, the winning men's team was from Kenya, with a time of 2:00:02 hours, and the women's team from Portugal, with 2:20:14 hours.

4523. Runner from the United States to win the men's marathon in the World Championships in Athletics was Mark Plaatjes, with a time of 2:13:57 hours in 1993 at Stuttgart, Germany.

4524. Runner from Africa to win the women's title in the New York Marathon was Tegla Loroupe of Kenya, who had a time of 2:28.06 hours to win in 1994. She would win again in 1995.

MARATHON—(1990-1999)—*continued*

4525. Runner to win three consecutive women's titles in the Boston Marathon was Uta Pippig of Germany. After winning in 1994 (with a course record of 2:21:45 hours) and 1995, she came back for her third straight title in 1996, with a time of 2:27:12 hours.

4526. Runner from Africa, and from Ethiopia, to win the women's marathon at the Olympic Games was Fatima Roba, who won on July 28, 1996, in Atlanta, Georgia, with a time of 2:26:5 hours.

4527. Runner from Africa to win the women's title in the Boston Marathon was Fatuma Roba of Ethiopia, with a time of 2:26:23 hours in 1997. She would win again in 1998 and 1999.

MARTIAL ARTS

4528. Development of judo was by Jigoro Kano, who in 1882 founded a school at the Eishoji Temple in Tokyo, Japan, to teach judo, drawing on several earlier martial arts and developing it into a sport.

4529. Formal instruction in karate was begun in the 1920s by Funakoshi Gichin in Japan. The self-defense sport had originally been developed in the 17th century on the island of Okinawa. It would become known as *karate* during the 1930s.

4530. School for aikido was the Aioi-ryu Aiki Bujutsu (later Aikido) school founded in 1928 by Morihei Ueshiba, a key figure in shaping and popularizing the martial art, who also founded Aiki-kai, a key association in the sport.

4531. International governing body for judo was the International Judo Federation, founded in 1951.

4532. World championships for judo were held in Tokyo, Japan, in 1956, and biennially from 1965.

4533. Men's middleweight judo event in the Olympic Games was in 1964 in Tokyo, Japan. The inaugural event was won by Isao Okano of Japan with a yoko-shiho-gatame hold.

4534. Men's lightweight judo event in the Olympic Games was in 1964 in Tokyo, Japan. Competing in the finals on October 20, Takehide Nakatani of Japan won on points.

4535. Men's heavyweight judo event in the Olympic Games was in 1964 in Tokyo, Japan. Isao Inokuma of Japan won a close decision over A. Douglas Rogers of Canada in the finals on October 22.

4536. Men's open judo event in the Olympic Games was held in 1964 in Tokyo, Japan. Two-time world champion Antonius Geesink of the Netherlands won the inaugural event with a kesa-gatame hold on October 23. The open event would be discontinued after 1984.

4537. World championships in karate were held in Tokyo, Japan, in 1970. They would come to be held biennially.

4538. Men's half-heavyweight judo event in the Olympic Games was in 1972 in Munich, West Germany. The winner of the inaugural event was Shota Chochoshvili of the Soviet Union, who en route to his victory had upset two-time world champion Fumio Sasahara of Japan.

4539. Men's half-middleweight judo event in the Olympic Games was in 1972 in Munich, West Germany. Toyokazu Nomura of Japan won the inaugural event on September 3.

4540. Judo artist to win two gold medals in a single Olympic Games was Willem Ruska of the Netherlands in 1972 in Munich, West Germany. On August 31, he won the men's heavyweight title with a harai-goshi throw. Then on September 9, he won the now-discontinued open event with a yoko-shiho-gatame hold.

4541. World championships in taekwondo were held in Seoul, South Korea, in 1973 and biennially thereafter, sponsored by the Korean Taekwondo Association. In that inaugural competition just two events were held, both for men only and both won by South Koreans. Lee Ki-hyung won the lightweight class and Kim Jeong-tae won the heavyweight class.

4542. National governing body for taekwondo in the United States was the United States Taekwondo Union, established in 1974.

4543. World championships in taekwondo to include additional weight classes for men were in 1975. The winners of the new events, all South Korean, were Whang Soo-yong in the finweight, Han You-Keun in the flyweight, Son Tae-whan in the bantamweight, Lee Gyeo-sung in the featherweight, Song Hur in the welterweight, and Yang Young-kwan in the middleweight.

4544. World championships in taekwondo to include light-middleweight and light-heavyweight classes for men were in 1979. Rainer Müller of West Germany won the light-middleweight crown, becoming the first non–South Korean to win a taekwondo world title, while Chung Chan of South Korea won the light-heavyweight competition.

4545. Men's extra-lightweight judo event held in the Olympic Games was in 1980 in Moscow, the Soviet Union. The inaugural winner was Thierry Ray of France, who won with a ko-soto-gari throw.

4546. World championships for judo to include women were held in 1980 in New York City, where Ingrid Berghmans of Belgium won the open class, the first of her six world titles (1980, 1982, 1984, and 1986 in the open class; 1984 and 1989 in the under 72 kilograms class).

4547. World championships in karate to include women were held in 1980. They would become biennial.

4548. Men's half-lightweight judo event held in the Olympic Games was in 1980 in Moscow, the Soviet Union. Nikolai Solodukhin of the Soviet Union won on July 31, after his opponent was heavily penalized for backpedaling.

4549. World championships in taekwondo to include women were sponsored by the World Taekwondo Federation in 1987, though women had competed unofficially starting in 1983. The inaugural winners in the eight weight classes for women were Jang Ei-suk of South Korea (finweight), Pai Yun-yao of Taiwan (flyweight), Tennur Yerlhsu of Turkey (bantamweight), Kim So-young of South Korea (featherweight), Lee Eun-young of South Korea (lightweight), Coral Bistuer of Spain (welterweight), Margaretha de Jongh of the Netherlands (middleweight), and Lynette Love of the United States (heavyweight).

4550. Judo artist to win two consecutive men's middleweight gold medals in the Olympic Games was Peter Seisenbacher of Austria. After winning his first men's in 1984, he went to Seoul, South Korea, for his second on September 29, 1988. Two days later Hitoshi Saito of Japan won his second heavyweight title.

4551. Judo artist to win two consecutive gold medals in the men's heavyweight title in the Olympic Games was Hitoshi Saito of Japan. After winning his first in 1984, he garnered his second on October 1, 1988, in Seoul, South Korea.

4552. Women's lightweight judo event held in the Olympic Games was in 1992 in Barcelona, Spain. Miriam Blasco Soto of Spain won the inaugural competition with a ko-soto-gake throw.

4553. Women's heavyweight judo event held in the Olympic Games was in 1992 in Barcelona, Spain. Using a kami-shiho-gatame hold, Zhuang Xiaoyan of China won the inaugural title on July 27.

4554. Women's half-heavyweight judo event held in the Olympic Games was in 1992 in Barcelona, Spain. The inaugural winner was Jim Mi-jung of South Korea on July 28.

4555. Judo artist to win gold medals in two different weight classes in the Olympic Games was Waldemar Legien of Poland. After winning the half-middleweight class in 1988, he went to Barcelona, Spain, where he won the middleweight title on July 29, 1992.

4556. Women's middleweight judo event held in the Olympic Games was in 1992 in Barcelona, Spain. Using an uchi-mata throw, Odalys Reve Jiménez of Cuba won the inaugural event on July 29.

4557. Women's half-middleweight judo event held in the Olympic Games was in 1992 in Barcelona, Spain. Catherine Fleury of France won on a referees' decision over Yael Arad of Israel in the finals on July 30, 1992.

4558. Women's half-lightweight judo event held in the Olympic Games was in 1992 in Barcelona, Spain. The final, on August 1, was won by Almudena Muñoz Martinez of Spain, with a tani-otoshi throw.

4559. Women's extra-lightweight judo event held in the Olympic Games was in 1992 in Barcelona, Spain. Winning the final on August 2, with a kochiki-taoshi throw, was Cécile Nowak of France.

4560. Men's taekwondo events held in the Olympic Games were in 2000 in Sydney, Australia. Steven Lopez of the United States won the flyweight title (for contestants up to 58 kilograms or 128 pounds) on September 27, and Michail Mouroutsos of Greece the featherweight (up to 68 kilograms or 150 pounds) on September 28. Angel Valodia Matos Fuentes of Cuba won the welterweight event (for fighters up to 80 kilograms or 176 pounds) on September 29, and Kim Kyong Hun of South Korea the heavyweight (over 80 kilograms or 176 pounds) on September 30.

4561. Women's taekwondo events held in the Olympic Games were in 2000 in Sydney, Australia. Lauren Burns of Australia won the flyweight title (for contestants up to up to 49 kilograms or 108 pounds) on September 27, Jung Jae-Eun Jung of South Korea the featherweight (up to 57 kilograms or 126 pounds) on Septem-

MARTIAL ARTS—*continued*

ber 28. Lee Sun-hee of South Korea won the welterweight event (for fighters up to 67 kilograms or 148 pounds) on September 29, and Chen Zhong of China the heavyweight (over 67 kilograms or 148 pounds) on September 30.

MOTORBOAT (POWERBOAT) RACING

4562. Gold Cup motorboat (powerboat) race was held at the Columbia Yacht Club on the Hudson River, in New York, in 1904, sponsored by the just-founded American Powerboat Association. The winner was C. C. Riotto, racing *Standard* at an average speed of 23.6 miles per hour. The race would be held annually, except in wartime.

4563. International motorboat (powerboat) race was held in Queenstown (now Cóbh), Ireland, in 1903, for the Harmsworth Trophy offered by Alfred Harmsworth (later Lord Northcliffe). The inaugural winner of the race, open to both men and women, was Dorothy Levitt of England in the *Napier I*, owned by S. F. Edge, with an average speed of 19.53 miles per hour. The race would be held annually, then irregularly until 1961, but was revived in 1977.

4564. National governing body for motorboat (powerboat) racing was the American Powerboat Association, founded in 1903 in the United States.

4565. Motorboat-racing event held in the Olympic Games was in London, England, on August 28–29, 1908, the only time the sport was included in the Olympics. Thomas Thornycroft, Bernard Redwood, and John Field-Richard of Great Britain won the 8-meter and under-60-foot events, while Émile Thubron of France won the open-class event.

4566. International governing body for motorboat (powerboat) racing was the Union Internationale Motonautique (UIM), founded in 1922.

4567. President's Cup motorboat (powerboat) race was held in 1926 in Washington, D.C. The inaugural winner was L. G. Hamersley in *Cigarette*, with an average speed of 55.20 miles per hour.

4568. Motorboat (powerboat) racer to go faster than 200 miles per hour was Donald Campbell, who reached 202.32 miles per hour in his *Bluebird* on July 23, 1955, on Ullswater, a lake in northern England. He would reach 275 mph by 1959.

MOTORCYCLE RACING

4569. Motorcycle race on record was on September 20, 1896, when eight contestants drove on a round trip between Paris and Nantes, France. With a time of 4:10:37 hours, M. Chevalier was the winner, driving a Michelin-Dion tricycle.

4570. Motorcycle race for two-wheeled vehicles was held on November 29, 1897, in Richmond, Surrey, England. Winning a one-mile race on an oval track was Charles Jarrott, driving a Fournier, with a time of 2:08 minutes.

4571. National governing body in motorcycle racing was the Auto-Cycle Union (ACU), founded in Great Britain in 1903.

4572. International governing body in motorcycle racing was the Fédération Internationale des Clubs Motorcyclistes, founded in 1904. It later became the Fédération Internationale Motorcycliste (FIM).

4573. Moto-cross trials riding competition was the Scottish Six Days Trial, begun in 1909 in Edinburgh, Scotland.

4574. International trials competition in moto-cross racing was the International Six Days Trial held in 1913.

4575. Moto-cross race was held in 1924 in Camberley, Surrey, England.

4576. World championships in dirt-track (speedway) motorcycle racing were held in 1936 in Wembley Stadium, London. Lionel Van Praag of Australia won the first individual short-track title. A team competition was added in 1960, pairs officially in 1970, and long-track in 1971.

4577. International moto-cross competition was the Moto-Cross des Nations established in 1947. A five-man team event for 500 cc motorcycles, it was won by Great Britain. It would be held annually, from 1984 for four-man teams.

4578. World championships in motorcycle racing were held in 1949, for four classes of vehicles and for vehicles with sidecars. The inaugural winners were Nello Pagani of Italy driving a Mondial in the 125 cc class, Bruno Ruffo of Italy driving a Guzzi in the 250 cc, Freddie Frith of Great Britain driving a Velocette in the 350 cc, Leslie Graham of Great Britain driving an AJS in the 500 cc, and Eric Oliver of Great Britain driving a Norton in the sidecar division.

4579. World championship in moto-cross racing was held in 1957. The inaugural winner of the men-only competition was Bill Nilsson of Sweden driving an AJS in the 500 cc class.

4580. Team event in the dirt-track (speedway) motorcycle racing world championships was in 1960, the first title being won by a team from Sweden. The event was discontinued after 1994.

4581. International moto-cross competition for 250 cc motorcycles was the Trophée des Nations, founded in 1961, when it was won by the five-man team from Great Britain. In 1976, it would merge with the Moto-Cross des Nations, for four-man teams.

4582. World championship in moto-cross racing to include the 250 cc class was in 1962, when that event was won by Torsten Hallman of Sweden driving a Husqvarna.

4583. World championships in ice speedway motorcycle racing were held in 1966, with the first individual champion being Gabdrahman Kadirov of the Soviet Union. Team competition was added in 1979.

4584. Motorcycle racer to win five individual dirt-track (speedway) world titles was Ove Fundin of Sweden, who won in the individual championships in 1956, 1960, 1961, 1963, and 1967.

4585. Pairs event in the dirt-track (speedway) motorcycle racing world championships was in 1970, when Ronnie Moore and Ivan Mauger of New Zealand won the title. Unofficial races had been held in 1968 and 1969, with the 1968 winners being Ove Fundin and Torbjörn Harryson of Sweden.

4586. Long-track event in the dirt-track (speedway) motorcycle racing world championships was in 1971. The first champion was Ivan Mauger of New Zealand, who would win the title again in 1972 and 1976.

4587. World championship in moto-cross racing to include the 125 cc class was in 1975. Gaston Rahier of Belgium won the event on a Suzuki.

4588. World championships in trials riding in moto-cross racing were held in 1975. Martin Lampkin of Great Britain was the winner, riding a Bultaco.

4589. Motorcycle racer to win six individual dirt-track (speedway) world titles was Ivan Mauger of New Zealand, who was the individual titlist in 1968, 1969, 1970, 1972, 1977, and 1979. He also won three long-track world titles in this period, in 1971, 1972, and 1976.

4590. Team event held in the ice speedway motorcycle racing world championships was in 1979. The team from the Soviet Union won that first title, and would win again 1980–1982, 1984, and 1986–1992, with Russia then winning in 1993–1994 and 1996–1998.

4591. World championship in moto-cross racing to include the sidecar class was in 1980. The winner was Reinhardt Bohler of West Germany aboard a Yamaha.

4592. World Endurance Championship in motorcycle racing was held in 1980, when Marc Fontan and Hervé Moineau of France won the event driving a Honda. It replaced an earlier competition called the Coupe d'Endurance.

4593. International moto-cross competition for 125 cc cycles was the Coupe des Nations, founded in 1982, when it was won by the team from Italy. From 1985, it would become part of the Moto-Cross des Nations.

4594. Motorcycle racer to win five individual long-track world titles was Simon Wigg of England, who was long-track champion in 1985, 1989, 1990, 1993, and 1994.

N

NETBALL

4595. Netball was developed in the United States in 1891, though it would become most popular in other countries. The 7-a-side game, derived from basketball, would come to be played primarily by women.

4596. National association for netball was founded in New Zealand in 1924.

4597. International governing body for netball was the International Federation of Netball Associations (IFNA), founded in 1960.

4598. World championships in netball were held in 1963, when the winning team was from Australia.

O

OLYMPIC GAMES (BEFORE 1900)
4599. Olympic Games were held in Olympia, Greece, from at least 776 BC, the date of the earliest recorded competition. Originally only one event was contested, a sprint, with the winner—Koroibos in 776—receiving an olive wreath, as well as a torch to light a fire to hon-

OLYMPIC GAMES—(BEFORE 1900)—_continued_

or the gods. Other sports were added later, among them wrestling, boxing, and horse racing. Women were barred from the Olympic Games, as both athletes and spectators. They later developed their own athletic competitions, the Heraea. The Games were held every four years until they were banned by Roman Emperor Theodosius in AD 393.

4600. Woman recorded as participating in the original Olympic Games in Olympia, Greece, was Cynisca of Sparta. Women were barred from competition as both athletes and spectators, but they were allowed to own chariots. Cynisca's chariot won the Olympic chariot race in 396 BC.

4601. Ban on the Olympic Games was in 393, when Roman Emperor Theodosius banned the quadrennial competitions as pagan. The Games would not be revived until 1896.

4602. Proposal to revive the Olympic Games in modern times was made by Baron Pierre de Coubertin of France in 1892, at a meeting of the Athletic Sports Union at the Sorbonne in Paris, France. His idea would become reality in 1896.

4603. Olympic Games at which Beethoven's "Ode to Joy" was sung were in 1896. At the request of Baron Pierre de Coubertin of France, who inspired the modern Olympic revival, it became a traditional part of the Opening Ceremony.

4604. Athlete, and the first from the United States, to win a gold medal in the modern Olympic Games was 27-year-old James Connolly, who won the triple jump at approximately 2 PM on April 6, 1896, in Athens, Greece. Denied leave by Harvard University, where he was a student, he dropped out to compete in the Olympics.

4605. Event held in the modern Olympic Games was a heat for the men's 100-meter race on April 6, 1896, in Athens, Greece. It was won by Francis Lane of the United States, with a time of 12.2 seconds. The final, four days later, would be won by his teammate, Thomas Burke.

4606. Modern Olympic Games were held on April 6–15, 1896, in Athens, Greece, the country of the original Olympics. (Under the old calendar then used in Greece, the starting date was March 24.) Competing in 43 events were 245 athletes—all male—from 14 countries. They competed as individuals, rather than on national teams, which would not be introduced until 1908. These first modern Olympic Games were sponsored privately, but from 1900 through 1980 they would be government financed.

4607. Athlete from Australia to win a gold medal in the modern Olympic Games was Edwin Flack, who won the men's 1500-meter track event on April 7, 1896, in Athens, Greece. Two days later he also won the 800-meter.

4608. Athlete from Denmark to win a gold medal in the Olympic Games was Viggo Jensen, who won the two-handed weightlifting title on April 7, 1896, in Athens, Greece.

4609. Athlete from France to win a gold medal in the Olympic Games was Eugène-Henri Gravelotte, who won the men's individual foil fencing title on April 7, 1896, in Athens, Greece.

4610. Athlete from Great Britain to win a gold medal in the Olympic Games was Launceston Elliot, who won the one-hand lift weightlifting competition on April 7, 1896, in Athens, Greece, with a lift of 71.0 kilograms.

4611. Athlete from Greece to win a gold medal in the modern Olympic Games was Leon Pyrgos, a professional fencer, who won the masters' foil individual event on April 7, 1896, in Athens, Greece.

4612. Athlete from Switzerland to win a gold medal in the Olympic Games was Louis Zutter, who won the men's side (pommel) horse gymnastics competition on April 9, 1896, in Athens, Greece.

4613. Brothers to win gold and silver medals in the same event in the Olympic Games were John Paine and Sumner Paine of the United States, who were gold and silver medalists, respectively, in the military revolver shooting competition on April 10, 1896, in Athens, Greece.

4614. Athlete from Hungary to win a gold medal in the modern Olympic Games was Alfréd Hajós (né Alfréd Guttmann), competing under a pseudonym, who won the men's 100-meter freestyle swimming event on April 11, 1896, in Athens, Greece. Later that day he also won the 1200-meter freestyle.

OLYMPIC GAMES (1900-1909)

4615. Olympic Games to include women athletes were in 1900 in Paris, France. Nineteen women competed, while the male contingent numbered 1206 in 87 events.

4616. Athlete from Belgium to win a gold medal in the Olympic Games was Aimé Haegeman, who won the individual jumping equestrian event on May 29, 1900, in London, England.

4617. Athlete from Cuba to win a gold medal in the Olympic Games was Ramón Fonst, who won the men's individual épée fencing title on June 14, 1900, in Paris, France. He would win it again in 1904, when he also won the men's individual foil fencing title.

4618. Athlete from Italy to win a gold medal in the Olympic Games was Antonio Conte, who won the masters sabre fencing competition on June 27, 1900, in Paris, France.

4619. Olympic Games in which animals were deliberately killed was in 1900, in Paris, France. For the only time, live pigeon shooting was included as an event, won by Léon de Lunden of Belgium on June 27.

4620. Woman to win a gold medal in the Olympic Games was Charlotte "Chattie" Cooper of Great Britain, who won the inaugural women's singles tennis competition on July 11, 1900, in Paris, France.

4621. Athlete from Canada to win a gold medal in the Olympic Games was George Orton, who won the men's 2500-meter steeplechase event on July 15, 1900, in Paris, France.

4622. Athletes from Sweden to win a gold medal in the Olympic Games were members of a combined team from Sweden and Denmark, who won the tug-of-war event in Paris, France, on July 16, 1900.

4623. Athlete 10 years old or under to earn a gold medal in the Olympic Games was a French boy whose name was unrecorded and whose age was estimated at 7–10 years. In the pair-oared shell with coxswain rowing competition, he was coxswain for the winning crew from the Netherlands in the final race on August 26, 1900, in Paris, France.

4624. Athletes from the Netherlands to win gold medals in the Olympic Games were François Antoine Brandt and Roelof Klein, who won the men's pair-oared shell with coxswain rowing event on August 26, 1900, in Paris, France.

4625. Woman from the United States to win a gold medal in the Olympic Games was Margaret Abbott, who on October 3, 1900, won the women's golf tournament in Paris, France, although she never realized that it was part of the Olympics.

4626. Olympic Games held in France, and outside Greece were in 1900 in Paris, France, the home of Baron Pierre de Coubertin, who had inspired the revival of the Olympics in modern times. Poorly organized, and somewhat overshadowed by the World Exhibition held there that year, the events were stretched out over five months, between May 20 and October 28.

4627. Athlete to win four gold medals in a single Olympic Games was Alvin Kraenzlein of the United States in 1900 in Paris, France, where he won the men's 110-meter hurdles on April 10, the long jump and the 60-meter hurdles on July 15, and the later-discontinued 200-meter hurdles on July 16.

4628. Olympic Games held in the United States were on July 1–November 23, 1904, in St. Louis, Missouri. Originally scheduled for Chicago, Illinois, they were shifted to St. Louis, that year the site of the Louisiana Purchase Exposition, or world fair. These third modern Olympics were both badly organized and ill attended, with some events including only U.S. contestants.

4629. Athlete of Black African ancestry to compete in the Olympic Games was George Poage of the United States, who placed sixth in the men's 400-meter track event in St. Louis, Missouri, on August 29, 1904.

4630. Black athletes from Africa to participate in the Olympic Games were Lentauw and Yamasani, two Zulus who were in the city for the Louisiana Purchase Exposition, as part of an "exhibit" on the Boer War in South Africa. They raced in the marathon on August 30, 1904, in St. Louis, Missouri.

4631. National team sent from the United States to the Olympic Games was in 1906, to the unofficial Olympics at Athens, Greece. Before then, athletes went to the Olympics as individuals.

4632. Olympic Games held after two years, instead of four were held in Athens, Greece, April 22–May 2, 1906. Called the Intercalated or Interim Olympics, this second Athens Olympics helped keep alive the Olympic movement, but many sports historians do not count the results of the 1906 Games as official.

4633. Athlete to win 10 gold medals in the Olympic Games was Raymond Ewry of the United States. They included four each in the standing high jump and standing long jump (1900, 1904, 1906, and 1908), and two in the standing triple jump (1900 and 1904), all now discontinued men's events. Some historians do not consider the 1906 Olympics official.

OLYMPIC GAMES—(1900-1909)—*continued*

4634. Olympic Games to include winter events were the 1908 Games held in London, England. Men's singles, women's singles, and pairs figure skating events were held because London had a rink with artificial ice. Skating would not be held again until 1920, when Antwerp, Belgium, also had an appropriate rink.

4635. Olympic Games to produce an Official Report of the results of the athletic events were in London, England, in 1908. Before—and sometimes after—that time, records were not always clearly kept.

4636. Olympic Games to include more than 2000 athletes, and more than 100 events, and to be held in Great Britain were between April 27 and October 31 in 1908, in London, England. In all, 2035 athletes participated in 109 events; only 36 of the contestants were women.

4637. Athletes from Norway to win official gold medals at the Olympic Games were members of the team that won the men's free rifle shooting event on April 28, 1908, in London, England. One of them, Gudbrand Skatteboe, won the individual men's free rifle title that same day. Norwegian athletes had won four gold medals in 1906, but some historians regard results from that Olympics as unofficial.

4638. Athlete from Africa, and from South Africa, to win a gold medal in the Olympic Games was Reginald Walker, who won the men's 100-meter track race on July 22, 1908.

4639. Athlete of Black African descent to win an Olympic gold medal was John Taylor of the United States, on July 25, 1908, in London, England. He ran the third leg on the winning 4 x 400-meter relay team. Just qualified as a veterinarian, "Doc" Taylor would die of typhoid less than five months later.

4640. Athlete from Russia to win a gold medal in the Olympic Games was figure skater Nikolai Kolomenkin, competing under the pseudonym Nikolai Panin, in London, England. He won his medal on October 29, 1908, in special figures, a competition involving tracing of set patterns on the ice, offered only that year.

4641. Athlete from Finland to win an official gold medal in the Olympic Games was Verner Weckman, who won the men's light heavyweight Greco-Roman wrestling title on July 22, 1908, in London, England. In the 1906 Olympics, not counted as official by some historians, he won the middleweight title on May 1; his teammate Verner Järvinen won the Greek-style discus event earlier that day, and so gained Finland's first gold medal, though unofficial.

OLYMPIC GAMES (1910-1919)

4642. Olympic Games held in Sweden, or in Scandinavia were in Stockholm on May 5–July 22, 1912, with 2547 athletes—2490 men and 57 women—from 28 countries participating in 102 events.

4643. Olympic Games to use electronic timing devices and a public address system were in Stockholm, Sweden, in 1912.

4644. Athlete to die while participating in the modern Olympic Games was Francisco Lazaro of Portugal. During the marathon race in Stockholm, Sweden, on July 14, 1912, he collapsed with sunstroke. Previously troubled by heart problems, he died on July 15.

4645. Native-American athlete to win a gold medal at the Olympic Games was Jim Thorpe of the United States, who won both the pentathlon and the decathlon at Stockholm, Sweden, the first on July 7, 1912, and the second on July 15.

4646. Modern Olympic Games to be canceled because of war were those originally scheduled for Berlin, Germany, in 1916, which were canceled because of World War I (1914–1918).

OLYMPIC GAMES (1920-1929)

4647. Flag showing five interlocking rings to symbolize the Olympic Games was flown at the 1920 Games in Antwerp, Belgium. Baron Pierre de Coubertin, founder of the modern Olympics, had designed the symbol in 1913, as well as the flag itself.

4648. Olympic Games held in Belgium were in Antwerp on April 20–September 12, 1920. The region was still much damaged from World War I.

4649. Modern Olympic Games at which member countries were barred from competing were in 1920, in Antwerp, Belgium, the first Olympics after World War I, when the losers—Germany, Austria, Hungary, Bulgaria, and Turkey—were not allowed to participate.

4650. Athlete from Brazil to win a gold medal in the Olympic Games was Guilherme Paraense, who won the men's rapid-fire pistol event on August 3, 1920, in Antwerp, Belgium.

4651. Athlete from Estonia to win a gold medal in the Olympic Games was Alfred Neuland, who won the men's lightweight weightlifting event on August 29, 1920, in Antwerp, Belgium.

4652. Athlete to win six medals overall in a single Olympic Games was Ville (Vilho) Ritola of Finland in 1924 in Paris, France. His four gold medals came in the men's 10,000-meters on July 6 (in a world record 30.23.2 minutes), the 3000-meter steeplechase on July 9, the 10,000-meter cross-country team race on July 12, and the 3000-meter team race on July 13; and his two silver in the 5000-meter race on July 10 and the 10,000-meter individual cross-country race on July 12, both behind his great teammate Paavo Nurmi.

4653. Olympic Winter Games were held in Chamonix, France, on January 25–February 4, 1924, with 281 men and 13 women from 16 countries participating in 14 events. Originally called International Sports Week 1924, the Winter Games would be held every four years through 1992. They were held again in 1994, after that alternating every two years with the Summer Games.

4654. Athlete to win a gold medal at the Olympic Winter Games was Charles Jewtraw of the United States, who won the men's 500-meter speed skating event at the first Winter Olympics at Chamonix, France, on January 26, 1924.

4655. Olympic Games in which more than 100 women participated were in Paris, France, on May 4–July 27, 1924, when 136 women (and 2956 men) from 44 countries participated in 126 events.

4656. Athletes from Uruguay to win gold medals in the Olympic Games were the members of the team that won the soccer (international football) title on June 9, 1924, in Paris, France.

4657. Athlete of Black African ancestry to win an individual gold medal in the Olympic Games was William DeHart Hubbard of the United States, who won the men's long jump on July 8, 1924, in Paris, France. With a jump of 24 feet 5 inches (7.44 meters), he bested his African-American teammate Edward Gourdin, then the world record-holder.

4658. Athlete to win five gold medals in a single Olympic Games was Paavo Nurmi of Finland in 1924 in Paris, France, when he won every race he entered: the men's 1500-meter race and, less than an hour later, the 5000 meters, on July 10; the individual and team cross-country titles on July 12, with the same race serving for both titles; and the 3000-meter team race on July 13. He might have won more but he was not entered in the 10,000-meter race, which he won in 1920 and 1928.

4659. Athletes from Argentina to win gold medals in the Olympic Games were the members of the team that won the polo title on July 12, 1924, in Paris, France: Arturo Kenny, Juan Nelson, Enrique Padilla, Juan Miles, and Guillermo Brooke Naylor.

4660. Athlete from Czechoslovakia to win a gold medal in the Olympic Games was Bedrich Supcik, who won the rope climbing gymnastics event on July 20, 1924, in Paris, France.

4661. Athlete from Yugoslavia to win a gold medal in the Olympic Games was Leon Stukelj, a Slovenian who won the men's all-around gymnastics title on July 20, 1924, in Paris, France. In 1992, at the age of 93, he watched athletes from newly independent Slovenia march under their own flag in the Olympics at Barcelona, Spain.

4662. Athlete from Egypt to win an Olympic gold medal was El Sayed Mohammed Nosseir, who won the men's light-heavyweight weightlifting title on July 29, 1928, in Amsterdam, the Netherlands.

4663. Olympic Winter Games held in a different country from the Summer Games were in 1928, when the Winter Games were held in St. Moritz, Switzerland, and the Summer Games in Amsterdam, the Netherlands.

4664. Olympic Winter Games held in Switzerland were held February 11–19, 1928, at St. Moritz. The first post–World War II Winter Games would also be held there in 1948.

4665. Athlete to win five individual gold medals, and seven medals overall, in the Olympic Winter Games all in speed skating, was A. Clas Thunberg of Finland. After winning the men's 1500- and 5000-meter races and the four-races combined event in 1924, he went to St. Moritz, Switzerland, in 1928, for a tie with Bernt Evensen of Norway in the 500-meter race on February 13, and finally a solo win over Evensen in the 1500-meter on February 14. In 1924, he had also taken silver in the 10,000-meter race and tied for bronze in the 500-meter.

OLYMPIC GAMES—(1920-1929)—*continued*

4666. Athlete to win three consecutive gold medals in the same event in the Olympic Winter Games was Gillis Grafström of Sweden. His third straight men's singles figure skating title came on February 17, 1928, at St. Moritz, Switzerland, after his first two wins in 1920 and 1924.

4667. Olympic Games to include track and field events for women were held in Amsterdam, the Netherlands, on May 17–August 12, 1928.

4668. Athletes from Asia, and from India, to win gold medals in the Olympic Games were the members of the team that won the men's field hockey title on May 26, 1928, in Amsterdam, the Netherlands. Led by Dhyan Chand as player and later coach, India would capture six straight titles in the event (1928–1956).

4669. Athlete to win 12 medals in the Olympic Games among them 9 gold, was Paavo Nurmi of Finland. His won his last medal, a gold, in the 10,000-meter race on July 29, 1928, in Amsterdam, the Netherlands; he had previously won the event in 1920. His other medals came in the 1500 meters (1924, gold), the 5000 meters (1920 and 1928, silver; 1924, gold), the individual cross-country (1920 and 1924, gold), the cross-country team race (1920 and 1924, gold), the 3000-meter steeplechase (1928, silver), and in the 3000-meter team race (gold, 1924). He might have won more but he was not entered in the 10,000-meter race in 1924, and he was suspended in 1932 for receiving more money than was deemed needed to cover his expenses on an exhibition tour.

4670. Athlete from Poland to win a gold medal in the Olympic Games was Halina Konopacka, who won the women's discus throw—the first women's track-and-field event held in the Olympic Games—on July 31, 1928, in Amsterdam, the Netherlands.

4671. Athlete from Japan to win a gold medal in the Olympic Games was Mikio Oda, who won the men's triple jump on August 2, 1928, in Amsterdam, the Netherlands.

4672. Athlete from New Zealand to win an Olympic gold medal was Edward Morgan, who won the welterweight boxing title on August 11, 1928, in Amsterdam, the Netherlands.

4673. Athletes from Spain to win gold medals in the Olympic Games were the members of the team that won the team jumping (Prix des Nations) equestrian event on August 12, 1928, in Amsterdam, the Netherlands: José Navarro Morenés, José Alvarez de las Asturias Bohorques y Goyeneche (de los Trujillos), and Julio Garcia Fernández.

OLYMPIC GAMES (1930-1939)

4674. Athlete to win gold medals in both the Summer and Winter Olympics was Edward Eagan of the United States. On August 24, 1920, he had won the light heavyweight boxing championships at Antwerp, Belgium, the last Olympics before summer and winter Games were separated. Then on February 15, 1932, he was on the winning four-man bobsled team at the Olympic Winter Games in Lake Placid, New York.

4675. Olympic Games to have medalists stand on a platform, and to play the gold medalist's national anthem were in 1932 in Los Angeles, California.

4676. Olympic Winter Games held in the United States were in 1932, at Lake Placid, New York, on February 4–15.

4677. Olympic Games to use automatic timing and photofinish cameras were in Los Angeles, California, on July 30–August 14, 1932.

4678. Result of an Olympic event to be changed after viewing of the film of the race was on August 3, 1932, at Los Angeles, California. After the viewing, Donald Finlay of Great Britain was given the bronze medal in the men's 100-meter hurdles, in place of Jack Keller of the United States.

4679. Jewish athlete to represent Germany in the 1936 Olympic Winter Games in Garmisch-Partenkirchen, Germany, was Rudi Ball. Ball had fled the country because of the Nazis' anti-Semitism campaigns, but had returned at the invitation of the Nazi government to lead the German ice hockey team, which placed fifth. Other Jewish athletes were barred from competing. Jews in many countries called for a boycott of the Olympics. As an alternative, the "People's Olympics" was scheduled for Barcelona, Spain, but then called off because of the Spanish Civil War.

4680. Olympic Games to be televised were in 1936 in Berlin, Germany. Television screens were set up in Berlin theaters, where visitors could view Olympic events.

4681. Olympic Games to have a torch relay were in 1936 in Berlin, Germany. The carrying of the torch from Olympia, Greece, to the site of each Olympiad would become a tradition.

4682. Olympic Winter Games held in Germany were in 1936, in the twin towns of Garmisch-Partenkirchen, February 6–16.

4683. Female athlete to win three consecutive titles in the same event in the Olympic Winter Games was Sonja Henie of Norway. Her third women's singles figure skating title came on February 15, 1936, at Garmisch-Partenkirchen, Germany, after her first two in 1928 and 1932.

4684. Olympic Games at which more than 4000 athletes participated was in Berlin, Germany, on August 1–16, 1936. Participating in the 116 events were 4066 athletes—3738 men and 328 women—from 49 countries. This was the last Olympics before World War II.

4685. Athlete from Turkey to win a gold medal in the Olympic Games was Yasar Erkan, who won the featherweight Greco-Roman wrestling title on August 9, 1936, in Berlin, Germany.

OLYMPIC GAMES (1940-1949)
4686. Olympic Winter Games to be canceled because of war were in 1940. They had originally been scheduled for Sapporo, Japan, but because of Japan's aggression in the Sino-Japanese War were to be switched to St. Moritz, Switzerland, or Garmisch-Partenkirchen, Germany. They were finally canceled altogether because of World War II (1939–1945), as were the 1944 Games, originally planned for London, England.

4687. Athlete to compete in seven Olympic Games was Ivan Osiier of Denmark, who competed in fencing in every Olympics between 1908 and 1932, and again in 1948, winning the silver medal in men's individual épée in 1912. His wife, Ellen Osiier, won the women's individual foil event in 1924.

4688. Athletes to compete in the Olympic Games over a period of 40 years were fencer Ivan Osiier of Denmark and sailor Magnus Konow of Norway, who both made their Olympic debuts in 1908 and their final appearances in 1948.

4689. Olympic Games at which athletes from Communist countries participated were in 1948 in London, England.

4690. Olympic Games attended by athletes of independent Korea were in 1948, in London, England. In 1936, Korea had been occupied by Japan, under whose flag Korean athletes had been forced to compete. Among them was Sohn Kee Chung (entered by Japan under the Japanese name Kitei Son), who won the gold medal in the marathon. He carried the South Korean flag in the 1948 Olympics and would later carry the Olympic torch in the 1988 Olympics in Seoul, South Korea.

4691. Athlete to win medals in the Olympic Winter Games 20 years apart was John Heaton of the United States. On February 4, 1948, at St. Moritz, Switzerland, he won the silver medal in the now-discontinued skeleton (Cresta run) luge event; he had previously won silver behind his brother, Jennison Heaton, in that event in 1928. Four days later, Richard Torriani won a bronze medal with the Swiss ice hockey team, as he had done 20 years before.

4692. Olympic Games at which athletes from more than 50 countries participated was the first post–World War II Games, held in London, England, July 29–August 14, 1948. There 4099 athletes—3714 men and 385 women—represented 59 countries in 136 events. Germany and Japan were not allowed to compete, following the precedent set after World War I.

4693. Athlete from Peru to win a gold medal in the Olympic Games was Edwin Vasquez Cam, who won the free pistol shooting event on August 2, 1948, in London, England.

4694. Asian-American athlete to win a gold medal in the Olympic Games was Korean-American Samuel Lee, who won his first of two consecutive men's platform diving titles on August 5, 1948, in London, England.

4695. Athlete from Jamaica to win a gold medal in the Olympic Games was Arthur Wint, who won the men's 400-meter track event on August 5, 1948, in London, England.

4696. Woman of Black African descent to win a gold medal in the Olympic Games was Alice Coachman of the United States, who won the women's high jump with an Olympic-record height of 5 feet 6 inches (1.68 meters) on August 7, 1948, in London, England.

4697. Athletes from Mexico to win gold medals in the Olympic Games were Humberto Mariles Cortés, Rubén Uriza, and Alberto Valdes, who won the team jumping (Prix des Nations) equestrian event in London, England, on August 14, 1948, the same day that Mariles Cortés also took the individual jumping title.

OLYMPIC GAMES (1950-1959)

4698. Olympic Games in which athletes from the Soviet Union participated were in 1952, at Helsinki, Finland. The Soviet team would leave Helsinki with 22 gold medals, 30 silver, and 19 bronze, second only to the United States.

4699. Olympic Winter Games held in Norway were at Oslo on February 14–25, 1952.

4700. Olympic event to be attended by 150,000 people was the men's individual 90-meter ski jump competition on February 24, 1952, in Oslo, Norway, won by one of the home team, Arnfinn Bergmann.

4701. Olympic Games held in Finland were at Helsinki, on July 19–August 3, 1952.

4702. Athlete from Romania to win a gold medal in the Olympic Games was Iosif Sarbu, who won the men's small-bore rifle (prone) event on July 29, 1952, in Helsinki, Finland.

4703. Olympic Games to be boycotted by member countries were in 1956 in Melbourne, Australia. Egypt, Iraq, and Lebanon boycotted over the Suez Canal crisis, and Spain, Switzerland, and the Netherlands over the Soviet Union's invasion of Hungary.

4704. Olympic Winter Games to be held in Italy, and the first to be televised were at Cortina d'Ampezzo, on January 26–February 5, 1956. The 1944 Games had been scheduled for Cortina, but then canceled because of World War II.

4705. Olympic Winter Games at which athletes from the Soviet Union participated were in 1956, at Cortina d'Ampezzo, Italy. The Soviet Union's first two Winter Olympic gold medals came on January 28, when Lyubov Kozyreva won the women's individual 10-kilometer Nordic (cross-country) skiing title and Yevgeny Grishin the 500-meter speed skating title. The Soviet team won seven gold medals and 16 medals altogether, more than any other country's team.

4706. Olympic Games held in the Southern Hemisphere, and in Australia were on November 22–December 8, 1956, in Melbourne, Australia. Because of Australia's quarantine laws, however, equestrian events were held in Stockholm, Sweden, on June 10–17. In this and the next two Olympics, West Germany and East Germany would be obliged to compete as a combined German team.

4707. Athlete from Bulgaria to win a gold medal in the Olympic Games was Nikola Stanchev, who won the middleweight freestyle wrestling title on December 1, 1956, in Melbourne, Australia.

4708. Olympic Games to have a formal closing ceremony were in 1956 in Melbourne, Australia. At the suggestion of John Ian Wing, an Australian of Chinese ancestry, athletes marched together on December 8, as a symbol of international unity, rather than being separated by country, as was traditional in the opening ceremony.

OLYMPIC GAMES (1960-1969)

4709. Athlete to win 13 medals in the Olympic Games was Edoardo Mangiarotti of Italy, all in fencing: men's individual foil (silver, 1952), team foil (silver, 1948, 1952, and 1960; gold, 1956), individual épée (bronze, 1948 and 1956; gold, 1952), and team épée (gold, 1936, 1952, 1956, and 1960; silver, 1952). His elder brother, Dario Mangiarotti, also won three medals—in individual épée (1952, silver) and team épée (silver, 1948; gold, 1952)—giving the family a total of 15 medals.

4710. Athlete from Ethiopia, and Black athlete from Africa, to win a gold medal at the Olympic Games was Abebe Bikila, who—running barefoot—won the men's marathon on September 10, 1960, in Rome, Italy.

4711. Athlete to win 18 medals in the Olympic Games was Larisa Latynina of the Soviet Union, all in gymnastics. In an Olympic career stretching from 1956 through 1964, she won nine gold, five silver, and four bronze medals, including two individual all-around titles in 1956 and 1960.

4712. Olympic Winter Games in which more than 1000 athletes competed were in Innsbruck, Austria, in 1964. Representing 36 nations were 986 men and 200 women, for a total of 1186.

4713. Olympic Winter Games at which an athlete was killed were in 1964, at Innsbruck, Austria, where Australian downhill skier Ross Milne was killed on January 25, during a practice run. A Polish-born luge slider, Kazimierz Kay-Skrzypeski of Great Britain, had been killed in practice two weeks before the Olympics officially began.

4714. Olympic Winter Games held in Austria were in 1964, at Innsbruck, January 29–February 9. Snow was severely lacking, however, so the Austrian army was mobilized to bring in tens of thousands of cubic meters of ice and snow for the competitions.

4715. Athlete to win four gold medals at a single Olympic Winter Games, and six Olympic gold medals overall was Lydia Skoblikova of the Soviet Union. In 1960, she had won the women's 1500- and 3000-meter speed skating events. In 1964, in Innsbruck, Austria, she won the 500-, 1000-, and 1500-meter titles, and then finally the 3000-meter, on February 2.

4716. Athlete to win nine medals in the Olympic Winter Games all of them in Nordic (cross-country) skiing, was Sixten Jernberg of Sweden. His ninth medal came on February 8, 1964, at Innsbruck, Austria, where he was part of the winning men's 4 x 10-kilometer relay team. He had won a bronze medal in the relay in 1956. His other medals had come in individual events: the 15-kilometer (silver, 1956 and 1960; bronze, 1964); the 30-kilometer (gold, 1960; silver, 1956); and the 50-kilometer (gold, 1956 and 1964).

4717. Wedding between Olympic athletes held at the Olympic Games was between long-jumper Diana Yorgova and gymnast Nikolai Prodanov, both of Bulgaria, who were married in the Olympic Village in Tokyo in October 1964.

4718. Olympic Games held in Asia, or in Japan were held in Tokyo on October 10–24, 1964.

4719. Athletes from the Bahamas to win gold medals in the Olympic Games were Durward Knowles and C. Cecil Cooke, who won the star-class sailboat race on October 21, 1964, in Tokyo, Japan.

4720. Olympic ban on drugs was made in 1967, when the International Olympic Committee's Medical Commission voted to outlaw some drugs.

4721. Athlete to be banned from the Olympic Games for taking drugs was Hans-Gunnar Liljenvall, a member of Sweden's pentathlon team. He was disqualified in 1968 for using alcohol.

4722. Olympic Games to include athletes from more than 100 countries were in 1968 in Mexico City, at which 5531 athletes—4750 men and 781 women—from 112 countries participated in 172 events. The high altitude (7347 feet) helped short-distance racers set many new records, but increased difficulty in longer-distance or endurance events.

4723. Olympic Games to institute sex tests for women athletes were the Olympic Winter Games at Grenoble, France, in 1968. Among the stunning discoveries was that—unknown to her—Erica Schinegger of Austria, the 1966 women's downhill skiing champion, had only male hormones and ingrown male organs. After surgery to become male, Schinegger took the name Eric and gave the 1966 gold medal to the original silver medalist, Marielle Goitschel.

4724. Olympic Games held in Mexico were held in Mexico City on October 12–27, 1968.

4725. Woman to carry the torch at the Olympic Games was Norma Enriqueta Basilio Satelo, who carried the torch into the stadium and lit the Olympic flame to signal the start of the Games in Mexico City on October 12, 1968.

4726. Sweep of the medals in an event by athletes of Black African ancestry at the Olympic Games was on October 14, 1968, in the 100-meter dash in Mexico City. James Hines of the United States set an Olympic record of 9.95 seconds, followed by Lennox Miller of Jamaica and Charles Greene of the United States.

4727. Athlete to win the gold medal in the same event in four consecutive Olympic Games was Alfred Oerter of the United States, who won the discus throw event in 1956, 1960, 1964, and finally on October 15, 1968, in Mexico City, setting an Olympic record each time.

4728. Athlete from Tunisia to win a gold medal in the Olympic Games was Mohamed Gammoudi, who won the men's 1500-meter track event on October 17, 1968, in Mexico City.

4729. Athlete from Venezuela to win a gold medal in the Olympic Games was Francisco Rodriguez, who won the first light flyweight boxing title on October 26, 1968, in Mexico City.

4730. Athletes from Pakistan to win gold medals in the Olympic Games were members of the team that won the men's field hockey title on October 26, 1968, in Mexico City, ending a streak of six straight Olympic wins by the team from India (1928–1956).

4731. Athlete from Iran to win a gold medal in the Olympic Games was Mohammad Nassiri Seresht, who won the men's bantamweight weightlifting event on October 13, 1968, in Mexico City. Another Iranian, Abdollah Movahhed Ardabilii, also won a gold medal, in men's lightweight freestyle wrestling, on October 20.

OLYMPIC GAMES—(1960-1969)—*continued*

4732. Athlete from Kenya to win a gold medal in the Olympic Games was Naftali Temu, who won the men's 10,000-meter track event on October 13, 1968, in Mexico City. Kenya had two more gold medalists at Mexico City: Amos Biwott won the men's 3000-meter steeplechase on October 16 and Kipchoge Keino the men's 1500-meter track event on October 20.

OLYMPIC GAMES (1970-1979)

4733. Athlete to compete in eight Olympic Games was Paul Elvström of Denmark, who competed in yachting between 1948 and 1960, and again in 1968 and finally 1972, in Munich, West Germany. His medals included four gold in the Finn class (1948, 1952, 1956, and 1960).

4734. Olympic Games at which organized drug testing was performed were in 1972 at Munich, West Germany. Athletes were tested for some kinds of stimulants, hormones, steroids, and sedatives. Seven male athletes had positive drug tests and were disqualified.

4735. Olympic Winter Games held in Asia were in 1972, at Sapporo, Japan, on February 3–13. The 1940 Winter Games had originally been scheduled for Sapporo, but were canceled because of World War II.

4736. Olympic Games at which more than 1000 women athletes participated were held at Munich, West Germany, on August 26–September 10, 1972. A total of 7123 athletes—1058 women and 6065 men—from 121 countries participated in 195 events.

4737. Athlete from North Korea to win a gold medal in the Olympic Games was Li Ho-jun, who won the men's small-bore rifle (prone) title on August 28, 1972, in Munich, West Germany.

4738. Athlete from Uganda to win a gold medal in the Olympic Games was John Akii-Bua, who won the men's 400-meter hurdles title on September 2, 1972, in Munich, West Germany.

4739. Olympic Games at which athletes were killed by terrorists were at Munich, West Germany, in 1972. Palestinian terrorists struck on September 5, killing two Israeli athletes and taking hostages. Nine Israeli hostages were later killed in a shootout at the Munich airport, along with three of the eight terrorists and one policeman. Olympic events were postponed, and a memorial service was held for the dead athletes.

4740. Athlete to win seven gold medals in a single Olympic Games all in swimming, was Mark Spitz of the United States in Munich, West Germany, in 1972. He set world records in winning all four individual medals: on August 28, the men's 200-meter butterfly with a time of 2:00.70 minutes; on August 29, the 200-meter freestyle in 1:52.78; on August 31, the 100-meter butterfly in 54.27 seconds; and on September 3, the 100-meter freestyle in 51.22. Added to these were three team gold medals: the men's 4 x 100-meter freestyle relay on August 28; the 4 x 200-meter freestyle relay on August 31; and the 4 x 100-meter medley relay on September 4, 1972. He had won the first two of those team events in 1968, giving him nine Olympic gold medals overall.

4741. Athlete to receive an Olympic medal 50 years after the competition was Anders Haugen of the United States. The Norwegian-born skier placed third in the 90-meter ski jump on February 4, 1924, at Chamonix, France, but his correct placement was not known until a computation error was discovered in 1974, after which he received his medal.

4742. Olympic Games to be voted down by the selected host region were in 1976. The Olympic Winter Games had been awarded to Denver, Colorado, but the citizens of that state objected and voted overwhelmingly to withhold public funds for the Games. As a result, the Winter Games went back to Innsbruck, Austria, where the 1964 Winter Games had been held.

4743. Woman athlete to be disqualified from the Olympic Games because of a positive drug test was Danuta Rosani, on Poland's shot put team, who tested positive for anabolic steroids in 1976 in Montreal, Quebec, Canada.

4744. Olympic Games held in Canada were in Montreal, Quebec, on July 17–August 1, 1976. Led by Tanzania, many African nations boycotted the Olympics because the New Zealand rugby team had visited South Africa, then under an Olympic ban because of its racist policies. The International Olympic Committee's protest that rugby was not an Olympic sport, and therefore not under its control, failed to end the boycott.

4745. Athlete from Trinidad and Tobago to win an Olympic gold medal was Hasely Crawford, who won the 100-meter dash on July 24, 1976, in Montreal, Quebec, Canada.

4746. Athlete from South Korea to win a gold medal in the Olympic Games was Yang Jung-mo, who won the featherweight freestyle wrestling competition on July 31, 1976, in Montreal, Quebec, Canada.

OLYMPIC GAMES (1980-1989)

4747. African-American athletes to compete in the Olympic Winter Games were Jeff Gadley and Willie Davenport, who were on a United States four-man bobsled team at Lake Placid, New York, in 1980, where they finished 12th. Davenport had won an Olympic gold medal in the 110-meter hurdles in 1968.

4748. Athlete to win five individual gold medals in a single Olympic Games was Eric Heiden of the United States, who in 1980 at the Olympic Winter Games at Lake Placid, New York, swept all five individual men's speed skating events 500, 1000, 1500, 5000, and 10,000 meters.

4749. Olympic Winter Games to be boycotted by a member country were on February 14–23, 1980, in Lake Placid, New York. In a bid to bring mainland China into the Olympic movement, the International Olympic Committee ordered Taiwan to compete under that name, rather than as the Republic of China. The Taiwanese boycotted the competition instead.

4750. Athlete from Liechtenstein to win an Olympic gold medal was Hanni Wenzel, who won the women's giant slalom skiing event on February 21, 1980, in Lake Placid, New York. That year she also won the women's slalom and took a silver medal in the downhill.

4751. Olympic Games held in the Soviet Union, and the first in a Communist country were in Moscow on July 19–August 3, 1980. The United States led a boycott against the Games to protest the Soviet invasion of Afghanistan, barring its athletes from participating under threat of losing their passports; athletes from some other countries could make individual decisions to participate. The Soviet Union would respond with a boycott of the 1984 Olympics in Los Angeles, California.

4752. Athletes from Zimbabwe to win gold medals in the Olympic Games were the members of the team that won the women's field hockey title on July 31, in 1980, in Moscow, the Soviet Union. It was an all-white team representing a country that had just recently come under black rule.

4753. Athlete who was paraplegic to compete in the Olympic Games was Neroli Fairhall of New Zealand. Paralyzed from the waist down after a motorbike accident, she competed in the women's individual archery event in the 1984 Olympics in Los Angeles, California, placing 35th.

4754. Olympic Winter Games held in Yugoslavia were in Sarajevo, on February 7–19, 1984. By 1992, the Olympic venue and much of the city itself would be largely destroyed in the Bosnian war of independence.

4755. Olympic Games to be privately financed, rather than government funded were held at Los Angeles, California, on July 2–August 12, 1984.

4756. Athlete from China to win a gold medal in the Olympic Games was Xu Haifeng, who won the free pistol shooting event on July 29, 1984, in Los Angeles, California. He had previously served as a "barefoot doctor" in the People's Republic of China.

4757. Athletes from China and Taiwan to share the medal platform in the Olympic Games were Chen Weiqiang of China and Tsai Wen-Yee of Taiwan, who won gold and bronze respectively in the featherweight class weightlifting competition on July 31, 1984, in Los Angeles, California.

4758. Athlete from Morocco to win a gold medal at the Olympic Games, and the first female athlete from an Islamic country to win an Olympic medal was Nawal El Moutawakel, who won the first women's 400-meter hurdles event at the Olympic Games in Los Angeles, California, on August 8, 1984. A second Moroccan gold-medalist that year was Saïd Aouita, who won the men's 5000-meter track event on August 11.

4759. Athlete to qualify for the finals of the same event in four Olympic Games was runner Pietro Mennea of Italy, in the men's 200-meter race. The world record-holder since 1979, he reached his fourth Olympic final in 1984, when he placed seventh on August 8, in Los Angeles, California. He had won the event in 1980, after placing third in 1972 and fourth in 1976.

4760. Athlete from Portugal to win a gold medal in the Olympic Games was Carlos Lopes, who won the men's marathon on August 12, 1984, in Los Angeles, California.

4761. Olympic Winter Games held in Canada were in Calgary, Alberta, on February 13–28, 1988.

OLYMPIC GAMES—(1980-1989)—*continued*

4762. Olympic Winter Games held on artificial snow were in Calgary, Alberta, Canada, on February 13–28, 1988. On February 25, Austrian surgeon Jörg Oberhammer was killed when he fell under a snow-grooming machine, after colliding with another skier between runs.

4763. African-American athlete to win a medal in the Olympic Winter Games was Debi Thomas, who won the bronze medal in the women's singles figure skating competition behind Katarina Witt and Elizabeth Manley on February 27, 1988, at Calgary, Alberta, Canada.

4764. Athlete to win eight medals in individual events in the Olympic Winter Games all in speed skating, was Karin Enke Kania of East Germany. Her eighth medal came on February 27, 1988, when she took silver in the 1500-meter event at Calgary, Alberta, Canada; she had won the event in 1984. Her other medals had come in the 500-meter (gold, 1980; silver, 1984; bronze, 1988); the 1000-meter (gold, 1984; silver, 1988), and the 3000-meter (silver, 1984).

4765. Olympic Games at which athletes from more than 150 countries participated were in Seoul, South Korea, on September 17–October 2, 1988, when 159 countries were represented by athletes—or 160, if you count Brunei, which sent an official but no athletes. Participating in 221 events were 6279 men and 2186 women.

4766. Olympic Games held in South Korea were in Seoul, on September 17–August 1, 1988.

4767. Athlete from Suriname to win a gold medal in the Olympic Games was Anthony Nesty, who won the men's 100-meter butterfly swimming title with an Olympic-record time of 53.00 seconds on September 21, 1988, in Seoul, South Korea.

4768. Athlete to win medals in both the Summer and Winter Olympic Games in the same year was Christa Luding-Rothenburger of East Germany. As Rothenburger, she won the women's 1000-meter speed skating competition in the Winter Games at Calgary, Alberta, Canada, on February 22, 1988. Then, seven months later, on September 24 (having married her coach, Ernst Luding), she won a silver medal in the 1000-meter match sprint cycling race in the Summer Games at Seoul, South Korea.

OLYMPIC GAMES (1990-1999)

4769. International society of Olympics researchers was the International Society of Olympic Historians, founded in London, England, on December 5, 1991.

4770. Female athlete from the United States to win three gold medals in the Olympic Winter Games was Bonnie Blair in 1992, at Albertville, France, where she won the 500-meter and 1000-meter speed skating titles, having already won the 500-meter event at the 1988 Olympics.

4771. Female athlete to win gold medals in two different sports in the Olympic Winter Games was Anfisa Reztsova of the Soviet Union. After winning her first as part of the cross-country relay skiing team in 1988, she came to Albertville, France, where on February 11, 1992, she won the inaugural women's 7.5-kilometer biathlon competition.

4772. Athlete to win ten medals in the Olympic Winter Games was Raisa Smetanina of the Soviet Union. Only 12 days short of being 40, she won her tenth medal on February 17, 1992, in Albertville, France, as part of the winning women's 4 x 5-kilometer relay Nordic (cross-country) skiing team. She had previously won three other relay medals (gold, 1976 and 1988; silver, 1980). Her other medals came in women's individual races: the 5-kilometer (silver, 1976; gold, 1980), the 10-kilometer (gold, 1976; silver, 1984 and 1988), and the 20-kilometer (bronze, 1988).

4773. Female athlete to win medals in the Olympic Winter Games 16 years apart was Raisa Smetanina of the Soviet Union. The last of her ten medals came on February 17, 1992, in the women's 4 x 5-kilometer relay Nordic (cross-country) skiing race. Her first three—two gold and one silver—had come in 1976.

4774. Athlete from the Southern Hemisphere to win a gold medal in the Olympic Winter Games was skier Annelise Coberger of New Zealand, who won the silver medal in the women's slalom on February 20, 1992, at Albertville, France.

4775. Olympic Games at which the number of female athletes was more than 40 percent of the number of male athletes were in Barcelona, Spain, on July 24–August 9, 1992. There the proportion of female to male athletes was 2708 to 6659, or 40.1 percent.

4776. Olympic Games held in Spain were in Barcelona, on July 24–August 9, 1992, where athletes from 169 countries participated in 257 events.

4777. Athlete from Indonesia to win a gold medal in the Olympic Games was Susi Susanti, who won the first women's individual title in badminton on August 4, 1992, in Barcelona, Spain. Later that day, Allan Budi Kusuma, her boyfriend and teammate, won the men's singles title.

4778. Athlete from newly independent Lithuania to win a gold medal in the Olympic Games was Romas Ubartas, who won the men's discus throw on August 5, 1992, in Barcelona, Spain.

4779. Athletes from South Africa to win medals in the Olympic Games, after the lifting of the ban on their country because of its racist policies were Wayne Ferreira and Piet Norval, who were silver-medalists in the men's doubles tennis competition on August 7, 1992, in Barcelona, Spain. Later that day Elana Meyer would be silver-medalist in the women's 10,000-meter track event.

4780. Black African woman to win an Olympic medal was Derartu Tulu of Ethiopia. On August 7, 1992, in Barcelona, Spain, she won the women's 10,000-meter title with a time of 31:06.02 minutes. The silver-medalist was Elana Meyer of South Africa, a country recently returned after a ban because of its racist policies. Signaling a new era, Tulu and Meyer held hands during a shared victory lap.

4781. Olympic Winter Games at which professional athletes were allowed to compete were in 1994 in Lillehammer, Norway, a ruling that primarily affected figure skating. Except for Ekaterina Gordeeva and Sergei Grinkov of the Soviet Union, who won their second gold medal in the pairs figure skating event, after their first in 1988, the returning professionals did not fare well.

4782. Olympic Winter Games not held in the same year as the Summer Games were in 1994 in Lillehammer, Norway. From then on the Olympic Winter Games would be held every four years, alternating every two years with the Summer Olympics.

4783. Athlete under the age of 14 to win a gold medal in the Olympic Winter Games was Kim Yoon-mi of South Korea, who was 13 years 83 days old when she was part of the women's 3000-meter short track speed skating team on February 22, 1994, at Lillehammer, Norway.

4784. Athlete from the United States to win six medals at the Olympic Winter Games, and the first female U.S. athlete to win five gold medals at the winter or summer Games was Bonnie Blair. After winning the women's 500-meter speed skating title in 1988 and 1992, she won it again on February 19, 1994, in Lille-hammer, Norway. In the women's 1000-meter event, she took bronze in 1988 and gold in 1992, winning again on February 23, 1994, for her fifth gold medal and sixth overall.

4785. Athlete from newly independent Uzbekistan to win a gold medal at the Olympic Games was Lina Cheryazova, who won the women's aerials freestyle skiing title on February 24, 1994, in Lillehammer, Norway.

4786. Athlete from newly independent Ukraine to win a gold medal at the Olympic Games was Oksana Baiul, who won the women's singles figure skating title on February 25, 1994, in Lillehammer, Norway.

4787. Athlete from newly independent Kazakhstan to win a gold medal at the Olympic Games was Vladimir Smirnov, who on February 27, 1994, won the men's 50-kilometer classical Nordic (cross-country) skiing title at Lillehammer, Norway.

4788. Athlete to participate in nine Olympic Games was Hubert Raudaschl of Austria, who competed in yachting in every Olympics between 1964 and 1996, winning the silver medal in the Finn class in 1968 and in the Star class in 1980, with Karl Ferstl.

4789. Olympic Games in which more than 10,000 athletes competed, and more than 50 percent were women were in Atlanta, Georgia, on July 19–August 9, 1996. Representing 197 nations were 6797 men and 3513 women, for a total of 10,310, with women making up 51.7 percent.

4790. Athlete from Costa Rica to win a gold medal in the Olympic Games was Claudia Poll, who won the women's 200-meter freestyle swimming event on July 21, 1996, in Atlanta, Georgia.

4791. Athlete from Armenia to win a gold medal in the Olympic Games was Armen Nazaryan, who won the men's flyweight Greco-Roman wrestling title on July 23, 1996, in Atlanta, Georgia.

4792. Athlete from Ecuador to win a gold medal in the Olympic Games was Jefferson Pérez, who won the men's 20-kilometer walk on July 26, 1996, in Atlanta, Georgia.

OLYMPIC GAMES—(1990-1999)—*continued*

4793. Woman athlete from the United States to win four gold medals at a single Olympic Games was Amy Van Dyken of the United States in 1996 at Atlanta, Georgia. Her fourth medal came on July 26 in the 50-meter freestyle swimming event. She had already won the 100-meter butterfly on July 23, and been on two winning relay teams, the 4 x 100 medley on July 24, and the 4 x 100 freestyle relay on July 22.

4794. Athlete from newly independent Belarus to win a gold medal in the Olympic Games was Yekaterina Knodotovich, who won the women's single sculls title on July 27, 1996, in Atlanta, Georgia.

4795. Athlete from the newly independent Slovak Republic to win a gold medal in the Olympic Games was Michael Martikan, who won the men's canoe slalom singles title on July 27, 1996, in Atlanta, Georgia.

4796. Athlete from Syria to win a gold medal in the Olympic Games was Ghada Shouaa, who won the women's heptathlon on July 28, 1996, in Atlanta, Georgia, after the two-time defending champion, Jacqueline Joyner-Kersee of the United States, had to withdraw because of injury.

4797. Athlete from Hong Kong to win a gold medal in the Olympic Games was Lee Lai-shan, who won the women's Mistral sailboarding race on July 29, 1996, in Atlanta, Georgia.

4798. Athlete from Nigeria to win a gold medal in the Olympic Games was Chioma Ajunwa, who won the women's long jump on August 2, 1996, in Atlanta, Georgia. The next day the Nigerian team would win the soccer gold medal.

4799. Athlete from Algeria to win a gold medal in the Olympic Games was Hocine Soltani, who won the lightweight men's boxing title on August 3, 1996, in Atlanta, Georgia. Some Algerians had earlier won competing for France.

4800. Athlete from Burundi to win a gold medal in the Olympic Games was Venuste Niyongabo, who won the men's 5000-meter steeplechase event on August 3, 1996, in Atlanta, Georgia.

4801. Athlete from Thailand to win a gold medal in the Olympic Games was Samluck Kamsing, who won the featherweight men's boxing title on August 4, 1996, in Atlanta, Georgia.

4802. Black African athlete from South Africa to win a gold medal in the Olympic Games was Josia Thugwane, who won the marathon on August 4, 1996, in Atlanta, Georgia, despite having injured his back the previous March.

4803. Olympic Winter Games in which more than 2000 athletes competed, and more than 55 percent were women were in Nagano, Japan, on February 7–22, 1998. Representing 72 nations—also a Winter Games record—were 1389 men and 787 women, for a total of 2176, with women making up 56.7 percent.

4804. Male athlete to win six individual gold medals in the Olympic Winter Games was Bjorn Dahlie of Norway. His sixth medal came on February 12, 1998, in Nagano, Japan, where he won his second straight men's 10-kilometer Nordic (cross-country) skiing title, after his first in 1994. His other gold medals came in the men's 50-kilometer freestyle (1992), the men's 4 x 10-kilometer relay (1994), and the men's combined pursuit (1992 and 1994).

ORIENTEERING

4805. Orienteering as a sport combining cross-country running with map-reading, was developed in Sweden in 1918 by Ernst Killander.

4806. National association for orienteering was the Svenska Orienteringföfundet, founded in Sweden in 1938.

4807. International governing body for orienteering was the International Orienteering Federation (IOF), founded in 1961.

4808. World championships in orienteering were held in 1966, and biennially thereafter, originally including long-distance and relay events only. The teams from Sweden won both the inaugural men's and women's relays. Åge Hadler of Norway won the men's individual title and Ulla Kindkvist of Sweden the women's.

4809. Ski orienteering world championships combining skiing and map-reading, were held in 1975. Athletes from Finland won all the top titles, including the men's and women's relays and the individual titles, Olavi Svanberg for the men and Sinikka Kukkonen for the women.

4810. Ski orienteering world championships to include sprint competitions were in 1988, when the inaugural winners were Hannu Koponen of Finland for the men and Ragnhild Bratberg of Norway for the women.

4811. World cup in orienteering was held in 1988. The winners of the series of races were both from Norway: Øyvin Thon on the men's side and Ragnhild Bratberg on the women's.

4812. World championships in orienteering to include short events were in 1991, when Petr Kazak and Jana Cieslarová, both of Czechoslovakia, respectively won the men's and women's short events.

P

PENTATHLON

4813. Pentathlon is believed to have been held in the Olympic Games in 708 BC, in Olympia, Greece, including five traditional events: discus, jump, javelin, sprint, and wrestling.

4814. Men's pentathlon held in the modern Olympic Games was in 1906, in the unofficial Olympics in Athens, Greece. On April 27, Hjalmar Mellander of Sweden was the winner of the five-part competition including the standing long jump, Greek-style discus throw, javelin throw, 192-meter race, and Greco-Roman wrestling match. The event was discontinued after 1924, but a modern pentathlon, involving different sports, was instituted in 1912.

4815. Men's modern pentathlon held in the Olympic Games was in 1912 in Stockholm, Sweden. Unlike the traditional pentathlon, this event involved shooting, swimming, fencing, riding, and running, and most contestants were from the military. Swedish athletes swept the top four spots, led by Gösta Lilliehöök. Fifth place was taken by George S. Patton, Jr., of the United States, later famed as a World War II general, who might have won the event except for his poor shooting.

4816. Pentathlete to hold the officially accepted world record in the women's pentathlon was Gisela Mauermayer of Germany, who won the benchmark event in London, England, on August 11, 1934. This type A pentathlon included the 100-meter race, javelin throw, high jump, long jump, and shot put. Events and scoring would change over the years.

4817. Pentathlete to achieve a perfect score in the shooting portion of the men's modern pentathlon in the Olympic Games was Charles Leonard of the United States, whose maximum 200 points placed him first in shooting and second in the overall competition on August 6, 1936, in Berlin, Germany.

4818. International pentathlon organization was the Union Internationale de Pentathlon Moderne (UIPM), founded in 1948 to foster support for the pentathlon. In 1957, it would also add the biathlon to its concerns, changing its name to Union Internationale de Pentathlon Moderne et Biathlon (UIPMB).

4819. Pentathlete to place first in three of the five events in the men's modern pentathlon in the Olympic Games was William Grut of Sweden, who won the overall competition on August 4, 1948, in London, England, leading all contestants in riding, fencing, and swimming.

4820. World championships in the pentathlon were held in 1949, under the auspices of the Union Internationale de Pentathlon Moderne (UIPM), founded in 1948. At the inaugural championships, for men only, Tage Bjurefelt of Sweden won the individual crown and his country took the team title. Women's championships would be held separately from 1981.

4821. Pentathlete to win two consecutive titles at the world pentathlon championships was Lars Hall of Sweden, who won in 1950 and 1951.

4822. Pentathlete to hold the officially accepted world record in the women's pentathlon (type B) was Fanny (Francina) Blankers-Koen, who won on September 16, 1951, in Amsterdam, the Netherlands. The two-day event then included the 200-meter race, 80-meter hurdles, high jump, long jump, and shot put.

4823. Men's modern pentathlon team event held in the Olympic Games was in 1952 in Helsinki, Finland. Taking home the honors on July 25 in the riding, fencing, shooting, swimming, and running competition was the team from Hungary: Gábor Benedek, István Szondy, and Aladár Kovácsi. The event would be discontinued after 1992.

4824. Pentathlete from a non-military background to win the men's modern pentathlon in the Olympic Games was Lars Hall, a carpenter from Sweden, who won the event on July 25, 1952, in Helsinki, Finland, after placing first in the riding and swimming portions of the competition.

4825. Pentathlete to win two consecutive titles in the men's modern pentathlon in the Olympic Games was Lars Hall of Sweden. After winning his first title in 1952, he won his second on November 28, 1956, in Melbourne, Australia.

PENTATHLON—continued

4826. Pentathlete to win three consecutive men's titles in the world pentathlon championships and then a fourth was Igor Novikov of the Soviet Union, who won in 1957, 1958, 1959, and 1961.

4827. Pentathlete to win two pentathlon gold medals in the same Olympic Games was Ferenc Németh of Hungary. On August 31, 1960, in Rome, Italy, he placed first in the men's individual riding, fencing, shooting, swimming, and running competitions. That same day, he and his teammates Imre Nagy and András Balczó won the team title. Balczó would lead a new Hungarian team to another gold medal in 1968, and would be individual gold-medalist again in 1972.

4828. Pentathlete to win two gold medals in the men's modern pentathlon team competition in the Olympic Games was Igor Novikov of the Soviet Union. He had led his team to victory in 1956, then with two new teammates, Albert Mokeyev and Viktor Mineyev, he did so again on October 15, 1964, in Tokyo, Japan.

4829. Women's pentathlon held in the Olympic Games was in 1964 in Tokyo, Japan. Iryna Press of the Soviet Union won the inaugural two-day five-event competition on October 17. The pentathlon would be replaced by the heptathlon in 1984. The sports and scoring would change over the years, so point totals are not comparable.

4830. Pentathlete to win five consecutive men's titles in the world pentathlon championships was András Balczó of Hungary, who won in 1963, 1965, 1966, 1967, and 1969. He would also win the men's individual pentathlon Olympic title in 1972.

4831. National team to sweep the medals in the women's pentathlon in the Olympic Games was from East Germany, which took the top three spots on July 26, 1976, in Montreal, Quebec, Canada. The competition was so close that the Siegrun Siegl, the gold-medalist, was tied with teammate Christiner Bodner Laser at 4745 points. Burglinde Pollak had 4740 points.

4832. World pentathlon championships for women were held in 1981 in London, England. Anne Ahlgren of Sweden won the first individual title, while Great Britain won the team honors.

4833. Pentathlete to win two consecutive titles at the women's world pentathlon championships was Irina Kiselyeva of the Soviet Union, who won in both 1986 and 1987.

4834. Pentathlete to win three, and then four, titles in the women's world championships was Eva Fjellerup of Denmark, who won in 1990, 1991, 1993, and 1994.

4835. Women's modern pentathlon event held in the Olympic Games was in 2000 in Sydney, Australia. Stephanie Cook of Britain, a physician, won the event on October 1, with a grand total of 5318 points. She sprinted ahead of seven other competitors in the final minute of the 3000-meter cross-country run, which followed an air-pistol shooting match, an épée fencing competition, a 200-meter freestyle swimming race, and a slow-jumping equestrian competition on horses picked by lot.

POLE VAULT

4836. Pole vault stand on record was at the Schnepfenthal School in Germany in 1791. It was believed to have been introduced by a teacher, Christian Carl Andre.

4837. Men's pole vault event held in the Olympic Games was on April 10, 1896, in Athens, Greece. William Welles Hoyt of the United States won it with a vault of 10 feet 10 inches (3.30 meters).

4838. National team to sweep the top spots in the men's pole vault in the Olympic Games was the United States, which took the top six spots on September 3, 1904, in St. Louis, Missouri, led by Charles Dvorak with an Olympic record of 11 feet 5¾ inches (3.50 meters). The United States would take every gold medal in the event (except for the unofficial 1906 Olympics) until 1972.

4839. Pole-vaulter to hold the officially accepted world record in the men's event was Marc Wright of the United States, with a height of 13 feet 2¼ inches (4.02 meters), set on June 8, 1912, in Cambridge, Massachusetts.

4840. Pole-vaulter to clear 14 feet was Sabin Carr of the United States with a vault of 14 feet 0 inches (4.27 meters) in the men's event on May 27, 1927, in Philadelphia, Pennsylvania.

4841. Pole-vaulter to clear 15 feet was Dutch (Cornelius) Warmerdam of the United States, who vaulted 15 feet 1 inch (4.60 meters) in the men's event on June 29, 1940, in Fresno, California. He would raise the record twice more, to 15 feet 7¾ inches (4.77 meters) on May 23, 1942, in Modesto, California.

4842. Fiberglass pole to be used in the men's pole vault event in the Olympic Games was on November 26, 1956, in Melbourne, Australia, introduced by bronze medalist Georgios Roubanis of Greece. Bob Mathias of the United States had first used it in the Olympics in 1952, in the decathlon.

4843. Pole-vaulter to win two consecutive titles in the men's event in the Olympic Games was Robert Richards of the United States. After winning in 1952, he returned to set an Olympic record with a vault of 14 feet, 11½ inches (4.56 meters), on November 26, 1956, in Melbourne, Australia.

4844. Pole-vaulter to clear 16 feet was John Uelses of the United States. He had an official vault of 16 feet ½ inch (4.89 meters) on March 31, 1962, in Santa Barbara, California. However, he had vaulted 16 feet ¼ inch unofficially on February 2, 1962, at Madison Square Garden in New York City.

4845. Pole-vaulter to clear 17 feet was John Pennell of the United States, who vaulted 17 feet ¾ inches (5.20 meters) on August 24, 1963, in Miami, Florida. A multiple world record-holder, he was unable to compete in the 1964 Olympics because of a back injury.

4846. Pole-vaulter to clear 18 feet was Christos Papanikolaou of Greece, who vaulted 18 feet ¼ inches (5.49 meters) in the men's event on October 24, 1970, in Athens, Greece.

4847. Pole-vaulter to clear 19 feet was Thierry Vigneron of France, who vaulted 19 feet ½ inch (5.80 meters) in the men's event on June 20, 1981, in Macon, France. He would raise that twice more, to 19 feet 4¾ inches on August 31, 1984, in Rome, Italy.

4848. Pole-vaulter to clear 6 meters was Sergey Bubka of the Soviet Union, with a vault of 6.00 meters (19 feet 8¼ inches) in the men's event on July 13, 1985, in Paris, France. Bubka would dominate the event into the late 1990s.

4849. Pole-vaulter to clear 20 feet was Sergey Bubka of the Soviet Union, with a vault of 20 feet ¼ inch (6.10 meters) in the men's event outdoors on August 5, 1991, in Malmö, Sweden. It was the 13th of his world outdoor records in the event.

4850. Pole-vaulter to hold the officially accepted world record in the women's event was Sun Caiyun of China. She set her benchmark height of 13 feet 3½ inches (4.05 meters) on May 21, 1992, in Nanjing, China.

4851. Pole-vaulter to break the 14-foot barrier in the women's event was Emma George of Australia, who vaulted 14 feet ½ inch (4.28 meters) on December 17, 1995, in Perth, Australia, in the second of numerous world records in the event.

4852. Women's pole vault event held in the Olympic Games was in 2000 in Sydney, Australia. Stacy Dragila of the United States took home the gold on September 25, with a vault of 15 feet 1 inch.

POLO

4853. Development of modern polo came in the 1850s, originally in the state of Manipur, in India. British military officers, especially Lieutenant (later Major General) John F. Sherer, developed the modern game. Similar stick-and-ball games had been played on horseback throughout central and western Asia for many centuries.

4854. Polo club was the Silchar Club, founded in 1859 by British military officers in Assam, India, where many British expatriates were introduced to the game.

4855. Introduction of polo in Europe was in 1869, when officers of the Tenth Hussars brought the game from India to England.

4856. Recorded polo match in England was in 1871 on Hounslow Heath between the Tenth Hussars and the Ninth Lancers.

4857. Governing body for polo was the Hurlingham Polo Association, which in 1875 drew up rules for the game, a year after the body was founded in Hurlingham, near London, England.

4858. Introduction of polo into Argentina was in around 1875, by British ranchers settling in the country.

4859. Champion Cup polo competition was played at Hurlingham, near London, England, in 1876. The tournament ended in 1939, being replaced by the British Open Championship from 1956.

4860. Polo competitions in the United States were in 1876, after newspaper publisher and sports enthusiast James Gordon Bennett saw the game in England and introduced it to America.

4861. Polo club in the United States was the Westchester Polo Club, founded in 1877 in Newport, Rhode Island.

POLO—*continued*

4862. International polo competition was between the United States and Great Britain for the Westchester Cup, established by the Westchester Club, in 1886. Played in Newport, Rhode Island, it was won by Great Britain. Competition lapsed in 1939, but multinational matches resumed in 1988.

4863. National polo organization in the United States was the Polo Association, founded in 1890, which became the American governing body for the sport.

4864. Argentine Open polo competition was held in 1893. Called the Polo Association of the River Plate Championship until 1923, it would become the most prestigious polo event in the world.

4865. Polo event held in the Olympic Games was in Paris, France, in 1900. The final, on June 2, was won by the Foxhunters, a team that included players from both Great Britain and the United States. Polo would be played at four more Olympics, but not after 1936.

4866. Polo team from the United States to win the Westchester Cup was in 1909, when Devereux Milburn, Harry Payne Whitney, Monty Waterbury, and Larry Waterbury defeated a British team at Hurlingham, near London, England.

4867. Cup of the Americas (Copa de las Americas) polo competition between the United States and Argentina, was held in 1928. The United States won in 1928 and 1932, but Argentina would dominate in later competitions.

4868. Avila Camacho Cup polo competition between the United States and Mexico, was held in 1941. The United States won the first competition for the cup offered by Mexican president General Manuel Avila Camacho.

4869. British Open Championship polo tournament was played in 1956 at Cowdray Park, Midhurst, Sussex, England. The Los Indios team won the inaugural competition, which replaced the earlier Champion Cup (1876–1939).

R

RACKETS

4870. Closed court for rackets was built in 1853 in London, England, at the Prince's Club. Derived from handball games played since at least medieval times, it had previously been played in the open, against the walls of buildings, especially prisons.

4871. International governing body for rackets was the Tennis and Rackets Association, founded in 1907.

4872. Rackets event held in the Olympic Games was in London, England, in 1908, the only time the sport was included. Players from Great Britain took all the top spots in both singles and doubles competition on April 27, the singles winner being Evan Noel and the doubles winners Vane Pennell and John Jacob Astor.

RACQUETBALL

4873. Racquetball game was developed in 1949 at the Young Men's Christian Association (YMCA) in Greenwich, Connecticut, by Joe Sobek. He developed a paddle for use in the game originally called *paddle rackets*, played on a handball and squash court.

4874. National organization for racquetball was the International Racquetball Association, founded in 1968 by Bob Kendler. It would become the American Amateur Racquetball Association (AARA) in 1980.

4875. Introduction of racquetball to England was in 1976 by Ian Wright. Using a slightly smaller court and a less active ball, the game would be called *racketball* in Britain.

4876. International governing body for racquetball was the International Racquetball Federation (IRF), established in 1979.

4877. World championships in racquetball were held in 1982, sponsored by the International Racquetball Federation (IRF). Ed Andrews won the men's singles title and Cindy Baxter the women's. Both were from the United States, which also won the men's, women's, and overall titles, and would continue to dominate in the sport.

RODEO

4878. Bronco-riding contest for cash prizes on record took place in 1869 in Deer Trail, Colorado.

4879. Professional rodeo involving cash prizes for the winners of roping and riding contests, was probably the Old Glory Blowout, staged by "Buffalo Bill" (William Frederick Cody) on July 4, 1882, in North Platte, Nebraska. This laid the basis for his first Wild West Show a year later, also in North Platte, which combined entertainment and rodeo, laying the basis for modern rodeos.

4880. Documented rodeo competition was the Cowboy Tournament, held on July 4, 1883, in Pecos, Texas. Winners in the roping and riding contests received $25 each. It would become known as the West of the Pecos Rodeo.

4881. Cheyenne Frontier Days rodeo was held on September 23, 1897, in Cheyenne, Wyoming. It would become the oldest continuing rodeo event.

4882. Pendleton Round-Up rodeo was held in Pendleton, Oregon, on September 10, 1910. It would remain one of the premier annual rodeos.

4883. Calgary Stampede rodeo was held in 1912, in Calgary, Alberta, Canada. Held annually from 1919, it would become a widely popular event.

4884. Madison Square Garden Rodeo was held in New York City in 1922. It became one of the largest indoor rodeos, inspiring many more for several decades.

4885. Cowboy to be named All-Around Cowboy by his professional rodeo peers was Earl Thode in 1929.

4886. Organization of rodeo producers in the United States was the Rodeo Association of America, founded in 1929, which set the first standards for the sport and for a system of world championships. Rodeo competitions for women were not included.

4887. Cowboy to be named All-Around Cowboy twice was Clay Carr, who won the honor in 1930 and again in 1933.

4888. National organization for rodeo cowboys was the Cowboys Turtle Association (CTA), founded in 1936. Founded in reaction to the rodeo producers' Rodeo Association of America, it later became the Professional Rodeo Cowboys Association (PRCA), the main governing body for rodeo competitions by 1955.

4889. Women-only rodeo was an "all-girl rodeo" held on June 26–29, 1942, at the Fannin County Fair Grounds in Bonham, Texas, organized by Fay Kirkwood. Others would follow, along with more women's competitions in formerly all-male rodeos.

4890. Cowboy to be named All-Around Cowboy twice consecutively was Louis Brooks, in 1943 and 1944.

4891. Organization for Australian rodeo cowboys was the Australian Rough Riders Association (ARRA), founded in 1945, which would become the Australian Professional Rodeo Association (APRA) in 1988.

4892. Girls' Rodeo Association was founded in 1948 in Texas. Becoming the Women's Professional Rodeo Association (WPRA), it would sponsor all-women rodeos and foster women's competitions in other rodeos.

4893. Agreement to encourage women's events in rodeos was made in 1955, when Jackie Worthington of the Women's Professional Rodeo Association (WPRA) and Bill Linderman of the Professional Rodeo Cowboys Association (PRCA) agreed to sanction women's competitions held in PRCA rodeos, which would come to include more women's contests, most often barrel racing.

4894. Cowboy to be named All-Around Cowboy four consecutive times, and five overall was Jim Shoulders, who won the title in 1949 and then in 1956–1959, the first year of the National Finals Rodeo (NFR). He also held 11 other world rodeo titles, giving him a record all-events total of 16.

4895. National Finals Rodeo (NFR) was held in 1959 in Dallas, Texas, with an inaugural purse of $50,000. Sponsored by the Professional Rodeo Cowboys Association (PRCA), and later co-sponsored by the Women's Professional Rodeo Association (WPRA), it would become the most prestigious rodeo in the United States.

4896. Cowboy to be named All-Around Cowboy five consecutive times, and six overall was Larry Mahan, who won the title 1966–1970 and then again in 1973.

4897. Rodeo cowboy to win more than $100,000 in a single season was Tom Ferguson in 1976, when he was in the midst of a six-year run as All-Around Cowboy (1974–1979).

4898. Cowboy to be named All-Around Cowboy six consecutive times was Tom Ferguson, who won the title 1974–1979.

4899. African-American cowboy to hold a world rodeo title was Charles Sampson, who in 1982 won the bull-riding championship of the Professional Rodeo Cowboys Association (PRCA).

4900. Rider to win ten consecutive women's barrel racing titles at the National Finals Rodeo (NFR) was Charmayne James Rodman of the United States, between 1984 and 1993.

ROLLER SKATING

4901. Roller skates were developed by Joseph Merlin of Belgium, who demonstrated the metal-wheeled devices in London, England, in 1760, though they would not become popular until nearly a century later.

ROLLER SKATING—continued

4902. Practical four-wheeled roller skates allowing some turning, were developed in 1863 by James Plimpton of Medford, Massachusetts. They quickly became popular, and were used for practice by early ice skaters.

4903. Roller-skating rink was established in Newport, Rhode Island, in 1866, by James Plimpton, who had developed the first practical skates three years earlier.

4904. International organization for roller skating and roller hockey was the Fédération Internationale de Patinage à Roulettes (FIPR), founded in 1924. Its successor was the Fédération Internationale de Roller Skating (FIRS), based in Barcelona, Spain.

4905. Roller derby was held on August 13, 1935, at the Chicago Coliseum, in Chicago, Illinois, organized by sports promoter Leo Seltzer.

4906. National speed skating championships in roller skating in the United States were held in Detroit, Michigan, in 1937.

4907. World speed skating championships for roller skating were held in 1937 in Monza, Italy, for men only. Women's events were not included until 1953.

4908. Roller derby to be televised was in 1947 in Chicago, Illinois, an event organized by sports promoter Leo Seltzer.

4909. World figure skating championships for roller skating were held in Washington, D.C., in 1947. In that inaugural competition, Donald Mounce of the United States won the men's combined figures and free skating competition and Ursula Wehrli of Switzerland the women's. The first pair's title was won by Fernand Leemans and Elvire Collin of Belgium, while Fred Ludwig and Barbara Gallagher of the United States took the dance title.

4910. In-line roller skates were developed in 1979 by Scott Olson of the United States, originally for use in off-season training by hockey players. They would be made and sold by the Rollerblade company from 1984.

ROWING (BEFORE 1900)

4911. Modern rowing competition on record was held on August 1, 1715, for watermen on the Thames River in London, England. Sponsored annually by Irish-born actor Thomas Doggett, and then by money from his will, the competition became the venerable Doggett's Coat and Badge race. However, rowing races had been held for many centuries before this era, back to early Greek and Roman times and perhaps earlier.

4912. Organized regatta, or series of boat races, on record was held in 1775 at Ranelagh Gardens, Putney, on the Thames River.

4913. University Boat Race was held on June 10, 1829, with teams from Oxford and Cambridge universities racing on the Thames River between Hambledon Lock and Henley Bridge, England. It would become an annual competition, generally between Putney and Mortlake on the Thames River. Oxford won the inaugural race, though Cambridge would hold a slight edge in wins at the end of the 20th century.

4914. Henley Regatta rowing races were held in 1839 on the Thames River in Henley, England, and would be held annually from then except in wartime. The event would be called the Henley Royal Regatta from 1851.

4915. Collegiate rowing competition, and the first intercollegiate athletic competition, on record in the United States was held on August 3, 1852, on Lake Winnipesaukee in New Hampshire, between teams from Harvard and Yale universities.

4916. National governing body for rowing in the United States was the National Association for Amateur Oarsmen, founded in 1872.

4917. Collegiate rowing program for women was established at Wellesley College in Wellesley, Massachusetts, in 1875.

4918. Dead heat on record in the University Boat Race between Oxford and Cambridge university teams occurred on March 24, 1877, when the annual race was held on its usual course on the Thames River between Putney and Mortlake, England.

4919. Diamond Challenge Sculls rowing race was held in 1884 at the Henley Regatta on the Thames River in Henley, England.

4920. International rowing competition was the unofficial European Championships held in 1890, sponsored by the Belgian Federation of Rowing Clubs. Edouard Lescrauwaet of Belgium won in the only class, the sculling outrigger.

4921. International governing body in rowing was the Fédération Internationale des Sociétés d'Aviron (FISA), founded in 1892.

4922. Officially sponsored international rowing championships were the European Championships held in 1893, sponsored by the Fédération Internationale des Sociétés d'Aviron (FISA), founded the previous year.

4923. Athletes to row across the Atlantic Ocean were George Harbo and Frank Samuelson, Norwegian-born rowers from the United States, in 1896. They left New York City on June 6 and arrived in Le Havre, France, 61 days later, after a day's rest on the Scilly Isles off Great Britain.

4924. Rower from the United States to win the Diamond Sculls at the Henley Regatta in Henley, England, was Ned Ten Eyck, who won in 1897.

ROWING (1900-1949)
4925. Men's eight-oared shell with coxswain rowing event held in the Olympic Games was on August 26, 1900, in Paris, France. The winners were from the Vesper Boat Club in Philadelphia, Pennsylvania: Louis Abell, Harry Debaecke, William Carr, John Exley, John Geiger, Edward Hedley, James Juvenal, Roscoe Lockwood, and Edward Marsh.

4926. Men's pair-oared shell with coxswain rowing event held in the Olympic Games was in 1900 in Paris, France. Representing the Minerva club in Amsterdam, the Netherlands, the winners were François Antoine Brandt, Roelof Klein, and Hermanus Brockmann, all from the Netherlands. However, in the final on August 26, Brockmann was replaced as coxswain by a French boy whose name was unrecorded and who, apparently no more than 10 years old, was probably the youngest gold-medalist ever in the Olympics. The event was discontinued after 1992.

4927. Men's single sculls rowing event held in the Olympic Games was on August 26, 1900, in Paris, France. The inaugural winner of the 1750-meter race was Henri Barrelet of France.

4928. Men's four-oared shell with coxswain rowing event held in the Olympic Games was in 1900 in Paris, France. Because of confusion and incompetence in the handling of the heats, two finals were held. The first, on August 26, was won by a team from the Cercle de l'Aviron de Roubaix, France. The second, on August 29, was won by members of the Ger-

mania Rowing Club, from Hamburg, Germany. Because the second finals did not include all who qualified, both teams were awarded medals. The event would be discontinued after 1992.

4929. Men's double sculls rowing event held in the Olympic Games was on July 30, 1904, in St. Louis, Missouri. Representing the Atalanta Boat Club of New York, John Mulcahy and William Varley won the event, with two other United States pairs taking the other medals.

4930. Men's four-oared shell without coxswain rowing event held in the Olympic Games was on July 30, 1904, in St. Louis, Missouri. The winning foursome was from St. Louis's Century Boat Club: George Dietz, August Erker, Albert Nasse, and Arthur Stockhoff.

4931. Men's pair-oared shell without coxswain rowing event held in the Olympic Games was on July 30, 1904, in St. Louis, Missouri. The winning pair, Robert Farnam and Joseph Ryan, were from the Seawanhaka Boat Club of Brooklyn, New York.

4932. National team to sweep the medals in the men's single sculls rowing event in the Olympic Games was from the United States. Winning the 2-mile race on July 30, 1904, in St. Louis, Missouri, were Frank Greer, James Juvenal, and Constance Titus, in that order.

4933. Rowers to win two consecutive gold medals in the men's eight-oared shell with coxswain competition in the Olympic Games were Louis Abell and John Exley. From the Vesper Boat Club in Philadelphia, Pennsylvania, they had won first in 1900, then with seven new teammates won again on July 30, 1904, in St. Louis, Missouri.

4934. Rowers to win two gold medals in pair-oared shell with coxswain rowing events in the same Olympic Games were Enrico Bruna, Emilio Fontanella, and Giorgio Cesana of Italy, from Bucintoro in Venice, Italy. Two races were held on April 26, 1906, in Athens, Greece—one of 1000 meters and one of 1609 meters—and the trio won them both. Two days earlier, joined by two others, they had also won the four-oared shell with coxswain event.

ROWING—(1900-1949)—*continued*

4935. Rowers to win two consecutive medals in the men's double sculls event in the Olympic Games were Jack (John) Kelly, Sr., and Paul Costello of the United States. After their first win in 1920, they returned for their second on July 17, 1924, in Paris, France. Costello would take a third in 1928. Kelly also won the men's single sculls gold medal in 1920; he was later better known as the father of Grace Kelly, who became Princess Grace of Monaco.

4936. Rower to win three consecutive medals in the men's double sculls event in the Olympic Games was Paul Costello of the United States. After winning in 1920 and 1924 with Jack (John) Kelly, Sr., he won again on July 17, 1928, in Amsterdam, the Netherlands, this time with Charles McIlvaine.

4937. Rower to win two consecutive men's single sculls rowing titles in the Olympic Games was Bobby (Henry) Pearce of Australia. His second win came on August 13, 1932, in Los Angeles, California. After his first win, in 1928, he had hoped to be able to row in the Diamond Sculls at the Henley Regatta in Henley, England, but was barred because he was a carpenter. He was only allowed to compete at Henley after he was given a job as a salesman, and so was no longer considered a "laborer."

4938. Woman to serve as coxswain on a men's varsity rowing team in the United States was Sally Stearns. On May 27, 1936, she led her Rollins College team in a race against Marietta College. Her first victory as coxswain came later that month against Manhattan College.

ROWING (1950-1999)
4939. Rower to win both the single and double sculls events at the Henley Regatta in Henley, England, was Stuart Mackenzie of Australia, in 1959.

4940. World championships in rowing were held in Lucerne, Switzerland, in 1962, originally for men only and quadrennial, but then annual except in Olympic years. Events for women would be included in 1974. At the inaugural competition, Vyacheslav Ivanov of the Soviet Union won the single sculls title; René Duhamel and Bernard Monnereau of France the double sculls; and Dieter Bender and Günther Zumkeller of West Germany the coxless pairs. The coxed pairs, coxless fours, coxed fours, and eights competitions were all won by teams from West Germany.

4941. Rower to win three consecutive men's single sculls rowing titles in the Olympic Games was Vyacheslav Ivanov of the Soviet Union. Following his wins in 1956 and 1960, Ivanov went to Tokyo to take his third title on October 15, 1964. Pertti Karppinen of Finland would also win three consecutive titles, in 1976, 1980, and 1984.

4942. Head of the Charles Regatta was held in Boston, Massachusetts, in 1965. Originally for rowers from colleges along the Charles River, it would become an international event.

4943. Rowers to win two consecutive titles in the men's four-oared shell without coxswain event in the Olympic Games were Frank Forberger, Dieter Grahn, Frank Rüle, and Dieter Schubert of East Germany. Following their first win in 1968 was their second on September 2, 1972, in Munich, West Germany.

4944. Men's quadruple sculls competition held in the world championships in rowing was in 1974, when the winning team was from East Germany.

4945. World championships in rowing to include women's competitions were in 1974. In the inaugural events, Christine Scheiblich of East Germany won the single sculls; Yelena Antonova and Galina Yermoleyeva of the Soviet Union the double sculls; and Marilena Ghita and Cornelia Neascu of Romania the coxless pairs. Teams from East Germany swept the quadruple sculls, the coxed fours, and the eights competitions.

4946. Women's double sculls event held in the Olympic Games was in 1976 in Montreal. Svetla Otsetova and Zdravka Yordanova of Bulgaria won that first competition, on July 24.

4947. Women's single sculls event held in the Olympic Games was in 1976 in Montreal. In the finals on July 24, the winner was Christine Scheiblich of East Germany.

4948. Men's quadruple sculls rowing event held in the Olympic Games was in 1976 in Montreal. Winning the event on July 25 was the team from East Germany: Wolfgang Güldenpfennig, Rüdiger Reiche, Karl-Heinz Bussert, and Michael Wolfgramm. Bussert was a last-minute replacement for Martin Winter, who had dropped out after an emergency appendectomy.

4949. Women's eight-oared shell with coxswain event held in the Olympic Games was on July 24, 1976, in Montreal, where the winning team was from East Germany. Three rowers from the team—Christiane Knetsch (later Kipke), Ilona Richter, and Marina Wilke—would win two consecutive medals in the event, winning with new teammates on July 26, 1980, in Moscow, the Soviet Union.

4950. Rowers to win two consecutive titles in the pair-oared shell without coxswain event in the Olympic Games were Jörg Landvoigt and Bernt Landvoigt, twins from East Germany. After their first win in 1976, they achieved their second on July 27, 1980, in Moscow, where the silver-medal-winning pair were also twins: Yuri Pimenov and Nikolai Pimenov of the Soviet Union.

4951. Woman to compete in the University Boat Race rowing competition between Oxford and Cambridge was Sandra Brown, who served as coxswain for the victorious Oxford team on April 4, 1981, repeating with another win in 1982.

4952. Team from the United States to win the women's eight-oared shell with coxswain event in the Olympic Games was on August 4, 1984, in Los Angeles, California.

4953. Rower to win gold medals in both the women's single and double sculls events in the Olympic Games was Elisabeta Oleniuc Lipa of Romania. On August 4, 1984, in Montreal, as Oleniuc, she won the double sculls event with teammate Marioara Popescu. Then on August 2, 1992, in Barcelona, Spain, she won the single sculls title.

4954. Women's coxless fours event held in the world championships in rowing was in 1986, when the event was won by a United States team.

4955. Women's quadruple sculls event held in the Olympic Games was in 1988 in Seoul, South Korea. Kerstin Förster, Kristina Mundt, Beate Schramm, and Jana Sorgers of East Germany won the inaugural competition on September 25.

4956. World Sculls Cup series of rowing races was held in 1990 and annually through 1995. Vaclav Chalupa of Czechoslovakia won the first men's title and Birgit Peter of East Germany the women's.

4957. Women's four-oared shell without coxswain event held in the Olympic Games was in 1992 in Barcelona, Spain, where Kirsten Barnes, Branda Taylor, Jessica Monroe, and Kay Worthington of Canada won the inaugural competition on August 1.

4958. Rowers to win two consecutive titles in the women's quadruple sculls in the Olympic Games were Kerstin Förster and Kristina Mundt of East Germany. After winning the initial competition in 1988, they went to Barcelona, Spain, to win again with two new partners on August 2, 1992.

4959. Men's lightweight double sculls rowing event held in the Olympic Games was in 1996 in Atlanta, Georgia, where Markus Gier and Michael Gier of Switzerland won on July 28.

4960. Men's lightweight four-oared shells without coxswain rowing event held in the Olympic Games was in 1996 in Atlanta, Georgia. Winning on July 28 were Niels Henriksen, Thomas Poulsen, Eskild Ebbesen, and Victor Feddersen of Denmark.

4961. Women's lightweight double sculls rowing event held in the Olympic Games was in 1996 in Atlanta, Georgia. Constanta Burcica and Camelia Macoviciuc of Romania won the inaugural event on July 28.

4962. World cup in rowing was held in 1997, with regattas in Munich, Germany; Paris, France; and Lucerne, Switzerland. The winning team was from Germany.

RUGBY

4963. Rugby Football Union (RFU) was founded in England in 1871, by some clubs who broke away from the Football Association, founded in 1863. It would become a prime organization in the sport.

4964. Rugby League was formed at Huddersfield, Yorkshire, England, in 1895, by a series of clubs from northern England who had seceded from the Rugby Football Union. Originally called the Northern Union, then the Northern Rugby League in 1922, it became the Rugby League in 1980.

4965. Rugby event held in the Olympic Games was in Paris, France, in 1900. The team from France won the inaugural competition on October 28. The sport would be included three more times, but not after 1924.

4966. Grey Cup awarded to the rugby football champion in Canada was offered in 1909, donated by Earl Grey, Governor General of Canada. Awarded annually, it was won in the first three years by teams from the University of Toronto. The Grey Cup would be awarded to the Canadian football champion from 1954, specifically the champion of the Canadian Football League after its founding in 1958.

RUGBY—*continued*

4967. Team from the United States to win the rugby event in the Olympic Games won on September 5, 1920, in Antwerp, Belgium. A U.S. team would win again in 1924, the last time rugby was included in the Olympics.

4968. Rugby players to win two Olympic gold medals in rugby were Charles Doe, John O'Neill, John Patrick, and Rudolph Scholz, who were all on the winning United States teams in 1920 and again on May 18, 1924, in Paris, France.

4969. World cup in rugby was held in France in 1954, where the winning team in the round-robin competition was from Great Britain. It would be replaced by the International Championship in 1977.

4970. International Championships in rugby were held in 1975, replacing the earlier world cup competition. After competitions at various world-wide sites, the team from Australia won the first championship.

RUNNING (BEFORE 1900)
4971. Evidence of organized running events dates from approximately 3800 BC in Egypt.

4972. Recorded steeplechase event for runners was held in Edinburgh, Scotland, in 1828. The distance of the course would vary until 1920, when it would be standardized at 3000 meters.

4973. Runner to race the 100-yard dash in under 10 seconds was John Owens of the United States, who raced the distance in 9.8 seconds on October 11, 1890, at the Amateur Athletic Union (AAU) championships in Washington, D.C.

4974. Men's 800-meter and 1500-meter running events held in the Olympic Games were in 1896, in the first modern Olympics, in Athens, Greece. Edwin Flack of Australia won both: the 1500-meter on April 7, with a time of 4:33.2 minutes; then the 800-meter on April 9, in 2:11.0.

4975. Men's 100- and 400-meter running events held in the Olympic Games were in 1896, in the first modern Olympics in Athens, Greece. Thomas Burke of the United States won both: the 400-meter in 54.2 seconds on April 7, then the 100-meter in 12.0 on April 10. Burke and teammate Thomas Curtis used a "crouch" start then unfamiliar to most Europeans.

RUNNING (1900-1909)
4976. Men's 60-meter running event held in the Olympic Games was on July 15, 1900, in Paris, France. Alvin Kraenzlein of the United States won with a world-record time of 7.0 seconds, for one of his four gold medals there.

4977. Men's steeplechase event held at the Olympic Games was in 1900. George Orton of Canada won the 2500-meter event with a time of 7:34.4 minutes on July 15 in Paris, France. Not until 1920 would the event be standardized at 3000 meters.

4978. Runner from Europe to win the men's 1500-meter title in the Olympic Games was Charles Bennett of Great Britain. Racing at Paris, France, on July 15, 1900, he had a world record time of 4:06.2 minutes.

4979. Men's 4000-meter steeplechase event held in the Olympic Games was in 1900 in Paris, France. John Thomas Rimmer won with a time of 12:58.4 minutes on July 16, the only time the event was held.

4980. Runner from Europe to win the men's 800-meter title in the Olympic Games was Alfred Tysoe of Great Britain. His time of 2:01.2 minutes won the event on July 16, 1900, in Paris, France.

4981. Men's 200-meter race held in the Olympic Games was in 1900, in Paris, France. John Walter Tewksbury of the United States won the event on July 22 with a time of 22.2 seconds.

4982. Men's 5000-meter team running event held in the Olympic Games was in Paris, France, in 1900. The British team, which included one Australian runner, won on July 22, the only time the event was held.

4983. Runner to hold the officially accepted world record in the men's 400-meter event was Maxey Long of the United States, who set a benchmark time of 47.8 seconds on September 29, 1900, in New York City. It would not be broken until May 27, 1916, by Ted (Edward) Meredith in Cambridge, Massachusetts.

4984. International Cross-Country Championships were held in Glasgow, Scotland, in 1903, originally for men from Great Britain only. The first champion was Alfred Shrubb of England. The event expanded from 1907 to include other countries and from 1967 would have women's races. In 1973 it became the World Cross-Country Championships, sponsored by the International Amateur Athletic Federation (IAAF).

4985. National team to sweep the top three medals in the men's 400-meter running event in the Olympic Games was from the United States. At St. Louis, Missouri, Harry Hillman, Frank Waller, and German Groman took the top three spots on August 29, 1904.

4986. Runner from the United States to win the men's steeplechase event at the Olympic Games was James Lightbody of the United States, who had a time of 7:39.6 minutes over the 2590-meter course on August 29, 1904, in St. Louis, Missouri. He also won the men's 800- and 1500-meter races in St. Louis.

4987. Runner from the United States to win the men's 800-meter race in the Olympic Games was James Lightbody with a time of 1:56.0 minutes, leading a United States sweep of the medals on September 1, 1904, in St. Louis, Missouri.

4988. Men's 4-mile team race held in the Olympic Games was on September 3, 1904, in St. Louis, Missouri. A team from the New York Athletic Club won, the only time the event was held.

4989. Runner from the United States to win the men's 1500-meter race in the Olympic Games was James Lightbody, who had a world record time of 4:05.4 minutes. He and two other members of the Chicago Athletic Association—William Frank Verner and Lacey Hearn—swept the medals on September 3, 1904, in St. Louis, Missouri. Lightbody would win the event again at the unofficial Olympics in 1906.

'4990. National team to sweep the top three medals in the men's 100- and 200-meter running events in the Olympic Games was from the United States. Racing at St. Louis, Missouri, Archie (Charles) Hahn, Nathaniel Cartmell, and William Hogenson placed in that order on August 31, 1904, in the 200-meter, and on September 3, in the 100-meter race.

4991. Runner to win both the men's 100- and 200-meter races in the same Olympic Games was Archie (Charles) Hahn of the United States in 1904 at St. Louis, Missouri. He won the 200-meters on August 31 with an Olympic record time of 21.6 seconds and the 100-meters on September 3 with 11.0 seconds. He also won the now-discontinued 60 meters on August 29, equaling the world record of 7.0 seconds.

4992. Men's 5-mile event held in the Olympic Games was on April 25, 1906, in the unofficial Games in Athens, Greece. The winner was Henry Hawtrey of Great Britain, with a time of 26:11.8 minutes. The event would be held only once more, in 1908.

4993. Runner to win both the men's 400- and 800-meter events in the same Olympic Games was Paul Pilgrim of the United States in 1906 in Athens, Greece. He won the 400-meter on April 29 with a time of 53.2 seconds, and the 800-meter the next day, in 2:01.5 minutes. Not part of the regular United States team, he paid his own way to Greece, where officials allowed him to compete.

4994. Men's 3-mile team race held in the Olympic Games was July 15, 1908, in London, England. The team of Joseph Deakin, Arthur Robertson, and Wilfred Coales of Great Britain won the event, the only time it was held.

4995. Runner from Africa to win the men's 100-meter race in the Olympic Games was Reginald Walker of South Africa, who won the event with a time of 10.8 seconds on July 22, 1908, in London, England. Walker was coached by Sam Mussabini, made famous in the 1981 film *Chariots of Fire*. Walker was the first runner from outside the United States to win the event.

4996. Runner from Canada to win the men's 200-meter race in the Olympic Games was Robert Kerr. An immigrant from Ireland, Kerr won the gold medal with a time of 22.6 seconds in London, England, on July 23, 1908.

4997. Men's 4 x 400-meter relay track event held in the Olympic Games was on July 25, 1908, in London, England, where the United States team of William Hamilton, Nathaniel Cartmell, John Taylor, and Melvin Sheppard won with a time of 3:29.4 minutes. Taylor was the first African-American, and the first athlete of Black African ancestry, to win an Olympic gold medal.

4998. Runner from Europe to win the men's 400-meter race in the Olympic Games was Wyndham Halswelle of Great Britain, who did so with a time of 50.0 seconds on July 25, 1908, in London, England. After controversy over the original final, one finalist was disqualified and two others refused to compete, so Halswelle raced the rerun alone.

RUNNING (1910-1919)

4999. Runner to hold the officially accepted world record in the men's 10,000-meter event was Jean Bouin of France. He was also the first to run the distance in under 31:00 minutes, with a time of 30:58.8 minutes set on November 16, 1911, in Paris, France.

5000. Runner to hold the officially accepted world record in the men's 1500-meter event sometimes called the European mile or the metric mile, was Russian-born Abel Kiviat of the United States. His record of 3:55.8 minutes, set on June 8, 1912, in Cambridge, Massachusetts, would stand until 1917.

5001. Runner to hold the officially accepted world record in the men's 100-meter dash was Donald Lippincott of the United States, who set a benchmark time of 10.6 seconds, in a semifinal race at the Olympic Games in Stockholm, Sweden, on July 6, 1912. In the final, after the field had seven false starts, he finished third. Lippincott's time would be equaled by Jackson Scholz in 1920, but not broken until 1921, by Charles Paddock.

5002. Runner to hold the officially accepted world record in the men's 800-meter event was Ted (Edward) Meredith of the United States. Racing in the Olympic Games in Stockholm, Sweden, on July 8, 1912, he set the record of 1:51.9 minutes. It would stand until July 3, 1926, when Otto Peltzer of Germany raced the distance in 1:51.6 minutes.

5003. Men's 4 x 100-meter relay track event held in the Olympic Games was on July 9, 1912, in Stockholm, Sweden. With a time of 42.4 seconds, the winning team was from Great Britain: David Jacobs, Henry Macintosh, Victor D'Arcy, and William Applegarth.

5004. Men's 3000-meter team running event held in the Olympic Games was on July 13, 1912, in Stockholm, Sweden. It was won by the United States team of Tel Berna, Norman Taber, and George Bonhag. The event would be held only twice more.

5005. Men's cross-country team track race held in the Olympic Games was on July 15, 1912, in Stockholm, Sweden, where the Swedish team won. The event would be held only twice more.

5006. Men's individual cross-country event held in the Olympic Games was on July 15, 1912, in Stockholm, Sweden. The winner was Johannes Kolehmainen of Finland, with a time of 45:11.6 minutes for the approximately 12,000-meter distance. He had previously won the 5000- and 10,000-meter races.

5007. Runner to win two consecutive gold medals in the men's 4 x 400-meter relay in the Olympic Games was Melvin Sheppard of the United States. He ran as anchor in winning the inaugural event in 1908, then took the first leg toward a world-record time of 3:16.6 minutes on July 15, 1912, in Stockholm, Sweden.

5008. Men's 5000- and 10,000-meter events held in the Olympic Games were in 1912 in Stockholm, Sweden. Johannes Kolehmainen of Finland won the events: the 10,000-meter race on July 8, with a time of 31:20.8 minutes, and the 5000-meter race on July 10, with a benchmark time of 14:36.6 minutes, to set the first official world record in the event. Also winner of the men's individual cross-country race, Kolehmainen would be the final runner in the torch relay for the 1952 Olympics, held in Helsinki, Finland. His world-record time for 5000 meters would not be broken until September 12, 1922, by his countryman Paavo Nurmi.

5009. Runner to hold the officially accepted world record in the men's mile race was John Paul Jones of the United States, who had a time of 4:14.4 minutes on May 31, 1913, in Cambridge, Massachusetts.

RUNNING (1920-1929)

5010. Runner from Africa to win the men's 400-meters title in the Olympic Games was Bevil Rudd of South Africa. He ran the distance in 49.6 seconds to win on August 20, 1920, in Antwerp, Belgium.

5011. Team from the United States to win the men's 4 x 100-meter relay track event in the Olympic Games consisted of Charles Paddock, Jackson Scholz, Loren Murchison, and Morris Kirksey. Racing on August 22, 1920, at Antwerp, Belgium, they set a world record of 42.2 seconds.

5012. Runner to race the men's 100-meter event in less than 10.5 seconds was Charles Paddock of the United States. On April 23, 1921, at Redlands, California, he ran the distance in 10.4 seconds, bettering the previous record of 10.6. His record would be equaled, but not bettered until 1930.

5013. Runner to hold the world record in both the men's 5000- and 10,000-meter events was Paavo Nurmi of Finland. He first gained the 10,000-meter record with a time of 30:40.2 minutes on June 22, 1921 in Stockholm, Sweden. He would lower that to 30:06.2 on August 31, 1924, a record that would stand until 1937. Also in Stockholm, he set his record of 14:35.4 minutes in the 5000-meter on September 12, 1922, the first of his two records in the event, which would stand until 1932. He also held world records in the 1500-meter and the mile.

5014. Runner from Europe to win the men's 100-meter title in the Olympic Games was Harold Abrahams of Great Britain, who led the field with a time of 10.6 seconds to win on July 7, 1924, at Paris, France. As portrayed in the 1981 film *Chariots of Fire*, he was coached by Sam Mussabini. Also featured in the film was his teammate Eric Liddell, who won the men's 400-meter track race.

5015. Runner to win two consecutive titles in the men's individual cross-country in the Olympic Games was Paavo Nurmi of Finland. After winning the approximately 8000-meter race in 1920, he returned to win a 10,000-meter event on July 12, 1924, in Paris, France, with a time of 32:54.8 minutes. So many racers collapsed in the heat on the difficult course that the event was discontinued.

5016. Runner to win two consecutive gold medals in the men's 4 x 100-meter relay in the Olympic Games was Loren Murchison from the United States. After being on the winning team in 1920, he went to Paris, France, to win another medal with the United States team on July 13, 1924, with a world-record time of 41.0 seconds in both the semifinal and final.

5017. Run across the United States was held in 1928, in a race sponsored by Charles C. Pyle. Andrew Payne was the first to cover the 3422 miles between Ascot Speedway in Los Angeles, California, and Madison Square Garden in New York City. His actual time on the road, not counting rest breaks, was a little over 573 hours.

5018. Runner from Canada to win the men's 100-meter race in the Olympic Games was Percy Williams, whose time of 10.8 seconds led the field on July 30, 1928, at Amsterdam, the Netherlands. He also won the 200-meter event on August 1.

5019. Runner to win two consecutive men's 800-meter titles in the Olympic Games was Douglas Lowe of Great Britain. After his earlier win in 1924, his second win came on July 31, 1928, in Amsterdam, the Netherlands, where he had an Olympic-record time of 1:51.8 minutes.

5020. Women's 100-meter running event, and the first women's track event, held in the Olympic Games was in 1928 at Amsterdam, the Netherlands. The winner was 16-year-old Betty (Elizabeth) Robinson of the United States, who equaled her own world record of 12.2 seconds on July 31.

5021. Runner to hold the officially accepted world record in the women's 800-meter event was Lina (Karoline) Radke (later Radke-Batschauer) of Germany, with a time of 2:16.8 minutes set at the Olympic Games in Amsterdam, the Netherlands, on August 2, 1928. It would stand until 1944.

5022. Women's 800-meter running event held in the Olympic Games was on August 2, 1928 in Amsterdam, the Netherlands. It was won by Lina (Karoline) Radke-Batschauer of Germany, with a world-record time of 2:16.8 minutes. Several women collapsed after the race (as also occurred in the men's races), and opponents of women's racing succeeded in banning women's races longer than 200 meters from international competitions for several decades, in the Olympics until 1960.

5023. Women's 4 x 100-meter relay running event held in the Olympic Games was on August 5, 1928, in Amsterdam, the Netherlands. Winning with a world-record time of 48.4 seconds was the team from Canada: Fanny Rosenfeld, Ethel Smith, Florence Bell, and Myrtle Cook.

5024. African-American runner to hold the record in the men's 100-meter dash was Eddie (Thomas) Tolan of the United States. He twice equaled Charles Paddock's time of 10.4 seconds, first on August 8, 1929, in Stockholm, Sweden, and again on August 25, in Copenhagen, Denmark, and later lowered his best time to 10.3 seconds.

RUNNING (1930-1939)

5025. Runner to complete the men's 1500-meter race in under 3:50 minutes was Jules Ladouméque of France, who posted a time of 3:49.2 minutes on October 5, 1930, in Paris, France.

5026. Runner to complete the men's mile race in under 4:10 minutes was Jules Ladoumèque of France. His record of 4:09.2 minutes was set at Paris, France, on October 4, 1931.

RUNNING—(1930-1939)—*continued*

5027. Runner to complete the men's 400-meter race in under 47 seconds was Ben Eastman of the United States, who had a time of 46.4 seconds on March 26, 1932, in Stanford, California. His record would be broken on August 5 in the Olympic Games in Los Angeles, California, by teammate William Carr, who cut the record to 46.2 seconds.

5028. Runner to race the men's 5000 meters in under 14:28.0 minutes was Lauri Lehtinen of Finland, who dropped the record to 14:17.0 on June 19, 1932, in Helsinki, Finland. The record would stand for seven years.

5029. Runner to complete the men's 800-meter race in under 1:50 minutes was Thomas Hampson of Great Britain. He broke the barrier with a 1:49.7 time on August 2, 1932, at the Olympic Games in Los Angeles, California. He was the first Briton to hold the 800-meter world record.

5030. Team from the United States to win the women's 4 x 100-meter relay running event in the Olympic Games won in 1932 at Los Angeles, California. Racing on August 7, the team of Mary Carew, Evelyn Furtsch, Annette Rogers, and Wilhelmina Von Bremen had a world-record time of 46.9 seconds.

5031. Team to race the men's 4 x 400-meter relay in under 3:10 minutes was from the United States, on August 7, 1932, in Los Angeles, California. Ivan Fuqua, Edgar Ablowich, Karl Warner, and William Carr set a new world record of 3:08.2 minutes.

5032. African-American runner to win the men's 100- and 200-meter titles in the Olympic Games was Eddie (Thomas) Tolan of the United States. He won the 100-meter title with an Olympic-record time of 10.3 seconds on August 1, 1932, in Los Angeles, California, in a photo finish with African-American teammate Ralph Metcalfe. Then on August 3, Tolan won the 200-meter race in 21.2 seconds, another Olympic record.

5033. Runner to hold the officially accepted world record in the women's 100-meter dash was Stanislawa Walasiewicz (Stella Walsh), who lived in the United States, but was born in and raced for Poland. Her time of 11.7 seconds was set in Warsaw, Poland, on August 26, 1934. She would lower it to 11.6 on August 1, 1937, a record that would stand until June 13, 1948. An autopsy at her death, in 1980, found that she was a hermaphrodite, who had both male and female sexual organs.

5034. Runner from Asia to hold the officially accepted world record in the men's 100-meter dash was Takayoshi Yoshioka of Japan. At an international meet in Tokyo, Japan, on June 15, 1935, he equaled the record of 10.3 seconds, set in 1930 by Percy Williams of Canada.

5035. Runner to hold the officially accepted world record in the women's 200 meters was Stanislawa Walasiewicz (Stella Walsh), a Polish-born United States resident competing for Poland, whose time of 23.6 seconds was set on August 4, 1935, in Warsaw, Poland. It would stand until 1952.

5036. Runner to race the men's 100-meter dash in 10.2 seconds was Jesse (James Cleveland) Owens of the United States. Set on June 20, 1936, in Chicago, Illinois, his record would be equaled but not bettered for more than 20 years.

5037. African-American runner to win the men's 800-meter title in the Olympic Games was John Woodruff, who won the event on August 4, 1936, in Berlin, Germany, with a time of 1:52.9 minutes.

5038. Runner from New Zealand to win the men's 1500-meter title at the Olympic Games and to hold the world record in the event was John Lovelock. He set a new world record with a time of 3:47.8 minutes on August 6, 1936, in Berlin, Germany.

5039. African-American runner to win the men's 400-meter title in the Olympic Games was Archie Williams, who won the event on August 7, 1936, in Berlin, Germany, with a time of 46.5 seconds.

5040. Runner to win three gold medals in the men's 4 x 100-meter relay in the Olympic Games was Frank Wykoff, who was a member of the winning United States teams in 1928, 1932, and 1936, equaling or setting a new world record all three times. The last was on August 9, 1936, in Berlin, Germany.

5041. Runner to win two gold medals in the women's 4 x 100-meter relay in the Olympic Games was Annette Rogers of the United States. After winning her first in 1932, she returned to take another on August 9, 1936, in Berlin, Germany, where she, Harriet Bland, Betty (Elizabeth) Robinson, and Helen Stephens had a time of 46.9 seconds.

5042. Team to race the men's 4 x 100-meter relay in under 40 seconds was from the United States. Racing at Berlin, Germany, on August 9, 1936, Jesse (James Cleveland) Owens, Ralph Metcalfe, Foy Draper, and Frank Wykoff did it in 39.8 seconds. Much to the consternation of German chancellor Adolf Hitler, African-American Owens also won three other gold medals in Berlin. He won the men's 100-meter event on August 3 with a time of 10.3 seconds and the 200-meter on August 5 with an Olympic-record time of 20.7 seconds (the silver medalist was Mack [Matthew] Robinson, older brother of baseball great Jackie Robinson). In between, on August 4, Owens won the long jump with an Olympic record of 26 feet 5½ inches (8.06 meters).

5043. Runner to race the men's 5000 meters in under 14:10 minutes was Taisto Mäki of Finland. Racing at Helsinki, Finland, on June 16, 1939, he cut the record to 14:08.8 minutes.

5044. Runner to race the men's 800 meters in under 1:48 minutes was Rudolf Harbig of Germany, who on July 15, 1939, in Milan, Italy, pared the record to 1:46.6 minutes, which would stand until 1955.

5045. Runner to race the men's 10,000 meters in under 30:00 minutes was Taisto Mäki of Finland. On September 17, 1939, in Helsinki, Finland, he set his new record of 29:52.6 minutes.

RUNNING (1940-1949)
5046. Runner to complete the men's mile race in under 4:05 minutes was Gunder Hägg of Sweden, whose time of 4:04.6 minutes was set at Stockholm, Sweden, on September 4, 1942. He would cut the time to 4:01.4 on July 17, 1945.

5047. Runner to race the men's 5000 meters in under 14:00 minutes was Gunder Hägg of Sweden. His new time of 13:58.2 minutes, set on September 20, 1942, in Gothenburg, Sweden, would stand for nearly 12 years.

5048. Runner to complete the men's 1500 meters in under 3:45.0 minutes was Gunder Hägg of Sweden, who sliced the time to 3:43.0 on July 7, 1944, in Gothenburg, Sweden. It would stand until 1954.

5049. Runner from Central or South America to set or equal a world track and field record was Lloyd LaBeach of Panama. On May 15, 1948, in Fresno, California, he matched Jesse Owens's 1936 record of 10.2 seconds in the men's 100 meters.

5050. Runner from the Caribbean to win the men's 400-meter title in the Olympic Games was Arthur Wint of Jamaica, a University of London medical student, who equaled the Olympic record with a time of 46.2 seconds on August 5, 1948, in London, England.

5051. Women's 200-meter race held in the Olympic Games was on August 6, 1948, in London, England. Fanny (Francina) Blankers-Koen of the Netherlands won the inaugural race with a time of 24.4 seconds. She would also win three other gold medals: in the women's 100-meter dash, 80-meter hurdles, and 4 x 100-meter relay.

5052. Runner to win both the women's 100- and 200-meter titles in the same Olympic Games was Fanny (Francina) Blankers-Koen of the Netherlands in 1948 in London, England. She raced the 100 meters in 11.9 seconds on August 2, and the 200 in an Olympic-record 24.4 seconds on August 6.

RUNNING (1950-1959)
5053. Runner to hold an officially accepted world record in the men's 200-meter race run on a curved track was Andy Stanfield of the United States, who had a record time of 20.6 seconds in Philadelphia, Pennsylvania, on May 26, 1951. The International Amateur Athletic Federation (IAAF) in that year voted to recognize only world records set on a curved track for the 400-meter race, so older records were no long acceptable.

5054. Runner to qualify for the finals men's of the 100-, 200-, and 400-meter races in the Olympic Games was Herbert McKenley of Jamaica, who did so in 1952 at Helsinki, Finland. He won silver medals in both the 100-meter and 400-meter events.

5055. Runner to race the women's 800 meters in under 2:10 minutes was Nina Pletneva Otkalenko of the Soviet Union. Racing on June 15, 1952, in Kiev, the Soviet Union, she had a time of 2:08.5 minutes, for the second of her five world records in the event.

5056. Runner to win two consecutive men's 10,000-meter titles in the Olympic Games was Emil Zátopek of Czechoslovakia. After winning the 1948 title, he returned to win at Helsinki, Finland, with a new Olympic-record time of 29.17.0 minutes, set on July 20, 1952.

5057. Runner from the United States to win the men's 3000-meter steeplechase title in the Olympic Games was Horace Ashenfelter, who had a world-record time of 8:45.4 minutes on July 25, 1952, in Helsinki, Finland.

RUNNING—(1950-1959)—*continued*

5058. African-American women to win gold medals in a track relay event in the Olympic Games were Mae Faggs, Barbara Jones, and Catherine Hardy of the United States who, with teammate Janet Moreau, set a world record time of 45.9 seconds in the women's 4 x 100-meter relay on July 27, 1952, in Helsinki, Finland.

5059. Runner from Australia to win the women's 100- and 200-meter titles in the Olympic Games was Marjorie Jackson. She equaled the world record of 11.5 seconds to win the 100-meter event on July 22, 1952, in Helsinki, Finland. Then on July 26, she won the 200-meter race with a time of 23.7 seconds.

5060. Runner to race the mile in under 4:00 minutes was Roger Bannister of Great Britain. Racing at Oxford, England, on May 6, 1954, he was the first to break that barrier, with a time of 3:59.4 minutes, retiring from racing later that year. He later became a neurologist and then master of Pembroke College, Oxford University.

5061. Runner to race the men's 10,000 meters in under 29:00 minutes was Emil Zátopek of Czechoslovakia. His time of 28:54.2 minutes—his fifth world record in the event—was set on June 1, 1954, in Brussels, Belgium.

5062. Runner to hold the officially accepted world record in the men's 5000-meter steeplechase was Sándor Rozsnyói of Hungary. His time of 8:49.6 minutes was set at the European Championships in Bern, Switzerland, on August 28, 1954. He would set another record at 8:35.6 minutes on September 16, 1956, in Budapest, Hungary.

5063. Runner to race the men's 100-meter dash in 10.1 seconds was Willie Williams of the United States. Racing on August 3, 1956, in Berlin, Germany, he broke Jesse Owens's 20-year-old record of 10.2 seconds.

5064. Runner to race the men's 5000-meter steeplechase in under 8:39 minutes was Semyon Rzhishchin of the Soviet Union, who set a time of 8:39.8 minutes on August 14, 1956, in Moscow, the Soviet Union.

5065. Runners to finish first and second in both the women's 100- and 200-meter races in the Olympic Games were Betty (Elizabeth) Cuthbert of Australia and Christa Stubrick of East Germany. Racing at Melbourne, Australia, they finished in that order in the 100-meter event on November 26, 1956, and in the 200-meter race on November 30.

5066. Runner to hold the officially accepted world record in the women's 400-meter event was Marlene Mathews of Australia, whose benchmark time of 57.0 seconds was set on January 6, 1957, in Sydney, Australia.

5067. Runner to complete the 1500-meter race in under 3:40 minutes was Stanislav Jungwirth of Czechoslovakia. His time of 3:38.1 minutes was set at Stara Boleslav, Czechoslovakia, on July 12, 1957.

5068. Runner to complete the men's mile race in under 3:55 minutes was Herb Elliott of Australia, who had a time of 3:54.5 minutes in Dublin, Ireland, on August 6, 1958.

RUNNING (1960-1969)

5069. African-American runner to win the women's 100- and 200-meter titles in the Olympic Games was Wilma Rudolph, in 1960, in Rome, Italy. She won the 100-meter race with a wind-aided time of 11.0 seconds on September 2 and then the 200-meter three days later in 24.0 seconds, well shy of her own world record of 22.9.

5070. Runner from New Zealand to win the men's 5000-meter title in the Olympic Games was Murray Halberg, who won on September 2, 1960, in Rome, Italy, with a time of 13:43.4 minutes.

5071. Runner from New Zealand to win the men's 800-meter title in the Olympic Games was Peter Snell, with an Olympic-record time of 1:46.3 minutes, set in Rome, Italy, on September 2, 1960. He would win the title again at the 1964 Olympics, where he also won the men's 1500-meter event.

5072. Runners to complete the men's 400-meter race in under 45 seconds were Otis Davis of the United States and Carl Kaufmann of West Germany, on September 6, 1960, at the Olympic Games in Rome, Italy. Both posted a time of 44.9 seconds, but Otis Davis broke the tape first and took the gold medal.

5073. Women's 800-meter race held in the Olympic Games after a 32-year ban was held in Rome, Italy, on September 7, 1960. It was won by Lyudmyla Shevtsova of the Soviet Union, who equaled the world-record time of 2:04.3 hours. No women's track event longer than 200 meters had been held in the Olympics between 1928 and 1960.

5074. Runner to complete the men's 800-meter race in under 1:45 minutes was Peter Snell of New Zealand. His new record of 1:44.3 minutes, set on February 3, 1962, in Christchurch, New Zealand, would stand until 1973.

5075. Runner to race the men's 5000-meter steeplechase in under 8:30.0 minutes was Gaston Roelants of Belgium. He broke the barrier with a time of 8:29.6 minutes on September 7, 1963, in Leuven, Belgium, and cut it further to 8:26.4 on August 7, 1965, in Brussels, Belgium.

5076. Women's 400-meter race held in the Olympic Games was on October 17, 1964, in Tokyo, Japan. The winner was Betty (Elizabeth) Cuthbert of Australia, setting an Olympic record of 52.0 seconds. She had won three gold medals at the 1956 Olympics, but had been forced out in 1960 by a pulled hamstring.

5077. Runner from the United States to win the men's 10,000-meter title at the Olympic Games was Billy (William) Mills, who set a new Olympic record on October 14, 1964, with a time of 28:24.4 minutes, at Tokyo, Japan.

5078. Runner from the United States to win the men's 5000-meter title at the Olympic Games was Robert Schul, with a time of 13:48.4 minutes, set on October 18, 1964, in Tokyo, Japan.

5079. Runner from Africa to hold the world record in the men's 5000 meters was Kip (H. Kipchoge) Keino of Kenya. Racing on November 30, 1965, in Auckland, New Zealand, he lowered the record time to 13:24.2 seconds.

5080. Runner to complete the men's mile race in under 3:53 minutes was Jim Ryun of the United States, who pared the record to 3:51.3 minutes on July 17, 1966, racing at Berkeley, California, dropping it further to 3:51.1 on June 23, 1967.

5081. International Cross-Country Championships to include a women's race were in 1967. Doris Brown of the United States won the women's cross-country race the first five times it was held (1967–1971).

5082. Runner to hold the officially accepted world record in the women's 1500 meters was Anne Smith of Great Britain. Her time of 4:17.3 minutes was set in London, England, on June 3, 1967.

5083. Runner to race the men's 1500 meters in less than 3:35 minutes was Jim Ryun of the United States. Racing in Los Angeles, California, on July 8, 1967, he set a new record 3:33.1, which would stand until 1974.

5084. Runner to race the men's 100-meter dash in under 10 seconds was Jim Hines of the United States. He broke that barrier on June 20, 1968, with a time of 9.9 seconds in the semifinals of an Amateur Athletic Union (AAU) race at Sacramento, California.

5085. Runner from Africa to win the men's 10,000-meter title at the Olympic Games was Naftali Temu of Kenya. Racing at Mexico City, he posted the winning time of 29:27.4 minutes on October 13, 1968.

5086. Runner to win two consecutive women's 200-meter titles in the Olympic Games was African-American Wyomia Tyus of the United States. After winning the first in 1964, she won her second with a world-record time of 11.08 seconds on October 15, 1968, in Mexico City.

5087. Runner from Africa to win the men's 3000-meter steeplechase title in the Olympic Games was Amos Biwott of Kenya, who had a time of 8:51.0 minutes on October 16, 1968, in Mexico City. The Kenyans would dominate the event from then on, though they boycotted the 1976 and 1980 Olympics.

5088. Runner to complete the men's 200-meter race in under 20 seconds was Tommie Smith of the United States, who broke that barrier with a time of 19.83 seconds on October 16, 1968, at the Olympic Games in Mexico City, where numerous track records were broken in the high, thin air. On the victory platform, he and bronze medalist teammate John Carlos raised their clenched, gloved fists in a Black Power salute, for which the two African-Americans were suspended by the United States Olympic Committee.

5089. Runner from Africa to win the men's 5000-meter title in the Olympic Games was Mohamed Gammoudi of Tunisia, with a time of 14:05.0 minutes on October 17, 1968, in Mexico City. He would be silver medalist in 1972.

5090. Runner to complete the men's 400-meter race in under 44 seconds was Lee Evans of the United States. He set a new world record of 43.86 seconds on October 18, 1968, in the Olympic Games at Mexico City. The record would stand until 1988, when Butch (Harry) Reynolds would lower it to 43.29 seconds.

5091. Runner from the United States to win the women's 800-meter title at the Olympic Games was Madeline Manning, whose Olympic-record time of 2:00.9 minutes was set on October 19, 1968, in Mexico City.

5092. Runner from Africa to win the men's 1500-meter title at the Olympic Games was Kip (H. Kipchoge) Keino of Kenya. Fighting a gall bladder infection that had caused him to drop out of the 10,000-meter race, he won with an Olympic-record time of 3:34.9 minutes on October 20, 1968, in Mexico City.

RUNNING (1970-1979)

5093. Runner to race the women's 800 meters in under 2:00 minutes was Hildegard Falck of West Germany. Her milestone time of 1:58.5 minutes was set in her homeland, in Stuttgart, on July 11, 1971.

5094. Women's 1500-meter event held in the Olympic Games was on September 9, 1972, in Munich, West Germany. The inaugural event was won by Lyudmila Bragina of the Soviet Union, with a world-record time of 4:01.4 hours.

5095. Women's 4 x 400-meter relay track event held in the Olympic Games was on September 10, 1972, in Munich, West Germany. That first event was won by Dagmar Käsling, Rita Kühne, Helga Seidler, and Monika Zehrt of East Germany, with a world-record time of 3:23.0 minutes.

5096. World Cross-Country Championships to have official world championship status was in 1973, when the International Amateur Athletic Federation (IAAF) took over the event from the International Cross-Country Union. Pekka Paivarinta of Finland was the first men's champion, with Paola Cacchi of Italy the women's champion.

5097. Runner to race the women's 100 meters in under 11.0 seconds was Renate Meissner Stecher of East Germany. After three times tying the 11.0 record, she broke the barrier on June 7, 1973, at Ostrava, Czechoslovakia, with a time of 10.9 seconds, which on July 20 she lowered to 10.8.

5098. Runner to race the men's 5000-meter steeplechase in under 8:20 minutes was Ben Jipcho of Kenya. On June 19, 1973, he set a time of 8:19.8 minutes, slashing it to 8:14.0 on June 27, both in Helsinki, Finland.

5099. Runner to complete the men's 800-meter race in under 1:44 minutes was Marcello Fiasconari of Italy, who shaved the record to 1:43.7 on June 27, 1973, at Milan, Italy.

5100. Runner to race the women's 400 meters in under 50 seconds was Irena Kirszenstein Szewinska of Poland. An Olympic medalist at shorter distances, she ran the 400 meters in 49.9 seconds on June 22, 1974, in Warsaw, Poland, in only her second 400-meter race. She would set two more records in 1976.

5101. Runner to hold the officially accepted world record in the women's 3000-meter event was Lyudmila Bragina of the Soviet Union. Her time of 8:52.8 minutes was set in Durham, North Carolina, on July 6, 1974. She set another world record, of 8:27.2 minutes, in 1976.

5102. Runner to race the men's 5000-meter steeplechase in under 8:10 minutes was Anders Gärderud of Sweden. For his third world record, he set a time of 8:09.8 minutes on July 1, 1975, in Stockholm, Sweden, which he would slice to 8:08.0 on July 28, 1976, at the Olympic Games in Montreal, Quebec, Canada.

5103. Runner to complete the men's mile race in under 3:50 minutes was John Walker of New Zealand, who shaved the record to 3:49.4 minutes on August 12, 1975, in Gothenburg, Sweden. By 1989 he would have run 100 sub-4-minute mile races, the first person to do so.

5104. Runner to race the women's 1500 meters in under 4 minutes was Tatyana Kazankina of the Soviet Union. She set her milestone of 3:56.0 minutes in Podolsk, the Soviet Union, on June 28, 1976, for the first of her three world records. Her 1980 time of 3:52.47 minutes would stand until 1993.

5105. Runner from the Caribbean to win the men's 100-meter dash at the Olympic Games was Hasely Crawford of Trinidad and Tobago, who posted a winning time of 10.06 seconds on July 24, 1976, in Montreal, Quebec, Canada.

5106. Runner from the Caribbean to win the men's 200-meter title at the Olympic Games was Donald Quarrie of Jamaica, who did so on July 26, 1976, with a time of 20.22 seconds, in Montreal, Quebec, Canada.

5107. Runner to win two consecutive men's 5000- and 10,000-meter titles at the Olympic Games was Lasse Viren of Finland. After winning both in 1972, Viren posted a time of 27:40.38 minutes to win his second straight 10,000-meter title on July 26, 1976, in Montreal, Quebec, Canada, despite falling at the 4-kilometer mark. Four days later he won his second 5000-meter title with a time of 13:24.76 minutes.

5108. Record in the men's 5000-meter steeplechase to last for more than 10 years was the time of 8:05.4 minutes set by Henry Rono of Kenya in Seattle, Washington, on May 13, 1978. It would stand until July 3, 1989, when his countryman Peter Koech ran the course in 8:05.35 minutes.

5109. Runner to race the women's 400 meters in under 49 seconds was Marita Koch of East Germany. In the third of her seven world records in the event, she posted a time of 48.94 on August 31, 1978, in Prague, Czechoslovakia. She would later lower that to 47.60 seconds, on October 6, 1985, in Canberra, Australia.

5110. Runner to race the women's 200 meters in under 22 seconds was Marita Koch of East Germany. She broke the 200-meter record with a time of 21.71 seconds, set on June 10, 1979, in Karl-Marx-Stadt, East Germany. It was the third of her four world records in the event.

5111. Runner to complete the men's 800-meter race in under 1:43 minutes was Sebastian Coe of Great Britain. He lowered the record to 1:42.33 on July 5, 1979, in Oslo, Norway, and lowered it further to 1:41.73 on June 10, 1981, at Florence, Italy.

5112. Runner to complete the men's 200-meter race in under 19.8 seconds was Pietro Mennea of Italy. On September 12, 1979, at the World University Games in Mexico City, he set the new world record of 19.72 seconds. It would last for 17 years, until it was broken by Michael Johnson with a time of 19.66 seconds on June 23, 1996, at the Olympic Trials in Atlanta, Georgia.

RUNNING (1980-1989)
5113. Runner to complete the men's mile race in under 3:49 minutes was Steve Ovett of Great Britain, who set a new record of 3:48.8 minutes on July 1, 1980, in Oslo, Norway. He would race it in 3:48.40 on August 26, 1981.

5114. National team to sweep the medals in the women's 800-meter race, or in any women's track event, at the Olympic Games was the Soviet Union. Led by Nadiya Olizarenko, with a world record time of 1:53.43 minutes, the Soviet team took the top three spots in the women's 800-meter race at the United States–boycotted Olympic Games in Moscow, the Soviet Union, on July 27, 1980.

5115. Women's 400-meter race in which the top three runners had times of under 50 seconds was on July 28, 1980, in Moscow, the Soviet Union. Marita Koch of East Germany led with an Olympic-record time of 48.88 seconds, followed by Jarmila Kratochvilova of Czechoslovakia and Christina Brehmer Lathan of East Germany.

5116. Runner to win two consecutive women's 200-meter titles at the Olympic Games was Bärbel Eckert Wöckel of East Germany. After winning her first title (as Eckert) in 1976, she returned to lower the Olympic record to 22.03 seconds on July 30, 1980, in Moscow, the Soviet Union.

5117. Runner to win two consecutive gold medals in the women's 4 x 100-meter relay in the Olympic Games was Bärbel Eckert Wöckel of East Germany. Anchor on the winning 1976 team (as Eckert), she returned on August 1, 1980, to run the second leg of her team's world-record race of 41.60 seconds in Moscow, the Soviet Union.

5118. Runner to win two consecutive titles in the women's 1500-meter race in the Olympic Games was Tatyana Kazankina of the Soviet Union. After winning in 1976, when she also won the 800-meter event, she returned on August 1, 1980, to win with an Olympic-record time of 3:56.6 minutes at the Olympic Games in Moscow, the Soviet Union.

5119. Runner to race the men's 1500 meters in under 3:32 minutes was Steve Ovett of Great Britain. Racing in Koblenz, West Germany, on August 27, 1980, he shaved his own record to 3:31.36 minutes. On September 4, 1983, he would cut it further, to 3:30.77.

5120. Runner to win the Jesse Owens International Award was Sebastian Coe of Great Britain in 1981.

5121. Runner to complete the men's mile race in under 3:48 minutes was Sebastian Coe of Great Britain. Racing in Brussels, Belgium, on August 28, 1981, he had a time of 3:47.33 minutes, his third world record in the event.

5122. Runner to hold the officially accepted world record in the women's 5000-meter race was Paula Fudge of Great Britain. Her inaugural time of 15:14.51 minutes was set on September 13, 1981, in Narvik, Norway.

5123. Runner to hold the officially accepted world record in the women's 10,000-meter race was Yelena Sipatova of the Soviet Union. Her time of 32:17.2 minutes was set on September 19, 1981, in Moscow, the Soviet Union.

5124. Runner from the United States to hold the world record in the women's 5000- and 10,000-meter races was Mary Decker (later Slaney). She set both milestones in Eugene, Oregon, in 1982: 15:08.26 minutes in the 5000 on June 5 and 31:35.3 minutes in the 10,000 on July 16.

RUNNING—(1980-1989)—*continued*

5125. Runner to win the men's 100-meter race held in the World Championships in Athletics was Carl Lewis of the United States, with a time of 10.07 seconds in 1983 in Helsinki, Finland.

5126. Runner to win the men's 10,000-meter race held in the World Championships in Athletics was Alberto Cova of Italy, who won the event with a time of 28:01.04 minutes in 1983 in Helsinki, Finland.

5127. Runner to win the men's 1500-meter race held in the World Championships in Athletics was Steve Cram of Great Britain, with a time of 3:41.59 minutes in 1983 in Helsinki, Finland.

5128. Runner to win the men's 200-meter race held in the World Championships in Athletics was Calvin Smith of the United States, who raced the distance in 20.14 seconds in 1983 in Helsinki, Finland.

5129. Runner to win the men's 3000-meter steeplechase held in the World Championships in Athletics was Patriz Ilg of West Germany, with a time of 8:15.06 minutes in 1983 in Helsinki, Finland.

5130. Runner to win the men's 400-meter race held in the World Championships in Athletics was Bert Cameron of Jamaica, who won the inaugural race in 45.05 seconds in 1983 in Helsinki, Finland.

5131. Runner to win the men's 5000-meter race held in the World Championships in Athletics was Eamonn Coghlan of Ireland, who won the event in 13:28.53 minutes in 1983 in Helsinki, Finland.

5132. Runner to win the men's 800-meter race held in the World Championships in Athletics was Willi Wülbeck of West Germany, who won the event with a time of 1:43.65 minutes in 1983 in Helsinki, Finland.

5133. Runner to win the women's 100-meter race in the World Championships in Athletics was Marlies Göhr of East Germany, who won the inaugural race in 10.97 seconds in 1983 in Helsinki, Finland.

5134. Runner to win the women's 1500-meter race in the World Championships in Athletics was Mary Decker (later Slaney) of the United States. She won the inaugural event with a time of 4:00.90 minutes in 1983 in Helsinki, Finland.

5135. Runner to win the women's 200-meter title in the World Championships in Athletics was Marita Koch of East Germany, who won the inaugural event in 22.13 seconds in 1983 in Helsinki, Finland.

5136. Runner to win the women's 400- and 800-meter events in the World Championships in Athletics was Jarmila Kratochvilová of Czechoslovakia. She won the inaugural 400-meter race with a time of 47.99 seconds and the 800-meter in 1:54.68 minutes, both in 1983 in Helsinki, Finland.

5137. Runner to race the women's 400 meters in under 48 seconds was Jarmila Kratochvilová of Czechoslovakia. At the first World Championships in Athletics in Helsinki, Finland, on August 10, 1983, she shaved the record to 47.99 seconds.

5138. Runner to race the women's 5000 meters in under 15 minutes was Ingrid Kristiansen of Norway. On June 28, 1984, in Oslo, Norway, she set a time of 14:58.89 minutes, the first of her two world records in the event.

5139. Runner from South America to win the men's 800-meter title at the Olympic Games was Joaquim Carvalho Cruz of Brazil, who had an Olympic-record run of 1:43.00 minutes on August 6, 1984, in Los Angeles, California.

5140. Women's 3000-meter race held at the Olympic Games was on August 10, 1984, in Los Angeles, California. The inaugural winner was Maricica Puica of Romania, with a time of 8:35.96 minutes. This was the notable race in which South African–born Zola Budd, competing for Great Britain, became entangled with Mary Decker (later Slaney) of the United States, with both falling out of the running. The event would be discontinued after 1992.

5141. Runner to win two consecutive officially accepted titles in the men's 1500-meters at the Olympic Games was Sebastian Coe of Great Britain. After winning in 1980, he posted an Olympic-record time of 3:32.53 on August 11, 1984, in Los Angeles, California. James Lightbody had won in 1904 and 1906, but the latter is considered an unofficial Olympics.

5142. Team from the United States to win the women's 4 x 400-meter relay at the Olympic Games won August 11, 1984, at the Soviet Union–boycotted Olympics in Los Angeles, California, with an Olympic-record time of 3:18.29 minutes. The team members were Lillie Leatherwood, Sherri Howard, Valerie Brisco-Hooks (for her third gold medal there, after the individual 200- and 400-meter titles), and Chandra Cheeseborough (for her second gold medal in an hour, after the 4 x 100-meter relay).

5143. Runner to win both the women's 200- and 400-meter titles at a single Olympic Games, and the first runner from the United States, or African-American, to win the 400-meter event was Valerie Brisco-Hooks of the United States. A young mother coming out of racing retirement, she set an Olympic record of 48.83 seconds in the 400-meter race on August 6, 1984, in Los Angeles, California, and then another Olympic record on August 9 with 21.81 seconds in the 200-meter.

5144. Runner to complete the men's 1500-meter race in under 3:30 minutes was Steve Cram of Great Britain, who set his record time of 3:29.67 minutes at Nice, France, on July 16, 1985.

5145. Runner to set seven world records in the women's 400 meters was Marita Koch of East Germany. Her first world record of 49.19 seconds was set on July 2, 1978, in Leipzig, East Germany. Her last was down to 47.60 seconds, set on October 6, 1985, in Canberra, Australia.

5146. Runner to win both the women's 100- and 200-meter titles in the World Championships in Athletics was Silke Gladisch of East Germany, who had a time of 10.90 seconds in the 100 meters and 21.74 seconds in the 200 meters in 1987 in Rome, Italy.

5147. Runner to win two, and then three, consecutive titles in the men's 100-meter event in the World Championships in Athletics was Carl Lewis of the United States. After winning the first event in 1983, he came in second to Ben Johnson in 1987 in Rome, Italy, but was awarded the title after Johnson was disqualified for having taken drugs. Lewis then won outright in 1991 in Tokyo, Japan.

5148. Runner to win two consecutive titles in the men's 200-meter event in the World Championships in Athletics was Calvin Smith of the United States. After winning in 1983, he won again with a time of 20.16 seconds in Rome, Italy, in 1987.

5149. Runner to race the men's 5000 meters in under 13:00 minutes was Saïd Aouita of Morocco. He broke that barrier on July 22, 1987, in Rome, Italy, with a time of 12:58.39 minutes.

5150. Runner to win two consecutive officially accepted men's 100-meter titles at the Olympic Games was Carl Lewis of the United States. After winning in 1984, he went back to win again in Seoul, South Korea, on September 24, 1988, with an Olympic-record time of 9.92 seconds. Ben Johnson of Canada had a better time of 9.79 seconds, but was disqualified because of drugs. Archie (Charles) Hahn of the United States had won the event in both 1904 and 1906, but the latter is not considered official.

5151. Runner from Africa to win the men's 800-meter title at the Olympic Games was Paul Ereng of Kenya, who posted a time of 1:43.45 minutes to lead the field at Seoul, South Korea, on September 26, 1988.

5152. Women's 10,000-meter running event held in the Olympic Games was on September 30, 1988, in Seoul, South Korea. It was won by Olga Bondarenko of the Soviet Union with a time of 31:05.21 minutes.

5153. Runner to race the women's 100 meters in under 10:50 seconds, and the 200 meters in under 21.50 seconds was Florence Griffith Joyner of the United States. Her record time of 10.49 seconds for 100 meters was set on July 16, 1988, in Indianapolis, Indiana. In the 200-meter event, she shaved her own record of 21.56 seconds down to 21.34 in the semifinals of the Olympic Games in Seoul, South Korea, on September 29, 1988. She won both events at the Seoul Olympics, and was also on the winning 4 x 100-meter relay team.

RUNNING (1990-1999)

5154. Runner to race the men's mile race in under 3:44.00 minutes was Hicham El Guerrouj of Morocco, who posted a record-shattering time of 3:43.13 minutes on July 7, 1999, in Rome, Italy.

5155. Runner to win two consecutive titles in the men's 800-meter event in the World Championships in Athletics was Billy Konchellah of Kenya. After winning in 1987, he won again in 1991 in Tokyo, Japan, with a time of 1:43.99 minutes.

RUNNING—(1990-1999)—*continued*

5156. Runner to race the men's 100 meters in under 9.9 seconds was Carl Lewis of the United States, who had a time of 9.86 seconds in the World Championships in Athletics at Tokyo, Japan, on August 25, 1991. It was his third straight world title in the event. It was also the first men's 100-meter race in which the top six runners all had times under 10.0 seconds.

5157. Runner to reach three consecutive finals in the men's 100-meter dash at the Olympic Games was Raymond Stewart of Jamaica. Sixth in 1984 in Los Angeles, California, and seventh in 1988 in Seoul, South Korea, he ran seventh again on August 1, 1992, in Barcelona, Spain.

5158. Runner from the Caribbean to win the women's 400-meter title in the Olympic Games was Marie-José Pérec, from the French island of Guadeloupe, racing for France. She won on August 5, 1992, in Barcelona, Spain, with a time of 48.83 seconds. She would win it again in 1996.

5159. Runner from Africa to win the women's 10,000-meter title, and the first Black African woman to win a medal, at the Olympic Games was Derartu Tulu of Ethiopia, with a time of 31:06.02 minutes on August 7, 1992, in Barcelona, Spain. Her victory lap was shared with silver medalist Elana Meyer, a white runner from South Africa, recently returned to the Olympics after a long ban because of its racist policies.

5160. Runner from Africa to win the women's 1500-meter title at the Olympic Games was Hassiba Boulmerka of Algeria, with a time of 3:55.30 minutes on August 8, 1992, in Barcelona, Spain. She became a heroine to many Islamic women, but was reviled by some Islamic fundamentalists for running bare-legged in view of men.

5161. Runner to win three consecutive gold medals in the women's 4 x 100-meter relay at the Olympic Games was Evelyn Ashford of the United States. After winning first in 1984 and 1988, she won her third gold medal on August 8, 1992, in Barcelona, Spain.

5162. Women's 1500-meter race in which the top four finishers all had times under 4 minutes was on August 8, 1992, at the Olympics in Barcelona, Spain, led by Hassiba Boulmerka of Algeria with a time of 3:55.30 minutes.

5163. Runner to race the men's 1500 meters in less than 3:29 minutes was Noureddine Morceli of Algeria, who pared the record to 3:28.86 minutes on September 6, 1992, in Rieti, Italy. He would lower it to 3:27.37 on July 12, 1995.

5164. Runner from the United States to win the women's 100-meter dash in the World Championships in Athletics was Gail Devers, with a time of 10.82 seconds in 1993 in Stuttgart, Germany.

5165. Runner from the United States to win the women's 400-meter race in the World Championships in Athletics was Jearl Miles, with a time of 49.82 seconds in 1993 in Stuttgart, Germany.

5166. Runner to win two, and then three, consecutive titles in the men's 1500-meter event in the World Championships in Athletics was Noureddine Morceli of Algeria. After winning in 1991, he came back in 1993 to win with 3:34.24 seconds in Stuttgart, Germany, and then again in 1995 with 3:33.73 seconds in Gothenburg, Sweden.

5167. Runner to win two, and then three, consecutive titles in the men's 3000-meter steeplechase in the World Championships in Athletics was Moses Kiptanui of Kenya. After winning first in 1991, he won in 1993 in Stuttgart, Germany, with a time of 8:06.36 minutes and then again in 1995 in Gothenburg, Sweden, with 8:04.16 minutes.

5168. Runner to race the men's 10,000 meters in under 27:00 minutes was Yobes Ondieki of Kenya. He lowered the record by almost 10 seconds, to 26:58.38 minutes, on July 10, 1993, in Oslo, Norway.

5169. Runner to race the women's 10,000 meters in under 30 minutes was Wang Junxia of China. Her landmark time of 29:31.78 minutes was set on September 8, 1993, in Beijing, China.

5170. Runner to complete the men's mile race in under 3:45 minutes was Noureddine Morceli of Algeria, who cut the record to 3:44.39 minutes on September 12, 1993, in Rieti, Italy.

5171. Runner to win both the men's 200- and 400-meter titles in the same World Championships in Athletics was Michael Johnson of the United States, who won them both in 1995 at Gothenburg, Sweden, with times of 19.79 seconds and 43.39 seconds respectively.

5172. Runner to win two consecutive titles in the men's 5000-meter event in the World Championships in Athletics was Ismael Kirui of Kenya. After first winning in 1993, he went back in 1995 to win in Gothenburg, Sweden, with a time of 13:16.77 minutes.

5173. Runner to win two consecutive titles in the women's 200-meter event in the World Championships in Athletics was Merlene Ottey of Jamaica. After winning in 1993, she did so again in 1995 in Gothenburg, Sweden, with a time of 22.12 seconds.

5174. Runner to win two, three, and then four consecutive titles in the men's 10,000-meter event in the World Championships in Athletics was Haile Gebrselassie of Ethiopia. After winning first in 1993, he won again at Gothenburg, Sweden, in 1995, with a time of 27:12.95 minutes; at Athens, Greece, in 1997, with 27:24.58; and at Seville, Spain, in 1999, with a time of 27.57.27.

5175. Runner to win two, three, and then four consecutive titles in the men's 400-meter event in the World Championships in Athletics was Michael Johnson of the United States. After winning first in 1993, he won again in 1995 in 43.39 seconds in Gothenburg, Sweden; in 1997 in 44.12 seconds in Athens, Greece; and in 1999 in a world-record 43.18 seconds in Seville, Spain.

5176. Runner to win two titles in the women's 1500-meter event in the World Championships in Athletics was Hassiba Boulmerka of Algeria. She had originally won in 1991, then won again in 1995 in Gothenburg, Sweden, with a time of 4:02.42 minutes.

5177. Runner to win two titles in the women's 400-meter event in the World Championships in Athletics was Marie-José Pérec, from the French island of Guadeloupe, racing for France. After winning first in 1991, she returned to win again in 1995 in Gothenburg, Sweden, with a time of 49.28 seconds.

5178. Runner to race the men's 5000-meter steeplechase in under 8:00 minutes was Moses Kiptanui of Kenya. Breaking his 1992 world record of 8:02.08 minutes, he set a time of 7:59.18 on August 16, 1995, in Zürich, Switzerland. For doing so, he was awarded $50,000 and a kilogram of gold. By 1997, he had lowered the record to 7:56.16.

5179. Runner to race the men's 5000 meters in under 12:55 minutes was Haile Gebrselassie of Ethiopia. Racing in Zürich, Switzerland, on August 16, 1995, he sliced the record to 12:44.39 minutes.

5180. Runner to race the women's 1000 meters in under 2:30 minutes was Maria Mutola of Mozambique, who shaved the record to 2:29.34 minutes on August 25, 1995, in Brussels, Belgium.

5181. Women's 5000-meter race held in the Olympic Games was in 1996 in Atlanta, Georgia. The winner was Wang Junxia of China, with a time of 14:59.88 minutes on July 28.

5182. Runner to win two consecutive titles in the women's 400-meter race in the Olympic Games was Marie-José Pérec of France's island of Guadeloupe. After winning in 1992, she set an Olympic record in 1996 with a time of 48.25 seconds on July 29 in Atlanta, Georgia. Two days later she also won the 200-meter event.

5183. Runner to complete the men's 200-meter race in under 19.7 seconds was Michael Johnson of the United States. He first broke Pietro Mennea's 17-year-old record of 19.72 with a time of 19.66 at the Olympic Trials in Atlanta, Georgia, on June 23, 1996, then shattered it with a 19.32 on August 1, at the Atlanta Olympics.

5184. Runner to win the men's 200- and 400-meter titles in the same Olympic Games was Michael Johnson of the United States, who won the 200-meter race with a world-record time of 19.32 seconds on August 1, 1996, in Atlanta, Georgia, and the 400-meter in an Olympic-record 43.49 seconds on July 29.

5185. Runner to win two consecutive titles in the women's 800-meter event in the World Championships in Athletics was Ana Quirot of Cuba. After her first win in 1995, she won again in 1997 in Athens, Greece, with a time of 1:57.14 minutes.

5186. Runner to race the men's 1500 meters in 3:26 minutes was Hicham El Gerrouj of Morocco, on July 14, 1998, in Rome, Italy, smashing the previous record of 3:29.91 minutes.

5187. Runner to win both the men's 100- and 200-meter titles in the same World Championships in Athletics was Maurice Greene of the United States. Competing at Seville, Spain, in 1999, he won the 100-meter event in 9.80 seconds and the 200-meter in 19.90 seconds. At the same meet, he also anchored the men's 4 x 100 relay team to a world-record time of 37.59 seconds.

RUNNING (2000-)

5188. Runner to win two consecutive men's 400-meter titles in the Olympic Games was Michael Johnson of the United States. On September 25, 2000, in Sydney, Australia, he won the 400 meters with a time of 43.84 seconds. That was well short of his Olympic-record 43.49 seconds for the same distance in the 1996 Games, where he had an unprecedented men's 200- and 400-meter double win. He was unable to defend his 200-meter title in 2000 because he pulled up lame in the trials for the event.

S

SAILBOARDING (WINDSURFING)

5189. Sailboard was developed in 1958 by 12-year-old Peter Chilvers of England. It would give rise to the sport variously called windsurfing, boardsailing, and sailboarding, developed in California from around 1968, primarily by Henry Hoyle Schweitzer and Jim Drake.

5190. World championships in sailboarding also called *boardsailing* or *windsurfing*, were held in 1973.

5191. Men's sailboarding event held in the Olympic Games was in 1984 in Los Angeles, California. Racing on August 8, Stephan van den Berg of the Netherlands won the inaugural event, which employed a 12-foot 9-inch board, with 70 square feet of sail.

5192. Women's sailboarding event held in the Olympic Games was in 1992 in Barcelona, Spain. Racing on August 2, the winner was Barbara Kendall of New Zealand. Her brother, Bruce Kendall, had won the 1988 men's event.

SAILBOAT AND YACHT RACING (BEFORE 1900)

5193. Sailing challenge race on record was in September 1, 1661, when England's King Charles II challenged his brother James, the Duke of York, to race on the Thames River from Greenwich to Gravesend for £100. Recently returned from exile in the Netherlands, where he had taken up yachting, the king won in his yacht *Mary*.

5194. Yacht club was the Cork Harbour Water Club (later the Royal Cork Yacht Club) of Cork, Ireland, established in 1720.

5195. Yacht club in England was the Cumberland Fleet, founded in 1775. It later became the Royal Thames Yacht Club.

5196. Yacht club in the United States was the Knickerbocker Club of New York City, founded in 1811. It survived for only a year.

5197. Organization of the New York Yacht Club which would later run the America's Cup challenge race, was in 1844.

5198. America's Cup was presented in 1851. Originally called the Hundred Guineas Cup, it was offered by Britain's Royal Yacht Squadron for a race circling the Isle of Wight, as part of England's Great Exhibition, a world's fair. The winner was the United States schooner *America*, which gave its name to the cup. It later became a challenge cup offered by the New York Yacht Club and was held against all challengers until 1983.

5199. Transatlantic sailing race was held in 1866, sponsored by the New York Yacht Club. Sailing from Sandy Hook, Connecticut, to Cowes, Isle of Wight, England, the *Henrietta*, owned by New York newspaper publisher James Gordon Bennett, won the three-yacht race.

5200. Single-handed sailing across the Atlantic was made in a 6-meter yacht in 1876 by Alfred Johnson, celebrating the centennial of the United States.

5201. Single-handed transatlantic race was in 1891, won by Si Lawlor of the United States.

5202. Sailor to complete a solo circumnavigation of the world was Joshua Slocum of Canada, in his 36-foot boat *Spray*. His journey began in Boston, Massachusetts, in April 1895 and ended in June 1898 when he arrived in Newport, Rhode Island, having sailed 46,000 miles in 3 years 2 months 2 days. A decade later he would be lost at sea en route to the Caribbean.

SAILBOAT AND YACHT RACING (1900-1949)

5203. Skipper to win the America's Cup sailing race twice in a row was James Barr in the United States yacht *Columbia*, which in 1899 and 1901 defeated English challengers *Shamrock* and then *Shamrock II*.

5204. Bermuda Race a 630-mile sailing race from Newport, Rhode Island, to Bermuda, was held in 1906 and has been held biennially since 1924, except in wartime, in alternate years from the Fastnet Race.

5205. 6-meter-class sailing event held in the Olympic Games was on July 29, 1908, in London, England, where the winners were Gilbert Laws, Thomas McMeekin, and Charles Crichton of Great Britain. The event would be held through 1952.

5206. 8-meter-class sailing event in the Olympic Games was on July 29, 1908, in London, England, where the winners were Blair Cochrane, Arthur Wood, Henry Sutton, John Rhodes, and Charles Campbell of Great Britain. The event would be discontinued after 1936.

5207. Woman to participate in an Olympic yachting event was Frances Clytie Rivett-Carnac of Great Britain in London, England, on July 29, 1908, when she was on the crew of the only boat entered in the 7-meter class, skippered by her husband, Charles Rivett-Carnac.

5208. Men's Finn-class sailing event in the Olympic Games was held in 1920 in Antwerp, Belgium. The original race was voided because of a dispute. A new race, held in the Netherlands because the remaining contestants were from there, was won by Johannes Hin and Franciscus Hin of the Netherlands on September 4.

5209. Fastnet Race was held in 1925. Held biennially, in alternate years from the Bermuda Race, this is a sailing race from Cowes, on England's Isle of Wight, along England's south coast to Ireland, around Fastnet Rock, and back to Plymouth, England.

5210. Woman to win an Olympic gold medal in sailing was Virginie Hériot of France, one of the crew in the winning boat in the 8-meter-class competition on August 9, 1928, in Amsterdam, the Netherlands.

5211. Sailing team from the United States to win the 8-meter-class event in the Olympic Games won on August 9, 1932, in Los Angeles, California.

5212. Star-class sailing event held in the Olympic Games was in 1932 in Los Angeles, California. Racing the two-person craft on August 12, Gilbert Gray and Andrew Libano of the United States emerged as the winners.

5213. Sailor to complete a solo circumnavigation of the world in under a year was Vito Dumas of Argentina, who did it in 272 days, with three stops, in 1942.

5214. Sydney-Hobart Race a 630-mile sailing race between Sydney, Australia, and Hobart, on the island of Tasmania, also part of Australia, was held in 1945. It traditionally starts on December 26.

5215. Father-and-son team to win the Star-class sailing event in the Olympic Games were Hilary Smart and his father, Paul Smart, on August 12, 1948, in London, England.

5216. Dragon-class sailing event held in the Olympic Games was in 1948 in London, England. The winners were Thor Thorvaldsen, Sigve Lie, and Håkon Barfod of Norway on August 12, who would win the event again on July 28, 1952, in Helsinki, Finland. This class event was discontinued after 1972.

SAILBOAT AND YACHT RACING (1950-1999)

5217. Sailors from the United States to win the 6-meter-class event in the Olympic Games were Herman Whiton, Alfred Loomis, James Weekes, James Smith, and Michael Mooney, on August 12, 1948, in London, England. Whiton would lead a new United States team to another win in 1952.

5218. 5.5-meter-class sailing event in the Olympic Games was on July 28, 1952, in Helsinki, Finland. The winners were Britton Chance, Sumner White, Edgar White, and Michael Schoettle of the United States. The event would be held through 1968.

5219. Sailor to win the men's Finn-class event two, three, and four times in the Olympic Games was Paul Elvström of Denmark. After his first win in 1948, he won again on July 28, 1952, in Helsinki, Finland; December 5, 1956, in Melbourne, Australia; and September 7, 1960, in Rome, Italy.

5220. Woman to sail across the Atlantic alone was Anne Davison of Great Britain in her yacht *Felicity Ann*. She completed her journey on August 13, 1953, in Miami, Florida, after starting on May 18, 1952, from Plymouth, England.

5221. Admiral's Cup race was held in 1957 in the English Channel, in the Solent off Cowes, Isle of Wight, base of Britain's Royal Yacht Squadron. An international race for three-boat national teams, it is held biennially. The English team was the first winner of the Admiral's Cup, offered by the Royal Ocean Racing Club.

5222. Single-Handed Transatlantic Race (STAR) was held in 1960. Sailing between Plymouth, England, and Newport, Rhode Island, the inaugural winner was Francis Chichester of Great Britain in his yacht *Gypsy Moth III*, with a time of 40 days 12 hours 30 minutes. The race would be held every four years from then on.

5223. Flying Dutchman–class sailing event held in the Olympic Games was on September 7, 1960, in Rome, Italy. The winners were Peder Lunde, Jr., and Björn Bergvall of Norway. The event would be discontinued after 1992.

SAILBOAT AND YACHT RACING—(1950-1999)—*continued*

5224. Single-handed, non-stop, round-the-world sailing race was the Golden Globe race, sponsored by London's *Sunday Times*, starting in 1968, inspired by British sailor Francis Chichester's 1966–1967 solo circumnavigation. The winner was Robin Knox-Johnston of England in his 32-foot boat *Suhaili*, in a 313-day journey.

5225. Sailors from the United States to win the Dragon-class event in the Olympic Games were George Friedrichs, Barton Jahncke, and Gerald Schreck, on October 21, 1968, in Mexico City.

5226. Woman to sail across the Pacific alone was Sharon Sites of the United States. On July 24, 1969, she arrived in San Diego, California, after leaving Yokohama, Japan, 74 days earlier.

5227. Sailor to complete a solo circumnavigation of the world from east to west against the prevailing winds, was Chay Blyth of England, in 1970.

5228. Sailor to win two consecutive gold medals in the Flying Dutchman–class event in the Olympic Games was Rodney Pattison of Great Britain. After winning in 1968 with Iain Macdonald-Smith, he returned to win again on September 8, 1972, in Munich, West Germany, this time with Christopher Davies.

5229. Soling-class sailing event held in the Olympic Games was in 1972 in Munich, West Germany. Racing the three-person boat on September 8, the winners were Buddy (Harry) Melges, William Bentsen, and William Allen of the United States.

5230. Tempest-class sailing event in the Olympic Games was on September 8, 1972, in Munich, West Germany, where the winners were Valentyn Mankin and Vitaly Dyrdyra of the Soviet Union. The event was discontinued after 1976.

5231. Sailor to complete a solo circumnavigation of the world in under 170 days was Alain Colas of France, who completed the journey in the multi-hull craft *Manuréva* in 169 days in 1973, with a single stop in Sydney, Australia.

5232. Whitbread Round-the-World Race was begun in August 1973. Sponsored by the Royal Naval Sailing Association and held every four years, the race began and ended at Portsmouth, England, and followed a route around the Cape of Good Hope and Cape Horn. Arriving back in Portsmouth in 1974, the winner of the multi-class handicap race was the yacht *Sayula II*, skippered by Ramon Carlin of Mexico, with a time of 152 days 9 hours. The fastest yacht, without a handicap, was *Great Britain II*, skippered by Chay Blyth, with 144 days 10 hours.

5233. International sailing championships for women were held in May 1974 in Quiberon, France, with 80 women from 11 countries participating. The first individual winner, in the dinghy class, was Martine Allix of France.

5234. Sailor to win the Single-Handed Transatlantic Race (STAR) twice was Éric Tabarly of France. After his first victory in 1964, Tabarly came back in 1976 to win again in his yacht *Pen Duick VI*, with a time of 23 days 20 hours 12 minutes.

5235. 470-class sailing event held at the Olympic Games was in 1976 in Montreal. Sailing the two-person craft on July 27, the winners were Frank Hübner and Harro Bode of West Germany. This event was open to both women and men until 1988, when a separate women's event was inaugurated.

5236. Tornado-class sailing event held in the Olympic Games was in 1976 in Montreal. Sailing the two-person catamaran on July 28, Reginald White and his brother-in-law John Osborn of Great Britain won the inaugural event.

5237. Woman to sail around the world alone was Krystyna Choynowska-Kiskiewicz of Poland. Leaving Las Palmas, in the Canary Islands, on March 28, 1976, she sailed westward, returning on March 26, 1978.

5238. Sailor from the United States to win the Single-Handed Transatlantic Race (STAR), and the first to make the crossing in under 20 hours was Phil Weld in his yacht *Moxie* in 1980, crossing in 17 days 23 hours 12 minutes.

5239. Sailor to win gold medals in three different sailing events in the Olympic Games was Valentyn Mankin of the Soviet Union. His wins came in the Finn class on October 21, 1968, in Mexico City; the Tempest class on September 8, 1972, in Munich, West Germany, with Vitaly Dyrdyra; and the Star class on July 29, 1980, in Moscow, the Soviet Union, with Aleksandr Muzicenko. The event was not held in 1976.

5240. BOC Challenge Race a solo round-the-world race for monohulled boats, was held in 1982. The first winner was Philippe Jeantot who completed the circumnavigation in 159 days 2 hours 26 minutes. He would win again in 1986. From 1998, the quadrennial race would be known as the Around Alone race.

5241. Sailor to win the Whitbread Round-the-World Race twice consecutively was Cornelis van Rietschoten of the Netherlands. After winning in 1978 in *Flyer*, he won again skippering *Flyer II* in 1982, with a time of 120 days 6 hours 35 minutes.

5242. America's Cup sailing race not won by the United States was in 1983, when the Australian boat *Australia II*, skippered by John Bertrand, first won the cup away from the Americans on September 26.

5243. Sailors from the United States to win the Flying Dutchman–class event in the Olympic Games were Jonathan McKee and William Carl Buchan, on August 8, 1984, in Los Angeles, California.

5244. Woman to be skipper of a boat in an Olympic competition was Catherine Foster of Great Britain in the 470-class sailing event, then open to both men and women, on August 8, 1984, in Los Angeles, California. She and Peter Newlands finished seventh.

5245. Sailor to complete a solo circumnavigation of the world in 150 days was Dodge Moran of the United States in 1985.

5246. Sailor to complete a solo circumnavigation of the world in under 130 days was Philippe Monet of France in 1985 in the trimaran *Kriter*. That would lowered to 125 days by Olivier de Kersauson in another trimaran in 1989.

5247. America's Cup won back by the United States after its loss in 1983, was in 1987, when the yacht *Stars and Stripes*, skippered by Dennis Conner, won it back over Australia's *Kookaburra III*.

5248. Sailor in the Single-Handed Transatlantic Race (STAR) to cross the Atlantic in under 11 days was Philippe Poupon of France in his yacht *Fleury Michon* in 1988, with a time of 10 days 9 hours 15 minutes.

5249. Women's 470-class sailing event held in the Olympic Games was in 1988 in Seoul, South Korea. Racing the two-person craft on September 27, Allison Jolly and Lynne Jewell of the United States won the inaugural event.

5250. Vendée Globe round-the-world challenge race was begun in 1989. Titouan Lamazou of France won the singlehanded, nonstop, real-time race in 109 days 8 hours 48 minutes and 50 seconds in his 60-foot yacht *Ecureuil d'Aquitaine*, leaving Les Sables d'Olonne, France, on November 26, 1989, and returning there on March 15, 1990, via the Cape of Good Hope and Cape Horn.

5251. Sailor to win two consecutive Tornado-class sailing titles in the Olympic Games was Nicolas Hénard of France. After winning in 1988 with Jean-Yves Le Déroff, he won again on August 2, 1992, in Barcelona, Spain, this time with Yves Loday.

5252. Women's Europe-class sailing event held in the Olympic Games was in 1992 in Barcelona, Spain. The winner was Linda Andersen of Norway on August 3.

5253. Sailor to win both the America's Cup and an Olympic gold medal in sailing was Buddy (Harry) Melges. Co-skipper of the victorious *America³* in the 1992 America's Cup race, he had been in the three-man crew that won the Olympic gold medal in the Soling class on September 8, 1972, in Munich, West Germany.

5254. America's Cup sailing race won by New Zealand was in 1995, when Russell Coutts skippered the *Black Magic* to a win over the United States yacht *Young America*.

5255. Sailor to win the Single-Handed Transatlantic Race (STAR) twice consecutively was Loïck Peyron of France. Sailing in his yacht *Fuijicolor II*, he won first in 1992 and then in 1996, the latter with a time of 10 days 10 hours 5 minutes.

5256. Laser-class sailing event held in the Olympic Games with crews including both women and men, was in 1996 in Atlanta, Georgia, where the winning yacht was captained by Robert Scheidt of Brazil on July 31.

5257. Sailor from the United States to win the Whitbread Round-the-World Race was Paul Cayard skippering the yacht *E. F. Language* in 1998. The winner was determined by points awarded by performance on various legs of the race.

SAILBOAT AND YACHT RACING (2000-)

5258. Open 49er-class sailing event held in the Olympic Games with crews open to both women and men, was in 2000 in Sydney, Australia. Thomas Johanson and Jyrki Jarvi of Finland won the gold medal on September 25 with a score of 55 points.

SHINTY (CAMANACHD)

5259. Formal organization for the game of shinty (*camanachd*) was the Camanachd Association, founded in Scotland in 1893. The 12-a-side team game, played with a curved stick (*caman*) and ball, may have been derived from hurling, a game brought to Scotland by immigrants from Ireland more than a dozen centuries earlier.

SHINTY (CAMANACHD)—*continued*

5260. Camanachd Association Challenge Cup for the sport of shinty (*camanachd*) was offered in Scotland in 1896, and annually since then. The winner of the first competition was the team from Kingussie.

SHOOTING (BEFORE 1900)
5261. Shooting club on record was the Lucerne Shooting Guild founded in approximately 1466 in Lucerne, Switzerland.

5262. Shooting tournament on record was held in Zürich, Switzerland, in 1472.

5263. National organization for shooting in Great Britain was the National Rifle Association of Great Britain, founded in 1860.

5264. Substitute for live birds in shooting competitions was a glass ball developed in England in around 1860.

5265. Use of glass ball targets in United States shooting competitions was in 1866, when they were introduced by Captain Adam H. Bogardus of Elkhart, Indiana.

5266. National governing body in shooting in the United States was the National Rifle Association, founded shortly after the Civil War, in 1871, by some National Guard officers. It would also govern Olympic shooting until 1995, when that role was taken over by USA Shooting.

5267. International rifle tournament held in the United States was on September 26, 1871, in Creedmor, Long Island, New York, sponsored by the recently founded National Rifle Association. Competing for a prize of $500, the competitors were the Irish Long Range Rifle Team, a team from the Ulster Rifle Club in northern Ireland, and a United States team from the New York Amateur Rifle Club in New York City, led by General George W. Wingate. The U.S. team won on the last shot, made by Colonel John Bodine.

5268. Clay pigeons for target shooting were developed in 1880 by George Ligowsky of Cincinnati, Ohio.

5269. Free rifle individual shooting event held in the Olympic Games was on April 9, 1896, in Athens, Greece. The winner of the inaugural competition was Pantelis Karasevdas, who led a Greek sweep of the top five positions. The event would be discontinued after 1908.

5270. Military revolver individual shooting event held in the Olympic Games was on April 10, 1896, in Athens, Greece. John Paine of the United States won the competition. The silver medalist was his brother, Sumner Paine, who would win the free pistol title the following day. The event was discontinued after 1906.

5271. Free pistol shooting individual event held in the Olympic Games was on April 11, 1896, in Athens, Greece. Sumner Paine of the United States won that first competition, though he had joined the U.S. contingent on a whim, joining his brother, John Paine, and other Boston Athletic Association members as they passed through Paris, France, where he was working.

5272. Rapid-fire pistol shooting individual event held in the Olympic Games was on April 11, 1896, in Athens, Greece. The winner of the inaugural competition was Ioannis Phrangoudis of Greece. The competition would be for men only until 1968.

5273. Free rifle (three position) individual shooting event held in the Olympic Games was on April 12, 1896, in Athens, Greece. Greek sharpshooter Georgios Orphanidis won that first competition. The day before he had been silver-medalist in the first rapid-fire pistol event. The event would be discontinued after 1972.

5274. World championships in shooting were the World Shooting Championships held in 1897 in Lyon, France, sponsored by five European countries.

SHOOTING (1900-1949)
5275. National trap shooting tournament in the United States was the Grand American Trapshoot held in 1900, sponsored by the Interstate Association of Trapshooters (IAT), later known as the American Trapshooting Association. The inaugural tournament was won by R. O. Heikes.

5276. Trap (clay pigeon) shooting individual event held in the Olympic Games was on July 15, 1900, in Paris, France. Roger de Barbarin led a French sweep of the top six spots.

5277. Moving target individual shooting event held in the Olympic Games was in 1900 in Paris, France. Louis Debray won the inaugural competition on July 17, leading a French sweep of the top six spots.

5278. National team to sweep the rapid-fire pistol individual shooting event in the Olympic Games was from France. Competing in Paris, France, Maurice Larrouy, Léon Moreaux, Eugène Balme, and Paul Moreau took the top four spots on August 4, 1900.

5279. Military rifle individual shooting event held in the Olympic Games was on August 5, 1900, in Paris, France. Emil Kellenberger of Switzerland won the 300-meter, three-position competition; Lars Jörgen Madsen of Denmark the 300-meter standing; Konrad Stäheli of Switzerland the 300-meter kneeling; and Achille Paroche of France the 300-meter prone. The competitions would be discontinued after 1920.

5280. Military revolver and military rifle team shooting events held in the Olympic Games were in 1900 in Paris, France, both won by teams from Switzerland. Winning the first revolver competition on August 1 were Conrad Karl Röderer, Konrad Stäheli, Louis Richardet, Friedrich Lüthi, and Paul Probst. On August 5, Stäheli, Richardet, Emil Kellenberger, Franz Böckli, and Alfred Grütter captured the rifle title. The revolver event would be discontinued after 1912 and the rifle after 1920.

5281. Free rifle team shooting event held in the Olympic Games was in 1906 in Athens, Greece. Winning that first competition on April 28 was the team from Switzerland: Konrad Stäheli, Jean Reich, Louis Richardet, Marcel Meyer de Stadelhofen, and Alfred Grütter.

5282. Dueling pistol shooting events held in the Olympic Games were in 1906 in Athens, Greece, with contestants shooting at dummies in full fancy dress. Léon Moreaux of France won the 20-meter competition on April 24 and Konstantinos Skarlatos of Greece the 25-meter on April 25. The events were never held again.

5283. International governing body in shooting was the Union Internationale de Tir (UIT), founded in Zürich, Switzerland, in 1907. It would become the International Shooting Sport Federation (ISSF) in 1998.

5284. Running deer (double shot) individual shooting event held in the Olympic Games was on July 11, 1908, in London, England. Walter Winans of the United States won that inaugural event, discontinued after 1924.

5285. Running deer (single shot) individual shooting event held in the Olympic Games was on July 11, 1908, in London, England. The gold medal went to 60-year-old Oscar Swahn. He won another gold medal in the team competition, as did his son Alfred Swahn, who would win the individual title in 1912. The event would be discontinued after 1924.

5286. Running deer (single shot) team shooting event held in the Olympic Games was on July 11, 1908, in London, England. The winning team was from Sweden: Oscar Swahn (the 1908 individual gold medalist in the event), Alfred Swahn (his son, and the 1912 individual gold medalist), Arvid Knöppel, and Ernst Rosell. The event would be discontinued after 1924.

5287. Shooters from the United States to win the military revolver team event in the Olympic Games were James Gorman, Ira Calkins, John Dietz, and Charles Axtell, who won the gold medal on July 11, 1908, in London, England.

5288. Shooters from the United States to win the military rifle team shooting title in the Olympic Games were William Leushner, William Martin, Charles Winder, Kellogg Kennon Casey, Albert Eastman, and Charles Benedict. They won the event on July 11, 1908 in London, England.

5289. Small-bore rifle moving and disappearing target individual shooting events held in the Olympic Games were in 1908 in London, England. On July 11, John Fleming led a British sweep of the top seven positions in the 25-yard moving target event, while William Styles led a British sweep of the top six spots in the 25-yard disappearing target competition. The events would be discontinued after 1920.

5290. Small-bore rifle (prone) individual shooting event held in the Olympic Games was in 1908 in London, England. That first competition was won by Arthur Carnell of Great Britain on July 11. He had actually been beaten by teammate Philip Plater, who was disqualified on a technicality: too many British shooters had been allowed to compete and, as the last shooter, Plater had his score nullified.

5291. Small-bore rifle team shooting event held in the Olympic Games was on July 11, 1908 in London, England, where the British team won: Michael Matthews, Harold Humby, William Pimm, and Edward Amoore.

SHOOTING—(1900-1949)—*continued*

5292. Trap (clay pigeon) team shooting event in the Olympic Games was on July 11, 1908, in London, England. The winning team was from Great Britain: Alexander Maunder, James Pike, Charles Palmer, John Postans, Frank Moore, and Philip Easte. It would be discontinued after 1924.

5293. Skeet shooting was developed for practice shooting by game hunters at the Glen Rock Kennels in Andover, Massachusetts, in 1910. Developed as a sport, it became widely popular after an influential 1926 article on skeet shooting, published in 1926 by William H. Foster, editor of *National Sportsman* and *Hunting and Fishing*.

5294. Shooters from the United States to win the trap (clay pigeon) team shooting event in the Olympic Games were Charles Billings, Ralph Spotts, John Hendrickson, James Graham, Edward Gleason, and Frank Hall, who won on July 1, 1912, in Stockholm, Sweden. Graham would win the individual title the following day.

5295. Shooter from the United States to win the men's trap (clay pigeon) individual shooting title in the Olympic Games was James Graham, who won on July 2, 1912, in Stockholm, Sweden.

5296. Shooter to win both the rapid-fire pistol and the free pistol individual events, and the first from the United States to win either event, in the Olympic Games was Alfred Lane. Competing in Stockholm, Sweden, he won the rapid-fire pistol title on June 29, 1912, and the free pistol on July 2, the same day he won a gold medal in the military revolver team event. In 1920, he would also win gold medals in the rapid-fire and free pistol team competitions, the only time they were held.

5297. Running deer (double shot) team shooting event held in the Olympic Games was on July 26, 1920, in Antwerp, Belgium. It was won by the team from Norway: Ole Andreas Lilloe-Olsen (who was also individual gold medalist in 1920 and 1924), Thorstein Johansen, Harald Natvig, Hans Nordvik, and Einar Liberg.

5298. Shooter to win five gold medals in shooting in the Olympic Games was Carl Osburn of the United States. On the winning military rifle team in 1912, he won two more military rifle team titles in 1920: in the 300 meters prone and the 300 + 600 meters prone, both on July 29, 1920, when he also won the individual military rifle competition (300 meters standing). Two days later he was on the gold-medal-winning free rifle team. He also won four silver and two bronze medals.

5299. Rapid-fire pistol and free pistol team events held in the Olympic Games were in 1920 at Antwerp, Belgium. United States teams won both events. On August 2, Karl Frederick, Alfred Lane, James Snook, Michael Kelly, and Raymond Bracken won the free pistol team title. The next day Lane, Frederick, Snook, Kelly, and Louis Harant won the rapid-fire pistol team competition. The team events were never held again.

5300. Shooters from the United States to win the small-bore rifle team title in the Olympic Games were Lawrence Nuesslein, Arthur Rothrock, Dennis Fenton, Willis Lee, and Ollie Schriver, who won on August 2, 1920, in Antwerp, Belgium.

5301. International governing body for trap shooting was the Fédération Internationale de Tir aux Armes Sportives de Chasse (FITASC), established in 1921. It would sponsor world and European championships from 1929.

5302. Shooter to win two consecutive titles in the men's free rifle (three positions) individual shooting event, and in the free rifle team event, in the Olympic Games was Morris Fisher of the United States. After winning medals in both the individual and team events in 1920, he won his second in each in Paris, France, on June 27, 1924. He also won a gold medal in the military rifle team competition in 1920.

5303. Shooter to win two consecutive titles in the running deer (double shot) individual shooting event in the Olympic Games was Ole Andreas Lilloe-Olsen. He first won in 1920, when he also was on the winning team in the event, and then captured his second individual gold medal on July 3, 1924, in Paris, France.

5304. National championships in skeet shooting were the American Skeet Shooting Championship held in 1935.

5305. Shooter to achieve a perfect score in international competition was Al Hemming of Detroit, Michigan, who had a perfect score of 300 on July 6, 1940, at the world pistol shooting championships.

SHOOTING (1950-1999)
5306. Woman to win the Grand American Trapshoot was Joan Pflueger at Vandalia, Ohio, in 1950, the only woman in the field. After breaking 100 consecutive clay pigeons, she won a five-person shootout.

5307. Shooter to win two consecutive men's rapid-fire pistol titles in the Olympic Games was Károly Takács of Hungary. After setting a world record in 1948, he won again on July 28, 1952, in Helsinki, Finland. His achievement was even more remarkable because he had been a pistol champion in 1938 when a grenade exploded in his right hand, his shooting hand. His Olympic medals were won after he then taught himself to shoot with his left hand.

5308. Running deer (single and double shot) individual shooting event held in the Olympic Games was on July 29, 1952, in Helsinki, Finland. The inaugural winner was John Larsen. It would be held only once more, in 1956.

5309. Small-bore rifle (three positions) individual shooting event held in the Olympic Games was in 1952 in Helsinki, Finland. Erling Kongshaug of Norway won the inaugural competition on July 29.

5310. Shooter from the United States to win the men's small-bore rifle (three positions) title in the Olympic Games was Lones Wigger, an Army captain, who set a world record in the competition on September 8, 1964, in Tokyo, Japan

5311. Women to compete in shooting events in the Olympic Games were Eulalia Rolinska of Poland and Gladys de Seminario of Peru in 1968, the first time that women were allowed to compete in what had previously been men-only events. Competing in Mexico City on August 28, Rolinska finished 22nd and de Seminario 31st in the small-bore rifle (prone) event. Separate women's events would be established in 1984.

5312. Skeet shooting individual event held in the Olympic Games was in 1968 in Mexico City, where Yevgeny Petroc of the Soviet Union won on October 22.

5313. Woman to win a medal in shooting at the Olympic Games was Margaret Murdock, a nurse from Kansas, who won a silver medal in the small-bore rifle (three positions) individual event. In the July 21, 1976, competition in Montreal, Quebec, Canada, Murdock was tied in points at the end with U.S. teammate Lanny Bassham, but lost the gold because of a tie-break rule: he had scored three 100s, and she had only two.

5314. World championships in sporting clay shooting were held in 1979, sponsored by the Fédération Internationale de Tir aux Armes Sportives de Chasse (FITASC).

5315. Shooting championships sponsored by the National Collegiate Athletic Association (NCAA) were in 1980, and held annually from then on.

5316. Women's sport pistol individual shooting event held in the Olympic Games was in 1984 in Los Angeles, California. Winning the inaugural event on July 29 was Linda Thom, a chef from Canada.

5317. Shooter to win two consecutive individual trap (clay pigeon) shooting titles in the Olympic Games was Luciano Giovannetti of Italy. After winning in 1980, the gun-shop owner won a second time on July 31, 1984, in Los Angeles, California.

5318. Women's air rifle individual shooting event in the Olympic Games was in 1984 in Los Angeles, California. Pat Spurgin of the United States won that first competition on July 31.

5319. Women's small-bore rifle (three positions) individual shooting event held in the Olympic Games was in 1984 in Los Angeles, California. Winning on August 2 was Wu Xiaoxuan of China, who had taken the bronze medal in the air rifle competition two days earlier.

5320. Air rifle shooting individual event held in the Olympic Games was in 1984 in Los Angeles, California. Philippe Hébérle, a firefighter from France, won the inaugural competition on August 3.

5321. Shooter from the United States to win the individual skeet-shooting title in the Olympic Games was Matthew Dryke, a trick shooter who won on August 4, 1984, in Los Angeles, California.

SHOOTING—(1950-1999)—*continued*

5322. Women's air pistol individual shooting event held in the Olympic Games was in 1988 in Seoul, South Korea. World champion Jasna Sekaric of Yugoslavia set a new world record in the inaugural competition on September 21.

5323. Shooter to win two consecutive titles in the small-bore rifle (three positions) individual event in the Olympic Games was Malcolm Cooper of Great Britain. After his initial win in 1984, he went to Seoul, South Korea, where he won again on September 22, 1988.

5324. Shooter from the United States to win the women's small-bore rifle (three positions) event at the Olympic Games was Launi Melli, who won on July 30, 1992, in Barcelona, Spain.

5325. Women's double trap (clay pigeon) individual shooting event held in the Olympic Games was in 1996 in Atlanta, Georgia. Kim Rhode of the United States won the first title on July 23.

5326. Men's double trap (clay pigeon) individual shooting event held in the Olympic Games was held in 1996 in Atlanta, Georgia. Winning the inaugural event on July 24 was Russell Mark of Australia.

SHOOTING (2000-)

5327. Women's trap shooting event held in the Olympic Games was in 2000 in Sydney, Australia. Daina Gudzineviciute of Lithuania took the gold medal with a score of 93.0 on September 18.

5328. Women's skeet shooting event held in the Olympic Games was in 2000 in Sydney, Australia. Zemfira Meftakhetdinova of Azerbaijan won the event with a score of 98.0 on September 21.

SHOT PUT

5329. Men's shot put event held in the Olympic Games was in 1896 in Athens, Greece. Winning that first event on April 7 was Robert Garrett of the United States, with a put of 36 feet 9¾ inches. He also won the first discus competition.

5330. National team to sweep the top spots in the men's shot put in the Olympic Games was the United States, on July 15, 1900, in Paris, France, led by Richard Sheldon with an Olympic-record distance of 46 feet 3¼ inches.

5331. Shot-putter to hold the officially accepted world record in the men's event was Ralph Rose of the United States with a put of 51 feet 0 inches (15.54 meters) on August 21, 1909, in San Francisco, California. It would stand until 1928.

5332. Men's shot put event for both hands held in the Olympic Games was in 1912 in Stockholm, Sweden. With a total distance of 90 feet 10½ inches (27.70 meters) for the two throws, Ralph Rose of the United States won on July 11, the only time the event was held.

5333. Shot-putter to break the 16-meter barrier was Emil Hirschfeld of Germany, with a put of 52 feet 7½ inches (16.04 meters) on August 26, 1928, in Bochum, Germany.

5334. Shot-putter to hold the officially accepted world record in the women's event was Gisela Mauermayer of Germany, who set her benchmark distance of 47 feet 2¼ inches (14.38 meters) on July 15, 1934, in Warsaw, Poland.

5335. Shot-putter to break the 17-meter barrier was Jack Torrance of the United States, with a put of 57 feet 1 inch (17.40 meters) on August 5, 1934, in Oslo, Norway. It was the third of his world records, all set in 1934.

5336. Women's shot put event held in the Olympic Games was on August 4, 1948, in London, England. The inaugural event was won with a put of 45 feet 1½ inches by Micheline Ostermeyer of France, a concert pianist who also won the discus and placed third in the high jump at the same Olympics.

5337. Shot-putter to break the 15-meter barrier in the women's event was Anna Andreyeva of the Soviet Union, who set a mark of 15.02 meters (49 feet 3¼ inches) on November 9, 1950, in Ploesti, Romania.

5338. Shot-putter to break the 50-foot barrier in the women's event was Galina Zybina of the Soviet Union, with a put of 50 feet 1⅛ inches (15.28 meters) at the Olympic Games in Helsinki, Finland, on July 26, 1952. It was the first of her eight world records in the event.

5339. Shot-putter to break the 16-meter barrier in the women's event was Galina Zybina of the Soviet Union. In the fourth of her eight world records, she had a put of 16.20 meters (53 feet 1⅛ inches) on October 9, 1953, in Malmö, Sweden.

5340. Shot-putter to break the 18- and 19-meter, and 60-foot, barriers was Parry O'Brien of the United States. His first world record came on May 9, 1953, at Compton, California, with a put of 59 feet ¾ inches (18.00 meters) in the men's event. His eighth world record came on September 3, 1956, in Eugene, Oregon, with a put of 62 feet 6¼ inches (19.06 meters), which he would extend to 63 feet 4 inches (19.38 meters) in 1959. In between, he first broke the 60-foot mark on May 8, 1954, with a put of 60 feet 5¼ inches in Los Angeles, California.

5341. Shot-putter to win two consecutive men's titles in the Olympic Games was Parry O'Brien of the United States. The world record-holder and 1952 Olympic medalist won his second Olympic title on November 28, 1956, in Melbourne, Australia, with an Olympic-record put of 60 feet 11¼ inches. O'Brien introduced to shot put the technique of starting the throw with his back turned, and rotating the body in the direction of the throw, a move developed in 1951 after an injury.

5342. Shot-putter to break the 17- and 18-meter, and 60-foot, barriers in the women's event was Tamara Press of the Soviet Union. In the first of her six world records, she had a distance of 17.25 meters (56 feet 7¼ inches) on April 26, 1959, in Nalchik, the Soviet Union. In her fourth, she had a put of 18.55 meters (60 feet 10¼ inches), on June 10, 1962, in Leipzig, East Germany.

5343. Shot-putter to break the 20-meter barrier was Bill Nieder of the United States. In the third of his world records, he had a put of 65 feet 10 inches (20.06 meters), on August 12, 1960, in Walnut, California.

5344. Shot-putter to win two consecutive titles in the women's event in the Olympic Games was Tamara Press of the Soviet Union. After winning first in 1960, she came back for another gold medal on October 20, 1964, with an Olympic-record put of 59 feet 6¼ inches in Tokyo, Japan, where she also won the discus throw.

5345. Shot-putter to break the 70-foot and 21-meter barriers was Randy (James Randel) Matson of the United States, with a put of 70 feet 7¼ inches (21.52 meters) on May 8, 1965, in College Station, Texas. He would be the Olympic gold medalist in 1968.

5346. Shot-putter to break the 19-meter barrier in the women's event was Margitta Helmboldt Gummel of East Germany. En route to the championship at the Mexico City Olympic Games, she had two record-shattering puts on October 20, 1968: one of 62 feet 6¼ inches (19.07 meters), the other of 64 feet 4 inches (19.61 meters).

5347. Shot-putter to break the 20- and 21-meter barriers in the women's event was Nadezhda Chizhova of the Soviet Union. She broke the first with a put of 20.09 meters (65 feet 11 inches), on July 13, 1969, in Chorzow, Poland, and the second with 21.03 meters (69 feet 0 inches) on September 7, 1972, in Munich, West Germany.

5348. Shot-putter to break the 70-foot barrier in the women's event was Marianne Adam of East Germany. Competing in Berlin, Germany, she had a put of 70 feet 10¼ inches (21.60 meters) on August 6, 1975.

5349. Shot-putter to break the 22-meter barrier was Aleksandr Baryshnikov of the Soviet Union, with a put of 72 feet 2¼ inches (22.00 meters) in the men's event on July 10, 1976, in Paris, France.

5350. Shot-putter to break the 23-meter barrier was Ulf Timmermann of East Germany, who had a distance of 75 feet 8 inches (23.06 meters) in Khania, on the island of Crete, in Greece, on May 22, 1988.

SKATEBOARDING

5351. Urethane wheel used on skateboards appeared in 1973. Giving much greater control, this made skateboards far more popular than they had ever been since they were first developed in the 1930s in California.

5352. National governing body for skateboarding was the National Skateboarding Association (NSA), founded in 1981, with an assist from the Boy Scouts of America.

SKIING (BEFORE 1900)

5353. Skiing manual was written in 1733 by Captain Jens Emmahausan of Norway.

5354. Organized Nordic (cross-country) ski races on record date to 1767 in Norway, where military skiers vied for cash prizes. Skis had been used for travel and transport from at least 2500 BC, but sport skiing developed only in the 18th century.

5355. Formally measured ski jump was by Sondre Norheim in Norway in 1860. Sometimes called the father of ski jumping, he developed ski bindings at around the same time.

245

SKIING—(BEFORE 1900)—*continued*

5356. Ski-jumping contest focusing on jumping alone rather than in combination with downhill or cross-country skiing, was held in 1862 in Trysil, Norway.

5357. Ski club in the United States was founded in Berlin, New Hampshire, in 1872. It would survive as the Nansen Ski Club, named after Norwegian explorer Fridtjof Nansen.

5358. National organization for skiing was founded in Norway in 1883.

5359. Organized ski-jumping competition in the United States was held on February 8, 1887, in Red Wing, Minnesota, sponsored by the Aurora Ski Club. Mikkel Hemmestvedt won the men's title.

SKIING (1900-1929)
5360. World championships for Nordic skiing were held in 1925, originally for men only, sponsored by the Fédération Internationale de Ski (FIS). Held annually, they were not considered "official" world championships until 1937. After World War II, they were held biennially.

5361. International governing body for competitive skiing was the International Skiing Commission, founded in 1910 in Oslo, Norway. It would be replaced in 1924 by the Fédération Internationale de Ski (FIS).

5362. Organized downhill ski race was held at Crans-Montana, Switzerland, in 1911, instituted by skier Arnold Lunn of Great Britain.

5363. Modern slalom course was created in 1922 by skier Arnold Lunn of Great Britain.

5364. Vasalopp long-distance ski race was held in March 1922, over a distance of 90 kilometers from Sälen to Mora, Sweden, commemorating a 1521 journey by Sweden's King Gustaf Vasa.

5365. Men's 50-kilometer freestyle Nordic (cross-country) skiing event held at the Olympic Winter Games was in 1924 in Chamonix, France. The inaugural event was won on January 30 by Thorleif Haug with a time of 3:44:32 hours, leading a Norwegian sweep of the top four spots.

5366. Men's individual 18-kilometer Nordic (cross-country) event held at the Olympic Winter Games was in Chamonix, France, in 1924. Thorleif Haug won the inaugural competition on February 2 with a time of 1:14:31.0 hours. The race would be changed to 15 kilometers in 1956 and was discontinued after 1988.

5367. Men's individual Nordic combined (cross-country and ski jump) event held in the Olympic Winter Games was in 1924 in Chamonix, France. Winning on February 4 with a combined total of 18.906 points was Thorleif Haug of Norway.

5368. Men's individual ski jump event held at the Olympic Winter Games was in 1924 in Chamonix, France. The winner was Jacob Tullin Thams of Norway, who scored a two-jump total of 18.960 points on February 4. The original 90-meter jump is now called the *large hill*; the 70-meter jump, added to the Olympics in 1964, is now the *normal hill*.

5369. National team to sweep the medals in the men's combined individual Nordic (cross-country) skiing event at the Olympic Winter Games was Norway, which took the top four spots on February 4, 1924, in Chamonix, France, led by Thorleif Haug.

5370. Skier for the United States to win a ski-jumping medal at the Olympic Winter Games was Norwegian-born Anders Haugen in 1924. In the first men's individual 90-meter ski jump event on February 4, in Chamonix, France, he placed third with a total of 17.916 points for two jumps. He did not receive his medal until 50 years later, however, when the 1974 discovery and correction of a computation error revealed that he had won the bronze medal, then awarded to him in a special ceremony.

5371. Men's 18-kilometer cross-country event held in the world championships of Nordic skiing was in 1925, where the first champion was Otokar Nemecky of Czechoslovakia. The event would be discontinued after 1950.

5372. Men's 50-kilometer cross-country event held in the world championships of Nordic skiing was in 1925, when Frantisek Donth of Czechoslovakia won the title.

5373. Men's ski jumping (normal hill) event held in the world championships of Nordic skiing was in 1925, when Willi Dick of Czechoslovakia won the title. Originally set at 90 meters, the "normal hill" would later be 70 meters.

5374. Nordic combined event held in the world championships of Nordic skiing was in 1925, when Otokar Nemecky of Czechoslovakia won the first title.

5375. Men's 30-kilometer cross-country event held in the world championships of Nordic skiing was in 1926, when Matti Raivo of Finland won the first title. It would not be held again until 1954.

5376. National team to sweep the medals in the men's 15-kilometer Nordic (cross-country) skiing event in the Olympic Winter Games was Norway, led by Johan Gröttumsbråten, on February 17, 1928, at St. Moritz, Switzerland.

SKIING (1930-1939)

5377. World championships in Alpine skiing were held in 1931 in Mürren, Switzerland. David Zogg of Switzerland won the inaugural men's slalom title, and Walter Prager of Switzerland the men's downhill. Esme MacKinnon of Great Britain won both events on the women's side. The championships were held annually until 1939, and again from 1995, but biennially from 1950 to 1993.

5378. Skier to win two consecutive men's individual Nordic combined titles in the Olympic Winter Games was Johan Gröttumsbråten of Norway. His second win came on February 11, 1932, at Lake Placid, New York, where he had a combined total (cross-country and ski jump) of 446.00 points. He had previously won in 1928.

5379. National team to sweep the medals in the men's 90-meter ski jump at the Olympic Winter Games was Norway, led by Birger Ruud, on February 12, 1932, in Lake Placid, New York.

5380. Men's 4 x 10-kilometer cross-country relay event held in the world championships of Nordic skiing was in 1933, when the team from Sweden won the title.

5381. Olympic Winter Games when ski instructors were barred from competition as professionals were in 1936 at Garmisch-Partenkirchen, Germany. After the International Olympic Committee ruling, Austrian and Swiss skiers boycotted the competition.

5382. Women's Alpine combined event held at the Olympic Winter Games was in 1936 at Garmisch-Partenkirchen, Germany. Christl Cranz of Germany won that first event with 97.06 points, on times of 5:23.4 minutes in the downhill and 2:22.1 minutes in the slalom.

5383. Men's Alpine combined event held at the Olympic Winter Games was in 1936 at Garmisch-Partenkirchen, Germany. The gold medal was won by Franc Pfnür of Germany on February 9. For his 4:51.8 minutes on the downhill run and 2:26.6 minutes on the two slalom runs, he earned a total of 99.25 points. From 1994 the event would be decided by combined time, rather than points.

5384. Men's 4 x 10-kilometer relay Nordic (cross-country) event held in the Olympic Winter Games was in 1936 at Garmisch-Partenkirchen, Germany. Posting a time of 2:41.33 hours, the team from Finland—Sulo Murmela, Klaes Karppinen, Matti Lähde, and Kalle Jalkanen—won on February 10.

5385. Skier to win two consecutive men's individual ski jump titles in the Olympic Winter Games was Birger Ruud of Norway, who won his second 90-meter jump title on February 16, 1936, at Garmisch-Partenkirchen, Germany, with a two-jump total of 232.0 points. He had previously won in 1932, and would take the silver medal 12 years later in 1948, after fighting in the Resistance during World War II.

SKIING (1940-1949)

5386. Men's downhill skiing event held at the Olympic Winter Games was in 1948 at St. Moritz, Switzerland. Henri Oreiller of France won on February 2 with a time of 2:55.0 minutes for the two-mile run. A member of the French Resistance during World War II, he later became a racing car driver.

5387. Women's downhill skiing event held at the Olympic Winter Games was in 1948 at St. Moritz, Switzerland. The winner of the inaugural event was Switzerland's own Hedy Schlunegger, whose time of 2:28.3 minutes led the field on February 2.

5388. Men's slalom event held at the Olympic Winter Games was in 1948, at St. Moritz, Switzerland. Winning on February 5 was Edi Reinalter of Switzerland, with a combined time for the two runs of 2:10.3 minutes.

5389. Women's slalom event held at the Olympic Winter Games was in 1948 at St. Moritz, Switzerland. The winner was Gretchen Fraser of the United States, with a two-run combined time of 1:57.2 minutes on February 5.

SKIING (1950-1959)

5390. Men's giant slalom event held in the Alpine skiing world championships was in 1950, won by Zeno Colò of Italy.

5391. Women's Alpine combination event held in the Alpine skiing world championships was in 1954, won by Ida Schöpfer of Switzerland.

5392. Women's events to be included in the Alpine skiing world championships were in 1950. They were the slalom and giant slalom, both won by Dagmar Rom of Austria, and the downhill, won by Trude Beiser-Jochum of Austria.

SKIING—(1950-1959)—*continued*

5393. Women's giant slalom event held at the Olympic Winter Games was in 1952 at Oslo, Norway. The winner of the inaugural competition was Andrea Mead Lawrence of the United States, who had a two-run combined time of 2:06.8 minutes on February 14. She also won the women's slalom six days later.

5394. Men's giant slalom event held at the Olympic Winter Games was in 1952 at Oslo, Norway. The winner was the host-country favorite, Stein Eriksen of Norway, with a two-run combined time of 2:25.0 minutes on February 15. Considered the first skiing "superstar," Eriksen became a ski instructor in the United States.

5395. National team to sweep the medals in the women's 10-kilometer Nordic (cross-country) skiing event in the Olympic Winter Games was Finland, led by Lydia Wideman, on February 23, 1952, in Oslo, Norway.

5396. Women's individual 10-kilometer Nordic (cross-country) event held at the Olympic Winter Games was in 1952 in Oslo, Norway. That first competition was won on February 23 by Lydia Wideman of Finland with a time of 41:40.0 minutes. The event would be discontinued after 1988.

5397. Skier from the United States to win two Olympic gold medals was Andrea Mead Lawrence, who won both at the 1952 Olympic Winter Games in Oslo, Norway. After winning the inaugural women's giant slalom competition on February 14, she won again on February 20, when she posted a two-run combined time of 2:10.6 minutes in the women's slalom.

5398. Men's 15-kilometer cross-country event held in the world championships of Nordic skiing was in 1954. Veikko Hakulinen of Finland won that first championship and the next in 1958. The event would be discontinued after 1991.

5399. Women's 10-kilometer cross-country event held in the world championships of Nordic skiing was in 1954, when Lyubov Kozyreva of the Soviet Union won the title. The event would be discontinued after 1991.

5400. Women's cross-country relay event held in the world championships of Nordic skiing was in 1954, when the team from the Soviet Union won the title. Originally 3 x 5 kilometers, the race would be 4 x 5 kilometers from 1974.

5401. Women's 3 x 5-kilometer relay Nordic (cross-country) skiing event held at the Olympic Winter Games was in 1956 at Cortina d'Ampezzo, Italy. Representing Finland, the team of Sirkka Polkunen, Mirja Hietamies, and Siiri Rantanen had the winning time of 1:09.01.0 hours on February 1. The event would become 4 x 5 kilometers in 1976.

5402. Men's 30-kilometer Nordic (cross-country) ski event held at the Olympic Winter Games was in 1956 at Cortina d'Ampezzo, Italy. The inaugural competition was won by Veikko Hakulinen of Finland on January 17, with a time of 1:44:06 hours.

5403. National team to sweep the medals in the men's giant slalom in the Olympic Winter Games was from Austria, led by Toni (Anton) Sailer, on January 29, 1956, at Cortina d'Ampezzo, Italy.

5404. Men's individual 15-kilometer Nordic (cross-country) event at the Olympic Winter Games was in 1956, at Cortina d'Ampezzo, Italy, where the distance was changed from 18-kilometers. Hallgeir Brenden of Norway won the first race at the new distance on January 30 with a time of 49:39.0 minutes. He had previously won at the 18-kilometer distance in 1952.

5405. Skiers from the Soviet Union to win the men's 4 x 10-kilometer relay Nordic (cross-country) title at the Olympic Winter Games were Fedor Terentyev, Pavel Kolchin, Nikolai Anikin, and Vladimir Kuzin. Their time of 2:15.30 hours won the event at Cortina d'Ampezzo, Italy, on February 4, 1956.

5406. Skier to sweep the men's individual Alpine events at the Olympic Winter Games was Toni (Anton) Sailer of Austria at Cortina d'Ampezzo, Italy, in 1956. He won the giant slalom on January 29, with a time of 3:00.1 minutes; the slalom on January 31, with a combined time for the two runs of 3:14.7 minutes; and the downhill on February 3, with a time of 2:52.2 minutes. In the downhill event, he raced with a borrowed strap tying his boot to its ski, since his own strap had broken just before the race.

SKIING (1960-1969)
5407. Men's ski jumping (large hill) event held in the world championships of Nordic skiing was in 1962, when the winner was Helmut Recknagel of East Germany. Originally 90 meters, the jump would be raised to 115 and then 120 meters.

5408. Women's 5-kilometer cross-country event held in the world championships of Nordic skiing was in 1962, when Alevtina Kolchina of the Soviet Union won the first of her two world titles in the event, the other coming in 1966.

5409. Skier to be killed during the Olympic Winter Games was Ross Milne of Australia, who died after sliding off the course and smashing into a tree on January 25, 1964, during a practice run for the men's downhill competition at Innsbruck, Austria.

5410. Men's individual 70-meter ski jump event held at the Olympic Winter Games was in 1964 at Innsbruck, Austria. Veikko Kankkonen of Finland won the first competition using the 70-meter hill (normal hill), with a total of 229.9 points combined for the two jumps, on January 31.

5411. Skier to win two titles in the men's 50-kilometer freestyle Nordic (cross-country) skiing at the Olympic Winter Games was Sixten Jernberg of Sweden. His second title in the event came on February 5, 1964, at Innsbruck, Austria, where he skied the course in 2:43:52.6 hours. His first 50-kilometer Olympic title had come eight years earlier, in 1956. He won another gold medal in 1964 as part of Sweden's 4 x 10-kilometer relay team.

5412. Women's individual 5-kilometer Nordic (cross-country) event in the Olympic Winter Games was in 1964 at Innsbruck, Austria. The winner of that first competition was Klaudia Boyarskikh of the Soviet Union, who had a time of 17:50.5 minutes on February 5. She swept the 1964 women's Nordic events, also winning the 10-kilometer Nordic title and winning the 3 x 5-kilometer relay.

5413. National team to sweep the medals in the women's downhill event in the Olympic Winter Games was from Austria, led by Christl Haas, on February 6, 1964, in Innsbruck, Austria.

5414. Skier to win both the men's individual 70- and 90-meter ski jumps in the same Olympic Winter Games was Toralf Engan of Norway in 1964 in Innsbruck, Austria. He first won the 90-meter jump on February 9, the first and only time the event was determined by the best two of three jumps. Then on February 11 he won the inaugural 70-meter competition.

5415. Freestyle skiing competition on record was held in 1966 in Attitash, New Hampshire.

5416. World cup series of competitions in Alpine skiing was in 1967. Jean-Claude Killy of France dominated the men's side, winning the downhill, slalom, giant slalom, and overall titles. On the women's side, Nancy Greene of Canada won the giant slalom and overall titles, while Marielle Goitschel of France won the downhill title and shared the slalom title with French teammate Annie Famose.

5417. Men's giant slalom to have two runs on separate days, rather than a single run, at the Olympic Winter Games was in 1968 at Grenoble, France. The winner of the redesigned event was Jean-Claude Killy, who posted a combined time of 3:29.28 minutes on February 12. Killy swept the Alpine events that year, also winning the men's downhill on February 9 and men's slalom on February 17.

5418. Nations' Cup for skiing awarded to the country whose athletes had the best overall performance in skiing's world cup, was awarded in 1969. The first winner was Austria, which would win again in 1973–1980, 1982, and 1990–1998.

SKIING (1970-1979)

5419. World ski flying championships were held in 1972. Walter Steiner of Switzerland won the first title in the competition, held biennially from 1973.

5420. National team to sweep the medals in the men's 70-meter ski jump at the Olympic Winter Games was from Japan, led by Yukio Kasaya, on February 6, 1972, in Sapporo, Japan.

5421. Skier to win both the women's downhill and giant slalom titles in the same Olympic Winter Games was Marie-Thérèse Nadig of Switzerland. Competing in Sapporo, Japan, she won the downhill on February 5, 1972, with a time of 1:36.68 minutes, and the giant slalom on February 8, with a time of 1:29.90 minutes.

SKIING—(1970-1979)—continued

5422. Organized competition for freestyle skiing was held in 1973 in New Hampshire.

5423. Skier to win two consecutive women's Nordic (cross-country) skiing titles in the Olympic Winter Games was Galina Kulakova of the Soviet Union. At Innsbruck, Austria, in 1976, the first year the event was a 4 x 5-kilometer relay, she and teammates Nina Baldycheva, Zinaida Amasova, and Raisa Smetanina posted the winning time of 1:07:49.75 hours on February 12. In 1972, she had been joined by Lyubov Mukhacheva and Alevtina Olunina in winning what was then the 3 x 5-kilometer relay race.

5424. Women's 20-kilometer cross-country event held in the world championships of Nordic skiing was in 1978, when the winner was Zinaida Amasova of the Soviet Union. The event would be discontinued after 1987.

5425. Skier to win 13 men's Alpine world cup races, and to win 10 in one category, in a single season was Ingemar Stenmark of Sweden, in the 1978–1979 season, when he won 10 giant slalom races and 13 overall.

5426. Skier to win seven women's downhill world cup titles was Annemarie Moser-Pröll of Austria, whose wins came in 1971–1975 and 1978–1979.

5427. Skier to win six women's overall world cup titles was Annemarie Moser-Pröll of Austria, who won five in a row (1971–1975) and then another in 1979.

5428. World cup for Nordic skiing was held in 1979. Oddvar Brå of Norway won the men's cross-country title and Galina Kulakova of the Soviet Union the women's.

5429. Worldloppet Cup a series of long-distance Nordic ski races held around the world, was held in 1979, for men only until 1989. The first champion was Matti Kuosku of Sweden, home of the longest race in the series, the Vasalopp.

SKIING (1980-1989)

5430. Ski jumping event held in the world cup for Nordic skiing was in 1980, when Hubert Neuper of Austria won the first men's title.

5431. World cup circuit for freestyle skiing was established in 1980, sponsored by the Fédération Internationale de Ski (FIS). Greg Athans of Canada won the men's overall championship and Marie-Claude Asselin of Canada the women's; she would win again in 1981 and 1982.

5432. Cross-country Nations' Cup in the world cup for Nordic skiing was given in 1981. The first award, for performance by both men and women, was won by the Soviet Union.

5433. Men's super giant slalom event which would be popularly called the Super G, was held in 1981.

5434. Ski jumping Nations' Cup in the world cup for Nordic skiing was in 1981, when Austria won the first title.

5435. Men's team Nordic combined event held in the world championships of Nordic skiing was in 1982, when the team from East Germany won the title.

5436. Men's team ski jumping event held in the world championships of Nordic skiing was in 1982, when the team from Norway won the title.

5437. Skier to introduce skating techniques into Nordic (cross-country) skiing in international competition was William Koch of the United States in 1982. The skating style was banned in 1983, but would be allowed in Olympic freestyle Nordic skiing competitions from 1988. He also introduced the practice of roughening, rather than waxing, the bottoms of the skis.

5438. Nordic combination event held in the world cup for Nordic skiing was in 1983, when the winner was Espen Andersen of Norway.

5439. Skier to win eight men's slalom world cup titles was Ingemar Stenmark of Sweden, who won a remarkable seven in a row (1975–1981) and then an eighth in 1983.

5440. Skier to win five men's downhill world cup titles was Franz Klammer of Austria, who won four times in a row (1975–1978) and again in 1983.

5441. Skier to win seven men's giant slalom world cup titles was Ingemar Stenmark of Sweden. His titles came in 1975, 1976, 1978–1981, and 1984, the latter in a tie with Pirmin Zurbriggen of Switzerland.

5442. Skier to win two consecutive men's 30-kilometer Nordic (cross-country) titles in the Olympic Winter Games was Nikolai Zimyatov of the Soviet Union. After his first win in 1980, his second win came on February 10, 1984, at Sarajevo, Yugoslavia, where he had a time of 1:28:56.3 hours.

5443. Skier to win three consecutive men's individual Nordic combined titles in the Olympic Winter Games was Ulrich Wehling of East Germany. His record-breaking third straight win came on February 12, 1984, at Sarajevo, Yugoslavia, where he had a combined (ski jump and cross-country) total of 422.595 points. He had previously won in 1976 and 1980, the only non–figure skater to win the same Winter Olympics event three straight times.

5444. Skier from the United States to win the men's downhill title at the Olympic Winter Games was Bill (William) Johnson, who led the field on February 16, 1984, with a time of 1:45.59 minutes, at Sarajevo, Yugoslavia.

5445. Women's individual 20-kilometer Nordic (cross-country) event held at the Olympic Winter Games was in 1984 at Sarajevo, Yugoslavia. The winner was Marja-Liisa Hämäläinen of Finland, who had a time of 1:01:45.0 hours on February 18. The event was run again in 1988, then discontinued.

5446. Skier from the United States to win the men's slalom title at the Olympic Winter Games was Phillip Mahre, on February 19, 1984, at Sarajevo, Yugoslavia. He posted a time for the combined runs of 1:39.41 minutes, which was just .21 seconds better than his twin brother, Steven Mahre, who took silver.

5447. Ski-jumper to spread the skis in a V formation in the air rather than keeping them parallel, was Jan Boklöv of Sweden in 1985. He was at first ridiculed, but his success and the results of aerodynamic tests sparked most ski-jumpers to adopt the V by the early 1990s.

5448. Men's super giant slalom to be included in the world cup for Alpine skiing was in 1986, when the event was won by Markus Wasmeier of West Germany.

5449. Skier to win five women's slalom world cup titles was Erika Hess of Switzerland, who won in 1981, 1982, 1983, 1985, and 1986, the last in a tie with Roswitha Steiner of Austria.

5450. Women's super giant slalom to be included in the world cup for Alpine skiing was in 1986, when Marina Kiehl of East Germany won the event.

5451. World championships for freestyle skiing were held in 1986, in Tignes, France. On the men's side, Richard Schabel of West Germany won the ballet title, Eric Berthon of France the moguls, Lloyd Langlois of Canada the aerials, and Alain Laroche of Canada the combined. For the women, Jan Bucher of the United States won the ballet championship, Mary Jo Tiampo of the United States the moguls, Maria Quintana of Cuba the aerials, and Connie Kissling of Switzerland the combined.

5452. Super giant slalom events held in the Alpine skiing world championships were in 1987. Pirmin Zurbriggen of Switzerland won the inaugural men's event, and Maria Walliser of East Germany the women's.

5453. Women's super giant slalom event held at the Olympic Winter Games was in 1988 at Calgary, Alberta, Canada. The winner of the inaugural event was Sigrid Wolf of Austria, who led with a time of 1:19.03 minutes.

5454. Men's super giant slalom event held at the Olympic Winter Games was on February 21, 1988, in Calgary, Alberta, Canada. Franck Piccard of France raced the course in 1:39.66 minutes to win the inaugural single-run event. Before that, Piccard had never won a World Cup race.

5455. Skier to win two consecutive titles in the men's 4 x 10-kilometer relay Nordic (cross-country) at the Olympic Winter Games was Thomas Wassberg of Sweden. After winning his initial gold medal in 1984, he teamed up with Jan Ottosson, Bunde Svan, and N. Torgny Mogren to win a second on February 22, 1988, at Calgary, Alberta, Canada, with a winning time of 1:43:58.6 hours.

5456. Men's Nordic combined team event held in the Olympic Winter Games was in 1988 at Calgary, Alberta, Canada. Hans-Peter Pohl, Hubert Schwarz, and Thomas Müller claimed the inaugural gold medal on February 23, after a first-place finish in the ski jump and an eighth in the cross-country.

5457. Men's team ski-jumping event held in the Olympic Winter Games was the 90-meter (large hill) jump introduced in 1988 in Calgary, Alberta, Canada. The winning team from Finland—Matti Nykänen, Ari-Pekka Nikkola, Jari Puikkonen, and Tuomo Yipulli—built a total of 634.4 points on February 24. Nykänen also won both men's individual ski jump competitions: the 70-meter on February 14 and the 90-meter on February 23.

SKIING—(1980-1989)—*continued*

5458. Skier of African ancestry to compete in the Olympic Winter Games was 14-year-old Seba Johnson of the U.S. Virgin Islands, who competed in the women's giant slalom on February 24, 1988, at Calgary, Alberta, Canada. Out of 64 skiers, only 29 completed the run, with Johnson placing 28th.

5459. National team to sweep the medals in the women's individual 20-kilometer Nordic (cross-country) event at the Olympic Winter Games was from the Soviet Union, led by Tamara Tikhonova, on February 25, 1988, at Calgary, Alberta, Canada.

5460. Skier to win two individual ski-jumping gold medals in the same Olympic Winter Games was Matti Nykänen of Finland in 1988 at Calgary, Alberta, Canada. He won the men's individual 70-meter jump on February 14, scoring 229.1 for the two jumps, and then on February 23, with a score of 224.0, he took the men's 90-meter jump. It was his second consecutive win in the 90-meter; in the 70-meter, he had won silver in 1984. He also won a third gold medal in 1988 in the inaugural 90-meter team ski-jump event, on February 24.

5461. Skier to win 14 women's Alpine World Cup races in a single season was Vreni Schneider of Switzerland in the 1988–1989 season, when she swept all seven slalom races, while winning seven other Alpine races.

5462. Women's 15-kilometer cross-country event held in the world championships of Nordic skiing was in 1989, when the winner was Marj Matikainen of Finland.

5463. Women's 30-kilometer cross-country event held in the world championships of Nordic skiing was in 1989, when Yelena Välbe of the Soviet Union won the title. The competition was freestyle until 1997, when it became classical.

5464. Worldloppet Cup to include women Nordic skiers was in 1989, when the women's champion was Ellen Holcomb of the United States.

SKIING (1990-1999)

5465. Skier to win four men's super giant slalom world cup titles was Pirmin Zurbriggen of Switzerland, who won four championships in a row: 1987–1990.

5466. Men's 10-kilometer cross-country (classical) event held in the world championships of Nordic skiing was in 1991, when Terje Langli of Norway won the event.

5467. Ski flying event held in the world cup for Nordic skiing was in 1991, when the winner was Stefan Zuend of Switzerland.

5468. Skier to win four women's super giant slalom world cup titles was Carole Merle of France, who won four times in a row: 1989–1992.

5469. Women's 30-kilometer Nordic (cross-country) skiing event held at the Olympic Winter Games was in 1992 at Albertville, France. Stefania Belmondo of Italy was the winner, with a time of 1:22.30.1 hours.

5470. Women's individual 15-kilometer Nordic (cross-country) skiing event at the Olympic Winter Games was in 1992 at Albertville, France. That first competition, held on February 9, was won by Lyubov Yegorova of the Soviet Union with a time of 42:20.8 minutes. She also won the women's combined pursuit Nordic titles in 1992 and 1994.

5471. National team to sweep the medals in the men's 30-kilometer Nordic (cross-country) skiing event at the Olympic Winter Games was Norway, led by Vegard Ulvang, on February 10, 1992, in Albertville, France.

5472. Men's 10-kilometer Nordic (cross-country) skiing event held at the Olympic Winter Games was in 1992 at Albertville, France. Vegard Ulvang of Norway won the cross-country event on February 13 with a time of 27:36.0 minutes, despite falling and breaking a pole, then finishing with a borrowed pole. Three days earlier, Ulvang had won the men's 30-kilometer title; he picked up a third gold medal as part of the 4 X 10-kilometer relay team on February 18.

5473. Men's moguls freestyle skiing event at the Olympic Winter Games was in 1992 at Albertville, France. The first winner was Edgar Grospiron of France, who racked up 25.81 points in his February 13 win. He would be the bronze medalist in 1994.

5474. Women's moguls freestyle skiing event held at the Olympic Winter Games was in 1992 in Albertville, France. The first winner of the title was Donna Weinbrecht of the United States, who on February 13 led the field with 23.69 points.

5475. Skier to win two medals in the men's 90-meter team ski-jumping event in the Olympic Winter Games was Ari-Pekka Nikkola of Finland. On the winning team in 1988, he won again on February 14, 1992, in Albertville, France, this time with Toni Nieminen, Risto Laakkonen, and Mika Laitinen.

5476. Men's combined pursuit Nordic (cross-country) skiing event held at the Olympic Winter Games was in 1992 at Albertville, France. Bjørn Dahlie of Norway won the competition on February 15, with a combined time (classical and freestyle) of 1:05:37.9 hours.

5477. Women's combined pursuit Nordic (cross-country) skiing event in the Olympic Winter Games was in 1992 at Albertville, France. Lyubov Yegorova won that first competition on February 15, with a combined (classical and freestyle) total of 40:07.7 minutes. She would win it again in 1994, also taking the women's individual 15-kilometer Nordic title in 1992.

5478. Skier to win four medals in the same Nordic skiing event in the Olympic Winter Games was Raisa Smetanina of the Soviet Union. Her fourth title in the women's 4 x 5-kilometer Nordic (cross-country) skiing relay came on February 17, 1992, at Albertville, France, where she and teammates Yelena Välbe, Larissa Lazutina, and Lyubov Yegorova posted the winning time of 59:34.8 minutes. She had earlier been on the winning teams in 1976 and 1988, and in second place in 1980. The 1992 title also gave her a record of 10 medals in the Winter Olympics.

5479. Skier to win two consecutive individual titles in an Alpine event in the Olympic Winter Games was Alberto Tomba of Italy. After his first win in the giant slalom in 1988, his second came in Albertville, France, on February 18, 1992, where he posted a time of 2:06.98 minutes, to lead the field.

5480. Skier to win both the women's slalom and the women's Alpine combination in the same Olympic Winter Games, and the first from Austria to win the Olympic women's slalom title was Petra Kronberger. Competing in Albertville, France, she won the Alpine combined event on February 13, 1992, then topped the women's slalom field on February 20, with a time of 1:32.68 minutes.

5481. Men's pursuit (10 kilometers classical and 15 kilometers freestyle) event held in the world championships of Nordic skiing was in 1993. The inaugural winner was Bjørn Dahlie of Norway, who would win again in 1997.

5482. Skier to win five men's overall titles in skiing's world cup was Marc Girardelli of Luxembourg, who won in 1985, 1986, 1989, 1991, and 1993.

5483. Women's pursuit (5 kilometers classical and 10 kilometers freestyle) event held in the world championships of Nordic skiing was in 1993, when the winner was Stefania Belmondo of Italy.

5484. Women's aerials freestyle skiing event held at the Olympic Winter Games was in 1994 at Lillehammer, Norway. The winner of this first competition was Lina Cheryazova of Uzbekistan, who built a total of 166.84 points to win on February 24, her country's first Olympic medal winner.

5485. Skier to win the 30-kilometer Nordic (cross-country) title in the Olympic Winter Games after it was converted from classical style to freestyle was Thomas Alsgaard of Norway. His time of 1:12:26.4 hours gave him an upset victory over teammate Bjørn Dahlie on February 14, 1994, in Lillehammer, Norway.

5486. Skier to win two consecutive women's combined pursuit Nordic (cross-country) skiing titles at the Olympic Winter Games was Lyubov Yegorova of Russia. Her second win came with a combined (classical and freestyle) time of 41:38.1 minutes on February 17, 1994, at Lillehammer, Norway. She had previously won the inaugural event in 1992.

5487. Male skier to win five gold medals in Nordic (cross-country) skiing in the Olympic Winter Games, and the first to win two consecutive men's combined pursuit titles was Bjørn Dahlie of Norway. His fifth Olympic gold medal and second consecutive combined pursuit title came on February 19, 1994, at Lillehammer, Norway, when he finished with a combined time (classical and freestyle) of 1:00:08.8 hours. In addition to his first combined pursuit title, in 1992, Dahlie's earlier gold medals were in the 50-kilometer freestyle (1992), the 4 x 10-kilometer relay (1994), and the 10-kilometer (1994). He would successfully defend the latter in 1998 for his sixth gold medal.

5488. Men's aerials freestyle skiing event at the Olympic Winter Games was in 1994 at Lillehammer, Norway. The inaugural competition was won by Sonny (Andreas) Schönbächler of Switzerland, who earned a total of 234.67 points for his aerial ski jumps on February 24.

SKIING—(1990-1999)—*continued*

5489. Skiers to win two consecutive men's Nordic combined team titles at the Olympic Winter Games were Takanori Kono and Kenju Ogiwara of Japan. With Masashi Abe, they won their second straight title on February 24, 1994, at Lillehammer, Norway, with a first-place showing in the ski jump and a third in the cross-country. Kono and Ogiwara had previously won in 1992 with Reiichi Mikata.

5490. National team to sweep the medals in the men's Alpine combined skiing event at the Olympic Winter Games was from Norway, led by Lasse Kjus, on February 25, 1994, at Lillehammer, Norway.

5491. Skier to win five medals in Alpine events at the Olympic Winter Games was Kjetil André Aamodt of Norway. His silver medal in the men's Alpine combined event in Lillehammer, Norway, on February 25, 1994, was his fifth. His other medals came in the men's super giant slalom (gold, 1992; silver 1994), the men's downhill (silver, 1994), and the men's giant slalom (bronze, 1992).

5492. Woman skier to win three gold medals, and to win five medals overall, in Alpine skiing at the Olympic Winter Games was Vreni Schneider of Switzerland. Her third Alpine title came on February 26, 1994, at Lillehammer, Norway, when she had the winning time of 1:56.01 minutes in the slalom, which she had first won in 1988. In the giant slalom, she had taken home the gold medal in 1988 and the bronze in 1994. Added to that was her silver medal in the Alpine combined in 1994.

5493. Skier to win the 50-kilometer Nordic (cross-country) title in the Olympic Winter Games after it was converted from freestyle to classical style was Vladimir Smirnov of Kazakhstan in 1994 at Lillehammer, Norway. His time of 2:07:20.3 hours won the gold medal on February 27, his country's first. Smirnov had previously competed for the Soviet Union, but had long trained in Sweden.

5494. Skier to win five women's giant slalom titles in skiing's world cup was Vreni Schneider of Switzerland, who won in 1986, 1987, 1989, 1991, and 1995.

5495. Skier to win six women's slalom titles in skiing's world cup was Vreni Schneider of Switzerland, whose titles came in 1989–1990 and 1992–1995.

5496. Skier to win five women's super giant slalom titles in skiing's world cup was Katja Seizinger of Germany, whose titles came in 1993–1996 and 1998.

5497. Skier from the United States to win the men's moguls freestyle skiing event in the Olympic Winter Games was Jonny Moseley, who won on February 11, 1998, in Nagano, Japan.

5498. Skier from the United States to win the women's super giant slalom at the Olympic Winter Games was Picabo Street, who won the event on February 11, 1998, in Nagano, Japan.

5499. Skier to win two consecutive men's 10-kilometer Nordic (cross-country) skiing titles, and the first male athlete to win six gold medals overall, at the Olympic Winter Games was Bjorn Dahlie of Norway. After winning his first men's 10-kilometer title in 1994, he returned for another title on February 12, 1998, at Nagano, Japan. His other four gold medals had come in the men's 50-kilometer freestyle (1992), the men's 4 x 10-kilometer relay (1994), and the men's combined pursuit (1992 and 1994).

5500. Skier from the United States to win the men's aerials freestyle skiing event in the Olympic Winter Games was Eric Bergoust, who won on February 18, 1998, in Nagano, Japan.

5501. Skier from the United States to win the women's aerials freestyle skiing event in the Olympic Winter Games was Nikki Stone, who won on February 18, 1998, in Nagano, Japan.

5502. Skier to win two consecutive titles in the women's giant slalom in the Olympic Winter Games was Deborah Compagnoni of Italy. After winning in 1994, she returned to win again on February 20, 1998, in Nagano, Japan.

5503. Skier to win two consecutive Olympic titles in the women's downhill, and the first to win both the downhill and Alpine combination events in the same Olympic Winter Games was Katja Seizinger of Germany. After winning her first downhill title in 1994, she won again on February 16, 1998, in Nagano, Japan, where she also won the Alpine combination on February 17.

SKY DIVING

5504. World sky diving championships were held at Lesce-Bled, Yugoslavia, in 1951. Both men and women competed at this first international sky diving competition, with Monique Laroche of France winning the women's title.

5505. Sky diver from the United States to win the men's title in the world sky diving championships was Jim Arender, who won the championship in 1960.

SLED DOG RACING

5506. Organized sled dog race on record was the All-Alaskan Sweepstake held in 1908, with sled dog racers, or mushers, following a round-trip course of approximately 408 miles between Candle and Nome, Alaska.

5507. World championships in sled dog racing were held in 1936. These short-course races would, however, be eclipsed by the Iditarod.

5508. International governing body for sled dog racing was the International Sled Dog Racing Association (ISDRA), founded in 1966.

5509. Iditarod sled dog race was run in 1973, on the Iditarod Trail between Anchorage and Nome, Alaska. Dick Wilmarth led the field of 22 mushers, with a time of 20 days, 49 minutes, and 41 seconds. Two shorter races had been run on the trail in 1967 and 1969, but this was the first full race, of approximately 1100 miles. Following a historic mail and supply route, the Iditarod commemorates a 1925 sled dog run that brought lifesaving serum to fight a diphtheria epidemic in Nome.

5510. Sled dog racer to complete the Iditarod in less than 15 days was Emmitt Peters, who in 1975 set a record of 14 days, 14 hours, 43 minutes, and 45 seconds for the approximately 1100-mile race between Anchorage and Nome, Alaska.

5511. Sled dog racer to win the Iditarod sled dog race four times, and the first to win it twice in a row was Rick Swenson. His fourth (and second consecutive) win came in 1982 and his fifth in 1991, after three earlier wins in 1977, 1979, and 1981. In the 1981 win, he posted a then-record of 12 days, 8 hours, 45 minutes, and 2 seconds for the approximately 1100-mile race between Anchorage and Nome, Alaska. He lost the 1978 race to Dick Mackey by just one second, or one dog's-length, in an extraordinary photo finish.

5512. Father and son to win the Iditarod sled dog race were Dick Mackey, who won in 1978, and his son Rick Mackey, who won the approximately 1100-mile race between Anchorage and Nome, Alaska in 1983.

5513. Yukon Quest sled dog race was run in 1984. The winner was Sonny Lindner, who completed the approximately 1000-mile course from Fairbanks, Alaska, to Whitehorse, in the Yukon Territory, Canada, in 12 days and 5 minutes.

5514. Sled dog racer to win both the Iditarod and the Yukon Quest sled dog races was Joe Runyan, who won the Yukon Quest in 1985 and the Iditarod in 1989.

5515. Woman sled dog racer to win the Iditarod sled dog race was Libby Riddles in 1985, who traversed the approximately 1100-mile course between Anchorage and Nome, Alaska in 18 days, 0 hours, 20 minutes, and 17 seconds.

5516. Sled dog racer to win three consecutive Iditarod races was Susan Butcher, who won in 1986, 1987, and 1988. Her 1986 time of 11 days, 15 hours, and 6 minutes set a record for the approximately 1100-mile race between Anchorage and Nome, Alaska, which she bettered in both 1988 and 1990, the latter being her fourth title.

5517. Woman sled dog racer to win the Iditarod sled dog race four times was Susan Butcher, who won her fourth Iditarod in 1990. She had previously won the approximately 1100-mile race between Anchorage and Nome, Alaska, three straight times, in 1986, 1987, and 1988. She retired from racing in 1993.

5518. Sled dog racer to win the Iditarod sled dog race five times, and the first to win across three decades was Rick Swenson. In the approximately 1100-mile race between Anchorage and Nome, he gained his fifth win in 1991, after four earlier wins in 1977, 1979, 1981, and 1982.

5519. Sled dog racer to win the Yukon Quest sled dog race twice was Charlie Boulding, who won his second in 1993, after an earlier win in 1991.

5520. Sled dog racer to complete the Iditarod sled dog race in less than 10 days was Doug Swingley, who in 1995 completed the approximately 1100-mile course between Anchorage and Nome, Alaska, in 9 days, 2 hours, 42 minutes, and 19 seconds.

SNOWBOARDING

5521. Snowboarding world championships were held in 1993, sponsored by the International Ski Federation (FIS). The men's champions were Alexis Parmentier of France in the slalom, Mosca Cla of Switzerland in the parallel slalom, and Terje Haakonsen of Norway in the halfpipe. In the women's events, Ashild Loftus of Norway won both the slalom and the parallel slalom, becoming the first athlete to win two snowboarding events in the same

SNOWBOARDING—*continued*
world championships, while Nicole Angelrath of Switzerland won the halfpipe. The men's combined winner was Kevin Delany and the women's Michelle Taggart, both from the United States.

5522. Snowboarder to win two consecutive titles in a world championship event was Terje Haakonsen of Norway, who won the halfpipe event in 1993 and again in 1995, the first two times it was held.

5523. Giant slalom and snowboard cross events held in the snowboarding world championships were in 1997. Thomas Prugger of Italy won the men's giant slalom and Sandra Van Ert of the United States the women's. In the snowboard cross, the men's winner was Helmut Pramstaller of Austria and the women's Karine Ruby of France.

5524. Men's giant slalom snowboarding event held at the Olympic Winter Games was in 1998 at Nagano, Japan. The inaugural winner was Ross Rebagliati of Canada on February 8.

5525. Women's giant slalom snow-boarding event held at the Olympic Winter Games was on February 10, 1998 at Nagano, Japan. Karine Ruby of France won the inaugural event.

5526. Men's halfpipe snowboarding event held at the Olympic Winter Games was on February 12, 1998, at Nagano, Japan. Gian Simmen of Switzerland was the inaugural winner.

5527. Women's halfpipe snowboarding event held at the Olympic Winter Games was on February 12, 1998, at Nagano, Japan. Nicola Thost of Germany took the gold medal.

SOCCER (INTERNATIONAL FOOTBALL)

5528. Written reference to football was in 1314 in England, where King Edward II banned the playing of football in London, because the players made too much noise. It was the first of many royal bans, all ineffective.

5529. Ban on football in Scotland was in 1424, when the Parliament of James I of Scotland forbade citizens from playing football (then often called *fut bawe*; in the United States later known as soccer) because it detracted from their focus on military training, especially archery. The ban was presumably not very successful, for it was repeated on several other occasions, including 1457 (when golf was also forbidden), 1470, and 1491.

5530. Code of rules for soccer (international football) was written in 1848 at Cambridge University in Cambridge, England. It was developed from earlier forms of football games dating back many centuries.

5531. Soccer (international football) club was the Sheffield Football Club, founded in Sheffield, England, on October 24, 1857.

5532. Football Association (FA) was founded in England in 1863. It would become the prime organization for the sport, which in the United States would be known as soccer, though various other football organizations would be founded throughout Great Britain.

5533. Soccer (international football) club outside Britain was probably the one established in Geneva, Switzerland, in 1869, by British students at La Châtelaine School. The game would be spread around the world by British people abroad, and then by people from other European countries as well.

5534. Football Association (FA) Challenge Cup for soccer (international football) was offered in 1872 to teams in Great Britain, sponsored by the Football Association. The Wanderers won the 15-team knockout competition, winning the final against the Royal Engineers before a crowd of 2000 at Kennington Oval, the event's main home through 1892.

5535. International championship in soccer (international football) was the Home International Championship contested by teams from England, Scotland, Wales, and Northern Ireland. The first championship, at the end of the 1883–1884 season, was won by the team from Scotland. This British championship would be held annually until 1984.

5536. National association for soccer (international football) in the United States was the American Football Association, founded in 1884.

5537. International soccer (international football) match involving the United States was against Canada on November 28, 1885.

5538. Soccer (international football) club in Germany was the SC Germania Hamburg, founded in 1887.

5539. Soccer (international football) league was the Football League, founded on April 17, 1888, at the Royal Hotel, in Manchester, England, after an initial March 22 meeting in London, England, organized by William McGregor of Aston Villa. The first season began in September 1888, with 12 teams.

5540. Team to win the championship in England's Football League was Preston North End in 1889, at the end of the first season, begun in September 1888. The international football (soccer) team would win again in 1890.

5541. Women's soccer (international football) game on record was in 1895 in England.

5542. National soccer (international football) league in Italy was the Italian League, founded in 1898. The team from Genoa won after a three-game season. From 1930 the league would be called Serie A.

5543. National soccer (international football) league in Germany was the Deutscher Fussball-Bund, founded in 1900, following establishment of regional leagues in 1898.

5544. Soccer (international football) event held in the Olympic Games was in 1900 in Paris, France. Representing Great Britain, the Upton Park Football Club won the inaugural competition on September 23. The event would be for men only; women's competition would not be introduced until 1996.

5545. Football Association Challenge Cup soccer (international football) tournament played before more than 100,000 spectators was in 1901, when Tottenham Hotspur bested Sheffield United at the Crystal Palace in England, before a crown of 110,810.

5546. International governing body for soccer (international football) was the Fédération Internationale de Football Association (FIFA), founded in Paris, France, in 1904.

5547. Soccer (international football) team from Britain to play in the United States was a team called the Pilgrims, which toured the United States in 1904, winning 21 of 23 games played.

5548. Soccer (international football) player to win two gold medals in the Olympic Games was Vivian Woodward of Great Britain. On the winning team in 1908, he joined a new set of teammates to win again on July 4, 1912, in Stockholm, Sweden.

5549. National Challenge Cup for soccer (international football) was awarded in 1913, originally open only to amateur teams in the United States, but later to professionals as well. The winner of the challenge match, played in New York City, was the New York Football Club, over the Hollywood Inn Football Club, both of Yonkers, New York. The cup had been donated the previous year by Thomas R. Dewar of Britain to the American Amateur Football Association.

5550. International soccer (international football) match played by women was in 1920, between teams from England and France.

5551. Football Association Challenge Cup tournament played at Wembley Stadium in London, England, was in 1923, when the Bolton Wanderers defeated West Ham United before 126,047 spectators.

5552. National Amateur Challenge Cup given to the top amateur soccer (international football) team in the United States, was awarded in 1924. The Fleisher Yarn Football Club from Philadelphia, Pennsylvania, won the inaugural competition. They had also been in the divisional finals the previous year, when the competition was called because of bad weather.

5553. World cup in soccer (international football) was held in 1930 in Montevideo, Uruguay, with 13 teams participating. (Some European teams boycotted the contest because it was being held in Uruguay.) In the final, Uruguay defeated Argentina 4–2 to win the Jules Rimet Trophy, named for the president of the Fédération Internationale de Football Association (FIFA). Uruguay would win again in 1950. The event would be held quadrennially from then on, except during war years. Qualifying tournaments were introduced in 1934.

5554. Soccer (international football) team from Italy to win the world cup was in 1934 in Rome, Italy, when Italy defeated Czechoslovakia 2–1. Italy would win again in 1938 and 1982.

5555. Soccer (international football) team to win the world cup twice in a row was from Italy. After their initial win in 1934, they won again in 1938, defeating Hungary 4–2 in Paris, France. Italy would win again in 1982.

5556. Soccer (international football) team from Germany to win the world cup was from West Germany, which defeated Hungary 3–2 in 1954 in Bern, Switzerland. The West Germans would win again in 1974 and 1990.

5557. Soccer (international football) team from Brazil to win the world cup won in 1958. Led by the great Pele, Brazil defeated Sweden 5–2 in Stockholm, Sweden. They would win again in 1962, 1970, and 1994.

5558. Football League Cup (later the English League Cup) was offered in 1961, to soccer (international football) teams from the Football League in Britain. The inaugural winner was Aston Villa, over Rotherham United.

SOCCER (INTERNATIONAL FOOTBALL)—*continued*

5559. Soccer (international football) team from England to win the world cup won in 1966, when England defeated West Germany 4–2 at Wembley Stadium, England.

5560. Professional soccer (international football) leagues in the United States were the North American Soccer League (NASL), organized by the United Soccer Association (USA), and the National Professional Soccer League (NPSL), which both began their first seasons in 1967. They merged later in the year, as a single North American Soccer League, which would last only a decade.

5561. Team to win the championship of the North American Soccer League was the Atlanta Chiefs, which defeated San Diego in 1968 at the end of the NASL's first season.

5562. Soccer (international football) team to win the world cup three times was Brazil. After winning first in 1958 and 1962, Brazil came back to win again in 1970 in Mexico City. The team would win again in 1994.

5563. Soccer (international football) team from Argentina to win the world cup won in 1978 in Buenos Aires, Argentina. The home team defeated the Netherlands 3–1 for their first world cup title; their second would come in 1986.

5564. Soccer (international football) player to be named World Footballer of the Year by *World Soccer* was Paolo Rossi of Juventus in Italy in 1982. He led Italy to its third world cup win that year in Madrid, Spain.

5565. Soccer (international football) player to be named World Footballer of the Year by the Fédération Internationale de Football Association (FIFA) was Lothar Matthäus of West Germany, who played for Internazionale Milan, in 1991.

5566. Women's World Cup in soccer (international football) was in 1991 in China. The United States team defeated Norway 2–1, to take the inaugural championship, for which 12 teams competed. The U.S. team would win again in 1999, to become the first to win two Women's World Cups.

5567. Soccer (international football) team to win the world cup four times was Brazil. After three earlier wins in 1958, 1962, and 1970, Brazil came back to win again in 1994 in Pasadena, California.

5568. Major League Soccer season was in 1996. The league was established in the United States by agreement with the Fédération Internationale de Football Association (FIFA), the sport's international governing body, after the 1994 World Cup was sited in the United States. The inaugural champions were D. C. United, which would win again in 1998 and 1999.

5569. Women's soccer event held in the Olympic Games was in 1996, in Atlanta, Georgia. The team from the United States won the inaugural title over China on August 1, led by Mia Hamm, Michelle Akers, and Carla Overbeck, with Shannon MacMillan and Tiffeny Milbrett scoring in the 2–1 final. The crowd of 76,481 was estimated to be the largest crowd ever for a women's sporting event.

5570. Team from Africa to win the men's soccer event in the Olympic Games was from Nigeria, which won the gold medal by defeating Argentina on August 3, 1996, in Atlanta, Georgia.

5571. Soccer (international football) team from France to win the world cup won in 1998 in Saint-Denis, France. With a score of 3–0, they defeated a strong Brazilian team going for its fifth world cup.

SOFTBALL (BEFORE 1900)

5572. Softball game a wholly improvised contest, was played at the gymnasium of the Farragut Boat Club, in Chicago, Illinois, on November 30, 1887. It was invented spontaneously by George Hancock, who with approximately 20 other young men had been watching a Harvard-Yale football game. At the end of the football game, Hancock turned a boxing glove into an impromptu "ball," and the group formed two teams that played the new "indoor baseball" game, as it was first called, on a diamond chalked on the gymnasium floor.

5573. Organized softball game, following George Hancock's rules, and with the diamond, ball, and bat he introduced was played at the gymnasium of the Farragut Boat Club, in Chicago, Illinois, on December 2, 1887. The game, called indoor baseball at the start, would later and in several variations be called indoor-outdoor baseball (when it moved outdoors), diamond baseball, kitten ball, playground ball, recreation ball, and finally softball. Softball's two major versions ultimately came to be called "fast-pitch" and "slow-pitch."

5574. Softball games played outdoors were in 1888, and the game was then sometimes known as indoor-outdoor baseball.

5575. Softball rules to be formally published were by George Hancock in 1889, as the game spread rapidly.

5576. Women's softball team was founded, at the West Division High School, Chicago, Illinois, in 1895.

SOFTBALL (1900-1949)

5577. Playground softball organization was founded in 1908, in Chicago, Illinois. It was the National Amateur Playground Ball Association of the United States, which published a new set of rules that differed substantially from those published by George Hancock in 1889.

5578. Introduction of the name "softball" was by Walter C. Hakanson of Denver, Colorado, in 1926, at a convention of the National Recreation Congress. The sport had until then been variously known as indoor baseball, indoor-outdoor baseball, kitten ball, mush ball, playground ball, and recreation ball.

5579. Amateur Softball Association of America (ASA) national championships were played at the Chicago World Fair, in 1933. The J. L. Friedman Boosters team, from Chicago, Illinois, won the first ASA Men's Major Fast Pitch title. The Women's Major Fast Pitch title was won by Chicago's Great Northerns.

5580. National governing body in softball was the Amateur Softball Association of America (ASA), founded in 1933 in Chicago, Illinois.

5581. Softball championship to be broadcast nationally on radio was the Amateur Softball Association of America Men's Major Fast Pitch National Championship, in 1937. It was won by the Briggs Manufacturing Company team, of Detroit, Michigan.

5582. Softball team to win two consecutive titles in the Amateur Softball Association Women's Major Fast Pitch National Championships was the National Screw and Manufacturing team of Cleveland, Ohio, in 1936 and 1937.

5583. National professional softball league was founded in 1939. It was the National Professional Indoor Baseball League, which lasted very briefly before failing.

5584. National Fastball League was founded in 1946, composed of many leading U.S. industrial teams.

5585. Softball team to win the Amateur Softball Association Women's Major Fast Pitch National Championships in three consecutive years was the Jax Maids team of New Orleans, from 1945 to 1947.

5586. Softball team to win three consecutive titles in the Amateur Softball Association Men's Major Fast Pitch national championships was the Fort Wayne Zollner Pistons, from 1945 to 1947.

5587. World championships in softball were held in Phoenix, Arizona, in 1947, sponsored by the International Softball Congress. The winner was Phoenix's Farm Fresh Market team.

SOFTBALL (1950-1959)

5588. Softball Hall of Fame opened in Oklahoma City, in 1957; sponsored by the Amateur Softball Association of America. The first members of the Hall of Fame, all selected in 1957, were all pitchers: Amy Peralta May, Sam Elliott, Marie Wadlow, and Harold Gears.

5589. International Softball Federation (ISF) was founded in 1950. The new body came to dominate international softball.

5590. Softball player to be batting champion of the Amateur Softball Association Major Fast Pitch league was Ed Tyranski of Detroit, Michigan, who batted .615 in 1950.

5591. Woman to become a licensed softball umpire was Madeleine Lorton of New York City, in 1951.

5592. Softball team to win the Amateur Softball Association Men's Slow Pitch National Championships was the Shields Construction team, of Newport, Kentucky, at Cincinnati, Ohio, in 1953.

5593. Softball player to win the Most Valuable Player Award in the Amateur Softball Association Major Fast Pitch National Tournament was John Hunter of the Clearwater Bombers, of Clearwater, Florida, in 1955.

5594. Amateur Softball Association Women's Major Slow Pitch National Championships were held in Richmond, Virginia, in 1959. The winner was the Pearl Laundry team, of Richmond.

5595. "Mixed" female-male softball team league was introduced by the Amateur Softball Association of America in Cleveland, Ohio, in 1959, with teams composed of equal numbers of women and men. The new mixed leagues were soon playing throughout the United States.

SOFTBALL (1960-1969)

5596. Softball team to win six consecutive titles in the International Softball Congress World Championships was the Long Beach Nitehawks, of Long Beach, California, from 1955 to 1960.

SOFTBALL—(1960-1969)—*continued*

5597. Softball player to win two consecutive Most Valuable Player Awards in the Amateur Softball Association Major Fast Pitch National Championships was Weldon Haney of the Clearwater Bombers, in 1962 and 1963. He would win it again in 1968.

5598. Softball team to win three consecutive titles at the Amateur Softball Association Major Slow Pitch National Championships was the Dana Gardens team, of Dana Gardens, Cincinnati, Ohio, in 1964.

5599. College softball player to win the Erv Lind Award as the top defensive player in the Amateur Softball Association Women's Major Fast Pitch National Championships, was Nera White, of Nashville, Tennessee, in 1965.

5600. Softball player to win two consecutive batting titles in the Amateur Softball Association Major Fast Pitch National League was Ned Wickersham of Aurora, Illinois, in 1964 and 1965.

5601. World championships in fast-pitch softball were held in 1965 in Melbourne, Australia, and were won by the Australian women's team. Sponsored by the International Softball Federation, they were for women only, with a men's competition being added the following year.

5602. World championships in fast-pitch softball to include men's teams were held in Mexico City in 1966. The Aurora Sealmasters, of Aurora, Illinois, won the first men's championship.

5603. Softball player to be named the top pitcher in the Amateur Softball Association Women's Major Fast Pitch National Championship was Bertha Tickey, of Stratford, Connecticut, in 1968. The award was later named after her.

5604. United States Slo-Pitch Softball Association meeting convened in Pittsburgh, Pennsylvania, in 1968.

5605. Batting title of the Amateur Softball Association Major Slow Pitch National Championship batting crown was awarded in 1969. It was shared by two players who were tied at .600: Emma Pope of Virginia Beach, Virginia, and Kay Smith of Little Rock, Arkansas.

SOFTBALL (1970-1979)

5606. Softball player to win three consecutive Erv Lind Awards as the top defensive player in the Amateur Softball Association Women's Major Fast Pitch National Championships, was Carole Spanks, of Orange, California, from 1968 to 1970.

5607. Softball player to be named Most Valuable Player of the United States Slo-Pitch Association World Series was James Mortl, of Milwaukee, Wisconsin, in 1971.

5608. Softball player to win three consecutive Bertha Tickey Awards as the top pitcher in the Amateur Softball Association Women's Major Fast Pitch National Championship, was Nancy Wellborn, of Orange, California, from 1969 to 1971.

5609. World Series of the United States Slo-Pitch Association was won by the Accurate Welding team, of Milwaukee, Wisconsin, at Las Vegas, Nevada, in 1971.

5610. Softball team to win 10 titles at the Amateur Softball Association Major Fast Pitch National Championships was the Clearwater Bombers, who won ten championships between 1950 and 1973.

5611. Little League Softball and Senior Little League Softball programs were organized by Little League Baseball in 1974. These were girls' programs within the Little Leagues; girls were still unable to play in Little League baseball games.

5612. International Women's Professional Softball Association (WPSA) teams began play on May 28, 1976.

5613. American Professional Slo-Pitch League teams began play in 1977.

5614. Softball player to win five Most Valuable Player Awards in the Amateur Softball Association Major Fast Pitch National Tournament was Ty Stofflet, of Reading, Pennsylvania, who won in 1971, 1974, 1975, 1977, and 1978.

5615. Softball team to win eight consecutive titles in the Amateur Softball Association Women's Major Fast Pitch National Championships was the Raybestos Brakettes, of Stratford, Connecticut, from 1971 to 1978. Between 1959 and 1983 the Brakettes won 18 national championships.

5616. Softball event held at the Pan-American Games was in 1979. The softball gold medal was won by the United States women's team.

SOFTBALL (1980-1989)

5617. Softball team to win the Amateur Softball Association Super Slow Pitch National Championships was the Howard's Western Steer team, of Denver, Colorado, at Burlington, North Carolina, in 1981.

5618. College women's softball team to win the National Collegiate Athletic Association (NCAA) Division I College World Series was the University of California at Los Angeles, at Omaha, Nebraska, in 1982. UCLA would dominate college softball for a decade, winning seven more NCAA College World Series between 1983 and 1994.

5619. World championships in slow pitch softball were held in 1987, sponsored by the International Softball Federation. The United States team won the first title.

5620. National Collegiate Athletic Association (NCAA) Division I women's softball player to pitch 50 wins in a single season was Debbie Nichols of Louisiana Tech University, in 1988.

SOFTBALL (1990-1999)

5621. National Collegiate Athletic Association (NCAA) Division I women's softball player to pitch 182 complete career games was Debbie Nichols of Louisiana Tech University, from 1987 to 1990.

5622. National Collegiate Athletic Association (NCAA) Division I women's softball player to hit .589 for a whole season was Sarah Graziano of Coastal Carolina (University of South Carolina), in 1994.

5623. National Collegiate Athletic Association (NCAA) Division I women's softball player to pitch 62 complete games in a single season was Jessica Acord of the University of Santa Clara, in 1994.

5624. National Collegiate Athletic Association (NCAA) Division I women's softball player to hit 37 home runs in a single season was Laura Espinoza of the University of Arizona, in 1995.

5625. National Collegiate Athletic Association (NCAA) Division I women's softball player to get seven hits in a single game was Michelle Lafomara of Cornell University, against Coppin State College, on March 19, 1995.

5626. Women's fast pitch softball event held in the Olympic Games was in 1996 in Atlanta, Georgia. The eight-team competition was won by the team from the United States on July 30.

5627. National Collegiate Athletic Association (NCAA) Division I women's softball player to get 132 hits in a single season was Alison McCutcheon of the University of Arizona, in 1997.

5628. National Collegiate Athletic Association (NCAA) Division I women's softball player to get 405 hits during her college career was Alison McCutcheon of the University of Arizona, from 1995 to 1998.

SPEED SKATING (BEFORE 1900)

5629. International speed skating competition was held in 1889, in Hamburg, Germany. The sport had long been popular in the Netherlands, spreading from there throughout Europe and across the sea to the British Isles, especially to the Fens district of England.

5630. World championship in speed skating was held in Amsterdam, the Netherlands, in 1893. The first world champion in men's long-distance speed skating was Jaap Eden of the Netherlands.

5631. Speed skater to skate the 500 meters in under 50 seconds was Alfred Naess of Norway, who did it in 49.4 at Hamar, Norway, on February 5, 1893.

5632. Speed skater to skate the 10,000 meters in under 20 minutes was Halfdan Nielsen of Norway, who did it in 19:47.4 at Stockholm, Sweden, on February 13, 1893.

5633. Speed skater to skate the 1500 meters in under 2:30 minutes was Einar Halvorsen of Norway, who skated it in 2:29.6 at Hamar, Norway, on February 24, 1894.

5634. Speed skater to skate the 5000 meters in under 9 minutes was Jaap Eden of the Netherlands, who did it in 8:37.6 at Hamar, Norway, on February 25, 1894.

5635. Speed skater to be world champion in men's long-distance speed skating twice, and then three times, in a row was Jaap Eden of the Netherlands, who won the title in 1895 and 1896, after having won the inaugural championship in 1893. Because of unclear rules, there was no winner in 1894.

5636. Speed skater to skate the 10,000 meters in under 18 minutes was Jaap Eden of the Netherlands, who shaved more than a minute off the previous record with a time of 17:56 at Hamar, Norway, on February 23, 1895.

SPEED SKATING (1900-1929)

5637. Speed skater to be world champion in men's long-distance speed skating five times was Oscar Mathisen of Norway, who won in 1908, 1909, 1912, 1913, and 1914.

SPEED SKATING—(1900-1929)—*continued*

5638. Speed skater to skate the 1500 meters in under 2:20 minutes was Oscar Mathisen of Norway, who posted a time of 2:19.4 at Kristiania (later Oslo), Norway, on January 11, 1914.

5639. Men's 500-meter speed skating event held at the Olympic Winter Games was in 1924, at Chamonix, France. Charles Jewtraw of the United States won the event on January 26, with a time of 44.0 seconds.

5640. Men's 5000-meter speed skating event held at the Olympic Winter Games was in 1924, at Chamonix, France. The winner was A. Clas Thunberg of Finland, who posted a time of 8:39.0 minutes on January 26. He would win four more Olympic gold medals in his career.

5641. Men's 10,000-meter speed skating event held in the Olympic Winter Games was in 1924 at Chamonix, France. Julius Skutnabb of Finland took the first title with a time of 18:04.8 minutes on January 27.

5642. Men's 1500-meter speed skating event held at the Olympic Winter Games was in 1924, at Chamonix, France. A. Clas Thunberg of Finland won the inaugural event on January 27, with a time of 2:20.8 minutes.

5643. Men's four races combined speed skating title offered at the Olympic Winter Games was in 1924 in Chamonix, France. A. Clas Thunberg of Finland won the title on January 27, the only time the combined medal was ever given in the Olympics. Thunberg had won gold medals in the 1500- and 5000-meter events and the silver in the 10,000-meter, and tied for the bronze in the 500-meter race.

5644. Men's 10,000-meter Olympic speed skating race to be voided was on February 14, 1928, in the Olympic Winter Games at St. Moritz, Switzerland. Irving Jaffee of the United States led the seven of ten skaters who had completed their heats when the temperature rose so high as to make continuation impossible. Officials called for the race to be cancelled and rerun, but the Norwegian participants, who acknowledged Jaffee as the winner, had already gone home.

5645. Speed skater to win two consecutive men's 1500-meter speed skating titles at the Olympic Winter Games was A. Clas Thunberg of Finland, who won his second at St. Moritz, Switzerland, on February 14, 1928, after taking his first in 1924.

SPEED SKATING (1930-1949)

5646. Speed skater to skate the 1000 meters in under 1:30 minutes was A. Clas Thunberg of Finland, who had a time of 1:28.4 at Davos, Switzerland, on January 11, 1930.

5647. Woman speed skater to skate the 500 meters in under 1 minute was Liselotte Landbeck of Austria, who had a time of 58.7 seconds at Davos, Switzerland, on January 9, 1932.

5648. Olympic speed skating events to be held as races, rather than in pairs as had been usual, were at the 1932 Olympics in Lake Placid, New York. A Lake Placid skater, John Shea, won the men's 500-meter title event on February 4. However, the great Finnish champion A. Clas Thunberg refused to participate under this "North American" approach, which was dropped in later Olympics.

5649. Speed skater from the United States to win the men's 1500-meter title at the Olympic Winter Games was John Shea, who won on February 5, 1932, at Lake Placid, New York. The race was won in a mass heat on the second run; the first run had been stopped in mid-race by the officials, who accused the skaters of "loafing."

5650. Speed skater to win the men's 10,000-meter title at the Olympic Winter Games was Irving Jaffee of the United States, who won on February 8, 1932, at Lake Placid, New York, with a time of 19:13.6 minutes. He would have been the first two-time winner of the event, but the 1928 race, which he led, was voided because of problems with the ice.

5651. Woman speed skater to skate the 1000 meters in under 2 minutes was Synnove Lie of Norway, who had a time of 1:51.2 at Brandbu, Norway, on March 20, 1932.

5652. Speed skater to skate the 3000 meters in under 5 minutes was Michael Staksrud of Norway, who did it in 4:59.1 at Hamar, Norway, on February 25, 1933.

5653. Woman speed skater to skate the 1500 meters in under 3 minutes was Verne Lesche of Finland, who had a time of 2:49.0 minutes at Helsinki, Finland, on February 26, 1933.

5654. Woman speed skater to skate the 500 meters in under 50 seconds was Laila Schou Nilsen of Norway, who skated the distance in 49.3 at Oslo, Norway, on February 27, 1935.

5655. Speed skater to win the women's title in the world championships was Kit Klein of the United States, who won the title at the first women's world championships, held in 1936.

5656. World championships in speed skating to include women skaters were in 1936.

5657. Speed skater to win two Olympic gold medals in men's 5000-meter speed skating was Ivar Ballangrud of Norway. His second win came on February 12, 1936, at Garmisch-Partenkirchen, Germany, with an Olympic record time of 8:19.6 minutes, though short of his own world record of 8:17.2. His first win in the event had come in 1928; he had placed only fifth in 1932.

5658. Speed skater to win three gold medals in speed skating at a single Olympic Winter Games was Ivar Ballangrud of Norway, at Garmisch-Partenkirchen, Germany. He won the men's 500-meter event on February 11, 1936; the 5000-meter on February 12; and the 10,000-meter on February 14. He also won the silver medal in the 1500-meter contest on February 13.

5659. Woman speed skater to skate the 3000 meters in under 6 minutes was Laila Schou Nilsen of Norway, who did it in 5:29.6 at Davos, Switzerland, on January 30, 1937.

5660. Woman speed skater to skate the 5000 meters in under 10 minutes was Laila Schou Nilsen of Norway, who cut some 47 seconds off the previous record with a time of 9:28.3 at Davos, Switzerland, on January 31, 1937.

5661. Speed skater to be women's world champion in speed skating twice in a row was Laila Schou Nilsen of Norway, who won the title in 1937 and 1938.

5662. Speed skater to skate the 10,000 meters in under 17 minutes was Hjalmar Andersen of Norway, who had a time of 16:57.4 at Davos, Switzerland, on February 6, 1949.

SPEED SKATING (1950-1969)
5663. Speed skater to win three consecutive women's titles in the world championships was Maria Isakova of the Soviet Union, who won the title in 1948, 1949, and 1950.

5664. Woman speed skater to skate the 1500 meters in under 2:30 minutes was Maria Isakova of the Soviet Union, who posted a time of 2:29.5 minutes for the distance at Medeo, Kazakhstan, then in the Soviet Union, on February 12, 1951.

5665. Speed skater to skate the 5000 meters in under 8 minutes was Boris Shilkov of the Soviet Union, who posted a time of 7:45.6 at Medeo, Kazakhstan, then in the Soviet Union, on January 9, 1955.

5666. Speed skater to skate the 1500 meters in under 2:10 minutes was Yevgeny Grishin of the Soviet Union, who did it in 2:09.8 at Medeo, Kazakhstan, then in the Soviet Union, on January 10, 1955.

5667. Women's 1000-meter speed skating event held at the Olympic Winter Games was in 1960, at Squaw Valley, California. The gold medal was won by Klara Guseva of the Soviet Union, with a time of 1:34.1 minutes.

5668. Women's 3000-meter speed skating event held at the Olympic Winter Games was in 1960 at Squaw Valley, California. The winner was Lydia Skoblikova of the Soviet Union, with a time of 5:14.3 minutes on February 12. She would win three more gold medals in 1960 and two in 1964.

5669. Women's 500-meter speed skating event held at the Olympic Winter Games was in 1960, at Squaw Valley, California. Helga Haase of East Germany won the inaugural event with a time of 45.9 seconds on February 20. She was the first East German athlete to win an Olympic gold medal.

5670. Women's 1500-meter speed skating event held at the Olympic Winter Games was in 1960 at Squaw Valley, California. Lydia Skoblikova of the Soviet Union won with a world record of 2:25.2 minutes on February 21. She would win five more gold medals in her career.

5671. Speed skater to win two consecutive titles in the men's 500 meters at the Olympic Winter Games was Yevgeny Grishin of the Soviet Union, who won his second title on February 24, 1960, at Squaw Valley, California, after winning his first in 1956, both times equaling his own world record of 40.2 seconds.

5672. Speed skater to skate the 10,000 meters in under 16 minutes was Knut Johannesen of Norway, who skated it in 15:46.6 on February 27, 1960, to take the gold medal in the Olympic Winter Games at Squaw Valley, California. The silver medalist, Viktor Kosichkin of the Soviet Union, also broke the 16-minute barrier in the event, with 15:49.2.

5673. Speed skater to skate the 500 meters in under 40 seconds was Yevgeny Grishin of the Soviet Union, who posted a time of 39.6 at Medeo, Kazakhstan, then in the Soviet Union, on January 27, 1963.

5674. Speed skater to skate the 3000 meters in under 4:30 minutes was Jonny Nilsson of Sweden, who skated it in 4:27.6 at Tolga, Norway, on March 23, 1963.

SPEED SKATING—(1950-1969)—*continued*

5675. National team to sweep the medals in the women's 500-meter speed-skating event at the Olympic Winter Games was the Soviet Union. Led by Lydia Skoblikova, they took the top spots on January 30, 1964, at Innsbruck, Austria.

5676. National team to sweep the medals in the men's 5000-meter speed-skating event at the Olympic Winter Games was Norway, led by Knut Johannesen, on February 5, 1964, at Innsbruck, Austria.

5677. Speed skater to win two consecutive women's 1500-meter and 3000-meter titles at the Olympic Winter Games was Lydia Skoblikova of the Soviet Union. She won her second straight 1500-meter title at Innsbruck, Austria, on January 31, 1964, with an Olympic record time of 2:22.6 minutes, and 3000-meter title on February 2, with a time of 5:14.9 minutes. She had won both titles previously in 1960.

5678. Speed skater to win four gold medals in speed skating in a single Olympic Winter Games was Lydia Skoblikova of the Soviet Union, at Innsbruck, Austria, in 1964. Setting three Olympic records, she won the 500 meters on January 30, with a time of 45.0 seconds; the 1500 meters in 2:22.6 minutes on January 31; and the 1000 meters with a time of 1:33.2 minutes on February 1. Then on February 2, she also won the 3000 meters with a time of 5:14.9 minutes. She had previously won the 1500- and 3000-meter titles at the 1960 Olympics, giving her a career total of six speed skating gold medals.

5679. Speed skater to skate the 3000 meters in under 4:20 minutes was Ard (Adrianus) Schenk of the Netherlands, who skated it in 4:18.4 at Inzell, Germany, on February 25, 1967. He would also be the first to break the 4:10 barrier, in 1972.

5680. Woman speed skater to skate the 3000 meters in under 5 minutes was Stien Kaiser of Norway, who had a time of 4:56.8 at Inzell, Germany, on March 5, 1967.

5681. Speed skater to skate the 1000 meters in under 1:20 minutes was Ivar Eriksen of Norway, who did it in 1:19.5 at Inzell, Germany, on March 1, 1969.

SPEED SKATING (1970-1979)

5682. Spring world championships in speed skating were held in 1970. Valeriy Muratov on the men's side and Lyudmila Titova, both from Soviet Union, took the men's and women's titles, respectively.

5683. Woman speed skater to skate the 1000 meters in under 1:30 minutes was Lyudmila Titova of the Soviet Union, who had a time of 1:29.5 minutes at Medeo, Kazakhstan, then in the Soviet Union, on January 9, 1970.

5684. Speed skater to skate the 1500 meters in under 2 minutes was Ard (Adrianus) Schenk of the Netherlands, who skated it in 1:58.7 minutes at Davos, Switzerland, on January 16, 1971. The following year, he would take the 1500-meter title at the Olympic Winter Games.

5685. Speed skater to skate the 10,000 meters in under 15 minutes was Ard (Adrianus) Schenk of the Netherlands, who skated it in 14:55.9 at Inzell, Germany, on March 14, 1971.

5686. Speed skaters to become world champions in speed skating sprints were Leo Linkovesi of Finland on the men's side and Monika Pflug of West Germany on the women's side, who led their respective fields at Eskilstuna, Sweden, in 1972.

5687. Speed skater from the United States to win the women's 1500-meter title at the Olympic Winter Games was Dianne Holum, who posted an Olympic record time of 2:20.85 minutes on February 9, 1972, at Sapporo, Japan. She also won the 1500-meter title and took silver in the 3000-meter. She would later coach Eric Heiden, who swept all five men's speed skating events in 1980.

5688. Speed skater from the United States to win the women's 500-meter title at the Olympic Winter Games was Anne Henning. The 16-year-old skater won on February 10, 1972, at Sapporo, Japan, with an Olympic record time of 43.33 seconds, though short of her world record of 42.5.

5689. Speed skater to skate the 3000 meters in under 4:10 minutes was Ard (Adrianus) Schenk of the Netherlands, who skated the distance in 4:08.3 at Inzell, Germany, on March 2, 1972.

5690. Speed skater to win four women's titles at the long-distance speed skating championships was Atje Keulen-Deelstra of the Netherlands, who won the title in 1970, 1972, 1973, and 1974.

5691. Speed skater to win three consecutive women's titles at the world speed skating championships was Sheila Young of the United States, who won her third title in Berlin, in 1976, after winning previously in 1973 and 1975.

5692. Men's 1000-meter speed skating event held in the Olympic Winter Games was on February 12, 1976, at Innsbruck, Austria. The inaugural winner was Peter Mueller of the United States, with a time of 1:19.32 minutes.

5693. Speed skater to skate the 5000 meters in under 7 minutes was Kav A. Stenshjemmet of Norway, who had a time of 6:56.9 at Medeo, Kazakhstan, then in the Soviet Union, on March 19, 1977.

5694. World championships in short track speed skating were held in 1978, when Jim Lynch of Australia and Sarah Docter of the United States took the men's and women's titles, respectively. The championships would not be officially recognized by the International Skating Union (ISU) until 1981.

SPEED SKATING (1980-1989)

5695. Speed skater to win four consecutive men's titles at the world speed skating sprint championships was Eric Heiden of the United States, who won his fourth consecutive title at West Allis, Wisconsin, in 1980, after taking the previous three titles in 1977, 1978, and 1979.

5696. Speed skater to sweep all five men's speed skating events in a single Olympic Winter Games was Eric Heiden of the United States at Lake Placid, New York, in 1980. He won the 500-meter title with 38.03 seconds on February 15, the 5000-meter with 7:02.29 minutes on February 16, the 1000-meter with 1:15.18 minutes on February 19, the 1500-meter with 1:55.44 minutes on February 21, and the 10,000-meter with 14.28.13 minutes on February 23, setting an Olympic record in each and a world record in the 10,000.

5697. World championships in short track speed skating to be officially recognized by the International Skating Union (ISU) were held in 1981, though unofficial world championships had been held since 1978. Benoit Baril of Canada was the 1981 men's champion and Miyoshi Kato of Japan took her second straight, and first official, women's title.

5698. Woman speed skater to skate the 3000 meters in under 4:30 minutes was Gabi Schonbrunn of East Germany, who skated the distance in 4:21.70 minutes at Medeo, Kazakhstan, then in the Soviet Union, on March 28, 1981.

5699. Woman speed skater to skate the 5000 meters in under 8 minutes was Andrea Mitscherlich Schöne of East Germany, who bettered the previous record by well over a minute, with a time of 7:40.97 at Heerenveen, the Netherlands, on January 23, 1983.

5700. Woman speed skater to skate the 500 meters in under 40 seconds was Christa Rothenburger (later Luding-Rothenburger) of East Germany, who had a time of 30.69 seconds at Medeo, Kazakhstan, then in the Soviet Union, on March 25, 1983.

5701. Woman speed skater to skate the 1000 meters in under 1:20 minutes was Natalia Petruseva of the Soviet Union, who had a time of 1:19.31 at Medeo, Kazakhstan, then in the Soviet Union, on March 26, 1983.

5702. National team to sweep the medals in the women's 3000-meter speed-skating event at the Olympic Winter Games was East Germany, led by Andrea Mitscherlich Schöne, on February 15, 1984, at Sarajevo, Yugoslavia.

5703. World Cup series of competitions for speed skating was held 1985–1986. Dan Jansen of the United States won the men's 500- and 1000-meter titles in the inaugural season, with Michael Hadschieff of Austria winning 1500-meter and Dave Silk of the United States the 5000-and 10,000-meter events. On the women's side, East German skaters dominated, with Christa Rothenburger (later Luding-Rothenburger) taking the 500-meter title, Karin Enke Kania the 1000-meter, and Andrea Ehrig the 3000-meter. Annette Carlén of Sweden won the first 1500-meter title.

5704. Woman speed skater to skate the 1500 meters in under 2 minutes was Karin Enke Kania of East Germany, who broke the barrier with a time of 1:59.30 minutes at Medeo, Kazakhstan, then in the Soviet Union, on March 22, 1986.

5705. Speed skater to win six women's titles in the world speed skating sprint championships was Karin Enke Kania of East Germany. She won her sixth title in 1987, at Sainte Foy, Quebec, Canada, after winning her earlier crowns in 1980, 1981, 1983, 1984, and 1986.

5706. Speed skater to skate the 3000 meters in under 4 minutes was Leo Visser of the Netherlands, who broke the barrier with a time of 3:59.27 at Heerenveen, the Netherlands, on March 19, 1987.

5707. Speed skater to skate the 10,000 meters in under 14 minutes was Geir Karlstad of Norway, who had a time of 13:48.51 minutes at Calgary, Alberta, Canada, on December 6, 1987.

5708. Speed skater to win five women's long-distance speed skating titles in the world championships was Karin Enke Kania of East Germany, who won the title in 1982, 1984, 1986, 1987, and 1988.

SPEED SKATING—(1980-1989)—*continued*

5709. Women's 5000-meter speed skating event held in the Olympic Winter Games was in 1988 at Calgary, Alberta, Canada. The inaugural winner was Yvonne van Gennip of the Netherlands, who broke her own world record with a time of 7:14.13 minutes on February 28. She was an upset winner in both the 5000- and 1500-meter events, having been in the hospital with a foot infection two months earlier.

5710. Speed skater to win two consecutive men's 5000-meter titles at the Olympic Winter Games was S. Tomas Gustafson of Sweden. After his first win in 1984, his second came on February 17, 1988, at Calgary, Alberta, Canada, with an Olympic record time of 6:44.63 minutes. He also won the 10,000-meter event at Calgary, with a world-record time of 13:48.20 minutes.

SPEED SKATING (1990-1999)
5711. Speed skater to win two consecutive women's 500-meter titles in the Olympic Winter Games was Bonnie Blair of the United States. Her second win came at Albertville, France, on February 10, 1992, with a time of 40.33 seconds. That was short of her own world-record time of 39.10, posted in her 1988 Olympic win. She would win again in 1994.

5712. Speed skater from the United States to win the women's 1000-meter title at the Olympic Winter Games was Bonnie Blair, who won with a time of 1:21.90 minutes on February 14, 1992, at Albertville, France.

5713. National team to sweep the medals in the women's 5000-meter speed-skating event at the Olympic Winter Games was Germany, led by Gunda Kleeman Niemann (later Niemann-Stirnemann), on February 17, 1992, at Albertville, France.

5714. Men's 1000-meter short track speed skating event held in the Olympic Winter Games was in 1992. Kim Ki-hoon of South Korea posted a world-record time of 1:30.76 minutes in the inaugural event on February 20 at Albertville, France. He won another gold medal with South Korea's short track 500-meter relay speed skating team.

5715. Women's 3000-meter short track relay speed skating event held at the Olympic Winter Games was in 1992, at Albertville, France. With a time of 4:36.62 minutes on February 20, the winning team was from Canada: Angela Cutrone, Sylvie Daigle, Nathalie Lambert, and Annie Perrault.

5716. Men's 5000-meter relay short track speed skating event held at the Olympic Winter Games was in 1992. Kim Ki-hoon, Lee Joon-ho, Song Jae-kun, and Mo Ji-su formed the winning team from South Korea, setting a world record of 7:14.02 minutes on February 22, in Albertville, France. Kim also won the men's 100-meter individual title.

5717. Women's 500-meter short track speed skating event held at the Olympic Winter Games was in 1992. The inaugural winner was Cathy Turner of the United States, who posted a time of 47.04 seconds on February 22 at Albertville, France.

5718. Speed skater to win six men's world speed skating sprint championships was Igor Zhelezovski of the Soviet Union, who took his sixth title in 1993 in Ikaho, Japan. His earlier titles had been won in 1985, 1986, 1989, 1991, and 1992.

5719. Speed skaters to be named *Sports Illustrated* Sportsmen of the Year were Johann Olav Koss of Norway and Bonnie Blair of the United States in 1994. Both had been outstanding at the 1994 Olympic Winter Games in Lillehammer, Norway, with Koss winning the men's 1500-, 5000-, and 10,000-meter individual titles, and Blair winning her third straight 500-meter and second straight 1000-meter titles.

5720. Speed skater to win two consecutive titles in the men's 1500-meters at the Olympic Winter Games was Johann Olav Koss of Norway. His second win came at Lillehammer, Norway, on February 16, 1994, with a world-record time of 1:51.29 minutes. His earlier 1500-meter win had come in 1992. Also at Lillehammer, he won the 5000- and 10,000-meter individual titles.

5721. Speed skater to win three consecutive women's 500-meter titles at the Olympic Winter Games was Bonnie Blair of the United States. Her third straight win came on February 19, 1994, at Lillehammer, Norway, with a time of 39.25 seconds. That was faster than in her 1992 Olympic win, but not as fast as her world-record 39.10 from the 1988 Olympics. She would break the 39-second barrier on March 26, 1994, with a time of 38.99, lowering that to 38.69 on February 2, 1995, both in Calgary, Alberta, Canada.

5722. Speed skater to win two consecutive men's 1000-meter short track titles at the Olympic Winter Games was Kim Ki-hoon of South Korea. He won his second straight title with a time of 1:34.57 minutes, on February 22, 1994, in Lillehammer, Norway. That was slower than his world record of 1:30.76, set at the 1994 Olympics, when the event was first held.

5723. Speed skater to win two consecutive women's 1000-meter speed skating titles at the Olympic Winter Games was Bonnie Blair of the United States. After winning her first in 1992, she garnered her second at Lillehammer, Norway, on February 23, 1994, with a time of 1:18.74 minutes.

5724. Speed skater to win two consecutive women's 500-meter short track titles at the Olympic Winter Games was Cathy Turner of the United States. After winning the inaugural title in 1992, she won her second on February 24, 1994, at Lillehammer, Norway, with an Olympic-record time of 45.98 seconds.

5725. Men's 500-meter short track speed skating event held in the Olympic Winter Games was in 1994. Chae Ji-hoon of South Korea posted the winning time of 43.45 seconds on February 26, at Lillehammer, Norway.

5726. Women's short track 1000-meter speed skating event held at the Olympic Winter Games was in 1994 at Lillehammer, Norway. The winner was Chun Lee-kyung of South Korea, with a time of 1:36.87 minutes, set on February 26.

5727. Speed skater to skate the 1500 meters in under 1:50 minutes was Ids Postma of the Netherlands, who posted a time of 1:49.81 minutes at Berlin on November 30, 1997.

5728. Speed skater to skate the 5000 meters in under 6:30 minutes was Gianni Romme of the Netherlands, who skated it in 6:22.20 on February 8, 1998, at Nagano, Japan, where he also won the 10,000-meter event.

5729. Speed skater to skate the 10,000 meters in under 13:30 minutes was Gianni Romme of the Netherlands, who did it in 13:15.33 on February 17, 1998, at the Olympic Games in Nagano, Japan, where he also won the 5000 meters.

5730. Speed skater to skate the women's 5000-meter event in under 7 minutes was Gunda Kleeman Niemann-Stirnemann of Germany. Skating at the Olympic Winter Games in Nagano, Japan, on February 20, 1998, she cut almost four seconds off the previous record, with a new time of 6:59.65—only to lose the gold medal when teammate Claudia Pechstein bettered that time by .04 seconds.

5731. Speed skater to win two consecutive women's 5000-meter titles in the Olympic Winter Games was Claudia Pechstein of Germany. She had won her first in 1994. Her second was harder: Skating at Nagano, Japan, on February 20, 1998, Pechstein won the event with a time of 6:59.61 minutes, after her teammate, Gunda Kleeman Niemann-Stirnemann, had skated the first sub-7-minute race, in 6:59.65.

5732. Speed skater to win two consecutive women's 1000-meter short track titles in the Olympic Winter Games was Chun Lee-kyung of South Korea. After winning the inaugural competition in 1994, she won again on February 21, 1998, in Nagano, Japan, with a time of 1:42.776 minutes.

5733. Speed skater to skate the 3000 meters in under 3:50 minutes was Bart Veldkamp of Belgium, who posted a time of 3:48.91 at Calgary, Alberta, Canada, on March 21, 1998.

5734. Speed skater to skate the 500 meters in under 35 seconds was Hiroyasu Shimizu of Japan, who did it in 34.82 at Calgary, Alberta, Canada, on March 28, 1998.

5735. Speed skater to skate the 1000 meters in under 1:10 minutes was Sylvain Bouchard of Canada, who sped to a time of 1:09.60 at Calgary, Alberta, Canada, on March 29, 1998.

5736. Speed skater to be women's world champion in long-distance speed skating eight times was Gunda Kleeman Niemann-Stirnemann of Germany, who was champion 1991–1993 and 1995–1999.

SPEEDBALL

5737. Speedball was developed in 1921 by E. D. Mitchell at the University of Michigan, drawing on football, soccer, and basketball. It became a popular intramural game. By the 1950s it had come to be played largely by girls and women, but it would later be overshadowed by the increasing popularity of soccer.

SPORTS, GENERAL

5738. Written reference to sports in Britain's American colonies was in May 1611, when Thomas Dale arrived by ship from England to find settlers playing *bowles*, a form of bowling, on the streets of Jamestown, Virginia.

5739. Collegiate sporting event at which admission was charged was a May 14, 1874, game of American-style football played at Cambridge, Massachusetts, at which Harvard University defeated Canada's McGill University by a score of 3–0.

5740. Major sporting goods business was started by Chicago White Stockings pitcher Albert Spalding in Chicago, Illinois, in February 1876. Spalding, who retired from playing professional baseball in 1877, built his business into A. G. Spalding and Brothers.

5741. Issue of *The Sporting News* was published on March 17, 1886. Originally focusing on baseball, the popular weekly would survive to become a major publication for many sports, among them baseball, football, basketball, and hockey.

5742. Amateur Athletic Union (AAU) was founded in 1888, as a United States national organization aiming to control and regulate amateur sports throughout the country.

5743. Film of a sporting event was made on June 14, 1894, of a fight between Jack Cushing and Mike Leonard. It was staged by Thomas Edison in his laboratory in West Orange, New Jersey, and shot with a single stationary camera. Admission was charged when it was first shown to the public approximately two months later.

5744. African-American Intercollegiate Athletic Association was the Central (then Colored) Intercollegiate Athletic Association (CIAA), founded in 1912.

5745. African-American Southern Intercollegiate Athletic Conference (SIAC) was founded in 1913.

5746. Sporting event at which the United States national anthem was played was Game 1 of baseball's World Series, between the Boston Red Sox and the Chicago Cubs, at Chicago, Illinois, on September 5, 1918, during World War I. "The Star-Spangled Banner" was played and sung during the seventh-inning stretch.

5747. Athlete to become a broadcaster after retiring was Jack Graney. After a 14-year career playing baseball with the Cleveland Indians, Graney began announcing Indians games in 1932, continuing until 1954.

5748. Sportswriter to win a Pulitzer Prize was William H. Taylor, yachting editor of New York's *Herald-Tribune*. He was honored in 1934 for his writings on the America's Cup races.

5749. Zamboni ice-resurfacing machine sold commercially was put into operation at the Pasadena Winter Garden, in Pasadena, California, in 1950. The first working model of the machine had been developed in 1949 by Frank J. Zamboni for use in his Iceland Skating Rink in Paramount, California.

5750. Sporting event to be televised in color in the United States was a horse race, the Molly Pitcher Handicap, from Monmouth Park, in Oceanport, New Jersey, on July 14, 1951, broadcast in color by the CBS television network.

5751. Federal legislation mandating equal opportunities for female athletes in the United States was passed by the U.S. Congress in 1972. Under the Title IX legislation, schools risked loss of federal funds if they failed to provide equal athletic opportunities for girls and women at all levels of education.

5752. All-sports television network was ESPN, which began broadcasting on September 7, 1979. Headquartered in Bristol, Connecticut, it would be widely imitated.

5753. Academic standards for college scholarship athletes in the United States were introduced by the National Collegiate Athletic Association (NCAA) in 1983, requiring as minimums a C average in high school, a score of 700 (out of 1600) on the Scholastic Aptitude Test, or a 15 (out of 36) on the American College Test. A minimum C or 2.0 average was required in college.

5754. National Senior Olympics were held in 1987 in St. Louis, Missouri, with competition in various sports for athletes over 50. Becoming biennial, it would later be called the National Senior Sports Classic, sponsored by the U.S. National Senior Sports Organization.

5755. Professional athlete to be named an All-Star in two sports, and the first to play with an artificial hip was Bo Jackson. On December 19, 1990, he was named to the National Football League's Pro Bowl, as a member of the Los Angeles Raiders. Earlier that year, he had played in major league baseball's All-Star Game, as a member of the Kansas City Royals. His football career would be ended by a hip injury in January 1991, but he would return to baseball in 1993 as a member of the Chicago White Sox, playing with an artificial hip.

SQUASH

5756. Development of squash (squash rackets) a game similar to rackets, but using a softer ball, was in 1817 at the Harrow School in England.

5757. National championships in squash were held in 1907, sponsored by the United States Squash Racquets Association founded earlier that year. The inaugural title, for men only, was won by John Miskey.

5758. National governing body for squash in England was the Squash Rackets Association, founded in 1928, which would help to popularize the sport.

5759. Women's squash association was the Women's Squash Rackets Association, founded in 1934.

5760. International governing body for squash was the International Squash Rackets Federation (ISRF), founded in 1967. It became the World Squash Federation (WSF) from 1992.

5761. World amateur championships in squash sponsored by the International Squash Rackets Federation (ISRF), were held in 1967. Geoff Hunt of Australia won the first title and the next two, in 1969 and 1971.

5762. World team championships in squash were held in 1967, when the team from Australia took its first of six team titles. Sponsored by the International Squash Rackets Federation (ISRF), it was for amateurs only until 1981, when professionals were allowed into the competition.

5763. World open championships in squash were held in 1976. Geoff Hunt of Australia won the men's title, as he would also the next three times it was contested, in 1977, 1979, and 1980. Heather McKay, also of Australia, won the initial women's title, repeating in 1979. The championships would be held annually for men from the start (except for 1978) and for women from 1990.

5764. Women's team competition in the world open squash championships was held in 1979, when the inaugural winner was the team from Great Britain.

5765. World cup in squash was held in 1984. Jahangir Khan of Pakistan won the men's singles title, while Ross Thorne and Dean Williams of Australia brought home the men's doubles title.

5766. Squash player to win six men's singles world open titles was Jahangir Khan of Pakistan, who won in 1981–1985 and again in 1988.

5767. Squash player to win five women's singles world open titles was Susan Devoy of New Zealand, who won in 1985, 1987, 1990, 1991, and 1992.

5768. Squash player to win eight men's singles world open titles was Jansher Khan of Pakistan, who won first in 1987, again in 1989 and 1990, and then five times in a row: 1992–1996.

STONE THROW

5769. Men's stone throw event held in the Olympic Games was in 1906, in the unofficial Olympics in Athens, Greece. The winner was Nicolaos Georgantas of Greece, with a throw of 65 feet $4\frac{1}{2}$ inches (19.925 meters) on April 27, the only time the event was held.

SURFING

5770. International Surfing Championships were held in 1954 in Makaha, Hawaii, sponsored by the Waikiki Surf Club. Surfing had developed centuries earlier in the Pacific, and the modern sport would develop especially in Hawaii, Australia, and California, from the 1950s using fiberglass to replace traditional all-wooden surfboards.

5771. Surfer not born in Hawaii to win the International Surfing Championships was Bernard Farrelly of Australia, who in 1962 won the annual event held in Makaha, Hawaii.

5772. International organization for surfing was the International Surfing Federation, founded in 1964, after the first World Surfing Championships, held in Manly, Australia.

5773. World Surfing Championships were held in Manly, Australia, in 1964. Bernard Farrelly of Australia won the first title.

5774. World professional championships in surfing were held in 1970. The men's champion was Robert Young of Australia. A women's championship was added in 1977.

5775. Women's competition to be included in the world professional championships in surfing was in 1977, when the winner was Margo Oberg of Hawaii, who would win again in 1980 and 1981.

5776. Surfer to win five men's professional world titles was Mark Richards of Australia, who won first in 1975 and then four times in a row (1979–1982).

5777. Surfer to win four women's professional world titles was Frieda Zamba of the United States, who won in 1984, 1985, 1986, and 1988.

SWIMMING (BEFORE 1900)

5778. Swimming races on record date from 36 BC in Japan.

5779. International swimming competition on record took place in St. Kilda, Australia, near Melbourne, on February 9, 1858, when Australian Joseph Bennet defeated Charles Steedman of England in a 100-yard race.

5780. National organization for swimming was the Metropolitan Swimming Clubs Association, founded in London, England, in 1869. It later became the Amateur Swimming Association (ASA).

5781. National swimming championship was held in England in 1869, sponsored by the newly founded Metropolitan Swimming Clubs Association. The first champion was Tom Morris, who won a mile race in the Thames River, between Putney and Hammersmith Bridge in London.

5782. Overarm swimming stroke was developed in 1873 by John Arthur Trudgen of England. It would develop into the Australian crawl, so-called because Australians first used it widely and successfully.

5783. Person to swim the English Channel was Matthew Webb, a British merchant captain. Using the breaststroke, he crossed from Dover, England, to Cap Gris-Nez, France, on August 24–25, 1875, taking 21 hours 45 minutes to do so. Jean-Maria Seletti, a French soldier who escaped from a British prison ship, is claimed to have swum from Dover, England, to Boulogne, France, in 1815, but that claim cannot be substantiated.

5784. National swimming championships in the United States were held in 1883, sponsored by the New York Athletic Club, in New York City. A. F. Camacho of the Manhattan Athletic Club won the first championships by swimming 100 yards in 88.25 seconds. The championships would be held annually, from 1887 under the auspices of the Amateur Athletic Union (AAU).

5785. Men's 100-meter freestyle swimming event held in the Olympic Games was on April 11, 1896, in Athens, Greece. Actually held outdoors in the Bay of Zea, the inaugural competition was won with a time of 1:22.2 minutes by Alfréd Hajós (Alfréd Guttmann) of Hungary, competing under a pseudonym, which he later took as his legal name. On the same day he won the 1200-meter freestyle.

5786. Men's 1200-meter freestyle swimming event held in the Olympic Games was on April 11, 1896, in Athens, Greece. Held in the 55-degree waters off Greece, the dangerous race was won by Alfréd Hajós (Alfréd Guttmann) of Hungary, who also won the men's 100-meter freestyle that day. The event would be held at various distances, finally becoming the 1500-meter freestyle.

5787. Men's 500-meter freestyle event held in the Olympic Games was on April 11, 1896, in Athens, Greece, won by Paul Neumann of Austria with a time of 8:12.6 minutes. The event would later become the 400-meter freestyle.

SWIMMING (1900-1909)

5788. Men's 200-meter backstroke swimming event held in the Olympic Games was on August 12, 1900, in Paris, France, where the first gold medal went to Ernst Hoppenberg of Germany, with a time of 2:47.0 minutes. Then discontinued, the event would not be revived in the Olympics until 1964.

5789. Men's 200-meter freestyle swimming event held in the Olympic Games was in 1900 in Paris, France. Winning the final on August 12 was Frederick Lane of Australia, with a time of 2:25.2 minutes—unusually fast because the race was held in the River Seine, going *with* the current. Dropped after 1904, the event would be revived in 1968.

5790. Men's obstacle swimming race held in the Olympic Games was on August 12, 1900, in Paris, France, and never again. Frederick Lane of Australia won the event, which involved—among other things—climbing over and swimming under boats. Lane also won the 200-meter freestyle title.

5791. Men's underwater swimming race held in the Olympic Games was on August 12, 1900, when the one-time-only event was won by Charles de Vendeville of France.

5792. Men's 4000-meter freestyle swimming event held in the Olympic Games was on August 19, 1900, in Paris, France. John Arthur Jarvis of Great Britain won the event, which was never held again.

5793. Swimmer to race 100 yards in one minute was Frederick Lane of Australia, who did so on July 24, 1902.

5794. Men's 100-yard (later 100-meter) backstroke swimming event held in the Olympic Games was on September 6, 1904, in St. Louis, Missouri. Germans swept the medals, led by Walter Brack with a time of 1:16.8 minutes.

5795. Men's 50-yard (later 50-meter) freestyle swimming event held in the Olympic Games was on September 6, 1904, in St. Louis, Missouri. Zoltan Halmay of Hungary won the event in a second final. The first had been declared a dead heat, though most observers—except a U.S. judge—thought Halmay had clearly beaten the silver medalist, United States swimmer J. Scott Leary. The event would be revived with a 50-meter distance in 1988. Halmay had also won the 100-meter freestyle the day before.

5796. Men's 440-yard (later 400-meter) breaststroke event held in the Olympic Games was on September 7, 1904, in St. Louis, Missouri. The winner was Georg Zacharias of Germany, but the most influential swimmer was the bronze medalist, Jam (H. Jamison) Handy of the United States, who helped shaped modern swimming by developing new techniques of breathing and backstrokes, and by painting lines on the pool floor to guide competitive swimmers. The event was discontinued after 1920.

5797. Men's 880-yard freestyle swimming event held in the Olympic Games was on September 7, 1904, in St. Louis, Missouri. Emil Rausch of Germany won the event, the only time it was held.

5798. Swimmer to win both the men's 220-yard (later 200-meter) and 440-yard (later 400-meter) freestyle events in a single Olympic Games was Charles Daniels of the United States in 1904. Competing in St. Louis, Missouri, he won the 220-yard in 2:44.2 minutes on September 6, and the 440-yard in 6:16.2 minutes the next day.

5799. Men's 4 x 250-meter (later 4 x 200-meter) freestyle relay swimming event held in the Olympic Games was on April 26, 1906, in Athens, Greece. Posting a time of 16:52.4 minutes, the winning team was from Hungary: Jószef Ónody, Henrik Hajós, Geza Kiss, and Zoltán Halmay, who also won the men's 50-yard freestyle swimming competition.

5800. International governing body for swimming was the Fédération Internationale de Natation Amateur (FINA), founded in 1908, which governs swimming, diving, and water polo.

5801. Men's 200-meter breaststroke event held in the Olympic Games was in 1908 in London, England. Competing on July 18, Frederick Holman of Great Britain won with a world-record time of 3:09.2 minutes.

5802. Swimmer to win two consecutive men's 100-meter freestyle titles in the Olympic Games was Charles Daniels of the United States. After winning his first title at the unofficial 1906 Olympics, he went to London, England, winning his second on July 20, 1908, with a world-record time of 1:05.6 minutes. He had won the men's 220-yard and 440-yard freestyle events in 1904.

5803. Swimmer to win two consecutive men's 1500-meter freestyle titles in the Olympic Games was Henry Taylor of Great Britain. After winning his first in 1906, he won his second in London, England, where he set a world record of 22:48.4 minutes on July 25, 1908. He had previously won the 400-meter freestyle on July 16 and was on the winning 4 x 200-meter freestyle relay team on July 24.

SWIMMING (1910-1919)

5804. Swimmer to race the women's 100-meter freestyle in under 1:20 minutes was Fanny (Sarah) Durack of Australia, who posted a 1:19.8 in a heat en route to her gold medal in the final on July 2, 1912, in the Olympic Games at Stockholm, Sweden.

5805. Women's 100-meter freestyle swimming event held in the Olympic Games was in 1912, in Stockholm, Sweden. Competing on July 2, Fanny (Sarah) Durack and Mina (Wilhelmina) Wylie of Australia placed first and second. They had had to raise their own fare, because the Australian Olympic authorities thought it not worthwhile to send women athletes.

5806. National team to sweep the medals in the men's 200-meter breaststroke event in the Olympic Games was from Germany. Competing in Stockholm, Sweden, on July 10, 1912. Walter Bathe led the field with a time of 3:01.8 minutes, followed by Wilhelm Lützow and Kurt Mahlisch.

5807. Swimmer from the United States to win the men's 100-meter backstroke title in the Olympic Games was Harry Hebner, who won on July 14, 1912, in Stockholm, Sweden, with a time of 1:21.2 minutes.

5808. Women's 4 x 100-meter freestyle relay swimming event in the Olympic Games was on July 15, 1912, in Stockholm, Sweden. The team from Great Britain—Isabella Moore, Jennie Fletcher, Annie Speirs, and Irene Steer—won with a world-record time of 5:52.8 minutes. Fanny (Sarah) Durack and Mina (Wilhelmina) Wylie of Australia had finished first and second in the individual race, but were barred from swimming two legs each in the relay, as they had wished.

SWIMMING (1920-1929)

5809. National team to sweep the medals in the men's 100-meter freestyle in the Olympic Games was from the United States, at Antwerp, Belgium, in 1920. Duke Paoa Kahanamoku and Pua Kela Keiloha, both from Hawaii, and William Harris finished in that order in both the first final and the second, held because the fourth-place finisher, William Herald of Australia, claimed he had been fouled in the first final. Kahanamoku and his younger brother, Samuel Kahanamoku, would be part of another U.S. sweep in 1924, behind Johnny Weissmuller.

5810. National team to sweep the medals in the women's 100-meter freestyle swimming event in the Olympic Games was from the United States. Competing on August 25, 1920, in Antwerp, Belgium, Ethelda Bleibtrey led the field with a world-record time of 1:13.6 minutes, followed by Irene Guest and Frances Schroth. In 1919, Bleibtrey had been arrested in New York City for "nude swimming," when she took off the stockings American women then generally wore while swimming.

5811. Swimmer from the United States to win the men's 1500-meter freestyle title in the Olympic Games was Norman Ross, who led the field on August 25, 1920, in Antwerp, Belgium.

5812. Women's 300-meter (later 400-meter) freestyle event held in the Olympic Games was on August 28, 1920, in Antwerp, Belgium. Ethelda Bleibtrey led a United States sweep of the medals with a world-record time of 4:34.0 minutes, one of the five world records she set in three events at Antwerp.

5813. Swimmer to win Olympic gold medals 8 years apart, and to win Olympic medals 12 years apart was Duke Paoa Kahanamoku of Hawaii, then a United States territory. After winning his first title in 1912, he led a U.S. medal sweep at Antwerp, Belgium, in the first post–World War I Olympics, where he set a world record of 1:00.4 minutes, on August 29, 1920. In 1924, he was silver-medalist behind Johnny Weissmuller, with his younger brother, Samuel Kahanamoku, taking the bronze. He also won a medal in the men's 4 x 200-meter freestyle relay in 1920.

5814. Swimmers from the United States to win the women's 4 x 100-meter freestyle relay title in the Olympic Games were Margaret Woodbridge, Frances Schroth, Irene Guest, and Ethelda Bleibtrey. They won the event on August 29, 1920, in Antwerp, Belgium, with a world-record time of 5:11.6 minutes.

5815. Swimmer to race the men's 100-meter freestyle in under one minute was Johnny Weissmuller of the United States, who swam the distance in 58.6 seconds on July 9, 1922, which he would lower to 57.4 seconds on February 17, 1924, a record that would stand for a decade. At the Olympic Games, Weissmuller won gold medals in the men's 100-meter freestyle (1924 and 1928), the 400-meter freestyle (1924), and the 4 x 200-meter freestyle relay (1924 and 1928). He later became a film star, playing Tarzan.

5816. Swimmer to swim across the English Channel from France to England was Enrique Tiraboschi of Italy on August 11, 1923, taking 16 hours 33 minutes to do so.

5817. Swimmer to win two consecutive men's 100-meter backstroke titles in the Olympic Games was Warren Paoa Kealoha of the United States. After winning first in 1920, he went to Paris, France, to win again, with an Olympic-record time of 1:13.2 minutes on July 8, 1924.

5818. Women's 200-meter breaststroke event held in the Olympic Games was in 1924 in Paris, France. In the final on July 18, the winner was Lucy Morton of Great Britain, with a time of 3:33.2 minutes.

5819. Women's 100-meter backstroke event held in the Olympic Games was in 1924 in Paris, France. The winner was Sybil Bauer of the United States, with a time of 1:23.2 minutes on July 20. She was undefeated in women's backstroke events up to her death of cancer in 1927.

5820. Woman to swim the English Channel was Gertrude Ederle of the United States, on August 6, 1926. Though widely criticized for even attempting the feat, she swam from Cap Gris-Nez, France, to Kingsdown, England, near Dover, in just 14 hours 34 minutes, nearly two hours faster than any male swimmer up to that time.

5821. Olympic men's 200-meter breaststroke event in which the medalists all had times under three minutes was on August 9, 1928, in Amsterdam, the Netherlands, led by Yoshiyuki Tsuruta of Japan with a time of 2:48.8 minutes.

5822. Swimmer to win two consecutive gold medals in the men's 4 x 200-meter freestyle relay swimming event in the Olympic Games was Johnny Weissmuller. Part of the winning team in 1924, he won another medal in Amsterdam, the Netherlands, with his teammates setting a new world record of 9:36.2 minutes on August 11, 1928.

SWIMMING (1930-1949)

5823. Olympic men's 400-meter freestyle event at which all the medalists had times under five minutes was on August 10, 1932, in Los Angeles, California. Buster (Clarence) Crabbe of the United States, later a film star, led the field with a thrilling come-from-behind win and a time of 4:48.4 seconds.

5824. Swimmer to win two women's 4 x 100-meter freestyle relay titles in the Olympic Games was Eleanor Garatti Saville of the United States. As Garatti she was on the world-record-setting team in 1928. She then joined Josephine McKim, Helen Johns, and Helene Madison in setting another world record, with 4:38.0 minutes, on August 12, 1932, in Los Angeles, California.

5825. Olympic men's 1500-meter freestyle event in which the medalists all had times under 20 minutes was on August 13, 1932, in Los Angeles, California, where the field was led by Kusuo Kitamura of Japan. At 14, he was the youngest individual gold-medalist in Olympic history.

5826. Swimmer to win two consecutive men's 200-meter breaststroke titles was Yoshiyuki Tsuruta of Japan. After winning first in 1928, he went to Los Angeles, California, to win again with a time of 2:45.5 minutes on August 13, 1932.

5827. Swimmer to swim the English Channel in both directions was Edward Temme, who swam from France to England in 1927, then from England to France in 1934.

5828. Butterfly stroke used in the Olympic Games was in 1936, at that time a controversial variation of the breaststroke. Separate competitions for the two strokes would be established after the 1952 Olympics.

5829. Use of underwater photography to determine the winner of a swimming event was on April 15, 1939, at the Amateur Athletic Union (AAU) national championships in Detroit, Michigan.

5830. Swimmer to swim across the Strait of Gibraltar was Daniel Carpio of Peru on July 22, 1948, taking 9 hours 20 minutes to swim from Spain to Morocco.

SWIMMING (1950-1959)

5831. Woman to swim the English Channel from England to France, and to swim it in both directions was Florence Chadwick of the United States. After swimming from France to England in 1950, she reversed her course to go from England to France on September 11, 1951, in 16 hours 19 minutes.

5832. Olympic men's 1500-meter freestyle event in which the medalists all had times under 19 minutes was on August 2, 1952, in Helsinki, Finland, where the field was led by Ford Konno of the United States, with a time of 18:30.0 minutes.

5833. Swimmer to race the women's 400-meter freestyle event in under five minutes was Lorraine Crapp of Australia, who had a time of 4:50.8 seconds on August 25, 1956.

5834. Men's 200-meter butterfly swimming event held in the Olympic Games was in 1956 in Melbourne, Australia. In the finals on December 1, William Yorzyk of the United States took the inaugural title with a time of 2:19.3 minutes.

5835. Women's 100-meter butterfly event held in the Olympic Games was in 1956 in Melbourne, Australia. Posting a time of 1:11.0 minutes, Shelly Mann led a United States sweep of the medals on December 5.

5836. Ban on underwater stroking in the breaststroke swimming events in international competition was in 1957.

SWIMMING (1960-1969)

5837. Swimmer to win two consecutive men's 400-meter freestyle titles in the Olympic Games was I. Murray Rose, a vegetarian from Australia. He won his first in his home country in 1956, then went on to Rome, Italy, to win his second on August 31, 1960, with an Olympic-record time of 4:18.3 minutes. He also won the 1500-meter freestyle in 1956, coming in second in 1960.

5838. Men's 4 x 100-meter medley relay swimming event held in the Olympic Games was in 1960 in Rome, Italy. Winning with a world-record time of 4:05.4 minutes on September 1 was the United States team: Frank McKinney, Paul Hait, Lance Larson, and F. Jeffrey Farrell. In the qualifying heats, even the backup U.S. team broke the world record.

5839. Olympic women's 400-meter freestyle event in which the medalists all had times under five minutes was on September 1, 1960, in Rome, Italy. There the top six finishers had sub-five-minute times, led by S. Christine Von Saltza of the United States, with 4:50.6 minutes.

5840. Women's 4 x 100-meter medley relay swimming event held in the Olympic Games was in 1960 in Rome, Italy. The final, on September 2, was won by the United States team— Lynn Burke, Patty Kempner, Carolyn Schuler, and S. Christine Von Saltza—with a world-record time of 4:41.1 minutes.

SWIMMING—(1960-1969)—*continued*

5841. Olympic men's 1500-meter freestyle event in which the medalists all had times under 18 minutes was on September 3, 1960, in Rome, Italy, where the field was led by world-record-holder John Konrads of Australia, with a time of 17:19.6 minutes

5842. Swimmer to win two and then three consecutive women's 100-meter freestyle titles in the Olympic Games was Dawn Fraser of Australia. After winning first in 1956 in Melbourne, Australia, with a world-record time of 1:02.0 minutes, she won again on August 29, 1960, in Rome, Italy, with 1:01.2. She then had an unprecedented third win in a swimming event when she swam for 59.5 seconds on October 13, 1964, in Tokyo.

5843. Swimmer to swim across the English Channel and back consecutively was Antonio Abertondo of Argentina on September 20–21, 1961. The total swim took 43 hours 10 minutes: 18 hours 50 minutes from England to France, 4 minutes rest, then 24 hours 16 minutes from France to England.

5844. Swimmer to race the women's 100-meter freestyle in under one minute was Dawn Fraser of Australia, who set a time of 59.9 seconds on October 27, 1962. She would later lower that to 58.9, a time that would stand for nearly eight years.

5845. Swimmer to win three consecutive titles in the same event in the Olympic Games was Dawn Fraser of Australia, who won the women's 100-meter freestyle titles in 1956, 1960, and 1964, all in world or Olympic record-setting times—though she had been in a serious automobile accident in March 1964, which had left her in a neck cast for six weeks, and in which her mother had been killed.

5846. National team to sweep the medals in the men's 200-meter backstroke event in the Olympic Games was from the United States. Competing in Tokyo on October 13, 1964, Jed Graef led the field with a world-record time of 2:10.3 minutes, followed by Gary Dilley and Robert Bennett.

5847. Men's 4 x 100-meter freestyle relay swimming event held in the Olympic Games was in 1964 in Tokyo. The final, on October 14, was won by the United States team: Stephen Clark, Michael Austin, Gary Ilman, and Donald Schollander, with a world-record time of 3:32.2 minutes.

5848. Men's 400-meter individual medley swimming event held in the Olympic Games was in 1964 in Tokyo. On October 14, Richard Roth of the United States won with a world-record time of 4:45.4 minutes, though he had chosen the dangerous course of foregoing both surgery and medicine for an attack of appendicitis three days earlier, choosing to be packed in ice instead.

5849. Women's 400-meter individual medley swimming event held in the Olympic Games was in 1964 in Tokyo. Leading a United States sweep on October 17 was Donna De Varona, with a time of 5:18.7 minutes, followed by Sharon Finneran and Martha Randall. She won another gold medal with the world-record-setting 4 x 100-meter freestyle relay team. De Varona later became a television sports commentator.

5850. Swimmer to win four gold medals in a single Olympic Games was Donald Schollander of the United States in 1964 in Tokyo. On October 12, he won the men's 100-meter freestyle with an Olympic-record time of 53.4 seconds; on October 15 he won the men's 400-meter freestyle with a world-record time of 4:12.2 minutes. He also won medals in the 4 x 100-meter freestyle relay on October 14 and in the 4 x 200-meter freestyle relay on October 16 (he would win another in 1968).

5851. Men's 100-meter breaststroke event held in the Olympic Games was in 1968 in Mexico City. The inaugural title was won on October 19 by Donald McKenzie of the United States, with a time of 1:07.7 minutes.

5852. Women's 100-meter breaststroke event held in the Olympic Games was in 1968 in Mexico City. Victorious in the inaugural finals on October 19 was Djurdjica Bjedov of Yugoslavia, with a time of 1:15.8 minutes.

5853. Men's 200-meter individual medley swimming event held in the Olympic Games was in 1968. Competing on October 20 in Mexico City, Charles Hickcox led a United States sweep of the medals with a time of 2:12.0 minutes. He also won the men's 400-meter individual medley on October 23 and was on the winning team in the 4 x 100-meter medley relay on October 26.

5854. Swimmer to win the women's 200- and 400-meter individual medley events in the same Olympic Games was Claudia Kolb of the United States. She won the inaugural 200-meter event on October 20, 1968, with a time of 2:24.7 minutes. Five days later, she won the 400-meter individual medley, in Olympic-record 5:08.5 minutes.

5855. Women's 200-meter individual medley swimming event held in the Olympic Games was in 1968 in Mexico City. In the finals, on October 20, Claudia Kolb of the United States had a time of 2:24.7 minutes, to lead a United States sweep in the event, which included the butterfly, backstroke, breaststroke, and freestyle. Susan Pedersen took silver and Jan Henne bronze.

5856. Men's 100-meter butterfly swimming event held in the Olympic Games was in 1968 in Mexico City. Competing on October 21, Douglas Russell led a United States sweep of the top medals, with a time of 55.9 seconds. Mark Spitz was silver-medalist at 56.4 seconds, though he earlier set a world record at 55.6 seconds.

5857. Women's 200-meter freestyle event held in the Olympic Games was in 1968 in Mexico City. Competing on October 22, Deborah Meyer of the United States won the inaugural competition with a time of 2:10.5 minutes. She also won the 400-meter freestyle on October 20 and the 800-meter freestyle on October 24.

5858. Swimmer from the United States to win the women's 200-meter breaststroke title in the Olympic Games was Sharon Wichman, who had an Olympic-record time of 2:44.4 minutes on October 23, 1968, in Mexico City.

5859. Women's 200-meter butterfly event held in the Olympic Games was in 1968 in Mexico City. The winner of the inaugural competition was Ada Kok of the Netherlands, with a time of 2:24.7 minutes on October 24.

5860. Women's 800-meter freestyle swimming event held in the Olympic Games was in 1968 in Mexico City. The inaugural event was won on October 24 by Deborah Meyer of the United States, with a time of 9:24.0 minutes.

5861. Women's 200-meter backstroke event held in the Olympic Games was in 1968 in Mexico City. That inaugural competition was won on October 25 by Pokey (Lillian) Watson of the United States, with a time of 2:24.8 minutes.

5862. Swimmer to win three individual gold medals in a single Olympic Games was Deborah Meyer of the United States at Mexico City in 1968. On October 20, she won the 400-meter freestyle with an Olympic-record time of 4:31.8 minutes. She then won the 200-meter freestyle on October 22 in 2:10.5 minutes, an Olympic record, and finally the 800-meter freestyle on October 24 in 9:24.0 minutes.

SWIMMING (1970-1979)

5863. Swimmer to win two consecutive men's 1500-meter freestyle titles in the Olympic Games was Michael Burton of the United States. After winning his first in 1968, he went to Munich, West Germany, to win his second on September 4, 1972, with a world-record time of 15:52.58 minutes. He had also won the 400-meter freestyle in 1968.

5864. National team to sweep the medals in the men's 200-meter butterfly swimming event in the Olympic Games was from the United States, led by Mark Spitz with a world-record time of 2:00.70 minutes on August 28, 1972, in Munich, West Germany.

5865. Swimmer to win two consecutive gold medals in the men's 4 x 100-meter freestyle relay in the Olympic Games was Mark Spitz of the United States. On the winning team in 1968, he led his team to another victory on August 28, 1972, in Munich, West Germany, setting world records both times. It was one of his record-breaking seven gold medals at the 1972 Games.

5866. Olympic men's 100-meter backstroke event in which the medalists all had times under one minute was on August 29, 1972, in Munich, West Germany, where the field was led by Roland Matthes of East Germany. His time of 56:58 seconds was short of his own world record of 56.3, but good enough for his second consecutive title in the Olympic event. In 1976, he finished third, despite having had an appendectomy six weeks earlier.

5867. Olympic women's 100-meter freestyle event in which the medalists all had times under one minute was on August 29, 1972, in Munich, West Germany, where the top six medalists had sub-60-second times, led by Sandra Neilson of the United States with 58.59 seconds.

5868. Swimmer from the United States to win the women's 100-meter breaststroke in the Olympic Games was Catherine Carr, who had a world-record time of 1:13.58 minutes on September 2, 1972, in Munich, West Germany.

5869. Swimmer to win two consecutive men's 200-meter backstroke titles in the Olympic Games was Roland Matthes of East Germany. After winning first in 1968, he won again on September 2, 1972, in Munich, West Germany, with a time of 2:02.82 minutes, equaling his own world record. He also won the 100-meter backstroke title both times.

SWIMMING—(1970-1979)—*continued*

5870. Men's 200-meter individual medley event in which the top four swimmers broke the world record was on September 3, 1972, in Munich, West Germany. Gunnar Larsson of Sweden broke his own world record of 2:09.3 minutes with a new time of 2:07.17, but so did three United States competitors: Tim (Alexander) McKee at 2:08.37, Steven Furniss at 2:08.45, and Gary Hall at 2:08.49. Larsson and McKee also finished in that order in the men's 400-meter individual medley.

5871. Olympic men's 1500-meter freestyle event in which the medalists all had times under 17 minutes was on September 4, 1972, in Munich, West Germany, where the field was led by Michael Burton of the United States, who had a world-record time of 15:52.58 minutes, en route to his second consecutive title in the Olympic event.

5872. National team to sweep the medals in the women's 200-meter butterfly in the Olympic Games was from the United States. On September 24, 1972, in Munich, West Germany, Karen Moe led the field with a world-record 2:15.57 minutes, followed by Lynn Colella and Ellie Daniel.

5873. Introduction of skin-tight Lycra bathing suits into women's international swimming competition was in 1973, when the East German team wore the suits at the world swimming championships in Belgrade, Yugoslavia. Developed in West Germany, the so-called "Belgrade suits" were soon adopted around the world.

5874. Men's 100-meter backstroke event held in the world championships was in 1973 in Belgrade, Yugoslavia, where Roland Matthes of East Germany won with a time of 57.47 seconds.

5875. Men's 100-meter breaststroke event held in the world championships was in 1973 in Belgrade, Yugoslavia. John Hencken of the United States won with a time of 1:04.02 minutes.

5876. Men's 100-meter butterfly event held in the world championships was in 1973 in Belgrade, Yugoslavia, where Bruce Robertson of Canada won with a time of 55.69 seconds.

5877. Men's 100-meter freestyle event held at the world championships was in 1973, at Belgrade, Yugoslavia. James Montgomery of the United States took the title with a time of 51.70 seconds.

5878. Men's 1500-meter freestyle event held at the world championships was in 1973 at Belgrade, Yugoslavia. Steve Holland of Australia won the event with a time of 15:31.85 minutes.

5879. Men's 200-meter backstroke event held in the world championships was in 1973 in Belgrade, Yugoslavia, where Roland Matthes of East Germany won with a time of 2:01.87 minutes.

5880. Men's 200-meter breaststroke event held in the world championships was in 1973 in Belgrade, Yugoslavia. The winner was David Wilkie of Great Britain, with a time of 2:19.28 minutes.

5881. Men's 200-meter butterfly event held in the world championships was in 1973 in Belgrade, Yugoslavia, where it was won by Robin Backhaus of the United States, with a time of 2:03.32 minutes.

5882. Men's 200-meter freestyle event held at the world championships was in 1973 at Belgrade, Yugoslavia. James Montgomery of the United States won the inaugural event with a time of 1:53.02 minutes.

5883. Men's 200-meter individual medley event held at the world championships was in 1973 in Belgrade, Yugoslavia, where it was won by Gunnar Larsson of Sweden, with a time of 2:08.26 minutes.

5884. Men's 4 x 100-meter freestyle swimming event held at the world championships was in 1973 at Belgrade, Yugoslavia. The United States won the event there and at every world championships through century's end.

5885. Men's 4 x 100-meter medley relay event held at the world championships was in 1973 in Belgrade, Yugoslavia. The United States won the event then and every time until 1998, when Australia won it.

5886. Men's 4 x 200-meter freestyle swimming event held at the world championships was in 1973 at Belgrade, Yugoslavia, where the United States team won the inaugural event.

5887. Men's 400-meter freestyle event held at the world championships was in 1973 at Belgrade, Yugoslavia. Rick DeMont of the United States won the inaugural competition with a time of 3:58.18 minutes.

5888. Men's 400-meter individual medley event held at the world championships was in 1973 in Belgrade, Yugoslavia. The winner was András Hargitay of Hungary, with a time of 4:31.11 minutes.

5889. Swimmer to hold both the women's 100- and 200-meter breaststroke world titles at the same time was Renate Vogel of East Germany, who won the inaugural titles in both events in 1973 in Belgrade, Yugoslavia.

5890. Swimmer to hold both the women's 100-meter freestyle and 100-meter butterfly world titles at the same time was Kornelia Ender of East Germany, who won them both in 1973 in East Germany.

5891. Swimmer to hold the world titles in both the men's 100-meter and 200-meter freestyle events at the same time was James Montgomery of the United States, who won both at the first world championships in 1973 in Belgrade, Yugoslavia.

5892. Swimmer to hold world titles in both the 100- and 200-meter backstroke at the same time was Roland Matthes of East Germany, who won both in the first championships, held in 1973, in Belgrade, Yugoslavia.

5893. Synchronized swimming team event held in the world championships was in 1973 in Belgrade, Yugoslavia, where the United States team won, as it would also in 1975, 1978, 1991, and 1994.

5894. Women's 100-meter backstroke event held in the world championships was in 1973 in Belgrade, Yugoslavia, where Ulrike Richter of East Germany had a time of 1:05.42 minutes to take her first of two straight titles.

5895. Women's 100-meter breaststroke event held in the world championships was in 1973 in Belgrade, Yugoslavia, when the title was won by Renate Vogel of East Germany, with a time of 1:13.74 minutes.

5896. Women's 100-meter butterfly event held in the world championships was in 1973 in Belgrade, Yugoslavia, where Kornelia Ender won her first of two straight titles, with a time of 1:02.53 minutes.

5897. Women's 100-meter freestyle swimming event held in the world championships was in 1973 in Belgrade, Yugoslavia, where Kornelia Ender of East Germany took the first title with a time of 57.54 seconds.

5898. Women's 200-meter backstroke event held in the world championships was in 1973 in Belgrade, Yugoslavia, where the winner was Melissa Belote of the United States, who had a time of 2:20.52 minutes.

5899. Women's 200-meter breaststroke event held in the world championships was in 1973 in Belgrade, Yugoslavia. Renate Vogel of East Germany won the title with a time of 2:40.01 minutes.

5900. Women's 200-meter butterfly event held in the world championships was in 1973 in Belgrade, Yugoslavia, where Rosemarie Kother of East Germany won with a time of 2:13.76 minutes, as she would again in 1975.

5901. Women's 200-meter freestyle swimming event held in the world championships was in 1973 in Belgrade, Yugoslavia, where the titlist was Keena Rothhammer of the United States, with a time of 2:04.99 minutes.

5902. Women's 200-meter individual medley swimming event held in the world championships was in 1973 in Belgrade, Yugoslavia. Angela Hübner of East Germany was the first champion, with a time of 2:20.51 minutes.

5903. Women's 4 x 100-meter freestyle swimming event held in the world championships was in 1973 in Belgrade, Yugoslavia, where team from East Germany won the title, as they would also in 1975, 1982, and 1986.

5904. Women's 4 x 100-meter medley relay swimming event held in the world championships was in 1973 in Belgrade, Yugoslavia, where the team from East Germany won, as it would again in 1975, 1982, and 1986.

5905. Women's 400-meter freestyle swimming event held in the world championships was in 1973 in Belgrade, Yugoslavia, where Heather Greenwood of the United States won the first title with a time of 4:20.28 minutes.

5906. Women's 400-meter individual medley swimming event held in the world championships was in 1973 in Belgrade, Yugoslavia, when Gudrun Wegner of East Germany won with a time of 4:57.31 minutes.

5907. Women's 800-meter freestyle swimming event held in the world championships was in 1973 in Belgrade, Yugoslavia. The first champion was Novella Calligaris of Italy, with a time of 8:52.97 minutes.

5908. Women's solo and duet synchronized swimming events held in the world championships were in 1973 in Belgrade, Yugoslavia. Teresa Andersen of the United States won the first individual title and also the duet title with Gail Johnson.

5909. World championships in swimming and diving apart from the Olympic Games, were held in 1973 in Belgrade, Yugoslavia. Under the auspices of the Fédération Internationale de Natation Amateur (FINA), they were held quadrennially from 1978 until 1998, and then biennially.

SWIMMING—(1970-1979)—*continued*

5910. Swimmer to hold both the women's 200- and 400-meter freestyle world titles at the same time was Shirley Babashoff of the United States, who won them both at Cali, Colombia, in 1975, with times of 2:02.50 minutes in the 200-meters and 4:16.87 in the 400-meters.

5911. Swimmer to hold the world titles in both the men's 200- and 400-meter individual medleys at the same time was András Hargitay of Hungary, who won them both at Cali, Colombia, in 1975. He had won the 400-meter title first in 1973.

5912. Swimmer to hold world titles in both the men's 100- and 200-meter breaststroke at the same time was David Wilkie of Great Britain. He won both in 1975 at Cali, Colombia, after previously winning the 200-meter contest, in 1973.

5913. Swimmer to hold world titles in the men's 200-, 400-, and 1500-meter freestyle at the same time was Tim Shaw of the United States, who won all three in 1975 at Cali, Colombia, with times of 1:51.04 minutes, 3:54.88 minutes, and 15:28.92 minutes respectively.

5914. Swimmer to win two consecutive men's 100-meter backstroke titles in the world championships was Roland Matthes of East Germany. He won the inaugural competition in 1973, then won again in Cali, Colombia, in 1975 with a time of 58.15 seconds.

5915. Swimmer to win two consecutive men's 200-meter breaststroke titles in the world championships was David Wilkie of Great Britain. After winning first in 1973, he went to Cali, Colombia, in 1975 to win his second, with 2:18.23 minutes.

5916. Swimmer to win two consecutive men's 400-meter individual medley titles at the world championships was András Hargitay of Hungary. After winning his first in 1973, he went to Cali, Colombia, for his second in 1975, posting a time of 4:32.57 minutes.

5917. Swimmer to win two consecutive women's 100-meter backstroke world titles was Ulrike Richter of East Germany. After winning the inaugural competition in 1973, she won again in 1975 in Cali, Colombia, with a time of 1:03.30 minutes.

5918. Swimmer to win two consecutive women's 100-meter butterfly world titles was Kornelia Ender of East Germany. After winning the inaugural competition in 1973, she won again in 1975 in Cali, Colombia, with a time of 1:01.24 minutes.

5919. Swimmer to win two consecutive women's 100-meter freestyle world titles was Kornelia Ender of East Germany. After winning the inaugural competition in 1973, she won her second straight title in 1975 in Cali, Colombia.

5920. Swimmer to win two consecutive women's 200-meter butterfly world titles was Rosemarie Kother of East Germany. After winning the first competition in 1973, she came back in 1975 for her second title in Cali, Colombia.

5921. National Team to sweep the medals in the men's 200-meter freestyle in the Olympic Games was from the United States. Taking home the medals on July 19, 1976, in Montreal, Quebec, Canada, were Bruce Furniss, who had a world-record time of 1:50.29 minutes, followed by John Naber and James Montgomery.

5922. Olympic men's 1500-meter freestyle event in which the medalists all had times under 16 minutes was on July 20, 1976, in Montreal, Quebec, Canada, where the field was led by Brian Goodell of the United States, who had a world-record time of 15:02.40 minutes.

5923. Olympic men's 400-meter freestyle event at which all the medalists had times under four minutes was on July 22, 1976, in Montreal, Quebec, Canada. Brian Goodell of the United States had a world-record time of 3:51.93 minutes, followed by five other sub-four-minute swimmers.

5924. Swimmer to break the two-minute barrier in the men's 200-meter backstroke event was John Naber of the United States, who had a time of 1:59.19 on July 24, 1976, at the Olympic Games in Montreal, Quebec, Canada, where he also won the 100-meter backstroke and was on the winning 4 x 200-meter freestyle and 4 x 100-meter medley relay teams.

5925. Women's 400-meter individual medley event in the Olympic Games in which all the medalists had times under five minutes was on July 24, 1976, in Montreal, Quebec, Canada. Ulrike Tauber of East Germany had a world-record time of 4:42.77 minutes, and the next five finishers also had times under five minutes.

5926. Swimmer to race the men's 100-meter freestyle in under 50 seconds was James Montgomery of the United States, who set his world-record time of 49.99 seconds on July 25, 1976, at the Olympic Games in Montreal, Quebec, Canada.

5927. Woman swimmer to win four gold medals at a single Olympic Games was Kornelia Ender of East Germany, in 1976 in Montreal, Quebec, Canada. She set or equaled world records with all four of her wins: the women's 100-meter butterfly with a time of 1:00.13 minutes on July 2; the women's 4 x 100-meter medley relay team event on July 18; the women's 100-meter freestyle in 55.65 seconds on July 19; and the women's 200-meter freestyle in 1:59.26 minutes on July 22.

5928. Woman to swim across the English Channel and back consecutively was Cynthia Nichols of Canada, who swam the round trip on September 7–8, 1977, in 19 hours 55 minutes.

5929. Swimmer to hold both the women's 100- and 200-meter backstroke world titles at the same time was Linda Jezek of the United States, who had times of 1:02.55 minutes and 2:11.93 minutes respectively to win them both in 1978 in West Berlin.

5930. Swimmer to hold both the women's 400- and 800-meter freestyle world titles at the same time was Tracey Wickham of Australia, who won them both in 1978 in West Berlin, with times of 4:06.28 minutes in the 400-meters and 8:24.94 in the 800-meters.

5931. Swimmer to hold the women's 200-meter butterfly and both the 200- and 400-meter individual medley world titles at the same time was Tracy Caulkins of the United States, who won all three in 1978 in West Berlin.

SWIMMING (1980-1989)

5932. Swimmer to race the women's 100-meter freestyle in under 55 seconds was Barbara Krause of East Germany, who set a time of 54.98 in a preliminary heat, en route to a gold medal with 54.79 seconds on July 21, 1980, in the Moscow Olympics. She also won the women's 200-meter freestyle at Moscow.

5933. Swimmer to race the men's 1500-meter freestyle in under 15 minutes was Vladimir Selnikov of the Soviet Union on July 22, 1980, in his home country in Moscow, where he had a world-record time of 14:58.27 minutes. He did not compete in the Soviet-boycotted 1984 Olympics, but won the event again in 1988.

5934. National team to sweep the medals in the men's 400-meter freestyle event in the Olympic Games was the Soviet Union at the United States–boycotted Moscow Games, led by Vladimir Salnikov on July 24, 1980.

5935. National team to sweep the medals in the women's 100-meter backstroke, and the women's 200-meter backstroke, in the Olympic Games was from East Germany. Competing at the United States–boycotted Moscow Olympics on July 23, 1980, Rica Reinisch had a world record time of 1:00.86 minutes in the 100-meter backstroke, well ahead of teammates Ina Kleber and Petra Riedel. On July 27, Reinisch set another world record in the 200 meters, with 2:11.77 minutes, leading Cornelia Polit and Birgit Treiber. On July 20, she had set an earlier world record in the backstroke leg of the women's 4 x 100-meter medley relay.

5936. Swimmer to hold world titles in both the men's 200-meter freestyle and butterfly at the same time, and to hold both twice consecutively was Michael Gross of East Germany, who won both titles first in 1982 in Guayaquil, Ecuador, and then in 1986 in Madrid, Spain.

5937. Swimmer to win two consecutive men's 1500-meter freestyle titles at the world championships was Vladimir Salnikov of the Soviet Union. Following his first title in 1978, he posted a time of 15:01.77 minutes in 1982, to win his second title at Guayaquil, Ecuador.

5938. Swimmer to win two consecutive men's 400-meter freestyle titles at the world championships was Vladimir Salnikov of the Soviet Union. After winning his first in 1978, he went to Guayaquil, Ecuador, to win his second in 1982, with a time of 3:51.30 minutes.

5939. Swimmers to win gold medals in the same event at the same Olympic Games were Nancy Hogshead and Carrie Steinseifer, both of the United States, who each swam the 100-meter freestyle in 55.92 seconds on July 29, 1984, in Los Angeles, California.

5940. Swimmer to win the women's 100-meter butterfly title in the Olympic Games with a time of under one minute was Mary T. Meagher of the United States, who had a time of 59.26 seconds on August 2, 1984, in Los Angeles, California. She had held a sub-minute world record in 1980, but missed the Moscow Olympics because of the United State boycott.

5941. Duet synchronized swimming event held in the Olympic Games was in 1984 in Los Angeles, California. Winning on August 9 were Candy Costie and Tracie Ruiz (later Ruiz-Conforto) of the United States. Ruiz also won the solo title three days later. The event was discontinued after 1992.

SWIMMING—(1980-1989)—*continued*

5942. Solo synchronized swimming event held in the Olympic Games was in 1984 in Los Angeles, California. The final, on August 12, was won by reigning world champion Tracie Ruiz (later Ruiz-Conforto) of the United States, who also was gold-medalist in the duet competition. The event was discontinued after 1992.

5943. Swimmer to win both the women's 100- and 200-meter butterfly titles in the same Olympic Games was Mary T. Meagher of the United States in Los Angeles, California, in 1984. After winning the 100-meter butterfly on August 2, with a time of 59.26 seconds, she won the 200 meters on August 4, with an Olympic-record 2:06.90 minutes. In between, she won another gold medal swimming the butterfly leg in the women's 4 x 100-meter medley relay.

5944. Men's 50-meter freestyle event held at the world championships was in Madrid, Spain, in 1986. Tom Jager of the United States won the event with a time of 22.49 seconds.

5945. Swimmer to win two consecutive men's 200-meter butterfly titles at the world championships was Michael Gross of West Germany. He took his first title in 1982, then gained his second in 1986 in Madrid, Spain, with a time of 1:56.53 minutes.

5946. Swimmer to win two consecutive men's 200-meter freestyle titles at the world championships was Michael Gross of West Germany. After winning his first title in 1982, he went to Madrid, Spain, to win his second in 1986, with a time of 1:47.92 minutes.

5947. Swimmer to win two consecutive women's 200-meter backstroke world titles was Cornelia Sirch of East Germany. After winning first in 1982, she went to Madrid, Spain, in 1986 to take her second, with a time of 2:11.37 minutes.

5948. Women's 4 x 200-meter freestyle swimming event held in the world championships was in 1986 in Madrid, Spain, where the team from East Germany led the field.

5949. Women's 50-meter freestyle swimming event held in the world championships was in 1986 in Madrid, Spain, when the inaugural winner was Tamara Costache of Romania, with a time of 25.28 seconds.

5950. Swimmer to race the women's 50-meter freestyle in under 25 seconds was Yang Wenyi of China, who had a time of 24.98 seconds on April 11, 1988. She came in second in the event at the 1988 Olympics, but won the gold medal on July 31, 1992, in Barcelona, Spain, with a new record of 24.79.

5951. Swimmer to race the men's 100-meter backstroke event in under 55 seconds was David Berkoff of the United States, who had times of 54.95 and 54.91 in the Olympic trials on August 13, 1988. However, at the Olympics themselves, he fell short and had to settle for silver.

5952. Olympic men's 100-meter freestyle swimming event in which all the medalists had times under 50 seconds was on September 22, 1988, in Seoul, South Korea, led by Matthew Biondi of the United States, with 48.63 seconds, short of his own world record of 48.42.

5953. Women's 100-meter butterfly event in the Olympic Games in which all the medalists had times under one minute was on September 23, 1988, in Seoul, South Korea. Kristin Otto of East Germany led the field with 59.00 seconds, followed by teammate Birte Weigang with 59.45 and Qian Hong of China with 59.52.

5954. Men's 50-meter freestyle swimming event held in the Olympic Games was in 1988 in Seoul, South Korea. Winning the final on September 24 was Matthew Biondi of the United States, with a world record swim of 22.14 seconds. He would be silver-medalist in 1992.

5955. Women's 50-meter freestyle swimming event held in the Olympic Games was in 1988 in Seoul, South Korea. The final, on September 25, was won by Kristin Otto of East Germany with a time of 25.49 seconds, for one of her six gold medals in Seoul.

5956. Woman swimmer to win Olympic medals 12 years apart was Jill Sterkel of the United States. On July 25, 1976, in Montreal, Quebec, Canada, she won a gold medal as part of the women's 4 x 100-meter freestyle relay team. A dozen years later, on September 25, 1988, she tied for third in the women's 50-meter freestyle event in Seoul, South Korea.

SWIMMING (1990-1999)
5957. Men's 25-kilometer river/sea swim event held in the world championships was in January 1991 in Perth, Australia. The winner of the inaugural event was Chad Hundeby of the United States, with a time of 5:01:45.78 hours.

5958. Swimmer to win two consecutive men's 100-meter freestyle titles at the world championships was Matthew Biondi of the United States. After his initial win in 1986, he won again in January 1991 in Perth, Australia, with a time of 49.18 seconds.

5959. Swimmer to win two consecutive men's 200-meter individual medley titles at the world championships was Tamás Darnyi of Hungary. After winning his first in 1986, he went to Perth, Australia, for his second in January 1991, with a time of 1:59.36 minutes.

5960. Swimmer to win two consecutive men's 50-meter freestyle titles at the world championships was Tom Jager of the United States, who won the initial competition in 1986 and then won again in January 1991 in Perth, Australia, with a time of 22.16 seconds.

5961. Women's 25-kilometer river/sea swim event held in the world championships was in January 1991 in Perth, Australia. Shelley Taylor-Smith of Australia won the inaugural title with a time of 5:21:05.53 hours.

5962. Swimmer to win two consecutive men's 400-meter individual medley titles in the Olympic Games was Tamás Darnyi of Hungary. After setting a world record of 4:14.75 minutes in 1988, he went to Barcelona, Spain, for a second title, with a time of 4:14.23 minutes on July 27, 1992. He also won the 200-meter individual medley both times.

5963. Olympic men's 200-meter backstroke event in which the medalists all had times under two minutes was on July 28, 1992, in Barcelona, Spain. Martin López-Zubero Purcell of Spain led the field with an Olympic-record time of 1:58.47 minutes.

5964. Swimmer to win three consecutive gold medals in the men's 4 x 100-meter freestyle relay in the Olympic Games was Matthew Biondi of the United States, who was on the winning teams in 1984, 1988, and finally on July 29, 1992, in Barcelona, Spain. He had also won gold medals in 1988 on the men's 4 x 200-meter freestyle relay and 4 x 100-meter medley relay teams.

5965. Swimmer to win two consecutive women's 800-meter freestyle titles in the Olympic Games was Janet Evans of the United States. After winning her first in 1988, she went to Barcelona, Spain, to win her second on July 30, 1992, with a time of 8:25.52 minutes. She tried for a third in 1996, but came in sixth. She also won the 400-meter freestyle in 1988 and was second in 1992.

5966. Swimmer to win two consecutive gold medals in the women's 200-meter backstroke in the Olympic Games was Krisztina Egerszegi of Hungary. After winning her first in 1988, she went to Barcelona, Spain, for her second with an Olympic-record time of 2:07.06 minutes on July 31, 1992. She would win the event again in 1996; with her two other individual gold medals, she would have a total of five, a women's record.

5967. Swimmer to win two consecutive men's 200-meter individual medley titles in the Olympic Games was Tamás Darnyi of Hungary. After winning with a world record 2:00.17 minutes in 1988, he went to Barcelona, Spain, to win again on July 31, 1992, with a time of 2:00.76. In between he broke the two-minute barrier, setting a new record of 1:59.36. He also won the 400-meter individual medley both times.

5968. Pairs of twins to take the top two spots in the synchronized swimming duet competition in the Olympic Games were Karen Josephson and Sarah Josephson of the United States and Penny Vilagos and Vicky Vilagos of Canada, who won gold and silver respectively on August 7, 1992, in Barcelona, Spain.

5969. World short-course championships in swimming using a 25-meter pool, were held in December 1993 in Palma de Mallorca, with competitions across the full range of swimming events.

5970. Swimmer to win two consecutive men's 100-meter breaststroke titles at the world championships was Norbert Rózsa of Hungary. After winning his first in 1991, he went to Rome, Italy, in 1994 to win his second, with a time of 1:01.24 minutes.

5971. Swimmer to win two consecutive women's 800-meter freestyle world titles was Janet Evans of the United States. After her first win in 1991, she won again in 1994 at Rome, Italy, with a time of 8:29.85 minutes. In between, in 1992, she won the Olympic 800-meter freestyle title, as she had in 1988.

5972. Swimmer to win five individual gold medals, and three consecutive medals in the women's 200-meter backstroke, in the Olympic Games was Krisztina Egerszegi of Hungary. After capturing the women's 200-meter backstroke title in 1988 and 1992, she won it again in Atlanta, Georgia, on July 25, 1996, with a time of 2:07.83 minutes. In 1992, she had also won the women's 400-meter individual medley and the 100-meter backstroke.

SWIMMING—(1990-1999)—*continued*

5973. Women's 4 x 200-meter freestyle relay swimming event held in the Olympic Games was in 1996 in Atlanta, Georgia. Winning the event on July 25 was a team from the United States: Trina Jackson, Sheila Taormina, Cristina Teuscher, and Jenny Thompson.

5974. Synchronized swimming event held in the Olympic Games was in 1996 in Atlanta, Georgia. The 8-swimmer team from the United States won, after receiving a perfect score of 10 from nine of the judges on August 2.

5975. Men's 5-kilometer river/sea swim event held in the world championships was in 1998 in Perth, Australia. The winner was Aleksey Akatiyev of Russia, with a time of 55:18.6 minutes.

5976. Swimmer to hold world titles in both the 5- and 25-kilometer river/sea swim at the same time was Aleksey Akatiyev of Russia, who won both titles in 1998, in Perth, Australia.

5977. Women's 5-kilometer river/sea swim event held in the world championships was in 1998 in Perth, Australia, where the inaugural title went to Erica Rose of the United States, who had a time of 59:23.5 minutes.

SWIMMING (2000-)

5978. Bodysuits for swimming events in the Olympic Games were approved in July 2000. They made their first appearance at the Games in Sydney, Australia, in September.

5979. Male swimmers to win gold medals in the same event at the same Olympic Games were Gary Hall, Jr., and Anthony Ervin, both of the United States, who both won gold medals for their identical times of 21.98 seconds in the 50-meter freestyle on September 22, 2000, at Sydney, Australia. Ervin was also the first African-American on the United States Olympic swimming team.

T

TABLE TENNIS

5980. Table tennis equipment on record was being sold in England in the 1880s. The celluloid ball was developed by James Gibb and manufactured by J. Jacques & Son, where the popular name "Ping-Pong" probably originated.

5981. National governing body in table tennis was the Ping Pong Association, founded in England in 1902. Later called the Table Tennis Association, it would in 1927 be replaced by the English Table Tennis Association.

5982. International governing body for table tennis was the International Table Tennis Federation (ITTF), founded in 1926. Ivor Montagu was its first president.

5983. Swaythling Cup was offered in 1926 to the winning men's team in the European (later world) table tennis championships. The first winner was the team from Hungary. The cup was offered by Lady Swaythling, the mother of Ivor Montagu, first president of the International Table Tennis Federation (ITTF).

5984. International championships in table tennis were the European championships held in December 1926, sponsored by the newly formed International Table Tennis Federation (ITTF). Athletes from Hungary swept the medals. Roland Jacobi won the men's singles title and also the men's doubles title, with Daniel Pécsi. Mária Mednyánszky (later Mednyánszky-Klucsik) won the women's singles title and the women's doubles title, with Erika Flamm, as well as the mixed doubles title with Zoltán Mechlovits. The European championships would come to be considered world championships, held annually in some periods and biennially from 1959.

5985. St. Bride Vase was offered by the St. Bride Institute Table Tennis Club of London, England, to the men's singles champion in the European (later considered world) championships starting in 1929. The first winner was Fred Perry of England, later better known as a three-time Wimbledon tennis champion.

5986. G. Geist Prize was offered by Dr. Gaspar Geist of the Hungarian Table Tennis Association to the women's singles champion in the European (later considered world) championships starting in 1931. The first winner was Mária Mednyánszky (later Mednyánszky-Klucsik), who won her fifth straight women's single title (1926, 1928–1931; no championships were held in 1927).

5987. Table tennis player to win five women's singles titles in the world championships was Mária Mednyánszky (later Mednyánszky-Klucsik), who won the first five titles offered (1926, 1928–1931). She also won seven women's doubles titles (1928, 1930–1935) and six mixed doubles titles (1927–1928, 1930–1931, 1933 [twice]).

5988. Marcel Corbillon Cup was offered in 1934 to the winning women's team in the European (later world) table tennis championships. The first winner was the team from Germany. The cup was offered by and named for the president of the French Table Tennis Association.

5989. Table tennis player to win five men's singles titles in the world championships was Viktor Barna of Hungary. After winning first in 1930, he came back to win four times in a row (1932–1935). He also won eight men's doubles titles (1929–1935, 1939).

5990. Iran Cup was offered by the Shah of Iran to the winning men's doubles team in the world table tennis championships starting in 1947. The first winners were Adolf Slár and Bohumil Vána of Czechoslovakia.

5991. Heydusek Prize was offered by Zdenek Heydusek of the Czechoslovak Table Tennis Association in 1948 to the winning mixed doubles team in the world table tennis championships. The first winners were Richard Miles and Thelma Thall of the United States.

5992. Pope Trophy was offered by W. J. Pope of the International Table Tennis Federation (ITTF) in 1948 to the winning women's doubles team in the world table tennis championships. The first winners were Margaret Franks and Vera Thomas of England.

5993. World cup in table tennis was held in 1980, originally for men's singles only. The inaugural winner was Guo Yuehua of China, who won again in 1982. Men's and women's doubles would be added in 1996 and women's singles in 1996.

5994. Men's doubles table tennis event held in the Olympic Games was in 1988 in Seoul, South Korea. In the finals on September 30, the winners were Chen Longcan and Wei Qingguang of China.

5995. Women's doubles table tennis event held in the Olympic Games was in 1988 in Seoul, South Korea. Winning on September 30 were a duo from South Korea: Hyun Jung-hwa and Yang Young-ja.

5996. Men's singles table tennis event held in the Olympic Games was in 1988 in Seoul, South Korea. After the top five seeded players were all upset, Yoo Nam-kyu of South Korea emerged as the inaugural winner on October 1.

5997. Women's singles table tennis event held in the Olympic Games was in 1988 in Seoul, South Korea. Two of China's top-ranked players had been left off the Olympic team, but nevertheless Chen Jing led a Chinese sweep of the medals on October 1.

5998. Men's and women's doubles events to be included in the world cup in table tennis were in 1990. The winners were all from South Korea: Yoo Nam-kyu and Kim Taek-soo won the men's doubles title, and Hyun Jung-hwa and Hong Cha-ok the women's.

5999. World team cup in table tennis was held in 1990. The team from Sweden won the men's team title and the team from China the women's.

6000. Table tennis player to win both singles and doubles titles in the Olympic Games was Deng Yaping of China. She first won the doubles title with Qiao Hong on August 3, 1992, in Barcelona, Spain, and then two days later defeated Qiao for the women singles title.

6001. Women's singles event to be included in the world cup in table tennis was in 1996, when the inaugural winner was Deng Yaping of China.

TENNIS (BEFORE 1900)

6002. Written reference to tennis was in *Dialogus miraculorum*, written ca. 1219–1223 by Caesarius of Heisterbach, a German monk. In France it was called *jeu de la paume* (game of the palm), for early versions were played with the palm of the hand, and later *jeu de paume*. When modern lawn tennis developed in the late 19th century, this earlier version of the sport, which survived, would be called *real tennis*. In the United States, real tennis would be called *court tennis*, and in Australia it was *royal tennis*.

6003. Development of the tennis racket strung with sheepgut, was in approximately 1500 in Europe. Before then, the ball was hit with the palm of the player's hand.

6004. International championships in tennis the version now called *real tennis*, took place in approximately 1750, when the winner was named Clergé (first name unknown) from France.

6005. Tennis game in its modern form was patented by Major Walter Wingfield of Belgrave Road, Pimlico, Middlesex County, England. After demonstrating it at a country house party in Nantclwyd, Wales, in 1873, he was granted a provisional patent for his outdoor "Portable Court for Playing Tennis" on Febru-

TENNIS—(BEFORE 1900)—*continued*

ary 23, 1874, and a formal patent on July 24. Wingfield also issued a book, *The Rules of the Game*, and developed the materials needed to set up the court and play the game, selling all as a complete package. The game was an instant success.

6006. Tennis club formed in the United States was the New Orleans Lawn Tennis Club, founded in 1876.

6007. Tennis tournament on record in the United States was played at Nahant, Massachusetts, near Boston, in 1876. It was organized primarily by Dr. James Dwight of the United States, who defeated his cousin, Fred Sears, in the finals to win the tournament.

6008. Tennis tournament played at Wimbledon was in 1877, at the All England Tennis and Croquet Club, previously the All England Croquet Club, on Worple Road, in Wimbledon, near London, England. Spencer Gore won on July 19, defeating William Marshall in the finals in straight sets, 6–1, 6–2, 6–4. The tournament would be held at the Worple Road location until 1922, and would then move to Church Road, Wimbledon, which remained its home. Originally a tournament for men's singles only, Wimbledon added women's singles and men's doubles in 1884, and women's doubles and mixed doubles in 1913.

6009. National tennis championships in Scotland were played in Edinburgh in 1878.

6010. National tennis championships in Ireland were played in Dublin, in 1879. Vere Goold won the men's singles title, and May Langrishe the women's.

6011. Tennis player to win two consecutive men's singles championships at Wimbledon was John Hartley of Great Britain, in 1879 and 1880.

6012. Men's doubles competition at the United States national tennis championships was held in 1881. The winners were Clarence Clark and Fred Taylor, both of the United States, who defeated Alexander Van Rensselaer and Arthur Newbold in straight sets, 6–5, 6–4, 6–5, at the Newport Casino, Newport, Rhode Island.

6013. Men's singles competition at the United States national tennis championships was in 1881, when Richard Sears of the United States, then a student at Harvard University, defeated William Glyn in straight sets, 6–0, 6–3, 6–2, at the Newport Casino, Newport, Rhode Island.

6014. United States national tennis championships were held in 1881, sponsored by the newly formed United States National Lawn Tennis Association at the Newport Casino in Newport, Rhode Island, originally with competitions for men's singles and men's doubles only. The tournament would be played at the Newport Casino until 1914; it would become the U.S. Open in 1968.

6015. United States intercollegiate tennis championships were held in the spring of 1883. Joseph Clark of Harvard University won the men's singles title. Clark and Howard Taylor, also of Harvard, teamed up for the first doubles title. Taylor won the men's singles title in autumn 1883, the only year in which two championship matches were played.

6016. Men's doubles tennis championship at Wimbledon was held in 1884. It was won by twin brothers William Renshaw and Ernest Renshaw, both of Great Britain, who had a 6–3, 6–1, 1–6, 6–4 win over Ernest Lewis and Edward Williams.

6017. Women's singles tennis championships at Wimbledon were held in 1884. Maud Watson of Great Britain was the first champion, defeating Lillian Watson 6–8, 6–3, 6–3. She would win the title again in 1885.

6018. Tennis player to win two consecutive women's singles championships at Wimbledon was Maud Watson of Great Britain, who won the event the first two times it was held, in 1884 and 1885. Her second win was over Blanche Bingley, 6–1, 7–5.

6019. Tennis player to win six consecutive men's singles championships at Wimbledon, and seven overall was William Renshaw of Great Britain, who was champion from 1881 to 1886, and again in 1889. Three of those wins (1882, 1883 and 1889) were over his twin brother and doubles partner, Ernest Renshaw.

6020. Tennis player to win seven consecutive men's singles titles at the United States national championships was Richard Sears of the United States, who was champion from 1881 to 1887, the first seven times the championships were held.

6021. Tennis player to win six consecutive men's doubles titles at the United States national championships was Richard Sears of the United States, from 1882 to 1887, partnered by Joseph Clark in 1885 and James Dwight in the other wins.

6022. Tennis player to win the women's singles title at the United States national championships was Ellen Hansell of the United States, who defeated Laura Knight in straight sets, 6–1, 6–0, at the Philadelphia Cricket Club, in Philadelphia, Pennsylvania, in 1887.

6023. United States national tennis championships to include women were held in 1887, at the Philadelphia Cricket Club, in Philadelphia, Pennsylvania.

6024. National organization for tennis in Great Britain was the Lawn Tennis Association, founded in 1888.

6025. Tennis player to win two consecutive women's singles titles at the United States national championships was Bertha Townsend of the United States, in 1888 and 1889.

6026. Tennis players to win five men's doubles championships at Wimbledon were twin brothers William Renshaw and Ernest Renshaw, both of Great Britain, who won in 1884, 1885, 1886, 1888, and 1889.

6027. United States women's doubles national tennis championships were held in 1889. Competing at the Philadelphia Cricket Club, in Philadelphia, Pennsylvania, Margarette Ballard and Bertha Townsend of the United States defeated Marion Wright and Laura Knight in straight sets, 6–0, 6–2.

6028. Sisters to win the women's doubles title at the United States national tennis championships were Grace Roosevelt and Ellen Roosevelt of the United States, who defeated Bertha Townsend and Margarette Ballard 6–1, 6–2, in 1890.

6029. French national tennis championships were held in 1891, for men only. Women's events would be added in 1897. The championships would be for citizens or residents of France only until 1925, when the event became international.

6030. United States national interscholastic boys singles tennis championships were held in 1891, when the winner was Robert Wrenn of the Cambridge Latin School, in Cambridge, Massachusetts.

6031. Tennis player to win two consecutive women's doubles titles at the United States national championships was Mabel Cahill of the United States, with Emma Leavitt Morgan in 1891 and Adeline McKinlay in 1892.

6032. United States national tennis championships to include mixed doubles competition were held in 1892. The first winners were Mabel Cahill and Clarence Hobart of the United States, who defeated Elisabeth Moore and Rod Beach 5–7, 6–1, 6–4, at the Philadelphia Cricket Club, in Philadelphia, Pennsylvania.

6033. Tennis player to win three consecutive Wimbledon women's singles championships, and five overall was Lottie (Charlotte) Dod of Great Britain. After winning the title in 1887 and 1888, she won it three straight times (1891–1893).

6034. Tennis player to win two consecutive mixed doubles titles at the United States national tennis championships was Clarence Hobart of the United States, with Mabel Cahill in 1892 and Ellen Roosevelt in 1893.

6035. Men's doubles tennis event held in the Olympic Games was in 1896 in Athens, Greece. In the April 11 finals, the winners were Fredrich "Fritz" Traun of Germany and John Boland of Great Britain, who had filled in at the last minute when Traun's partner became ill. Boland also won the singles title on the same day. The event would be held through 1924, then not again until 1988.

6036. Men's singles tennis event held in the Olympic Games was in 1896 in Athens, Greece. Winning the inaugural competition on April 11 was John Boland of Great Britain, who had originally traveled to the Olympics simply as a spectator. He also won the first doubles title that day, as a fill-in for a sick competitor. The event would be held through 1924, then not again until 1988.

6037. Tennis player to win five consecutive women's doubles titles at the United States national championships was Juliette Atkinson of the United States, who won in 1894 and 1895 with Helen Hellwig, in 1896 with Elisabeth Moore, and in 1897 and 1898 with her sister Kathleen Atkinson. Atkinson also won the U.S. women's doubles title in 1901 and 1902.

TENNIS (1900-1919)

6038. Davis Cup match took place at the Longwood Cricket Club, in Boston, Massachusetts, in 1900, and was won by Great Britain, which defeated the United States team 3–0, with Britain winning first possession of the Cup, formally named the International Lawn Tennis Challenge Trophy.

TENNIS—(1900-1919)—*continued*

6039. Mixed doubles tennis event held in the Olympic Games was in 1900 in Paris, France. Winning on July 11 were Charlotte "Chattie" Cooper, also the women's individual champion, and Reginald Doherty, the men's bronze-medalist by default, both of Great Britain. The event would be discontinued after 1924.

6040. National team to sweep the medals in the men's singles tennis event in the Olympic Games was from Great Britain, which took the top four spots on July 11, 1900, in Paris. Laurie (Hugh) Doherty won the final over Harold Mahoney. Reginald Doherty placed third, after declining to play his younger brother in the semifinals.

6041. Women's singles tennis event held in the Olympic Games was in 1900 in Paris. Winning the competition on July 11 was Charlotte "Chattie" Cooper of Great Britain, the first woman to win an Olympic gold medal. The event would be held through 1924, then not again until 1988.

6042. Tennis player to win two men's doubles titles in the Olympic Games was Reginald Doherty of Great Britain. After winning his first doubles title in 1900 with his brother, Laurie (Hugh) Doherty, he won his second on July 15, 1908, in London, England, with a new partner, George Hillyard.

6043. National team to sweep the medals in the men's doubles tennis event in the Olympic Games was from the United States. Leading the sweep on September 3, 1904, in St. Louis, Missouri, were Edgar Leonard and Beals Wright, who also won the singles title.

6044. Tennis player from the United States to win the men's singles title in the Olympic Games was Beals Wright, who led a United States sweep of the medals on September 3, 1904, in St. Louis, Missouri. He also won the doubles title.

6045. Australian national tennis championships were held at Warehouseman's Grounds, in Melbourne, Australia, in 1905. The first men's singles title was won by Rodney Heath of Australia, who defeated A. H. Curtis 4–6, 6–3, 6–4, 6–4. The inaugural doubles champions were Randolph Lycett and Tom Tachell, both of Australia, who defeated E. T. Barnard and B. Spence 11–9, 8–6, 1–6, 4–6, 6–1. Women's singles, women's doubles, and mixed doubles championships would be introduced in 1922.

6046. Tennis player to win four women's singles titles at the United States national championships was Elisabeth Moore of the United States, who won in 1896, 1901, 1903, and 1905.

6047. Tennis players to win eight Wimbledon men's doubles championships were brothers Laurie (Hugh) Doherty and Reginald Doherty of Great Britain, who won from 1897 to 1901, were runners-up in 1902, and then won again from 1903 to 1905.

6048. Tennis player to win three gold medals in tennis in the same Olympic Games was Max Decugis of France in 1906. In the unofficial Olympics in Athens, Greece, he won the men's singles title on April 23; the men's doubles on April 25, with Maurice Germot; and the mixed doubles on April 26, with Marie Decugis. He would win the latter again in 1920 with Suzanne Lenglen.

6049. Jeu de paume (court tennis or real tennis) event in the Olympic Games was in 1908, the only time the event was included in the Olympics. Winning in London, England, on May 28, was Jay Gould of the United States.

6050. Tennis player to win two Australian national men's singles championships was Rodney Heath of Australia, in 1905 and 1910.

6051. Tennis player to win three consecutive women's singles titles at the United States national championships was Hazel Hotchkiss (later Wightman) of the United States, from 1909 to 1911.

6052. Tennis player to win two Australian national men's doubles championships was Rodney Heath of Australia, who won with Tony Wilding in 1905 and Randolph Lycett in 1911.

6053. Mixed doubles championships at Wimbledon were held in 1913. The inaugural winners were Agnes Daniell Tuckey and Hope Crisp, both of Great Britain, who defeated Ethel Thomson Lacombe and James Parke. Tuckey and Crisp had lost the first set 3–6, but were leading 5–3 in the second set when their opponents had to retire.

6054. Women's doubles championships at Wimbledon were held in 1913. Winifred Slocock McNair and Dora Boothby, both of Great Britain, won the first title 4–6, 2–4. The losers, Charlotte Sterry and Dorothea Douglass Chambers, won the first set, but were forced to retire in the second.

6055. International governing body for tennis was the International Lawn Tennis Federation, later the International Tennis Federation (ITF), founded on March 1, 1913, in Paris, France.

6056. Tennis player to win seven Wimbledon women's singles championships was Dorothea Douglass Chambers of Great Britain, who won in 1903, 1904, and 1906 as Douglass, and again in 1910, 1911, 1913, and 1914.

6057. United States men's singles tennis national championship matches played at the West Side Tennis Club in Forest Hills, Queens, New York, were in 1915, when Bill Johnston of the United States defeated Maurice McLoughlin 1–6, 6–0, 7–6, 10–8. From its inception, in 1881, the tournament had been played at the Newport Casino in Newport, Rhode Island.

6058. Tennis player to win four straight women's singles titles at the United States national championships was Norwegian-born Molla Bjurstedt (later Mallory) of the United States, from 1915 to 1918. She would later win four more: in 1920, 1921, 1922 and 1926.

TENNIS (1920-1939)
6059. Tennis player to win six United States mixed doubles titles was Hazel Hotchkiss Wightman of the United States. As Hotchkiss, she won in 1909 and 1911 with Wallace Johnson and in 1910 with Joseph Carpenter. Then as Wightman, she won in 1915 with Harry Johnson, in 1918 with Irving Wright, and finally in 1920 with Wallace Johnson again.

6060. Women's doubles tennis event held in the Olympic Games was in 1920 in Antwerp, Belgium. In the finals on August 24, the winners were Winifred McNair and Kitty (Kathleen) McKane of Great Britain. The event would be discontinued after 1924 and would resume only in 1988.

6061. Australian mixed doubles national tennis championships were in 1922, when the inaugural winners were Esna Boyd and John Hawkes of Australia, who defeated Lorna Utz and H. S. Utz in straight sets, 6–1, 6–1.

6062. Australian women's doubles national tennis championships were in 1922. Esna Boyd and Marjorie Mountain of Australia won the event, defeating Floris St. George and Lorna Utz 1–6, 6–4, 7–5.

6063. Australian women's singles national tennis championships were held in 1922. The winner was Mall Molesworth of Australia, who defeated Esna Boyd in straight sets, 6–3, 10–8.

6064. Wimbledon tennis tournament at a new site was held in 1922, when the All England Club tournament moved into a larger facility in the town of Wimbledon. Center Court at the new Wimbledon site seated 14,750.

6065. Tennis player to win five consecutive Wimbledon women's singles championships was Suzanne Lenglen of France, from 1919 to 1923. She would win again in 1925.

6066. Tennis player to win two consecutive Australian national women's doubles championships was Esna Boyd of Australia, who won with Marjorie Mountain in 1922 and Sylvia Lance in 1923. Boyd would win a third doubles title in 1928.

6067. Tennis player to win two consecutive Australian national women's singles tennis championships was Mall Molesworth of Australia, who won in 1923, after taking the inaugural title in 1922, both times defeating Esna Boyd.

6068. Tennis players to win five consecutive Wimbledon women's doubles championships were Suzanne Lenglen of France and Elizabeth Ryan of the United States, from 1919 to 1923. They would also win in 1925, and Ryan would win again in 1926, 1927, and 1930 with different partners.

6069. United States men's singles national tennis championship matches played at the new West Side Tennis Club stadium in Forest Hills, Queens, New York, were in 1924. Bill Tilden of the United States, the dominant men's player of the 1920s, defeated Bill Johnston in straight sets, 6–1, 9–7, 6–2, to win the championship. It was the fifth of Tilden's six consecutive United States men's singles titles. The tournament had been played at Forest Hills from 1915 to 1920, then moved to the Germantown Cricket Club in Pennsylvania from 1921 to 1923.

6070. Tennis players from the United States to win the women's doubles title in the Olympic Games were Hazel Hotchkiss Wightman and Helen Wills (later Moody), who won the title on July 19, 1924, in Paris, France, the last time the event was held until 1988.

6071. Tennis player from the United States to win the women's singles tennis title in the Olympic Games was Helen Wills (later Moody), who won the competition on July 20, 1924, in Paris, France. Tennis competitions would not be held again in the Olympics until 1988.

TENNIS—(1920-1939)—*continued*

6072. Tennis players from the United States to win the mixed doubles event in the Olympic Games were Hazel Hotchkiss Wightman and Richard Norris Williams, who won on July 21, 1924, in Paris, France, the last time the event was held in the Olympics.

6073. Wightman Cup tennis tournament was held at the new West Side Tennis Club stadium at Forest Hills, Queens, New York, starting on August 10, 1924. The United States team defeated the British team 7–0.

6074. French national tennis championships open to those who were not citizens or residents of France were in 1925. Until then, only French citizens or residents were admitted into title play.

6075. Tennis player to win 98 straight men's singles matches was Bill Tilden of the United States, during the 1924 and 1925 seasons.

6076. Tennis player to win a French national men's singles championship after the event became international was René Lacoste of France, who defeated Jean Borotra in straight sets, 7–5, 6–1, 6–4, in 1925.

6077. Tennis player to win the French national women's singles championship after the event became international was Suzanne Lenglen of France, who defeated Kitty (Kathleen) McKane in straight sets, 6–1, 6–2, in 1925. Lenglen also won the title in 1926, becoming the first to win it in two consecutive years.

6078. Tennis players to win a French national mixed doubles championship after the event became international were Suzanne Lenglen and Jacques Brugnon, both of France, who defeated Didi Vlasto and Henri Cochet in straight sets, 5–2, 6–2, in 1925. Lenglen and Brugnon won the title again in 1926, becoming the first to win the titles twice consecutively.

6079. Tennis players to win the French national men's doubles championship after the event became international were Jean Borotra and René Lacoste, both of France, who defeated Henri Cochet and Jacques Brugnon 7–5, 4–6, 6–3, 2–6, 6–3, in 1925. The duo would win again in 1929, becoming the first to win the event twice, and Borotra would win in 1928 with another partner, becoming the first to win it three times.

6080. Tennis players to win the French national women's doubles championship after the event became international were Suzanne Lenglen and Didi Vlasto, both of France, who defeated Evelyn Coler and Kitty (Kathleen) McKane 6–1, 9–11, 6–2, in 1925. Lenglen and Vlasto defeated the same opponents in 1926, becoming the first to win the event twice.

6081. Tennis star to turn professional was Suzanne Lenglen of France, in 1926. She became the chief attraction of the first professional tour, in a touring group that included Vinnie Richards and Mary K. Browne. They played their first exhibition matches at Madison Square Garden, in New York City, on October 9, 1926, and went on to tour the United States and Canada into early 1927.

6082. Tennis players to win three Australian national mixed doubles championships were Esna Boyd and John Hawkes of Australia, who won in 1922, 1926, and 1927.

6083. Tennis player to win two consecutive Wimbledon mixed doubles championships was Elizabeth Ryan of the United States, who won with Frank Hunter in 1927 and Pat Spence in 1928. She had earlier won in 1919, 1921, and 1923, and would win again in 1930 and 1932, with different partners, for a total of seven mixed doubles titles.

6084. Tennis player to win eight women's singles titles at the United States national championships was Norwegian-born Molla Bjurstedt (later Mallory) of the United States. As Bjurstedt, she won in 1915–1918, and then as Mallory she won again in 1920–1922 and 1929.

6085. Tennis player to win four Australian national mixed doubles titles was Daphne Akhurst of Australia, who won in 1924 and 1925 with John Willard, in 1928 with Jean Borotra, and in 1929 with Gar Moon.

6086. Tennis player to win three French national men's singles championships after the event became international was René Lacoste of France, in 1925, 1927, and 1929. Lacoste introduced short-sleeved cotton tennis shirts, now called polo shirts, with his famous trademark crocodile logo.

6087. Tennis player to win five Australian national women's singles championships, and the first to win three in a row was Daphne Akhurst of Australia, who won in 1925, 1926, and 1928–1930.

6088. Tennis player to win nine Wimbledon women's doubles titles was Elizabeth Ryan of the United States, who won in 1919–1923 and 1925 with Suzanne Lenglen, in 1926 with Mary K. Browne, and in 1927 and 1930 with Helen Wills (later Moody).

6089. Tennis player to win three, four, and then five French national men's doubles championships after the event became international was Jacques Brugnon of France, who won with Henri Cochet in 1927, 1930, and 1932, and with Jean Borotra in 1928 and 1934.

6090. Tennis player to win four French national men's singles championships after the event became international was Henri Cochet of France, who won in 1926, 1928, 1930, and 1932.

6091. Tennis player to win seven Wimbledon mixed doubles championships was Elizabeth Ryan of the United States, who won in 1919, 1921, 1923, 1927–1928, 1930, and 1932, the first three with Randolph Lycett, and the rest each with a different partner.

6092. Tennis player to win three consecutive French national women's singles championships, and then four overall, after the event became international was Helen Wills Moody of the United States, who won from 1928 to 1930, the first two times as Wills, and then again in 1932.

6093. Tennis player to win 158 straight women's singles matches was Helen Wills Moody of the United States, whose winning streak extended from 1926 to 1933.

6094. Tennis player to win three consecutive Australian national men's singles championships, and four overall was Jack Crawford of Australia, who won 1931–1933. He also won a fourth men's singles title, in 1935.

6095. United States national women's and men's singles tennis championships to both be played at the West Side Tennis Club stadium in Forest Hills, Queens, New York, were in 1935. The women's singles had been played at Forest Hills since 1921, but separately and at different times from the men's event, which had been played at Forest Hills since 1924. In the 1935 women's event, Helen Jacobs of the United States defeated Sarah Palfrey Fabyan in straight sets, 6–2, 6–4. Wilmer Allison of the United States won the men's singles, defeating Sidney Wood in straight sets, 6–2, 6–2, 6–3.

6096. Tennis player to win three consecutive Wimbledon mixed doubles championships was Dorothy Round of Great Britain, who won in 1934 with Ryuki Miki and in 1935 and 1936 with Fred Perry.

6097. Tennis tournament to be televised in Great Britain was the Wimbledon tournament in 1937.

6098. Tennis player to achieve a Grand Slam winning the United States, British (Wimbledon), French, and Australian national men's singles championships in a single year, was Don Budge of the United States, in 1938.

6099. Tennis player to win the Wimbledon women's singles championship eight times was Helen Wills Moody of the United States, in 1927–1930, 1932–1933, 1936, and 1938, the first three as Wills.

6100. Tennis tournament to be televised in the United States was the Davis Cup tournament of 1938, played in Rye, New York.

6101. Tennis player to win six French national women's doubles championships after the event became international, and four times consecutively was Simone Passemard Mathieu of France, who was partnered with Elizabeth Ryan in 1933 and 1934, with Billie (Adeline) Yorke in 1936–1938, and with Jadwiga Jedrzejowska in 1939.

TENNIS (1940-1959)

6102. Tennis player to win 10 consecutive Australian national men's doubles championships was Adrian Quist of Australia. He won his first two in 1936 and 1937, with Don Turnbull, and the rest with John Bromwich (1938–1940 and 1946–1950). The tournament was not held from 1941 to 1945 because of World War II.

6103. Tennis player to win four consecutive Australian national women's singles championships was Nancye Wynne Bolton of Australia. As Wynne, she won in 1940. Then, after the 1941–1945 break for World War II, she won again in 1946–1948, as Bolton. She also won 10 women's doubles titles and 4 mixed doubles titles.

6104. Tennis players to win five consecutive Australian national women's doubles championships were Thelma Coyne (later Long) and Nancye Wynne (later Bolton), both of Australia, from 1936 to 1940. After the 1941–1945 break for the war, Long and Bolton would win the title five more times (1947–1949, 1951, and 1952), for a record 10 titles as a team. Long upped her record to 12 by winning with Mary Bevis Hawton in 1956 and 1958.

TENNIS—(1940-1959)—*continued*

6105. Tennis player to win four consecutive United States mixed doubles national championships, and nine overall was Margaret Osborne duPont of the United States. As Osborne, she won from 1943 to 1946 with Bill Tilden. As duPont, she also won in 1950 with Ken McGregor, in 1956 with Ken Rosewall, and in 1958–1960 with Neale Fraser, for a total of nine mixed doubles titles in all. She also won 13 women's doubles titles and three women's singles titles.

6106. Tennis player to win 10 consecutive women's doubles titles at the United States national championships, and 13 overall was Margaret Osborne duPont of the United States. After winning in 1941 with Sarah Palfrey Fabyan, she won nine straight with Louise Brough of the United States (1942–1950), the latter three years as duPont. The duPont-Brough duo also won in 1955–1957, giving duPont 13 women's doubles titles—to go with her nine mixed doubles titles and three women's singles titles.

6107. Woman tennis player to achieve a Grand Slam winning the United States, British (Wimbledon), French, and Australian women's singles national championships in a single year, was Maureen Connolly of the United States, in 1953.

6108. United States National Tennis Hall of Fame was opened in 1955, at the Newport Casino, at Newport, Rhode Island, the site of the first United States national championships in 1881. The organization became the International Tennis Hall of Fame in 1975.

6109. African-American tennis player to win a Grand Slam event was Althea Gibson, who won the French women's singles national championship in 1956, when she also won the French women's doubles title. Her third Grand Slam title of 1956 was the women's doubles championship at Wimbledon, with Angela Buxton.

6110. African-American tennis player to win the women's singles championship at Wimbledon was Althea Gibson, who defeated Darlene Hard 6–3, 6–2, in 1957. Gibson went on to win the 1957 United States women's singles national championships, her first of two consecutive titles at Forest Hills, Queens, New York, where she also won the 1957 mixed doubles title with Kurt Nielsen.

6111. United States intercollegiate women's singles and women's doubles national championships were held in 1958. Darlene Hard of Pomona College, California, won the singles titles. Sue Metzger and Erika Puetz Webster won the doubles.

TENNIS (1960-1969)

6112. Federation Cup championships were held at the Queen's Club, London, England, in 1963. The United States women's team, which included Billie Jean King and Darlene Hard, defeated Australia 2–1. This first Federation Cup tournament included teams from 16 nations.

6113. Tennis player to win six consecutive French national men's doubles championships after the event became international was Roy Emerson of Australia, who won with Neale Fraser in 1960 and 1962, Rod Laver in 1961, Manuel Santana in 1963, Ken Fletcher in 1964, and Fred Stolle in 1965.

6114. Tennis player to win seven consecutive Australian national women's singles championships, and 11 overall was Margaret Smith of Australia, from 1960 to 1966. As Margaret Smith Court, she also won the title in 1969–1971 and 1973, for a total of 11.

6115. Steel tennis rackets came into widespread use in 1967, after their adoption by several tennis stars, most notably Billie Jean King of the United States.

6116. Tennis player to win five consecutive Australian national men's singles championships, and six overall was Roy Emerson of Australia, who won from 1963 to 1967, after an earlier win in 1961.

6117. French Open men's doubles tennis match was won by Ken Rosewall and Fred Stolle, both of Australia, who defeated Roy Emerson and Rod Laver in straight sets, 6–3, 6–4, 6–3, at Stade Roland Garros, in Paris, France, in 1968.

6118. French Open men's singles tennis match was won by Ken Rosewall of Australia, who defeated Rod Laver 6-3, 6-1, 2-6, 6-2, at Stade Roland Garros, in Paris, France, in 1968.

6119. French Open mixed doubles tennis match was won by Françoise Durr and Jean Claude Barclay, both of France, who defeated Billie Jean King and Owen Davidson 6–1, 6–4, at Stade Roland Garros, in Paris, France, in 1968.

6120. French Open tennis tournament was held at Stade Roland Garros, in Paris, France, in 1968, as what had been the amateurs-only French national championships became for the first time a tournament open to both professionals and amateurs, with cash payments to the winners.

6121. French Open women's doubles tennis match was won by Françoise Durr of France and Ann Haydon Jones of Great Britain, who defeated Rosie Casals and Billie Jean King 7–5, 4–6, 6–4, at Stade Roland Garros, in Paris, France, in 1968.

6122. French Open women's singles tennis match was won by Nancy Richey of the United States, who defeated Ann Haydon Jones 5–7, 6–4, 6–1, at Stade Roland Garros, in Paris, France, in 1968.

6123. Tennis player to win the United States interscholastic girls' singles national championship was Linda Tuero, in 1968.

6124. U.S. Open men's doubles tennis title was won by Bob Lutz and Stan Smith, both of the United States, who defeated Arthur Ashe and Andres Gimeno in straight sets, 11-9, 6-1, 7-5, at Forest Hills, Queens, New York, in 1968.

6125. U.S. Open mixed doubles tennis title was won by Mary Ann Eisel of the United States and Peter Curtis of Great Britain, who defeated Tory Ann Fretz and Robert Perry in straight sets, 6–4, 7–5, at Forest Hills, Queens, New York, in 1968.

6126. U.S. Open tennis tournament was held at Forest Hills, Queens, New York, in 1968, as what had been the amateurs-only U.S. national championships became a tournament open to both professionals and amateurs, with cash payments to the winners for the first time.

6127. U.S. Open women's doubles tennis title was won by Maria Bueno of Brazil and Margaret Smith Court of Australia, who defeated Billie Jean King and Rosie Casals 4–6, 9–7, 8–6, at Forest Hills, Queens, New York, in 1968.

6128. U.S. Open women's singles tennis title was won by Virginia Wade of Great Britain, who defeated Billie Jean King in straight sets, 6–4, 6–2, at Forest Hills, Queens, New York, in 1968.

6129. Wimbledon Open men's doubles tennis title was won by John Newcombe and Tony Roche, both of Australia, who defeated Ken Rosewall and Fred Stolle 3–6, 8–6, 5–7, 14–12, 6–3 at Wimbledon, England, in 1968.

6130. Wimbledon Open men's singles tennis title was won by Rod Laver of Australia, who defeated Tony Roche in straight sets, 6–3, 6–4, 6–2, at Wimbledon, England, in 1968. He would win it again in 1969.

6131. Wimbledon Open mixed doubles tennis title was won by Margaret Smith Court and Ken Fletcher, both of Australia, in straight sets, 6–1, 14–12, at Wimbledon, England, in 1968.

6132. Wimbledon Open tennis tournament was held at Wimbledon, near London, England, in 1968, with the formerly amateurs-only tournament open to professionals and amateurs and with cash payments to the winners for the first time.

6133. Wimbledon Open women's doubles tennis title was won by Billie Jean King and Rosie Casals, both of the United States, who defeated Françoise Durr and Haydon Jones, 6–2, 6–3, at Wimbledon, England, 1968.

6134. Wimbledon Open women's singles tennis match was won by Billie Jean King of the United States in straight sets, 9–7, 7–5, over Judy Tegart (later Dalton) at Wimbledon, England, in 1968.

6135. U.S. Open men's singles title, and the first men's singles Grand Slam title won by an African-American was won by Arthur Ashe of the United States, who defeated Tom Okker 14–12, 5–7, 6–3, 3–6, 6–3, at Forest Hills, Queens, New York, on September 9, 1968.

6136. Australian Open men's doubles tennis title was won by Roy Emerson and Rod Laver, both of Australia, who defeated Ken Rosewall and Fred Stolle, 6–4, 6–4, at the National Tennis Centre (Flinders Park), in Melbourne, Australia, in 1969.

6137. Australian Open men's singles tennis title was won by Rod Laver of Australia, who defeated Andres Gimeno in straight sets, 6–3, 6–4, 7–5, at the National Tennis Centre (Flinders Park), in Melbourne, Australia, in 1969.

6138. Australian Open tennis tournament was held at the National Tennis Centre (Flinders Park), in Melbourne, Australia, in 1969, as what had been the amateurs-only Australian national championships became a tournament open to both professionals and amateurs, with cash payments to the winners for the first time.

6139. Australian Open women's doubles tennis title was won by Margaret Smith Court and Judy Tegart Dalton, both of Australia, who defeated Rosie Casals and Billie Jean King 6–4, 6–4, at the National Tennis Centre (Flinders Park), in Melbourne, Australia, in 1969.

TENNIS—(1960-1969)—*continued*

6140. Australian Open women's singles tennis title was won by Margaret Smith Court of Australia, who defeated Billie Jean King in straight sets, 6–4, 6–1, at the National Tennis Centre (Flinders Park), Melbourne, Australia, in 1969.

6141. Tennis player to win 17 men's singles tournaments in one season was Rod Laver of Australia, in 1969.

6142. Tennis player to win two Grand Slams by twice winning the men's singles titles at the United States, Wimbledon (British), French, and Australian national championships (later opens) in a single year, was Rod Laver of Australia, in 1962 and 1969.

TENNIS (1970-1979)

6143. African-American tennis player to win the men's singles title at the Australian Open was Arthur Ashe of the United States, in 1970.

6144. Tennis player to win 21 women's singles tournaments in a single season was Margaret Smith Court of Australia, in 1970.

6145. Tie-breaker rule at the U.S. Open was adopted by the United States Lawn Tennis Association in 1970. The new rule was aimed at ending sets that reached a 6–6 tie score, and until 1974 provided a 9-point tie-breaking game, with victory to the player who first reached 5 points. In 1974, that became a 12-point game, with victory going to the player who first reaches 7 points and is ahead 2 points. This was in conformance with International Tennis Association tie-breaker rules.

6146. Native Australian tennis player to win a Grand Slam event was Evonne Goolagong (later Cawley), who won the women's singles titles at Wimbledon and at the French Open in 1971. In the same year, she had a Grand Slam win in the Australian doubles. She went on to win the women's singles title at Wimbledon in 1980, and four times at the Australian Open, with many more Grand Slam doubles wins.

6147. Tennis player to win 112 women's singles matches in a single season was Billie Jean King of United States, in 1971.

6148. Tie-breaker rule at the Australian Open was adopted in 1971, providing for a 12-point tie-breaking game to conclude a set tied 6–6, with victory to the player who first reaches 7 points and is ahead by 2 points. Australia, however, did not apply the tie-breaker rule to the final set in a match.

6149. Successful organization of male tennis professionals was the Association of Tennis Professionals (ATP), founded at Wimbledon in 1972, which became a major force in professional tennis.

6150. Tie-breaker rule adopted at Wimbledon was in 1972, differing somewhat from the International Tennis Association rule until 1979, when it fell in line with the rest of the world. It provided for a 12-point tie-breaking game to conclude a set tied 6–6, with victory to the player who first reaches 7 points and is ahead by 2 points. Wimbledon, however, did not apply the tie-breaker rule to the final set in a match.

6151. Davis Cup to be a full open tournament for professionals and amateurs was played in 1973, at Cleveland, Ohio. The Australian team, which included Rod Laver, Ken Rosewall, and John Newcombe, won 5–0.

6152. Successful organization of women tennis professionals was the Women's Tennis Association (WTA), founded at Wimbledon, England, in 1973, which would make a major contribution to the rapid development of women's tennis.

6153. Tennis player classified as "non-white" by South Africa's then-racist government to win a South African tennis tournament was Arthur Ashe of the United States, in 1973. Ashe made a substantial contribution to the long battle for equality and against apartheid during his highly publicized visit to South Africa.

6154. Tennis player of the modern era to win the United States women's singles title five times was Margaret Smith Court of Australia, in 1962, 1965, 1969, 1970, and 1973, bridging from the all-amateur era to the Open era. She also won the U.S. amateur title in 1968.

6155. Tie-breaker rule at the French Open was adopted in 1973, providing for a 12-point tie-breaking game to conclude a set tied 6–6, with victory to the player who first reaches 7 points and is also ahead by 2 points.

6156. Women's Tennis Association (WTA) championships then called the Virginia Slims Championships after their first sponsor, were held at Boca Raton, Florida, in 1973. The winner was Chris Evert of the United States, who defeated Kerry Melville Reid in straight sets, 7–5, 6–4.

6157. Tennis player to be ranked number one in the Association of Tennis Professionals (ATP) rankings when they went into effect on August 23, 1973, was Ilie Nastase of Romania.

6158. African-American tennis player to win the men's singles championship at Wimbledon was Arthur Ashe of the United States, in 1975.

6159. Night tennis games played at the U.S. Open in Forest Hills, Queens, New York, were in 1975, as public interest in the game soared and attendance grew.

6160. Tennis player to be named Association of Tennis Professionals (ATP) Player of the Year was Arthur Ashe of the United States, in 1975.

6161. Tennis player to be ranked number one in the Women's Tennis Association (WTA) rankings when they went into effect in November 1975 was Chris Evert of the United States.

6162. Player to be named Women's Tennis Association (WTA) Player of the Year was Virginia Wade of Great Britain, in 1977.

6163. Tennis player to win 145 men's singles matches in a single season was Guillermo Vilas of Argentina, in 1977.

6164. Tennis player to win the Women's Tennis Association (WTA) championship four times was Chris Evert of the United States, in 1972, 1973, 1975, and 1977.

6165. Tennis player to be ranked number one in the Association of Tennis Professionals (ATP) rankings for 160 consecutive weeks was Jimmy Connors of the United States, from July 29, 1974, to August 23, 1977.

6166. Tennis player to win the U.S. Open women's singles title four consecutive times was Chris Evert of the United States, from 1975 to 1978.

6167. United States National Tennis Center opened on August 30, 1978, on the site of the 1964 World's Fair, at Flushing, Queens, New York. Its major court was Louis Armstrong Stadium, which seated 22,000.

TENNIS (1980-1989)

6168. Tennis player of the Open era to win the Wimbledon men's singles title five consecutive times was Bjorn Borg of Sweden, from 1976 to 1980.

6169. Tennis player to win the French Open men's singles title six times was Bjorn Borg of Sweden, in 1974, 1975, and from 1978 to 1981.

6170. Tennis player to win the U.S. Open men's singles title three consecutive times was John McEnroe of the United States, from 1979 to 1981. McEnroe would win it again in 1984.

6171. Tennis player to win the U.S. Open men's singles title five times was Jimmy Connors of the United States, in 1974, 1976, 1978, 1982, and 1983.

6172. Unseeded tennis player to win the men's singles title at Wimbledon was Boris Becker of Germany, in 1985.

6173. Tennis player to be ranked number one in the Women's Tennis Association (WTA) rankings for 156 consecutive weeks was Martina Navratilova, born in Czechoslovakia but later a United States citizen. She was number one from June 14, 1982, to June 9, 1985.

6174. Tennis player to win the French Open women's singles title seven times was Chris Evert of the United States. She won as Evert in 1974 and 1975; as Chris Evert Lloyd 1979–1980, 1983, and 1985; then again as Evert in 1986.

6175. Tennis player to win the Wimbledon women's singles title six consecutive times was Czech-born Martina Navratilova of the United States, from 1982 to 1987. Navratilova had previously won the title in 1978 and 1979, and would win it again in 1990.

6176. Tennis player to win the French Open women's doubles title five consecutive times was Czech-born Martina Navratilova of the United States, from 1984 to 1988, with Andrea Temesvari in 1986 and Pam Shriver the other years. Navratilova had also won the title in 1982, with Anne Smith.

6177. Tennis player to win the Women's Tennis Association (WTA) championship eight times was Czech-born Martina Navratilova of the United States, in 1978, 1979, 1981, 1983–1985, and twice (spring and fall) in 1988.

6178. Tennis player to win the men's singles title in the Olympic Games after tennis competition resumed in 1988 was Miloslav Mecir of Czechoslovakia, who won on September 30, 1988, in Seoul, South Korea.

6179. Tennis players to win the women's doubles title in the Olympic Games after tennis competition resumed in 1988 were Pam Shriver and Zina Garrison of the United States, who won on September 30, 1988, in Seoul, South Korea.

TENNIS—(1980-1989)—*continued*

6180. Tennis player to win the women's singles title in the Olympic Games after tennis competition resumed in 1988 was Steffi Graf of Germany, who won on October 1, 1988, in Seoul, South Korea.

6181. Tennis players to win the men's doubles title in the Olympic Games after tennis competition resumed in 1988 were Kenneth Flach and Robert Seguso of the United States, who won on October 1, 1988, in Seoul, South Korea.

TENNIS (1990-1999)

6182. Grand Slam Cup sponsored by the International Tennis Federation (ITF), was played in 1990. The winner was Pete Sampras of the United States, who in the final defeated Brad Gilbert in straight sets, 6–3, 5–4, 6–2.

6183. Tennis player (man or woman) to be ranked number one in the world for 186 consecutive weeks was Steffi Graf of Germany, who was atop the Women's Tennis Association (WTA) rankings from August 17, 1987, to March 10, 1991.

6184. Tennis player to win 1,438 women's singles matches during her career was Czech-born Martina Navratilova of the United States, between 1973 and 1994.

6185. Tennis player to win 167 women's singles tournaments during her career was Czech-born Martina Navratilova, between 1973 and 1994.

6186. Tennis player to win at least four women's singles titles at each of the four Grand Slam tournaments was Steffi Graf of Germany. She completed that quadruple circuit in 1995 with her fourth U.S. Open title. She had previously won that title in 1988, 1989, and 1993, and would win it again in 1996. Her other Grand Slam wins were at Wimbledon (1988, 1989, 1991–1993, 1995, and 1996), the French Open (1987, 1988, 1993, 1995, 1996, and 1999), and the Australian Open (1988–1990 and 1994).

6187. Tennis player to win 109 men's singles tournaments during his career was Jimmy Connors of the United States, between 1970 and 1996.

6188. Tennis players to win five Wimbledon men's doubles titles in the Open era were Todd Woodbridge and Mark Woodforde, both of Australia, from 1993 to 1997.

6189. Sisters to win the women's doubles tennis title at the U.S. Open were Serena Williams and Venus Williams of the United States, in 1999.

6190. Tennis player to win six Wimbledon men's singles championships in the Open era was Pete Sampras of the United States, in 1993, 1994, 1995, 1997, 1998, and 1999.

6191. Sisters to face each other in the finals of a professional tennis tournament were Venus Williams and Serena Williams, African-American siblings, in a match on March 28, 1999, during the finals of the Lipton Championships in Key Biscayne, Florida. Venus, the elder sister, won.

TENNIS (2000-)

6192. Sisters to each win a women's singles grand slam title in tennis were Venus Williams and Serena Williams. In 1999, Serena won the U.S. Open, and in 2000 Venus won both the Wimbledon and the U.S. Open. As doubles partners, the sisters also won grand slam titles at the French Open (1999), the U.S. Open (1999), Wimbledon (2000), and also the 2000 Olympic Games in Sydney, Australia, where Venus also took the women's singles gold medal.

6193. Tennis player to win 13 men's singles grand slam titles was Pete Sampras of the United States. His 13th win came at Wimbledon in 2000, where he broke Roy Emerson's previous record of 12. Sampras's previous grand slam titles had been at the Australian Open (1994, 1997), Wimbledon (1993, 1994, 1995, 1997, 1998, 2000), and the U.S. Open (1990, 1993, 1995, 1996). One major tournament not in his win column was the French Open.

TENNIS, PADDLE

6194. Invention of paddle tennis was in 1898 by Frank E. Beal in Michigan, originally to help prepare children for standard tennis.

6195. National organization for paddle tennis was the American Paddle Tennis Association, founded in 1923. It was later renamed the American Platform Tennis Association.

TENNIS, PLATFORM

6196. Invention of platform tennis was in 1928, in Scarsdale, New York, by Fessenden S. Blanchard and James K. Cogswell, originally to provide a cold-weather outside court for tennis, badminton, and other such games.

TRACK AND FIELD (ATHLETICS)

6197. Track event in the Olympic Games was held in the first Olympics on record, in 776 BC in Olympia, Greece. The sprint of approximately 200 yards was won by Koroibos.

6198. Indoor track meet on record was held in Cincinnati, Ohio, in 1861.

6199. National track and field (athletics) championships were held in England in 1866, organized by the Amateur Athletic Club.

6200. Major track and field competition in the United States was held in 1868 in New York City, sponsored by the recently established New York Athletic Club.

6201. National championships in track and field (athletics) in the United States were in 1876, sponsored by the New York Athletic Club for men only. They would be held annually, from 1888 under the auspices of the Amateur Athletic Union (AAU). In the inaugural championships, F. C. Saportas won the 100-yard race with a time of 10.5 seconds; Edward Merritt the 440-yard race in 54.5 seconds; H. Lambe the 880-yard race in 2:10 minutes and the mile in 4:51.2 minutes; George Hitchcock the 120-yard high hurdles in 19 seconds; H. E. Ficken the high jump with 5 feet 5 inches; I. Frazier the long jump with 17 feet 4 inches; H. E. Buermeyer the shot put with 32 feet 5 inches; and William B. Curtis the hammer throw (16 pound) with 76 feet 4 inches.

6202. National governing body for track and field (athletics) in England was the Amateur Athletic Association, founded in 1880. It would become the key national organization for track and field events, sponsoring national championships.

6203. National governing body for track and field (athletics) in the United States was the Amateur Athletic Union (AAU), founded in 1888, which sponsored competitions for amateurs.

6204. International governing organization for track and field (athletics) was the International Amateur Athletic Federation (IAAF), founded in Stockholm, Sweden, in 1912, after the Olympic Games ended on July 22.

6205. List of officially accepted world records in track and field (athletics) was published by the International Amateur Athletic Federation (IAAF) in 1914.

6206. National collegiate track and field (athletics) championships sponsored by the National Collegiate Athletic Association (NCAA) were held in 1921 in Chicago, Illinois. The championships would be held annually from then on, with indoor championships added in 1965. At the inaugural championships, the University of Illinois won the team honors. In individual events, Leonard Paulu of Grinnell College won the 100-yard race; Eric C. Wilson of the University of Iowa the 220-yard race; Frank J. Shea of the University of Pittsburgh the 440-yard race; Earl Eby of the University of Pennsylvania the 880-yard race; Ray Watson of Kansas State University the mile race; John Romig of Pennsylvania State University the two-mile race; Earl J. Thomson of Dartmouth College the 120-yard high hurdles; August Desch of the University of Notre Dame the 220-yard low hurdles; Gaylord Stinchcomb of Ohio State University the long jump; John Murphy of the University of Notre Dame the high jump; Gus Pope of the University of Washington the shot put and discus throw; and Charles Redmon of the University of Chicago the hammer throw. The pole vault was a four-way tie.

6207. National track and field (athletics) championships for women in the United States were held in 1923 and annually thereafter, sponsored by the Amateur Athletic Union (AAU). At the inaugural championships, Frances Rupert won the 100-meter race with a time of 12 seconds; Hazel Kirk the 80-meter hurdles with 9.6 seconds; Catherine Wright the high jump with 4 feet 7½ inches; Helen Dinnehy the long jump with 15 feet 4 inches; Bertha Christophel the shot put (8 pound) with 30 feet 10½ inches; Babe Wolbert the discus throw with 71 feet, 9½ inches; Roberta Ranck the javelin throw with 59 feet 7¾ inches; and a team from the Meadowbrook Club the 400-meter relay with 52.4 seconds.

6208. Use of the metric system by the Amateur Athletic Union (AAU) instead of the traditional yards, feet, and inches, was in 1931. The AAU originally used the metric system for outdoor events only.

6209. Track world record for which there was an official wind-speed reading was on July 16, 1932, at the Olympic Trials in Stanford, California, where Jack Keller of the United States set a record of 14.4 seconds in the 110-meter hurdles, with a wind speed of -0.2 meters per second.

TRACK AND FIELD (ATHLETICS)—*continued*

6210. Track-and-field star to set five new world records and equal a sixth in less than an hour was Jesse (James Cleveland) Owens at the Big Ten championship in Ann Arbor, Michigan, on May 25, 1935. He started at 3:15 PM by equaling the 9.4-second record for the 100-yard dash. At 3:25 he leapt 26 feet 8¼ inches in the long jump, setting a record that would stand for more than 25 years. Ten minutes later, he ran the 200-yard dash in a record 20.3 seconds; his time also set a record in the 200-meter dash. Finally, at 4 PM, he ran the 220-yard low hurdles in 22.6 seconds, becoming the first runner to break the 23-second barrier, and also breaking the record for the 200-meter low hurdles.

6211. College track and field (athletics) meet to be televised was a meet sponsored by the Amateur Athletic Union (AAU) on March 5, 1940, at Madison Square Garden in New York City. In a field of 23 colleges, New York University emerged the winner.

6212. Woman athlete to win four gold medals in track and field in a single Olympic Games was Fanny (Francina) Blankers-Koen of the Netherlands in 1948 in London, England. The mother of two, thought by many to be "too old" at 30, she first won the women's 100-meter event in 11.9 seconds on August 2. Two days later she set an Olympic record in the 80-meter hurdles with 11.2 seconds. On August 6, she won the first women's 200-meter race in 24.4 seconds. Finally, on August 7, she anchored the Dutch team to a win in the women's 4 x 100-meter relay, with a time of 47.5 seconds. She also held the world record in the long jump but was not entered in that event in London.

6213. Father and son to both win gold medals in track and field in the Olympic Games were Imre Németh of Hungary, who won the men's hammer throw event on July 31, 1948, in London, England; and his son Miklos Németh, who won the men's javelin throw event on July 25, 1976, in Montreal, Quebec, Canada.

6214. Woman athlete to win seven track and field medals in the Olympic Games was Shirley Strickland de la Hunty. Her seventh came on November 28, 1956, at Melbourne, Australia, where she won the women's 80-meter hurdles. She had won gold in the same event in 1952 and the bronze in 1948. Her other medals came in the women's 100-meter dash (bronze, 1948 and 1952) and the women's 4 x 100-meter relay (silver, 1948; gold, 1956).

6215. European Cup pitting national track and field (athletics) teams from European countries, was held in 1965. At the inaugural event, the winning men's and women's teams were both from the Soviet Union. Originally biennial, the Cup was held annually from 1994.

6216. Indoor track and field competition sponsored by the National Collegiate Athletic Association (NCAA) was held in 1965, when the winning Division I collegiate team was from the University of Missouri.

6217. Athlete to compete in track and field events in six Olympic Games was Lia Manoliu of Romania. She competed in six consecutive women's discus-throw events, from 1952, when she placed sixth, to 1972, when she placed ninth. She won the event in 1968.

6218. Track and field (athletics) meet to be televised nationally was a professional meet held at El Paso, Texas, in 1974.

6219. Switch to metric distances in international track and field events was in 1977. From then on, all distances accepted by the International Amateur Athletic Federation (IAAF) were measured in meters, except the mile.

6220. World Cup in track and field (athletics) sponsored by the International Amateur Athletic Federation (IAAF) was held in 1977 in Düsseldorf, West Germany, pitting teams of athletes representing the continents, with a separate team from the United States, and with Europe represented by the top European Cup teams. Staged irregularly for some years, it was held every four years from 1994.

6221. Mandated use of automatic electronic timing devices in official track and field events was from January 1, 1977. From then on, the use of handheld watches was ended, for the purposes of official results, in favor of devices that could record times to 0.01 second and even more accurately.

6222. Separate world championships for track and field events were the World Championships in Athletics, first held in 1983 at Olympic Stadium in Helsinki, Finland. They would be held every four years until 1991, then every two years.

6223. International Amateur Athletic Federation (IAAF) Grand Prix was introduced in 1985, with a series of men's and women's events held in international venues. Doug Padilla and Mary Decker Slaney, both of the United States, were the inaugural winners in the Grand Prix, which became an annual competition.

6224. World indoor track and field (athletics) championships called the World Indoor Games, were held in Bercy, Paris, France, on January 19–20, 1985. They would be held biennially from then on.

6225. World indoor records recognized by the International Amateur Athletic Federation (IAAF) were from January 1, 1987. To be accepted as official, indoor races must be run around a turn on a track not exceeding 200 meters.

TRAMPOLINING

6226. Trampoline was invented in 1936 by George Nissen in Cedar Rapids, Iowa, though similar equipment had been used in circuses for years before.

6227. Trampolining tournament was held in 1947 in the United States.

6228. World championships in trampolining were held in 1964, under the auspices of the newly founded Fédération International de Trampoline (FIT). They would be held annually until 1968, then biennially. Danny Millman and Judy Wills, both of the United States, won the men's and women's individual titles, respectively. Wills would win the next four individual titles as well as the first two tumbling (1965–1966) and synchronized pairs (1966–1967) titles.

6229. World championships in trampolining to include individual tumbling and synchronized pairs competitions were in 1965. Athletes from the United States won all the inaugural events. Frank Schmitz and Judy Wills respectively won the first men's and women's tumbling titles. Gary Irwin and Frank Smith won the inaugural synchronized pairs competition for men. Women's synchronized pairs competition was introduced the next year and won by Judy Wills and Nancy Smith of the United States.

6230. World championships in trampolining to include double mini trampoline competitions were in 1976. Ron Merriott and Leigh Hennessy, both of the United States, respectively won the inaugural men's and women's titles.

6231. World cup in trampolining was held in 1980, becoming a biennial series of competitions.

6232. Women's trampoline event held in the Olympic Games was in 2000 in Sydney, Australia. Irina Karavaeva of Russia won the event with 38.90 points on September 22.

6233. Men's trampoline event held in the Olympic Games was in 2000 in Sydney, Australia. Alexandre Moskalenko of Russia had retired from trampolining in 1994 but returned to win the gold medal with 41.70 points on September 23.

TRIATHLON

6234. Men's triathlon event held in the Olympic Games was in 1904 in St. Louis, Missouri, the three events being the long jump, the shot put, and the 100-yard dash. The only time the event was held, it was won by Max Emmerich of the United States on July 2.

6235. Hawaii Ironman triathlon was held on February 18, 1978, in Oahu, Hawaii. Competitors swam 2.4 miles, cycled 112 miles, and then ran a full marathon. The inaugural winner was Gordon Haller of the United States, with a time of 11:46:58 hours.

6236. Hawaii Ironman triathlon to include women was held in Oahu, Hawaii, in 1979. The inaugural women's champion was Lyn Lemaire of the United States, with a time of 12:55:38 hours.

6237. Athlete to win the men's Hawaii Ironman triathlon two, three, four, five, and six times was Dave Scott of the United States. After first winning in 1980, he won it again in 1982, 1983, 1984, 1986, and 1987, the last five times at Kona, Hawaii.

6238. Athlete to win two consecutive women's Hawaii Ironman triathlons was Sylviane Puntous of Canada in 1983 and 1984, both at Kona, Hawaii.

6239. Athlete to win the women's Hawaii Ironman triathlon three and up to eight times was Paula Newby-Fraser of Zimbabwe. Her wins came in 1986, 1988, 1989, 1991–1994, and 1996, all at Kona, Hawaii.

6240. World championships in the triathlon were held in 1989, at Avignon, France, under the auspices of L'Union Internationale de Triathlon (UIT), founded the year before. The competition involved swimming 1.5 kilometers, cycling 40 kilometers, and running 10 kilometers. The men's individual competition was won by Mark Allen of the United States, who that year also won his first of six Hawaii Ironman triathlon titles. Erin Baker of New Zealand took the women's title, and the United States won both team titles.

6241. World cup in the triathlon was held in 1991. Winning the series of 11 events in the inaugural season were Leandro Macedo of Brazil on the men's side and Karen Smyers of the United States on the women's.

TRIATHLON—*continued*

6242. Athlete to win the men's Hawaii Ironman triathlon competition four, and then five, times consecutively, and six times overall was Mark Allen of the United States, who won 1989–1993, and would return for a sixth win in 1995, all in Kona, Hawaii.

6243. Athlete to win two consecutive women's titles in the world triathlon championships was Michellie Jones of Australia, who won in 1992 and 1993.

6244. Athlete to win two consecutive men's titles in the world triathlon championships was Spencer Smith of Great Britain, who won in 1993 and 1994.

6245. World long-distance triathlon championships were held in 1994. In its first two years the competitors swam 4 kilometers (later 1.9 km), cycled 120 km (later 90 km), and ran 32 km (later 21.6 km). Rob Barel of the Netherlands won the inaugural men's title, with a time of 5:59:47 hours; Isabelle Mouthan of France took the women's crown, in 6:41:50 hours.

6246. Athlete to win three men's titles in the world triathlon championships was Simon Lessing of Great Britain. After winning first in 1992, he came back to win again in 1995 and 1996. He also won the men's world long-distance championship in 1995.

6247. Women's triathlon event held in the Olympic Games was in 2000 in Sydney, Australia. The winner was Brigitte McMahon of Switzerland, with a time of 2:00:40.52 hours on September 15. She sprinted past Australia's Michellie Jones, the world champion, in the last 100 meters of the 10,000-meter run, following a 1500-meter swim and a 40-kilometer bicycle race.

6248. Men's modern triathlon event held in the Olympic Games was in 2000 in Sydney, Australia. The winner was Simon Whitfield of Canada, who won the event with an overall time of 1:48.24.02 hours on September 16, taking the lead with a big kick in the final 200 meters of the 10,000-meter running segment, which followed a 1500-meter swim and a 40-kilometer bicycle race.

TRIPLE JUMP

6249. Men's triple jump event held in the Olympic Games was in 1896, in Athens, Greece. The winner was James Connolly of the United States, who won the first gold medal of the modern Olympics with a triple jump of 44 feet 11¾ inches on April 6.

6250. Men's standing triple jump event held in the Olympic Games was on July 16, 1900, in Paris, France. Raymond Ewry of the United States won the event then and in 1904, the only other time it was held.

6251. National team to sweep the top spots in the men's triple jump in the Olympic Games was the United States, on July 16, 1900, in Paris, France. The U.S. team would do so again in 1904, on September 1 in St. Louis, Missouri, both times led by Meyer Prinstein.

6252. Triple-jumper to win two consecutive men's titles in the Olympic Games was Meyer Prinstein of the United States. After winning it first in 1900, he had a distance of 47 feet 1 inch on September 1, 1904, at St. Louis, Missouri, when he led the second straight United States sweep in the event.

6253. Triple-jumper to hold the officially accepted world record in the men's event was Daniel Ahearn of the United States, with a distance of 50 feet 11 inches on May 30, 1911, in New York City. It would be equaled in 1924, but not bettered until 1931.

6254. Triple-jumper to reach a distance of 16 meters in the men's event was Naoto Tajima of Japan, who posted 52 feet 6 inches (16.00 meters) on August 6, 1936, in Berlin, Germany.

6255. Triple-jumper of Black African ancestry to win the men's title in the Olympic Games was Adhemar Ferreira da Silva of Brazil. Already the world record-holder, he set a new world record of 53 feet 2¼ inches on July 23, 1952 in Helsinki, Finland. It was his fourth of five world records—and his second set that day, for he had earlier jumped for a record 52 feet 10¼ inches. He would win the event again in 1956.

6256. Triple-jumper to win two consecutive men's titles in the Olympic Games was Adhemar Ferreira da Silva of Brazil. World record-holder and Olympic champion from 1952, he again won in Melbourne, Australia, with an Olympic-record distance of 53 feet 7¼ inches on November 27, 1956. He later starred in the 1958 film *Black Orpheus*.

6257. Triple-jumper to break both the 55-foot and 17-meter barriers was Józef Schmidt of Poland, with a triple jump of 55 feet 10¼ inches (17.03 meters) on August 5, 1960, at Olsztyn, Poland.

6258. Triple-jumper to break the 58-foot barrier was João Carlos de Oliveira of Brazil, with a distance of 58 feet 8½ inches (17.89 meters) on October 15, 1975, at the Pan American Games in Mexico City. He would be only third in the 1976 and 1980 Olympics, however.

6259. Triple-jumper to win three consecutive men's titles in the Olympic Games was Viktor Saneyev of the Soviet Union. After winning in 1968 and 1972, he won again on July 30, 1976, with a distance of 56 feet 8¾ inches in Montreal, Quebec, Canada. He would come close again in 1980, but had to settle for silver.

6260. Triple-jumper from the United States, and the first African-American, to win the men's event in the Olympic Games was Al (Alfrederick) Joyner, with a wind-aided distance of 56 feet 7½ inches on August 4, 1984, in Los Angeles, California. He bested the favorite, teammate Michael Conley, who would later win in 1992. The older brother of heptathlon great Jackie Joyner-Kersee, Joyner later married sprint star Florence Griffith-Joyner.

6261. Triple-jumper to hold the officially accepted world record in the women's event was Li Huirong of China. Her benchmark distance of 14.54 meters (47 feet 8½ inches) was set on August 25, 1990, in Sapporo, Japan.

6262. Triple-jumper to break the 15-meter barrier in the women's event was Ana Biryukova of Russia. Her distance of 15.09 meters (49 feet 6½ inches) was set on August 21, 1993, in Stuttgart, Germany.

6263. Triple-jumper to break the 50-foot barrier in the women's event was Inessa Kravets of Ukraine. She reached 50 feet 10¼ inches (15.50 meters) on August 10, 1995, in Gothenburg, Sweden. She had previously set a world record competing for the Soviet Union in 1991.

6264. Triple-jumper to break the 18-meter and 60-foot barriers was Jonathan Edwards of Great Britain. His first world record came on July 18, 1995, at Salamanca, Spain, with a distance of 59 feet 0 inches (17.98 meters). Then on August 7, 1995, in Gothenburg, Sweden, he broke the record twice, with distances of 59 feet 7 inches (18.16 meters) and then 60 feet ¼ inch (18.29 meters).

6265. Women's triple jump event held in the Olympic Games was in 1996, in Atlanta, Georgia. The inaugural winner was Inessa Kravets of Ukraine, who won with a distance of 50 feet 3¼ inches (15.33 meters), well short of her own world record, on July 31.

TUG-OF-WAR

6266. Code of rules for tug-of-war was established in New York City in 1879 by the New York Athletic Club.

6267. Tug-of-war event held in the Olympic Games was in Paris, France, on July 16, 1900. A combined team from Sweden and Denmark emerged victorious. The sport would be included in the Olympics through 1920.

6268. National team to win two Olympic gold medals in the tug-of-war competition was Great Britain. A team from the City of London Police had first won in 1908. Another British team won on August 18, 1920, in Antwerp, Belgium, the last time the sport was included in the Olympics.

6269. Governing body solely for tug-of-war events was the Tug-of-War Association, founded in 1958. The Tug-of-War International Federation (TWIF) would be founded two years later.

6270. World championships in tug-of-war were held in 1975, for men only until 1986. Teams from England won the competitions in both the 640- and 720-kilogram classes.

6271. World championships in tug-of-war to include women were in 1986, when teams from Sweden won both events open to women.

V

VOLLEYBALL

6272. Volleyball originally called Mintonette, was developed in 1895 in Holyoke, Massachusetts, by William G. Morgan, director of the local Young Men's Christian Association (YMCA), inspired by James Naismith, who had a few years earlier invented basketball.

6273. International competition in volleyball was in 1913, when the sport was included in the Far Eastern Games held in Manila, the Philippines.

6274. National championships in volleyball in the United States were held in 1922 in Brooklyn, New York, at the Central Branch of the Young Men's Christian Association (YMCA), where the Pittsburgh, Pennsylvania, YMCA team emerged victorious.

6275. Beach volleyball was developed in 1930 in Santa Monica, California.

6276. Organized tournament in beach volleyball was held in 1948 at State Beach, California.

VOLLEYBALL—*continued*

6277. World championships in volleyball were held in 1949 and quadrennially from then on, sponsored by the International Volleyball Federation (FIVB), founded in 1947. The inaugural competition, for men only, was won by the team from the Soviet Union.

6278. World championships in volleyball to include women were in 1952. The team from the Soviet Union won that first competition.

6279. Men's volleyball event held in the Olympic Games was in 1964 in Tokyo, where the Soviet team won in the finals on October 23.

6280. Women's volleyball event held in the Olympic Games was in 1964 in Tokyo, where the team from Japan won on October 23. Of its 12 members, 10 were from the Nichibo spinning mill near Osaka, where their coach—noted for his harsh training methods—was manager of the office supplies department.

6281. World cup in volleyball was held in 1965, and quadrennially from then on. The Soviet Union won the initial competition, for men only.

6282. Volleyball players to win two consecutive men's gold medals in the Olympic Games were Ivans Bugajenkovs and Georgy Mondzolevsky. Both members of the inaugural winning Soviet team in 1964, they went to Mexico City with new teammates to win again on October 26, 1968.

6283. Volleyball players to win two consecutive women's gold medals in the Olympic Games were Inna Ryskal, Vera Galushka Douiounova, Nina Smoleyeva, Roza Salikhova, Lyudmila Buldakova, Galina Leontyeva, and Tatyana Sarycheva of the Soviet Union. Members of the winning team in 1968, they formed the core of the team that won again on September 7, 1972, in Munich, West Germany.

6284. World cup in volleyball to include women was held in 1973, when the team from the Soviet Union won the event.

6285. Volleyball team from the United States to win the men's title in the Olympic Games did so on August 11, 1984, at the Soviet-boycotted Olympics in Los Angeles, California. Four members of the team—David Saunders, Stephen Timmons, Craig Buck, and Charles "Karch" Kiraly—would return to win again in 1988.

6286. Beach volleyball event held in the Olympic Games was in 1996 in Atlanta, Georgia. The inaugural 2-a-side men's event was won by Charles "Karch" Kiraly and Kent Steffers of the United States on July 28, while Jackie Silva and Sandra Pires of Brazil won the women's title on July 27.

W

WALKING

6287. Walker to be considered a professional was Edward Payson Weston of the United States. He made and won a bet that he could walk from Boston, Massachusetts, to Washington, D.C., in 10 days straight, arriving on March 4, 1861, in time for the inauguration of President Abraham Lincoln. His feat won enormous attention, establishing walking (*pedestrianism*) as a sport, and he turned professional.

6288. Men's 3000-meter walk event held in the Olympic Games was in the unofficial 1906 Games in Athens, Greece. György Sztantics of Hungary won on May 1 with a time of 15:13.2 minutes.

6289. Men's 3500-meter and 10-mile walks held in the Olympic Games were in 1908 in London, England. George Larner of Great Britain won both events the only time they were held: the 3500-meter on July 14 and the 10-mile on July 17.

6290. Men's 10,000-meter walk held in the Olympic Games was in 1912 in Stockholm, Sweden. The winner of the inaugural event, on July 11, was English-born George Goulding of Canada.

6291. Men's 50,000-meter walk held in the Olympic Games was in 1932 in Los Angeles, California. The winner was Thomas Green of Great Britain, who had a time of 4:50:10 hours on August 3, despite having been badly wounded and gassed during World War I.

6292. Men's 20,000-meter walk event held in the Olympic Games was in 1956 in Melbourne, Australia. Racing on November 28, the winner was Leonid Spirin of the Soviet Union, with a time of 1:31:27.4 hours.

6293. Walker to win two titles in the men's 20,000-meter walk in the Olympic Games was Volodymyr Holubnychy of the Soviet Union. After winning first in 1960, he returned in 1968 to win again, with a time of 1:27:05.0 hours on October 14 in Mexico City.

6294. World Race Walking Cup sponsored by the International Amateur Athletic Federation (IAAF) was held in 1977. The Lugano Trophy, awarded to the winning men's national teams, was first won by Mexico. The Eschborn Cup for women would be offered starting in 1979.

6295. Eschborn Cup offered to the winning women's national team at the World Race Walking Cup, was in 1979. Sponsored by the International Amateur Athletic Federation (IAAF), it was won by the team from Great Britain.

6296. Women's 10,000-meter walk held in the Olympic Games was on August 3, 1992, in Barcelona, Spain. The inaugural winner was Chen Yueling of China, with a time of 44.32 minutes, after Alina Ivanova of Ukraine was disqualified.

6297. Women's 20-kilometer walk event held in the Olympic Games was in 2000 in Sydney, Australia. With a time of 1.29.5 hours on September 27, Wang Liping of China was ultimately the winner, after three walkers in front of her were disqualified.

WATER POLO

6298. Development of water polo originally called "water soccer" and "football in the water," was in 1869 in Great Britain.

6299. Code of rules for water polo was written at the London Swimming Club in England in 1870.

6300. International water polo match was in 1890, when the team from Scotland defeated England 4–1.

6301. Water polo event held in the Olympic Games was in 1900 in Paris, France. Representing the Osborne Swimming Club, in Manchester, England, Arthur Robertson, Thomas Coe, Eric Robinson, Peter Kemp, George Wilkinson, John Derbyshire, and William Lister won the event on August 12.

6302. Water polo team from the United States to win the title at the Olympic Games was from the New York Athletic Club. Winning the finals on September 6, 1904, in St. Louis, Missouri, were David Bratton, George Van Cleef, Leo "Budd" Goodwin, Louis Handley, David Hesser, Joseph Ruddy, and James Steen.

6303. Water polo player to win two, and then three, gold medals in the Olympic Games was George Wilkinson of Great Britain. A member of the Osborne Swimming Club team, from Manchester, England, that won in 1900, Wilkinson returned with new teammates to win again on July 22, 1908, in London, England, and on July 13, 1912, in Stockholm, Sweden.

6304. Water polo player to win medals in five different Olympic Games was Dezsö Gyarmati of Hungary. After winning a silver medal in 1948, he won gold medals in 1952 and 1956, a bronze in 1960, and a final gold medal on October 18, 1964, in Tokyo, at the age of 37.

6305. World championships for water polo were held in 1973, under the auspices of the Fédération International de Natation Amateur (FINA). The team from Hungary won the first title. For men only until 1986, the competitions would be held quadrennially from 1978.

6306. World cup for water polo sponsored by the Fédération International de Natation Amateur (FINA), was held in 1979. The team from Hungary won the first men's title, and that from the United States the women's.

6307. World championships for water polo to include women were in 1986, when the team from Australia won the inaugural title.

6308. Women's water polo event held in the Olympic Games was in 2000 in Sydney, Australia. With two last-minute scores, the Australian team defeated the United States team 4–3 on September 23.

WATER-SKIING

6309. Water-skiing using motorized boats was developed in approximately 1922, primarily by Ralph Samuelson on Lake Pepin, off Lake City, Minnesota.

6310. Water-ski jump was made in 1925 by water-skiing pioneer Ralph Samuelson off a ramp on Lake Pepin, Minnesota.

6311. Water-skiing tournament was held in Massapequa, New York, in 1936, where Jack Andresen won the inaugural competition.

6312. National governing body for water-skiing was the American Water Ski Association (ASWA), founded in 1939, primarily by Dan Haines of the United States. It would sponsor national championships starting that year.

WATER-SKIING—*continued*

6313. National water-skiing championships were held in 1939 at Jones Beach on Long Island, New York, sponsored by the newly founded American Water Ski Association. Esther Yates won the first women's all-around title.

6314. International governing body in water-skiing was the Union Internationale de Ski Nautique, founded in Geneva, Switzerland, in 1946. It would become the World Water Ski Union (WWSU) and then the International Water Ski Federation (IWSF).

6315. Water-skier known to have skied barefoot was Dick Pope, Jr., on March 6, 1947, on Lake Eloise, Florida.

6316. World championships in water-skiing were held in 1949, then becoming biennial. At the inaugural championships, held at Juan Les Pins, France, Christian Jourdan of France and Guy de Clercq of Belgium shared the men's overall title. Jourdan also won the men's slalom, de Clercq the men's jumping, and Pierre Gouin of France the men's tricks titles. Willa Worthington (later McGuire) of the United States took the women's overall crown (her first of three), as well as the women's slalom and women's jumping titles. The women's tricks title was taken by Madeleine Boutellier of France.

6317. Water-skier to win two, and then three, women's titles at the world championships was Willa Worthington McGuire of the United States. After winning the inaugural title in 1949 as Worthington, she came back to win again in 1953 and 1955.

6318. Water-skier to win two consecutive men's titles at the world championships was Alfredo Mendoza of the United States, who won in 1953 and 1955.

6319. World championships in barefoot water-skiing were held in 1978. Australians dominated the inaugural event, winning the team title, as Brett Wing took the men's overall crown, his first of three in a row, and Colleen Wilkinson the women's.

6320. World championships in water-ski-racing were held in 1979. The top individual winners were from Australia: Wayne Ritchie took the men's title and Bronwyn Wright the women's.

6321. Water-skier to win three, and then four, consecutive men's overall titles at the world championships was Sammy Duvall of the United States, who won four times in a row: 1981, 1983, 1985, and 1987.

6322. Water-skier to win five consecutive men's overall titles at the world championships was Patrice Martin of France, who won in 1989, 1991, 1993, 1995, and 1997.

WEIGHT THROW

6323. Men's 56-pound weight throw event held in the Olympic Games was in 1904 in St. Louis, Missouri. The winner was Étienne Desmarteau of Canada, with a throw of 34 feet four inches on September 1. He would die of typhoid the following year, at just 34. The event would be held again in 1920, then discontinued.

6324. Thrower from the United States to win the men's 56-pound weight throw in the Olympic Games was 42-year-old Patrick McDonald. He had a throw of 36 feet 11½ inches to win on August 21, 1920, in Antwerp, Belgium, the second and last time the event was held.

WEIGHTLIFTING

6325. Unlimited weight weightlifting events held in the Olympic Games were in 1896 in Athens, Greece. Launceston Elliot of Great Britain won the one-hand lift competition, with a lift of 71.0 kilograms on April 7. In the two-hand lift competition, Elliot and Viggo Jensen both lifted 111.5 kg, but Jensen won the gold medal on style, because Elliot had shifted a foot during the lift. These events would later be classed as super heavyweight.

6326. Weightlifter to win two medals in the same Olympic Games, and the first from the United States to win a weightlifting Olympic gold medal was Oscar Osthoff. On September 3, 1904, in St. Louis, Missouri, he won the silver medal in the two-hand lift and the gold in the all-around dumbbell competition.

6327. International governing body in weightlifting was the Fédération Haltérophile Internationale, founded in 1920. It would later become the International Weightlifting Federation (IWF).

6328. Featherweight weightlifting event held in the Olympic Games was in 1920 in Antwerp, Belgium. Belgian contestant François de Haes won the event on August 29 with a total weight of 220.0 kilograms.

6329. Lightweight weightlifting event held in the Olympic Games was in 1920 in Antwerp, Belgium. In the finals on August 29, the winner was Alfred Neuland of Estonia, with a total weight of 257.5 kilograms.

6330. Middleweight weightlifting event held in the Olympic Games was in 1920 in Antwerp, Belgium. Henri Gance of France won the inaugural competition with a total weight of 245.0 kilograms on August 29.

6331. Light heavyweight weightlifting event held in the Olympic Games was in 1920 in Antwerp, Belgium. Winning the finals on August 31 was Ernest Cadine of France, with a total weight of 295.0 kilograms.

6332. World championships in weightlifting for men only, were held in Tallinn, Estonia, in 1922. Sponsored by the organization that became the International Weightlifting Federation (IWF), they would be held irregularly, but then annually from 1946 (except 1967), with the Olympic Games being regarded as world championships.

6333. Weightlifter to win two consecutive light heavyweight titles in the Olympic Games was Louis Hostin of France. After winning his first in 1932, he won his second in Berlin, Germany, on August 3, 1936, with a total weight of 372.5 kilograms.

6334. Bantamweight weightlifting event held in the Olympic Games was in 1948 in London, England. Competing on August 9, Joseph Di Pietro of the United States won with a new world-record total of 307.5 kilograms, breaking his own previous record of 300 kg—though he was less than five feet tall.

6335. Weightlifter from the United States to win the middleweight title in the Olympic Games was Frank Spellman, who had an Olympic-record total weight of 390.0 kilograms on August 10, 1948, in London, England.

6336. Weightlifter from the United States to win the light heavyweight title in the Olympic Games was Stanley Stanczyk, who won with an Olympic-record total of 417.5 kilograms on August 11, 1948. Silver-medalist was his teammate Harold Sakata, who later became an actor, best known for playing the villain Oddjob in the 1964 James Bond movie *Goldfinger*.

6337. Weightlifter from the United States to win the lightweight weightlifting title in the Olympic Games was Tamio "Tommy" Kono, who had an Olympic-record weight of 362.5 kilograms on July 26, 1952, in Helsinki, Finland. He would win another gold medal in the light heavyweight class in 1956 and a silver in the middleweight class in 1960.

6338. Middle heavyweight weightlifting event held in the Olympic Games was in 1952 in Helsinki, Finland. Winning that first competition on July 27 was Norbert Schemansky of the United States, with a world-record total weight of 445.0 kilograms.

6339. Weightlifter to win two consecutive titles in the unlimited weight (super heavyweight) competition in the Olympic Games was John Davis of the United States. After winning his first in 1948, he won his second in Helsinki, Finland, on July 27, 1952, with an Olympic-record total weight of 460.0 kilograms. From 1938 to 1953, he was undefeated in competition.

6340. Weightlifter from the United States to win the featherweight title in the Olympic Games was Isaac Berger, who had a world record total of 352.5 kilograms on November 23, 1956, in Melbourne, Australia.

6341. Weightlifter to win two consecutive bantamweight titles in the Olympic Games was Charles Vinci of the United States. After winning first in 1956 with a world record, he equaled another world record with a total of 345.0 kilograms on September 7, 1960, in Rome, Italy.

6342. Weightlifter to win two consecutive middle heavyweight titles in the Olympic Games was Arkady Vorobyov of the Soviet Union. After having a world record total weight of 462.5 kilograms in 1956, he went to Rome, Italy, to win his second title with another world record, 472.5 kg, on September 9, 1960.

6343. Weightlifter to win two consecutive featherweight titles in the Olympic Games was Yoshinobu Miyake of Japan. After winning first in 1964 with a world record total of 397.5 kilograms, he won again on October 14, 1968, with 392.5 kilograms in Mexico City. The bronze-medalist was his younger brother Yoshiyuki Miyake.

6344. Weightlifter to win two consecutive lightweight titles in the Olympic Games was Waldemar Baszanowski of Poland. After setting a new world record of 432.5 kilograms on October 13, 1964, in Tokyo, he returned to win again on October 15, 1968, in Mexico City, with an Olympic-record 437.5 kg. Even that was short of his own world record of 440 kg, which he would later up to 450 kg.

6345. Flyweight weightlifting event held in the Olympic Games was in 1972 in Munich, West Germany. The winner at the August 31 finals was Zygmunt Smalcerz of Poland, with a total of 337.5 kilograms.

WEIGHTLIFTING—*continued*

6346. Heavyweight weightlifting event held in the Olympic Games was in 1972 in Munich, West Germany. The winner was Jaan Talts of the Soviet Union, with a total weight of 580.0 kilograms on September 22.

6347. Weightlifter to compete in five Olympic Games was Imre Földi of Hungary. Competing in the men's bantamweight event, he placed sixth in 1960, took silver in 1964 and 1968, won the gold medal in 1972, and finally was fifth on July 19, 1976, in Montreal, Quebec, Canada.

6348. World cup in weightlifting a series of international competitions, was offered in 1980. The winner of the first championship was György Szalai of Hungary, while János Sólyomnári, also of Hungary, won the season-ending world cup gala. The event would be for men only until 1991.

6349. First Heavyweight weightlifting event held in the Olympic Games was in 1980 in Moscow, the Soviet Union. Ota Zaremba of Czechoslovakia won the inaugural competition on July 28, with a total weight of 395.0 kilograms.

6350. World championships for women's weightlifting were held in 1987 at Daytona Beach, Florida. Weightlifters from China won most weight classes: Cai Jun took the 44 kilogram, Huang Xiaoyu the 49 kg, Yan Zangqun the 52 kg, Cui Aihong the 56 kg, Zeng Xinling the 60 kg, Gao Lijuan the 67.5 kg, Li Hongling the 75 kg, Han Changmei the 82.5+ kg. The only other class was the 82.5 kg, won by Karyn Marshall of the United States.

6351. World cup in weightlifting to include women was held in 1991. Sun Caiyun of China won the world cup championships, as well as the season-ending gala event.

6352. Weightlifter to win three gold medals in the Olympic Games was Naim Suleymanoğlu of Turkey. He was born Naim Suleimanov in Bulgaria, but was forced to compete under the Bulgarian name Naum Shalamanov, winning two world championships (1985 and 1986). He then was granted political asylum in Turkey, and as Suleymanoğlu won the featherweight titles in 1988 and 1992. He then came back for an astonishing third title on July 23, 1996, in Atlanta, Georgia, where he also set a new world record. Less than five feet tall, he was nicknamed the Pocket Hercules.

6353. Women's weightlifting events held in the Olympic Games were in 2000 in Sydney, Australia. Tara Nott of the United States received the gold medal in the flyweight competition (for contestants weighing up to 48 kilograms or 106 pounds) on September 17 with an average lift of 185.0 kilograms, after Izabela Dragneva of Bulgaria was stripped of the gold medal for failing a drug test. On September 18, Yang Xia of China won the featherweight title (for athletes weighing up to 53 kilograms or 117 pounds) with an average lift of 225.0 kilograms, and Soraya Jimenez Mendivil of Mexico the lightweight (for athletes up to 58 kilograms or 128 pounds) with an average lift of 222.5 kilograms. On September 19, Xiaomin Chen of China won the middleweight title (for contestants weighing up to 63 kilograms or 139 pounds) with a world-record average lift of 242.5 kilograms, and Lin Weining the light heavyweight (up to 69 kilograms or 152.5 pounds), also with an average lift of 242.5 kilograms. On September 20, Maria Isabel Urrutia of Colombia won the heavyweight title (for contestants weighing up to 75 kilograms or 165.5 pounds) with an average lift of 245.0 pounds. Two days later, Ding Meiyuan of China won the super heavyweight title (for athletes over 75 kilograms or 165.5 pounds) with an average lift of 300.0 kilograms.

WRESTLING (BEFORE 1900)

6354. Depictions of wrestling matches date back to at least 3000 BC in Egypt and elsewhere in the Near East.

6355. Wrestling event in the Olympic Games is believed to have been held in 708 BC in Olympia, Greece.

6356. Sumo wrestling matches on record date from 821, when annual tournaments were held at the imperial court in Kyoto, Japan, though the sport clearly has far older roots. Sumo matches would be held from then until the 12th century, when they petered out.

6357. Sumo wrestling organization to achieve national recognition was in 1773, when sumo wrestling groups (*heya*) were officially recognized by Japan's ruling shogun. From this would eventually develop the Nihon Sumo Kaikyo (Japanese Sumo Association).

6358. Unlimited weight (super heavyweight) Greco-Roman wrestling event held in the Olympic Games was in 1896 in Athens, Greece. Carl Schuhmann of Germany won with a fall on April 11. No maximum weight would be established for wrestlers until 1988.

WRESTLING (1900-1949)

6359. Intercollegiate wrestling match in the United States was in 1900, between teams from Yale University and the University of Pennsylvania.

6360. Organization of professional wrestlers in the United States was the National Wrestling Alliance, founded in 1904. Professional wrestlers had been touring the country for decades by then, with purses of $1000 or more being offered. Later in the 20th century, professional wrestling would degenerate into staged entertainments, rather than actual bouts.

6361. World championships in Greco-Roman wrestling were held in 1904 in Vienna, Austria, though the 1904 results are now regarded as unofficial.

6362. Bantamweight freestyle wrestling event held in the Olympic Games was in 1904 in St. Louis, Missouri. Winning with a fall on October 15, Jack (Isidor) Niflot led a United States sweep of the medals.

6363. Featherweight freestyle wrestling event held in the Olympic Games was in 1904 in St. Louis, Missouri. Winning by a decision on October 15, Benjamin Bradshaw led a United States sweep of the medals.

6364. Flyweight freestyle wrestling event held in the Olympic Games was in 1904 in St. Louis, Missouri. Winning by a decision on October 15, George Mehnert led a United States sweep of the medals. The event would not be held again until 1948.

6365. Light flyweight freestyle wrestling event held in the Olympic Games was in 1904 in St. Louis, Missouri, where Robert Curry, winning with a fall, led a United States sweep of the medals on October 15. The event would not be held again unil 1972.

6366. Lightweight freestyle wrestling event held in the Olympic Games was in 1904 in St. Louis, Missouri. Winning by a decision on October 15, Otto Roehm led a United States sweep of the medals.

6367. Super heavyweight freestyle wrestling event held in the Olympic Games was in 1904 in St. Louis, Missouri. Winning with a fall on October 15 was Bernhuff Hansen, who led a United States sweep of the medals.

6368. Welterweight freestyle wrestling event held in the Olympic Games was in 1904 in St. Louis, Missouri. Leading a United States sweep of the medals was Charles Erickson, who won by a decision on October 15.

6369. All-around wrestling title awarded in the Olympic Games was in 1906 in Athens, Greece, where the honor was given on May 1 to Soren Marius Jensen of Denmark, winner of the unlimited weight (later called super heavyweight) division.

6370. Lightweight Greco-Roman wrestling event held in the Olympic Games was in 1906 in Athens, Greece, where Rudolf Watzl of Austria won the inaugural competition on May 1.

6371. Middleweight Greco-Roman wrestling event held in the Olympic Games was in 1906 in Athens, Greece, where Verner Wekman of Finland won that first competition on May 1.

6372. Middleweight freestyle wrestling event held in the Olympic Games was in 1908 in London, England. Winning by a decision on July 21, Stanley Bacon led a British sweep of the medals.

6373. Light heavyweight Greco-Roman wrestling event held in the Olympic Games was in 1908 in London, England. In the final on July 22, Verner Weckman of Finland emerged victorious. He had won the middleweight Olympic title in 1906.

6374. International governing body for wrestling was the Fédération Inter-nationale des Luttes Amateurs (FILA), the International Amateur Wrestling Federation, founded in 1912.

6375. Wrestling event in the Olympic Games to have no gold-medalist was on July 14, 1912, in Stockholm, Sweden. The light heavyweight Greco-Roman match between Anders Ahlgren of Sweden and Ivar Böhling of Finland went for nine hours before it was declared a draw. Because neither contestant won, under Olympic rules they were declared joint silver-medalists. After 1921, new rules limited the length of Greco-Roman wrestling matches.

6376. Wrestler to win two consecutive lightweight Greco-Roman titles in the Olympic Games was Eemil Wäre of Finland, who won his first in 1912, then won again in Antwerp, Belgium, after World War I on August 19, 1920.

6377. Light heavyweight freestyle wrestling event held in the Olympic Games was in 1920 in Antwerp, Belgium. Anders Larsson of Sweden won the title on August 27 after a forfeit.

305

WRESTLING—(1900-1949)—*continued*

6378. Wrestler to win gold medals in three different divisions in the Olympic Games was Carl Westergren of Sweden. Competing in Antwerp, Belgium, he won the middleweight title on August 19, 1920. On July 10, 1924, he won the light heavyweight title in Paris, France, but would lose in the first round in 1928. Moving up to the super heavyweight class, he won again on August 7, 1932, in Los Angeles, California, when he was 36.

6379. World championships in Greco-Roman wrestling regarded as official were held in 1921 in Helsinki, Finland, and in 1922, but not again until 1950.

6380. Bantamweight Greco-Roman wrestling event held in the Olympic Games was in 1924 in Paris. Eduard Pütsep of Estonia won the inaugural competition on July 10.

6381. Intercollegiate wrestling tournament sponsored by the National Collegiate Athletic Association (NCAA) was held in 1927, under rules written the previous year by R. G. Clapp of the University of Nebraska.

6382. Wrestler to win two super heavyweight freestyle titles in the Olympic Games was Johan Richthoff of Sweden. After winning his first in 1928, he won his second in Los Angeles, California, on August 3, 1932, at the age of 34.

6383. Welterweight Greco-Roman wrestling event held in the Olympic Games was in 1932 in Los Angeles, California, where Ivar Johansson of Sweden won the event on August 7.

6384. Wrestler to win two consecutive middleweight Greco-Roman titles in the Olympic Games was Väinö Kokkinen of Finland. After winning his first in 1928, he went to Los Angeles, California, to take his second on August 7, 1932.

6385. Wrestler to win heavyweight titles in both freestyle and Greco-Roman wrestling in the Olympic Games was Kristian Palusalu of Estonia. Competing in Berlin, Germany, he won the super heavyweight freestyle title on August 4, 1936, and the heavyweight Greco-Roman on August 9.

6386. Wrestler from the United States to win the middleweight freestyle wrestling title in the Olympic Games was Glen Brand, who won the event on July 31, 1948, in London, England.

6387. Flyweight Greco-Roman wrestling event held in the Olympic Games was in 1948 in London, England. Winning that first competition on August 6 was Pietro Lombardi of Italy.

WRESTLING (1950-1999)

6388. World championships in Greco-Roman wrestling held on a regular basis began in 1950. Wrestlers from Sweden won four titles: Bengt Johansson the flyweight, Olle Anderberg the featherweight, Axel Brönberg the middleweight, and Bertil Antonsson the heavyweight. Ali Mahmoud Hassan of Egypt took the bantamweight title, József Gál of Hungary the lightweight, Matti Simanainen of Finland the welterweight, and Muharrem Candas of Turkey the light heavyweight.

6389. World championships in freestyle wrestling were held in 1951 in Helsinki, Finland. Wrestlers from Turkey took six titles: Ali Yücel won the flyweight, Nasuh Akar the bantamweight, Haydar Zafer the featherweight, Celál Atik the welterweight, Haydar Zafer the middleweight, and Yasar Dogu the light heavyweight. Sweden had two champions: Olle Anderberg won the lightweight and Bertil Antonsson the heavyweight.

6390. Wrestler to win two consecutive welterweight Greco-Roman titles in the Olympic Games was Mithat Bayrak of Turkey, who won his second title on August 31, 1960, in Rome, Italy, after winning his first in 1956.

6391. Wrestler to win two consecutive light heavyweight Greco-Roman titles in the Olympic Games was Boyan Radev of Bulgaria. After winning his first in 1964, he went to Mexico City to win his second on October 26, 1968.

6392. Wrestler to win two consecutive super heavyweight Greco-Roman titles in the Olympic Games was István Kozma of Hungary, who won his first in 1964, then took his second on October 26, 1968, in Mexico City.

6393. Light flyweight event held in the world freestyle wrestling championships was in 1969, when Aleksandr Medved of the Soviet Union won the first of his three straight titles in the event (1969–1971).

6394. Light flyweight event held in the world Greco-Roman wrestling championships was in 1969, when Gheorghe Berceanu of Romania won the title, as he would also in 1970.

6395. Light flyweight freestyle wrestling event held in the world wrestling championships was in 1969, when the inaugural title was won by Ebrahim Javadi of Iran, who would win again in 1970 and 1971.

6396. Super heavyweight event held in the world Greco-Roman wrestling championships was in 1969, when Anatoliy Roshin of the Soviet Union won his first title. He would repeat in 1970.

6397. Heavyweight freestyle wrestling event held in the Olympic Games was in 1972 in Munich, West Germany. The winner of the inaugural competition on August 31 was Ivan Yarygin of the Soviet Union, who would win again in 1976.

6398. Wrestler to win the light flyweight freestyle competition in the Olympic Games when it resumed in 1972 was Roman Dmitriev of the Soviet Union, who won in the final round on August 31, 1972, in Munich, West Germany.

6399. Wrestler to win two consecutive super heavyweight freestyle titles in the Olympic Games, and wrestling gold medals in three consecutive Olympic Games was Aleksandr Medved of the Soviet Union. In 1964, he won the light heavyweight freestyle wrestling title. Moving up to the super heavyweight class, he won his second gold medal in 1968, successfully defending it on August 31, 1972, in Munich, West Germany, for his third gold medal.

6400. Heavyweight Greco-Roman wrestling event held in the Olympic Games was in 1972 in Munich, West Germany, where the competition was won by Nicolae Martinescu of Romania on September 10.

6401. Light flyweight Greco-Roman wrestling event held in the Olympic Games was in 1972 in Munich, West Germany. The inaugural competition was won by Gheorghe Berceanu of Romania on September 10.

6402. Wrestler to win two consecutive flyweight Greco-Roman wrestling titles in the Olympic Games was Peter Kirov of Bulgaria. His second title was won on September 10, 1972, in Munich, West Germany, following his first in 1968.

6403. Wrestler to win two consecutive heavyweight freestyle wrestling titles in the Olympic Games was Ivan Yarygin of the Soviet Union. After winning his first in 1972, he captured his second on July 31, 1976, in Montreal, Quebec, Canada.

6404. Twin brothers to win gold medals in wrestling in the same Olympic Games were Anatoly Bilohlazov, who won the flyweight freestyle wrestling title on July 30, 1980, in Moscow, the Soviet Union, and his twin, Serhei Bilohlazov, who won the bantamweight freestyle title on July 31. Both represented the Soviet Union.

6405. Wrestler from the United States to win a Greco-Roman title in the Olympic Games was Steven Fraser, a Michigan deputy sheriff who won the light heavyweight title on August 1, 1984, in Los Angeles, California.

6406. Wrestler from the United States to win the super heavyweight Greco-Roman title in the Olympic Games was Jeffrey Blatnick, who won on August 2, 1984, in Los Angeles, California. He was only the second (by a day) U.S. wrestler to win an Olympic Greco-Roman title, and was an enormous surprise because he was considered "over the hill" and was also suffering from Hodgkin's disease, a form of cancer for which he began treatment immediately following the Olympics.

6407. Wrestler from the United States to win the heavyweight freestyle wrestling title in the Olympic Games was Louis Banach, who won with a fall on August 11, 1984, in Los Angeles, California. His twin brother, Ed Banach, won the light heavyweight title.

6408. Wrestler to win two consecutive light flyweight Greco-Roman wrestling titles in the Olympic Games was Vincenzo Maenza of Italy. Following his first title in 1984, he won again on September 20, 1988, in Seoul, South Korea.

6409. Wrestler of Black African descent to win a gold medal in wrestling in the Olympic Games was Kenneth Monday of the United States, who defeated world champion Adlan Varayev of the Soviet Union to take the welterweight freestyle wrestling title on September 30, 1988, in Seoul, South Korea.

6410. Wrestler to win two bantamweight freestyle wrestling titles in the Olympic Games was Serhei Bilohlazov of the Soviet Union. He won the first in 1980, but was unable to defend it in 1984 because of the Soviet Olympic boycott. Six-time world champion, he went to Seoul, South Korea, to win again on October 1, 1988.

6411. Wrestler to win two consecutive lightweight freestyle wrestling titles in the Olympic Games was Arsen Fadzayev. After winning his first for the Soviet Union in 1988, he went to Barcelona, Spain, to win his second for Russia, on August 5, 1992.

WRESTLING—(1950-1999)—*continued*

6412. Wrestler from the United States to win two super heavyweight freestyle titles in the Olympic Games was Bruce Baumgartner. Following his first in 1984, he dropped to silver in 1988, but then went back to gold at Barcelona, Spain, where he won on August 6, 1992.

6413. Wrestler to win two consecutive featherweight freestyle wrestling titles in the Olympic Games was John Smith of the United States. After winning first in 1988, he went to Barcelona, Spain, to take his second on August 7, 1992.

6414. Wrestler to win two consecutive light heavyweight freestyle wrestling titles in the Olympic Games was Makharbek Khadartsev. He won his first competing for the Soviet Union in 1988, then went to Barcelona, Spain, for Russia, winning his second title on August 7, 1992.

6415. Sumo wrestler born outside Japan to be named grand champion (yokozuna) was Chad Rowan of the United States, who wrestled under the name of Akebono, meaning Rising Sun. Born in Hawaii, he was so honored in January 1993.

Subject Index

The Subject Index is an alphabetical listing of the subjects mentioned in the main text of the book. Each index entry includes key information about the "first" and a 4-digit number in italics. That number directs you to the full entry in the main text, where entries are numbered in order, starting with 1001.

To find the full entry, look in the main text for the entry tagged with that 4-digit number. For example, to find the entry on admission fees first being charged at a baseball game, look for the entry numbered 1192 in the main text.

Note that most names of people and places are not included in this index, but instead are listed separately in the Personal Name Index and the Geographical Index. For example, references to Jesse Owens will be found in the Personal Name Index. However, references to the Jesse Owens International Award are given in the Subject Index.

For more information, see "How to Use This Book," on page ix.

---

athlete from Ethiopia, and Black athlete from Africa, to win gold medal at Olympic games, *4710*

athlete of Black African ancestry to compete in Olympic Games, *4629*

athlete to win long jump, or any field event, in Olympic Games, *4444*

Black athlete from South Africa to win gold medal in Olympic Games, *4802*

Black athletes to participate in Olympic Games, *4630*

runner from Africa, and from Ethiopia, to win women's marathon at Olympic Games, *4526*

runner from Africa to hold world record in men's 5000 meters, *5079*

runner from Africa to win men's 10,000-meter title at Olympic Games, *5085*

runner from Africa to win men's 100-meter race in Olympic Games, *4995*

runner from Africa to win men's 1500-meter title at Olympic Games, *5092*

runner from Africa to win men's 3000-meter steeplechase title in Olympic Games, *5087*

runner from Africa to win men's 400-meters title in Olympic Games, *5010*

runner from Africa to win men's 5000-meter title in Olympic Games, *5089*

runner from Africa to win men's 800-meter title at Olympic Games, *5151*

runner from Africa to win men's title at Olympic Games, and to hold world record in the event, *4487*

runner from Africa to win men's title in Boston Marathon, *4518*

runner from Africa to win men's title in New York Marathon, *4516*

runner from Africa to win women's 10,000 meters, and first Black African woman to win a medal, at Olympic Games, *5159*

runner from Africa to win women's 1500-meter title at Olympic Games, *5160*

runner from Africa to win women's title in Boston Marathon, *4527*

runner from Africa to win women's title in New York Marathon, *4524*

skier of African ancestry to compete in Olympic Winter Games, *5458*

woman of Black African descent to win a gold medal in Olympic Games, *4696*

aikido
school for, *4530*

Air Canada Centre
Toronto Maple Leafs regular season hockey game played at, *4234*

Toronto Raptors regular season basketball game played at, *2419*
> *See also*
> air races

air pistol shooting
women's individual event held in Olympic Games, *5322*

air rifle shooting
Olympic Games
> individual event held in, *5320*
> women's individual event in, *5318*

airplane races
Bendix Trophy, *1009*
> Jet Division, pilot to win, *1014*
> pilot to win Thompson Trophy and, *1010*
> pilot to win three times in a row, *1016*
> woman to fly in, *1011*
> woman to win, *1012*

international, *1001*
> in U.S., *1002*
> Schneider Cup, *1004*

national, *1006*

Pulitzer Trophy, *1005*

Thompson Trophy, *1008*
> Jet Division, pilot to win, *1015*
> pilot to win, twice, and then three times, *1013*
> pilot to win Bendix Trophy and, *1010*

Women's Air Derby, *1007*

Alabama, University of
football team to win three consecutive Sugar Bowl games, *3364*

win in Rose Bowl, *3156*

Alamo Bowl
football game, *3458*

Alamodome
San Antonio Spurs regular season basketball game played at, *2329*

All-African Games, *4376*

All America Football Conference (AAFC)
championship, *3199*

player to be named Most Valuable Player of, *3202*

season, *3200*

All-American athletes
African-American basketball player to be named, *1951*

athlete to be named All-American in both basketball and football, *1147*

All American Red Heads, *1893*

All-American teams
college football
> African-American, *3137*
> African-American player named to Walter Camp's, *3124*
> lineman to be named to Walter Camp's, *3143*
> named by Grantland Rice, *3153*
> named by Walter Camp, *3121*
> running back to be named to Walter Camp's, *3139*

women's college basketball

Arizona Diamondbacks
    regular season baseball game played at Bank One Ballpark, *1850*

Arizona State University
    football team in a major bowl game to gain total of 718 yards, *3326*
    team to win three consecutive Fiesta Bowl games, *3333*

Arkansas, University of
    championship in National Collegiate Athletic Association (NCAA) Men's Basketball National Tournament, *2338*

Arlington Stadium
    Texas Rangers regular season baseball game played, *1725*

Army-Navy football game, *3123*

Arrowhead Stadium
    Kansas City Chiefs regular season football game played at, *3325*

artificial hip
    professional athlete to be named All-Star in two sports, and first to play with, *5755*

artificial ice
    ice skating rink using, *2954*
        in Great Britain, *2955*
    open-air rink featuring, *2981*

Asahi Marathon, *4481*

Asian-Americans
    athlete to win gold medal in Olympic Games, *4694*
    figure skater to win singles title at U.S. national championships, *3088*
    golfer of African-American or Asian-American descent to win U.S. Amateur Championship, *3879*
    golfer of Asian-American or Native American descent to be named *Sports Illustrated* Sportsman of the Year, *1161*

Asian Games, *4372*

Asians
    jumper to hold officially accepted world record in women's event, and first female athlete from Asia to set world track and field record, *4431*
    runner from Asia to hold officially accepted world record in men's 100-meter dash, *5034*

asphalt roadway
    Southern 500 automobile race, *1075*

assists (basketball)
    basketball player to have 1,076, during his Division I National Collegiate Athletic Association (NCAA) career, *2321*
    player to average 13.3, per game during single Division I National Collegiate Athletic Association (NCAA) season, *2262*
    player to have 1,184, in single National Basketball Association (NBA) season, *2300*

player to have 115, in National Basketball Association (NBA) playoffs, *2263*
player to have 14, in single quarter of National Basketball Association (NBA) game, *2206*
player to have 19, in a single half of an NBA game, *1986*
player to have 21, in National Basketball Association (NBA) Finals game, *2207*
player to have 22, during single Division I National Collegiate Athletic Association (NCAA) game, *2258*
player to have 30, in single National Basketball Association (NBA) game, *2299*
player to have 406, during single Division I National Collegiate Athletic Association (NCAA) season, *2247*
player to have 868, in his rookie year in the National Basketball Association (NBA), *2266*
player to have 95, in National Basketball Association (NBA) Finals series, *2195*
player to have average of 14, per game in National Basketball Association (NBA) Finals series, *2211*
player to have average of 14.5, per game in single National Basketball Association (NBA) season, *2289*
player to have average of 17.6, per game in National Basketball Association (NBA) playoff series, *2212*
player to lead National Basketball Association (NBA) in, for nine consecutive years, *2365*
player to make more than 13,000, in his National Basketball Association (NBA) career, *2414*
team to have 196, in National Basketball Association (NBA) Finals series, *2198*
team to have 233, in single set of National Basketball Association (NBA) playoffs, *2138*
team to have 44, in single National Basketball Association (NBA) Finals game, *2075*
team to have 51, and 56 defensive rebounds, in single National Basketball Association (NBA) playoff game, *2192, 2192*
team to have 53, in single National Basketball Association (NBA) game, *2145*
team to have average of 31.4, per game in single National Basketball Association (NBA) season, *2217*
women's basketball player to have 23, in single Division I National Collegiate Athletic Association (NCAA) game, *2307*
women's basketball player to have 355, in single Division I National Collegiate Athletic Association (NCAA) season, *2253*

B

baseball stadiums and parks—*Continued*

Florida Marlins regular season baseball game played at, *1823*

Kauffman Stadium
Kansas City Royals regular season baseball game at, *1732*

Lakefront Park
Chicago White Stockings regular season game at, *1243*

League Park II
Cleveland Indians regular season baseball game played at, *1400*

Max M. Brown Memorial Park
Little League World Series, *1555*

Memorial Coliseum
Los Angeles Dodgers regular season game played at, *1633*

Memorial Stadium
Baltimore Orioles regular season baseball game played at, *1607*

Metropolitan Stadium
Minnesota Twins regular season game played at, *1647*

Mile High Stadium
Colorado Rockies regular season baseball game played at, *1824*

Municipal Stadium
Kansas City Athletics regular season baseball game played at, *1614*
Kansas City Royals regular season baseball game played at, *1708*

New Comiskey Park
Chicago White Sox regular season baseball game played at, *1816*

Oakland Alameda County Coliseum
Athletics regular season baseball game played at, *1700*

Olympic Stadium
Montreal Expos regular season baseball game played, *1746*

Pacific Bell Park
San Francisco Giants regular season game played at, *1860*

Palace of the Fans
Reds regular season game played at, *1346*

Polo Grounds I
New York Giants regular season game played at, *1268*
professional stadium in Manhattan, *1253*

Polo Grounds II
New York Giants regular season game played at, *1297*

Polo Grounds III
New York Giants regular season game played at, *1303*
New York Mets regular season game played at, *1657*

Recreation Park

Philadelphia Phillies regular season game played at, *1269*

RFK Stadium
Washington Senators regular season baseball game played at, *1654*

Riverfront Stadium
Cincinnati Reds regular season baseball game played at, *1716*

SAFECO Field
Seattle Mariners regular season baseball game played at, *1855*

Seals Stadium
San Francisco Giants regular season baseball game played at, *1632*

Seattle Kingdome
Mariners regular season baseball game played at, *1744*

Shea Stadium
New York Mets regular season baseball game played, *1671*

Shibe Park
Philadelphia Athletics regular season game played at, *1393*

Skydome
Toronto Blue Jays regular season baseball game played at, *1807*

South End Grounds
Boston Red Stockings regular season game played at, *1220*

Sportsman's Park I
St. Louis Browns (future Cardinals) regular season game played at, *1261*
St. Louis Browns (future Orioles) regular season game played at, *1347*

Sportsman's Park II
St. Louis Cardinals regular season game played at, *1445*

State Street Grounds
Chicago White Stockings regular season game at, *1226*

Three Rivers Stadium
Pittsburgh Pirates regular season baseball game played at, *1717*

Tiger Stadium
Detroit Tigers regular season game at, *1414*

Tropicana Field
Tampa Bay Devil Rays regular season baseball game played at, *1851*

Turner Field
Atlanta Braves regular season baseball game played at, *1844*

Veterans Stadium
Philadelphia Phillies regular season baseball game played at, *1721*

Washington Park
Brooklyn Dodgers regular season game played at, *1277*

Washington Park II

Boston Red Sox—*Continued*

player to lead American League in runs scored in two consecutive years, *1360*

regular season baseball game played at Fenway Park, *1413*

regular season game played at Huntington Avenue Grounds, *1340*

team to hit three home runs in one inning of World Series game, *1695*

team to win two consecutive American League pennants, *1364*

woman known to have played for a major league baseball team, *1462*

World Series victory, *1349*

Boston Red Stockings

hit made in National League, *1221*

major league player to hit four doubles in one game, *1252*

National League game, *1222*

player to score 6 runs in 9-inning National League game, *1271*

professional game played in Boston, Mass., *1210*

professional pitcher to win 200 games, *1216*

regular season game played at South End Grounds I and II, *1220*

teams from U.S. to tour England and Ireland, *1214*

two consecutive home runs by different players to open major league game, *1305*

bowl games (football)

African-American player in, *3158*

Alamo Bowl, *3458*

Aloha Bowl, *3376*

Carquest Bowl, *3445*

Copper Bowl, *3435*

Cotton Bowl, *3180*

    player to pass for or himself score total of six touchdowns in, *3203*

    team to win two consecutive games, *3303*

Fiesta Bowl, *3320*

    team to win three consecutive games, *3333*

Gator Bowl, *3204*

    team to win two consecutive, *3495*

Hall of Fame Bowl, *3406*

Heritage Bowl, *3446*

Humanitarian Bowl, *3485*

Independence Bowl, *3351*

Las Vegas Bowl, *3455*

Liberty Bowl, *3250*

    team to win two consecutive games, *3256*

Motor City Bowl, *3484*

Music City Bowl, *3502*

Orange Blossom Classic, *3163*

Orange Bowl, *3169*

    African-American football players to appear in, *3239*

team to win three consecutive games, *3330*

team to win two consecutive games, *3249*

Peach Bowl, *3294*

player to complete 19 consecutive passes in a major, *3494*

player to gain 280 yards rushing in major, *3432*

player to gain 359 all-purpose yards in a major bowl game, *3469*

player to gain 594 all-purpose yards in major, *3433*

player to kick five field goals in, *3385*

player to pass for six touchdowns in a major, *3397*

player to receive 20 passes in a major game, *3292*

player to receive for 252 yards in a major, *3427*

player to score 30 points in a major, *3423*

player to score five rushing touchdowns in major, *3130*

Pro Bowl, *3186*

    National Football League game between two All-Star teams, *3229*

    National Football League player to be named Most Valuable Player in, for two consecutive years, *3258*

Rose Bowl, *3133*

    African-American player to play in, *3140*

    African-American player to score touchdown in, *3212*

    African-American quarterback to appear in, *3260*

    Columbia University win in, *3166*

    Georgia Tech win in, *3159*

    Harvard University win in, *3145*

    Northwestern University win in, *3223*

    Notre Dame University win in, *3154*

    Oregon State University win in, and only Rose Bowl not played in Pasadena, California, *3191*

    Purdue University win in, *3281*

    Stanford University win in, *3157*

    University of Alabama win in, *3156*

    University of California at Los Angeles win in, *3275*

    University of California win in, *3149*

    University of Georgia win in, *3192*

    University of Illinois win in, *3214*

    University of Iowa win in, *3244*

    University of Michigan win in, *3220*

    University of Minnesota win in, *3266*

    University of Oregon win in, *3142*

    University of Pittsburgh win in, *3181*

    University of Southern California win in, *3152*

Brooklyn Dodgers (baseball)—*Continued*
regular season game played at Washington Park II, *1318*
World Series victory, *1612*
Brooklyn Dodgers (football)
African-American professional player to join, *3206*
Brooklyn Excelsiors, *1194*
shutout game on record, *1195*
Brooklyn's Smart Set Club
OAL title, *1881*
brother-and-sister pairs
figure skaters to win title at U.S. national championships, *3017*
international figure skating competition in which all medalists were, *3041*
Brotherhood of Ballplayers, *1284*
Buffalo Bills
American Football Conference championship, *3452*
American Football League championship, *3272*
regular season football game played at Rich Stadium, *3332*
Team to win four consecutive American Football Conference championships, *3457*
Buffalo Braves
player to be named National Basketball Association (NBA) Most Valuable Player of the Year, *2109*
Buffalo Sabres
regular season hockey game played at Marine Midland Arena, *4227*
regular season hockey game played at Memorial Auditorium, *4157*
Busch Memorial Stadium
St. Louis Cardinals regular season baseball game played at, *1689*
Butkus Award, *3398*
college football player to win Butkus Award, *3417*
butterfly stroke
used in Olympic Games, *5828*

C

Calgary Flames
regular season hockey game played at the Olympic Saddledome, *4186*
Calgary Stampede rodeo, *4883*
California, University of
win in Rose Bowl, *3149*
California Angels
player to be named Most Valuable Player, *1751*

player to be named Rookie of the Year, *1821*
regular season baseball game played at Anaheim Stadium, *1688*
California at Los Angeles, University of (UCLA)
championship in National Collegiate Athletic Association (NCAA) Men's Basketball National Tournament, *2026*
team to win seven consecutive Division I National Collegiate Athletic Association (NCAA) championships, *2096*
win in Rose Bowl, *3275*
camanachd
See
shinty
Camanachd Association Challenge Cup, *5260*
Cambridge University
cricket match on record between teams from Oxford University and, *2645*
university golf clubs, *3589*
Camden Yards
Baltimore Orioles regular season baseball game played at, *1819*
cameras
electric-eye photo finish
use of, in horse racing, *4294*
instant replay
football, American, *3269*
Canada Cup golf tournament, *3732*
national golf team that won, twice, *3748*
national team to win five consecutive, *3776*
Canada Cup ice hockey competition, *4173*
Canadian football
See
football, Canadian
Canadian Grand Prix auto race, *1112*
cancer
cyclist to win Tour de France after recovering from, *2727*
Candlestick Park
San Francisco 49ers regular season football game played at, *3318*
San Francisco Giants regular season game played at, *1643*
canoe polo
world championships, *2627*
canoe racing
international governing body for canoeing, *2595*
marathon world championships, *2624*
Olympic Games
canoer to win three titles in men's Canadian pairs 1000-meter event in, *2622*
canoer to win two men's Canadian pairs 1000-meter titles in, *2602*
men's Canadian pairs 1000-meter event held in, *2596*

men's Canadian pairs 500-meter event held in, *2618*

men's Canadian singles 1000-meter event held in, *2597*

men's Canadian singles 500-meter event held in, *2616*

racer to win five gold medals, and eight medals overall, in women's events in, *2628*

racer to win gold medal in both singles and pairs in women's 500 meters in, *2620*

racer to win six gold medals, and eight medals overall, in, *2609*

racer to win three gold medals in a single, *2621*

racer to win two consecutive men's Canadian singles 1000-meter titles in, *2605*

slalom world championships, *2604*

wild-water world championships, *2608*

world championships, *2600*

canoe sailing

world championships, *2601*

Caribbean Cup

bobsledding, *2476*

Carolina Hurricanes

regular season hockey game played at Raleigh Entertainment and Sports Arena, *4237*

Carolina Panthers

regular season football game played at Ericsson Stadium, *3477*

Carquest Bowl

football game, *3445*

carriage driving

world championships, *2878*

Cartwright's Rules

baseball game on record played under, *1185*

baseball team on record, *1184*

inter-club baseball game on record played under, *1187*

person to introduce baseball as played by, to California, *1188*

person to introduce baseball as played under, to Hawaii, *1189.*

Catawba College

football team to win two consecutive Tangerine Bowl games, *3219*

catcher (baseball)

to hit 38 home runs, *1600*

catcher's mask

used in National League game, *1237*

Champion Cup polo competition, *4859*

Champion Hurdle horse race, *4293*

Championship Auto Racing Teams (CART)

Indy Car national championship, *1051*

Charlotte Coliseum

Charlotte Hornets regular season game played at, *2276*

Charlotte Hornets

player to be named National Basketball Association (NBA) Rookie of the Year, *2314*

regular season game played at Charlotte Coliseum, *2276*

team to have .428 field goal percentage for single National Basketball Association (NBA) season, *2383*

Cheltenham Gold Cup horse race, *4291*

chest protector

used in baseball, *1233*

Cheyenne Frontier Days rodeo, *4881*

Chicago Bears

National Football Conference championship, *3403*

regular season football game played at Soldier Field, *3315*

team to win two consecutive league championships, *3189*

win in Super Bowl, *3405*

Chicago Blackhawks

National Hockey League Stanley Cup championship, *4110*

regular season game played in United Center, *4218*

Chicago Bulls

National Basketball Association (NBA) championship, *2304*

player to be named National Basketball Association (NBA) Defensive Player of the Year, *2269*

player to be named National Basketball Association (NBA) Most Valuable Player of the Year, *2270*

player to be named National Basketball Association (NBA) Rookie of the Year, *2016*

regular season game played in United Center, *2341*

team to have .878 winning percentage for National Basketball Association (NBA) season, *2369*

team to have a defensive rebound percentage of .952 in single National Basketball Association (NBA) playoff game, *2116*

team to win 44 straight National Basketball Association (NBA) home games, *2370*

Chicago Cardinals

National Football League championship, *3215*

Chicago Cubs

National League team to top 1 million paying customers at home in a single season, *1478*

pitcher to lead National League in winning percentage for three consecutive years, *1378*

Chicago Cubs—*Continued*
  pitcher to throw two shutouts in one day, *1381*
  pitcher to win the Cy Young Award, *1719*
  player to be named Most Valuable Player, *1515*
  player to be named Rookie of the Year, *1645*
  player to lead the National League in bases on balls for two consecutive years, *1408*
  regular season game played at Wrigley Field, *1425*
  team to win two consecutive World Series, *1379*
  World Series between two teams from same city, *1372*
  World Series victory, *1376*
Chicago Marathon, *4500*
Chicago Rockets
  African-American professional football player to join, *3207*
Chicago White Sox
  African-American player to play for, *1583*
  American league baseball game, *1331*
  pitcher to win Cy Young Award, *1636*
  player to be named Most Valuable Player, *1635*
  player to be named Rookie of the Year, *1618*
  player widely recognized as black to play for, *1588*
  regular season baseball game played at New Comiskey Park, *1816*
  regular season game played at Comiskey Park, *1401*
  regular season game played at Southside Park, *1332*
  two home runs in single American League game, *1338*
  World Series between two teams from same city, *1372*
  World Series victory, *1371*
Chicago White Stockings
  championship game in professional baseball, *1211*
  major league baseball team to win 21 games in a row, *1250*
  National League championship, *1232*
  pitcher to pitch shutout in National league, *1223*
  player to hit home run in National League, *1225*
  player to lead National League in batting average, *1217*
  professional pitcher to win 200 games, *1216*
  regular season game played at State Street Grounds, *1226*
  regular season game played at West Side Grounds, *1309*

regular season game played at West Side Park, *1282*
  sudden death rule to end baseball games, *1247*
  team to score 35 runs in single game, *1264*
  team to win three consecutive pennants, *1267*
chole
  introduction to British Isles, *2630*
  written reference to, *2629*
Cincinnati, University of
  championship in National Collegiate Athletic Association (NCAA) Men's Basketball National Tournament, *2007*
Cincinnati Bengals
  American Football Conference championship, *3371*
  regular season football game played at Paul Brown Stadium, *3514*
  regular season football game played at Riverfront Stadium, *3308*
Cincinnati Red Stockings
  loss as a professional baseball team, and the end of the first winning streak in professional baseball, *1204*
  professional baseball team, *1203*
Cincinnati Reds
  African-American player to play for, *1608*
  major league game played on Sunday, *1236*
  player to be named Most Valuable Player, *1526*
  player to be named Rookie of the Year, *1619*
  player to lead the National League in stolen bases for four consecutive years, *1409*
  player to lead the National League in triples in two consecutive years, *1397*
  regular season baseball game played at Riverfront Stadium, *1716*
  regular season game played at Bank Street Grounds, *1246*
  regular season game played at Crosley Field, *1412*
  regular season game played at The Palace of the Fans, *1346*
  scheduled Sunday game in National League, *1307*
  team to hit nine home runs in single National League game, *1856*
  World Series victory, *1436*
Cincinnati Royals
  player to be named National Basketball Association (NBA) Most Valuable Player, *2025*
  player to be named National Basketball Association (NBA) Rookie of the Year, *2006*
Cinergy Field
  Cincinnati Reds regular season baseball game played at Riverfront Stadium, later, *1716*

Circle City Classic
African-American college football game, *3386*

circumnavigation of the world
balloonists to complete, *1183*
sailor to complete solo, *5202*
sailor to complete solo, from east to west, *5227*
sailor to complete solo, in 150 days, *5245*
sailor to complete solo, in under 130 days, *5246*
sailor to complete solo, in under 170 days, *5231*
sailor to complete solo, in under a year, *5213*
single-handed, non-stop, round-the-world sailing race, *5224*
Vendée Globe challenge race, *5250*
Whitbread Race, *5232*
  sailor from U.S. to win, *5257*
  sailor to win twice consecutively, *5241*
woman to sail alone, *5237*

City College of New York
championship in the National Collegiate Athletic Association (NCAA) Men's Basketball National Tournament, *1928*

clay pigeons
for target shooting, *5268*
  See also
  trap shooting

Cleveland Blues
American league baseball game, *1331*

Cleveland Broncos
player to lead American League in batting average for two consecutive years, *1359*
player to lead the American League in triples in three consecutive years, *1375*
three consecutive home runs in single inning of an American League game, *1348*
unassisted triple play of 20th century in major league baseball, *1395*

Cleveland Browns
African-American professional football player to join, *3197*
National Football League championship, *3226*
regular season football game played at Municipal Stadium, *3205*
regular season game played in Cleveland Browns Stadium, *3510*

Cleveland Cavaliers
regular season game played in Gund Arena, *2342*

Cleveland Indians
Brothers to play on opposing teams in World Series, *1447*
pitcher to win Cy Young Award, *1723*
player to be named Most Valuable Player, *1567*

player to be named Rookie of the Year, *1613*
regular season baseball game played at Jacobs Field, *1827*
regular season baseball game played at League Park II, *1400*
regular season game played at League Park I, *1336*
team to hit four successive home runs in American League game, *1666*
World Series victory, *1438*

Cleveland Rams
National Football League championship, *3196*

closed courts
for rackets, *4870*

Coach of the Year
American Basketball Association
  coach to be named by, *2057*
American Football Coaches Association
  college football coach to be named by, *3241*
  college football coach to be named by, three times, *3328*
Associated Press (AP)
  women's college basketball coach to be named by, *2349*
Football Writers Association
  college football coach to be named by, *3168*
Naismith Award
  women's college basketball coach to receive, four times, *2408*
National Basketball Association (NBA)
  coach to be named by, *2023*
  coach to be named by, three times, *2315*
  coach to be named by, twice, *2158*
National Football League (NFL)
  coach to be named by, *3211*
National Hockey League (NHL)
  coach to be named by, *4164*
  coach to be named by, twice in a row, *4197*
United States Basketball Writers Association
  women's college basketball coach to be named by, *2335*
Women's National Basketball Association (WNBA)
  coach to be named by, *2388*

Colisée de Québec
Quebec Nordiques regular season hockey game played at, *4163*

college baseball
African-American league, *1315*
American College Baseball Association, *1286*
coach to win 10 National Collegiate World Championships, *1748*
game between Yale and Princeton, *1200*
intercollegiate game, *1193*

NCAA major team to have 44 consecutive winning seasons, *3161*

player to be awarded Heisman Trophy, *3171*

player to be awarded Outland Trophy twice, *3377*

player to be win Maxwell Award, *3178*

player to receive the *Sports Illustrated* Sportsman of the Year Award, *3264*

player to rush for 1,000 yards or more in single season, *3179*

player to win Associated Press (AP) Athlete of the Year Award, *3185*

player to win Lombardi Award, *3299*

player to win Maxwell Award twice, *3235*

player to win Outland Trophy, *3201*

player to win Sullivan Award, *3194*

team to be named national champions by Associated Press (AP) Sportswriters Poll, *3174*

team to be named national champions by United Press International (UPI) Sportwriters Poll, *3224*

use of numbers on uniforms, *3136*
> *See also*
> bowl games (football)
> National Collegiate Athletic Association (NCAA)
> Rose Bowl

college ice hockey
National Collegiate Athletic Association (NCAA) championship, *4121*

player to score five goals in a single "Frozen Four" tournament game, *4125*

player to score seven points in a single "Frozen Four" tournament game, *4133*

team to win "Frozen Four" tournament in three consecutive years, *4129*

team to win the "Frozen Four" tournament seven times, *4146*

United States collegiate women's hockey league, *4188*

women's, Player of the Year Award, *4214*

college rowing
collegiate competition, and first intercollegiate athletic competition, on record in U.S., *4915*

program for women, *4917*

University Boat Race, *4913*
> dead heat on record in, *4918*
> woman to compete in, *4951*

woman to serve as coxswain on men's varsity team in U.S., *4938*

college softball
> *See*
> women's college softball

college sports
> *See*
> names of sports, as college football; National Collegiate Athletic Association (NCAA)

college track and field
meet to be televised, *6211*

College World Series (baseball)
player to bat in 17 runs in, *1758*

player to have 15 hits in, *1846*

player to hit four home runs in, *1664*

player to pitch 20 bases on balls in, *1576*

player to pitch 38 strikeouts in, *1652*

player to score 11 runs in, *1590*

player to steal eight bases in, *1778*

College World Series (women's college softball)
team to win, *5618*

Collegiate Basketball Officials Association
African-American to become a member of, *1974*

Colombian baseball players, *1344*

Colorado Avalanche
National Hockey League Stanley Cup championship, *4221*

regular season hockey game played at Pepsi Center, *4235*

Colorado Rockies
player to be named Most Valuable Player, *1838*

regular season baseball game played at Coors Field, *1831*

regular season baseball game played at Mile High Stadium, *1824*

team to top 4 million paying customers at home in single season, *1822*

Colored Intercollegiate Baseball Association (CIBA), *1410*

Columbia Park
Athletics regular season game played at, *1335*

Columbia University
win in Rose Bowl, *3166*

Comerica Park
Detroit Tigers regular season baseball game played at, *1858*

Comiskey Park
Chicago White Sox regular season baseball game played at, *1401*

Chicago White Sox regular season baseball game played at New, *1816*

Commissioner of Baseball, *1456*

Communist countries
boxer from, to turn professional, *2561*

Olympic Games at which athletes from, participated, *4689*

Olympic Games held in Soviet Union, and first in, *4751*

Conn Smythe Trophy
National Hockey League player to win, as Most Valuable Player of the playoffs, *4147*

Connecticut, University of
championship in National Collegiate Athletic Association (NCAA) Women's Basketball National Tournament, *2355*

Conseco Fieldhouse
Indiana Pacers regular season basketball game played at, *2426*
See also
International games; Olympic Games
names of individual sports and organizations, eg.

Coors Field
Colorado Rockies regular season baseball game played at, *1831*

Copper Bowl
football game, *3435*

corporate title sponsor
for professional golf tournament, *3696*

Cotton Bowl
football game, *3180*
player to pass for or himself score total of six touchdowns in major bowl game, *3203*
team to win two consecutive games, *3303*

County Stadium
Milwaukee Braves regular season baseball game played at, *1597*
Milwaukee Brewers regular season baseball game played at, *1715*

cowboys
African-American, to hold world rodeo title, *4899*
national organization for rodeo, *4888*
organization for Australian rodeo, *4891*
to be named All-Around Cowboy, *4885*
five consecutive times, and six overall, *4896*
four consecutive times, and five overall, *4894*
six consecutive times, *4898*
twice, *4887*
twice consecutively, *4890*
to win more than $100,000 in single season, *4897*
See also
rodeo

cricket
code of rules, *2635*
game on record played outside British Isles, *2632*
game to be broadcast on television, *2658*
governing body, *2638*
ground set aside for play, *2634*
International Cricket Conference (ICC) competition, *2662*
international match outside Great Britain, *2647*
international organization, *2654*
match at which admission was charged, and first game to be fully documented, *2636*

match on record at current location of Lord's Cricket Ground, *2642*
match on record at Lord's Cricket Ground, *2639*
match on record between teams from Oxford and Cambridge universities, *2645*
men's world cup, *2661*
Olympic Games
event at, *2653*
professional touring team, *2648*
protective gear worn by players, *2643*
radio broadcast of a game, *2655*
record of, being played in West Indies, *2641*
reference, *2631*
reference in North America, *2633*
team from outside British Isles to tour England, *2649*
team from outside England to play in England, *2646*
test match, *2650*
women's
international organization, *2659*
match, *2637*
national organization, *2656*
test match, *2657*
touring team, *2652*
world cup, *2660*

cricket clubs
in Australia, *2644*
in India, *2640*
women's, *2651*

croquet
All England Croquet Club, *2666*
club in U.S., *2664*
events at Olympic Games, *2670*
governing body for, in U.S., *2667*
open championship, *2665*
organization for, in Britain, *2669*
rules for roque, *2668*

croquet sets, *2663*

Crosley Field
night game in major league baseball played at, *1517*
Reds regular season game played at, *1412*

cross-country running
International Cross-Country Championships, *4984*
International Cross-Country Championships to include women's race, *5081*
men's cross-country team track race held in Olympic Games, *5005*
men's individual cross-country event held in Olympic Games, *5006*
runner to win two consecutive titles in men's individual event in Olympic Games, *5015*
World Cross-Country Championships, *5096*

cross-country skiing
20-kilometer event held in world championships of Nordic skiing, *5424*

women's points race event held in, *2722*
women's road race event in, *2708*
women's road time trial event held in, *2726*
Primavera race, *2690*
Race Across America (RAAM) bicycle marathon, *2705*
race on record, *2682*
races to include both amateurs and professionals, *2720*
Tour de France, *2689*
  cyclist from U.S. to win, *2712*
  cyclist to win, after recovering from cancer, *2727*
  cyclist to win, five times, *2721*
  cyclist to win, five times, and four times consecutively, *2701*
  cyclist to win, three consecutive times, *2699*
  cyclist to win, three times, *2694*
  cyclist to win, twice consecutively, *2691*
  women racers, *2706*
Tour of Italy (Giro d'Italia), *2693*
Tour of Spain (Vuelta a España), *2697*
world championships, *2684*
  to include women racers, *2700*
world cup in, *2715*
cycling clubs, *2681*

D

Dallas Cowboys
National Football Conference championship, *3313*
regular season football game played at Texas Stadium, *3319*
win in Super Bowl, *3324*
Dallas Mavericks
player to be named National Basketball Association (NBA) Rookie of the Year, *2352*
regular season game played at Reunion Arena, *2164*
team to average 8.96 3-point goals per game in single National Basketball Association (NBA) season, *2367*
team to have an .894 free throw percentage in single set of National Basketball Association (NBA) playoffs, *2200*
Dallas Stars
regular season hockey game played at Reunion Arena, *4207*
Dallas Texans
American Football League championship, *3267*
darts
modern, rules for, *2734*
playing of, on record in North America, *2733*

world professional championships, *2735*
Davey O'Brien National Quarterback Award, *3354*
Davis Cup tennis match, *6038*
to be a full professional-amateur Open, *6151*
Daytona auto races
24 hours of, *1103*
500, *1098*
deaths and accidents
athlete to die while participating in modern Olympics, *4644*
athlete to die while participating in Olympic Winter Games, *4713*
athletes to be killed by terrorists during Olympic Games, *4739*
baseball player to die of injuries suffered during a major league game, *1446*
golfer to die in accident, *3542*
ice-skating accident on record, *2946*
decathlon
African-Americans
  decathlete to win men's title in Olympic Games, *2743*
athlete to win both men's, and pentathlon in Olympic Games, and first Native American to win Olympic gold medal, *2738*
athlete to win Olympic gold medal, or to hold world record, in both men's, and individual track and field event, *2741*
championship on record, *2736*
decathlete from U.S. to hold world record in men's, *2740*
decathlete to hold officially accepted world record in men's, *2739*
decathlete to score 8,891 points in men's, *2745*
decathlete to score more than 8500 points in men's, *2744*
decathlete to win two consecutive titles in men's decathlon in Olympic Games, *2742*
men's event held in Olympic Games, *2737*
defenseman (ice hockey)
National Hockey League player to be named outstanding, *4131*
National Hockey League player to be named outstanding, eight times in a row, *4167*
National Hockey League player to be named outstanding, four times in a row, *4137*
National Hockey League player to have 102 assists in a single season, *4159*
National Hockey League player to have 25 assists in a single set of Stanley Cup playoffs, *4189*
National Hockey League player to score 12 goals in a single set of Stanley Cup playoffs, *4190*
National Hockey League player to score 37 points in a single set of Stanley Cup playoffs, *4191*

defenseman (ice hockey)—*Continued*

National Hockey League player to score 48 goals in a single season, *4193*

Defensive Player of the Year

National Basketball Association (NBA)

Chicago Bulls player to be named, *2269*

Denver Nuggets player to be named, *2353*

Detroit Pistons player to be named, *2292*

Houston Rockets player to be named, *2325*

Los Angeles Lakers player to be named, *2245*

player to be named, *2184*

player to be named, three times, *2401*

player to be named twice, *2196*

San Antonio Spurs player to be named, *2239*

Utah Jazz player to be named, *2221*

National Football League (NFL) player to be named, *3276*

Women's National Basketball Association (WNBA), *2389*

Delta Center

Utah Jazz regular season basketball game played at, *2309*

Denver Broncos

American Football Conference championship, *3358*

regular season football game played at Mile High Stadium, *3255*

win in Super Bowl, *3496*

Denver Nuggets

player to be named National Basketball Association (NBA) Defensive Player of the Year, *2353*

regular season game played at McNichols Sports Arena, *2117*

team to have 71 blocked shots in single set of National Basketball Association (NBA) playoffs, *2334*

team to have average of 18.54 offensive rebounds per game in single National Basketball Association (NBA) season, *2303*

team to score average of 126.5 points per game in single National Basketball Association (NBA) season, *2174*

Derby horse race, *4261*

horse bred and trained in U.S. to win England's, *4281*

jockey who won five, at Epsom Downs, *4266*

jockey who won seven, eight, and nine, at Epsom Downs, *4311*

jockey who won six, at Epsom Downs, *4269*

jockey who won three, at Epsom Downs, *4262*

designated hitter

baseball player to appear as, during regular season game, *1731*

baseball player to come to bat as, *1730*

Detroit Lions

African-American professional football players to join, in modern period, *3218*

National Football League championship, *3172, 3233*

regular season football game played at Pontiac Silverdome, *3346*

Detroit Pistons

National Basketball Association (NBA) championship, *2287*

player to be named National Basketball Association (NBA) Defensive Player of the Year, *2292*

player to be named National Basketball Association (NBA) Rookie of the Year, *2047*

regular season game played at The Palace of Auburn Hills, *2277*

team to have offensive rebound average of .556 in single National Basketball Association (NBA) Finals game, *2274*

team to score 186 points, and 74 field goals, in single National Basketball Association (NBA) game, *2193*

teams to have combined total of 188 rebounds in a single National Basketball Association (NBA) game, *1999*

Detroit Red Wings

National Hockey League Stanley Cup championship, *4114*

regular season hockey game played at Joe Louis Arena, *4177*

Detroit Tigers

American League pennant, *1377*

manager to be named Manager of the Year, *1772*

pitcher to win Cy Young Award, *1698*

player to be named Most Valuable Player, *1511*

player to be named Rookie of the Year, *1593*

player to hit more than .400 in two consecutive years in the American league, *1406*

player to lead the American League in hits in three consecutive years, *1382*

player to lead the American League in runs batted in for three consecutive years, *1383*

player to lead the American League in runs scored in three consecutive years, *1404*

player to lead the American League in slugging average for six consecutive years, *1407*

player to lead the American League in total bases for three consecutive years, *1384*

player widely recognized as black to play for, *1634*

F

facemasks

National Hockey League goaltender to wear, in a scheduled game, *4101*

Fastnet Race, *5209*

federal legislation

mandating equal opportunities for female athletes in U.S., *5751*

Federation Cup championships, *6112*

Fédération Internationale de Football Association (FIFA)

soccer player to be named World Footballer of the Year by, *5565*

Fédération Internationale de l'Automobile, *1048*

Fédération Internationale de Tir à l'Arc, *1029*

world championships in archery involving FITA rounds, *1033*

fencing

épée

fencer to win both men's masters épée and masters sabre competitions in Olympic Games, *2907*

fencer to win men's individual and team titles in same Olympic Games, *2908*

fencer to win three men's épée titles in world championships, *2927*

fencer to win two, three, and four men's team titles in Olympic Games, *2931*

fencer to win two consecutive men's titles in world championships, *2924*

fencer to win two consecutive women's titles in world championships, *2942*

men's amateurs and masters competition held in Olympic Games, *2904*

men's individual competition held in Olympic Games, *2902*

men's masters competition held in Olympic Games, *2903*

men's team competition held in Olympic Games, *2910*

national team to sweep top honors in men's individual competition in Olympic Games, *2913*

women's competition held in world championships of, *2941*

women's individual and team competitions held in Olympic Games, *2944*

fencer to win 13 medals in Olympic Games, *2934*

foil

fencer to win five gold medals in single Olympic Games, and to win two consecutive men's individual foil titles in Olympic Games, *2916*

fencer to win five men's titles in world championships, *2939*

fencer to win three, and then four, men's titles in world championships, *2932*

fencer to win three consecutive women's titles in world championships, *2930*

fencer to win two, and then three, women's titles in world championships, *2925*

fencer to win two consecutive men's individual titles in Olympic Games, *2933*

fencer to win two consecutive men's team titles in Olympic Games, *2926*

fencer to win two consecutive men's titles in world championships, *2922*

fencer to win two consecutive women's individual titles in Olympic Games, *2929*

fencer to win two consecutive women's titles in world championships, *2928*

fencers to win three gold medals in women's team competition in Olympic Games, *2938*

fencers to win two gold medals in women's team competition in Olympic Games, *2937*

men's competition held in world championships of fencing, *2921*

men's individual competition held in Olympic Games, *2897*

men's masters competition held in Olympic Games, *2898*

men's team competition held in Olympic Games, *2906*

national team to sweep medals in men's individual competition in Olympic Games, *2900*

national team to sweep medals in men's masters event in Olympic Games, *2901*

national team to sweep medals in women's individual fencing competition in Olympic Games, *2940*

women's individual competition held in Olympic Games, *2920*

women's team fencing competition held in Olympic Games, *2935*

international governing body, *2915*

sabre

fencer to win both men's sabre and épée titles in Olympic Games, *2912*

fencer to win consecutive men's individual titles, and men's team titles, in Olympic Games, *2914*

fencer to win four men's titles in world championships, *2943*

fencer to win three men's titles in world championships, *2936* fencer to win two consecutive men's titles in world championships, *2919*

masters competition held in Olympic Games, *2905*

men's competition held in world championships of fencing, *2918*

men's individual competition held in Olympic Games, *2899*

men's team competition held in Olympic Games, *2911*

world championships, *2917*

to include women, *2923*

Fenway Park

Boston Red Sox regular season game played at, *1413*

field goals (basketball)

player to have 17 3-point, in National Basketball Association (NBA) Finals series, *2322*

player to have a .739 field goal percentage in National Basketball Association (NBA) Finals series, *2108*

player to have an average of 95.5 percent in a single Division I National Collegiate Athletic Association (NCAA) Final Four championship series game, *2092*

player to have average of .599 over his National Basketball Association (NBA) career, *2267*

player to have average percentage of .727 in a single National Basketball Association (NBA) season, *2093*

player to have percentage of .783 in single set of National Basketball Association (NBA) playoffs, *2404*

player to have perfect field goal percentage in Division I NCAA game, *2331*

player to lead National Basketball Association (NBA) in, for five successive years, *2063*

player to lead National Basketball Association (NBA) in rebounds for 11 seasons, and in field-goal percentage nine times, *2095*

player to make 11 3-point field goals in single National Basketball Association (NBA) game, *2373*

player to make 113, in one set of, *2024*

player to make 18 consecutive, in single National Basketball Association (NBA) game, *2048*

player to make 267 3-point, in single National Basketball Association (NBA) season, *2366*

player to make 35 consecutive, in National Basketball Association (NBA) playoffs, *2248*

player to make all his attempts in National Basketball Association (NBA) Finals game, *2225*

player to make eight consecutive 3-point field goals in National Basketball Association (NBA) in single gam, *2343*

player to make more than 1,700 3-point, in his National Basketball Association (NBA) career, *2415*

player to make nine 3-point, in single National Basketball Association (NBA) playoff game, *2393*

player to make seven consecutive 3-point, in single National Basketball Association (NBA) playoff game, *2394*

player to miss on 17 consecutive attempts in single National Basketball Association (NBA) game, *2312*

player to score 13, in a single quarter of National Basketball Association (NBA) game, *2141*

player to score 16 consecutive field goals in a single NCAA game, *2053*

player to score 75, in Division I National Collegiate Athletic Association (NCAA) series, *2282*

player to score eleven 3-point, in single Division I National Collegiate Athletic Association (NCAA) championship series game, *2291*

player to score ten 3-point, in single Division I National Collegiate Athletic Association (NCAA) championship series game, *2249*

player to shoot 11 consecutive 3-point, during single Division I National Collegiate Athletic Association (NCAA) game, *2257*

player to shoot 15 3-point, in single Division I National Collegiate Athletic Association (NCAA) game, *2377*

player to shoot 158 3-point, during single Division I National Collegiate Athletic Association (NCAA) season, *2250*

player to shoot 413, during single Division I National Collegiate Athletic Association (NCAA) season, *2251*

team to have 20 3-point field goals in single National Basketball Association (NBA) playoff game, *2374*

team to have a .428 field goal percentage for single National Basketball Association (NBA) season, *2383*

team to have a .545 percentage in single National Basketball Association (NBA) season, *2215*

team to have a .600 percentage in National Basketball Association (NBA) playoffs, *2216*

team to have a .707 percentage in single National Basketball Association (NBA) game, *2191*

field goals (basketball)—*Continued*

team to have an .851 percentage in National Basketball Association (NBA) Finals series, *2368*

team to have percentage of .617 in single National Basketball Association (NBA) Finals game, *2308*

team to make 333, in one set of National Basketball Association (NBA) playoffs, *2022*

team to score 148 points, and 62, in single National Basketball Association (NBA) Finals game, *2226*

team to score 186 points, and 74, in single National Basketball Association (NBA) game, *2193*

team to score 41 3-point, in National Basketball Association (NBA) Finals series, *2347*

women's basketball player to score 27, in single Division I National Collegiate Athletic Association (NCAA) game, *2204*

women's player to score 17 consecutive, in single Division I National Collegiate Athletic Association (NCAA) game, *2244*

field goals (football)

National Collegiate Athletic Association college football player to kick 67-yard, *3356*

National Collegiate Athletic Association major college football player to kick 29, in a single season, *3387*

National Collegiate Athletic Association major college football player to kick 80, during his college career, *3402*

National Football League kicker to reach 420 career, *3492*

National Football League player to kick 37, in a single season, *3475*

National Football League player to kick 63-yard, *3309*

National Football League player to kick at least one, in 31 consecutive games, *3310*

National Football League player to kick seven, in a single game, *3284*

player to kick five, in major bowl game, *3385*

player to kick four, in a single Super Bowl game, *3289*

field hockey

See

hockey, field

Fiesta Bowl

football game, *3320*

team to win three consecutive games, *3333*

Fighter of the Year

boxer named, by *Ring* magazine, *2548*

two, three, and four times, *2551*

figure skating

Champion Series in, *3112*

competition at Olympic Games, *2974*

Ice Capades

season for, *3026*

ice dancing

skater to win five consecutive titles at U.S. national championships, *3027*

skaters for France to win title in world championships, *3096*

skaters from Canada to win medal in at Olympic Winter Games, *3093*

skaters from Czechoslovakia to win title in world championships, *3061*

skaters from Hungary to win title in world championship, *3083*

skaters from Soviet Union to win title in world championships, *3066*

skaters from United States to win Olympic medal in ice dancing, *3074*

skaters to win five consecutive ice dancing titles with same partner at U.S. national championships, *3068*

skaters to win five consecutive titles with same partner at U.S. national championships, *3068*

skaters to win gold medal in ice dancing in U.S. national championships, *2989*

skaters to win title at U.S. national championships, *3021*

skaters to win title in Olympic Winter Games, *3076*

skaters to win title in world championships, and first to win it two, three, and four times, *3046*

skaters to win two consecutive ice dancing titles at U.S. national championships, *3023*

skaters to win two consecutive titles at Olympic Winter Games, *3114*

skaters to win unanimous top scores for artistic impression, and first from Great Britain to win ice dancing title at Olympic Winter Games, *3087*

international competition, *2960*

international competition at which recorded music was standard, *2996*

International Skating Union (ISU) events to offer cash prizes to amateurs, *3113*

men's

national team to sweep singles figure skating medals at Olympic Winter Games, *2979*

skater from Austria to win men's singles titles in Olympic Winter Games, *3012*

skater from Canada to win singles title at world championships, *3058*

skater from Czechoslovakia to win singles title at Olympic Winter Games, *3070*

skater from Czechoslovakia to win singles title at world championships, *3067*

women's player to score 275, in single Division I National Collegiate Athletic Association (NCAA) season, *2175*

French Grand Prix auto race, *1082*

French national tennis championships
See
tennis

French Open
men's doubles tennis match, *6118*
mixed doubles tennis match, *6119*
tennis tournament, *6120*
tie-breaker rule at, *6155*
women's doubles tennis match, *6121*
women's singles tennis match, *6122*

Frisbee, *3525*
international tournament, *3526*
Ultimate, *3527*
intercollegiate match, *3528*
World Flying Disc Conference, *3529*

"Frozen Four" NCAA hockey tournament
player to score five assists in a single game, *4155*
player to score five goals in a single game, *4125*
player to score seven points in a single game, *4133*
team to win, seven times, *4146*

Fukuoka Marathon, *4484*

G

Gaelic football
See
football, Gaelic

Gator Bowl
football game, *3204*
team to win two consecutive, *3495*

Gay Games, *4378*

Geist Prize (table tennis), *5986*

General Motors Palace
Vancouver Canucks regular season hockey game played at, *4220*

Georgetown University
championship in National Collegiate Athletic Association (NCAA) Men's Basketball National Tournament, *2202*

Georgia, University of
win in Rose Bowl, *3192*

Georgia Dome
Atlanta Falcons regular season football game played at, *3454*

Georgia Tech
African-American player to become a quarterback at, *3298*
win in Rose Bowl, *3159*

German Grand Prix auto race, *1063*
to be part of Formula One Grand Prix circuit, *1084*

Giants Stadium
New York Giants regular season football game played at, *3350*
New York Jets regular season football game played at, *3396*

Girls' Rodeo Association, *4892*

Giro d'Italia cycling race, *2693*

Glaciarium (London, England), *2955*

gliding (soaring)
international governing body for competitions, *3530*
national championships for, in U.S., *3532*
world championships, *3531*
See also
hang gliding

gloves
baseball, on record, *1215*

goal posts
international game of American-style football, and first to use, *3118*

goaltender
National Hockey League, to be credited with 22 shutouts in a single season, *4100*
National Hockey League, to have six consecutive shutouts, *4095*
National Hockey League, to reach 300 career wins, *4127*
National Hockey League, to reach 400 career wins, *4148*
National Hockey League, to reach 50 career shutouts, *4097*
National Hockey League, to reach a career total of 103 shutouts, *4154*
National Hockey League, to wear facemask in a scheduled game, *4101*
National Hockey League goaltender to be credited with four shutouts in a single set of Stanley Cup playoffs, *4091*
National Hockey League player to be named outstanding, *4089*
National Hockey League player to be named outstanding, five times in a row, *4139*
National Hockey League player to be named outstanding, four times in a row, *4120*
National Hockey League player to be named outstanding, six times, *4124*
National Hockey League player to be named outstanding, two, and then three, consecutive times, *4092*
woman, to be credited with a win in a professional hockey game, *4211*

Gold Cup race
for motorboat racing, *4562*

Golden Glove matches, *2546*

national team to win five consecutive, *3776*

Championship Meeting, *3572*

    in employing individual match play format, *3573*

confirmation of public's right to play, *3538*

    and other sports on Sundays, *3540*

corporate title sponsor for professional golf tournament, *3696*

Curtis Cup match, *3695*

    British win of, *3730*

    played in U.S., *3697*

death in golf accident, *3542*

Du Maurier Classic, *3823*

event to be broadcast live on network television in prime time, *3898*

father and son to win tournaments on same day, *3896*

game on record in North America, *3560*

golfer born in U.S. to win U.S. national championship, *3627*

golfer from United States to win British Amateur Championship, *3638*

golfer to be full-time tournament professional in U.S., *3661*

golfer to be named *Sports Illustrated* Sportsman of the Year, *3760*

golfer to earn more than $1 million in single season in official prize money, *3858*

golfer to earn more than $100,000 in official prize money during single year, *3769*

golfer to earn more than $500,000 in official prize money in a single season, *3825*

golfer to hold record low scores in all four Professional Golfers' Association (PGA) major tournaments, *3899*

golfer to score under 80 at Old Course at St. Andrews, Scotland, *3574*

golfer to win $100,000 in single tournament, *3805*

golfer to win 100 professional tournaments, *3883*

golfer to win 32 straight matches, *3699*

golfer to win all four major tournaments, *3700*

golfer to win four U.S. Amateur titles, *3654*

golfer to win more than $10 million in official prize money during a career, *3885*

golfer to win more than 10 titles in four major tournaments, *3689*

golfer to win more than $2.5 million in official prize money in a single season, *3889*

golfer to win more than $2 million in official prize money during his career, *3801*

golfer to win more than $2 million in official prize money in a single season, *3886*

golfer to win more than $200,000 in official prize money in a single season, *3792*

golfer to win more than $3 million in official prize money during his career, *3812*

golfer to win more than $300,000 in official prize money in a single season, *3798*

golfer to win more than $4 million in official prize money during his career, *3840*

golfer to win more than $5 million in official prize money during his career, *3859*

golfer to win more than $6 million in official prize money during his career, *3866*

golfer to win more than $7 million in official prize money in a single season, *3894*

grand slams

    golfer to complete, *3693*

    golfer to have a double, and then triple, winning golf's four major tournaments twice, and then three times, each, *3797*

Hale America tournaments, *3711*

intercollegiate association in U.S., *3620*

intercollegiate tournament in U.S., *3621*

international championship, *3602*

international match, *3545*

JCPenney Classic tournament, *3761*

Legends of Golf tournament, *3817*

magazine in North America, *3618*

Masters tournament, *3698*

    golfer to win, *3807*

    golfer to win, four times, *3775*

    golfer to win, in under 280 for 72 holes, *3709*

    golfer to win, twice in a row, *3783*

    golfer to win 18 titles in golf's four major tournaments, and six, *3850*

    golfer to win three times, *3728, 3742*

    golfer to win two, *3702*

match reported in newspaper, *3547*

match to charge fees for spectators, *3601*

national championship in U.S., *3608*

national governing body in U.S., *3609*

Olympic Games

    men's event in, *3629*

    women's event in, *3630*

open competition, *3550*

    at St. Andrews, Scotland, *3553*

package, *3765*

practice range, *3665*

Presidents Cup Match, *3880*

    won by international team, *3893*

professional-amateur tournament, *3705*

Professional Golfers' Association (PGA) Seniors' Championship, *3706*

Professional Golfers' Association (PGA) Tour

    season purse to top $500,000, *3737*

purchase of equipment, *3536*

reference on record in England, *3537*

reigning monarch to play in national championship, *3710*

rules, *3551*

    to be published, *3552*

rules of committee of, *3619*

Ryder Cup match, *3687*

Grand Prix auto races—*Continued*

Japanese race to be part of Formula One Grand Prix circuit, *1122*

Mexican race to be part of Formula One Grand Prix circuit, *1106*

Monacan race, *1064*

to be part of Formula One Grand Prix circuit, *1078*

Pescara race, *1059, 1059*

racer to be world champion on the Formula One Grand Prix circuit, *1092*

racer to have 25 wins on Formula One Grand Prix circuit, *1113*

racer to have 6 wins in single season on Formula One Grand Prix circuit, *1087*

racer to have 7 wins in a single season on Formula One Grand Prix circuit, *1105*

racer to have 8 wins in single season on Formula One Grand Prix circuit, *1136*

racer to have 9 consecutive wins over two seasons on Formula One Grand Prix circuit, *1089*

racer to have 9 wins in single season on Formula One Grand Prix circuit, *1141*

racer to have more than 20 wins on Formula One circuit, *1096*

racer to have more than 50 wins on Formula One Grand Prix circuit, *1143*

Spanish race to be part of Formula One Grand Prix circuit, *1085*

Swiss race, *1065*

to be part of Formula One Grand Prix circuit, *1080*

woman racer to compete in, eligible for world-championship points, *1097*

woman racer to win world-championship points in, *1119*

Grand Prix du Paris horse race, *4275*

Grand Slam Cup (tennis), *6182*

grand slams (baseball)

game to include three, *1791*

home run in World Series history, *1448*

in major league baseball, *1256*

player in American League to hit four, in a single season, *1434*

player to hit, home runs in two consecutive games, *1314*

player to hit 13, in National League, *1629*

player to hit 23 grand slam home runs, *1528*

player to hit six, in single season, *1795*

rookie to hit grand slam home run in World Series, *1589*

grand slams (figure skating)

skaters to complete, winning European, world, and Olympic titles in same year, *3010*

grand slams (golf)

golfer to complete, *3693*

golfer to have a double, and then triple, winning golf's four major tournaments twice, and then three times, each, *3797*

grand slams (tennis)

African-American tennis player to win, *6109*

men's singles title, and first men's singles title won by an African-American, *6135*

Native Australian tennis player to win, *6146*

player to win 13, *6193*

player to win at least four women's singles titles at each of four Grand Slam tournaments, *6186*

player to win two, *6142*

tennis player to achieve, *6098*

woman tennis player to achieve, *6107*

Great Western Forum

Los Angeles Lakers regular season basketball game played at, *2054*

Greco-Roman wrestling

Olympic Games

bantamweight event held in, *6380*

flyweight event held in, *6387*

heavyweight event held in, *6400*

light flyweight event held in, *6401*

light heavyweight Greco-Roman event held in, *6373*

lightweight event held in, *6370*

middleweight event held in, *6371*

unlimited weight (super heavyweight) event held in, *6358*

welterweight event held in, *6383*

wrestler from U.S. to win super heavyweight title in, *6406*

wrestler from U.S. to win title in, *6405*

wrestler to win heavyweight titles in both freestyle and Greco-Roman wrestling in, *6385*

wrestler to win two consecutive flyweight titles in, *6402*

wrestler to win two consecutive light flyweight titles in, *6408*

wrestler to win two consecutive light heavyweight titles in, *6391*

wrestler to win two consecutive lightweight Greco-Roman titles in, *6376*

wrestler to win two consecutive middleweight titles in, *6384*

wrestler to win two consecutive super heavyweight titles in, *6392*

wrestler to win two consecutive welterweight titles in, *6390*

world championships, *6361*

held on a regular basis, *6388*

light flyweight event held in, *6394*

regarded as official, *6379*

super heavyweight event held in, *6396*

Green Bay Packers

National Football Conference championship, *3480*

H

Heisman Trophy
African-American college football player to win, *3257*
college football player to be awarded Heisman Trophy, *3171*
player to win it twice, *3347*

Henley Regatta, *4914*
rower from U.S. to win Diamond Sculls at, *4924*
rower to win both single and double sculls events at, *4939*

heptathlon
heptathlete from United States, and first African-American, to hold world record in women's event, *4014*
heptathlete from United States, and first African-American, to win women's event at Olympic Games world record in women's, *4015*
heptathlete to hold world record in women's, *4012*
heptathlete to win two consecutive women's titles in Olympic Games, *4016*
women's, event held in Olympic Games, *4013*

Heritage Bowl
African-American college football game, *3446*

Hershey Chocolate Company
corporate title sponsor for professional golf tournament, *3696*

Heydusek Prize
in table tennis, *5991*

high jump
African-American high-jumper to win men's title in Olympic Games, *4024*
high-jumper to clear seven feet, *4025*
high-jumper to clear six feet, *4017*
high-jumper to clear six feet in women's event, *4026*
high-jumper to hold officially accepted world record in men's event, *4021*
high-jumper to reach, and then break, 8-foot barrier, *4032*
high-jumper to set more than 10 world records in women's event, *4028*
high-jumper to set or equal four world records in men's event in a single year, *4027*
high-jumper to set six world records in men's event, *4029*
high-jumper to use "Fosbury flop" jumping method, *4031*
high-jumper to win two consecutive women's titles in Olympic Games, *4030*
high-jumpers to hold officially accepted world record in women's event, and first from U.S. to win women's event in Olympic Games, *4023*
men's event held in Olympic Games, *4019*

men's standing high-jump event held in Olympic Games, *4020*
organized women's competitions, *4018*
women's event held in Olympic Games, *4022*

Hilltop Park (N.Y.)
Highlanders regular season game played at, *1353*

Hispanics
baseball player widely recognized as black to play for Detroit Tigers, *1634*
baseball player widely recognized as black to play for the Chicago White Sox, *1588*
baseball player widely recognized as black to play for the Washington Senators, *1610*
Colombian major league baseball player, *1344*
Cuban, and first Hispanic-American to play in World Series game, *1435*
Cuban major league baseball player, *1205*
Cuban professional baseball league, *1240*
Dominican major league baseball player, *1620*
Dominican pitcher to pitch a no-hitter in the major leagues, *1665*
Dominican to be inducted into baseball's Hall of Fame, *1769*
Hispanic-American All-Star Game in major league baseball, *1667*
Hispanic-American baseball player to be named Rookie of the Year, *1621*
Hispanic-American major league baseball player to play in All-Star Game, *1584*
Hispanic-born baseball star to appear on U.S. postage stamp, *1779*
Hispanic-born major league baseball manager to be named Manager of the Year, *1829*
Hispanic-born major league baseball player to become a member of baseball's Hall of Fame, *1729*
Honduran major league baseball player, *1792*
major league baseball team consisting of nine black players, *1722*
Mexican-American boxer to win lightweight title in Olympic Games, *2589*
Mexican major league baseball player, *1505*
Mexican major league baseball player to win a batting title, *1603*
Puerto Rican baseball league, *1527*
Puerto Rican major league baseball player, *1543*
season in which both major league Most Valuable Player Awards went to, *1849*
Venezuelan major league baseball player, *1534*

· hits, in baseball
American League player to have 6, in 9-inning game, *1341*

hockey stadiums (ice hockey)—*Continued*
Tampa Bay Lightning regular season hockey game played at, *4206*
United Center
Chicago Blackhawks regular season game played in, *4218*
US Air Arena
Washington Capitals regular season hockey game played at, *4166*
Winnipeg Arena
Winnipeg Jets regular season hockey game played at, *4176*

Holy Cross College
championship in National Collegiate Athletic Association (NCAA) Men's Basketball National Tournament, *1917*

home runs
African-American player to hit, in American League, *1562*
American League player to steal 40 bases and hit 40 home runs in a season, *1797*
baseball rookie to hit 49 home runs in single season, *1793*
by a pitcher in a World Series, *1449*
catcher to hit 38 home runs, *1600*
college baseball player to hit four, in College World Series, *1664*
college baseball player to hit four, in single game, *1786*
game to include three grand slam, *1791*
grand slam in major league baseball, *1256*
grand slam in World Series history, *1448*
hit by Babe Ruth as New York Yankee, *1442*
in American League, *1334*
major league baseball club to hit total of 10,000, *1801*
major league game in which 11, were hit, *1581*
major league pitcher to hit two, in single game, *1270*
major league player to hit 60, in a single season, *1481*
player in American League to hit four grand slams in a single season, *1434*
player to hit, as a pinch hitter in World Series, *1565*
player to hit, in a National League night game, *1519*
player to hit, in an American League night game, *1536*
player to hit, in major league All-Star Game, *1508*
player to hit, in National League, *1225*
player to hit, the first time he came to bat in American League game, *1486*
player to hit 13 grand slams in National League, *1629*
player to hit 23 grand slams, *1528*
player to hit 27, in single season, *1275*

player to hit 500, *1487*
player to hit 59, in a single season, *1459*
player to hit 61, in single season, *1649*
player to hit 70 home runs in single season, *1853*
player to hit 700, *1513*
player to hit 714, *1518*
player to hit 715, *1738*
player to hit at least 60, in two consecutive seasons, *1857*
player to hit five, in doubleheader, *1609*
player to hit four, in 9-inning game, *1312*
player to hit four, in a single regular season American League game, *1504*
player to hit grand slam in two consecutive games, *1314*
player to hit home run on season's first pitch, *1788*
player to hit six grand slam, in single season, *1795*
player to hit triple and, in same inning, *1310*
player to hit two home runs in first major league game, *1298*
player to lead American League in, *1322*
player to lead American League in, for six consecutive years, *1496*
player to lead American League in, in four consecutive years, *1374*
player to lead the National League in, in three consecutive years, *1421*
player to reach a career total of 700, *1501*
player to steal 40 bases and hit 40 home runs in a season in National League, *1833*
player to steal more than 30 bases and hit more than 30, in a National League season, *1617*
player to steal more than 30 bases and hit more than 30 home runs in a single season in American League, *1461*
rookie to hit grand slam in World Series, *1589*
team to hit four successive, in American League game, *1666*
team to hit nine, in single National League game, *1856*
team to hit three home runs in one inning of World Series game, *1695*
three consecutive, in single inning of an American League game, *1348*
two, in single American League game, *1338*
two consecutive, by different players to open major league game, *1305*
World Series, *1357*

horizontal bar (men's gymnastics)
event held in Olympic Games, *3902*
gymnast to win two consecutive titles in Olympic Games, *3947*
to win three consecutive titles in world championships, *3920*

horse shows
National Horse Show, *2840*
Royal International Horse Show, *2842*

horse vault
men's, gymnast to win two consecutive titles in world championships, *3914*
women's, gymnast to win two consecutive women's titles in world championships, *3953*

horseshoes
club on record, *4320*
international tournament, *4321*

Houston, University of
team to score 11 passing touchdowns in a single game, *3443*

Houston Astrodome
Astros regular season baseball game played at, *1680*
Houston Oilers regular season football game played at, *3291*

Houston Astros
pitcher to win Cy Young Award, *1787*
player to be named Most Valuable Player, *1825*
player to be named Rookie of the Year, *1813*
regular season baseball game played at Houston Astrodome, *1680*
regular season game played at Enron Field, *1859*

Houston Comets
team to win Women's National Basketball Association (WNBA) championship twice in a row, *2411*
Women's National Basketball Association (WNBA) championship, *2396*
Women's National Basketball Association (WNBA) team to win league championship three times, and in three consecutive years, *2422*

Houston Oilers
American Football League team to win two consecutive conference championships, *3262*
regular season football game played at Houston Astrodome, *3291*

Houston Rockets
National Basketball Association (NBA) championship, *2337*
player to be named National Basketball Association (NBA) Defensive Player of the Year, *2325*
player to be named National Basketball Association (NBA) Most Valuable Player of the Year, *2148*
regular season game played at The Summit, *2118*
team to get 246 defensive rebounds in single set of National Basketball Association (NBA) playoffs, *2333*

team to have 28 offensive rebounds in single National Basketball Association (NBA) Finals game, *2171*
team to score 14 3-point goals in single National Basketball Association (NBA) Finals game, *2357*

Howard University
African-American basketball team at, *1882*

Hubert H. Humphrey Metrodome
Minnesota Twins regular season baseball game played at, *1766*
Minnesota Vikings regular season football game played at, *3374*

Humanitarian Bowl
football game, *3485*

Huntington Avenue Grounds (Boston, Mass.)
Red Sox regular season game played at, *1340*

Huntington Street Grounds (Philadelphia, Pa.)
Philadelphia Phillies regular season baseball game played at, *1289*

hurdles
electronically timed world record in men's 110-meter, *4343*
hurdler to hold officially accepted world record in men's 110-meter hurdles, and to set 110-meter hurdle record that would stand for more than 10 years, *4327*
hurdler to hold officially accepted world record in men's 400-meter hurdles, and to set 400-meter hurdle record that would stand for more than 10 years, *4326*
hurdler to hold officially accepted world record in women's 100-meter, *4342*
hurdler to hold officially accepted world record in women's 400-meter, *4344*
hurdler to hold officially accepted world record in women's 80-meter event, *4333*
hurdler to hold world record in both men's 110- and 400-meter events, *4331*
hurdler to race 400-meter hurdles in under 55 seconds, *4328*
hurdler to race men's 110-meter hurdles in under 13 seconds, *4346*
hurdler to race men's 110-meter hurdles in under 14 seconds, *4335*
hurdler to race men's 400-meter hurdles in under 47 seconds, *4353*
hurdler to race men's 400-meter hurdles in under 49 seconds, *4341*
hurdler to race men's 400-meter hurdles in under 50 seconds, *4337*
hurdler to race men's 400-meter hurdles in under 52 seconds, *4334*
hurdler to race men's 400-meter hurdles in under 53 seconds, *4330*
hurdler to race men's 400-meter hurdles in under 54 seconds, *4329*

hurdler to set four new world records in men's 400-meter hurdles, *4349*

Olympic Games

African-American hurdler to win men's 100-meter titles in Olympic Games, *4336*

African-American hurdler to win men's 400-meter title in, *4345*

hurdler to win two consecutive titles in men's 110-meter hurdles in, *4340*

hurdler to win two consecutive titles in men's 400-meter hurdles in, *4339*

hurdler to win two consecutive titles in women's 80-meter hurdles in, *4338*

men's 110-meter event held in, *4322*

men's 200-meter event held in, *4325*

men's 400-meter event held in, *4324*

national team to sweep medals in men's 110-meter event in, *4323*

women's 400-meter hurdles event held in, *4350*

women's 80-meter hurdles event held in, *4332*

World Championships in Athletics

hurdler from Great Britain to win men's title in 400-meter event in, *4354*

hurdler to win men's 110-meter event in, *4347*

hurdler to win men's 400-meter hurdles held in, *4348*

hurdler to win two, and then three, consecutive titles in men's 110-meter event in, *4351*

hurdler to win two consecutive titles in men's 400-meter event in, *4352*

hurling

All-Ireland Championship in, *4358*

ban on, *4355*

national organization for, *4356*

standardization of rules of, *4357*

hydro-aeroplane race

Schneider Cup international seaplane race, *1004*

I

ice boating

in U.S., *4359*

Ice Capades

season for, *3026*

ice dancing

skater to win five consecutive titles at U.S. national championships, *3027*

skaters for France to win title in world championships, *3096*

skaters from Canada to win medal in at Olympic Winter Games, *3093*

skaters from Czechoslovakia to win title in world championships, *3061*

skaters from Hungary to win title in world championship, *3083*

skaters from Soviet Union to win title in world championships, *3066*

skaters from United States to win Olympic medal in ice dancing, *3074*

skaters to win five consecutive titles with same partner at U.S. national championships, *3068*

skaters to win gold medal in ice dancing in U.S. national championships, *2989*

skaters to win title at U.S. national championships, *3021*

skaters to win title in Olympic Winter Games, *3076*

skaters to win title in world championships, and first to win it two, three, and four times, *3046*

skaters to win two consecutive ice dancing titles at U.S. national championships, *3023*

skaters to win two consecutive titles at Olympic Winter Games, *3114*

skaters to win unanimous top scores for artistic impression, and first from Great Britain to win ice dancing title at Olympic Winter Games, *3087*

See also

college ice hockey

National Hockey League

Ice Palace

Tampa Bay Lightning regular season hockey game played at, *4228*

ice skate sailing

competition, *4360*

icewing sail for, *4361*

world ice and snow sailing championship, *4362*

ice skating

accident, *2946*

book on techniques, *2950*

international governing body for, *2962*

iron skates

in England, *2948*

on record, *2947*

literary reference to, *2945*

organizations

in North America, *2957*

national, in Great Britain, *2959*

national, in U.S., *2961*

skates with steel blades, *2952*

See also

figure skating

ice dancing

speed skating

ice skating clubs, *2949*

in mainland Europe, *2953*

in U.S., *2951*

J

javelin throw—*Continued*
> thrower to break 230-foot and 70-meter barriers, *4388*
> thrower to break 230-foot barrier in women's event, *4405*
> thrower to break 240- and 250-foot barriers, *4391*
> thrower to break 240-foot barrier in women's event, *4406*
> thrower to break 250-foot barrier in women's event, *4408*
> thrower to break 260-foot and 80-meter barriers, and first from U.S. to hold world record in men's event, *4394*
> thrower to break 260-foot barrier, and to reach 80-meter barrier, in women's event, *4410*
> thrower to break 270-foot barrier, *4396*
> thrower to break 280-foot barrier and to hold world record in men's event, *4397*
> thrower to break 290-foot barrier with the new javelin, *4411*
> thrower to break 300-foot and 90-meter barriers in men's event, *4399*
> thrower to break 300-foot and 90-meter barriers with the new javelin, *4412*
> thrower to break 310- and 320-foot barriers with the new javelin, *4413*
> thrower to break 310-foot barrier, *4403*
> thrower to break 330- and 340-foot and 100-meter barriers in men's event, *4407*
> thrower to break 70-meter barrier in women's event, *4404*
> thrower to hold officially accepted world record in men's event, *4384*
> thrower to hold officially accepted world record in women's event, *4389*
> thrower to reach 190-foot barrier in women's event, *4398*

JCPenney Classic golf tournament, *3761*
Jesse Owens International Award
> African-American athlete to win, *1159*
> African-American woman athlete to win, *1160*
> athlete to win, *1157*
> athlete to win two, *1162*
> cyclist to win, *2717*
> diver to win, *2817*
> runner to win, *5120*
> speed skater to win, *1157*
> woman athlete to win, *1158*

jeu de paume (court tennis or real tennis)
> in Olympic Games, *6049*
Jews
> athlete to represent Germany in the 1936 Olympic Winter Games, *4679*
> major league baseball manager, *1234*
> major league baseball player, *1218*
> Olympic Games at which athletes were killed by terrorists, *4739*

Jim Thorpe Award, *3401*
jockey clubs
> establishment of North American Jockey Club, *4284*
> in England, *4255*
> in North America, *4254*
jockeys
> African-American, known by name, *4265*
> African-American woman to win Thoroughbred race in U.S., *4309*
> to be named *Sports Illustrated* Sportsman of the Year, *4312*
> to win 8,834 horse races, *4319*
> to win America's Triple Crown, *4289*
> to win America's Triple Crown twice, *4300*
> to win five Derbys at Epsom Downs, *4266*
> to win Kentucky Derby, *4279*
> to win Kentucky Derby five times, *4301*
> to win nine races in a single day, *4316*
> to win seven, eight, and nine Derbys at Epsom Downs, *4311*
> to win six Derbys at Epsom Downs, *4269*
> to win three Derbys at Epsom Downs, *4262*
> to win three Kentucky Derbys, and first to win two in a row, *4283*
> wearing of racing colors by, *4257*
> woman, on record, *4264*
> woman to be licensed as, in U.S., *4304*
> woman to race at pari-mutuel track in U.S., *4305*
> woman to ride in Kentucky Derby, *4307*
> woman to win one of America's Triple Crown races, *4317*

Joe Louis Arena
> Detroit Red Wings regular season hockey game played at, *4177*
Joe Robbie Stadium
> Florida Marlins regular season baseball game played at, *1823*
> Miami Dolphins regular season football game played at, *3415*
Johnny Unitas Golden Arm Award, *3407*
judo
> development of, *4528*
> international governing body for, *4531*
> Olympic Games
>> artist to win gold medals in two different weight classes in, *4555*
>> artist to win two consecutive gold medals in men's heavyweight title in, *4551*
>> artist to win two consecutive men's middleweight gold medals in, *4550*
>> artist to win two gold medals in single, *4540*
>> men's extra-lightweight event held in, *4545*
>> men's half-heavyweight event in, *4538*
>> men's half-lightweight event held in, *4548*
>> men's half-middleweight event in, *4539*

men's heavyweight event in, *4535*
men's lightweight event in, *4534*
men's middleweight event in, *4533*
men's open event in, *4536*
women's extra-lightweight event held in, *4559*
women's half-heavyweight event held in, *4554*
women's half-lightweight event held in, *4558*
women's half-middleweight event held in, *4557*
women's heavyweight event held in, *4553*
women's lightweight event held in, *4552*
women's middleweight event held in, *4556*
world championships in, *4532*
to include women, *4546*

Junior League Baseball
leagues organized by Little League, *1752*

K

Kansas, University of
championship in NCAA Men's Basketball National Tournament, *1935*

Kansas City Athletics
regular season baseball game played at Municipal Stadium, *1614*

Kansas City Chiefs
American Football League championship, *3280, 3304*
regular season football game played at Arrowhead Stadium, *3325*
win in Super Bowl, *3306*

Kansas City Kings
player to be named National Basketball Association (NBA) Rookie of the Year, *2149*

Kansas City Rotary Club Trophy
National Air Races, *1006*

Kansas City Royals
American League pennant, *1754*
pitcher to win Cy Young Award, *1780*
player to be named Most Valuable Player, *1755*
player to be named Rookie of the Year, *1704*
regular season baseball game at Kauffman Stadium, *1732*
regular season baseball game played at Municipal Stadium, *1708*
World Series win, *1781*

karate
competition to include women, *4547*
formal instruction in, *4529*
world championships in, *4537*

Kauffman Stadium
Kansas City Royals regular season baseball game at, *1732*

kayak racing
Olympic Games
men's fours 1000-meter event held in, *2611*
men's kayak slalom white-water canoeing events held in, *2615, 2615*
men's pairs 500-meter event held in, *2617*
men's singles 100-meter event held in, *2599*
men's singles 500-meter event held in, *2619*
racer from U.S. to win men's singles 1000-meter event, and to win a gold medal in any kayaking event, in, *2626*
racer to win two, and then three, consecutive titles in men's singles 1000-meter kayak event, in, *2607*
racer to win two consecutive titles in women's 500-meter singles event, *2612*
racers to win both men's 1000- and 10,000-meter pairs kayak events, *2606*
racers to win two consecutive titles in men's pairs 500-meter event in, *2625*
racers to win two consecutive women's 500-meter kayak pairs event in, *2613*
women's 500-meter fours event held in, *2623*
women's 500-meter pairs kayaking event held in, *2610*
women's 500-meter singles event held in, *2603*
women's slalom singles event held in, *2614*

Kentucky, University of
team to win two consecutive National Collegiate Athletic Association (NCAA) national college basketball tournaments, *1922*

Kentucky Derby, *4279*
jockey to win, *4279*
jockey to win, five times, *4301*
jockey to win three, and first to win two in a row, *4283*
woman jockey to ride in, *4307*

Key Arena
Seattle SuperSonics regular season game played in, *2361*

Kiel Center
St. Louis Blues regular season hockey game played at, *4238*

King George V Gold Cup, *2844*

kolven
written reference to, *4414*
in North America, *4415*

L

La Salle University
championship in National Collegiate Athletic Association (NCAA) Men's Basketball National Tournament, *1948*
lacrosse
collegiate team in U.S., *4418*
event held in Olympic Games, *4420*
Intercollegiate Lacrosse Association, *4419*
international governing body for, *4422*
national organizations, *4417*
organization, *4416*
Wilson Wingate Trophy, *4423*
women's organization, *4421*
world championships
men's, *4424*
women's, *4425*
Ladies' Day baseball game, *1272*
Ladies Professional Golf Association (LPGA)
Championships, *3746*
golfer to win, in a sudden-death playoff, *3749*
golfer to win, with score under 280, *3774*
golfer to win two, and then three, *3762*
Player of the Year
golfer to be named, *3782*
golfer to be named, seven times, *3800*
President of, *3722*
Tour
African-American woman to play on, *3786*
golfer named Rookie of the Year on, *3766*
golfer on, to win four consecutively scheduled tournaments, *3768*
golfer to have 15 consecutive seasons with victory on, *3779*
golfer to win 10 major tournaments recognized by, *3738*
golfer to win 10 titles recognized by, in a single season, *3752*
golfer to win 13 titles recognized by, in a single season, *3773*
golfer to win her first tournament on, *3729*
golfer to win more than $1 million in her rookie year on, *3884*
golfer to win three major tournaments, and six titles overall, on, in a single season, *3725*
golfer to win two of golf's major tournaments in her rookie year on, *3844*
golfer to win Vare Trophy for lowest average score on, *3736*
season purse to top $1 million, *3804*
season purse to top $10 million, *3851*
season purse to top $100,000, *3731*
season purse to top $20 million, *3873*
season purse to top $200,000, *3758*
season purse to top $5 million, *3828*
season purse to top $500,000, *3785*
tournament to be nationally televised, *3772*
tournament to be nationally televised for all four rounds, *3839*
Lady Byng Memorial Trophy
National Hockey League player to win, as most gentlemanly player, *4085*
National Hockey League player to win, seven times, as most gentlemanly player, *4113*
Lakefront Park
Chicago White Stockings regular season game at, *1243*
Lambeau Field
Green Bay Packers regular season football game played at, *3245*
Las Vegas Bowl
football game, *3455*
laws
legal off-track betting operation in U.S., *4308*
relating to archery, *1017*
Le Mans 24-hours sports car race, *1057*
League Park I
Indians regular season game played at, *1336*
League Park II
Cleveland Indians regular season baseball game played at, *1400*
Legends of Golf tournament, *3817*
Leondi Big Five, *1883*
Liberty Bowl
football game, *3250*
team to win two consecutive games, *3256*
Lincoln Giants, *1299*
line of scrimmage
system in American-style football, *3119*
Little All-America teams
African-American football player from African-American college to be named to Associated Press (AP), *3234*
Little Brown Jug harness race, *4299*
Little League
baseball league, *1533*
girl from U.S. to appear in World Series, *1806*
in Canada, and first outside U.S., *1585*
Junior League Baseball leagues organized by, *1752*
national agreement to fully admit girls, *1734*
perfect game in World Series, *1578*
Senior Leagues for 13-year-old to 15-year-old players organized by, *1653*
team to win World Series in five consecutive years, *1757*

teams in new Challenger division, *1773*
World Series, *1555*
World Series to be televised, *1594*
World Series won by an East Asian team, *1692*
World Series won by Korean team, *1774*
World Series won by team from outside U.S., *1624*

Little League Softball
program, *5611*

Lloyd Street Park (Milwaukee, Wisc.)
Brewers regular season game played at, *1339*

Lombardi Award
African-American college football player to win, *3321*
college football player to win, *3299*

London Marathon, *4507*

London Prize Ring Rules, *2510*
title fight under, *2511*

Long Beach State College (California)
women's basketball team to score 149 points in single Division I National Collegiate Athletic Association (NCAA) game, *2260*

long horse vault (gymnastics)
event held in Olympic Games, *3903*
gymnast to win two consecutive titles in, in Olympic Games, *3965*

long jump
athlete to hold world record in both men's long jump and triple jump, *4433*
jumper from U.S. to set or equal world record in women's event, *4441*
jumper to break 20-foot and 6-meter barriers in women's event, *4435*
jumper to break 25-foot barrier, *4430*
jumper to break 26-foot barrier, *4432*
jumper to break 27-foot barrier, *4438*
jumper to break 7-meter barrier in women's event, *4440*
jumper to hold officially accepted world record in men's event, *4428*
jumper to hold officially accepted world record in women's event, and first female athlete from Asia to set world track and field record, *4431*
Olympic Games
  athlete from Africa to win long jump, or any field event, in, *4444*
  jumper from U.S. to win women's event in, *4442*
  jumper to break 28- and 29-foot barriers, *4439*
  jumper to win three, and then four, consecutive men's titles in, *4443*
  jumper to win two consecutive men's titles in, *4429*
  men's event held in, *4426*

men's event in which top four contestants jumped more than 26 feet, *4437*
women's event held in, *4436*
record to stand for more than 25 years, *4434*

Lord's Cricket Ground
cricket match on record at, *2639*
cricket match on record at current location of, *2642*

Los Angeles Angels
pitcher to win Cy Young Award, *1668*
regular season game played at Dodger Stadium, *1658*
regular season game played at Wrigley Field, *1648*

Los Angeles Clippers
regular season basketball game played at Memorial Sports Arena, *2209*
regular season game played in Staples Center, *2423*

Los Angeles Dodgers
National League team to top 3 million paying customers at home in single season, *1749*
regular season game played at Dodger Stadium, *1655*
regular season game played at Memorial Coliseum, *1633*

Los Angeles Dons
African-American professional football player to join, *3208*

Los Angeles Kings
regular season game played in Staples Center, *4236*

Los Angeles Lakers
National Basketball Association (NBA) championship, *2082*
player to be named National Basketball Association (NBA) Defensive Player of the Year, *2245*
player to be named National Basketball Association (NBA) Most Valuable Player of the Year, *2120*
regular season game played at Great Western Forum, *2054*
regular season game played in Staples Center, *2424*
team to have, *2215, 2242*
team to have 196 assists in National Basketball Association (NBA) Finals series, *2198*
team to have 44 assists in single National Basketball Association (NBA) Finals game, *2075*
team to have .580 rebound percentage in National Basketball Association (NBA) Finals series, *2156*
team to have .600 field goal percentage in National Basketball Association (NBA) playoffs, *2216*

Los Angeles Lakers—*Continued*

team to have .782 defensive rebound percentage in National Basketball Association (NBA) Finals series, *2157*

team to have a .652 rebound percentage in National Basketball Association (NBA) playoffs, *2233*

team to have a defensive rebound percentage of .921 in single National Basketball Association (NBA) Finals game, *2227*

team to have a road game winning percentage of .816 in single NBA season, *2083*

team to have average of 31.4 assists per game in single National Basketball Association (NBA) season, *2217*

team to win 16 consecutive road games in National Basketball Association (NBA), *2086*

team to win 33 consecutive games in the National Basketball Association (NBA), *2087*

Los Angeles Memorial Coliseum

Los Angeles Raiders regular season football game played at, *3375*

Los Angeles Raiders

American Football Conference championship, *3393*

regular season football game played at Los Angeles Memorial Coliseum, *3375*

win in Super Bowl, *3394*

Los Angeles Rams

African-American professional football players to play in National Football League in modern period, and first to play with, *3198*

National Football Conference championship, *3365*

National Football League championship, *3231*

regular season football game played at Anaheim Stadium, *3367*

losing streaks

major league baseball 26-game, *1295*

Lou Groza Collegiate Place Kicker Award, *3453*

Louisiana Superdome

New Orleans Saints regular season football game played at, *3345*

Louisiana Tech University

championship in National Collegiate Athletic Association (NCAA) Women's Basketball National Tournament, *2272*

women's basketball team to have 54-game winning streak, *2180*

women's basketball team to win National Collegiate Athletic Association (NCAA) national tournament, *2179*

Louisville, University of

championship in the National Collegiate Athletic Association (NCAA) Men's Basketball National Tournament, *2161*

Louisville Colonels

26-game losing streak, *1295*

luge

Grand National race, *4449*

international competition, *4447*

international governing body specifically for, *4454*

Olympic Games

coed event in, *4464*

men's singles event held in, *4455*

men's skeleton luge event at Olympic Games, *4452*

national team to sweep medals in men's singles event at, *4459*

national team to sweep medals in women's singles event at, *4460*

slider to win two, and then three, consecutive men's singles titles in, *4465*

slider to win two consecutive women's singles titles at, *4463*

sliders to win two consecutive titles at, *4462*

two-seater event at, *4456*

two-seater event to have two pairs of gold medalists in a single, *4458*

women's singles event held in, *4457*

skeleton, *4448*

men's event at Olympic Games, *4452*

slider to ride Cresta Run luge face forward, *4450*

sliding seat developed for, *4451*

specially built runs, *4446*

world championships, *4453*

world cup in, *4461*

written reference to tobogganing, *4445*

M

Madison Square Garden

indoor ice skating rink, *2958*

New York Knicks regular season basketball game played at, *2059*

New York Rangers regular season hockey game played at, *4151*

women's basketball game played in, *2114*

Madison Square Garden rodeo, *4884*

Major League Soccer

season, *5568*

Manager of the Year

American League manager to be named, *1768*

Baltimore Orioles manager to be named, *1804*

martial arts—*Continued*

See also

judo

Maryland Hunt Cup Race, *4285*

Masters golf tournament, *3698*

African-American golfer to play in, *3808*

golfer to win, four times, *3775*

golfer to win, in under 280 for 72 holes, *3709*

golfer to win, twice in a row, *3783*

golfer to win 18 titles in golf's four major tournaments, and six, *3850*

golfer to win five, *3807*

golfer to win three times, *3728, 3742*

golfer to win two, *3702*

golfer to win U.S. Open, Masters, and British Open in same year, and first to score under 275 for 72 holes, *3735*

Max M. Brown Memorial Park

Little League World Series, *1555*

Maxwell Award

African-American college football player to win, *3286*

college football player to win, *3178*

college football player to win, twice, *3235*

MCI Center

Washington Capitals regular season hockey game played at, *4229*

Washington Wizards regular season basketball game played at, *2398*

McNichols Sports Arena

Denver Nuggets regular season game played at, *2117*

mechanical rabbit

used in dog racing, *2834*

Melbourne Cup horse race, *4274*

Memorial Auditorium

Buffalo Sabres regular season hockey game played at, *4157*

Memorial Coliseum (Los Angeles, Calif.)

Los Angeles Dodgers regular season game played at, *1633*

Memorial Coliseum (Portland, Ore.)

Portland Trail Blazers regular season basketball game played at, *2076*

Memorial Sports Arena

Los Angeles Clippers regular season basketball game played at, *2209*

Memorial Stadium

Baltimore Orioles regular season baseball game played at, *1607*

Metropolitan Stadium

Minnesota Twins regular season game played at, *1647*

Mexican Grand Prix auto race

to be part of Formula One Grand Prix circuit, *1106*

Miami Arena

Florida Panthers regular season hockey game played at, *4209*

Miami Heat regular season basketball game played at, *2278*

Miami Dolphins

American Football Conference championship, *3323*

National Football League team to win 14 consecutive games in a single season, and to have an undefeated season, *3322*

regular season football game played at Joe Robbie Stadium, *3415*

team to win three consecutive American Football Conference championships, *3329*

win in Super Bowl, *3331*

Miami Heat

regular season basketball game played at Miami Arena, *2278*

Michigan, University of

National Collegiate Athletic Association hockey team to win "Frozen Four" tournament in three consecutive years, *4129*

win in Rose Bowl, *3220*

Michigan State University

championship in the National Collegiate Athletic Association (NCAA) Men's Basketball National Tournament, *2150*

Mighty Ducks of Anaheim

regular season hockey game played at The Pond of Anaheim, *4208*

Mile High Stadium

Colorado Rockies regular season baseball game played at, *1824*

Denver Broncos regular season football game played at, *3255*

Milwaukee Braves

pitcher to win Cy Young Award, *1625*

regular season baseball game played at County Stadium, *1597*

team to top 2 million paying customers at home in single season, *1604*

Milwaukee Brewers

American League pennant, *1765*

player to be named Most Valuable Player, and to win the Cy Young Award, *1760*

player to be named Rookie of the Year, *1817*

regular season baseball game played at County Stadium, *1715*

regular season game played at Lloyd Street Park, *1339*

Milwaukee Bucks

African-American to become general manager of a team in major professional sport, *2081*

player to be named National Basketball Association (NBA) Most Valuable Player of the Year, *2079* player to be named National Basketball Association (NBA) Rookie of the Year, *2072*

regular season basketball game played at Bradley Center, *2279*

team to have 233 assists in single set of National Basketball Association (NBA) playoffs, *2138*

team to have 53 assists in single National Basketball Association (NBA) game, *2145*

Milwaukee Hawks

player to be named National Basketball Association (NBA) Rookie of the Year, *1955*

miniature golf course, *3657*

Minneapolis Lakers

player to be named National Basketball Association (NBA) Rookie of the Year, *1985*

team to win three consecutive National Basketball Association (NBA) championships, *1946*

team to win two consecutive National Basketball Association (NBA) championships, *1927*

Minnesota, University of

win in Rose Bowl, *3266*

Minnesota Timberwolves

regular season basketball game played at Target Center, *2298*

Minnesota Twins

manager to be named Manager of the Year, *1815*

pitcher to win Cy Young Award, *1712*

player to be named Most Valuable Player, *1679*

regular season baseball game played at Hubert H. Humphrey Metrodome, *1766*

regular season game played at Metropolitan Stadium, *1647*

Minnesota Vikings

National Football Conference championship, *3334*

National Football League championship, *3305*

regular season football game played at Hubert H. Humphrey Metrodome, *3374*

Molson Center

Montreal Canadiens regular season hockey game played at, *4224*

Monaco Grand Prix auto race, *1064*

to be part of Formula One Grand Prix circuit, *1078*

Monday Night Football, *3300*

Monte Carlo Rally, *1053*

Montreal Amateur Athletic Association

ice hockey team to win Stanley Cup three times, *4052*

team to win Stanley Cup, *4045*

team to win Stanley Cup twice in a row, *4046*

Montreal Canadiens

National Hockey League Stanley Cup championship for, *4080*

National Hockey League team to win 60 games in a single season, *4171*

National Hockey League team to win Stanley Cup five times in a row, *4140*

National Hockey League team to win Stanley Cup more than 20 times, *4172*

regular season hockey game played at Molson Center, *4224*

Montreal Expos

baseball team situated in Canada, *1705*

pitcher to win Cy Young Award, *1842*

player to be named Rookie of the Year, *1713*

regular season baseball game played at Jarry Park, *1710*

regular season baseball game played at Olympic Stadium, *1746*

Montreal Maroons

National Hockey League Stanley Cup championship for, *4088*

moon

golf shot taken on, *3795*

Most Valuable Player

baseball

African-American player to be named, in American League, *1663*

African-American player to be named, in National League, *1568*

Baltimore Orioles player to be named, *1669*

Boston Braves player to be named, *1553*

Boston Red Sox player to be named, *1525*

Brooklyn Dodgers player to be named, *1541*

California Angels player to be named, *1751*

Chicago Cubs player to be named, *1515*

Chicago White Sox player to be named, *1635*

Cincinnati Reds player to be named, *1526*

Cleveland Indians player to be named, *1567*

Colorado Rockies player to be named, *1838*

Detroit Tigers player to be named, *1511*

Houston Astros player to be named, *1825*

Kansas City Royals player to be named, *1755*

Milwaukee Brewers player to be named, and to win the Cy Young Award, *1760*

Minnesota Twins player to be named, *1679*

New York Giants player to be named, *1506*

Most Valuable Player—*Continued*

New York Yankees player to be named, *1479*

Philadelphia Athletics player to be named, *1497*

Philadelphia Phillies player to be named, *1503*

Pittsburgh Pirates player to be named, *1641*

player from Canada to be named, in either league, *1840*

player to be named, in both major leagues, *1690*

player to be named American League Rookie of the Year and, in consecutive years, *1770*

players to be named, of their leagues, *1405*

San Diego Padres player to be named, *1834*

season in which both major league baseball awards went to Hispanic players, *1849*

Seattle Mariners player to be named, *1843*

St. Louis Cardinals player to be named, *1498*

Texas Rangers player to be named, *1736*

Toronto Blue Jays player to be named, *1794*

basketball

Baltimore Bullets player to be named, of National Basketball Association (NBA), *2060*

Boston Celtics player to be named, of NBA, *1969*

Buffalo Braves player to be named, of NBA, *2109*

Chicago Bulls player to be named, of NBA, *2270*

Cincinnati Royals player to be named, of NBA, *2025*

Houston Rockets player to be named, of NBA, *2148*

Los Angeles Lakers player to be named, of NBA, *2120*

Milwaukee Bucks player to be named, of NBA, *2079*

New York Knicks player to be named, of NBA, *2074*

Philadelphia Warriors player to be named, of NBA, *1993*

Phoenix Suns player to be named, of NBA, *2327*

player to be named, in NBA All-Star game, *1930*

player to be named, of NBA Finals, *2062*

player to be named, of NBA Finals six times, *2400*

player to be named, of NBA Finals three times, *2246*

player to be named, of NBA Finals twice, *2090*

player to win American Basketball Association award, *2055*

player to win American Basketball Association award in three consecutive years, *2121*

player to win National Basketball Association (NBA) award as, *1962*

player to win NBA award as, five times, *2032*

player to win NBA award as, six times, *2154*

player to win three consecutive NBA awards as, *2021*

Portland Trail Blazers player to be named, of NBA, *2140*

San Antonio Spurs player to be named, of NBA, *2354*

Utah Jazz player to be named, of NBA, *2385*

Women's National Basketball Association (WNBA) player to be named, *2390*

Women's National Basketball Association (WNBA) player to be named, twice in a row, *2402*

college baseball

team to have two consecutive winners, *1799*

college basketball

player to be named, of National Collegiate Athletic Association (NCAA) Final Four three times in a row, *2061*

player to be named, of NCAA Division I Final Four, *1899*

player to be named, of NCAA Division I Final Four twice in a row, *1908*

football

African-American player to be named, in Super Bowl, *3343*

National Football League player, and first African-American football player, to win Associated Press (AP) award as, *3243*

National Football League player to be named, at season-ending Pro Bowl, *3228*

National Football League player to be named, by Professional Football Writers Association, *3340*

National Football League player to be named, of American Football Conference, *3301*

National Football League player to be named, of National Football Conference, *3302*

N

National Basketball Association (NBA)—Continued

Chicago Bulls player to be named, 2270

Cincinnati Royals player to be named, 2025

Houston Rockets player to be named, 2148

Los Angeles Lakers player to be named, 2120

Milwaukee Bucks player to be named, 2079

New York Knicks player to be named, 2074

Philadelphia Warriors player to be named, 1993

Phoenix Suns player to be named, 2327

player to be named, 1962

player to be named, five times, 2032

player to be named, of NBA Finals, 2062

player to be named, six times, 2154

player to be named, three times in a row, 2021

Portland Trail Blazers player to be named, 2140

San Antonio Spurs player to be named, 2354

Utah Jazz player to be named, 2385

New York Knicks championship, 2073

player to average 2.71 steals per game in his career, 2363

player to average more than 50 points per game in single season in, 2009

player to capture 587 offensive rebounds in single season, 2146

player to get 23,924 career rebounds, and to average 22.9 rebounds per game, in his career, 2091

player to get 55 rebounds in a single game, 1998

player to go from high school into, without attending college, 2102

player to grab 2,149 rebounds in a single season, 2003

player to grab 32 rebounds in single half of NBA game, 1973

player to have 1,111 defensive rebounds in single season, 2127

player to have 1,184 assists in single season, 2300

player to have 10,117 defensive rebounds in his National Basketball Association (NBA) career, 2381

player to have 11 steals in single game, 2119

player to have 14 assists in single quarter of a game, 2206

player to have 17 blocked shots in single game, 2099

player to have 18 rebounds in single quarter of NBA game, 2035

player to have 19 assists in a single half of a game, 1986

player to have 21 offensive rebounds in single game, 2181

player to have 3,582 blocked shots in his career, 2412

player to have 30 assists in single game, 2299

player to have 301 steals in single season, 2232

player to have 456 blocked shots, and average of 5.56 blocked shots, in single season, 2210

player to have 6,371 offensive rebounds in his career, 2344

player to have 8,551 free throws in his career, 2345

player to have 868 assists in his rookie year in, 2266

player to have .958 free throw average in single season, 2166

player to have a .904 free throw average in his career, 2403

player to have a career average of 9.8 defensive rebounds per game in, 2185

player to have average field-goal percentage of .727 in single season, 2093

player to have average of 14.5 assists per game in single season, 2289

player to have field goal average of .599 over his career, 2267

player to have more than 2,700 steals in his career, 2413

player to lead, for three consecutive years in blocked shots, 2364

player to lead, for three years in steals, 2213

player to lead, in assists for nine consecutive years, 2365

player to lead, in field goal percentage for five successive years, 2063

player to lead, in free throw percentage for five consecutive years, 1964

player to lead, in offensive rebounds for eight years, 2290

player to lead, in offensive rebounds for seven consecutive years, 2186

player to lead, in rebounds for seven consecutive seasons, 2405

player to lead, in scoring for seven consecutive years, 2037

player to lead, in scoring in three consecutive years, 1931

player to lead, in scoring ten times, 2406

player to lead, in single season scoring, 1915

player to lead in free throw percentage for seven years, 2004

National Basketball Association (NBA)—*Continued*

team to have 97 rebounds in a single game, *1995*

team to have a .600 field goal percentage in, *2216*

team to have a .652 rebound percentage in, *2233*

team to have a.723 rebound percentage in a single game, *2242*

team to have a defensive rebound percentage of .952 in single game, *2116*

team to have an .894 free throw percentage in a single set of, *2200*

team to have offensive rebounding percentage of .609 in single game, *2340*

team to make 22 steals in a single game, *2115*

team to make 333 field goals in one set of, *2022*

team to score 157 points in single game, *2296*

team to score 869 points in one set of, *1984*

Portland Trail Blazers championship, *2132*

Rochester Royals championship, *1932*

Rookie of the Year

Baltimore Bullets player to be named, *1942*

Boston Celtics player to be named, *1970*

Charlotte Hornets player to be named, *2314*

Chicago Bulls player to be named, *2016*

Dallas Mavericks player to be named, *2352*

Indiana Pacers player to be name, *2255*

Kansas City Kings player to be named, *2149*

Milwaukee Bucks player to be named, *2072*

Milwaukee Hawks player to be named, *1955*

Minneapolis Lakers player to be named, *1985*

New Jersey Nets player to be named, *2177*

New York Knicks player to be named, *2034*

Orlando Magic player to be named, *2326*

Philadelphia Warriors player to be named, *1978*

Phoenix Suns player to be named, *2124*

player to be named, *1937, 2006, 2041, 2047*

Portland Trail Blazers player to be named, *2080*

Rochester Royals player to be named, *1963*

San Diego Clippers player to be named, *2190*

Toronto Raptors player to be named, *2371*

Utah Jazz player to be named, *2169*

San Antonio Spurs championship, *2417*

Seattle SuperSonics championship, *2151*

Sixth Man Award

player to win, *2187*

player to win, twice in a row, *2214*

St. Louis Hawks championship, *1979*

Syracuse Nationals championship, *1956*

team to average 12.9 steals per game in single season, *2137*

team to average 31.9 free throws per game in a season, *1977*

team to average 37.5 rebounds per game in single season, *2104*

team to average 8.96 three-point goals per game in single season, *2367*

team to get 39 offensive rebounds in single game, *2098*

team to get 61 defensive rebounds in single game, *2106*

team to have 19 three-point goals in single game, *2378*

team to have 22 blocked shots in single game, *2311*

team to have 27 steals in single game, *2392*

team to have 53 assists in single game, *2145*

team to have 57 free throws in a single playoff game, *1939*

team to have .878 winning percentage for NBA season, *2369*

team to have a .428 field goal percentage for a single season, *2383*

team to have a .545 field goal percentage in a single season, *2215*

team to have a .707 field goal percentage in single game, *2191*

team to have a .976 home game winning percentage for single season, *2234*

team to have a road game winning percentage of .816 in single season, *2083*

team to have average of 18.54 offensive rebounds per game in single season, *2303*

team to have average of 31.4 assists per game in single season, *2217*

team to have average of 8.7 blocked shots per game in single season, *2235*

team to lead, with average of 71.5 rebounds per game, *1991*

team to make 244 free throws in one set of playoffs, *1966*

team to make 39 consecutive free throws in single game, *2182*

team to make 61 free throws in single game, *2295*

team to score 186 points, and 74 field goals, in single game, *2193* team to score 25 points in single overtime period of NBA game, *2376*

team to score average of 126.5 points per game in single season, *2174*

team to win 16 consecutive road games in, *2086*

team to win 33 consecutive games in, *2087*

team to win 44 straight home games, *2370*

team to win eight consecutive titles, *2040*

team to win the championship of, *1916*

team to win three consecutive championships, *1946*

team to win two consecutive championships, *1927*

teams to have combined total of 188 rebounds in a single game, *1999*

three-point goal scored in NBA game, *2153*

woman basketball player to sign with NBA team, *2152*

women referees in, *2386*

National Car Rental Center

Florida Panthers regular season hockey game played at, *4231*

National Challenge Cup (soccer), *5549*

National Collegiate Athletic Association (NCAA)

academic standards for scholarship athletes in U.S., *5753*

basketball—Division I

consensus All-American college basketball team, *1890*

player in to receive Wooden Award as Player of the Year, *2126*

player to average 13.3 assists per game during single season, *2262*

player to average 23.3 rebounds in championship series, *2020*

player to average 44.5 points per game in single season, *2066*

player to average 5.0 steals per game during single season, *2228*

player to average 52.7 points per game in, championship series, *2067*

player to be named, United Press International (UPI) Player of the Year, *1952*

player to be named, United States Basketball Writers Association Player of the Year in three consecutive years, *2101*

player to be named Associated Press (AP) Player of the Year, *2001*

player to be named Associated Press (AP) Player of the Year in three consecutive years, *2183*

player to be named Associated Press (AP) Player of the Year in two consecutive years, *2010*

player to be named Most Valuable Player, in Final Four, *1899*

player to be named Most Valuable Player in Final Four, twice in a row, *1908*

player to be named Most Valuable Player of Final Four three times in a row, *2061*

player to be named United Press International (UPI) Player of the Year three consecutive times, *1989*

player to block 11 shots in single championship series game, *2313*

player to have 1,076 assists during his career, *2321*

player to have 1,224 rebounds during his career, *2077*

player to have 1,751 rebounds during his career, *1953*

player to have 13 steals during single game, *2261*

player to have 14 rebounds during single game, *2241*

player to have 150 steals during single season, *2264*

player to have 207 rebounds during single season, *2230*

player to have 22 assists during single game, *2258*

player to have 23 blocked shots in a series, *2231*

player to have 23 steals in a championship series, *2265*

player to have 27 rebounds in single Final Four championship series game, *1960*

player to have 34 rebounds in NCAA game, *1961*

player to have 376 steals during his college career, *2301*

player to have 406 assists during single season, *2247*

player to have 51 rebounds during single game, *1938*

player to have 734 rebounds during single season, *1936*

player to have a field goal average of 95.5 percent in a single Final Four championship series game, *2092*

player to have an average of 25.6 rebounds per game during single season, *1954*

player to have eight steals in championship series game, *2324*

player to have perfect field goal percentage in NCAA game, *2331*

player to have six blocked shots in single Final Four championship series game, *2268*

player to make 18 free throws in single Final Four championship series game, *2028*

National Collegiate Athletic Association (NCAA)—*Continued*

player to make 30 free throws in a single game, *2065*

player to score 1,381 points in single season, *2068*

player to score 100 points in a single game, *1949*

player to score 16 consecutive field goals in single game, *2053*

player to score 184 points in, series, *2281*

player to score 23 free throws in a game, *1943*

player to score 3,122 points during her career, *2285*

player to score 55 free throws in a series, *1944*

player to score 58 points in single Final Four championship series game, *2030*

player to score 61 points in single championship series game, *2069*

player to score 75 field goals in, series, *2282*

player to score eleven 3-point field goals in single championship series game, *2291*

player to score ten 3-point field goals in single championship series game, *2249*

player to shoot 11 consecutive 3-point field goals during single game, *2257*

player to shoot 15 3-point field goals in single game, *2377*

player to shoot 158 3-point field goals during single season, *2250*

player to shoot 24 consecutive free throws, and to shoot 100 percent in free throws, during a single game, *1987*

player to shoot 355 free throws during single Division I National Collegiate Athletic Association (NCAA) season, *1945*

player to shoot 413 field goals during single season, *2251*

team to win seven consecutive championships, *2096*

team to win two consecutive basketball championships, *1910*

tournament basketball championship game, *1898*

tournament basketball game, *1897*

tournament championship basketball game to be televised, *1909*

women's basketball player to block 15 shots in single game, *2319*

women's basketball player to have 1,887 rebounds in single career, *2236*

women's basketball player to have 151 blocked shots, and 5.6 rebounds per game, in single season, *2284*

women's basketball player to have 191 steals, and an average of 6.4 steals per game, in single season, *2351*

women's basketball player to have 23 assists in single game, *2307*

women's basketball player to have 355 assists in single season, *2253*

women's basketball player to have 40 rebounds in single game, *2188*

women's basketball player to have 534 rebounds in single season, *2218*

women's basketball player to have average of 18.5 rebounds per game in single season, *2219*

women's basketball player to score 12 3-point goals in single game, *2356*

women's basketball player to score 126 3-point goals in single season, *2305*

women's basketball player to score 17 consecutive field goals in single game, *2244*

women's basketball player to score 20 consecutive free throws in single game, *2379*

women's basketball player to score 23 free throws in single game, *2310*

women's basketball player to score 27 field goals in single game, *2204*

women's basketball player to score 275 free throws in single season, *2175*

women's basketball player to score 392 points in single season, *2176*

women's basketball player to score 60 points in single game, *2259*

women's basketball player to score 974 points in single season, *2254*

women's basketball player to score average of 28.4 points per game during her career, *2286*

women's basketball player to score nine consecutive 3-point goals in single game, *2273*

women's basketball team to have 39 wins in single season, *2410*

women's basketball team to score 149 points in single game, *2260*

women's basketball team to score 18 3-point goals in single game, *2399*

basketball—Men's Basketball National Tournament, *1907*

championship win by team with all-African-American starting lineup in final game, and first championship for Texas Western, in, *2043*

City College of New York championship in, *1928*

Duke University championship in, *2306*

Georgetown University championship in, *2202*

National Collegiate Athletic Association (NCAA)—*Continued*

player to kick 71 consecutive points after touchdown in a single season, *3464*

player to receive 141 passes in a single season, *3425*

player to receive 23 passes in single game, *3462*

player to receive 295 passes during his college career, *3488*

player to rush for 6,279 college career yards, *3489*

player to rush for 6,397 college career yards, *3503*

player to score eight rushing touchdowns in a single game, *3441*

player to score touchdowns on pass receptions in 12 consecutive games, *3478*

team to gain 1,021 all-purpose yards in a single game, *3430*

team to gain 6,874 all-purpose yards in a single season, *3426*

team to gain 768 yards rushing in a single game, *3422*

team to score 11 passing touchdowns in a single game, *3443*

team to win 47 consecutive games, *3242*

gymnastics

national championships sponsored by, *3969*

hockey, ice

championship, *4121*

player to score five assists in a single "Frozen Four" tournament game, *4155*

player to score five goals in a single "Frozen Four" tournament game, *4125*

player to score seven points in a single "Frozen Four" tournament game, *4133*

team to win the "Frozen Four" tournament in three consecutive years, *4129*

team to win the "Frozen Four" tournament seven times, *4146*

shooting

championships sponsored by, *5315*

softball—Division I

women's softball player to get 132 hits in a single season, *5627*

women's softball player to get 405 hits during her college career, *5628*

women's softball player to get seven hits in a single game, *5625*

women's softball player to hit 37 home runs in a single season, *5624*

women's softball player to pitch 182 complete career games, *5621*

women's softball player to pitch 50 wins in a single season, *5620*

women's softball player to pitch 62 complete games in a single season, *5623*

women's softball team to win World Series, *5618*

track and field

indoor competition sponsored by, *6216*

national championships sponsored by, *6206*

wrestling

intercollegiate tournament sponsored by, *6381*

National Collegiate World Championships (baseball)

coach to win 10, *1748*

team to win, *1554*

team to win five consecutive, *1735*

team to win two consecutive, *1577*

National Colored League

baseball game, *1290*

organizing meeting, *1288*

National Fastball League, *5584*

National Finals Rodeo (NFR), *4895*

National Football Conference (NFC)

African-American professional football player to be named Most Valuable Player of, *3311*

Atlanta Falcons championship, *3508*

Chicago Bears championship, *3403*

Dallas Cowboys championship, *3313*

Green Bay Packers championship, *3480*

Los Angeles Rams championship, *3365*

Minnesota Vikings championship, *3334*

National Football League player to be named Most Valuable Player of, *3302*

New York Giants championship, *3413*

Philadelphia Eagles championship, *3369*

San Francisco 49ers championship, *3372*

Washington Redskins championship, *3327*

National Football League (NFL)

African-American player to be named Player of the Year by Pro Football Writers Association, *3353*

African-American player to be named Rookie of the Year, *3240*

African-American player to play in championship game, *3252*

African-American professional football players to play in, in modern period, and first to play with Los Angeles Rams, *3198*

Baltimore Colts championship, *3246*

championship, *3164*

Chicago Cardinals championship, *3215*

Cleveland Browns championship, *3226*

Cleveland Rams championship, *3196*

Coach of the Year, *3211*

college draft, *3176*

defensive player to reach 192.5 career sacks, *3490*

defensive player to reach 22 sacks in a single season, *3388*

Detroit Lions championship, *3172, 3233*

game played in Australia, *3509*

New York Giants (football)—*Continued*
regular season football game played at Giants Stadium, *3350*
win in Super Bowl, *3414*

New York Highlanders
major league game played by, *1351*
pitcher to pitch 30 consecutive complete games, *1366*
player of 20th century to pitch for more than 40 wins in single season, *1365*
player to lead American League in singles in three consecutive years, *1369*
regular season game played at Hilltop Park, *1353*
> *See also*
> New York Yankees

New York Islanders
National Hockey League Stanley Cup championship, *4179*
regular season hockey game played at Nassau Veterans Memorial Coliseum, *4162*

New York Jets
American Football League championship, *3293*
regular season football game played at Giants Stadium, *3396*
win in Super Bowl, *3296*

New York Knickerbockers (baseball)
African-Americans
to join, *1925*
baseball team on record, *1184*
baseball uniform, *1186*
game on record to go into extra innings, *1190*
game played under Cartwright's Rules, *1185*
inter-club game on record played under Cartwright's Rules, *1187*
National Association of Base Ball Players convention, *1191*

New York Knicks (basketball), *2059*
National Basketball Association (NBA) championship, *2073*
player to be named National Basketball Association (NBA) Most Valuable Player of the Year, *2074*
player to be named National Basketball Association (NBA) Rookie of the Year, *2034*
team to average 31.9 free throws per game in a season, *1977*
team to have offensive rebounding percentage of .609 in single National Basketball Association (NBA) playoff game, *2340*
team to score 332 field goals in National Basketball Association (NBA) Finals series, *2071*

New York Marathon, *4493*
course to traverse New York City's five boroughs, *4499*

runner from Africa to win men's title in, *4516*
runner from Africa to win women's title in, *4524*
runner to be woman's champion in, *4494*
runner to win four consecutive, *4504*
runner to win men's title in both Boston Marathon and, in same year, *4503*
runner to win women's title in both Boston Marathon and, in same year, *4501*

New York Mets
pitcher to win Cy Young Award, *1706*
player to be named Rookie of the Year, *1693*
regular season game played at Polo Grounds, *1657*
regular season game played at Shea Stadium, *1671*
World Series victory, *1707*

New York Mutuals
triple play in baseball's National League, *1227*

New York Rangers
National Hockey League Stanley Cup championship, *4093*
regular season hockey game played at Madison Square Garden, *4151*

New York Yacht Club
organization of, *5197*

New York Yankees
African-American to play for, *1615*
American League pennant, *1454*
American League team to top 2 million paying customers at home in a single season, *1549*
home run hit by Babe Ruth as, *1442*
pitcher to win Cy Young Award, *1630*
player to be named Most Valuable Player, *1479*
player to be named Rookie of the Year, *1587*
regular season game played at Yankee Stadium, *1467*
team to play 14 games in the World Series without suffering a defeat, *1863*
team to win 25 World Series in the 20th century, *1854*
team to win five consecutive American League pennants, *1592*
team to win four consecutive American League pennants, *1532*
team to win three consecutive World Series, *1529*
World Series victory, *1465*
> *See also*
> New York Highlanders

New York Yankees (football)
African-American professional football player to join, *3210*

Olympic Games—*Continued*

in which more than 1000 athletes competed, *4712*

in which more than 2000 athletes competed, and more than 55 percent were women, *4803*

Jewish athlete to represent Germany in 1936, *4679*

not held in the same year as Summer Games, *4782*

to be boycotted by a member country, *4749*

to be canceled because of war, *4686*

to be held in Italy, and first to be televised, *4704*

woman athlete from U.S. to win six medals at Winter Games, and first female U.S. athlete to win five gold medals at Winter or Summer Games, *4784*

woman athlete from U.S. to win three gold medals in, *4770*

woman athlete to win medals in, 16 years apart, *4773*

woman athlete to win three consecutive titles in same event in, *4683*

woman athlete from U.S. to win four gold medals at a single, *4793*

woman athlete from U.S. to win gold medal in, *4625*

woman athlete to be disqualified from, because of positive drug test, *4743*

woman athlete to win a gold medal in, *4620*

woman of Black African descent to win a gold medal in, *4696*

woman to carry torch at, *4725*

women recorded as participating in original, *4600*

　　See also

African-Americans, Olympic Games international games

names of individual Olympic sports, e.g. biathlon, marathon

women, Olympic Games

Olympic ice hockey team, U.S. (1980)
team to be named *Sports Illustrated* Sportsman of the Year, *1156*

Olympic Saddledome
Calgary Flames regular season hockey game played at, *4186*

Olympic Stadium
Montreal Expos regular season baseball game played, *1746*

Omni, The
Atlanta Hawks regular season basketball game played at, *2089*

One Thousand Guineas horse race, *4268*

Orange Blossom Classic, *3163*

Orange Bowl
African-American football players to appear in, *3239*

football game, *3169*

team to win three consecutive games, *3330*

team to win two consecutive games, *3249*

Oregon, University of
win in Rose Bowl, *3142*

Oregon State University
win in college football's Rose Bowl, and only Rose Bowl not played in Pasadena, California, *3191*

orienteering
developed as a sport, *4805*

international governing body for, *4807*

national association for, *4806*

ski

　　world championships, *4809*

　　world championships to include sprint competitions, *4810*

world championships, *4808*

　　to include short events, *4812*

world cup in, *4811*

Original English Lady Cricketers
women's touring team, *2652*

Oriole Park
Baltimore Orioles regular season game played at, *1330*

Orlando Arena
Orlando Magic regular season basketball game played at, *2288*

Orlando Magic
player to be named National Basketball Association (NBA) Rookie of the Year, *2326*

regular season basketball game played at Orlando Arena, *2288*

team to score 41 3-point field goals in National Basketball Association (NBA) Finals series, *2347*

Ottawa Civic Center
Ottawa Senators regular season hockey game played at, *4205*

Ottawa Senators
National Hockey League Stanley Cup championship, *4071*

National Hockey League team to win 25 games in a single season, *4090*

regular season hockey game played at Ottawa Civic Center, *4205*

regular season hockey game played at Palladium, *4223*

team to win Stanley Cup twice in a row, *4074*

Ottawa Silver Seven
ice hockey team to win Stanley Cup three times in a row, *4055*

Outland Trophy
African-American college football player to win, *3237*

college football player to be awarded, *3201*

college football player to be awarded Outland Trophy twice, *3377*

Outstanding Player Award
college baseball player to win, *1573*
oversized golf clubs, *3870*
Owens International Award
See
Jesse Owens International Award
Oxford University
cricket match on record between teams from, and Cambridge university, *2645*
university golf clubs, *3589*
Oyakazu archery contest, *1018*

P

Pacific Bell Park
San Francisco Giants regular season baseball game played at, *1860*
Pacific Coast Hockey Association
championship, *4060*
Pacific Coliseum
Vancouver Canucks regular season hockey game played at, *4156*
paddle tennis
invention of, *6194*
national organization, *6195*
Palace of Auburn Hills, The
Detroit Pistons regular season game played at, *2277*
Palace of the Fans
Cincinnati Reds regular season game played at, *1346*
Palio horse race, *4248*
Palladium
Ottawa Senators regular season hockey game played at, *4223*
Pan-American Games, *4370*
softball event held at, *5616*
U.S. women's basketball team to play in, *1957*
Pan-Arab Games, *4373*
parallel bars (gymnastics)
gymnast to win two consecutive men's parallel bars titles in Olympic Games, *3963*
gymnast to win two consecutive men's titles in world championships, *3915*
men's competitions, held in Olympic Games, *3906*
pass interceptions
National Collegiate Athletic Association major college football player to intercept 14 passes in a single season, *3288*
National Collegiate Athletic Association major college football player to intercept 29 passes during his college career, *3232*
National Football League player to reach 81 career, *3359*

pass receptions
college football player to receive 20 passes in a major bowl game, *3292*
football player to gain 215 yards receiving in a single Super Bowl game, *3428*
National Collegiate Athletic Association football player to gain 1,996 yards receiving in a single season, *3487*
National Collegiate Athletic Association football player to gain 405 yards receiving in a single game, *3497*
National Collegiate Athletic Association football player to receive 295 passes during his college career, *3488*
National Collegiate Athletic Association major college football player to gain 4,518 yards receiving during his college career, *3474*
National Collegiate Athletic Association major college football player to receive 141 passes in a single season, *3425*
National Collegiate Athletic Association major college football player to score six touchdowns on, in a single game, *3297*
National Football League player to lead league eight times in, *3195*
National Football League player to reach career total of 1,206 passes received, *3505*
National Football League player to receive 18 completed passes in single game, *3225*
National Football League player to receive a pass in 193 consecutive games, *3501*
National Football League player to receive for 336 yards in a single game, *3431*
player to receive at least one touchdown pass in 13 consecutive games, *3416*
player to receive for 252 yards in a major bowl game, *3427*
passing yardage
National Football League player to pass for 554 yards in a single game, *3230*
patents
for dimple-patterned golf balls, *3642*
for golf ball, *3541*
Paul Brown Stadium
Cincinnati Bengals regular season football game played at, *3514*
Peach Bowl
football game, *3294*
Pendleton Round-Up rodeo, *4882*
pentathlon, *4813*
international organization, *4818*
Olympic Games
athlete to win both men's decathlon and pentathlon in, and first Native American to win Olympic gold medal, *2738*
men's event held in, *4814*
men's modern event in, *4815*
men's modern team event held in, *4823*

national team to sweep medals in women's pentathlon, in, *4831*

pentathlete from a non-military background to win men's modern pentathlon in, *4824*

pentathlete to achieve perfect score in shooting portion of men's modern pentathlon in, *4817*

pentathlete to place first in three of five events in men's modern pentathlon in, *4819*

pentathlete to win two consecutive titles in men's modern pentathlon in, *4825*

pentathlete to win two gold medals in men's modern team competition in, *4828*

pentathlete to win two gold medals in same, *4827*

women's modern pentathlon held in, *4835*

women's pentathlon held in, *4829*

pentathlete to hold officially accepted world record in women's type A pentathlon, *4816*

pentathlete to hold officially accepted world record in women's type B pentathlon, *4822*

world championships
  for men, *4820*
  for women, *4832*
  pentathlete to win five consecutive men's titles in, *4830*
  pentathlete to win three, and then four, consecutive men's titles in, *4826*
  pentathlete to win three, and then four, women's titles in, *4834*
  pentathlete to win two consecutive men's titles at, *4821*
  pentathlete to win two consecutive women's titles at, *4833*

"People's Olympics"
Jewish athlete to represent Germany in 1936 Olympic Winter Games, *4679*

Pepsi Center
Colorado Avalanche regular season hockey game played at, *4235*

perfect games
in the Little League World Series, *1578*
in World Series, *1623*

Pescara, Circuit
auto race at, *1058*

Philadelphia 76ers
regular season basketball game played at First Union Center, *2375*
regular season game played at The Spectrum, *2052*
team to get 93 rebounds in single National Basketball Association (NBA) Finals game, *2050*

team to have 20 blocked shots in single National Basketball Association (NBA) playoff game, *2170*
team to have 80 blocked shots in National Basketball Association (NBA) Finals series, *2155*

Philadelphia Athletics
African-American to play for, *1601*
American League pennant, *1345*
baseball teams from U.S. to tour England and Ireland, *1214*
championship game in professional baseball, *1211*
National League game, *1222*
pitcher to lead the American League in strikeouts for six consecutive years, *1373*
player to be named Most Valuable Player, *1497*
player to be named Rookie of the Year, *1591*
player to have 6 hits in 9-inning National League game, *1228*
player to hit for the cycle (single, double, triple, and home run) in a single game, *1342*
player to lead American League in batting average, *1321*
player to lead American League in home runs, *1322*
player to lead American League in home runs in four consecutive years, *1374*
player to lead American League in runs scored, *1323*
player to lead American League in slugging average, *1324*
player to lead American League in total bases, *1325*
regular season game played at Columbia Park, *1335*
regular season game played at Shibe Park, *1393*
Triple Crown hitter in American League, *1328*
World series victory, *1398*

Philadelphia Eagles
National Football Conference championship, *3369*
National Football League championship, *3221*
regular season football game played at Veterans Stadium, *3317*

Philadelphia Flyers
National Hockey League Stanley Cup championship, *4165*
regular season hockey game played at First Union Center, *4225*
regular season hockey game played at The Spectrum, *4150*

Philadelphia Phillies
African-American player to play for, *1627*

Q

quadruple jumps
figure skater to perform quadruple jump in competition, *3091*
figure skater to perform quadruple jump in Olympic Games, *3101*
skater to land three, and two different ones, in single international competition, *3116*

quadruple twist lift
skaters to perform, in competition, *3078*

Qualcomm Stadium
San Diego Padres regular season baseball game played at Jack Murphy Stadium later, *1709*

Quebec Nordiques
regular season hockey game played at the Colisée de Québec, *4163*

Queen Elizabeth II Cup (show jumping)
winner, *2861*

Queensberry Rules (boxing), *2512*
boxer to be heavyweight champion under, *2518*

R

RAC Grand Prix, *1062*

Race Across America (RAAM) bicycle marathon, *2705*

race tracks (automobile)
paved, *1052*
paved with asphalt, *1075*

race tracks (foot)
curved, *5053*

race tracks (horse)
public, in Britain, *4246*
to hold harness race at night, *4282*
to hold regular night harness races, *4297*

race walking
World Race Walking Cup, *6294*

Racing Calendar, *4258*

rackets
closed court for, *4870*
event held in Olympic Games, *4872*
international governing body for, *4871*

racquetball
game, *4873*
international governing body for, *4876*
introduction of, to England, *4875*
national organization for, *4874*
world championships in, *4877*

radio broadcasts
boxing match to be broadcast, *2540*
college football game to be broadcast, *3148*
college football game to be broadcast nationally, *3151*
cricket game to be broadcast, *2655*
heavyweight bout to be broadcast, *2541*
major league baseball game to be broadcast, *1458*
softball championship to be broadcast, *5581*
World Series game to be broadcast, *1460*
World Series game to be broadcast nationally, *1466*

Raleigh Entertainment and Sports Arena
Carolina Hurricanes regular season hockey game played at, *4237*

Raymond James Stadium
Tampa Bay Buccaneers regular season football game played at, *3499*

RCA Dome
Indianapolis Colts regular season football game played at, *3395*

rebounds
player to average 23.3, in Division I National Collegiate Athletic Association (NCAA) championship series, *2020*
player to average 29.5, per game in National Basketball Association (NBA) Finals series, *1982*
player to capture 587 offensive, in a single National Basketball Association (NBA) season, *2146*
player to collect 189, in National Basketball Association (NBA) Finals series, *2011*
player to collect 40, in a single National Basketball Association (NBA) Finals game, *1996*
player to get 220, in one set of National Basketball Association (NBA) playoffs, *2027*
player to get 23,924 career, and to average 22.9, per game, in his National Basketball Association (NBA) career, *2091*
player to get 55, in a single National Basketball Association (NBA) game, *1998*
player to get an average of 32, in National Basketball Association (NBA) playoff series, *2046*
player to grab 2,149, in a single National Basketball Association (NBA) season, *2003*
player to grab 32, in single half of NBA game, *1973*
player to grab 41, in single National Basketball Association (NBA) playoff game, *2049*
player to have 1,111 defensive, in single National Basketball Association (NBA) season, *2127*
player to have 1,224, during his Division I National Collegiate Athletic Association (NCAA) college career, *2078*

rebounds—*Continued*

player to have 1,751, during his Division I National Collegiate Athletic Association (NCAA) career, *1953*

player to have 10,117 defensive, in his National Basketball Association (NBA) career, *2381*

player to have 14, during single Division I National Collegiate Athletic Association (NCAA) game, *2241*

player to have 18, in single quarter of National Basketball Association (NBA) game, *2035*

player to have 207, during single Division I National Collegiate Athletic Association (NCAA) season, *2230*

player to have 21 offensive, in single National Basketball Association (NBA) game, *2181*

player to have 27, in single Division I National Collegiate Athletic Association (NCAA) Final Four championship series game, *1960*

player to have 34, in Division I National Collegiate Athletic Association (NCAA) game, *1961*

player to have 46 offensive, in single set of National Basketball Association (NBA) playoffs, and in NBA Finals, *2165*

player to have 51, during single Division I National Collegiate Athletic Association (NCAA) game, *1938*

player to have 6,371 offensive, in his National Basketball Association (NBA) career, *2344*

player to have 734, during single Division I National Collegiate Athletic Association (NCAA) season, *1936*

player to have 91 defensive, in National Basketball Association (NBA) Finals series, *2128*

player to have 95 defensive, in single set of National Basketball Association (NBA) playoffs, *2129*

player to have a career average of 9.8 defensive, per game in National Basketball Association (NBA), *2185*

player to have an average of 25.6, per game during single Division I National Collegiate Athletic Association (NCAA) season, *1954*

player to lead National Basketball Association (NBA) in, for 11 seasons, and in field-goal percentage nine times, *2094*

player to lead National Basketball Association (NBA) in, for seven consecutive seasons, *2405*

player to lead National Basketball Association (NBA) in offensive, for eight years, *2290*

player to lead National Basketball Association (NBA) in offensive, for seven consecutive years, *2186*

team to average 37.5, per game in single National Basketball Association (NBA) season, *2104*

team to get 246 defensive in single set of National Basketball Association (NBA) playoffs, *2333*

team to get 39 offensive, in single National Basketball Association (NBA) game, *2098*

team to get 61 defensive, in single National Basketball Association (NBA) game, *2106*

team to get 93 rebounds in single National Basketball Association (NBA) Finals game, *2050*

team to have, *2242*

team to have 131 offensive, in National Basketball Association (NBA) Finals series, *2197*

team to have 142 offensive, in single set of National Basketball Association (NBA) playoffs, *2147*

team to have 240 defensive, in a National Basketball Association (NBA) Finals series, *2122*

team to have 28 offensive, in single National Basketball Association (NBA) Finals game, *2171*

team to have 30 offensive, in single National Basketball Association (NBA) playoff game, *2143*

team to have .410 offensive average in National Basketball Association (NBA) Finals series, *2167*

team to have 46 defensive, in single National Basketball Association (NBA) Finals game, *2133*

team to have 487, in one National Basketball Association (NBA) Finals series, *1965*

team to have 51 assists and 56 defensive, in single National Basketball Association (NBA) playoff game, *2192*

team to have 525, in one set of National Basketball Association (NBA) playoffs, *1983*

team to have .580 percentage in National Basketball Association (NBA) Finals series, *2156*

team to have .782 defensive percentage in National Basketball Association (NBA) Finals series, *2157*

team to have 97, in a single National Basketball Association (NBA) playoff game, *1995*

team to have a .652 rebound percentage in National Basketball Association (NBA) playoffs, *2233* team to have a defensive percentage of .921 in single National Basketball Association (NBA) Finals game, *2227*

team to have a defensive percentage of .952 in a single National Basketball Association (NBA) playoff game, *2116*

team to have a percentage of .667 in a single National Basketball Association (NBA) Finals game, *1997*

team to have average of 18.54 offensive, per game in single National Basketball Association (NBA) season, *2303*

team to have offensive average of .556 in single National Basketball Association (NBA) Finals game, *2274*

team to have offensive percentage of .609 in single National Basketball Association (NBA) playoff game, *2340*

team to lead National Basketball Association (NBA) with average of 71.5, per game, *1991*

teams to have combined total of 188, in a single National Basketball Association (NBA) game, *1999*

women's basketball player to have 1,887, in single Division I National Collegiate Athletic Association (NCAA) career, *2236*

women's basketball player to have 151 blocked shots, and 5.6, per game, in single Division I National Collegiate Athletic Association (NCAA) season, *2284*

women's basketball player to have 40, in single Division I National Collegiate Athletic Association (NCAA) game, *2188*

women's basketball player to have 534, in single Division I National Collegiate Athletic Association (NCAA) season, *2218*

women's basketball player to have average of 18.5 per game in single Division I National Collegiate Athletic Association (NCAA) season, *2219*

Recreation Park

Philadelphia Phillies regular season game played at, *1269*

referees

women, in National Basketball Association (NBA), *2386*

Renaissance Big Five, *1886*

African-American professional team to win world championship, *1892*

"reserve clause"

successful set of actions against major league baseball's, *1714*

Reunion Arena

Dallas Mavericks regular season game played at, *2164*

Dallas Stars regular season hockey game played at, *4207*

RFK Memorial Stadium

Washington Redskins regular season football game played at, *3261*

Washington Senators regular season baseball game played at, *1654*

rhythmic sportive gymnastics

Olympic Games

all-around individual competition held in, *3974*

competition held in, *3979*

world championships, *3949*

gymnast to win all-around title two, and then three, times in, *3957*

world cup, *3970*

Rich Stadium

Buffalo Bills regular season football game played at, *3332*

rifle shooting

international tournament held in U.S., *5267*

Olympic Games

free, individual shooting event held in, *5269*

free, team event held in, *5281*

military, individual event held in, *5279*

military revolver and, team events held in, *5280*

shooter from U.S. to win men's small-bore (three positions) title in, *5310*

shooter from U.S. to win women's small-bore (three positions) event at, *5324*

shooter to win two consecutive titles in men's free (three positions) individual event, and in free rifle team event, in, *5302*

shooter to win two consecutive titles in small-bore (three positions) individual event in, *5323*

shooters from U.S. to win military rifle team shooting title in, *5288*

shooters from U.S. to win small-bore team title in, *5300*

small-bore, moving and disappearing target individual events held, *5289*

small-bore, team event held in, *5291*

small-bore (prone), individual event held in, *5290*

small-bore (three positions) individual event held in, *5309*

women's small-bore (three positions) individual event held in, *5319*

***Ring* magazine**

boxer named Fighter of the Year by, *2548*

boxer named Fighter of the Year by, two, three, and four times, *2551*

rings (gymnastics)

gymnast to win three, and then four, men's titles in world championships, *3977*

gymnast to win two consecutive men's titles in Olympic Games, *3948*

rings (gymnastics)—*Continued*
  gymnast to win two consecutive men's titles in world championships, *3925*
  men's competition held in the Olympic Games, *3904*

rink hockey
  See
  roller hockey

Riverfront Stadium
  Cincinnati Bengals regular season football game played at, *3308*
  Cincinnati Reds regular season baseball game played at, *1716*

road games
  basketball team to win 16 consecutive, in the National Basketball Association (NBA), *2086*
  team to have winning percentage of .816 in single NBA season, *2083*

Rochester Royals
  National Basketball Association (NBA) championship, *1932*
  player to be named NBA's Rookie of the Year, *1963*

rodeo
  African-American cowboy to hold world title, *4899*
  agreement to encourage women's events in, *4893*
  bronco-riding contest for cash prizes, *4878*
  Calgary Stampede, *4883*
  Cheyenne Frontier Days, *4881*
  cowboy to be named All-Around Cowboy, *4885*
    five consecutive times, and six overall, *4896*
    four consecutive times, and five overall, *4894*
    six consecutive times, *4898*
    twice, *4887*
    twice consecutively, *4890*
  cowboy to win more than $100,000 in single season, *4897*
  documented competition, *4880*
  Girls' Rodeo Association, *4892*
  Madison Square Garden, *4884*
  National Finals Rodeo (NFR), *4895*
  national organization for rodeo cowboys, *4888*
  organization for Australian cowboys, *4891*
  organization of producers, *4886*
  Pendleton Round-Up, *4882*
  professional, *4879*
  rider to win consecutive women's barrel racing titles, *4900*
  women-only, *4889*

roller derby, *4905*
  to be televised, *4908*

roller hockey
  international organization for, *4904*
  national organization, *4239*
  world championships, *4240*
    played with in-line skates, *4242*
    women's, *4241*

roller skating
  international organization for, *4904*
  national championships in speed skating in U.S., *4906*
  national speed skating championships in, in U.S., *4906*
  rink, *4903*
  roller derby, *4905*
    to be televised, *4908*
  roller skates, *4901*
    in-line, *4910*
    practical four-wheeled, *4902*
  world championships for speed skating, *4907*
  world figure skating championships for, *4909*
  world speed skating championships for, *4907*

Rookie of the Year (baseball)
  Baltimore Orioles player to be named, *1571*
  Boston Braves player to be named, *1566*
  Boston Red Sox player to be named, *1575*
  California Angels player to be named, *1821*
  Chicago Cubs player to be named, *1645*
  Chicago White Sox player to be named, *1618*
  Cincinnati Reds player to be named, *1619*
  Cleveland Indians player to be named, *1613*
  Detroit Tigers player to be named, *1593*
  Hispanic-American player to be named, *1621*
  Houston Astros player to be named, *1813*
  Kansas City Royals player to be named, *1704*
  Milwaukee Brewers player to be named, *1817*
  Montreal Expos player to be named, *1713*
  New York Giants player to be named, *1586*
  New York Mets player to be named, *1693*
  New York Yankees player to be named, *1587*
  Philadelphia Athletics player to be named, *1591*
  Philadelphia Phillies player to be named, *1626*
  player to be named, and the first African-American to win the award, *1556*
  player to be named American League, and Most Valuable Player in consecutive years, *1770*
  Seattle Mariners baseball player to be named, *1776*
  Texas Rangers baseball player to be named, *1737*

Washington Senators player to be named, *1631*

Rookie of the Year (basketball)
American Basketball Association (ABA) player to win award, *2056*
National Basketball Association (NBA)
Baltimore Bullets player to be named, *1942*
Boston Celtics player to be named, *1970*
Charlotte Hornets player to be named, *2314*
Chicago Bulls player to be named, *2016*
Cincinnati Royals player to be named, *2006*
Dallas Mavericks player to be named, *2352*
Detroit Pistons player to be named, *2047*
Indiana Pacers player to be named, *2255*
Kansas City Kings player to be named, *2149*
Milwaukee Bucks player to be named, *2072*
Milwaukee Hawks player to be named, *1955*
Minneapolis Lakers player to be named, *1985*
New Jersey Nets player to be named, *2177*
New York Knicks player to be named, *2034*
Orlando Magic player to be named, *2326*
Philadelphia Warriors player to be named, *1978*
Phoenix Suns player to be named, *2124*
player to be named, *1937*
Portland Trail Blazers player to be named, *2080*
Rochester Royals player to be named, *1963*
San Diego Clippers player to be named, *2190*
San Francisco Warriors player to be named, *2041*
Utah Jazz player to be named, *2169*

Rookie of the Year (football)
African-American player to be named National Football League's, *3240*
National Football League player to be named, *3238*

Rookie of the Year (golf)
golfer named, on Ladies Professional Golf Association (LPGA) Tour, *3766*
golfer on Professional Golfers' Association (PGA) Tour to be named, *3751*
golfer to be named, and Player of the Year, and to win Vare Trophy for lowest scoring average, in same year, *3816*

golfer to be named, and Player of the Year on Senior Professional Golfers' Association (PGA) Tour, *3864*

Rookie of the Year (ice hockey)
National Hockey League player to be named, *4108*

rookies
baseball
to hit grand slam home run in World Series, *1589*

rope climbing (gymnastics)
men's competition, held in Olympic Games, *3907*

roque (variation on croquet)
event at Olympic Games, *2671*
rules for, *2668*

Rose Bowl, *3133*
African-American player to play in, *3140*
African-American player to score touchdown in, *3212*
African-American quarterback to appear in, *3260*
Columbia University win in, *3166*
Georgia Tech win in, *3159*
Harvard University win in, *3145*
Northwestern University win in, *3223*
Notre Dame University win in, *3154*
Oregon State University win in college football's, and only Rose Bowl not played in Pasadena, California, *3191*
Purdue University win in, *3281*
Stanford University win in, *3157*
University of Alabama win in, *3156*
University of California at Los Angeles win in, *3275*
University of California win in, *3149*
University of Georgia win in, *3192*
University of Illinois win in, *3214*
University of Iowa win in, *3244*
University of Michigan win in, *3220*
University of Minnesota win in, *3266*
University of Oregon win in, *3142*
University of Pittsburgh win in, *3181*
University of Southern California win in, *3152*
Washington State University win in, *3141*

Rose Garden, The
Portland Trail Blazers regular season basketball game played at, *2360*

Rotterdam Marathon, *4506*
runner to win women's championship in, *4509*

rowing
athletes to row across Atlantic Ocean, *4923*
collegiate competition, and first intercollegiate athletic competition, on record in U.S., *4915*
collegiate program for women, *4917*
Head of the Charles Regatta, *4942*
Henley Regatta races, *4914*

running—*Continued*

runner to win two consecutive gold medals in men's 4 x 100-meter relay in, *5016*

runner to win two consecutive gold medals in men's 4 x 400-meter relay in, *5007*

runner to win two consecutive men's 10,000-meter titles in, *5056*

runner to win two consecutive men's 400-meter titles, *5188*

runner to win two consecutive men's 5000- and 10,000-meter titles at, *5107*

runner to win two consecutive men's 800-meter titles in, *5019*

runner to win two consecutive officially accepted men's 100-meter titles at, *5150*

runner to win two consecutive officially accepted titles in men's 1500-meters at, *5141*

runner to win two consecutive titles in men's individual cross-country in, *5015*

team from U.S. to win men's 4 x 100-meter relay track event in, *5011*

run across U.S., *5017*

runner from Africa to hold world record in men's 5000 meters, *5079*

runner from Asia to hold officially accepted world record in men's 100-meter dash, *5034*

runner from Central or South America to set or equal a world track and field record, *5049*

runner to complete 1500-meter race in under 3:40 minutes, *5067*

runner to complete men's 1500-meter race in under 3:30 minutes, *5144*

runner to complete men's 1500-meter race in under 3:45.0 minutes, *5048*

runner to complete men's 1500-meter race in under 3:50 minutes, *5025*

runner to complete men's 200-meter race in under 19.8 seconds, *5112*

runner to complete men's 200-meter race in under 20 seconds, *5088*

runner to complete men's 400-meter race in under 44 seconds, *5090*

runner to complete men's 400-meter race in under 47 seconds, *5027*

runner to complete men's 800-meter race in under 1:43 minutes, *5111*

runner to complete men's 800-meter race in under 1:44 minutes, *5099*

runner to complete men's 800-meter race in under 1:45 minutes, *5074*

runner to complete men's 800-meter race in under 1:50 minutes, *5029*

runner to complete men's mile race in under 3:45 minutes, *5170*

runner to complete men's mile race in under 3:48 minutes, *5121*

runner to complete men's mile race in under 3:49 minutes, *5113*

runner to complete men's mile race in under 3:53 minutes, *5080*

runner to complete men's mile race in under 3:55 minutes, *5068*

runner to complete men's mile race in under 4:05 minutes, *5046*

runner to complete men's mile race in under 4:10 minutes, *5026*

runner to hold officially accepted world record in men's 200-meter race run on curved track, *5053*

runner to hold officially accepted world record in men's 400-meter event, *4983*

runner to hold officially accepted world record in men's mile race, *5009*

runner to hold world record in both men's 5000 and 10,000 meters, *5013*

runner to race 100-yard dash in under 10 seconds, *4973*

runner to race 5000-meter, under 8:10 minutes, *5103*

runner to race men's 10,000 meters in under 27:00 minutes, *5168*

runner to race men's 10,000 meters in under 29:00 minutes, *5061*

runner to race men's 10,000 meters in under 30:00 minutes, *5045*

runner to race men's 100-meter dash in 10.1 seconds, *5063*

runner to race men's 100-meter dash in 10.2 seconds, *5036*

runner to race men's 100-meter dash in under 10 seconds, *5084*

runner to race men's 100 meters in less than 10.5 seconds, *5012*

runner to race men's 100 meters in under 9.9 seconds, *5156*

runner to race men's 1500 meters in 3:26 minutes, *5186*

runner to race men's 1500 meters in less than 3:29 minutes, *5163*

runner to race men's 1500 meters in less than 3:35 minutes, *5083*

runner to race men's 1500 meters in under 3:32 minutes, *5119*

runner to race men's 5000 meters in under 12:55 minutes, *5179*

runner to race men's 5000 meters in under 13:00 minutes, *5149*

runner to race men's 5000 meters in under 14:00 minutes, *5047*

runner to race men's 5000 meters in under 14:10 minutes, *5043*

runner to race men's 5000 meters in under 14:28.0 minutes, *5028*

San Diego Clippers
player to be named National Basketball Association (NBA) Rookie of the Year, *2190*

San Diego Padres
National League pennant, *1775*
pitcher to win the Cy Young Award, *1743*
player to be named Most Valuable Player, *1834*
regular season baseball game played at Jack Murphy Stadium (later Qualcomm Stadium), *1709*

San Francisco, University of
championship in National Collegiate Athletic Association (NCAA) Men's Basketball National Tournament, *1958*

San Francisco 49ers
African-American professional football player to join, *3217*
National Football Conference championship, *3372*
National Football League team to win 15 games in a single season, *3392*
regular season football game played at Candlestick Park, *3318*
win in Super Bowl, *3373*

San Francisco Giants
pitcher to win Cy Young Award, *1694*
regular season baseball game played at Pacific Bell Park, *1860*
regular season game played at Candlestick Park, *1643*
regular season game played at Seals Stadium, *1632*

San Francisco Warriors
player to be named National Basketball Association (NBA) Rookie of the Year, *2041*
regular season basketball game played at the Oakland Coliseum, *2044*

San Jose Arena
San Jose Sharks regular season hockey game played at, *4210*

San Jose Sharks
regular season hockey game played at San Jose Arena, *4210*

Santa Clara University
team to win the Sugar Bowl in two consecutive years, *3184*

Schneider Cup international seaplane (hydro-aeroplane) race, *1004*

schools
boxing, *2505*

Scottish Highland Gathering, *4364*

Seals Stadium
San Francisco Giants regular season baseball game played at, *1632*

seaplanes
Schneider Cup international race, *1004*

Seattle Kingdome
Mariners regular season baseball game played at, *1744*
Seattle Seahawks regular season football game played at, *3348*

Seattle Mariners
baseball player to be named Most Valuable Player, *1843*
pitcher to win the Cy Young Award, *1830*
player to be named Rookie of the Year, *1776*
regular season baseball game played at SAFECO Field, *1855*
regular season baseball game played at Seattle Kingdome, *1744*

Seattle Metropolitans
team from outside Canada to win Stanley Cup, *4063*

Seattle Seahawks
regular season football game played at Seattle Kingdome, *3348*

Seattle SuperSonics
National Basketball Association (NBA) championship, *2151*
regular season game played in Key Arena, *2361*
team to have 20 3-point field goals in single National Basketball Association (NBA) playoff game, *2374*
team to have 27 steals in single National Basketball Association (NBA) game, *2392*
team to have 30 offensive rebounds in single National Basketball Association (NBA) playoff game, *2143*
team to have an .851 percentage in National Basketball Association (NBA) Finals series, *2368*

Senior Little League Softball
program, *5611*

Senior Professional Golfers' Association (PGA) Tour, *3830*
African-American golfer to win an event in, *3834*
golfer on, to win more than $100,000 in a season, *3837*
golfer to be named Rookie of the Year and Player of the Year on, *3864*
golfer to win more than $1 million in a single season on, *3865*
tournament on, *3832*

Shea Stadium
New York Mets regular season baseball game played, *1671*

Shibe Park
Philadelphia Athletics regular season baseball game played at, *1393*

shinty (*camanachd*)
Camanachd Association Challenge Cup for, *5260*

formal organization for game of, *5259*

shooting

air rifle

individual event held in Olympic Games, *5320*

club, *5261*

international governing body in, *5283*

moving target individual event held in Olympic Games, *5277*

National Collegiate Athletic Association (NCAA)

championships sponsored by, *5315*

national governing body in U.S., *5266*

national organization for

in Great Britain, *5263*

pistol and revolver

free individual event held in Olympic Games, *5271*

military, individual event held in Olympic Games, *5270*

national team to sweep rapid-fire, individual event in Olympic Games, *5278*

rapid-fire pistol and free pistol team events held in Olympic Games, *5299*

shooter to win both rapid-fire pistol and free pistol individual events, and first from U.S. to win either event, in Olympic Games, *5296*

shooter to win two consecutive men's rapid-fire titles in Olympic Games, *5307*

shooters from U.S. to win military, team event in Olympic Games, *5287*

pistol and revolver shooting

dueling events held in Olympic Games, *5282*

rapid-fire, individual event held in Olympic Games, *5272*

rifle

free, team event held in Olympic Games, *5281*

free individual shooting event held in Olympic Games, *5269*

international tournament held in U.S., *5267*

military, individual event held in Olympic Games, *5279*

military revolver and, team events held in Olympic Games, *5280*

shooter from U.S. to win men's small-bore (three positions) title in Olympic Games, *5310*

shooter to win two consecutive titles in men's free (three positions) individual event, and in free rifle team event, in Olympic Games, *5302*

shooter to win two consecutive titles in small-bore (three positions) individual event in Olympic Games, *5323*

shooters from U.S. to win military, team title in Olympic Games, *5288*

shooters from U.S. to win small-bore team title in Olympic Games, *5300*

small-bore, moving and disappearing target individual events held in Olympic Games, *5289*

small-bore, team event held in Olympic Games, *5291*

small-bore (prone), individual event held in Olympic Games, *5290*

small-bore (three positions) individual event held in Olympic Games, *5309*

running deer

double shot individual event held in Olympic Games, *5284*

double shot team event held in Olympic Games, *5297*

shooter to win two consecutive titles in running deer (double shot) individual event in Olympic Games, *5303*

single and double shot individual event held in Olympic Games, *5308*

single shot individual event held in Olympic Games, *5285*

single shot team event held in Olympic Games, *5286*

shooter to achieve perfect score in international competition, *5305*

shooter to win five gold medals in Olympic Games, *5298*

skeet, *5293*

individual event held in Olympic Games, *5312*

national championships, *5304*

shooter from U.S. to win individual title in Olympic Games, *5321*

women's event held in Olympic Games, *5328*

sporting clay

world championships, *5314*

targets

clay pigeons, *5268*

substitutes (glass balls) for live birds in competitions, *5264*

use of glass balls in U.S. competitions, *5265*

tournament on record, *5262*

trap shooting

individual event held in Olympic Games, *5276*

international governing body for, *5301*

men's double trap (clay pigeon) individual event held in Olympic Games, *5326*

national tournament in U.S., *5275*

shooter from U.S. to win men's individual title in Olympic Games, *5295*

shooter to win two consecutive individual titles in Olympic Games, *5317*

shooting—*Continued*

shooters from U.S. to win team event in Olympic Games, *5294*

team event in Olympic Games, *5292*

women's event held in Olympic Games, *5327*

women's

air pistol individual event held in Olympic Games, *5322*

air rifle individual event in Olympic Games, *5318*

double trap (clay pigeon) individual event held in Olympic Games, *5325*

shooter from U.S. to win small-bore rifle (three positions) event at Olympic Games, *5324*

small-bore rifle (three positions) individual event held in Olympic Games, *5319*

sport pistol individual event held in Olympic Games, *5316*

woman to win Grand American Trapshoot, *5306*

woman to win medal in shooting at Olympic Games, *5313*

women to compete in events in Olympic Games, *5311*

world championships, *5274*

shot put

Olympic Games

men's event held in, *5329*

men's shot put event for both hands held in, *5332*

national team to sweep top spots in men's shot put in, *5330*

shot-putter to win two consecutive men's titles in, *5341*

shot-putter to win two consecutive women's titles in, *5344*

women's event held in, *5336*

shot-putter to break 16-meter barrier, *5333*

shot-putter to break 17-meter barrier, *5335*

shot-putter to break 18- and 19-meter, and 60-foot, barriers, *5340*

shot-putter to break 20-meter barrier, *5343*

shot-putter to break 22-meter barrier, *5349*

shot-putter to break 23-meter barrier, *5350*

shot-putter to break 70-foot and 21-meter barriers, *5345*

shot-putter to hold officially accepted world record in men's event, *5331*

women's

event held in Olympic Games, *5336*

shot-putter to break 15-meter barrier in, *5337*

shot-putter to break 16-meter barrier in, *5339*

shot-putter to break 17- and 18-meter, and 60-foot, barriers in, *5342*

shot-putter to break 19-meter barrier in, *5346*

shot-putter to break 20- and 21-meter barriers in, *5347*

shot-putter to break 50-foot barrier in, *5338*

shot-putter to break 70-foot barrier in, *5348*

shot-putter to hold officially accepted world record in, *5334*

shot-putter to win two consecutive titles in event in Olympic Games, *5344*

show jumping

competition, *2837*

held in England, *2839*

held in France, *2838*

Queen Elizabeth II Cup, *2861*

world championships, *2865*

to include women riders, *2870*

World Cup, *2882*

woman to win, *2883*

shutouts

baseball game on record, *1195*

eighteen-inning, in major league baseball, *1265*

in a major league baseball All-Star Game, *1540*

on record in professional baseball, *1209*

pitcher to lead American League in, for two consecutive years, *1358*

pitcher to lead National League in, for three consecutive years, *1427*

pitcher to lead the American League in, for three consecutive years, *1419*

pitcher to pitch, in National League, *1223*

pitcher to pitch six successive, *1701*

pitcher to throw two, in one day, *1381*

player of the 20th century to pitch 16, in a single season, *1424*

player to pitch four consecutive, *1293*

side horse (gymnastics)

gymnast to win three consecutive men's titles in world championships, *3956*

gymnast to win two consecutive men's titles in Olympic Games, *3955*

men's competition held in Olympic Games, *3905*

side horse vault (gymnastics)

gymnast to win two consecutive women's titles in Olympic Games, *3954*

women's competition held in Olympic Games, *3937*

Single-Handed Transatlantic Race (STAR), *5222*

sailor from U.S. to win, and first to make crossing in under 20 hours, *5238*

sailor in, to cross Atlantic in under 11 days, *5248*

sailor to win, twice, *5234*

sailor to win twice consecutively, *5256*

skiing—*Continued*

men's combined pursuit event held at
Olympic Winter Games, *5476*

men's individual 15-kilometer event at
Olympic Winter Games, *5404*

men's individual 18-kilometer event
held at Olympic Winter Games, *5366*

men's individual Nordic combined event
held in Olympic Winter Games, *5367*

men's Nordic combined team event held
in Olympic Winter Games, *5456*

men's pursuit (10 kilometers classical
and 15 kilometers freestyle) event held
in world championships of Nordic skiing, *5481*

men's team combined event held in
world championships of Nordic skiing,
5435

national team to sweep medals in men's
15-kilometer event in Olympic Winter
Games, *5376*

national team to sweep medals in men's
30-kilometer event at Olympic Winter
Games, *5471*

national team to sweep medals in men's
combined individual Nordic event at
Olympic Winter Games, *5369*

organized races, *5354*

skier to introduce skating techniques
into, in international competition, *5437*

skier to win 30-kilometer title in Olympic Winter Games after it was converted from classical style to freestyle,
5485

skier to win 50-kilometer title in Olympic Winter Games after it was converted from freestyle to classical style,
5493

skier to win four medals in same event
in Olympic Winter Games, *5478*

skier to win three consecutive men's individual combined titles in Olympic
Winter Games, *5443*

skier to win two consecutive men's 10-
kilometer titles, and first male athlete
to win six gold medals overall, at
Olympic Winter Games, *5499*

skier to win two consecutive men's 30-
kilometer titles in Olympic Winter
Games, *5442*

skier to win two consecutive men's individual combined titles in Olympic Winter Games, *5378*

skier to win two consecutive titles in
men's 4 x 10-kilometer relay at Olympic Winter Games, *5455*

skier to win two titles in men's 50-
kilometer freestyle at Olympic Winter
Games, *5411*

skiers from Soviet Union to win men's
4 x 10-kilometer relay title at Olympic
Winter Games, *5405*

skiers to win two consecutive men's
combined team titles at Olympic Winter Games, *5489*

women's 10-kilometer event held in
world championships of, *5399*

women's individual 5-kilometer event in
Olympic Winter Games, *5412*

world championships for, *5360*

downhill

men's Alpine combined event held at
Olympic Winter Games, *5383*

men's event held at Olympic Winter
Games, *5386*

national team to sweep medals in men's
Alpine combined skiing event at Olympic Winter Games, *5490*

organized race, *5362*

skier from U.S. to win men's title at
Olympic Winter Games, *5444*

skier to sweep men's individual Alpine
events at Olympic Winter Games, *5406*

skier to win 13 men's Alpine world cup
races, and to win 10 in one category, in
a single season, *5425*

skier to win five medals in Alpine
events at Olympic Winter Games, *5491*

skier to win five men's world cup titles,
5440

skier to win two consecutive individual
titles in Alpine event in Olympic Winter Games, *5479*

world championships in Alpine skiing,
5377

World cup series of competitions in Alpine skiing, *5416*

freestyle

competition on record, *5415*

men's aerials freestyle event at Olympic
Winter Games, *5488*

men's moguls freestyle event at Olympic Winter Games, *5473*

organized competition, *5422*

skier from U.S. to win men's aerials
freestyle skiing event in Olympic Winter Games, *5500*

skier from U.S. to win men's moguls
freestyle event in Olympic Winter
Games, *5497*

world championships, *5451*

world cup circuit for, *5431*

international governing body for, *5361*

manual, *5353*

national organization for, *5358*

Nations' Cup, *5418*

cross-country, in world cup for Nordic
skiing, *5432*

team to win two consecutive titles in Amateur Softball Association Major Fast Pitch National Championships, *5582*

world championships in fast-pitch softball, *5601*

world championships in fast-pitch softball to include men's teams, *5602*

world championships, *5587*

See also
  college softball

softball leagues
  Amateur Softball Association Major Fast Pitch league
    player to be batting champion of, *5590*
  American Professional Slo-Pitch League teams, *5613*
  Little League Softball and Senior Little League Softball programs, *5611*
  "Mixed" female-male, *5595*
  National Fastball league, *5584*
  national professional league, *5583*

Soldier Field
  Chicago Bears regular season football game played at, *3315*

Solheim Cup golf competition, *3869*

South African Professional Golfers' Association (PGA) Open
  African-American golfer to play in, *3791*

South Africans
  athlete from Africa, and from South Africa, to win gold medal in Olympic Games, *4638*
  athletes from South Africa to win medals in Olympic Games, after lifting of ban on their country because of its racist policies, *4779*
  Black African athlete from South Africa to win gold medal in Olympic Games, *4802*

South-East Asia Games, *4374*

South End Grounds
  regular season baseball game played at, *1220*

Southern 500 automobile race, *1075*

Southern California, University of
  win in Rose Bowl, *3152*
  women's basketball team to win National Collegiate Athletic Association (NCAA) national championship in two consecutive years, *2201*

Southside Park
  White Sox regular season game played at, *1332*

Spanish Grand Prix auto race, *1085*

Special Olympics, *2752*

Spectrum, The
  Philadelphia 76ers regular season game played at, *2052*

Philadelphia Flyers regular season hockey game played at, *4150*

speed skating
  international competition, *5629*
  Olympic Games
    10,000-meter event held in Winter Games, *5641*
    10,000-meter race to be voided, *5644*
    1500-meter event held at Winter Games, *5642*
    500-meter event held at Winter Games, *5639*
    5000-meter event held at Winter Games, *5640*
    5000-meter relay short track event held at Winter Games, *5716*
    events to be held as races, rather than in pairs, *5648*
    four races combined title offered at Winter Games, *5643*
    men's 1000-meter event held in Winter Games, *5692*
    men's 1000-meter short track event held in Winter Games, *5714*
    men's 500-meter short track event held in Winter Games, *5725*
    national team to sweep medals in men's 5000-meter event at Winter Games, *5676*
    skater from U.S. to win men's 1500-meter title at Winter Games, *5649*
    skater to sweep all five men's events in a single Winter Games, *5696*
    skater to win four gold medals in a single Winter Games, *5678*
    skater to win men's 10,000-meter title at Winter Games, *5650*
    skater to win three gold medals at a single, *5658*
    skater to win two consecutive men's 1000-meter short track titles at Olympic Winter Games, *5722*
    skater to win two consecutive men's 1500-meter titles at Winter Games, *5645*
    skater to win two consecutive men's 5000-meter titles at Winter Games, *5710*
    skater to win two consecutive titles in men's 1500-meters at Olympic Winter Games, *5720*
    skater to win two consecutive titles in men's 500 meters at Winter Games, *5671*
  skater to be world champion in men's long-distance speed skating five times, *5637*
  skater to be world champion in men's long-distance speed skating twice, and then three times, in a row, *5635*

speed skating—*Continued*

skater to skate 10,000 meters in under 13:30 minutes, *5729*

skater to skate 10,000 meters in under 14 minutes, *5707*

skater to skate 10,000 meters in under 15 minutes, *5685*

skater to skate 10,000 meters in under 16 minutes, *5672*

skater to skate 10,000 meters in under 18 minutes, *5636*

skater to skate 1000 meters in under 1:10 minutes, *5735*

skater to skate 1000 meters in under 1:20 minutes, *5681*

skater to skate 1000 meters in under 1:30 minutes, *5646*

skater to skate 1500 meters in under 1:50 minutes, *5727*

skater to skate 1500 meters in under 2 minutes, *5684*

skater to skate 1500 meters in under 2:10 minutes, *5666*

skater to skate 1500 meters in under 2:30 minutes, *5633*

skater to skate 3000 meters in under 3:50 minutes, *5734, 5733*

skater to skate 3000 meters in under 4 minutes, *5706*

skater to skate 3000 meters in under 4:10 minutes, *5689*

skater to skate 3000 meters in under 4:20 minutes, *5679*

skater to skate 3000 meters in under 4:30 minutes, *5674*

skater to skate 500 meters in under 40 seconds, *5673*

skater to skate 500 meters in under 50 seconds, *5631*

skater to skate 5000 meters in under 6:30 minutes, *5728*

skater to skate 5000 meters in under 7 minutes, *5693*

skater to skate 5000 meters in under 8 minutes, *5665*

skater to skate 5000 meters in under 9 minutes, *5634*

skater to skate the 10,000 meters in under 20 minutes, *5632*

skater to skate the 1500 meters in under 2:20 minutes, *5638*

skater to skate the 3000 meters in under 5 minutes, *5652*

skater to win four consecutive men's titles at world sprint championships, *5695*

skater to win six men's world sprint championships, *5718*

skaters to be named *Sports Illustrated* Sportsmen of the Year, *5719*

skaters to become world champions in sprints, *5686*

Spring world championships in, *5682*

women's

1000-meter speed skating event held at Olympic Winter Games, *5667*

1500-meter speed skating event held at Olympic Winter Games, *5670*

3000-meter short track relay event held at Olympic Winter Games, *5715*

3000-meter speed skating held at Olympic Winter Games, *5668*

500-meter short track event held at Olympic Winter Games, *5717*

500-meter speed skating event held at Olympic Winter Games, *5669*

5000-meter event held in Olympic Winter Games, *5709*

national team to sweep medals in 3000-meter event at Olympic Winter Games, *5702*

national team to sweep medals in 500-meter event at Olympic Winter Games, *5675*

national team to sweep medals in 5000-meter event at Olympic Winter Games, *5713*

short track 1000-meter event held at Olympic Winter Games, *5726*

skater from U.S. to win 1000-meter title at Olympic Winter Games, *5712*

skater from U.S. to win 1500-meter title at Olympic Winter Games, *5687*

skater from U.S. to win 500-meter title at Olympic Winter Games, *5688*

skater to be world champion in, twice in a row, *5661*

skater to be world champion in long-distance speed skating eight times, *5736*

skater to skate 10,000 meters in under 17 minutes, *5662*

skater to skate 1000 meters in under 1:20 minutes, *5701*

skater to skate 1000 meters in under 1:30 minutes, *5683*

skater to skate 1000 meters in under 2 minutes, *5651*

skater to skate 1500 meters in under 2:30 minutes, *5664*

skater to skate 3000 meters in under 4:30 minutes, *5698*

skater to skate 3000 meters in under 5 minutes, *5680*

skater to skate 3000 meters in under 6 minutes, *5659*

skater to skate 500 meters in under 1 minute, *5647*

skater to skate 500 meters in under 40 seconds, *5700*

player to kick four field goals in a single game, *3289*

player to kick seven points after touchdown in a single game, *3439*

player to rush for 204 yards in a single game, *3420*

player to score 18 points in a single game, *3400*

Saint Louis Rams win in, *3513*

San Francisco 49ers win in, *3373*

team to win two consecutive games, *3290*

Washington Redskins win in, *3383*

surfing

international championships, *5770*
    surfer not born in Hawaii to win, *5771*

international organization, *5772*

surfer to win five men's professional world titles, *5776*

surfer to win four women's professional world titles, *5777*

World Championships, *5773*

world professional championships, *5774*
    women's competition to be included in, *5775*

Swaythling Cup

in table tennis, *5983*

swimming

athlete to win Olympic medals in both diving and, *2798*

backstroke
    men's 100-yard (later 100-meter) event held in Olympic Games, *5794*
    men's 200-meter event held in Olympic Games, *5788*
    national team to sweep medals in men's 200-meter event in Olympic Games, *5846*
    Olympic men's 100-meter backstroke event in which medalists all had times under one minute, *5866*
    Olympic men's 200-meter backstroke event in which medalists all had times under two minutes, *5963*
    swimmer from U.S. to win men's 100-meter title in Olympic Games, *5807*
    swimmer to break two-minute barrier in men's 200-meter event, *5924*
    swimmer to hold world titles in both 100- and 200-meter at same time, *5892*
    swimmer to race men's 100-meter event in under 55 seconds, *5951*
    swimmer to win two consecutive men's 100-meter titles in Olympic Games, *5817*
    swimmer to win two consecutive men's 200-meter titles in Olympic Games, *5869*

breaststroke
    ban on underwater stroking in events in international competition, *5836*

men's 100-meter event held in Olympic Games, *5851*

men's 200-meter event held in Olympic Games, *5801*

men's 440-yard (later 400-meter) event held in Olympic Games, *5796*

national team to sweep medals in men's 200-meter event in Olympic Games, *5806*

Olympic men's 200-meter event in which medalists all had times under three minutes, *5821*

swimmer to hold world titles in both men's 100- and 200-meter at same time, *5912*

swimmer to win two consecutive men's 100-meter titles at world championships, *5970*

swimmer to win two consecutive men's 200-meter titles, *5826*

butterfly stroke
    men's 100-meter event held in Olympic Games, *5856*
    men's 200-meter event held in Olympic Games, *5834*
    national team to sweep medals in men's 200-meter event in Olympic Games, *5864*
    used in Olympic Games, *5828*

English Channel
    person to swim, *5783*
    swimmer to swim, across and back consecutively, *5843*
    swimmer to swim, in both directions, *5827*
    swimmer to swim across, from France to England, *5816*
    woman to swim, *5820*
    woman to swim, across and back consecutively, *5928*
    woman to swim, from England to France, and to swim it in both directions, *5831*

freestyle
    men's 100-meter event held in Olympic Games, *5785*
    men's 1200-meter event held in Olympic Games, *5786*
    men's 200-meter event held in Olympic Games, *5789*
    men's 4 x 100-meter relay event held in Olympic Games, *5847*
    men's 4 x 250-meter (later 4 x 200-meter) relay event held in Olympic Games, *5799*
    men's 4000-meter event held in Olympic Games, *5792*
    men's 50-meter event held in Olympic Games, *5954*

races on record, *5778*

Strait of Gibraltar
    swimmer to swim across, *5830*

swimmer to hold world titles in both 5- and 25-kilometer river-sea swim at same time, *5976*

swimmer to hold world titles in both men's 200- and 400-meter individual medleys at same time, *5911*

swimmer to race 100 yards in one minute, *5793*

underwater
    race held in Olympic Games, *5791*

use of underwater photography to determine winner of an event, *5829*

women's
    100-meter backstroke event held in Olympic Games, *5819*
    100-meter backstroke event held in world championships, *5894*
    100-meter breaststroke event held in Olympic Games, *5852*
    100-meter breaststroke event held in world championships, *5895*
    100-meter butterfly event held in Olympic Games, *5835*
    100-meter butterfly event held in world championships, *5896*
    100-meter butterfly event in Olympic Games in which all medalists had times under one minute, *5953*
    100-meter freestyle event held in Olympic Games, *5805*
    100-meter freestyle event held in world championships, *5897*
    200-meter backstroke event held in Olympic Games, *5818, 5861*
    200-meter backstroke event held in world championships, *5898*
    200-meter breaststroke event held in world championships, *5899*
    200-meter butterfly event held in Olympic Games, *5859*
    200-meter butterfly event held in world championships, *5900*
    200-meter freestyle event held in Olympic Games, *5857*
    200-meter freestyle event held in world championships, *5901*
    200-meter individual medley event held in Olympic Games, *5855*
    200-meter individual medley event held in world championships, *5902*
    25-kilometer river, *5961*
    300-meter (later 400-meter) event held in Olympic Games, *5812*
    4 x 100-meter freestyle event held in world championships, *5903*
    4 x 100-meter freestyle relay event in Olympic Games, *5808*

4 x 100-meter medley relay event held in Olympic Games, *5840*

4 x 100-meter medley relay event held in world championships, *5904*

4 x 200-meter freestyle event held in world championships, *5948*

4 x 200-meter freestyle relay event held in Olympic Games, *5973*

400-meter freestyle event held in world championships, *5905*

400-meter individual medley event held in Olympic Games, *5849*

400-meter individual medley event held in world championships, *5906*

400-meter individual medley event in Olympic Games in which all medalists had times under five minutes, *5925*

5-kilometer river, *5977*

50-meter freestyle event held in Olympic Games, *5955*

50-meter freestyle swimming event held in world championships, *5949*

800-meter freestyle event held in world championships, *5907*

800-meter freestyle swimming event held in Olympic Games, *5860*

duet synchronized swimming event held in Olympic Games, *5941*

introduction of skin-tight Lycra bathing suits into international swimming competition, *5873*

national team to sweep medals in 100-meter backstroke, and 200-meter backstroke, in Olympic Games, *5935*

national team to sweep medals in 100-meter freestyle event in Olympic Games, *5810*

national team to sweep medals in 200-meter butterfly in Olympic Games, *5872*

Olympic 100-meter freestyle event in which medalists all had times under one minute, *5867*

Olympic 400-meter freestyle event in which medalists all had times under five minutes, *5839*

pairs of twins to take top two spots in synchronized swimming duet competition in Olympic Games, *5968*

solo and duet synchronized swimming events held in world championships, *5908*

solo synchronized event held in Olympic Games, *5942*

swimmer from U.S. to win 100-meter breaststroke in Olympic Games, *5868*

swimmer from U.S. to win 200-meter breaststroke title in Olympic Games, *5858*

swimming—*Continued*

swimmer to hold 200-meter butterfly and both 200- and 400-meter individual medley world titles at same time, *5931*

swimmer to hold both 100- and 200-meter backstroke world titles at same time, *5929*

swimmer to hold both 100- and 200-meter breaststroke world titles at same time, *5889*

swimmer to hold both 200- and 400-meter freestyle world titles at same time, *5910*

swimmer to hold both 400- and 800-meter freestyle world titles at same time, *5930*

swimmer to race 100-meter freestyle in under 1:20 minutes, *5804*

swimmer to race 100-meter freestyle in under 55 seconds, *5932*

swimmer to race 100-meter freestyle in under one minute, *5844*

swimmer to race 400-meter freestyle event in under five minutes, *5833*

swimmer to race 50-meter freestyle in under 25 seconds, *5950*

swimmer to win 100-meter butterfly title in Olympic Games with time of under one minute, *5940*

swimmer to win 200- and 400-meter individual medley events in same Olympic Games, *5854*

swimmer to win both 100- and 200-meter butterfly titles in same Olympic Games, *5943*

swimmer to win five individual gold medals, and three consecutive medals in 200-meter backstroke, in Olympic Games, *5972*

swimmer to win four gold medals at a single Olympic Games, *5927*

swimmer to win Olympic medals 12 years apart, *5956*

swimmer to win two 4 x 100-meter freestyle relay titles in Olympic Games, *5824*

swimmer to win two and then three consecutive 100-meter freestyle titles in Olympic Games, *5842*

swimmer to win two consecutive 100-meter backstroke world titles, *5917*

swimmer to win two consecutive 100-meter butterfly world titles, *5918*

swimmer to win two consecutive 100-meter freestyle world titles, *5919*

swimmer to win two consecutive 200-meter backstroke world titles, *5947*

swimmer to win two consecutive 200-meter butterfly world titles, *5920*

swimmer to win two consecutive 800-meter freestyle titles in Olympic Games, *5965*

swimmer to win two consecutive 800-meter freestyle world titles, *5971*

swimmer to win two consecutive gold medals in 200-meter backstroke in Olympic Games, *5966*

swimmers from U.S. to win 4 x 100-meter freestyle relay title in Olympic Games, *5814*

swimmers to win gold medals in the same event at the same Olympic Games, *5939*

synchronized swimming event held in Olympic Games, *5974*

synchronized team event held in world championships, *5893*

world championships, *5909*

men's 100-meter breaststroke event held in, *5875*

men's 100-meter butterfly event held in, *5876*

men's 100-meter event held in backstroke event, *5874*

men's 100-meter freestyle event held at, *5877*

men's 1500-meter freestyle event held at, *5878*

men's 200-meter backstroke event held in, *5879*

men's 200-meter breaststroke event held in, *5880*

men's 200-meter butterfly event held in, *5881*

men's 200-meter freestyle event held at, *5882*

men's 200-meter individual medley event held at, *5883*

men's 25-kilometer river, *5957*

men's 4 x 100-meter freestyle event held at, *5884*

men's 4 x 100-meter medley relay event held at, *5885*

men's 4 x 200-meter freestyle event held at, *5886*

men's 400-meter freestyle event held at, *5887*

men's 400-meter individual medley event held at, *5888*

men's 5-kilometer river, *5975*

men's 50-meter freestyle event held at, *5944*

swimmer to win two consecutive men's 100-meter freestyle titles at, *5958*

swimmer to win two consecutive men's 100-meter titles in, *5914*

swimmer to win two consecutive men's 1500-meter freestyle titles at, *5937* swimmer to win two consecutive men's 200-meter breaststroke titles in, *5915*

swimmer to win two consecutive men's 200-meter butterfly titles at, *5945*

swimmer to win two consecutive men's 200-meter freestyle titles at, *5946*

swimmer to win two consecutive men's 200-meter individual medley titles at, *5959*

swimmer to win two consecutive men's 400-meter freestyle titles at, *5938*

swimmer to win two consecutive men's 400-meter individual medley titles at, *5916*

swimmer to win two consecutive men's 50-meter freestyle titles at, *5960*

world short-course championships in, *5969*

Swiss Grand Prix automobile race, *1065*

Sydney–Hobart Race, *5214*

Syracuse Nationals

NBA championship, *1956*

T

table tennis

equipment, *5980*

Geist Prize, *5986*

Heydusek Prize, *5991*

international championships, *5984*

international governing body in, *5982*

Iran Cup, *5990*

Marcel Corbillon Cup, *5988*

national governing body in, *5981*

Olympic Games

men's doubles event in, *5994*

men's singles event held in, *5996*

player to win both singles and doubles titles in, *6000*

women's doubles event held in, *5995*

women's singles table tennis event held in, *5997*

Pope Trophy, *5992*

St. Bride Vase, *5985*

Swaythling Cup, *5983*

world championships

player to win five men's singles titles in, *5989*

player to win five women's singles titles in, *5987*

world cup, *5993*

men's and women's doubles events to be included in, *5998*

women's singles event to be included in, *6001*

world team cup in, *5999*

taekwondo

national governing body for, in U.S., *4542*

Olympic Games

to include events for men, *4560*

to include events for women, *4561*

world championships, *4541*

to include additional weight classes for men, *4543*

to include light-middleweight and light-heavyweight classes for men, *4544*

to include women, *4549*

Tailteann Games

establishment of, *4363*

Talladega 500 auto race, *1115*

Tampa Bay Buccaneers

regular season football game played at Raymond James Stadium, *3499*

regular season football game played at Tampa Stadium, *3349*

Tampa Bay Devil Rays

regular season baseball game played at Tropicana Field, *1851*

Tampa Bay Lightning

regular season hockey game played at Ice Palace, *4228*

regular season hockey game played at Thunderdome, *4206*

Tampa Stadium

Tampa Bay Buccaneers regular season football game played at, *3349*

Tangerine Bowl

football game, *3213*

team to win two consecutive games, *3219*

tano lutz jump

figure skater to perform, in competition, *3092*

Target Center

Minnesota Timberwolves regular season basketball game played at, *2298*

targets (shooting)

clay pigeons for, *5268*

glass balls substituted for live birds, *5264*

glass balls used in U.S., *5265*

televised broadcasts

automobile racing

NASCAR race of 500 miles to be televised live from start to finish, *1128*

NASCAR race to be televised, *1102*

baseball

baseball game to be televised, *1537*

Little League World Series to be televised, *1594*

major league games, *1539*

World Series to be televised, *1564*

basketball

college game to be televised, *1901*

National Collegiate Athletic Association (NCAA) Division I tournament championship game to be televised, *1909*

bowler to bowl 300 game in televised match, *2496*

447

Texas Western—*Continued*

championship win by team with all-African-American starting lineup in final game, and first championship for, in National Collegiate Athletic Association (NCAA) Men's Basketball National Tournament, *2043*

Thomas Cup

world team, badminton championships for men, *1169*

Thompson Trophy airplane race, *1008*

Jet Division

pilot to win, *1015*

pilot to win, twice and then three times, *1013*

pilot to win Bendix Trophy and, *1010*

Three Rivers Stadium

Pittsburgh Pirates regular season baseball game played at, *1717*

Pittsburgh Steelers regular season football game played at, *3307*

Three-Tour Challenge, *3874*

ThreeCom Park

San Francisco Giants regular season game played at Candlestick Park later called, *1643*

Thunderdome

Tampa Bay Lightning regular season hockey game played at, *4206*

Tiger Stadium

Detroit Tigers regular game played at, *1414*

tobogganing

See

luge

torch relay

Olympic Games to have, *4681*

woman to carry torch at Olympic Games, *4725*

Toronto Arenas

National Hockey League team to win Stanley Cup, *4067*

Toronto Blue Jays

baseball player to be named Most Valuable Player, *1794*

pitcher to win Cy Young Award, *1835*

regular season baseball game played at Exhibition Stadium, *1745*

regular season baseball game played at the Skydome, *1807*

World Series victory, *1818*

Toronto Graduates

national team to win three consecutive ice hockey titles at Olympic Winter Games, *4096*

Toronto Granites

national team to win two consecutive ice hockey titles at Olympic Winter Games, *4083*

Toronto Maple Leafs

National Hockey League Stanley Cup championship, *4106*

National Hockey League team to win Stanley Cup three times in a row, *4123*

regular season hockey game played at Air Canada Centre, *4234*

regular season hockey game played at Maple Leaf Gardens, *4104*

Toronto Raptors

player to be named National Basketball Association (NBA) Rookie of the Year, *2371*

regular season basketball game played at Air Canada Centre, *2419*

Toronto St. Patricks

National Hockey League Stanley Cup championship, *4076*

total bases

player to lead American League in, *1325*

player to lead American League in, for three consecutive years, *1384*

player to lead National League in, for four consecutive years, *1389*

touchdowns

college football player to pass for six, in major bowl game, *3397*

National Collegeiate Athletic Association major college team to score a total of 84, rushing and passing, in a single season, *3380*

National Collegiate Athletic Association college football player to complete 54, passes in a single season, *3437*

National Collegiate Athletic Association college football player to score, on pass receptions in 12 consecutive games, *3478*

National Collegiate Athletic Association college football player to score eight rushing, in a single game, *3441*

National Collegiate Athletic Association college team to score 11 passing, in a single game, *3443*

National Collegiate Athletic Association major college football player to score six, on pass receptions in a single game, *3297*

National Collegiate Athletic Association major college team to score 89, in a single season, *3379*

National Collegiate Athletic Association player to pass for or himself score total of six, in major bowl game, *3203*

National Football League player to lead league in passing, for four consecutive years, *3253*

National Football League player to lead league in rushing touchdowns five times, *3273*

National Football League player to pass for 48, in a single season, *3390*

U

player to be named Most Valuable Player of, *5607*

United States teams
to play women's basketball in Pan American Games, *1957*
to sweep medals in men's 110-meter event in Olympic Games, *4323*
to sweep top honors in men's horizontal bar, long horse vault, side (pommel) horse, and rings gymnastics competitions in Olympic Games, *3913*
to sweep top spots in men's discus throw in Olympic Games, *2758*
to sweep top spots in men's shot put in Olympic Games, *5330*
to sweep top three medals in men's 100- and 200-meter running events in Olympic Games, *4990*
to sweep top three medals in men's 400-meter running event in Olympic Games, *4985*
to win eight-oared shell with coxswain women's rowing event in Olympic Games, *4952*
to win ice hockey title at Olympic Winter Games, *4141*
to win men's 4 x 100-meter relay track event in Olympic Games, *5011*
to win men's baseball title in Olympic Games, *1861*
to win rugby event in Olympic Games, *4967*
to win women's 4 x 100-meter relay running event in the Olympic Games, *5030*
to win women's 4 x 400-meter relay running event at Olympic Games, *5142*
to win women's basketball title in non-boycotted Olympic Games, *2275*
to win women's basketball title in Olympic Games, *2208*
to win women's gymnastics team title in Olympic Games, *3978*

United States Trotting Association
establishment of, *4295*

United States Women's Amateur Championship, *3615*
golfer to win both British Women's Amateur and, *3647*
golfer to win four, and then five, *3688*
golfer to win six, *3701*
golfer to win twice, and then three times, in a row, *3622*

United States Women's Open golf tournament, *3715*
amateur golfer to win, *3787*
golfer to win, four times, *3778*
golfer to win, in a playoff, *3739*
golfer to win, three times, *3744*
golfer to win two, *3726*
golfer to win two consecutive, *3757*
to be won in sudden-death playoff, *3892*

Universiade, *4375*
universities
See
entered under place name, eg. California at Los Angeles, University of
University Boat Race, *4913*
dead heat on record in, *4918*
university golf
match, *3591*
university golf clubs, *3589*
US Air Arena
Washington Bullets regular season game played at, *2100*
Washington Capitals regular season hockey game played at, *4166*
USA Boxing
women's amateur boxing match sponsored by, *2590*
Utah, University of
championship in National Collegiate Athletic Association (NCAA) Men's Basketball National Tournament, *1906*
Utah Jazz
player to be named National Basketball Association (NBA) Defensive Player of the Year, *2221*
player to be named National Basketball Association (NBA) Most Valuable Player of the Year, *2385*
player to be named National Basketball Association (NBA) Rookie of the Year, *2169*
regular season basketball game played at the Delta Center, *2309*
team to make 39 consecutive free throws in single National Basketball Association (NBA) game, *2182*

V

Val Barker Cup
boxer to win, *2549*
Vancouver Canucks
regular season hockey game played at General Motors Palace, *4220*
regular season hockey game played at Pacific Coliseum, *4156*
Vancouver Grizzlies
regular season basketball game played at Bear Country at General Motors Place, *2362*
Vardon Trophy, *3704*
African-American golfer to win, for lowest stroke average on Professional Golfers' Association (PGA) Tour, *3842*

Vare Trophy

golfer to be named Rookie of the Year and Player of the Year, and to win, for lowest scoring average, in same year, *3816*

golfer to win, for lowest average score on Ladies Professional Golf Association (LPGA) Tour, *3736*

Vasalopp long-distance ski race, *5364*

Vassar College

women's college baseball team on record, *1198*

vaulting (equestrian event)

world championships, *2888*

vélocipéde

first practical bicycle, *2681*

Vendée Globe round-the-world challenge race, *5250*

Venezuelans

baseball player, *1534*

Veterans Stadium

Philadelphia Eagles regular season football game played at, *3317*

Philadelphia Phillies regular season baseball game played at, *1721*

Victorian Football Association

state organization for Australian rules football, *3516*

Vienna Ice Club, *2953*

Villanova University

championship in National Collegiate Athletic Association (NCAA) Men's Basketball National Tournament, *2222*

women's college basketball team to score 18 3-point goals in single Division I National Collegiate Athletic Association (NCAA) game, *2399*

volleyball, *6272*

beach, *6275*

  held in Olympic Games, *6286*

  organized tournament in, *6276*

international competition in, *6273*

national championships in, in U.S., *6274*

Olympic Games

  men's event held in, *6279*

  players to win two consecutive men's gold medals in, *6282*

  players to win two consecutive women's gold medals in, *6283*

  team from U.S. to win men's title in, *6285*

  women's event held in, *6280*

world championships, *6277*

  to include women, *6278*

world cup, *6281*

  to include women, *6284*

Vuelta a España cycling race, *2697*

W

Walker Cup golf match, *3673*

British win of, *3707*

played in Britain, *3676*

walking

Eschborn Cup, *6295*

Olympic Games

  men's 10,000-meter walk held in, *6290*

  men's 20,000-meter walk event held in, *6292*

  men's 3000-meter event held in, *6288*

  men's 3500-meter and 10-mile walks held in, *6289*

  men's 50,000-meter walk held in, *6291*

  walker to win two titles in men's 20,000-meter walk in, *6293*

  women's 10,000-meter walk held in, *6296*

  women's 20-kilometer walk held in, *6297*

walker to be considered a professional, *6287*

World Race Walking Cup, *6294*

walks, in baseball

major league baseball player to have 170, in a single season, *1464*

pitcher to walk eight players in single inning, *1396*

Walter Payton Player of the Year Award, *3412*

war

modern Olympic Games canceled because of, *4646*

Olympic Winter Games canceled because of, *4686*

Washington Bullets

regular season game played at the US Air Arena, *2100*

team to have 142 offensive rebounds in single set of National Basketball Association (NBA) playoffs, *2147*

team to have average of 8.7 blocked shots per game in single National Basketball Association (NBA) season, *2235*

Washington Capitals

regular season hockey game played at MCI Center, *4229*

regular season hockey game played at US Air Arena, *4166*

Washington Capitols

African-Americans basketball player to join, *1926*

Washington Park

Brooklyn Dodgers regular season game played at, *1277*

Washington Park II

Brooklyn Dodgers regular season game played at, *1318*

women's college basketball—*Continued*

player to score 126 3-point goals in single Division I National Collegiate Athletic Association (NCAA) season, *2305*

player to score 17 consecutive field goals in single Division I National Collegiate Athletic Association (NCAA) game, *2244*

player to score 20 consecutive free throws in single Division I National Collegiate Athletic Association (NCAA) game, *2379*

player to score 27 field goals in single Division I National Collegiate Athletic Association (NCAA) game, *2204*

player to score 275 free throws in single Division I National Collegiate Athletic Association (NCAA) season, *2175*

player to score 3,122 points during her National Collegiate Athletic Association (NCAA) Division I career, *2285*

player to score 392 points in single Division I National Collegiate Athletic Association (NCAA) season, *2176*

player to score 60 points in single Division I National Collegiate Athletic Association (NCAA) game, *2259*

player to score 974 points in single Division I National Collegiate Athletic Association (NCAA) season, *2254*

player to score average of 28.4 points per game during her Division I National Collegiate Athletic Association (NCAA) career, *2286*

player to score more than 3,500 points during her college career, *2168*

player to score nine consecutive 3-point goals in single Division I National Collegiate Athletic Association (NCAA) game, *2273*

player to win Broderick Cup as top college woman athlete of the year, *2130*

player to win Margaret Wade Trophy, awarded to the Player of the Year, *2136*

player to win the Broderick Cup in two consecutive years, *2160*

player to win *The Sporting News* Player of the Year Award, *2409*

Purdue University championship in National Collegiate Athletic Association (NCAA) Women's Basketball National Tournament, *2416*

small college National Invitation Tournament, *2113*

Stanford University championship in National Collegiate Athletic Association (NCAA) Women's Basketball National Tournament, *2293*

team in South, *1870*

team to have 54-game winning streak, *2180*

team to score 149 points in single Division I National Collegiate Athletic Association (NCAA) game, *2260*

team to score 18 3-point goals in single Division I National Collegiate Athletic Association (NCAA) game, *2399*

team to win National Collegiate Athletic Association (NCAA) national championship in two consecutive years, *2201*

team to win National Collegiate Athletic Association (NCAA) national tournament, *2179*

Texas Tech University championship in National Collegiate Athletic Association (NCAA) Women's Basketball National Tournament, *2328*

United States Basketball Writers Association All-American first team, *2271*

United States Basketball Writers Association Coach of the Year Award, *2335*

United States Basketball Writers Association Player of the Year Award, *2336*

United States National Tournament, *2085*

University of North Carolina championship in National Collegiate Athletic Association (NCAA) Women's Basketball National Tournament, *2339*

University of Tennessee championship in National Collegiate Athletic Association (NCAA) Women's Basketball National Tournament, *2256*

University of Texas championship in National Collegiate Athletic Association (NCAA) Women's Basketball National Tournament, *2240*

women's college softball

player to win Erv Lind Award, *5599*

team to win the National Collegiate Athletic Association (NCAA) Division I College World Series, *5618*

women's cricket

club, *2651*

international organization, *2659*

match, *2637*

national organization, *2656*

test match, *2657*

touring team, *2652*

world cup, *2660*

women's cycling

cycling world championships to include, *2700*

Olympic Games

1000-meter match sprint cycling event held in, *2713*

3000-meter individual pursuit cycling event in, *2719*

500-meter time trial event in, *2728*

cross-country race held in, *2724*

cyclist to win two consecutive titles in 1000-meter match sprint in, *2718*

women's figure skating—*Continued*

skater from Hungary to win singles title in world championships, *2972*

skater from Japan to win singles title in world championships, *3094*

skater from Netherlands to win singles title at Olympic Winter Games, *3065*

skater from Netherlands to win singles title in world championships, *3059*

skater from Norway to win singles title at Olympic Winter Games, *3007*

skater from Norway to win singles title in world championships, *3006*

skater from Sweden to win singles title in Olympic Games, *2997*

skater from Switzerland to win singles title in world championships, *3086*

skater from Ukraine to win singles title at Olympic Winter Games, *3108*

skater from Ukraine to win singles title in world championships, *3103*

skater from United States to win singles title at Olympic Winter Games, *3053*

skater from United States to win singles title in world championships, *3048*

skater to be stripped of U.S. national singles title, *3104*

skater to perform an axel in competition, *2985*

skater to perform sit spin, *2969*

skater to perform triple lutz in competition, *3081*

skater to win 10 consecutive singles titles in world championships, *3019*

skater to win five consecutive singles championships, *3004*

skater to win singles title at Olympic Games, *2977*

skater to win singles title at U.S. national championships, *2988, 3099*

skater to win singles title in world championships, *2968*

skater to win singles U.S., world, and Olympic championships in same year, *3056*

skater to win six consecutive singles titles, and nine overall, at U.S. national championships, *3016*

skater to win three and then four consecutive singles titles in world championships, *2982*

skater to win two, and then three, consecutive singles titles at Olympic Winter Games, *3014*

skater to win two consecutive singles titles in world championships, *2971*

skater to win two straight singles titles at U.S. national championships, *2994*

skaters from United States to sweep singles medals in world championships, *3097*

women's golf

British Ladies' Open Amateur championship, *3604*

British Women's Amateur Championship golfer from U.S. to win, *3717*

club for African-Americans, *3684*

competition, *3562*

course for, in U.S., *3607*

Dinah Shore tournament, *3799*

golfer to be named Rookie of the Year and Player of the Year, and to win Vare Trophy for lowest scoring average, in same year, *3816*

golfer to earn more than $100,000 in official prize money in a season, *3810*

golfer to earn more than $2 million in official prize money during her career, *3852*

golfer to earn more than $3 million in official prize money during her career, *3867*

golfer to earn more than $300,000 in a single season, *3838*

golfer to earn more than $400,000 in official prize money in a single season, *3846*

golfer to earn more than $500,000 in official prize money in a season, *3861*

golfer to earn more than $600,000 in official prize money in a single season, *3868*

golfer to have season scoring average of under 70, *3891*

golfer to score 20 below par in 72 holes, *3847*

golfer to win five straight tournaments in which she played, *3820*

golfer to win more than $5 million, and then $6 million, in official prize money during her career, *3882*

international match between female golfers, *3641*

Ladies Professional Golf Association (LPGA)

golfer to be named Player of the Year, *3782*

golfer to be named Player of the Year seven times, *3800*

President of, *3722*

tournament to be nationally televised, *3772*

Ladies Professional Golf Association (LPGA) Championship, *3746*

golfer to win, with score under 280, *3774*

Ladies Professional Golf Association (LPGA) Championships

golfer to win two, and then three, *3762*

Ladies Professional Golf Association (LPGA) Tour

African-American woman to play on, *3786*

golfer named Rookie of the Year on, *3766*

golfer on, to win four consecutively scheduled tournaments, *3768*

golfer to have 15 consecutive seasons with victory on, *3779*

golfer to win 10 major tournaments recognized by, *3738*

golfer to win 10 titles recognized by, in a single season, *3752*

golfer to win 13 titles recognized by, in a single season, *3773*

golfer to win her first tournament on, *3729*

golfer to win more than $1 million in her rookie year on, *3884*

golfer to win three major tournaments, and six titles overall, on, in a single season, *3725*

golfer to win two of golf's major tournaments in her rookie year on, *3844*

golfer to win Vare Trophy for lowest average score on, *3736*

season purse to top $1 million, *3804*

season purse to top $10 million, *3851*

season purse to top $100,000, *3731*

season purse to top $20 million, *3873*

season purse to top $200,000, *3758*

season purse to top $5 million, *3828*

season purse to top $500,000, *3785*

tournament to be nationally televised for all four rounds, *3839*

Olympic Games

event in, *3630*

organization for professionals in U.S., *3712*

professional, *3646*

to earn more than $1 million in official prize money during her career, *3835*

U.S. Women's Amateur Championships, *3615*

golfer to win both British Women's Amateur and, *3647*

golfer to win four and then five, *3688*

golfer to win six, *3701*

golfer to win twice, and then three times, in a row, *3622*

U.S. Women's Open, *3715*

amateur golfer to win, *3787*

golfer to win, four times, *3778*

golfer to win, in a playoff, *3739*

golfer to win, three times, *3744*

golfer to win two, *3726*

golfer to win two consecutive, *3757*

to be won in sudden-death playoff, *3892*

Women's Professional Golfers' Association (WPGA)European Tour, *3822*

Women's World Amateur Team Championship, *3777*

World Championship of, *3829*

golfer to win, twice in a row, and then three times, *3836*

women's gymnastics

national competition in U.S. to include, *3927*

Olympic Games

all-around gymnastics competition held in, *3934*

balance beam gymnastics competition held in, *3935*

floor exercises competition held in, *3936*

gymnast from U.S. to win all-around women's title in, *3973*

gymnast to receive a perfect score of 10 in, *3960*

gymnast to win 10 medals in, *3940*

gymnast to win two consecutive all-around titles in, *3944*

gymnast to win two consecutive floor exercise titles in, *3941*

gymnast to win two consecutive side horse vault titles in, *3954*

gymnast to win two consecutive titles in balance beam competition in, *3966*

gymnast to win two consecutive titles in uneven (asymmetrical) bars in, *3952*

gymnasts from U.S. to win team title in, *3978*

gymnasts to win two consecutive gold medals in team combined exercises, *3945*

national team to sweep top medals in all-around gymnastics competition in, *3946*

side horse vault competition held in, *3937*

team combined exercises competition held in, *3926*

uneven (asymmetrical) bars gymnastics competition held in, *3938*

world championships

gymnast to win two, and then three, consecutive uneven (asymmetrical) bars titles in, *3968*

gymnast to win two balance beam titles in, *3975*

gymnast to win two consecutive all-around titles in world championships, *3931*

gymnast to win two consecutive horse vault titles in, *3953*

to award women's titles in specific events, *3932*

world championships in gymnastics to include women, *3930*

women's hammer throw

event included in Olympic Games, *3998*

thrower to hold officially accepted world record in women's event, *3997*

women's handball

Olympic Games

women's handball—*Continued*

players to win two consecutive gold medals in team handball in, *4008*
team event held in, *4007*
world handball championships to include women, *4006*

women's heptathlon

event held in Olympic Games, *4013*
heptathlete from United States, and first African-American, to hold world record in, *4014*
heptathlete from United States, and first African-American, to win title at Olympic Games world record in women's, *4015*
heptathlete to hold world record in, *4012*
heptathlete to win two consecutive titles in Olympic Games, *4016*

women's high jump

event held in the Olympic Games, *4022*
high-jumper to clear six feet in women's event, *4026*
high-jumper to set more than 10 world records in women's event, *4028*
high-jumper to win two consecutive titles in Olympic Games, *4030*
high-jumpers to hold officially accepted world record in women's event, and first from U.S. to win women's event in Olympic Games, *4023*
organized competitions, *4018*

women's hurdles

400-meter hurdles event held in Olympic Games, *4350*
80-meter hurdles event held in the Olympic Games, *4332*
hurdler to hold officially accepted world record in 100-meter, *4342*
hurdler to hold officially accepted world record in 400-meter, *4344*
hurdler to hold officially accepted world record in 80-meter event, *4333*
hurdler to win two consecutive titles in 80-meter hurdles in, *4338*

women's ice hockey

college hockey Player of the Year Award, *4214*
event held in Olympic Games, *4230*
state to recognize high school, as a varsity sport, *4213*
United States collegiate league, *4188*
world championships in, *4200*

women's javelin throw

thrower to break 160- and 170-foot and 50-meter barriers in, *4392*
thrower to break 180-foot barrier in, *4395*
thrower to break 200-foot and 60-meter barriers in, *4400*
thrower to break 210- and 220-foot barriers in, *4401*
thrower to break 230-foot barrier in, *4405*

thrower to break 240-foot barrier in, *4406*
thrower to break 250-foot barrier in, *4409*
thrower to break 260-foot barrier, and to reach 80-meter barrier, in, *4410*
thrower to break 70-meter barrier in, *4404*
thrower to hold officially accepted world record in, *4389*
thrower to reach 190-foot barrier in, *4398*
thrower to win two consecutive women's titles in Olympic Games, *4402*
women's event held in Olympic Games, *4390*

women's judo

extra-lightweight event held in Olympic Games, *4559*
half-heavyweight event held in Olympic Games, *4554*
half-lightweight event held in Olympic Games, *4558*
half-middleweight event held in Olympic Games, *4557*
heavyweight event held in Olympic Games, *4553*
lightweight event held in Olympic Games, *4552*
middleweight event held in Olympic Games, *4556*
world championships to include women, *4546*

women's karate

world championships in karate to include women, *4547*

women's lacrosse

organization, *4421*
world championships for, *4425*

women's long jump

event held in Olympic Games, *4436*
jumper from U.S. to set or equal world record in, *4441*
jumper from U.S. to win event in Olympic Games, *4442*
jumper to break 20-foot and 6-meter barriers in, *4435*
jumper to break 7-meter barrier in, *4440*
jumper to hold officially accepted world record in, and first female athlete from Asia to set world track and field record, *4431*

women's luge

national team to sweep medals in singles event at Olympic Winter Games, *4460*
singles event held in Olympic Games, *4457*

women's marathon

Boston Marathon to include women, as official participants, *4496*
champion of wheelchair division in Boston Marathon, *4502*
held in Olympic Games, *4512*

women's running—*Continued*

African-American women to win gold medals in track relay event in, *5058*

national team to sweep medals in 800-meter race, or in any women's track event, at, *5114*

runner from Africa to win 10,000 meters, and first Black African woman to win a medal, at, *5159*

runner from Africa to win 1500-meter title at, *5160*

runner from Australia to win 100- and 200-meter titles in, *5059*

runner from Caribbean to win 400-meter title in, *5158*

runner from U.S. to win 800-meter title at, *5091*

runner to win both 100- and 200- meter titles in, *5052*

runner to win both 200-and 400-meter titles at, and first runner from U.S., or African-American, to win 400-meters, *5143*

runner to win three consecutive gold medals in 4 x 100-meter relay at, *5161*

runner to win two consecutive 200-meter titles at, *5116*

runner to win two consecutive gold medals in women's 4 x 100-meter relay in, *5117*

runner to win two consecutive titles in 400 meters in, *5182*

runner to win two consecutive women's 200-meter titles in, *5086*

runner to win two gold medals in 4 x 100-meter relay in, *5041*

runners to finish first and second in both 100- and 200-meter races in, *5065*

team from U.S. to win 4 x 100-meter relay running event in, *5030*

team from U.S. to win 4 x 400-meter relay at, *5142*

women's 4 x 100-meter relay running event held in, *5023*

women's 800-meter running event held in, *5022*

runner from U.S. to hold world record in 5000 and 10,000 meters, *5124*

runner to hold officially accepted world record in 100-meter dash, *5033*

runner to hold officially accepted world record in 1500 meters, *5082*

runner to hold officially accepted world record in 200 meters, *5035*

runner to hold officially accepted world record in 3000 meters, *5101*

runner to hold officially accepted world record in 400 meters, *5066*

runner to hold officially accepted world record in 800 meters, *5021*

runner to hold officially accepted world record in women's 10,000 meters, *5123*

runner to hold officially accepted world record in women's 5000 meters, *5122*

runner to race 100 meters in under 10:50 seconds, and the 200 meters in under 21.50 seconds, *5153*

runner to race 200 meters in under 22 seconds, *5110*

runner to race 400 meters in under 48 seconds, *5137*

runner to race 400 meters in under 49 seconds, *5109*

runner to race 400 meters in under 50 seconds, *5100*

runner to race 800 meters in under 2:10 minutes, *5055*

runner to race women's 10,000 meters in under 30 minutes, *5169*

runner to race women's 100 meters in under 11.0 seconds, *5097*

runner to race women's 1000 meters in under 2:30 minutes, *5180*

runner to race women's 1500 meters in under 4 minutes, *5104*

runner to race women's 5000 meters in under 15 minutes, *5138*

runner to race women's 800 meters in under 2:00 minutes, *5093*

runner to set seven world records in women's 400 meters, *5145*

runner to win two consecutive titles in 1500 meters in, *5118*

World Championships in Athletics

runner from U.S. to win women's 100 meters in, *5164*

runner from U.S. to win women's 400 meters in, *5165*

runner to win 200 meters in, *5135*

runner to win both 100- and 200-meter titles in, *5146*

runner to win t 100 meters in, *5133*

runner to win two consecutive titles in women's 800 meters in, *5185*

runner to win two titles in 1500 meters in, *5176*

women's sailboarding

event held in the Olympic Games, *5192*

women's sailboat and yacht racing

Europe-class sailing event held in Olympic Games, *5252*

Olympic Games

470-class sailing event held in, *5249*

woman to win gold medal in, *5210*

women's sailing

international championships, *5233*

women's shooting

Olympic Games

air pistol individual event held in, *5322*

air rifle individual event in, *5318*

light heavyweight freestyle wrestling event held in, *6377*

light heavyweight Greco-Roman event held in, *6373*

lightweight freestyle event held in, *6366*

lightweight Greco-Roman event held in, *6370*

middleweight freestyle event held in, *6372*

middleweight Greco-Roman event held in, *6371*

super heavyweight freestyle event held in, *6367*

twin brothers to win gold medals in same, *6404*

unlimited weight (super heavyweight) Greco-Roman event held in, *6358*

welterweight freestyle event held in, *6368*

welterweight Greco-Roman event held in, *6383*

wrestler from U.S. to win Greco-Roman title in, *6405*

wrestler from U.S. to win heavyweight freestyle title in, *6407*

wrestler from U.S. to win middleweight freestyle title in, *6386*

wrestler from U.S. to win super heavyweight Greco-Roman title in, *6406*

wrestler from U.S. to win two super heavyweight freestyle titles in, *6412*

wrestler of Black African descent to win a gold medal in, *6409*

wrestler to win gold medals in three different divisions in, *6378*

wrestler to win heavyweight titles in both freestyle and Greco-Roman wrestling in, *6385*

wrestler to win light flyweight freestyle competition in, when it resumed in 1972, *6398*

wrestler to win two bantamweight freestyle titles in, *6410*

wrestler to win two consecutive featherweight freestyle titles in, *6413*

wrestler to win two consecutive flyweight Greco-Roman titles in, *6402*

wrestler to win two consecutive heavyweight freestyle titles in, *6403*

wrestler to win two consecutive light flyweight Greco-Roman titles in, *6408*

wrestler to win two consecutive light heavyweight freestyle titles in, *6414*

wrestler to win two consecutive light heavyweight Greco-Roman titles in, *6391*

wrestler to win two consecutive lightweight freestyle titles in, *6411*

wrestler to win two consecutive lightweight Greco-Roman titles in, *6376*

wrestler to win two consecutive middleweight Greco-Roman titles in, *6384*

wrestler to win two consecutive super heavyweight freestyle titles in, and gold medals in three consecutive, *6399*

wrestler to win two consecutive super heavyweight Greco-Roman titles in, *6392*

wrestler to win two consecutive welterweight Greco-Roman titles in, *6390*

wrestler to win two super heavyweight freestyle titles in, *6382*

organization of professional wrestlers in U.S., *6360*

sumo

matches, *6356*

organization to achieve national recognition, *6357*

wrestler born outside Japan to be named grand champion (yokozuna), *6415*

world championships

in freestyle wresting, *6389*

in Greco-Roman wrestling, *6361*

in Greco-Roman wrestling held on a regular basis, *6388*

in Greco-Roman wrestling regarded as official, *6379*

light flyweight event held in freestyle wrestling championships, *6393*

light flyweight event held in Greco-Roman championships, *6394*

light flyweight freestyle event held in, *6395*

super heavyweight event held in Greco-Roman championships, *6396*

Wrigley Field (Chicago, Ill.)

Chicago Cubs regular season game played at, *1425*

Wrigley Field (Los Angeles, Calif.)

Los Angeles Angels regular season baseball game played at, *1648*

Wyoming, University of

championship in National Collegiate Athletic Association (NCAA) Men's Basketball National Tournament, *1904*

Y

yacht clubs, *5194*

in England, *5195*

in U.S., *5196*

yacht racing

See

sailboat and yacht racing

Yale University

African-American player to be captain of football team at, *3216*

Z

Index by Year

The Index by Year is a chronological listing of key information from the main text of the book, organized by year starting with the earliest. Each index entry includes key information about the "first" and a 4-digit number in italics. That number directs you to the full entry in the main text, where entries are numbered in order, starting with 1001.

To find the full entry, look in the main text for the entry tagged with that 4-digit number. For example, to find the entry relating to the year 1219, about the first written reference to tennis, look for the entry numbered 6002 in the main text.

Note that entries containing specific dates (such as March 14) are also indexed separately in the Index by Month and Day.

For more information, see "How to Use This Book," on page ix.

1396

Ice skating accident, *2946*

1421

Introduction of *chole* to the British Isles, *2630*

1424

Ban on football in Scotland, *5529*

1429

Written reference to billiards, *2443*

1457

Written reference to golf, *3535*

1466

Shooting club, *5261*

1472

Shooting tournament on record, *5262*

1482

Palio horse race, *4248*

1500

Development of the tennis racket, *6003*

1502

Purchase of golf equipment, *3536*

1513

Golf reference on record in England, *3537*

1520

Written reference to tobogganing, *4445*

1552

Confirmation of the public's right to play golf, *3538*

1567

Woman golfer on record, *3539*

1572

Iron skates on record, *2947*

1598

Cricket reference, *2631*

1606

Oyakazu archery contest, *1018*

1611

Written reference to sports in Britain's American colonies, *5738*

1618

Confirmation of people's right to play golf and other sports on Sundays, *3540*
Patent for a golf ball, *3541*

1620

Playing of darts on record in North America, *2733*

1632

Death in a golf accident, *3542*

1636

Golf book, *3543*

1642

License for producing golf balls, *3544*

1651

Documented horse race, *4249*

1659

Written reference to *kolven* in North America, *4415*

1660

Iron skates in England, *2948*
Rules for horse racing, *4250*

1661

Sailing challenge race on record, *5193*

1665

Newmarket Town Four Mile Race, *4251*
Organized horse races in colonial North America, *4252*

1668

Silver trophy known to be awarded at a sporting event in North America, *1146*

1673

Scorton Arrow Contest, *1019*

1676

Cricket game on record played outside the British Isles, *2632*

1682

International golf match, *3545*

1709

Cricket reference in North America, *2633*

1715

Modern rowing competition on record, *4911*

1719

Boxing school, *2505*

1720

Yacht club, *5194*

1721

Golf course in the west of Scotland, *3546*

1724

Golf match reported in a newspaper, *3547*

1727

Organized record of match race performances, *4253*

1731

Cricket ground set aside for play, *2634*

1733

Skiing manual, *5353*

1734

Jockey club in North America, *4254*

1742

Ice skating club, *2949*

1743

Boxing code of rules, *2506*
Literary work about golf, *3548*

1744

Code of rules for cricket, *2635*
Cricket match at which admission was charged, and the first cricket game to be fully documented, *2636*
Golf club, *3549*
Golf rules, *3551*
Open competition in golf, *3550*

1745

Women's cricket match, *2637*

1750

International championships in tennis, *6004*
Jockey Club in England, *4255*

1752

Steeplechase horse race, *4256*

1754

Golf rules to be published, *3552*
Open golf competition at St. Andrews, Scotland, *3553*

1759

Stroke play game recorded in golf, *3554*

1760

Curling games in the Americas, *2672*
Roller skates, *4901*

1762

Wearing of racing colors by jockeys, *4257*

1764

Golf course with 18 holes, *3555*
Restriction of golf competition to club members, *3556*

1766

Golf club outside Scotland, *3557*

1767

Organized Nordic (cross-country) ski races, *5354*
Skiing and shooting competition (later known as biathlon), *2427*

1768

Golf clubhouse, *3558*

1772

Book on ice skating techniques, *2950*

1773

Racing Calendar, *4258*
Sumo wrestling organization to achieve national recognition, *6357*

1774

Golf course professional, *3559*

1775

Organized regatta, or series of boat races, on record, *4912*
Yacht club in England, *5195*

1776

Dog racing club, *2830*
Gymnastics school to teach the modern sport, *3900*
St. Leger horse race, *4259*

1779

Golf game on record in North America, *3560*

1779—*continued*

Oaks horse race, *4260*

1780

Derby horse race, *4261*

1781

Organization for archery as a sport, *1020*

1783

People to fly in a balloon, *1176*

1784

Woman to fly in a hot-air balloon, *1177*

1785

Flyers to cross the English Channel in a balloon, *1178*

Jockey who won three Derbys at Epsom Downs, *4262*

1786

Golf club in the Americas, and the first outside Great Britain, *3561*

1787

Archery organization to admit women as members, *1021*

Cricket match on record at Lord's Cricket Ground, *2639*

Governing body in cricket, *2638*

1791

Pole vault stand, *4836*

Stud book for horse racing, *4263*

1792

Cricket club in India, *2640*

1793

Balloon flight in the United States, *1179*

1804

Woman jockey on record, *4264*

1805

African-American boxer to fight in a title bout, *2507*

1806

African-American jockey known by name, *4265*

Record of cricket being played in the West Indies, *2641*

1807

Jockey who won five Derbys at Epsom Downs, *4266*

1809

2000 Guineas horse race, *4267*

1810

African-American boxer to fight in a title bout, *2507*

1811

Golf competition for women, *3562*

Yacht club in the United States, *5196*

1814

1000 Guineas horse race, *4268*

Cricket match on record at the current location of Lord's Cricket Ground, *2642*

1816

Boxing match under English rules held in the United States, *2508*

1817

Development of squash (squash rackets), *5756*

1818

Protective gear worn by cricket players, *2643*

1822

Boxer to be barred by a boxing authority for throwing a fight, *2509*

1825

Importation of North American hickory to Britain for golf clubs, *3563*

Woman to fly solo in a hot-air balloon in the United States, *1180*

1826

Cricket club in Australia, *2644*

1827

Cricket match on record between teams from Oxford and Cambridge universities, *2645*

1828

Archery club in the United States, *1022*

Recorded steeplechase event for runners, *4972*

1829

Golf club in Asia, *3564*

University Boat Race, *4913*

1832

Curling organization in the United States, *2673*

1860

Baseball club tour, *1194*
British Open golf tournament, *3576*
Formally measured ski jump, *5355*
Golfer to win the British Open, *3577*
National organization for shooting in Great Britain, *5263*
Shutout baseball game on record, *1195*
Substitute for live birds in shooting competitions, *5264*

1861

British Open golf championship open to amateurs, *3578*
Football game on record in Canada, *3520*
Indoor track meet, *6198*
Melbourne Cup horse race, *4274*
Ski and shooting club, *2428*
Walker to be considered a professional, *6287*

1862

Enclosed baseball field to which admission was charged, *1196*
Golfer to win the British Open championship twice in a row, *3579*
Ski-jumping contest focusing on jumping alone, *5356*

1863

Football Association (FA), *5532*
Grand Prix du Paris horse race, *4275*
Practical four-wheeled roller skates, *4902*

1864

Croquet club in the United States, *2664*
Equestrian show jumping competition, *2837*

1865

Ice boating club in the United States, *4359*

1866

Equestrian show jumping competition held in France, *2838*
National track and field (athletics) championships, *6199*
Roller-skating rink, *4903*
Rule in baseball establishing the pitcher's box, *1197*
Transatlantic sailing race, *5199*
Use of glass ball targets in United States shooting competitions, *5265*
Women's college baseball teams on record, *1198*

1867

Baseball box score, *1199*
Baseball game between Princeton and Yale, *1200*

Belmont Stakes horse race, *4276*
Cycling club, *2681*
Golf club for women, *3580*
Golfer to win four British Open championships, *3581*
Ice skating club in mainland Europe, *2953*
National organization for lacrosse, *4417*
Open championship in croquet, *2665*

1868

Cricket team from outside the British Isles to tour England, *2649*
Cycling race on record, *2682*
Golfer under the age of 20 to win the British Open championship, *3582*
Major track and field competition in the United States, *6200*
Non-collegiate women's baseball team, *1201*
Rule establishing that no baseball game can be completed until five innings have been played by both teams, *1202*

1869

All England Croquet Club, *2666*
Bronco-riding contest for cash prizes, *4878*
Development of water polo, *6298*
Equestrian show jumping competition held in England, *2839*
Intercollegiate football game in the United States, *3117*
Introduction of polo in Europe, *4855*
National organization for swimming, *5780*
National swimming championship, *5781*
Professional baseball team, *1203*
Soccer (international football) club outside Britain, *5533*

1870

Cincinnati Red Stockings loss as a professional baseball team, and the end of the first winning streak in professional baseball, *1204*
Code of rules for water polo, *6299*
Golf club in Australia, *3583*
Golfer to win the British Open championship three times in a row, *3584*
Ice skating rink using artificial ice, *2954*
Standardized rules for badminton, *1164*
World professional championships in billiards, *2444*

1871

All-professional baseball game on record, *1207*
Championship game in professional baseball, *1211*
Cuban major league baseball player, *1205*
Hit in an all-professional baseball game, *1208*
International rifle tournament held in the United States, *5267*
National governing body in shooting in the United States, *5266*

Professional baseball game played in Boston, Massachusetts, *1210*
Professional baseball league, *1206*
Recorded polo match in England, *4856*
Rugby Football Union (RFU), *4963*
Shutout on record in professional baseball, *1209*

1872

Football Association (FA) Challenge Cup for soccer (international football), *5534*
Golfer to win the British Open championship four times in a row, *3585*
National governing body for rowing in the United States, *4916*
Ski club in the United States, *5357*

1873

British Open golf championship held at the Old Course at St. Andrews, Scotland, *3586*
Golf club in Canada, *3587*
Grand Circuit series of harness horse races, *4277*
Overarm swimming stroke, *5782*
Preakness Stakes horse race, *4278*

1874

Baseball teams from the United States to tour England and Ireland, *1214*
Batter's box in baseball, *1212*
British Open golf championship held at Musselburgh, Scotland, *3588*
Collegiate sporting event at which admission was charged, *5739*
International game of American-style football, and the first to use football goal posts, *3118*
Rules against professional baseball players betting on either their own or the opposing team, *1213*
Tennis game in its modern form, *6005*

1875

Baseball glove on record, *1215*
Collegiate rowing program for women, *4917*
Governing body for polo, *4857*
Ice hockey game, *4041*
Introduction of polo into Argentina, *4858*
Kentucky Derby horse race, *4279*
National governing body for bowling in the United States, *2479*
National governing body for field hockey, *4033*
Person to swim the English Channel, *5783*
Professional baseball pitcher to win 200 games, *1216*
Snooker game on record, *2445*
University golf clubs, *3589*

1876

Balloon race in the United States, *1181*

Baseball player to have 6 hits in a 9-inning National League game, *1228*
Baseball player to hit a home run in the National League, *1225*
Baseball player to lead the National League in batting average, *1217*
Boston Red Stockings regular season baseball game played at South End Grounds, *1220*
Boxing match between women on record in the United States, *2513*
Champion Cup polo competition, *4859*
Chicago White Stockings regular season baseball game played at the State Street Grounds, *1226*
Cincinnati Red Stockings regular season baseball game played at the Avenue Grounds, *1224*
Doubleheader in baseball's National League, *1230*
Golfer to win the British Open after a default in a playoff, *3590*
High-jumper to clear six feet, *4017*
Hit made in baseball's National League, *1221*
Ice skating rink in Great Britain to use artificial ice, *2955*
Jewish major league baseball player, *1218*
Major sporting goods business, *5740*
National championships in track and field (athletics) in the United States, *6201*
National League baseball game, *1222*
National League championship, *1232*
National League was organized, *1219*
National organization for harness (trotting) horse owners in the United States, *4280*
No-hitter pitched in baseball's National League, *1229*
Pitcher in baseball's National League to pitch and win two games on the same day, *1231*
Pitcher to pitch a shutout in baseball's National League, *1223*
Polo competitions in the United States, *4860*
Single-handed sailing across the Atlantic, *5200*
Tennis club formed in the United States, *6006*
Tennis tournament on record in the United States, *6007*
Triple play in baseball's National League, *1227*

1877

Baseball chest protector, *1233*
Catcher's mask used in a National League game, *1237*
Collegiate lacrosse team in the United States, *4418*
Dead heat on record in the University Boat Race, *4918*
Ice skating rink in Switzerland, *2956*
Jewish major league baseball manager, *1234*
Left-handed pitcher in the National League, *1235*

1877—*continued*

Major league baseball game played on Sunday, *1236*

Polo club in the United States, *4861*

State organization for Australian rules football, *3516*

Tennis tournament played at Wimbledon, *6008*

Test match in cricket, *2650*

1878

African-American baseball player known to have played professionally with a previously all-white team, *1238*

Automobile race on record, *1041*

Baseball team to win two consecutive National League pennants, *1239*

Chicago White Stockings regular season baseball game played at Lakefront Park, *1243*

Cuban professional baseball league, *1240*

National ice skating organization in North America, *2957*

National tennis championships in Scotland, *6009*

Pitcher to lead the National League in winning percentage for two consecutive years, *1241*

Three-cushion billiards, *2446*

Unassisted triple play in major league baseball, *1242*

University golf match, *3591*

1879

Code of rules for tug-of-war, *6266*

Indoor ice skating rink, *2958*

Inter-state game in Australian rules football, *3517*

Major league baseball player born in Canada, *1244*

National archery tournament in the United States, *1024*

National ice skating organization in Great Britain, *2959*

National organization for archery in the United States, *1023*

National organization for hurling, *4356*

National tennis championships in Ireland, *6010*

Reserve agreement among major league baseball club owners, *1245*

Specially built luge (toboggan) runs, *4446*

1880

Cincinnati Reds regular season baseball game played at the Bank Street Grounds, *1246*

Clay pigeons for target shooting, *5268*

Golf balls manufactured with "dimples", *3592*

Major league baseball player to hit four doubles in one game, *1252*

Major league baseball team to win 21 games in a row, *1250*

National boxing organization, *2514*

National governing body for track and field (athletics) in England, *6202*

Night baseball game on record, *1251*

Perfect game in professional baseball, *1249*

Professional baseball stadium in Manhattan, *1253*

"Rotating" pitchers in major league baseball, *1248*

Sudden death rule to end games in major league baseball, *1247*

Table tennis equipment, *5980*

Tennis player to win two consecutive men's singles championships at Wimbledon, *6011*

1881

American Association of Professionals, *1257*

Grand slam home run in major league baseball, *1256*

Horse bred and trained in the United States to win England's Derby, *4281*

Major league baseball player to steal seven bases in a single game, *1255*

Men's doubles competition at the United States national tennis championships, *6012*

Men's singles competition at the United States national tennis championships, *6013*

Pitcher to lead the National League in wins and in losses in the same season, *1254*

United States national tennis championships, *6014*

1882

Boxer to be undisputed world heavyweight champion, *2515*

Development of judo, *4528*

Eighteen-inning shutout in major league baseball, *1265*

Governing body for croquet in the United States, *2667*

Intercollegiate Lacrosse Association, *4419*

International figure skating competition, *2960*

Line of scrimmage system in American-style football, *3119*

Major league baseball professional umpire staff, *1258*

Major league pitcher to pitch left-handed and right-handed in the same game, *1263*

National League player to hit for the cycle (single, double, triple, and home run) in a single game, *1262*

National League player to lead the league in doubles in two consecutive years, *1259*

National League team to score 35 runs in a single game, *1264*

Professional rodeo, *4879*

St. Louis Browns regular season baseball game played at a field called Sportsman's Park, *1261*

Umpire to be barred from major league baseball for dishonesty, *1260*

1883

Baseball player to lead the National League in batting average for two consecutive years, *1266*

Baseball player to score 6 runs in a 9-inning National League game, *1271*

Diving tournament on record, *2787*

Documented rodeo competition, *4880*

Golfer to win the British Open in a playoff, *3593*

International luge (toboggan) competition, *4447*

Ladies' Day baseball game, *1272*

Major league pitcher to hit two home runs in a single game, *1270*

National Horse Show, *2840*

National League team to win three consecutive pennants, *1267*

National organization for skiing, *5358*

National swimming championships in the United States, *5784*

New York Giants regular season baseball game played at Polo Grounds I, *1268*

Philadelphia Phillies regular season baseball game played at Recreation Park, *1269*

Union Association in baseball, *1273*

United States intercollegiate tennis championships, *6015*

1884

African-American major league baseball player, *1274*

Boxer to be world middleweight champion, *2516*

Brooklyn Dodgers regular season baseball game played at Washington Park, *1277*

Code of rules for Gaelic football, *3523*

Diamond Challenge Sculls rowing race, *4919*

Eastern League convention in baseball, *1276*

International championship in soccer (international football), *5535*

International curling competition between Canada and the United States, *2675*

Major league baseball player to hit 27 home runs in a single season, *1275*

Major league pitcher to strike out 19 batters in a single 9-inning game, *1278*

Men's doubles tennis championship at Wimbledon, *6016*

National association for soccer (international football) in the United States, *5536*

Skeleton luge (toboggan), *4448*

Standardization of the rules of hurling, *4357*

Women's singles tennis championships at Wimbledon, *6017*

World championship in billiards, *2447*

1885

African-American professional baseball team, *1279*

Batting and fielding cage in baseball, *1280*

Boxer to be world heavyweight champion under the Queensberry rules, *2517*

British Amateur Championship, *3594*

Chicago White Stockings regular season baseball game played at West Side Park, *1282*

Field hockey club established in India, *4034*

Golf club in Africa, *3595*

Grand National luge (toboggan) race, *4449*

Intercollegiate ice hockey game, *4042*

International soccer (international football) match involving the United States, *5537*

Major league baseball player to get four triples, and five extra-base hits, in a single game, *1283*

Major league baseball players' union, *1284*

National governing body for billiards and snooker, *2448*

Official code of rules for billiards, *2449*

St. Louis Browns American Association pennant, *1281*

Tennis player to win two consecutive women's singles championships at Wimbledon, *6018*

1886

Boxer to be undisputed world lightweight champion, *2518*

Canadian ice hockey league, *4043*

International ice hockey tournament, *4044*

International polo competition, *4862*

Issue of *The Sporting News*, *5741*

National ice skating organization in the United States, *2961*

National League baseball game to be played in Kansas City, *1285*

Tennis player to win six consecutive men's singles championships at Wimbledon, and seven overall, *6019*

1887

All-Ireland championships in Gaelic football, *3524*

All-Ireland Championships in hurling, *4358*

American College Baseball Association, *1286*

Automobile race on record in Europe, *1042*

Ice skate sailing competition, *4360*

International court (four-wall) handball competition, *3999*

Major league baseball team to score more than 1,000 runs in a single season, *1287*

Meeting of the Boston Athletic Association, *4466*

National Colored League baseball game, *1290*

National Colored League organizing meeting, *1288*

Organized ski-jumping competition in the United States, *5359*

Organized softball game, following George Hancock's rules, and with the diamond, ball, and bat he introduced, *5573*

1887—*continued*

Philadelphia Phillies regular season baseball game played at Huntington Street Grounds, *1289*

Soccer (international football) club in Germany, *5538*

Softball game, *5572*

Tennis player to win seven consecutive men's singles titles at the United States national championships, *6020*

Tennis player to win six consecutive men's doubles titles at the United States national championships, *6021*

Tennis player to win the women's singles title at the United States national championships, *6022*

United States national tennis championships to include women, *6023*

Women's cricket club, *2651*

1888

Amateur Athletic Union (AAU), *5742*

Colored Championships of America tournament, *1291*

Harness race held at night, *4282*

Major league baseball player to pitch four consecutive shutouts, *1293*

National governing body for track and field (athletics) in the United States, *6203*

National organization for tennis in Great Britain, *6024*

New York Giants National League pennant, *1292*

Slider to ride the skeleton (Cresta Run) luge (toboggan) face forward, *4450*

Soccer (international football) league, *5539*

Softball games played outdoors, *5574*

United States baseball team to tour the world, and to visit Australia, *1294*

1889

African-American college football player, *3120*

All-America college football team named by Walter Camp, *3121*

Baseball player to hit two home runs in his first major league game, *1298*

Formally organized diving competition, *2788*

Golf course in the United States, *3596*

International speed skating competition, *5629*

Major league baseball 26-game losing streak, *1295*

New York Giants regular season baseball game played at Polo Grounds II, *1297*

Players' League, *1296*

Rules for roque (a variation on croquet), *2668*

Softball rules to be formally published, *5575*

Team to win the championship in England's Football League, *5540*

Tennis player to win two consecutive women's singles titles at the United States national championships, *6025*

Tennis players to win five men's doubles championships at Wimbledon, *6026*

United States women's doubles national tennis championships, *6027*

1890

African-American football player to captain an otherwise largely white college team, *3122*

African-American professional baseball team west of the Mississippi, *1299*

Amateur, and the first non-Scot, to win the British Open golf championship, *3597*

Army-Navy football game, *3123*

Bogey as a score in golf, *3598*

Boxer of African descent to win a national boxing title, *2519*

Boxer to be world featherweight champion, *2520*

Brooklyn Dodgers National League pennant, *1300*

International rowing competition, *4920*

International water polo match, *6300*

Major league baseball player to play in 577 consecutive games, *1301*

National polo organization in the United States, *4863*

Runner to race the 100-yard dash in under 10 seconds, *4973*

Sisters to win the women's doubles title at the United States national tennis championships, *6028*

Women's touring cricket team, *2652*

1891

Baseball player to lead the National League in stolen bases for two consecutive years, *1302*

Basketball game, *1864*

Boxer of African descent to win a United States boxing title, and probably the first athlete of African descent to hold a U.S. title in any sport, *2521*

Brooklyn Dodgers regular season baseball game played at Eastern Park, *1304*

French national tennis championships, *6029*

International governing body for gymnastics, *3901*

Jockey to win three Kentucky Derbys, and the first to win two in a row, *4283*

Netball, *4595*

New York Giants regular season baseball game played at Polo Grounds III, *1303*

Scheduled Sunday games in the National League were authorized, *1306*

Single-handed transatlantic race, *5201*

Two consecutive home runs by different players to open a major league baseball game, *1305*

United States national interscholastic boys singles tennis championships, *6030*

1892

African-American college football player named to Walter Camp's All-America team, *3124*

Article reporting on basketball's first game, *1867*

Basketball team, *1865*

Boxer of African descent to win a world boxing title, *2523*

Boxer to be undisputed world welterweight champion, *2522*

British Open championship held at Muirfield, Scotland, *3599*

College football game between two African-American colleges, *3126*

College women's basketball game, *1868*

Golf clubhouse in the United States, *3600*

Golf match to charge fees for spectators, *3601*

Horseshoe club on record, *4320*

International cycling organization, *2683*

International golf championship, *3602*

International governing body for ice skating, *2962*

International governing body in rowing, *4921*

President of the United States to attend a major league baseball game, *1308*

Professional football player, *3125*

Proposal to revive the Olympic Games in modern times, *4602*

Scheduled Sunday game in the National League, *1307*

Tennis player to win two consecutive women's doubles titles at the United States national championships, *6031*

United States national tennis championships to include mixed doubles competition, *6032*

Women's basketball program, *1866*

1893

Argentine Open polo competition, *4864*

British Ladies' Open Amateur golf championship, *3604*

Chicago White Stockings regular season baseball game played at the West Side Grounds, *1309*

Formal organization for the game of shinty (*camanachd*), *5259*

Golf course for women in the United States, *3603*

Ice hockey team to win the Stanley Cup, *4045*

Intercollegiate men's basketball game, *1869*

Major league baseball player to hit a triple and a home run in the same inning, *1310*

National governing body for badminton, *1165*

Officially sponsored international rowing championships, *4922*

Organized automobile race in the United States, *1043*

Speed skater to skate the 10,000 meters in under 20 minutes, *5632*

Speed skater to skate the 500 meters in under 50 seconds, *5631*

Tennis player to win three consecutive Wimbledon women's singles championships, and five overall, *6033*

Tennis player to win two consecutive mixed doubles titles at the United States national tennis championships, *6034*

Women's college basketball team in the South, *1870*

World championship in speed skating, *5630*

World championships in cycling, *2684*

1894

Automobile track race on record, *1044*

British Open golf tournament held in England, *3605*

Establishment of the North American Jockey Club, *4284*

Film of a sporting event, *5743*

Golf clubs made in the United States, *3606*

Ice hockey team to win the Stanley Cup twice in a row, *4046*

Major league baseball player to hit .440 in a single season, *1311*

Major league baseball player to hit five times in five at-bats during his first major league game, *1313*

Major league baseball player to hit grand slam home runs in two consecutive games, *1314*

Maryland Hunt Cup Race, *4285*

National golf championship in the United States, *3608*

National governing body for golf in the United States, *3609*

National League player to hit 4 home runs in a 9-inning baseball game, *1312*

Separate golf course for women in the United States, *3607*

Speed skater to skate the 1500 meters in under 2:30 minutes, *5633*

Speed skater to skate the 5000 meters in under 9 minutes, *5634*

1895

Code of rules for modern bowling, *2480*

Eighteen-hole golf course in the United States, *3610*

Establishment of the American Bowling Congress (ABC), *2481*

Golf book published in the United States, *3611*

Golf club on the West Coast of North America, *3612*

Ice hockey exhibition game in Great Britain, *4047*

Modern handball, *4000*

National diving competition, *2789*

1895—*continued*

National organization for steeplechase racing in the United States, *4286*

Organized long-distance automobile race, *1045*

Organized women's high jump competitions, *4018*

Professional football player who acknowledged being a professional, *3127*

Rugby League, *4964*

Speed skater to be world champion in men's long-distance speed skating twice, and then three times, in a row, *5635*

Speed skater to skate the 10,000 meters in under 18 minutes, *5636*

U.S. Amateur golf tournament, *3613*

U.S. Open golf tournament, *3614*

U.S. Women's Amateur golf tournament, *3615*

Volleyball, *6272*

Women's basketball game in the South that was open to the public, *1871*

Women's basketball published set of rules, *1872*

Women's soccer (international football) game, *5541*

Women's softball team, *5576*

1896

African-American college baseball league, *1315*

Athlete, and the first from the United States, to win a gold medal in the modern Olympic Games, *4604*

Athlete from Australia to win a gold medal in the modern Olympic Games, *4607*

Athlete from Denmark to win a gold medal in the Olympic Games, *4608*

Athlete from France to win a gold medal in the Olympic Games, *4609*

Athlete from Great Britain to win a gold medal in the Olympic Games, *4610*

Athlete from Greece to win a gold medal in the modern Olympic Games, *4611*

Athlete from Hungary to win a gold medal in the modern Olympic Games, *4614*

Athlete from Switzerland to win a gold medal in the Olympic Games, *4612*

Athletes to row across the Atlantic Ocean, *4923*

Brothers to win gold and silver medals in the same event in the Olympic Games, *4613*

Camanachd Association Challenge Cup for the sport of shinty (*camanachd*), *5260*

Cyclist to win the men's 12-hour cycling race in the Olympic Games, *2687*

Cyclist to win two, and then three, cycling gold medals in the Olympic Games, *2688*

Event held in the modern Olympic Games, *4605*

Figure skater to win the men's singles title at the world championships, *2963*

Free pistol shooting individual event held in the Olympic Games, *5271*

Free rifle individual shooting event held in the Olympic Games, *5269*

Free rifle (three position) individual shooting event held in the Olympic Games, *5273*

Fully professional football team, *3128*

Marathon runner to be stripped of his medal, *4467*

Men's 100- and 400-meter running events held in the Olympic Games, *4975*

Men's 100-meter freestyle swimming event held in the Olympic Games, *5785*

Men's 1000-meter match sprint cycling race held in the Olympic Games, *2685*

Men's 110-meter hurdles event held in the Olympic Games, *4322*

Men's 1200-meter freestyle swimming event held in the Olympic Games, *5786*

Men's 500-meter freestyle event held in the Olympic Games, *5787*

Men's 800-meter and 1500-meter running events held in the Olympic Games, *4974*

Men's discus throw event held in the Olympic Games, *2754*

Men's doubles tennis event held in the Olympic Games, *6035*

Men's high jump event held in the Olympic Games, *4019*

Men's horizontal bar gymnastics competitions held in the Olympic Games, *3902*

Men's individual foil fencing competition held in the Olympic Games, *2897*

Men's individual sabre fencing competition held in the Olympic Games, *2899*

Men's long horse vault gymnastics competition held in the Olympic Games, *3903*

Men's long jump event held in the Olympic Games, *4426*

Men's marathon race held in the Olympic Games, *4468*

Men's masters foil fencing competition held in the Olympic Games, *2898*

Men's parallel bars gymnastics competitions held in the Olympic Games, *3906*

Men's pole vault event held in the Olympic Games, *4837*

Men's rings gymnastics competition held in the Olympic Games, *3904*

Men's road race cycling event held in the Olympic Games, *2686*

Men's rope climbing gymnastics competition held in the Olympic Games, *3907*

Men's shot put event held in the Olympic Games, *5329*

Men's side (pommel) horse gymnastics competition held in the Olympic Games, *3905*

Men's singles tennis event held in the Olympic Games, *6036*

Men's triple jump event held in the Olympic Games, *6249*

Military revolver individual shooting event held in the Olympic Games, *5270*
Modern Olympic Games, *4606*
Motorcycle race on record, *4569*
Olympic Games at which Beethoven's "Ode to Joy" was sung, *4603*
Organization for croquet in Britain, *2669*
Professional basketball game, *1874*
Professional basketball team, *1873*
Rapid-fire pistol shooting individual event held in the Olympic Games, *5272*
Rules for modern darts, *2734*
Unlimited weight (super heavyweight) Greco-Roman wrestling event held in the Olympic Games, *6358*
Unlimited weight weightlifting events held in the Olympic Games, *6325*
World championships in figure skating, *2964*

1897

Amateur golfer to win two British Open championships, *3616*
Basketball rules setting the number of players on each team at five, *1875*
Boston Marathon, *4469*
Cheyenne Frontier Days rodeo, *4881*
Golfer to win the U.S. Amateur Championship twice in a row, *3617*
Golfer to win the U.S. Women's Amateur Championship twice, and then three times, in a row, *3622*
Golfing magazine in North America, *3618*
Grand final for Australian rules football, *3518*
Intercollegiate golf association in the United States, *3620*
Intercollegiate golf tournament in the United States, *3621*
Motorcycle race for two-wheeled vehicles, *4570*
National Amateur Athletic Union (AAU) basketball tournament, *1876*
National championships in gymnastics held in the United States, *3908*
National League player to hit 4 triples in a 9-inning baseball game, *1316*
National organization for dog racing in the United States, *2833*
Native American major league baseball player, *1317*
Rower from the United States to win the Diamond Sculls at the Henley Regatta, *4924*
Rules of Golf committee, *3619*
Stud book for horse racing published in North America, *4287*
World championships in 18.1 balkline billiards, *2450*
World championships in shooting, *5274*

1898

Brooklyn Dodgers regular season baseball game played at Washington Park II, *1318*

Invention of paddle tennis, *6194*
National organization for roller hockey (rink hockey), *4239*
National soccer (international football) league in Italy, *5542*
Professional basketball league, *1877*
Rubber-cored golf ball, and the first golf ball manufactured in the United States, *3623*
Sailor to complete a solo circumnavigation of the world, *5202*
Tennis player to win five consecutive women's doubles titles at the United States national championships, *6037*
U.S. Open to use a 72-hole format, *3624*
United States ice hockey league, *4048*
Woman automobile racer, *1046*

1899

All-England Championships in badminton, *1166*
American Amateur Hockey League championship, *4049*
Figure skater to win two, and then three, men's singles titles at the world championships, *2965*
Golf tee, *3625*
Golfer born in the United States to win a U.S. national championship, *3627*
Ice hockey game on record in Russia, *4050*
Professional ice hockey player of Black African ancestry on record, *4051*
Western Open, *3626*

1900

All-England Championships in badminton to include individual competitions, *1167*
Archer to win four Olympic gold medals in a single Olympic Games, and six overall, *1026*
Archery events held in the Olympic Games, *1025*
Athlete 10 years old or under to earn a gold medal in the Olympic Games, *4623*
Athlete from Belgium to win a gold medal in the Olympic Games, *4616*
Athlete from Canada to win a gold medal in the Olympic Games, *4621*
Athlete from Cuba to win a gold medal in the Olympic Games, *4617*
Athlete from Italy to win a gold medal in the Olympic Games, *4618*
Athlete to win four gold medals in a single Olympic Games, *4627*
Athletes from Sweden to win a gold medal in the Olympic Games, *4622*
Athletes from the Netherlands to win gold medals in the Olympic Games, *4624*
Cricket event at the Olympic Games, *2653*
Croquet events at the Olympic Games, *2670*
Davis Cup match, *6038*
Decathlon championship on record, *2736*

1900—*continued*

Fencer to win both the men's individual sabre and épée titles in the Olympic Games, *2912*

Golfer to win both the U.S. Open and British Open, *3628*

Hammer-throw event held at the Olympic Games, *3981*

Individual jumping equestrian event held in the Olympic Games, *2841*

Intercollegiate wrestling match in the United States, *6359*

Masters sabre fencing competition held in the Olympic Games, *2905*

Men's 200-meter backstroke swimming event held in the Olympic Games, *5788*

Men's 200-meter freestyle swimming event held in the Olympic Games, *5789*

Men's 200-meter hurdles event held in the Olympic Games, *4325*

Men's 200-meter race held in the Olympic Games, *4981*

Men's 400-meter hurdles event held in the Olympic Games, *4324*

Men's 4000-meter freestyle swimming event held in the Olympic Games, *5792*

Men's 4000-meter steeplechase event held in the Olympic Games, *4979*

Men's 5000-meter team running event held in the Olympic Games, *4982*

Men's 60-meter running event held in the Olympic Games, *4976*

Men's all-around gymnastics competition held in the Olympic Games, *3909*

Men's amateurs and masters épée fencing competition held in the Olympic Games, *2904*

Men's eight-oared shell with coxswain rowing event held in the Olympic Games, *4925*

Men's four-oared shell with coxswain rowing event held in the Olympic Games, *4928*

Men's golf event in the Olympic Games, *3629*

Men's individual épée fencing competition held in the Olympic Games, *2902*

Men's masters épée fencing competition held in the Olympic Games, *2903*

Men's obstacle swimming race held in the Olympic Games, *5790*

Men's pair-oared shell with coxswain rowing event held in the Olympic Games, *4926*

Men's single sculls rowing event held in the Olympic Games, *4927*

Men's standing high jump event held in the Olympic Games, *4020*

Men's standing long jump event held in the Olympic Games, *4427*

Men's standing triple jump event held in the Olympic Games, *6250*

Men's steeplechase event held at the Olympic Games, *4977*

Men's underwater swimming race held in the Olympic Games, *5791*

Military revolver and military rifle team shooting events held in the Olympic Games, *5280*

Military rifle individual shooting event held in the Olympic Games, *5279*

Mixed doubles tennis event held in the Olympic Games, *6039*

Moving target individual shooting event held in the Olympic Games, *5277*

National soccer (international football) league in Germany, *5543*

National team to sweep the medals in the men's 110-meter hurdles in the Olympic Games, *4323*

National team to sweep the medals in the men's individual foil fencing competition in the Olympic Games, *2900*

National team to sweep the medals in the men's masters foil fencing event in the Olympic Games, *2901*

National team to sweep the medals in the men's singles tennis event in the Olympic Games, *6040*

National team to sweep the rapid-fire pistol individual shooting event in the Olympic Games, *5278*

National team to sweep the top spots in the men's shot put in the Olympic Games, *5330*

National team to sweep the top spots in the men's triple jump in the Olympic Games, *6251*

National trap shooting tournament in the United States, *5275*

Official code of rules for snooker, *2451*

Olympic Games held in France, and outside Greece, *4626*

Olympic Games in which animals were deliberately killed, *4619*

Olympic Games to include women athletes, *4615*

Polo event held in the Olympic Games, *4865*

Rugby event held in the Olympic Games, *4965*

Runner from Europe to win the men's 1500-meter title in the Olympic Games, *4978*

Runner from Europe to win the men's 800-meter title in the Olympic Games, *4980*

Runner to hold the officially accepted world record in the men's 400-meter event, *4983*

Soccer (international football) event held in the Olympic Games, *5544*

Tennis player to win two men's doubles titles in the Olympic Games, *6042*

Trap (clay pigeon) shooting individual event held in the Olympic Games, *5276*

Tug-of-war event held in the Olympic Games, *6267*

Water polo event held in the Olympic Games, *6301*

Woman from the United States to win a gold medal in the Olympic Games, *4625*

Woman to win a gold medal in the Olympic Games, *4620*

Women's golf event in the Olympic Games, *3630*

Women's singles tennis event held in the Olympic Games, *6041*

1901

American League baseball game, *1331*

American League convention, *1329*

American League player to have 6 hits in a 9-inning baseball game, *1341*

American League player to hit for the cycle (single, double, triple, and home run) in a single game, *1342*

Association of professional golfers, *3631*

Baltimore Orioles regular season baseball game played at Oriole Park, *1330*

Baseball pitcher to lead the American League in strikeouts, *1320*

Baseball player to lead the American League in batting average, *1321*

Baseball player to lead the American League in home runs, *1322*

Baseball player to lead the American League in runs scored, *1323*

Baseball player to lead the American League in slugging average, *1324*

Baseball player to lead the American League in total bases, *1325*

Baseball team to win an American League pennant, *1326*

Boston Red Sox regular season baseball game played at the Huntington Avenue Grounds, *1340*

Chicago White Sox regular season baseball game played at Southside Park, *1332*

Cleveland Indians regular season baseball game played at League Park I, *1336*

Detroit Tigers regular season baseball game played at Bennett Park, *1333*

Football Association Challenge Cup soccer (international football) tournament played before more than 100,000 spectators, *5545*

Golf course developed on cleared land, with grass grown entirely from seed, *3632*

Golfer to win a major tournament with a rubber-cored golf ball, *3633*

Golfer to win the U.S. Open in a playoff, *3634*

Governing body for diving, *2790*

Home run in the American League, *1334*

Introduction of field hockey into the United States, *4035*

Long-jumper to hold the officially accepted world record in the men's event, *4428*

Milwaukee Brewers regular season baseball game played at Lloyd Street Park, *1339*

National bowling championships in the United States, *2482*

Nordic Games, *4365*

Philadelphia Athletics regular season baseball game played at Columbia Park, *1335*

Pittsburgh Pirates National League pennant, *1327*

Runner to win two consecutive Boston Marathons, *4470*

Skipper to win the America's Cup sailing race twice in a row, *5203*

Sliding seat developed for the luge (toboggan), *4451*

Triple Crown hitter in the American League, *1328*

Two home runs in a single American League game, *1338*

Washington Senators regular season baseball game played in American League Park, *1337*

1902

African-American boxer born in the United States to win a world boxing title, *2524*

African-American professional football player, *3129*

Baseball player to lead the American League in triples in two consecutive years, *1343*

Cincinnati Reds regular season baseball game played at The Palace of the Fans, *1346*

College football player to score five rushing touchdowns in a major bowl game, *3130*

Colombian major league baseball player, *1344*

Golfer to shoot under 80 in all four rounds of the U.S. Open, *3635*

Ice hockey team to win the Stanley Cup three times, *4052*

National governing body in table tennis, *5981*

Philadelphia Athletics American League pennant, *1345*

Professional football game played at night, *3131*

Professional football league, *3132*

Rose Bowl football game, *3133*

Runs specially built for bobsleds, *2465*

St. Louis Browns regular season baseball game played at Sportsman's Park, *1347*

Swimmer to race 100 yards in one minute, *5793*

Three consecutive home runs in a single inning of an American League game, *1348*

Woman figure skater to compete in a world championship, and to win a world figure skating medal, *2966*

1903

Boston Red Sox World Series victory, *1349*

Boxer to hold the undisputed world light heavyweight title, *2525*

Boxer to hold world titles in three different weight classes, *2526*

Football stadium, built specifically for the sport, *3134*

1903—*continued*

Golfer to win three men's U.S. Amateur titles, *3636*

Golfer to win two U.S. Open championships, *3637*

International Cross-Country Championships, *4984*

International motorboat (powerboat) race, *4563*

Major league baseball game played by the New York Highlanders, *1351*

National governing body for motorboat (powerboat) racing, *4564*

National governing body in motorcycle racing, *4571*

New York Highlanders regular season baseball game played at Hilltop Park, *1353*

Pitcher to pitch five complete games in a World Series, *1350*

Pitcher to win a World Series game, *1354*

Professional ice hockey club in the United States, *4053*

Strathcona Cup curling competition, *2676*

Tour de France cycling race, *2689*

Washington Senators regular season baseball game played at Griffith Stadium, *1352*

Woman driver to win an automobile race, *1047*

World championships in gymnastics, *3910*

World Series, *1355*

World Series game, *1356*

World Series home run, *1357*

1904

Archery events for women held in the Olympic Games, *1027*

Athlete of Black African ancestry to compete in the Olympic Games, *4629*

Bantamweight and featherweight boxing events held in the Olympic Games, and the first boxer to win two gold medals in a single Olympic Games, *2527*

Bantamweight freestyle wrestling event held in the Olympic Games, *6362*

Baseball pitcher to lead the American League in shutouts for two consecutive years, *1358*

Baseball player to lead the American League in batting average for two consecutive years, *1359*

Baseball player to lead the American League in runs scored in two consecutive years, *1360*

Baseball player to lead the American League in slugging average for two consecutive years, *1361*

Baseball player to lead the National League in hits in three consecutive years, *1362*

Baseball player to lead the National League in singles in three consecutive years, *1363*

Baseball team to win two consecutive American League pennants, *1364*

Black athletes from Africa to participate in the Olympic Games, *4630*

Discus throw event in the Olympic Games to be decided by a throw-off, *2755*

Featherweight freestyle wrestling event held in the Olympic Games, *6363*

Flyweight boxing event in the Olympic Games, *2528*

Flyweight freestyle wrestling event held in the Olympic Games, *6364*

Golfer from the United States to win the British Amateur Championship, *3638*

Golfer to win the British Open golf championship in under 300 for 72 holes, *3639*

Gymnast with a wooden leg to win a medal in the Olympic Games, *3912*

Heavyweight boxing event held in the Olympic Games, *2529*

International automobile racing organization, *1048*

International governing body for soccer (international football), *5546*

International governing body in motorcycle racing, *4572*

International professional ice hockey league, *4054*

Jai alai game in the United States, *4380*

Lacrosse event held in the Olympic Games, *4420*

Light flyweight freestyle wrestling event held in the Olympic Games, *6365*

Lightweight boxing event held in the Olympic Games, *2530*

Lightweight freestyle wrestling event held in the Olympic Games, *6366*

Major league baseball player of the 20th century to pitch for more than 40 wins in a single season, *1365*

Major league pitcher to pitch 30 consecutive complete games, *1366*

Men's 100-yard (later 100-meter) backstroke swimming event held in the Olympic Games, *5794*

Men's 4-mile team race held in the Olympic Games, *4988*

Men's 440-yard (later 400-meter) breaststroke event held in the Olympic Games, *5796*

Men's 50-yard (later 50-meter) freestyle swimming event held in the Olympic Games, *5795*

Men's 56-pound weight throw event held in the Olympic Games, *6323*

Men's 880-yard freestyle swimming event held in the Olympic Games, *5797*

Men's decathlon event held in the Olympic Games, *2737*

Men's double sculls rowing event held in the Olympic Games, *4929*

Men's four-oared shell without coxswain rowing event held in the Olympic Games, *4930*

Men's pair-oared shell without coxswain rowing event held in the Olympic Games, *4931*

Men's platform diving event held in the Olympic Games, *2791*

Men's team combined exercises gymnastics competition in the Olympic Games, *3911*

Men's team foil fencing competition held in the Olympic Games, *2906*

Men's triathlon event held in the Olympic Games, *6234*

Middleweight boxing event held in the Olympic Games, *2531*

National team to sweep the medals in the men's doubles tennis event in the Olympic Games, *6043*

National team to sweep the medals in the men's single sculls rowing event in the Olympic Games, *4932*

National team to sweep the top honors in the men's horizontal bar, long horse vault, side (pommel) horse, and rings gymnastics competitions in the Olympic Games, *3913*

National team to sweep the top spots in the men's pole vault in the Olympic Games, *4838*

National team to sweep the top spots in the men's triple jump in the Olympic Games, *6251*

National team to sweep the top three medals in the men's 100- and 200-meter running events in the Olympic Games, *4990*

National team to sweep the top three medals in the men's 400-meter running event in the Olympic Games, *4985*

Olympic Games held in the United States, *4628*

Organization of professional wrestlers in the United States, *6360*

Roque event (a type of croquet) at the Olympic Games, *2671*

Rowers to win two consecutive gold medals in the men's eight-oared shell with coxswain competition in the Olympic Games, *4933*

Runner for the United States to win the men's marathon at the Olympic Games, *4471*

Runner from the United States to win the men's 1500-meter race in the Olympic Games, *4989*

Runner from the United States to win the men's 800-meter race in the Olympic Games, *4987*

Runner from the United States to win the men's steeplechase event at the Olympic Games, *4986*

Runner to win both the men's 100- and 200-meter races in the same Olympic Games, *4991*

Soccer (international football) team from Britain to play in the United States, *5547*

Super heavyweight freestyle wrestling event held in the Olympic Games, *6367*

Swimmer to win both the men's 220-yard (later 200-meter) and 440-yard (later 400-meter) freestyle events in a single Olympic Games, *5798*

Team archery event held in the Olympic Games, *1028*

Tennis player from the United States to win the men's singles title in the Olympic Games, *6044*

Triple-jumper to win two consecutive men's titles in the Olympic Games, *6252*

Water polo team from the United States to win the title at the Olympic Games, *6302*

Weightlifter to win two medals in the same Olympic Games, and the first from the United States to win a weightlifting Olympic gold medal, *6326*

Welterweight boxing event held in the Olympic Games, *2532*

Welterweight freestyle wrestling event held in the Olympic Games, *6368*

World championships in Greco-Roman wrestling, *6361*

1905

African-American basketball club in the New York City area, *1878*

Australian national tennis championships, *6045*

Baseball pitcher to lead the National League in strikeouts for three consecutive years, *1367*

Boxer to retire undefeated as world heavyweight champion, *2533*

Figure skater to win five consecutive men's singles titles at the world championships, *2967*

Golfer to win the U.S. Open championship four times, and two and three times consecutively, *3640*

Gymnast to win two consecutive men's horse vault titles in the world championships, *3914*

Gymnast to win two consecutive men's parallel bar titles in the world championships, *3915*

Ice hockey team to win the Stanley Cup three times in a row, *4055*

International governing body for bowls, *2483*

International governing body for gliding (soaring) competitions, *3530*

International match between female golfers, *3641*

New York Giants World Series victory, *1368*

Patent for dimple-patterned golf balls, *3642*

Tennis player to win four women's singles titles at the United States national championships, *6046*

Tennis players to win eight Wimbledon men's doubles championships, *6047*

World Professional Basketball Championship, *1879*

1906

African-American basketball league in the New York City area, *1880*

All-around wrestling title awarded in the Olympic Games, *6369*

Athlete from Finland to win an official gold medal in the Olympic Games, *4641*

Baseball player to lead the American League in singles in three consecutive years, *1369*

Bermuda Race, *5204*

Chicago White Sox World Series victory, *1371*

Discus-thrower to win two, and then three, consecutive men's titles in the Olympic Games, *2757*

Dueling pistol shooting events held in the Olympic Games, *5282*

Fencer to win both the men's individual sabre and épée titles in the Olympic Games, *2912*

Fencer to win both the men's masters épée and masters sabre competitions in the Olympic Games, *2907*

Fencer to win men's individual and team épée titles in the same Olympic Games, *2908*

Fencer to win two men's individual sabre titles in the Olympic Games, *2909*

Figure skater to win the women's singles title in the world championships, *2968*

Free rifle team shooting event held in the Olympic Games, *5281*

Golf ball with compressed air inside the rubber core, *3643*

Golfer to win the U.S. Open with a 72-hole score under 300, *3644*

Grand Prix automobile race, *1049*

International balloon race, *1182*

Lightweight Greco-Roman wrestling event held in the Olympic Games, *6370*

Long-jumper to win two consecutive men's titles in the Olympic Games, *4429*

Major league pitcher of the 20th century to strike out four batters in a single inning, *1370*

Men's 3000-meter walk event held in the Olympic Games, *6288*

Men's 4 x 250-meter (later 4 x 200-meter) freestyle relay swimming event held in the Olympic Games, *5799*

Men's 5-mile event held in the Olympic Games, *4992*

Men's freestyle javelin event held in the Olympic Games, *4381*

Men's Greek-style discus throw event held in the Olympic Games, *2756*

Men's pentathlon held in the modern Olympic Games, *4814*

Men's stone throw event held in the Olympic Games, *5769*

Men's team épée fencing competition held in the Olympic Games, *2910*

Men's team sabre fencing competition held in the Olympic Games, *2911*

Middleweight Greco-Roman wrestling event held in the Olympic Games, *6371*

National team sent from the United States to the Olympic Games, *4631*

Olympic Games held after two years, instead of four, *4632*

Rowers to win two gold medals in pair-oared shell with coxswain rowing events in the same Olympic Games, *4934*

Runner to win both the men's 400- and 800-meter events in the same Olympic Games, *4993*

Tennis player to win three gold medals in tennis in the same Olympic Games, *6048*

Use of the forward pass in American-style football, *3135*

Woman figure skater to perform the sit spin, *2969*

World Series between two teams from the same city, *1372*

1907

Baseball pitcher to lead the American League in strikeouts for six consecutive years, *1373*

Baseball player to lead the American League in home runs in four consecutive years, *1374*

Baseball player to lead the American League in triples in three consecutive years, *1375*

Bowling league for women in the United States, *2484*

Chicago Cubs World Series victory, *1376*

Detroit Tigers American League pennant, *1377*

Figure skater to perform the salchow jump in competition, *2970*

Figure skater to win two consecutive women's singles titles in the world championships, *2971*

Golfer from outside Great Britain to win the British Open, *3645*

Ice hockey game played in Australia, *4056*

International and transcontinental automobile race, *1050*

International governing body for rackets, *4871*

International governing body in shooting, *5283*

National championships in squash, *5757*

Olympian Athletic League (OAL) title, *1881*

Primavera cycling race, *2690*

Royal International Horse Show, *2842*

1908

6-meter-class sailing event held in the Olympic Games, *5205*

8-meter-class sailing event in the Olympic Games, *5206*

Athlete from Africa, and from South Africa, to win a gold medal in the Olympic Games, *4638*

1908—*continued*

Running deer (single shot) team shooting event held in the Olympic Games, *5286*

Shooters from the United States to win the military revolver team event in the Olympic Games, *5287*

Shooters from the United States to win the military rifle team shooting title in the Olympic Games, *5288*

Small-bore rifle moving and disappearing target individual shooting events held in the Olympic Games, *5289*

Small-bore rifle (prone) individual shooting event held in the Olympic Games, *5290*

Small-bore rifle team shooting event held in the Olympic Games, *5291*

Swimmer to win two consecutive men's 100-meter freestyle titles in the Olympic Games, *5802*

Swimmer to win two consecutive men's 1500-meter freestyle titles in the Olympic Games, *5803*

Trap (clay pigeon) team shooting event in the Olympic Games, *5292*

Use of numbers on college football uniforms, *3136*

Water polo player to win two, and then three, gold medals in the Olympic Games, *6303*

Woman golf professional, *3646*

Woman to participate in an Olympic yachting event, *5207*

Golfer to win both the British Women's Amateur and the U.S. Women's Amateur titles, *3647*

Grey Cup awarded to the rugby football champion in Canada, *4966*

Gymnast to win two men's horizontal bar titles in the world championships, *3916*

International airplane races, *1001*

International cricket organization, *2654*

International horseshoe tournament, *4321*

Major league baseball pitcher to walk eight players in a single inning, *1396*

Moto-cross trials riding competition, *4573*

National championship in Indy Car racing, *1051*

Nations Cup equestrian team event, *2843*

Open-air rink featuring artificial ice, *2981*

Paved automobile racing track, *1052*

Philadelphia Athletics regular season baseball game played at Shibe Park, *1393*

Pittsburgh Pirates regular season baseball game played at Forbes Field, *1394*

Pittsburgh Pirates World Series victory, *1392*

Polo team from the United States to win the Westchester Cup, *4866*

Runner to complete the men's marathon in under 2:55 hours, *4473*

Shot-putter to hold the officially accepted world record in the men's event, *5331*

Tour of Italy (Giro d'Italia) cycling race, *2693*

Unassisted triple play of the 20th century in major league baseball, *1395*

1909

Baseball player to lead the American League in hits in three consecutive years, *1382*

Baseball player to lead the American League in runs batted in for three consecutive years, *1383*

Baseball player to lead the American League in total bases for three consecutive years, *1384*

Baseball player to lead the National League in batting average for four consecutive years, *1385*

Baseball player to lead the National League in doubles in four consecutive years, *1386*

Baseball player to lead the National League in runs batted in for four consecutive years, *1387*

Baseball player to lead the National League in slugging average for three consecutive years, *1388*

Baseball player to lead the National League in total bases for four consecutive years, *1389*

Baseball team to win three consecutive American League pennants, *1390*

Cork-centered baseball, *1391*

Figure skaters from Great Britain, and the first married couple, to win the pairs title in the world championships, *2980*

1910

Baseball player to lead the National League in triples in two consecutive years, *1397*

Chicago White Sox regular season baseball game played at Comiskey Park, *1401*

Cleveland Indians regular season baseball game played at League Park II, *1400*

English Ice Hockey League Championship, *4058*

Figure skater to win three and then four consecutive women's singles titles in the world championships, *2982*

Golf club with a steel shaft, *3648*

Golfer to win five British Open championships, *3649*

International air race in the United States, *1002*

International governing body for competitive skiing, *5361*

Pendleton Round-Up rodeo, *4882*

Philadelphia Athletics World Series victory, *1398*

Skeet shooting, *5293*

Tennis player to win two Australian national men's singles championships, *6050*

United States President to throw out the first ball in a major league baseball opening day game, *1399*

1911

African-American All-America team, *3137*

African-American All-Star Team in professional baseball, *1402*

African-American basketball team at Howard University, *1882*

Baseball pitcher to lead the American League in winning percentage for two consecutive years, *1403*

Baseball player to lead the American League in runs scored in three consecutive years, *1404*

Figure skater to win 10 men's singles titles at the world championships, *2983*

Figure skaters from Finland to win the pairs title in the world championships, *2984*

Golfer born in the United States to win the U.S. Open, *3650*

Golfer to win British Open titles in three decades, *3651*

Indianapolis 500, *1054*

Inter-Empire Sports tournament, *4366*

International governing body for boxing, *2535*

King George V Gold Cup, *2844*

Major league baseball players to be named Most Valuable Players of their leagues, *1405*

Monte Carlo Rally, *1053*

Organized downhill ski race, *5362*

Pommel horse competition held at the world championships in gymnastics, *3917*

Professional ice hockey league on North America's West Coast, *4059*

Runner to hold the officially accepted world record in the men's 10,000-meter event, *4999*

Tennis player to win three consecutive women's singles titles at the United States national championships, *6051*

Tennis player to win two Australian national men's doubles championships, *6052*

Triple-jumper to hold the officially accepted world record in the men's event, *6253*

1912

African-American Intercollegiate Athletic Association, *5744*

Athlete to die while participating in the modern Olympic Games, *4644*

Athlete to win both the men's decathlon and pentathlon in the Olympic Games, and the first Native American to win an Olympic gold medal, *2738*

Baseball player to hit more than .400 in two consecutive years in the American League, *1406*

Baseball player to lead the American League in slugging average for six consecutive years, *1407*

Baseball player to lead the National League in bases on balls for two consecutive years, *1408*

Baseball player to lead the National League in stolen bases for four consecutive years, *1409*

Boston Red Sox regular season baseball game played at Fenway Park, *1413*

Calgary Stampede rodeo, *4883*

Cincinnati Reds regular season baseball game played at Crosley Field, *1412*

Colored Intercollegiate Baseball Association (CIBA), *1410*

Detroit Tigers regular season baseball game played at Tiger Stadium, *1414*

Discus-thrower to hold the officially accepted world record in the men's event, *2760*

Equestrian to win both individual and team gold medals in the three-day event competitions in the Olympic Games, *2846*

Fencer to win two consecutive men's individual sabre titles, and men's team sabre titles, in the Olympic Games, *2914*

Golfer to win eight British Amateur championships, *3652*

Gymnast to win two consecutive men's all-around titles in the Olympic Games, *3918*

High-jumper to hold the officially accepted world record in the men's event, *4021*

Individual dressage equestrian competition held in the Olympic Games, *2845*

Individual skiing-and-shooting competition, *2429*

International governing body for wrestling, *6374*

International governing organization for track and field (athletics), *6204*

Javelin-thrower to hold the officially accepted world record in the men's event, *4384*

Men's 10,000-meter walk held in the Olympic Games, *6290*

Men's 3000-meter team running event held in the Olympic Games, *5004*

Men's 4 x 100-meter relay track event held in the Olympic Games, *5003*

Men's 5000- and 10,000-meter events held in the Olympic Games, *5008*

Men's cross-country team track race held in the Olympic Games, *5005*

Men's discus throw event for both hands held in the Olympic Games, *2761*

Men's individual cross-country event held in the Olympic Games, *5006*

Men's javelin event for both hands held in the Olympic Games, *4383*

Men's modern pentathlon held in the Olympic Games, *4815*

Men's plain high dive event held in the Olympic Games, *2795*

Men's shot put event for both hands held in the Olympic Games, *5332*

National team to sweep the medals in the men's 200-meter breaststroke event in the Olympic Games, *5806*

1912—*continued*

National team to sweep the top medals in men's springboard diving in the Olympic Games, *2794*

Native-American athlete to win a gold medal at the Olympic Games, *4645*

Olympic Games held in Sweden, or in Scandinavia, *4642*

Olympic Games to use electronic timing devices and a public address system, *4643*

Pacific Coast Hockey Association championship, *4060*

Pole-vaulter to hold the officially accepted world record in the men's event, *4839*

Runner to hold the officially accepted world record in the men's 100-meter dash, *5001*

Runner to hold the officially accepted world record in the men's 1500-meter event, *5000*

Runner to hold the officially accepted world record in the men's 800-meter event, *5002*

Runner to win two consecutive gold medals in the men's 4 x 400-meter relay in the Olympic Games, *5007*

Shooter from the United States to win the men's trap (clay pigeon) individual shooting title in the Olympic Games, *5295*

Shooter to win both the rapid-fire pistol and the free pistol individual events, and the first from the United States to win either event, in the Olympic Games, *5296*

Shooters from the United States to win the trap (clay pigeon) team shooting event in the Olympic Games, *5294*

Soccer (international football) player to win two gold medals in the Olympic Games, *5548*

Swimmer from the United States to win the men's 100-meter backstroke title in the Olympic Games, *5807*

Swimmer to race the women's 100-meter freestyle in under 1:20 minutes, *5804*

Team jumping (Prix des Nations) equestrian event held in the Olympic Games, *2847*

Three-day event individual equestrian competition held in the Olympic Games, *2848*

Three-day event team equestrian competition held in the Olympic Games, *2849*

Triple Crown hitter in the National League, *1411*

Use of the double-wing formation in football, *3138*

Water polo player to win two, and then three, gold medals in the Olympic Games, *6303*

Woman figure skater to perform an axel in competition, *2985*

Woman pilot to fly across the English Channel, *1003*

Women's 100-meter freestyle swimming event held in the Olympic Games, *5805*

Women's 4 x 100-meter freestyle relay swimming event in the Olympic Games, *5808*

Women's lacrosse organization, *4421*

Wrestling event in the Olympic Games to have no gold-medalist, *6375*

1913

African-American Southern Intercollegiate Athletic Conference (SIAC), *5745*

Amateur golfer to win the U.S. Open, *3653*

Bowler to win four titles in the American Bowling Congress (ABC) national championships, *2485*

Boxer to be undisputed world flyweight champion, *2536*

Brooklyn Dodgers regular season baseball game played at Ebbets Field, *1415*

Far Eastern Games, *4367*

Figure skaters from Austria to win the pairs title in the world championships, *2986*

Floor exercise competition held at the world championships in gymnastics, *3919*

Golfer to win four U.S. Amateur titles, *3654*

Gymnast to win three consecutive men's horizontal bar titles in the world championships, *3920*

Gymnast to win two consecutive men's pommel horse titles in the world championships, *3921*

Hammer-thrower to hold the officially accepted world record in the men's event, *3982*

International competition in volleyball, *6273*

International governing body for fencing, *2915*

International governing body for tennis, *6055*

International trials competition in moto-cross racing, *4574*

Leondi Big Five, *1883*

Mixed doubles championships at Wimbledon, *6053*

National Challenge Cup for soccer (international football), *5549*

Runner to hold the officially accepted world record in the men's mile race, *5009*

Schneider Cup international seaplane (hydroaeroplane) race, *1004*

Women's doubles championships at Wimbledon, *6054*

1914

Baseball team to sweep the World Series, *1418*

Boston Braves World Series victory, *1416*

Figure skater to win the men's singles title in the U.S. national championships, *2987*

Figure skater to win the women's singles title at the U.S. national championships, *2988*

Figure skaters to win a gold medal in ice dancing in the U.S. national championships, *2989*

Figure skaters to win the pairs title in the U.S. national championships, *2990*

Golf club in Japan, *3655*

Golfer to win six British Open golf championships, *3656*

List of officially accepted world records in track and field (athletics), *6205*

Major league baseball pitcher of the 20th century to have an earned run average of less than 1.0 for a season, *1417*

National figure skating championships in the United States, *2991*

Speed skater to be world champion in men's long-distance speed skating five times, *5637*

Speed skater to skate the 1500 meters in under 2:20 minutes, *5638*

Tennis player to win seven Wimbledon women's singles championships, *6056*

1915

African-American college football running back to be named to Walter Camp's All-America team, *3139*

Baseball pitcher to lead the American League in shutouts for three consecutive years, *1419*

Baseball player to lead the American League in batting average for nine consecutive years, *1420*

Baseball player to lead the National League in home runs in three consecutive years, *1421*

Boston Braves regular season baseball game played at Braves Field, *1423*

Philadelphia Phillies National League pennant, *1422*

United States men's singles tennis national championship matches played at the West Side Tennis Club, *6057*

1916

African-American college football player to play in the Rose Bowl, *3140*

Chicago Cubs regular season baseball game played at Wrigley Field, *1425*

Golfer to win both the U.S. Amateur and U.S. Open championships in the same year, and to win the U.S. Open in under 290 for 72 holes, *3659*

Major league baseball player of the 20th century to pitch 16 shutouts in a single season, *1424*

Miniature golf course, *3657*

Modern Olympic Games to be canceled because of war, *4646*

National bowling championships for women in the United States, *2486*

National bowling organization for women in the United States, *2487*

New York Celtics semiprofessional basketball team, *1884*

Professional Golfers' Association (PGA) Championship, *3658*

Washington State University win in college football's Rose Bowl, *3141*

1917

Baseball pitcher to lead the National League in earned run average for three consecutive years, *1426*

Baseball pitcher to lead the National League in shutouts for three consecutive years, *1427*

Baseball pitcher to lead the National League in strikeouts for four consecutive years, *1428*

Baseball player to lead the American League in stolen bases for three consecutive years, *1429*

Baseball player to lead the National League in runs scored in two consecutive years, *1430*

Four teams in the National Hockey League, *4061*

Hockey player from the United States to play in the National Hockey League, *4062*

Hockey team from outside Canada to win the Stanley Cup, *4063*

Major league baseball pitcher of the 20th century to pitch 19 straight wins, *1431*

National Hockey League game, *4064*

National Hockey League goal, *4065*

University of Oregon win in college football's Rose Bowl, *3142*

1918

African-American lineman to be named to Walter Camp's All-America football team, *3143*

Boston Marathon to be canceled, *4474*

Hockey player to lead the National Hockey League in scoring, *4066*

National Hockey League shutout, *4068*

National Hockey League team to win the Stanley Cup, *4067*

New York Celtics fully professional basketball team, *1885*

Orienteering as a sport, *4805*

Sporting event at which the United States national anthem was played, *5746*

Tennis player to win four straight women's singles titles at the United States national championships, *6058*

1919

African-American professional football coach, *3144*

Baseball pitcher to lead the American League in earned run average for two consecutive years, *1432*

Baseball pitcher to lead the American League in strikeouts for eight consecutive years, *1433*

Baseball player in the American League to hit four grand slam home runs in a single season, *1434*

Cincinnati Reds World Series victory, *1436*

Cuban, and first Hispanic-American, to play in a World Series game, *1435*

1919—*continued*

Golf book to use high-speed sequential photographs, *3660*

Golfer to be a full-time tournament professional in the United States, *3661*

Golfer to win two straight Professional Golfers' Association (PGA) Championships, *3662*

Horse to win America's Triple Crown, *4289*

Javelin-thrower to break the 210-foot barrier, *4385*

Mechanical rabbit used in dog racing, *2834*

Stanley Cup hockey playoffs to be canceled, *4069*

United States national four-wall handball championships, *4001*

1920

American League team to top 1 million paying customers at home in a single season, *1437*

American Professional Football League convention, *3146*

American Professional Football League game, *3147*

Athlete from Brazil to win a gold medal in the Olympic Games, *4650*

Athlete from Estonia to win a gold medal in the Olympic Games, *4651*

Athlete to win gold medals in both the Summer and Winter Olympics, *4674*

Baseball player to die of injuries suffered during a major league baseball game, *1446*

Bowler to win two all-events titles in the American Bowling Congress (ABC) championships, *2488*

British Open golf championship to be administered by the Royal and Ancient Golf Club of St. Andrews, *3664*

Brothers to play on opposing teams in a World Series, *1447*

Cleveland Indians World Series victory, *1438*

College football game to be broadcast on radio, *3148*

Convention of the Negro National League, *1441*

Cyclist to win the Tour de France three times, *2694*

Cyclo-cross races, *2695*

Diver from the United States to win the men's springboard diving event in the Olympic Games, *2796*

Equestrian to win two consecutive medals in the team jumping (Prix des Nations) event in the Olympic Games, *2851*

Featherweight weightlifting event held in the Olympic Games, *6328*

Fencer to win five gold medals in a single Olympic Games, and to win two consecutive men's individual foil titles in the Olympic Games, *2916*

Figure riding individual and team events held in the Olympic Games, *2850*

Figure skater from Sweden to win the women's singles title in the Olympic Games, *2997*

Figure skaters from Finland to win the pairs title in the Olympic Games, *2999*

Flag showing five interlocking rings to symbolize the Olympic Games, *4647*

Formal instruction in karate, *4529*

Golf practice range, *3665*

Governing body for boxing in the United States, *2537*

Grand slam home run in World Series history, *1448*

Gymnasts to win two consecutive gold medals in the men's team combined exercises in the Olympic Games, *3922*

Harvard University win in college football's Rose Bowl, *3145*

Home run by a pitcher in a World Series, *1449*

Home run hit by Babe Ruth as a New York Yankees player, *1442*

Hurdler to race the 400-meter hurdles in under 55 seconds, *4328*

Ice hockey event to be held in the Olympic Games, *4073*

International figure skating competition at which recorded music was standard, *2996*

International governing body in weightlifting, *6327*

International soccer (international football) match played by women, *5550*

Light heavyweight boxing event held in the Olympic Games, *2538*

Light heavyweight freestyle wrestling event held in the Olympic Games, *6377*

Light heavyweight weightlifting event held in the Olympic Games, *6331*

Lightweight weightlifting event held in the Olympic Games, *6329*

Major league baseball player to get 257 hits in a single season, *1439*

Men's Finn-class sailing event in the Olympic Games, *5208*

Men's world championships in ice hockey, *4070*

Middleweight weightlifting event held in the Olympic Games, *6330*

Modern Olympic Games at which member countries were barred from competing, *4649*

National Hockey League player to score seven goals in a single game, *4072*

National League game to last 26 innings, *1443*

National team to sweep the medals in the men's 100-meter freestyle in the Olympic Games, *5809*

National team to sweep the medals in the women's 100-meter freestyle swimming event in the Olympic Games, *5810*

National team to win two Olympic gold medals in the tug-of-war competition, *6268*

Negro National League game, *1444*

Olympic Games held in Belgium, *4648*

Ottawa Senators National Hockey League Stanley Cup championship, *4071*

Prix de l'Arc de Triomphe horse race, *4290*

Pulitzer Trophy airplane race, *1005*

Rapid-fire pistol and free pistol team events held in the Olympic Games, *5299*

Runner from Africa to win the men's 400-meters title in the Olympic Games, *5010*

Running deer (double shot) team shooting event held in the Olympic Games, *5297*

Shooter to win five gold medals in shooting in the Olympic Games, *5298*

Shooters from the United States to win the small-bore rifle team title in the Olympic Games, *5300*

St. Louis Cardinals regular season baseball game played at Sportsman's Park II, *1445*

Swimmer from the United States to win the men's 1500-meter freestyle title in the Olympic Games, *5811*

Swimmer to win Olympic gold medals 8 years apart, and to win Olympic medals 12 years apart, *5813*

Swimmers from the United States to win the women's 4 x 100-meter freestyle relay title in the Olympic Games, *5814*

Team from the United States to win the men's 4 x 100-meter relay track event in the Olympic Games, *5011*

Team from the United States to win the rugby event in the Olympic Games, *4967*

Tennis player to win six United States mixed doubles titles, *6059*

Thrower from the United States to win the men's 56-pound weight throw in the Olympic Games, *6324*

Unassisted triple play in the World Series, *1440*

Woman figure skater to perform a full-revolution jump, the salchow, in competition, *2998*

Women's 300-meter (later 400-meter) freestyle event held in the Olympic Games, *5812*

Women's doubles tennis event held in the Olympic Games, *6060*

Women's springboard diving event held in the Olympic Games, *2797*

Wrestler to win gold medals in three different divisions in the Olympic Games, *6378*

Wrestler to win two consecutive lightweight Greco-Roman titles in the Olympic Games, *6376*

1921

American Professional Football League champions, *3150*

Baseball player to have 100 extra-base hits in a single American League season, *1450*

Baseball player to lead the American League in bases on balls for two consecutive years, *1451*

Baseball player to lead the National League in bases on balls for three consecutive years, *1452*

Boxer to hold the super-featherweight (junior lightweight) title, *2542*

Boxing match to be broadcast on radio, *2540*

Boxing match to have a $1 million gate, and the first heavyweight bout to be broadcast on radio, *2541*

Commissioner of Baseball, *1456*

Golfer born in the United States to win the Professional Golfers' Association (PGA) Championship, *3666*

Golfer who was a United States citizen to win the British Open, *3667*

International governing body for equestrian competitions, *2852*

International governing body for trap shooting, *5301*

International hockey game played in Sweden, *4075*

Italian Grand Prix automobile race, *1055*

Long-jumper to break the 25-foot barrier, *4430*

Major league baseball game to be broadcast on radio, *1458*

Major league baseball player of the 20th century to score 177 runs in a single season, *1453*

Major league baseball player to hit 59 home runs in a single season, *1459*

National collegiate track and field (athletics) championships sponsored by the National Collegiate Athletic Association (NCAA), *6206*

National governing body for boxing in the United States, *2539*

National Hockey League team to win the Stanley Cup twice in a row, *4074*

New York Yankees American League pennant, *1454*

No-hitter on record in Negro League history, *1457*

Ruling limiting the size and weight of a golf ball, *3668*

Runner to hold the world record in both the men's 5000- and 10,000-meter events, *5013*

Runner to race the men's 100-meter event in less than 10.5 seconds, *5012*

Speedball, *5737*

University of California win in college football's Rose Bowl, *3149*

World championships in fencing, *2917*

World championships in Greco-Roman wrestling regarded as official, *6379*

1921—*continued*

World Series game to be broadcast by radio, *1460*

World Series to be won by a team that lost the first two games of the Series, *1455*

1922

Amateur Public Links Championship, *3669*

Australian mixed doubles national tennis championships, *6061*

Australian women's doubles national tennis championships, *6062*

Australian women's singles national tennis championships, *6063*

Baseball player to steal more than 30 bases and hit more than 30 home runs in a single season in the American League, *1461*

Boxer to be undisputed world super-bantamweight (junior featherweight) champion, *2543*

Boxer to hold the world super-lightweight (junior welterweight) title, *2544*

College football game to be broadcast nationally on radio, *3151*

Decathlete to hold the officially accepted world record in the men's decathlon, *2739*

Golfer born in the United States to win the British Open, *3670*

Golfer to win the U.S. Open and the Professional Golfers' Association (PGA) Championship in the same year, *3674*

Gymnast to win two consecutive men's all-around titles in the world championships, *3923*

International governing body for motorboat (powerboat) racing, *4566*

Madison Square Garden Rodeo, *4884*

Men's sabre competition held in the world championships of fencing, *2918*

Modern slalom course, *5363*

National championships in volleyball in the United States, *6274*

National field hockey organization in the United States, *4037*

National Hockey League goaltender to score at least one goal in 16 consecutive games, *4078*

National Hockey League tie game, *4077*

Professional golfer to found a company selling clubs under his own name, *3671*

Radio broadcast of a cricket game, *2655*

Runner to hold the world record in both the men's 5000- and 10,000-meter events, *5013*

Swimmer to race the men's 100-meter freestyle in under one minute, *5815*

Toronto St. Patricks National Hockey League Stanley Cup championship, *4076*

U.S. Open golf tournament to charge admission to spectators, *3672*

Vasalopp long-distance ski race, *5364*

Walker Cup golf match, *3673*

Water-skiing, *6309*

Wimbledon tennis tournament at a new site, *6064*

Woman known to have played for a major league baseball team, *1462*

World championships in weightlifting, *6332*

1923

African-American professional basketball team, *1886*

Automobile racer to win the Indianapolis 500 twice, *1056*

Baseball player to lead the American League in doubles in four consecutive years, *1463*

Fencer to win two consecutive men's sabre titles in the world championships, *2919*

Football Association Challenge Cup tournament, *5551*

Governing body for bobsled events, *2466*

Le Mans 24-hours sports car race, *1057*

Major league baseball player to have 170 walks in a single season, *1464*

National Hockey League game played without any penalties being assessed, *4079*

National organization for paddle tennis, *6195*

National track and field (athletics) championships for women in the United States, *6207*

New York Yankees regular season baseball game played at Yankee Stadium, *1467*

New York Yankees World Series victory, *1465*

Swimmer to swim across the English Channel from France to England, *5816*

Tennis player to win five consecutive Wimbledon women's singles championships, *6065*

Tennis player to win two consecutive Australian national women's doubles championships, *6066*

Tennis player to win two consecutive Australian national women's singles tennis championships, *6067*

Tennis players to win five consecutive Wimbledon women's doubles championships, *6068*

Texas Open golf tournament, *3675*

University of Southern California win in college football's Rose Bowl, *3152*

Walker Cup golf match played in Britain, *3676*

World championships in bowling, *2489*

World Series to be broadcast nationally on radio, *1466*

World Series to reach total receipts of more than $1 million, *1468*

1924

Athlete from Czechoslovakia to win a gold medal in the Olympic Games, *4660*

Athlete from Yugoslavia to win a gold medal in the Olympic Games, *4661*

Athlete of Black African ancestry to win an individual gold medal in the Olympic Games, *4657*

Athlete to receive an Olympic medal 50 years after the competition, *4741*

Athlete to win a gold medal at the Olympic Winter Games, *4654*

Athlete to win an Olympic gold medal, or to hold the world record, in both the men's decathlon and an individual track and field event, *2741*

Athlete to win five gold medals in a single Olympic Games, *4658*

Athlete to win Olympic medals in both diving and swimming, *2798*

Athlete to win six medals overall in a single Olympic Games, *4652*

Athletes from Argentina to win gold medals in the Olympic Games, *4659*

Athletes from Uruguay to win gold medals in the Olympic Games, *4656*

Automobile race at the Circuit Pescara, *1058*

Bantamweight Greco-Roman wrestling event held in the Olympic Games, *6380*

Baseball player to lead the American League in slugging average for seven consecutive years, *1469*

Baseball team to win four consecutive National League pennants, *1470*

Bobsled event held at the Olympic Winter Games, *2467*

Bowler to bowl two consecutive 300 games, *2490*

Boxer to win two consecutive middleweight titles in the Olympic Games, *2545*

Cheltenham Gold Cup horse race, *4291*

Decathlete from the United States to hold the world record in the men's decathlon, *2740*

Diver to win both the men's springboard and platform diving titles in the same Olympic Games, *2799*

Figure skater from Austria to win the women's singles title at the Olympic Games, *3000*

Figure skater to win two, and then three, consecutive men's singles titles in the Olympic Games, *3001*

Figure skaters from Austria to win the pairs title at the Olympic Winter Games, *3002*

Golfer to win two straight individual titles at the U.S. intercollegiate golf championships, *3677*

Gymnast to win three consecutive gold medals in the men's team combined exercises in the Olympic Games, *3924*

Hammer-thrower born in the United States to win the men's event in the Olympic Games, *3983*

International governing body for canoeing, *2595*

International organization for athletes with disabilities, *2746*

International organization for roller skating and roller hockey, *4904*

International tournament for athletes with disabilities, *2747*

International Universities Games, *4368*

Javelin-thrower to win two consecutive men's titles in the Olympic Games, *4386*

Men's 10,000-meter speed skating event held in the Olympic Winter Games, *5641*

Men's 1500-meter speed skating event held at the Olympic Winter Games, *5642*

Men's 50-kilometer freestyle Nordic (cross-country) skiing event held at the Olympic Winter Games, *5365*

Men's 500-meter speed skating event held at the Olympic Winter Games, *5639*

Men's 5000-meter speed skating event held at the Olympic Winter Games, *5640*

Men's four races combined speed skating title offered at the Olympic Winter Games, *5643*

Men's individual 18-kilometer Nordic (cross-country) event held at the Olympic Winter Games, *5366*

Men's individual Nordic combined (cross-country and ski jump) event held in the Olympic Winter Games, *5367*

Men's individual ski jump event held at the Olympic Winter Games, *5368*

Montreal Canadiens National Hockey League Stanley Cup championship, *4080*

Moto-cross race, *4575*

National Amateur Challenge Cup, *5552*

National association for netball, *4596*

National Hockey League 0–0 tie, *4084*

National Hockey League player to win the Hart Memorial Trophy as the league's Most Valuable Player, *4081*

National team to sweep the medals in the men's combined individual Nordic (cross-country) skiing event at the Olympic Winter Games, *5369*

National team to win two consecutive ice hockey titles at the Olympic Winter Games, *4083*

Negro Leagues World Series, *1472*

Olympic Games in which more than 100 women participated, *4655*

Olympic Winter Games, *4653*

Pescara Grand Prix automobile race, *1059*

Rowers to win two consecutive medals in the men's double sculls event in the Olympic Games, *4935*

Rugby players to win two Olympic gold medals in rugby, *4968*

Runner from Europe to win the men's 100-meter title in the Olympic Games, *5014*

Runner to win three consecutive Boston Marathons, *4476*

Runner to win two consecutive gold medals in the men's 4 x 100-meter relay in the Olympic Games, *5016*

505

1924—*continued*

Runner to win two consecutive titles in the men's individual cross-country in the Olympic Games, *5015*

Shooter to win two consecutive titles in the men's free rifle (three positions) individual shooting event, and in the free rifle team event, in the Olympic Games, *5302*

Shooter to win two consecutive titles in the running deer (double shot) individual shooting event in the Olympic Games, *5303*

Skier for the United States to win a ski-jumping medal at the Olympic Winter Games, *5370*

Standardization of the marathon distance, *4475*

Swimmer to win two consecutive men's 100-meter backstroke titles in the Olympic Games, *5817*

Team from the United States to join the National Hockey League, *4082*

Tennis player from the United States to win the women's singles tennis title in the Olympic Games, *6071*

Tennis players from the United States to win the mixed doubles event in the Olympic Games, *6072*

Tennis players from the United States to win the women's doubles title in the Olympic Games, *6070*

United States men's singles national tennis championship matches played at the new West Side Tennis Club stadium, *6069*

Washington Senators World Series victory, *1471*

Wightman Cup tennis tournament, *6073*

Women's 100-meter backstroke event held in the Olympic Games, *5819*

Women's 200-meter breaststroke event held in the Olympic Games, *5818*

Women's individual foil fencing competition held in the Olympic Games, *2920*

Wrestler to win gold medals in three different divisions in the Olympic Games, *6378*

1925

Automobile racer to win the Indianapolis 500 with an average speed of more than 100 miles per hour, *1060*

Baseball player to lead the National League in batting average for six consecutive years, *1473*

Baseball player to lead the National League in slugging average for six consecutive years, *1474*

Belgian Grand Prix automobile race, *1061*

College football All-America team named by Grantland Rice, *3153*

Fastnet Race, *5209*

Figure skater to win both the singles and pairs title at the same world championships, *3003*

French national tennis championships open to those who were not citizens or residents of France, *6074*

Goalie to have 20 career shutouts in the National Hockey League, *4086*

Golfer to win three Professional Golfers' Association (PGA) Championships, *3678*

Harlem Globetrotters professional basketball game, *1887*

Hurdler to race the men's 400-meter hurdles in under 54 seconds, *4329*

International team handball match, *4002*

Irrigation system for fairways on a golf course, *3679*

Men's 18-kilometer cross-country event held in the world championships of Nordic skiing, *5371*

Men's 50-kilometer cross-country event held in the world championships of Nordic skiing, *5372*

Men's ski jumping (normal hill) event held in the world championships of Nordic skiing, *5373*

National Hockey League player to win the Lady Byng Memorial Trophy as the most gentlemanly player, *4085*

Nordic combined event held in the world championships of Nordic skiing, *5374*

Notre Dame University win in college football's Rose Bowl, *3154*

Runner to complete the men's marathon in under 2:30 hours, *4477*

Tennis player to win 98 straight men's singles matches, *6075*

Tennis player to win a French national men's singles championship after the event became international, *6076*

Tennis player to win the French national women's singles championship after the event became international, *6077*

Tennis players to win a French national mixed doubles championship after the event became international, *6078*

Tennis players to win the French national men's doubles championship after the event became international, *6079*

Tennis players to win the French national women's doubles championship after the event became international, *6080*

Triple Crown hitter in two seasons in the National League, *1475*

Water-ski jump, *6310*

1926

American Division was formed in the National Hockey League, *4087*

American Football League season, *3155*

British Grand Prix automobile race, *1062*

Figure skater to win five consecutive women's singles championships, *3004*

Figure skaters from France to win the pairs title in the world championships, *3005*

German Grand Prix automobile race, *1063*

Golf tournament to offer a $10,000 purse, *3680*

Golfer born in the United States to win the British Amateur Championship, *3681*

Golfer to win both the U.S. Open and the British Open in the same year, *3682*

Gymnast to win two consecutive men's rings titles in the world championships, *3925*

Hambletonian Stakes harness race, *4292*

International championships in table tennis, *5984*

International governing body for table tennis, *5982*

Introduction of the name "softball", *5578*

Major league baseball player to score four runs in a single World Series game, *1477*

Men's 30-kilometer cross-country event held in the world championships of Nordic skiing, *5375*

Men's foil competition held in the world championships of fencing, *2921*

Montreal Maroons National Hockey League Stanley Cup championship, *4088*

National Air Races, *1006*

National cricket organization for women, *2656*

National golf organization founded by African-Americans, *3683*

President's Cup motorboat (powerboat) race, *4567*

Professional basketball major league, *1888*

Runner to hold the officially accepted world record in the women's marathon, *4478*

St. Louis Cardinals World Series victory, *1476*

Swaythling Cup, *5983*

Tennis star to turn professional, *6081*

University of Alabama win in college football's Rose Bowl, *3156*

Woman to swim the English Channel, *5820*

Women's basketball national championship played largely by men's rules, *1889*

World amateur championships in billiards, *2452*

World professional championships in snooker, *2453*

1927

Boxer to win both Olympic and professional world championships, *2547*

Champion Hurdle horse race, *4293*

Figure skater from Norway to win the women's singles title in the world championships, *3006*

Golden Gloves matches, *2546*

Golf club for African-American women, *3684*

Golfer to win the British Open golf championship in under 290 for 72 holes, *3685*

Golfer to win the Professional Golfers' Association (PGA) Championship four times in a row, and five times overall, *3686*

Hurdler to hold the world record in both the men's 110- and 400-meter events, *4331*

Hurdler to race the men's 400-meter hurdles in under 53 seconds, *4330*

Intercollegiate wrestling tournament sponsored by the National Collegiate Athletic Association (NCAA), *6381*

Javelin-thrower to break the 220-foot barrier, *4387*

Major league baseball player of the 20th century to reach 4,000 hits, *1480*

Major league baseball player to hit 60 home runs in a single season, *1481*

National governing body for duck pin bowling, *2491*

National Hockey League player to be named outstanding goaltender, *4089*

National Hockey League team to win 25 games in a single season, *4090*

National League team to top 1 million paying customers at home in a single season, *1478*

New York Yankees baseball player to be named Most Valuable Player, *1479*

Pole-vaulter to clear 14 feet, *4840*

Ryder Cup golf match, *3687*

Tennis players to win three Australian national mixed doubles championships, *6082*

1928

Athlete from Egypt to win an Olympic gold medal, *4662*

Athlete from independent Ireland to win a gold medal in the Olympic Games, *3984*

Athlete from Japan to win a gold medal in the Olympic Games, *4671*

Athlete from New Zealand to win an Olympic gold medal, *4672*

Athlete from Poland to win a gold medal in the Olympic Games, *4670*

Athlete to be named an All-American in both basketball and football, *1147*

Athlete to win 12 medals in the Olympic Games, *4669*

Athlete to win five individual gold medals, and seven medals overall, in the Olympic Winter Games, *4665*

Athlete to win three consecutive gold medals in the same event in the Olympic Winter Games, *4666*

Athletes from Asia, and from India, to win gold medals in the Olympic Games, *4668*

Athletes from Spain to win gold medals in the Olympic Games, *4673*

Baseball pitcher to lead the National League in strikeouts for seven consecutive years, *1482*

Baseball player to lead the American League in bases on balls for three consecutive years, *1483*

1928—*continued*

Bobsledders from the United States to win the five-man bobsled title at the Olympic Winter Games, *2468*

Boston Bruins regular season hockey game played at Boston Garden, *4098*

Boxer named Fighter of the Year by *Ring* magazine, *2548*

Cup of the Americas (Copa de las Americas) polo competition, *4867*

Equestrian to win both an individual and a team medal in dressage in the Olympic Games, *2853*

Equestrian to win the individual jumping event in the Olympic Games without a single fault, *2856*

Equestrians to win two consecutive three-day event team titles, *2854*

Figure skater from Norway to win the women's singles title at the Olympic Winter Games, *3007*

Figure skaters from France to win the pairs title in the Olympic Winter Games, *3008*

Hammer-thrower representing Ireland to win the men's event in the Olympic Games, *3985*

International governing organization for lacrosse, *4422*

International government body in handball, *4003*

International hockey game between Sweden and Finland, *4094*

Invention of platform tennis, *6196*

Javelin-thrower to break the 230-foot and 70-meter barriers, *4388*

Long-jumper to break the 26-foot barrier, *4432*

Long-jumper to hold the officially accepted world record in the women's event, and the first female athlete from Asia to set a world track and field record, *4431*

Major league baseball player to hit for a World Series average of .625, *1484*

Major league baseball player to steal home 50 times in the course of his career, *1485*

Men's 1000-meter time trial cycling event held in the Olympic Games, *2696*

Men's 10,000-meter Olympic speed skating race to be voided, *5644*

Men's skeleton luge event at the Olympic Winter Games, *4452*

National Award tournament in duck pin bowling, *2492*

National governing body for squash in England, *5758*

National Hockey League goaltender to be credited with four shutouts in a single set of Stanley Cup playoffs, *4091*

National Hockey League goaltender to have six consecutive shutouts, *4095*

National Hockey League goaltender to reach 50 career shutouts, *4097*

National Hockey League player to be named outstanding goaltender two, and then three, consecutive times, *4092*

National team to sweep the medals in the men's 15-kilometer Nordic (cross-country) skiing event in the Olympic Winter Games, *5376*

National team to win three consecutive ice hockey titles at the Olympic Winter Games, *4096*

New York Rangers National Hockey League Stanley Cup championship, *4093*

Olympic Games to include track and field events for women, *4667*

Olympic men's 200-meter breaststroke event in which the medalists all had times under three minutes, *5821*

Olympic Winter Games held in a different country from the Summer Games, *4663*

Olympic Winter Games held in Switzerland, *4664*

Rower to win three consecutive medals in the men's double sculls event in the Olympic Games, *4936*

Run across the United States, *5017*

Runner from Canada to win the men's 100-meter race in the Olympic Games, *5018*

Runner to hold the officially accepted world record in the women's 800-meter event, *5021*

Runner to win two consecutive men's 800-meter titles in the Olympic Games, *5019*

School for aikido, *4530*

Shot-putter to break the 16-meter barrier, *5333*

Speed skater to win two consecutive men's 1500-meter speed skating titles at the Olympic Winter Games, *5645*

Stanford University win in college football's Rose Bowl, *3157*

Swimmer to win two consecutive gold medals in the men's 4 x 200-meter freestyle relay swimming event in the Olympic Games, *5822*

Team dressage equestrian event held in the Olympic Games, *2855*

Tennis player to win two consecutive Wimbledon mixed doubles championships, *6083*

Woman to win an Olympic gold medal in sailing, *5210*

Women's 100-meter running event, and the first women's track event, held in the Olympic Games, *5020*

Women's 4 x 100-meter relay running event held in the Olympic Games, *5023*

Women's 800-meter running event held in the Olympic Games, *5022*

Women's discus throw event, and the first women's field event, held in the Olympic Games, *2762*

Women's high jump event held in the Olympic Games, *4022*

Women's team combined exercises gymnastics competition held in the Olympic Games, *3926*

World championships for three-cushion billiards (carom), *2454*

1929

African-American college football bowl game, *3158*

African-American runner to hold the record in the men's 100-meter dash, *5024*

Baseball player to hit a home run the first time he came to bat in an American League game, *1486*

Boston Bruins National Hockey League Stanley Cup championship, *4099*

Cowboy to be named All-Around Cowboy, *4885*

Discus-thrower to break the 160-foot and 50-meter barriers, *2763*

Fencer to win two consecutive men's foil titles in the world championships, *2922*

Georgia Tech win in college football's Rose Bowl, *3159*

Golfer to win four, and then five and six, U.S. Women's Amateur Championships, *3688*

Golfer to win more than 10 titles in golf's four major tournaments, *3689*

Major league baseball player to hit 500 home runs, *1487*

Monaco Grand Prix automobile race, *1064*

National Collegiate Athletic Association (NCAA) consensus Division I All-American college basketball team, *1890*

National Hockey League goaltender to be credited with 22 shutouts in a single season, *4100*

Organization of rodeo producers, *4886*

Professional football player to score all 40 of his team's points, *3160*

Ryder Cup golf match played in Britain, *3690*

St. Bride Vase, *5985*

Tennis player to win eight women's singles titles at the United States national championships, *6084*

Tennis player to win four Australian national mixed doubles titles, *6085*

Tennis player to win three French national men's singles championships after the event became international, *6086*

Woman bowler to bowl a 300 game, *2493*

Women's Air Derby, *1007*

World championships in fencing to include women, *2923*

1930

Amateur golfer to win three British Open championships, *3691*

Baseball player to have 100 extra-base hits in a season in the National League, *1489*

Beach volleyball, *6275*

British Empire Games (later the British Commonwealth Games), *4369*

Discus-thrower to break the 160-foot and 50-meter barriers, *2763*

Fencer to win two consecutive men's épée titles in the world championships, *2924*

Golfer to complete a grand slam, *3693*

Golfer to win five U.S. Amateur titles, *3692*

Major league baseball player to bat in 190 runs in a single season, *1490*

Major league baseball player to earn $80,000 per year, *1491*

National Hockey League goaltender to wear a facemask in a scheduled game, *4101*

Negro League game played at Yankee Stadium, *1493*

Professional baseball game played at night under lights, *1492*

Runner to complete the men's 1500-meter race in under 3:50 minutes, *5025*

Runner to win seven Boston Marathons, *4479*

Speed skater to skate the 1000 meters in under 1:30 minutes, *5646*

Sullivan Award, *1148*

Tennis player to win five Australian national women's singles championships, and the first to win three in a row, *6087*

Tennis player to win nine Wimbledon women's doubles titles, *6088*

Tennis player to win three, four, and then five French national men's doubles championships after the event became international, *6089*

Thompson Trophy airplane race, *1008*

World championships in bobsledding, *2469*

World cup in soccer (international football), *5553*

1931

African-American women's basketball team, *1891*

All-Star National Hockey League Team selected by the Professional Hockey Writers' Association, *4102*

Athlete to hold the world record in both the men's long jump and triple jump, *4433*

Baseball pitcher to lead the American League in winning percentage for three consecutive years, *1494*

Baseball player to be named Associated Press Athlete of the Year, *1495*

Baseball player to lead the American League in home runs for six consecutive years, *1496*

Bendix Trophy airplane race, *1009*

Bobsled run in the United States, *2470*

Fencer to win two, and then three, women's foil titles in the world championships, *2925*

Figure skaters from Hungary to win the pairs title in the world championships, *3009*

509

1931—*continued*

G. Geist Prize, *5986*

Golfer to win a major tournament using steel-shafted golf clubs, *3694*

International governing body for archery, *1029*

Major league baseball player to reach a career total of 600 home runs, *1501*

National gymnastics competition in the United States to include women, *3927*

National Hockey League game in which three assists were credited on a single goal, *4103*

Philadelphia Athletics baseball player to be named Most Valuable Player, *1497*

Runner to complete the men's mile race in under 4:10 minutes, *5026*

St. Louis Cardinals baseball player to be named Most Valuable Player, *1498*

Table tennis player to win five women's singles titles in the world championships, *5987*

Toronto Maple Leafs regular season hockey game played at Maple Leaf Gardens, *4104*

Use of the metric system by the Amateur Athletic Union (AAU), *6208*

Woman baseball team owner, *1499*

Woman to pitch against a major league baseball team, *1500*

Women's world amateur championships in billiards, *2455*

World championships in Alpine skiing, *5377*

World championships in target archery, *1030*

1932

African-American professional basketball team to win a world championship, *1892*

African-American runner to win the men's 100- and 200-meter titles in the Olympic Games, *5032*

Archer to win two, and then up to seven, women's individual world championships, *1031*

Athlete to become a broadcaster after retiring, *5747*

Athlete to hold the world record in both the men's long jump and triple jump, *4433*

Athlete to win gold medals in both the Summer and Winter Olympics, *4674*

Baseball player to hit four home runs in a single regular season American League game, *1504*

Bobsledders to win two straight titles in the four-man bobsled at the Olympic Winter Games, *2472*

Curtis Cup golf match, *3695*

Discus-thrower from the United States to win the women's event in the Olympic Games, *2764*

Equestrian to win two consecutive three-day event individual titles, *2857*

Fencer to win two men's team foil titles in the Olympic Games, *2926*

Field hockey players to win two gold medals in the Olympic Games, *4038*

Figure skater from Austria to win the men's singles titles in the Olympic Winter Games, *3012*

Figure skater to win two, and then three, consecutive women's singles titles at the Olympic Winter Games, *3014*

Figure skaters to complete a grand slam, winning the European, world, and Olympic titles in the same year, *3010*

Figure skaters to win four pairs titles in the world championships, *3011*

Figure skaters to win two consecutive pairs titles at the Olympic Winter Games, *3013*

High-jumpers to hold the officially accepted world record in the women's event, and the first from the United States to win the women's event in the Olympic Games, *4023*

Javelin-thrower to break the 240- and 250-foot barriers, *4391*

Javelin-thrower to hold the officially accepted world record in the women's event, *4389*

Major league baseball manager to win pennants in both the American and National Leagues, *1502*

Men's 50,000-meter walk held in the Olympic Games, *6291*

Men's floor exercises gymnastics competition held in the Olympic Games, *3928*

Men's tumbling gymnastics competition held in the Olympic Games, *3929*

National Collegiate Athletic Association major college football team to have 44 consecutive winning seasons, *3161*

National Football League game played indoors, *3162*

National Hockey League player to be named the league's Most Valuable Player twice in a row, *4105*

National team to sweep the medals in the men's 90-meter ski jump at the Olympic Winter Games, *5379*

National team to sweep the top medals in the women's platform diving event in the Olympic Games, *2800*

National team to win four consecutive ice hockey titles at the Olympic Winter Games, *4107*

Olympic Games to have medalists stand on a platform, and to play the gold medalist's national anthem, *4675*

Olympic Games to use automatic timing and photofinish cameras, *4677*

Olympic men's 1500-meter freestyle event in which the medalists all had times under 20 minutes, *5825*

Olympic men's 400-meter freestyle event at which all the medalists had times under five minutes, *5823*

Olympic speed skating events to be held as races, rather than in pairs, *5648*

Olympic Winter Games held in the United States, *4676*

Philadelphia Phillies baseball player to be named Most Valuable Player, *1503*

Result of an Olympic event to be changed after viewing of the film of the race, *4678*

Rower to win two consecutive men's single sculls rowing titles in the Olympic Games, *4937*

Runner to complete the men's 400-meter race in under 47 seconds, *5027*

Runner to complete the men's 800-meter race in under 1:50 minutes, *5029*

Runner to race the men's 5000 meters in under 14:28.0 minutes, *5028*

Sailing team from the United States to win the 8-meter-class event in the Olympic Games, *5211*

Skier to win two consecutive men's individual Nordic combined titles in the Olympic Winter Games, *5378*

Speed skater from the United States to win the men's 1500-meter title at the Olympic Winter Games, *5649*

Speed skater to win the men's 10,000-meter title at the Olympic Winter Games, *5650*

Star-class sailing event held in the Olympic Games, *5212*

Swimmer to win two consecutive men's 200-meter breaststroke titles, *5826*

Swimmer to win two women's 4 x 100-meter freestyle relay titles in the Olympic Games, *5824*

Team from the United States to win the women's 4 x 100-meter relay running event in the Olympic Games, *5030*

Team to race the men's 4 x 400-meter relay in under 3:10 minutes, *5031*

Tennis player to win four French national men's singles championships after the event became international, *6090*

Tennis player to win seven Wimbledon mixed doubles championships, *6091*

Tennis player to win three consecutive French national women's singles championships, and then four overall, after the event became international, *6092*

Toronto Maple Leafs National Hockey League Stanley Cup championship, *4106*

Track world record for which there was an official wind-speed reading, *6209*

Two-man bobsled competition held in the Olympic Games, *2471*

Welterweight Greco-Roman wrestling event held in the Olympic Games, *6383*

Woman speed skater to skate the 1000 meters in under 2 minutes, *5651*

Woman speed skater to skate the 500 meters in under 1 minute, *5647*

Women's 80-meter hurdles event held in the Olympic Games, *4332*

Women's javelin-throw event held in the Olympic Games, *4390*

Wrestler to win gold medals in three different divisions in the Olympic Games, *6378*

Wrestler to win two consecutive middleweight Greco-Roman titles in the Olympic Games, *6384*

Wrestler to win two super heavyweight freestyle titles in the Olympic Games, *6382*

1933

Amateur Softball Association of America (ASA) national championships, *5579*

Baseball player to hit a home run in major league baseball's All-Star Game, *1508*

Corporate title sponsor for a professional golf tournament, *3696*

Cowboy to be named All-Around Cowboy twice, *4887*

Fencer to win three men's épée titles in the world championships, *2927*

Figure skater to win six, and then seven, consecutive men's singles titles in the U.S. national championships, *3015*

Figure skater to win six consecutive women's singles titles, and nine overall, at the U.S. national championships, *3016*

Major league baseball All-Star Game, *1509*

Men's 4 x 10-kilometer cross-country relay event held in the world championships of Nordic skiing, *5380*

Mexican major league baseball player, *1505*

National Football League championship, *3164*

National governing body in softball, *5580*

National Hockey League player to be named Rookie of the Year, *4108*

National Hockey League player to reach 250 career goals, *4109*

Negro League East-West All-Star Game, *1510*

New York Giants baseball player to be named Most Valuable Player, *1506*

Orange Blossom Classic, *3163*

Revived Negro National League, *1507*

Speed skater to skate the 3000 meters in under 5 minutes, *5652*

Tennis player to win 158 straight women's singles matches, *6093*

Tennis player to win three consecutive Australian national men's singles championships, and four overall, *6094*

Woman speed skater to skate the 1500 meters in under 3 minutes, *5653*

Women's world amateur championships in snooker, *2456*

1934

Brother-and-sister figure skaters to win the pairs title at the U.S. national championships, *3017*

Chicago Blackhawks National Hockey League Stanley Cup championship, *4110*

College football All-Star Game, *3165*

Columbia University win in college football's Rose Bowl, *3166*

Curtis Cup golf match played in the United States, *3697*

Detroit Tigers baseball player to be named Most Valuable Player, *1511*

Discus-thrower to break the 170-foot barrier, *2765*

Figure skaters to win two, and then three, consecutive pairs titles in the world championships, *3018*

Hurdler to hold the officially accepted world record in the women's 80-meter event, *4333*

Hurdler to race the men's 400-meter hurdles in under 52 seconds, *4334*

International governing body for badminton, *1168*

Javelin-thrower to break the 240- and 250-foot barriers, *4391*

Major league baseball player to hit 700 home runs, *1513*

Major league baseball player to reach a total of 2,000 bases on balls, *1514*

Marcel Corbillon Cup, *5988*

Masters golf tournament, *3698*

National Hockey League All-Star Game, *4111*

New York Giants National Football League championship, *3167*

Night baseball games authorized by the National League, *1512*

Pentathlete to hold the officially accepted world record in the women's pentathlon, *4816*

Pilot to win both the Thompson Trophy and Bendix Trophy airplane races, *1010*

Runner to hold the officially accepted world record in the women's 100-meter dash, *5033*

Shot-putter to break the 17-meter barrier, *5335*

Shot-putter to hold the officially accepted world record in the women's event, *5334*

Soccer (international football) team from Italy to win the world cup, *5554*

Sportswriter to win a Pulitzer Prize, *5748*

Swimmer to swim the English Channel in both directions, *5827*

Swiss Grand Prix automobile race, *1065*

Women's squash association, *5759*

Women's test match in cricket, *2657*

World championships in gymnastics to include women, *3930*

1935

Baseball player to hit a home run in a National League night game, *1519*

Chicago Cubs baseball player to be named Most Valuable Player, *1515*

College football coach to be named Coach of the Year, *3168*

College football player to be awarded the Heisman Trophy, *3171*

Detroit Lions National Football League championship, *3172*

Detroit Tigers World Series victory, *1516*

Fencer to win two consecutive women's foil titles in the world championships, *2928*

Golfer to win 32 straight matches, *3699*

Golfer to win all four of golf's major tournaments, *3700*

Golfer to win six U.S. Women's Amateur championships, *3701*

Long-jump record to stand for more than 25 years, *4434*

Major league baseball night game, *1517*

Major league baseball player to hit 714 home runs, *1518*

National championships in skeet shooting, *5304*

National Hockey League player to lead the league in scoring twice in a row, *4112*

National Hockey League player to win the Lady Byng Memorial Trophy as the most gentlemanly player seven times, *4113*

Orange Bowl football game, *3169*

Record in the men's marathon to stand for more than 10 years, *4480*

Roller derby, *4905*

Runner from Asia to hold the officially accepted world record in the men's 100-meter dash, *5034*

Runner to hold the officially accepted world record in the women's 200 meters, *5035*

Sugar Bowl football game, *3170*

Table tennis player to win five men's singles titles in the world championships, *5989*

Tour of Spain (Vuelta a España) cycling race, *2697*

Track-and-field star to set five new world records and equal a sixth in less than an hour, *6210*

United States national women's and men's singles tennis championships to both be played at the West Side Tennis Club stadium, *6095*

Woman speed skater to skate the 500 meters in under 50 seconds, *5654*

Woman to fly in the Bendix Trophy airplane race, *1011*

1936

African-American coach of a Big Ten college football team, *3173*

African-American high-jumper to win the men's title in the Olympic Games, *4024*

African-American runner to win the men's 400-meter title in the Olympic Games, *5039*

1936—*continued*

Woman figure skater to complete a double jump in competition, *3022*

Woman to serve as coxswain on a men's varsity rowing team in the United States, *4938*

Woman to win the Bendix Trophy airplane race, *1012*

Women's Alpine combined event held at the Olympic Winter Games, *5382*

World championships in dirt-track (speedway) motorcycle racing, *4576*

World championships in roller hockey (rink hockey), *4240*

World championships in sled dog racing, *5507*

World championships in speed skating to include women skaters, *5656*

Wrestler to win heavyweight titles in both freestyle and Greco-Roman wrestling in the Olympic Games, *6385*

1937

Automobile racer to win the Indianapolis 500 with an average speed of more than 110 miles per hour, *1066*

Boxer to win three different world boxing titles within one year, *2550*

College football player to receive the Maxwell Award, *3178*

College football player to rush for 1,000 yards or more in a single season, *3179*

Cotton Bowl football game, *3180*

Golfer over 50 to win a Professional Golfers' Association (PGA) recognized tournament, *3703*

Golfer to win the Vardon Trophy, *3704*

National Hockey League player to reach 250 career assists, *4116*

National speed skating championships in roller skating in the United States, *4906*

Negro American League operations began, *1523*

Night baseball games were authorized by the American League, *1524*

Officially timed drag races, *1067*

Professional-amateur golf tournament, *3705*

Professional Golfers' Association (PGA) Seniors' Championship, *3706*

Softball championship to be broadcast nationally on radio, *5581*

Softball team to win two consecutive titles in the Amateur Softball Association Women's Major Fast Pitch National Championships, *5582*

Tennis tournament to be televised in Great Britain, *6097*

University of Pittsburgh win in college football's Rose Bowl, *3181*

Washington Redskins National Football League championship, *3182*

Woman speed skater to skate the 3000 meters in under 6 minutes, *5659*

Woman speed skater to skate the 5000 meters in under 10 minutes, *5660*

World championships in gliding (soaring), *3531*

World speed skating championships for roller skating, *4907*

1938

Basketball team to win college basketball's National Invitation Tournament, *1895*

Boston Red Sox baseball player to be named Most Valuable Player, *1525*

Boxer named Fighter of the Year by *Ring* magazine two, three, and four times, *2551*

Boxer to win three different world boxing titles within one year, *2550*

British win of the Walker Cup golf tournament, *3707*

Canoe racing world championships, *2600*

Canoe sailing world championships, *2601*

Cincinnati Reds baseball player to be named Most Valuable Player, *1526*

College football team to win the Sugar Bowl in two consecutive years, *3184*

Cricket game to be broadcast on television, *2658*

Figure skaters to win two consecutive ice dancing titles at the U.S. national championships, *3023*

Gymnast to win two consecutive women's all-around titles in the world championships, *3931*

Hammer-thrower to break the 190-foot barrier, *3986*

Intercollegiate golf tournament for African-American players, *3708*

Major league baseball player to hit 23 grand slam home runs, *1528*

Major league baseball player to pitch two successive no-hitters, *1530*

Major league baseball team to win three consecutive World Series, *1529*

National association for orienteering, *4806*

National Football League player to be named the league's Most Valuable Player, *3183*

National Hockey League European tour, *4117*

Pilot to win the Thompson Trophy airplane race twice, and then three times, *1013*

Puerto Rican Professional Baseball League, *1527*

Soccer (international football) team to win the world cup twice in a row, *5555*

Speed skater to be women's world champion in speed skating twice in a row, *5661*

Tennis player to achieve a Grand Slam, *6098*

Tennis player to win the Wimbledon women's singles championship eight times, *6099*

Tennis tournament to be televised in the United States, *6100*

Woman bobsledder to win the U.S. national bobsled championship, *2473*

World championships in gymnastics to award women's titles in specific events, *3932*

World championships in handball, *4005*

1939

Baseball game to be televised, *1537*

Baseball pitcher to lead the American League in earned run average for six consecutive years, *1531*

Baseball player to hit a home run in an American League night game, *1536*

Baseball team to win four consecutive American League pennants, *1532*

Boxing match to be broadcast on television in the United States, *2552*

College football game to be televised, *3187*

College football player to win the Associated Press (AP) Athlete of the Year Award, *3185*

Establishment of the United States Trotting Association, *4295*

Figure skater from Great Britain to win the men's singles title at the world championships, *3024*

Figure skaters to win four consecutive pairs titles in the world championships, *3025*

Golfer to win the Masters in under 280 for 72 holes, *3709*

Little League baseball league, *1533*

Long-jumper to break the 20-foot and 6-meter barriers in the women's event, *4435*

Major league baseball games to be televised, *1539*

Major league baseball player to play 2,130 consecutive games, *1535*

Major league baseball player whose uniform number was retired at the end of his career, *1538*

National Collegiate Athletic Association (NCAA) Division I tournament basketball championship game, *1898*

National Collegiate Athletic Association (NCAA) Division I tournament basketball game, *1897*

National Football League Pro Bowl, *3186*

National governing body for water-skiing, *6312*

National professional softball league, *5583*

National water-skiing championships, *6313*

Professional football game to be televised, *3188*

Reigning monarch to play in a national golf championship, *3710*

Runner to race the men's 10,000 meters in under 30:00 minutes, *5045*

Runner to race the men's 5000 meters in under 14:10 minutes, *5043*

Runner to race the men's 800 meters in under 1:48 minutes, *5044*

Tennis player to win six French national women's doubles championships after the event became international, and four times consecutively, *6101*

Use of underwater photography to determine the winner of a swimming event, *5829*

Venezuelan major league baseball player, *1534*

World Tournament of professional basketball, *1896*

1940

Automobile racer to win the Indianapolis 500 three times, and to win it twice in a row, *1068*

Basketball player to be named Most Valuable Player of the Division I National Collegiate Athletic Association (NCAA) Final Four, *1899*

College basketball games to be televised, *1901*

College track and field (athletics) meet to be televised, *6211*

Horse to be named Horse of the Year twice consecutively, *4296*

Indiana University championship in the National Collegiate Athletic Association (NCAA) Men's Basketball National Tournament, *1900*

Olympic Winter Games to be canceled because of war, *4686*

Pole-vaulter to clear 15 feet, *4841*

Regularly held night harness racing, *4297*

Season for the Ice Capades, *3026*

Shooter to achieve a perfect score in international competition, *5305*

Shutout in a major league baseball All-Star Game, *1540*

Tennis players to win five consecutive Australian national women's doubles championships, *6104*

Woman to be licensed as a boxing referee, *2553*

1941

Avila Camacho Cup polo competition, *4868*

Brooklyn Dodgers baseball player to be named Most Valuable Player, *1541*

Figure skater to win five consecutive ice dancing titles at the U.S. national championships, *3027*

Iroquois Steeplechase horse race, *4298*

Major league baseball player to hit safely in 56 consecutive games, *1542*

National Football League team to win two consecutive league championships, *3189*

University of Wisconsin championship in the National Collegiate Athletic Association (NCAA) Men's Basketball National Tournament, *1902*

1942

Batting helmet in professional baseball, *1544*

515

1942—*continued*

Hale America golf tournaments, *3711*

National Football League player to win two consecutive Most Valuable Player Awards, *3190*

Oregon State University win in college football's Rose Bowl, and the only Rose Bowl not played in Pasadena, California, *3191*

Puerto Rican major league baseball player, *1543*

Runner to complete the men's mile race in under 4:05 minutes, *5046*

Runner to race the men's 5000 meters in under 14:00 minutes, *5047*

Sailor to complete a solo circumnavigation of the world in under a year, *5213*

Stanford University championship in the National Collegiate Athletic Association (NCAA) Men's Basketball National Tournament, *1903*

Women-only rodeo, *4889*

1943

Baseball player to lead the American League in stolen bases for five consecutive years, *1545*

National Football League player to pass for seven touchdowns in a single game, *3193*

University of Georgia win in college football's Rose Bowl, *3192*

University of Wyoming championship in the National Collegiate Athletic Association (NCAA) Men's Basketball National Tournament, *1904*

Women's professional baseball league, *1546*

1944

College basketball team to win two consecutive college basketball National Invitation Tournaments, *1905*

Cowboy to be named All-Around Cowboy twice consecutively, *4890*

National Hockey League player to score five goals in a single Stanley Cup playoff game, *4118*

Organization for women golf professionals in the United States, *3712*

Runner to complete the men's 1500 meters in under 3:45.0 minutes, *5048*

St. Louis Browns American League pennant, *1547*

University of Utah championship in the National Collegiate Athletic Association (NCAA) Men's Basketball National Tournament, *1906*

Woman to win the Sullivan Award, *1149*

1945

African-American baseball player of the 20th century to join the previously all-white mainstream baseball leagues, *1548*

Cleveland Rams National Football League championship, *3196*

College football player to win the James E. Sullivan Memorial Award, *3194*

Golfer to score under 260 for 72 holes in a Professional Golfers' Association (PGA)–recognized event, *3713*

Golfer to win more than 10 straight titles, and to win 18 titles overall during a single year, on the Professional Golfers' Association (PGA) Tour, *3714*

National Football League player to lead the league eight times in pass receptions, *3195*

National Hockey League player to score 50 goals in a single season, *4119*

Oklahoma State University championship in the National Collegiate Athletic Association (NCAA) Men's Basketball National Tournament, *1907*

Organization for Australian rodeo cowboys, *4891*

Sydney-Hobart Race, *5214*

1946

African-American baseball player in the International League in the 20th century, *1550*

African-American professional football player to join the Cleveland Browns, *3197*

African-American professional football players to play in the National Football League in the modern period, and the first to play with the Los Angeles Rams, *3198*

All America Football Conference (AAFC) championship, *3199*

All America Football Conference (AAFC) season, *3200*

American League team to top 2 million paying customers at home in a single season, *1549*

Baseball player to score 6 runs in a 9-inning American League game, *1551*

Basketball Association of America (BAA) founding meeting, *1911*

Basketball Association of America (BAA) season, *1912*

Basketball player to be named Most Valuable Player of the Division I National Collegiate Athletic Association (NCAA) Final Four twice in a row, *1908*

Boston Celtics regular season basketball game played at Boston Garden, *1913*

Cleveland Browns regular season football game played at Municipal Stadium, *3205*

College football player to be awarded the Outland Trophy, *3201*

College football player to pass for or himself score a total of six touchdowns in a major bowl game, *3203*

Discus-thrower to break the 180-foot barrier, *2767*

Football player to be named Most Valuable Player of the All America Football Conference (AAFC), *3202*

Gator Bowl football game, *3204*

Heavyweight boxing match to be broadcast on television, and the first at which top-price tickets cost $100, *2554*

International governing body in water-skiing, *6314*

Little Brown Jug harness race, *4299*

Major league baseball playoff series, *1552*

National Collegiate Athletic Association (NCAA) Division I tournament championship basketball game to be televised, *1909*

National Collegiate Athletic Association (NCAA) team to win two consecutive Division I basketball championships, *1910*

National Fastball League, *5584*

Pilot to win the Bendix Trophy–Jet Division airplane race, *1014*

Pilot to win the Thompson Trophy–Jet Division airplane race, *1015*

Tennis player to win four consecutive United States mixed doubles national championships, and nine overall, *6105*

U.S. Women's Open golf championship, *3715*

1947

African-American baseball player in the American League, *1560*

African-American baseball player in the modern major leagues, *1558*

African-American baseball player to hit a home run in the American League, *1562*

African-American baseball player to play for the St. Louis Browns, *1559*

African-American college football player to score a touchdown in the Rose Bowl, *3212*

African-American player to be a pitcher in major league baseball, *1563*

African-American professional football player to join the Brooklyn Dodgers, *3206*

African-American professional football player to join the Chicago Rockets, *3207*

African-American professional football player to join the Los Angeles Rams, *3208*

African-American professional football player to join the New York Giants in the modern period, *3209*

African-American professional football player to join the New York Yankees, *3210*

All–National Basketball Association (NBA) First Team, *1914*

Asahi Marathon, *4481*

Basketball player to lead the National Basketball Association (NBA) in single season scoring, *1915*

Basketball team to win the championship of the National Basketball Association (NBA), *1916*

Boston Braves baseball player to be named Most Valuable Player, *1553*

Chicago Cardinals National Football League championship, *3215*

College baseball team to win the National Collegiate World Championship, *1554*

Figure skater from Canada and from the Americas to win the women's singles title in the world championships, *3028*

Figure skater from Switzerland to win the men's singles title at the world championships, *3029*

Figure skater to perform the flying camel spin, *3030*

Figure skaters from Belgium to win the pairs title in the world championships, *3031*

Formula Two automobile racing circuit, *1069*

Golf tournament to be shown on television, *3716*

Golfer from the United States to win the British Women's Amateur Championship, *3717*

Holy Cross College championship in the National Collegiate Athletic Association (NCAA) Men's Basketball National Tournament, *1917*

International moto-cross competition, *4577*

Iran Cup, *5990*

Little League World Series, *1555*

Major league baseball player to be named Rookie of the Year, and the first African-American to win the award, *1556*

Major league baseball player to hit a home run as a pinch hitter in the World Series, *1565*

National Basketball Association (NBA) draft, *1918*

National Football League Coach of the Year, *3211*

National Hockey League player to be named outstanding goaltender four times in a row, *4120*

Roller derby to be televised, *4908*

Runner officially representing South Korea to hold the world record in the men's marathon, and to win the Boston Marathon, *4482*

Softball team to win the Amateur Softball Association Women's Major Fast Pitch National Championships in three consecutive years, *5585*

Softball team to win three consecutive titles in the Amateur Softball Association Men's Major Fast Pitch national championships, *5586*

Tangerine Bowl football game, *3213*

Trampolining tournament, *6227*

Triple Crown hitter in 2 seasons in the American League, *1557*

Two African-American major league baseball players to play for the same club in the same game, *1561*

University of Illinois win in college football's Rose Bowl, *3214*

1947—*continued*

Water-skier known to have skied barefoot, *6315*

World championships in softball, *5587*

World figure skating championships for roller skating, *4909*

World Series broadcast on television, *1564*

1948

African-American basketball player on an Olympic team, *1919*

African-American basketball player to win an Olympic gold medal, *1921*

African-American golfers to play in a Professional Golfers' Association (PGA)–recognized event, *3720*

African-American player to be captain of the football team at Yale University, *3216*

African-American professional football player to join the San Francisco 49ers, *3217*

African-American professional football players to join the Detroit Lions in the modern period, *3218*

Asian-American athlete to win a gold medal in the Olympic Games, *4694*

Athlete from Jamaica to win a gold medal in the Olympic Games, *4695*

Athlete from Peru to win a gold medal in the Olympic Games, *4693*

Athlete to compete in seven Olympic Games, *4687*

Athlete to win medals in the Olympic Winter Games 20 years apart, *4691*

Athletes from Mexico to win gold medals in the Olympic Games, *4697*

Athletes to compete in the Olympic Games over a period of 40 years, *4688*

Automobile race sponsored by the National Association for Stock Car Auto Racing (NASCAR), *1070*

Baltimore Bullets National Basketball Association (NBA) championship, *1920*

Bantamweight weightlifting event held in the Olympic Games, *6334*

Boston Braves baseball player to be named Rookie of the Year, *1566*

Canoer to win two men's Canadian pairs 1000-meter titles in the Olympic Games, *2602*

Cleveland Indians baseball player to be named Most Valuable Player, *1567*

College football team to win two consecutive Tangerine Bowl games, *3219*

Discus-thrower to break the 50-meter and 160-, 170-, and 180-foot barriers in the women's event, *2768*

Diver to win both the women's springboard and platform diving titles in the same Olympic Games, *2802*

Dragon-class sailing event held in the Olympic Games, *5216*

Equestrian to be stripped of his dressage title because he was not a commissioned officer, *2860*

Father-and-son team to win the Star-class sailing event in the Olympic Games, *5215*

Father and son to both win gold medals in track and field in the Olympic Games, *6213*

Fencer to win two consecutive women's individual foil titles in the Olympic Games, *2929*

Figure skater from Canada or from the Americas to win the women's singles title at the Olympic Winter Games, *3032*

Figure skater from the United States to win the men's singles title at the world championships, *3033*

Figure skater from the United States to win the men's singles titles in the Olympic Games, *3035*

Figure skater to win the men's singles U.S., world, and Olympic championships in the same year, and then twice in a row, *3034*

Figure skaters from Belgium to win the pairs title at the Olympic Winter Games, *3036*

Flyweight Greco-Roman wrestling event held in the Olympic Games, *6387*

Girls' Rodeo Association, *4892*

Golfer to win the U.S. Open in under 280 for 72 holes, *3718*

Heydusek Prize, *5991*

International pentathlon organization, *4818*

Jockey to win America's Triple Crown twice, *4300*

Men's downhill skiing event held at the Olympic Winter Games, *5386*

Men's slalom event held at the Olympic Winter Games, *5388*

National Association for Stock Car Auto Racing (NASCAR), *1071*

National Collegiate Athletic Association college hockey championship, *4121*

National team to win five ice hockey titles at the Olympic Winter Games, *4122*

Olympic Games at which athletes from Communist countries participated, *4689*

Olympic Games at which athletes from more than 50 countries participated, *4692*

Olympic Games attended by athletes of independent Korea, *4690*

Organized tournament in beach volleyball, *6276*

Pentathlete to place first in three of the five events in the men's modern pentathlon in the Olympic Games, *4819*

Philadelphia Eagles National Football League championship, *3221*

Pilot to win the Bendix Trophy race three times in a row, *1016*

Pope Trophy, *5992*

Runner from Central or South America to set or equal a world track and field record, *5049*

Runner from the Caribbean to win the men's 400-meter title in the Olympic Games, *5050*

Runner to win both the women's 100- and 200-meter titles in the same Olympic Games, *5052*

Sailors from the United States to win the 6-meter-class event in the Olympic Games, *5217*

Swimmer to swim across the Strait of Gibraltar, *5830*

U.S. Junior Amateur golf championship, *3719*

University of Michigan win in college football's Rose Bowl, *3220*

Weightlifter from the United States to win the light heavyweight title in the Olympic Games, *6336*

Weightlifter from the United States to win the middleweight title in the Olympic Games, *6335*

Wheelchair sports tournaments, *2748*

Woman athlete to win four gold medals in track and field in a single Olympic Games, *6212*

Woman of Black African descent to win a gold medal in the Olympic Games, *4696*

Women's 200-meter race held in the Olympic Games, *5051*

Women's 500-meter singles kayaking event held in the Olympic Games, *2603*

Women's downhill skiing event held at the Olympic Winter Games, *5387*

Women's long jump event held in the Olympic Games, *4436*

Women's shot put event held in the Olympic Games, *5336*

Women's slalom event held at the Olympic Winter Games, *5389*

Wrestler from the United States to win the middleweight freestyle wrestling title in the Olympic Games, *6386*

1949

African-American baseball player to be named Most Valuable Player in the National League, *1568*

African-American baseball player to lead one of the major leagues in batting average, *1569*

African-American baseball player to play for the New York Giants, *1570*

African-American football player from an African-American college to join a major professional football team, *3222*

African-American major league baseball players to appear in an All-Star Game, *1574*

Automobile racer to win the Indianapolis 500 with an average speed of more than 120 miles per hour, *1072*

Baltimore Orioles baseball player to be named Rookie of the Year, *1571*

Baseball player to lead the American League in bases on balls for four consecutive years, *1572*

Basketball team to win two consecutive National Collegiate Athletic Association (NCAA) national college basketball tournaments, *1922*

Boxer to hold a world boxing title for more than 10 years, and to defend a world boxing title 25 times, *2555*

Canoe slalom world championships, *2604*

College baseball player to win the Outstanding Player Award, *1573*

Figure skater from Czechoslovakia to win the women's singles title in the world championships, *3037*

Figure skater to perform the double loop–double loop combination jump in competition, *3038*

Figure skater to win the James E. Sullivan Award, *3039*

Golfer from the British Commonwealth to win the British Open, *3721*

Javelin-thrower to break the 160- and 170-foot and 50-meter barriers in the women's event, *4392*

National Association for Stock Car Auto Racing (NASCAR) Winston Cup (Grand National) Series, *1073*

National Hockey League team to win the Stanley Cup three times in a row, *4123*

National organization for basketball players in wheelchairs, *2749*

Northwestern University win in college football's Rose Bowl, *3223*

President of the Ladies Professional Golf Association (LPGA), *3722*

Queen Elizabeth II Cup, *2861*

Racquetball game, *4873*

Speed skater to skate the 10,000 meters in under 17 minutes, *5662*

Sudden-death playoff in golf that ran more than 10 holes, *3723*

World championships in handball to include women, *4006*

World championships in motorcycle racing, *4578*

World championships in the pentathlon, *4820*

World championships in volleyball, *6277*

World championships in water-skiing, *6316*

World team Thomas Cup badminton championships for men, *1169*

1950

African-American baseball player to play for the Boston Braves, *1579*

African-American baseball players to join the New York Yankees organization, *1582*

African-American basketball player to be drafted into the National Basketball Association (NBA), *1923*

1950—continued

African-American basketball player to join the Boston Celtics of the National Basketball Association (NBA), 1924

African-American basketball player to join the New York Knickerbockers of the National Basketball Association (NBA), 1925

African-American basketball player to join the Washington Capitols of the National Basketball Association (NBA), 1926

Archer to win two, three, and four men's individual world championships, 1032

Basketball team to win two consecutive National Basketball Association (NBA) championships, 1927

Belgian Grand Prix automobile race to be part of the Formula One Grand Prix circuit, 1081

Boston Red Sox baseball player to be named Rookie of the Year, 1575

British Grand Prix automobile race to be part of the Formula One Grand Prix circuit, 1077

City College of New York championship in the National Collegiate Athletic Association (NCAA) Men's Basketball National Tournament, 1928

Cleveland Browns National Football League championship, 3226

College baseball player to pitch 20 bases on balls in a College World Series, 1576

College baseball player to pitch a no-hitter, 1580

College baseball team to win two consecutive National Collegiate World Championships, 1577

College football team to be named national champions by the United Press International (UPI) Sportwriters Poll, 3224

Fencer to win three consecutive women's foil titles in the world championships, 2930

Figure skaters from the United States to win the pairs title in the world championships, 3040

French Grand Prix automobile race to be part of the Formula One Grand Prix circuit, 1082

Golfer to win the British Open golf championship in under 280 for 72 holes, 3724

Golfer to win three major tournaments, and six titles overall, on the Ladies Professional Golf Association (LPGA) Tour in a single season, 3725

Golfer to win two U.S. Women's Open championships, 3726

Governing body for drag racing, 1074

Indianapolis 500 automobile race to be part of the Formula One Grand Prix circuit, 1079

International pairs figure skating competition in which all the medalists were brother-and-sister pairs, 3041

International Softball Federation (ISF), 5589

Italian Grand Prix automobile race to be part of the Formula One Grand Prix circuit, 1083

Major league baseball game in which 11 home runs were hit, 1581

Monaco Grand Prix automobile race to be part of the Formula One Grand Prix circuit, 1078

National Basketball Association (NBA) game in which a total of only 37 points was scored, 1929

National Collegiate Athletic Association hockey player to score five goals in a single "Frozen Four" tournament game, 4125

National Football League player to receive 18 completed passes in a single game, 3225

National Hockey League All-Star Game to be televised, 4126

National Hockey League goaltender to reach 300 career wins, 4127

National Hockey League player to be named outstanding goaltender six times, 4124

Perfect game in the Little League World Series, 1578

Runners from a single country outside the United States to take the top three spots in the Boston Marathon, 4483

Shot-putter to break the 15-meter barrier in the women's event, 5337

Softball player to be batting champion of the Amateur Softball Association Major Fast Pitch league, 5590

Southern 500 automobile race, 1075

Speed skater to win three consecutive women's titles in the world championships, 5663

Swiss Grand Prix automobile race to be part of the Formula One Grand Prix circuit, 1080

Tennis player to win 10 consecutive women's doubles titles at the United States national championships, and 13 overall, 6106

Uneven (asymmetrical) bars competition held in the world championships for gymnastics, 3933

Woman to win the Grand American Trapshoot, 5306

Women's events to be included in the Alpine skiing world championships, 5392

World championship for automobile racers, 1076

World championships in cyclo-cross, 2698

World championships in Greco-Roman wrestling held on a regular basis, 6388

Zamboni ice-resurfacing machine sold commercially, 5749

1951

African-American baseball player to play for the Chicago White Sox, 1583

Asian Games, 4372

Basketball player to be named Most Valuable Player of the National Basketball Association (NBA) All-Star Game, 1930

1952

1952—*continued*

Fencer to win two, three, and four men's team épée titles in the Olympic Games, *2931*

Figure skater from France to win the women's singles title in the world championships, *3043*

Figure skater to perform a triple jump in competition, *3047*

Figure skater to perform a triple loop–triple loop combination jump in competition, *3044*

Figure skaters from the United States to sweep the men's singles medals in the world championships, *3045*

Figure skaters to win the ice dancing title in the world championships, and the first to win it two, three, and four times, *3046*

Hammer-thrower to break the 200-foot barrier, *3988*

Hammer-thrower to break the 60-meter barrier, *3987*

Heavyweight boxing match to be broadcast nationally on television, *2556*

Individual and team dressage equestrian competitions open to women, and to men other than commissioned military officers, in the Olympic Games, *2862*

Javelin-thrower from the United States to win the men's event in the Olympic Games, *4393*

Ladies Professional Golf Association (LPGA) Tour season purse to top $100,000, *3731*

Light middleweight boxing event held in the Olympic Games, *2558*

Light welterweight boxing event, and the first match between a Soviet and a United States boxer, in the Olympic Games, *2559*

Men's giant slalom event held at the Olympic Winter Games, *5394*

Men's modern pentathlon team event held in the Olympic Games, *4823*

Middle heavyweight weightlifting event held in the Olympic Games, *6338*

National Collegiate Athletic Association major college football player to intercept 29 passes during his college career, *3232*

National team to sweep the medals in the women's 10-kilometer Nordic (cross-country) skiing event in the Olympic Winter Games, *5395*

National team to win six ice hockey titles at the Olympic Winter Games, *4128*

Olympic event to be attended by 150,000 people, *4700*

Olympic Games held in Finland, *4701*

Olympic Games in which athletes from the Soviet Union participated, *4698*

Olympic men's 1500-meter freestyle event in which the medalists all had times under 19 minutes, *5832*

Olympic Winter Games held in Norway, *4699*

Pentathlete from a non-military background to win the men's modern pentathlon in the Olympic Games, *4824*

Philadelphia Athletics baseball player to be named Rookie of the Year, *1591*

Runner from Australia to win the women's 100- and 200-meter titles in the Olympic Games, *5059*

Runner from the United States to win the men's 3000-meter steeplechase title in the Olympic Games, *5057*

Runner to qualify for the finals men's of the 100-, 200-, and 400-meter races in the Olympic Games, *5054*

Runner to race the women's 800 meters in under 2:10 minutes, *5055*

Runner to win two consecutive men's 10,000-meter titles in the Olympic Games, *5056*

Running deer (single and double shot) individual shooting event held in the Olympic Games, *5308*

Sailor to win the men's Finn-class event two, three, and four times in the Olympic Games, *5219*

Shooter to win two consecutive men's rapid-fire pistol titles in the Olympic Games, *5307*

Shot-putter to break the 50-foot barrier in the women's event, *5338*

Skier from the United States to win two Olympic gold medals, *5397*

Small-bore rifle (three positions) individual shooting event held in the Olympic Games, *5309*

Triple-jumper of Black African ancestry to win the men's title in the Olympic Games, *6255*

University of Kansas championship in the National Collegiate Athletic Association (NCAA) Men's Basketball National Tournament, *1935*

Weightlifter from the United States to win the lightweight weightlifting title in the Olympic Games, *6337*

Weightlifter to win two consecutive titles in the unlimited weight (super heavyweight) competition in the Olympic Games, *6339*

Woman equestrian to win a team dressage medal in the Olympic Games, *2863*

Woman equestrian to win an individual dressage medal in the Olympic Games, *2864*

Women's all-around gymnastics competition held in the Olympic Games, *3934*

Women's balance beam gymnastics competition held in the Olympic Games, *3935*

Women's floor exercises gymnastics competition held in the Olympic Games, *3936*

Women's giant slalom event held at the Olympic Winter Games, *5393*

Women's individual 10-kilometer Nordic (cross-country) event held at the Olympic Winter Games, *5396*

Women's side horse vault gymnastics competition held in the Olympic Games, *3937*

Women's uneven (asymmetrical) bars gymnastics competition held in the Olympic Games, *3938*

World championships in volleyball to include women, *6278*

1953

African-American baseball player to play for the Philadelphia Athletics, *1601*

African-American football player from an African-American college to be named to the Associated Press (AP) Little All-America Team, *3234*

Argentine Grand Prix automobile race, *1091*

Automobile racer to have nine consecutive wins over two seasons on the Formula One Grand Prix circuit, *1089*

Automobile racer to win more than 10 races in a single season in the National Association for Stock Car Auto Racing (NASCAR) Winston Cup series, *1090*

Baseball team to win five consecutive American League pennants, *1592*

Basketball player to have 51 rebounds during a single Division I National Collegiate Athletic Association (NCAA) game, *1938*

Basketball player to have 734 rebounds during a single Division I National Collegiate Athletic Association (NCAA) season, *1936*

Basketball team to have 57 free throws in a single National Basketball Association (NBA) playoff game, *1939*

Canada Cup golf tournament, *3732*

College football player to win the Maxwell Award twice, *3235*

Detroit Tigers baseball player to be named Rookie of the Year, *1593*

Discus-thrower to break the 190-foot barrier, *2769*

Fencer to win three, and then four, men's foil titles in the world championships, *2932*

Figure skater from the United States to win the women's singles title in the world championships, *3048*

Golf tournament to be televised nationally, *3733*

Golfer to win 10 major tournaments recognized by the Ladies Professional Golf Association (LPGA) Tour, *3738*

Golfer to win the Tournament of Champions, *3734*

Golfer to win the U.S. Open, the Masters, and the British Open in the same year, and the first to score under 275 for 72 holes, *3735*

Golfer to win the U.S. Women's Open in a playoff, *3739*

Golfer to win the Vare Trophy for the lowest average score on the Ladies Professional Golf Association (LPGA) Tour, *3736*

Javelin-thrower to break the 260-foot and 80-meter barriers, and the first from the United States to hold the world record in the men's event, *4394*

Little League World Series to be televised, *1594*

Major league baseball catcher to hit 38 home runs, *1600*

Major league baseball pitcher to strike out eight consecutive opposing batters, *1599*

Milwaukee Braves regular season baseball game played at County Stadium, *1597*

National Basketball Association (NBA) player to be named Rookie of the Year, *1937*

National Collegiate Athletic Association hockey team to win the "Frozen Four" tournament in three consecutive years, *4129*

National Hockey League coach to reach 600 career wins, *4130*

Native-American major league baseball player to be named to baseball's Hall of Fame, *1595*

Pan-Arab Games, *4373*

Professional Golfers' Association (PGA) Tour season purse to top $500,000, *3737*

Runner to complete the men's marathon in under 2:20 hours, *4485*

Shot-putter to break the 16-meter barrier in the women's event, *5339*

Shot-putter to break the 18- and 19-meter, and 60-foot, barriers, *5340*

Softball team to win the Amateur Softball Association Men's Slow Pitch National Championships, *5592*

Twin major league baseball players to play in the same game on the same team, *1598*

Water-skier to win two, and then three, women's titles at the world championships, *6317*

Woman tennis player to achieve a Grand Slam, *6107*

Woman to play as a fully recognized regular on a men's major league baseball team, *1596*

Woman to sail across the Atlantic alone, *5220*

World championships in show jumping, *2865*

1954

Adoption of the "24-second" rule by the National Basketball Association (NBA), *1940*

African-American athlete to win the Sullivan Award, *1150*

African-American baseball player to be named Associated Press Athlete of the Year, *1602*

African-American baseball player to play for the Cincinnati Reds, *1608*

African-American baseball player to play for the Pittsburgh Pirates, *1605*

1954—_continued_

African-American baseball player to play for the St. Louis Cardinals, _1606_

African-American college basketball team to win a national title, _1941_

Athlete to be named _Sports Illustrated_ Sportsman of the Year, _1151_

Automobile racer to be world champion on the Formula One Grand Prix circuit two, three, four, and five times; the first to win the title three and four times consecutively; and the first from Argentina to be world champion, _1092_

Automobile racer to win the Indianapolis 500 with an average speed of more than 130 miles per hour, _1093_

Baltimore Bullets player to be named National Basketball Association (NBA) Rookie of the Year, _1942_

Baltimore Orioles regular season baseball game played at Memorial Stadium in Baltimore, _1607_

Basketball player to score 100 points in a single Division I National Collegiate Athletic Association (NCAA) game, _1949_

Basketball player to score 23 free throws in a Division I National Collegiate Athletic Association (NCAA) game, _1943_

Basketball player to score 55 free throws in a Division I National Collegiate Athletic Association (NCAA) championship series, _1944_

Basketball player to shoot 355 free throws during a single Division I National Collegiate Athletic Association (NCAA) season, _1945_

Basketball team to win three consecutive National Basketball Association (NBA) championships, _1946_

Bowler to bowl a 300 game in a televised match, _2496_

Figure skater from Germany to win the women's singles title in the world championships, _3049_

Figure skaters from Canada to win the pairs title in the world championships, _3050_

Golf tournament to offer a $100,000 purse, _3740_

Golfer to score under 190 for three consecutive 18-hole rounds in a Professional Golfers' Association (PGA) recognized event, _3741_

Golfer to win the Masters tournament three times, _3742_

Golfer to win the U.S. Women's Open three times, _3744_

Hammer-thrower to break the 210-foot barrier, _3989_

International Surfing Championships, _5770_

Javelin-thrower to break the 180-foot barrier in the women's event, _4395_

La Salle University championship in the National Collegiate Athletic Association (NCAA) Men's Basketball National Tournament, _1948_

Limit on the number of fouls per period in the National Basketball Association (NBA), _1947_

Major league baseball player to hit five home runs in a doubleheader, _1609_

Major league baseball player widely recognized as black to play for the Washington Senators, _1610_

Men's 15-kilometer cross-country event held in the world championships of Nordic skiing, _5398_

Mexican major league baseball player to win a batting title, _1603_

National Collegiate Athletic Association hockey player to score seven points in a single "Frozen Four" tournament game, _4133_

National Football League player to win _The Sporting News_ Most Valuable Player Award, _3236_

National Hockey League player to be named outstanding defenseman, _4131_

National Hockey League player to lead the league in scoring four times in a row, _4132_

National Hockey League player to reach 400 career goals, _4134_

National League team to top 2 million paying customers at home in a single season, _1604_

Runner to hold the officially accepted world record in the men's 5000-meter steeplechase, _5062_

Runner to race the men's 10,000 meters in under 29:00 minutes, _5061_

Runner to race the mile in under 4:00 minutes, _5060_

Shot-putter to break the 18- and 19-meter, and 60-foot, barriers, _5340_

Soccer (international football) team from Germany to win the world cup, _5556_

U.S. Open golf tournament to be televised nationally, _3743_

Women's 10-kilometer cross-country event held in the world championships of Nordic skiing, _5399_

Women's cross-country relay event held in the world championships of Nordic skiing, _5400_

World cup in rugby, _4969_

1955

Adoption of a lane-widening rule by the National Basketball Association (NBA), _1950_

African-American baseball player to play for the New York Yankees, _1615_

African-American college football player to win the Outland Trophy, _3237_

African-American football players to appear in the Orange Bowl, _3239_

1956—*continued*

Golfer to win the Ladies Professional Golf Association (LPGA) Championship in a sudden-death playoff, *3749*

Golfer to win the Tournament of Champions twice, and then three times, in a row, *3747*

Gymnast to win two consecutive women's floor exercise titles in the Olympic Games, *3941*

Hammer-thrower to break the 220-foot barrier, *3990*

High-jumper to clear seven feet, *4025*

Hispanic-American major league baseball player to be named Rookie of the Year, *1621*

Hurdler to race the men's 400-meter hurdles in under 50 seconds, *4337*

Hurdler to win two consecutive titles in the women's 80-meter hurdles in the Olympic Games, *4338*

Ice hockey team from the Soviet Union to win the gold medal at the Olympic Winter Games, *4135*

Javelin-thrower to break the 270-foot barrier, *4396*

Javelin-thrower to break the 280-foot barrier and to hold the world record in the men's event, *4397*

Major league baseball pitcher to win the Cy Young Award, *1622*

Male gymnast to win more than 10 medals in the Olympic Games, *3939*

Men's 200-meter butterfly swimming event held in the Olympic Games, *5834*

Men's 20,000-meter walk event held in the Olympic Games, *6292*

Men's 30-kilometer Nordic (cross-country) ski event held at the Olympic Winter Games, *5402*

Men's individual 15-kilometer Nordic (cross-country) event at the Olympic Winter Games, *5404*

National golf team that won the Canada Cup twice, *3748*

National team to sweep the medals in the men's giant slalom in the Olympic Winter Games, *5403*

Olympic Games held in the Southern Hemisphere, and in Australia, *4706*

Olympic Games to be boycotted by member countries, *4703*

Olympic Games to have a formal closing ceremony, *4708*

Olympic Winter Games at which athletes from the Soviet Union participated, *4705*

Olympic Winter Games to be held in Italy, and the first to be televised, *4704*

Pentathlete to win two consecutive titles in the men's modern pentathlon in the Olympic Games, *4825*

Perfect game in the World Series, *1623*

Pole-vaulter to win two consecutive titles in the men's event in the Olympic Games, *4843*

Precision team figure skating event, *3052*

Rochester Royals player to be named National Basketball Association (NBA) Rookie of the Year, *1963*

Runner to race the men's 100-meter dash in 10.1 seconds, *5063*

Runner to race the men's 5000-meter steeplechase in under 8:39 minutes, *5064*

Runners to finish first and second in both the women's 100- and 200-meter races in the Olympic Games, *5065*

Sailor to win the men's Finn-class event two, three, and four times in the Olympic Games, *5219*

Shot-putter to break the 18- and 19-meter, and 60-foot, barriers, *5340*

Shot-putter to win two consecutive men's titles in the Olympic Games, *5341*

Skier to sweep the men's individual Alpine events at the Olympic Winter Games, *5406*

Skiers from the Soviet Union to win the men's 4 x 10-kilometer relay Nordic (cross-country) title at the Olympic Winter Games, *5405*

Swimmer to race the women's 400-meter freestyle event in under five minutes, *5833*

Triple-jumper to win two consecutive men's titles in the Olympic Games, *6256*

Weightlifter from the United States to win the featherweight title in the Olympic Games, *6340*

Woman athlete to win seven track and field medals in the Olympic Games, *6214*

Woman gymnast to win 10 medals in the Olympic Games, *3940*

Women's 100-meter butterfly event held in the Olympic Games, *5835*

Women's 3 x 5-kilometer relay Nordic (cross-country) skiing event held at the Olympic Winter Games, *5401*

World championships for judo, *4532*

1957

Admiral's Cup race, *5221*

African-American baseball player to play for the Philadelphia Phillies, *1627*

African-American golfer to win a title in a significant predominantly white tournament, *3750*

African-American tennis player to win the women's singles championship at Wimbledon, *6110*

Automobile racer to win two consecutive championships on the National Association for Stock Car Auto Racing (NASCAR) Winston Cup circuit, *1094*

Automobile racer to win two, three, and four Argentine Grand Prix races, *1095*

Ban on underwater stroking in the breaststroke swimming events in international competition, 5836

Baseball player to hit 13 grand slam home runs in the National League, 1629

Basketball player to grab 32 rebounds in a single half of a National Basketball Association (NBA) game, 1973

Basketball player to lead the National Basketball Association (NBA) in free throw percentage for five consecutive years, 1964

Basketball team to have 487 rebounds in one National Basketball Association (NBA) Finals series, 1965

Basketball team to make 244 free throws in one set of National Basketball Association (NBA) playoffs, 1966

Basketball team to make 45 free throws in a single National Basketball Association (NBA) Finals game, 1972

Basketball team to score 827 points in a National Basketball Association (NBA) Finals series, 1967

Boston Celtics National Basketball Association (NBA) championship, 1968

Boston Celtics player to be named National Basketball Association (NBA) Most Valuable Player of the Year, 1969

Boston Celtics player to be named National Basketball Association (NBA) Rookie of the Year, 1970

Boston Marathon winner who was a member of the Boston Athletic Association, 4486

Boxer from a Communist country to turn professional, 2561

College football coach to be named Coach of the Year, 3241

Golfer on the Professional Golfers' Association (PGA) Tour to be named Rookie of the Year, 3751

Golfer to win 10 titles recognized by the Ladies Professional Golf Association (LPGA) Tour in a single season, 3752

Green Bay Packers regular season football game played at Lambeau Field, 3245

International governing body specifically for luge events, 4454

Little League World Series won by a team from outside the United States, 1624

Milwaukee Braves pitcher to win the Cy Young Award, 1625

National Collegiate Athletic Association major college football team to win 47 consecutive games, 3242

National Football League player, and the first African-American football player, to win the Associated Press (AP) Most Valuable Player Award, 3243

National Hockey League player to reach 500 career goals, 4136

National League baseball player to play in 823 consecutive games, 1628

Philadelphia Phillies baseball player to be named Rookie of the Year, 1626

Runner to complete the 1500-meter race in under 3:40 minutes, 5067

Runner to hold the officially accepted world record in the women's 400-meter event, 5066

University of Iowa win in college football's Rose Bowl, 3244

University of North Carolina championship in the National Collegiate Athletic Association (NCAA) Men's Basketball National Tournament, 1971

Whitbread Gold Cup horse race, 4302

World championship in moto-cross racing, 4579

World championships in archery involving FITA rounds, 1033

World team Uber Cup badminton championships for women, 1170

1958

African-American athlete to be named *Sports Illustrated* Sportsman of the Year, 1152

African-American to become a member of the Collegiate Basketball Officials Association, 1974

African-American to play in the National Hockey League, 4138

Automobile racer to have more than 20 wins on the Formula One Grand Prix circuit, 1096

Baltimore Colts National Football League championship, 3246

Basketball Hall of Fame, 1975

Basketball player to make 19 free throws in a National Basketball Association (NBA) Finals game, 1980

Basketball player to score more than 2,000 points in a single National Basketball Association (NBA) season, 1976

Basketball team to average 31.9 free throws per game in a single National Basketball Association (NBA) season, 1977

Frisbee, 3525

Golfer to win the Professional Golfers' Association (PGA) Championship after it was converted into a stroke play tournament, 3753

Governing body solely for tug-of-war events, 6269

Gymnast to win two consecutive men's floor exercise titles in the world championships, 3942

High-jumper to clear six feet in the women's event, 4026

International cricket organization for women, 2659

International Frisbee Tournament, 3526

Los Angeles Dodgers regular season baseball game played at Los Angeles Memorial Coliseum, 1633

1958—*continued*

Major league baseball player widely recognized as black to play for the Detroit Tigers, *1634*

Married figure skaters to win the pairs title at the U.S. national championships, *3054*

National Football League game to be nationally televised, *3247*

National Hockey League player to be named outstanding defenseman four times in a row, *4137*

National tournament for athletes in wheelchairs held in the United States, *2750*

New York Yankees pitcher to win the Cy Young Award, *1630*

Philadelphia Warriors player to be named National Basketball Association (NBA) Rookie of the Year, *1978*

Professional league for Canadian-style football, *3521*

Runner to complete the men's mile race in under 3:55 minutes, *5068*

Sailboard, *5189*

San Francisco Giants regular season baseball game played at Seals Stadium, *1632*

Soccer (international football) team from Brazil to win the world cup, *5557*

St. Louis Hawks National Basketball Association (NBA) championship, *1979*

Sudden death overtime game in the National Football League, *3248*

Total purse on the Professional Golfers' Association (PGA) Tour to top $1 million, *3754*

United States intercollegiate women's singles and women's doubles national championships, *6111*

Washington Senators Rookie of the Year, *1631*

Woman automobile racer to compete in a Grand Prix race eligible for world-championship points, *1097*

World Biathlon Championships, *2430*

1959

African-American baseball player to play for the Boston Red Sox, *1639*

African-American basketball players to be named to an All–National Basketball Association (NBA) first team, *1981*

African-American golfer to be classified as an "approved player" on the Professional Golfers' Association (PGA) Tour, *3755*

African-American golfer to win a national championship, *3756*

Amateur Softball Association Women's Major Slow Pitch National Championships, *5594*

Basketball player to average 29.5 rebounds per game in an National Basketball Association (NBA) Finals series, *1982*

Basketball player to have 19 assists in a single half of a National Basketball Association (NBA) game, *1986*

Basketball player to shoot 24 consecutive free throws, and to shoot 100 percent in free throws, during a single Division I National Collegiate Athletic Association (NCAA) game, *1987*

Basketball team to have 525 rebounds in one set of National Basketball Association (NBA) playoffs, *1983*

Basketball team to score 869 points in one set of National Basketball Association (NBA) playoffs, *1984*

Boxer to be named *Sports Illustrated* Sportsman of the Year, *2562*

Chicago White Sox baseball player to be named Most Valuable Player, *1635*

Chicago White Sox pitcher to win the Cy Young Award, *1636*

College baseball player to score five runs in a single game, *1638*

College football team to win two consecutive Orange Bowl games, *3249*

Cowboy to be named All-Around Cowboy four consecutive times, and five overall, *4894*

Daytona 500 automobile race, *1098*

Golfer to win two consecutive U.S. Women's Open titles, *3757*

Ladies Professional Golf Association (LPGA) Tour season purse to top $200,000, *3758*

Liberty Bowl football game, *3250*

Lifting of the "no blacks allowed" clause from the constitution of the Professional Golfers' Association (PGA), *3759*

Major league baseball player to be a unanimous All-Star Game selection, *1637*

Minneapolis Lakers player to be named National Basketball Association (NBA) Rookie of the Year, *1985*

"Mixed" female-male softball team league, *5595*

National Finals Rodeo (NFR), *4895*

Pentathlete to win three consecutive men's titles in the world pentathlon championships and then a fourth, *4826*

Rower to win both the single and double sculls events at the Henley Regatta, *4939*

Shot-putter to break the 17- and 18-meter, and 60-foot, barriers in the women's event, *5342*

South-East Asia Games, *4374*

United States Grand Prix automobile race to be part of the Formula One Grand Prix circuit, *1099*

Wild-water world championships, *2608*

World championships in curling, *2677*

World championships in cycling to include women racers, *2700*

World field archery championships, *1034*

1960

African-American assistant coach in the National Basketball Association (NBA), *1988*

1960—*continued*

National Hockey League player to be named outstanding goaltender five times in a row, *4139*

National Hockey League player to reach 1,000 career points, *4142*

National Hockey League team to win the Stanley Cup five times in a row, *4140*

National team to sweep the top medals in the women's all-around gymnastics competition in the Olympic Games, *3946*

Ohio State University championship in the National Collegiate Athletic Association (NCAA) Men's Basketball National Tournament, *1992*

Olympic men's 1500-meter freestyle event in which the medalists all had times under 18 minutes, *5841*

Olympic Winter Games host city to refuse to build a bobsled run, *2474*

Olympic women's 400-meter freestyle event in which the medalists all had times under five minutes, *5839*

Olympics-like tournament for athletes with disabilities, *2751*

Pentathlete to win two pentathlon gold medals in the same Olympic Games, *4827*

Philadelphia Warriors player to be named National Basketball Association (NBA) Most Valuable Player of the Year, *1993*

Pittsburgh Pirates baseball player to be named Most Valuable Player, *1641*

Pittsburgh Pirates pitcher to win the Cy Young Award, *1642*

Runner from New Zealand to win the men's 5000-meter title in the Olympic Games, *5070*

Runner from New Zealand to win the men's 800-meter title in the Olympic Games, *5071*

Runners to complete the men's 400-meter race in under 45 seconds, *5072*

Sailor to win the men's Finn-class event two, three, and four times in the Olympic Games, *5219*

San Francisco Giants regular season baseball game played at Candlestick Park (later 3Com Park), *1643*

Shot-putter to break the 20-meter barrier, *5343*

Single-Handed Transatlantic Race (STAR), *5222*

Sky diver from the United States to win the men's title in the world sky diving championships, *5505*

Softball team to win six consecutive titles in the International Softball Congress World Championships, *5596*

Speed skater to skate the 10,000 meters in under 16 minutes, *5672*

Speed skater to win two consecutive titles in the men's 500 meters at the Olympic Winter Games, *5671*

Swimmer to win two and then three consecutive women's 100-meter freestyle titles in the Olympic Games, *5842*

Swimmer to win two consecutive men's 400-meter freestyle titles in the Olympic Games, *5837*

Team event in the dirt-track (speedway) motorcycle racing world championships, *4580*

Triple-jumper to break both the 55-foot and 17-meter barriers, *6257*

Weightlifter to win two consecutive bantamweight titles in the Olympic Games, *6341*

Weightlifter to win two consecutive middle heavyweight titles in the Olympic Games, *6342*

Women's 1000-meter speed skating event held at the Olympic Winter Games, *5667*

Women's 1500-meter speed skating event held at the Olympic Winter Games, *5670*

Women's 3000-meter speed skating event held at the Olympic Winter Games, *5668*

Women's 4 x 100-meter medley relay swimming event held in the Olympic Games, *5840*

Women's 500-meter pairs kayaking event held in the Olympic Games, *2610*

Women's 500-meter speed skating event held at the Olympic Winter Games, *5669*

Women's 800-meter race held in the Olympic Games after a 32-year ban, *5073*

Women's team foil fencing competition held in the Olympic Games, *2935*

World 600 automobile race, *1101*

Wrestler to win two consecutive welterweight Greco-Roman titles in the Olympic Games, *6390*

1961

African-American college football player to win the Heisman Trophy, *3257*

African-American golfer to play in a Professional Golfers' Association (PGA) Tour tournament in the South, *3763*

African-American professional basketball coach, *2000*

African-American quarterback to appear in the Rose Bowl college football game, *3260*

African-American woman to win the Sullivan Award, *1153*

American Football Conference championship, *3259*

American Football League team to win two consecutive conference championships, *3262*

Basketball player to be named Division I National Collegiate Athletic Association (NCAA) Associated Press (AP) Player of the Year, *2001*

Basketball player to be named *Sports Illustrated* Sportsman of the Year, *2002*

1962—continued

Figure skater from the Netherlands to win the women's singles title in the world championships, *3059*

Figure skater to land a triple lutz jump in competition, *3060*

Figure skaters from Czechoslovakia to win the ice dancing title in the world championships, *3061*

Figure skaters from the Soviet Union to win the pairs title in the world championships, *3062*

Golf package, *3765*

Golfer named Rookie of the Year on the Ladies Professional Golf Association (LPGA) Tour, *3766*

Golfer on the Ladies Professional Golf Association (LPGA) Tour to win four consecutively scheduled tournaments, *3768*

Los Angeles Angels regular season baseball game played at Dodger Stadium, *1658*

Los Angeles Dodgers regular season baseball game played at Dodger Stadium, *1655*

Major league baseball player to have 104 steals in one season, *1662*

Major league baseball player to reach 5,864 bases, *1660*

Men's ski jumping (large hill) event held in the world championships of Nordic skiing, *5407*

National Football League player to win the *Pro Football Weekly* Most Valuable Player Award, *3265*

National Hockey League player to be named Most Valuable Player of the NHL All-Star Game, *4143*

New York Mets regular season baseball game played at the Polo Grounds, *1657*

Pole-vaulter to clear 16 feet, *4844*

Runner to complete the men's 800-meter race in under 1:45 minutes, *5074*

Senior Leagues for 13-year-old to 15-year-old players organized by Little League Baseball, *1653*

Shot-putter to break the 17- and 18-meter, and 60-foot, barriers in the women's event, *5342*

Surfer not born in Hawaii to win the International Surfing Championships, *5771*

Swimmer to race the women's 100-meter freestyle in under one minute, *5844*

Tournament of Champions in bowling, *2497*

Universiade (World Student Games), *4375*

University of Minnesota win in college football's Rose Bowl, *3266*

Washington Senators regular season baseball game played at DC Stadium, *1654*

Women's 5-kilometer cross-country event held in the world championships of Nordic skiing, *5408*

World championship in moto-cross racing to include the 250 cc class, *4582*

World championships in rowing, *4940*

World Series of Golf, *3767*

1963

African-American baseball player to be named Most Valuable Player in the American League, *1663*

All–National Basketball Association (NBA) Rookie Team, *2019*

Automobile racer to have seven wins in a single season on the Formula One Grand Prix circuit, *1105*

Baseball team to hit four successive home runs in an American League game, *1666*

Basketball player to average 23.3 rebounds in a Division I National Collegiate Athletic Association (NCAA) championship series, *2020*

Basketball player to win three consecutive National Basketball Association (NBA) Most Valuable Player Awards, *2021*

Basketball team to make 333 field goals in one set of National Basketball Association (NBA) playoffs, *2022*

Coach to be named National Basketball Association (NBA) Coach of the Year, *2023*

College baseball player to hit four home runs in a College World Series, *1664*

Dominican pitcher to pitch a no-hitter in the major leagues, *1665*

Federation Cup championships, *6112*

Golfer to earn more than $100,000 in official prize money during a single year, *3769*

Golfer to win 13 titles recognized by the Ladies Professional Golf Association (LPGA) Tour in a single season, *3773*

Golfer to win the World Series of Golf twice in a row, *3770*

High-jumper to set six world records in the men's event, *4029*

Hispanic-American All-Star Game in major league baseball, *1667*

Instant replay, *3269*

Ladies Professional Golf Association (LPGA) tournament to be nationally televised, *3772*

Mexican Grand Prix automobile race to be part of the Formula One Grand Prix circuit, *1106*

National Hockey League Amateur Draft, *4145*

National Hockey League player to be named the league's Most Valuable Player six times, *4144*

Pole-vaulter to clear 17 feet, *4845*

Pro Football Hall of Fame, *3268*

Runner to break the 1926 record in the women's marathon, and the first from the United States to hold the world record in the event, *4488*

Runner to race the men's 5000-meter steeplechase in under 8:30.0 minutes, *5075*

Softball player to win two consecutive Most Valuable Player Awards in the Amateur Softball Association Major Fast Pitch National Championships, *5597*

Speed skater to skate the 3000 meters in under 4:30 minutes, *5674*

Speed skater to skate the 500 meters in under 40 seconds, *5673*

Sports commissioner to be named *Sports Illustrated* Sportsman of the Year, *1154*

Total purse on the Professional Golfers' Association (PGA) Tour to top $2 million, *3771*

World amateur snooker championships, *2457*

World championships in bowling to include women, *2498*

World championships in netball, *4598*

World championships in rhythmic sportive gymnastics, *3949*

1964

African-American college football player to become a quarterback at Harvard University, *3270*

Athlete to win 18 medals in the Olympic Games, *4711*

Athlete to win four gold medals at a single Olympic Winter Games, and six Olympic gold medals overall, *4715*

Athlete to win nine medals in the Olympic Winter Games, *4716*

Athletes from the Bahamas to win gold medals in the Olympic Games, *4719*

Austrian Grand Prix automobile race to be part of the Formula One Grand Prix circuit, *1107*

Baltimore Orioles baseball player to be named Most Valuable Player, *1669*

Baseball player from Japan to play in United States major league baseball, *1674*

Baseball player to lead the American League in stolen bases for nine consecutive years, *1670*

Basketball player to make 113 field goals in one set of National Basketball Association (NBA) playoffs, *2024*

Boxer to win the world heavyweight championship three times, *2566*

Buffalo Bills American Football League championship, *3272*

Cincinnati Royals player to be named National Basketball Association (NBA) Most Valuable Player, *2025*

Cyclist to win the Tour de France five times, and four times consecutively, *2701*

Discus-thrower to break the 210-foot barrier, *2774*

Drag racer to reach a speed of over 200, and then 250, miles per hour, *1108*

Equestrian to win three consecutive titles in team jumping in the Olympic Games, *2869*

Figure skater from Germany to win the men's singles title at the Olympic Winter Games, *3063*

Figure skater from the Netherlands to win the women's singles title at the Olympic Winter Games, *3065*

Figure skaters from the Soviet Union to win the pairs title at the Olympic Winter Games, *3064*

Golfer to win the Ladies Professional Golf Association (LPGA) Championship with a score under 280, *3774*

Golfer to win the Masters tournament four times, *3775*

Golfer to win the U.S. Women's Open four times, *3778*

Gymnast to win 9 gold medals and 18 medals overall in the Olympics Games, *3950*

Gymnast to win three consecutive gold medals in the team combined exercises in the Olympic Games, *3951*

Gymnast to win two consecutive titles in the women's uneven (asymmetrical) bars in the Olympic Games, *3952*

High-jumper to win two consecutive women's titles in the Olympic Games, *4030*

Horse to be named Horse of the Year three, four, and five times consecutively, *4303*

International organization for surfing, *5772*

Javelin-thrower to break the 200-foot and 60-meter barriers in the women's event, *4400*

Javelin-thrower to break the 300-foot and 90-meter barriers in the men's event, *4399*

Los Angeles Angels pitcher to win the Cy Young Award, *1668*

Major league baseball pitcher to pitch a losing 9-inning no-hitter, *1672*

Men's 4 x 100-meter freestyle relay swimming event held in the Olympic Games, *5847*

Men's 400-meter individual medley swimming event held in the Olympic Games, *5848*

Men's 4000-meter individual pursuit cycling event held in the Olympic Games, *2702*

Men's fours 1000-meter kayaking event held in the Olympic Games, *2611*

Men's heavyweight judo event in the Olympic Games, *4535*

Men's individual 70-meter ski jump event held at the Olympic Winter Games, *5410*

Men's lightweight judo event in the Olympic Games, *4534*

Men's middleweight judo event in the Olympic Games, *4533*

Men's open judo event in the Olympic Games, *4536*

Men's singles luge (toboggan) event held in the Olympic Winter Games, *4455*

Men's volleyball event held in the Olympic Games, *6279*

1964—*continued*

National Collegiate Athletic Association college hockey team to win the "Frozen Four" tournament seven times, *4146*

National golf team to win five consecutive Canada Cup tournaments, *3776*

National League game to run 7 hours and 25 minutes over 23 innings, *1673*

National team to sweep the medals in the men's 200-meter backstroke event in the Olympic Games, *5846*

National team to sweep the medals in the men's 5000-meter speed-skating event at the Olympic Winter Games, *5676*

National team to sweep the medals in the women's 500-meter speed-skating event at the Olympic Winter Games, *5675*

National team to sweep the medals in the women's downhill event in the Olympic Winter Games, *5413*

New York Mets regular season baseball game played at Shea Stadium, *1671*

Olympic Games held in Asia, or in Japan, *4718*

Olympic light heavyweight boxing champion to become world heavyweight champion, *2565*

Olympic Winter Games at which an athlete was killed, *4713*

Olympic Winter Games held in Austria, *4714*

Olympic Winter Games in which more than 1000 athletes competed, *4712*

Pentathlete to win two gold medals in the men's modern pentathlon team competition in the Olympic Games, *4828*

Rower to win three consecutive men's single sculls rowing titles in the Olympic Games, *4941*

Runner from the United States to win the men's 10,000-meter title at the Olympic Games, *5077*

Runner from the United States to win the men's 5000-meter title at the Olympic Games, *5078*

Runner to win two consecutive marathon titles in the Olympic Games, *4489*

San Diego Chargers American Football League championship, *3271*

Shooter from the United States to win the men's small-bore rifle (three positions) title in the Olympic Games, *5310*

Shot-putter to win two consecutive titles in the women's event in the Olympic Games, *5344*

Skier to be killed during the Olympic Winter Games, *5409*

Skier to win both the men's individual 70- and 90-meter ski jumps in the same Olympic Winter Games, *5414*

Skier to win two titles in the men's 50-kilometer freestyle Nordic (cross-country) skiing at the Olympic Winter Games, *5411*

Softball team to win three consecutive titles at the Amateur Softball Association Major Slow Pitch National Championships, *5598*

Speed skater to win four gold medals in speed skating in a single Olympic Winter Games, *5678*

Speed skater to win two consecutive women's 1500-meter and 3000-meter titles at the Olympic Winter Games, *5677*

Swimmer to win four gold medals in a single Olympic Games, *5850*

Swimmer to win three consecutive titles in the same event in the Olympic Games, *5845*

Swimmer to win two and then three consecutive women's 100-meter freestyle titles in the Olympic Games, *5842*

Two-seater luge (toboggan) event at the Olympic Winter Games, *4456*

University of California at Los Angeles championship in the National Collegiate Athletic Association (NCAA) Men's Basketball National Tournament, *2026*

Water polo player to win medals in five different Olympic Games, *6304*

Wedding between Olympic athletes held at the Olympic Games, *4717*

Woman to compete in the three-day event individual equestrian competition in the Olympic Games, *2868*

Women's 400-meter individual medley swimming event held in the Olympic Games, *5849*

Women's 400-meter race held in the Olympic Games, *5076*

Women's individual 5-kilometer Nordic (cross-country) event in the Olympic Winter Games, *5412*

Women's pentathlon held in the Olympic Games, *4829*

Women's singles luge (toboggan) event held in the Olympic Winter Games, *4457*

Women's volleyball event held in the Olympic Games, *6280*

Women's World Amateur Team Championship, *3777*

World championships in trampolining, *6228*

World Surfing Championships, *5773*

1965

African-American to become a major league baseball broadcaster, *1675*

African-American to win a world title in billiards, *2458*

All-African Games, *4376*

Automobile racer to win the Indianapolis 500 with an average speed of over 150 miles per hour, *1109*

Baseball player chosen in major league baseball's first free draft, *1682*

Baseball player to be named Associated Press Athlete of the Year twice, *1676*

Baseball player to lead the National League in stolen bases for six consecutive years, *1677*

Baseball player to win batting titles in his first two major league years, *1678*

Basketball player to get 220 rebounds in one set of National Basketball Association (NBA) playoffs, *2027*

Basketball player to have 18 rebounds in a single quarter of a National Basketball Association (NBA) game, *2035*

Basketball player to make 18 free throws in a single Division I National Collegiate Athletic Association (NCAA) Final Four championship series game, *2028*

Basketball player to make 86 free throws in one set of National Basketball Association (NBA) playoffs, *2029*

Basketball player to score 58 points in a single Division I National Collegiate Athletic Association (NCAA) Final Four championship series game, *2030*

Basketball player to score an average of 46.5 points in one set of National Basketball Association (NBA) playoffs, *2031*

Basketball player to win the National Basketball Association (NBA) Most Valuable Player Award five times, *2032*

College basketball player to receive the James E. Sullivan Memorial Award, *2033*

College softball player to win the Erv Lind Award, *5599*

European Cup, *6215*

Golfer to have 15 consecutive seasons with a victory on the Ladies Professional Golf Association (LPGA) Tour, *3779*

Golfer to win more than 80 tournaments on the Professional Golfers' Association (PGA) Tour, and to win the same PGA event eight times, *3780*

Hammer-thrower to break the 240-foot barrier, *3992*

Head of the Charles Regatta, *4942*

Houston Astros regular season baseball game played at the Houston Astrodome, *1680*

Indoor track and field competition sponsored by the National Collegiate Athletic Association (NCAA), *6216*

Major league baseball game played indoors and on an artificial surface, *1681*

Major league baseball pitcher to reach 382 strikeouts in a single season, *1683*

Minnesota Twins baseball player to be named Most Valuable Player, *1679*

National Football League player to lead the league in rushing touchdowns five times, *3273*

National Football League player to lead the league in rushing yards eight times, *3274*

National Hockey League goaltender to reach 400 career wins, *4148*

National Hockey League player to win the Conn Smythe Trophy as the Most Valuable Player of the playoffs, *4147*

New York Knicks player to be named National Basketball Association (NBA) Rookie of the Year, *2034*

Qualifying School of the Professional Golfers' Association (PGA) Tour, *3781*

Runner from Africa to hold the world record in the men's 5000 meters, *5079*

Shot-putter to break the 70-foot and 21-meter barriers, *5345*

Softball player to win two consecutive batting titles in the Amateur Softball Association Major Fast Pitch National League, *5600*

Tennis player to win six consecutive French national men's doubles championships after the event became international, *6113*

University of California at Los Angeles win in college football's Rose Bowl, *3275*

World championships in fast-pitch softball, *5601*

World championships in show jumping to include women riders, *2870*

World championships in trampolining to include individual tumbling and synchronized pairs competitions, *6229*

World cup in volleyball, *6281*

1966

African-American National Basketball Association (NBA) head coach, *2036*

African-American to work as an umpire in major league baseball, *1686*

Atlanta Braves regular season baseball game played at Atlanta–Fulton County Stadium, *1687*

Baltimore Orioles World Series victory, *1684*

Baseball pitcher to lead the National League in earned run average for five consecutive years, *1685*

Baseball player to be named Most Valuable Player in both major leagues, *1690*

Basketball player to lead the National Basketball Association (NBA) in scoring for seven consecutive years, *2037*

Basketball player to make 14 free throws in a single quarter of a National Basketball Association (NBA) game, *2045*

Basketball player to make 840 free throws in a single National Basketball Association (NBA) season, *2038*

Basketball team to score 827 points in a National Basketball Association (NBA) Finals series, *2039*

Basketball team to win eight consecutive National Basketball Association (NBA) titles, *2040*

1966—*continued*

California Angels regular season baseball game played at Anaheim Stadium, *1688*

Championship win by a team with an all-African-American starting lineup in the final game, and the first championship for Texas Western, in the National Collegiate Athletic Association (NCAA) Men's Basketball National Tournament, *2043*

Fencer to win three men's sabre titles in the world championships, *2936*

Freestyle skiing competition on record, *5415*

Golfer to be named Ladies Professional Golf Association (LPGA) Player of the Year, *3782*

Golfer to win the Masters tournament twice in a row, *3783*

Golfer to win the Tournament of Champions in a playoff, *3784*

Gymnast to win two consecutive women's horse vault titles in the world championships, *3953*

International governing body for sled dog racing, *5508*

International governing organization for curling, *2678*

Ladies Professional Golf Association (LPGA) Tour season purse to top $500,000, *3785*

National Football League player to be named Defensive Player of the Year, *3276*

Runner to complete the men's mile race in under 3:53 minutes, *5080*

San Francisco Warriors player to be named National Basketball Association (NBA) Rookie of the Year, *2041*

San Francisco Warriors regular season basketball game played at the Oakland Coliseum, *2044*

Season in which the National Football League (NFL) and American Football League (AFL) were merged, *3277*

Soccer (international football) team from England to win the world cup, *5559*

St. Louis Cardinals regular season baseball game played at Busch Memorial Stadium, *1689*

Tennis player to win seven consecutive Australian national women's singles championships, and 11 overall, *6114*

Texas Western championship in the National Collegiate Athletic Association (NCAA) Men's Basketball National Tournament, *2042*

Woman to race in the Boston Marathon, *4490*

World championships in dressage, *2871*

World championships in fast-pitch softball to include men's teams, *5602*

World championships in ice speedway motorcycle racing, *4583*

World championships in orienteering, *4808*

World championships in three-day event equestrian competition, *2872*

World outdoor championships in bowls, *2499*

1967

African-American professional football player to be named to the Pro Football Hall of Fame, *3278*

African-American woman to play on the Ladies Professional Golf Association (LPGA) tour, *3786*

Amateur golfer to win the U.S. Women's Open, *3787*

American Basketball Association season, *2051*

Automobile racer to earn more than $100,000 in a single season in the National Association for Stock Car Auto Racing (NASCAR) Winston Cup series, *1110*

Automobile racer to win more than 20 races in a single season in the National Association for Stock Car Auto Racing (NASCAR) Winston Cup series, *1111*

Baseball team to hit three home runs in one inning of a World Series game, *1695*

Basketball player to get an average of 32 rebounds in a National Basketball Association (NBA) playoff series, *2046*

Basketball player to grab 41 rebounds in a single National Basketball Association (NBA) playoff game, *2049*

Basketball player to make 18 consecutive field goals in a single National Basketball Association (NBA) game, *2048*

Basketball player to score 16 consecutive field goals in a single Division I National Collegiate Athletic Association (NCAA) game, *2053*

Basketball team to get 93 rebounds in a single National Basketball Association (NBA) Finals game, *2050*

Boston Red Sox pitcher to win the Cy Young Award, *1691*

Canadian Grand Prix automobile race, *1112*

Detroit Pistons player to be named National Basketball Association (NBA) Rookie of the Year, *2047*

Discus-thrower to break the 60-meter and 200-foot barriers in the women's event, *2775*

International Cross-Country Championships to include a women's race, *5081*

International governing body for squash, *5760*

Kansas City Chiefs American Football League championship, *3280*

Little League World Series won by an East Asian team, *1692*

Los Angeles Lakers regular season basketball game played at the Forum, *2054*

Motorcycle racer to win five individual dirt-track (speedway) world titles, *4584*

National Football League player to kick seven field goals in a single game, *3284*

New York Mets baseball player to be named Rookie of the Year, *1693*

Oakland Raiders American Football League championship, *3285*

Olympic ban on drugs, *4720*

Philadelphia 76ers regular season basketball game played at The Spectrum, *2052*

Philadelphia Flyers regular season hockey game played at The Spectrum, *4150*

Pittsburgh Penguins regular season hockey game played at the Pittsburgh Civic Arena, *4149*

Professional soccer (international football) leagues in the United States, *5560*

Purdue University win in college football's Rose Bowl, *3281*

Runner to hold the officially accepted world record in the women's 1500 meters, *5082*

Runner to race the men's 1500 meters in less than 3:35 minutes, *5083*

Runner to race the men's marathon in under 2:12 hours, and the first representing Australia to hold the world record in the event, *4492*

San Diego Chargers regular season football game played at San Diego Stadium, *3283*

San Francisco Giants pitcher to win the Cy Young Award, *1694*

Speed skater to skate the 3000 meters in under 4:20 minutes, *5679*

Steel tennis rackets came into widespread use, *6115*

Super Bowl, *3282*

Team to win three consecutive National Football League championships, *3279*

Tennis player to win five consecutive Australian national men's singles championships, and six overall, *6116*

Woman speed skater to skate the 3000 meters in under 5 minutes, *5680*

Woman to run in the Boston Marathon wearing an official number, *4491*

World amateur championships in squash, *5761*

World championships for men's lacrosse, *4424*

World cup series of competitions in Alpine skiing, *5416*

World team championships in squash, *5762*

1968

African-American college football player to receive the Maxwell Award, *3286*

African-American quarterback to play regularly on a professional football team, *3287*

Athlete from Iran to win a gold medal in the Olympic Games, *4731*

Athlete from Kenya to win a gold medal in the Olympic Games, *4732*

Athlete from Tunisia to win a gold medal in the Olympic Games, *4728*

Athlete from Venezuela to win a gold medal in the Olympic Games, *4729*

Athlete to be banned from the Olympic Games for taking drugs, *4721*

Athlete to win the gold medal in the same event in four consecutive Olympic Games, *4727*

Athletes from Pakistan to win gold medals in the Olympic Games, *4730*

Automobile racer to have 25 wins on the Formula One Grand Prix circuit, *1113*

Baseball player to be named *The Sporting News* Sportsman of the Year, *1696*

Basketball player to win the American Basketball Association Most Valuable Player Award, *2055*

Basketball player to win the American Basketball Association Rookie of the Year Award, *2056*

Big League Baseball leagues for 16-year-old to 18-year-old players, *1697*

Boxer to win two consecutive light middleweight titles in the Olympic Games, *2568*

Boxer to win two consecutive light welterweight titles in the Olympic Games, *2569*

Canoe racer to win two consecutive titles in the women's 500-meter singles kayak event, *2612*

Canoe racers to win two consecutive women's 500-meter kayak pairs event in the Olympic Games, *2613*

Coach to win the American Basketball Association Coach of the Year Award, *2057*

College football player to receive 20 passes in a major bowl game, *3292*

Detroit Tigers pitcher to win the Cy Young Award, *1698*

Discus-thrower to break the 220-foot barrier, *2776*

Discus-thrower to win four consecutive men's titles in the Olympic Games, and the first to win any Olympic event four consecutive times, *2777*

Equestrian from the United States to win the individual jumping title in the Olympic Games, *2873*

Fencers to win two gold medals in the women's team foil competition in the Olympic Games, *2937*

French Open men's doubles tennis match, *6117*

French Open men's singles tennis match, *6118*

French Open mixed doubles tennis match, *6119*

French Open tennis tournament, *6120*

French Open women's doubles tennis match, *6121*

French Open women's singles tennis match, *6122*

1968—*continued*

Golfer to win more than $1 million in official prize money on the Professional Golfers' Association (PGA) Tour during his career, *3788*

Gymnast to win two consecutive men's side (pommel) horse titles in the Olympic Games, *3955*

Gymnast to win two consecutive women's side horse vault titles in the Olympic Games, *3954*

High-jumper to use the "Fosbury flop" jumping method, *4031*

Houston Oilers regular season football game played at the Houston Astrodome, *3291*

Hurdler to race the men's 400-meter hurdles in under 49 seconds, *4341*

Light flyweight boxing event held in the Olympic Games, *2570*

Long-jumper to break the 28- and 29-foot barriers, *4439*

Major league pitcher to pitch 54 consecutive scoreless innings, *1702*

Major league pitcher to pitch six successive shutouts, *1701*

Men's 100-meter breaststroke event held in the Olympic Games, *5851*

Men's 100-meter butterfly swimming event held in the Olympic Games, *5856*

Men's 200-meter individual medley swimming event held in the Olympic Games, *5853*

Men's 4 x 7.5-kilometer relay biathlon team event held at the Olympic Winter Games, *2432*

Men's giant slalom to have two runs on separate days, rather than a single run, at the Olympic Winter Games, *5417*

National Collegiate Athletic Association major college football player to intercept 14 passes in a single season, *3288*

National organization for racquetball, *4874*

New York Jets American Football League championship, *3293*

New York Knicks regular season basketball game played at Madison Square Garden, *2059*

New York Rangers regular season hockey game played at Madison Square Garden, *4151*

Oakland Athletics regular season baseball game played at the Oakland Alameda County Coliseum, *1700*

Olympic Games held in Mexico, *4724*

Olympic Games to include athletes from more than 100 countries, *4722*

Olympic Games to institute sex tests for women athletes, *4723*

Olympic heavyweight boxing champion to become world heavyweight champion, *2567*

Peach Bowl football game, *3294*

Professional basketball player to be named *Sports Illustrated* Sportsman of the Year, *2058*

Professional football player to be named Most Valuable Player in the Super Bowl twice in a row, *3295*

Professional football player to kick four field goals in a single Super Bowl game, *3289*

Professional football team to win two consecutive Super Bowl games, *3290*

Runner from Africa to win the men's 10,000-meter title at the Olympic Games, *5085*

Runner from Africa to win the men's 1500-meter title at the Olympic Games, *5092*

Runner from Africa to win the men's 3000-meter steeplechase title in the Olympic Games, *5087*

Runner from Africa to win the men's 5000-meter title in the Olympic Games, *5089*

Runner from the United States to win the women's 800-meter title at the Olympic Games, *5091*

Runner to complete the men's 200-meter race in under 20 seconds, *5088*

Runner to complete the men's 400-meter race in under 44 seconds, *5090*

Runner to race the men's 100-meter dash in under 10 seconds, *5084*

Runner to win two consecutive women's 200-meter titles in the Olympic Games, *5086*

Sailor to win gold medals in three different sailing events in the Olympic Games, *5239*

Sailors from the United States to win the Dragon-class event in the Olympic Games, *5225*

Shot-putter to break the 19-meter barrier in the women's event, *5346*

Single-handed, non-stop, round-the-world sailing race, *5224*

Skeet shooting individual event held in the Olympic Games, *5312*

Softball player to be named the top pitcher, *5603*

Special Olympics, *2752*

St. Louis Cardinals pitcher to win the Cy Young Award, *1699*

Sweep of the medals in an event by athletes of Black African ancestry at the Olympic Games, *4726*

Swimmer from the United States to win the women's 200-meter breaststroke title in the Olympic Games, *5858*

Swimmer to win the women's 200- and 400-meter individual medley events in the same Olympic Games, *5854*

Swimmer to win three individual gold medals in a single Olympic Games, *5862*

Team to win the championship of the North American Soccer League, *5561*

1969

1969—*continued*

Light flyweight event held in the world Greco-Roman wrestling championships, *6394*

Light flyweight freestyle wrestling event held in the world wrestling championships, *6395*

Major league baseball team situated in Canada, *1705*

Montreal Expos regular season baseball game played at Jarry Park, *1710*

National Collegiate Athletic Association major college football player to score six touchdowns on pass receptions in a single game, *3297*

National Hockey League player to score 100 points in a single season, *4152*

Nations' Cup for skiing, *5418*

New York Jets win in the National Football League's Super Bowl, *3296*

New York Mets pitcher to win the Cy Young Award, *1706*

New York Mets World Series victory, *1707*

Pentathlete to win five consecutive men's titles in the world pentathlon championships, *4830*

San Diego Padres regular season baseball game played at San Diego Stadium, *1709*

Shot-putter to break the 20- and 21-meter barriers in the women's event, *5347*

Speed skater to skate the 1000 meters in under 1:20 minutes, *5681*

Super heavyweight event held in the world Greco-Roman wrestling championships, *6396*

Talladega 500 automobile race, *1115*

Tennis player to win 17 men's singles tournaments in one season, *6141*

Tennis player to win two Grand Slams, *6142*

Woman jockey to race at a pari-mutuel track in the United States, *4305*

Woman jockey to win a professional horse race in the United States, *4306*

Woman to sail across the Pacific alone, *5226*

World championships for women's lacrosse, *4425*

World outdoor championships in bowls to include women players, *2501*

1970

African-American college football player to become a quarterback at Georgia Tech, *3298*

African-American tennis player to win the men's singles title at the Australian Open, *6143*

Basketball player to average 44.5 points per game in a single Division I National Collegiate Athletic Association (NCAA) season, *2066*

Basketball player to average 52.7 points per game in a Division I National Collegiate Athletic Association (NCAA) championship series, *2067*

Basketball player to score 1,381 points in a single Division I National Collegiate Athletic Association (NCAA) season, *2068*

Basketball player to score 61 points in a single Division I National Collegiate Athletic Association (NCAA) championship series game, *2069*

Basketball player to score a total of 3,667 points during his college career, *2070*

Basketball team to have 44 assists in a single National Basketball Association (NBA) Finals game, *2075*

Basketball team to score 332 field goals in a National Basketball Association (NBA) Finals series, *2071*

Buffalo Sabres regular season hockey game played at Memorial Auditorium, *4157*

Cincinnati Bengals regular season football game played at Riverfront Stadium, *3308*

Cincinnati Reds regular season baseball game played at Riverfront Stadium (later Cinergy Field), *1716*

College football player to win the Lombardi Award, *3299*

College football team to win two consecutive Cotton Bowl games, *3303*

Cowboy to be named All-Around Cowboy five consecutive times, and six overall, *4896*

Figure skaters from the Soviet Union to win the ice dancing title in the world championships, *3066*

Hockey player to be named *Sports Illustrated* Sportsman of the Year, *4153*

Kansas City Chiefs American Football League championship, *3304*

Kansas City Chiefs win in professional football's Super Bowl, *3306*

Milwaukee Brewers regular season baseball game played at County Stadium, *1715*

Milwaukee Bucks player to be named National Basketball Association (NBA) Rookie of the Year, *2072*

Minnesota Twins pitcher to win the Cy Young Award, *1712*

Minnesota Vikings National Football League championship, *3305*

Monday Night Football, *3300*

Montreal Expos baseball player to be named Rookie of the Year, *1713*

National Collegiate Athletic Association college hockey player to score five assists in a single "Frozen Four" tournament game, *4155*

National Football League player to be named Most Valuable Player of the American Football Conference, *3301*

National Football League player to be named Most Valuable Player of the National Football Conference, *3302*

National Football League player to kick a 63-yard field goal, *3309*

National Football League player to kick at least one field goal in 31 consecutive games, *3310*

National Hockey League goaltender to reach a career total of 103 shutouts, *4154*

National Hockey League player to reach 1,000 career assists, *4158*

New York Knicks National Basketball Association (NBA) championship, *2073*

New York Knicks player to be named National Basketball Association (NBA) Most Valuable Player of the Year, *2074*

New York Marathon, *4493*

Pairs event in the dirt-track (speedway) motorcycle racing world championships, *4585*

Pittsburgh Pirates regular season baseball game played at Three Rivers Stadium, *1717*

Pittsburgh Steelers regular season football game played at Three Rivers Stadium, *3307*

Pole-vaulter to clear 18 feet, *4846*

Portland Trail Blazers regular season basketball game played at the Memorial Coliseum, *2076*

Sailor to complete a solo circumnavigation of the world from east to west, *5227*

Soccer (international football) team to win the world cup three times, *5562*

Softball player to win three consecutive Erv Lind Awards, *5606*

Spring world championships in speed skating, *5682*

Successful set of actions against major league baseball's "reserve clause", *1714*

Tennis player to win 21 women's singles tournaments in a single season, *6144*

Tie-breaker rule at the U.S. Open, *6145*

Vancouver Canucks regular season hockey game played at the Pacific Coliseum, *4156*

Woman jockey to ride in the Kentucky Derby, *4307*

Woman rider to win the world championships in dressage, *2876*

Woman speed skater to skate the 1000 meters in under 1:30 minutes, *5683*

Woman to win the world championships in the three-day event equestrian competition, *2877*

World championships in karate, *4537*

World professional championships in surfing, *5774*

1971

African-American golfer to play in the South African Professional Golfers' Association (PGA) Open, *3791*

African-American major league baseball player to win the American League's Cy Young Award, *1718*

African-American professional football player to be named Most Valuable Player of the National Football Conference, *3311*

African-American woman to win a Thoroughbred horse race in the United States, *4309*

Automobile racer to win three, four, five, six, and seven championships on the National Association for Stock Car Auto Racing (NASCAR) Winston Cup circuit, *1116*

Baltimore Colts American Football Conference championship, *3312*

Baltimore Colts win in professional football's Super Bowl, *3314*

Basketball player to have 1,224 rebounds during his Division I National Collegiate Athletic Association (NCAA) college career, *2077*

Chicago Bears regular season football game played at Soldier Field, *3315*

Chicago Cubs pitcher to win the Cy Young Award, *1719*

Dallas Cowboys National Football Conference championship, *3313*

Dallas Cowboys regular season football game played at Texas Stadium, *3319*

Discus-thrower to break the 210-foot barrier in the women's event, *2778*

Fiesta Bowl football game, *3320*

Figure skater from Czechoslovakia to win the men's singles title at the world championships, *3067*

Golf shot taken on the moon, *3795*

Golfer to win more than $200,000 in official prize money in a single season, *3792*

Golfer to win the U.S., Canadian, and British Opens in the same year, *3793*

Golfer to win two Professional Golfers' Association (PGA) Championships, after the tournament was converted to a stroke play format, *3794*

Gymnast to win the all-around title two, and then three, times in the world championships of rhythmic sportive gymnastics, *3957*

Hammer-thrower to break the 250-foot and 260-foot barriers, *3993*

Legal off-track betting operation in the United States, *4308*

Long-track event in the dirt-track (speedway) motorcycle racing world championships, *4586*

Major league baseball team consisting of nine black players, *1722*

Milwaukee Bucks National Basketball Association (NBA) championship, *2078*

Milwaukee Bucks player to be named National Basketball Association (NBA) Most Valuable Player of the Year, *2079*

National Hockey League defenseman to have 102 assists in a single season, *4159*

National Hockey League player to be named Most Valuable Player of the NHL All-Star Game twice in a row, *4160*

Native Australian tennis player to win a Grand Slam event, *6146*

1971—*continued*

New England Patriots regular season football game played at Foxboro Stadium, *3316*

Oakland Athletics pitcher to win the Cy Young Award, *1720*

Philadelphia Eagles regular season football game played at Veterans Stadium, *3317*

Philadelphia Phillies regular season baseball game played at Veterans Stadium, *1721*

Portland Trail Blazers player to be named National Basketball Association (NBA) Rookie of the Year, *2080*

Runner to race the women's 800 meters in under 2:00 minutes, *5093*

San Francisco 49ers regular season football game played at Candlestick Park, *3318*

Softball player to be named Most Valuable Player of the United States Slo-Pitch Association World Series, *5607*

Softball player to win three consecutive Bertha Tickey Awards, *5608*

Speed skater to skate the 10,000 meters in under 15 minutes, *5685*

Speed skater to skate the 1500 meters in under 2 minutes, *5684*

Tennis player to win 112 women's singles matches in a single season, *6147*

Tie-breaker rule at the Australian Open, *6148*

Woman to be women's champion in the New York Marathon, *4494*

Woman to race the marathon in under 3:00 hours, *4495*

World Series of the United States Slo-Pitch Association, *5609*

1972

African-American college football player to win the Lombardi Award, *3321*

African-American to become the general manager of a team in a major professional sport, *2081*

Athlete from North Korea to win a gold medal in the Olympic Games, *4737*

Athlete from Uganda to win a gold medal in the Olympic Games, *4738*

Athlete to compete in eight Olympic Games, *4733*

Athlete to compete in track and field events in six Olympic Games, *6217*

Athlete to win seven gold medals in a single Olympic Games, *4740*

Athlete to win two consecutive gold medals in the biathlon in the Olympic Winter Games, *2433*

Atlanta Hawks regular season basketball game played at The Omni, *2089*

Automobile racer to win the Indianapolis 500 with an average speed of more than 160 miles per hour, *1117*

Basketball team from the Soviet Union to win the men's title in the Olympic Games, *2088*

Basketball team to have a road game winning percentage of .816 in a single National Basketball Association (NBA) season, *2083*

Basketball team to win 16 consecutive road games in the National Basketball Association (NBA), *2086*

Basketball team to win 33 consecutive games in the National Basketball Association (NBA), *2087*

Boston Marathon to include women as official participants, *4496*

Cleveland Indians pitcher to win the Cy Young Award, *1723*

College baseball player to steal five bases in a single game, *1726*

College basketball coach to be named *Sports Illustrated* Sportsman of the Year, *2084*

College football team in a major bowl game to gain a total of 718 yards, *3326*

College women's basketball United States National Tournament, *2085*

Cyclist to win two consecutive men's titles in the 1000-meter match sprint in the Olympic Games, *2703*

Dallas Cowboys win in professional football's Super Bowl, *3324*

Dinah Shore golf tournament, *3799*

Discus-thrower to break the 220-foot barrier in the women's event, *2779*

Electronically timed world record in the men's 110-meter hurdles, *4343*

Equestrian to win four titles in team jumping in the Olympic Games, *2880*

Federal legislation mandating equal opportunities for female athletes in the United States, *5751*

Fencers to win three gold medals in the women's team foil competition in the Olympic Games, *2938*

Figure skater from Czechoslovakia to win the men's singles title at the Olympic Winter Games, *3070*

Figure skaters to win five consecutive ice dancing titles with the same partner at the U.S. national championships, *3068*

Flyweight weightlifting event held in the Olympic Games, *6345*

Golf tournaments held on the Professional Golfers' Association (PGA) European Tour, *3796*

Golfer to have a double, and then triple, grand slam, winning golf's four major tournaments twice, and then three times, each, *3797*

Golfer to win more than $300,000 in official prize money in a single season, *3798*

Heavyweight freestyle wrestling event held in the Olympic Games, *6397*

Heavyweight Greco-Roman wrestling event held in the Olympic Games, *6400*

Heavyweight weightlifting event held in the Olympic Games, *6346*

Ice hockey competition in the Olympic Winter Games to be boycotted, *4161*

Intercollegiate Ultimate match, *3528*

Javelin-thrower to break the 210- and 220-foot barriers in the women's event, *4401*

Judo artist to win two gold medals in a single Olympic Games, *4540*

Kansas City Chiefs regular season football game played at Arrowhead Stadium, *3325*

Light flyweight Greco-Roman wrestling event held in the Olympic Games, *6401*

Los Angeles Lakers National Basketball Association (NBA) championship, *2082*

Major league baseball player to bat in 13 runs in a doubleheader, *1727*

Major league baseball players' strike to stop the opening of a season, *1728*

Men's 200-meter individual medley event in which the top four swimmers broke the world record, *5870*

Men's half-heavyweight judo event in the Olympic Games, *4538*

Men's half-middleweight judo event in the Olympic Games, *4539*

Men's individual archery event in the modern format held in the Olympic Games, *1035*

Men's kayak slalom white-water canoeing events held in the Olympic Games, *2615*

Miami Dolphins American Football Conference championship, *3323*

National Football League team to win 14 consecutive games in a single season, and to have an undefeated season, *3322*

National team to sweep the medals in the men's 200-meter butterfly swimming event in the Olympic Games, *5864*

National team to sweep the medals in the men's 70-meter ski jump at the Olympic Winter Games, *5420*

National team to sweep the medals in the men's singles luge (toboggan) event at the Olympic Winter Games, *4459*

National team to sweep the medals in the women's 200-meter butterfly in the Olympic Games, *5872*

National team to sweep the medals in the women's singles luge (toboggan) event at the Olympic Winter Games, *4460*

New York Islanders regular season hockey game played at the Nassau Veterans Memorial Coliseum, *4162*

Olympic Games at which athletes were killed by terrorists, *4739*

Olympic Games at which more than 1000 women athletes participated, *4736*

Olympic Games at which organized drug testing was performed, *4734*

Olympic men's 100-meter backstroke event in which the medalists all had times under one minute, *5866*

Olympic men's 1500-meter freestyle event in which the medalists all had times under 17 minutes, *5871*

Olympic Winter Games held in Asia, *4735*

Olympic women's 100-meter freestyle event in which the medalists all had times under one minute, *5867*

Philadelphia Phillies pitcher to win the Cy Young Award, *1724*

Quebec Nordiques regular season hockey game played at the Colisée de Québec, *4163*

Rowers to win two consecutive titles in the men's four-oared shell without coxswain event in the Olympic Games, *4943*

Sailor to win gold medals in three different sailing events in the Olympic Games, *5239*

Sailor to win two consecutive gold medals in the Flying Dutchman–class event in the Olympic Games, *5228*

Shot-putter to break the 20- and 21-meter barriers in the women's event, *5347*

Skier to win both the women's downhill and giant slalom titles in the same Olympic Winter Games, *5421*

Soling-class sailing event held in the Olympic Games, *5229*

Speed skater from the United States to win the women's 1500-meter title at the Olympic Winter Games, *5687*

Speed skater from the United States to win the women's 500-meter title at the Olympic Winter Games, *5688*

Speed skater to skate the 3000 meters in under 4:10 minutes, *5689*

Speed skaters to become world champions in speed skating sprints, *5686*

Sports Illustrated Sportsman of the Year award to be given to a woman and to be shared, *1155*

Successful organization of male tennis professionals, *6149*

Swimmer from the United States to win the women's 100-meter breaststroke in the Olympic Games, *5868*

Swimmer to win two consecutive gold medals in the men's 4 x 100-meter freestyle relay in the Olympic Games, *5865*

Swimmer to win two consecutive men's 200-meter backstroke titles in the Olympic Games, *5869*

Tempest-class sailing event in the Olympic Games, *5230*

Texas Rangers regular season baseball game played at Arlington Stadium, *1725*

Tie-breaker rule adopted at Wimbledon, *6150*

1972—*continued*

Two-seater luge (toboggan) event to have two pairs of gold medalists in a single Olympic Winter Games, *4458*

Volleyball players to win two consecutive women's gold medals in the Olympic Games, *6283*

Washington Redskins National Football Conference championship, *3327*

Woman equestrian to win the individual dressage title in the Olympic Games, *2879*

Woman figure skater to perform a triple salchow in competition, *3069*

Women's 1500-meter event held in the Olympic Games, *5094*

Women's 4 x 400-meter relay track event held in the Olympic Games, *5095*

Women's individual archery event in the modern format held in the Olympic Games, *1036*

Women's slalom singles kayaking event held in the Olympic Games, *2614*

World championships in carriage driving, *2878*

World ski flying championships, *5419*

Wrestler to win the light flyweight freestyle competition in the Olympic Games when it resumed in 1972, *6398*

Wrestler to win two consecutive flyweight Greco-Roman wrestling titles in the Olympic Games, *6402*

Wrestler to win two consecutive super heavyweight freestyle titles in the Olympic Games, and wrestling gold medals in three consecutive Olympic Games, *6399*

1973

African-American to serve as a manager in baseball's major leagues, *1733*

Automobile racer to be named *Sports Illustrated* Sportsman of the Year, *1118*

Basketball player to be named Most Valuable Player of the National Basketball Association (NBA) Finals twice, *2090*

Basketball player to get 23,924 career rebounds, and to average 22.9 rebounds per game, in his National Basketball Association (NBA) career, *2091*

Basketball player to have 17 blocked shots in a single National Basketball Association (NBA) game, *2099*

Basketball player to have a field goal average of 95.5 percent in a single Division I National Collegiate Athletic Association (NCAA) Final Four championship series game, *2092*

Basketball player to have an average field-goal percentage of .727 in a single National Basketball Association (NBA) season, *2093*

Basketball player to lead the National Basketball Association (NBA) in rebounds for 11 seasons, and in field-goal percentage nine times, *2094*

Basketball player to score 50 points or more in 118 games during his National Basketball Association (NBA) career, *2095*

Basketball team to get 39 offensive rebounds in a single National Basketball Association (NBA) game, *2098*

Basketball team to win seven consecutive Division I National Collegiate Athletic Association (NCAA) championships, *2096*

Buffalo Bills regular season football game played at Rich Stadium, *3332*

College football coach to be named Coach of the Year three times, *3328*

College football team to win three consecutive Fiesta Bowl games, *3333*

College football team to win three consecutive Orange Bowl games, *3330*

Davis Cup to be a full open tournament for professionals and amateurs, *6151*

Golfer to be named Ladies Professional Golf Association (LPGA) Player of the Year seven times, *3800*

Golfer to win $100,000 in a single tournament, *3805*

Golfer to win more than $2 million in official prize money during his career, *3801*

Golfer to win the Tournament of Champions four and five times, *3802*

Golfer to win three straight individual titles at the U.S. intercollegiate golf championships, *3803*

Hispanic-born major league baseball player to become a member of baseball's Hall of Fame, *1729*

Icewing sail for ice skate sailing, *4361*

Iditarod sled dog race, *5509*

Introduction of skin-tight Lycra bathing suits into women's international swimming competition, *5873*

Kansas City Royals regular season baseball game at Kauffman Stadium, *1732*

Ladies Professional Golf Association (LPGA) Tour season purse to top $1 million, *3804*

Little League baseball national agreement to fully admit girls, *1734*

Major league baseball player to appear as a designated hitter during a regular season game, *1731*

Major league baseball player to come to bat as a designated hitter, *1730*

Men's 100-meter backstroke event held in the world championships, *5874*

Men's 100-meter breaststroke event held in the world championships, *5875*

Men's 100-meter butterfly event held in the world championships, *5876*

Men's 100-meter freestyle event held at the world championships, *5877*

Men's 1500-meter freestyle event held at the world championships, *5878*

1973—*continued*

Women's Tennis Association (WTA) championships, *6156*

World championships for water polo, *6305*

World championships in sailboarding, *5190*

World championships in swimming and diving, *5909*

World championships in taekwondo, *4541*

World Cross-Country Championships, *5096*

World cup in volleyball to include women, *6284*

World cup in women's cricket, *2660*

1974

Athlete to receive an Olympic medal 50 years after the competition, *4741*

Basketball player to be named Division I National Collegiate Athletic Association (NCAA) United States Basketball Writers Association Player of the Year in three consecutive years, *2101*

Basketball player to go from high school into the American Basketball Association (ABA) without attending college, *2102*

Basketball player to play 345 minutes in a single set of National Basketball Association (NBA) playoffs, *2103*

Basketball team to average 37.5 rebounds per game in a single National Basketball Association (NBA) season, *2104*

Basketball team to get 61 defensive rebounds in a single National Basketball Association (NBA) game, *2106*

Bayou Classic African-American college football game, *3335*

Boxer to win the world heavyweight championship three times, *2566*

College baseball team to win five consecutive National Collegiate World Championships, *1735*

Free agents in major league baseball, *1740*

Gymnast to win two consecutive women's floor exercise titles in the world championships, *3958*

Hurdler to hold the officially accepted world record in the women's 400-meter hurdles, *4344*

Indiana Pacers regular season game played at Market Square Arena, *2107*

International sailing championships for women, *5233*

Javelin-thrower to break the 210- and 220-foot barriers in the women's event, *4401*

Little League Softball and Senior Little League Softball programs, *5611*

Major league baseball player to have 118 steals in a single season, *1739*

Major league baseball player to hit 715 career home runs, *1738*

Men's quadruple sculls competition held in the world championships in rowing, *4944*

National governing body for taekwondo in the United States, *4542*

National Hockey League coach to be named Coach of the Year, *4164*

North Carolina State University championship in the National Collegiate Athletic Association (NCAA) Men's Basketball National Tournament, *2105*

Philadelphia Flyers National Hockey League Stanley Cup championship, *4165*

Pittsburgh Steelers American Football Conference championship, *3338*

Runner to hold the officially accepted world record in the women's 3000-meter event, *5101*

Runner to race the women's 400 meters in under 50 seconds, *5100*

Speed skater to win four women's titles at the long-distance speed skating championships, *5690*

Texas Rangers baseball player to be named Most Valuable Player, *1736*

Texas Rangers baseball player to be named Rookie of the Year, *1737*

Tournament Players Championship, *3806*

Track and field (athletics) meet to be televised nationally, *6218*

Washington Capitals regular season hockey game played at the US Air Arena, *4166*

Woman to complete the Boston Marathon in under 3:00 hours, *4497*

Women's professional football league, *3336*

World amateur boxing championships, *2571*

World championships in rowing to include women's competitions, *4945*

World Football League championship, *3337*

1975

African-American golfer to play in the Masters tournament, *3808*

African-American professional football player from an African-American college to be inducted into the Pro Football Hall of Fame, *3339*

African-American professional football player to be named Most Valuable Player in the Super Bowl, *3343*

African-American tennis player to win the men's singles championship at Wimbledon, *6158*

African-American to be named manager of a major league baseball team, *1741*

Basketball player to have 11 steals in a single National Basketball Association (NBA) game, *2119*

Basketball player to have a .739 field goal percentage in a National Basketball Association (NBA) Finals series, *2108*

1975—*continued*

Women's basketball game played in Madison Square Garden, *2114*

Women's basketball small college National Invitation Tournament, *2113*

World championship in moto-cross racing to include the 125 cc class, *4587*

World championships in taekwondo to include additional weight classes for men, *4543*

World championships in trials riding in moto-cross racing, *4588*

World championships in tug-of-war, *6270*

World cup in gymnastics, *3959*

World cup in men's cricket, *2661*

1976

470-class sailing event held at the Olympic Games, *5235*

African-American hurdler to win the men's 400-meter title in the Olympic Games, *4345*

Athlete from South Korea to win a gold medal in the Olympic Games, *4746*

Athlete from Trinidad and Tobago to win an Olympic gold medal, *4745*

Basketball player to win the American Basketball Association Most Valuable Player Award, *2121*

Basketball team to have 240 defensive rebounds in a National Basketball Association (NBA) Finals series, *2122*

Basketball team to have 94 steals in a single set of National Basketball Association (NBA) playoffs, *2123*

Boxer to win two, and then three, consecutive heavyweight titles, and three boxing titles in a single class, in the Olympic Games, *2575*

Brothers to win Olympic boxing titles on the same day, *2574*

Cyclist to win two consecutive titles in the men's 4000-meter team pursuit in the Olympic Games, *2704*

Decathlete to score more than 8500 points in the men's decathlon, *2744*

Discus-thrower to break the 230-feet and 70-meter barriers in the men's event, *2781*

Diver to win three consecutive men's platform diving titles in the Olympic Games, *2811*

Equestrians from the United States to win the three-day event individual competition, and team competition, in the Olympic Games, *2881*

Father and son to both win gold medals in track and field in the Olympic Games, *6213*

Figure skater, and the first female athlete, to sign a contract for $1 million a year, *3072*

Figure skater from Great Britain to win the men's singles title at the Olympic Winter Games, *3077*

Figure skater to perform a back flip in competition, *3073*

Figure skater to win a pairs title in the Olympic Winter Games with two different partners, *3075*

Figure skaters from the United States to win an Olympic medal in ice dancing, *3074*

Figure skaters to win the ice dancing title in the Olympic Winter Games, *3076*

Golfer to win the World Series of Golf in its new 72-hole format, *3809*

Gymnast to receive a perfect score of 10 in the Olympic Games, *3960*

Gymnast to win two consecutive men's floor exercises titles in the Olympic Games, *3962*

Gymnast to win two consecutive men's parallel bars titles in the Olympic Games, *3963*

Independence Bowl football game, *3351*

International Women's Professional Softball Association (WPSA) teams, *5612*

Introduction of racquetball to England, *4875*

Japanese Grand Prix automobile race, *1122*

Javelin-thrower to break the 310-foot barrier, *4403*

Javelin-thrower to win two consecutive women's titles in the Olympic Games, *4402*

Jockey who won seven, eight, and nine Derbys at Epsom Downs, *4311*

Los Angeles Lakers player to be named National Basketball Association (NBA) Most Valuable Player of the Year, *2120*

Male gymnast to win 8 gold medals, and 12 medals overall, in the Olympics Games, *3961*

Men's 1000-meter speed skating event held in the Olympic Winter Games, *5692*

Men's Canadian pairs 500-meter canoeing event held in the Olympic Games, *2618*

Men's Canadian singles 500-meter canoeing event held in the Olympic Games, *2616*

Men's pairs 500-meter kayaking event held in the Olympic Games, *2617*

Men's quadruple sculls rowing event held in the Olympic Games, *4948*

Men's singles 500-meter kayak event held in the Olympic Games, *2619*

National Hockey League player to score 19 goals in a single set of Stanley Cup playoffs, *4170*

National Team to sweep the medals in the men's 200-meter freestyle in the Olympic Games, *5921*

National team to sweep the medals in the women's pentathlon in the Olympic Games, *4831*

New York Giants regular season football game played at Giants Stadium, *3350*

New York Marathon to traverse New York City's five boroughs, *4499*

Nicaraguan major league baseball player, *1742*

Oakland Raiders American Football Conference championship, *3352*

Olympic Games held in Canada, *4744*

1977

1977—*continued*

British Open golf championship in which the top ten golfers were all from the United States, *3811*

Champion of the women's wheelchair division in the Boston Marathon, *4502*

Chicago Marathon, *4500*

Davey O'Brien Award, *3354*

Figure skaters to perform a quadruple twist lift in competition, *3078*

Golfer to score under 60 in an 18-hole round in a Professional Golfers' Association (PGA) recognized event, *3815*

Golfer to win more than $3 million in official prize money during his career, *3812*

Golfer to win the British Open golf championship in under 270 for 72 holes, *3813*

Jockey to be named *Sports Illustrated* Sportsman of the Year, *4312*

Mandated use of automatic electronic timing devices in official track and field events, *6221*

Marquette University championship in the National Collegiate Athletic Association (NCAA) Men's Basketball National Tournament, *2131*

Montreal Expos regular season baseball game played at Olympic Stadium, *1746*

National Collegiate Athletic Association major college football player to kick a 67-yard field goal, *3356*

National Football League rusher to gain 275 yards in a single game, *3357*

National Hockey League team to win 60 games in a single season, *4171*

Oakland Raiders win in professional football's Super Bowl, *3355*

Player to be named Women's Tennis Association (WTA) Player of the Year, *6162*

Portland Trail Blazers National Basketball Association (NBA) championship, *2132*

Runner to win the women's title in both the Boston Marathon and the New York Marathon in the same year, *4501*

Seattle Mariners regular season baseball game played at the Seattle Kingdome, *1744*

Speed skater to skate the 5000 meters in under 7 minutes, *5693*

Sudden-death playoff in one of golf's major tournaments, *3814*

Switch to metric distances in international track and field events, *6219*

Tennis player to be ranked number one in the Association of Tennis Professionals (ATP) rankings for 160 consecutive weeks, *6165*

Tennis player to win 145 men's singles matches in a single season, *6163*

Tennis player to win the Women's Tennis Association (WTA) championship four times, *6164*

Toronto Blue Jays regular season baseball game played at Exhibition Stadium, *1745*

Woman automobile racer to race in the Indianapolis 500, *1124*

Woman boxing judge to officiate at a world championship bout, *2576*

Woman to swim across the English Channel and back consecutively, *5928*

Women's competition to be included in the world professional championships in surfing, *5775*

World championships in badminton, *1171*

World cup in luge (toboggan), *4461*

World Cup in track and field (athletics), *6220*

World Race Walking Cup, *6294*

World rally championship for drivers, *1125*

1978

All-Star Classic (All-American Classic) in women's college basketball, *2135*

Automobile racer to earn more than $500,000 in a single season in the National Association for Stock Car Auto Racing (NASCAR) Winston Cup series, *1126*

Baseball pitcher to win the Cy Young Award in both leagues, *1747*

Basketball player to score 13 field goals in a single quarter of a National Basketball Association (NBA) game, *2141*

Basketball player to score 33 points in a single quarter of a National Basketball Association (NBA) game, *2142*

Basketball player to win the Margaret Wade Trophy, awarded to the women's college basketball Player of the Year, *2136*

Basketball team to average 12.9 steals per game in a single National Basketball Association (NBA) season, *2137*

Basketball team to have 233 assists in a single set of National Basketball Association (NBA) playoffs, *2138*

Basketball team to have 30 offensive rebounds in a single National Basketball Association (NBA) playoff game, *2143*

Basketball team to have 53 assists in a single National Basketball Association (NBA) game, *2145*

Boxer to win the world heavyweight championship three times, *2566*

College baseball coach to win 10 National Collegiate World Championships, *1748*

Denver Broncos American Football Conference championship, *3358*

Diver to hold women's world titles in both springboard and highboard platform diving at the same time, *2812*

Diver to win two consecutive women's world titles in springboard diving, *2813*

Figure skater to perform a triple axel in competition, *3079*

1979

1979—*continued*

Kansas City Kings player to be named National Basketball Association (NBA) Rookie of the Year, *2149*

Michigan State University championship in the National Collegiate Athletic Association (NCAA) Men's Basketball National Tournament, *2150*

Motorcycle racer to win six individual dirt-track (speedway) world titles, *4589*

National Association for Stock Car Auto Racing (NASCAR) automobile race of 500 miles to be televised live from start to finish, *1128*

National Football League player to reach 81 career interceptions, *3359*

National Football League player to rush for 200 or more yards in six different games during his career, *3360*

Professional football player to play 282 consecutive games, *3361*

Runner to complete the men's 200-meter race in under 19.8 seconds, *5112*

Runner to complete the men's 800-meter race in under 1:43 minutes, *5111*

Runner to race the women's 200 meters in under 22 seconds, *5110*

Runner to race the women's marathon in under 2:30 hours, *4505*

Runner to win both the women's title in the Boston Marathon and the women's marathon in the Olympic Games, *4513*

Runner to win four consecutive New York Marathons, *4504*

Ryder Cup to include players from the European mainland, *3821*

Seattle SuperSonics National Basketball Association (NBA) championship, *2151*

Skier to win 13 men's Alpine world cup races, and to win 10 in one category, in a single season, *5425*

Skier to win seven women's downhill world cup titles, *5426*

Skier to win six women's overall world cup titles, *5427*

Softball event held at the Pan-American Games, *5616*

Team event held in the ice speedway motorcycle racing world championships, *4590*

Three-point goal scored in a National Basketball Association (NBA) game, *2153*

Winnipeg Jets regular season hockey game played at the Winnipeg Arena, *4176*

Woman basketball player to sign with a National Basketball Association (NBA) team, *2152*

Women's Professional Golfers' Association (WPGA) European Tour, *3822*

Women's team competition in the world open squash championships, *5764*

Women's world championships in curling, *2679*

World championships in sporting clay shooting, *5314*

World championships in taekwondo to include light-middleweight and light-heavyweight classes for men, *4544*

World championships in water-ski-racing, *6320*

World cup for Nordic skiing, *5428*

World cup for water polo, *6306*

World cup in diving, *2814*

World Cup in show jumping, *2882*

World indoor championships in bowls, *2502*

Worldloppet Cup, *5429*

1980

African-American athletes to compete in the Olympic Winter Games, *4747*

African-American golfer to win a Senior Professional Golfers' Association (PGA) Tour event, *3834*

Athlete from Liechtenstein to win an Olympic gold medal, *4750*

Athlete to win eight medals in a single Olympic Games, *3967*

Athlete to win five individual gold medals in a single Olympic Games, *4748*

Athletes from Zimbabwe to win gold medals in the Olympic Games, *4752*

Basketball player to score 42 points in a National Basketball Association (NBA) Finals game in his rookie year, *2162*

Basketball player to win the National Basketball Association (NBA) Most Valuable Player Award six times, *2154*

Basketball team from Yugoslavia to win the men's title in the Olympic Games, *2163*

Basketball team to have 80 blocked shots in a National Basketball Association (NBA) Finals series, *2155*

Basketball team to have a .580 rebound percentage in a National Basketball Association (NBA) Finals series, *2156*

Basketball team to have a .782 defensive rebound percentage in a National Basketball Association (NBA) Finals series, *2157*

Boxer to be world super-flyweight (junior bantamweight) champion, *2578*

Boxer to compete in four Olympic Games, *2579*

Boxer to win two, and then three, consecutive heavyweight titles, and three boxing titles in a single class, in the Olympic Games, *2575*

Canoe racer to win a gold medal in both the singles and pairs in the women's 500 meters in the Olympic Games, *2620*

Canoe racer to win three gold medals in a single Olympic Games, *2621*

Coach to be named National Basketball Association (NBA) Coach of the Year twice, *2158*

College football team to win three consecutive Sugar Bowl games, *3364*

1980—continued

Swimmer to race the women's 100-meter freestyle in under 55 seconds, 5932

Team to be named *Sports Illustrated* Sportsman of the Year, 1156

Tennis player of the Open era to win the Wimbledon men's singles title five consecutive times, 6168

Tournament on the Senior Professional Golfers' Association (PGA) Tour, 3832

Twin brothers to win gold medals in wrestling in the same Olympic Games, 6404

U.S. Senior Open golf tournament, 3833

University of Louisville championship in the National Collegiate Athletic Association (NCAA) Men's Basketball National Tournament, 2161

Women to be caddies at the U.S. Open golf tournament, 3831

Women's 400-meter race in which the top three runners had times of under 50 seconds, 5115

Women's eight-oared shell with coxswain event held in the Olympic Games, 4949

Women's field hockey event held in the Olympic Games, 4040

World championship in moto-cross racing to include the sidecar class, 4591

World Championship of Women's Golf, 3829

World championships for judo to include women, 4546

World championships in karate to include women, 4547

World cup circuit for freestyle skiing, 5431

World cup in table tennis, 5993

World cup in trampolining, 6231

World cup in weightlifting, 6348

World Endurance Championship in motorcycle racing, 4592

World ice and snow sailing championships, 4362

1981

Athlete to win the Jesse Owens International Award, 1157

Baseball team to win the Little League World Series in five consecutive years, 1757

Basketball player to have 46 offensive rebounds in the National Basketball Association (NBA) Finals, 2165

Basketball player to have a .958 free throw average in a single National Basketball Association (NBA) season, 2166

Basketball team to have 20 blocked shots in a single National Basketball Association (NBA) playoff game, 2170

Basketball team to have 28 offensive rebounds in a single National Basketball Association (NBA) Finals game, 2171

Basketball team to have a .410 offensive rebound average in a National Basketball Association (NBA) Finals series, 2167

College baseball player to bat in 17 runs in a College World Series, 1758

Cross-country Nations' Cup in the world cup for Nordic skiing, 5432

Figure skater from Switzerland to win the women's singles title in the world championships, 3086

Golfer to win the World Championship of Women's Golf twice in a row, 3836

Gymnast to win two, and then three, consecutive women's uneven (asymmetrical) bars titles in the world championships, 3968

Heptathlete to hold the world record in the women's heptathlon, 4012

Hurdler to race the men's 110-meter hurdles in under 13 seconds, 4346

Japan Cup horse race, 4314

Javelin-thrower to break the 230-foot barrier in the women's event, 4405

London Marathon, 4507

Long-term baseball strike to completely shut down both major leagues, 1761

Major college women's basketball player to score more than 3,500 points during her college career, 2168

Major league baseball rookie to win the Cy Young Award, 1759

Men's super giant slalom event, 5433

Milwaukee Brewers baseball player to be named Most Valuable Player, and to win the Cy Young Award, 1760

National Collegiate Athletic Association major college football player to rush 403 times in a single season, 3368

National governing body for skateboarding, 5352

New Jersey Nets regular season basketball game played at the Brendan Byrne Arena, 2173

Philadelphia Eagles National Football Conference championship, 3369

Pole-vaulter to clear 19 feet, 4847

Rotterdam Marathon, 4506

Runner to complete the men's mile race in under 3:48 minutes, 5121

Runner to hold the officially accepted world record in the women's 10,000-meter race, 5123

Runner to hold the officially accepted world record in the women's 5000-meter race, 5122

Runner to win the Jesse Owens International Award, 5120

Ski jumping Nations' Cup in the world cup for Nordic skiing, 5434

Softball team to win the Amateur Softball Association Super Slow Pitch National Championships, 5617

1982

1982—continued

Runner from the United States to hold the world record in the women's 5000- and 10,000-meter races, 5124

Sailor to win the Whitbread Round-the-World Race twice consecutively, 5241

San Francisco 49ers National Football Conference championship, 3372

San Francisco 49ers win in professional football's Super Bowl, 3373

Skier to introduce skating techniques into Nordic (cross-country) skiing in international competition, 5437

Sled dog racer to win the Iditarod sled dog race four times, and the first to win it twice in a row, 5511

Soccer (international football) player to be named World Footballer of the Year, 5564

Surfer to win five men's professional world titles, 5776

Swimmer to hold world titles in both the men's 200-meter freestyle and butterfly at the same time, and to hold both twice consecutively, 5936

Swimmer to win two consecutive men's 1500-meter freestyle titles at the world championships, 5937

Swimmer to win two consecutive men's 400-meter freestyle titles at the world championships, 5938

Woman golfer to earn more than $300,000 in a single season, 3838

Woman show jumper to win the World Cup, 2883

Women's Basketball Coaches Association convention, 2178

Women's basketball team to win the the National Collegiate Athletic Association (NCAA) national tournament, 2179

World championships in racquetball, 4877

1983

Academic standards for college scholarship athletes in the United States, 5753

American League manager to be named Manager of the Year, 1768

America's Cup sailing race not won by the United States, 5242

Basketball player to be named Division I National Collegiate Athletic Association (NCAA) Associated Press (AP) Player of the Year in three consecutive years, 2183

Basketball player to be named National Basketball Association (NBA) Defensive Player of the Year, 2184

Basketball player to have a career average of 9.8 defensive rebounds per game in the National Basketball Association (NBA), 2185

Basketball player to lead the National Basketball Association (NBA) in offensive rebounds for seven consecutive years, 2186

Basketball player to win the National Basketball Association (NBA) Sixth Man Award, 2187

Basketball team to have 51 assists, and 56 defensive rebounds, in a single National Basketball Association (NBA) playoff game, 2192

Basketball team to have a .707 field goal percentage in a single National Basketball Association (NBA) game, 2191

Basketball team to score 186 points, and 74 field goals, in a single National Basketball Association (NBA) game, 2193

Calgary Flames regular season hockey game played at the Olympic Saddledome, 4186

College football player to be awarded the Outland Trophy twice, 3377

College football player to kick five field goals in a major bowl game, 3385

College women's basketball player to have 40 rebounds in a single Division I National Collegiate Athletic Association (NCAA) game, 2188

College women's basketball player to receive the Naismith Award, 2189

Discus-thrower to break the 240-foot barrier, 2783

Dominican to be inducted into baseball's Hall of Fame, 1769

Father and son to win the Iditarod sled dog race, 5512

Fencer to win five men's foil titles in the world championships, 2939

Golfer to win more than $4 million in official prize money during his career, 3840

Hurdler to set four new world records in the men's 400-meter hurdles, 4349

Hurdler to win the men's 110-meter event in the World Championships in Athletics, 4347

Hurdler to win the men's 400-meter hurdles held in the World Championships in Athletics, 4348

Major league baseball player to be named the American League Rookie of the Year and Most Valuable Player in consecutive years, 1770

National Basketball Association (NBA) game in which a total of 370 points was scored, 2194

National Collegiate Athletic Association major college team to score 624 points in a single season, 3378

National Collegiate Athletic Association major college team to score 89 touchdowns in a single season, 3379

1984

1984—*continued*

Basketball player to score 14 points in an overtime period in the National Basketball Association (NBA), *2205*

Basketball player to win the National Basketball Association (NBA) Defensive Player of the Year Award twice, *2196*

Basketball team from the United States to win the women's title in the Olympic Games, *2208*

Basketball team to have 131 offensive rebounds in a National Basketball Association (NBA) Finals series, *2197*

Basketball team to have 196 assists in a National Basketball Association (NBA) Finals series, *2198*

Basketball team to have 65 steals in a National Basketball Association (NBA) Finals series, *2199*

Basketball team to have an .894 free throw percentage in a single set of National Basketball Association (NBA) playoffs, *2200*

Boxer to hold the world super middleweight title, *2580*

Canoer to win three titles in the men's Canadian pairs 1000-meter event in the Olympic Games, *2622*

Circle City Classic African-American college football game, *3386*

College football player to pass for six touchdowns in a major bowl game, *3397*

College women's basketball player to score 27 field goals in a single Division I National Collegiate Athletic Association (NCAA) game, *2204*

College women's basketball team to win the National Collegiate Athletic Association (NCAA) national championship in two consecutive years, *2201*

Cyclist from the United States to win the men's 1000-meter match sprint in the Olympic Games, *2710*

Cyclist from the United States to win the men's 4000-meter individual pursuit in the Olympic Games, *2709*

Cyclist from the United States to win the men's road race in the Olympic Games, *2707*

Detroit Tigers manager to be named Manager of the Year, *1772*

Duet synchronized swimming event held in the Olympic Games, *5941*

Edmonton Oilers National Hockey League Stanley Cup championship, *4187*

Figure skaters to win unanimous top scores for artistic impression, and the first from Great Britain to win the ice dancing title, at the Olympic Winter Games, *3087*

Georgetown University championship in the National Collegiate Athletic Association (NCAA) Men's Basketball National Tournament, *2202*

Golfer to win two of golf's major tournaments in her rookie year on the Ladies Professional Golf Association (LPGA) Tour, *3844*

Gymnast from the United States to win the all-around women's title in the Olympic Games, *3973*

Gymnast to be named *Sports Illustrated* Sportsman of the Year, *3971*

Gymnasts from the United States to win the men's combined exercises title in the Olympic Games, *3972*

Hammer-thrower to break the 280-foot barrier, *3996*

Heavyweight boxing event with a limited weight held in the Olympic Games, *2581*

Indianapolis Colts regular season football game played at the RCA Dome, *3395*

Javelin-thrower to break the 330- and 340-foot and 100-meter barriers in the men's event, *4407*

Little League baseball teams in the new Challenger division, *1773*

Little League World Series won by a Korean team, *1774*

Los Angeles Clippers regular season basketball game played at the Memorial Sports Arena, *2209*

Los Angeles Raiders American Football Conference championship, *3393*

Los Angeles Raiders win in professional football's Super Bowl, *3394*

Men's points cycling race held in the Olympic Games, *2711*

Men's sailboarding event held in the Olympic Games, *5191*

National Basketball Association (NBA) draft lottery, *2203*

National Collegiate Athletic Association major college football player to kick 29 field goals in a single season, *3387*

National Football League defensive player to reach 22 sacks in a single season, *3388*

National Football League player to complete passes totaling 5,084 yards in a single season, *3389*

National Football League player to pass for 48 touchdowns in a single season, *3390*

National Football League player to rush for 2,105 yards in a single season, *3391*

National Football League team to win 15 games in a single season, *3392*

National team to sweep the medals in the women's 3000-meter speed-skating event at the Olympic Winter Games, *5702*

New York Jets regular season football game played at Giants Stadium, *3396*

1984—*continued*

World Biathlon Championships to include women's competitions, *2436*

World cup in bobsledding, *2475*

World cup in squash, *5765*

World four-wall handball championships, *4010*

Wrestler from the United States to win a Greco-Roman title in the Olympic Games, *6405*

Wrestler from the United States to win the heavyweight freestyle wrestling title in the Olympic Games, *6407*

Wrestler from the United States to win the super heavyweight Greco-Roman title in the Olympic Games, *6406*

Yukon Quest sled dog race, *5513*

1985

African-American golfer to win the Tournament Players Championship, *3845*

Asian-American figure skater to win the women's singles title at the U.S. national championships, *3088*

Australian Grand Prix automobile race, *1132*

Automobile racer to win more than $1 million in a single season in the National Association for Stock Car Auto Racing (NASCAR) Winston Cup series, *1129*

Automobile racer to win the Brazilian Grand Prix three, four, five, and six times, *1130*

Basketball player to have 456 blocked shots, and an average of 5.56 blocked shots, in a single National Basketball Association (NBA) season, *2210*

Basketball player to have an average of 14 assists per game in a National Basketball Association (NBA) Finals series, *2211*

Basketball player to have an average of 17.6 assists per game in a National Basketball Association (NBA) playoff series, *2212*

Basketball player to have ten blocked shots in a single National Basketball Association (NBA) playoff game, *2224*

Basketball player to lead the National Basketball Association (NBA) for three years in steals, *2213*

Basketball player to make all his field goal attempts in a National Basketball Association (NBA) Finals game, *2225*

Basketball player to win the National Basketball Association (NBA) Sixth Man Award twice in a row, *2214*

Basketball team to have a .545 field goal percentage in a single National Basketball Association (NBA) season, *2215*

Basketball team to have a .600 field goal percentage in the National Basketball Association (NBA) playoffs, *2216*

Basketball team to have a defensive rebound percentage of .921 in a single National Basketball Association (NBA) Finals game, *2227*

Basketball team to have an average of 31.4 assists per game in a single National Basketball Association (NBA) season, *2217*

Basketball team to score 148 points, and 62 field goals, in a single National Basketball Association (NBA) Finals game, *2226*

Butkus Award, *3398*

College baseball player to steal eight bases in a College World Series, *1778*

College women's basketball player to have 534 rebounds in a single Division I National Collegiate Athletic Association (NCAA) season, *2218*

College women's basketball player to have an average of 18.5 rebounds per game in a single Division I National Collegiate Athletic Association (NCAA) season, *2219*

European Formula 3000 automobile racing circuit, *1131*

Hispanic-born major league baseball star to appear on a U.S. postage stamp, *1779*

International Amateur Athletic Federation (IAAF) Grand Prix, *6223*

Introduction of the "skating" technique to biathlon, *2437*

Kansas City Royals pitcher to win the Cy Young Award, *1780*

Kansas City Royals World Series win, *1781*

Major league baseball player to reach 4,192 career hits, *1783*

Major league pitcher to reach 4,000 career strikeouts, *1782*

National Football League player to gain a total of 2,535 yards running in a single season, *3399*

National Hockey League defenseman to have 25 assists in a single set of Stanley Cup playoffs, *4189*

National Hockey League defenseman to score 12 goals in a single set of Stanley Cup playoffs, *4190*

National Hockey League defenseman to score 37 points in a single set of Stanley Cup playoffs, *4191*

National Hockey League player to score 47 points in a single set of Stanley Cup playoffs, *4192*

Old Dominion University championship in the National Collegiate Athletic Association (NCAA) Women's Basketball National Tournament, *2220*

Pole-vaulter to clear 6 meters, *4848*

Professional football player to score 18 points in a single Super Bowl game, *3400*

Runner to complete the men's 1500-meter race in under 3:30 minutes, *5144*

Runner to set seven world records in the women's 400 meters, *5145*

Sailor to complete a solo circumnavigation of the world in 150 days, *5245*

Sailor to complete a solo circumnavigation of the world in under 130 days, *5246*

Ski-jumper to spread the skis in a V formation in the air, *5447*

Sled dog racer to win both the Iditarod and the Yukon Quest sled dog races, *5514*

Tennis player to be ranked number one in the Women's Tennis Association (WTA) rankings for 156 consecutive weeks, *6173*

Unseeded tennis player to win the men's singles title at Wimbledon, *6172*

Utah Jazz player to be named National Basketball Association (NBA) Defensive Player of the Year, *2221*

Villanova University championship in the National Collegiate Athletic Association (NCAA) Men's Basketball National Tournament, *2222*

Water-skier to win three, and then four, consecutive men's overall titles at the world championships, *6321*

Woman basketball player to sign with the Harlem Globetrotters, *2223*

Woman golfer to earn more than $400,000 in official prize money in a single season, *3846*

Woman golfer to score 20 below par in 72 holes, *3847*

Woman sled dog racer to win the Iditarod sled dog race, *5515*

World Cup Marathon, *4514*

World Cup series of competitions for speed skating, *5703*

World Flying Disc Conference, *3529*

World indoor track and field (athletics) championships, *6224*

1986

African-American figure skater to win the women's singles title at the U.S. national championships, *3089*

African-American figure skater to win the women's singles title in the world championships, *3090*

African-American golfer to win the Tournament of Champions, *3848*

Automobile racer to win the Indianapolis 500 with an average speed of more than 170 miles per hour, *1133*

Automobile racer to win three Austrian Grand Prix races, *1134*

Basketball player to average 5.0 steals per game during a single Division I National Collegiate Athletic Association (NCAA) season, *2228*

Basketball player to be named National Basketball Association (NBA) Most Improved Player of the Year, *2229*

Basketball player to have 14 rebounds during a single Division I National Collegiate Athletic Association (NCAA) game, *2241*

Basketball player to have 207 rebounds during a single Division I National Collegiate Athletic Association (NCAA) season, *2230*

Basketball player to have 23 blocked shots in a Division I National Collegiate Athletic Association (NCAA) championship series, *2231*

Basketball player to have 301 steals in a single National Basketball Association (NBA) season, *2232*

Basketball player to score 63 points in a single National Basketball Association (NBA) playoff game, *2243*

Basketball team to have a .652 rebound percentage in the National Basketball Association (NBA) playoffs, *2233*

Basketball team to have a .723 rebound percentage in a single National Basketball Association (NBA) playoff game, *2242*

Basketball team to have a .976 home game winning percentage for a single National Basketball Association (NBA) season, *2234*

Basketball team to have an average of 8.7 blocked shots per game in a single National Basketball Association (NBA) season, *2235*

Boston Marathon to offer prize money, *4515*

Boston Red Sox manager to be named Manager of the Year, *1784*

Chicago Bears National Football Conference championship, *3403*

Chicago Bears win in professional football's Super Bowl, *3405*

College baseball player to bat in nine runs in a single game, *1785*

College baseball player to have six hits in a single game, *1790*

College baseball player to hit four home runs in a single game, *1786*

College women's basketball player to have 1,887 rebounds in a single Division I National Collegiate Athletic Association (NCAA) career, *2236*

College women's basketball player to receive the Broderick Cup in three consecutive years, *2237*

College women's basketball player to receive the Naismith Award in three consecutive years, *2238*

College women's basketball player to score 17 consecutive field goals in a single Division I National Collegiate Athletic Association (NCAA) game, *2244*

Cyclist from the United States to win the Tour de France, *2712*

Discus-thrower to break the 240-foot barrier in the men's event, *2784*

Diver to win three consecutive men's highboard platform diving titles in the world championships, *2816*

Golf tournament to offer a purse of $1 million, *3849*

1986—*continued*

Golfer to win 18 titles in golf's four major tournaments, and six Masters championships, *3850*

Goodwill Games, *4379*

Hall of Fame Bowl football game, *3406*

Heptathlete from the United States, and the first African-American, to hold the world record in the women's event, *4014*

Houston Astros pitcher to win the Cy Young Award, *1787*

Javelin-throw world record set using the new javelin in the men's event, *4409*

Javelin-thrower to break the 250-foot barrier in the women's event, *4408*

Jim Thorpe Award, *3401*

Ladies Professional Golf Association (LPGA) Tour season purse to top $10 million, *3851*

Major league baseball game to include three grand slam home runs, *1791*

Major league baseball player to hit a home run on the season's first pitch, *1788*

Major league pitcher to pitch 20 strikeouts in a single game, *1789*

Men's 50-meter freestyle event held at the world championships, *5944*

Men's super giant slalom to be included in the world cup for Alpine skiing, *5448*

National Collegiate Athletic Association major college football player to kick 80 field goals during his college career, *3402*

National Hockey League defenseman to score 48 goals in a single season, *4193*

National Hockey League player to have 163 assists in a single season, *4194*

New England Patriots American Football Conference championship, *3404*

San Antonio Spurs player to be named National Basketball Association (NBA) Defensive Player of the Year, *2239*

Skier to win five women's slalom world cup titles, *5449*

Swimmer to win two consecutive men's 200-meter butterfly titles at the world championships, *5945*

Swimmer to win two consecutive men's 200-meter freestyle titles at the world championships, *5946*

Swimmer to win two consecutive women's 200-meter backstroke world titles, *5947*

Tennis player to win the French Open women's singles title seven times, *6174*

University of Texas championship in the National Collegiate Athletic Association (NCAA) Women's Basketball National Tournament, *2240*

Woman golfer to earn more than $2 million in official prize money during her career, *3852*

Woman speed skater to skate the 1500 meters in under 2 minutes, *5704*

Women's 4 x 200-meter freestyle swimming event held in the world championships, *5948*

Women's 50-meter freestyle swimming event held in the world championships, *5949*

Women's coxless fours event held in the world championships in rowing, *4954*

Women's super giant slalom to be included in the world cup for Alpine skiing, *5450*

World championships for freestyle skiing, *5451*

World championships for water polo to include women, *6307*

World championships in endurance riding, *2887*

World championships in tug-of-war to include women, *6271*

World championships in vaulting, *2888*

World cup in dressage, *2889*

1987

America's Cup won back by the United States, *5247*

Automobile racer to win more than $2 million, and then $3 million, in a single season in the National Association for Stock Car Auto Racing (NASCAR) Winston Cup series, *1135*

Basketball player to be named Most Valuable Player of the National Basketball Association (NBA) Finals three times, *2246*

Basketball player to have 13 steals during a single Division I National Collegiate Athletic Association (NCAA) game, *2261*

Basketball player to have 22 assists during a single Division I National Collegiate Athletic Association (NCAA) game, *2258*

Basketball player to have 406 assists during a single Division I National Collegiate Athletic Association (NCAA) season, *2247*

Basketball player to make 35 consecutive field goals in the National Basketball Association (NBA) playoffs, *2248*

Basketball player to score ten 3-point field goals in a single Division I National Collegiate Athletic Association (NCAA) championship series game, *2249*

Basketball player to shoot 11 consecutive 3-point field goals during a single Division I National Collegiate Athletic Association (NCAA) game, *2257*

Basketball player to shoot 158 3-point field goals during a single Division I National Collegiate Athletic Association (NCAA) season, *2250*

Basketball player to shoot 413 field goals during a single Division I National Collegiate Athletic Association (NCAA) season, *2251*

College women's basketball Naismith Coach of the Year Award, *2252*

College women's basketball player to have 355 assists in a single Division I National Collegiate Athletic Association (NCAA) season, *2253*

1988

1988—*continued*

African-American college football player to win the Butkus Award, *3417*

African-American quarterback to play in and to win football's Super Bowl, *3419*

American League player to steal 40 bases and hit 40 home runs in a season, *1797*

American League team to top 3 million paying customers at home in a single season, *1798*

Archer to win two titles in women's events in a single Olympic Games, *1038*

Athlete from Suriname to win a gold medal in the Olympic Games, *4767*

Athlete to win eight medals in individual events in the Olympic Winter Games, *4764*

Athlete to win medals in both the Summer and Winter Olympic Games in the same year, *4768*

Athlete to win two biathlon gold medals at a single Olympic Winter Games, *2438*

Automobile racer to have eight wins in a single season on the Formula One Grand Prix circuit, *1136*

Automobile racer to win two Australian Grand Prix races, *1137*

Basketball player to average 13.3 assists per game during a single Division I National Collegiate Athletic Association (NCAA) season, *2262*

Basketball player to have 115 assists in the National Basketball Association (NBA) playoffs, *2263*

Basketball player to have 150 steals during a single Division I National Collegiate Athletic Association (NCAA) season, *2264*

Basketball player to have 23 steals in a Division I National Collegiate Athletic Association (NCAA) championship series, *2265*

Basketball player to have 868 assists in his rookie year in the National Basketball Association (NBA), *2266*

Basketball player to have a field goal average of .599 over his National Basketball Association (NBA) career, *2267*

Basketball player to have six blocked shots in a single Division I National Collegiate Athletic Association (NCAA) Final Four championship series game, *2268*

Basketball team from the United States to win the women's title in a non-boycotted Olympic Games, *2275*

Basketball team to have an offensive rebound average of .556 in a single National Basketball Association (NBA) Finals game, *2274*

Black African-born boxer to win a boxing title in the Olympic Games, *2585*

Boxer to hold the undisputed world cruiserweight (junior heavyweight) title, *2583*

Boxer to hold world titles in five different weight classes, *2584*

Canoe marathon world championships, *2624*

Canoe racer from the United States to win the men's singles 1000-meter kayak event, and to win a gold medal in any kayaking event, in the Olympic Games, *2626*

Canoe racers to win two consecutive titles in the men's pairs 500-meter kayak event in the Olympic Games, *2625*

Caribbean Cup, *2476*

Charlotte Hornets regular season game played at the Charlotte Coliseum, *2276*

Chicago Bulls player to be named National Basketball Association (NBA) Defensive Player of the Year, *2269*

Chicago Bulls player to be named National Basketball Association (NBA) Most Valuable Player of the Year, *2270*

College baseball team to have two consecutive Most Valuable Player Award winners, *1799*

College football player to score 30 points in a major bowl game, *3423*

College women's basketball player to score nine consecutive 3-point goals in a single Division I National Collegiate Athletic Association (NCAA) game, *2273*

College women's basketball United States Basketball Writers Association All-American first team, *2271*

Detroit Pistons regular season game played at The Palace of Auburn Hills, *2277*

Discus-thrower to break the 250-foot barrier, *2785*

Diver to win both the men's platform and springboard diving titles in two consecutive Olympic Games, *2818*

Figure skater to perform a quadruple jump in competition, *3091*

Figure skater to perform the tano lutz jump in competition, *3092*

Figure skaters from Canada to win a medal in ice dancing at the Olympic Winter Games, *3093*

Golf course in China, *3857*

Golfer to earn more than $1 million in a single season in official prize money, *3858*

Golfer to win more than $5 million in official prize money during his career, *3859*

Golfer to win the Tour Championship in a playoff, *3860*

Heptathlete from the United States, and the first African-American, to win the women's heptathlon in the Olympic Games, *4015*

Individual dressage equestrian competition in the Olympic Games in which women riders swept the top medals, *2890*

Javelin-thrower to break the 260-foot barrier, and to reach the 80-meter barrier, in the women's event, *4410*

1988—*continued*

Swimmer to race the men's 100-meter backstroke event in under 55 seconds, *5951*

Swimmer to race the women's 50-meter freestyle in under 25 seconds, *5950*

Tennis player to win the French Open women's doubles title five consecutive times, *6176*

Tennis player to win the men's singles title in the Olympic Games after tennis competition resumed in 1988, *6178*

Tennis player to win the women's singles title in the Olympic Games after tennis competition resumed in 1988, *6180*

Tennis player to win the Women's Tennis Association (WTA) championship eight times, *6177*

Tennis players to win the men's doubles title in the Olympic Games after tennis competition resumed in 1988, *6181*

Tennis players to win the women's doubles title in the Olympic Games after tennis competition resumed in 1988, *6179*

Woman swimmer to win Olympic medals 12 years apart, *5956*

Woman to play on a men's college baseball team, *1800*

Women's 100-meter butterfly event in the Olympic Games in which all the medalists had times under one minute, *5953*

Women's 1000-meter match sprint cycling event held in the Olympic Games, *2713*

Women's 10,000-meter running event held in the Olympic Games, *5152*

Women's 470-class sailing event held in the Olympic Games, *5249*

Women's 50-meter freestyle swimming event held in the Olympic Games, *5955*

Women's 5000-meter speed skating event held in the Olympic Winter Games, *5709*

Women's air pistol individual shooting event held in the Olympic Games, *5322*

Women's doubles table tennis event held in the Olympic Games, *5995*

Women's quadruple sculls event held in the Olympic Games, *4955*

Women's singles table tennis event held in the Olympic Games, *5997*

Women's super giant slalom event held at the Olympic Winter Games, *5453*

Women's world indoor championships in bowls, *2503*

World cup in orienteering, *4811*

World matchplay championships in snooker, *2463*

Wrestler of Black African descent to win a gold medal in wrestling in the Olympic Games, *6409*

Wrestler to win two bantamweight freestyle wrestling titles in the Olympic Games, *6410*

Wrestler to win two consecutive light flyweight Greco-Roman wrestling titles in the Olympic Games, *6408*

1989

African-American to become president of a major baseball league, *1803*

African-American woman to win the Jesse Owens International Award, *1160*

Athlete to win the women's Hawaii Ironman triathlon three and up to eight times, *6239*

Baltimore Orioles manager to be named Manager of the Year, *1804*

Basketball player to score 184 points in a Division I National Collegiate Athletic Association (NCAA) championship series, *2281*

Basketball player to score 75 field goals in a Division I National Collegiate Athletic Association (NCAA) championship series, *2282*

Basketball player to score more than 38,000 points in his National Basketball Association (NBA) career, *2283*

Boxer to hold the undisputed world heavyweight title after 1980, *2586*

College football player to gain 280 yards rushing in a major bowl game, *3432*

College football player to gain 594 all-purpose yards in a major bowl game, *3433*

College football player to receive for 252 yards in a major bowl game, *3427*

College football team to gain 576 yards passing in a major bowl game, *3434*

College women's basketball player to have 151 blocked shots, and 5.6 rebounds per game, in a single Division I National Collegiate Athletic Association (NCAA) season, *2284*

College women's basketball player to score 3,122 points during her National Collegiate Athletic Association (NCAA) Division I career, *2285*

College women's basketball player to score an average of 28.4 points per game during her Division I National Collegiate Athletic Association (NCAA) career, *2286*

Copper Bowl football game, *3435*

Cyclist to be named *Sports Illustrated* Sportsman of the Year, *2714*

Detroit Pistons National Basketball Association (NBA) championship, *2287*

Drag racer to reach a speed over 290 miles per hour, *1138*

Father and son to play at the same time in major league baseball, *1805*

Figure skater from Japan to win the women's singles title in the world championships, *3094*

Figure skaters to win Emmy awards for a television special, *3095*

Girl from the United States to appear in a Little League baseball World Series, *1806*

Gymnast to win two women's balance beam titles in the world championships, *3975*

High-jumper to reach, and then break, the 8-foot barrier, *4032*

Major league pitcher to reach 5,000 career strikeouts, *1808*

National Collegiate Athletic Association major college football player to gain 510 yards in a single half of a game, *3424*

National Collegiate Athletic Association major college football player to receive 141 passes in a single season, *3425*

National Collegiate Athletic Association major college team to gain 1,021 all-purpose yards in a single game, *3430*

National Collegiate Athletic Association major college team to gain 6,874 all-purpose yards in a single season, *3426*

National Football League player to receive for 336 yards in a single game, *3431*

Orlando Magic regular season basketball game played at the Orlando Arena, *2288*

Professional football player to gain 215 yards receiving in a single Super Bowl game, *3428*

Professional football player to gain 357 yards passing in a single Super Bowl game, *3429*

Skier to win 14 women's Alpine World Cup races in a single season, *5461*

Sudirman Trophy awarded at the badminton world championships, *1172*

Toronto Blue Jays regular season baseball game played at the Skydome, *1807*

Vendée Globe round-the-world challenge race, *5250*

Woman golfer to earn more than $500,000 in official prize money in a season, *3861*

Women's 15-kilometer cross-country event held in the world championships of Nordic skiing, *5462*

Women's 30-kilometer cross-country event held in the world championships of Nordic skiing, *5463*

Women's épée competition held in the world championships of fencing, *2941*

World championships in the triathlon, *6240*

World cup in cycling, *2715*

World Series game to be canceled by an earthquake, *1809*

Worldloppet Cup to include women Nordic skiers, *5464*

1990

Automobile racer to win the Indianapolis 500 with an average speed of more than 180 miles per hour, *1139*

Basketball player to have 30 assists in a single National Basketball Association (NBA) game, *2299*

Basketball player to have an average of 14.5 assists per game in a single National Basketball Association (NBA) season, *2289*

Basketball player to lead the National Basketball Association (NBA) in offensive rebounds for eight years, *2290*

Basketball player to make 15 consecutive free throws in a National Basketball Association (NBA) Finals game, *2297*

Basketball player to score eleven 3-point field goals in a single Division I National Collegiate Athletic Association (NCAA) championship series game, *2291*

Basketball team to make 61 free throws in a single National Basketball Association (NBA) game, *2295*

Basketball team to score 157 points in a single National Basketball Association (NBA) playoff game, *2296*

Ben Hogan Tour, *3863*

Carquest Bowl football game, *3445*

Detroit Pistons player to be named National Basketball Association (NBA) Defensive Player of the Year, *2292*

Doak Walker National Running Back Award, *3436*

Father and son to play as teammates in major league baseball, *1810*

Golfer to be named Rookie of the Year and Player of the Year on the Senior Professional Golfers' Association (PGA) Tour, *3864*

Golfer to win more than $1 million in a single season on the Senior Professional Golfers' Association (PGA) Tour, *3865*

Golfer to win more than $6 million in official prize money during his career, *3866*

Grand Slam Cup, *6182*

Javelin-thrower to break the 290-foot barrier with the new javelin, *4411*

Major league baseball player of the 20th century to pitch 57 saves in a single season, *1811*

Male rider to win the world cup in dressage, *2891*

Men's and women's doubles events to be included in the world cup in table tennis, *5998*

Minnesota Timberwolves regular season basketball game played at the Target Center, *2298*

National Collegiate Athletic Association major college football player to complete 54 touchdown passes in a single season, *3437*

National Collegiate Athletic Association major college football player to gain 5,221 yards in a single year, *3444*

National Collegiate Athletic Association major college football player to gain more than 400 yards per game in five consecutive games, *3438*

1990—*continued*

National Collegiate Athletic Association major college football player to score eight rushing touchdowns in a single game, *3441*

National Collegiate Athletic Association major college team to score 11 passing touchdowns in a single game, *3443*

National Collegiate Athletic Association (NCAA) Division I women's softball player to pitch 182 complete career games, *5621*

National Football League player to make seven sacks in a single game, *3442*

National Hockey League player to be named Most Valuable Player of the NHL All-Star Game three times, *4201*

Professional athlete to be named an All-Star in two sports, and the first to play with an artificial hip, *5755*

Professional football player to complete 13 consecutive passes in a single Super Bowl game, *3440*

Professional football player to kick seven points after touchdown in a single Super Bowl game, *3439*

Runner to win two consecutive women's titles in the Boston Marathon, and three overall, *4519*

Skier to win four men's super giant slalom world cup titles, *5465*

Solheim Cup golf competition, *3869*

Stanford University championship in the National Collegiate Athletic Association (NCAA) Women's Basketball National Tournament, *2293*

Triple-jumper to hold the officially accepted world record in the women's event, *6261*

University of Nevada at Las Vegas championship in the National Collegiate Athletic Association (NCAA) Men's Basketball National Tournament, *2294*

Vendée Globe round-the-world challenge race, *5250*

Woman golfer to earn more than $3 million in official prize money during her career, *3867*

Woman golfer to earn more than $600,000 in official prize money in a single season, *3868*

Woman sled dog racer to win the Iditarod sled dog race four times, *5517*

Women's world championships in ice hockey, *4200*

World championships for nine-ball pool, *2464*

World championships in duathlon, *2835*

World championships in mountain biking, *2716*

World Equestrian Games, *2892*

World Sculls Cup series of rowing races, *4956*

World team cup in table tennis, *5999*

1991

African-American golfer to win the U.S. Junior Amateur title, *3871*

American League team to top 4 million paying customers at home in a single season, *1812*

Automobile racer to win five Belgian Grand Prix races, *1140*

Basketball player to have 1,164 assists in a single National Basketball Association (NBA) season, *2300*

Basketball player to have 376 steals during his Division I National Collegiate Athletic Association (NCAA) college career, *2301*

Basketball player to miss on 17 consecutive field goal attempts in a single National Basketball Association (NBA) game, *2312*

Basketball player to receive the Associated Press (AP) Athlete of the Year Award, *2302*

Basketball team to have 22 blocked shots in a single National Basketball Association (NBA) game, *2311*

Basketball team to have a field goal percentage of .617 in a single National Basketball Association (NBA) Finals game, *2308*

Basketball team to have an average of 18.54 offensive rebounds per game in a single National Basketball Association (NBA) season, *2303*

Boxer to hold world titles in six different weight classes, *2587*

Buffalo Bills American Football Conference championship, *3452*

Chicago Bulls National Basketball Association (NBA) championship, *2304*

Chicago White Sox regular season baseball game played at New Comiskey Park, *1816*

College women's basketball player to have 23 assists in a single Division I National Collegiate Athletic Association (NCAA) game, *2307*

College women's basketball player to score 126 3-point goals in a single Division I National Collegiate Athletic Association (NCAA) season, *2305*

College women's basketball player to score 23 free throws in a single Division I National Collegiate Athletic Association (NCAA) game, *2310*

Cyclist to win the Jesse Owens International Award, *2717*

Diver to be awarded more than 100 points on a single dive, *2819*

Diver to hold the women's world titles in both the one- and three-meter springboard diving at the same time, *2820*

Duke University championship in the National Collegiate Athletic Association (NCAA) Men's Basketball National Tournament, *2306*

Father and son to be named Most Valuable Player of the National Hockey League, *4202*

Figure skaters for France to win the ice dancing title in the world championships, *3096*

1992

1992—*continued*

Boxing competitions in the Olympic Games to use computer scoring, *2588*

Charlotte Hornets player to be named National Basketball Association (NBA) Rookie of the Year, *2314*

Coach to be named National Basketball Association (NBA) Coach of the Year three times, *2315*

College women's basketball player to block 15 shots in a single Division I National Collegiate Athletic Association (NCAA) game, *2319*

Cyclist to win two consecutive women's titles in the 1000-meter match sprint in the Olympic Games, *2718*

Decathlete to score 8,891 points in the men's decathlon, *2745*

Drag racer to reach a speed over 300 miles per hour, *1142*

Female athlete from the United States to win three gold medals in the Olympic Winter Games, *4770*

Female athlete to win gold medals in two different sports in the Olympic Winter Games, *4771*

Female athlete to win medals in the Olympic Winter Games 16 years apart, *4773*

Fencer to win two consecutive women's épée titles in the world championships, *2942*

Figure skater from Ukraine to win the men's singles title at the Olympic Winter Games, *3100*

Figure skater from Ukraine to win the men's singles title at the world championships, *3098*

Figure skater to perform a quadruple jump in the Olympic Games, *3101*

Gymnast to win six gold medals in a single Olympic Games, *3976*

Handball player to win two consecutive gold medals in men's team handball in the Olympic Games, *4011*

Heptathlete to win two consecutive women's heptathlon titles in the Olympic Games, *4016*

Hurdler to race the men's 400-meter hurdles in under 47 seconds, *4353*

Japanese-American figure skater to win the women's singles title at the Olympic Winter Games, *3102*

Japanese-American figure skater to win the women's singles title at the U.S. national championships, *3099*

Javelin-thrower to break the 300-foot and 90-meter barriers with the new javelin, *4412*

Judo artist to win gold medals in two different weight classes in the Olympic Games, *4555*

Ladies Professional Golf Association (LPGA) Tour season purse to top $20 million, *3873*

Las Vegas Bowl football game, *3455*

Long-jumper to win three, and then four, consecutive men's titles in the Olympic Games, *4443*

Lou Groza Collegiate Place Kicker Award, *3453*

Male figure skater to win the pairs title at the Olympic Winter Games with two different partners, *3115*

Men's 10-kilometer Nordic (cross-country) skiing event held at the Olympic Winter Games, *5472*

Men's 1000-meter short track speed skating event held in the Olympic Winter Games, *5714*

Men's 5000-meter relay short track speed skating event held at the Olympic Winter Games, *5716*

Men's combined pursuit Nordic (cross-country) skiing event held at the Olympic Winter Games, *5476*

Men's moguls freestyle skiing event at the Olympic Winter Games, *5473*

Mexican-American boxer to win the lightweight title in the Olympic Games, *2589*

Milwaukee Brewers baseball player to be named Rookie of the Year, *1817*

National team to sweep the medals in the men's 30-kilometer Nordic (cross-country) skiing event at the Olympic Winter Games, *5471*

National team to sweep the medals in the women's 5000-meter speed-skating event at the Olympic Winter Games, *5713*

Olympic basketball competition to include openly professional athletes, *2316*

Olympic Games at which the number of female athletes was more than 40 percent of the number of male athletes, *4775*

Olympic Games held in Spain, *4776*

Olympic men's 200-meter backstroke event in which the medalists all had times under two minutes, *5963*

Ottawa Senators regular season hockey game played at the Ottawa Civic Center, *4205*

Pairs of twins to take the top two spots in the synchronized swimming duet competition in the Olympic Games, *5968*

Phoenix Suns regular season basketball game played at the America West Arena, *2318*

Pole-vaulter to hold the officially accepted world record in the women's event, *4850*

Rower to win gold medals in both the women's single and double sculls events in the Olympic Games, *4953*

Rowers to win two consecutive titles in the women's quadruple sculls in the Olympic Games, *4958*

1992—*continued*

Women's middleweight judo event held in the Olympic Games, *4556*

Women's moguls freestyle skiing event held at the Olympic Winter Games, *5474*

Women's sailboarding event held in the Olympic Games, *5192*

Women's world championships in roller hockey (rink hockey), *4241*

World Half Marathon Championship, *4521*

World Road Relay Championship, *4522*

Wrestler from the United States to win two super heavyweight freestyle titles in the Olympic Games, *6412*

Wrestler to win two consecutive featherweight freestyle wrestling titles in the Olympic Games, *6413*

Wrestler to win two consecutive light heavyweight freestyle wrestling titles in the Olympic Games, *6414*

Wrestler to win two consecutive lightweight freestyle wrestling titles in the Olympic Games, *6411*

1993

Alamo Bowl football game, *3458*

Athlete to win the men's Hawaii Ironman triathlon competition four, and then five, times consecutively, and six times overall, *6242*

Athlete to win two consecutive women's titles in the world triathlon championships, *6243*

Automobile racer to have more than 50 wins on the Formula One Grand Prix circuit, *1143*

Basketball player to have 1,076 assists during his Division I National Collegiate Athletic Association (NCAA) career, *2321*

Basketball player to have 17 3-point field goals in a National Basketball Association (NBA) Finals series, *2322*

Basketball player to have a perfect field goal percentage in a Division I National Collegiate Athletic Association (NCAA) game, *2331*

Basketball player to have an average of 41 points per game in a National Basketball Association (NBA) Finals series, *2323*

Basketball player to have eight steals in a Division I National Collegiate Athletic Association (NCAA) championship series game, *2324*

Basketball player to make 97 consecutive free throws in the National Basketball Association (NBA), *2330*

Bronko Nagurski Award, *3456*

California Angels baseball player to be named Rookie of the Year, *1821*

Colorado Rockies regular season baseball game played at Mile High Stadium, *1824*

Cycling races to include both amateurs and professionals, *2720*

Dallas Stars regular season hockey game played at the Reunion Arena, *4207*

Figure skater from Ukraine to win the women's singles title in the world championships, *3103*

Florida Marlins regular season baseball game played at Joe Robbie Stadium, *1823*

Florida Panthers regular season hockey game played at Miami Arena, *4209*

Golfer to win the British Open in 267 for 72 holes, *3875*

High-jumper to reach, and then break, the 8-foot barrier, *4032*

Houston Rockets player to be named National Basketball Association (NBA) Defensive Player of the Year, *2325*

Hurdler from Great Britain to win the men's title in the 110-meter hurdles in the World Championships in Athletics, *4354*

Javelin-thrower to break the 310- and 320-foot barriers with the new javelin, *4413*

Men's pursuit (10 kilometers classical and 15 kilometers freestyle) event held in the world championships of Nordic skiing, *5481*

Mighty Ducks of Anaheim regular season hockey game played at The Pond of Anaheim, *4208*

National League team to top 4 million paying customers at home in a single season, *1822*

Orlando Magic player to be named National Basketball Association (NBA) Rookie of the Year, *2326*

Pentathlete to win three, and then four, titles in the women's world championships, *4834*

Phoenix Suns player to be named National Basketball Association (NBA) Most Valuable Player of the Year, *2327*

Rider to win ten consecutive women's barrel racing titles, *4900*

Runner from the United States to win the men's marathon in the World Championships in Athletics, *4523*

Runner from the United States to win the women's 100-meter dash in the World Championships in Athletics, *5164*

Runner from the United States to win the women's 400-meter race in the World Championships in Athletics, *5165*

Runner to complete the men's mile race in under 3:45 minutes, *5170*

Runner to race the men's 10,000 meters in under 27:00 minutes, *5168*

Runner to race the women's 10,000 meters in under 30 minutes, *5169*

Runner to win two, and then three, consecutive titles in the men's 1500-meter event in the World Championships in Athletics, *5166*

Runner to win two, and then three, consecutive titles in the men's 3000-meter steeplechase in the World Championships in Athletics, *5167*

San Antonio Spurs regular season basketball game played at the Alamodome, *2329*

San Jose Sharks regular season hockey game played at San Jose Arena, *4210*

Skier to win five men's overall titles in skiing's world cup, *5482*

Sled dog racer to win the Yukon Quest sled dog race twice, *5519*

Snowboarding world championships, *5521*

Speed skater to win six men's world speed skating sprint championships, *5718*

Sumo wrestler born outside Japan to be named grand champion (yokozuna), *6415*

Team to win four consecutive American Football Conference championships, *3457*

Texas Tech University championship in the National Collegiate Athletic Association (NCAA) Women's Basketball National Tournament, *2328*

Total purse on the Professional Golfers' Association (PGA) Tour to top $50 million, *3876*

Triple-jumper to break the 15-meter barrier in the women's event, *6262*

Woman goaltender to be credited with a win in a professional hockey game, *4211*

Woman jockey to win one of America's Triple Crown horse races, *4317*

Women's pursuit (5 kilometers classical and 10 kilometers freestyle) event held in the world championships of Nordic skiing, *5483*

World short-course championships in swimming, *5969*

1994

Athlete from newly independent Kazakhstan to win a gold medal at the Olympic Games, *4787*

Athlete from newly independent Ukraine to win a gold medal at the Olympic Games, *4786*

Athlete from newly independent Uzbekistan to win a gold medal at the Olympic Games, *4785*

Athlete from the United States to win six medals at the Olympic Winter Games, and the first female U.S. athlete to win five gold medals at the winter or summer Games, *4784*

Athlete to win two consecutive men's titles in the world triathlon championships, *6244*

Athlete under the age of 14 to win a gold medal in the Olympic Winter Games, *4783*

Basketball player to have 38 blocked shots in a single set of National Basketball Association (NBA) playoffs, *2332*

Basketball player to make eight consecutive 3-point field goals in the National Basketball Association (NBA) in a single game, *2343*

Basketball team to get 246 defensive rebounds in a single set of National Basketball Association (NBA) playoffs, *2333*

Basketball team to have 71 blocked shots in a single set of National Basketball Association (NBA) playoffs, *2334*

Basketball team to have an offensive rebounding percentage of .609 in a single National Basketball Association (NBA) playoff game, *2340*

Bobsledders to win two consecutive two-man bobsled titles at the Olympic Winter Games, *2477*

Canoe polo world championships, *2627*

Chicago Bulls regular season game played in the United Center, *2341*

Cleveland Cavaliers regular season game played in the Gund Arena, *2342*

Cleveland Indians regular season baseball game played at Jacobs Field, *1827*

Coed luge (toboggan) event in the Olympic Winter Games, *4464*

College women's basketball United States Basketball Writers Association Coach of the Year Award, *2335*

College women's basketball United States Basketball Writers Association Player of the Year, *2336*

Diver to win two consecutive women's highboard platform diving titles at the world championships, *2823*

Eco-Challenge extreme sports race, *2895*

Figure skater from Russia to win the men's singles title at the Olympic Winter Games, *3107*

Figure skater from Ukraine to win the women's singles title at the Olympic Winter Games, *3108*

Figure skater to be stripped of the U.S. national women's singles title, *3104*

Fred Biletnikoff Receiver Award, *3459*

Golfer of African-American or Asian-American descent to win the U.S. Amateur Championship, *3879*

Golfer to win the Professional Golfers' Association (PGA) Championship in under 270, *3877*

Golfer to win the U.S. Open in a sudden-death playoff, *3878*

Golfer to win the World Championship of Women's Golf twice in a row, *3836*

Hammer-thrower to hold the officially accepted world record in the women's event, *3997*

Houston Astros baseball player to be named Most Valuable Player, *1825*

Houston Rockets National Basketball Association (NBA) championship, *2337*

Ice hockey team from Sweden to win the title at the Olympic Winter Games, *4215*

1994—*continued*

International precision team figure skating competition officially recognized by the International Skating Union (ISU), *3105*

Major league baseball postseason playoffs to be canceled because of a players' strike, *1826*

Male skier to win five gold medals in Nordic (cross-country) skiing in the Olympic Winter Games, and the first to win two consecutive men's combined pursuit titles, *5487*

Men's 500-meter short track speed skating event held in the Olympic Winter Games, *5725*

Men's aerials freestyle skiing event at the Olympic Winter Games, *5488*

Motorcycle racer to win five individual long-track world titles, *4594*

National Collegiate Athletic Association major college football player to gain 347 yards in a single quarter, *3461*

National Collegiate Athletic Association major college football player to receive 23 passes in a single game, *3462*

National Collegiate Athletic Association (NCAA) Division I women's softball player to hit .589 for a whole season, *5622*

National Collegiate Athletic Association (NCAA) Division I women's softball player to pitch 62 complete games in a single season, *5623*

National Football League player to complete 45 passes in a single game, *3463*

National Hockey League player to lead the league in scoring 10 times, *4212*

National Hockey League player to reach 802 career goals, *4216*

National team to sweep the medals in the men's Alpine combined skiing event at the Olympic Winter Games, *5490*

Olympic Winter Games at which professional athletes were allowed to compete, *4781*

Olympic Winter Games not held in the same year as the Summer Games, *4782*

Presidents Cup Match in golf, *3880*

Professional figure skaters to win a gold medal in the Olympic Winter Games after being reinstated to amateur competition, *3106*

Professional football player to complete 31 passes in a single Super Bowl game, *3460*

Runner from Africa to win the women's title in the New York Marathon, *4524*

Skier to win five medals in Alpine events at the Olympic Winter Games, *5491*

Skier to win the 30-kilometer Nordic (cross-country) title in the Olympic Winter Games after it was converted from classical style to freestyle, *5485*

Skier to win the 50-kilometer Nordic (cross-country) title in the Olympic Winter Games after it was converted from freestyle to classical style, *5493*

Skier to win two consecutive women's combined pursuit Nordic (cross-country) skiing titles at the Olympic Winter Games, *5486*

Skiers to win two consecutive men's Nordic combined team titles at the Olympic Winter Games, *5489*

Slider to win two, and then three, consecutive men's singles luge (toboggan) titles in the Olympic Winter Games, *4465*

Soccer (international football) team to win the world cup four times, *5567*

Speed skater to win three consecutive women's 500-meter titles at the Olympic Winter Games, *5721*

Speed skater to win two consecutive men's 1000-meter short track titles at the Olympic Winter Games, *5722*

Speed skater to win two consecutive titles in the men's 1500-meters at the Olympic Winter Games, *5720*

Speed skater to win two consecutive women's 1000-meter speed skating titles at the Olympic Winter Games, *5723*

Speed skater to win two consecutive women's 500-meter short track titles at the Olympic Winter Games, *5724*

Speed skaters to be named *Sports Illustrated* Sportsmen of the Year, *5719*

State to recognize women's high school ice hockey as a varsity sport, *4213*

Swimmer to win two consecutive men's 100-meter breaststroke titles at the world championships, *5970*

Swimmer to win two consecutive women's 800-meter freestyle world titles, *5971*

Tennis player to win 1,438 women's singles matches during her career, *6184*

Tennis player to win 167 women's singles tournaments during her career, *6185*

Texas Rangers regular season baseball game played at The Ballpark, *1828*

University of Arkansas championship in the National Collegiate Athletic Association (NCAA) Men's Basketball National Tournament, *2338*

University of North Carolina championship in the National Collegiate Athletic Association (NCAA) Women's Basketball National Tournament, *2339*

Woman skier to win three gold medals, and to win five medals overall, in Alpine skiing at the Olympic Winter Games, *5492*

Woman to win gold medals in two biathlon events in the same Olympic Winter Games, *2442*

Women's aerials freestyle skiing event held at the Olympic Winter Games, *5484*

Women's amateur boxing match sponsored by USA Boxing, *2590*

Women's college hockey Player of the Year Award, *4214*

Women's short track 1000-meter speed skating event held at the Olympic Winter Games, *5726*

World long-distance triathlon championships, *6245*

1995

America's Cup sailing race won by New Zealand, *5254*

Automobile racer to earn more than $4 million in a single season in the National Association for Stock Car Auto Racing (NASCAR) Winston Cup series, *1144*

Basketball player to have 6,371 offensive rebounds in his National Basketball Association (NBA) career, *2344*

Basketball player to have 8,551 free throws in his National Basketball Association (NBA) career, *2345*

Basketball player to have seven steals in a single National Basketball Association (NBA) Finals game, *2358*

Basketball player to score 28 3-point goals in a single set of National Basketball Association (NBA) playoffs, *2346*

Basketball team to score 14 3-point goals in a single National Basketball Association (NBA) Finals game, *2357*

Basketball team to score 41 3-point field goals in a National Basketball Association (NBA) Finals series, *2347*

Boston Bruins regular season hockey game played at the FleetCenter, *4219*

Boston Celtics regular season basketball game played at the FleetCenter, *2359*

Chicago Blackhawks regular season game played in the United Center, *4218*

College football player to gain 359 all-purpose yards in a major bowl game, *3469*

College women's basketball Associated Press (AP) All-American first team, *2348*

College women's basketball Associated Press (AP) Coach of the Year Award, *2349*

College women's basketball Associated Press (AP) Player of the Year, *2350*

College women's basketball player to have 191 steals, and an average of 6.4 steals per game, in a single Division I National Collegiate Athletic Association (NCAA) season, *2351*

College women's basketball player to score 12 3-point goals in a single Division I National Collegiate Athletic Association (NCAA) game, *2356*

Colorado Rockies regular season baseball game played at Coors Field, *1831*

Cyclist to win the Tour de France five consecutive times, *2721*

Dallas Mavericks player to be named National Basketball Association (NBA) Rookie of the Year, *2352*

Denver Nuggets player to be named National Basketball Association (NBA) Defensive Player of the Year, *2353*

Extreme Games, *2896*

Fencer to win four men's sabre titles in the world championships, *2943*

Figure skater from China to win the women's singles title in the world championships, *3109*

Figure skaters from the Czech Republic to win the pairs title in the world championships, *3110*

Figure skaters to receive six perfect scores (6.0) for artistic impression in the U.S. national pairs competition, *3111*

Golf course to host the British Open championship 25 times, *3881*

Gymnast to win three, and then four, men's rings titles in the world championships, *3977*

Hispanic-born major league baseball manager to be named Manager of the Year, *1829*

Jacksonville Jaguars regular season football game played at the ALLTEL Stadium, *3470*

Major league baseball player to top Lou Gehrig's record of 2,130 consecutive games played, *1832*

National Collegiate Athletic Association major college football player to complete 55 passes in a single game, *3471*

National Collegiate Athletic Association major college football player to kick 71 consecutive points after touchdown in a single season, *3464*

National Collegiate Athletic Association (NCAA) Division I women's softball player to get seven hits in a single game, *5625*

National Collegiate Athletic Association (NCAA) Division I women's softball player to hit 37 home runs in a single season, *5624*

National Football League player to gain a total of 404 yards running in a single game, *3473*

National Football League player to receive 123 passes in a single season, *3465*

National Football League player to receive for 1,848 yards in a single season, *3466*

National Football League player to score 25 touchdowns rushing in a single season, *3467*

New Jersey Devils National Hockey League Stanley Cup championship, *4217*

Pole-vaulter to break the 14-foot barrier in the women's event, *4851*

Portland Trail Blazers regular season basketball game played at The Rose Garden, *2360*

1995—*continued*

Professional football coach to win 328 games, *3468*

Runner to race the men's 5000-meter steeplechase in under 8:00 minutes, *5178*

Runner to race the men's 5000 meters in under 12:55 minutes, *5179*

Runner to race the women's 1000 meters in under 2:30 minutes, *5180*

Runner to win both the men's 200- and 400-meter titles in the same World Championships in Athletics, *5171*

Runner to win two consecutive titles in the men's 5000-meter event in the World Championships in Athletics, *5172*

Runner to win two consecutive titles in the women's 200-meter event in the World Championships in Athletics, *5173*

Runner to win two, three, and then four consecutive titles in the men's 10,000-meter event in the World Championships in Athletics, *5174*

Runner to win two, three, and then four consecutive titles in the men's 400-meter event in the World Championships in Athletics, *5175*

Runner to win two titles in the women's 1500-meter event in the World Championships in Athletics, *5176*

Runner to win two titles in the women's 400-meter event in the World Championships in Athletics, *5177*

San Antonio Spurs player to be named National Basketball Association (NBA) Most Valuable Player of the Year, *2354*

Seattle Mariners pitcher to win the Cy Young Award, *1830*

Seattle SuperSonics regular season game played in the Key Arena, *2361*

Skier to win five women's giant slalom titles in skiing's world cup, *5494*

Skier to win six women's slalom titles in skiing's world cup, *5495*

Sled dog racer to complete the Iditarod sled dog race in less than 10 days, *5520*

Snowboarder to win two consecutive titles in a world championship event, *5522*

St. Louis Blues regular season hockey game played at the Kiel Center, *4238*

St. Louis Rams regular season football game played at the Trans World Dome, *3472*

Tennis player to win at least four women's singles titles at each of the four Grand Slam tournaments, *6186*

Triple-jumper to break the 18-meter and 60-foot barriers, *6264*

Triple-jumper to break the 50-foot barrier in the women's event, *6263*

University of Connecticut championship in the National Collegiate Athletic Association (NCAA) Women's Basketball National Tournament, *2355*

Vancouver Canucks regular season hockey game played at General Motors Place, *4220*

Vancouver Grizzlies regular season basketball game played at Bear Country at General Motors Place, *2362*

Woman golfer to win more than $5 million, and then $6 million, in official prize money during her career, *3882*

World championships for roller hockey (rink hockey) played with in-line skates, *4242*

1996

Archer from the United States to win the men's individual gold medal in the Olympic Games, *1039*

Archers from the United States to win a gold medal in the team event in the Olympic Games, *1040*

Athlete from Africa to win the long jump, or any field event, in the Olympic Games, *4444*

Athlete from Algeria to win a gold medal in the Olympic Games, *4799*

Athlete from Armenia to win a gold medal in the Olympic Games, *4791*

Athlete from Burundi to win a gold medal in the Olympic Games, *4800*

Athlete from Costa Rica to win a gold medal in the Olympic Games, *4790*

Athlete from Ecuador to win a gold medal in the Olympic Games, *4792*

Athlete from Hong Kong to win a gold medal in the Olympic Games, *4797*

Athlete from newly independent Belarus to win a gold medal in the Olympic Games, *4794*

Athlete from Nigeria to win a gold medal in the Olympic Games, *4798*

Athlete from Syria to win a gold medal in the Olympic Games, *4796*

Athlete from Thailand to win a gold medal in the Olympic Games, *4801*

Athlete from the newly independent Slovak Republic to win a gold medal in the Olympic Games, *4795*

Athlete of Asian or Native American descent to be named *Sports Illustrated* Sportsman of the Year, *1161*

Athlete to participate in nine Olympic Games, *4788*

Athlete to win three men's titles in the world triathlon championships, *6246*

Athlete to win two Jesse Owens International Awards, *1162*

Badminton event for mixed doubles in the Olympic Games, *1175*

Baseball event held in the Olympic Games, *1820*

1996—*continued*

Ottawa Senators regular season hockey game played at the Palladium, *4223*

Philadelphia 76ers regular season basketball game played at the First Union Center, *2375*

Philadelphia Flyers regular season hockey game played at the First Union Center, *4225*

Phoenix Coyotes regular season hockey game played at the America West Arena, *4226*

Rhythmic gymnastics team competition held in the Olympic Games, *3979*

Runner from Africa, and from Ethiopia, to win the women's marathon at the Olympic Games, *4526*

Runner to complete the men's 200-meter race in under 19.7 seconds, *5183*

Runner to win the men's 200- and 400-meter titles in the same Olympic Games, *5184*

Runner to win three consecutive women's titles in the Boston Marathon, *4525*

Runner to win two consecutive titles in the women's 400-meter race in the Olympic Games, *5182*

Sailor to win the Single-Handed Transatlantic Race (STAR) twice consecutively, *5255*

San Diego Padres baseball player to be named Most Valuable Player, *1834*

Squash player to win eight men's singles world open titles, *5768*

Swimmer to win five individual gold medals, and three consecutive medals in the women's 200-meter backstroke, in the Olympic Games, *5972*

Synchronized swimming event held in the Olympic Games, *5974*

Tampa Bay Lightning regular season hockey game played at the Ice Palace, *4228*

Team from Africa to win the men's soccer event in the Olympic Games, *5570*

Tennis player to win 109 men's singles tournaments during his career, *6187*

Tennis players to win five Wimbledon men's doubles titles in the Open era, *6188*

Toronto Blue Jays pitcher to win the Cy Young Award, *1835*

Toronto Raptors player to be named National Basketball Association (NBA) Rookie of the Year, *2371*

Weightlifter to win three gold medals in the Olympic Games, *6352*

Woman athlete from the United States to win four gold medals at a single Olympic Games, *4793*

Women's 4 x 200-meter freestyle relay swimming event held in the Olympic Games, *5973*

Women's 5000-meter race held in the Olympic Games, *5181*

Women's boxing match to be watched by more than 1 million television viewers, *2593*

Women's cross-country cycling race held in the Olympic Games, *2724*

Women's double trap (clay pigeon) individual shooting event held in the Olympic Games, *5325*

Women's fast pitch softball event held in the Olympic Games, *5626*

Women's individual and team épée competitions held in the Olympic Games, *2944*

Women's lightweight double sculls rowing event held in the Olympic Games, *4961*

Women's National Basketball Association (WNBA), *2372*

Women's points race cycling event held in the Olympic Games, *2722*

Women's road time trial cycling event held in the Olympic Games, *2726*

Women's singles event to be included in the world cup in table tennis, *6001*

Women's soccer event held in the Olympic Games, *5569*

Women's triple jump event held in the Olympic Games, *6265*

World Cup in ice hockey, *4222*

1997

Atlanta Braves regular season baseball game played at Turner Field, *1844*

Baseball player to lead the National League in bases on balls for four consecutive years, *1837*

Basketball player to have 10,117 defensive rebounds in his National Basketball Association (NBA) career, *2381*

Basketball player to make nine 3-point field goals in a single National Basketball Association (NBA) playoff game, *2393*

Basketball player to make seven consecutive 3-point field goals in a single National Basketball Association (NBA) playoff game, *2394*

Basketball player to play 21 seasons in the National Basketball Association (NBA), *2382*

Basketball player to play more than 900 consecutive games in the National Basketball Association (NBA), *2397*

Basketball team to have 27 steals in a single National Basketball Association (NBA) game, *2392*

Basketball team to have a .428 field goal percentage for a single National Basketball Association (NBA) season, *2383*

College baseball player to pitch 21 strikeouts in a single game, *1845*

College women's basketball team to score 18 3-point goals in a single Division I National Collegiate Athletic Association (NCAA) game, *2399*

Colorado Rockies baseball player to be named Most Valuable Player, *1838*

Florida Marlins World Series victory, *1839*

1998

1998—*continued*

College baseball player to have 15 hits in a College World Series, *1846*

College football player to complete 19 consecutive passes in a major bowl game, *3494*

College football team to win two consecutive Gator Bowl games, *3495*

College women's basketball coach to receive the Naismith Coach of the Year Award four times, *2408*

College women's basketball player to win *The Sporting News* Player of the Year Award, *2409*

College women's basketball team to have 39 wins in a single National Collegiate Athletic Association (NCAA) season, *2410*

Curling event held in the Olympic Games, *2680*

Denver Broncos win in professional football's Super Bowl, *3496*

Drag racer to reach a speed over 320 miles per hour, *1145*

Figure skaters to win two consecutive ice dancing titles at the Olympic Winter Games, *3114*

Florida Panthers regular season hockey game played at the National Car Rental Center, *4231*

Golfer to win more than $2.5 million in official prize money in a single season, *3889*

Golfer to win more than $400,000 in the Skins Game, *3890*

Major league baseball pitcher to pitch 1,071 games during his career, *1847*

Major league baseball pitcher to win five Cy Young Awards, *1848*

Major league baseball player to hit 70 home runs in a single season, *1853*

Major league baseball player to play in 2,632 consecutive games, *1852*

Male athlete to win six individual gold medals in the Olympic Winter Games, *4804*

Male figure skater to win the pairs title at the Olympic Winter Games with two different partners, *3115*

Men's 5-kilometer river/sea swim event held in the world championships, *5975*

Men's giant slalom snowboarding event held at the Olympic Winter Games, *5524*

Men's halfpipe snowboarding event held at the Olympic Winter Games, *5526*

Music City Bowl football game, *3502*

Nashville Predators regular season hockey game played at the Nashville Arena, *4232*

National Collegiate Athletic Association major college football player to complete 23 consecutive passes in a single game, *3500*

National Collegiate Athletic Association major college football player to complete 400 passes in a single season, *3486*

National Collegiate Athletic Association major college football player to gain 1,996 yards receiving in a single season, *3487*

National Collegiate Athletic Association major college football player to gain 405 yards receiving in a single game, *3497*

National Collegiate Athletic Association major college football player to receive 295 passes during his college career, *3488*

National Collegiate Athletic Association major college football player to rush for 6,279 college career yards, *3489*

National Collegiate Athletic Association (NCAA) Division I women's softball player to get 405 hits during her college career, *5628*

National Football League defensive player to reach 192.5 career sacks, *3490*

National Football League kicker to have a perfect season, *3491*

National Football League kicker to reach 420 career field goals, *3492*

National Football League player to gain 1,000 or more yards rushing in ten consecutive years, *3493*

National Football League player to receive a pass in 193 consecutive games, *3501*

Olympic Winter Games in which more than 2000 athletes competed, and more than 55 percent were women, *4803*

Presidents Cup Match won by the international team, *3893*

Runner to race the men's 1500 meters in 3:26 minutes, *5186*

Sailor from the United States to win the Whitbread Round-the-World Race, *5257*

Season in which both major league baseball Most Valuable Player Awards went to Hispanic players, *1849*

Skier from the United States to win the men's aerials freestyle skiing event in the Olympic Winter Games, *5500*

Skier from the United States to win the men's moguls freestyle skiing event in the Olympic Winter Games, *5497*

Skier from the United States to win the women's aerials freestyle skiing event in the Olympic Winter Games, *5501*

Skier from the United States to win the women's super giant slalom at the Olympic Winter Games, *5498*

Skier to win five women's super giant slalom titles in skiing's world cup, *5496*

Skier to win two consecutive men's 10-kilometer Nordic (cross-country) skiing titles, and the first male athlete to win six gold medals overall, at the Olympic Winter Games, *5499*

1999—*continued*

National Collegiate Athletic Association (NCAA) major college football player to rush for 6,397 college career yards, *3503*

National Football League game played in Australia, *3509*

National Football League player to pass for 60,000 career yards, *3512*

National Football League player to reach 18,442 career receiving yards, *3504*

National Football League player to reach a career total of 1,206 passes received, *3505*

National Football League player to receive 169 career touchdowns, *3506*

National Football League player to score 136 career touchdowns rushing, *3507*

People to circle the globe in a balloon, *1183*

Purdue University championship in the National Collegiate Athletic Association (NCAA) Women's Basketball National Tournament, *2416*

Runner to win both the men's 100- and 200-meter titles in the same World Championships in Athletics, *5187*

San Antonio Spurs National Basketball Association (NBA) championship, *2417*

Seattle Mariners regular season baseball game played at SAFECO Field, *1855*

Sisters to face each other in the finals of a professional tennis tournament, *6191*

Sisters to win the women's doubles tennis title at the U.S. Open, *6189*

Speed skater to be women's world champion in long-distance speed skating eight times, *5736*

Tennessee Titans regular season football game played at the Adelphia Coliseum, *3511*

Tennis player to win six Wimbledon men's singles championships in the Open era, *6190*

Toronto Maple Leafs regular season hockey game played at Air Canada Centre, *4234*

Toronto Raptors regular season basketball game played at the Air Canada Centre, *2419*

Total purse on the Professional Golfers' Association (PGA) Tour to top $100 million, *3895*

Women's National Basketball Association (WNBA) All-Star Game, *2421*

Women's National Basketball Association (WNBA) players union league contract, *2418*

Women's National Basketball Association (WNBA) team to win the league championship three times, and in three consecutive years, *2422*

Women's team to be named *Sports Illustrated* Sportsman of the Year, *1163*

2000

Baseball team to play 14 games in the World Series without suffering a defeat, *1863*

Basketball player to win three, and then four, gold medals in the Olympic Games, *2380*

Bodysuits for swimming events in the Olympic Games, *5978*

Cincinnati Bengals regular season football game played at Paul Brown Stadium, *3514*

Cycling team to break the 4-minute mark in the men's 4000-meter team pursuit race in the Olympic Games, *2730*

Detroit Tigers regular season baseball game played at Comerica Park, *1858*

Golfer to hold the record low (under-par) scores in all four Professional Golfers Association (PGA) major tournaments, *3899*

Gymnasts from China to win the men's team title at the Olympic Games, *3980*

Houston Astros regular season baseball game played at Enron Field, *1859*

Male swimmers to win gold medals in the same event at the same Olympic Games, *5979*

Men's Keirin cycling event held in the Olympic Games, *2731*

Men's Madison cycling event held in the Olympic Games, *2732*

Men's modern triathlon event held in the Olympic Games, *6248*

Men's Olympic sprint cycling event held in the Olympic Games, *2729*

Men's synchronized platform diving event held in the Olympic Games, *2826*

Men's synchronized springboard diving event held in the Olympic Games, *2828*

Men's taekwondo events held in the Olympic Games, *4560*

Men's trampoline event held in the Olympic Games, *6233*

Open 49er-class sailing event held in the Olympic Games, *5258*

Runner to win two consecutive men's 400-meter titles in the Olympic Games, *5188*

San Francisco Giants regular season baseball game played at Pacific Bell Park, *1860*

Sisters to each win a women's singles grand slam title in tennis, *6192*

St. Louis Rams Super Bowl win, *3513*

Tennis player to win 13 men's singles grand slam titles, *6193*

United States team to win the men's baseball title in the Olympic Games, *1861*

Women's 20-kilometer walk event held in the Olympic Games, *6297*

Women's 500-meter time trial cycling event held in the Olympic Games, *2728*

Women's hammer-throw event held in the Olympic Games, *3998*

Women's modern pentathlon event held in the Olympic Games, *4835*

Women's pole vault event held in the Olympic Games, *4852*

Index by Month and Day

The Index by Month and Day is a chronological listing of key information from the main text of the book, organized by month and day, starting with the earliest. Each index entry includes key information about the "first" and a 4-digit number in italics. That number directs you to the full entry in the main text, where entries are numbered in order, starting with 1001.

To find the full entry, look in the main text for the entry tagged with that 4-digit number. For example, to find the entry relating to January 1, 1902, about the first Rose Bowl football game, look for the entry numbered 3133 in the main text.

Note that some entries do not contain month or day information, so they are not included in this index. Entries that contain only month, but not day, information are listed first under each month.

For more information, see "How to Use This Book," on page ix.

January 1—*continued*

1943   University of Georgia win in college football's Rose Bowl, *3192*

1946   College football player to pass for or himself score a total of six touchdowns in a major bowl game, *3203*

Gator Bowl football game, *3204*

1947   African-American college football player to score a touchdown in the Rose Bowl, *3212*

Tangerine Bowl football game, *3213*

University of Illinois win in college football's Rose Bowl, *3214*

1948   College football team to win two consecutive Tangerine Bowl games, *3219*

University of Michigan win in college football's Rose Bowl, *3220*

1949   Northwestern University win in college football's Rose Bowl, *3223*

1955   African-American football players to appear in the Orange Bowl, *3239*

1957   University of Iowa win in college football's Rose Bowl, *3244*

1959   College football team to win two consecutive Orange Bowl games, *3249*

1961   American Football Conference championship, *3259*

1962   University of Minnesota win in college football's Rose Bowl, *3266*

1965   University of California at Los Angeles win in college football's Rose Bowl, *3275*

1967   Kansas City Chiefs American Football League championship, *3280*

1973   College football team to win three consecutive Orange Bowl games, *3330*

1977   Mandated use of automatic electronic timing devices in official track and field events, *6221*

1978   Denver Broncos American Football Conference championship, *3358*

1980   College football team to win three consecutive Sugar Bowl games, *3364*

1987   World indoor records recognized by the International Amateur Athletic Federation (IAAF), *6225*

1989   College football player to receive for 252 yards in a major bowl game, *3427*

1998   College football player to complete 19 consecutive passes in a major bowl game, *3494*

College football team to win two consecutive Gator Bowl games, *3495*

January 2

1928   Stanford University win in college football's Rose Bowl, *3157*

1961   African-American quarterback to appear in the Rose Bowl college football game, *3260*

1967   Purdue University win in college football's Rose Bowl, *3281*

1995   College football player to gain 359 all-purpose yards in a major bowl game, *3469*

1996   College football team to gain 524 yards rushing in a major bowl game, *3476*

January 3

1971   Baltimore Colts American Football Conference championship, *3312*

Dallas Cowboys National Football Conference championship, *3313*

1972   Miami Dolphins American Football Conference championship, *3323*

1983   National Football League player to rush for 99 yards from the line of scrimmage, *3382*

January 4

1884   Eastern League convention in baseball, *1276*

1970   Kansas City Chiefs American Football League championship, *3304*

Minnesota Vikings National Football League championship, *3305*

1986   Basketball player to have 14 rebounds during a single Division I National Collegiate Athletic Association (NCAA) game, *2241*

January 5

1964   San Diego Chargers American Football League championship, *3271*

January 6

1957   Runner to hold the officially accepted world record in the women's 400-meter event, *5066*

1980   Los Angeles Rams National Football Conference championship, *3365*

1984   College women's basketball player to score 27 field goals in a single Division I National Collegiate Athletic Association (NCAA) game, *2204*

January 7

1785   Flyers to cross the English Channel in a balloon, *1178*

1925   Harlem Globetrotters professional basketball game, *1887*

January 16—*continued*

1980 Senior Professional Golfers' Association (PGA) Tour, *3830*

January 17

1956 Men's 30-kilometer Nordic (cross-country) ski event held at the Olympic Winter Games, *5402*

1971 Baltimore Colts win in professional football's Super Bowl, *3314*

1996 Ottawa Senators regular season hockey game played at the Palladium, *4223*

1999 Atlanta Falcons National Football Conference championship, *3508*

January 18

1953 Argentine Grand Prix automobile race, *1091*

1958 African-American to play in the National Hockey League, *4138*

January 19

1885 Boxer to be world heavyweight champion under the Queensberry rules, *2517*

1985 World indoor track and field (athletics) championships, *6224*

January 20

1925 Goalie to have 20 career shutouts in the National Hockey League, *4086*

1985 Professional football player to score 18 points in a single Super Bowl game, *3400*

1991 Buffalo Bills American Football Conference championship, *3452*

January 21

1921 Commissioner of Baseball, *1456*

1927 Boxer to win both Olympic and professional world championships, *2547*

1990 National Hockey League player to be named Most Valuable Player of the NHL All-Star Game three times, *4201*

January 22

1857 National Association of Base Ball Players convention, *1191*

1984 Los Angeles Raiders win in professional football's Super Bowl, *3394*

1989 Professional football player to gain 215 yards receiving in a single Super Bowl game, *3428*

Professional football player to gain 357 yards passing in a single Super Bowl game, *3429*

January 23

1879 National organization for archery in the United States, *1023*

1983 Woman speed skater to skate the 5000 meters in under 8 minutes, *5699*

January 24

1982 San Francisco 49ers win in professional football's Super Bowl, *3373*

January 25

1924 Olympic Winter Games, *4653*

1960 Basketball player to score 58 points in a single National Basketball Association (NBA) game, *1994*

1964 Olympic Winter Games at which an athlete was killed, *4713*

Skier to be killed during the Olympic Winter Games, *5409*

1987 New York Giants win in professional football's Super Bowl, *3414*

1992 Javelin-thrower to break the 300-foot and 90-meter barriers with the new javelin, *4412*

1995 Chicago Blackhawks regular season game played in the United Center, *4218*

1998 Denver Broncos win in professional football's Super Bowl, *3496*

January 26

1924 Athlete to win a gold medal at the Olympic Winter Games, *4654*

Men's 500-meter speed skating event held at the Olympic Winter Games, *5639*

Men's 5000-meter speed skating event held at the Olympic Winter Games, *5640*

1956 Olympic Winter Games to be held in Italy, and the first to be televised, *4704*

1977 Figure skaters to perform a quadruple twist lift in competition, *3078*

1986 Chicago Bears win in professional football's Super Bowl, *3405*

1995 St. Louis Blues regular season hockey game played at the Kiel Center, *4238*

1997 National Football League player to gain 99 yards with a single Super Bowl punt return, *3481*

February—continued

1994 Athlete under the age of 14 to win a gold medal in the Olympic Winter Games, *4783*

Women's aerials freestyle skiing event held at the Olympic Winter Games, *5484*

Women's amateur boxing match sponsored by USA Boxing, *2590*

1996 Match between women boxers to be televised live, *2592*

February 1

1964 Men's singles luge (toboggan) event held in the Olympic Winter Games, *4455*

Speed skater to win four gold medals in speed skating in a single Olympic Winter Games, *5678*

Two-seater luge (toboggan) event at the Olympic Winter Games, *4456*

1978 Figure skaters to perform simultaneous triple jumps in competition, *3082*

February 2

1876 National League was organized, *1219*

1924 Men's individual 18-kilometer Nordic (cross-country) event held at the Olympic Winter Games, *5366*

1948 Men's downhill skiing event held at the Olympic Winter Games, *5386*

Women's downhill skiing event held at the Olympic Winter Games, *5387*

1956 Figure skater from the United States to win the women's singles title at the Olympic Winter Games, *3053*

1962 Pole-vaulter to clear 16 feet, *4844*

1964 Athlete to win four gold medals at a single Olympic Winter Games, and six Olympic gold medals overall, *4715*

Figure skater from the Netherlands to win the women's singles title at the Olympic Winter Games, *3065*

Speed skater to win four gold medals in speed skating in a single Olympic Winter Games, *5678*

Speed skater to win two consecutive women's 1500-meter and 3000-meter titles at the Olympic Winter Games, *5677*

February 3

1924 Bobsled event held at the Olympic Winter Games, *2467*

1956 Skier to sweep the men's individual Alpine events at the Olympic Winter Games, *5406*

1962 Runner to complete the men's 800-meter race in under 1:45 minutes, *5074*

1972 Olympic Winter Games held in Asia, *4735*

February 4

1924 Athlete to receive an Olympic medal 50 years after the competition, *4741*

Men's individual Nordic combined (cross-country and ski jump) event held in the Olympic Winter Games, *5367*

Men's individual ski jump event held at the Olympic Winter Games, *5368*

National team to sweep the medals in the men's combined individual Nordic (cross-country) skiing event at the Olympic Winter Games, *5369*

Skier for the United States to win a ski-jumping medal at the Olympic Winter Games, *5370*

1932 Olympic speed skating events to be held as races, rather than in pairs, *5648*

Olympic Winter Games held in the United States, *4676*

1948 Athlete to win medals in the Olympic Winter Games 20 years apart, *4691*

1956 Ice hockey team from the Soviet Union to win the gold medal at the Olympic Winter Games, *4135*

Skiers from the Soviet Union to win the men's 4 x 10-kilometer relay Nordic (cross-country) title at the Olympic Winter Games, *5405*

1964 Women's singles luge (toboggan) event held in the Olympic Winter Games, *4457*

1965 National Hockey League goaltender to reach 400 career wins, *4148*

February 5

1893 Speed skater to skate the 500 meters in under 50 seconds, *5631*

1932 Speed skater from the United States to win the men's 1500-meter title at the Olympic Winter Games, *5649*

1948 Figure skater from the United States to win the men's singles titles in the Olympic Games, *3035*

Men's slalom event held at the Olympic Winter Games, *5388*

February 9—*continued*

1992   Women's individual 15-kilometer Nordic (cross-country) skiing event at the Olympic Winter Games, *5470*

1995   College women's basketball player to score 12 3-point goals in a single Division I National Collegiate Athletic Association (NCAA) game, *2356*

1998   Slider to win two, and then three, consecutive men's singles luge (toboggan) titles in the Olympic Winter Games, *4465*

February 10

1932   Two-man bobsled competition held in the Olympic Games, *2471*

1936   Men's 4 x 10-kilometer relay Nordic (cross-country) event held in the Olympic Winter Games, *5384*

1972   Speed skater from the United States to win the women's 500-meter title at the Olympic Winter Games, *5688*

1984   Skier to win two consecutive men's 30-kilometer Nordic (cross-country) titles in the Olympic Winter Games, *5442*

1989   Boxer to hold the undisputed world heavyweight title after 1980, *2586*

1992   National team to sweep the medals in the men's 30-kilometer Nordic (cross-country) skiing event at the Olympic Winter Games, *5471*

        Speed skater to win two consecutive women's 500-meter titles in the Olympic Winter Games, *5711*

1998   Male figure skater to win the pairs title at the Olympic Winter Games with two different partners, *3115*

        Women's giant slalom snow-boarding event held at the Olympic Winter Games, *5525*

February 11

1922   National Hockey League tie game, *4077*

1928   Olympic Winter Games held in Switzerland, *4664*

1932   Skier to win two consecutive men's individual Nordic combined titles in the Olympic Winter Games, *5378*

1936   Speed skater to win three gold medals in speed skating at a single Olympic Winter Games, *5658*

1964   Skier to win both the men's individual 70- and 90-meter ski jumps in the same Olympic Winter Games, *5414*

1972   Figure skater from Czechoslovakia to win the men's singles title at the Olympic Winter Games, *3070*

1976   Figure skater from Great Britain to win the men's singles title at the Olympic Winter Games, *3077*

1982   Basketball player to have 21 offensive rebounds in a single National Basketball Association (NBA) game, *2181*

1989   Drag racer to reach a speed over 290 miles per hour, *1138*

1992   Female athlete to win gold medals in two different sports in the Olympic Winter Games, *4771*

        Male figure skater to win the pairs title at the Olympic Winter Games with two different partners, *3115*

        Women's 7.5-kilometer biathlon competition held in the Olympic Winter Games, *2439*

1998   Skier from the United States to win the men's moguls freestyle skiing event in the Olympic Winter Games, *5497*

        Skier from the United States to win the women's super giant slalom at the Olympic Winter Games, *5498*

February 12

1839   Boxing title fight under the London Prize Ring Rules, *2511*

1909   Runner to complete the men's marathon in under 2:55 hours, *4473*

1932   Figure skaters to win two consecutive pairs titles at the Olympic Winter Games, *3013*

        National team to sweep the medals in the men's 90-meter ski jump at the Olympic Winter Games, *5379*

1936   Speed skater to win three gold medals in speed skating at a single Olympic Winter Games, *5658*

        Speed skater to win two Olympic gold medals in men's 5000-meter speed skating, *5657*

1951   Woman speed skater to skate the 1500 meters in under 2:30 minutes, *5664*

1960   Women's 3000-meter speed skating event held at the Olympic Winter Games, *5668*

1968   Men's giant slalom to have two runs on separate days, rather than a single run, at the Olympic Winter Games, *5417*

1976   Men's 1000-meter speed skating event held in the Olympic Winter Games, *5692*

February 15—*continued*

1932 Athlete to win gold medals in both the Summer and Winter Olympics, *4674*

Bobsledders to win two straight titles in the four-man bobsled at the Olympic Winter Games, *2472*

1936 Female athlete to win three consecutive titles in the same event in the Olympic Winter Games, *4683*

1948 Automobile race sponsored by the National Association for Stock Car Auto Racing (NASCAR), *1070*

National Association for Stock Car Auto Racing (NASCAR), *1071*

1952 Men's giant slalom event held at the Olympic Winter Games, *5394*

1953 Figure skater from the United States to win the women's singles title in the world championships, *3048*

1968 Men's 4 x 7.5-kilometer relay biathlon team event held at the Olympic Winter Games, *2432*

1980 Speed skater to sweep all five men's speed skating events in a single Olympic Winter Games, *5696*

1984 National team to sweep the medals in the women's 3000-meter speed-skating event at the Olympic Winter Games, *5702*

1992 Figure skater from Ukraine to win the men's singles title at the Olympic Winter Games, *3100*

Figure skater to perform a quadruple jump in the Olympic Games, *3101*

Men's combined pursuit Nordic (cross-country) skiing event held at the Olympic Winter Games, *5476*

Women's combined pursuit Nordic (cross-country) skiing event in the Olympic Winter Games, *5477*

1994 Professional figure skaters to win a gold medal in the Olympic Winter Games after being reinstated to amateur competition, *3106*

1998 Curling event held in the Olympic Games, *2680*

February 16

1936 Ice hockey team from Great Britain to win the gold medal at the Olympic Winter Games, *4115*

Skier to win two consecutive men's individual ski jump titles in the Olympic Winter Games, *5385*

1980 Speed skater to sweep all five men's speed skating events in a single Olympic Winter Games, *5696*

1984 Skier from the United States to win the men's downhill title at the Olympic Winter Games, *5444*

1987 College women's basketball player to score 60 points in a single Division I National Collegiate Athletic Association (NCAA) game, *2259*

College women's basketball team to score 149 points in a single Division I National Collegiate Athletic Association (NCAA) game, *2260*

1988 Slider to win two consecutive women's singles luge (toboggan) titles at the Olympic Winter Games, *4463*

1994 Speed skater to win two consecutive titles in the men's 1500-meters at the Olympic Winter Games, *5720*

1998 Figure skaters to win two consecutive ice dancing titles at the Olympic Winter Games, *3114*

Skier to win two consecutive Olympic titles in the women's downhill, and the first to win both the downhill and Alpine combination events in the same Olympic Winter Games, *5503*

February 17

1928 Athlete to win three consecutive gold medals in the same event in the Olympic Winter Games, *4666*

Men's skeleton luge event at the Olympic Winter Games, *4452*

National team to sweep the medals in the men's 15-kilometer Nordic (cross-country) skiing event in the Olympic Winter Games, *5376*

1955 Golfer to score 257 for 72 holes in a Professional Golfers' Association (PGA) recognized event, *3745*

1980 Figure skater to win three consecutive medals in pairs competition at the Olympic Winter Games, *3084*

1988 Speed skater to win two consecutive men's 5000-meter titles at the Olympic Winter Games, *5710*

1992 Athlete to win ten medals in the Olympic Winter Games, *4772*

Female athlete to win medals in the Olympic Winter Games 16 years apart, *4773*

National team to sweep the medals in the women's 5000-meter speed-skating event at the Olympic Winter Games, *5713*

Skier to win four medals in the same Nordic skiing event in the Olympic Winter Games, *5478*

1994 Skier to win two consecutive women's combined pursuit Nordic (cross-country) skiing titles at the Olympic Winter Games, *5486*

1998 Skier to win two consecutive Olympic titles in the women's downhill, and the first to win both the downhill and Alpine combination events in the same Olympic Winter Games, *5503*

Speed skater to skate the 10,000 meters in under 13:30 minutes, *5729*

Women's ice hockey event held in the Olympic Games, *4230*

February 18

1885 Grand National luge (toboggan) race, *4449*

1918 National Hockey League shutout, *4068*

1928 Bobsledders from the United States to win the five-man bobsled title at the Olympic Winter Games, *2468*

Figure skater from Norway to win the women's singles title at the Olympic Winter Games, *3007*

National Hockey League goaltender to have six consecutive shutouts, *4095*

1968 New York Rangers regular season hockey game played at Madison Square Garden, *4151*

1978 Hawaii Ironman triathlon, *6235*

1984 Women's individual 20-kilometer Nordic (cross-country) event held at the Olympic Winter Games, *5445*

1992 Skier to win two consecutive individual titles in an Alpine event in the Olympic Winter Games, *5479*

1994 Woman to win gold medals in two biathlon events in the same Olympic Winter Games, *2442*

1998 Skier from the United States to win the men's aerials freestyle skiing event in the Olympic Winter Games, *5500*

Skier from the United States to win the women's aerials freestyle skiing event in the Olympic Winter Games, *5501*

February 19

1928 Figure skaters from France to win the pairs title in the Olympic Winter Games, *3008*

1958 National team to win three consecutive ice hockey titles at the Olympic Winter Games, *4096*

International cricket organization for women, *2659*

1960 Figure skaters from Canada to win the pairs title at the Olympic Winter Games, *3055*

1980 Men's 10-kilometer biathlon competition at the Olympic Winter Games, *2435*

Sliders to win two consecutive luge (toboggan) titles at the Olympic Winter Games, *4462*

Speed skater to sweep all five men's speed skating events in a single Olympic Winter Games, *5696*

1984 Skier from the United States to win the men's slalom title at the Olympic Winter Games, *5446*

1992 Women's 15-kilometer biathlon competition held in the Olympic Winter Games, *2441*

1994 Figure skater from Russia to win the men's singles title at the Olympic Winter Games, *3107*

Male skier to win five gold medals in Nordic (cross-country) skiing in the Olympic Winter Games, and the first to win two consecutive men's combined pursuit titles, *5487*

Speed skater to win three consecutive women's 500-meter titles at the Olympic Winter Games, *5721*

February 20

1930 National Hockey League goaltender to wear a facemask in a scheduled game, *4101*

1952 Skier from the United States to win two Olympic gold medals, *5397*

1960 Women's 500-meter speed skating event held at the Olympic Winter Games, *5669*

1988 Athlete to win two biathlon gold medals at a single Olympic Winter Games, *2438*

1992 Athlete from the Southern Hemisphere to win a gold medal in the Olympic Winter Games, *4774*

Men's 1000-meter short track speed skating event held in the Olympic Winter Games, *5714*

Skier to win both the women's slalom and the women's Alpine combination in the same Olympic Winter Games, and the first from Austria to win the Olympic women's slalom title, *5480*

February 20—*continued*

Women's 3000-meter short track relay speed skating event held at the Olympic Winter Games, *5715*

1994 Bobsledders to win two consecutive two-man bobsled titles at the Olympic Winter Games, *2477*

1998 Skier to win two consecutive titles in the women's giant slalom in the Olympic Winter Games, *5502*

Speed skater to skate the women's 5000-meter event in under 7 minutes, *5730*

Speed skater to win two consecutive women's 5000-meter titles in the Olympic Winter Games, *5731*

February 21

1952 Figure skater to perform a triple jump in competition, *3047*

1960 Men's 20-kilometer biathlon competition at the Olympic Winter Games, *2431*

Women's 1500-meter speed skating event held at the Olympic Winter Games, *5670*

1980 Athlete from Liechtenstein to win an Olympic gold medal, *4750*

Speed skater to sweep all five men's speed skating events in a single Olympic Winter Games, *5696*

1988 Men's super giant slalom event held at the Olympic Winter Games, *5454*

1992 Japanese-American figure skater to win the women's singles title at the Olympic Winter Games, *3102*

1998 Speed skater to win two consecutive women's 1000-meter short track titles in the Olympic Winter Games, *5732*

1999 Toronto Raptors regular season basketball game played at the Air Canada Centre, *2419*

February 22

1886 International ice hockey tournament, *4044*

1969 Woman jockey to win a professional horse race in the United States, *4306*

1975 Women's basketball game played in Madison Square Garden, *2114*

1988 Athlete to win medals in both the Summer and Winter Olympic Games in the same year, *4768*

Skier to win two consecutive titles in the men's 4 x 10-kilometer relay Nordic (cross-country) at the Olympic Winter Games, *5455*

1992 Men's 5000-meter relay short track speed skating event held at the Olympic Winter Games, *5716*

Women's 500-meter short track speed skating event held at the Olympic Winter Games, *5717*

1994 Speed skater to win two consecutive men's 1000-meter short track titles at the Olympic Winter Games, *5722*

February 23

1874 Tennis game in its modern form, *6005*

1895 Speed skater to skate the 10,000 meters in under 18 minutes, *5636*

1952 National team to sweep the medals in the women's 10-kilometer Nordic (cross-country) skiing event in the Olympic Winter Games, *5395*

Women's individual 10-kilometer Nordic (cross-country) event held at the Olympic Winter Games, *5396*

1960 Figure skater to win the women's singles U.S., world, and Olympic championships in the same year, *3056*

1980 Figure skater from Germany to win the women's singles title at the Olympic Winter Games, *3085*

Speed skater to sweep all five men's speed skating events in a single Olympic Winter Games, *5696*

1988 Athlete to win two biathlon gold medals at a single Olympic Winter Games, *2438*

Figure skaters from Canada to win a medal in ice dancing at the Olympic Winter Games, *3093*

Men's Nordic combined team event held in the Olympic Winter Games, *5456*

Skier to win two individual ski-jumping gold medals in the same Olympic Winter Games, *5460*

1994 Athlete from the United States to win six medals at the Olympic Winter Games, and the first female U.S. athlete to win five gold medals at the winter or summer Games, *4784*

Hammer-thrower to hold the officially accepted world record in the women's event, *3997*

Speed skater to win two consecutive women's 1000-meter speed skating titles at the Olympic Winter Games, *5723*

Woman to win gold medals in two biathlon events in the same Olympic Winter Games, *2442*

February 24

February 25

February 26

February 27

February 28

February 28—*continued*

1988 Women's 5000-meter speed skating event held in the Olympic Winter Games, *5709*

March

1883 International luge (toboggan) competition, *4447*
1922 Vasalopp long-distance ski race, *5364*
1966 Championship win by a team with an all-African-American starting lineup in the final game, and the first championship for Texas Western, in the National Collegiate Athletic Association (NCAA) Men's Basketball National Tournament, *2043*
1974 Basketball team to get 61 defensive rebounds in a single National Basketball Association (NBA) game, *2106*
1975 Woman to become a boxing judge, *2573*
1995 National Collegiate Athletic Association (NCAA) Division I women's softball player to get seven hits in a single game, *5625*

March 1

1913 International governing body for tennis, *6055*
1969 Speed skater to skate the 1000 meters in under 1:20 minutes, *5681*

March 2

1874 Batter's box in baseball, *1212*
Rules against professional baseball players betting on either their own or the opposing team, *1213*
1951 National Basketball Association (NBA) All-Star Game, *1934*
1962 Basketball player to score 100 points in a single National Basketball Association (NBA) game, *2017*
1969 National Hockey League player to score 100 points in a single season, *4152*
1972 Speed skater to skate the 3000 meters in under 4:10 minutes, *5689*

March 3

1875 Ice hockey game, *4041*
1927 National Hockey League team to win 25 games in a single season, *4090*

March 4

1861 Walker to be considered a professional, *6287*

1968 Olympic heavyweight boxing champion to become world heavyweight champion, *2567*

March 5

1924 Bowler to bowl two consecutive 300 games, *2490*
1940 College track and field (athletics) meet to be televised, *6211*
1967 Woman speed skater to skate the 3000 meters in under 5 minutes, *5680*

March 6

1947 Water-skier known to have skied barefoot, *6315*
1973 Major league baseball player to come to bat as a designated hitter, *1730*

March 7

1744 Golf rules, *3551*
1959 Basketball player to shoot 24 consecutive free throws, and to shoot 100 percent in free throws, during a single Division I National Collegiate Athletic Association (NCAA) game, *1987*

March 8

1930 Major league baseball player to earn $80,000 per year, *1491*
1951 Asian Games, *4372*

March 9

1929 Discus-thrower to break the 160-foot and 50-meter barriers, *2763*
1937 National Hockey League player to reach 250 career assists, *4116*

March 10

1991 Tennis player (man or woman) to be ranked number one in the world for 186 consecutive weeks, *6183*

March 11

1945 Golfer to win more than 10 straight titles, and to win 18 titles overall during a single year, on the Professional Golfers' Association (PGA) Tour, *3714*
1954 National Collegiate Athletic Association hockey player to score seven points in a single "Frozen Four" tournament game, *4133*

March 14

1887 National Colored League organizing meeting, *1288*

599

March 26—*continued*

1978 Woman to sail around the world alone, *5237*

1983 Woman speed skater to skate the 1000 meters in under 1:20 minutes, *5701*

March 27

1939 National Collegiate Athletic Association (NCAA) Division I tournament basketball championship game, *1898*

March 28

1981 Woman speed skater to skate the 3000 meters in under 4:30 minutes, *5698*

1998 Speed skater to skate the 500 meters in under 35 seconds, *5734*

1999 Father and son to win golf tournaments on the same day, *3896*
Sisters to face each other in the finals of a professional tennis tournament, *6191*

March 29

1960 Basketball player to collect 40 rebounds in a single National Basketball Association (NBA) Finals game, *1996*

1981 London Marathon, *4507*

1998 Speed skater to skate the 1000 meters in under 1:10 minutes, *5735*

March 30

1889 Golf course in the United States, *3596*

1932 African-American professional basketball team to win a world championship, *1892*

March 31

1891 Boxer of African descent to win a United States boxing title, and probably the first athlete of African descent to hold a U.S. title in any sport, *2521*

1962 Pole-vaulter to clear 16 feet, *4844*

1998 Arizona Diamondbacks regular season baseball game played at the Bank One Ballpark, *1850*
Tampa Bay Devil Rays regular season baseball game played at Tropicana Field, *1851*

April

1846 Baseball uniform, *1186*

April 1

1931 Woman to pitch against a major league baseball team, *1500*

1972 Major league baseball players' strike to stop the opening of a season, *1728*

1982 Ladies Professional Golf Association (LPGA) Tour tournament to be nationally televised for all four rounds, *3839*

April 4

1981 Woman to compete in the University Boat Race, *4951*

1994 Cleveland Indians regular season baseball game played at Jacobs Field, *1827*

April 5

1967 Basketball player to grab 41 rebounds in a single National Basketball Association (NBA) playoff game, *2049*

1981 Basketball team to have 20 blocked shots in a single National Basketball Association (NBA) playoff game, *2170*

1993 Florida Marlins regular season baseball game played at Joe Robbie Stadium, *1823*

April 6

1896 Athlete, and the first from the United States, to win a gold medal in the modern Olympic Games, *4604*
Event held in the modern Olympic Games, *4605*
Men's discus throw event held in the Olympic Games, *2754*
Men's triple jump event held in the Olympic Games, *6249*
Modern Olympic Games, *4606*

1901 Baltimore Orioles regular season baseball game played at Oriole Park, *1330*

1913 Schneider Cup international seaplane (hydro-aeroplane) race, *1004*

1973 Major league baseball player to appear as a designated hitter during a regular season game, *1731*

1977 Seattle Mariners regular season baseball game played at the Seattle Kingdome, *1744*

1982 Minnesota Twins regular season baseball game played at the Hubert H. Humphrey Metrodome, *1766*

1992 Baltimore Orioles regular season baseball game played at Camden Yards, *1819*

1993 Javelin-thrower to break the 310- and 320-foot barriers with the new javelin, *4413*

April 7

1896 Athlete from Australia to win a gold medal in the modern Olympic Games, *4607*

Athlete from Denmark to win a gold medal in the Olympic Games, *4608*

Athlete from France to win a gold medal in the Olympic Games, *4609*

Athlete from Great Britain to win a gold medal in the Olympic Games, *4610*

Athlete from Greece to win a gold medal in the modern Olympic Games, *4611*

Men's 100- and 400-meter running events held in the Olympic Games, *4975*

Men's 800-meter and 1500-meter running events held in the Olympic Games, *4974*

Men's individual foil fencing competition held in the Olympic Games, *2897*

Men's long jump event held in the Olympic Games, *4426*

Men's masters foil fencing competition held in the Olympic Games, *2898*

Men's shot put event held in the Olympic Games, *5329*

Unlimited weight weightlifting events held in the Olympic Games, *6325*

1970 Milwaukee Brewers regular season baseball game played at County Stadium, *1715*

1971 Legal off-track betting operation in the United States, *4308*

1977 Toronto Blue Jays regular season baseball game played at Exhibition Stadium, *1745*

1986 Major league baseball player to hit a home run on the season's first pitch, *1788*

2000 Houston Astros regular season baseball game played at Enron Field, *1859*

April 8

1969 Kansas City Royals regular season baseball game played at Municipal Stadium, *1708*

San Diego Padres regular season baseball game played at San Diego Stadium, *1709*

1974 Major league baseball player to hit 715 career home runs, *1738*

1982 National Hockey League player to have six assists in a single Stanley Cup playoffs game, *4184*

1984 Golfer to win two of golf's major tournaments in her rookie year on the Ladies Professional Golf Association (LPGA) Tour, *3844*

April 9

1896 Athlete from Switzerland to win a gold medal in the Olympic Games, *4612*

Free rifle individual shooting event held in the Olympic Games, *5269*

Men's 800-meter and 1500-meter running events held in the Olympic Games, *4974*

Men's horizontal bar gymnastics competitions held in the Olympic Games, *3902*

Men's individual sabre fencing competition held in the Olympic Games, *2899*

Men's long horse vault gymnastics competition held in the Olympic Games, *3903*

Men's rings gymnastics competition held in the Olympic Games, *3904*

Men's side (pommel) horse gymnastics competition held in the Olympic Games, *3905*

1958 Basketball player to make 19 free throws in a National Basketball Association (NBA) Finals game, *1980*

1960 Basketball team to have a rebound percentage of .667 in a single National Basketball Association (NBA) Finals game, *1997*

1962 Washington Senators regular season baseball game played at DC Stadium, *1654*

1978 Basketball player to score 13 field goals in a single quarter of a National Basketball Association (NBA) game, *2141*

Basketball player to score 33 points in a single quarter of a National Basketball Association (NBA) game, *2142*

1990 Basketball team to make 61 free throws in a single National Basketball Association (NBA) game, *2295*

1993 Colorado Rockies regular season baseball game played at Mile High Stadium, *1824*

April 10

1896 Brothers to win gold and silver medals in the same event in the Olympic Games, *4613*

April 10—*continued*

Marathon runner to be stripped of his medal, *4467*

Men's 100- and 400-meter running events held in the Olympic Games, *4975*

Men's 110-meter hurdles event held in the Olympic Games, *4322*

Men's high jump event held in the Olympic Games, *4019*

Men's marathon race held in the Olympic Games, *4468*

Men's parallel bars gymnastics competitions held in the Olympic Games, *3906*

Men's pole vault event held in the Olympic Games, *4837*

Men's rope climbing gymnastics competition held in the Olympic Games, *3907*

Military revolver individual shooting event held in the Olympic Games, *5270*

1900 Athlete to win four gold medals in a single Olympic Games, *4627*

1961 Washington Senators regular season baseball game played at Griffith Stadium, *1646*

1962 Los Angeles Dodgers regular season baseball game played at Dodger Stadium, *1655*

1973 Kansas City Royals regular season baseball game at Kauffman Stadium, *1732*

1975 African-American golfer to play in the Masters tournament, *3808*

April 11

1896 Athlete from Hungary to win a gold medal in the modern Olympic Games, *4614*

Cyclist to win two, and then three, cycling gold medals in the Olympic Games, *2688*

Free pistol shooting individual event held in the Olympic Games, *5271*

Men's 100-meter freestyle swimming event held in the Olympic Games, *5785*

Men's 1000-meter match sprint cycling race held in the Olympic Games, *2685*

Men's 1200-meter freestyle swimming event held in the Olympic Games, *5786*

Men's 500-meter freestyle event held in the Olympic Games, *5787*

Men's doubles tennis event held in the Olympic Games, *6035*

Men's singles tennis event held in the Olympic Games, *6036*

Rapid-fire pistol shooting individual event held in the Olympic Games, *5272*

Unlimited weight (super heavyweight) Greco-Roman wrestling event held in the Olympic Games, *6358*

1921 Boxing match to be broadcast on radio, *2540*

1966 African-American to work as an umpire in major league baseball, *1686*

1988 Swimmer to race the women's 50-meter freestyle in under 25 seconds, *5950*

1994 Texas Rangers regular season baseball game played at The Ballpark, *1828*

2000 San Francisco Giants regular season baseball game played at Pacific Bell Park, *1860*

April 12

1896 Cyclist to win two, and then three, cycling gold medals in the Olympic Games, *2688*

Free rifle (three position) individual shooting event held in the Olympic Games, *5273*

Men's road race cycling event held in the Olympic Games, *2686*

1909 Philadelphia Athletics regular season baseball game played at Shibe Park, *1393*

1955 Kansas City Athletics regular season baseball game played at Muncipal Stadium, *1614*

1960 San Francisco Giants regular season baseball game played at Candlestick Park (later 3Com Park), *1643*

1965 Houston Astros regular season baseball game played at the Houston Astrodome, *1680*

Major league baseball game played indoors and on an artificial surface, *1681*

1966 Atlanta Braves regular season baseball game played at Atlanta–Fulton County Stadium, *1687*

April 13

1896 Cyclist to win the men's 12-hour cycling race in the Olympic Games, *2687*

1953 Milwaukee Braves regular season baseball game played at County Stadium, *1597*

April 18—*continued*

1946 African-American baseball player in the International League in the 20th century, *1550*

1950 African-American baseball player to play for the Boston Braves, *1579*

1958 Los Angeles Dodgers regular season baseball game played at Los Angeles Memorial Coliseum, *1633*

1991 Chicago White Sox regular season baseball game played at New Comiskey Park, *1816*

1996 Basketball player to make 11 3-point field goals in a single National Basketball Association (NBA) game, *2373*

April 19

1897 Boston Marathon, *4469*

1901 Runner to win two consecutive Boston Marathons, *4470*

1913 Brooklyn Dodgers regular season baseball game played at Ebbets Field, *1415*

1924 Runner to win three consecutive Boston Marathons, *4476*

1930 Runner to win seven Boston Marathons, *4479*

1947 Runner officially representing South Korea to hold the world record in the men's marathon, and to win the Boston Marathon, *4482*

1950 Runners from a single country outside the United States to take the top three spots in the Boston Marathon, *4483*

1957 Boston Marathon winner who was a member of the Boston Athletic Association, *4486*

1966 California Angels regular season baseball game played at Anaheim Stadium, *1688*

Woman to race in the Boston Marathon, *4490*

1967 Woman to run in the Boston Marathon wearing an official number, *4491*

1971 Philadelphia Phillies regular season baseball game played at Veterans Stadium, *1721*

1972 Boston Marathon to include women as official participants, *4496*

1974 Woman to complete the Boston Marathon in under 3:00 hours, *4497*

1975 Wheelchair entrant in the Boston Marathon, *4498*

1977 Champion of the women's wheelchair division in the Boston Marathon, *4502*

1978 Runner to win the men's title in both the Boston Marathon and the New York Marathon in the same year, *4503*

1979 Runner to win both the women's title in the Boston Marathon and the women's marathon in the Olympic Games, *4513*

1983 Runner to win two official women's championships in the Boston Marathon, *4511*

1986 Boston Marathon to offer prize money, *4515*

1988 Runner from Africa to win the men's title in the Boston Marathon, *4518*

Runner to win two consecutive women's titles in the Boston Marathon, and three overall, *4519*

1990 Runner to win two consecutive women's titles in the Boston Marathon, and three overall, *4519*

1991 Runner to race in more than 60 Boston Marathons, *4520*

1996 Runner to win three consecutive women's titles in the Boston Marathon, *4525*

1997 Runner from Africa to win the women's title in the Boston Marathon, *4527*

April 20

1887 Automobile race on record in Europe, *1042*

1903 Major league baseball game played by the New York Highlanders, *1351*

1912 Boston Red Sox regular season baseball game played at Fenway Park, *1413*

Detroit Tigers regular season baseball game played at Tiger Stadium, *1414*

1916 Chicago Cubs regular season baseball game played at Wrigley Field, *1425*

1986 Basketball player to score 63 points in a single National Basketball Association (NBA) playoff game, *2243*

1988 Major league baseball club to hit a total of 10,000 home runs, *1801*

1995 Colorado Rockies regular season baseball game played at Coors Field, *1831*

April 21

1910 Cleveland Indians regular season baseball game played at League Park II, *1400*

April 27

1891 Brooklyn Dodgers regular season baseball game played at Eastern Park, *1304*

1906 Long-jumper to win two consecutive men's titles in the Olympic Games, *4429*

Men's pentathlon held in the modern Olympic Games, *4814*

Men's stone throw event held in the Olympic Games, *5769*

1908 Olympic Games to include more than 2000 athletes, and more than 100 events, and to be held in Great Britain, *4636*

Rackets event held in the Olympic Games, *4872*

1961 Los Angeles Angels regular season baseball game played at Wrigley Field, *1648*

April 28

1906 Fencer to win both the men's individual sabre and épée titles in the Olympic Games, *2912*

Fencer to win both the men's masters épée and masters sabre competitions in the Olympic Games, *2907*

Fencer to win men's individual and team épée titles in the same Olympic Games, *2908*

Fencer to win two men's individual sabre titles in the Olympic Games, *2909*

Free rifle team shooting event held in the Olympic Games, *5281*

Men's team épée fencing competition held in the Olympic Games, *2910*

Men's team sabre fencing competition held in the Olympic Games, *2911*

1908 Athletes from Norway to win official gold medals at the Olympic Games, *4637*

1930 Professional baseball game played at night under lights, *1492*

1990 Basketball team to score 157 points in a single National Basketball Association (NBA) playoff game, *2296*

April 29

1901 Cleveland Indians regular season baseball game played at League Park I, *1336*

Washington Senators regular season baseball game played in American League Park, *1337*

1906 Runner to win both the men's 400- and 800-meter events in the same Olympic Games, *4993*

1986 Major league pitcher to pitch 20 strikeouts in a single game, *1789*

April 30

1886 National League baseball game to be played in Kansas City, *1285*

1887 Philadelphia Phillies regular season baseball game played at Huntington Street Grounds, *1289*

1898 Brooklyn Dodgers regular season baseball game played at Washington Park II, *1318*

1906 Runner to win both the men's 400- and 800-meter events in the same Olympic Games, *4993*

1921 American Professional Football League champions, *3150*

1940 Woman to be licensed as a boxing referee, *2553*

1960 High-jumper to set or equal four world records in the men's event in a single year, *4027*

1975 Basketball team to have a defensive rebound percentage of .952 in a single National Basketball Association (NBA) playoff game, *2116*

May

1611 Written reference to sports in Britain's American colonies, *5738*

1974 International sailing championships for women, *5233*

1976 Woman automobile racer to compete in a major stock car race, *1121*

May 1

1880 Cincinnati Reds regular season baseball game played at the Bank Street Grounds, *1246*

Sudden death rule to end games in major league baseball, *1247*

1883 New York Giants regular season baseball game played at Polo Grounds I, *1268*

Philadelphia Phillies regular season baseball game played at Recreation Park, *1269*

1890 Major league baseball player to play in 577 consecutive games, *1301*

1901 Two home runs in a single American League game, *1338*

1903 New York Highlanders regular season baseball game played at Hilltop Park, *1353*

1906 All-around wrestling title awarded in the Olympic Games, *6369*

May 9

1953 Shot-putter to break the 18- and 19-meter, and 60-foot, barriers, *5340*

1984 American League game to last more than 8 hours, *1777*

May 10

1876 Chicago White Stockings regular season baseball game played at the State Street Grounds, *1226*

1941 Iroquois Steeplechase horse race, *4298*

1953 Twin major league baseball players to play in the same game on the same team, *1598*

1981 Basketball team to have 28 offensive rebounds in a single National Basketball Association (NBA) Finals game, *2171*

May 12

1806 Record of cricket being played in the West Indies, *2641*

1902 African-American boxer born in the United States to win a world boxing title, *2524*

1966 St. Louis Cardinals regular season baseball game played at Busch Memorial Stadium, *1689*

May 13

1876 Triple play in baseball's National League, *1227*

1891 Jockey to win three Kentucky Derbys, and the first to win two in a row, *4283*

1897 Intercollegiate golf tournament in the United States, *3621*

1950 British Grand Prix automobile race to be part of the Formula One Grand Prix circuit, *1077*

1978 Record in the men's 5000-meter steeplechase to last for more than 10 years, *5108*

1999 Basketball player to have 10 steals in a single National Basketball Association (NBA) playoff game, *2420*

May 14

1874 Collegiate sporting event at which admission was charged, *5739*
International game of American-style football, and the first to use football goal posts, *3118*

1878 Chicago White Stockings regular season baseball game played at Lakefront Park, *1243*

1893 Chicago White Stockings regular season baseball game played at the West Side Grounds, *1309*

1978 Golfer to win five straight tournaments in which she played, *3820*

May 15

1862 Enclosed baseball field to which admission was charged, *1196*

1906 Major league pitcher of the 20th century to strike out four batters in a single inning, *1370*

1941 Major league baseball player to hit safely in 56 consecutive games, *1542*

1948 Runner from Central or South America to set or equal a world track and field record, *5049*

May 16

1871 Professional baseball game played in Boston, Massachusetts, *1210*

1939 Baseball player to hit a home run in an American League night game, *1536*

1980 Basketball player to score 42 points in a National Basketball Association (NBA) Finals game in his rookie year, *2162*

May 17

1875 Kentucky Derby horse race, *4279*

1928 Olympic Games to include track and field events for women, *4667*

1930 Discus-thrower to break the 160-foot and 50-meter barriers, *2763*

1939 Baseball game to be televised, *1537*

1998 Drag racer to reach a speed over 320 miles per hour, *1145*

May 18

1897 National League player to hit 4 triples in a 9-inning baseball game, *1316*

1912 High-jumper to hold the officially accepted world record in the men's event, *4021*

1924 Rugby players to win two Olympic gold medals in rugby, *4968*

1962 Discus-thrower to break the 200-foot barrier, *2773*

May 19

1962 Baseball player to reach 3,431 hits in the National League, *1659*

May 20

1880 "Rotating" pitchers in major league baseball, *1248*

May 30—*continued*

1911 Indianapolis 500, *1054*

Triple-jumper to hold the officially accepted world record in the men's event, *6253*

1950 Indianapolis 500 automobile race to be part of the Formula One Grand Prix circuit, *1079*

1985 Basketball team to have a defensive rebound percentage of .921 in a single National Basketball Association (NBA) Finals game, *2227*

May 31

1913 Runner to hold the officially accepted world record in the men's mile race, *5009*

1930 Golfer to complete a grand slam, *3693*

1938 Boxer to win three different world boxing titles within one year, *2550*

1964 National League game to run 7 hours and 25 minutes over 23 innings, *1673*

June

1965 Baseball player chosen in major league baseball's first free draft, *1682*

1973 World cup in women's cricket, *2660*

1980 Women to be caddies at the U.S. Open golf tournament, *3831*

1995 Extreme Games, *2896*

June 1

1939 Boxing match to be broadcast on television in the United States, *2552*

1954 Runner to race the men's 10,000 meters in under 29:00 minutes, *5061*

1959 College baseball player to score five runs in a single game, *1638*

June 2

1900 Polo event held in the Olympic Games, *4865*

1972 College baseball player to steal five bases in a single game, *1726*

June 3

1927 Ryder Cup golf match, *3687*

1932 Baseball player to hit four home runs in a single regular season American League game, *1504*

1967 Runner to hold the officially accepted world record in the women's 1500 meters, *5082*

1977 Basketball team to have 46 defensive rebounds in a single National Basketball Association (NBA) Finals game, *2133*

1984 Basketball player to have 21 assists in a National Basketball Association (NBA) Finals game, *2207*

1996 Nine-inning American League baseball game to take as long as 4 hours and 20 minutes, *1836*

June 4

1827 Cricket match on record between teams from Oxford and Cambridge universities, *2645*

1950 Swiss Grand Prix automobile race to be part of the Formula One Grand Prix circuit, *1080*

1955 College baseball player to pitch 17 bases on balls in a single game, *1616*

1968 Major league pitcher to pitch six successive shutouts, *1701*

1982 Hammer-thrower to break the 270-foot barrier, *3995*

1989 Toronto Blue Jays regular season baseball game played at the Skydome, *1807*

June 5

1952 Heavyweight boxing match to be broadcast nationally on television, *2556*

1963 National Hockey League Amateur Draft, *4145*

1977 Basketball player to have 8 blocked shots in a National Basketball Association (NBA) Finals game, *2134*

1982 Runner from the United States to hold the world record in the women's 5000- and 10,000-meter races, *5124*

1991 Basketball team to have a field goal percentage of .617 in a single National Basketball Association (NBA) Finals game, *2308*

1993 Woman jockey to win one of America's Triple Crown horse races, *4317*

1994 Basketball team to have an offensive rebounding percentage of .609 in a single National Basketball Association (NBA) playoff game, *2340*

June 6

1885 Chicago White Stockings regular season baseball game played at West Side Park, *1282*

June 14—*continued*

1992 Basketball team to have a perfect free throw record in a National Basketball Association (NBA) Finals game, *2317*

June 15

1900 Men's amateurs and masters épée fencing competition held in the Olympic Games, *2904*

1928 Major league baseball player to steal home 50 times in the course of his career, *1485*

1935 Runner from Asia to hold the officially accepted world record in the men's 100-meter dash, *5034*

1938 Major league baseball player to pitch two successive no-hitters, *1530*

1952 Runner to race the women's 800 meters in under 2:10 minutes, *5055*

1958 Woman automobile racer to compete in a Grand Prix race eligible for world-championship points, *1097*

1963 Dominican pitcher to pitch a no-hitter in the major leagues, *1665*

June 16

1883 Ladies' Day baseball game, *1272*

1939 Runner to race the men's 5000 meters in under 14:10 minutes, *5043*

1956 Equestrian to win two consecutive individual and team dressage titles in the Olympic Games, *2866*

1988 Basketball team to have an offensive rebound average of .556 in a single National Basketball Association (NBA) Finals game, *2274*

June 17

1901 Golfer to win the U.S. Open in a playoff, *3634*

June 18

1932 Javelin-thrower to hold the officially accepted world record in the women's event, *4389*

1950 Belgian Grand Prix automobile race to be part of the Formula One Grand Prix circuit, *1081*

2000 Golfer to hold the record low (under-par) scores in all four Professional Golfers Association (PGA) major tournaments, *3899*

June 19

1846 Inter-club baseball game on record under Cartwright's Rules, *1187*

1867 Belmont Stakes horse race, *4276*

1932 Runner to race the men's 5000 meters in under 14:28.0 minutes, *5028*

1946 Heavyweight boxing match to be broadcast on television, and the first at which top-price tickets cost $100, *2554*

1950 College baseball player to pitch a no-hitter, *1580*

1973 Runner to race the men's 5000-meter steeplechase in under 8:20 minutes, *5098*

June 20

1930 Golfer to complete a grand slam, *3693*

1936 Runner to race the men's 100-meter dash in 10.2 seconds, *5036*

1968 Runner to race the men's 100-meter dash in under 10 seconds, *5084*

1969 Hurdler to hold the officially accepted world record in the women's 100-meter hurdles, *4342*

1981 Pole-vaulter to clear 19 feet, *4847*

June 21

1979 International Cricket Conference (ICC) competition, *2662*

1997 Women's National Basketball Association (WNBA) began its first season of play, *2395*

June 22

1814 Cricket match on record at the current location of Lord's Cricket Ground, *2642*

1889 Major league baseball 26-game losing streak, *1295*

1921 Runner to hold the world record in both the men's 5000- and 10,000-meter events, *5013*

1962 Major league baseball player to reach 5,864 bases, *1660*

1974 Runner to race the women's 400 meters in under 50 seconds, *5100*

1980 Tournament on the Senior Professional Golfers' Association (PGA) Tour, *3832*

June 23

1950 Major league baseball game in which 11 home runs were hit, *1581*

1996 Runner to complete the men's 200-meter race in under 19.7 seconds, *5183*

June 24

1901   American League player to have 6 hits in a 9-inning baseball game, *1341*

1938   Cricket game to be broadcast on television, *2658*

1956   Golfer to win the Ladies Professional Golf Association (LPGA) Championship in a sudden-death playoff, *3749*

        Javelin-thrower to break the 270-foot barrier, *4396*

1960   High-jumper to set or equal four world records in the men's event in a single year, *4027*

June 25

1881   Major league baseball player to steal seven bases in a single game, *1255*

1885   Major league baseball player to get four triples, and five extra-base hits, in a single game, *1283*

1891   Two consecutive home runs by different players to open a major league baseball game, *1305*

1900   Fencer to win both the men's individual sabre and épée titles in the Olympic Games, *2912*

June 26

1920   Hurdler to race the 400-meter hurdles in under 55 seconds, *4328*

1942   Women-only rodeo, *4889*

June 27

1876   Baseball player to have 6 hits in a 9-inning National League game, *1228*

1890   Boxer of African descent to win a national boxing title, *2519*

1892   Boxer of African descent to win a world boxing title, *2523*

1900   Athlete from Italy to win a gold medal in the Olympic Games, *4618*

        Masters sabre fencing competition held in the Olympic Games, *2905*

        Olympic Games in which animals were deliberately killed, *4619*

1924   Shooter to win two consecutive titles in the men's free rifle (three positions) individual shooting event, and in the free rifle team event, in the Olympic Games, *5302*

1932   Javelin-thrower to break the 240- and 250-foot barriers, *4391*

1953   Golfer to win the U.S. Women's Open in a playoff, *3739*

1973   Runner to complete the men's 800-meter race in under 1:44 minutes, *5099*

June 28

1976   Runner to race the women's 1500 meters in under 4 minutes, *5104*

1981   Heptathlete to hold the world record in the women's heptathlon, *4012*

1984   Runner to race the women's 5000 meters in under 15 minutes, *5138*

June 29

1912   Shooter to win both the rapid-fire pistol and the free pistol individual events, and the first from the United States to win either event, in the Olympic Games, *5296*

1940   Pole-vaulter to clear 15 feet, *4841*

1956   High-jumper to clear seven feet, *4025*

        Hurdler to race the men's 400-meter hurdles in under 50 seconds, *4337*

1980   U.S. Senior Open golf tournament, *3833*

June 30

1854   Baseball game on record to go into extra innings, *1190*

1860   Baseball club tour, *1194*

1894   Major league baseball player to hit five times in five at-bats during his first major league game, *1313*

1902   Three consecutive home runs in a single inning of an American League game, *1348*

1909   Pittsburgh Pirates regular season baseball game played at Forbes Field, *1394*

1916   Golfer to win both the U.S. Amateur and U.S. Open championships in the same year, and to win the U.S. Open in under 290 for 72 holes, *3659*

1934   Hurdler to race the men's 400-meter hurdles in under 52 seconds, *4334*

1968   Major league pitcher to pitch 54 consecutive scoreless innings, *1702*

1970   Cincinnati Reds regular season baseball game played at Riverfront Stadium (later Cinergy Field), *1716*

July

1897   Native American major league baseball player, *1317*

1900   Croquet events at the Olympic Games, *2670*

1947   African-American baseball player to play for the St. Louis Browns, *1559*

1950   African-American baseball players to join the New York Yankees organization, *1582*

613

July—*continued*

1980 Twin brothers to win gold medals in wrestling in the same Olympic Games, *6404*

1991 African-American golfer to win the U.S. Junior Amateur title, *3871*

July 1

1859 Intercollegiate baseball game, *1193*

1904 Olympic Games held in the United States, *4628*

1910 Chicago White Sox regular season baseball game played at Comiskey Park, *1401*

1912 Shooters from the United States to win the trap (clay pigeon) team shooting event in the Olympic Games, *5294*

1920 St. Louis Cardinals regular season baseball game played at Sportsman's Park II, *1445*

1941 Major league baseball player to hit safely in 56 consecutive games, *1542*

1947 National Basketball Association (NBA) draft, *1918*

1951 Golfer to win her first tournament on the Ladies Professional Golf Association (LPGA) Tour, *3729*

1960 High-jumper to set or equal four world records in the men's event in a single year, *4027*

1975 Runner to race the men's 5000-meter steeplechase in under 8:10 minutes, *5102*

1980 Runner to complete the men's mile race in under 3:49 minutes, *5113*

July 2

1904 Men's team combined exercises gymnastics competition in the Olympic Games, *3911*

Men's triathlon event held in the Olympic Games, *6234*

1912 Shooter from the United States to win the men's trap (clay pigeon) individual shooting title in the Olympic Games, *5295*

Shooter to win both the rapid-fire pistol and the free pistol individual events, and the first from the United States to win either event, in the Olympic Games, *5296*

Swimmer to race the women's 100-meter freestyle in under 1:20 minutes, *5804*

Women's 100-meter freestyle swimming event held in the Olympic Games, *5805*

1921 Boxing match to have a $1 million gate, and the first heavyweight bout to be broadcast on radio, *2541*

1927 Hurdler to race the men's 400-meter hurdles in under 53 seconds, *4330*

1950 French Grand Prix automobile race to be part of the Formula One Grand Prix circuit, *1082*

1976 Woman swimmer to win four gold medals at a single Olympic Games, *5927*

July 3

1924 Shooter to win two consecutive titles in the running deer (double shot) individual shooting event in the Olympic Games, *5303*

1954 Golfer to win the U.S. Women's Open three times, *3744*

1984 Hammer-thrower to break the 280-foot barrier, *3996*

July 4

1882 Professional rodeo, *4879*

1883 Documented rodeo competition, *4880*

1889 Players' League, *1296*

1904 Men's decathlon event held in the Olympic Games, *2737*

1912 Soccer (international football) player to win two gold medals in the Olympic Games, *5548*

1924 Women's individual foil fencing competition held in the Olympic Games, *2920*

1939 Major league baseball player whose uniform number was retired at the end of his career, *1538*

1942 Batting helmet in professional baseball, *1544*

1960 Golfer to win two, and then three, Ladies Professional Golf Association (LPGA) Championships, *3762*

July 5

1947 African-American baseball player in the American League, *1560*

1979 Runner to complete the men's 800-meter race in under 1:43 minutes, *5111*

1998 U.S. Women's Open to be won in a sudden-death playoff, *3892*

July 6

1912 Runner to hold the officially accepted world record in the men's 100-meter dash, *5001*

1933 Baseball player to hit a home run in major league baseball's All-Star Game, *1508*

Major league baseball All-Star Game, *1509*

1940 Shooter to achieve a perfect score in international competition, *5305*

1974 Runner to hold the officially accepted world record in the women's 3000-meter event, *5101*

July 7

1904 Lacrosse event held in the Olympic Games, *4420*

1912 Athlete to win both the men's decathlon and pentathlon in the Olympic Games, and the first Native American to win an Olympic gold medal, *2738*

Native-American athlete to win a gold medal at the Olympic Games, *4645*

1924 Athlete to win an Olympic gold medal, or to hold the world record, in both the men's decathlon and an individual track and field event, *2741*

Runner from Europe to win the men's 100-meter title in the Olympic Games, *5014*

1944 Runner to complete the men's 1500 meters in under 3:45.0 minutes, *5048*

1986 Heptathlete from the United States, and the first African-American, to hold the world record in the women's event, *4014*

July 8

1880 Major league baseball team to win 21 games in a row, *1250*

1889 New York Giants regular season baseball game played at Polo Grounds II, *1297*

1899 Golfer born in the United States to win a U.S. national championship, *3627*

1912 Men's 5000- and 10,000-meter events held in the Olympic Games, *5008*

Runner to hold the officially accepted world record in the men's 800-meter event, *5002*

1924 Athlete of Black African ancestry to win an individual gold medal in the Olympic Games, *4657*

Swimmer to win two consecutive men's 100-meter backstroke titles in the Olympic Games, *5817*

1967 Runner to race the men's 1500 meters in less than 3:35 minutes, *5083*

July 9

1912 Men's 4 x 100-meter relay track event held in the Olympic Games, *5003*

Men's javelin event for both hands held in the Olympic Games, *4383*

National team to sweep the top medals in men's springboard diving in the Olympic Games, *2794*

1922 Swimmer to race the men's 100-meter freestyle in under one minute, *5815*

1930 Negro League game played at Yankee Stadium, *1493*

1978 Hammer-thrower to break the 80-meter barrier, *3994*

1988 Discus-thrower to break the 250-foot barrier, *2785*

July 10

1901 American League player to hit for the cycle (single, double, triple, and home run) in a single game, *1342*

1912 Men's 5000- and 10,000-meter events held in the Olympic Games, *5008*

National team to sweep the medals in the men's 200-meter breaststroke event in the Olympic Games, *5806*

1924 Athlete to win five gold medals in a single Olympic Games, *4658*

Bantamweight Greco-Roman wrestling event held in the Olympic Games, *6380*

Hammer-thrower born in the United States to win the men's event in the Olympic Games, *3983*

Wrestler to win gold medals in three different divisions in the Olympic Games, *6378*

1935 Baseball player to hit a home run in a National League night game, *1519*

1976 Shot-putter to break the 22-meter barrier, *5349*

1993 Runner to race the men's 10,000 meters in under 27:00 minutes, *5168*

1999 Women's team to be named *Sports Illustrated* Sportsman of the Year, *1163*

July 11

1900 Mixed doubles tennis event held in the Olympic Games, *6039*

National team to sweep the medals in the men's singles tennis event in the Olympic Games, *6040*

Woman to win a gold medal in the Olympic Games, *4620*

Women's singles tennis event held in the Olympic Games, *6041*

July 11—*continued*

1908
Running deer (double shot) individual shooting event held in the Olympic Games, *5284*

Running deer (single shot) individual shooting event held in the Olympic Games, *5285*

Running deer (single shot) team shooting event held in the Olympic Games, *5286*

Shooters from the United States to win the military revolver team event in the Olympic Games, *5287*

Shooters from the United States to win the military rifle team shooting title in the Olympic Games, *5288*

Small-bore rifle moving and disappearing target individual shooting events held in the Olympic Games, *5289*

Small-bore rifle (prone) individual shooting event held in the Olympic Games, *5290*

Small-bore rifle team shooting event held in the Olympic Games, *5291*

Trap (clay pigeon) team shooting event in the Olympic Games, *5292*

1912
Men's 10,000-meter walk held in the Olympic Games, *6290*

Men's plain high dive event held in the Olympic Games, *2795*

Men's shot put event for both hands held in the Olympic Games, *5332*

1936
Discus-thrower to hold the officially accepted world record in the women's event, *2766*

1953
Discus-thrower to break the 190-foot barrier, *2769*

1964
Golfer to win the U.S. Women's Open four times, *3778*

1971
Runner to race the women's 800 meters in under 2:00 minutes, *5093*

1985
Major league pitcher to reach 4,000 career strikeouts, *1782*

July 12

1731
Cricket ground set aside for play, *2634*

1912
Gymnast to win two consecutive men's all-around titles in the Olympic Games, *3918*

1924
Athlete to win an Olympic gold medal, or to hold the world record, in both the men's decathlon and an individual track and field event, *2741*

Athletes from Argentina to win gold medals in the Olympic Games, *4659*

Decathlete from the United States to hold the world record in the men's decathlon, *2740*

Runner to win two consecutive titles in the men's individual cross-country in the Olympic Games, *5015*

1949
African-American major league baseball players to appear in an All-Star Game, *1574*

1957
Runner to complete the 1500-meter race in under 3:40 minutes, *5067*

1980
Javelin-thrower to break the 70-meter barrier in the women's event, *4404*

July 13

1912
Men's 3000-meter team running event held in the Olympic Games, *5004*

Men's discus throw event for both hands held in the Olympic Games, *2761*

Water polo player to win two, and then three, gold medals in the Olympic Games, *6303*

1924
Runner to win two consecutive gold medals in the men's 4 x 100-meter relay in the Olympic Games, *5016*

1934
Major league baseball player to hit 700 home runs, *1513*

1969
Shot-putter to break the 20- and 21-meter barriers in the women's event, *5347*

1974
Hurdler to hold the officially accepted world record in the women's 400-meter hurdles, *4344*

1985
Pole-vaulter to clear 6 meters, *4848*

July 14

1900
National team to sweep the medals in the men's 110-meter hurdles in the Olympic Games, *4323*

1908
Men's 3500-meter and 10-mile walks held in the Olympic Games, *6289*

1912
Athlete to die while participating in the modern Olympic Games, *4644*

Swimmer from the United States to win the men's 100-meter backstroke title in the Olympic Games, *5807*

Wrestling event in the Olympic Games to have no gold-medalist, *6375*

Sporting event to be televised in color in the United States, *5750*

1951

1998
Runner to race the men's 1500 meters in 3:26 minutes, *5186*

1999
Women's National Basketball Association (WNBA) All-Star Game, *2421*

July 15

July 16

July 17

1900 Moving target individual shooting event held in the Olympic Games, *5277*

1908 Men's 3500-meter and 10-mile walks held in the Olympic Games, *6289*

Men's 4000-meter team pursuit cycling event held in the Olympic Games, *2692*

Men's javelin-throw event held at the Olympic Games, *4382*

1912 Equestrian to win both individual and team gold medals in the three-day event competitions in the Olympic Games, *2846*

Team jumping (Prix des Nations) equestrian event held in the Olympic Games, *2847*

Three-day event individual equestrian competition held in the Olympic Games, *2848*

Three-day event team equestrian competition held in the Olympic Games, *2849*

1924 Diver to win both the men's springboard and platform diving titles in the same Olympic Games, *2799*

Rowers to win two consecutive medals in the men's double sculls event in the Olympic Games, *4935*

1928 Rower to win three consecutive medals in the men's double sculls event in the Olympic Games, *4936*

1934 Major league baseball player to reach a total of 2,000 bases on balls, *1514*

1955 Ladies Professional Golf Association (LPGA) Championship, *3746*

1966 Runner to complete the men's mile race in under 3:53 minutes, *5080*

1976 Olympic Games held in Canada, *4744*

July 18

1882 Major league pitcher to pitch left-handed and right-handed in the same game, *1263*

1908 Discus-thrower from the United States to win the men's Greek-style title in the Olympic Games, *2759*

Men's 200-meter breaststroke event held in the Olympic Games, *5801*

Men's springboard diving event held in the Olympic Games, *2792*

1924 Women's 200-meter breaststroke event held in the Olympic Games, *5818*

1927 Major league baseball player of the 20th century to reach 4,000 hits, *1480*

1965 All-African Games, *4376*

1976 Woman swimmer to win four gold medals at a single Olympic Games, *5927*

1995 Triple-jumper to break the 18-meter and 60-foot barriers, *6264*

1999 Golfer to come from 10 strokes behind to win a Professional Golfers' Association (PGA) recognized tournament, *3897*

July 19

1877 Tennis tournament played at Wimbledon, *6008*

1909 Unassisted triple play of the 20th century in major league baseball, *1395*

1924 Tennis players from the United States to win the women's doubles title in the Olympic Games, *6070*

1952 Olympic Games held in Finland, *4701*

1976 National Team to sweep the medals in the men's 200-meter freestyle in the Olympic Games, *5921*

Weightlifter to compete in five Olympic Games, *6347*

Woman swimmer to win four gold medals at a single Olympic Games, *5927*

1980 Olympic Games held in the Soviet Union, and the first in a Communist country, *4751*

1996 Olympic Games in which more than 10,000 athletes competed, and more than 50 percent were women, *4789*

1997 Women's national championships in boxing, *2594*

July 20

1858 Baseball game on record at which admission was charged, *1192*

1908 Swimmer to win two consecutive men's 100-meter freestyle titles in the Olympic Games, *5802*

1924 Athlete from Czechoslovakia to win a gold medal in the Olympic Games, *4660*

Athlete from Yugoslavia to win a gold medal in the Olympic Games, *4661*

Athlete to win Olympic medals in both diving and swimming, *2798*

Boxer to win two consecutive middleweight titles in the Olympic Games, *2545*

Diver to win both the men's springboard and platform diving titles in the same Olympic Games, *2799*

Gymnast to win three consecutive gold medals in the men's team combined exercises in the Olympic Games, *3924*

Tennis player from the United States to win the women's singles tennis title in the Olympic Games, *6071*

Women's 100-meter backstroke event held in the Olympic Games, *5819*

1947 Two African-American major league baseball players to play for the same club in the same game, *1561*

1952 Runner to win two consecutive men's 10,000-meter titles in the Olympic Games, *5056*

1963 Ladies Professional Golf Association (LPGA) tournament to be nationally televised, *3772*

1976 Olympic men's 1500-meter freestyle event in which the medalists all had times under 16 minutes, *5922*

1984 Javelin-thrower to break the 330- and 340-foot and 100-meter barriers in the men's event, *4407*

July 21

1908 Middleweight freestyle wrestling event held in the Olympic Games, *6372*

1924 Tennis players from the United States to win the mixed doubles event in the Olympic Games, *6072*

1959 African-American baseball player to play for the Boston Red Sox, *1639*

1963 High-jumper to set six world records in the men's event, *4029*

1976 Woman to win a medal in shooting at the Olympic Games, *5313*

1980 Swimmer to race the women's 100-meter freestyle in under 55 seconds, *5932*

1996 Athlete from Costa Rica to win a gold medal in the Olympic Games, *4790*

July 22

1900 Men's 200-meter race held in the Olympic Games, *4981*

Men's 5000-meter team running event held in the Olympic Games, *4982*

1908 Athlete from Africa, and from South Africa, to win a gold medal in the Olympic Games, *4638*

Athlete from Finland to win an official gold medal in the Olympic Games, *4641*

Hurdler to hold the officially accepted world record in the men's 400-meter hurdles, and to set a 400-meter hurdle record that would stand for more than 10 years, *4326*

Light heavyweight Greco-Roman wrestling event held in the Olympic Games, *6373*

Runner from Africa to win the men's 100-meter race in the Olympic Games, *4995*

Water polo player to win two, and then three, gold medals in the Olympic Games, *6303*

1912 International governing organization for track and field (athletics), *6204*

1948 Swimmer to swim across the Strait of Gibraltar, *5830*

1952 Runner from Australia to win the women's 100- and 200-meter titles in the Olympic Games, *5059*

1976 Olympic men's 400-meter freestyle event at which all the medalists had times under four minutes, *5923*

Woman swimmer to win four gold medals at a single Olympic Games, *5927*

1980 Athlete to win eight medals in a single Olympic Games, *3967*

Swimmer to race the men's 1500-meter freestyle in under 15 minutes, *5933*

1987 Runner to race the men's 5000 meters in under 13:00 minutes, *5149*

July 23

1908 Runner from Canada to win the men's 200-meter race in the Olympic Games, *4996*

1921 Long-jumper to break the 25-foot barrier, *4430*

1952 Javelin-thrower from the United States to win the men's event in the Olympic Games, *4393*

Triple-jumper of Black African ancestry to win the men's title in the Olympic Games, *6255*

Women's all-around gymnastics competition held in the Olympic Games, *3934*

Women's balance beam gymnastics competition held in the Olympic Games, *3935*

Women's floor exercises gymnastics competition held in the Olympic Games, *3936*

Women's side horse vault gymnastics competition held in the Olympic Games, *3937*

July 23—*continued*

Women's uneven (asymmetrical) bars gymnastics competition held in the Olympic Games, *3938*

1955 Motorboat (powerboat) racer to go faster than 200 miles per hour, *4568*

1976 Gymnast to win two consecutive men's floor exercises titles in the Olympic Games, *3962*

Gymnast to win two consecutive men's parallel bars titles in the Olympic Games, *3963*

1980 National team to sweep the medals in the women's 100-meter backstroke, and the women's 200-meter backstroke, in the Olympic Games, *5935*

1996 Athlete from Armenia to win a gold medal in the Olympic Games, *4791*

Gymnasts from the United States to win the women's team title in the Olympic Games, *3978*

Weightlifter to win three gold medals in the Olympic Games, *6352*

Women's double trap (clay pigeon) individual shooting event held in the Olympic Games, *5325*

2000 Golfer to hold the record low (under-par) scores in all four Professional Golfers Association (PGA) major tournaments, *3899*

July 24

1874 Tennis game in its modern form, *6005*

1882 National League team to score 35 runs in a single game, *1264*

1902 Swimmer to race 100 yards in one minute, *5793*

1908 National team to sweep the top honors in the men's individual épée competition in the Olympic Games, *2913*

National team to sweep the top medals in men's platform diving in the Olympic Games, *2793*

Runner to hold the officially accepted world record in the men's marathon, and the first United States runner to win the Olympic marathon, *4472*

1952 African-American hurdler to win the men's 110-meter titles in the Olympic Games, *4336*

Hammer-thrower to break the 60-meter barrier, *3987*

1969 Woman to sail across the Pacific alone, *5226*

1976 Athlete from Trinidad and Tobago to win an Olympic gold medal, *4745*

Cyclist to win two consecutive titles in the men's 4000-meter team pursuit in the Olympic Games, *2704*

Javelin-thrower to win two consecutive women's titles in the Olympic Games, *4402*

Runner from the Caribbean to win the men's 100-meter dash at the Olympic Games, *5105*

Swimmer to break the two-minute barrier in the men's 200-meter backstroke event, *5924*

Women's 400-meter individual medley event in the Olympic Games in which all the medalists had times under five minutes, *5925*

Women's double sculls event held in the Olympic Games, *4946*

Women's eight-oared shell with coxswain event held in the Olympic Games, *4949*

Women's single sculls event held in the Olympic Games, *4947*

1980 Athlete to win eight medals in a single Olympic Games, *3967*

Male gymnast to receive a perfect score of 10 in the Olympic Games, *3964*

National team to sweep the medals in the men's 400-meter freestyle event in the Olympic Games, *5934*

1992 Olympic Games at which the number of female athletes was more than 40 percent of the number of male athletes, *4775*

Olympic Games held in Spain, *4776*

1996 Men's double trap (clay pigeon) individual shooting event held in the Olympic Games, *5326*

July 25

1908 Athlete of Black African descent to win an Olympic gold medal, *4639*

Hurdler to hold the officially accepted world record in the men's 110-meter hurdles, and to set a 110-meter hurdle record that would stand for more than 10 years, *4327*

Men's 4 x 400-meter relay track event held in the Olympic Games, *4997*

Runner from Europe to win the men's 400-meter race in the Olympic Games, *4998*

Swimmer to win two consecutive men's 1500-meter freestyle titles in the Olympic Games, *5803*

July 27—*continued*

National team to sweep the medals in the women's 800-meter race, or in any women's track event, at the Olympic Games, *5114*

Rowers to win two consecutive titles in the pair-oared shell without coxswain event in the Olympic Games, *4950*

1992 Swimmer to win two consecutive men's 400-meter individual medley titles in the Olympic Games, *5962*

Women's heavyweight judo event held in the Olympic Games, *4553*

1993 High-jumper to reach, and then break, the 8-foot barrier, *4032*

1996 Athlete from newly independent Belarus to win a gold medal in the Olympic Games, *4794*

Athlete from the newly independent Slovak Republic to win a gold medal in the Olympic Games, *4795*

Beach volleyball event held in the Olympic Games, *6286*

July 28

1952 5.5-meter-class sailing event in the Olympic Games, *5218*

Canoe racer to win two, and then three, consecutive titles in the men's singles 1000-meter kayak event in the Olympic Games, *2607*

Canoe racer to win two consecutive men's Canadian singles 1000-meter titles in the Olympic Games, *2605*

Canoe racers to win both the men's 1000- and 10,000-meter pairs kayak events in the Olympic Games, *2606*

Dragon-class sailing event held in the Olympic Games, *5216*

Sailor to win the men's Finn-class event two, three, and four times in the Olympic Games, *5219*

Shooter to win two consecutive men's rapid-fire pistol titles in the Olympic Games, *5307*

1976 Men's pairs 500-meter kayaking event held in the Olympic Games, *2617*

Tornado-class sailing event held in the Olympic Games, *5236*

Women's team handball event held in the Olympic Games, *4007*

1980 Canoe racer to win three gold medals in a single Olympic Games, *2621*

First Heavyweight weightlifting event held in the Olympic Games, *6349*

Women's 400-meter race in which the top three runners had times of under 50 seconds, *5115*

1984 Olympic Games to be privately financed, rather than government funded, *4755*

1992 Olympic men's 200-meter backstroke event in which the medalists all had times under two minutes, *5963*

Women's half-heavyweight judo event held in the Olympic Games, *4554*

1996 Athlete from Syria to win a gold medal in the Olympic Games, *4796*

Men's lightweight double sculls rowing event held in the Olympic Games, *4959*

Men's lightweight four-oared shells without coxswain rowing event held in the Olympic Games, *4960*

Runner from Africa, and from Ethiopia, to win the women's marathon at the Olympic Games, *4526*

Women's 5000-meter race held in the Olympic Games, *5181*

Women's lightweight double sculls rowing event held in the Olympic Games, *4961*

Women's points race cycling event held in the Olympic Games, *2722*

July 29

1839 Cricket team from outside England to play in England, *2646*

1908 6-meter-class sailing event held in the Olympic Games, *5205*

8-meter-class sailing event in the Olympic Games, *5206*

Woman to participate in an Olympic yachting event, *5207*

1928 Athlete to win 12 medals in the Olympic Games, *4669*

1948 Olympic Games at which athletes from more than 50 countries participated, *4692*

1951 German Grand Prix automobile race to be part of the Formula One Grand Prix circuit, *1084*

1952 Athlete from Romania to win a gold medal in the Olympic Games, *4702*

Running deer (single and double shot) individual shooting event held in the Olympic Games, *5308*

Small-bore rifle (three positions) individual shooting event held in the Olympic Games, *5309*

Woman equestrian to win a team dressage medal in the Olympic Games, *2863*

Woman equestrian to win an individual dressage medal in the Olympic Games, *2864*

1979 Du Maurier Classic, *3823*

July 30—*continued*

Women's cross-country cycling race held in the Olympic Games, *2724*

Women's fast pitch softball event held in the Olympic Games, *5626*

July 31

1920 Shooter to win five gold medals in shooting in the Olympic Games, *5298*

1928 Athlete from Poland to win a gold medal in the Olympic Games, *4670*

Runner to win two consecutive men's 800-meter titles in the Olympic Games, *5019*

Women's 100-meter running event, and the first women's track event, held in the Olympic Games, *5020*

Women's discus throw event, and the first women's field event, held in the Olympic Games, *2762*

1932 Women's javelin-throw event held in the Olympic Games, *4390*

1948 Father and son to both win gold medals in track and field in the Olympic Games, *6213*

Wrestler from the United States to win the middleweight freestyle wrestling title in the Olympic Games, *6386*

1963 Baseball team to hit four successive home runs in an American League game, *1666*

1976 Athlete from South Korea to win a gold medal in the Olympic Games, *4746*

Boxer to win two, and then three, consecutive heavyweight titles, and three boxing titles in a single class, in the Olympic Games, *2575*

Brothers to win Olympic boxing titles on the same day, *2574*

Wrestler to win two consecutive heavyweight freestyle wrestling titles in the Olympic Games, *6403*

1980 Athletes from Zimbabwe to win gold medals in the Olympic Games, *4752*

Men's half-lightweight judo event held in the Olympic Games, *4548*

Twin brothers to win gold medals in wrestling in the same Olympic Games, *6404*

Women's field hockey event held in the Olympic Games, *4040*

1981 Long-term baseball strike to completely shut down both major leagues, *1761*

1984 Athletes from China and Taiwan to share the medal platform in the Olympic Games, *4757*

Gymnasts from the United States to win the men's combined exercises title in the Olympic Games, *3972*

Shooter to win two consecutive individual trap (clay pigeon) shooting titles in the Olympic Games, *5317*

Women's air rifle individual shooting event in the Olympic Games, *5318*

1992 Cyclist to win two consecutive women's titles in the 1000-meter match sprint in the Olympic Games, *2718*

Gymnast to win six gold medals in a single Olympic Games, *3976*

Swimmer to win two consecutive gold medals in the women's 200-meter backstroke in the Olympic Games, *5966*

Swimmer to win two consecutive men's 200-meter individual medley titles in the Olympic Games, *5967*

Women's 3000-meter individual pursuit cycling event in the Olympic Games, *2719*

1996 Laser-class sailing event held in the Olympic Games, *5256*

Women's triple jump event held in the Olympic Games, *6265*

August

1952 Automatic pin-setter to be used in a bowling alley, *2495*

August 1

1715 Modern rowing competition on record, *4911*

1900 Military revolver and military rifle team shooting events held in the Olympic Games, *5280*

1932 African-American runner to win the men's 100- and 200-meter titles in the Olympic Games, *5032*

Fencer to win two men's team foil titles in the Olympic Games, *2926*

1936 Olympic Games at which more than 4000 athletes participated, *4684*

1952 Diver to win two consecutive men's platform diving titles in the Olympic Games, *2803*

1957 Baseball player to hit 13 grand slam home runs in the National League, *1629*

1964 Drag racer to reach a speed of over 200, and then 250, miles per hour, *1108*

1972 Major league baseball player to bat in 13 runs in a doubleheader, *1727*

August 2—*continued*

Rower to win gold medals in both the women's single and double sculls events in the Olympic Games, *4953*

Rowers to win two consecutive titles in the women's quadruple sculls in the Olympic Games, *4958*

Sailor to win two consecutive Tornado-class sailing titles in the Olympic Games, *5251*

Woman rider, and the first horse, to win two consecutive gold medals in the individual dressage competition, and in team dressage, in the Olympic Games, *2893*

Women's extra-lightweight judo event held in the Olympic Games, *4559*

Women's sailboarding event held in the Olympic Games, *5192*

1996 Archers from the United States to win a gold medal in the team event in the Olympic Games, *1040*

Athlete from Africa to win the long jump, or any field event, in the Olympic Games, *4444*

Athlete from Nigeria to win a gold medal in the Olympic Games, *4798*

Baseball event held in the Olympic Games, *1820*

Rhythmic gymnastics team competition held in the Olympic Games, *3979*

Synchronized swimming event held in the Olympic Games, *5974*

1999 Golf event to be broadcast live on network television in prime time, *3898*

August 3

1852 Collegiate rowing competition, and the first intercollegiate athletic competition, on record in the United States, *4915*

1874 Baseball teams from the United States to tour England and Ireland, *1214*

1920 Athlete from Brazil to win a gold medal in the Olympic Games, *4650*

1932 African-American runner to win the men's 100- and 200-meter titles in the Olympic Games, *5032*

Men's 50,000-meter walk held in the Olympic Games, *6291*

Result of an Olympic event to be changed after viewing of the film of the race, *4678*

Wrestler to win two super heavyweight freestyle titles in the Olympic Games, *6382*

1936

1948 Weightlifter to win two consecutive light heavyweight titles in the Olympic Games, *6333*

Diver to win both the women's springboard and platform diving titles in the same Olympic Games, *2802*

1956 Runner to race the men's 100-meter dash in 10.1 seconds, *5063*

1984 Air rifle shooting individual event held in the Olympic Games, *5320*

Cyclist from the United States to win the men's 1000-meter match sprint in the Olympic Games, *2710*

Gymnast from the United States to win the all-around women's title in the Olympic Games, *3973*

Men's points cycling race held in the Olympic Games, *2711*

Women to win medals in the three-day individual equestrian event in the Olympic Games, *2885*

1992 Table tennis player to win both singles and doubles titles in the Olympic Games, *6000*

Women's 10,000-meter walk held in the Olympic Games, *6296*

Women's Europe-class sailing event held in the Olympic Games, *5252*

1996 Athlete from Algeria to win a gold medal in the Olympic Games, *4799*

Athlete from Burundi to win a gold medal in the Olympic Games, *4800*

Canoe racer to win five gold medals, and eight medals overall, in women's events in the Olympic Games, *2628*

Freestyle dressage equestrian event held in the Olympic Games, *2894*

Men's road time trial cycling event held in the Olympic Games, *2725*

Team from Africa to win the men's soccer event in the Olympic Games, *5570*

Women's road time trial cycling event held in the Olympic Games, *2726*

August 4

1900 National team to sweep the rapid-fire pistol individual shooting event in the Olympic Games, *5278*

1932 Athlete to hold the world record in both the men's long jump and triple jump, *4433*

Women's 80-meter hurdles event held in the Olympic Games, *4332*

1935 Runner to hold the officially accepted world record in the women's 200 meters, *5035*

1936 African-American runner to win the men's 800-meter title in the Olympic Games, *5037*

Discus-thrower to hold the officially accepted world record in the women's event, *2766*

Team to race the men's 4 x 100-meter relay in under 40 seconds, *5042*

Wrestler to win heavyweight titles in both freestyle and Greco-Roman wrestling in the Olympic Games, *6385*

1945 Golfer to win more than 10 straight titles, and to win 18 titles overall during a single year, on the Professional Golfers' Association (PGA) Tour, *3714*

1948 Pentathlete to place first in three of the five events in the men's modern pentathlon in the Olympic Games, *4819*

Woman athlete to win four gold medals in track and field in a single Olympic Games, *6212*

Women's long jump event held in the Olympic Games, *4436*

Women's shot put event held in the Olympic Games, *5336*

1984 Rower to win gold medals in both the women's single and double sculls events in the Olympic Games, *4953*

Shooter from the United States to win the individual skeet-shooting title in the Olympic Games, *5321*

Swimmer to win both the women's 100- and 200-meter butterfly titles in the same Olympic Games, *5943*

Team from the United States to win the women's eight-oared shell with coxswain event in the Olympic Games, *4952*

Triple-jumper from the United States, and the first African-American, to win the men's event in the Olympic Games, *6260*

Women's heptathlon event held in the Olympic Games, *4013*

1992 Athlete from Indonesia to win a gold medal in the Olympic Games, *4777*

Badminton events held in the Olympic Games as medal sports, *1174*

1996 Athlete from Thailand to win a gold medal in the Olympic Games, *4801*

Basketball player to win three, and then four, gold medals in the Olympic Games, *2380*

Black African athlete from South Africa to win a gold medal in the Olympic Games, *4802*

August 5

1900 Archer to win four Olympic gold medals in a single Olympic Games, and six overall, *1026*

Military revolver and military rifle team shooting events held in the Olympic Games, *5280*

Military rifle individual shooting event held in the Olympic Games, *5279*

1901 Long-jumper to hold the officially accepted world record in the men's event, *4428*

1921 Major league baseball game to be broadcast on radio, *1458*

1928 Women's 4 x 100-meter relay running event held in the Olympic Games, *5023*

Women's high jump event held in the Olympic Games, *4022*

1934 Shot-putter to break the 17-meter barrier, *5335*

1936 Team to race the men's 4 x 100-meter relay in under 40 seconds, *5042*

1948 Asian-American athlete to win a gold medal in the Olympic Games, *4694*

Athlete from Jamaica to win a gold medal in the Olympic Games, *4695*

Runner from the Caribbean to win the men's 400-meter title in the Olympic Games, *5050*

1949 Javelin-thrower to break the 160- and 170-foot and 50-meter barriers in the women's event, *4392*

1960 Triple-jumper to break both the 55-foot and 17-meter barriers, *6257*

1984 Runner to win both the women's title in the Boston Marathon and the women's marathon in the Olympic Games, *4513*

Women's marathon held in the Olympic Games, *4512*

1991 Pole-vaulter to clear 20 feet, *4849*

1992 Athlete from newly independent Lithuania to win a gold medal in the Olympic Games, *4778*

Baseball event held in the Olympic Games, *1820*

Runner from the Caribbean to win the women's 400-meter title in the Olympic Games, *5158*

August 5—*continued*

Woman rider, and the first horse, to win two consecutive gold medals in the individual dressage competition, and in team dressage, in the Olympic Games, *2893*

Wrestler to win two consecutive lightweight freestyle wrestling titles in the Olympic Games, *6411*

August 6

1926   Woman to swim the English Channel, *5820*

1936   Pentathlete to achieve a perfect score in the shooting portion of the men's modern pentathlon in the Olympic Games, *4817*

Runner from New Zealand to win the men's 1500-meter title at the Olympic Games and to hold the world record in the event, *5038*

Triple-jumper to reach a distance of 16 meters in the men's event, *6254*

1948   Diver to win both the women's springboard and platform diving titles in the same Olympic Games, *2802*

Flyweight Greco-Roman wrestling event held in the Olympic Games, *6387*

Runner to win both the women's 100- and 200-meter titles in the same Olympic Games, *5052*

Woman athlete to win four gold medals in track and field in a single Olympic Games, *6212*

Women's 200-meter race held in the Olympic Games, *5051*

1958   Runner to complete the men's mile race in under 3:55 minutes, *5068*

1975   Shot-putter to break the 70-foot barrier in the women's event, *5348*

1984   Runner from South America to win the men's 800-meter title at the Olympic Games, *5139*

Runner to win both the women's 200-and 400-meter titles at a single Olympic Games, and the first runner from the United States, or African-American, to win the 400-meter event, *5143*

1986   Major league baseball game to include three grand slam home runs, *1791*

1992   Hurdler to race the men's 400-meter hurdles in under 47 seconds, *4353*

Long-jumper to win three, and then four, consecutive men's titles in the Olympic Games, *4443*

Wrestler from the United States to win two super heavyweight freestyle titles in the Olympic Games, *6412*

August 7

1894   Major league baseball player to hit grand slam home runs in two consecutive games, *1314*

1928   Men's 1000-meter time trial cycling event held in the Olympic Games, *2696*

1932   High-jumpers to hold the officially accepted world record in the women's event, and the first from the United States to win the women's event in the Olympic Games, *4023*

Team from the United States to win the women's 4 x 100-meter relay running event in the Olympic Games, *5030*

Team to race the men's 4 x 400-meter relay in under 3:10 minutes, *5031*

Welterweight Greco-Roman wrestling event held in the Olympic Games, *6383*

Wrestler to win gold medals in three different divisions in the Olympic Games, *6378*

Wrestler to win two consecutive middleweight Greco-Roman titles in the Olympic Games, *6384*

1936   African-American runner to win the men's 400-meter title in the Olympic Games, *5039*

1948   Woman athlete to win four gold medals in track and field in a single Olympic Games, *6212*

Woman of Black African descent to win a gold medal in the Olympic Games, *4696*

1984   Basketball team from the United States to win the women's title in the Olympic Games, *2208*

Woman equestrian to win a medal in team jumping in the Olympic Games, *2886*

1992   Athletes from South Africa to win medals in the Olympic Games, after the lifting of the ban on their country because of its racist policies, *4779*

Black African woman to win an Olympic medal, *4780*

Pairs of twins to take the top two spots in the synchronized swimming duet competition in the Olympic Games, *5968*

Runner from Africa to win the women's 10,000-meter title, and the first Black African woman to win a medal, at the Olympic Games, *5159*

Wrestler to win two consecutive featherweight freestyle wrestling titles in the Olympic Games, *6413*

Wrestler to win two consecutive light heavyweight freestyle wrestling titles in the Olympic Games, *6414*

1995 Triple-jumper to break the 18-meter and 60-foot barriers, *6264*

August 8

1877 Catcher's mask used in a National League game, *1237*

1929 African-American runner to hold the record in the men's 100-meter dash, *5024*

1932 Men's floor exercises gymnastics competition held in the Olympic Games, *3928*

1936 Men's Canadian pairs 1000-meter canoeing event held in the Olympic Games, *2596*

Men's Canadian singles 1000-meter canoeing event held in the Olympic Games, *2597*

Men's pairs 1000-meter kayaking event held in the Olympic Games, *2598*

Men's singles 100-meter kayak event held in the Olympic Games, *2599*

1948 Discus-thrower to break the 50-meter and 160-, 170-, and 180-foot barriers in the women's event, *2768*

1953 Javelin-thrower to break the 260-foot and 80-meter barriers, and the first from the United States to hold the world record in the men's event, *4394*

1984 Athlete from Morocco to win a gold medal at the Olympic Games, and the first female athlete from an Islamic country to win an Olympic medal, *4758*

Athlete to qualify for the finals of the same event in four Olympic Games, *4759*

Men's sailboarding event held in the Olympic Games, *5191*

Sailors from the United States to win the Flying Dutchman–class event in the Olympic Games, *5243*

Woman to be skipper of a boat in an Olympic competition, *5244*

Women's 400-meter hurdles event held in the Olympic Games, *4350*

1992 Handball player to win two consecutive gold medals in men's team handball in the Olympic Games, *4011*

Mexican-American boxer to win the lightweight title in the Olympic Games, *2589*

Runner from Africa to win the women's 1500-meter title at the Olympic Games, *5160*

Runner to win three consecutive gold medals in the women's 4 x 100-meter relay at the Olympic Games, *5161*

Women's 1500-meter race in which the top four finishers all had times under 4 minutes, *5162*

1999 National Football League game played in Australia, *3509*

August 9

1928 Olympic men's 200-meter breaststroke event in which the medalists all had times under three minutes, *5821*

Woman to win an Olympic gold medal in sailing, *5210*

1932 Sailing team from the United States to win the 8-meter-class event in the Olympic Games, *5211*

1936 Athlete from Turkey to win a gold medal in the Olympic Games, *4685*

Runner to win three gold medals in the men's 4 x 100-meter relay in the Olympic Games, *5040*

Runner to win two gold medals in the women's 4 x 100-meter relay in the Olympic Games, *5041*

Team to race the men's 4 x 100-meter relay in under 40 seconds, *5042*

Team to race the men's 4 x 100-meter relay in under 40 seconds, *5042*

Wrestler to win heavyweight titles in both freestyle and Greco-Roman wrestling in the Olympic Games, *6385*

1948 Bantamweight weightlifting event held in the Olympic Games, *6334*

1984 Duet synchronized swimming event held in the Olympic Games, *5941*

Runner to win both the women's 200- and 400-meter titles at a single Olympic Games, and the first runner from the United States, or African-American, to win the 400-meter event, *5143*

629

August 10

1907 International and transcontinental automobile race, *1050*

1924 Wightman Cup tennis tournament, *6073*

1928 Women's team combined exercises gymnastics competition held in the Olympic Games, *3926*

1932 Men's tumbling gymnastics competition held in the Olympic Games, *3929*

Olympic men's 400-meter freestyle event at which all the medalists had times under five minutes, *5823*

1948 Weightlifter from the United States to win the middleweight title in the Olympic Games, *6335*

1980 Canoe racer to win a gold medal in both the singles and pairs in the women's 500 meters in the Olympic Games, *2620*

1981 Long-term baseball strike to completely shut down both major leagues, *1761*

1983 Runner to race the women's 400 meters in under 48 seconds, *5137*

1984 Women's 3000-meter race held at the Olympic Games, *5140*

1995 Triple-jumper to break the 50-foot barrier in the women's event, *6263*

August 11

1923 Swimmer to swim across the English Channel from France to England, *5816*

1928 Athlete from New Zealand to win an Olympic gold medal, *4672*

Equestrian to win both an individual and a team medal in dressage in the Olympic Games, *2853*

Equestrians to win two consecutive three-day event team titles, *2854*

Swimmer to win two consecutive gold medals in the men's 4 x 200-meter freestyle relay swimming event in the Olympic Games, *5822*

Team dressage equestrian event held in the Olympic Games, *2855*

1929 Major league baseball player to hit 500 home runs, *1487*

1932 Field hockey players to win two gold medals in the Olympic Games, *4038*

1934 Hurdler to hold the officially accepted world record in the women's 80-meter event, *4333*

Pentathlete to hold the officially accepted world record in the women's pentathlon, *4816*

1948 Weightlifter from the United States to win the light heavyweight title in the Olympic Games, *6336*

1961 Discus-thrower to break the 60-meter barrier, *2771*

1984 Canoer to win three titles in the men's Canadian pairs 1000-meter event in the Olympic Games, *2622*

Heavyweight boxing event with a limited weight held in the Olympic Games, *2581*

Rhythmic gymnastics all-around individual competition held in the Olympic Games, *3974*

Runner to win two consecutive officially accepted titles in the men's 1500-meters at the Olympic Games, *5141*

Superheavyweight boxing event in the Olympic Games, *2582*

Team from the United States to win the women's 4 x 400-meter relay at the Olympic Games, *5142*

Volleyball team from the United States to win the men's title in the Olympic Games, *6285*

Women's 500-meter fours kayaking event held in the Olympic Games, *2623*

Wrestler from the United States to win the heavyweight freestyle wrestling title in the Olympic Games, *6407*

August 12

1879 National archery tournament in the United States, *1024*

1900 Men's 200-meter backstroke swimming event held in the Olympic Games, *5788*

Men's 200-meter freestyle swimming event held in the Olympic Games, *5789*

Men's obstacle swimming race held in the Olympic Games, *5790*

Men's underwater swimming race held in the Olympic Games, *5791*

Water polo event held in the Olympic Games, *6301*

1928 Athletes from Spain to win gold medals in the Olympic Games, *4673*

Equestrian to win the individual jumping event in the Olympic Games without a single fault, *2856*

1932 National team to sweep the top medals in the women's platform diving event in the Olympic Games, *2800*

Star-class sailing event held in the Olympic Games, *5212*

August 17

1882 Eighteen-inning shutout in major league baseball, *1265*

1913 Hammer-thrower to hold the officially accepted world record in the men's event, *3982*

1920 Fencer to win five gold medals in a single Olympic Games, and to win two consecutive men's individual foil titles in the Olympic Games, *2916*

1938 Boxer to win three different world boxing titles within one year, *2550*

1952 Dutch Grand Prix automobile race to be part of the Formula One Grand Prix circuit, *1088*

August 18

1915 Boston Braves regular season baseball game played at Braves Field, *1423*

1920 Fencer to win five gold medals in a single Olympic Games, and to win two consecutive men's individual foil titles in the Olympic Games, *2916*

National team to win two Olympic gold medals in the tug-of-war competition, *6268*

1922 Golfer to win the U.S. Open and the Professional Golfers' Association (PGA) Championship in the same year, *3674*

1929 Women's Air Derby, *1007*

1978 Long-jumper to break the 7-meter barrier in the women's event, *4440*

August 19

1900 Men's 4000-meter freestyle swimming event held in the Olympic Games, *5792*

1920 Wrestler to win gold medals in three different divisions in the Olympic Games, *6378*

Wrestler to win two consecutive lightweight Greco-Roman titles in the Olympic Games, *6376*

1962 Golfer on the Ladies Professional Golf Association (LPGA) Tour to win four consecutively scheduled tournaments, *3768*

1973 Whitbread Round-the-World Race, *5232*

1981 Hurdler to race the men's 110-meter hurdles in under 13 seconds, *4346*

August 20

1900 Cricket event at the Olympic Games, *2653*

1920 Runner from Africa to win the men's 400-meters title in the Olympic Games, *5010*

1938 Major league baseball player to hit 23 grand slam home runs, *1528*

1975 Discus-thrower to break the 230-foot and 70-meter barriers, *2780*

1993 Hurdler from Great Britain to win the men's title in the 110-meter hurdles in the World Championships in Athletics, *4354*

2000 Golfer to hold the record low (under-par) scores in all four Professional Golfers Association (PGA) major tournaments, *3899*

August 21

1909 Shot-putter to hold the officially accepted world record in the men's event, *5331*

1920 Fencer to win five gold medals in a single Olympic Games, and to win two consecutive men's individual foil titles in the Olympic Games, *2916*

Thrower from the United States to win the men's 56-pound weight throw in the Olympic Games, *6324*

1931 Major league baseball player to reach a career total of 600 home runs, *1501*

1993 Triple-jumper to break the 15-meter barrier in the women's event, *6262*

August 22

1909 International airplane races, *1001*

1920 Team from the United States to win the men's 4 x 100-meter relay track event in the Olympic Games, *5011*

1989 Major league pitcher to reach 5,000 career strikeouts, *1808*

August 23

1912 Fencer to win two consecutive men's individual sabre titles, and men's team sabre titles, in the Olympic Games, *2914*

1964 Austrian Grand Prix automobile race to be part of the Formula One Grand Prix circuit, *1107*

1973 Tennis player to be ranked number one in the Association of Tennis Professionals (ATP) rankings, *6157*

1977 Tennis player to be ranked number one in the Association of Tennis Professionals (ATP) rankings for 160 consecutive weeks, *6165*

1981 Golfer to win the World Championship of Women's Golf twice in a row, *3836*

August 28—*continued*

1972 Athlete from North Korea to win a gold medal in the Olympic Games, *4737*

Athlete to win seven gold medals in a single Olympic Games, *4740*

Men's kayak slalom white-water canoeing events held in the Olympic Games, *2615*

National team to sweep the medals in the men's 200-meter butterfly swimming event in the Olympic Games, *5864*

Swimmer to win two consecutive gold medals in the men's 4 x 100-meter freestyle relay in the Olympic Games, *5865*

1981 Runner to complete the men's mile race in under 3:48 minutes, *5121*

1986 Javelin-thrower to break the 250-foot barrier in the women's event, *4408*

1994 Golfer of African-American or Asian-American descent to win the U.S. Amateur Championship, *3879*

August 29

1900 Men's four-oared shell with coxswain rowing event held in the Olympic Games, *4928*

1904 Athlete of Black African ancestry to compete in the Olympic Games, *4629*

National team to sweep the top three medals in the men's 400-meter running event in the Olympic Games, *4985*

Runner from the United States to win the men's steeplechase event at the Olympic Games, *4986*

Runner to win both the men's 100- and 200-meter races in the same Olympic Games, *4991*

1920 Athlete from Estonia to win a gold medal in the Olympic Games, *4651*

Featherweight weightlifting event held in the Olympic Games, *6328*

Lightweight weightlifting event held in the Olympic Games, *6329*

Middleweight weightlifting event held in the Olympic Games, *6330*

Swimmer to win Olympic gold medals 8 years apart, and to win Olympic medals 12 years apart, *5813*

Swimmers from the United States to win the women's 4 x 100-meter freestyle relay title in the Olympic Games, *5814*

Women's springboard diving event held in the Olympic Games, *2797*

1960 Canoe racer to win six gold medals, and eight medals overall, in the Olympic Games, *2609*

Swimmer to win two and then three consecutive women's 100-meter freestyle titles in the Olympic Games, *5842*

Women's 500-meter pairs kayaking event held in the Olympic Games, *2610*

1972 Athlete to win seven gold medals in a single Olympic Games, *4740*

Olympic men's 100-meter backstroke event in which the medalists all had times under one minute, *5866*

Olympic women's 100-meter freestyle event in which the medalists all had times under one minute, *5867*

1998 National Collegiate Athletic Association major college football player to gain 405 yards receiving in a single game, *3497*

August 30

1904 Black athletes from Africa to participate in the Olympic Games, *4630*

Runner for the United States to win the men's marathon at the Olympic Games, *4471*

1927 Major league baseball player to hit 60 home runs in a single season, *1481*

1972 Men's kayak slalom white-water canoeing events held in the Olympic Games, *2615*

Women's slalom singles kayaking event held in the Olympic Games, *2614*

1978 United States National Tennis Center, *6167*

1997 Women's National Basketball Association (WNBA) championship, *2396*

August 31

1846 Professional touring cricket team, *2648*

1904 National team to sweep the top three medals in the men's 100- and 200-meter running events in the Olympic Games, *4990*

Runner to win both the men's 100- and 200-meter races in the same Olympic Games, *4991*

1920 Light heavyweight weightlifting event held in the Olympic Games, *6331*

1960 Pentathlete to win two pentathlon gold medals in the same Olympic Games, *4827*

September 2—*continued*

Swimmer from the United States to win the women's 100-meter breast-stroke in the Olympic Games, *5868*

Swimmer to win two consecutive men's 200-meter backstroke titles in the Olympic Games, *5869*

September 3

1894 National golf championship in the United States, *3608*

1904 Discus throw event in the Olympic Games to be decided by a throw-off, *2755*

Men's 4-mile team race held in the Olympic Games, *4988*

National team to sweep the medals in the men's doubles tennis event in the Olympic Games, *6043*

National team to sweep the top spots in the men's pole vault in the Olympic Games, *4838*

National team to sweep the top three medals in the men's 100- and 200-meter running events in the Olympic Games, *4990*

Runner from the United States to win the men's 1500-meter race in the Olympic Games, *4989*

Runner to win both the men's 100- and 200-meter races in the same Olympic Games, *4991*

Tennis player from the United States to win the men's singles title in the Olympic Games, *6044*

Weightlifter to win two medals in the same Olympic Games, and the first from the United States to win a weightlifting Olympic gold medal, *6326*

1925 International team handball match, *4002*

1950 Italian Grand Prix automobile race to be part of the Formula One Grand Prix circuit, *1083*

1956 Shot-putter to break the 18- and 19-meter, and 60-foot, barriers, *5340*

1960 Olympic men's 1500-meter freestyle event in which the medalists all had times under 18 minutes, *5841*

Women's team foil fencing competition held in the Olympic Games, *2935*

1962 Golfer on the Ladies Professional Golf Association (LPGA) Tour to win four consecutively scheduled tournaments, *3768*

1972 Athlete to win seven gold medals in a single Olympic Games, *4740*

Men's 200-meter individual medley event in which the top four swimmers broke the world record, *5870*

Men's half-middleweight judo event in the Olympic Games, *4539*

1974 Javelin-thrower to break the 210- and 220-foot barriers in the women's event, *4401*

1995 Jacksonville Jaguars regular season football game played at the ALLTEL Stadium, *3470*

September 4

1920 Men's Finn-class sailing event in the Olympic Games, *5208*

1948 Pilot to win the Bendix Trophy race three times in a row, *1016*

1965 Hammer-thrower to break the 240-foot barrier, *3992*

1971 Hammer-thrower to break the 250-foot and 260-foot barriers, *3993*

1972 Athlete to win seven gold medals in a single Olympic Games, *4740*

Olympic men's 1500-meter freestyle event in which the medalists all had times under 17 minutes, *5871*

September 5

1918 Sporting event at which the United States national anthem was played, *5746*

1920 Team from the United States to win the rugby event in the Olympic Games, *4967*

1960 Boxer from the United States to win the light middleweight title in the Olympic Games, *2563*

Discus-thrower to win two titles in the women's event in the Olympic Games, *2770*

Hurdler to win two consecutive titles in the men's 110-meter hurdles in the Olympic Games, *4340*

1972 Olympic Games at which athletes were killed by terrorists, *4739*

1992 Decathlete to score 8,891 points in the men's decathlon, *2745*

1999 Baseball team to hit nine home runs in a single National League game, *1856*

Women's National Basketball Association (WNBA) team to win the league championship three times, and in three consecutive years, *2422*

September 6

1904 Men's 100-yard (later 100-meter) backstroke swimming event held in the Olympic Games, *5794*

Men's 50-yard (later 50-meter) freestyle swimming event held in the Olympic Games, *5795*

Swimmer to win both the men's 220-yard (later 200-meter) and 440-yard (later 400-meter) freestyle events in a single Olympic Games, *5798*

Water polo team from the United States to win the title at the Olympic Games, *6302*

1946 Cleveland Browns regular season football game played at Municipal Stadium, *3205*

1953 Major league baseball catcher to hit 38 home runs, *1600*

1954 Major league baseball player widely recognized as black to play for the Washington Senators, *1610*

1960 Runners to complete the men's 400-meter race in under 45 seconds, *5072*

1984 New York Jets regular season football game played at Giants Stadium, *3396*

1992 Atlanta Falcons regular season football game played at the Georgia Dome, *3454*

Runner to race the men's 1500 meters in less than 3:29 minutes, *5163*

1995 Major league baseball player to top Lou Gehrig's record of 2,130 consecutive games played, *1832*

1998 Baltimore Ravens regular season game played in the PSINet Stadium, *3498*

September 7

1904 Men's 440-yard (later 400-meter) breaststroke event held in the Olympic Games, *5796*

Men's 880-yard freestyle swimming event held in the Olympic Games, *5797*

Men's platform diving event held in the Olympic Games, *2791*

Swimmer to win both the men's 220-yard (later 200-meter) and 440-yard (later 400-meter) freestyle events in a single Olympic Games, *5798*

1934 Javelin-thrower to break the 240- and 250-foot barriers, *4391*

1960 Flying Dutchman–class sailing event held in the Olympic Games, *5223*

Sailor to win the men's Finn-class event two, three, and four times in the Olympic Games, *5219*

Weightlifter to win two consecutive bantamweight titles in the Olympic Games, *6341*

1963 Women's 800-meter race held in the Olympic Games after a 32-year ban, *5073*

Runner to race the men's 5000-meter steeplechase in under 8:30.0 minutes, *5075*

1972 Electronically timed world record in the men's 110-meter hurdles, *4343*

Shot-putter to break the 20- and 21-meter barriers in the women's event, *5347*

Volleyball players to win two consecutive women's gold medals in the Olympic Games, *6283*

Woman equestrian to win the individual dressage title in the Olympic Games, *2879*

1973 Little League baseball national agreement to fully admit girls, *1734*

1977 Woman to swim across the English Channel and back consecutively, *5928*

1979 All-sports television network, *5752*

1980 Los Angeles Rams regular season football game played at Anaheim Stadium, *3367*

September 8

1895 Establishment of the American Bowling Congress (ABC), *2481*

1904 Men's team foil fencing competition held in the Olympic Games, *2906*

1960 Gymnast to win two consecutive women's all-around titles in the Olympic Games, *3944*

Gymnasts to win two consecutive gold medals in the women's team combined exercises, *3945*

National team to sweep the top medals in the women's all-around gymnastics competition in the Olympic Games, *3946*

1964 Shooter from the United States to win the men's small-bore rifle (three positions) title in the Olympic Games, *5310*

1968 Houston Oilers regular season football game played at the Houston Astrodome, *3291*

1972 Fencers to win three gold medals in the women's team foil competition in the Olympic Games, *2938*

Sailor to win gold medals in three different sailing events in the Olympic Games, *5239*

Sailor to win two consecutive gold medals in the Flying Dutchman–class event in the Olympic Games, *5228*

September 8—*continued*

Soling-class sailing event held in the Olympic Games, *5229*

Tempest-class sailing event in the Olympic Games, *5230*

1992 Sailor to win both the America's Cup and an Olympic gold medal in sailing, *5253*

1993 Runner to race the women's 10,000 meters in under 30 minutes, *5169*

September 9

1876 Doubleheader in baseball's National League, *1230*

Pitcher in baseball's National League to pitch and win two games on the same day, *1231*

1916 Golfer to win both the U.S. Amateur and U.S. Open championships in the same year, and to win the U.S. Open in under 290 for 72 holes, *3659*

1928 Long-jumper to break the 26-foot barrier, *4432*

1960 Fencer to win two, three, and four men's team épée titles in the Olympic Games, *2931*

Weightlifter to win two consecutive middle heavyweight titles in the Olympic Games, *6342*

1967 San Diego Chargers regular season football game played at San Diego Stadium, *3283*

1968 U.S. Open men's singles title, and the first men's singles Grand Slam title won by an African-American, *6135*

1972 Judo artist to win two gold medals in a single Olympic Games, *4540*

Women's 1500-meter event held in the Olympic Games, *5094*

1988 Javelin-thrower to break the 260-foot barrier, and to reach the 80-meter barrier, in the women's event, *4410*

September 10

1881 Grand slam home run in major league baseball, *1256*

1910 Pendleton Round-Up rodeo, *4882*

1933 Negro League East-West All-Star Game, *1510*

1960 Athlete from Ethiopia, and Black athlete from Africa, to win a gold medal at the Olympic Games, *4710*

Black African runner to win the men's marathon title at the Olympic Games, and to hold the world record in the event, *4487*

Gymnast to win two consecutive men's horizontal bar titles in the Olympic Games, *3947*

Gymnast to win two consecutive titles in the men's rings competition in the Olympic Games, *3948*

1972 Basketball team from the Soviet Union to win the men's title in the Olympic Games, *2088*

Heavyweight Greco-Roman wrestling event held in the Olympic Games, *6400*

Light flyweight Greco-Roman wrestling event held in the Olympic Games, *6401*

Men's individual archery event in the modern format held in the Olympic Games, *1035*

Women's 4 x 400-meter relay track event held in the Olympic Games, *5095*

Women's individual archery event in the modern format held in the Olympic Games, *1036*

Wrestler to win two consecutive flyweight Greco-Roman wrestling titles in the Olympic Games, *6402*

2000 Cincinnati Bengals regular season football game played at Paul Brown Stadium, *3514*

September 11

1920 Figure riding individual and team events held in the Olympic Games, *2850*

1951 Woman to swim the English Channel from England to France, and to swim it in both directions, *5831*

1960 Equestrians to win two consecutive titles in team jumping in the Olympic Games, *2867*

1968 Hurdler to race the men's 400-meter hurdles in under 49 seconds, *4341*

1972 Equestrian to win four titles in team jumping in the Olympic Games, *2880*

1985 Major league baseball player to reach 4,192 career hits, *1783*

September 12

1883 Union Association in baseball, *1273*

1920 Equestrian to win two consecutive medals in the team jumping (Prix des Nations) event in the Olympic Games, *2851*

1922 Runner to hold the world record in both the men's 5000- and 10,000-meter events, *5013*

639

September 19—*continued*

1976   Tampa Bay Buccaneers regular season football game played at Tampa Stadium, *3349*

1981   Runner to hold the officially accepted world record in the women's 10,000-meter race, *5123*

2000   Cycling team to break the 4-minute mark in the men's 4000-meter team pursuit race in the Olympic Games, *2730*

     Women's weightlifting events held in the Olympic Games, *6353*

September 20

1896   Motorcycle race on record, *4569*

1942   Runner to race the men's 5000 meters in under 14:00 minutes, *5047*

1961   Swimmer to swim across the English Channel and back consecutively, *5843*

1970   Pittsburgh Steelers regular season football game played at Three Rivers Stadium, *3307*

1988   Diver to win both the men's platform and springboard diving titles in two consecutive Olympic Games, *2818*

     Wrestler to win two consecutive light flyweight Greco-Roman wrestling titles in the Olympic Games, *6408*

1998   Major league baseball player to play in 2,632 consecutive games, *1852*

     Tampa Bay Buccaneers regular season football game played at Raymond James Stadium, *3499*

2000   Women's weightlifting events held in the Olympic Games, *6353*

September 21

1904   Team archery event held in the Olympic Games, *1028*

1970   Cincinnati Bengals regular season football game played at Riverfront Stadium, *3308*

1986   Javelin-throw world record set using the new javelin in the men's event, *4409*

1988   Athlete from Suriname to win a gold medal in the Olympic Games, *4767*

     Women's air pistol individual shooting event held in the Olympic Games, *5322*

2000   Men's Keirin cycling event held in the Olympic Games, *2731*

     Men's Madison cycling event held in the Olympic Games, *2732*

     Women's skeet shooting event held in the Olympic Games, *5328*

September 22

1904   Bantamweight and featherweight boxing events held in the Olympic Games, and the first boxer to win two gold medals in a single Olympic Games, *2527*

     Flyweight boxing event in the Olympic Games, *2528*

     Heavyweight boxing event held in the Olympic Games, *2529*

     Lightweight boxing event held in the Olympic Games, *2530*

     Middleweight boxing event held in the Olympic Games, *2531*

     Welterweight boxing event held in the Olympic Games, *2532*

1972   Heavyweight weightlifting event held in the Olympic Games, *6346*

1988   National team to sweep the medals in the women's individual foil fencing competition in the Olympic Games, *2940*

     Olympic men's 100-meter freestyle swimming event in which all the medalists had times under 50 seconds, *5952*

     Shooter to win two consecutive titles in the small-bore rifle (three positions) individual event in the Olympic Games, *5323*

1990   National Collegiate Athletic Association major college football player to score eight rushing touchdowns in a single game, *3441*

2000   Male swimmers to win gold medals in the same event at the same Olympic Games, *5979*

     Women's trampoline event held in the Olympic Games, *6232*

     Women's weightlifting events held in the Olympic Games, *6353*

September 23

1897   Cheyenne Frontier Days rodeo, *4881*

1900   Soccer (international football) event held in the Olympic Games, *5544*

1972   Discus-thrower to break the 220-foot barrier in the women's event, *2779*

1988   Women's 100-meter butterfly event in the Olympic Games in which all the medalists had times under one minute, *5953*

2000   Men's synchronized platform diving event held in the Olympic Games, *2826*

     Men's trampoline event held in the Olympic Games, *6233*

     Women's synchronized springboard diving event held in the Olympic Games, *2827*

Women's water polo event held in the Olympic Games, *6308*

September 24

1844 International cricket match outside Great Britain, *2647*

1967 National Football League player to kick seven field goals in a single game, *3284*

1972 National team to sweep the medals in the women's 200-meter butterfly in the Olympic Games, *5872*

1988 Athlete to win medals in both the Summer and Winter Olympic Games in the same year, *4768*

Heptathlete from the United States, and the first African-American, to win the women's heptathlon in the Olympic Games, *4015*

Men's 50-meter freestyle swimming event held in the Olympic Games, *5954*

Runner to win two consecutive officially accepted men's 100-meter titles at the Olympic Games, *5150*

Women's 1000-meter match sprint cycling event held in the Olympic Games, *2713*

September 25

1988 Woman swimmer to win Olympic medals 12 years apart, *5956*

Women's 50-meter freestyle swimming event held in the Olympic Games, *5955*

Women's quadruple sculls event held in the Olympic Games, *4955*

2000 Gymnasts from China to win the men's team title at the Olympic Games, *3980*

Open 49er-class sailing event held in the Olympic Games, *5258*

Runner to win two consecutive men's 400-meter titles in the Olympic Games, *5188*

Women's pole vault event held in the Olympic Games, *4852*

September 26

1871 International rifle tournament held in the United States, *5267*

1876 National League championship, *1232*

1908 Major league pitcher to throw two shutouts in one day, *1381*

1971 Philadelphia Eagles regular season football game played at Veterans Stadium, *3317*

1982 Javelin-thrower to break the 240-foot barrier in the women's event, *4406*

1983 America's Cup sailing race not won by the United States, *5242*

1988 Runner from Africa to win the men's 800-meter title at the Olympic Games, *5151*

September 27

1988 Diver to win both the men's platform and springboard diving titles in two consecutive Olympic Games, *2818*

Individual dressage equestrian competition in the Olympic Games in which women riders swept the top medals, *2890*

Women's 470-class sailing event held in the Olympic Games, *5249*

1998 Major league baseball player to hit 70 home runs in a single season, *1853*

2000 Men's taekwondo events held in the Olympic Games, *4560*

United States team to win the men's baseball title in the Olympic Games, *1861*

Women's 20-kilometer walk event held in the Olympic Games, *6297*

Women's taekwondo events held in the Olympic Games, *4561*

September 28

1951 National Football League player to pass for 554 yards in a single game, *3230*

1975 New Orleans Saints regular season football game played at the Louisiana Superdome, *3345*

1988 Major league pitcher to pitch 59 consecutive regular season scoreless innings, *1802*

2000 Men's synchronized springboard diving event held in the Olympic Games, *2828*

Men's taekwondo events held in the Olympic Games, *4560*

Women's synchronized platform diving event held in the Olympic Games, *2829*

Women's taekwondo events held in the Olympic Games, *4561*

September 29

1880 Professional baseball stadium in Manhattan, *1253*

1900 Runner to hold the officially accepted world record in the men's 400-meter event, *4983*

1912 Javelin-thrower to hold the officially accepted world record in the men's event, *4384*

1957 Green Bay Packers regular season football game played at Lambeau Field, *3245*

1974 Major league baseball player to have 118 steals in a single season, *1739*

1977 Woman boxing judge to officiate at a world championship bout, *2576*

1987 Major league baseball player to hit six grand slam home runs in a single season, *1795*

1988 Basketball team from the United States to win the women's title in a non-boycotted Olympic Games, *2275*

Judo artist to win two consecutive men's middleweight gold medals in the Olympic Games, *4550*

Long-jumper from the United States to win the women's event in the Olympic Games, *4442*

Runner to race the women's 100 meters in under 10:50 seconds, and the 200 meters in under 21.50 seconds, *5153*

2000 Men's taekwondo events held in the Olympic Games, *4560*

Women's hammer-throw event held in the Olympic Games, *3998*

Women's taekwondo events held in the Olympic Games, *4561*

September 30

1939 College football game to be televised, *3187*

1947 World Series broadcast on television, *1564*

1973 Buffalo Bills regular season football game played at Rich Stadium, *3332*

1988 Archer to win two titles in women's events in a single Olympic Games, *1038*

Canoe racers to win two consecutive titles in the men's pairs 500-meter kayak event in the Olympic Games, *2625*

Men's doubles table tennis event held in the Olympic Games, *5994*

Tennis player to win the men's singles title in the Olympic Games after tennis competition resumed in 1988, *6178*

Tennis players to win the women's doubles title in the Olympic Games after tennis competition resumed in 1988, *6179*

Women's 10,000-meter running event held in the Olympic Games, *5152*

Women's doubles table tennis event held in the Olympic Games, *5995*

Wrestler of Black African descent to win a gold medal in wrestling in the Olympic Games, *6409*

2000 Basketball player to win three, and then four, gold medals in the Olympic Games, *2380*

October

1908 Figure skating competition at the Olympic Games, *2974*

1964 Wedding between Olympic athletes held at the Olympic Games, *4717*

1967 American Basketball Association season, *2051*

1969 American League and National League championships, *1711*

1975 African-American to be named manager of a major league baseball team, *1741*

1987 Sport of Kings Challenge steeplechase horse race, *4315*

October 1

1903 Pitcher to win a World Series game, *1354*

World Series, *1355*

World Series game, *1356*

World Series home run, *1357*

1946 Major league baseball playoff series, *1552*

1950 Golfer to win three major tournaments, and six titles overall, on the Ladies Professional Golf Association (LPGA) Tour in a single season, *3725*

Golfer to win two U.S. Women's Open championships, *3726*

1961 Major league baseball player to hit 61 home runs in a single season, *1649*

Washington Redskins regular season football game played at DC Stadium, *3261*

1977 National Collegiate Athletic Association major college football player to kick a 67-yard field goal, *3356*

1988 Archer to win two titles in women's events in a single Olympic Games, *1038*

Black African-born boxer to win a boxing title in the Olympic Games, *2585*

Canoe racer from the United States to win the men's singles 1000-meter kayak event, and to win a gold medal in any kayaking event, in the Olympic Games, *2626*

October 7—*continued*

1995 Boston Bruins regular season hockey game played at the FleetCenter, *4219*

October 8

1805 African-American boxer to fight in a title bout, *2507*

1927 Javelin-thrower to break the 220-foot barrier, *4387*

1950 National Hockey League All-Star Game to be televised, *4126*

1956 Perfect game in the World Series, *1623*

1960 Major league baseball player to bat in six runs in a single World Series game, *1644*

1993 Mighty Ducks of Anaheim regular season hockey game played at The Pond of Anaheim, *4208*

October 9

1889 Baseball player to hit two home runs in his first major league game, *1298*

1906 Chicago White Sox World Series victory, *1371*

World Series between two teams from the same city, *1372*

1919 Cincinnati Reds World Series victory, *1436*

1926 Tennis star to turn professional, *6081*

1932 Figure skater to win two, and then three, consecutive women's singles titles at the Olympic Winter Games, *3014*

1938 Major league baseball team to win three consecutive World Series, *1529*

1951 Rookie to hit a grand slam home run in the World Series, *1589*

1953 Shot-putter to break the 16-meter barrier in the women's event, *5339*

1967 Baseball team to hit three home runs in one inning of a World Series game, *1695*

1970 Vancouver Canucks regular season hockey game played at the Pacific Coliseum, *4156*

1995 Vancouver Canucks regular season hockey game played at General Motors Place, *4220*

1998 Florida Panthers regular season hockey game played at the National Car Rental Center, *4231*

October 10

1920 Grand slam home run in World Series history, *1448*

Home run by a pitcher in a World Series, *1449*

1964 Olympic Games held in Asia, or in Japan, *4718*

1971 San Francisco 49ers regular season football game played at Candlestick Park, *3318*

1976 New York Giants regular season football game played at Giants Stadium, *3350*

1996 Phoenix Coyotes regular season hockey game played at the America West Arena, *4226*

October 11

1890 Runner to race the 100-yard dash in under 10 seconds, *4973*

1911 Major league baseball players to be named Most Valuable Players of their leagues, *1405*

1967 Pittsburgh Penguins regular season hockey game played at the Pittsburgh Civic Arena, *4149*

1975 Drag racer to reach a speed of over 200, and then 250, miles per hour, *1108*

1980 Dallas Mavericks regular season game played at Reunion Arena, *2164*

1987 Miami Dolphins regular season football game played at Joe Robbie Stadium, *3415*

October 12

1925 Runner to complete the men's marathon in under 2:30 hours, *4477*

1963 Hispanic-American All-Star Game in major league baseball, *1667*

1964 Swimmer to win four gold medals in a single Olympic Games, *5850*

1968 Olympic Games held in Mexico, *4724*

Woman to carry the torch at the Olympic Games, *4725*

1979 Three-point goal scored in a National Basketball Association (NBA) game, *2153*

1982 Major league baseball player to get five hits in a single World Series game, *1767*

1993 Florida Panthers regular season hockey game played at Miami Arena, *4209*

1996 Buffalo Sabres regular season hockey game played at Marine Midland Arena, *4227*

October 13

1914 Baseball team to sweep the World Series, *1418*

October 14

October 15

October 15—*continued*
1988 National Collegiate Athletic Association major college team to gain 768 yards rushing in a single game, *3422*

October 16

1964 Javelin-thrower to break the 200-foot and 60-meter barriers in the women's event, *4400*

Swimmer to win four gold medals in a single Olympic Games, *5850*

1968 Athlete from Kenya to win a gold medal in the Olympic Games, *4732*

Runner from Africa to win the men's 3000-meter steeplechase title in the Olympic Games, *5087*

Runner to complete the men's 200-meter race in under 20 seconds, *5088*

1970 Portland Trail Blazers regular season basketball game played at the Memorial Coliseum, *2076*

October 17

1860 British Open golf tournament, *3576*

Golfer to win the British Open, *3577*

1964 Men's 4000-meter individual pursuit cycling event held in the Olympic Games, *2702*

Women's 400-meter individual medley swimming event held in the Olympic Games, *5849*

Women's pentathlon held in the Olympic Games, *4829*

1968 Athlete from Tunisia to win a gold medal in the Olympic Games, *4728*

Runner from Africa to win the men's 5000-meter title in the Olympic Games, *5089*

1987 World Series game to be played indoors, *1796*

1989 World Series game to be canceled by an earthquake, *1809*

1994 Golfer to win the World Championship of Women's Golf twice in a row, *3836*

1999 National Football League player to pass for 60,000 career yards, *3512*

October 18

1952 Discus-thrower to break the 50-meter and 160-, 170-, and 180-foot barriers in the women's event, *2768*

1958 High-jumper to clear six feet in the women's event, *4026*

1964 Runner from the United States to win the men's 5000-meter title at the Olympic Games, *5078*

Water polo player to win medals in five different Olympic Games, *6304*

1967 Philadelphia 76ers regular season basketball game played at The Spectrum, *2052*

1968 Long-jumper to break the 28- and 29-foot barriers, *4439*

Runner to complete the men's 400-meter race in under 44 seconds, *5090*

1974 Indiana Pacers regular season game played at Market Square Arena, *2107*

October 19

1957 National Hockey League player to reach 500 career goals, *4136*

1964 Woman to compete in the three-day event individual equestrian competition in the Olympic Games, *2868*

1967 Philadelphia Flyers regular season hockey game played at The Spectrum, *4150*

1968 Men's 100-meter breaststroke event held in the Olympic Games, *5851*

Runner from the United States to win the women's 800-meter title at the Olympic Games, *5091*

Women's 100-meter breaststroke event held in the Olympic Games, *5852*

October 20

1964 Men's lightweight judo event in the Olympic Games, *4534*

Shot-putter to win two consecutive titles in the women's event in the Olympic Games, *5344*

1968 Athlete from Iran to win a gold medal in the Olympic Games, *4731*

Athlete from Kenya to win a gold medal in the Olympic Games, *4732*

High-jumper to use the "Fosbury flop" jumping method, *4031*

Men's 200-meter individual medley swimming event held in the Olympic Games, *5853*

Runner from Africa to win the men's 1500-meter title at the Olympic Games, *5092*

Shot-putter to break the 19-meter barrier in the women's event, *5346*

Swimmer to win the women's 200- and 400-meter individual medley events in the same Olympic Games, *5854*

Swimmer to win three individual gold medals in a single Olympic Games, *5862*

Women's 200-meter individual medley swimming event held in the Olympic Games, *5855*

1973 Basketball team to get 39 offensive rebounds in a single National Basketball Association (NBA) game, *2098*

1999 Los Angeles Kings regular season game played in the Staples Center, *4236*

October 21

1964 Athletes from the Bahamas to win gold medals in the Olympic Games, *4719*

Gymnast to win three consecutive gold medals in the team combined exercises in the Olympic Games, *3951*

Runner to win two consecutive marathon titles in the Olympic Games, *4489*

1968 Men's 100-meter butterfly swimming event held in the Olympic Games, *5856*

Sailor to win gold medals in three different sailing events in the Olympic Games, *5239*

Sailors from the United States to win the Dragon-class event in the Olympic Games, *5225*

1979 Runner to race the women's marathon in under 2:30 hours, *4505*

1989 National Collegiate Athletic Association major college team to gain 1,021 all-purpose yards in a single game, *3430*

1996 Tampa Bay Lightning regular season hockey game played at the Ice Palace, *4228*

2000 World Series game to last 4 hours and 51 minutes, *1862*

October 22

1883 National Horse Show, *2840*

1885 Major league baseball players' union, *1284*

1939 Professional football game to be televised, *3188*

1953 National Hockey League coach to reach 600 career wins, *4130*

1956 Hammer-thrower to break the 220-foot barrier, *3990*

1964 Gymnast to win two consecutive titles in the women's uneven (asymmetrical) bars in the Olympic Games, *3952*

Men's fours 1000-meter kayaking event held in the Olympic Games, *2611*

1968 Men's heavyweight judo event in the Olympic Games, *4535*

Skeet shooting individual event held in the Olympic Games, *5312*

Swimmer to win three individual gold medals in a single Olympic Games, *5862*

Women's 200-meter freestyle event held in the Olympic Games, *5857*

1978 Runner to win the men's title in both the Boston Marathon and the New York Marathon in the same year, *4503*

2000 Baseball team to play 14 games in the World Series without suffering a defeat, *1863*

October 23

1945 African-American baseball player of the 20th century to join the previously all-white mainstream baseball leagues, *1548*

1964 Men's open judo event in the Olympic Games, *4536*

Men's volleyball event held in the Olympic Games, *6279*

Women's volleyball event held in the Olympic Games, *6280*

1968 Equestrian from the United States to win the individual jumping title in the Olympic Games, *2873*

Swimmer from the United States to win the women's 200-meter breaststroke title in the Olympic Games, *5858*

Woman equestrian to win an individual jumping medal in the Olympic Games, *2874*

October 24

1857 Soccer (international football) club, *5531*

1964 Equestrian to win three consecutive titles in team jumping in the Olympic Games, *2869*

1968 Fencers to win two gold medals in the women's team foil competition in the Olympic Games, *2937*

Swimmer to win three individual gold medals in a single Olympic Games, *5862*

Woman equestrian to win a gold medal in team dressage in the Olympic Games, *2875*

Women's 200-meter butterfly event held in the Olympic Games, *5859*

Women's 800-meter freestyle swimming event held in the Olympic Games, *5860*

October 24—*continued*
1970 Pole-vaulter to clear 18 feet, *4846*
1971 Dallas Cowboys regular season football game played at Texas Stadium, *3319*
1976 Japanese Grand Prix automobile race, *1122*

October 25

1968 Canoe racer to win two consecutive titles in the women's 500-meter singles kayak event, *2612*
Canoe racers to win two consecutive women's 500-meter kayak pairs event in the Olympic Games, *2613*
Gymnast to win two consecutive women's side horse vault titles in the Olympic Games, *3954*
Women's 200-meter backstroke event held in the Olympic Games, *5861*
1973 National championships for gliding (soaring) in the United States, *3532*
1975 Denver Nuggets regular season game played at McNichols Sports Arena, *2117*

October 26

1968 Athlete from Venezuela to win a gold medal in the Olympic Games, *4729*
Athletes from Pakistan to win gold medals in the Olympic Games, *4730*
Boxer to win two consecutive light middleweight titles in the Olympic Games, *2568*
Boxer to win two consecutive light welterweight titles in the Olympic Games, *2569*
Gymnast to win two consecutive men's side (pommel) horse titles in the Olympic Games, *3955*
Light flyweight boxing event held in the Olympic Games, *2570*
Volleyball players to win two consecutive men's gold medals in the Olympic Games, *6282*
Wrestler to win two consecutive light heavyweight Greco-Roman titles in the Olympic Games, *6391*
Wrestler to win two consecutive super heavyweight Greco-Roman titles in the Olympic Games, *6392*

October 27

1931 Athlete to hold the world record in both the men's long jump and triple jump, *4433*

1962 Swimmer to race the women's 100-meter freestyle in under one minute, *5844*
1963 Mexican Grand Prix automobile race to be part of the Formula One Grand Prix circuit, *1106*

October 28

1900 Olympic Games held in France, and outside Greece, *4626*
Rugby event held in the Olympic Games, *4965*
1904 Gymnast with a wooden leg to win a medal in the Olympic Games, *3912*
National team to sweep the top honors in the men's horizontal bar, long horse vault, side (pommel) horse, and rings gymnastics competitions in the Olympic Games, *3913*
1922 College football game to be broadcast nationally on radio, *3151*
1951 Spanish Grand Prix automobile race to be part of the Formula One Grand Prix circuit, *1085*
1973 Basketball player to have 17 blocked shots in a single National Basketball Association (NBA) game, *2099*
1995 National Collegiate Athletic Association major college football player to complete 55 passes in a single game, *3471*

October 29

1886 Boxer to be undisputed world lightweight champion, *2518*
1908 Athlete from Russia to win a gold medal in the Olympic Games, *4640*
Figure skater to win the men's singles title in the Olympic Games, *2975*
Figure skater to win the title for special figures in the Olympic Games, *2976*
Figure skater to win the women's singles title at the Olympic Games, *2977*
Figure skaters to win the pairs title at the Olympic Games, *2978*
National team to sweep the men's singles figure skating medals at the Olympic Winter Games, *2979*
1937 Boxer to win three different world boxing titles within one year, *2550*
1970 National Hockey League player to reach 1,000 career assists, *4158*
1999 Carolina Hurricanes regular season hockey game played at the Raleigh Entertainment and Sports Arena, *4237*

November 5—*continued*

1995 Vancouver Grizzlies regular season basketball game played at Bear Country at General Motors Place, *2362*

November 6

1869 Intercollegiate football game in the United States, *3117*
1972 Intercollegiate Ultimate match, *3528*
1999 Indiana Pacers regular season basketball game played at the Conseco Fieldhouse, *2426*

November 7

1896 Professional basketball game, *1874*
1991 Utah Jazz regular season basketball game played at the Delta Center, *2309*
1992 Phoenix Suns regular season basketball game played at the America West Arena, *2318*

November 8

1860 Shutout baseball game on record, *1195*
1966 Baseball player to be named Most Valuable Player in both major leagues, *1690*
1970 National Football League player to kick a 63-yard field goal, *3309*
1988 Sacramento Kings regular season basketball game played at the ARCO Arena, *2280*
1994 Cleveland Cavaliers regular season game played in the Gund Arena, *2342*

November 9

1912 Use of the double-wing formation in football, *3138*
1950 Shot-putter to break the 15-meter barrier in the women's event, *5337*
1993 Basketball player to make 97 consecutive free throws in the National Basketball Association (NBA), *2330*

November 11

1990 National Football League player to make seven sacks in a single game, *3442*

November 12

1892 Professional football player, *3125*
1931 Toronto Maple Leafs regular season hockey game played at Maple Leaf Gardens, *4104*

1995 St. Louis Rams regular season football game played at the Trans World Dome, *3472*

November 13

1988 Automobile racer to win two Australian Grand Prix races, *1137*
1994 National Football League player to complete 45 passes in a single game, *3463*

November 14

1903 Football stadium, built specifically for the sport, *3134*
1943 National Football League player to pass for seven touchdowns in a single game, *3193*

November 15

1920 College football game to be broadcast on radio, *3148*

November 16

1911 Runner to hold the officially accepted world record in the men's 10,000-meter event, *4999*
1946 Boston Celtics regular season basketball game played at Boston Garden, *1913*
1957 Basketball player to grab 32 rebounds in a single half of a National Basketball Association (NBA) game, *1973*
1980 African-American golfer to win a Senior Professional Golfers' Association (PGA) Tour event, *3834*
1990 Solheim Cup golf competition, *3869*

November 17

1973 Golfer to win $100,000 in a single tournament, *3805*
1990 National Collegiate Athletic Association major college team to score 11 passing touchdowns in a single game, *3443*

November 18

1892 College women's basketball game, *1868*
1921 Boxer to hold the super-featherweight (junior lightweight) title, *2542*

November 20

1928 Boston Bruins regular season hockey game played at Boston Garden, *4098*

November 30—*continued*

1991 College women's basketball player to score 23 free throws in a single Division I National Collegiate Athletic Association (NCAA) game, *2310*

1996 Basketball team to score 25 points in a single overtime period of a National Basketball Association (NBA) game, *2376*

1997 Speed skater to skate the 1500 meters in under 1:50 minutes, *5727*

December

1888 United States baseball team to tour the world, and to visit Australia, *1294*

1891 Basketball game, *1864*
Scheduled Sunday games in the National League were authorized, *1306*

1926 International championships in table tennis, *5984*

1951 Fukuoka Marathon, *4484*

1993 World short-course championships in swimming, *5969*

December 1

1810 African-American boxer to fight in a title bout, *2507*

1956 Athlete from Bulgaria to win a gold medal in the Olympic Games, *4707*
Boxer to win three gold medals, and two consecutive light middleweight titles, in the Olympic Games, *2560*
Canoe racer to win two, and then three, consecutive titles in the men's singles 1000-meter kayak event in the Olympic Games, *2607*
Men's 200-meter butterfly swimming event held in the Olympic Games, *5834*

December 2

1887 Organized softball game, following George Hancock's rules, and with the diamond, ball, and bat he introduced, *5573*

1973 Washington Bullets regular season game played at the US Air Arena, *2100*
Woman to race the marathon in under 3:00 hours, *4495*

1975 Football player to win the Heisman Trophy twice, *3347*

1990 National Collegiate Athletic Association major college football player to gain 5,221 yards in a single year, *3444*

1997 Washington Wizards regular season basketball game played at the MCI Center, *2398*

December 3

1950 National Football League player to receive 18 completed passes in a single game, *3225*

1967 Runner to race the men's marathon in under 2:12 hours, and the first representing Australia to hold the world record in the event, *4492*

December 4

1956 Diver to win two consecutive titles in both springboard and platform diving events, and the first to win four gold medals in diving, in the Olympic Games, *2804*

December 5

1956 Gymnast to win two consecutive women's floor exercise titles in the Olympic Games, *3941*
Sailor to win the men's Finn-class event two, three, and four times in the Olympic Games, *5219*
Women's 100-meter butterfly event held in the Olympic Games, *5835*

1970 National Football League player to kick at least one field goal in 31 consecutive games, *3310*

1971 Woman to race the marathon in under 3:00 hours, *4495*

1991 International society of Olympics researchers, *4769*

1997 Washington Capitals regular season hockey game played at the MCI Center, *4229*

December 6

1966 Basketball player to make 14 free throws in a single quarter of a National Basketball Association (NBA) game, *2045*

1967 Basketball player to score 16 consecutive field goals in a single Division I National Collegiate Athletic Association (NCAA) game, *2053*

1987 Speed skater to skate the 10,000 meters in under 14 minutes, *5707*

December 7

1956 Diver to win two consecutive titles in both springboard and platform diving events, and the first to win four gold medals in diving, in the Olympic Games, *2804*

December 19—*continued*

National Hockey League goal, *4065*

1959 Liberty Bowl football game, *3250*

1990 Professional athlete to be named an All-Star in two sports, and the first to play with an artificial hip, *5755*

December 20

1950 National Hockey League goaltender to reach 300 career wins, *4127*

1992 College women's basketball player to block 15 shots in a single Division I National Collegiate Athletic Association (NCAA) game, *2319*

1997 College women's basketball team to score 18 3-point goals in a single Division I National Collegiate Athletic Association (NCAA) game, *2399*

December 21

1849 Ice skating club in the United States, *2951*

1941 National Football League team to win two consecutive league championships, *3189*

1973 College football team to win three consecutive Fiesta Bowl games, *3333*

1997 National Football League player to rush for 100 or more yards in ten consecutive games, *3483*

December 22

1894 National governing body for golf in the United States, *3609*

1969 Basketball player to make 30 free throws during a single Division I National Collegiate Athletic Association (NCAA) game, *2065*

December 23

1951 Los Angeles Rams National Football League championship, *3231*

1962 Dallas Texans American Football League championship, *3267*

1972 College football team in a major bowl game to gain a total of 718 yards, *3326*

1986 Hall of Fame Bowl football game, *3406*

December 24

1924 National Hockey League 0–0 tie, *4084*

1950 Cleveland Browns National Football League championship, *3226*

1960 Basketball teams to have a combined total of 188 rebounds in a single National Basketball Association (NBA) game, *1999*

1961 American Football League team to win two consecutive conference championships, *3262*

December 25

1982 Aloha Bowl football game, *3376*

December 26

1908 Boxer of African descent to become world heavyweight champion, *2534*

1945 Sydney-Hobart Race, *5214*

1964 Buffalo Bills American Football League championship, *3272*

1975 Basketball player to have 11 steals in a single National Basketball Association (NBA) game, *2119*

1976 Oakland Raiders American Football Conference championship, *3352*

1978 Basketball team to have 53 assists in a single National Basketball Association (NBA) game, *2145*

1997 Motor City Bowl football game, *3484*

December 27

1892 College football game between two African-American colleges, *3126*

1968 College football player to receive 20 passes in a major bowl game, *3292*

1971 Fiesta Bowl football game, *3320*

1979 Detroit Red Wings regular season hockey game played at Joe Louis Arena, *4177*

1987 National Football League player to receive at least one touchdown pass in 13 consecutive games, *3416*

1991 Basketball player to miss on 17 consecutive field goal attempts in a single National Basketball Association (NBA) game, *2312*

1992 Three-Tour Challenge, *3874*

1998 National Football League player to receive a pass in 193 consecutive games, *3501*

December 28

1933 National Hockey League player to reach 250 career goals, *4109*

1934 Women's test match in cricket, *2657*

1947 Chicago Cardinals National Football League championship, *3215*

1948 Philadelphia Eagles National Football League championship, *3221*

1952 Detroit Lions National Football League championship in the modern era, *3233*

Personal Name Index

The Personal Name Index is a listing of personal names mentioned in the main text of the book, arranged alphabetically by last name. Each index entry includes key information about the "first" and a 4-digit number in italics. That number directs you to the full entry in the main text, where entries are numbered in order, starting with 1001.

To find the full entry, look in the main text for the entry tagged with that 4-digit number. For example, to find the entry on Margaret Abbott, the first woman from the United States to win the gold medal in the Olympic Games, look for the entry numbered 4625 in the main text.

For more information, see "How to Use This Book," on page ix.

Acord, Jessica: National Collegiate Athletic Association (NCAA) Division I women's softball player to pitch 62 complete games in a single season, *5623*

Adam, Marianne: Shot-putter to break the 70-foot barrier in the women's event, *5348*

Adams, Alvan: Phoenix Suns player to be named National Basketball Association (NBA) Rookie of the Year, *2124*

Adams, D. L.: National Association of Base Ball Players convention, *1191*

Adams, George: National golf organization founded by African-Americans, *3683*

Adkins, Charles: Light welterweight boxing event, and the first match between a Soviet and a United States boxer, in the Olympic Games, *2559*

Adlercreutz, Nils: Three-day event team equestrian competition held in the Olympic Games, *2849*

Adlerz, Erik: Men's plain high dive event held in the Olympic Games, *2795*

Ahearn, Daniel: Triple-jumper to hold the officially accepted world record in the men's event, *6253*

Ahlgren, Anders: Wrestling event in the Olympic Games to have no gold-medalist, *6375*

Ahlgren, Anne: World pentathlon championships for women, *4832*

Aitken, Brett: Men's Madison cycling event held in the Olympic Games, *2732*

Ajunwa, Chioma: Athlete from Africa to win the long jump, or any field event, in the Olympic Games, *4444*

Athlete from Nigeria to win a gold medal in the Olympic Games, *4798*

Akar, Nasuh: World championships in freestyle wrestling, *6389*

Akatiyev, Aleksey: Men's 5-kilometer river/sea swim event held in the world championships, *5975*

Swimmer to hold world titles in both the 5- and 25-kilometer river/sea swim at the same time, *5976*

Akebono (Chad Rowan): Sumo wrestler born outside Japan to be named grand champion (yokozuna), *6415*

Akers, Michelle: Women's soccer event held in the Olympic Games, *5569*

Akhurst, Daphne: Tennis player to win five Australian national women's singles championships, and the first to win three in a row, *6087*

Tennis player to win four Australian national mixed doubles titles, *6085*

Akii-Bua, John: Athlete from Uganda to win a gold medal in the Olympic Games, *4738*

Albright, Tenley: Figure skater from the United States to win the women's singles title at the Olympic Winter Games, *3053*

Figure skater from the United States to win the women's singles title in the world championships, *3048*

Alcindor, Lew *See* Abdul-Jabbar, Kareem

Alcivar, Patricia: Women's national championships in boxing, *2594*

Alcott, Amy: Du Maurier Classic, *3823*

Alexander, Grover Cleveland: Baseball pitcher to lead the National League in earned run average for three consecutive years, *1426*

Baseball pitcher to lead the National League in shutouts for three consecutive years, *1427*

Baseball pitcher to lead the National League in strikeouts for four consecutive years, *1428*

Major league baseball player of the 20th century to pitch 16 shutouts in a single season, *1424*

Alexander, Kristeena: College women's basketball player to score 20 consecutive free throws in a single Division I National Collegiate Athletic Association (NCAA) game, *2379*

Ali, Muhammad: Boxer to win the world heavyweight championship three times, *2566*

Olympic light heavyweight boxing champion to become world heavyweight champion, *2565*

Woman boxing judge to officiate at a world championship bout, *2576*

Alibert, Gaston: National team to sweep the top honors in the men's individual épée competition in the Olympic Games, *2913*

Allen, Dick: Houston Astros regular season baseball game played at the Houston Astrodome, *1680*

Allen, Forrest Claire ("Phog"): Basketball Hall of Fame, *1975*

Allen, Marcus: Los Angeles Raiders win in professional football's Super Bowl, *3394*

National Collegiate Athletic Association major college football player to rush 403 times in a single season, *3368*

Allen, Mark: Athlete to win the men's Hawaii Ironman triathlon competition four, and then five, times consecutively, and six times overall, *6242*

World championships in the triathlon, *6240*

Allen, Richard: Field hockey players to win three gold medals in the Olympic Games, *4039*

Field hockey players to win two gold medals in the Olympic Games, *4038*

Allen, William: Soling-class sailing event held in the Olympic Games, *5229*

Allison, Joe: Lou Groza Collegiate Place Kicker Award, *3453*

Allison, Wilmer: United States national women's and men's singles tennis championships to both be played at the West Side Tennis Club stadium, *6095*

Allix, Martine: International sailing championships for women, *5233*

Almada, Baldomero: Mexican major league baseball player, *1505*

Alomar, Sandy: Milwaukee Brewers regular season baseball game played at County Stadium, *1715*

Alou, Felipe: Hispanic-born major league baseball manager to be named Manager of the Year, *1829*
St. Louis Cardinals regular season baseball game played at Busch Memorial Stadium, *1689*

Alou, Jesus: San Diego Padres regular season baseball game played at San Diego Stadium, *1709*

Alsgaard, Thomas: Skier to win the 30-kilometer Nordic (cross-country) title in the Olympic Winter Games after it was converted from classical style to freestyle, *5485*

Alston, Tom: African-American baseball player to play for the St. Louis Cardinals, *1606*

Amaral, Rich: Cleveland Indians regular season baseball game played at Jacobs Field, *1827*

Amasova, Zinaida: Skier to win two consecutive women's Nordic (cross-country) skiing titles in the Olympic Winter Games, *5423*
Women's 20-kilometer cross-country event held in the world championships of Nordic skiing, *5424*

Amato, Joe: Drag racer to reach a speed over 320 miles per hour, *1145*

Ambers, Lou: Boxer to win three different world boxing titles within one year, *2550*

Ameche, Alan: National Football League player to be named Rookie of the Year, *3238*

Amend, Rolf-Dieter: Men's kayak slalom white-water canoeing events held in the Olympic Games, *2615*

Ames, Knowlton: All-America college football team named by Walter Camp, *3121*

Amoore, Edward: Small-bore rifle team shooting event held in the Olympic Games, *5291*

Amyot, Francis: Men's Canadian singles 1000-meter canoeing event held in the Olympic Games, *2597*

Anderberg, Olle: World championships in freestyle wrestling, *6389*

World championships in Greco-Roman wrestling held on a regular basis, *6388*

Andersen, Espen: Nordic combination event held in the world cup for Nordic skiing, *5438*

Andersen, Hjalmar: Speed skater to skate the 10,000 meters in under 17 minutes, *5662*

Andersen, Linda: Women's Europe-class sailing event held in the Olympic Games, *5252*

Andersen, Teresa: Women's solo and duet synchronized swimming events held in the world championships, *5908*

Anderson, Gary: National Football League kicker to have a perfect season, *3491*
National Football League kicker to reach 420 career field goals, *3492*

Anderson, Sparky: Detroit Tigers manager to be named Manager of the Year, *1772*

Anderson, Willie: Golfer to win the U.S. Open championship four times, and two and three times consecutively, *3640*
Golfer to win the U.S. Open in a playoff, *3634*
Golfer to win two U.S. Open championships, *3637*
National Football League player to receive for 336 yards in a single game, *3431*

Andersson, Agneta: Canoe racer to win a gold medal in both the singles and pairs in the women's 500 meters in the Olympic Games, *2620*

Andersson, Harald: Discus-thrower to break the 170-foot barrier, *2765*

Andersson, Robert: National team to sweep the top medals in men's platform diving in the Olympic Games, *2793*

Andre, Christian Carl: Pole vault stand, *4836*

Andresen, Jack: Water-skiing tournament, *6311*

Andretti, Mario: Japanese Grand Prix automobile race, *1122*

Andrews, Ed: World championships in racquetball, *4877*

Andreyeva, Anna: Shot-putter to break the 15-meter barrier in the women's event, *5337*

Andriakopoulous, Nikolaos: Men's rope climbing gymnastics competition held in the Olympic Games, *3907*

Andrianov, Nikolai: Gymnast to win two consecutive men's floor exercises titles in the Olympic Games, *3962*
Gymnast to win two consecutive titles in the men's long horse vault in the Olympic Games, *3965*
World cup in gymnastics, *3959*

Angelrath, Nicole: Snowboarding world championships, *5521*

659

Anikin, Nikolai: Skiers from the Soviet Union to win the men's 4 x 10-kilometer relay Nordic (cross-country) title at the Olympic Winter Games, *5405*

Anquetil, Jacques: Cyclist to win the Tour de France five times, and four times consecutively, *2701*

Ansar, Anders: Icewing sail for ice skate sailing, *4361*

Anson, Cap: "Rotating" pitchers in major league baseball, *1248*

Anthony, Eric: Cleveland Indians regular season baseball game played at Jacobs Field, *1827*

Antley, Chris: Jockey to win nine races in a single day, *4316*

Antonova, Yelena: World championships in rowing to include women's competitions, *4945*

Antonsson, Bertil: World championships in freestyle wrestling, *6389*
World championships in Greco-Roman wrestling held on a regular basis, *6388*

Aouita, Saïd: Athlete from Morocco to win a gold medal at the Olympic Games, and the first female athlete from an Islamic country to win an Olympic medal, *4758*
Runner to race the men's 5000 meters in under 13:00 minutes, *5149*

Aowei, Xing *See* Xing Aowei

Aparicio, Luis: Baseball player to lead the American League in stolen bases for nine consecutive years, *1670*
Chicago White Sox baseball player to be named Rookie of the Year, *1618*
Hispanic-American major league baseball player to be named Rookie of the Year, *1621*

Applebee, Constance: Introduction of field hockey into the United States, *4035*

Applegarth, William: Men's 4 x 100-meter relay track event held in the Olympic Games, *5003*

Arcaro, Eddie: Jockey to win America's Triple Crown twice, *4300*
Jockey to win the Kentucky Derby five times, *4301*

Archer, Fred: Horse bred and trained in the United States to win England's Derby, *4281*

Arender, Jim: Sky diver from the United States to win the men's title in the world sky diving championships, *5505*

Arledge, Missouri: African-American woman college basketball player to be named an All-American, *1951*

Arlin, Harold: Major league baseball game to be broadcast on radio, *1458*

Armstrong, Gloria: JCPenney Classic golf tournament, *3761*

Armstrong, Henry: Boxer to win three different world boxing titles within one year, *2550*

Armstrong, Lance: Cyclist to win the Tour de France after recovering from cancer, *2727*

Arnull, John: Jockey who won five Derbys at Epsom Downs, *4266*

Arnull, Sam: Derby horse race, *4261*

Ascari, Alberto: Argentine Grand Prix automobile race, *1091*
Automobile racer to have nine consecutive wins over two seasons on the Formula One Grand Prix circuit, *1089*
Automobile racer to have six wins in a single season on the Formula One Grand Prix circuit, *1087*
Dutch Grand Prix automobile race to be part of the Formula One Grand Prix circuit, *1088*
German Grand Prix automobile race to be part of the Formula One Grand Prix circuit, *1084*

Ashe, Arthur: African-American tennis player to win the men's singles championship at Wimbledon, *6158*
African-American tennis player to win the men's singles title at the Australian Open, *6143*
Tennis player classified as "non-white" by South Africa's then-racist government to win a South African tennis tournament, *6153*
Tennis player to be named Association of Tennis Professionals (ATP) Player of the Year, *6160*
U.S. Open men's doubles tennis title, *6124*
U.S. Open men's singles title, and the first men's singles Grand Slam title won by an African-American, *6135*

Ashenfelter, Horace: Runner from the United States to win the men's 3000-meter steeplechase title in the Olympic Games, *5057*

Ashford, Emmett: African-American to work as an umpire in major league baseball, *1686*

Ashford, Evelyn: Runner to win three consecutive gold medals in the women's 4 x 100-meter relay at the Olympic Games, *5161*

Ashley, Alicia: Women's national championships in boxing, *2594*

Asmussen, Cash: Japan Cup horse race, *4314*

Aspromonte, Bob: Houston Astros regular season baseball game played at the Houston Astrodome, *1680*

Asselin, Marie-Claude: World cup circuit for freestyle skiing, *5431*

Astakhova, Polina: Gymnast to win two consecutive titles in the women's uneven (asymmetrical) bars in the Olympic Games, *3952*

National team to sweep the top medals in the women's all-around gymnastics competition in the Olympic Games, *3946*

Astor, John Jacob: Rackets event held in the Olympic Games, *4872*

Athans, Greg: World cup circuit for freestyle skiing, *5431*

Atik, Celál: World championships in freestyle wrestling, *6389*

Atkinson, Jess: College football player to kick five field goals in a major bowl game, *3385*

Atkinson, Juliette: Tennis player to win five consecutive women's doubles titles at the United States national championships, *6037*

Atkinson, Kathleen: Tennis player to win five consecutive women's doubles titles at the United States national championships, *6037*

Atwood, Donna: Season for the Ice Capades, *3026*

Auchterlonie, Laurie: Golfer to shoot under 80 in all four rounds of the U.S. Open, *3635*

Golfer to win a major tournament with a rubber-cored golf ball, *3633*

Auerbach, Red (Arnold): Coach to be named National Basketball Association (NBA) Coach of the Year, *2023*

Auriemma, Geno: College women's basketball Associated Press (AP) Coach of the Year Award, *2349*

Austin, Michael: Men's 4 x 100-meter freestyle relay swimming event held in the Olympic Games, *5847*

Averill, Earl: Baseball player to hit a home run the first time he came to bat in an American League game, *1486*

Avila, Bobby (Roberto): Mexican major league baseball player to win a batting title, *1603*

Avila Camacho, Manuel: Avila Camacho Cup polo competition, *4868*

Axtell, Charles: Shooters from the United States to win the military revolver team event in the Olympic Games, *5287*

Ayat, Albert: Men's amateurs and masters épée fencing competition held in the Olympic Games, *2904*

Men's individual épée fencing competition held in the Olympic Games, *2902*

Men's masters épée fencing competition held in the Olympic Games, *2903*

Azaryan, Albert: Gymnast to win two consecutive titles in the men's rings competition in the Olympic Games, *3948*

B

Babashoff, Shirley: Swimmer to hold both the women's 200- and 400-meter freestyle world titles at the same time, *5910*

Backhaus, Robin: Men's 200-meter butterfly event held in the world championships, *5881*

Backley, Steve: Javelin-thrower to break the 300-foot and 90-meter barriers with the new javelin, *4412*

Bacon, Charles: Hurdler to hold the officially accepted world record in the men's 400-meter hurdles, and to set a 400-meter hurdle record that would stand for more than 10 years, *4326*

Bacon, Stanley: Middleweight freestyle wrestling event held in the Olympic Games, *6372*

Badger, Sherwin: Figure skater to win two consecutive men's singles titles in the U.S. national championships, *2993*

Badmann, Natascha: World championships in long-distance duathlon, *2836*

Baer, Clara Gregory: Women's basketball game in the South that was open to the public, *1871*

Women's basketball published set of rules, *1872*

Women's college basketball team in the South, *1870*

Baer, Max: Boxing match to be broadcast on television in the United States, *2552*

Bagby, Jim: Home run by a pitcher in a World Series, *1449*

Bagwell, Jeff: Houston Astros baseball player to be named Most Valuable Player, *1825*

Houston Astros baseball player to be named Rookie of the Year, *1813*

Baier, Ernst: Figure skaters to win four consecutive pairs titles in the world championships, *3025*

Bailey, Ace: National Hockey League All-Star Game, *4111*

Bailey, Jerry: Dubai World Cup horse race, *4318*

Baiul, Oksana: Athlete from newly independent Ukraine to win a gold medal at the Olympic Games, *4786*

Figure skater from Ukraine to win the women's singles title at the Olympic Winter Games, *3108*

Baiul, Oksana:—*continued*

Figure skater from Ukraine to win the women's singles title in the world championships, *3103*

Baker, Buck: Automobile racer to win two consecutive championships on the National Association for Stock Car Auto Racing (NASCAR) Winston Cup circuit, *1094*

Baker, Erin: World championships in the triathlon, *6240*

Baker, Terry: College football player to receive the *Sports Illustrated* Sportsman of the Year Award, *3264*

Bakken, Jim: National Football League player to kick seven field goals in a single game, *3284*

Seattle Seahawks regular season football game played at the Seattle Kingdome, *3348*

Balas, Iolanda: High-jumper to clear six feet in the women's event, *4026*

High-jumper to set more than 10 world records in the women's event, *4028*

High-jumper to win two consecutive women's titles in the Olympic Games, *4030*

Balczó, András: Pentathlete to win five consecutive men's titles in the world pentathlon championships, *4830*

Pentathlete to win two pentathlon gold medals in the same Olympic Games, *4827*

Baldycheva, Nina: Skier to win two consecutive women's Nordic (cross-country) skiing titles in the Olympic Winter Games, *5423*

Ball, John: Golfer to win eight British Amateur championships, *3652*

Ball, John, Jr.: Amateur, and the first non-Scot, to win the British Open golf championship, *3597*

Ball, Neal: Unassisted triple play of the 20th century in major league baseball, *1395*

Ball, Rudi: Jewish athlete to represent Germany in the 1936 Olympic Winter Games, *4679*

Ballanger, Felicia: Women's 500-meter time trial cycling event held in the Olympic Games, *2728*

Ballangrud, Ivar: Speed skater to win three gold medals in speed skating at a single Olympic Winter Games, *5658*

Speed skater to win two Olympic gold medals in men's 5000-meter speed skating, *5657*

Ballard, Margarette: Sisters to win the women's doubles title at the United States national tennis championships, *6028*

United States women's doubles national tennis championships, *6027*

Balme, Eugène: National team to sweep the rapid-fire pistol individual shooting event in the Olympic Games, *5278*

Balzer, Karin: Hurdler to hold the officially accepted world record in the women's 100-meter hurdles, *4342*

Banach, Ed: Wrestler from the United States to win the heavyweight freestyle wrestling title in the Olympic Games, *6407*

Banach, Louis: Wrestler from the United States to win the heavyweight freestyle wrestling title in the Olympic Games, *6407*

Banaszak, Pete: New England Patriots regular season football game played at Foxboro Stadium, *3316*

Bankhead, Dan: African-American player to be a pitcher in major league baseball, *1563*

Banks, Ernie: African-American to serve as a manager in baseball's major leagues, *1733*

Banks, Freddie: Basketball player to score ten 3-point field goals in a single Division I National Collegiate Athletic Association (NCAA) championship series game, *2249*

Bannister, Roger: Athlete to be named *Sports Illustrated* Sportsman of the Year, *1151*

Runner to race the mile in under 4:00 minutes, *5060*

Bannon, Jimmy: Major league baseball player to hit grand slam home runs in two consecutive games, *1314*

Barbarie, Bret: Florida Marlins regular season baseball game played at Joe Robbie Stadium, *1823*

Barbarin, Roger de: Trap (clay pigeon) shooting individual event held in the Olympic Games, *5276*

Barbee, G.: Preakness Stakes horse race, *4278*

Barber, Miller: Golfer on the Senior Professional Golfers' Association (PGA) Tour to win more than $100,000 in a season, *3837*

Golfer to win $100,000 in a single tournament, *3805*

Barber, Red: Major league baseball games to be televised, *1539*

Barclay, Jean Claude: French Open mixed doubles tennis match, *6119*

Bardauskiene, Vilma: Long-jumper to break the 7-meter barrier in the women's event, *4440*

Barel, Rob: World long-distance triathlon championships, *6245*

Barfod, Håkon: Dragon-class sailing event held in the Olympic Games, *5216*

Baril, Benoit: World championships in short track speed skating to be officially recognized, *5697*

Barkley, Charles: Olympic basketball competition to include openly professional athletes, *2316*

Phoenix Suns player to be named National Basketball Association (NBA) Most Valuable Player of the Year, *2327*

Barksdale, Don: African-American basketball player on an Olympic team, *1919*

African-American basketball player to win an Olympic gold medal, *1921*

Barlois, Valerie: Women's individual and team épée competitions held in the Olympic Games, *2944*

Barna, Petr: Figure skater to perform a quadruple jump in the Olympic Games, *3101*

Barna, Viktor: Table tennis player to win five men's singles titles in the world championships, *5989*

Barnard, E. T.: Australian national tennis championships, *6045*

Barnekow, Marten von: Equestrian to win gold medals in both individual and team jumping in the same Olympic Games, *2859*

Barnes, Frank: African-American baseball players to join the New York Yankees organization, *1582*

Barnes, James: Golf book to use high-speed sequential photographs, *3660*

Golfer over 50 to win a Professional Golfers' Association (PGA) recognized tournament, *3703*

Golfer to win two straight Professional Golfers' Association (PGA) Championships, *3662*

Professional Golfers' Association (PGA) Championship, *3658*

Barnes, Kirsten: Women's four-oared shell without coxswain event held in the Olympic Games, *4957*

Barnes, Ross: Baseball player to hit a home run in the National League, *1225*

Baseball player to lead the National League in batting average, *1217*

Barr, James: Skipper to win the America's Cup sailing race twice in a row, *5203*

Barragon, Jimmy: College baseball player to have six hits in a single game, *1790*

Barrelet, Henri: Men's single sculls rowing event held in the Olympic Games, *4927*

Barry, Rick: Basketball player to make 14 free throws in a single quarter of a National Basketball Association (NBA) game, *2045*

San Francisco Warriors player to be named National Basketball Association (NBA) Rookie of the Year, *2041*

Bartko, Robert: Cycling team to break the 4-minute mark in the men's 4000-meter team pursuit race in the Olympic Games, *2730*

Barton, Gregory: Canoe racer from the United States to win the men's singles 1000-meter kayak event, and to win a gold medal in any kayaking event, in the Olympic Games, *2626*

Barty, Ceal: College women's basketball United States Basketball Writers Association Coach of the Year Award, *2335*

Bary, Jacob Erckrath de: Men's team sabre fencing competition held in the Olympic Games, *2911*

Baryshnikov, Aleksandr: Shot-putter to break the 22-meter barrier, *5349*

Basilio Satelo, Norma Enriqueta: Woman to carry the torch at the Olympic Games, *4725*

Bass, Bill: African-American professional football player to join the Chicago Rockets, *3207*

Bassham, Lanny: Woman to win a medal in shooting at the Olympic Games, *5313*

Baszanowski, Waldemar: Weightlifter to win two consecutive lightweight titles in the Olympic Games, *6344*

Bathe, Walter: National team to sweep the medals in the men's 200-meter breaststroke event in the Olympic Games, *5806*

Battle, Ken: World championships in hang gliding, *3533*

Bau, Sabine: National team to sweep the medals in the women's individual foil fencing competition in the Olympic Games, *2940*

Bauer, Sybil: Women's 100-meter backstroke event held in the Olympic Games, *5819*

Baugh, Sammy: Pro Football Hall of Fame, *3268*

Baugniet, Pierre: Figure skaters from Belgium to win the pairs title at the Olympic Winter Games, *3036*

Figure skaters from Belgium to win the pairs title in the world championships, *3031*

Bauman, Lorri: College women's basketball player to score 27 field goals in a single Division I National Collegiate Athletic Association (NCAA) game, *2204*

College women's basketball player to score 275 free throws in a single Division I National Collegiate Athletic Association (NCAA) season, *2175*

Baumgartner, Bruce: Wrestler from the United States to win two super heavyweight freestyle titles in the Olympic Games, *6412*

Baxter, Cindy: World championships in racquetball, *4877*

Bayard, Louis, Jr.: Intercollegiate golf tournament in the United States, *3621*

Baylor, Don: California Angels baseball player to be named Most Valuable Player, *1751*

Baylor, Elgin: African-American basketball players to be named to an All–National Basketball Association (NBA) first team, *1981*

Baylor, Elgin:—*continued*
Basketball player to score 284 points in a National Basketball Association (NBA) Finals series, *2012*
Basketball player to score 30 points or more in 11 consecutive National Basketball Association (NBA) playoff games, *2013*
Basketball player to score 61 points in a National Basketball Association (NBA) Finals game, *2018*
Minneapolis Lakers player to be named National Basketball Association (NBA) Rookie of the Year, *1985*

Bayrak, Mithat: Wrestler to win two consecutive welterweight Greco-Roman titles in the Olympic Games, *6390*

Beach, Rod: United States national tennis championships to include mixed doubles competition, *6032*

Beal, Frank E.: Invention of paddle tennis, *6194*

Beall, Johnny: Chicago Cubs regular season baseball game played at Wrigley Field, *1425*

Beames, Adrienne: Woman to race the marathon in under 3:00 hours, *4495*

Beamon, Robert: Long-jumper to break the 28- and 29-foot barriers, *4439*
Long-jumper to win three, and then four, consecutive men's titles in the Olympic Games, *4443*

Beardsley, Dick: London Marathon, *4507*

Beasley, Tom: Boxing match under English rules held in the United States, *2508*

Beaty, Zelmo: All–National Basketball Association (NBA) Rookie Team, *2019*

Beauchamp, Johnny: Daytona 500 automobile race, *1098*

Beaufort family: Standardized rules for badminton, *1164*

Beaumont, Ginger: Baseball player to lead the National League in hits in three consecutive years, *1362*
Baseball player to lead the National League in singles in three consecutive years, *1363*

Bebble, Bert: Little League baseball league, *1533*

Bebble, George: Little League baseball league, *1533*

Beck, Erve: Home run in the American League, *1334*

Becke, Daniel: Cycling team to break the 4-minute mark in the men's 4000-meter team pursuit race in the Olympic Games, *2730*

Becker, Boris: Unseeded tennis player to win the men's singles title at Wimbledon, *6172*

Bédard, Myriam: Woman to win gold medals in two biathlon events in the same Olympic Winter Games, *2442*

Beethoven, Ludwig von: Olympic Games at which Beethoven's "Ode to Joy" was sung, *4603*

Behmann, Angelika: Women's slalom singles kayaking event held in the Olympic Games, *2614*

Behrens, Kurt: National team to sweep the top medals in men's springboard diving in the Olympic Games, *2794*

Beiser-Jochum, Trude: Women's events to be included in the Alpine skiing world championships, *5392*

Belita (Gladys Lynne Jepson-Turner): Season for the Ice Capades, *3026*

Beliveau, Jean: National Hockey League player to win the Conn Smythe Trophy as the Most Valuable Player of the playoffs, *4147*

Bell, Bert: Pro Football Hall of Fame, *3268*

Bell, Florence: Women's 4 x 100-meter relay running event held in the Olympic Games, *5023*

Bell, George: Toronto Blue Jays baseball player to be named Most Valuable Player, *1794*

Bell, Judy: Woman to be elected to the executive committee of the United States Golf Association (USGA), *3856*

Bell, Robin: World championships for nine-ball pool, *2464*

Bellamy, Walt: Chicago Bulls player to be named National Basketball Association (NBA) Rookie of the Year, *2016*

Bellan, Esteban: Cuban major league baseball player, *1205*

Belle, Albert: Major league baseball player to earn $10 million a year, *1841*

Bellingham, Norman: Canoe racer from the United States to win the men's singles 1000-meter kayak event, and to win a gold medal in any kayaking event, in the Olympic Games, *2626*

Belmondo, Stefania: Women's 30-kilometer Nordic (cross-country) skiing event held at the Olympic Winter Games, *5469*
Women's pursuit (5 kilometers classical and 10 kilometers freestyle) event held in the world championships of Nordic skiing, *5483*

Belmont, August: Belmont Stakes horse race, *4276*

Belokas, Spiridon: Marathon runner to be stripped of his medal, *4467*

Belote, Melissa: Women's 200-meter backstroke event held in the world championships, *5898*

Belousova, Ludmila: Figure skaters from the Soviet Union to win the pairs title at the Olympic Winter Games, *3064*

Figure skaters from the Soviet Union to win the pairs title in the world championships, *3062*

Bender, Chief (Charles): Baseball pitcher to lead the American League in winning percentage for two consecutive years, *1403*

Native-American major league baseball player to be named to baseball's Hall of Fame, *1595*

Bender, Dieter: World championships in rowing, *4940*

Benedek, Gábor: Men's modern pentathlon team event held in the Olympic Games, *4823*

Benedict, Charles: Shooters from the United States to win the military rifle team shooting title in the Olympic Games, *5288*

Benedict, Clint: Goalie to have 20 career shutouts in the National Hockey League, *4086*

National Hockey League goaltender to be credited with four shutouts in a single set of Stanley Cup playoffs, *4091*

National Hockey League goaltender to wear a facemask in a scheduled game, *4101*

Benirschke, Rolf: Los Angeles Raiders regular season football game played at the Los Angeles Memorial Coliseum, *3375*

Bennet, Joseph: International swimming competition on record, *5779*

Bennett, Charles: Runner from Europe to win the men's 1500-meter title in the Olympic Games, *4978*

Bennett, James Gordon: International airplane races, *1001*

International balloon race, *1182*

Polo competitions in the United States, *4860*

Transatlantic sailing race, *5199*

Bennett, Robert: National team to sweep the medals in the men's 200-meter backstroke event in the Olympic Games, *5846*

Benoit (later Samuelson), Joan: Runner to win both the women's title in the Boston Marathon and the women's marathon in the Olympic Games, *4513*

Runner to win two official women's championships in the Boston Marathon, *4511*

Women's marathon held in the Olympic Games, *4512*

Bentsen, William: Soling-class sailing event held in the Olympic Games, *5229*

Berceanu, Gheorghe: Light flyweight event held in the world Greco-Roman wrestling championships, *6394*

Light flyweight Greco-Roman wrestling event held in the Olympic Games, *6401*

Berg, Patty: Golfer to win 10 major tournaments recognized by the Ladies Professional Golf Association (LPGA) Tour, *3738*

Golfer to win the Ladies Professional Golf Association (LPGA) Championship in a sudden-death playoff, *3749*

Golfer to win the Vare Trophy for the lowest average score on the Ladies Professional Golf Association (LPGA) Tour, *3736*

President of the Ladies Professional Golf Association (LPGA), *3722*

U.S. Women's Open golf championship, *3715*

Berg, Stephan Van den: Men's sailboarding event held in the Olympic Games, *5191*

Berger, Alfred: Figure skaters from Austria to win the pairs title at the Olympic Winter Games, *3002*

Figure skaters from Austria to win the pairs title in the world championships, *2986*

Berger, Isaac: Weightlifter from the United States to win the featherweight title in the Olympic Games, *6340*

Berger, Samuel: Heavyweight boxing event held in the Olympic Games, *2529*

Berghmans, Ingrid: World championships for judo to include women, *4546*

Bergmann, Arnfinn: Olympic event to be attended by 150,000 people, *4700*

Bergoust, Eric: Skier from the United States to win the men's aerials freestyle skiing event in the Olympic Winter Games, *5500*

Bergvall, Björn: Flying Dutchman–class sailing event held in the Olympic Games, *5223*

Berkoff, David: Swimmer to race the men's 100-meter backstroke event in under 55 seconds, *5951*

Berna, Tel: Men's 3000-meter team running event held in the Olympic Games, *5004*

Bernhard, Silke: World championships in vaulting, *2888*

Bernstein, Kenny: Drag racer to reach a speed over 300 miles per hour, *1142*

Berra, Yogi: Major league baseball player to hit a home run as a pinch hitter in the World Series, *1565*

Berthon, Eric: World championships for freestyle skiing, *5451*

Bertrand, John: America's Cup sailing race not won by the United States, *5242*

Berwanger, Jay: College football player to be awarded the Heisman Trophy, *3171*

Berwick, William: Patent for a golf ball, *3541*

Bescher, Bob: Baseball player to lead the National League in stolen bases for four consecutive years, *1409*

Besselink, Al: Golfer to win the Tournament of Champions, *3734*

Betley, Bob: Women to be caddies at the U.S. Open golf tournament, *3831*

Betley, Jane: Women to be caddies at the U.S. Open golf tournament, *3831*

Bettis, Jerome: St. Louis Rams regular season football game played at the Trans World Dome, 3472

Betts, W. Rossiter: Golfer to win the U.S. Amateur Championship twice in a row, 3617

Bianchi, Pietro: Gymnasts to win two consecutive gold medals in the men's team combined exercises in the Olympic Games, 3922

Bief, Jacqueline du See du Bief, Jacqueline

Biellmann, Denise: Figure skater from Switzerland to win the women's singles title in the world championships, 3086

Woman figure skater to perform a triple lutz in competition, 3081

Biggs, Tyrell: Superheavyweight boxing event in the Olympic Games, 2582

Bikila, Abebe: Athlete from Ethiopia, and Black athlete from Africa, to win a gold medal at the Olympic Games, 4710

Black African runner to win the men's marathon title at the Olympic Games, and to hold the world record in the event, 4487

Runner to win two consecutive marathon titles in the Olympic Games, 4489

Biletnikoff, Fred: Fred Biletnikoff Receiver Award, 3459

Oakland Raiders win in professional football's Super Bowl, 3355

Billings, Charles: Shooters from the United States to win the trap (clay pigeon) team shooting event in the Olympic Games, 5294

Bilohlazov, Anatoly: Twin brothers to win gold medals in wrestling in the same Olympic Games, 6404

Bilohlazov, Serhei: Twin brothers to win gold medals in wrestling in the same Olympic Games, 6404

Wrestler to win two bantamweight freestyle wrestling titles in the Olympic Games, 6410

Bing, Dave: Detroit Pistons player to be named National Basketball Association (NBA) Rookie of the Year, 2047

Bingley, Blanche: Tennis player to win two consecutive women's singles championships at Wimbledon, 6018

Biondi, Matthew: Men's 50-meter freestyle swimming event held in the Olympic Games, 5954

Olympic men's 100-meter freestyle swimming event in which all the medalists had times under 50 seconds, 5952

Swimmer to win three consecutive gold medals in the men's 4 x 100-meter freestyle relay in the Olympic Games, 5964

Swimmer to win two consecutive men's 100-meter freestyle titles at the world championships, 5958

Bird, Larry: Olympic basketball competition to include openly professional athletes, 2316

Biryukova, Ana: Triple-jumper to break the 15-meter barrier in the women's event, 6262

Biryulina, Tatyana: Javelin-thrower to break the 70-meter barrier in the women's event, 4404

Bistuer, Coral: World championships in taekwondo to include women, 4549

Bithorn, Hiram: Puerto Rican major league baseball player, 1543

Biwott, Amos: Athlete from Kenya to win a gold medal in the Olympic Games, 4732

Runner from Africa to win the men's 3000-meter steeplechase title in the Olympic Games, 5087

Bjedov, Djurdjica: Women's 100-meter breaststroke event held in the Olympic Games, 5852

Bjurefelt, Tage: World championships in the pentathlon, 4820

Bjurstedt, Molla See Mallory, Molla Bjurstedt

Blair, Bonnie: Athlete from the United States to win six medals at the Olympic Winter Games, and the first female U.S. athlete to win five gold medals at the winter or summer Games, 4784

Female athlete from the United States to win three gold medals in the Olympic Winter Games, 4770

Speed skater from the United States to win the women's 1000-meter title at the Olympic Winter Games, 5712

Speed skater to win three consecutive women's 500-meter titles at the Olympic Winter Games, 5721

Speed skater to win two consecutive women's 1000-meter speed skating titles at the Olympic Winter Games, 5723

Speed skater to win two consecutive women's 500-meter titles in the Olympic Winter Games, 5711

Speed skaters to be named *Sports Illustrated* Sportsmen of the Year, 5719

Blake, Toe: National Hockey League team to win the Stanley Cup five times in a row, 4140

Blalock, Jane: Dinah Shore golf tournament, 3799

Blanchard, Doc (Felix): College football player to win the James E. Sullivan Memorial Award, 3194

Blanchard, Fessenden S.: Invention of platform tennis, 6196

Blanchard, Jean Pierre: Balloon flight in the United States, *1179*
Balloon flight in the United States, *1179*
Flyers to cross the English Channel in a balloon, *1178*
Woman to fly in a hot-air balloon, *1177*
Blanchard, Marie Sophie: Woman to fly in a hot-air balloon, *1177*
Blanchard, Theresa Weld: Figure skater to win the women's singles title at the U.S. national championships, *2988*
Figure skater to win two straight women's singles titles at the U.S. national championships, *2994*
Figure skaters to win a gold medal in ice dancing in the U.S. national championships, *2989*
Figure skaters to win the pairs title in the U.S. national championships, *2990*
Woman figure skater to perform a full-revolution jump, the salchow, in competition, *2998*
Bland, Harriet: Runner to win two gold medals in the women's 4 x 100-meter relay in the Olympic Games, *5041*
Blanda, George: National Football League player to be named Most Valuable Player of the American Football Conference, *3301*
Professional football player to play for 26 seasons in major league football, *3341*
Professional football player to score a career total of 2,002 points, *3342*
Blankers-Koen, Fanny (Francina): Pentathlete to hold the officially accepted world record in the women's pentathlon (type B), *4822*
Woman athlete to win four gold medals in track and field in a single Olympic Games, *6212*
Women's 200-meter race held in the Olympic Games, *5051*
Women's long jump event held in the Olympic Games, *4436*
Blasco Soto, Miriam: Women's lightweight judo event held in the Olympic Games, *4552*
Blasingame, Don: San Francisco Giants regular season baseball game played at Candlestick Park (later 3Com Park), *1643*
Blask, Erwin: Hammer-thrower to break the 190-foot barrier, *3986*
Blatnick, Jeffrey: Wrestler from the United States to win the super heavyweight Greco-Roman title in the Olympic Games, *6406*
Blaylock, Mookie: Basketball player to have 13 steals during a single Division I National Collegiate Athletic Association (NCAA) game, *2261*

Basketball player to have 150 steals during a single Division I National Collegiate Athletic Association (NCAA) season, *2264*
Basketball player to have 23 steals in a Division I National Collegiate Athletic Association (NCAA) championship series, *2265*
Blazejowski, Carol: Basketball player to win the Margaret Wade Trophy, awarded to the women's college basketball Player of the Year, *2136*
Major college women's basketball player to score more than 3,000 points during her college career, *2139*
Bledsoe, Drew: National Football League player to complete 45 passes in a single game, *3463*
Bleibtrey, Ethelda: National team to sweep the medals in the women's 100-meter freestyle swimming event in the Olympic Games, *5810*
Swimmers from the United States to win the women's 4 x 100-meter freestyle relay title in the Olympic Games, *5814*
Women's 300-meter (later 400-meter) freestyle event held in the Olympic Games, *5812*
Bleriot, Louis: International airplane races, *1001*
Blomberg, Ron: Major league baseball player to appear as a designated hitter during a regular season game, *1731*
Blue, Vida: African-American major league baseball player to win the American League's Cy Young Award, *1718*
Oakland Athletics pitcher to win the Cy Young Award, *1720*
Blyth, Chay: Sailor to complete a solo circumnavigation of the world from east to west, *5227*
Whitbread Round-the-World Race, *5232*
Bobet, Louison: Cyclist to win the Tour de France three consecutive times, *2699*
Bobo, Mike: College football player to complete 19 consecutive passes in a major bowl game, *3494*
Bocharova, Nina: Women's balance beam gymnastics competition held in the Olympic Games, *3935*
Böckli, Franz: Military revolver and military rifle team shooting events held in the Olympic Games, *5280*
Bode, Harro: 470-class sailing event held at the Olympic Games, *5235*
Bodén, Patrik: Javelin-thrower to break the 290-foot barrier with the new javelin, *4411*
Bodine, John: International rifle tournament held in the United States, *5267*
Bogardus, Adam H.: Use of glass ball targets in United States shooting competitions, *5265*

Boggs, Phil: Diver to win two, and then three, consecutive men's springboard diving titles in the world championships, *2809*

Men's springboard diving event held at the world championships, *2806*

Bohler, Reinhardt: World championship in moto-cross racing to include the sidecar class, *4591*

Böhling, Ivar: Wrestling event in the Olympic Games to have no gold-medalist, *6375*

Bohorques y Goyeneche (de los Trujillos), José Alvarez de las Asturias: Athletes from Spain to win gold medals in the Olympic Games, *4673*

Boitano, Brian: Figure skater to perform the tano lutz jump in competition, *3092*

Figure skaters to win Emmy awards for a television special, *3095*

Boklöv, Jan: Ski-jumper to spread the skis in a V formation in the air, *5447*

Boland, John: Men's doubles tennis event held in the Olympic Games, *6035*

Men's singles tennis event held in the Olympic Games, *6036*

Boltenstern, Gustav-Adolf, Jr.: Equestrian to be stripped of his dressage title because he was not a commissioned officer, *2860*

Bolton, Nancye Wynne: Tennis player to win four consecutive Australian national women's singles championships, *6103*

Tennis players to win five consecutive Australian national women's doubles championships, *6104*

Bolton-Holifield, Ruthie: Women's National Basketball Association (WNBA) All-WNBA First Team, *2387*

Bond, Tommy: Pitcher to lead the National League in winning percentage for two consecutive years, *1241*

Bondarenko, Olga: Women's 10,000-meter running event held in the Olympic Games, *5152*

Bonde, Carl: Individual dressage equestrian competition held in the Olympic Games, *2845*

Bonds, Barry: Baseball player to lead the National League in bases on balls for four consecutive years, *1837*

Baseball player to steal 40 bases and hit 40 home runs in a season in the National League, *1833*

Bonhag, George: Men's 3000-meter team running event held in the Olympic Games, *5004*

Bonner, Beth: Woman to be women's champion in the New York Marathon, *4494*

Woman to race the marathon in under 3:00 hours, *4495*

Booker, Pete: African-American All-Star Team in professional baseball, *1402*

Boothby, Dora: Women's doubles championships at Wimbledon, *6054*

Borden, Amanda: Gymnasts from the United States to win the women's team title in the Olympic Games, *3978*

Borg, Bjorn: Tennis player of the Open era to win the Wimbledon men's singles title five consecutive times, *6168*

Tennis player to win the French Open men's singles title six times, *6169*

Borghese, Prince Scipione: International and transcontinental automobile race, *1050*

Boros, Julius: Senior Professional Golfers' Association (PGA) Tour, *3830*

Borotra, Jean: Tennis player to win a French national men's singles championship after the event became international, *6076*

Tennis player to win four Australian national mixed doubles titles, *6085*

Tennis player to win three, four, and then five French national men's doubles championships after the event became international, *6089*

Tennis players to win the French national men's doubles championship after the event became international, *6079*

Bossert, Gary: Basketball player to shoot 11 consecutive 3-point field goals during a single Division I National Collegiate Athletic Association (NCAA) game, *2257*

Bossi, Carmelo: Boxer from the United States to win the light middleweight title in the Olympic Games, *2563*

Boston, Ralph: Long-jump record to stand for more than 25 years, *4434*

Long-jumper to break the 27-foot barrier, *4438*

Men's long jump event in which the top four contestants jumped more than 26 feet, *4437*

Bosworth, Brian: Butkus Award, *3398*

Bott (first name unknown): Sliding seat developed for the luge (toboggan), *4451*

Bouchard, Sylvain: Speed skater to skate the 1000 meters in under 1:10 minutes, *5735*

Boucher, Frank: National Hockey League player to reach 250 career assists, *4116*

National Hockey League player to win the Lady Byng Memorial Trophy as the most gentlemanly player seven times, *4113*

Bouckaert (first name unknown): Figure riding individual and team events held in the Olympic Games, *2850*

Boudreau, Lou: Cleveland Indians baseball player to be named Most Valuable Player, *1567*

Bouin, Jean: Runner to hold the officially accepted world record in the men's 10,000-meter event, *4999*

Boulding, Charlie: Sled dog racer to win the Yukon Quest sled dog race twice, *5519*

Boulenger, Marcel Jacques: National team to sweep the medals in the men's individual foil fencing competition in the Olympic Games, *2900*

Boulmerka, Hassiba: Runner from Africa to win the women's 1500-meter title at the Olympic Games, *5160*

Runner to win two titles in the women's 1500-meter event in the World Championships in Athletics, *5176*

Women's 1500-meter race in which the top four finishers all had times under 4 minutes, *5162*

Boutellier, Madeleine: World championships in water-skiing, *6316*

Bowa, Larry: Philadelphia Phillies regular season baseball game played at Veterans Stadium, *1721*

Bowden, Norris: Figure skaters from Canada to win the pairs title in the world championships, *3050*

Boyarskikh, Klaudia: Women's individual 5-kilometer Nordic (cross-country) event in the Olympic Winter Games, *5412*

Boyd, Esna: Australian mixed doubles national tennis championships, *6061*

Australian women's doubles national tennis championships, *6062*

Australian women's singles national tennis championships, *6063*

Tennis player to win two consecutive Australian national women's doubles championships, *6066*

Tennis player to win two consecutive Australian national women's singles tennis championships, *6067*

Tennis players to win three Australian national mixed doubles championships, *6082*

Brå, Oddvar: World cup for Nordic skiing, *5428*

Brabham, Jack: Automobile racer to have five consecutive wins in a single season on the Formula One Grand Prix circuit, *1100*

Canadian Grand Prix automobile race, *1112*

Brack, Walter: Men's 100-yard (later 100-meter) backstroke swimming event held in the Olympic Games, *5794*

Bracken, Raymond: Rapid-fire pistol and free pistol team events held in the Olympic Games, *5299*

Bradley, Bill (baseball player): Three consecutive home runs in a single inning of an American League game, *1348*

Bradley, Bill (basketball player): Basketball player to score 58 points in a single Division I National Collegiate Athletic Association (NCAA) Final Four championship series game, *2030*

College basketball player to receive the James E. Sullivan Memorial Award, *2033*

Bradley, George: No-hitter pitched in baseball's National League, *1229*

Bradley, Pat: Woman golfer to earn more than $2 million in official prize money during her career, *3852*

Woman golfer to earn more than $3 million in official prize money during her career, *3867*

Bradshaw, Benjamin: Featherweight freestyle wrestling event held in the Olympic Games, *6363*

Brady, Mike: Golfer born in the United States to win the U.S. Open, *3650*

Brady, Neal: Ottawa Senators regular season hockey game played at the Ottawa Civic Center, *4205*

Bragina, Lyudmila: Runner to hold the officially accepted world record in the women's 3000-meter event, *5101*

Women's 1500-meter event held in the Olympic Games, *5094*

Braglia, Alberto: Gymnast to win two consecutive men's all-around titles in the Olympic Games, *3918*

Braid, James: Golfer to win five British Open championships, *3649*

Brallier, John: Professional football player who acknowledged being a professional, *3127*

Brand, Glen: Wrestler from the United States to win the middleweight freestyle wrestling title in the Olympic Games, *6386*

Brandt, François Antoine: Athletes from the Netherlands to win gold medals in the Olympic Games, *4624*

Men's pair-oared shell with coxswain rowing event held in the Olympic Games, *4926*

Brandt, Heinz: Equestrian to win gold medals in both individual and team jumping in the same Olympic Games, *2859*

Brann, William L.: Horse to be named Horse of the Year twice consecutively, *4296*

Brasher, Christopher: London Marathon, *4507*

Bratberg, Ragnhild: Ski orienteering world championships to include sprint competitions, *4810*

World cup in orienteering, *4811*

Bratton, David: Water polo team from the United States to win the title at the Olympic Games, *6302*

Brébeuf, Jean de: Lacrosse organization, *4416*

Bredow, Reinhard: Two-seater luge (toboggan) event to have two pairs of gold medalists in a single Olympic Winter Games, *4458*

Bremen, Wilhelmina Von *See* Von Bremen, Wilhelmina

669

Brenden, Hallgeir: Men's individual 15-kilometer Nordic (cross-country) event at the Olympic Winter Games, *5404*

Brentjens, Bart Jan: Men's cross-country (mountain bike) race held in the Olympic Games, *2723*

Brett, George: Kansas City Royals baseball player to be named Most Valuable Player, *1755*

Brewer, Gay: Golfer to win the Tournament of Champions in a playoff, *3784*

Briand, Anne: Women's 4 x 7.5-kilometer biathlon relay competition held in the Olympic Winter Games, *2440*

Brickhouse, Richard: Talladega 500 automobile race, *1115*

Bridges, Cheryl: Woman to race the marathon in under 3:00 hours, *4495*

Brill, Frank: National bowling championships in the United States, *2482*

Brisco-Hooks, Valerie: Runner to win both the women's 200-and 400-meter titles at a single Olympic Games, and the first runner from the United States, or African-American, to win the 400-meter event, *5143*

Team from the United States to win the women's 4 x 400-meter relay at the Olympic Games, *5142*

Briscoe, Mark: Kansas City Chiefs regular season football game played at Arrowhead Stadium, *3325*

Briscoe, Marlin: African-American quarterback to play regularly on a professional football team, *3287*

Brittman, Darron: Basketball player to average 5.0 steals per game during a single Division I National Collegiate Athletic Association (NCAA) season, *2228*

Broadbent, Harry: National Hockey League goaltender to score at least one goal in 16 consecutive games, *4078*

Brock, Lou: Major league baseball player to have 118 steals in a single season, *1739*

Brocklin, Norm Van *See* Van Brocklin, Norm

Brockmann, Hermanus: Men's pair-oared shell with coxswain rowing event held in the Olympic Games, *4926*

Broda, Turk: National Hockey League goaltender to reach 300 career wins, *4127*

Brodie, John: National Football League player to be named Most Valuable Player of the National Football Conference, *3302*

Brogna, Rico: Colorado Rockies regular season baseball game played at Coors Field, *1831*

Bromwich, John: Tennis player to win 10 consecutive Australian national men's doubles championships, *6102*

Brönberg, Axel: World championships in Greco-Roman wrestling held on a regular basis, *6388*

Brooks, Louis: Cowboy to be named All-Around Cowboy twice consecutively, *4890*

Brooks, Marshall Jones: High-jumper to clear six feet, *4017*

Brooks, Nathan: African-American boxers to win gold medals in the Olympic Games, *2557*

Brosky, Al: National Collegiate Athletic Association major college football player to intercept 29 passes during his college career, *3232*

Broten, Neal: Dallas Stars regular season hockey game played at the Reunion Arena, *4207*

Brough, Louise: Tennis player to win 10 consecutive women's doubles titles at the United States national championships, and 13 overall, *6106*

Broughton, Jack: Boxing code of rules, *2506* London Prize Ring Rules for boxing, *2510*

Brousse, Roger: Boxer to win two consecutive middleweight titles in the Olympic Games, *2545*

Brouthers, Dan: Baseball player to lead the National League in batting average for two consecutive years, *1266*

Brown, Cindy: College women's basketball player to score 60 points in a single Division I National Collegiate Athletic Association (NCAA) game, *2259*

College women's basketball player to score 974 points in a single Division I National Collegiate Athletic Association (NCAA) season, *2254*

Brown, David: Golfer to win two U.S. Open championships, *3637*

Brown, Dewey: African-American golfer to be a member of the Professional Golfers' Association (PGA), *3663*

Brown, Doris: International Cross-Country Championships to include a women's race, *5081*

Brown, Ed: Green Bay Packers regular season football game played at Lambeau Field, *3245*

Brown, Jim: National Football League player, and the first African-American football player, to win the Associated Press (AP) Most Valuable Player Award, *3243*

National Football League player to lead the league in rushing yards eight times, *3274*

Brown, Mrs. Charles (first name unknown): U.S. Women's Amateur golf tournament, *3615*

Brown, Mrs. S. (first name unknown): National archery tournament in the United States, *1024*

Brown, Roosevelt: African-American professional football player from an African-American college to be inducted into the Pro Football Hall of Fame, *3339*

Brown, Sandra: Woman to compete in the University Boat Race, *4951*

Brown, Tom: Two consecutive home runs by different players to open a major league baseball game, *1305*

Brown, Willard: African-American baseball player to hit a home run in the American League, *1562*

African-American baseball player to play for the St. Louis Browns, *1559*

Two African-American major league baseball players to play for the same club in the same game, *1561*

Browne, Mary K.: Tennis player to win nine Wimbledon women's doubles titles, *6088*

Tennis star to turn professional, *6081*

Browning, Kurt: Figure skater to perform a quadruple jump in competition, *3091*

Bruckner, Victoria: Girl from the United States to appear in a Little League baseball World Series, *1806*

Brugnon, Jacques: Tennis player to win three, four, and then five French national men's doubles championships after the event became international, *6089*

Tennis players to win a French national mixed doubles championship after the event became international, *6078*

Tennis players to win the French national men's doubles championship after the event became international, *6079*

Brumel, Valeriy: High-jumper to set six world records in the men's event, *4029*

Bruna, Enrico: Rowers to win two gold medals in pair-oared shell with coxswain rowing events in the same Olympic Games, *4934*

Brundage, Avery: International government body in handball, *4003*

Brunet, Andrée Joly: Figure skaters from France to win the pairs title in the Olympic Winter Games, *3008*

Figure skaters from France to win the pairs title in the world championships, *3005*

Figure skaters to win four pairs titles in the world championships, *3011*

Figure skaters to win two consecutive pairs titles at the Olympic Winter Games, *3013*

Brunet, Pierre: Figure skaters from France to win the pairs title in the Olympic Winter Games, *3008*

Figure skaters from France to win the pairs title in the world championships, *3005*

Figure skaters to win four pairs titles in the world championships, *3011*

Figure skaters to win two consecutive pairs titles at the Olympic Winter Games, *3013*

Bryant, Bear (Paul W.): College football coach to be named Coach of the Year three times, *3328*

Bryant, Charles: African-American football players to appear in the Orange Bowl, *3239*

Bryant, David: World indoor championships in bowls, *2502*

World outdoor championships in bowls, *2499*

Brzak-Felix, Jan: Canoer to win two men's Canadian pairs 1000-meter titles in the Olympic Games, *2602*

Men's Canadian pairs 1000-meter canoeing event held in the Olympic Games, *2596*

Bubka, Sergey: Pole-vaulter to clear 20 feet, *4849*

Pole-vaulter to clear 6 meters, *4848*

Buchan, William Carl: Sailors from the United States to win the Flying Dutchman–class event in the Olympic Games, *5243*

Buchard, Georges: Fencer to win three men's épée titles in the world championships, *2927*

Bucher, Jan: World championships for freestyle skiing, *5451*

Buck, Craig: Volleyball team from the United States to win the men's title in the Olympic Games, *6285*

Budd, Zola: Women's 3000-meter race held at the Olympic Games, *5140*

Buddo, Thomas: Golfer to score under 80 at the Old Course at St. Andrews, Scotland, *3574*

Budge, Don: Tennis player to achieve a Grand Slam, *6098*

Bueno, Maria: U.S. Open women's doubles tennis title, *6127*

Buermeyer, H. E.: National championships in track and field (athletics) in the United States, *6201*

"Buffalo Bill" (William Frederick Cody): Professional rodeo, *4879*

Bugajenkovs, Ivans: Volleyball players to win two consecutive men's gold medals in the Olympic Games, *6282*

Buldakova, Lyudmila: Volleyball players to win two consecutive women's gold medals in the Olympic Games, *6283*

Bulkely, Morgan: National League was organized, *1219*

Bullock, Frank: Prix de l'Arc de Triomphe horse race, *4290*

Bulpetts, W. H.: Skeleton luge (toboggan), *4448*

Burcica, Constanta: Women's lightweight double sculls rowing event held in the Olympic Games, *4961*

Burden, Michelle: College women's basketball player to have 23 assists in a single Division I National Collegiate Athletic Association (NCAA) game, *2307*

Burger, Heinrich: Figure skaters to win the pairs title at the Olympic Games, *2978*

Figure skaters to win the pairs title in the world championships, and the first to win two titles, *2973*

Burke, Billy: Golfer to win a major tournament using steel-shafted golf clubs, *3694*

Burke, James "Deaf": Boxing title fight under the London Prize Ring Rules, *2511*

Burke, Lynn: Women's 4 x 100-meter medley relay swimming event held in the Olympic Games, *5840*

Burke, Miles: Flyweight boxing event in the Olympic Games, *2528*

Burke, Thomas: Event held in the modern Olympic Games, *4605*

Men's 100- and 400-meter running events held in the Olympic Games, *4975*

Burnan, Bill: National Hockey League player to be named outstanding goaltender four times in a row, *4120*

National Hockey League player to be named outstanding goaltender six times, *4124*

Burns, George: Baseball player to lead the National League in bases on balls for three consecutive years, *1452*

Baseball player to lead the National League in runs scored in two consecutive years, *1430*

New York Yankees regular season baseball game played at Yankee Stadium, *1467*

Burns, Lauren: Women's taekwondo events held in the Olympic Games, *4561*

Burns, Tommy: Boxer of African descent to become world heavyweight champion, *2534*

Burroughs, Jeff: Texas Rangers baseball player to be named Most Valuable Player, *1736*

Burton, Michael: Olympic men's 1500-meter freestyle event in which the medalists all had times under 17 minutes, *5871*

Busch, Gundi: Figure skater from Germany to win the women's singles title in the world championships, *3049*

Bush, Carolyn: College women's basketball All-America team, *2110*

Bush, George Herbert Walker: Walker Cup golf match, *3673*

Bushnell, E. W.: Ice skates with steel blades, *2952*

Bussert, Karl-Heinz: Men's quadruple sculls rowing event held in the Olympic Games, *4948*

Butcher, Susan: Sled dog racer to win three consecutive Iditarod races, *5516*

Woman sled dog racer to win the Iditarod sled dog race four times, *5517*

Butkus, Dick: Butkus Award, *3398*

Butler, Brett: Colorado Rockies regular season baseball game played at Coors Field, *1831*

Button, Dick: Figure skater from the United States to win the men's singles title at the world championships, *3033*

Figure skater from the United States to win the men's singles titles in the Olympic Games, *3035*

Figure skater to perform a double axel in competition, *3042*

Figure skater to perform a triple jump in competition, *3047*

Figure skater to perform a triple loop–triple loop combination jump in competition, *3044*

Figure skater to perform the double loop–double loop combination jump in competition, *3038*

Figure skater to perform the flying camel spin, *3030*

Figure skater to win the James E. Sullivan Award, *3039*

Figure skater to win the men's singles U.S., world, and Olympic championships in the same year, and then twice in a row, *3034*

Figure skaters from the United States to sweep the men's singles medals in the world championships, *3045*

Buxton, Angela: African-American tennis player to win a Grand Slam event, *6109*

Byrd, Harry: Philadelphia Athletics baseball player to be named Rookie of the Year, *1591*

Byrd, William, the Younger: Cricket reference in North America, *2633*

Byron, Red: Automobile race sponsored by the National Association for Stock Car Auto Racing (NASCAR), *1070*

National Association for Stock Car Auto Racing (NASCAR) Winston Cup (Grand National) Series, *1073*

C

Cacchi, Paola: World Cross-Country Championships, *5096*

Cada, Josef: Gymnast to win three consecutive men's horizontal bar titles in the world championships, *3920*

Cadine, Ernest: Light heavyweight weightlifting event held in the Olympic Games, *6331*

Caesarius of Heisterbach: Written reference to tennis, *6002*

Caffery, John: Runner to win two consecutive Boston Marathons, *4470*

Cahill, Mabel: Tennis player to win two consecutive mixed doubles titles at the United States national tennis championships, *6034*

Tennis player to win two consecutive women's doubles titles at the United States national championships, *6031*

United States national tennis championships to include mixed doubles competition, *6032*

Cai Jun: World championships for women's weightlifting, *6350*

Calder, Frank: National Hockey League player to be named Rookie of the Year, *4108*

Calhoun, Lee: Hurdler to win two consecutive titles in the men's 110-meter hurdles in the Olympic Games, *4340*

Calkins, Ira: Shooters from the United States to win the military revolver team event in the Olympic Games, *5287*

Calligaris, Novella: Women's 800-meter freestyle swimming event held in the world championships, *5907*

Camacho, A. F. (swimmer): National swimming championships in the United States, *5784*

Camel, Marvin: Boxer to hold the world cruiserweight title, *2577*

Cameron, Bert: Runner to win the men's 400-meter race held in the World Championships in Athletics, *5130*

Camilli, Dolph: Brooklyn Dodgers baseball player to be named Most Valuable Player, *1541*

Caminiti, Ken: San Diego Padres baseball player to be named Most Valuable Player, *1834*

Camp, Walter: African-American college football player named to Walter Camp's All-America team, *3124*

African-American college football running back to be named to Walter Camp's All-America team, *3139*

African-American lineman to be named to Walter Camp's All-America football team, *3143*

All-America college football team named by Walter Camp, *3121*

Line of scrimmage system in American-style football, *3119*

Campanella, Roy: African-American major league baseball players to appear in an All-Star Game, *1574*

Major league baseball catcher to hit 38 home runs, *1600*

Campbell, Charles: 8-meter-class sailing event in the Olympic Games, *5206*

Campbell, Donald: Motorboat (powerboat) racer to go faster than 200 miles per hour, *4568*

Campbell, Earl: Davey O'Brien Award, *3354*

Campbell, Howard: National Award tournament in duck pin bowling, *2492*

Campbell, Milton: African-American decathlete to win the men's title in the Olympic Games, *2743*

Candas, Muharrem: World championships in Greco-Roman wrestling held on a regular basis, *6388*

Canmore, Malcolm: Scottish Highland Gathering, *4364*

Canseco, José: American League player to steal 40 bases and hit 40 home runs in a season, *1797*

Capece, Bill: Minnesota Vikings regular season football game played at the Hubert H. Humphrey Metrodome, *3374*

Carauna, Frank: Bowler to bowl two consecutive 300 games, *2490*

Carew, Mary: Team from the United States to win the women's 4 x 100-meter relay running event in the Olympic Games, *5030*

Carey, Paul: College baseball team to have two consecutive Most Valuable Player Award winners, *1799*

Carlin, Ramon: Whitbread Round-the-World Race, *5232*

Carlos, John: Runner to complete the men's 200-meter race in under 20 seconds, *5088*

Carlton, Steve: Major league baseball pitcher to win four Cy Young Awards, *1762*

Philadelphia Phillies pitcher to win the Cy Young Award, *1724*

Carnell, Arthur: Small-bore rifle (prone) individual shooting event held in the Olympic Games, *5290*

Carner, Joanne Gunderson: Woman golfer to earn more than $2 million in official prize money during her career, *3852*

Woman golfer to earn more than $300,000 in a single season, *3838*

Carney, Bob: Basketball player to score 23 free throws in a Division I National Collegiate Athletic Association (NCAA) game, *1943*

Basketball player to score 55 free throws in a Division I National Collegiate Athletic Association (NCAA) championship series, *1944*

Carpenter, Joseph: Tennis player to win six United States mixed doubles titles, *6059*

Carpenter-Phinney, Connie: Women's road race cycling event held in the Olympic Games, *2708*

Carpentier, Georges: Boxing match to have a $1 million gate, and the first heavyweight bout to be broadcast on radio, *2541*

Carpio, Daniel: Swimmer to swim across the Strait of Gibraltar, *5830*

Carr, Austin: Basketball player to average 52.7 points per game in a Division I National Collegiate Athletic Association (NCAA) championship series, *2067*

Basketball player to score 61 points in a single Division I National Collegiate Athletic Association (NCAA) championship series game, *2069*

Carr, Catherine: Swimmer from the United States to win the women's 100-meter breaststroke in the Olympic Games, *5868*

Carr, Clay: Cowboy to be named All-Around Cowboy twice, *4887*

Carr, Joe: Pro Football Hall of Fame, *3268*

Carr, Sabin: Pole-vaulter to clear 14 feet, *4840*

Carr, William: Men's eight-oared shell with coxswain rowing event held in the Olympic Games, *4925*

Runner to complete the men's 400-meter race in under 47 seconds, *5027*

Team to race the men's 4 x 400-meter relay in under 3:10 minutes, *5031*

Carrasquel, Alejandro: Venezuelan major league baseball player, *1534*

Carrasquel, Alfonso "Chico": Hispanic-American major league baseball player to play in the All-Star Game, *1584*

Carrora, Giuseppe *See* Dundee, Johnny

Carter, Anson: Los Angeles Kings regular season game played in the Staples Center, *4236*

Carter, Butch: Basketball player to score 14 points in an overtime period in the National Basketball Association (NBA), *2205*

Cartmell, Nathaniel: Men's 4 x 400-meter relay track event held in the Olympic Games, *4997*

National team to sweep the top three medals in the men's 100- and 200-meter running events in the Olympic Games, *4990*

Cartwright, Alexander: Baseball team on record, *1184*

Person to introduce baseball as played under Cartwright's Rules to Hawaii, *1189*

Person to take the new sport of baseball west, *1188*

Carvalho Cruz, Joaquim: Runner from South America to win the men's 800-meter title at the Olympic Games, *5139*

Casals, Rosie: Australian Open women's doubles tennis title, *6139*

French Open women's doubles tennis match, *6121*

U.S. Open women's doubles tennis title, *6127*

Wimbledon Open women's doubles tennis title, *6133*

Casanova, Gaby: Women's world championships in curling, *2679*

Case, George: Baseball player to lead the American League in stolen bases for five consecutive years, *1545*

Casey, Kellogg Kennon: Shooters from the United States to win the military rifle team shooting title in the Olympic Games, *5288*

Casey, Phil: International court (four-wall) handball competition, *3999*

Cash, Dave: Montreal Expos regular season baseball game played at Olympic Stadium, *1746*

Caslavska, Vera: Gymnast to win two consecutive women's horse vault titles in the world championships, *3953*

Gymnast to win two consecutive women's side horse vault titles in the Olympic Games, *3954*

Casmir, Gustav: Men's team sabre fencing competition held in the Olympic Games, *2911*

Casparsson, Ernst: Three-day event team equestrian competition held in the Olympic Games, *2849*

Castella, Robert de *See* de Castella, Robert

Castilla, Vinny: Arizona Diamondbacks regular season baseball game played at the Bank One Ballpark, *1850*

Castro, Luis: Colombian major league baseball player, *1344*

Catherine of Aragon, Queen of England: Golf reference on record in England, *3537*

Catherwood, Ethel: Women's high jump event held in the Olympic Games, *4022*

Cator, Silvio: Long-jumper to break the 26-foot barrier, *4432*

Cattiau, Philippe: Fencer to win two consecutive men's épée titles in the world championships, *2924*

Fencer to win two men's team foil titles in the Olympic Games, *2926*

Caulkins, Tracy: Swimmer to hold the women's 200-meter butterfly and both the 200- and 400-meter individual medley world titles at the same time, *5931*

Cauthen, Steve: Jockey to be named *Sports Illustrated* Sportsman of the Year, *4312*

Cawley, Evonne Goolagong *See* Goolagong, Evonne

Cayard, Paul: Sailor from the United States to win the Whitbread Round-the-World Race, *5257*

Cazzeta, Vince: Coach to win the American Basketball Association Coach of the Year Award, *2057*

Cerar, Miroslav: Gymnast to win three consecutive men's side (pommel) horse titles in the world championships, *3956*

Gymnast to win two consecutive men's side (pommel) horse titles in the Olympic Games, *3955*

Cerda, Antonio: Canada Cup golf tournament, *3732*

Cesana, Giorgio: Rowers to win two gold medals in pair-oared shell with coxswain rowing events in the same Olympic Games, *4934*

Chadwick, Florence: Woman to swim the English Channel from England to France, and to swim it in both directions, *5831*

Chadwick, Henry: Baseball box score, *1199*

Chae Ji-hoon: Men's 500-meter short track speed skating event held in the Olympic Winter Games, *5725*

Chalupa, Vaclav: World Sculls Cup series of rowing races, *4956*

Chamberlain, Neville: Snooker game on record, *2445*

Chamberlain, Wilt: Basketball player to average more than 50 points per game in a single season in the National Basketball Association (NBA), *2009*

Basketball player to get 220 rebounds in one set of National Basketball Association (NBA) playoffs, *2027*

Basketball player to get 23,924 career rebounds, and to average 22.9 rebounds per game, in his National Basketball Association (NBA) career, *2091*

Basketball player to get 55 rebounds in a single National Basketball Association (NBA) game, *1998*

Basketball player to get an average of 32 rebounds in a National Basketball Association (NBA) playoff series, *2046*

Basketball player to grab 2,149 rebounds in a single National Basketball Association (NBA) season, *2003*

Basketball player to grab 41 rebounds in a single National Basketball Association (NBA) playoff game, *2049*

Basketball player to have an average field-goal percentage of .727 in a single National Basketball Association (NBA) season, *2093*

Basketball player to lead the National Basketball Association (NBA) in field goal percentage for five successive years, *2063*

Basketball player to lead the National Basketball Association (NBA) in rebounds for 11 seasons, and in field-goal percentage nine times, *2094*

Basketball player to lead the National Basketball Association (NBA) in scoring for seven consecutive years, *2037*

Basketball player to make 113 field goals in one set of National Basketball Association (NBA) playoffs, *2024*

Basketball player to make 18 consecutive field goals in a single National Basketball Association (NBA) game, *2048*

Basketball player to score 100 points in a single National Basketball Association (NBA) game, *2017*

Basketball player to score 50 or more points in 45 games during a single National Basketball Association (NBA) season, *2014*

Basketball player to score 50 or more points in seven consecutive National Basketball Association (NBA) games, *2008*

Basketball player to score 50 points or more in 118 games during his National Basketball Association (NBA) career, *2095*

Basketball player to score 58 points in a single National Basketball Association (NBA) game, *1994*

Basketball player to score more than 2,700 points in his rookie season in the National Basketball Association (NBA), *1990*

Basketball player to score more than 3,000 points in a single National Basketball Association (NBA) season, *2005*

Basketball player to score more than 4,000 points in a single National Basketball Association (NBA) season, *2015*

Philadelphia Warriors player to be named National Basketball Association (NBA) Most Valuable Player of the Year, *1993*

Chambers, Bill: Basketball player to have 51 rebounds during a single Division I National Collegiate Athletic Association (NCAA) game, *1938*

Chambers, Dorothea Douglass: Tennis player to win seven Wimbledon women's singles championships, *6056*

Women's doubles championships at Wimbledon, *6054*

Chambers, John Graham: Queensberry rules for boxing, *2512*

Chambers, Robert: Championship Meeting in golf employing the individual match play format, *3573*

Chance, Britton: 5.5-meter-class sailing event in the Olympic Games, *5218*

Chance, Dean: Los Angeles Angels pitcher to win the Cy Young Award, *1668*

Chancellor, Van: Women's National Basketball Association (WNBA) Coach of the Year, *2388*

Chand, Dhyan: Athletes from Asia, and from India, to win gold medals in the Olympic Games, *4668*

Field hockey players to win three gold medals in the Olympic Games, *4039*

Field hockey players to win two gold medals in the Olympic Games, *4038*

Chandler, Don: Professional football player to kick four field goals in a single Super Bowl game, *3289*

Channing, R. H.: All-America college football team named by Walter Camp, *3121*

Chapman, Raymond: Baseball player to die of injuries suffered during a major league baseball game, *1446*

Chapman, Rex: Basketball player to make nine 3-point field goals in a single National Basketball Association (NBA) playoff game, *2393*

Charles, Ezzard: Heavyweight boxing match to be broadcast nationally on television, *2556*

Charles I, King of England: Confirmation of people's right to play golf and other sports on Sundays, *3540*

Charles II, King of England: Newmarket Town Four Mile Race, *4251*

Rules for horse racing, *4250*

Sailing challenge race on record, *5193*

Chase, Ralph: College football All-America team named by Grantland Rice, *3153*

Chase, Sue: Match between women boxers to be televised live, *2592*

Chechi, Yuri: Gymnast to win three, and then four, men's rings titles in the world championships, *3977*

Cheeseborough, Chandra: Team from the United States to win the women's 4 x 400-meter relay at the Olympic Games, *5142*

Chen Jing: Women's singles table tennis event held in the Olympic Games, *5997*

Chen Longcan: Men's doubles table tennis event held in the Olympic Games, *5994*

Chen Lu: Figure skater from China to win the women's singles title in the world championships, *3109*

Chen Weiqiang: Athletes from China and Taiwan to share the medal platform in the Olympic Games, *4757*

Chen Yueling: Women's 10,000-meter walk held in the Olympic Games, *6296*

Chen Zhong: Women's taekwondo events held in the Olympic Games, *4561*

Cheny, John: Organized record of match race performances, *4253*

Chernyshova, Venera: World Biathlon Championships to include women's competitions, *2436*

Cheryazova, Lina: Athlete from newly independent Uzbekistan to win a gold medal at the Olympic Games, *4785*

Women's aerials freestyle skiing event held at the Olympic Winter Games, *5484*

Chesbro, Jack: Major league baseball player of the 20th century to pitch for more than 40 wins in a single season, *1365*

Major league pitcher to have the best winning record in both the American League and the National League, *1319*

Major league pitcher to pitch 30 consecutive complete games, *1366*

Chevalier, Jeanne: Figure skaters to win the pairs title in the U.S. national championships, *2990*

Chevalier, M.: Motorcycle race on record, *4569*

Chiavacci, Giorgio: Men's foil competition held in the world championships of fencing, *2921*

Chichester, Francis: Single-handed, non-stop, round-the-world sailing race, *5224*

Single-Handed Transatlantic Race (STAR), *5222*

Chilvers, Peter: Sailboard, *5189*

Chin, Tiffany: Asian-American figure skater to win the women's singles title at the U.S. national championships, *3088*

Chizhova, Nadezhda: Shot-putter to break the 20- and 21-meter barriers in the women's event, *5347*

Chochoshvili, Shota: Men's half-heavyweight judo event in the Olympic Games, *4538*

Chow, Amy: Gymnasts from the United States to win the women's team title in the Olympic Games, *3978*

Choynowska-Kiskiewicz, Krystyna: Woman to sail around the world alone, *5237*

Christophel, Bertha: National track and field (athletics) championships for women in the United States, *6207*

Chuasiriporn, Jenny: U.S. Women's Open to be won in a sudden-death playoff, *3892*

Chubina, Maria: Women's 500-meter pairs kayaking event held in the Olympic Games, *2610*

Chukarin, Viktor: Male gymnast to win more than 10 medals in the Olympic Games, *3939*

Chukhray, Serhei: Canoe racer to win three gold medals in a single Olympic Games, *2621*

Chun In-soo: Men's team archery event held in the Olympic Games, *1037*

Chun Lee-kyung: Speed skater to win two consecutive women's 1000-meter short track titles in the Olympic Winter Games, *5732*

Women's short track 1000-meter speed skating event held at the Olympic Winter Games, *5726*

Chung Chan: World championships in taekwondo to include light-middleweight and light-heavyweight classes for men, *4544*

Chung So-young: Badminton events held in the Olympic Games as medal sports, *1174*

Chuzhykov, Mykola: Men's fours 1000-meter kayaking event held in the Olympic Games, *2611*

Cieslarová, Jana: World championships in orienteering to include short events, *4812*

Cla, Mosca: Snowboarding world championships, *5521*

Clancy, King: All-Star National Hockey League Team selected by the Professional Hockey Writers' Association, *4102*

Clapp, R. G.: Intercollegiate wrestling tournament sponsored by the National Collegiate Athletic Association (NCAA), *6381*

Clark, Arlen: Basketball player to shoot 24 consecutive free throws, and to shoot 100 percent in free throws, during a single Division I National Collegiate Athletic Association (NCAA) game, *1987*

Clark, Clarence: Men's doubles competition at the United States national tennis championships, *6012*

Clark, Dutch (Earl): Pro Football Hall of Fame, *3268*

Clark, Elky: Boxer to win both Olympic and professional world championships, *2547*

Clark, Ellery: Men's high jump event held in the Olympic Games, *4019*

Men's long jump event held in the Olympic Games, *4426*

Clark, James: Runner to complete the men's marathon in under 2:55 hours, *4473*

Clark, Jim: Automobile racer to have 25 wins on the Formula One Grand Prix circuit, *1113*

Automobile racer to have seven wins in a single season on the Formula One Grand Prix circuit, *1105*

Automobile racer to win the Indianapolis 500 with an average speed of over 150 miles per hour, *1109*

Mexican Grand Prix automobile race to be part of the Formula One Grand Prix circuit, *1106*

Clark, Joseph: Tennis player to win six consecutive men's doubles titles at the United States national championships, *6021*

United States intercollegiate tennis championships, *6015*

Clark, Stephen: Men's 4 x 100-meter freestyle relay swimming event held in the Olympic Games, *5847*

Clark, Tony: Tampa Bay Devil Rays regular season baseball game played at Tropicana Field, *1851*

Clarke, Fred: Major league baseball player to hit five times in five at-bats during his first major league game, *1313*

Clarke, William: Professional touring cricket team, *2648*

Clatto, Thomas: Death in a golf accident, *3542*

Claudel, Véronique: Women's 4 x 7.5-kilometer biathlon relay competition held in the Olympic Winter Games, *2440*

Clay, Cassius *See* Ali, Muhammad

Clayton, Derek: Runner to race the men's marathon in under 2:12 hours, and the first representing Australia to hold the world record in the event, *4492*

Cleef, George Van *See* Van Cleef, George

Clemens, Roger: Major league baseball pitcher to win five Cy Young Awards, *1848*

Major league baseball player to earn $5 million a year, *1814*

Major league pitcher to pitch 20 strikeouts in a single game, *1789*

Major league pitcher to strike out 19 batters in a single 9-inning game, *1278*

Clemente, Roberto: Hispanic-born major league baseball player to become a member of baseball's Hall of Fame, *1729*

Hispanic-born major league baseball star to appear on a U.S. postage stamp, *1779*

Clercq, Guy de: World championships in water-skiing, *6316*

Clergé (first name unknown): International championships in tennis, *6004*

Clifton, Nat "Sweetwater": African-American basketball player to join the New York Knickerbockers of the National Basketball Association (NBA), *1925*

Cline, Ty: Pittsburgh Pirates regular season baseball game played at Three Rivers Stadium, *1717*

Coachman, Alice: Woman of Black African descent to win a gold medal in the Olympic Games, *4696*

Coakes (later Mould), Marion: Woman equestrian to win an individual jumping medal in the Olympic Games, *2874*

World championships in show jumping to include women riders, *2870*

Coales, Wilfred: Men's 3-mile team race held in the Olympic Games, *4994*

Cobb, Ty: Baseball player to hit more than .400 in two consecutive years in the American League, *1406*

Baseball player to lead the American League in batting average for nine consecutive years, *1420*

Baseball player to lead the American League in hits in three consecutive years, *1382*

Baseball player to lead the American League in runs batted in for three consecutive years, *1383*

Baseball player to lead the American League in runs scored in three consecutive years, *1404*

Cobb, Ty:—*continued*

Baseball player to lead the American League in slugging average for six consecutive years, *1407*

Baseball player to lead the American League in stolen bases for three consecutive years, *1429*

Baseball player to lead the American League in total bases for three consecutive years, *1384*

Major league baseball player of the 20th century to reach 4,000 hits, *1480*

Major league baseball player to have 104 steals in one season, *1662*

Major league baseball player to reach 4,192 career hits, *1783*

Major league baseball player to steal home 50 times in the course of his career, *1485*

Major league baseball players to be named Most Valuable Players of their leagues, *1405*

Major league baseball players to be named to the Baseball Hall of Fame, *1520*

Coberger, Annelise: Athlete from the Southern Hemisphere to win a gold medal in the Olympic Winter Games, *4774*

Cochet, Henri: Tennis player to win four French national men's singles championships after the event became international, *6090*

Tennis player to win three, four, and then five French national men's doubles championships after the event became international, *6089*

Tennis players to win a French national mixed doubles championship after the event became international, *6078*

Tennis players to win the French national men's doubles championship after the event became international, *6079*

Cochran, Jacqueline: Woman to fly in the Bendix Trophy airplane race, *1011*

Cochrane, Blair: 8-meter-class sailing event in the Olympic Games, *5206*

Cochrane, Mickey: Detroit Tigers baseball player to be named Most Valuable Player, *1511*

Cody, William Frederick See "Buffalo Bill" (William Frederick Cody)

Coe, Sebastian: Runner to complete the men's 800-meter race in under 1:43 minutes, *5111*

Runner to complete the men's mile race in under 3:48 minutes, *5121*

Runner to win the Jesse Owens International Award, *5120*

Runner to win two consecutive officially accepted titles in the men's 1500-meters at the Olympic Games, *5141*

Coe, Thomas: Water polo event held in the Olympic Games, *6301*

Cofer, Mike: Professional football player to kick seven points after touchdown in a single Super Bowl game, *3439*

Coffen, LaKiea: Women's national championships in boxing, *2594*

Coffey, Paul: National Hockey League defenseman to have 25 assists in a single set of Stanley Cup playoffs, *4189*

National Hockey League defenseman to score 12 goals in a single set of Stanley Cup playoffs, *4190*

National Hockey League defenseman to score 37 points in a single set of Stanley Cup playoffs, *4191*

National Hockey League defenseman to score 48 goals in a single season, *4193*

Coffin, Edmund: Equestrians from the United States to win the three-day event individual competition, and team competition, in the Olympic Games, *2881*

Coghlan, Eamonn: Runner to win the men's 5000-meter race held in the World Championships in Athletics, *5131*

Cogswell, James K.: Invention of platform tennis, *6196*

Cohen, Fred: Basketball player to have 34 rebounds in a Division I National Collegiate Athletic Association (NCAA) game, *1961*

Colas, Alain: Sailor to complete a solo circumnavigation of the world in under 170 days, *5231*

Colbert, Nate: Major league baseball player to bat in 13 runs in a doubleheader, *1727*

Colella, Lynn: National team to sweep the medals in the women's 200-meter butterfly in the Olympic Games, *5872*

Coleman, Georgia: National team to sweep the top medals in the women's platform diving event in the Olympic Games, *2800*

Coler, Evelyn: Tennis players to win the French national women's doubles championship after the event became international, *6080*

Colledge, Cecilia: Woman figure skater to complete a double jump in competition, *3022*

Collett, Glenna See Vare, Glenna Collett

Collin, Elvire: World figure skating championships for roller skating, *4909*

Colò, Zeno: Men's giant slalom event held in the Alpine skiing world championships, *5390*

Comaneci, Nadia: Gymnast to receive a perfect score of 10 in the Olympic Games, *3960*

Gymnast to win two consecutive titles in the women's balance beam competition in the Olympic Games, *3966*

Compagnoni, Deborah: Skier to win two consecutive titles in the women's giant slalom in the Olympic Winter Games, *5502*

Conacher, Charlie: National Hockey League player to lead the league in scoring twice in a row, *4112*

Condie, George: Amateur golf championship, *3575*

Conley, Michael: Triple-jumper from the United States, and the first African-American, to win the men's event in the Olympic Games, *6260*

Conn, Billy: Heavyweight boxing match to be broadcast on television, and the first at which top-price tickets cost $100, *2554*

Connell, Alex: National Hockey League 0–0 tie, *4084*

National Hockey League goaltender to have six consecutive shutouts, *4095*

National Hockey League goaltender to reach 50 career shutouts, *4097*

Conner, Bart: Gymnasts from the United States to win the men's combined exercises title in the Olympic Games, *3972*

Conner, Dennis: America's Cup won back by the United States, *5247*

Connolly, Harold: Hammer-thrower to break the 70-meter and 230-foot barriers, *3991*

Connolly, James: Athlete, and the first from the United States, to win a gold medal in the modern Olympic Games, *4604*

Men's triple jump event held in the Olympic Games, *6249*

Connolly, Maureen: Woman tennis player to achieve a Grand Slam, *6107*

Connor, George: College football player to be awarded the Outland Trophy, *3201*

Connor, Roger: Grand slam home run in major league baseball, *1256*

Connors, Jimmy: Tennis player to be ranked number one in the Association of Tennis Professionals (ATP) rankings for 160 consecutive weeks, *6165*

Tennis player to win 109 men's singles tournaments during his career, *6187*

Tennis player to win the U.S. Open men's singles title five times, *6171*

Constantin, Agafia Buhaev: Women's 500-meter fours kayaking event held in the Olympic Games, *2623*

Conte, Antonio: Athlete from Italy to win a gold medal in the Olympic Games, *4618*

Masters sabre fencing competition held in the Olympic Games, *2905*

Conzelman, Jimmy: National Football League Coach of the Year, *3211*

Cook, Bill: All-Star National Hockey League Team selected by the Professional Hockey Writers' Association, *4102*

Cook, Myrtle: Women's 4 x 100-meter relay running event held in the Olympic Games, *5023*

Cook, Stephanie: Women's modern pentathlon event held in the Olympic Games, *4835*

Cook, William: World professional championships in billiards, *2444*

Cooke, C. Cecil: Athletes from the Bahamas to win gold medals in the Olympic Games, *4719*

Cooke, Emma: Archery events for women held in the Olympic Games, *1027*

Coolidge, Thornton: Figure skater to win six consecutive women's singles titles, and nine overall, at the U.S. national championships, *3016*

Cooper, Charlotte "Chattie": Mixed doubles tennis event held in the Olympic Games, *6039*

Woman to win a gold medal in the Olympic Games, *4620*

Women's singles tennis event held in the Olympic Games, *6041*

Cooper, Chuck: African-American basketball player to join the Boston Celtics of the National Basketball Association (NBA), *1924*

Cooper, Cynthia: Basketball player to be named Women's National Basketball Association (WNBA) Most Valuable Player twice in a row, *2402*

Basketball team from the United States to win the women's title in a non-boycotted Olympic Games, *2275*

Basketball team to win the Women's National Basketball Association (WNBA) championship twice in a row, *2411*

Women's National Basketball Association (WNBA) All-WNBA First Team, *2387*

Women's National Basketball Association (WNBA) championship, *2396*

Women's National Basketball Association (WNBA) Most Valuable Player, *2390*

Women's National Basketball Association (WNBA) team to win the league championship three times, and in three consecutive years, *2422*

Cooper, Denise: Canoe marathon world championships, *2624*

Cooper, Harry: Golfer to win the Vardon Trophy, *3704*

Cooper, Malcolm: Shooter to win two consecutive titles in the small-bore rifle (three positions) individual event in the Olympic Games, *5323*

Cooper, Michael: Los Angeles Lakers player to be named National Basketball Association (NBA) Defensive Player of the Year, *2245*

Copeland, Lillian: Discus-thrower from the United States to win the women's event in the Olympic Games, *2764*

Corbin, Vern: National Collegiate Athletic Association (NCAA) consensus Division I All-American college basketball team, *1890*

Corcoran, Larry: "Rotating" pitchers in major league baseball, *1248*

Costache, Tamara: Women's 50-meter freestyle swimming event held in the world championships, *5949*

Coste, Emile: National team to sweep the medals in the men's individual foil fencing competition in the Olympic Games, *2900*

Costello, Paul: Rower to win three consecutive medals in the men's double sculls event in the Olympic Games, *4936*

Rowers to win two consecutive medals in the men's double sculls event in the Olympic Games, *4935*

Costie, Candy: Duet synchronized swimming event held in the Olympic Games, *5941*

Coubertin, Pierre de: Flag showing five interlocking rings to symbolize the Olympic Games, *4647*

Olympic Games at which Beethoven's "Ode to Joy" was sung, *4603*

Olympic Games held in France, and outside Greece, *4626*

Proposal to revive the Olympic Games in modern times, *4602*

Couch, Tim: National Collegiate Athletic Association major college football player to complete 400 passes in a single season, *3486*

Court, Margaret Smith: Australian Open women's doubles tennis title, *6139*

Australian Open women's singles tennis title, *6140*

Tennis player of the modern era to win the United States women's singles title five times, *6154*

Tennis player to win 21 women's singles tournaments in a single season, *6144*

Tennis player to win seven consecutive Australian national women's singles championships, and 11 overall, *6114*

U.S. Open women's doubles tennis title, *6127*

Wimbledon Open mixed doubles tennis title, *6131*

Cousy, Bob: Basketball player to have 19 assists in a single half of a National Basketball Association (NBA) game, *1986*

Boston Celtics player to be named National Basketball Association (NBA) Most Valuable Player of the Year, *1969*

Coutts, Russell: America's Cup sailing race won by New Zealand, *5254*

Cova, Alberto: Runner to win the men's 10,000-meter race held in the World Championships in Athletics, *5126*

Covaliov, Serghei: Canoer to win three titles in the men's Canadian pairs 1000-meter event in the Olympic Games, *2622*

Cowan, Hector: All-America college football team named by Walter Camp, *3121*

Cowens, Dave: Basketball player to have a career average of 9.8 defensive rebounds per game in the National Basketball Association (NBA), *2185*

Portland Trail Blazers player to be named National Basketball Association (NBA) Rookie of the Year, *2080*

Cox, Fred: National Football League player to kick at least one field goal in 31 consecutive games, *3310*

Coyne, Thelma *See* Long, Thelma Coyne

Crabbe, Buster (Clarence): Olympic men's 400-meter freestyle event at which all the medalists had times under five minutes, *5823*

Craig, Roger: Professional football player to score 18 points in a single Super Bowl game, *3400*

Cram, Steve: Runner to complete the men's 1500-meter race in under 3:30 minutes, *5144*

Runner to win the men's 1500-meter race held in the World Championships in Athletics, *5127*

Cranston, John: All-America college football team named by Walter Camp, *3121*

Cranz, Christl: Women's Alpine combined event held at the Olympic Winter Games, *5382*

Crapp, Lorraine: Swimmer to race the women's 400-meter freestyle event in under five minutes, *5833*

Cravath, Gavvy: Baseball player to lead the National League in home runs in three consecutive years, *1421*

Crawford, Hasely: Athlete from Trinidad and Tobago to win an Olympic gold medal, *4745*

Runner from the Caribbean to win the men's 100-meter dash at the Olympic Games, *5105*

Crawford, Jack: Tennis player to win three consecutive Australian national men's singles championships, and four overall, *6094*

Crawford, Marjorie: College women's basketball All-America team, *2110*

Creighton, James: Ice hockey game, *4041*

Crenshaw, Ben: Golfer to win three straight individual titles at the U.S. intercollegiate golf championships, *3803*

Cribb, Tom: African-American boxer to fight in a title bout, *2507*

Crichton, Charles: 6-meter-class sailing event held in the Olympic Games, *5205*

Cridlan, May: World outdoor championships in bowls to include women players, *2501*

Crisp, Hope: Mixed doubles championships at Wimbledon, *6053*

Cross, Art: Automobile racer to be named Rookie of the Year in the Indianapolis 500, *1086*

Croteau, Julie: Woman to play on a men's college baseball team, *1800*

Crump, Diane: Woman jockey to race at a pari-mutuel track in the United States, *4305*

Woman jockey to ride in the Kentucky Derby, *4307*

Woman to be licensed as a jockey in the United States, *4304*

Cruz, Julio: Minnesota Twins regular season baseball game played at the Hubert H. Humphrey Metrodome, *1766*

Csermák, József: Hammer-thrower to break the 60-meter barrier, *3987*

Cuddihy, George: National Air Races, *1006*

Cuellar, Mike: Baltimore Orioles pitcher to win the Cy Young Award, *1703*

Cui Aihong: World championships for women's weightlifting, *6350*

Cummings, Candy: Doubleheader in baseball's National League, *1230*

Pitcher in baseball's National League to pitch and win two games on the same day, *1231*

Cummings, Dexter: Golfer to win two straight individual titles at the U.S. intercollegiate golf championships, *3677*

Cummings, Terry: San Diego Clippers player to be named National Basketball Association (NBA) Rookie of the Year, *2190*

Cummock, Arthur: All-America college football team named by Walter Camp, *3121*

Cunningham, Joe: San Francisco Giants regular season baseball game played at Candlestick Park (later 3Com Park), *1643*

Curry, John: Figure skater from Great Britain to win the men's singles title at the Olympic Winter Games, *3077*

Curry, Robert: Light flyweight freestyle wrestling event held in the Olympic Games, *6365*

Curtis, A. H.: Australian national tennis championships, *6045*

Curtis, Ann: Woman to win the Sullivan Award, *1149*

Curtis, Glenn: International airplane races, *1001*

Curtis, Harriot: Curtis Cup golf match, *3695*

Curtis, Isaac: New Orleans Saints regular season football game played at the Louisiana Superdome, *3345*

Curtis, Margaret: Curtis Cup golf match, *3695*

Curtis, Peter: U.S. Open mixed doubles tennis title, *6125*

Curtis, Thomas: Men's 100- and 400-meter running events held in the Olympic Games, *4975*

Men's 110-meter hurdles event held in the Olympic Games, *4322*

Curtis, William B.: National championships in track and field (athletics) in the United States, *6201*

Cushing, Jack: Film of a sporting event, *5743*

Cuthbert, Betty (Elizabeth): Runners to finish first and second in both the women's 100- and 200-meter races in the Olympic Games, *5065*

Women's 400-meter race held in the Olympic Games, *5076*

Cutrone, Angela: Women's 3000-meter short track relay speed skating event held at the Olympic Winter Games, *5715*

Cynisca: Woman recorded as participating in the original Olympic Games, *4600*

D

da Silva, Adhemar Ferreira: Triple-jumper of Black African ancestry to win the men's title in the Olympic Games, *6255*

Triple-jumper to win two consecutive men's titles in the Olympic Games, *6256*

Dafoe, Frances: Figure skaters from Canada to win the pairs title in the world championships, *3050*

Daggett, Timothy: Gymnasts from the United States to win the men's combined exercises title in the Olympic Games, *3972*

Dahlie, Bjorn: Male athlete to win six individual gold medals in the Olympic Winter Games, *4804*

Male skier to win five gold medals in Nordic (cross-country) skiing in the Olympic Winter Games, and the first to win two consecutive men's combined pursuit titles, *5487*

Men's combined pursuit Nordic (cross-country) skiing event held at the Olympic Winter Games, *5476*

Men's pursuit (10 kilometers classical and 15 kilometers freestyle) event held in the world championships of Nordic skiing, *5481*

Skier to win the 30-kilometer Nordic (cross-country) title in the Olympic Winter Games after it was converted from classical style to freestyle, *5485*

Dahlie, Bjorn:—*continued*

Skier to win two consecutive men's 10-kilometer Nordic (cross-country) skiing titles, and the first male athlete to win six gold medals overall, at the Olympic Winter Games, *5499*

Daigle, Sylvie: Women's 3000-meter short track relay speed skating event held at the Olympic Winter Games, *5715*

Dale, Thomas: Written reference to sports in Britain's American colonies, *5738*

d'Alençon, Pierre: Canoe slalom world championships, *2604*

Daler, Jiri: Men's 4000-meter individual pursuit cycling event held in the Olympic Games, *2702*

Dalipagic, Drazen: Basketball team from Yugoslavia to win the men's title in the Olympic Games, *2163*

Dalton, Judy Tegart: Australian Open women's doubles tennis title, *6139*

Wimbledon Open women's singles tennis match, *6134*

Daly, John: Golf course to host the British Open championship 25 times, *3881*

Damiani, Francesco: Superheavyweight boxing event in the Olympic Games, *2582*

Danek, Ludvik: Discus-thrower to break the 210-foot barrier, *2774*

Daniel, Beth: Golfer to win the World Championship of Women's Golf twice in a row, *3836*

Woman golfer to earn more than $600,000 in official prize money in a single season, *3868*

World Championship of Women's Golf, *3829*

Daniel, Ellie: National team to sweep the medals in the women's 200-meter butterfly in the Olympic Games, *5872*

Daniels, Charles: Swimmer to win both the men's 220-yard (later 200-meter) and 440-yard (later 400-meter) freestyle events in a single Olympic Games, *5798*

Swimmer to win two consecutive men's 100-meter freestyle titles in the Olympic Games, *5802*

Daniels, Mel: Basketball player to win the American Basketball Association Rookie of the Year Award, *2056*

Danielsen, Egil: Javelin-thrower to break the 280-foot barrier and to hold the world record in the men's event, *4397*

Danner, Christian: European Formula 3000 automobile racing circuit, *1131*

D'Arcy, Victor: Men's 4 x 100-meter relay track event held in the Olympic Games, *5003*

Dark, Alvin: Boston Braves baseball player to be named Rookie of the Year, *1566*

d'Arlandes, Marquis: People to fly in a balloon, *1176*

Darnyi, Tamás: Swimmer to win two consecutive men's 200-meter individual medley titles at the world championships, *5959*

Swimmer to win two consecutive men's 200-meter individual medley titles in the Olympic Games, *5967*

Swimmer to win two consecutive men's 400-meter individual medley titles in the Olympic Games, *5962*

Davenport, Willie: African-American athletes to compete in the Olympic Winter Games, *4747*

Davidson, Bruce: Equestrians from the United States to win the three-day event individual competition, and team competition, in the Olympic Games, *2881*

Davidson, Owen: French Open mixed doubles tennis match, *6119*

Davies, Christopher: Sailor to win two consecutive gold medals in the Flying Dutchman–class event in the Olympic Games, *5228*

Davis, Alvin: Seattle Mariners baseball player to be named Rookie of the Year, *1776*

Davis, Dale: Basketball player to have a field goal percentage of .783 in a single set of National Basketball Association (NBA) playoffs, *2404*

Davis, Ernest: African-American college football player to win the Heisman Trophy, *3257*

Davis, George: Major league baseball player to hit a triple and a home run in the same inning, *1310*

Davis, Glenn: Hurdler to race the men's 400-meter hurdles in under 50 seconds, *4337*

Hurdler to win two consecutive titles in the men's 400-meter hurdles in the Olympic Games, *4339*

Davis, Harry: American League player to hit for the cycle (single, double, triple, and home run) in a single game, *1342*

Baseball player to lead the American League in home runs in four consecutive years, *1374*

Davis, Jason: National Collegiate Athletic Association major college football player to gain 347 yards in a single quarter, *3461*

Davis, Joe: World professional championships in snooker, *2453*

Davis, John: Weightlifter to win two consecutive titles in the unlimited weight (super heavyweight) competition in the Olympic Games, *6339*

Davis, Otis: Runners to complete the men's 400-meter race in under 45 seconds, *5072*

Davis, Steve: World matchplay championships in snooker, *2463*

Davis, Terrell: Denver Broncos win in professional football's Super Bowl, *3496*

Davison, Anne: Woman to sail across the Atlantic alone, *5220*

Dawes, Dominique: Gymnasts from the United States to win the women's team title in the Olympic Games, *3978*

Dawson, Len: Kansas City Chiefs win in professional football's Super Bowl, *3306*

Day, Boots: Philadelphia Phillies regular season baseball game played at Veterans Stadium, *1721*

Day, Hap: National Hockey League team to win the Stanley Cup three times in a row, *4123*

Dayne, Ron: National Collegiate Athletic Association (NCAA) major college football player to rush for 6,397 college career yards, *3503*

de Barbarin, Roger *See* Barbarin, Roger de

de Bary, Jacob Erckrath *See* Bary, Jacob Erckrath de

de Brébeuf, Jean *See* Brébeuf, Jean de

de Castella, Robert: Boston Marathon to offer prize money, *4515*

Runner to win the men's marathon in the World Championships in Athletics, *4508*

de Clercq, Guy *See* Clercq, Guy de

de Coubertin, Pierre *See* Coubertin, Pierre de

de Dion de Malfiance, Count Jules Felix Philippe Albert *See* Dion de Malfiance, Count Jules Felix Philippe Albert de

de Filippis, Maria Teresa *See* Filippis, Maria Teresa de

de Hase, François *See* Hase, François de

de Jaeghere, G. *See* Jaeghere, G. de

de Jong, Adrianus *See* Jong, Adrianus de

de Jongh, Margaretha *See* Jongh, Margaretha de

de Kersauson, Olivier *See* Kersauson, Olivier de

de la Falaise, Georges *See* Falaise, Georges de la

De La Hoya, Oscar: Mexican-American boxer to win the lightweight title in the Olympic Games, *2589*

de la Hunty, Shirley Strickland: Hurdler to win two consecutive titles in the women's 80-meter hurdles in the Olympic Games, *4338*

Woman athlete to win seven track and field medals in the Olympic Games, *6214*

de Lunden, Léon *See* Lunden, Léon de

de Oliveira, João Carlos *See* Oliveira, João Carlos de

de Seminario, Gladys *See* Seminario, Gladys de

de Stadelhofen, Marcel Meyer *See* Stadelhofen, Marcel Meyer de

De Varona, Donna: Women's 400-meter individual medley swimming event held in the Olympic Games, *5849*

de Vendeville, Charles *See* Vendeville, Charles de

de Vicenzo, Roberto: Canada Cup golf tournament, *3732*

U.S. Senior Open golf tournament, *3833*

Deakin, Joseph: Men's 3-mile team race held in the Olympic Games, *4994*

Dean, Christopher: Figure skaters from the Soviet Union to win the ice dancing title in the world championships, *3066*

Figure skaters to win unanimous top scores for artistic impression, and the first from Great Britain to win the ice dancing title, at the Olympic Winter Games, *3087*

Debaecke, Harry: Men's eight-oared shell with coxswain rowing event held in the Olympic Games, *4925*

Debray, Louis: Moving target individual shooting event held in the Olympic Games, *5277*

DeBusschere, Dave: All–National Basketball Association (NBA) Rookie Team, *2019*

Decker, Mary *See* Slaney, Mary Decker

Deckert, Merv: World four-wall handball championships, *4010*

Decugis, Marie: Tennis player to win three gold medals in tennis in the same Olympic Games, *6048*

Decugis, Max: Tennis player to win three gold medals in tennis in the same Olympic Games, *6048*

Dedeaux, Rod: College baseball coach to win 10 National Collegiate World Championships, *1748*

Dekanova, Vlasta: Gymnast to win two consecutive women's all-around titles in the world championships, *3931*

World championships in gymnastics to award women's titles in specific events, *3932*

World championships in gymnastics to include women, *3930*

Delaney, Tim: National Collegiate Athletic Association major college football player to score six touchdowns on pass receptions in a single game, *3297*

Delany, Kevin: Snowboarding world championships, *5521*

Delfs, Flemming: World championships in badminton, *1171*

Dellsperger, Urs: World championships in long-distance duathlon, *2836*

Delour, Gustave: Tour of Spain (Vuelta a España) cycling race, *2697*

DeMar, Clarence: Runner to win seven Boston Marathons, *4479*

Runner to win three consecutive Boston Marathons, *4476*

Demaret, Jimmy: Golfer to win the Masters three times, *3728*

National golf team to win five consecutive Canada Cup tournaments, *3776*

Demers, Jacques: National Hockey League coach to be named Coach of the Year twice in a row, *4197*

Demmy, Laurence: Figure skaters to win the ice dancing title in the world championships, and the first to win it two, three, and four times, *3046*

DeMont, Rick: Men's 400-meter freestyle event held at the world championships, *5887*

Dempsey, Jack (the Nonpareil): Boxer to be world middleweight champion, *2516*

Boxing match to have a $1 million gate, and the first heavyweight bout to be broadcast on radio, *2541*

Dempsey, Jack (William Harrison): Boxing match to have a $1 million gate, and the first heavyweight bout to be broadcast on radio, *2541*

Dempsey, Tom: National Football League player to kick a 63-yard field goal, *3309*

Deng Yaping: Table tennis player to win both singles and doubles titles in the Olympic Games, *6000*

Women's singles event to be included in the world cup in table tennis, *6001*

Dennistoun, Alexander: Golf club in Canada, *3587*

Densimo, Belayneh: Runner to race the men's marathon in under 2:7 hours, *4517*

Dent, Jim: Women to be caddies at the U.S. Open golf tournament, *3831*

Dent, Richard: Chicago Bears win in professional football's Super Bowl, *3405*

DePaolo, Peter: Automobile racer to win the Indianapolis 500 with an average speed of more than 100 miles per hour, *1060*

Derbyshire, John: Water polo event held in the Olympic Games, *6301*

Desch, August: National collegiate track and field (athletics) championships sponsored by the National Collegiate Athletic Association (NCAA), *6206*

Desmarteau, Étienne: Men's 56-pound weight throw event held in the Olympic Games, *6323*

Desmond, Tracy: Women's amateur boxing match sponsored by USA Boxing, *2590*

Detmer, Ty: College football player to gain 594 all-purpose yards in a major bowl game, *3433*

National Collegiate Athletic Association major college football player to gain 15,397 college career yards, *3447*

National Collegiate Athletic Association major college football player to gain more than 400 yards per game in five consecutive games, *3438*

National Collegiate Athletic Association major college football player to gain more than 4,000 yards per season three times, *3448*

Deutgen, Hans: Archer to win two, three, and four men's individual world championships, *1032*

Devers, Gail: Runner from the United States to win the women's 100-meter dash in the World Championships in Athletics, *5164*

Devine, Cindy: World championships in mountain biking, *2716*

Devoy, Susan: Squash player to win five women's singles world open titles, *5767*

Dewar, Thomas R.: National Challenge Cup for soccer (international football), *5549*

Dewey, Katherine: Woman bobsledder to win the U.S. national bobsled championship, *2473*

deWit, William: Heavyweight boxing event with a limited weight held in the Olympic Games, *2581*

d'Hugues, Pierre *See* Hugues, Pierre d'

Di Pietro, Joseph: Bantamweight weightlifting event held in the Olympic Games, *6334*

Diaz, Manuel: Men's team foil fencing competition held in the Olympic Games, *2906*

Diba, Vasile: Men's singles 500-meter kayak event held in the Olympic Games, *2619*

Dibiasi, Carlo: Diver to win three consecutive men's platform diving titles in the Olympic Games, *2811*

Dibiasi, Klaus: Diver to win three consecutive men's platform diving titles in the Olympic Games, *2811*

Diver to win two consecutive men's highboard platform diving titles at the world championships, *2810*

Men's highboard platform diving event held at the world championships, *2805*

Dick, Willi: Men's ski jumping (normal hill) event held in the world championships of Nordic skiing, *5373*

Dickerson, Eric: National Football League player to rush for 2,105 yards in a single season, *3391*

Dickey, Curtis: Indianapolis Colts regular season football game played at the RCA Dome, *3395*

Dickey, Derrek: Basketball player to have a .739 field goal percentage in a National Basketball Association (NBA) Finals series, *2108*

Dickinson, Gardner: Legends of Golf tournament, *3817*

Senior Professional Golfers' Association (PGA) Tour, *3830*

Dickson, John: License for producing golf balls, *3544*

Didrikson, Babe (Mildred) *See* Zaharias, Babe Didrikson

Diehl, Carl: College football All-America team named by Grantland Rice, *3153*

Dietz, George: Men's four-oared shell without coxswain rowing event held in the Olympic Games, *4930*

Dietz, John: Shooters from the United States to win the military revolver team event in the Olympic Games, *5287*

Dijkstra, Sjoukje: Figure skater from the Netherlands to win the women's singles title at the Olympic Winter Games, *3065*

Figure skater from the Netherlands to win the women's singles title in the world championships, *3059*

Dillard, Harrison: African-American hurdler to win the men's 110-meter titles in the Olympic Games, *4336*

Dilley, Gary: National team to sweep the medals in the men's 200-meter backstroke event in the Olympic Games, *5846*

DiMaggio, Joe: Major league baseball player to hit safely in 56 consecutive games, *1542*

Ding Meiyuan: Women's weightlifting events held in the Olympic Games, *6353*

Dinnehy, Helen: National track and field (athletics) championships for women in the United States, *6207*

Dion de Malfiance, Count Jules Felix Philippe Albert de: Automobile race on record in Europe, *1042*

Dischinger, Terry: All–National Basketball Association (NBA) Rookie Team, *2019*

Dittmar, Heini: World championships in gliding (soaring), *3531*

Dityatin, Aleksandr: Athlete to win eight medals in a single Olympic Games, *3967*

Male gymnast to receive a perfect score of 10 in the Olympic Games, *3964*

Dixon, George: Boxer of African descent to win a national boxing title, *2519*

Boxer of African descent to win a United States boxing title, and probably the first athlete of African descent to hold a U.S. title in any sport, *2521*

Boxer of African descent to win a world boxing title, *2523*

Dmitriev, Artur: Male figure skater to win the pairs title at the Olympic Winter Games with two different partners, *3115*

Dmitriev, Roman: Wrestler to win the light flyweight freestyle competition in the Olympic Games when it resumed in 1972, *6398*

Dobbs, Glenn: Football player to be named Most Valuable Player of the All America Football Conference (AAFC), *3202*

Doby, Larry: African-American baseball player in the American League, *1560*

African-American major league baseball players to appear in an All-Star Game, *1574*

Docter, Sarah: World championships in short track speed skating, *5694*

Dod, Lottie (Charlotte): Tennis player to win three consecutive Wimbledon women's singles championships, and five overall, *6033*

Doe, Charles: Rugby players to win two Olympic gold medals in rugby, *4968*

Doggett, Thomas: Modern rowing competition on record, *4911*

Dogu, Yasar: World championships in freestyle wrestling, *6389*

Doherty, Laurie (Hugh): National team to sweep the medals in the men's singles tennis event in the Olympic Games, *6040*

Tennis player to win two men's doubles titles in the Olympic Games, *6042*

Tennis players to win eight Wimbledon men's doubles championships, *6047*

Doherty, Reginald: Mixed doubles tennis event held in the Olympic Games, *6039*

National team to sweep the medals in the men's singles tennis event in the Olympic Games, *6040*

Tennis player to win two men's doubles titles in the Olympic Games, *6042*

Tennis players to win eight Wimbledon men's doubles championships, *6047*

Dolore, Terry: World championships in hang gliding, *3533*

Domenichelli, Giuseppe: Gymnasts to win two consecutive gold medals in the men's team combined exercises in the Olympic Games, *3922*

Donlin, Mike: American League player to have 6 hits in a 9-inning baseball game, *1341*

Donohue, Mark: Automobile racer to win the Indianapolis 500 with an average speed of more than 160 miles per hour, *1117*

Donovan, Ann: College women's basketball player to receive the Naismith Award, *2189*

Donth, Frantisek: Men's 50-kilometer cross-country event held in the world championships of Nordic skiing, *5372*

Doolittle, Jimmy: Bendix Trophy airplane race, *1009*

Dorais, Gus: Use of the forward pass in American-style football, *3135*

Dorfner, Alfons: Men's pairs 1000-meter kayaking event held in the Olympic Games, *2598*

Dorgan, Mike: Catcher's mask used in a National League game, *1237*

d'Oriola, Christian: Fencer to win three, and then four, men's foil titles in the world championships, *2932*

Fencer to win two consecutive men's individual foil titles in the Olympic Games, *2933*

Dörre, Katrin: World Cup Marathon, *4514*

Dorsett, Tony: National Football League player to rush for 99 yards from the line of scrimmage, *3382*

Doubleday, Abner: Baseball team on record, *1184*

Dougherty, Charles: African-American All-Star Team in professional baseball, *1402*

Dougherty, Patsy: Baseball player to lead the American League in runs scored in two consecutive years, *1360*

Douglas, Buster (James): Boxer to hold the undisputed world heavyweight title after 1980, *2586*

Douglas, Findlay S.: Golfer born in the United States to win a U.S. national championship, *3627*

Douglass (later Chambers), Dorothea: Tennis player to win seven Wimbledon women's singles championships, *6056*

Douiounova, Vera Galushka: Volleyball players to win two consecutive women's gold medals in the Olympic Games, *6283*

Doyle, Gladys: World outdoor championships in bowls to include women players, *2501*

Dragila, Stacy: Women's pole vault event held in the Olympic Games, *4852*

Dragneva, Izabela: Women's weightlifting events held in the Olympic Games, *6353*

Drake, Jim: Sailboard, *5189*

Draper, Foy: Team to race the men's 4 x 100-meter relay in under 40 seconds, *5042*

Draves, Victoria: Diver to win both the women's springboard and platform diving titles in the same Olympic Games, *2802*

Drechsler, Heike Daute: Long-jumper from the United States to set or equal the world record in the women's event, *4441*

Dropo, Walt: Boston Red Sox baseball player to be named Rookie of the Year, *1575*

Dryke, Matthew: Shooter from the United States to win the individual skeet-shooting title in the Olympic Games, *5321*

Drysdale, Don: Major league pitcher to pitch 54 consecutive scoreless innings, *1702*

Major league pitcher to pitch six successive shutouts, *1701*

du Bief, Jacqueline: Figure skater from France to win the women's singles title in the world championships, *3043*

Dubey, August: World championships in carriage driving, *2878*

Duchesnay, Isabelle: Figure skaters for France to win the ice dancing title in the world championships, *3096*

Duchesnay, Paul: Figure skaters for France to win the ice dancing title in the world championships, *3096*

Duffy, Hugh: Major league baseball player to hit .440 in a single season, *1311*

Duffy, Paddy: Boxer to be undisputed world welterweight champion, *2522*

Duhamel, René: World championships in rowing, *4940*

Dukes, Walt: Basketball player to have 734 rebounds during a single Division I National Collegiate Athletic Association (NCAA) season, *1936*

Duller, George: Champion Hurdle horse race, *4293*

Dumas, Charles: High-jumper to clear seven feet, *4025*

Dumas, Vito: Sailor to complete a solo circumnavigation of the world in under a year, *5213*

Dumbadze, Nina: Discus-thrower to break the 50-meter and 160-, 170-, and 180-foot barriers in the women's event, *2768*

Duncan, Frank: African-American All-Star Team in professional baseball, *1402*

Duncan, George: British Open golf championship to be administered by the Royal and Ancient Golf Club of St. Andrews, *3664*

Duncan, James: Discus-thrower to hold the officially accepted world record in the men's event, *2760*

Dundee, Johnny: Boxer to hold the super-featherweight (junior lightweight) title, *2542*

Boxing match to be broadcast on radio, *2540*

Dunkle, Nancy: College women's basketball All-America team, *2110*

Dupont, Helen: Woman to compete in the three-day event individual equestrian competition in the Olympic Games, *2868*

duPont, Margaret Osborne: Tennis player to win 10 consecutive women's doubles titles at the United States national championships, and 13 overall, *6106*

Tennis player to win four consecutive United States mixed doubles national championships, and nine overall, *6105*

duPont, Mrs. R. C.: Horse to be named Horse of the Year three, four, and five times consecutively, *4303*

Durack, Fanny (Sarah): Swimmer to race the women's 100-meter freestyle in under 1:20 minutes, *5804*

Women's 100-meter freestyle swimming event held in the Olympic Games, *5805*

Women's 4 x 100-meter freestyle relay swimming event in the Olympic Games, *5808*

Durr, Francoise: French Open mixed doubles tennis match, *6119*

French Open women's doubles tennis match, *6121*

Wimbledon Open women's doubles tennis title, *6133*

Duval, Bob: Father and son to win golf tournaments on the same day, *3896*

Duval, David: Father and son to win golf tournaments on the same day, *3896*

Golf event to be broadcast live on network television in prime time, *3898*

Golfer to win more than $2.5 million in official prize money in a single season, *3889*

Golfer to win more than $7 million in official prize money in a single season, *3894*

Duvall, Sammy: Water-skier to win three, and then four, consecutive men's overall titles at the world championships, *6321*

Dvorak, Charles: National team to sweep the top spots in the men's pole vault in the Olympic Games, *4838*

Dwight, James: Tennis player to win six consecutive men's doubles titles at the United States national championships, *6021*

Tennis tournament on record in the United States, *6007*

Dyrdyra, Vitaly: Sailor to win gold medals in three different sailing events in the Olympic Games, *5239*

Tempest-class sailing event in the Olympic Games, *5230*

E

Eagan, Edward: Athlete to win gold medals in both the Summer and Winter Olympics, *4674*

Bobsledders to win two straight titles in the four-man bobsled at the Olympic Winter Games, *2472*

Light heavyweight boxing event held in the Olympic Games, *2538*

Eagan, James: Lightweight boxing event held in the Olympic Games, *2530*

Earlham, Joe: World amateur championships in billiards, *2452*

Earnhardt, Dale: Automobile racer to win more than $2 million, and then $3 million, in a single season in the National Association for Stock Car Auto Racing (NASCAR) Winston Cup series, *1135*

East, Henry: Whitbread Gold Cup horse race, *4302*

Easte, Philip: Trap (clay pigeon) team shooting event in the Olympic Games, *5292*

Eastman, Albert: Shooters from the United States to win the military rifle team shooting title in the Olympic Games, *5288*

Eastman, Ben: Runner to complete the men's 400-meter race in under 47 seconds, *5027*

Eaton, Mark: Basketball player to have 456 blocked shots, and an average of 5.56 blocked shots, in a single National Basketball Association (NBA) season, *2210*

Basketball player to have ten blocked shots in a single National Basketball Association (NBA) playoff game, *2224*

Utah Jazz player to be named National Basketball Association (NBA) Defensive Player of the Year, *2221*

Ebbesen, Eskild: Men's lightweight four-oared shells without coxswain rowing event held in the Olympic Games, *4960*

Eby, Earl: National collegiate track and field (athletics) championships sponsored by the National Collegiate Athletic Association (NCAA), *6206*

Eckersley, Dennis: Major league baseball pitcher to pitch 1,071 games during his career, *1847*

Eckert, Bärbel *See* Wöckel, Bärbel Eckert

Eden, Jaap: Speed skater to be world champion in men's long-distance speed skating twice, and then three times, in a row, *5635*

Speed skater to skate the 10,000 meters in under 18 minutes, *5636*

Speed skater to skate the 5000 meters in under 9 minutes, *5634*

World championship in speed skating, *5630*

Ederle, Gertrude: Woman to swim the English Channel, *5820*

Edge, S. F.: International motorboat (powerboat) race, *4563*

Edison, Thomas: Film of a sporting event, *5743*

Edmiston, Bart: National Collegiate Athletic Association major college football player to kick 71 consecutive points after touchdown in a single season, *3464*

Edward II, King of England: Written reference to football, *5528*

Edwards, Billy: Grand Circuit series of harness horse races, *4277*

Edwards, Jonathan: Triple-jumper to break the 18-meter and 60-foot barriers, *6264*

Edwards, Michelle: College women's basketball United States Basketball Writers Association All-American first team, *2271*

Edwards, Teresa: Basketball player to win three, and then four, gold medals in the Olympic Games, *2380*

Edwards, Teresa:—*continued*

Basketball team from the United States to win the women's title in a non-boycotted Olympic Games, *2275*

Basketball team from the United States to win the women's title in the Olympic Games, *2208*

Edwards, Troy: National Collegiate Athletic Association major college football player to gain 1,996 yards receiving in a single season, *3487*

National Collegiate Athletic Association major college football player to gain 405 yards receiving in a single game, *3497*

Egan, Walter E.: Golfer to win three men's U.S. Amateur titles, *3636*

Egerszegi, Krisztina: Swimmer to win five individual gold medals, and three consecutive medals in the women's 200-meter backstroke, in the Olympic Games, *5972*

Swimmer to win two consecutive gold medals in the women's 200-meter backstroke in the Olympic Games, *5966*

Ehrler, Jim: College baseball player to pitch a no-hitter, *1580*

Eiben, Reinhard: Men's kayak slalom whitewater canoeing events held in the Olympic Games, *2615*

Eilers, Ludovika *See* Jakobsson, Ludovika Eilers

Eisel, Mary Ann: U.S. Open mixed doubles tennis title, *6125*

Eisenhower, Dwight D.: Use of the double-wing formation in football, *3138*

Eiterer, Othmar: Canoe slalom world championships, *2604*

El Guerrouj, Hicham: Runner to race the men's 1500 meters in 3:26 minutes, *5186*

Runner to race the men's mile race in under 3:44.00 minutes, *5154*

El Moutawakel, Nawal: Athlete from Morocco to win a gold medal at the Olympic Games, and the first female athlete from an Islamic country to win an Olympic medal, *4758*

Women's 400-meter hurdles event held in the Olympic Games, *4350*

Elder, Lee: African-American golfer to play in the Masters tournament, *3808*

African-American golfer to play in the South African Professional Golfers' Association (PGA) Open, *3791*

African-American golfer to represent the United States in the Ryder Cup tournament, *3824*

Elek, Ilona: Fencer to win two consecutive women's foil titles in the world championships, *2928*

Fencer to win two consecutive women's individual foil titles in the Olympic Games, *2929*

Elkington, Steve: Golfer to win the Professional Golfers' Association (PGA) Championship in under 270, *3877*

Elliot, Launceston: Athlete from Great Britain to win a gold medal in the Olympic Games, *4610*

Unlimited weight weightlifting events held in the Olympic Games, *6325*

Elliott, Bob: Boston Braves baseball player to be named Most Valuable Player, *1553*

Elliott, Herb: Runner to complete the men's mile race in under 3:55 minutes, *5068*

Elliott, Sam: Softball Hall of Fame opened, *5588*

Elm, George Von *See* Von Elm, George

Elphinstone, Alexander: Golf match reported in a newspaper, *3547*

Els, Ernie: Golfer to win the U.S. Open in a sudden-death playoff, *3878*

Elvström, Paul: Athlete to compete in eight Olympic Games, *4733*

Sailor to win the men's Finn-class event two, three, and four times in the Olympic Games, *5219*

Embry, Wayne: African-American to become the general manager of a team in a major professional sport, *2081*

Emerson, Roy: Australian Open men's doubles tennis title, *6136*

French Open men's doubles tennis match, *6117*

Tennis player to win five consecutive Australian national men's singles championships, and six overall, *6116*

Tennis player to win six consecutive French national men's doubles championships after the event became international, *6113*

Emmahausan, Jens: Skiing manual, *5353*

Emmerich, Max: Men's triathlon event held in the Olympic Games, *6234*

Ender, Kornelia: Swimmer to hold both the women's 100-meter freestyle and 100-meter butterfly world titles at the same time, *5890*

Swimmer to win two consecutive women's 100-meter butterfly world titles, *5918*

Swimmer to win two consecutive women's 100-meter freestyle world titles, *5919*

Woman swimmer to win four gold medals at a single Olympic Games, *5927*

Women's 100-meter butterfly event held in the world championships, *5896*

Women's 100-meter freestyle swimming event held in the world championships, *5897*

Enderlein, Ortrun: Women's singles luge (toboggan) event held in the Olympic Winter Games, *4457*

Engan, Toralf: Skier to win both the men's individual 70- and 90-meter ski jumps in the same Olympic Winter Games, *5414*

Engelhard, Ruth: Hurdler to hold the officially accepted world record in the women's 80-meter event, *4333*

Engelmann, Edward: Open-air rink featuring artificial ice, *2981*

Engelmann, Helene: Figure skaters from Austria to win the pairs title at the Olympic Winter Games, *3002*
Figure skaters from Austria to win the pairs title in the world championships, *2986*

Engle, Dave: Minnesota Twins regular season baseball game played at the Hubert H. Humphrey Metrodome, *1766*

Engram, Bobb: Fred Biletnikoff Receiver Award, *3459*

Enke, Karin *See* Kania, Karin Enke

Ereng, Paul: Runner from Africa to win the men's 800-meter title at the Olympic Games, *5151*

Erickson, Charles: Welterweight freestyle wrestling event held in the Olympic Games, *6368*

Eriksen, Ivar: Speed skater to skate the 1000 meters in under 1:20 minutes, *5681*

Eriksen, Stein: Men's giant slalom event held at the Olympic Winter Games, *5394*

Erkan, Yasar: Athlete from Turkey to win a gold medal in the Olympic Games, *4685*

Erker, August: Men's four-oared shell without coxswain rowing event held in the Olympic Games, *4930*

Erne, Frank: African-American boxer born in the United States to win a world boxing title, *2524*

Ert, Sandra Van *See* Van Ert, Sandra

Ervin, Anthony: Male swimmers to win gold medals in the same event at the same Olympic Games, *5979*

Erving, Julius: Basketball player to win the American Basketball Association Most Valuable Player Award, *2121*

Erxleben, Russell: National Collegiate Athletic Association major college football player to kick a 67-yard field goal, *3356*

Escalera, Nino: African-American baseball player to play for the Cincinnati Reds, *1608*

Espinoza, Laura: National Collegiate Athletic Association (NCAA) Division I women's softball player to hit 37 home runs in a single season, *5624*

Esposito, Phil: National Hockey League player to score 100 points in a single season, *4152*

Esser, Roswitha: Canoe racers to win two consecutive women's 500-meter kayak pairs event in the Olympic Games, *2613*

Evans, Chick (Charles, Jr.): Golfer to win both the U.S. Amateur and U.S. Open championships in the same year, and to win the U.S. Open in under 290 for 72 holes, *3659*

Evans, Dwight: Major league baseball player to hit a home run on the season's first pitch, *1788*

Evans, Janet: Swimmer to win two consecutive women's 800-meter freestyle titles in the Olympic Games, *5965*
Swimmer to win two consecutive women's 800-meter freestyle world titles, *5971*

Evans, Lee: Runner to complete the men's 400-meter race in under 44 seconds, *5090*

Evensen, Bernt: Athlete to win five individual gold medals, and seven medals overall, in the Olympic Winter Games, *4665*

Everett, Thomas: Jim Thorpe Award, *3401*

Evert, Chris: Tennis player to be ranked number one in the Women's Tennis Association (WTA) rankings, *6161*
Tennis player to win the French Open women's singles title seven times, *6174*
Tennis player to win the U.S. Open women's singles title four consecutive times, *6166*
Tennis player to win the Women's Tennis Association (WTA) championship four times, *6164*
Women's Tennis Association (WTA) championships, *6156*

Ewing, Patrick: National Basketball Association (NBA) draft lottery, *2203*

Ewry, Raymond: Athlete to win 10 gold medals in the Olympic Games, *4633*
Men's standing high jump event held in the Olympic Games, *4020*
Men's standing long jump event held in the Olympic Games, *4427*
Men's standing triple jump event held in the Olympic Games, *6250*

Exley, John: Men's eight-oared shell with coxswain rowing event held in the Olympic Games, *4925*
Rowers to win two consecutive gold medals in the men's eight-oared shell with coxswain competition in the Olympic Games, *4933*

Eyser, George: Gymnast with a wooden leg to win a medal in the Olympic Games, *3912*
National team to sweep the top honors in the men's horizontal bar, long horse vault, side (pommel) horse, and rings gymnastics competitions in the Olympic Games, *3913*

F

Fabyan, Sarah Palfrey: Tennis player to win 10 consecutive women's doubles titles at the United States national championships, and 13 overall, *6106*

United States national women's and men's singles tennis championships to both be played at the West Side Tennis Club stadium, *6095*

Fadzayev, Arsen: Wrestler to win two consecutive lightweight freestyle wrestling titles in the Olympic Games, *6411*

Faggs, Mae: African-American women to win gold medals in a track relay event in the Olympic Games, *5058*

Fagioli, Luigi: French Grand Prix automobile race to be part of the Formula One Grand Prix circuit, *1082*

Fairhall, Neroli: Athlete who was paraplegic to compete in the Olympic Games, *4753*

Fairley, Tony: Basketball player to have 22 assists during a single Division I National Collegiate Athletic Association (NCAA) game, *2258*

Falaise, Georges de la: Fencer to win both the men's individual sabre and épée titles in the Olympic Games, *2912*

Fencer to win men's individual and team épée titles in the same Olympic Games, *2908*

Men's team épée fencing competition held in the Olympic Games, *2910*

Falck, Hildegard: Runner to race the women's 800 meters in under 2:00 minutes, *5093*

Famose, Annie: World cup series of competitions in Alpine skiing, *5416*

Fangio, Juan Manuel: Automobile racer to be world champion on the Formula One Grand Prix circuit two, three, four, and five times; the first to win the title three and four times consecutively; and the first from Argentina to be world champion, *1092*

Automobile racer to have more than 20 wins on the Formula One Grand Prix circuit, *1096*

Automobile racer to win two, three, and four Argentine Grand Prix races, *1095*

Belgian Grand Prix automobile race to be part of the Formula One Grand Prix circuit, *1081*

French Grand Prix automobile race to be part of the Formula One Grand Prix circuit, *1082*

Monaco Grand Prix automobile race to be part of the Formula One Grand Prix circuit, *1078*

Spanish Grand Prix automobile race to be part of the Formula One Grand Prix circuit, *1085*

Farber, Bea: International Women's Driving Tournament, *4313*

Farina, Nino (Giuseppe): British Grand Prix automobile race to be part of the Formula One Grand Prix circuit, *1077*

Italian Grand Prix automobile race to be part of the Formula One Grand Prix circuit, *1083*

Swiss Grand Prix automobile race to be part of the Formula One Grand Prix circuit, *1080*

World championship for automobile racers, *1076*

Farnam, Henry: International airplane races, *1001*

Farnam, Robert: Men's pair-oared shell without coxswain rowing event held in the Olympic Games, *4931*

Farnie, H. B.: Book about how to play golf, *3571*

Farrell, F. Jeffrey: Men's 4 x 100-meter medley relay swimming event held in the Olympic Games, *5838*

Farrelly, Bernard: Surfer not born in Hawaii to win the International Surfing Championships, *5771*

World Surfing Championships, *5773*

Fears, Tom: National Football League player to receive 18 completed passes in a single game, *3225*

Feddersen, Victor: Men's lightweight four-oared shells without coxswain rowing event held in the Olympic Games, *4960*

Feerick, Bob: All–National Basketball Association (NBA) First Team, *1914*

Feistmantl, Josef: Two-seater luge (toboggan) event at the Olympic Winter Games, *4456*

Felix, Ray: Baltimore Bullets player to be named National Basketball Association (NBA) Rookie of the Year, *1942*

Felke, Petra: Javelin-thrower to break the 260-foot barrier, and to reach the 80-meter barrier, in the women's event, *4410*

Feller, Bob: Baseball pitcher to have 17 strikeouts in a single American League game, *1522*

Fenton, Dennis: Shooters from the United States to win the small-bore rifle team title in the Olympic Games, *5300*

Ferguson, Ian: Canoe racers to win two consecutive titles in the men's pairs 500-meter kayak event in the Olympic Games, *2625*

Ferguson, Robert: Golfer to win the British Open in a playoff, *3593*

Ferguson, Tom: Cowboy to be named All-Around Cowboy six consecutive times, *4898*

Rodeo cowboy to win more than $100,000 in a single season, *4897*

Fernie, Willie: Golfer to win the British Open in a playoff, *3593*

Ferreira, Wayne: Athletes from South Africa to win medals in the Olympic Games, after the lifting of the ban on their country because of its racist policies, *4779*

Fewster, Chick: New York Yankees regular season baseball game played at Yankee Stadium, *1467*

Fiasconari, Marcello: Runner to complete the men's 800-meter race in under 1:44 minutes, *5099*

Fichjtel, Anja: National team to sweep the medals in the women's individual foil fencing competition in the Olympic Games, *2940*

Ficken, H. E.: National championships in track and field (athletics) in the United States, *6201*

Field-Richard, John: Motorboat-racing event held in the Olympic Games, *4565*

Fielder, Cecil: Chicago White Sox regular season baseball game played at New Comiskey Park, *1816*

Figg, James: Boxing school, *2505*

Fikotová, Olga: Hammer-thrower to break the 70-meter and 230-foot barriers, *3991*

Filippis, Maria Teresa de: Woman automobile racer to compete in a Grand Prix race eligible for world-championship points, *1097*

Finet (first name unknown): Figure riding individual and team events held in the Olympic Games, *2850*

Fingers, Rollie: Milwaukee Brewers baseball player to be named Most Valuable Player, and to win the Cy Young Award, *1760*

Finlay, Donald: Result of an Olympic event to be changed after viewing of the film of the race, *4678*

Finnegan, George: Bantamweight and featherweight boxing events held in the Olympic Games, and the first boxer to win two gold medals in a single Olympic Games, *2527*

Flyweight boxing event in the Olympic Games, *2528*

Finneran, Sharon: Women's 400-meter individual medley swimming event held in the Olympic Games, *5849*

Finterswald, Dow: Golfer to win the Professional Golfers' Association (PGA) Championship after it was converted into a stroke play tournament, *3753*

Fischer, Birgit *See* Schmidt, Birgit Fischer

Fischer, Johnny: Golf club with a steel shaft, *3648*

Fisher, Morris: Shooter to win two consecutive titles in the men's free rifle (three positions) individual shooting event, and in the free rifle team event, in the Olympic Games, *5302*

Fiske, William: Bobsledders from the United States to win the five-man bobsled title at the Olympic Winter Games, *2468*

Bobsledders to win two straight titles in the four-man bobsled at the Olympic Winter Games, *2472*

Fitch, Bill: Coach to be named National Basketball Association (NBA) Coach of the Year twice, *2158*

Fitch, Robert: Discus-thrower to break the 180-foot barrier, *2767*

Fitzgerald, Darren: Basketball player to shoot 158 3-point field goals during a single Division I National Collegiate Athletic Association (NCAA) season, *2250*

Fitzsimmons, Bob: Boxer to hold world titles in three different weight classes, *2526*

Boxer to retire undefeated as world heavyweight champion, *2533*

Fitzsimmons, James: Horse to be named Horse of the Year, *4288*

Fjellerup, Eva: Pentathlete to win three, and then four, titles in the women's world championships, *4834*

Flach, Kenneth: Tennis players to win the men's doubles title in the Olympic Games after tennis competition resumed in 1988, *6181*

Flack, Edwin: Athlete from Australia to win a gold medal in the modern Olympic Games, *4607*

Men's 800-meter and 1500-meter running events held in the Olympic Games, *4974*

Flamm, Erika: International championships in table tennis, *5984*

Flanagan, John: Hammer-throw event held at the Olympic Games, *3981*

Flatow, Alfred: Men's parallel bars gymnastics competitions held in the Olympic Games, *3906*

Fleming, John: Small-bore rifle moving and disappearing target individual shooting events held in the Olympic Games, *5289*

Flessel, Laura: Women's individual and team épée competitions held in the Olympic Games, *2944*

Fletcher, Jennie: Women's 4 x 100-meter freestyle relay swimming event in the Olympic Games, *5808*

Fletcher, Ken: Tennis player to win six consecutive French national men's doubles championships after the event became international, *6113*

Wimbledon Open mixed doubles tennis title, *6131*

Fleury, Catherine: Women's half-middleweight judo event held in the Olympic Games, *4557*

Flick, Elmer: Baseball player to lead the American League in triples in three consecutive years, *1375*

Flint, William: Woman jockey on record, *4264*

Flood, Curt: Successful set of actions against major league baseball's "reserve clause", *1714*

Földi, Imre: Weightlifter to compete in five Olympic Games, *6347*

Foley, Curry: National League player to hit for the cycle (single, double, triple, and home run) in a single game, *1262*

Follis, Charles W.: African-American professional football player, *3129*

Fonst, Ramón: Athlete from Cuba to win a gold medal in the Olympic Games, *4617*

Men's amateurs and masters épée fencing competition held in the Olympic Games, *2904*

Men's individual épée fencing competition held in the Olympic Games, *2902*

Men's masters épée fencing competition held in the Olympic Games, *2903*

Men's team foil fencing competition held in the Olympic Games, *2906*

Fontan, Marc: World Endurance Championship in motorcycle racing, *4592*

Fontanella, Emilio: Rowers to win two gold medals in pair-oared shell with coxswain rowing events in the same Olympic Games, *4934*

Forberger, Frank: Rowers to win two consecutive titles in the men's four-oared shell without coxswain event in the Olympic Games, *4943*

Forbes, Jake: National Hockey League 0–0 tie, *4084*

Forbes, Robert J.: African-American professional basketball team, *1886*

Force, Dave: Baseball player to have 6 hits in a 9-inning National League game, *1228*

Ford, Chris: Three-point goal scored in a National Basketball Association (NBA) game, *2153*

Ford, Phil: Kansas City Kings player to be named National Basketball Association (NBA) Rookie of the Year, *2149*

Ford, Wanda: College women's basketball player to have 1,887 rebounds in a single Division I National Collegiate Athletic Association (NCAA) career, *2236*

College women's basketball player to have 534 rebounds in a single Division I National Collegiate Athletic Association (NCAA) season, *2218*

Foreman, George: Boxer to win the world heavyweight championship three times, *2566*

Förster, Kerstin: Rowers to win two consecutive titles in the women's quadruple sculls in the Olympic Games, *4958*

Women's quadruple sculls event held in the Olympic Games, *4955*

Fosbury, Richard: High-jumper to use the "Fosbury flop" jumping method, *4031*

Foster, Catherine: Woman to be skipper of a boat in an Olympic competition, *5244*

Foster, George: Major league baseball player to earn $2 million a year, *1763*

Foster, Greg: Hurdler to win the men's 110-meter event in the World Championships in Athletics, *4347*

Hurdler to win two, and then three, consecutive titles in the men's 110-meter hurdles in the World Championships in Athletics, *4351*

Foster, Rube: African-American All-Star Team in professional baseball, *1402*

Convention of the Negro National League, *1441*

Foster, William H.: Skeet shooting, *5293*

Foulon, Emmanual: Archery events held in the Olympic Games, *1025*

Fowler, John W.: African-American baseball player known to have played professionally with a previously all-white team, *1238*

Fox, Nellie: Baseball player to lead the American League in singles in seven consecutive years, *1640*

Chicago White Sox baseball player to be named Most Valuable Player, *1635*

Foxx, Jimmie: Boston Red Sox baseball player to be named Most Valuable Player, *1525*

Foyt, A. J.: Automobile racer to win the Indianapolis 500 four times, *1123*

France, Bill, Sr.: National Association for Stock Car Auto Racing (NASCAR), *1071*

Frank, Clint: College football player to receive the Maxwell Award, *3178*

Franks, Margaret: Pope Trophy, *5992*

Fraser, Dawn: Swimmer to race the women's 100-meter freestyle in under one minute, *5844*

Swimmer to win three consecutive titles in the same event in the Olympic Games, *5845*

Swimmer to win two and then three consecutive women's 100-meter freestyle titles in the Olympic Games, *5842*

Fraser, Gretchen: Women's slalom event held at the Olympic Winter Games, *5389*

Fraser, Neale: Tennis player to win four consecutive United States mixed doubles national championships, and nine overall, *6105*

Tennis player to win six consecutive French national men's doubles championships after the event became international, *6113*

Fraser, Steven: Wrestler from the United States to win a Greco-Roman title in the Olympic Games, *6405*

Frazier, I.: National championships in track and field (athletics) in the United States, *6201*

Frazier, Joe: Olympic heavyweight boxing champion to become world heavyweight champion, *2567*

Frederick, Karl: Rapid-fire pistol and free pistol team events held in the Olympic Games, *5299*

Fredriksson, Gert: Canoe racer to win six gold medals, and eight medals overall, in the Olympic Games, *2609*

Canoe racer to win two, and then three, consecutive titles in the men's singles 1000-meter kayak event in the Olympic Games, *2607*

Fregosi, Carlo: Gymnasts to win two consecutive gold medals in the men's team combined exercises in the Olympic Games, *3922*

Fretz, Ann: U.S. Open mixed doubles tennis title, *6125*

Friedrichs, George: Sailors from the United States to win the Dragon-class event in the Olympic Games, *5225*

Frisch, Frank: St. Louis Cardinals baseball player to be named Most Valuable Player, *1498*

Frisch, Toni: Detroit Lions regular season football game played at the Pontiac Silverdome, *3346*

Frith, Freddie: World championships in motorcycle racing, *4578*

Fryer, Jeff: Basketball player to score eleven 3-point field goals in a single Division I National Collegiate Athletic Association (NCAA) championship series game, *2291*

Fu Mingxia: Diver to win two consecutive women's highboard platform diving titles at the world championships, *2823*

Fuchs, Gilbert: Figure skater to win the men's singles title at the world championships, *2963*

World championships in figure skating, *2964*

Fuchs, Jenö: Fencer to win two consecutive men's individual sabre titles, and men's team sabre titles, in the Olympic Games, *2914*

Fuchs, Ruth: Javelin-thrower to break the 210- and 220-foot barriers in the women's event, *4401*

Javelin-thrower to win two consecutive women's titles in the Olympic Games, *4402*

Fudge, Paula: Runner to hold the officially accepted world record in the women's 5000-meter race, *5122*

Fuentes, Angel Valodia Matos: Men's taekwondo events held in the Olympic Games, *4560*

Fuist, Guido: Cycling team to break the 4-minute mark in the men's 4000-meter team pursuit race in the Olympic Games, *2730*

Fulks, Joe: All–National Basketball Association (NBA) First Team, *1914*

Basketball player to lead the National Basketball Association (NBA) in single season scoring, *1915*

Fulljames, George: Boxer to be world middleweight champion, *2516*

Fundin, Ove: Motorcycle racer to win five individual dirt-track (speedway) world titles, *4584*

Pairs event in the dirt-track (speedway) motorcycle racing world championships, *4585*

Fung, Lori: Rhythmic gymnastics all-around individual competition held in the Olympic Games, *3974*

Funkenhauser, Zita-Eva: National team to sweep the medals in the women's individual foil fencing competition in the Olympic Games, *2940*

Fuqua, Ivan: Team to race the men's 4 x 400-meter relay in under 3:10 minutes, *5031*

Furgol, Ed: National golf team that won the Canada Cup twice, *3748*

U.S. Open golf tournament to be televised nationally, *3743*

Furniss, Bruce: National Team to sweep the medals in the men's 200-meter freestyle in the Olympic Games, *5921*

Furniss, Steven: Men's 200-meter individual medley event in which the top four swimmers broke the world record, *5870*

Furtado, Julie: World championships in mountain biking, *2716*

Furtsch, Evelyn: Team from the United States to win the women's 4 x 100-meter relay running event in the Olympic Games, *5030*

G

Gadley, Jeff: African-American athletes to compete in the Olympic Winter Games, *4747*

Gaines, Joseph *See* Gans, Joe

Gál, József: World championships in Greco-Roman wrestling held on a regular basis, *6388*

Galindo, Rudy: Japanese-American figure skater to win the women's singles title at the U.S. national championships, *3099*

Gallagher, Barbara: World figure skating championships for roller skating, *4909*

Gallatin, Harry: Coach to be named National Basketball Association (NBA) Coach of the Year, *2023*

Galloway, Hipple: Professional ice hockey player of Black African ancestry on record, *4051*

Galushka Douiounova, Vera: Volleyball players to win two consecutive women's gold medals in the Olympic Games, *6283*

Gamble, Kenny: Walter Payton Player of the Year Award, *3412*

Gamlin, Brian: Rules for modern darts, *2734*

Gammoudi, Mohamed: Athlete from Tunisia to win a gold medal in the Olympic Games, *4728*

Runner from Africa to win the men's 5000-meter title in the Olympic Games, *5089*

Gance, Henri: Middleweight weightlifting event held in the Olympic Games, *6330*

Gane, Laurent: Men's Olympic sprint cycling event held in the Olympic Games, *2729*

Ganna, Luigi: Tour of Italy (Giro d'Italia) cycling race, *2693*

Gans, Joe: African-American boxer born in the United States to win a world boxing title, *2524*

Gao Lijuan: World championships for women's weightlifting, *6350*

Gao Min: Diver to hold the women's world titles in both the one- and three-meter springboard diving at the same time, *2820*

Women's one-meter springboard diving event held at the world championships, *2822*

Garatti, Eleanor *See* Saville, Eleanor Garatti

Garcia Fernández, Julio: Athletes from Spain to win gold medals in the Olympic Games, *4673*

Gärderud, Anders: Runner to race the men's 5000-meter steeplechase in under 8:10 minutes, *5102*

Gardiner, Charles: All-Star National Hockey League Team selected by the Professional Hockey Writers' Association, *4102*

Gardner, George: Boxer to hold the undisputed world light heavyweight title, *2525*

Garibaldi, Bob: College baseball player to pitch 38 strikeouts in a College World Series, *1652*

Garilhe, Renée: Fencer to win three consecutive women's foil titles in the world championships, *2930*

Garin, Maurice: Tour de France cycling race, *2689*

Garlits, Don: Drag racer to reach a speed of over 200, and then 250, miles per hour, *1108*

Garrett, Robert: Men's discus throw event held in the Olympic Games, *2754*

Men's shot put event held in the Olympic Games, *5329*

Garrison, Zina: Tennis players to win the women's doubles title in the Olympic Games after tennis competition resumed in 1988, *6179*

Gary Hall, Jr.: Male swimmers to win gold medals in the same event at the same Olympic Games, *5979*

Gastineau, Mark: National Football League defensive player to reach 22 sacks in a single season, *3388*

Gatewood, Bill: No-hitter on record in Negro League history, *1457*

Gatewood, Randy: National Collegiate Athletic Association major college football player to receive 23 passes in a single game, *3462*

Gaudin, Lucien: World championships in fencing, *2917*

Gayden, Cornelia: College women's basketball player to score 12 3-point goals in a single Division I National Collegiate Athletic Association (NCAA) game, *2356*

Gaylord, Mitchell: Gymnasts from the United States to win the men's combined exercises title in the Olympic Games, *3972*

Gears, Harold: Softball Hall of Fame opened, *5588*

Gebrselassie, Haile: Runner to race the men's 5000 meters in under 12:55 minutes, *5179*

Runner to win two, three, and then four consecutive titles in the men's 10,000-meter event in the World Championships in Athletics, *5174*

Gedó, György: Boxer to compete in four Olympic Games, *2579*

Geesink, Antonius: Men's open judo event in the Olympic Games, *4536*

Gehrig, Lou: Baseball player to hit four home runs in a single regular season American League game, *1504*

Major league baseball player to hit 23 grand slam home runs, *1528*

Major league baseball player to play 2,130 consecutive games, *1535*

Major league baseball player to top Lou Gehrig's record of 2,130 consecutive games played, *1832*

Major league baseball player whose uniform number was retired at the end of his career, *1538*

New York Yankees baseball player to be named Most Valuable Player, *1479*

Woman to pitch against a major league baseball team, *1500*

Geiberger, Al: Golfer to score under 60 in an 18-hole round in a Professional Golfers' Association (PGA) recognized event, *3815*

Geiger, Gary: St. Louis Cardinals regular season baseball game played at Busch Memorial Stadium, *1689*

Geiger, John: Men's eight-oared shell with coxswain rowing event held in the Olympic Games, *4925*

Geist, Gaspar: G. Geist Prize, *5986*

Gennip, Yvonne van: Women's 5000-meter speed skating event held in the Olympic Winter Games, *5709*

Georgantas, Nicolaos: Men's stone throw event held in the Olympic Games, *5769*

George, Emma: Pole-vaulter to break the 14-foot barrier in the women's event, *4851*

George, William: All-America college football team named by Walter Camp, *3121*

George V, King of England: Inter-Empire Sports tournament, *4366*

Georgiadis, Ioannis: Fencer to win two men's individual sabre titles in the Olympic Games, *2909*
Men's individual sabre fencing competition held in the Olympic Games, *2899*

Geran, Jerry: Hockey player from the United States to play in the National Hockey League, *4062*

Germot, Maurice: Tennis player to win three gold medals in tennis in the same Olympic Games, *6048*

Gerschwiler, Hans: Figure skater from Switzerland to win the men's singles title at the world championships, *3029*

Gervin, George: Basketball player to score 33 points in a single quarter of a National Basketball Association (NBA) game, *2142*

Ghita, Marilena: World championships in rowing to include women's competitions, *4945*

Gibb, James: Table tennis equipment, *5980*

Gibb, Roberta: Woman to race in the Boston Marathon, *4490*

Gibson, Althea: African-American tennis player to win a Grand Slam event, *6109*
African-American tennis player to win the women's singles championship at Wimbledon, *6110*
African-American woman to play on the Ladies Professional Golf Association (LPGA) tour, *3786*

Gibson, Bob: St. Louis Cardinals pitcher to win the Cy Young Award, *1699*

Gibson, Florent: Boxing match to be broadcast on radio, *2540*

Gibson, J. L.: Professional ice hockey club in the United States, *4053*

Gibson, John: Hurdler to race the men's 400-meter hurdles in under 53 seconds, *4330*

Gichin, Funakoshi: Formal instruction in karate, *4529*

Gier, Markus: Men's lightweight double sculls rowing event held in the Olympic Games, *4959*

Gier, Michael: Men's lightweight double sculls rowing event held in the Olympic Games, *4959*

Gigova, Maria: Gymnast to win the all-around title two, and then three, times in the world championships of rhythmic sportive gymnastics, *3957*

Gil Young-ah: Badminton event for mixed doubles in the Olympic Games, *1175*

Gilbert, Brad: Grand Slam Cup, *6182*

Gill, Charles O.: All-America college football team named by Walter Camp, *3121*

Gillette, Walker: College football player to receive 20 passes in a major bowl game, *3292*

Gilmore, Artis: Basketball player to have 1,224 rebounds during his Division I National Collegiate Athletic Association (NCAA) college career, *2077*
Basketball player to have a field goal average of .599 over his National Basketball Association (NBA) career, *2267*

Gilpatrick, J.: Belmont Stakes horse race, *4276*

Gimeno, Andres: Australian Open men's singles tennis title, *6137*
U.S. Open men's doubles tennis title, *6124*

Gindele, Nan: Javelin-thrower to hold the officially accepted world record in the women's event, *4389*

Giovannetti, Luciano: Shooter to win two consecutive individual trap (clay pigeon) shooting titles in the Olympic Games, *5317*

Girardelli, Marc: Skier to win five men's overall titles in skiing's world cup, *5482*

Gladisch, Silke: Runner to win both the women's 100- and 200-meter titles in the World Championships in Athletics, *5146*

Glass, Hermann: National team to sweep the top honors in the men's horizontal bar, long horse vault, side (pommel) horse, and rings gymnastics competitions in the Olympic Games, *3913*

Gleason, Edward: Shooters from the United States to win the trap (clay pigeon) team shooting event in the Olympic Games, *5294*

Glennie, George: Championship Meeting in golf, *3572*

Glover, Rich: African-American college football player to win the Lombardi Award, *3321*

Glyn, William: Men's singles competition at the United States national tennis championships, *6013*

Gnauck, Maxi: Gymnast to win two, and then three, consecutive women's uneven (asymmetrical) bars titles in the world championships, *3968*

Goalby, Bob: Golfer to score eight consecutive birdies in a Professional Golfers' Association (PGA) recognized event, *3764*

Senior Professional Golfers' Association (PGA) Tour, *3830*

Goebel, Timothy: Figure skater to land three quadruple jumps, and two different ones, in a single international competition, *3116*

Gogarty, Deirdre: Women's boxing match to be watched by more than 1 million television viewers, *2593*

Göhr, Marlies: Runner to win the women's 100-meter race in the World Championships in Athletics, *5133*

Goitschel, Marielle: Olympic Games to institute sex tests for women athletes, *4723*

World cup series of competitions in Alpine skiing, *5416*

Gola, Tom: Basketball player to be named Division I National Collegiate Athletic Association (NCAA) United Press International (UPI) Player of the Year, *1952*

Basketball player to have 1,751 rebounds during his Division I National Collegiate Athletic Association (NCAA) career, *1953*

Golden, Hayden: Intercollegiate golf tournament for African-American players, *3708*

Goldsmith, Fred: "Rotating" pitchers in major league baseball, *1248*

Gonzalez, Juan: Season in which both major league baseball Most Valuable Player Awards went to Hispanic players, *1849*

Gonzalez, Luis: Tampa Bay Devil Rays regular season baseball game played at Tropicana Field, *1851*

Goodell, Brian: Olympic men's 1500-meter freestyle event in which the medalists all had times under 16 minutes, *5922*

Olympic men's 400-meter freestyle event at which all the medalists had times under four minutes, *5923*

Goodrich, Gail: Basketball player to make 18 free throws in a single Division I National Collegiate Athletic Association (NCAA) Final Four championship series game, *2028*

Goodwin, Leo "Budd": Water polo team from the United States to win the title at the Olympic Games, *6302*

Goolagong, Evonne: Native Australian tennis player to win a Grand Slam event, *6146*

Goold, Vere: National tennis championships in Ireland, *6010*

Gorchakova, Yelena: Javelin-thrower to break the 200-foot and 60-meter barriers in the women's event, *4400*

Gordeeva, Ekaterina: Olympic Winter Games at which professional athletes were allowed to compete, *4781*

Professional figure skaters to win a gold medal in the Olympic Winter Games after being reinstated to amateur competition, *3106*

Gordien, Fortune: Discus-thrower to break the 190-foot barrier, *2769*

Gordon, Bridgette: College women's basketball United States Basketball Writers Association All-American first team, *2271*

Gordon, Jeff: Automobile racer to earn more than $4 million in a single season in the National Association for Stock Car Auto Racing (NASCAR) Winston Cup series, *1144*

Gordon-Watson, Mary: Woman to win the world championships in the three-day event equestrian competition, *2877*

Gore, George: Major league baseball player to steal seven bases in a single game, *1255*

Gore, Spencer: Tennis tournament played at Wimbledon, *6008*

Gorman, James: Shooters from the United States to win the military revolver team event in the Olympic Games, *5287*

Gorman, Miki (Michiko): New York Marathon to traverse New York City's five boroughs, *4499*

Runner to win the women's title in both the Boston Marathon and the New York Marathon in the same year, *4501*

Woman to complete the Boston Marathon in under 3:00 hours, *4497*

Woman to race the marathon in under 3:00 hours, *4495*

Gorokhova, Galina: Fencers to win three gold medals in the women's team foil competition in the Olympic Games, *2938*

Fencers to win two gold medals in the women's team foil competition in the Olympic Games, *2937*

Women's team foil fencing competition held in the Olympic Games, *2935*

Gorshkov, Aleksandr: Figure skaters from the Soviet Union to win the ice dancing title in the world championships, *3066*

Figure skaters from the United States to win an Olympic medal in ice dancing, *3074*

Figure skaters to win the ice dancing title in the Olympic Winter Games, *3076*

Gorski, Mark: Cyclist from the United States to win the men's 1000-meter match sprint in the Olympic Games, *2710*

Gossett, Bruce: San Francisco 49ers regular season football game played at Candlestick Park, *3318*

Gouin, Pierre: World championships in water-skiing, *6316*

Gould, Jay: Jeu de paume (court tennis or real tennis) event in the Olympic Games, *6049*

Goulding, George: Men's 10,000-meter walk held in the Olympic Games, *6290*

Gourdin, Edward: Athlete of Black African ancestry to win an individual gold medal in the Olympic Games, *4657*

Long-jumper to break the 25-foot barrier, *4430*

Goyoago, Francisco: World championships in show jumping, *2865*

Graef, Jed: National team to sweep the medals in the men's 200-meter backstroke event in the Olympic Games, *5846*

Graeme, Miss (first name unknown): All-England Championships in badminton, *1166*

Graf, Steffi: Tennis player (man or woman) to be ranked number one in the world for 186 consecutive weeks, *6183*

Tennis player to win at least four women's singles titles at each of the four Grand Slam tournaments, *6186*

Tennis player to win the women's singles title in the Olympic Games after tennis competition resumed in 1988, *6180*

Grafström, Gillis: Athlete to win three consecutive gold medals in the same event in the Olympic Winter Games, *4666*

Figure skater from Austria to win the men's singles titles in the Olympic Winter Games, *3012*

Figure skater to win two, and then three, consecutive men's singles titles in the Olympic Games, *3001*

Graham, David: Presidents Cup Match in golf, *3880*

Graham, James: Shooter from the United States to win the men's trap (clay pigeon) individual shooting title in the Olympic Games, *5295*

Shooters from the United States to win the trap (clay pigeon) team shooting event in the Olympic Games, *5294*

Graham, John: Rotterdam Marathon, *4506*

Graham, Leslie: World championships in motorcycle racing, *4578*

Graham, Otto: National Football League player to be named Most Valuable Player at the season-ending Pro Bowl, *3228*

National Football League player to be named the league's Most Valuable Player by United Press International (UPI), *3227*

Grahame-White, Claude: International air race in the United States, *1002*

Grahn, Dieter: Rowers to win two consecutive titles in the men's four-oared shell without coxswain event in the Olympic Games, *4943*

Graney, Jack: Athlete to become a broadcaster after retiring, *5747*

Grange, Red (Harold): College football All-America team named by Grantland Rice, *3153*

National Football League game played indoors, *3162*

Pro Football Hall of Fame, *3268*

Granger, Hoyle: Houston Oilers regular season football game played at the Houston Astrodome, *3291*

Grant, George F.: Golf tee, *3625*

Gravelotte, Eugène-Henri: Athlete from France to win a gold medal in the Olympic Games, *4609*

Men's individual foil fencing competition held in the Olympic Games, *2897*

Gray, Clifford: Bobsledders from the United States to win the five-man bobsled title at the Olympic Winter Games, *2468*

Bobsledders to win two straight titles in the four-man bobsled at the Olympic Winter Games, *2472*

Gray, Gilbert: Star-class sailing event held in the Olympic Games, *5212*

Gray, James: College football player to gain 280 yards rushing in a major bowl game, *3432*

Gray, William: Baseball chest protector, *1233*

Major league baseball pitcher to walk eight players in a single inning, *1396*

Grayson, Doug: Basketball player to score 16 consecutive field goals in a single Division I National Collegiate Athletic Association (NCAA) game, *2053*

Graziano, Sarah: National Collegiate Athletic Association (NCAA) Division I women's softball player to hit .589 for a whole season, *5622*

Green, A. C.: Basketball player to play more than 900 consecutive games in the National Basketball Association (NBA), *2397*

Green, Hubert: World Series of Golf won in a playoff, *3819*

Green, Pete: National Hockey League team to win the Stanley Cup twice in a row, *4074*

Green, Pumpsie (Elijah): African-American baseball player to play for the Boston Red Sox, *1639*

Green, Thomas: Men's 50,000-meter walk held in the Olympic Games, *6291*

Greene, Charles: Sweep of the medals in an event by athletes of Black African ancestry at the Olympic Games, *4726*

Greene, Maurice: Runner to win both the men's 100- and 200-meter titles in the same World Championships in Athletics, *5187*

Greene, Nancy: World cup series of competitions in Alpine skiing, *5416*

Greene, Shaunda: College women's basketball player to score 23 free throws in a single Division I National Collegiate Athletic Association (NCAA) game, *2310*

Greenough-Smith, Dorothy: Woman figure skater to perform an axel in competition, *2985*

Greenwood, Heather: Women's 400-meter freestyle swimming event held in the world championships, *5905*

Greer, Frank: National team to sweep the medals in the men's single sculls rowing event in the Olympic Games, *4932*

Gretzky, Wayne: Hockey player to be named the National Hockey League's Most Valuable Player eight consecutive times, and nine overall, *4195*

Hockey player to win the Associated Press Athlete of the Year Award, *4181*

National Hockey League player to have 163 assists in a single season, *4194*

National Hockey League player to have 31 assists in a single set of Stanley Cup playoffs, *4198*

National Hockey League player to lead the league in scoring 10 times, *4212*

National Hockey League player to lead the league in scoring seven times in a row, *4196*

National Hockey League player to reach 802 career goals, *4216*

National Hockey League player to score 200 points in a single season, *4183*

National Hockey League player to score 47 points in a single set of Stanley Cup playoffs, *4192*

National Hockey League player to score 92 goals in a single season, *4182*

Grewal, Alexi: Cyclist from the United States to win the men's road race in the Olympic Games, *2707*

Grey, Albert Henry George, 4th Earl Grey: Grey Cup awarded to the rugby football champion in Canada, *4966*

Grey, Leon: Pilot to win the Bendix Trophy–Jet Division airplane race, *1014*

Griffey, Ken, Jr.: Baltimore Orioles manager to be named Manager of the Year, *1804*

Father and son to play as teammates in major league baseball, *1810*

Father and son to play at the same time in major league baseball, *1805*

Seattle Mariners baseball player to be named Most Valuable Player, *1843*

Griffey, Ken, Sr.: Baltimore Orioles manager to be named Manager of the Year, *1804*

Father and son to play as teammates in major league baseball, *1810*

Father and son to play at the same time in major league baseball, *1805*

Griffin, Archie: Football player to win the Heisman Trophy twice, *3347*

Griffin, Ellen: Organization for women golf professionals in the United States, *3712*

Griffith, Darrell: Utah Jazz player to be named National Basketball Association (NBA) Rookie of the Year, *2169*

Griffith, Emile: Boxer to become world super-welterweight (junior middleweight) champion, *2564*

Griffith, Howard: National Collegiate Athletic Association major college football player to score eight rushing touchdowns in a single game, *3441*

Griffith-Joyner, Florence: African-American woman to win the Jesse Owens International Award, *1160*

Triple-jumper from the United States, and the first African-American, to win the men's event in the Olympic Games, *6260*

Griffiths, Albert: Boxer to be world featherweight champion, *2520*

Grinkov, Sergei: Olympic Winter Games at which professional athletes were allowed to compete, *4781*

Professional figure skaters to win a gold medal in the Olympic Winter Games after being reinstated to amateur competition, *3106*

Grishin, Anatoly: Men's fours 1000-meter kayaking event held in the Olympic Games, *2611*

Grishin, Yevgeny: Olympic Winter Games at which athletes from the Soviet Union participated, *4705*

Speed skater to skate the 1500 meters in under 2:10 minutes, *5666*

Speed skater to skate the 500 meters in under 40 seconds, *5673*

Speed skater to win two consecutive titles in the men's 500 meters at the Olympic Winter Games, *5671*

Gritschuk, Oksana *See* Gritschuk, Pasha

Gritschuk, Pasha: Champions Series in figure skating, *3112*

Figure skaters to win two consecutive ice dancing titles at the Olympic Winter Games, *3114*

Groat, Dick: Pittsburgh Pirates baseball player to be named Most Valuable Player, *1641*

Grogan, James: Figure skaters from the United States to sweep the men's singles medals in the world championships, *3045*

Groman, German: National team to sweep the top three medals in the men's 400-meter running event in the Olympic Games, *4985*

Groomes, Mel: African-American professional football players to join the Detroit Lions in the modern period, *3218*

Grospiron, Edgar: Men's moguls freestyle skiing event at the Olympic Winter Games, *5473*

Gross, Michael: Swimmer to hold world titles in both the men's 200-meter freestyle and butterfly at the same time, and to hold both twice consecutively, *5936*

Swimmer to win two consecutive men's 200-meter butterfly titles at the world championships, *5945*

Swimmer to win two consecutive men's 200-meter freestyle titles at the world championships, *5946*

Gröttumsbråten, Johan: National team to sweep the medals in the men's 15-kilometer Nordic (cross-country) skiing event in the Olympic Winter Games, *5376*

Skier to win two consecutive men's individual Nordic combined titles in the Olympic Winter Games, *5378*

Grove, Lefty: Baseball pitcher to lead the American League in winning percentage for three consecutive years, *1494*

Philadelphia Athletics baseball player to be named Most Valuable Player, *1497*

Groza, Lou: Lou Groza Collegiate Place Kicker Award, *3453*

National Football League player to win *The Sporting News* Most Valuable Player Award, *3236*

Grumiaux, Emile: Archery events held in the Olympic Games, *1025*

Grut, William: Pentathlete to place first in three of the five events in the men's modern pentathlon in the Olympic Games, *4819*

Grütter, Alfred: Free rifle team shooting event held in the Olympic Games, *5281*

Military revolver and military rifle team shooting events held in the Olympic Games, *5280*

Gudzineviciute, Daina: Women's trap shooting event held in the Olympic Games, *5327*

Guest, Irene: National team to sweep the medals in the women's 100-meter freestyle swimming event in the Olympic Games, *5810*

Swimmers from the United States to win the women's 4 x 100-meter freestyle relay title in the Olympic Games, *5814*

Guldahl, Ralph: Golfer to win the Masters in under 280 for 72 holes, *3709*

Güldenpfennig, Wolfgang: Men's quadruple sculls rowing event held in the Olympic Games, *4948*

Gummel, Margitta Helmboldt: Shot-putter to break the 19-meter barrier in the women's event, *5346*

Gundartsev, Vladimir: Men's 4 x 7.5-kilometer relay biathlon team event held at the Olympic Winter Games, *2432*

Gunter, Madison: Lifting of the "no blacks allowed" clause from the constitution of the Professional Golfers' Association (PGA), *3759*

Günther, Paul: National team to sweep the top medals in men's springboard diving in the Olympic Games, *2794*

Guo Yuehua: World cup in table tennis, *5993*

Gurney, Dan: 24 Hours of Daytona automobile race, *1103*

Guseva, Klara: Women's 1000-meter speed skating event held at the Olympic Winter Games, *5667*

Gustaf I, King of Sweden (Gustaf Vasa): Vasalopp long-distance ski race, *5364*

Gustafson, S. Tomas: Speed skater to win two consecutive men's 5000-meter titles at the Olympic Winter Games, *5710*

Guthrie, Janet: Woman automobile racer to compete in a major stock car race, *1121*

Woman automobile racer to race in the Indianapolis 500, *1124*

Guttmann, Alfréd *See* Hajós, Alfréd (Alfréd Guttmann)

Gyarmati, Dezső: Water polo player to win medals in five different Olympic Games, *6304*

Gyarmati, Olga: Women's long jump event held in the Olympic Games, *4436*

H

Haakonsen, Terje: Snowboarder to win two consecutive titles in a world championship event, *5522*

Snowboarding world championships, *5521*

Haas, Christl: National team to sweep the medals in the women's downhill event in the Olympic Winter Games, *5413*

Haase, Helga: Women's 500-meter speed skating event held at the Olympic Winter Games, *5669*

Hackl, Georg: Slider to win two, and then three, consecutive men's singles luge (toboggan) titles in the Olympic Winter Games, *4465*

Hadler, Åge: World championships in orienteering, *4808*

Hadschieff, Michael: World Cup series of competitions for speed skating, *5703*

Haegeman, Aimé: Athlete from Belgium to win a gold medal in the Olympic Games, *4616*

Individual jumping equestrian event held in the Olympic Games, *2841*

Hagen, Walter: Golfer born in the United States to win the British Open, *3670*

Golfer born in the United States to win the Professional Golfers' Association (PGA) Championship, *3666*

Golfer to be a full-time tournament professional in the United States, *3661*

Golfer to win 18 titles in golf's four major tournaments, and six Masters championships, *3850*

Golfer to win more than 10 titles in golf's four major tournaments, *3689*

Golfer to win the Professional Golfers' Association (PGA) Championship four times in a row, and five times overall, *3686*

Golfer to win three Professional Golfers' Association (PGA) Championships, *3678*

Professional golfer to found a company selling clubs under his own name, *3671*

Hägg, Gunder: Runner to complete the men's 1500 meters in under 3:45.0 minutes, *5048*

Runner to complete the men's mile race in under 4:05 minutes, *5046*

Runner to race the men's 5000 meters in under 14:00 minutes, *5047*

Hagge, Marlene Bauer: Golfer to win the Ladies Professional Golf Association (LPGA) Championship in a sudden-death playoff, *3749*

Hahn, Archie (Charles): National team to sweep the top three medals in the men's 100- and 200-meter running events in the Olympic Games, *4990*

Runner to win both the men's 100- and 200-meter races in the same Olympic Games, *4991*

Runner to win two consecutive officially accepted men's 100-meter titles at the Olympic Games, *5150*

Hahn, Norbert: Sliders to win two consecutive luge (toboggan) titles at the Olympic Winter Games, *4462*

Hailiang, Xiao *See* Xiao Hailiang

Haines, Dan: National governing body for water-skiing, *6312*

Haines, Jackson: Ice skating club in mainland Europe, *2953*

National ice skating organization in North America, *2957*

Hainsworth, George: National Hockey League goaltender to be credited with 22 shutouts in a single season, *4100*

National Hockey League player to be named outstanding goaltender, *4089*

National Hockey League player to be named outstanding goaltender two, and then three, consecutive times, *4092*

Hairston, Sam: African-American baseball player to play for the Chicago White Sox, *1583*

Hait, Paul: Men's 4 x 100-meter medley relay swimming event held in the Olympic Games, *5838*

Haizia Zheng: Women's National Basketball Association (WNBA) player to win the league's Sportsmanship Award, *2391*

Hajós, Alfréd (Alfréd Guttmann): Athlete from Hungary to win a gold medal in the modern Olympic Games, *4614*

Men's 100-meter freestyle swimming event held in the Olympic Games, *5785*

Men's 1200-meter freestyle swimming event held in the Olympic Games, *5786*

Hajós, Henrik: Men's 4 x 250-meter (later 4 x 200-meter) freestyle relay swimming event held in the Olympic Games, *5799*

Hakanson, Walter C.: Introduction of the name "softball", *5578*

Hakulinen, Veikko: Men's 15-kilometer cross-country event held in the world championships of Nordic skiing, *5398*

Men's 30-kilometer Nordic (cross-country) ski event held at the Olympic Winter Games, *5402*

Halas, George: Pro Football Hall of Fame, *3268*

Halberg, Murray: Runner from New Zealand to win the men's 5000-meter title in the Olympic Games, *5070*

Haldeman, Lon: Race Across America (RAAM) bicycle marathon, *2705*

Hall, Bob: Wheelchair entrant in the Boston Marathon, *4498*

Hall, Charley: Boston Red Sox regular season baseball game played at Fenway Park, *1413*

Hall, Frank: Shooters from the United States to win the trap (clay pigeon) team shooting event in the Olympic Games, *5294*

Hall, Gary: Men's 200-meter individual medley event in which the top four swimmers broke the world record, *5870*

Hall, Jane: Canoe marathon world championships, *2624*

Hall, Lars: Pentathlete from a non-military background to win the men's modern pentathlon in the Olympic Games, *4824*

Pentathlete to win two consecutive titles at the world pentathlon championships, *4821*

Pentathlete to win two consecutive titles in the men's modern pentathlon in the Olympic Games, *4825*

Haller, Frank: Bantamweight and featherweight boxing events held in the Olympic Games, and the first boxer to win two gold medals in a single Olympic Games, *2527*

Haller, Gordon: Hawaii Ironman triathlon, *6235*

Hallman, Torsten: World championship in moto-cross racing to include the 250 cc class, *4582*

Halmay, Zoltán: Men's 4 x 250-meter (later 4 x 200-meter) freestyle relay swimming event held in the Olympic Games, *5799*

Men's 50-yard (later 50-meter) freestyle swimming event held in the Olympic Games, *5795*

Halswelle, Wyndham: Runner from Europe to win the men's 400-meter race in the Olympic Games, *4998*

Halvorsen, Einar: Speed skater to skate the 1500 meters in under 2:30 minutes, *5633*

Hämäläinen, Marja-Liisa: Women's individual 20-kilometer Nordic (cross-country) event held at the Olympic Winter Games, *5445*

Hamersley, L. G.: President's Cup motorboat (powerboat) race, *4567*

Hamill, Dorothy: Figure skater, and the first female athlete, to sign a contract for $1 million a year, *3072*

Hamilton, Billy: Baseball player to lead the National League in stolen bases for two consecutive years, *1302*

Hamilton, Bishop: Confirmation of the public's right to play golf, *3538*

Hamilton, William: Men's 4 x 400-meter relay track event held in the Olympic Games, *4997*

Hamm, Mia: Women's soccer event held in the Olympic Games, *5569*

Hammond, Leslie: Field hockey players to win two gold medals in the Olympic Games, *4038*

Hampson, Thomas: Runner to complete the men's 800-meter race in under 1:50 minutes, *5029*

Han Changmei: World championships for women's weightlifting, *6350*

Han You-Keun: World championships in taekwondo to include additional weight classes for men, *4543*

Hancock, George: Playground softball organization, *5577*

Softball game, *5572*

Softball rules to be formally published, *5575*

Handley, Louis: Water polo team from the United States to win the title at the Olympic Games, *6302*

Handy, Jam (H. Jamison): Men's 440-yard (later 400-meter) breaststroke event held in the Olympic Games, *5796*

Haney, Weldon: Softball player to win two consecutive Most Valuable Player Awards in the Amateur Softball Association Major Fast Pitch National Championships, *5597*

Hanford, C.: Horse to be named Horse of the Year three, four, and five times consecutively, *4303*

Hansell, Ellen: Tennis player to win the women's singles title at the United States national championships, *6022*

Hansen, Bernhuff: Super heavyweight freestyle wrestling event held in the Olympic Games, *6367*

Hansen, Villy Falck: Men's 1000-meter time trial cycling event held in the Olympic Games, *2696*

Hanson, Beverly: Golfer to win her first tournament on the Ladies Professional Golf Association (LPGA) Tour, *3729*

Ladies Professional Golf Association (LPGA) Championship, *3746*

Harant, Louis: Rapid-fire pistol and free pistol team events held in the Olympic Games, *5299*

Harbert, Chick: National golf team that won the Canada Cup twice, *3748*

Harbig, Rudolf: Runner to race the men's 800 meters in under 1:48 minutes, *5044*

Harbo, George: Athletes to row across the Atlantic Ocean, *4923*

Hard, Darlene: African-American tennis player to win the women's singles championship at Wimbledon, *6110*

Federation Cup championships, *6112*

United States intercollegiate women's singles and women's doubles national championships, *6111*

Hardaway, Tim: Basketball player to miss on 17 consecutive field goal attempts in a single National Basketball Association (NBA) game, *2312*

Hardin, Glenn: Hurdler to race the men's 400-meter hurdles in under 52 seconds, *4334*

Harding, Tonya: Figure skater to be stripped of the U.S. national women's singles title, *3104*

Figure skaters from the United States to sweep the women's singles medals in the world championships, *3097*

Hardy, Catherine: African-American women to win gold medals in a track relay event in the Olympic Games, *5058*

Hargitay, András: Men's 400-meter individual medley event held at the world championships, *5888*

Hargitay, András:—*continued*
Swimmer to hold the world titles in both the men's 200- and 400-meter individual medleys at the same time, *5911*
Swimmer to win two consecutive men's 400-meter individual medley titles at the world championships, *5916*

Hargrove, Mike: Texas Rangers baseball player to be named Rookie of the Year, *1737*

Harland, Rose: Boxing match between women on record in the United States, *2513*

Harmsworth, Alfred *See* Northcliffe, Alfred Charles William Harmsworth, 1st Viscount

Harper, Chandler: Golfer to score under 190 for three consecutive 18-hole rounds in a Professional Golfers' Association (PGA) recognized event, *3741*

Harriman, Herbert M.: Golfer born in the United States to win a U.S. national championship, *3627*

Harris, Albert: National golf organization founded by African-Americans, *3683*

Harris, Elmore: African-American professional football player to join the Brooklyn Dodgers, *3206*

Harris, Franco: African-American professional football player to be named Most Valuable Player in the Super Bowl, *3343*
Pittsburgh Steelers win in professional football's Super Bowl, *3344*

Harris, Homer: African-American coach of a Big Ten college football team, *3173*

Harris, Lusia: Basketball player to win the Broderick Cup as top college woman athlete of the year, *2130*
College women's basketball All-America team, *2110*

Harris, Marcus: National Collegiate Athletic Association major college football player to gain 4,518 yards receiving during his college career, *3474*

Harris, Nate: African-American All-Star Team in professional baseball, *1402*

Harris, William: National team to sweep the medals in the men's 100-meter freestyle in the Olympic Games, *5809*

Harrison, Benjamin: President of the United States to attend a major league baseball game, *1308*

Harrison, Henry Colden: Australian rules football, *3515*

Harroun, Ray: Indianapolis 500, *1054*

Harryson, Torbjörn: Pairs event in the dirt-track (speedway) motorcycle racing world championships, *4585*

Hartel, Lis: Woman equestrian to win an individual dressage medal in the Olympic Games, *2864*

Hartley, John: Tennis player to win two consecutive men's singles championships at Wimbledon, *6011*

Hartnett, Gabby: Chicago Cubs baseball player to be named Most Valuable Player, *1515*

Hartshorne, Harold: Figure skater to win five consecutive ice dancing titles at the U.S. national championships, *3027*
Figure skaters to win two consecutive ice dancing titles at the U.S. national championships, *3023*

Hartung, James: Gymnasts from the United States to win the men's combined exercises title in the Olympic Games, *3972*

Harvey, Doug: National Hockey League player to be named outstanding defenseman four times in a row, *4137*

Hase, François de: Featherweight weightlifting event held in the Olympic Games, *6328*

Haskell, Coburn: Rubber-cored golf ball, and the first golf ball manufactured in the United States, *3623*

Hassan, Ali Mahmoud: World championships in Greco-Roman wrestling held on a regular basis, *6388*

Hasse, Kurt: Equestrian to win gold medals in both individual and team jumping in the same Olympic Games, *2859*

Haug, Thorleif: Men's 50-kilometer freestyle Nordic (cross-country) skiing event held at the Olympic Winter Games, *5365*
Men's individual 18-kilometer Nordic (cross-country) event held at the Olympic Winter Games, *5366*
Men's individual Nordic combined (cross-country and ski jump) event held in the Olympic Winter Games, *5367*
National team to sweep the medals in the men's combined individual Nordic (cross-country) skiing event at the Olympic Winter Games, *5369*

Haugen, Anders: Athlete to receive an Olympic medal 50 years after the competition, *4741*
Skier for the United States to win a ski-jumping medal at the Olympic Winter Games, *5370*

Havemeyer, Theodore A.: National governing body for golf in the United States, *3609*

Havlicek, John: All–National Basketball Association (NBA) Rookie Team, *2019*

Hawkes, John: Australian mixed doubles national tennis championships, *6061*
Tennis players to win three Australian national mixed doubles championships, *6082*

Hawkins, Connie: Basketball player to win the American Basketball Association Most Valuable Player Award, *2055*

Hawkins, Darrell: Basketball player to have eight steals in a Division I National Collegiate Athletic Association (NCAA) championship series game, *2324*

Hawkins, Robert: National golf organization founded by African-Americans, *3683*

Hawton, Mary Bevis: Tennis players to win five consecutive Australian national women's doubles championships, *6104*

Hawtrey, Henry: Men's 5-mile event held in the Olympic Games, *4992*

Hayes, Frankie: Baseball player to hit a home run in an American League night game, *1536*

Hayes, John: Runner to hold the officially accepted world record in the men's marathon, and the first United States runner to win the Olympic marathon, *4472*

Hayes, Woody: College football coach to be named Coach of the Year, *3241*

Haynes, Abner: African-American professional football player to be named American Football Conference Player of the Year, *3251*

Hazard, Manny: National Collegiate Athletic Association major college football player to receive 141 passes in a single season, *3425*

Hearn, Lacey: Runner from the United States to win the men's 1500-meter race in the Olympic Games, *4989*

Hearns, Thomas: Boxer to hold world titles in six different weight classes, *2587*

Heath, Rodney: Australian national tennis championships, *6045*
Tennis player to win two Australian national men's doubles championships, *6052*
Tennis player to win two Australian national men's singles championships, *6050*

Heaton, Jennison: Athlete to win medals in the Olympic Winter Games 20 years apart, *4691*
Men's skeleton luge event at the Olympic Winter Games, *4452*

Heaton, John: Athlete to win medals in the Olympic Winter Games 20 years apart, *4691*
Men's skeleton luge event at the Olympic Winter Games, *4452*

Héberle, Philippe: Air rifle shooting individual event held in the Olympic Games, *5320*

Hebner, Harry: Swimmer from the United States to win the men's 100-meter backstroke title in the Olympic Games, *5807*

Hebner, Richie: Pittsburgh Pirates regular season baseball game played at Three Rivers Stadium, *1717*

Hedley, Edward: Men's eight-oared shell with coxswain rowing event held in the Olympic Games, *4925*

Heeney, Tom: Boxer named Fighter of the Year by *Ring* magazine, *2548*

Heffelfinger, William "Pudge": All-America college football team named by Walter Camp, *3121*
Professional football player, *3125*

Hegg, Steve: Cyclist from the United States to win the men's 4000-meter individual pursuit in the Olympic Games, *2709*

Heida, Anton: National team to sweep the top honors in the men's horizontal bar, long horse vault, side (pommel) horse, and rings gymnastics competitions in the Olympic Games, *3913*

Heiden, Eric: Athlete to win five individual gold medals in a single Olympic Games, *4748*
Athlete to win the Jesse Owens International Award, *1157*
Speed skater from the United States to win the women's 1500-meter title at the Olympic Winter Games, *5687*
Speed skater to sweep all five men's speed skating events in a single Olympic Winter Games, *5696*
Speed skater to win four consecutive men's titles at the world speed skating sprint championships, *5695*

Heikes, R. O.: National trap shooting tournament in the United States, *5275*

Hein, Mel: National Football League player to be named the league's Most Valuable Player, *3183*
Pro Football Hall of Fame, *3268*

Heinsohn, Tom: Boston Celtics player to be named National Basketball Association (NBA) Rookie of the Year, *1970*

Heisman, John William: College football player to be awarded the Heisman Trophy, *3171*

Heiss (later Jenkins), Carol: Figure skater to win the women's singles U.S., world, and Olympic championships in the same year, *3056*

Held, Bud: Javelin-thrower to break the 260-foot and 80-meter barriers, and the first from the United States to hold the world record in the men's event, *4394*

Held, Edmund R.: Amateur Public Links Championship, *3669*

Hellwig, Helen: Tennis player to win five consecutive women's doubles titles at the United States national championships, *6037*

Hemmestvedt, Mikkel: Organized ski-jumping competition in the United States, *5359*

Hemming, Al: Shooter to achieve a perfect score in international competition, *5305*

Hénard, Nicolas: Sailor to win two consecutive Tornado-class sailing titles in the Olympic Games, *5251*

Hencken, John: Men's 100-meter breaststroke event held in the world championships, *5875*

Henderson, Rickey: Major league baseball player to reach 130 steals in a single season, *1764*

Hendrickson, John: Shooters from the United States to win the trap (clay pigeon) team shooting event in the Olympic Games, *5294*

Henie, Sonja: Female athlete to win three consecutive titles in the same event in the Olympic Winter Games, *4683*

Figure skater from Norway to win the women's singles title at the Olympic Winter Games, *3007*

Figure skater from Norway to win the women's singles title in the world championships, *3006*

Figure skater to win 10 consecutive women's singles titles in the world championships, *3019*

Figure skater to win two, and then three, consecutive women's singles titles at the Olympic Winter Games, *3014*

Figure skaters to complete a grand slam, winning the European, world, and Olympic titles in the same year, *3010*

Henne, Jan: Women's 200-meter individual medley swimming event held in the Olympic Games, *5855*

Hennessy, Leigh: World championships in trampolining to include double mini trampoline competitions, *6230*

Hennig, Edward: National team to sweep the top honors in the men's horizontal bar, long horse vault, side (pommel) horse, and rings gymnastics competitions in the Olympic Games, *3913*

Henning, Anne: Speed skater from the United States to win the women's 500-meter title at the Olympic Winter Games, *5688*

Henriksen, Niels: Men's lightweight four-oared shells without coxswain rowing event held in the Olympic Games, *4960*

Henry, Pete (Wilbur): Pro Football Hall of Fame, *3268*

Henry, Peter: Caribbean Cup, *2476*

Hentgen, Pat: Toronto Blue Jays pitcher to win the Cy Young Award, *1835*

Hentges, François: World championships in gymnastics, *3910*

Herald, William: National team to sweep the medals in the men's 100-meter freestyle in the Olympic Games, *5809*

Herber, Maxi: Figure skaters to win four consecutive pairs titles in the world championships, *3025*

Herbold, Greg: World championships in mountain biking, *2716*

Herd, Fred: U.S. Open to use a 72-hole format, *3624*

Herd, Sandy: Rubber-cored golf ball, and the first golf ball manufactured in the United States, *3623*

Herd, Sandy (Alexander): Golfer to win a major tournament with a rubber-cored golf ball, *3633*

Hériot, Virginie: Woman to win an Olympic gold medal in sailing, *5210*

Herman, Babe: Baseball player to hit a home run in a National League night game, *1519*

Hérouin, Henri: Archery events held in the Olympic Games, *1025*

Hershiser, Oral: Major league pitcher to pitch 59 consecutive regular season scoreless innings, *1802*

Herz, Jenny: Woman figure skater to perform the sit spin, *2969*

Hess, Edwin: College football All-America team named by Grantland Rice, *3153*

Hess, Erika: Skier to win five women's slalom world cup titles, *5449*

Hesser, David: Water polo team from the United States to win the title at the Olympic Games, *6302*

Heydusek, Zdenek: Heydusek Prize, *5991*

Hickcox, Charles: Men's 200-meter individual medley swimming event held in the Olympic Games, *5853*

Hickman, Charles "Piano Legs": Three consecutive home runs in a single inning of an American League game, *1348*

Hicks, Betty: Organization for women golf professionals in the United States, *3712*

Hicks, Thomas: Runner for the United States to win the men's marathon at the Olympic Games, *4471*

Hietamies, Mirja: Women's 3 x 5-kilometer relay Nordic (cross-country) skiing event held at the Olympic Winter Games, *5401*

Hietanen, Yrjö: Canoe racers to win both the men's 1000- and 10,000-meter pairs kayak events in the Olympic Games, *2606*

Higham, Dick: Triple play in baseball's National League, *1227*

Umpire to be barred from major league baseball for dishonesty, *1260*

Hildgartner, Paul: Two-seater luge (toboggan) event to have two pairs of gold medalists in a single Olympic Winter Games, *4458*

Hill, Calvin: Philadelphia Eagles regular season football game played at Veterans Stadium, *3317*

Hill, Dorothy Poynton *See* Poynton, Dorothy

Hill, Drew: Los Angeles Rams regular season football game played at Anaheim Stadium, *3367*

Hill, George: Figure skater to win six consecutive women's singles titles, and nine overall, at the U.S. national championships, *3016*

Hill, Grant: Dallas Mavericks player to be named National Basketball Association (NBA) Rookie of the Year, *2352*

Hill, Pete: African-American All-Star Team in professional baseball, *1402*

Hillman, Harry: National team to sweep the top three medals in the men's 400-meter running event in the Olympic Games, *4985*

Hillyard, George: Tennis player to win two men's doubles titles in the Olympic Games, *6042*

Hilton, Harold: Amateur golfer to win two British Open championships, *3616*

British Open championship held at Muirfield, Scotland, *3599*

Hin, Franciscus: Men's Finn-class sailing event in the Olympic Games, *5208*

Hin, Johannes: Men's Finn-class sailing event in the Olympic Games, *5208*

Hines, James: Sweep of the medals in an event by athletes of Black African ancestry at the Olympic Games, *4726*

Hines, Jim: Runner to race the men's 100-meter dash in under 10 seconds, *5084*

Hines, Paul: Unassisted triple play in major league baseball, *1242*

Hirschfeld, Emil: Shot-putter to break the 16-meter barrier, *5333*

Hisle, Larry: Major league baseball player to come to bat as a designated hitter, *1730*

Hitchcock, George: National championships in track and field (athletics) in the United States, *6201*

Hitler, Adolf: African-American high-jumper to win the men's title in the Olympic Games, *4024*

Team to race the men's 4 x 100-meter relay in under 40 seconds, *5042*

Hitomi, Kinue: Long-jumper to hold the officially accepted world record in the women's event, and the first female athlete from Asia to set a world track and field record, *4431*

Hobart, Clarence: Tennis player to win two consecutive mixed doubles titles at the United States national tennis championships, *6034*

United States national tennis championships to include mixed doubles competition, *6032*

Hodges, Gil: Baseball player to hit 13 grand slam home runs in the National League, *1629*

Hoff, John: College baseball player to pitch 17 bases on balls in a single game, *1616*

Hoff, Karen: Women's 500-meter singles kayaking event held in the Olympic Games, *2603*

Hofmann, Walter: Men's kayak slalom whitewater canoeing events held in the Olympic Games, *2615*

Hogan, Ben: Ben Hogan Tour, *3863*

Golfer to win the U.S. Open championship four times, and two and three times consecutively, *3640*

Golfer to win the U.S. Open in under 280 for 72 holes, *3718*

Golfer to win the U.S. Open, the Masters, and the British Open in the same year, and the first to score under 275 for 72 holes, *3735*

National golf team that won the Canada Cup twice, *3748*

Hogenson, William: National team to sweep the top three medals in the men's 100- and 200-meter running events in the Olympic Games, *4990*

Hogshead, Nancy: Swimmers to win gold medals in the same event at the same Olympic Games, *5939*

Hohn, Uwe: Javelin-thrower to break the 330- and 340-foot and 100-meter barriers in the men's event, *4407*

Holcomb, Ellen: Worldloppet Cup to include women Nordic skiers, *5464*

Holdsclaw, Chamique: College women's basketball player to win *The Sporting News* Player of the Year Award, *2409*

Holecek, Josef: Canoe racer to win two consecutive men's Canadian singles 1000-meter titles in the Olympic Games, *2605*

Holgate, Virginia: Women to win medals in the three-day individual equestrian event in the Olympic Games, *2885*

Holland, Bill: Automobile racer to win the Indianapolis 500 with an average speed of more than 120 miles per hour, *1072*

Holland, Steve: Men's 1500-meter freestyle event held at the world championships, *5878*

Hollowell, Bud: College baseball player to hit four home runs in a College World Series, *1664*

Holman, Charles: Thompson Trophy airplane race, *1008*

Holman, Frederick: Men's 200-meter breaststroke event held in the Olympic Games, *5801*

Holmes, Alfred: Intercollegiate golf tournament for African-American players, *3708*

Holmes, Stan: College baseball player to bat in 17 runs in a College World Series, *1758*

Holubnychy, Volodymyr: Walker to win two titles in the men's 20,000-meter walk in the Olympic Games, *6293*

Holum, Dianne: Speed skater from the United States to win the women's 1500-meter title at the Olympic Winter Games, *5687*

Holyfield, Evander: Boxer to hold the undisputed world cruiserweight (junior heavyweight) title, *2583*

Homans, Eugene V.: Golfer to win five U.S. Amateur titles, *3692*

Hong Cha-ok: Men's and women's doubles events to be included in the world cup in table tennis, *5998*

Hoppenberg, Ernst: Men's 200-meter backstroke swimming event held in the Olympic Games, *5788*

Horine, George: High-jumper to hold the officially accepted world record in the men's event, *4021*

Horn, Sam: Baltimore Orioles regular season baseball game played at Camden Yards, *1819*

Horn, Siegbert: Men's kayak slalom whitewater canoeing events held in the Olympic Games, *2615*

Hornacek, Jeff: Basketball player to make eight consecutive 3-point field goals in the National Basketball Association (NBA) in a single game, *2343*

Hörnlein, Horst: Two-seater luge (toboggan) event to have two pairs of gold medalists in a single Olympic Winter Games, *4458*

Hornsby, Rogers: Baseball player to lead the National League in batting average for six consecutive years, *1473*

Baseball player to lead the National League in slugging average for six consecutive years, *1474*

Major league baseball player to get 257 hits in a single season, *1439*

Triple Crown hitter in two seasons in the National League, *1475*

Hornung, Paul: National Football League player to score a total of 176 points in a single season, *3254*

Horokhovska, Maria: Women's all-around gymnastics competition held in the Olympic Games, *3934*

Women's balance beam gymnastics competition held in the Olympic Games, *3935*

Horry, Robert: Basketball player to have seven steals in a single National Basketball Association (NBA) Finals game, *2358*

Basketball player to make seven consecutive 3-point field goals in a single National Basketball Association (NBA) playoff game, *2394*

Horváth, Marianne: Fencer to win two consecutive women's épée titles in the world championships, *2942*

Hoskins, Patricia: College women's basketball player to score 3,122 points during her National Collegiate Athletic Association (NCAA) Division I career, *2285*

College women's basketball player to score an average of 28.4 points per game during her Division I National Collegiate Athletic Association (NCAA) career, *2286*

Hosoya, Sky: Women's national championships in boxing, *2594*

Hostin, Louis: Weightlifter to win two consecutive light heavyweight titles in the Olympic Games, *6333*

Hotchkiss, Hazel *See* Wightman, Hazel Hotchkiss

Howard, Desmond: National Football League player to gain 99 yards with a single Super Bowl punt return, *3481*

Howard, Elston: African-American baseball player to be named Most Valuable Player in the American League, *1663*

African-American baseball player to play for the New York Yankees, *1615*

African-American baseball players to join the New York Yankees organization, *1582*

Howard, John: Race Across America (RAAM) bicycle marathon, *2705*

Howard, Sherri: Team from the United States to win the women's 4 x 400-meter relay at the Olympic Games, *5142*

Howe, Gordie: Hockey player to play for more than 25 seasons in the National Hockey League, *4174*

Hockey player to play more than 1,700 games in the National Hockey League, *4178*

National Hockey League player to be named the league's Most Valuable Player six times, *4144*

National Hockey League player to lead the league in scoring four times in a row, *4132*

National Hockey League player to reach 1,000 career assists, *4158*

National Hockey League player to reach 1,000 career points, *4142*

National Hockey League player to reach 802 career goals, *4216*

Howell, Lida: Archery events for women held in the Olympic Games, *1027*

Howley, Chuck: Baltimore Colts win in professional football's Super Bowl, *3314*

Hoy, Dummy: Two home runs in a single American League game, *1338*

Hoya, Oscar De La *See* De La Hoya, Oscar

Hoyt, Beatrix: Golfer to win the U.S. Women's Amateur Championship twice, and then three times, in a row, *3622*

Golfer to win three men's U.S. Amateur titles, *3636*

Hoyt, William Welles: Men's pole vault event held in the Olympic Games, *4837*

Hradetzky, Gregor: Men's singles 100-meter kayak event held in the Olympic Games, *2599*

Huang Hwa: World cup/grand prix competition in badminton, *1173*

Huang Xiaoyu: World championships for women's weightlifting, *6350*

Huang Xu: Gymnasts from China to win the men's team title at the Olympic Games, *3980*

Hubbard, Cal: Pro Football Hall of Fame, *3268*

Hubbard, William DeHart: Athlete of Black African ancestry to win an individual gold medal in the Olympic Games, *4657*

Hubbell, Carl: New York Giants baseball player to be named Most Valuable Player, *1506*

Hubler, Anna: Figure skaters to win the pairs title at the Olympic Games, *2978*

Figure skaters to win the pairs title in the world championships, and the first to win two titles, *2973*

Hübner, Angela: Women's 200-meter individual medley swimming event held in the world championships, *5902*

Hübner, Frank: 470-class sailing event held at the Olympic Games, *5235*

Huffman, Marv: Basketball player to be named Most Valuable Player of the Division I National Collegiate Athletic Association (NCAA) Final Four, *1899*

Hugel, Gustav: Figure skater to win two, and then three, men's singles titles at the world championships, *2965*

Hugues, Pierre d': Men's team épée fencing competition held in the Olympic Games, *2910*

Huish, Justin: Archer from the United States to win the men's individual gold medal in the Olympic Games, *1039*

Archers from the United States to win a gold medal in the team event in the Olympic Games, *1040*

Hulbert, William: National League was organized, *1219*

Hull, Bobby: Father and son to be named Most Valuable Player of the National Hockey League, *4202*

Father and son to be named Most Valuable Player of the National Hockey League All-Star Game, *4180*

National Hockey League player to be named Most Valuable Player of the NHL All-Star Game twice in a row, *4160*

Hull, Brett: Father and son to be named Most Valuable Player of the National Hockey League, *4202*

Father and son to be named Most Valuable Player of the National Hockey League All-Star Game, *4180*

Hulse, David: Texas Rangers regular season baseball game played at The Ballpark, *1828*

Humby, Harold: Small-bore rifle team shooting event held in the Olympic Games, *5291*

Hundeby, Chad: Men's 25-kilometer river/sea swim event held in the world championships, *5957*

Hundley, Charles: Jockey who won three Derbys at Epsom Downs, *4262*

Hunt, Geoff: World amateur championships in squash, *5761*

World open championships in squash, *5763*

Hunter, Brian: Tampa Bay Devil Rays regular season baseball game played at Tropicana Field, *1851*

Hunter, Frank: Tennis player to win two consecutive Wimbledon mixed doubles championships, *6083*

Hunter, Harold: African-American basketball player to be drafted into the National Basketball Association (NBA), *1923*

Hunter, John: Softball player to win the Most Valuable Player Award, *5593*

Hunty, Shirley Strickland de la *See* de la Hunty, Shirley Strickland

Hurley, Bobby: Basketball player to have 1,076 assists during his Division I National Collegiate Athletic Association (NCAA) career, *2321*

Hussein, Ibrahim: Runner from Africa to win the men's title in the Boston Marathon, *4518*

Runner from Africa to win the men's title in the New York Marathon, *4516*

Hutchinson, Jock: Golfer born in the United States to win the British Open, *3670*

Golfer who was a United States citizen to win the British Open, *3667*

Professional Golfers' Association (PGA) Championship, *3658*

Professional Golfers' Association (PGA) Seniors' Championship, *3706*

Hutson, Don: National Football League player to lead the league eight times in pass receptions, *3195*

National Football League player to win two consecutive Most Valuable Player Awards, *3190*

Pro Football Hall of Fame, *3268*

Hwang Hye-young: Badminton events held in the Olympic Games as medal sports, *1174*

Hyatt, Charley: National Collegiate Athletic Association (NCAA) consensus Division I All-American college basketball team, *1890*

Hyer, Jacob: Boxing match under English rules held in the United States, *2508*

Hyun Jung-hwa: Men's and women's doubles events to be included in the world cup in table tennis, *5998*

Women's doubles table tennis event held in the Olympic Games, *5995*

I

Ignatova, Lilia: World cup in rhythmic sportive gymnastics, *3970*

Ikangaa, Juma: Runner from Africa to win the men's title in the Boston Marathon, *4518*

Ilegems, Roger: Men's points cycling race held in the Olympic Games, *2711*

Ilg, Patriz: Runner to win the men's 3000-meter steeplechase held in the World Championships in Athletics, *5129*

Ilina, Vera: Women's synchronized springboard diving event held in the Olympic Games, *2827*

Ilman, Gary: Men's 4 x 100-meter freestyle relay swimming event held in the Olympic Games, *5847*

Induráin, Miguel: Cyclist to win the Tour de France five consecutive times, *2721*

Men's road time trial cycling event held in the Olympic Games, *2725*

Inkster, Juli: Golfer to win two of golf's major tournaments in her rookie year on the Ladies Professional Golf Association (LPGA) Tour, *3844*

Inness, Simeon: Discus-thrower to break the 190-foot barrier, *2769*

Innis, Hubert van: Archer to win four Olympic gold medals in a single Olympic Games, and six overall, *1026*

Archery events held in the Olympic Games, *1025*

Inokuma, Isao: Men's heavyweight judo event in the Olympic Games, *4535*

Ionescu, Nastasia: Women's 500-meter fours kayaking event held in the Olympic Games, *2623*

Ionov, Vyacheslav: Men's fours 1000-meter kayaking event held in the Olympic Games, *2611*

Irby, Jan: College women's basketball All-America team, *2110*

Irvin, Dick: National Hockey League coach to reach 600 career wins, *4130*

Irwin, Gary: World championships in trampolining to include individual tumbling and synchronized pairs competitions, *6229*

Irwin, Hale: Presidents Cup Match in golf, *3880*

Isakova, Maria: Speed skater to win three consecutive women's titles in the world championships, *5663*

Woman speed skater to skate the 1500 meters in under 2:30 minutes, *5664*

Isam, Ricky: Miami Dolphins regular season football game played at Joe Robbie Stadium, *3415*

Ito, Midori: Figure skater from Japan to win the women's singles title in the world championships, *3094*

Ivanov, Vyacheslav: Rower to win three consecutive men's single sculls rowing titles in the Olympic Games, *4941*

World championships in rowing, *4940*

Ivanova, Alina: Women's 10,000-meter walk held in the Olympic Games, *6296*

Iverson, Allen: Basketball player to have 10 steals in a single National Basketball Association (NBA) playoff game, *2420*

J

Jackson, Bo: Professional athlete to be named an All-Star in two sports, and the first to play with an artificial hip, *5755*

Jackson, Colin: Hurdler from Great Britain to win the men's title in the 110-meter hurdles in the World Championships in Athletics, *4354*

Jackson, Donald: Figure skater from Canada to win the men's singles title at the world championships, *3058*

Figure skater to land a triple lutz jump in competition, *3060*

Jackson, Frank: International horseshoe tournament, *4321*

Jackson, Harry: National golf organization founded by African-Americans, *3683*

Jackson, Joe: Detroit Tigers regular season baseball game played at Tiger Stadium, *1414*

Jackson, John: African-American baseball player known to have played professionally with a previously all-white team, *1238*

Jackson, Levi: African-American player to be captain of the football team at Yale University, *3216*

Jackson, Marjorie: Runner from Australia to win the women's 100- and 200-meter titles in the Olympic Games, *5059*

Jackson, Mark: Basketball player to have 868 assists in his rookie year in the National Basketball Association (NBA), *2266*

Jackson, Sonny: Cincinnati Reds regular season baseball game played at Riverfront Stadium (later Cinergy Field), *1716*

Jackson, Trina: Women's 4 x 200-meter freestyle relay swimming event held in the Olympic Games, *5973*

Jackson, William Tecumseh Sherman: African-American college football player, *3120*

Jacobi, Roland: International championships in table tennis, *5984*

Jacobs, David: Men's 4 x 100-meter relay track event held in the Olympic Games, *5003*

Jacobs, Helen: United States national women's and men's singles tennis championships to both be played at the West Side Tennis Club stadium, *6095*

Jacobs, Rose: Woman bowler to bowl a 300 game, *2493*

Jacobus, Charles: Roque event (a type of croquet) at the Olympic Games, *2671*

Jacoby, John: Canoe marathon world championships, *2624*

Jaeger, Jeff: National Collegiate Athletic Association major college football player to kick 80 field goals during his college career, *3402*

Tampa Bay Buccaneers regular season football game played at Raymond James Stadium, *3499*

Jaeghere, G. de: Gymnast to win two consecutive men's horse vault titles in the world championships, *3914*

World championships in gymnastics, *3910*

Jaffee, Irving: Men's 10,000-meter Olympic speed skating race to be voided, *5644*

Speed skater to win the men's 10,000-meter title at the Olympic Winter Games, *5650*

Jager, Tom: Men's 50-meter freestyle event held at the world championships, *5944*

Swimmer to win two consecutive men's 50-meter freestyle titles at the world championships, *5960*

Jahl, Evelin Schlaak: Discus-thrower to win two consecutive women's titles in the Olympic Games, *2782*

Jahncke, Barton: Sailors from the United States to win the Dragon-class event in the Olympic Games, *5225*

Jakobsson, Ludovika Eilers: Figure skaters from Austria to win the pairs title at the Olympic Winter Games, *3002*

Figure skaters from Finland to win the pairs title in the Olympic Games, *2999*

Figure skaters from Finland to win the pairs title in the world championships, *2984*

Figure skaters to win three pairs titles in the world championships, *2995*

Jakobsson, Walter: Figure skaters from Austria to win the pairs title at the Olympic Winter Games, *3002*

Figure skaters from Finland to win the pairs title in the Olympic Games, *2999*

Figure skaters from Finland to win the pairs title in the world championships, *2984*

Figure skaters to win three pairs titles in the world championships, *2995*

Jalkanen, Kalle: Men's 4 x 10-kilometer relay Nordic (cross-country) event held in the Olympic Winter Games, *5384*

James, Calvin: College baseball player to steal eight bases in a College World Series, *1778*

James, Lionel: National Football League player to gain a total of 2,535 yards running in a single season, *3399*

James I, King of England (James VI, King of Scotland): Confirmation of people's right to play golf and other sports on Sundays, *3540*

Patent for a golf ball, *3541*

James I, King of Scotland: Ban on football in Scotland, *5529*

James II, King of England (Duke of York): International golf match, *3545*

Sailing challenge race on record, *5193*

James II, King of Scotland: Written reference to golf, *3535*

James IV, King of Scotland: Golf reference on record in England, *3537*

Purchase of golf equipment, *3536*

Jameson, Betty: Golfer to win the Vare Trophy for the lowest average score on the Ladies Professional Golf Association (LPGA) Tour, *3736*

Jang Ei-suk: World championships in taekwondo to include women, *4549*

Jansen, Dan: World Cup series of competitions for speed skating, *5703*

January, Don: Senior Professional Golfers' Association (PGA) Tour, *3830*

Tournament on the Senior Professional Golfers' Association (PGA) Tour, *3832*

Jaques, Jean: Croquet sets, *2663*

Jarasinski, Kurt: Equestrian to win three consecutive titles in team jumping in the Olympic Games, *2869*

Jaross-Szabo, Herma: Figure skater from Austria to win the women's singles title at the Olympic Games, *3000*

Figure skater from Austria to win the women's singles title in the world championships, *2992*

Figure skater to win both the singles and pairs title at the same world championships, *3003*

Jaross-Szabo, Herma:—*continued*
Figure skater to win five consecutive women's singles championships, *3004*

Jarrott, Charles: Motorcycle race for two-wheeled vehicles, *4570*

Jarv, Jyrki: Open 49er-class sailing event held in the Olympic Games, *5258*

Järvinen, Matti: Javelin-thrower to break the 240- and 250-foot barriers, *4391*
Men's Greek-style discus throw event held in the Olympic Games, *2756*

Järvinen, Verner: Athlete from Finland to win an official gold medal in the Olympic Games, *4641*
Javelin-thrower to break the 240- and 250-foot barriers, *4391*
Men's Greek-style discus throw event held in the Olympic Games, *2756*

Jarvis, John Arthur: Men's 4000-meter freestyle swimming event held in the Olympic Games, *5792*

Javadi, Ebrahim: Light flyweight freestyle wrestling event held in the world wrestling championships, *6395*

Jeantot, Philippe: BOC Challenge Race, *5240*

Jedrzejowska, Jadwiga: Tennis player to win six French national women's doubles championships after the event became international, and four times consecutively, *6101*

Jeffries, J.: Flyers to cross the English Channel in a balloon, *1178*

Jeffries, James J.: Boxer to retire undefeated as world heavyweight champion, *2533*

Jenkins, David: Figure skaters to take all three medals in the same order in the U.S., world, and Olympic men's singles competitions, *3051*

Jenkins, Ferguson: Chicago Cubs pitcher to win the Cy Young Award, *1719*

Jenkins, Hayes Allen: Figure skaters from the United States to sweep the men's singles medals in the world championships, *3045*
Figure skaters to take all three medals in the same order in the U.S., world, and Olympic men's singles competitions, *3051*

Jensen, Anne Grethe: World cup in dressage, *2889*

Jensen, Soren Marius: All-around wrestling title awarded in the Olympic Games, *6369*

Jensen, Viggo: Athlete from Denmark to win a gold medal in the Olympic Games, *4608*
Unlimited weight weightlifting events held in the Olympic Games, *6325*

Jepson-Turner, Gladys Lynne *See* Belita (Gladys Lynne Jepson-Turner)

Jernberg, Sixten: Athlete to win nine medals in the Olympic Winter Games, *4716*

Skier to win two titles in the men's 50-kilometer freestyle Nordic (cross-country) skiing at the Olympic Winter Games, *5411*

Jethroe, Sam: African-American baseball player to play for the Boston Braves, *1579*

Jewell, Lynne: Women's 470-class sailing event held in the Olympic Games, *5249*

Jewtraw, Charles: Athlete to win a gold medal at the Olympic Winter Games, *4654*
Men's 500-meter speed skating event held at the Olympic Winter Games, *5639*

Jezek, Linda: Swimmer to hold both the women's 100- and 200-meter backstroke world titles at the same time, *5929*

Jim Mi-jung: Women's half-heavyweight judo event held in the Olympic Games, *4554*

Jimenez Mendivil, Soraya *See* Mendivil, Soraya Jimenez

Jipcho, Ben: Runner to race the men's 5000-meter steeplechase in under 8:20 minutes, *5098*

Johannesen, Knut: National team to sweep the medals in the men's 5000-meter speed-skating event at the Olympic Winter Games, *5676*
Speed skater to skate the 10,000 meters in under 16 minutes, *5672*

Johansen, Thorstein: Running deer (double shot) team shooting event held in the Olympic Games, *5297*

Johanson, Thomas: Open 49er-class sailing event held in the Olympic Games, *5258*

Johansson, Bengt: World championships in Greco-Roman wrestling held on a regular basis, *6388*

Johansson, Hjalmar: National team to sweep the top medals in men's platform diving in the Olympic Games, *2793*

Johansson, Ingemar: Boxer to be named *Sports Illustrated* Sportsman of the Year, *2562*

Johansson, Ivar: Welterweight Greco-Roman wrestling event held in the Olympic Games, *6383*

Johns, Helen: Swimmer to win two women's 4 x 100-meter freestyle relay titles in the Olympic Games, *5824*

Johnson, Alex: Milwaukee Brewers regular season baseball game played at County Stadium, *1715*

Johnson, Alfred: Single-handed sailing across the Atlantic, *5200*

Johnson, Avery: Basketball player to average 13.3 assists per game during a single Division I National Collegiate Athletic Association (NCAA) season, *2262*

Johnson, Ban: American League convention, *1329*

Johnson, Ben: Runner to win two, and then three, consecutive titles in the men's 100-meter event in the World Championships in Athletics, *5147*

Runner to win two consecutive officially accepted men's 100-meter titles at the Olympic Games, *5150*

Johnson, Bill (William): Skier from the United States to win the men's downhill title at the Olympic Winter Games, *5444*

Johnson, Cornelius: African-American high-jumper to win the men's title in the Olympic Games, *4024*

Johnson, Earvin "Magic": Basketball player to be named Most Valuable Player of the National Basketball Association (NBA) Finals three times, *2246*

Basketball player to have 21 assists in a National Basketball Association (NBA) Finals game, *2207*

Basketball player to have 95 assists in a National Basketball Association (NBA) Finals series, *2195*

Basketball player to have an average of 14 assists per game in a National Basketball Association (NBA) Finals series, *2211*

Basketball player to have an average of 17.6 assists per game in a National Basketball Association (NBA) playoff series, *2212*

Basketball player to score 42 points in a National Basketball Association (NBA) Finals game in his rookie year, *2162*

Olympic basketball competition to include openly professional athletes, *2316*

Johnson, Fred: Boxer of African descent to win a world boxing title, *2523*

Johnson, Gail: Women's solo and duet synchronized swimming events held in the world championships, *5908*

Johnson, Harry: Tennis player to win six United States mixed doubles titles, *6059*

Johnson, Jack (John Arthur): Boxer of African descent to become world heavyweight champion, *2534*

Boxer to retire undefeated as world heavyweight champion, *2533*

Johnson, James: Figure skaters from Great Britain, and the first married couple, to win the pairs title in the world championships, *2980*

Johnson, Joe Lee: World 600 automobile race, *1101*

Johnson, John Arthur *See* Johnson, Jack (John Arthur)

Johnson, Ken: Major league baseball pitcher to pitch a losing 9-inning no-hitter, *1672*

Johnson, Larry: Charlotte Hornets player to be named National Basketball Association (NBA) Rookie of the Year, *2314*

Johnson, Madame (first name unknown): Woman to fly solo in a hot-air balloon in the United States, *1180*

Johnson, Marques: Basketball player in Division I of the National Collegiate Athletic Association (NCAA) to receive the Wooden Award as Player of the Year, *2126*

Johnson, Michael: Athlete to win two Jesse Owens International Awards, *1162*

Runner to complete the men's 200-meter race in under 19.7 seconds, *5183*

Runner to complete the men's 200-meter race in under 19.8 seconds, *5112*

Runner to win both the men's 200- and 400-meter titles in the same World Championships in Athletics, *5171*

Runner to win the men's 200- and 400-meter titles in the same Olympic Games, *5184*

Runner to win two consecutive men's 400-meter titles in the Olympic Games, *5188*

Runner to win two, three, and then four consecutive titles in the men's 400-meter event in the World Championships in Athletics, *5175*

Johnson, Niesa: College women's basketball Associated Press (AP) All-American first team, *2348*

Johnson, Norm: Atlanta Falcons regular season football game played at the Georgia Dome, *3454*

Baltimore Ravens regular season game played in the PSINet Stadium, *3498*

Johnson, Phyllis Squire: Figure skaters from Great Britain, and the first married couple, to win the pairs title in the world championships, *2980*

Johnson, Rafer: African-American athlete to be named *Sports Illustrated* Sportsman of the Year, *1152*

African-American decathlete to win the men's title in the Olympic Games, *2743*

Johnson, Randy: Seattle Mariners pitcher to win the Cy Young Award, *1830*

Johnson, Richard: Archers from the United States to win a gold medal in the team event in the Olympic Games, *1040*

Johnson, Scott: Gymnasts from the United States to win the men's combined exercises title in the Olympic Games, *3972*

Johnson, Seba: Skier of African ancestry to compete in the Olympic Winter Games, *5458*

Johnson, Wallace: Tennis player to win six United States mixed doubles titles, *6059*

Johnson, Walter: Baseball pitcher to lead the American League in earned run average for two consecutive years, *1432*

Baseball pitcher to lead the American League in shutouts for three consecutive years, *1419*

Johnson, Walter:—*continued*

Baseball pitcher to lead the American League in strikeouts for eight consecutive years, *1433*

Major league baseball players to be named to the Baseball Hall of Fame, *1520*

Johnston, Bill: United States men's singles national tennis championship matches played at the new West Side Tennis Club stadium, *6069*

United States men's singles tennis national championship matches played at the West Side Tennis Club, *6057*

Johnston, Jimmy: Brothers to play on opposing teams in a World Series, *1447*

Johnston, Wheeler: Brothers to play on opposing teams in a World Series, *1447*

Johnston, Margaret: Women's world indoor championships in bowls, *2503*

Johnstone, Jay: Montreal Expos regular season baseball game played at Olympic Stadium, *1746*

Joliet, Aurel: All-Star National Hockey League Team selected by the Professional Hockey Writers' Association, *4102*

Jolly, Allison: Women's 470-class sailing event held in the Olympic Games, *5249*

Jones, Alan: Automobile racer to win two Austrian Grand Prix races, *1127*

Jones, Ann Haydon: French Open women's doubles tennis match, *6121*

French Open women's singles tennis match, *6122*

Wimbledon Open women's doubles tennis title, *6133*

Jones, Barbara: African-American women to win gold medals in a track relay event in the Olympic Games, *5058*

Jones, Benjamin: Men's 4000-meter team pursuit cycling event held in the Olympic Games, *2692*

Jones, Bobby (Robert T., Jr.): Amateur golfer to win three British Open championships, *3691*

Golfer to complete a grand slam, *3693*

Golfer to win both the U.S. Open and the British Open in the same year, *3682*

Golfer to win five U.S. Amateur titles, *3692*

Golfer to win the British Open golf championship in under 290 for 72 holes, *3685*

Golfer to win the U.S. Open championship four times, and two and three times consecutively, *3640*

Masters golf tournament, *3698*

Sullivan Award, *1148*

Jones, Brian: People to circle the globe in a balloon, *1183*

Jones, Calvin: African-American college football player to win the Outland Trophy, *3237*

Jones, Chipper: Atlanta Braves regular season baseball game played at Turner Field, *1844*

Jones, John Paul: Runner to hold the officially accepted world record in the men's mile race, *5009*

Jones, Michellie: Athlete to win two consecutive women's titles in the world triathlon championships, *6243*

Jones, Randy: San Diego Padres pitcher to win the Cy Young Award, *1743*

Jones, Robert: Book on ice skating techniques, *2950*

Jones, Robert Trent, Jr.: Presidents Cup Match in golf, *3880*

Jones, Robert Tyre, Jr. *See* Jones, Bobby (Robert T., Jr.)

Jong, Adrianus de: Fencer to win two consecutive men's sabre titles in the world championships, *2919*

Men's sabre competition held in the world championships of fencing, *2918*

Jongejans, Edwin: Men's one-meter springboard diving event held at the world championships, *2821*

Jongh, Margaretha de: World championships in taekwondo to include women, *4549*

Jordan, Michael: Basketball player to be named Most Valuable Player of the National Basketball Association (NBA) Finals six times, *2400*

Basketball player to have an average of 41 points per game in a National Basketball Association (NBA) Finals series, *2323*

Basketball player to lead the National Basketball Association (NBA) in scoring ten times, *2406*

Basketball player to make 20 free throws in a single half of a National Basketball Association (NBA) game, *2320*

Basketball player to receive the Associated Press (AP) Athlete of the Year Award, *2302*

Basketball player to score 63 points in a single National Basketball Association (NBA) playoff game, *2243*

Chicago Bulls National Basketball Association (NBA) championship, *2304*

Chicago Bulls player to be named National Basketball Association (NBA) Defensive Player of the Year, *2269*

Chicago Bulls player to be named National Basketball Association (NBA) Most Valuable Player of the Year, *2270*

Olympic basketball competition to include openly professional athletes, *2316*

Joseph, Joe: Tournament of Champions in bowling, *2497*

Josephson, Karen: Pairs of twins to take the top two spots in the synchronized swimming duet competition in the Olympic Games, *5968*

Josephson, Sarah: Pairs of twins to take the top two spots in the synchronized swimming duet competition in the Olympic Games, *5968*

Jourdan, Christian: World championships in water-skiing, *6316*

Jousseaume, André: Equestrian to win two consecutive titles in team dressage in the Olympic Games, *2858*

Joyce, Bill: National League player to hit 4 triples in a 9-inning baseball game, *1316*
Two consecutive home runs by different players to open a major league baseball game, *1305*

Joyner, Al (Alfrederick): Triple-jumper from the United States, and the first African-American, to win the men's event in the Olympic Games, *6260*

Joyner, Florence Griffith: Runner to race the women's 100 meters in under 10:50 seconds, and the 200 meters in under 21.50 seconds, *5153*

Joyner-Kersee, Jacqueline: Athlete from Syria to win a gold medal in the Olympic Games, *4796*
Heptathlete from the United States, and the first African-American, to hold the world record in the women's event, *4014*
Heptathlete from the United States, and the first African-American, to win the women's heptathlon in the Olympic Games, *4015*
Heptathlete to win two consecutive women's heptathlon titles in the Olympic Games, *4016*
Long-jumper from the United States to set or equal the world record in the women's event, *4441*
Long-jumper from the United States to win the women's event in the Olympic Games, *4442*
Triple-jumper from the United States, and the first African-American, to win the men's event in the Olympic Games, *6260*

Julin-Mauroy, Magda: Figure skater from Sweden to win the women's singles title in the Olympic Games, *2997*

Junfeng, Xiao *See* Xiao Junfeng

Jung Jae-Eun: Women's taekwondo events held in the Olympic Games, *4561*

Jungwirth, Stanislav: Runner to complete the 1500-meter race in under 3:40 minutes, *5067*

Juvenal, James: Men's eight-oared shell with coxswain rowing event held in the Olympic Games, *4925*

National team to sweep the medals in the men's single sculls rowing event in the Olympic Games, *4932*

K

Kacperczyk, Krystyna: Hurdler to hold the officially accepted world record in the women's 400-meter hurdles, *4344*

Kadirov, Gabdrahman: World championships in ice speedway motorcycle racing, *4583*

Kahanamoku, Duke Paoa: National team to sweep the medals in the men's 100-meter freestyle in the Olympic Games, *5809*
Swimmer to win Olympic gold medals 8 years apart, and to win Olympic medals 12 years apart, *5813*

Kahanamoku, Samuel: National team to sweep the medals in the men's 100-meter freestyle in the Olympic Games, *5809*
Swimmer to win Olympic gold medals 8 years apart, and to win Olympic medals 12 years apart, *5813*

Kainz, Adolf: Men's pairs 1000-meter kayaking event held in the Olympic Games, *2598*

Kaiser, Stien: Woman speed skater to skate the 3000 meters in under 5 minutes, *5680*

Kalinchuk, Yekaterina: Women's side horse vault gymnastics competition held in the Olympic Games, *3937*

Kalinina, Irina: Diver to hold women's world titles in both springboard and highboard platform diving at the same time, *2812*
Diver to win two consecutive women's world titles in springboard diving, *2813*

Kalitta, Connie: Drag racer to reach a speed over 290 miles per hour, *1138*

Kamsing, Samluck: Athlete from Thailand to win a gold medal in the Olympic Games, *4801*

Kania, Karin Enke: Athlete to win eight medals in individual events in the Olympic Winter Games, *4764*
Speed skater to win five women's long-distance speed skating titles in the world championships, *5708*
Woman speed skater to skate the 1500 meters in under 2 minutes, *5704*
World Cup series of competitions for speed skating, *5703*

Kankkonen, Veikko: Men's individual 70-meter ski jump event held at the Olympic Winter Games, *5410*

Kano, Jigoro: Development of judo, *4528*

Kanon, Larry: Basketball player to have 11 steals in a single National Basketball Association (NBA) game, *2119*

Kantner, Dee: Women referees in the National Basketball Association (NBA), *2386*

Karasevdas, Pantelis: Free rifle individual shooting event held in the Olympic Games, *5269*

Karavaeva, Irina: Women's trampoline event held in the Olympic Games, *6232*

Karlova, Larysa: Handball players to win two consecutive gold medals in women's team handball in the Olympic Games, *4008*

Karlstad, Geir: Speed skater to skate the 10,000 meters in under 14 minutes, *5707*

Karppinen, Klaes: Men's 4 x 10-kilometer relay Nordic (cross-country) event held in the Olympic Winter Games, *5384*

Karppinen, Pertti: Rower to win three consecutive men's single sculls rowing titles in the Olympic Games, *4941*

Kasaya, Yukio: National team to sweep the medals in the men's 70-meter ski jump at the Olympic Winter Games, *5420*

Kasey, John: National Football League player to kick 37 field goals in a single season, *3475*

Kasko, Eddie: Los Angeles Dodgers regular season baseball game played at Dodger Stadium, *1655*

Käsling, Dagmar: Women's 4 x 400-meter relay track event held in the Olympic Games, *5095*

Kato, Miyoshi: World championships in short track speed skating to be officially recognized, *5697*

Kato, Sawao: Gymnast to win two consecutive men's parallel bars titles in the Olympic Games, *3963*

Male gymnast to win 8 gold medals, and 12 medals overall, in the Olympics Games, *3961*

Kaufmann, Carl: Runners to complete the men's 400-meter race in under 45 seconds, *5072*

Kay-Skrzypeski, Kazimierz: Men's singles luge (toboggan) event held in the Olympic Winter Games, *4455*

Olympic Winter Games at which an athlete was killed, *4713*

Kazak, Petr: World championships in orienteering to include short events, *4812*

Kazakova, Oksana: Male figure skater to win the pairs title at the Olympic Winter Games with two different partners, *3115*

Kazankina, Tatyana: Runner to race the women's 1500 meters in under 4 minutes, *5104*

Runner to win two consecutive titles in the women's 1500-meter race in the Olympic Games, *5118*

Kealoha, Warren Paoa: Swimmer to win two consecutive men's 100-meter backstroke titles in the Olympic Games, *5817*

Kee Yong Ham: Runners from a single country outside the United States to take the top three spots in the Boston Marathon, *4483*

Keeler, Willy: Baseball player to lead the American League in singles in three consecutive years, *1369*

Keiloha, Pua Kela: National team to sweep the medals in the men's 100-meter freestyle in the Olympic Games, *5809*

Keino, Kip (H. Kipchoge): Athlete from Kenya to win a gold medal in the Olympic Games, *4732*

Runner from Africa to hold the world record in the men's 5000 meters, *5079*

Runner from Africa to win the men's 1500-meter title at the Olympic Games, *5092*

Keleti, Agnes: Gymnast to win two consecutive women's floor exercise titles in the Olympic Games, *3941*

Woman gymnast to win 10 medals in the Olympic Games, *3940*

Women's floor exercises gymnastics competition held in the Olympic Games, *3936*

Kellenberger, Emil: Military revolver and military rifle team shooting events held in the Olympic Games, *5280*

Military rifle individual shooting event held in the Olympic Games, *5279*

Keller, Jack: Result of an Olympic event to be changed after viewing of the film of the race, *4678*

Track world record for which there was an official wind-speed reading, *6209*

Kelley, John A.: Runner to race in more than 60 Boston Marathons, *4520*

Kelley, John J.: Boston Marathon winner who was a member of the Boston Athletic Association, *4486*

Kelly, Geoff: World outdoor championships in bowls, *2499*

Kelly, Grace: Rowers to win two consecutive medals in the men's double sculls event in the Olympic Games, *4935*

Kelly, Jack (John, Sr.): Rower to win three consecutive medals in the men's double sculls event in the Olympic Games, *4936*

Rowers to win two consecutive medals in the men's double sculls event in the Olympic Games, *4935*

Kelly, Jim: Professional football player to complete 31 passes in a single Super Bowl game, *3460*

Kelly, King: National League player to lead the league in doubles in two consecutive years, *1259*

Kelly, Michael: Rapid-fire pistol and free pistol team events held in the Olympic Games, *5299*

Kelly, Red: National Hockey League player to be named outstanding defenseman, *4131*

Kelly, Sean: World cup in cycling, *2715*

Kelly, Tom: Minnesota Twins manager to be named Manager of the Year, *1815*

Kemp, Peter: Water polo event held in the Olympic Games, *6301*

Kempner, Patty: Women's 4 x 100-meter medley relay swimming event held in the Olympic Games, *5840*

Kendall, Barbara: Women's sailboarding event held in the Olympic Games, *5192*

Kendall, Bruce: Women's sailboarding event held in the Olympic Games, *5192*

Kendler, Bob: National organization for racquetball, *4874*

Kennedy, Barbara: College women's basketball player to score 392 points in a single Division I National Collegiate Athletic Association (NCAA) season, *2176*

Kennedy, Hugh: Introduction of *chole* to the British Isles, *2630*

Kennedy, John: African-American baseball player to play for the Philadelphia Phillies, *1627*

Kennedy, Karol: Figure skaters from the United States to win the pairs title in the world championships, *3040*

International pairs figure skating competition in which all the medalists were brother-and-sister pairs, *3041*

Kennedy, Peter: Figure skaters from the United States to win the pairs title in the world championships, *3040*

International pairs figure skating competition in which all the medalists were brother-and-sister pairs, *3041*

Kenny, Arturo: Athletes from Argentina to win gold medals in the Olympic Games, *4659*

Keogh, Rod: College baseball player to pitch 20 bases on balls in a College World Series, *1576*

Kerr, Robert: Runner from Canada to win the men's 200-meter race in the Olympic Games, *4996*

Kerrigan, Nancy: Figure skater to be stripped of the U.S. national women's singles title, *3104*

Figure skaters from the United States to sweep the women's singles medals in the world championships, *3097*

Kersauson, Olivier de: Sailor to complete a solo circumnavigation of the world in under 130 days, *5246*

Kersee, Bob: Heptathlete from the United States, and the first African-American, to win the women's heptathlon in the Olympic Games, *4015*

Keulen-Deelstra, Atje: Speed skater to win four women's titles at the long-distance speed skating championships, *5690*

Khadartsev, Makharbek: Wrestler to win two consecutive light heavyweight freestyle wrestling titles in the Olympic Games, *6414*

Khan, Jahangir: Squash player to win six men's singles world open titles, *5766*

World cup in squash, *5765*

Khan, Jansher: Squash player to win eight men's singles world open titles, *5768*

Khvedosyuk, Pinayeva Lyudmila *See* Pinayeva, Lyudmila Khvedosyuk

Ki Yoon Song: Runners from a single country outside the United States to take the top three spots in the Boston Marathon, *4483*

Kicanovic, Dragan: Basketball team from Yugoslavia to win the men's title in the Olympic Games, *2163*

Kidd, Jason: Dallas Mavericks player to be named National Basketball Association (NBA) Rookie of the Year, *2352*

Kidd, Tom: British Open golf championship held at the Old Course at St. Andrews, Scotland, *3586*

Kiehl, Marina: Women's super giant slalom to be included in the world cup for Alpine skiing, *5450*

Kiely, Thomas: Men's decathlon event held in the Olympic Games, *2737*

Kienzl, Karla: World championships in luge (toboggan), *4453*

Killander, Ernst: Orienteering as a sport, *4805*

Killefer, Red: Chicago Cubs regular season baseball game played at Wrigley Field, *1425*

Killett, Iris: Queen Elizabeth II Cup, *2861*

Killy, Jean-Claude: Men's giant slalom to have two runs on separate days, rather than a single run, at the Olympic Winter Games, *5417*

World cup series of competitions in Alpine skiing, *5416*

Kilman, Gustaf: Team jumping (Prix des Nations) equestrian event held in the Olympic Games, *2847*

Kim, Dong-moon: Badminton event for mixed doubles in the Olympic Games, *1175*

Kim, Jeong-tae: World championships in taekwondo, *4541*

Kim, Ki-hoon: Men's 1000-meter short track speed skating event held in the Olympic Winter Games, *5714*

Men's 5000-meter relay short track speed skating event held at the Olympic Winter Games, *5716*

Speed skater to win two consecutive men's 1000-meter short track titles at the Olympic Winter Games, *5722*

Kim, Kyong Hun: Men's taekwondo events held in the Olympic Games, *4560*

Kim, Moon-soo: Badminton events held in the Olympic Games as medal sports, *1174*

Kim, Nelli: Gymnast to receive a perfect score of 10 in the Olympic Games, *3960*

Kim, So-young: World championships in taekwondo to include women, *4549*

Kim, Soo-nyung: Archer to win two titles in women's events in a single Olympic Games, *1038*

Kim, Taek-soo: Men's and women's doubles events to be included in the world cup in table tennis, *5998*

Kim, Yoon-mi: Athlete under the age of 14 to win a gold medal in the Olympic Winter Games, *4783*

Kindkvist, Ulla: World championships in orienteering, *4808*

King, Betsy: Woman golfer to earn more than $500,000 in official prize money in a season, *3861*

Woman golfer to win more than $5 million, and then $6 million, in official prize money during her career, *3882*

King, Billie Jean: Australian Open women's doubles tennis title, *6139*

Australian Open women's singles tennis title, *6140*

Federation Cup championships, *6112*

French Open mixed doubles tennis match, *6119*

French Open women's doubles tennis match, *6121*

Sports Illustrated Sportsman of the Year award to be given to a woman and to be shared, *1155*

Steel tennis rackets came into widespread use, *6115*

Tennis player to win 112 women's singles matches in a single season, *6147*

U.S. Open women's doubles tennis title, *6127*

U.S. Open women's singles tennis title, *6128*

Wimbledon Open women's doubles tennis title, *6133*

Wimbledon Open women's singles tennis match, *6134*

King, William "Dolly": African-American to become a member of the Collegiate Basketball Officials Association, *1974*

Kingsbury, Clarence: Men's 4000-meter team pursuit cycling event held in the Olympic Games, *2692*

Kinnick, Niles: College football player to win the Associated Press (AP) Athlete of the Year Award, *3185*

Kipke, Christiane Knetsch: Women's eight-oared shell with coxswain event held in the Olympic Games, *4949*

Kiptanui, Moses: Runner to race the men's 5000-meter steeplechase in under 8:00 minutes, *5178*

Runner to win two, and then three, consecutive titles in the men's 3000-meter steeplechase in the World Championships in Athletics, *5167*

Kiraly, Karch (Charles): Beach volleyball event held in the Olympic Games, *6286*

Volleyball team from the United States to win the men's title in the Olympic Games, *6285*

Kirchhoffer, Alphonse: National team to sweep the medals in the men's masters foil fencing event in the Olympic Games, *2901*

Kirienko, Grigoriy: Fencer to win four men's sabre titles in the world championships, *2943*

Kirk, Hazel: National track and field (athletics) championships for women in the United States, *6207*

Kirk, Oliver: Bantamweight and featherweight boxing events held in the Olympic Games, and the first boxer to win two gold medals in a single Olympic Games, *2527*

Kirksey, Morris: Team from the United States to win the men's 4 x 100-meter relay track event in the Olympic Games, *5011*

Kirkwood, Fay: Women-only rodeo, *4889*

Kirov, Peter: Wrestler to win two consecutive flyweight Greco-Roman wrestling titles in the Olympic Games, *6402*

Kirui, Ismael: Runner to win two consecutive titles in the men's 5000-meter event in the World Championships in Athletics, *5172*

Kiselyeva, Irina: Pentathlete to win two consecutive titles at the women's world pentathlon championships, *4833*

Kiss, Geza: Men's 4 x 250-meter (later 4 x 200-meter) freestyle relay swimming event held in the Olympic Games, *5799*

Kissling, Connie: World championships for freestyle skiing, *5451*

Kitamura, Kusuo: Olympic men's 1500-meter freestyle event in which the medalists all had times under 20 minutes, *5825*

Kite, Tom: Golfer to win the Tour Championship in a playoff, *3860*

Golfer to win three straight individual titles at the U.S. intercollegiate golf championships, *3803*

Kiviat, Abel: Runner to hold the officially accepted world record in the men's 1500-meter event, *5000*

Kjus, Lasse: National team to sweep the medals in the men's Alpine combined skiing event at the Olympic Winter Games, *5490*

Klammer, Franz: Skier to win five men's downhill world cup titles, *5440*

Kleber, Ina: National team to sweep the medals in the women's 100-meter backstroke, and the women's 200-meter backstroke, in the Olympic Games, *5935*

Klein, Chuck: Baseball player to have 100 extra-base hits in a season in the National League, *1489*

Philadelphia Phillies baseball player to be named Most Valuable Player, *1503*

Klein, Kit: Speed skater to win the women's title in the world championships, *5655*

Klein, Roelof: Athletes from the Netherlands to win gold medals in the Olympic Games, *4624*

Men's pair-oared shell with coxswain rowing event held in the Olympic Games, *4926*

Klimki, Reiner: Woman equestrian to win a gold medal in team dressage in the Olympic Games, *2875*

Klingler, David: National Collegiate Athletic Association major college football player to complete 54 touchdown passes in a single season, *3437*

National Collegiate Athletic Association major college football player to gain 5,221 yards in a single year, *3444*

Kluge, H. L.: Book on diving, *2786*

Klumberg, Aleksandr: Decathlete to hold the officially accepted world record in the men's decathlon, *2739*

Knape, Ulrike: Women's highboard platform diving event held in the world championships, *2807*

Knetsch (later Kipke), Christiane: Women's eight-oared shell with coxswain event held in the Olympic Games, *4949*

Knight, Arthur F.: Golf club with a steel shaft, *3648*

Knight, Laura: Tennis player to win the women's singles title at the United States national championships, *6022*

United States women's doubles national tennis championships, *6027*

Knodotovich, Yekaterina: Athlete from newly independent Belarus to win a gold medal in the Olympic Games, *4794*

Knöppel, Arvid: Running deer (single shot) team shooting event held in the Olympic Games, *5286*

Knowles, Durward: Athletes from the Bahamas to win gold medals in the Olympic Games, *4719*

Knox-Johnston, Robin: Single-handed, non-stop, round-the-world sailing race, *5224*

Koch, Lars: Canoe marathon world championships, *2624*

Koch, Marita: Runner to race the women's 200 meters in under 22 seconds, *5110*

Runner to race the women's 400 meters in under 49 seconds, *5109*

Runner to set seven world records in the women's 400 meters, *5145*

Runner to win the women's 200-meter title in the World Championships in Athletics, *5135*

Women's 400-meter race in which the top three runners had times of under 50 seconds, *5115*

Koch, William: Skier to introduce skating techniques into Nordic (cross-country) skiing in international competition, *5437*

Kocherhina, Tetyana Makarets: Handball players to win two consecutive gold medals in women's team handball in the Olympic Games, *4008*

Koech, Peter: Record in the men's 5000-meter steeplechase to last for more than 10 years, *5108*

Koester, Mrs. A. J.: National bowling championships for women in the United States, *2486*

Kohler, Christine: Women's springboard diving event held at the world championships, *2808*

Köhler, Thomas: Men's singles luge (toboggan) event held in the Olympic Winter Games, *4455*

Kok, Ada: Women's 200-meter butterfly event held in the Olympic Games, *5859*

Kokkinen, Väinö: Wrestler to win two consecutive middleweight Greco-Roman titles in the Olympic Games, *6384*

Kolar, Gertchen: Uneven (asymmetrical) bars competition held in the world championships for gymnastics, *3933*

Kolb, Claudia: Swimmer to win the women's 200- and 400-meter individual medley events in the same Olympic Games, *5854*

Women's 200-meter individual medley swimming event held in the Olympic Games, *5855*

Kolchin, Pavel: Skiers from the Soviet Union to win the men's 4 x 10-kilometer relay Nordic (cross-country) title at the Olympic Winter Games, *5405*

Kolchina, Alevtina: Women's 5-kilometer cross-country event held in the world championships of Nordic skiing, *5408*

Kolehmainen, Johannes: Men's 5000- and 10,000-meter events held in the Olympic Games, *5008*

Men's individual cross-country event held in the Olympic Games, *5006*

Kolomenkin, Nikolai: Athlete from Russia to win a gold medal in the Olympic Games, *4640*

Figure skater to win the title for special figures in the Olympic Games, *2976*

Konchellah, Billy: Runner to win two consecutive titles in the men's 800-meter event in the World Championships in Athletics, *5155*

Kongshaug, Erling: Small-bore rifle (three positions) individual shooting event held in the Olympic Games, *5309*

König, Regina: World cup in luge (toboggan), *4461*

Konno, Ford: Olympic men's 1500-meter freestyle event in which the medalists all had times under 19 minutes, *5832*

Kono, Takanori: Skiers to win two consecutive men's Nordic combined team titles at the Olympic Winter Games, *5489*

Kono, Tamio "Tommy": Weightlifter from the United States to win the lightweight weightlifting title in the Olympic Games, *6337*

Konopacka, Halina: Athlete from Poland to win a gold medal in the Olympic Games, *4670*

Women's discus throw event, and the first women's field event, held in the Olympic Games, *2762*

Konow, Magnus: Athletes to compete in the Olympic Games over a period of 40 years, *4688*

Konrads, John: Olympic men's 1500-meter freestyle event in which the medalists all had times under 18 minutes, *5841*

Konstantinidis, Aristidis: Men's road race cycling event held in the Olympic Games, *2686*

Konyayeva, Nadezhda: Javelin-thrower to break the 180-foot barrier in the women's event, *4395*

Koponen, Hannu: Ski orienteering world championships to include sprint competitions, *4810*

Köppen, Lene: World championships in badminton, *1171*

Koroibos: Olympic Games, *4599*

Track event in the Olympic Games, *6197*

Korondi, Margit: Women's uneven (asymmetrical) bars gymnastics competition held in the Olympic Games, *3938*

Kosichkin, Viktor: Speed skater to skate the 10,000 meters in under 16 minutes, *5672*

Koss, Johann Olav: Speed skater to win two consecutive titles in the men's 1500-meters at the Olympic Winter Games, *5720*

Speed skaters to be named *Sports Illustrated* Sportsmen of the Year, *5719*

Koster, John: Bowler to win four titles in the American Bowling Congress (ABC) national championships, *2485*

Kother, Rosemarie: Swimmer to win two consecutive women's 200-meter butterfly world titles, *5920*

Women's 200-meter butterfly event held in the world championships, *5900*

Koufax, Sandy: Baseball pitcher to lead the National League in earned run average for five consecutive years, *1685*

Baseball player to be named Associated Press Athlete of the Year twice, *1676*

Major league baseball pitcher to reach 382 strikeouts in a single season, *1683*

Kovácsi, Aladár: Men's modern pentathlon team event held in the Olympic Games, *4823*

Kovarikova, Radka: Figure skaters from the Czech Republic to win the pairs title in the world championships, *3110*

Kozma, István: Wrestler to win two consecutive super heavyweight Greco-Roman titles in the Olympic Games, *6392*

Kozyreva, Lyubov: Olympic Winter Games at which athletes from the Soviet Union participated, *4705*

Women's 10-kilometer cross-country event held in the world championships of Nordic skiing, *5399*

Kraenzlein, Alvin: Athlete to win four gold medals in a single Olympic Games, *4627*

Men's 200-meter hurdles event held in the Olympic Games, *4325*

Men's 60-meter running event held in the Olympic Games, *4976*

National team to sweep the medals in the men's 110-meter hurdles in the Olympic Games, *4323*

Kratochvilová, Jarmila: Runner to race the women's 400 meters in under 48 seconds, *5137*

Runner to win the women's 400- and 800-meter events in the World Championships in Athletics, *5136*

Women's 400-meter race in which the top three runners had times of under 50 seconds, *5115*

Krause, Barbara: Swimmer to race the women's 100-meter freestyle in under 55 seconds, *5932*

Krause, Charles: National team to sweep the top honors in the men's horizontal bar, long horse vault, side (pommel) horse, and rings gymnastics competitions in the Olympic Games, *3913*

Krause, Paul: National Football League player to reach 81 career interceptions, *3359*

Krausner, Hans: World championships in luge (toboggan), *4453*

Kravets, Inessa: Triple-jumper to break the 50-foot barrier in the women's event, *6263*

Women's triple jump event held in the Olympic Games, *6265*

Krenz, Eric: Discus-thrower to break the 160-foot and 50-meter barriers, *2763*

Kristiansen, Ingrid: Boston Marathon to offer prize money, *4515*

Runner to race the women's 5000 meters in under 15 minutes, *5138*

Krivonosov, Mikhail: Hammer-thrower to break the 220-foot barrier, *3990*

Kronberger, Lily: Figure skater from Hungary to win the women's singles title in the world championships, *2972*

Figure skater to win three and then four consecutive women's singles titles in the world championships, *2982*

Kronberger, Petra: Skier to win both the women's slalom and the women's Alpine combination in the same Olympic Winter Games, and the first from Austria to win the Olympic women's slalom title, *5480*

Krone, Julie: Woman jockey to win one of America's Triple Crown horse races, *4317*

Krumbhaar, Edward B.: National field hockey organization in the United States, *4037*

Kruyuff, Charles Gerard de: Equestrians to win two consecutive three-day event team titles, *2854*

Kubicka, Terry: Figure skater to perform a back flip in competition, *3073*

Kudma, Bohumil: Canoer to win two men's Canadian pairs 1000-meter titles in the Olympic Games, *2602*

Kuehn, Louis: Diver from the United States to win the men's springboard diving event in the Olympic Games, *2796*

Kuenn, Harvey: Detroit Tigers baseball player to be named Rookie of the Year, *1593*

Kühne, Rita: Women's 4 x 400-meter relay track event held in the Olympic Games, *5095*

Kukkonen, Sinikka: Ski orienteering world championships, *4809*

Kulakova, Galina: Skier to win two consecutive women's Nordic (cross-country) skiing titles in the Olympic Winter Games, *5423*

World cup for Nordic skiing, *5428*

Kulej, Jerzy: Boxer to win two consecutive light welterweight titles in the Olympic Games, *2569*

Kuosku, Matti: Worldloppet Cup, *5429*

Kurkowska, Janina: Archer to win two, and then up to seven, women's individual world championships, *1031*

World championships in target archery, *1030*

Kurland, Bob: Basketball player to be named Most Valuable Player of the Division I National Collegiate Athletic Association (NCAA) Final Four twice in a row, *1908*

Kuscsik, Nina: Boston Marathon to include women as official participants, *4496*

Kusner, Kathy: Woman to be licensed as a jockey in the United States, *4304*

Kusuma, Allan Budi: Athlete from Indonesia to win a gold medal in the Olympic Games, *4777*

Badminton events held in the Olympic Games as medal sports, *1174*

Kuzenkova, Olga: Hammer-thrower to hold the officially accepted world record in the women's event, *3997*

Kuzin, Vladimir: Skiers from the Soviet Union to win the men's 4 x 10-kilometer relay Nordic (cross-country) title at the Olympic Winter Games, *5405*

Kwan, Michelle: Champions Series in figure skating, *3112*

L

La Russa, Tony: American League manager to be named Manager of the Year, *1768*

Laakkonen, Risto: Skier to win two medals in the men's 90-meter team ski-jumping event in the Olympic Winter Games, *5475*

LaBarba, Fidel: Boxer to win both Olympic and professional world championships, *2547*

LaBeach, Lloyd: Runner from Central or South America to set or equal a world track and field record, *5049*

Lacombe, Ethel Thomson: Mixed doubles championships at Wimbledon, *6053*

Lacoste, Catherine: Amateur golfer to win the U.S. Women's Open, *3787*

Lacoste, René: Amateur golfer to win the U.S. Women's Open, *3787*

Tennis player to win a French national men's singles championship after the event became international, *6076*

Tennis player to win three French national men's singles championships after the event became international, *6086*

Tennis players to win the French national men's doubles championship after the event became international, *6079*

Ladoumèque, Jules: Runner to complete the men's 1500-meter race in under 3:50 minutes, *5025*

Runner to complete the men's mile race in under 4:10 minutes, *5026*

Lafomara, Michelle: National Collegiate Athletic Association (NCAA) Division I women's softball player to get seven hits in a single game, *5625*

Lagache, André: Le Mans 24-hours sports car race, *1057*

Lagutin, Boris: Boxer to win two consecutive light middleweight titles in the Olympic Games, *2568*

Lähde, Matti: Men's 4 x 10-kilometer relay Nordic (cross-country) event held in the Olympic Winter Games, *5384*

Lainonen, Mikko: National Hockey League player to have six assists in a single Stanley Cup playoffs game, *4184*

Laitinen, Mika: Skier to win two medals in the men's 90-meter team ski-jumping event in the Olympic Winter Games, *5475*

Lajoie, Napoleon: Baseball player to lead the American League in batting average, *1321*

Baseball player to lead the American League in batting average for two consecutive years, *1359*

Baseball player to lead the American League in home runs, *1322*

Baseball player to lead the American League in runs scored, *1323*

Baseball player to lead the American League in slugging average, *1324*

Baseball player to lead the American League in slugging average for two consecutive years, *1361*

Baseball player to lead the American League in total bases, *1325*

Detroit Tigers regular season baseball game played at Tiger Stadium, *1414*

Three consecutive home runs in a single inning of an American League game, *1348*

Triple Crown hitter in the American League, *1328*

Lamazou, Titouan: Vendée Globe round-the-world challenge race, *5250*

Lambe, H.: National championships in track and field (athletics) in the United States, *6201*

Lambeau, Curly (Earl): Pro Football Hall of Fame, *3268*

Lambert, Nathalie: Women's 3000-meter short track relay speed skating event held at the Olympic Winter Games, *5715*

Lampkin, Martin: World championships in trials riding in moto-cross racing, *4588*

Lance, Sylvia: Tennis player to win two consecutive Australian national women's doubles championships, *6066*

Lancien, Nathalie: Women's points race cycling event held in the Olympic Games, *2722*

Landale, Bailie William: Open golf competition at St. Andrews, Scotland, *3553*

Landbeck, Liselotte: Woman speed skater to skate the 500 meters in under 1 minute, *5647*

Landis, Kenesaw Mountain: Cincinnati Reds World Series victory, *1436*

Commissioner of Baseball, *1456*

Landvoigt, Bernt: Rowers to win two consecutive titles in the pair-oared shell without coxswain event in the Olympic Games, *4950*

Landvoigt, Jörg: Rowers to win two consecutive titles in the pair-oared shell without coxswain event in the Olympic Games, *4950*

Lane, Alfred: Rapid-fire pistol and free pistol team events held in the Olympic Games, *5299*

Shooter to win both the rapid-fire pistol and the free pistol individual events, and the first from the United States to win either event, in the Olympic Games, *5296*

Lane, Francis: Event held in the modern Olympic Games, *4605*

Lane, Frederick: Men's 200-meter freestyle swimming event held in the Olympic Games, *5789*

Men's obstacle swimming race held in the Olympic Games, *5790*

Swimmer to race 100 yards in one minute, *5793*

Lane, Jason: College baseball player to have 15 hits in a College World Series, *1846*

Langen-Parow, Carl Friedrich Freiherr von: Equestrian to win both an individual and a team medal in dressage in the Olympic Games, *2853*

Team dressage equestrian event held in the Olympic Games, *2855*

Langli, Terje: Men's 10-kilometer cross-country (classical) event held in the world championships of Nordic skiing, *5466*

Langlois, Lloyd: World championships for freestyle skiing, *5451*

Langrishe, May: National tennis championships in Ireland, *6010*

Lannoy, Micheline: Figure skaters from Belgium to win the pairs title at the Olympic Winter Games, *3036*

Figure skaters from Belgium to win the pairs title in the world championships, *3031*

Lansing, Mike: Arizona Diamondbacks regular season baseball game played at the Bank One Ballpark, *1850*

Larner, George: Men's 3500-meter and 10-mile walks held in the Olympic Games, *6289*

Laroche, Alain: World championships for freestyle skiing, *5451*

Laroche, Monique: World sky diving championships, *5504*

Larrouy, Maurice: National team to sweep the rapid-fire pistol individual shooting event in the Olympic Games, *5278*

Larsen, Don: Perfect game in the World Series, *1623*

Larsen, John: Running deer (single and double shot) individual shooting event held in the Olympic Games, *5308*

Larson, Lance: Men's 4 x 100-meter medley relay swimming event held in the Olympic Games, *5838*

Larsson, Anders: Light heavyweight freestyle wrestling event held in the Olympic Games, *6377*

Larsson, Gunnar: Men's 200-meter individual medley event held at the world championships, *5883*

Men's 200-meter individual medley event in which the top four swimmers broke the world record, *5870*

LaRue, Rusty: National Collegiate Athletic Association major college football player to complete 55 passes in a single game, *3471*

Laser, Christiner Bodner: National team to sweep the medals in the women's pentathlon in the Olympic Games, *4831*

Lashko, Irina: Women's synchronized three-meter springboard diving event held at the world championships, *2825*

Lasorda, Tommy: National League manager to be named Manager of the Year, *1771*

United States team to win the men's baseball title in the Olympic Games, *1861*

Lathan, Christina Brehmer Lathan: Women's 400-meter race in which the top three runners had times of under 50 seconds, *5115*

Lattner, John: College football player to win the Maxwell Award twice, *3235*

Latynina, Larisa: Athlete to win 18 medals in the Olympic Games, *4711*

Gymnast to win 9 gold medals and 18 medals overall in the Olympics Games, *3950*

Gymnast to win three consecutive gold medals in the team combined exercises in the Olympic Games, *3951*

Gymnast to win two consecutive women's all-around titles in the Olympic Games, *3944*

Gymnasts to win two consecutive gold medals in the women's team combined exercises, *3945*

National team to sweep the top medals in the women's all-around gymnastics competition in the Olympic Games, *3946*

Laumaille, Madame (first name unknown): Woman automobile racer, *1046*

Laurie, Louis: Boxer to be awarded the Val Barker Cup, *2549*

Laver, Rod: Australian Open men's doubles tennis title, *6136*

Australian Open men's singles tennis title, *6137*

Davis Cup to be a full open tournament for professionals and amateurs, *6151*

French Open men's doubles tennis match, *6117*

French Open men's singles tennis match, *6118*

Tennis player to win 17 men's singles tournaments in one season, *6141*

Tennis player to win six consecutive French national men's doubles championships after the event became international, *6113*

Tennis player to win two Grand Slams, *6142*

Wimbledon Open men's singles tennis title, *6130*

Lavrov, Andrei: Handball player to win two consecutive gold medals in men's team handball in the Olympic Games, *4011*

Law, Vernon: Pittsburgh Pirates pitcher to win the Cy Young Award, *1642*

Lawlor, Si: Single-handed transatlantic race, *5201*

Lawrence, Andrea Mead: Skier from the United States to win two Olympic gold medals, *5397*

Women's giant slalom event held at the Olympic Winter Games, *5393*

Lawrence, Carl: National Collegiate Athletic Association hockey player to score five goals in a single "Frozen Four" tournament game, *4125*

Lawrence, Charles: Cricket team from outside the British Isles to tour England, *2649*

Lawrence, W. B.: National golf championship in the United States, *3608*

Lawrie, Paul: Golfer to come from 10 strokes behind to win a Professional Golfers' Association (PGA) recognized tournament, *3897*

Laws, Gilbert: 6-meter-class sailing event held in the Olympic Games, *5205*

Layne, Bobby: College football player to pass for or himself score a total of six touchdowns in a major bowl game, *3203*

Lazaro, Francisco: Athlete to die while participating in the modern Olympic Games, *4644*

Lazutina, Larissa: Skier to win four medals in the same Nordic skiing event in the Olympic Winter Games, *5478*

Le Déroff, Jean-Yves: Sailor to win two consecutive Tornado-class sailing titles in the Olympic Games, *5251*

Leach, Reggie: National Hockey League player to score 19 goals in a single set of Stanley Cup playoffs, *4170*

Leary, J. Scott: Men's 50-yard (later 50-meter) freestyle swimming event held in the Olympic Games, *5795*

Leatherwood, Lillie: Team from the United States to win the women's 4 x 400-meter relay at the Olympic Games, *5142*

Leden, Judy: World championships in hang gliding for women, *3534*

Lee, Eun-young: World championships in taekwondo to include women, *4549*

Lee, Gyeo-sung: World championships in taekwondo to include additional weight classes for men, *4543*

Lee, Han-sup: Men's team archery event held in the Olympic Games, *1037*

Lee, James: Golf book published in the United States, *3611*

Lee, James T.: All-America college football team named by Walter Camp, *3121*

Lee, John: National Collegiate Athletic Association major college football player to kick 29 field goals in a single season, *3387*

Lee, Joon-ho: Men's 5000-meter relay short track speed skating event held at the Olympic Winter Games, *5716*

Lee, Ki-hyung: World championships in taekwondo, *4541*

Lee, Lai-shan: Athlete from Hong Kong to win a gold medal in the Olympic Games, *4797*

Lee, Norvel: African-American boxers to win gold medals in the Olympic Games, *2557*

Lee, Samuel: Asian-American athlete to win a gold medal in the Olympic Games, *4694*
Diver to win two consecutive men's platform diving titles in the Olympic Games, *2803*

Lee, Sun-hee: Women's taekwondo events held in the Olympic Games, *4561*

Lee, Willis: Shooters from the United States to win the small-bore rifle team title in the Olympic Games, *5300*

Leemans, Fernand: World figure skating championships for roller skating, *4909*

Legien, Waldemar: Judo artist to win gold medals in two different weight classes in the Olympic Games, *4555*

Lehmann, Jens: Cycling team to break the 4-minute mark in the men's 4000-meter team pursuit race in the Olympic Games, *2730*

Lehtinen, Lauri: Runner to race the men's 5000 meters in under 14:28.0 minutes, *5028*

Lemaire, Lyn: Hawaii Ironman triathlon to include women, *6236*

Lemieux, Mario: National Hockey League player to be named Most Valuable Player of the NHL All-Star Game three times, *4201*

Lemming, Erik: Javelin-thrower to hold the officially accepted world record in the men's event, *4384*

Men's freestyle javelin event held in the Olympic Games, *4381*

Men's javelin-throw event held at the Olympic Games, *4382*

LeMond, Greg: Cyclist from the United States to win the Tour de France, *2712*

Cyclist to be named *Sports Illustrated* Sportsman of the Year, *2714*

Cyclist to win the Jesse Owens International Award, *2717*

Lenglen, Suzanne: Tennis player to win five consecutive Wimbledon women's singles championships, *6065*

Tennis player to win nine Wimbledon women's doubles titles, *6088*

Tennis player to win the French national women's singles championship after the event became international, *6077*

Tennis player to win three gold medals in tennis in the same Olympic Games, *6048*

Tennis players to win a French national mixed doubles championship after the event became international, *6078*

Tennis players to win five consecutive Wimbledon women's doubles championships, *6068*

Tennis players to win the French national women's doubles championship after the event became international, *6080*

Tennis star to turn professional, *6081*

Lentauw: Black athletes from Africa to participate in the Olympic Games, *4630*

Lenzi, Mark: Diver to be awarded more than 100 points on a single dive, *2819*

Leonard, Charles: Pentathlete to achieve a perfect score in the shooting portion of the men's modern pentathlon in the Olympic Games, *4817*

Leonard, Dutch: Major league baseball pitcher of the 20th century to have an earned run average of less than 1.0 for a season, *1417*

Leonard, Edgar: National team to sweep the medals in the men's doubles tennis event in the Olympic Games, *6043*

Leonard, Justin: Golfer to come from 10 strokes behind to win a Professional Golfers' Association (PGA) recognized tournament, *3897*

Leonard, Mike: Film of a sporting event, *5743*

Leonard, René: Le Mans 24-hours sports car race, *1057*

Leonard, Sugar Ray (Ray Charles): Boxer to hold world titles in five different weight classes, *2584*

Leontyeva, Galina: Volleyball players to win two consecutive women's gold medals in the Olympic Games, *6283*

Leopold, King of Belgium: Reigning monarch to play in a national golf championship, *3710*

Ligowsky, George: Clay pigeons for target shooting, *5268*

Lihui, Zheng *See* Zheng Lihui

Lilienthal, Otto: International governing body for gliding (soaring) competitions, *3530*

Liljenvall, Hans-Gunnar: Athlete to be banned from the Olympic Games for taking drugs, *4721*

Lilliehöök, Gösta: Men's modern pentathlon held in the Olympic Games, *4815*

Lilloe-Olsen, Ole Andreas: Running deer (double shot) team shooting event held in the Olympic Games, *5297*

Shooter to win two consecutive titles in the running deer (double shot) individual shooting event in the Olympic Games, *5303*

Lillywhite, James: Test match in cricket, *2650*

Lincoln, Abraham: Walker to be considered a professional, *6287*

Lind, Dean: U.S. Junior Amateur golf championship, *3719*

Lindenbach, Hermann: Team dressage equestrian event held in the Olympic Games, *2855*

Linderman, Bill: Agreement to encourage women's events in rodeos, *4893*

Linderman, Earl: National championships in gymnastics held in the United States, *3908*

Lindner, Sonny: Yukon Quest sled dog race, *5513*

Lindstrom, Dorinda: College women's basketball player to score 17 consecutive field goals in a single Division I National Collegiate Athletic Association (NCAA) game, *2244*

Linkovesi, Leo: Speed skaters to become world champions in speed skating sprints, *5686*

Linsenhoff, Liselott: Woman equestrian to win a gold medal in team dressage in the Olympic Games, *2875*

Woman equestrian to win the individual dressage title in the Olympic Games, *2879*

Lipa, Elisabeta Oleniuc: Rower to win gold medals in both the women's single and double sculls events in the Olympic Games, *4953*

Liping, Wang *See* Wang Liping

Lippincott, Donald: Runner to hold the officially accepted world record in the men's 100-meter dash, *5001*

Lippmann, Alexandre: National team to sweep the top honors in the men's individual épée competition in the Olympic Games, *2913*

Lipps, Louis: New York Jets regular season football game played at Giants Stadium, *3396*

Listach, Pat: Milwaukee Brewers baseball player to be named Rookie of the Year, *1817*

Texas Rangers regular season baseball game played at The Ballpark, *1828*

Lister, William: Water polo event held in the Olympic Games, *6301*

Liston, Sonny: Boxer to win the world heavyweight championship three times, *2566*

Olympic light heavyweight boxing champion to become world heavyweight champion, *2565*

Little, Sally: Ladies Professional Golf Association (LPGA) Tour tournament to be nationally televised for all four rounds, *3839*

Little, W. Lawson: Golfer to win 32 straight matches, *3699*

Littler, Gene: Golfer to win the Tournament of Champions twice, and then three times, in a row, *3747*

Sudden-death playoff in one of golf's major tournaments, *3814*

U.S. Open golf tournament to be televised nationally, *3743*

Litvinov, Sergey: Hammer-thrower to break the 270-foot barrier, *3995*

Lloyd, Chris Evert *See* Evert, Chris

Lloyd, Earl: African-American assistant coach in the National Basketball Association (NBA), *1988*

African-American basketball player to join the Washington Capitols of the National Basketball Association (NBA), *1926*

Lloyd, John Henry: African-American All-Star Team in professional baseball, *1402*

Lobo, Rebecca: College women's basketball Associated Press (AP) All-American first team, *2348*

College women's basketball Associated Press (AP) Player of the Year, *2350*

Locke, Bobby: Golfer from the British Commonwealth to win the British Open, *3721*

Golfer to win the British Open golf championship in under 280 for 72 holes, *3724*

Lockwood, Roscoe: Men's eight-oared shell with coxswain rowing event held in the Olympic Games, *4925*

Loday, Yves: Sailor to win two consecutive Tornado-class sailing titles in the Olympic Games, *5251*

Lofton, Kenny: Baltimore Orioles regular season baseball game played at Camden Yards, *1819*

Loftus, Ashild: Snowboarding world championships, *5521*

Loftus, John: Horse to win America's Triple Crown, *4289*

Logan, Tiffany: Women's national championships in boxing, *2594*

Loi, Francesco: Gymnasts to win two consecutive gold medals in the men's team combined exercises in the Olympic Games, *3922*

Lombardi, Ernie: Cincinnati Reds baseball player to be named Most Valuable Player, *1526*

Lombardi, Lelia: Woman automobile racer to win world-championship points in a Grand Prix race, *1119*

Lombardi, Pietro: Flyweight Greco-Roman wrestling event held in the Olympic Games, *6387*

Lombardi, Vince: College football player to win the Lombardi Award, *3299*

Lonborg, Jim: Boston Red Sox pitcher to win the Cy Young Award, *1691*

Long, Chuck: College football player to pass for six touchdowns in a major bowl game, *3397*

Long, Maxey: Runner to hold the officially accepted world record in the men's 400-meter event, *4983*

Long, Thelma Coyne: Tennis players to win five consecutive Australian national women's doubles championships, *6104*

Loomis, Alfred: Sailors from the United States to win the 6-meter-class event in the Olympic Games, *5217*

Lopes, Carlos: Athlete from Portugal to win a gold medal in the Olympic Games, *4760*

Lopez, Nancy: Golfer to be named Rookie of the Year and Player of the Year, and to win the Vare Trophy for lowest scoring average in the same year, *3816*

Golfer to win five straight tournaments in which she played, *3820*

Three-Tour Challenge, *3874*

Woman golfer to earn more than $400,000 in official prize money in a single season, *3846*

Woman golfer to score 20 below par in 72 holes, *3847*

Lopez, Steven: Men's taekwondo events held in the Olympic Games, *4560*

Loroupe, Tegla: Runner from Africa to win the women's title in the New York Marathon, *4524*

Lorton, Madeleine: Woman to become a licensed softball umpire, *5591*

Lotzbeck, Eugen Freiherr von: Team dressage equestrian event held in the Olympic Games, *2855*

Louganis, Gregory: Diver to hold the men's world titles in both springboard diving and highboard platform diving at the same time, *2815*

Diver to win both the men's platform and springboard diving titles in two consecutive Olympic Games, *2818*

Diver to win the Jesse Owens International Award, *2817*

Diver to win three consecutive men's highboard platform diving titles in the world championships, *2816*

Loughran, Beatrix: Figure skater to win two consecutive men's singles titles in the U.S. national championships, *2993*

Louis, Joe: Boxer named Fighter of the Year by *Ring* magazine two, three, and four times, *2551*

Boxer to hold a world boxing title for more than 10 years, and to defend a world boxing title 25 times, *2555*

Heavyweight boxing match to be broadcast on television, and the first at which top-price tickets cost $100, *2554*

Louis, Spiridon: Men's marathon race held in the Olympic Games, *4468*

Louis XVI, King of France: Documented horse race, *4249*

Loukachine, Igor: Men's synchronized platform diving event held in the Olympic Games, *2826*

Love, Lynette: World championships in taekwondo to include women, *4549*

Lovelock, John: Runner from New Zealand to win the men's 1500-meter title at the Olympic Games and to hold the world record in the event, *5038*

Lowe, Bobby: National League player to hit 4 home runs in a 9-inning baseball game, *1312*

Lowe, Douglas: Runner to win two consecutive men's 800-meter titles in the Olympic Games, *5019*

Lowe, Paul: San Diego Chargers regular season football game played at San Diego Stadium, *3283*

Luber, Hans: National team to sweep the top medals in men's springboard diving in the Olympic Games, *2794*

Lucas, Jerry: Basketball player to be named Division I National Collegiate Athletic Association (NCAA) Associated Press (AP) Player of the Year, *2001*

Basketball player to be named Division I National Collegiate Athletic Association (NCAA) Associated Press (AP) Player of the Year in two consecutive years, *2010*

Basketball player to be named *Sports Illustrated* Sportsman of the Year, *2002*

Lucas, John: Basketball player to have 14 assists in a single quarter of a National Basketball Association (NBA) game, *2206*

Lucas, Meriel: All-England Championships in badminton, *1166*

Luckman, Sid: National Football League player to pass for seven touchdowns in a single game, *3193*

Luddington, Nancy Rouillard: Married figure skaters to win the pairs title at the U.S. national championships, *3054*

Luddington, Ronald: Married figure skaters to win the pairs title at the U.S. national championships, *3054*

Luding, Ernst: Athlete to win medals in both the Summer and Winter Olympic Games in the same year, *4768*

Luding-Rothenburger, Christa: Athlete to win medals in both the Summer and Winter Olympic Games in the same year, *4768*

Woman speed skater to skate the 500 meters in under 40 seconds, *5700*

World Cup series of competitions for speed skating, *5703*

Ludwig, Fred: World figure skating championships for roller skating, *4909*

Luisetti, Hank (Angelo): Basketball Hall of Fame, *1975*

Lunde, Peder, Jr.: Flying Dutchman–class sailing event held in the Olympic Games, *5223*

Lunden, Léon de: Olympic Games in which animals were deliberately killed, *4619*

Lundquist, Amy: College women's basketball player to block 15 shots in a single Division I National Collegiate Athletic Association (NCAA) game, *2319*

Lundquist, Gus: Pilot to win the Thompson Trophy–Jet Division airplane race, *1015*

Lundqvist, Erik: Javelin-thrower to break the 230-foot and 70-meter barriers, *4388*

Lunn, Arnold: Modern slalom course, *5363*

Organized downhill ski race, *5362*

Luque, Adolfo: Cuban, and first Hispanic-American, to play in a World Series game, *1435*

Lüthi, Friedrich: Military revolver and military rifle team shooting events held in the Olympic Games, *5280*

Lutrick, Denise: Women's national championships in boxing, *2594*

Lutz, Bob: U.S. Open men's doubles tennis title, *6124*

Lutz, Tomas: Figure skater to land a triple lutz jump in competition, *3060*

Lützow, Wilhelm: National team to sweep the medals in the men's 200-meter breaststroke event in the Olympic Games, *5806*

Lux, Jos: World championships in gymnastics, *3910*

Luyendyk, Arie: Automobile racer to win the Indianapolis 500 with an average speed of more than 180 miles per hour, *1139*

Luzinski, Greg: Montreal Expos regular season baseball game played at Olympic Stadium, *1746*

Lycett, Randolph: Australian national tennis championships, *6045*

Tennis player to win seven Wimbledon mixed doubles championships, *6091*

Tennis player to win two Australian national men's doubles championships, *6052*

Lydwina of Schiedam, Saint: Ice skating accident, *2946*

Lynch, Jim: World championships in short track speed skating, *5694*

Lynn, William: Grand National Steeplechase horse race, *4271*

M

Macdonald, Charles Blair: Eighteen-hole golf course in the United States, *3610*

U.S. Amateur golf tournament, *3613*

MacDonald, Paul: Canoe racers to win two consecutive titles in the men's pairs 500-meter kayak event in the Olympic Games, *2625*

MacDonald, Sandy: Figure skater to win five consecutive ice dancing titles at the U.S. national championships, *3027*

Figure skaters to win two consecutive ice dancing titles at the U.S. national championships, *3023*

Macdonald-Smith, Iain: Sailor to win two consecutive gold medals in the Flying Dutchman–class event in the Olympic Games, *5228*

Macedo, Leandro: World cup in the triathlon, *6241*

Macfie, A. F.: British Amateur Championship, *3594*

Macintosh, Henry: Men's 4 x 100-meter relay track event held in the Olympic Games, *5003*

Mack, Connie: Philadelphia Athletics American League pennant, *1345*

Mackenzie, Alister: Masters golf tournament, *3698*

Mackenzie, Stuart: Rower to win both the single and double sculls events at the Henley Regatta, *4939*

Mackey, Dick: Father and son to win the Iditarod sled dog race, *5512*

Sled dog racer to win the Iditarod sled dog race four times, and the first to win it twice in a row, *5511*

Mackey, Rick: Father and son to win the Iditarod sled dog race, *5512*

MacKinnon, Esme: World championships in Alpine skiing, *5377*

MacMillan, Shannon: Women's soccer event held in the Olympic Games, *5569*

Macoviciuc, Camelia: Women's lightweight double sculls rowing event held in the Olympic Games, *4961*

Madden, Grace: Brother-and-sister figure skaters to win the pairs title at the U.S. national championships, *3017*

Madden, J. Lester: Brother-and-sister figure skaters to win the pairs title at the U.S. national championships, *3017*

Madison, Helene: Swimmer to win two women's 4 x 100-meter freestyle relay titles in the Olympic Games, *5824*

Madsen, Lars Jörgen: Military rifle individual shooting event held in the Olympic Games, *5279*

Maenza, Vincenzo: Wrestler to win two consecutive light flyweight Greco-Roman wrestling titles in the Olympic Games, *6408*

Mahan, Larry: Cowboy to be named All-Around Cowboy five consecutive times, and six overall, *4896*

Mahlisch, Kurt: National team to sweep the medals in the men's 200-meter breast-stroke event in the Olympic Games, *5806*

Mahoney, Harold: National team to sweep the medals in the men's singles tennis event in the Olympic Games, *6040*

Mahre, Phillip: Skier from the United States to win the men's slalom title at the Olympic Winter Games, *5446*

Mahre, Steven: Skier from the United States to win the men's slalom title at the Olympic Winter Games, *5446*

Majerle, Dan: Basketball player to have 17 3-point field goals in a National Basketball Association (NBA) Finals series, *2322*

Majowska, Marta: World championships in gymnastics to award women's titles in specific events, *3932*

Mäki, Taisto: Runner to race the men's 10,000 meters in under 30:00 minutes, *5045*
Runner to race the men's 5000 meters in under 14:10 minutes, *5043*

Mallin, Henry: Boxer to win two consecutive middleweight titles in the Olympic Games, *2545*

Mallory, Molla Bjurstedt: Tennis player to win eight women's singles titles at the United States national championships, *6084*
Tennis player to win four straight women's singles titles at the United States national championships, *6058*

Malmström, Karl: National team to sweep the top medals in men's platform diving in the Olympic Games, *2793*

Malone, Joe: Hockey player to lead the National Hockey League in scoring, *4066*
National Hockey League player to score seven goals in a single game, *4072*

Malone, Karl: Basketball player to score more than 2,000 points in 11 consecutive National Basketball Association (NBA) seasons, *2407*
Olympic basketball competition to include openly professional athletes, *2316*
Utah Jazz player to be named National Basketball Association (NBA) Most Valuable Player of the Year, *2385*

Malone, Moses: Basketball player to capture 587 offensive rebounds in a single National Basketball Association (NBA) season, *2146*
Basketball player to go from high school into the American Basketball Association (ABA) without attending college, *2102*
Basketball player to have 21 offensive rebounds in a single National Basketball Association (NBA) game, *2181*
Basketball player to have 46 offensive rebounds in the National Basketball Association (NBA) Finals, *2165*
Basketball player to have 6,371 offensive rebounds in his National Basketball Association (NBA) career, *2344*
Basketball player to have 8,551 free throws in his National Basketball Association (NBA) career, *2345*
Basketball player to lead the National Basketball Association (NBA) in offensive rebounds for eight years, *2290*
Basketball player to lead the National Basketball Association (NBA) in offensive rebounds for seven consecutive years, *2186*
Houston Rockets player to be named National Basketball Association (NBA) Most Valuable Player of the Year, *2148*

Mamatov, Victor: Men's 4 x 7.5-kilometer relay biathlon team event held at the Olympic Winter Games, *2432*

Mangiarotti, Dario: Athlete to win 13 medals in the Olympic Games, *4709*
Fencer to win 13 medals in the Olympic Games, *2934*

Mangiarotti, Edoardo: Athlete to win 13 medals in the Olympic Games, *4709*
Fencer to win 13 medals in the Olympic Games, *2934*
Fencer to win two, three, and four men's team épée titles in the Olympic Games, *2931*

Mangrum, Lloyd: Sudden-death playoff in golf that ran more than 10 holes, *3723*

Mankin, Valentyn: Sailor to win gold medals in three different sailing events in the Olympic Games, *5239*
Tempest-class sailing event in the Olympic Games, *5230*

Manley, Elizabeth: African-American athlete to win a medal in the Olympic Winter Games, *4763*

Mann, Bob: African-American professional football players to join the Detroit Lions in the modern period, *3218*

Mann, Shelly: Women's 100-meter butterfly event held in the Olympic Games, *5835*

Manning, Danny: Basketball player to have six blocked shots in a single Division I National Collegiate Athletic Association (NCAA) Final Four championship series game, *2268*

Manning, Madeline: Runner from the United States to win the women's 800-meter title at the Olympic Games, *5091*

Manoliu, Lia: Athlete to compete in track and field events in six Olympic Games, *6217*

Mansell, Nigel: Automobile racer to have nine wins in a single season on the Formula One Grand Prix circuit, *1141*

Mantz, Johnny: Southern 500 automobile race, *1075*

Mantz, Paul: Pilot to win the Bendix Trophy race three times in a row, *1016*

Mara, Tim: Pro Football Hall of Fame, *3268*

Maravich, Pete: Basketball player to average 44.5 points per game in a single Division I National Collegiate Athletic Association (NCAA) season, *2066*
Basketball player to make 30 free throws during a single Division I National Collegiate Athletic Association (NCAA) game, *2065*
Basketball player to score 1,381 points in a single Division I National Collegiate Athletic Association (NCAA) season, *2068*
Basketball player to score a total of 3,667 points during his college career, *2070*

Marichal, Juan: Dominican pitcher to pitch a no-hitter in the major leagues, *1665*
Dominican to be inducted into baseball's Hall of Fame, *1769*

Mariles Cortés, Humberto: Athletes from Mexico to win gold medals in the Olympic Games, *4697*

Marinescu, Tecia: Women's 500-meter fours kayaking event held in the Olympic Games, *2623*

Marino, Dan: National Football League player to complete passes totaling 5,084 yards in a single season, *3389*
National Football League player to lead the league six times in completed passes, *3479*
National Football League player to pass for 48 touchdowns in a single season, *3390*
National Football League player to pass for 60,000 career yards, *3512*

Marino, John: Race Across America (RAAM) bicycle marathon, *2705*

Maris, Roger: Major league baseball player to hit 61 home runs in a single season, *1649*
Major league baseball player to hit 70 home runs in a single season, *1853*

Mark, Russell: Men's double trap (clay pigeon) individual shooting event held in the Olympic Games, *5326*

Marquand, Rube: Major league baseball pitcher of the 20th century to pitch 19 straight wins, *1431*

Marsh, Edward: Men's eight-oared shell with coxswain rowing event held in the Olympic Games, *4925*

Marshall, George Preston: Pro Football Hall of Fame, *3268*

Marshall, Jim: Professional football player to play 282 consecutive games, *3361*

Marshall, Karyn: World championships for women's weightlifting, *6350*

Marshall, Penny: Women's professional baseball league, *1546*

Marshall, William: Tennis tournament played at Wimbledon, *6008*

Martell, Belle: Woman to be licensed as a boxing referee, *2553*

Martikan, Michael: Athlete from the newly independent Slovak Republic to win a gold medal in the Olympic Games, *4795*

Martin, Christy: Match between women boxers to be televised live, *2592*
Women's boxing match to be watched by more than 1 million television viewers, *2593*

Martin, Marianne: Women's Tour de France cycling race, *2706*

Martin, Patrice: Water-skier to win five consecutive men's overall titles at the world championships, *6322*

Martin, Pepper: Baseball player to be named Associated Press Athlete of the Year, *1495*

Martin, Robert: Golfer to win the British Open after a default in a playoff, *3590*

Martin, Steffi *See* Walker, Steffi Martin

Martin, Tee: National Collegiate Athletic Association major college football player to complete 23 consecutive passes in a single game, *3500*

Martin, William: Shooters from the United States to win the military rifle team shooting title in the Olympic Games, *5288*

Martinescu, Nicolae: Heavyweight Greco-Roman wrestling event held in the Olympic Games, *6400*

Martinez, Dennis: Nicaraguan major league baseball player, *1742*

Martinez, Joseph: Gymnast to win two consecutive men's parallel bar titles in the world championships, *3915*
Gymnast to win two men's horizontal bar titles in the world championships, *3916*

World championships in gymnastics, *3910*

Martinez, Patricia: Women's national championships in boxing, *2594*

Martinez, Pedro: Montreal Expos pitcher to win the Cy Young Award, *1842*

Mary, Queen of Scots: Woman golfer on record, *3539*

Mason, Geoffrey: Bobsledders from the United States to win the five-man bobsled title at the Olympic Winter Games, *2468*

Mason, Jem: Grand National Steeplechase horse race, *4271*

Massey, Arnaud: Golfer from outside Great Britain to win the British Open, *3645*

Massey, Stewart: All-England Championships in badminton, *1166*

Masson, Henri: National team to sweep the medals in the men's individual foil fencing competition in the Olympic Games, *2900*

Masson, Paul: Cyclist to win two, and then three, cycling gold medals in the Olympic Games, *2688*

Men's 1000-meter match sprint cycling race held in the Olympic Games, *2685*

Masya, Benson: World Half Marathon Championship, *4521*

Mathews, Marlene: Runner to hold the officially accepted world record in the women's 400-meter event, *5066*

Mathewson, Christy: Baseball pitcher to lead the National League in strikeouts for three consecutive years, *1367*

Major league baseball players to be named to the Baseball Hall of Fame, *1520*

New York Giants World Series victory, *1368*

Mathias, Bob (Robert): Decathlete to win two consecutive titles in the men's decathlon in the Olympic Games, *2742*

Fiberglass pole to be used in the men's pole vault event in the Olympic Games, *4842*

Mathieu, Simone Passemard: Tennis player to win six French national women's doubles championships after the event became international, and four times consecutively, *6101*

Mathis, Buster: Olympic heavyweight boxing champion to become world heavyweight champion, *2567*

Mathisen, Oscar: Speed skater to be world champion in men's long-distance speed skating five times, *5637*

Speed skater to skate the 1500 meters in under 2:20 minutes, *5638*

Mathison, Thomas: Literary work about golf, *3548*

Matikainen, Marj: Women's 15-kilometer cross-country event held in the world championships of Nordic skiing, *5462*

Matos Fuentes, Angel Valodia *See* Fuentes, Angel Valodia Matos

Matson, Randy (James Randel): Shot-putter to break the 70-foot and 21-meter barriers, *5345*

Mattern, Joachim: Men's pairs 500-meter kayaking event held in the Olympic Games, *2617*

Matthäus, Lothar: Soccer (international football) player to be named World Footballer of the Year by the Fédération Internationale de Football Association (FIFA), *5565*

Matthes, Roland: Men's 100-meter backstroke event held in the world championships, *5874*

Men's 200-meter backstroke event held in the world championships, *5879*

Olympic men's 100-meter backstroke event in which the medalists all had times under one minute, *5866*

Swimmer to hold world titles in both the 100- and 200-meter backstroke at the same time, *5892*

Swimmer to win two consecutive men's 100-meter backstroke titles in the world championships, *5914*

Swimmer to win two consecutive men's 200-meter backstroke titles in the Olympic Games, *5869*

Matthews, Bobby: Shutout on record in professional baseball, *1209*

Matthews, Michael: Small-bore rifle team shooting event held in the Olympic Games, *5291*

Mattingly, Don: Major league baseball player to hit six grand slam home runs in a single season, *1795*

Mauermayer, Gisela: Discus-thrower to hold the officially accepted world record in the women's event, *2766*

Pentathlete to hold the officially accepted world record in the women's pentathlon, *4816*

Shot-putter to hold the officially accepted world record in the women's event, *5334*

Mauger, Ivan: Long-track event in the dirt-track (speedway) motorcycle racing world championships, *4586*

Motorcycle racer to win six individual dirt-track (speedway) world titles, *4589*

Pairs event in the dirt-track (speedway) motorcycle racing world championships, *4585*

Maunder, Alexander: Trap (clay pigeon) team shooting event in the Olympic Games, *5292*

Maxson, Louis: Team archery event held in the Olympic Games, *1028*

May, Amy Peralta: Softball Hall of Fame opened, *5588*

May, Carl: Baseball player to die of injuries suffered during a major league baseball game, *1446*

Mayasich, John: National Collegiate Athletic Association hockey player to score seven points in a single "Frozen Four" tournament game, *4133*

Mayberry, John: Kansas City Royals regular season baseball game at Kauffman Stadium, *1732*

Mayer, Charles: Heavyweight boxing event held in the Olympic Games, *2529*

Middleweight boxing event held in the Olympic Games, *2531*

Mayer, Helene: Fencer to win two, and then three, women's foil titles in the world championships, *2925*

World championships in fencing to include women, *2923*

Mayes, Gayl: Canoe marathon world championships, *2624*

Mays, Willie: African-American baseball player to be named Associated Press Athlete of the Year, *1602*

Baseball player to steal more than 30 bases and hit more than 30 home runs in a National League season, *1617*

New York Giants baseball player to be named Rookie of the Year, *1586*

McAdoo, Bob: Buffalo Braves player to be named National Basketball Association (NBA) Most Valuable Player of the Year, *2109*

McAshan, Eddie: African-American college football player to become a quarterback at Georgia Tech, *3298*

McAuliffe, Jack: Boxer to be undisputed world lightweight champion, *2518*

McCall, Robert: Figure skaters from Canada to win a medal in ice dancing at the Olympic Winter Games, *3093*

McCartan, Jack: Ice hockey team from the United States to win the title at the Olympic Winter Games, *4141*

McCarthy, Cal: Boxer of African descent to win a United States boxing title, and probably the first athlete of African descent to hold a U.S. title in any sport, *2521*

McCarthy, Joseph: Major league baseball manager to win pennants in both the American and National Leagues, *1502*

McCauley, Ed: Basketball player to be named Most Valuable Player of the National Basketball Association (NBA) All-Star Game, *1930*

McClelland, Dan: African-American All-Star Team in professional baseball, *1402*

McClinick, Cora Lee: Intercollegiate golf tournament for African-American players, *3708*

McClure, Wilbert "Skeeter": Boxer from the United States to win the light middleweight title in the Olympic Games, *2563*

McClusky, John: African-American college football player to become a quarterback at Harvard University, *3270*

McColgan, Liz: World Half Marathon Championship, *4521*

McConnell, Suzie: College women's basketball player to have 355 assists in a single Division I National Collegiate Athletic Association (NCAA) season, *2253*

College women's basketball United States Basketball Writers Association All-American first team, *2271*

McCormick, Mike: San Francisco Giants pitcher to win the Cy Young Award, *1694*

McCormick, Patricia: Diver to win two consecutive titles in both springboard and platform diving events, and the first to win four gold medals in diving, in the Olympic Games, *2804*

McCormick (first name unknown): Slider to ride the skeleton (Cresta Run) luge (toboggan) face forward, *4450*

McCray, Nikki: College women's basketball Associated Press (AP) All-American first team, *2348*

McCutcheon, Alison: National Collegiate Athletic Association (NCAA) Division I women's softball player to get 132 hits in a single season, *5627*

National Collegiate Athletic Association (NCAA) Division I women's softball player to get 405 hits during her college career, *5628*

McDermott, John: Golfer born in the United States to win the U.S. Open, *3650*

McDermott, John J.: Boston Marathon, *4469*

McDonald, Elsie: World outdoor championships in bowls to include women players, *2501*

McDonald, Patrick: Thrower from the United States to win the men's 56-pound weight throw in the Olympic Games, *6324*

McDougald, Gil: New York Yankees baseball player to be named Rookie of the Year, *1587*

Rookie to hit a grand slam home run in the World Series, *1589*

McEnroe, John: Tennis player to win the U.S. Open men's singles title three consecutive times, *6170*

McFarland, Denny: Two home runs in a single American League game, *1338*

McGonigal, Elizabeth: Women's national championships in boxing, *2594*

McGregor, Ken: Tennis player to win four consecutive United States mixed doubles national championships, and nine overall, *6105*

McGregor, William: Soccer (international football) league, *5539*

McGriff, Fred: Toronto Blue Jays regular season baseball game played at the Skydome, *1807*

McGrory, Scott: Men's Madison cycling event held in the Olympic Games, *2732*

McGuire, Willa Worthington: Water-skier to win two, and then three, women's titles at the world championships, *6317*

World championships in water-skiing, *6316*

McGwire, Mark: Major league baseball player to hit 70 home runs in a single season, *1853*

Major league baseball rookie to hit 49 home runs in a single season, *1793*

McHale, Kevin: Basketball player to win the National Basketball Association (NBA) Sixth Man Award twice in a row, *2214*

McIlvaine, Charles: Rower to win three consecutive medals in the men's double sculls event in the Olympic Games, *4936*

McKane, Kitty (Kathleen): Tennis player to win the French national women's singles championship after the event became international, *6077*

Tennis players to win the French national women's doubles championship after the event became international, *6080*

Women's doubles tennis event held in the Olympic Games, *6060*

McKay, Heather: World open championships in squash, *5763*

McKee, Jonathan: Sailors from the United States to win the Flying Dutchman–class event in the Olympic Games, *5243*

McKee, Tim (Alexander): Men's 200-meter individual medley event in which the top four swimmers broke the world record, *5870*

McKenley, Herbert: Runner to qualify for the finals men's of the 100-, 200-, and 400-meter races in the Olympic Games, *5054*

McKenzie, Donald: Men's 100-meter breaststroke event held in the Olympic Games, *5851*

McKim, Josephine: Swimmer to win two women's 4 x 100-meter freestyle relay titles in the Olympic Games, *5824*

McKinney, Bones: All–National Basketball Association (NBA) First Team, *1914*

McKinney, Frank: Men's 4 x 100-meter medley relay swimming event held in the Olympic Games, *5838*

McLain, Denny: Baltimore Orioles pitcher to win the Cy Young Award, *1703*

Baseball player to be named *The Sporting News* Sportsman of the Year, *1696*

Detroit Tigers pitcher to win the Cy Young Award, *1698*

McLaren, Bruce: United States Grand Prix automobile race to be part of the Formula One Grand Prix circuit, *1099*

McLendon, Johnny B.: African-American college basketball team to win a national title, *1941*

African-American professional basketball coach, *2000*

McLeod, Fred: Golfer to win two straight Professional Golfers' Association (PGA) Championships, *3662*

McLoughlin, Maurice: United States men's singles tennis national championship matches played at the West Side Tennis Club, *6057*

McMahon, Brigitte: Women's triathlon event held in the Olympic Games, *6247*

McMeekin, Thomas: 6-meter-class sailing event held in the Olympic Games, *5205*

McMillan, Edward: College football All-America team named by Grantland Rice, *3153*

McMullen, Lisa: College women's basketball player to score 126 3-point goals in a single Division I National Collegiate Athletic Association (NCAA) season, *2305*

McNair, Steve: Tennessee Titans regular season football game played at the Adelphia Coliseum, *3511*

McNair, Winifred Slocock: Women's doubles championships at Wimbledon, *6054*

Women's doubles tennis event held in the Olympic Games, *6060*

McNally, Blood (Johnny): Pro Football Hall of Fame, *3268*

McNally, Dave: Free agents in major league baseball, *1740*

McNamara, John: Boston Red Sox manager to be named Manager of the Year, *1784*

McNamee, Graham: World Series game to be broadcast by radio, *1460*

McPherson, Dan: Johnny Unitas Golden Arm Award, *3407*

McQuade, Bernard: International court (four-wall) handball competition, *3999*

McRae, Brian: Atlanta Braves regular season baseball game played at Turner Field, *1844*

McWilliams, Jon: African-American football players to appear in the Orange Bowl, *3239*

Meagher, Mary T.: Swimmer to win both the women's 100- and 200-meter butterfly titles in the same Olympic Games, *5943*

Meagher, Mary T.:—*continued*
Swimmer to win the women's 100-meter butterfly title in the Olympic Games with a time of under one minute, *5940*

Mechlovits, Zoltán: International championships in table tennis, *5984*

Mecir, Miloslav: Tennis player to win the men's singles title in the Olympic Games after tennis competition resumed in 1988, *6178*

Mednov, Viktor: Light welterweight boxing event, and the first match between a Soviet and a United States boxer, in the Olympic Games, *2559*

Mednyánszky, Maria: G. Geist Prize, *5986*
International championships in table tennis, *5984*
Table tennis player to win five women's singles titles in the world championships, *5987*

Mednyánszky-Klucski, Maria *See* Mednyánszky, Maria

Medved, Aleksandr: Light flyweight event held in the world freestyle wrestling championships, *6393*
Wrestler to win two consecutive super heavyweight freestyle titles in the Olympic Games, and wrestling gold medals in three consecutive Olympic Games, *6399*

Meftakhetdinova, Zemfira: Women's skeet shooting event held in the Olympic Games, *5328*

Mehnert, George: Flyweight freestyle wrestling event held in the Olympic Games, *6364*

Meineke, Don: National Basketball Association (NBA) player to be named Rookie of the Year, *1937*

Meistrik, Karl: Figure skaters from Austria to win the pairs title in the world championships, *2986*

Melges, Buddy (Harry): Sailor to win both the America's Cup and an Olympic gold medal in sailing, *5253*
Soling-class sailing event held in the Olympic Games, *5229*

Mellander, Hjalmar: Men's pentathlon held in the modern Olympic Games, *4814*

Melli, Launi: Shooter from the United States to win the women's small-bore rifle (three positions) event at the Olympic Games, *5324*

Melnik, Faina: Discus-thrower to break the 210-foot barrier in the women's event, *2778*
Discus-thrower to break the 230-foot and 70-meter barriers, *2780*

Mendis, Duleep: International Cricket Conference (ICC) competition, *2662*

Mendivil, Soraya Jimenez: Women's weightlifting events held in the Olympic Games, *6353*

Mendoza, Alfredo: Water-skier to win two consecutive men's titles at the world championships, *6318*

Menis, Argentina: Discus-thrower to break the 220-foot barrier in the women's event, *2779*

Mennea, Pietro: Athlete to qualify for the finals of the same event in four Olympic Games, *4759*
Runner to complete the men's 200-meter race in under 19.8 seconds, *5112*

Meno, Jenni: Figure skaters to receive six perfect scores (6.0) for artistic impression in the U.S. national pairs competition, *3111*

Merchant, John: African-American golfers to become members of the executive committee of the United States Golf Association (USGA), *3872*

Meredith, Leonard: Men's 4000-meter team pursuit cycling event held in the Olympic Games, *2692*

Meredith, Ted (Edward): Runner to hold the officially accepted world record in the men's 400-meter event, *4983*
Runner to hold the officially accepted world record in the men's 800-meter event, *5002*

Mérignac, Lucien: National team to sweep the medals in the men's masters foil fencing event in the Olympic Games, *2901*

Merle, Carole: Skier to win four women's super giant slalom world cup titles, *5468*

Merlin, Joseph: Roller skates, *4901*

Merriott, Ron: World championships in trampolining to include double mini trampoline competitions, *6230*

Merritt, Edward: National championships in track and field (athletics) in the United States, *6201*

Merz, William: National team to sweep the top honors in the men's horizontal bar, long horse vault, side (pommel) horse, and rings gymnastics competitions in the Olympic Games, *3913*

Messersmith, Andy: Free agents in major league baseball, *1740*

Metcalfe, Ralph: African-American runner to win the men's 100- and 200-meter titles in the Olympic Games, *5032*
Team to race the men's 4 x 100-meter relay in under 40 seconds, *5042*

Metzger, Sue: United States intercollegiate women's singles and women's doubles national championships, *6111*

Meyer, Deborah: Swimmer to win three individual gold medals in a single Olympic Games, *5862*

Women's 200-meter freestyle event held in the Olympic Games, *5857*

Women's 800-meter freestyle swimming event held in the Olympic Games, *5860*

Meyer, Elana: Athletes from South Africa to win medals in the Olympic Games, after the lifting of the ban on their country because of its racist policies, *4779*

Black African woman to win an Olympic medal, *4780*

Runner from Africa to win the women's 10,000-meter title, and the first Black African woman to win a medal, at the Olympic Games, *5159*

Meyers, Ann: College women's basketball All-America team, *2110*

Woman basketball player to sign with a National Basketball Association (NBA) team, *2152*

Meynell, Alicia: Woman jockey on record, *4264*

Miasek, Stan: All–National Basketball Association (NBA) First Team, *1914*

Michaux, Ernest: Cycling club, *2681*

Michaux, Pierre: Cycling club, *2681*

Michelsen, Albert: Runner to complete the men's marathon in under 2:30 hours, *4477*

Middlecoff, Cary: Sudden-death playoff in golf that ran more than 10 holes, *3723*

Mikan, George: American Basketball Association season, *2051*

Basketball Hall of Fame, *1975*

Basketball player to lead the National Basketball Association (NBA) in scoring in three consecutive years, *1931*

Mikata, Reiichi: Skiers to win two consecutive men's Nordic combined team titles at the Olympic Winter Games, *5489*

Miki, Ryuki: Tennis player to win three consecutive Wimbledon mixed doubles championships, *6096*

Milbrett, Tiffeny: Women's soccer event held in the Olympic Games, *5569*

Milburn, Devereux: Polo team from the United States to win the Westchester Cup, *4866*

Milburn, Glyn: National Football League player to gain a total of 404 yards running in a single game, *3473*

Milburn, Rod: Electronically timed world record in the men's 110-meter hurdles, *4343*

Miles, Jearl: Runner from the United States to win the women's 400-meter race in the World Championships in Athletics, *5165*

Miles, Juan: Athletes from Argentina to win gold medals in the Olympic Games, *4659*

Miles, Richard: Heydusek Prize, *5991*

Millan, Felix: Cincinnati Reds regular season baseball game played at Riverfront Stadium (later Cinergy Field), *1716*

Miller, Cheryl: Basketball team from the United States to win the women's title in the Olympic Games, *2208*

College women's basketball player to receive the Broderick Cup in three consecutive years, *2237*

College women's basketball player to receive the Naismith Award in three consecutive years, *2238*

Miller, Lennox: Sweep of the medals in an event by athletes of Black African ancestry at the Olympic Games, *4726*

Miller, Nannie: Non-collegiate women's baseball team, *1201*

Miller, Reggie: Basketball player to make more than 1,700 3-point field goals in his National Basketball Association (NBA) career, *2415*

Miller, Shannon: Gymnasts from the United States to win the women's team title in the Olympic Games, *3978*

Millman, Danny: World championships in trampolining, *6228*

Millns, Jim: Figure skaters from the United States to win an Olympic medal in ice dancing, *3074*

Mills, Billy (William): Runner from the United States to win the men's 10,000-meter title at the Olympic Games, *5077*

Mills, Mary: Golfer named Rookie of the Year on the Ladies Professional Golf Association (LPGA) Tour, *3766*

Golfer to win the Ladies Professional Golf Association (LPGA) Championship with a score under 280, *3774*

Ladies Professional Golf Association (LPGA) tournament to be nationally televised, *3772*

Milne, Ross: Olympic Winter Games at which an athlete was killed, *4713*

Skier to be killed during the Olympic Winter Games, *5409*

Milton, Tommy: Automobile racer to win the Indianapolis 500 twice, *1056*

Mimiague, Jean-Baptiste: National team to sweep the medals in the men's masters foil fencing event in the Olympic Games, *2901*

Minch, Peter: International luge (toboggan) competition, *4447*

Minenkov, Andrei: Figure skaters from the United States to win an Olympic medal in ice dancing, *3074*

Mineyev, Viktor: Pentathlete to win two gold medals in the men's modern pentathlon team competition in the Olympic Games, *4828*

Mingo, Eugene: Denver Broncos regular season football game played at Mile High Stadium, *3255*

Minnea, Pietro: Runner to complete the men's 200-meter race in under 19.7 seconds, *5183*

Minoso, Minnie (Saturnino): Major league baseball player widely recognized as black to play for the Chicago White Sox, *1588*

Mischou, Irene: National Award tournament in duck pin bowling, *2492*

Misersky, Antje: Women's 15-kilometer biathlon competition held in the Olympic Winter Games, *2441*

Mishkutenok, Natalia: Male figure skater to win the pairs title at the Olympic Winter Games with two different partners, *3115*

Miskey, John: National championships in squash, *5757*

Mitchell, Bobby (baseball player): Left-handed pitcher in the National League, *1235*

Mitchell, Bobby (football player): African-American professional football player to join the Washington Redskins, *3263*

Mitchell, E. D.: Speedball, *5737*

Mitchell, Jackie (Virne): Woman to pitch against a major league baseball team, *1500*

Mitchell, Mike: Baseball player to lead the National League in triples in two consecutive years, *1397*

Mitchell, Pinkey: Boxer to hold the world super-lightweight (junior welterweight) title, *2544*

Mitchell, Thomas: National Collegiate Athletic Association (NCAA) consensus Division I All-American college basketball team, *1890*

Mitchell, William: Code of rules for bowls, *2478*

Mitropoulous, Ioannis: Men's rings gymnastics competition held in the Olympic Games, *3904*

Miyake, Yoshinobu: Weightlifter to win two consecutive featherweight titles in the Olympic Games, *6343*

Miyake, Yoshiyuki: Weightlifter to win two consecutive featherweight titles in the Olympic Games, *6343*

Mo Ji-su: Men's 5000-meter relay short track speed skating event held at the Olympic Winter Games, *5716*

Moceanu, Dominique: Gymnasts from the United States to win the women's team title in the Olympic Games, *3978*

Mochrie, Dottie *See* Pepper, Dottie

Moe, Karen: National team to sweep the medals in the women's 200-meter butterfly in the Olympic Games, *5872*

Moeller, Brenda: College women's basketball All-America team, *2110*

Mogren, N. Torgny: Skier to win two consecutive titles in the men's 4 x 10-kilometer relay Nordic (cross-country) at the Olympic Winter Games, *5455*

Mohr, Georges Dillon-Kavanagh: Men's team épée fencing competition held in the Olympic Games, *2910*

Moineau, Hervé: World Endurance Championship in motorcycle racing, *4592*

Moiseeva, Irina: Figure skaters from the United States to win an Olympic medal in ice dancing, *3074*

Mokeyev, Albert: Pentathlete to win two gold medals in the men's modern pentathlon team competition in the Olympic Games, *4828*

Molesworth, Mall: Australian women's singles national tennis championships, *6063*
Tennis player to win two consecutive Australian national women's singles tennis championships, *6067*

Molineaux, Tom: African-American boxer to fight in a title bout, *2507*

Molitor, Paul: Major league baseball player to get five hits in a single World Series game, *1767*
Toronto Blue Jays regular season baseball game played at the Skydome, *1807*

Monahan, Garry: National Hockey League Amateur Draft, *4145*

Moncrief, Sidney: Basketball player to be named National Basketball Association (NBA) Defensive Player of the Year, *2184*
Basketball player to win the National Basketball Association (NBA) Defensive Player of the Year Award twice, *2196*

Monday, Kenneth: Wrestler of Black African descent to win a gold medal in wrestling in the Olympic Games, *6409*

Monday, Rick: Baseball player chosen in major league baseball's first free draft, *1682*

Mondzolevsky, Georgy: Volleyball players to win two consecutive men's gold medals in the Olympic Games, *6282*

Monet, Philippe: Sailor to complete a solo circumnavigation of the world in under 130 days, *5246*

Money, Don: Philadelphia Phillies regular season baseball game played at Veterans Stadium, *1721*

Monnereau, Bernard: World championships in rowing, *4940*

Monroe, Jessica: Women's four-oared shell without coxswain event held in the Olympic Games, *4957*

Montagu, Ivor: International governing body for table tennis, *5982*
Swaythling Cup, *5983*

Montana, Joe: Professional football player to complete 13 consecutive passes in a single Super Bowl game, *3440*
Professional football player to gain 357 yards passing in a single Super Bowl game, *3429*
San Francisco 49ers win in professional football's Super Bowl, *3373*
Montgolfier, Jacques Etienne: People to fly in a balloon, *1176*
Montgolfier, Joseph: People to fly in a balloon, *1176*
Montgomerie, Colin: Golfer to win the Professional Golfers' Association (PGA) Championship in under 270, *3877*
Golfer to win the U.S. Open in a sudden-death playoff, *3878*
Montgomery, James: Men's 100-meter freestyle event held at the world championships, *5877*
Men's 200-meter freestyle event held at the world championships, *5882*
National Team to sweep the medals in the men's 200-meter freestyle in the Olympic Games, *5921*
Swimmer to hold the world titles in both the men's 100-meter and 200-meter freestyle events at the same time, *5891*
Swimmer to race the men's 100-meter freestyle in under 50 seconds, *5926*
Moody, Helen *See* Wills, Helen
Moon, Warren: National Football League player to complete 404 passes in a single season, *3449*
Mooney, Michael: Sailors from the United States to win the 6-meter-class event in the Olympic Games, *5217*
Moore, Elisabeth: Tennis player to win five consecutive women's doubles titles at the United States national championships, *6037*
Tennis player to win four women's singles titles at the United States national championships, *6046*
United States national tennis championships to include mixed doubles competition, *6032*
Moore, Frank: Trap (clay pigeon) team shooting event in the Olympic Games, *5292*
Moore, Harry: African-American All-Star Team in professional baseball, *1402*
Moore, Herman: National Football League player to receive 123 passes in a single season, *3465*
Moore, Isabella: Women's 4 x 100-meter freestyle relay swimming event in the Olympic Games, *5808*
Moore, James: Cycling race on record, *2682*

Moore, Lenny: African-American professional football player to be named National Football League Rookie of the Year, *3240*
Moore, Ronnie: Pairs event in the dirt-track (speedway) motorcycle racing world championships, *4585*
Moran, Dodge: Sailor to complete a solo circumnavigation of the world in 150 days, *5245*
Moratorio, Carlos: World championships in three-day event equestrian competition, *2872*
Morceli, Noureddine: Runner to complete the men's mile race in under 3:45 minutes, *5170*
Runner to race the men's 1500 meters in less than 3:29 minutes, *5163*
Runner to win two, and then three, consecutive titles in the men's 1500-meter event in the World Championships in Athletics, *5166*
Moreau, Janet: African-American women to win gold medals in a track relay event in the Olympic Games, *5058*
Moreau, Paul: National team to sweep the rapid-fire pistol individual shooting event in the Olympic Games, *5278*
Moreaux, Léon: Dueling pistol shooting events held in the Olympic Games, *5282*
National team to sweep the rapid-fire pistol individual shooting event in the Olympic Games, *5278*
Morelon, Daniel: Cyclist to win two consecutive men's titles in the 1000-meter match sprint in the Olympic Games, *2703*
Morenz, Howie (Howard): All-Star National Hockey League Team selected by the Professional Hockey Writers' Association, *4102*
National Hockey League player to be named the league's Most Valuable Player twice in a row, *4105*
National Hockey League player to reach 250 career goals, *4109*
Moresee-Pichot, Sophie: Women's individual and team épée competitions held in the Olympic Games, *2944*
Morgan, Edward: Athlete from New Zealand to win an Olympic gold medal, *4672*
Morgan, Gil: World Series of Golf won in a playoff, *3819*
Morgan, William G.: Volleyball, *6272*
Morgenstern, Sonya: Woman figure skater to perform a triple salchow in competition, *3069*
Morozov, Volodymyr: Men's fours 1000-meter kayaking event held in the Olympic Games, *2611*
Morris, Ed: Major league baseball player to pitch four consecutive shutouts, *1293*

Morris, Tom, Jr. "Young Tom" (golfer): British Open golf championship open to amateurs, *3578*

Course specifically designed for golf, *3568*

Golfer to win four British Open championships, *3581*

Golfer to win the British Open championship four times in a row, *3585*

Golfer to win the British Open championship three times in a row, *3584*

Golfer to win the British Open championship twice in a row, *3579*

Golfer under the age of 20 to win the British Open championship, *3582*

Morris, Tom, Sr. "Old Tom" (golfer): British Open golf championship open to amateurs, *3578*

Course specifically designed for golf, *3568*

Golfer to win four British Open championships, *3581*

Golfer to win the British Open championship four times in a row, *3585*

Golfer to win the British Open championship three times in a row, *3584*

Golfer to win the British Open championship twice in a row, *3579*

Golfer under the age of 20 to win the British Open championship, *3582*

Morris, Tom (swimmer): National swimming championship, *5781*

Morrison, Fred: Frisbee, *3525*

Mortanges, Charles Pahud de: Equestrian to win two consecutive three-day event individual titles, *2857*

Equestrians to win two consecutive three-day event team titles, *2854*

Mortl, James: Softball player to be named Most Valuable Player of the United States Slo-Pitch Association World Series, *5607*

Morton, Carl: Montreal Expos baseball player to be named Rookie of the Year, *1713*

Morton, Lucy: Women's 200-meter breaststroke event held in the Olympic Games, *5818*

Moseley, Corliss: Pulitzer Trophy airplane race, *1005*

Moseley, Jonny: Skier from the United States to win the men's moguls freestyle skiing event in the Olympic Winter Games, *5497*

Moser-Pröll, Annemarie: Skier to win seven women's downhill world cup titles, *5426*

Skier to win six women's overall world cup titles, *5427*

Moses, Edwin: African-American hurdler to win the men's 400-meter title in the Olympic Games, *4345*

Gymnast to be named *Sports Illustrated* Sportsman of the Year, *3971*

Hurdler to set four new world records in the men's 400-meter hurdles, *4349*

Hurdler to win the men's 400-meter hurdles held in the World Championships in Athletics, *4348*

Hurdler to win two consecutive titles in the men's 400-meter hurdles in the World Championships in Athletics, *4352*

Moskalenko, Alexandre: Men's trampoline event held in the Olympic Games, *6233*

Moss, Randy: National Collegiate Athletic Association major college football player to score touchdowns on pass receptions in 12 consecutive games, *3478*

Mota, Rosa: Runner to win the women's championship in the Rotterdam Marathon, *4509*

Runner to win two consecutive women's titles in the Boston Marathon, and three overall, *4519*

Motley, Marion: African-American professional football player to join the Cleveland Browns, *3197*

African-American professional football player to play in a National Football League championship game, *3252*

Mougin, Eugène: Archery events held in the Olympic Games, *1025*

Mounce, Donald: World figure skating championships for roller skating, *4909*

Mountain, Marjorie: Australian women's doubles national tennis championships, *6062*

Tennis player to win two consecutive Australian national women's doubles championships, *6066*

Mouroutsos, Michail: Men's taekwondo events held in the Olympic Games, *4560*

Mouthan, Isabelle: World long-distance triathlon championships, *6245*

Moyer, Denny: Boxer to become world super-welterweight (junior middleweight) champion, *2564*

Mueller, Peter: Men's 1000-meter speed skating event held in the Olympic Winter Games, *5692*

Muhrcke, Gary: New York Marathon, *4493*

Mukhacheva, Lyubov: Skier to win two consecutive women's Nordic (cross-country) skiing titles in the Olympic Winter Games, *5423*

Mulcahy, John: Men's double sculls rowing event held in the Olympic Games, *4929*

Muldowney, Shirley: Woman automobile racer to win a national tournament of the National Hot Rod Association (NHRA), *1120*

Mullane, Tony: Major league pitcher to pitch left-handed and right-handed in the same game, *1263*

Müller, Anna-Maria: National team to sweep the medals in the women's singles luge (toboggan) event at the Olympic Winter Games, *4460*

Müller, Rainer: World championships in taekwondo to include light-middleweight and light-heavyweight classes for men, *4544*

Müller, Thomas: Men's Nordic combined team event held in the Olympic Winter Games, *5456*

Müller-Preiss, Ellen: Fencer to win three consecutive women's foil titles in the world championships, *2930*

Munari, Sandro: World rally championship for drivers, *1125*

Mundt, Kristina: Rowers to win two consecutive titles in the women's quadruple sculls in the Olympic Games, *4958*
Women's quadruple sculls event held in the Olympic Games, *4955*

Muñoz Martinez, Almudena: Women's half-lightweight judo event held in the Olympic Games, *4558*

Murakami, Masanori: Baseball player from Japan to play in United States major league baseball, *1674*

Muratov, Valentin: Gymnast to win two consecutive men's floor exercise titles in the world championships, *3942*

Muratov, Valeriy: Spring world championships in speed skating, *5682*

Muratova, Sofia: Gymnasts to win two consecutive gold medals in the women's team combined exercises, *3945*
National team to sweep the top medals in the women's all-around gymnastics competition in the Olympic Games, *3946*

Murchison, Loren: Runner to win two consecutive gold medals in the men's 4 x 100-meter relay in the Olympic Games, *5016*
Team from the United States to win the men's 4 x 100-meter relay track event in the Olympic Games, *5011*

Murdoch, Eric: Basketball player to have 376 steals during his Division I National Collegiate Athletic Association (NCAA) college career, *2301*

Murdock, Margaret: Woman to win a medal in shooting at the Olympic Games, *5313*

Murmela, Sulo: Men's 4 x 10-kilometer relay Nordic (cross-country) event held in the Olympic Winter Games, *5384*

Murphy, Calvin: Basketball player to have a .958 free throw average in a single National Basketball Association (NBA) season, *2166*

Murphy, Charles: National Collegiate Athletic Association (NCAA) consensus Division I All-American college basketball team, *1890*

Murphy, Cicero: African-American to win a world title in billiards, *2458*

Murphy, Elizabeth: Woman known to have played for a major league baseball team, *1462*

Murphy, Isaac: Jockey to win three Kentucky Derbys, and the first to win two in a row, *4283*

Murphy, Joe: Chicago Blackhawks regular season game played in the United Center, *4218*

Murphy, John: National collegiate track and field (athletics) championships sponsored by the National Collegiate Athletic Association (NCAA), *6206*

Murphy, "Torpedo" Billy: Boxer to be world featherweight champion, *2520*

Musial, Stan: Baseball player in the National League to reach 1,862 runs batted in, *1661*
Baseball player to reach 3,431 hits in the National League, *1659*
Baseball player to score 1,869 runs in the National League, *1656*
Major league baseball player to hit five home runs in a doubleheader, *1609*
Major league baseball player to reach 5,864 bases, *1660*
National League baseball player to play in 823 consecutive games, *1628*

Mussabini, Sam: Runner from Africa to win the men's 100-meter race in the Olympic Games, *4995*
Runner from Europe to win the men's 100-meter title in the Olympic Games, *5014*

Musso, Luigi: Automobile racer to win two, three, and four Argentine Grand Prix races, *1095*

Mutola, Maria: Runner to race the women's 1000 meters in under 2:30 minutes, *5180*

Mutombo, Dikembe: Basketball player to be named National Basketball Association (NBA) Defensive Player of the Year three times, *2401*
Basketball player to have 38 blocked shots in a single set of National Basketball Association (NBA) playoffs, *2332*
Basketball player to lead the National Basketball Association (NBA) for three consecutive years in blocked shots, *2364*
Denver Nuggets player to be named National Basketball Association (NBA) Defensive Player of the Year, *2353*

Muzicenko, Aleksandr: Sailor to win gold medals in three different sailing events in the Olympic Games, *5239*

Myers, Carlotta (Mary H.): Woman to fly solo in a hot-air balloon in the United States, *1180*

Myyrä, Jonni: Javelin-thrower to break the 210-foot barrier, *4385*
Javelin-thrower to win two consecutive men's titles in the Olympic Games, *4386*

N

Na, Li *See* Li Na

Naber, John: National Team to sweep the medals in the men's 200-meter freestyle in the Olympic Games, *5921*

Swimmer to break the two-minute barrier in the men's 200-meter backstroke event, *5924*

Nadi, Nedo: Fencer to win five gold medals in a single Olympic Games, and to win two consecutive men's individual foil titles in the Olympic Games, *2916*

Nadig, Marie-Thérèse: Skier to win both the women's downhill and giant slalom titles in the same Olympic Winter Games, *5421*

Naess, Alfred: Speed skater to skate the 500 meters in under 50 seconds, *5631*

Nagel, Ida von: Woman equestrian to win a team dressage medal in the Olympic Games, *2863*

Nagurski, Bronko: Bronko Nagurski Award, *3456*

National Football League game played indoors, *3162*

Pro Football Hall of Fame, *3268*

Nagy, Imre: Pentathlete to win two pentathlon gold medals in the same Olympic Games, *4827*

Nagy, Laszlo: International pairs figure skating competition in which all the medalists were brother-and-sister pairs, *3041*

Nagy, Marianne: International pairs figure skating competition in which all the medalists were brother-and-sister pairs, *3041*

Nagy, Steven: Bowler to bowl a 300 game in a televised match, *2496*

Naismith, James: Article reporting on basketball's first game, *1867*

Basketball game, *1864*

Basketball Hall of Fame, *1975*

Volleyball, *6272*

Nakatani, Takehide: Men's lightweight judo event in the Olympic Games, *4534*

Namath, Joe: New York Jets win in the National Football League's Super Bowl, *3296*

Nambu, Chuhei: Athlete to hold the world record in both the men's long jump and triple jump, *4433*

Nansen, Fridtjof: Ski club in the United States, *5357*

Nasse, Albert: Men's four-oared shell without coxswain rowing event held in the Olympic Games, *4930*

Nastase, Ilie: Tennis player to be ranked number one in the Association of Tennis Professionals (ATP) rankings, *6157*

Natvig, Harald: Running deer (double shot) team shooting event held in the Olympic Games, *5297*

Naumov, Vadim: Champions Series in figure skating, *3112*

Navarro Morenés, Julio: Athletes from Spain to win gold medals in the Olympic Games, *4673*

Navratilova, Martina: Tennis player to be ranked number one in the Women's Tennis Association (WTA) rankings for 156 consecutive weeks, *6173*

Tennis player to win 1,438 women's singles matches during her career, *6184*

Tennis player to win 167 women's singles tournaments during her career, *6185*

Tennis player to win the French Open women's doubles title five consecutive times, *6176*

Tennis player to win the Wimbledon women's singles title six consecutive times, *6175*

Tennis player to win the Women's Tennis Association (WTA) championship eight times, *6177*

Naylor, Guillermo Brooke: Athletes from Argentina to win gold medals in the Olympic Games, *4659*

Nazaryan, Armen: Athlete from Armenia to win a gold medal in the Olympic Games, *4791*

Neascu, Cornelia: World championships in rowing to include women's competitions, *4945*

Neckermann, Josef: Woman equestrian to win a gold medal in team dressage in the Olympic Games, *2875*

World championships in dressage, *2871*

Nehemiah, Renaldo: Hurdler to race the men's 110-meter hurdles in under 13 seconds, *4346*

Neilson, Sandra: Olympic women's 100-meter freestyle event in which the medalists all had times under one minute, *5867*

Nelson, Byron: Golfer to score under 190 for three consecutive 18-hole rounds in a Professional Golfers' Association (PGA) recognized event, *3741*

Golfer to score under 260 for 72 holes in a Professional Golfers' Association (PGA)–recognized event, *3713*

Golfer to win more than 10 straight titles, and to win 18 titles overall during a single year, on the Professional Golfers' Association (PGA) Tour, *3714*

Nelson, Dave: Kansas City Royals regular season baseball game at Kauffman Stadium, *1732*

Nelson, Don: Coach to be named National Basketball Association (NBA) Coach of the Year three times, *2315*

Nelson, Juan: Athletes from Argentina to win gold medals in the Olympic Games, *4659*

Nemcova, Eva: Women's National Basketball Association (WNBA) All-WNBA First Team, *2387*

Nemecky, Otokar: Men's 18-kilometer cross-country event held in the world championships of Nordic skiing, *5371*

Nordic combined event held in the world championships of Nordic skiing, *5374*

Németh, Ferenc: Pentathlete to win two pentathlon gold medals in the same Olympic Games, *4827*

Németh, Imre: Father and son to both win gold medals in track and field in the Olympic Games, *6213*

Javelin-thrower to break the 310-foot barrier, *4403*

Németh, Miklos: Father and son to both win gold medals in track and field in the Olympic Games, *6213*

Javelin-thrower to break the 310-foot barrier, *4403*

Neneniene, Aldona Cesaityte: Handball players to win two consecutive gold medals in women's team handball in the Olympic Games, *4008*

Nepala, Ondrej: Figure skater from Czechoslovakia to win the men's singles title at the Olympic Winter Games, *3070*

Figure skater from Czechoslovakia to win the men's singles title at the world championships, *3067*

Nesty, Anthony: Athlete from Suriname to win a gold medal in the Olympic Games, *4767*

Neubert, Romana: Heptathlete to hold the world record in the women's heptathlon, *4012*

Neuland, Alfred: Athlete from Estonia to win a gold medal in the Olympic Games, *4651*

Lightweight weightlifting event held in the Olympic Games, *6329*

Neumann, Paul: Men's 500-meter freestyle event held in the Olympic Games, *5787*

Neuper, Hubert: Ski jumping event held in the world cup for Nordic skiing, *5430*

Nevers, Ernie: College football All-America team named by Grantland Rice, *3153*

Pro Football Hall of Fame, *3268*

Professional football player to score all 40 of his team's points, *3160*

Neveu, Alfred: Bobsled event held at the Olympic Winter Games, *2467*

Newbold, Arthur: Men's doubles competition at the United States national tennis championships, *6012*

Newby-Fraser, Paula: Athlete to win the women's Hawaii Ironman triathlon three and up to eight times, *6239*

Newcombe, Don: African-American major league baseball players to appear in an All-Star Game, *1574*

Major league baseball pitcher to win the Cy Young Award, *1622*

Newcombe, John: Davis Cup to be a full open tournament for professionals and amateurs, *6151*

Wimbledon Open men's doubles tennis title, *6129*

Newhouse, Robert: New York Giants regular season football game played at Giants Stadium, *3350*

Newlands, Peter: Woman to be skipper of a boat in an Olympic competition, *5244*

Ni, Xiong *See* Xiong Ni

Nichols, Cynthia: Woman to swim across the English Channel and back consecutively, *5928*

Nichols, Dave: College baseball player to steal five bases in a single game, *1726*

Nichols, Debbie: National Collegiate Athletic Association (NCAA) Division I women's softball player to pitch 182 complete career games, *5621*

National Collegiate Athletic Association (NCAA) Division I women's softball player to pitch 50 wins in a single season, *5620*

Nicklaus, Jack: Golfer to have a double, and then triple, grand slam, winning golf's four major tournaments twice, and then three times, each, *3797*

Golfer to win 100 professional tournaments, *3883*

Golfer to win 18 titles in golf's four major tournaments, and six Masters championships, *3850*

Golfer to win five Masters tournaments, *3807*

Golfer to win five Professional Golfers' Association (PGA) Championships, *3826*

Golfer to win more than $2 million in official prize money during his career, *3801*

Golfer to win more than $200,000 in official prize money in a single season, *3792*

Golfer to win more than $3 million in official prize money during his career, *3812*

Golfer to win more than $300,000 in official prize money in a single season, *3798*

Golfer to win more than $4 million in official prize money during his career, *3840*

Golfer to win more than $5 million in official prize money during his career, *3859*

Golfer to win more than $6 million in official prize money during his career, *3866*

Nicklaus, Jack:—*continued*

Golfer to win the Masters tournament twice in a row, *3783*

Golfer to win the Tournament of Champions four and five times, *3802*

Golfer to win the U.S. Open championship four times, and two and three times consecutively, *3640*

Golfer to win the U.S. Open in under 275, and to win the U.S. Open twice on the same course, *3827*

Golfer to win the World Series of Golf in its new 72-hole format, *3809*

Golfer to win the World Series of Golf twice in a row, *3770*

Golfer to win two Professional Golfers' Association (PGA) Championships, after the tournament was converted to a stroke play format, *3794*

National golf team to win five consecutive Canada Cup tournaments, *3776*

Presidents Cup Match won by the international team, *3893*

Tournament Players Championship, *3806*

World Series of Golf, *3767*

Nicks, Jennifer: International pairs figure skating competition in which all the medalists were brother-and-sister pairs, *3041*

Nicks, John: International pairs figure skating competition in which all the medalists were brother-and-sister pairs, *3041*

Nicolls, Richard: Organized horse races in colonial North America, *4252*

Silver trophy known to be awarded at a sporting event in North America, *1146*

Nieder, Bill: Shot-putter to break the 20-meter barrier, *5343*

Nielsen, Halfdan: Speed skater to skate the 10,000 meters in under 20 minutes, *5632*

Nielsen, Kurt: African-American tennis player to win the women's singles championship at Wimbledon, *6110*

Nielsen, Thor: Canoe marathon world championships, *2624*

Niemann, Gunda Kleeman *See* Niemann-Stirnemann, Gunda Kleeman

Niemann-Stirnemann, Gunda Kleeman: National team to sweep the medals in the women's 5000-meter speed-skating event at the Olympic Winter Games, *5713*

Speed skater to be women's world champion in long-distance speed skating eight times, *5736*

Speed skater to skate the women's 5000-meter event in under 7 minutes, *5730*

Nieminen, Toni: Skier to win two medals in the men's 90-meter team ski-jumping event in the Olympic Winter Games, *5475*

Niflot, Jack (Isidor): Bantamweight freestyle wrestling event held in the Olympic Games, *6362*

Nighbor, Frank: National Hockey League player to win the Hart Memorial Trophy as the league's Most Valuable Player, *4081*

National Hockey League player to win the Lady Byng Memorial Trophy as the most gentlemanly player, *4085*

Nikkinen, Soini: Javelin-thrower to break the 270-foot barrier, *4396*

Nikkola, Ari-Pekka: Men's team ski-jumping event held in the Olympic Winter Games, *5457*

Skier to win two medals in the men's 90-meter team ski-jumping event in the Olympic Winter Games, *5475*

Nikolayeva, Marharyta: National team to sweep the top medals in the women's all-around gymnastics competition in the Olympic Games, *3946*

Niles, Nathaniel: Figure skater to win the women's singles title at the U.S. national championships, *2988*

Figure skater to win two straight women's singles titles at the U.S. national championships, *2994*

Figure skaters to win a gold medal in ice dancing in the U.S. national championships, *2989*

Figure skaters to win the pairs title in the U.S. national championships, *2990*

Nilsen, Laila Schou: Speed skater to be women's world champion in speed skating twice in a row, *5661*

Woman speed skater to skate the 3000 meters in under 6 minutes, *5659*

Woman speed skater to skate the 500 meters in under 50 seconds, *5654*

Woman speed skater to skate the 5000 meters in under 10 minutes, *5660*

Nilsson, Bill: World championship in motocross racing, *4579*

Nilsson, Dave: Texas Rangers regular season baseball game played at The Ballpark, *1828*

Nilsson, Jonny: Speed skater to skate the 3000 meters in under 4:30 minutes, *5674*

Niogret, Corinne: Women's 4 x 7.5-kilometer biathlon relay competition held in the Olympic Winter Games, *2440*

Nissen, George: Trampoline, *6226*

Niyongabo, Venuste: Athlete from Burundi to win a gold medal in the Olympic Games, *4800*

Noel, Evan: Rackets event held in the Olympic Games, *4872*

Noisy, Geoff: National Collegiate Athletic Association major college football player to receive 295 passes during his college career, *3488*

Noll, Chuck: National Football League coach to lead his team to four wins in the Super Bowl, *3363*

Nomura, Toyokazu: Men's half-middleweight judo event in the Olympic Games, *4539*

Nordlander, Axel: Equestrian to win both individual and team gold medals in the three-day event competitions in the Olympic Games, *2846*

Three-day event individual equestrian competition held in the Olympic Games, *2848*

Three-day event team equestrian competition held in the Olympic Games, *2849*

Nordvik, Hans: Running deer (double shot) team shooting event held in the Olympic Games, *5297*

Norheim, Sondre: Formally measured ski jump, *5355*

Norman, Greg: Golfer to win more than $10 million in official prize money during a career, *3885*

Golfer to win the British Open in 267 for 72 holes, *3875*

Northcliffe, Alfred Charles William Harmsworth, 1st Viscount: International motorboat (powerboat) race, *4563*

Norton, John: Hurdler to race the 400-meter hurdles in under 55 seconds, *4328*

Norval, Piet: Athletes from South Africa to win medals in the Olympic Games, after the lifting of the ban on their country because of its racist policies, *4779*

Nosseir, El Sayed Mohammed: Athlete from Egypt to win an Olympic gold medal, *4662*

Nott, Tara: Women's weightlifting events held in the Olympic Games, *6353*

Nova, Lou: Boxing match to be broadcast on television in the United States, *2552*

Novikov, Igor: Pentathlete to win three consecutive men's titles in the world pentathlon championships and then a fourth, *4826*

Pentathlete to win two gold medals in the men's modern pentathlon team competition in the Olympic Games, *4828*

Novotny, Rene: Figure skaters from the Czech Republic to win the pairs title in the world championships, *3110*

Nowak, Cécile: Women's extra-lightweight judo event held in the Olympic Games, *4559*

Nuesslein, Lawrence: Shooters from the United States to win the small-bore rifle team title in the Olympic Games, *5300*

Nunn, Glynis: Women's heptathlon event held in the Olympic Games, *4013*

Nurmi, Paavo: Athlete to win 12 medals in the Olympic Games, *4669*

Athlete to win five gold medals in a single Olympic Games, *4658*

Athlete to win six medals overall in a single Olympic Games, *4652*

Men's 5000- and 10,000-meter events held in the Olympic Games, *5008*

Runner to hold the world record in both the men's 5000- and 10,000-meter events, *5013*

Runner to win two consecutive titles in the men's individual cross-country in the Olympic Games, *5015*

Nyenashev, Stanislav: Hammer-thrower to break the 210-foot barrier, *3989*

Nykänen, Matti: Men's team ski-jumping event held in the Olympic Winter Games, *5457*

Skier to win two individual ski-jumping gold medals in the same Olympic Winter Games, *5460*

O

Oakes, D.: All-England Championships in badminton, *1166*

Oberg, Margo: Women's competition to be included in the world professional championships in surfing, *5775*

Oberhammer, Jörg: Olympic Winter Games held on artificial snow, *4762*

Oberlander, Andy: College football All-America team named by Grantland Rice, *3153*

O'Brien, Dan: Decathlete to score 8,891 points in the men's decathlon, *2745*

O'Brien, Davey: Davey O'Brien Award, *3354*

O'Brien, Edward: Twin major league baseball players to play in the same game on the same team, *1598*

O'Brien, Jay: Bobsledders to win two straight titles in the four-man bobsled at the Olympic Winter Games, *2472*

O'Brien, John: Twin major league baseball players to play in the same game on the same team, *1598*

O'Brien, Parry: Shot-putter to break the 18- and 19-meter, and 60-foot, barriers, *5340*

Shot-putter to win two consecutive men's titles in the Olympic Games, *5341*

O'Callaghan, Patrick: Athlete from independent Ireland to win a gold medal in the Olympic Games, *3984*

Hammer-thrower representing Ireland to win the men's event in the Olympic Games, *3985*

O'Connor, Colleen: Figure skaters from the United States to win an Olympic medal in ice dancing, *3074*

O'Connor, Peter: Long-jumper to hold the officially accepted world record in the men's event, *4428*

Oda, Mikio: Athlete from Japan to win a gold medal in the Olympic Games, *4671*

Odynokova, Lyubov Berezhnaya: Handball players to win two consecutive gold medals in women's team handball in the Olympic Games, *4008*

Oerter, Alfred: Discus-thrower to win four consecutive men's titles in the Olympic Games, and the first to win any Olympic event four consecutive times, *2777*

Oerter, Alfred: Discus-thrower to break the 200-foot barrier, *2773*

Offerman, José: Florida Marlins regular season baseball game played at Joe Robbie Stadium, *1823*

Ogiwara, Kenju: Skiers to win two consecutive men's Nordic combined team titles at the Olympic Winter Games, *5489*

Oing, Debbie: College women's basketball All-America team, *2110*

Okano, Isao: Men's middleweight judo event in the Olympic Games, *4533*

Okker, Tom: U.S. Open men's singles title, and the first men's singles Grand Slam title won by an African-American, *6135*

Olajuwon, Hakeem: Basketball player to have 3,582 blocked shots in his National Basketball Association (NBA) career, *2412*

Houston Rockets player to be named National Basketball Association (NBA) Defensive Player of the Year, *2325*

Olbricht, Bernd: Men's pairs 500-meter kayaking event held in the Olympic Games, *2617*

Oleniuc (later Lipa), Elisabeta: Rower to win gold medals in both the women's single and double sculls events in the Olympic Games, *4953*

Oliva, Tony (Pedro): Baseball player to win batting titles in his first two major league years, *1678*

Oliveira, João Carlos de: Triple-jumper to break the 58-foot barrier, *6258*

Oliver, Eric: World championships in motorcycle racing, *4578*

Olivier, Eugène: National team to sweep the top honors in the men's individual épée competition in the Olympic Games, *2913*

Olizarenko, Nadiya: National team to sweep the medals in the women's 800-meter race, or in any women's track event, at the Olympic Games, *5114*

Olson, Scott: In-line roller skates, *4910*

Olsson, Anna: Canoe racer to win a gold medal in both the singles and pairs in the women's 500 meters in the Olympic Games, *2620*

Olunina, Alevtina: Skier to win two consecutive women's Nordic (cross-country) skiing titles in the Olympic Winter Games, *5423*

O'Meara, Mark: Golfer to win more than $400,000 in the Skins Game, *3890*

Omlie, Phoebe Fairgrave: Women's Air Derby, *1007*

Ondieki, Yobes: Runner to race the men's 10,000 meters in under 27:00 minutes, *5168*

O'Neal, Shaquille: Basketball player to block 11 shots in a single Division I National Collegiate Athletic Association (NCAA) championship series game, *2313*

Orlando Magic player to be named National Basketball Association (NBA) Rookie of the Year, *2326*

O'Neill, John: Rugby players to win two Olympic gold medals in rugby, *4968*

O'Neill, John "Buck": African-American to become a major league baseball coach, *1651*

Ono, Takashi: Gymnast to win two consecutive men's horizontal bar titles in the Olympic Games, *3947*

Ónody, Jószef: Men's 4 x 250-meter (later 4 x 200-meter) freestyle relay swimming event held in the Olympic Games, *5799*

Oosterbaan, Bennie: Athlete to be named an All-American in both basketball and football, *1147*

College football All-America team named by Grantland Rice, *3153*

Oreiller, Henri: Men's downhill skiing event held at the Olympic Winter Games, *5386*

Orford, Lord: Dog racing club, *2830*

O'Rhee, Willie: African-American to play in the National Hockey League, *4138*

Orono, Rafael: Boxer to be world superflyweight (junior bantamweight) champion, *2578*

O'Rourke, Jim: Hit made in baseball's National League, *1221*

O'Rourke, John: Major league baseball player to hit four doubles in one game, *1252*

Orphanidis, Georgios: Free rifle (three position) individual shooting event held in the Olympic Games, *5273*

Orr, Bobby: Hockey player to be named *Sports Illustrated* Sportsman of the Year, *4153*

National Hockey League defenseman to have 102 assists in a single season, *4159*

National Hockey League player to be named outstanding defenseman eight times in a row, *4167*

Orr, Vickie: College women's basketball United States Basketball Writers Association All-American first team, *2271*

Orser, Brian: Figure skaters to win Emmy awards for a television special, *3095*

Orton, George: Athlete from Canada to win a gold medal in the Olympic Games, *4621*
Men's steeplechase event held at the Olympic Games, *4977*

Osborn, Harold: Athlete to win an Olympic gold medal, or to hold the world record, in both the men's decathlon and an individual track and field event, *2741*
Decathlete from the United States to hold the world record in the men's decathlon, *2740*

Osborn, John: Tornado-class sailing event held in the Olympic Games, *5236*

Osborne (later duPont), Margaret: Tennis player to win 10 consecutive women's doubles titles at the United States national championships, and 13 overall, *6106*
Tennis player to win four consecutive United States mixed doubles national championships, and nine overall, *6105*

Osburn, Carl: Shooter to win five gold medals in shooting in the Olympic Games, *5298*

Osiier, Ellen: Women's individual foil fencing competition held in the Olympic Games, *2920*

Osiier, Ivan: Athlete to compete in seven Olympic Games, *4687*
Athletes to compete in the Olympic Games over a period of 40 years, *4688*
Women's individual foil fencing competition held in the Olympic Games, *2920*

Ostermeyer, Micheline: Women's shot put event held in the Olympic Games, *5336*

Osthoff, Oscar: Weightlifter to win two medals in the same Olympic Games, and the first from the United States to win a weightlifting Olympic gold medal, *6326*

Otkalenko, Nina Pletneva: Runner to race the women's 800 meters in under 2:10 minutes, *5055*

Otsetova, Svetla: Women's double sculls event held in the Olympic Games, *4946*

Ott, Dietmar: World championships in vaulting, *2888*

Ottey, Merlene: Runner to win two consecutive titles in the women's 200-meter event in the World Championships in Athletics, *5173*

Otto, Kristin: Women's 100-meter butterfly event in the Olympic Games in which all the medalists had times under one minute, *5953*
Women's 50-meter freestyle swimming event held in the Olympic Games, *5955*

Otto-Crépin, Margit: Individual dressage equestrian competition in the Olympic Games in which women riders swept the top medals, *2890*

Ottosson, Jan: Skier to win two consecutive titles in the men's 4 x 10-kilometer relay Nordic (cross-country) at the Olympic Winter Games, *5455*

Ouimet, Francis: Amateur golfer to win the U.S. Open, *3653*
Golfer from the United States to become captain of the Royal and Ancient Golf Club of St. Andrews, *3727*

Overbeck, Carla: Women's soccer event held in the Olympic Games, *5569*

Overend, Ted: World championships in mountain biking, *2716*

Ovett, Steve: Runner to complete the men's mile race in under 3:49 minutes, *5113*
Runner to race the men's 1500 meters in under 3:32 minutes, *5119*

Owen, Gary: World amateur snooker championships, *2457*

Owen, Laurence: World figure skating championship to be canceled other than because of war, *3057*

Owen, Maribel Vinson: Figure skater to win six consecutive women's singles titles, and nine overall, at the U.S. national championships, *3016*
World figure skating championship to be canceled other than because of war, *3057*

Owen, Maribel Y.: World figure skating championship to be canceled other than because of war, *3057*

Owens, Jesse (James Cleveland): Long-jump record to stand for more than 25 years, *4434*
Runner from Central or South America to set or equal a world track and field record, *5049*
Runner to race the men's 100-meter dash in 10.1 seconds, *5063*
Runner to race the men's 100-meter dash in 10.2 seconds, *5036*
Team to race the men's 4 x 100-meter relay in under 40 seconds, *5042*
Track-and-field star to set five new world records and equal a sixth in less than an hour, *6210*

Owens, John: Runner to race the 100-yard dash in under 10 seconds, *4973*

Ozolina, Elvira: Javelin-thrower to reach the 190-foot barrier in the women's event, *4398*

P

Paddock, Charles: African-American runner to hold the record in the men's 100-meter dash, *5024*

Runner to hold the officially accepted world record in the men's 100-meter dash, *5001*

Runner to race the men's 100-meter event in less than 10.5 seconds, *5012*

Team from the United States to win the men's 4 x 100-meter relay track event in the Olympic Games, *5011*

Padilla, Doug: International Amateur Athletic Federation (IAAF) Grand Prix, *6223*

Padilla, Enrique: Athletes from Argentina to win gold medals in the Olympic Games, *4659*

Pae Gil-su: Gymnast to win six gold medals in a single Olympic Games, *3976*

Pagani, Nello: World championships in motorcycle racing, *4578*

Page, Alan: African-American professional football player to be named Most Valuable Player of the National Football Conference, *3311*

Page, James: Ice skating club in the United States, *2951*

Pai Yun-yao: World championships in taekwondo to include women, *4549*

Paine, Andrew: African-American All-Star Team in professional baseball, *1402*

Paine, John: Brothers to win gold and silver medals in the same event in the Olympic Games, *4613*

Free pistol shooting individual event held in the Olympic Games, *5271*

Military revolver individual shooting event held in the Olympic Games, *5270*

Paine, Sumner: Brothers to win gold and silver medals in the same event in the Olympic Games, *4613*

Free pistol shooting individual event held in the Olympic Games, *5271*

Military revolver individual shooting event held in the Olympic Games, *5270*

Paivarinta, Pekka: World Cross-Country Championships, *5096*

Pak, Se Ri: U.S. Women's Open to be won in a sudden-death playoff, *3892*

Pakhalina, Yuliya: Women's synchronized springboard diving event held in the Olympic Games, *2827*

Women's synchronized three-meter springboard diving event held at the world championships, *2825*

Pakhomova, Ludmila: Figure skaters from the Soviet Union to win the ice dancing title in the world championships, *3066*

Figure skaters from the United States to win an Olympic medal in ice dancing, *3074*

Figure skaters to win the ice dancing title in the Olympic Winter Games, *3076*

Palazzi, Osvaldo: Gymnast to win two consecutive men's pommel horse titles in the world championships, *3921*

Pommel horse competition held at the world championships in gymnastics, *3917*

Palfrey, Sarah *See* Fabyan, Sarah Palfrey

Palfyova, Matylda: World championships in gymnastics to award women's titles in specific events, *3932*

Palm, Bert: World outdoor championships in bowls, *2499*

Palmer, Arnold: Golf course in China, *3857*

Golfer to be named *Sports Illustrated* Sportsman of the Year, *3760*

Golfer to earn more than $100,000 in official prize money during a single year, *3769*

Golfer to win 100 professional tournaments, *3883*

Golfer to win more than $1 million in official prize money on the Professional Golfers' Association (PGA) Tour during his career, *3788*

Golfer to win the Masters tournament four times, *3775*

Golfer to win the Tournament of Champions in a playoff, *3784*

National golf team to win five consecutive Canada Cup tournaments, *3776*

Palmer, Charles: Trap (clay pigeon) team shooting event in the Olympic Games, *5292*

Palmer, Violet: Women referees in the National Basketball Association (NBA), *2386*

Palusalu, Kristian: Wrestler to win heavyweight titles in both freestyle and Greco-Roman wrestling in the Olympic Games, *6385*

Panin, Nikolai *See* Kolomenkin, Nikolai

Papanikolaou, Christos: Pole-vaulter to clear 18 feet, *4846*

Papp, László: Boxer from a Communist country to turn professional, *2561*

Boxer to win three gold medals, and two consecutive light middleweight titles, in the Olympic Games, *2560*

Light middleweight boxing event held in the Olympic Games, *2558*

Paraense, Guilherme: Athlete from Brazil to win a gold medal in the Olympic Games, *4650*

Parent, Bernie: National Hockey League player to be named the Most Valuable Player of the playoffs twice in a row, *4168*

Parfenovich, Vladimir: Canoe racer to win three gold medals in a single Olympic Games, *2621*

Parish, Robert: Basketball player to have 10,117 defensive rebounds in his National Basketball Association (NBA) career, *2381*
Basketball player to play 21 seasons in the National Basketball Association (NBA), *2382*
Park, Joo-bong: Badminton events held in the Olympic Games as medal sports, *1174*
Park, Mungo: Golfer to win the British Open, *3577*
Park, Sung-soo: Men's team archery event held in the Olympic Games, *1037*
Park, Willie, Jr.: Golfer to win the British Open, *3577*
Park, Willie, Sr.: British Open golf tournament, *3576*
Golfer to win the British Open, *3577*
Parke, James: Mixed doubles championships at Wimbledon, *6053*
Parke, Richard: Bobsledders from the United States to win the five-man bobsled title at the Olympic Winter Games, *2468*
Parker (later Smith), Marjorie: Figure skaters to win the ice dancing title at the U.S. national championships, *3021*
Parmentier, Alexis: Snowboarding world championships, *5521*
Paroche, Achille: Military rifle individual shooting event held in the Olympic Games, *5279*
Parsons, Johnnie: Indianapolis 500 automobile race to be part of the Formula One Grand Prix circuit, *1079*
Patak, Fred: Kansas City Royals regular season baseball game at Kauffman Stadium, *1732*
Paterson, John: International golf match, *3545*
Patrick, Frank: Professional ice hockey league on North America's West Coast, *4059*
Patrick, John: Rugby players to win two Olympic gold medals in rugby, *4968*
Patrick, Lester: Professional ice hockey league on North America's West Coast, *4059*
Patterson, James: Golf ball made of gutta-percha, *3567*
Pattison, Rodney: Sailor to win two consecutive gold medals in the Flying Dutchman–class event in the Olympic Games, *5228*
Patton, George S., Jr.: Men's modern pentathlon held in the Olympic Games, *4815*
Patzaichin, Ivan: Canoer to win three titles in the men's Canadian pairs 1000-meter event in the Olympic Games, *2622*
Paul, Robert: Figure skaters from Canada to win the pairs title at the Olympic Winter Games, *3055*
Paula, Carlos: Major league baseball player widely recognized as black to play for the Washington Senators, *1610*

Paulsen, Axel: Figure skater to perform a double axel in competition, *3042*
Woman figure skater to perform an axel in competition, *2985*
Paulu, Leonard: National collegiate track and field (athletics) championships sponsored by the National Collegiate Athletic Association (NCAA), *6206*
Pavano, Carl: Major league baseball player to hit 70 home runs in a single season, *1853*
Pawlowski, Jerzy: Fencer to win three men's sabre titles in the world championships, *2936*
Payne, Andrew: Run across the United States, *5017*
Payne, Ernest: Men's 4000-meter team pursuit cycling event held in the Olympic Games, *2692*
Payssé, Pierre: World championships in gymnastics, *3910*
Payton, Walter: African-American professional football player to be named National Football League Player of the Year by the Pro Football Writers Association, *3353*
National Football League player to gain a career total of 16,726 yards rushing, *3408*
National Football League player to gain a career total of 21,803 yards running, *3409*
National Football League player to rush for 100 yards or more in 77 games, *3411*
National Football League rusher to gain 275 yards in a single game, *3357*
Walter Payton Player of the Year Award, *3412*
Pearce, Bobby (Henry): Rower to win two consecutive men's single sculls rowing titles in the Olympic Games, *4937*
Pearson, Albie: Washington Senators Rookie of the Year, *1631*
Pearson, David: National Association for Stock Car Auto Racing (NASCAR) race to be televised, *1102*
Pearson, Rosina: College women's basketball player to have an average of 18.5 rebounds per game in a single Division I National Collegiate Athletic Association (NCAA) season, *2219*
Pechacek, Frantisek: Gymnast to win two consecutive men's all-around titles in the world championships, *3923*
Pechstein, Claudia: Speed skater to skate the women's 5000-meter event in under 7 minutes, *5730*
Speed skater to win two consecutive women's 5000-meter titles in the Olympic Winter Games, *5731*
Pécsi, Daniel: International championships in table tennis, *5984*

Pedersen, Susan: Women's 200-meter individual medley swimming event held in the Olympic Games, *5855*

Pederson, Terje: Javelin-thrower to break the 300-foot and 90-meter barriers in the men's event, *4399*

Peete, Calvin: African-American golfer to win the Tournament of Champions, *3848*

African-American golfer to win the Tournament Players Championship, *3845*

African-American golfer to win the Vardon Trophy for the lowest stroke average on the Professional Golfers' Association (PGA) Tour, *3842*

Pele: Soccer (international football) team from Brazil to win the world cup, *5557*

Pelle, István: Men's floor exercises gymnastics competition held in the Olympic Games, *3928*

Pennell, John: Pole-vaulter to clear 17 feet, *4845*

Pennell, Vane: Rackets event held in the Olympic Games, *4872*

Penttilä, Eino: Javelin-thrower to break the 220-foot barrier, *4387*

Pepper, Dottie: Three-Tour Challenge, *3874*

Pérec, Marie-José: Runner from the Caribbean to win the women's 400-meter title in the Olympic Games, *5158*

Runner to win two consecutive titles in the women's 400-meter race in the Olympic Games, *5182*

Runner to win two titles in the women's 400-meter event in the World Championships in Athletics, *5177*

Pérez, Jefferson: Athlete from Ecuador to win a gold medal in the Olympic Games, *4792*

Perez, Tony: Pittsburgh Pirates regular season baseball game played at Three Rivers Stadium, *1717*

Perrault, Annie: Women's 3000-meter short track relay speed skating event held at the Olympic Winter Games, *5715*

Perry, Fred: St. Bride Vase, *5985*

Tennis player to win three consecutive Wimbledon mixed doubles championships, *6096*

Perry, Gaylord: Baseball pitcher to win the Cy Young Award in both leagues, *1747*

Cleveland Indians pitcher to win the Cy Young Award, *1723*

Perry, Jim: Minnesota Twins pitcher to win the Cy Young Award, *1712*

Perry, Joe: African-American professional football player to join the San Francisco 49ers, *3217*

Perry, Robert: U.S. Open mixed doubles tennis title, *6125*

Person, Chuck: Indiana Pacers player to be named National Basketball Association (NBA) Rookie of the Year, *2255*

Persson, Gehnäll: Equestrian to be stripped of his dressage title because he was not a commissioned officer, *2860*

Pesky, Johnny: Baseball player to score 6 runs in a 9-inning American League game, *1551*

Peter, Birgit: World Sculls Cup series of rowing races, *4956*

Peters, Emmitt: Sled dog racer to complete the Iditarod in less than 15 days, *5510*

Peters, Jim: Runner to complete the men's marathon in under 2:20 hours, *4485*

Peterson, Alexander: Caribbean Cup, *2476*

Pétervári, Pál: Canoe marathon world championships, *2624*

Petit-Breton, Lucien: Cyclist to win the Tour de France twice consecutively, *2691*

Petrenko, Serhei: Men's Canadian pairs 500-meter canoeing event held in the Olympic Games, *2618*

Petrenko, Tatyana *See* Samusenko, Tatyana Petrenko

Petrenko, Viktor: Figure skater from Ukraine to win the men's singles title at the Olympic Winter Games, *3100*

Figure skater from Ukraine to win the men's singles title at the world championships, *3098*

Figure skater from Ukraine to win the women's singles title in the world championships, *3103*

Petri, August: Men's team sabre fencing competition held in the Olympic Games, *2911*

Petrie, Geoff: Portland Trail Blazers player to be named National Basketball Association (NBA) Rookie of the Year, *2080*

Petroc, Yevgeny: Skeet shooting individual event held in the Olympic Games, *5312*

Petruseva, Natalia: Woman speed skater to skate the 1000 meters in under 1:20 minutes, *5701*

Pettersson, Anna: Uneven (asymmetrical) bars competition held in the world championships for gymnastics, *3933*

Pettersson, Sten: Hurdler to hold the world record in both the men's 110- and 400-meter events, *4331*

Hurdler to race the men's 400-meter hurdles in under 54 seconds, *4329*

Pettit, Bob: Basketball player to make 19 free throws in a National Basketball Association (NBA) Finals game, *1980*

Basketball player to win the National Basketball Association (NBA) Most Valuable Player Award, *1962*

Milwaukee Hawks player to be named National Basketball Association (NBA) Rookie of the Year, *1955*

Petty, Lee: Daytona 500 automobile race, *1098*

Petty, Richard: Automobile racer to earn more than $100,000 in a single season in the National Association for Stock Car Auto Racing (NASCAR) Winston Cup series, *1110*

Automobile racer to win more than 20 races in a single season in the National Association for Stock Car Auto Racing (NASCAR) Winston Cup series, *1111*

Automobile racer to win three, four, five, six, and seven championships on the National Association for Stock Car Auto Racing (NASCAR) Winston Cup circuit, *1116*

National Association for Stock Car Auto Racing (NASCAR) automobile race of 500 miles to be televised live from start to finish, *1128*

Petuchkova, Yelena: Woman rider to win the world championships in dressage, *2876*

Petway, Bruce: African-American All-Star Team in professional baseball, *1402*

Peyron, Loïck: Sailor to win the Single-Handed Transatlantic Race (STAR) twice consecutively, *5255*

Pezzo, Paola: Women's cross-country cycling race held in the Olympic Games, *2724*

Pflueger, Joan: Woman to win the Grand American Trapshoot, *5306*

Pflug, Monika: Speed skaters to become world champions in speed skating sprints, *5686*

Pfnür, Franc: Men's Alpine combined event held at the Olympic Winter Games, *5383*

Pheidippides: Men's marathon race held in the Olympic Games, *4468*

Phelps, Jaycie: Gymnasts from the United States to win the women's team title in the Olympic Games, *3978*

Phillippe, Deacon: Pitcher to pitch five complete games in a World Series, *1350*

Pitcher to win a World Series game, *1354*

Phillips, Bill: Major league baseball player born in Canada, *1244*

Phillips, Tony: Chicago White Sox regular season baseball game played at New Comiskey Park, *1816*

Phrangoudis, Ioannis: Rapid-fire pistol shooting individual event held in the Olympic Games, *5272*

Piccard, Bertrand: People to circle the globe in a balloon, *1183*

Piccard, Franck: Men's super giant slalom event held at the Olympic Winter Games, *5454*

Piercy, Violet: Runner to hold the officially accepted world record in the women's marathon, *4478*

Pietri, Dorando: Runner to hold the officially accepted world record in the men's marathon, and the first United States runner to win the Olympic marathon, *4472*

Pietro, Joseph Di *See* Di Pietro, Joseph

Piggott, Bert: African-American professional football player to join the Los Angeles Rams, *3208*

Piggott, Lester: Jockey who won seven, eight, and nine Derbys at Epsom Downs, *4311*

Pike, James: Trap (clay pigeon) team shooting event in the Olympic Games, *5292*

Pike, Lipman: Jewish major league baseball manager, *1234*

Jewish major league baseball player, *1218*

Pilâtre de Rozier, Jean-François: People to fly in a balloon, *1176*

Pilgrim, Paul: Runner to win both the men's 400- and 800-meter events in the same Olympic Games, *4993*

Pillwein, Hedi: Canoe slalom world championships, *2604*

Pimenov, Nikolai: Rowers to win two consecutive titles in the pair-oared shell without coxswain event in the Olympic Games, *4950*

Pimenov, Yuri: Rowers to win two consecutive titles in the pair-oared shell without coxswain event in the Olympic Games, *4950*

Pimm, William: Small-bore rifle team shooting event held in the Olympic Games, *5291*

Pinayeva, Lyudmila Khvedosyuk: Canoe racer to win two consecutive titles in the women's 500-meter singles kayak event, *2612*

Pincay, Laffit, Jr.: Jockey to win 8,834 horse races, *4319*

Pinckney, George: Major league baseball player to play in 577 consecutive games, *1301*

Piniella, Lou: Kansas City Royals baseball player to be named Rookie of the Year, *1704*

Pinniger, Broome Eric: Field hockey players to win two gold medals in the Olympic Games, *4038*

Pippig, Uta: Runner to win three consecutive women's titles in the Boston Marathon, *4525*

Pires, Sandra: Beach volleyball event held in the Olympic Games, *6286*

Plaatjes, Mark: Runner from the United States to win the men's marathon in the World Championships in Athletics, *4523*

Plaikner, Walter: Two-seater luge (toboggan) event to have two pairs of gold medalists in a single Olympic Winter Games, *4458*

Planck-Szabo, Herma *See* Jaross-Szabo, Herma

Plante, Jacques: National Hockey League player to be named outstanding goaltender five times in a row, *4139*

Plater, Philip: Small-bore rifle (prone) individual shooting event held in the Olympic Games, *5290*

Platov, Evgeny: Champions Series in figure skating, *3112*

Figure skaters to win two consecutive ice dancing titles at the Olympic Winter Games, *3114*

Player, Gary: Skins Game, *3841*

Plemel, Lee: College baseball team to have two consecutive Most Valuable Player Award winners, *1799*

Plimpton, James: Practical four-wheeled roller skates, *4902*

Roller-skating rink, *4903*

Plumb, J. Michael: Equestrians from the United States to win the three-day event individual competition, and team competition, in the Olympic Games, *2881*

Poage, George: Athlete of Black African ancestry to compete in the Olympic Games, *4629*

Podoloff, Maurice: Basketball Association of America (BAA) founding meeting, *1911*

Basketball player to win the National Basketball Association (NBA) Most Valuable Player Award, *1962*

Podres, Johnny: Baseball player to be named *Sports Illustrated* Sportsman of the Year, *1611*

Poe, Edgar Allen: All-America college football team named by Walter Camp, *3121*

Poetzsch, Anett: Figure skater from Germany to win the women's singles title at the Olympic Winter Games, *3085*

Pohl, Hans-Peter: Men's Nordic combined team event held in the Olympic Winter Games, *5456*

Polis, Carol: Woman to become a boxing judge, *2573*

Polit, Cornelia: National team to sweep the medals in the women's 100-meter backstroke, and the women's 200-meter backstroke, in the Olympic Games, *5935*

Polkunen, Sirkka: Women's 3 x 5-kilometer relay Nordic (cross-country) skiing event held at the Olympic Winter Games, *5401*

Poll, Claudia: Athlete from Costa Rica to win a gold medal in the Olympic Games, *4790*

Pollak, Burglinde: National team to sweep the medals in the women's pentathlon in the Olympic Games, *4831*

Pollard, Fritz (Frederick Douglass): African-American college football player to play in the Rose Bowl, *3140*

African-American college football running back to be named to Walter Camp's All-America team, *3139*

African-American professional football coach, *3144*

Pollenroth, Bob: National Collegiate Athletic Association college hockey player to score five assists in a single "Frozen Four" tournament game, *4155*

Pollock, Jessie: Archery events for women held in the Olympic Games, *1027*

Ponomaryeva, Nina Romaschkova: Discus-thrower to win two titles in the women's event in the Olympic Games, *2770*

Pope, Dick, Jr.: Water-skier known to have skied barefoot, *6315*

Pope, Emma: Batting title of the Amateur Softball Association Major Slow Pitch National Championship batting crown, *5605*

Pope, Gus: National collegiate track and field (athletics) championships sponsored by the National Collegiate Athletic Association (NCAA), *6206*

Pope, W. J.: Pope Trophy, *5992*

Popescu, Marioara: Rower to win gold medals in both the women's single and double sculls events in the Olympic Games, *4953*

Poradnyk, Lyudmila Bobrus: Handball players to win two consecutive gold medals in women's team handball in the Olympic Games, *4008*

Porteous, John: Golf match reported in a newspaper, *3547*

Porter, Terry: Basketball player to make 15 consecutive free throws in a National Basketball Association (NBA) Finals game, *2297*

Posey, Cumberland: Leondi Big Five, *1883*

Post, Albertson Van Zo *See* Van Zo Post, Albertson

Post, Wally: Los Angeles Dodgers regular season baseball game played at Dodger Stadium, *1655*

Postans, John: Trap (clay pigeon) team shooting event in the Olympic Games, *5292*

Postma, Ids: Speed skater to skate the 1500 meters in under 1:50 minutes, *5727*

Poulsen, Thomas: Men's lightweight four-oared shells without coxswain rowing event held in the Olympic Games, *4960*

Poupon, Philippe: Sailor in the Single-Handed Transatlantic Race (STAR) to cross the Atlantic in under 11 days, *5248*

Powell, Boog: Oakland Athletics regular season baseball game played at the Oakland Alameda County Coliseum, *1700*

Powell, Mike: Long-jumper to break the 28- and 29-foot barriers, *4439*

Long-jumper to win three, and then four, consecutive men's titles in the Olympic Games, *4443*

Powell, Renee: African-American woman to play on the Ladies Professional Golf Association (LPGA) tour, *3786*

Poynton, Dorothy: Diver to win two consecutive women's platform diving titles in the Olympic Games, *2801*

National team to sweep the top medals in the women's platform diving event in the Olympic Games, *2800*

Praag, Lionel Van *See* Van Praag, Lionel

Prager, Walter: World championships in Alpine skiing, *5377*

Pramstaller, Helmut: Giant slalom and snowboard cross events held in the snowboarding world championships, *5523*

Prantell, Nettie: Figure skater to win five consecutive ice dancing titles at the U.S. national championships, *3027*

Figure skaters to win two consecutive ice dancing titles at the U.S. national championships, *3023*

Press, Iryna: Women's pentathlon held in the Olympic Games, *4829*

Press, Tamara: Discus-thrower to break the 190-foot barrier in the women's event, *2772*

Shot-putter to break the 17- and 18-meter, and 60-foot, barriers in the women's event, *5342*

Shot-putter to win two consecutive titles in the women's event in the Olympic Games, *5344*

Prevost, Maurice: Schneider Cup international seaplane (hydro-aeroplane) race, *1004*

Price, Mark: Basketball player to have a .904 free throw average in his National Basketball Association (NBA) career, *2403*

Price, Nick: Golfer to win the Professional Golfers' Association (PGA) Championship in under 270, *3877*

Prinstein, Meyer: Long-jumper to win two consecutive men's titles in the Olympic Games, *4429*

National team to sweep the top spots in the men's triple jump in the Olympic Games, *6251*

Triple-jumper to win two consecutive men's titles in the Olympic Games, *6252*

Probst, Paul: Military revolver and military rifle team shooting events held in the Olympic Games, *5280*

Prodanov, Nikolai: Wedding between Olympic athletes held at the Olympic Games, *4717*

Prost, Alain: Automobile racer to have more than 50 wins on the Formula One Grand Prix circuit, *1143*

Automobile racer to win the Brazilian Grand Prix three, four, five, and six times, *1130*

Automobile racer to win three Austrian Grand Prix races, *1134*

Automobile racer to win two Australian Grand Prix races, *1137*

Protopopov, Oleg: Figure skaters from the Soviet Union to win the pairs title at the Olympic Winter Games, *3064*

Figure skaters from the Soviet Union to win the pairs title in the world championships, *3062*

Prudskova, Valentina: Women's team foil fencing competition held in the Olympic Games, *2935*

Prugger, Thomas: Giant slalom and snowboard cross events held in the snowboarding world championships, *5523*

Puica, Maricica: Women's 3000-meter race held at the Olympic Games, *5140*

Puikkonen, Jari: Men's team ski-jumping event held in the Olympic Winter Games, *5457*

Puliti, Oreste: Fencer to win two consecutive men's foil titles in the world championships, *2922*

Pung, Jackie: Golfer to win the U.S. Women's Open in a playoff, *3739*

Puntous, Sylviane: Athlete to win two consecutive women's Hawaii Ironman triathlons, *6238*

Purcell, Martin López-Zubero: Olympic men's 200-meter backstroke event in which the medalists all had times under two minutes, *5963*

Pusanov, Nikolai: Men's 4 x 7.5-kilometer relay biathlon team event held at the Olympic Winter Games, *2432*

Pütsep, Eduard: Bantamweight Greco-Roman wrestling event held in the Olympic Games, *6380*

Pyle, Charles C.: Run across the United States, *5017*

Pyrgos, Leon: Athlete from Greece to win a gold medal in the modern Olympic Games, *4611*

Men's masters foil fencing competition held in the Olympic Games, *2898*

Q

Qian Hong: Women's 100-meter butterfly event in the Olympic Games in which all the medalists had times under one minute, *5953*

Qiao Hong: Table tennis player to win both singles and doubles titles in the Olympic Games, *6000*

Quarrie, Donald: Runner from the Caribbean to win the men's 200-meter title at the Olympic Games, *5106*

Queensberry, John Sholto Douglas, 8th Marquess of: Queensberry rules for boxing, *2512*

Quimby, Harriet: Woman pilot to fly across the English Channel, *1003*

Quintana, Maria: World championships for freestyle skiing, *5451*

Quirot, Ana: Runner to win two consecutive titles in the women's 800-meter event in the World Championships in Athletics, *5185*

Quist, Adrian: Tennis player to win 10 consecutive Australian national men's doubles championships, *6102*

R

Rabic, V.: Floor exercise competition held at the world championships in gymnastics, *3919*

Radev, Boyan: Wrestler to win two consecutive light heavyweight Greco-Roman titles in the Olympic Games, *6391*

Radke-Batschauer, Lina (Karoline): Runner to hold the officially accepted world record in the women's 800-meter event, *5021*

Women's 800-meter running event held in the Olympic Games, *5022*

Ragan, Dave, Jr.: Golfer to win 13 titles recognized by the Ladies Professional Golf Association (LPGA) Tour in a single season, *3773*

Rahal, Bobby: Automobile racer to win the Indianapolis 500 with an average speed of more than 170 miles per hour, *1133*

Rahier, Gaston: World championship in motocross racing to include the 125 cc class, *4587*

Rahn, Sharon: Champion of the women's wheelchair division in the Boston Marathon, *4502*

Raivo, Matti: Men's 30-kilometer cross-country event held in the world championships of Nordic skiing, *5375*

Ramsey, Kirk: African-American bowler to bowl a 300 game in an American Bowling Congress (ABC) tournament, *2494*

Ranck, Roberta: National gymnastics competition in the United States to include women, *3927*

National track and field (athletics) championships for women in the United States, *6207*

Randall, Martha: Women's 400-meter individual medley swimming event held in the Olympic Games, *5849*

Rankin, Judy: Woman golfer to earn more than $100,000 in official prize money in a season, *3810*

Rankin, Thomas L.: Indoor ice skating rink, *2958*

Ranst, (first name unknown) van: Figure riding individual and team events held in the Olympic Games, *2850*

Rantanen, Siiri: Women's 3 x 5-kilometer relay Nordic (cross-country) skiing event held at the Olympic Winter Games, *5401*

Rastvorova, Valentina: Women's team foil fencing competition held in the Olympic Games, *2935*

Rattray, John: Open competition in golf, *3550*

Raudaschl, Hubert: Athlete to participate in nine Olympic Games, *4788*

Rausch, Emil: Men's 880-yard freestyle swimming event held in the Olympic Games, *5797*

Rawlins, Horace: U.S. Open golf tournament, *3614*

Rawls, Betsy: Golfer to have 15 consecutive seasons with a victory on the Ladies Professional Golf Association (LPGA) Tour, *3779*

Golfer to win 10 titles recognized by the Ladies Professional Golf Association (LPGA) Tour in a single season, *3752*

Golfer to win the U.S. Women's Open in a playoff, *3739*

Ray, Johnny: Boxing match to be broadcast on radio, *2540*

Ray, Nat: Hambletonian Stakes harness race, *4292*

Ray, Ted (Edward): Amateur golfer to win the U.S. Open, *3653*

Ray, Thierry: Men's extra-lightweight judo event held in the Olympic Games, *4545*

Reardon, Ray: Grand Prix in snooker, *2462*

World rankings for snooker, *2461*

Rebagliati, Ross: Men's giant slalom snowboarding event held at the Olympic Winter Games, *5524*

Recknagel, Helmut: Men's ski jumping (large hill) event held in the world championships of Nordic skiing, *5407*

Redmon, Charles: National collegiate track and field (athletics) championships sponsored by the National Collegiate Athletic Association (NCAA), *6206*

Redmond, John Lee: Perfect game in professional baseball, *1249*

Redwood, Bernard: Motorboat-racing event held in the Olympic Games, *4565*

Reed, Willis: Basketball player to be named Most Valuable Player of the National Basketball Association (NBA) Finals twice, *2090*

New York Knicks player to be named National Basketball Association (NBA) Most Valuable Player of the Year, *2074*

New York Knicks player to be named National Basketball Association (NBA) Rookie of the Year, *2034*

Rees, Dick: Cheltenham Gold Cup horse race, *4291*

Rees, Leighton: World professional darts championships, *2735*

Regoczy, Kristina: Figure skaters from Hungary to win the ice dancing title in the world championships, *3083*

Reich, Jean: Free rifle team shooting event held in the Olympic Games, *5281*

Reichardt, Rich: California Angels regular season baseball game played at Anaheim Stadium, *1688*

Reiche, Rüdiger: Men's quadruple sculls rowing event held in the Olympic Games, *4948*

Reid, John T.: Golf course in the United States, *3596*

Reid, Kerry Melville: Women's Tennis Association (WTA) championships, *6156*

Reilly, Charles: Baseball player to hit two home runs in his first major league game, *1298*

Reinalter, Edi: Men's slalom event held at the Olympic Winter Games, *5388*

Reinisch, Rica: National team to sweep the medals in the women's 100-meter backstroke, and the women's 200-meter backstroke, in the Olympic Games, *5935*

Reinsch, Gabriele: Discus-thrower to break the 250-foot barrier, *2785*

Remy, Jerry: Seattle Mariners regular season baseball game played at the Seattle Kingdome, *1744*

Renshaw, Ernest: Men's doubles tennis championship at Wimbledon, *6016*

Tennis player to win six consecutive men's singles championships at Wimbledon, and seven overall, *6019*

Tennis players to win five men's doubles championships at Wimbledon, *6026*

Renshaw, William: Men's doubles tennis championship at Wimbledon, *6016*

Tennis player to win six consecutive men's singles championships at Wimbledon, and seven overall, *6019*

Tennis players to win five men's doubles championships at Wimbledon, *6026*

Rensselaer, Alexander Van *See* Van Rensselaer, Alexander

Retton, Mary Lou: Gymnast from the United States to win the all-around women's title in the Olympic Games, *3973*

Gymnast to be named *Sports Illustrated* Sportsman of the Year, *3971*

Reulbach, Ed: Baseball pitcher to lead the National League in winning percentage for three consecutive years, *1378*

Major league pitcher to throw two shutouts in one day, *1381*

Reve Jiménez, Odalys: Women's middleweight judo event held in the Olympic Games, *4556*

Revere, Paul: Boston Marathon, *4469*

Reynolds, Bill: College baseball player to bat in nine runs in a single game, *1785*

College baseball player to hit four home runs in a single game, *1786*

Reynolds, Butch (Harry): Runner to complete the men's 400-meter race in under 44 seconds, *5090*

Reztsova, Anfisa: Female athlete to win gold medals in two different sports in the Olympic Winter Games, *4771*

Women's 7.5-kilometer biathlon competition held in the Olympic Winter Games, *2439*

Rheaume, Manon: Woman to play in a professional hockey game, *4204*

Rhode, Kim: Women's double trap (clay pigeon) individual shooting event held in the Olympic Games, *5325*

Rhodes, John: 8-meter-class sailing event in the Olympic Games, *5206*

Rhodes, Ted: African-American golfers to play in a Professional Golfers' Association (PGA)–recognized event, *3720*

Lifting of the "no blacks allowed" clause from the constitution of the Professional Golfers' Association (PGA), *3759*

Rice, Glen: Basketball player to score 184 points in a Division I National Collegiate Athletic Association (NCAA) championship series, *2281*

Basketball player to score 75 field goals in a Division I National Collegiate Athletic Association (NCAA) championship series, *2282*

Rice, Grantland: College football All-America team named by Grantland Rice, *3153*

Rice, Jerry: National Football League player to reach 18,442 career receiving yards, *3504*

National Football League player to reach a career total of 1,206 passes received, *3505*

National Football League player to receive 169 career touchdowns, *3506*

National Football League player to receive a pass in 193 consecutive games, *3501*

Rice, Jerry:—*continued*

National Football League player to receive at least one touchdown pass in 13 consecutive games, *3416*

National Football League player to receive for 1,848 yards in a single season, *3466*

National Football League player to receive for 22 touchdowns in a single season, *3410*

Professional football player to gain 215 yards receiving in a single Super Bowl game, *3428*

Richard, Maurice: National Hockey League player to reach 400 career goals, *4134*

National Hockey League player to reach 500 career goals, *4136*

National Hockey League player to score 50 goals in a single season, *4119*

National Hockey League player to score five goals in a single Stanley Cup playoff game, *4118*

Richardet, Louis: Free rifle team shooting event held in the Olympic Games, *5281*

Military revolver and military rifle team shooting events held in the Olympic Games, *5280*

Richards, Mark: Surfer to win five men's professional world titles, *5776*

Richards, Robert: Pole-vaulter to win two consecutive titles in the men's event in the Olympic Games, *4843*

Richards, Vinnie: Tennis star to turn professional, *6081*

Richardson, Bobby: Major league baseball player to bat in six runs in a single World Series game, *1644*

Richardson, Ernie: World championships in curling, *2677*

Richardson, Micheal Ray: Basketball player to lead the National Basketball Association (NBA) for three years in steals, *2213*

Richey, Nancy: French Open women's singles tennis match, *6122*

Richie, Leroy: African-American golfers to become members of the executive committee of the United States Golf Association (USGA), *3872*

Richmond, William: African-American boxer to fight in a title bout, *2507*

Richter, Ilona: Women's eight-oared shell with coxswain event held in the Olympic Games, *4949*

Richter, Ulrike: Swimmer to win two consecutive women's 100-meter backstroke world titles, *5917*

Women's 100-meter backstroke event held in the world championships, *5894*

Richthoff, Johan: Wrestler to win two super heavyweight freestyle titles in the Olympic Games, *6382*

Rickey, Branch: African-American baseball player of the 20th century to join the previously all-white mainstream baseball leagues, *1548*

Riddles, Libby: Woman sled dog racer to win the Iditarod sled dog race, *5515*

Riedel, Petra: National team to sweep the medals in the women's 100-meter backstroke, and the women's 200-meter backstroke, in the Olympic Games, *5935*

Rietschoten, Cornelis van: Sailor to win the Whitbread Round-the-World Race twice consecutively, *5241*

Riggin, Aileen: Athlete to win Olympic medals in both diving and swimming, *2798*

Women's springboard diving event held in the Olympic Games, *2797*

Riggins, John: National Football League player to score at least one touchdown in 13 consecutive games, *3384*

Washington Redskins win in professional football's Super Bowl, *3383*

Riley, Mrs. Jack: National bowling championships for women in the United States, *2486*

Rimington, Dave: College football player to be awarded the Outland Trophy twice, *3377*

Rimmer, John Thomas: Men's 4000-meter steeplechase event held in the Olympic Games, *4979*

Rinn, Hans: Sliders to win two consecutive luge (toboggan) titles at the Olympic Winter Games, *4462*

Riotto, C. C.: Gold Cup motorboat (powerboat) race, *4562*

Ripken, Cal, Jr.: Major league baseball player to be named the American League Rookie of the Year and Most Valuable Player in consecutive years, *1770*

Major league baseball player to play in 2,632 consecutive games, *1852*

Major league baseball player to play in 577 consecutive games, *1301*

Major league baseball player to top Lou Gehrig's record of 2,130 consecutive games played, *1832*

Riskiyev, Rufat: Brothers to win Olympic boxing titles on the same day, *2574*

Rison, Andre: College football player to receive for 252 yards in a major bowl game, *3427*

Ritchie, Dave: National Hockey League goal, *4065*

Ritchie, Wayne: World championships in water-ski-racing, *6320*

Ritola, Ville (Vilho): Athlete to win six medals overall in a single Olympic Games, *4652*

Rivett-Carnac, Charles: Woman to participate in an Olympic yachting event, *5207*

Robinson, Jackie (John Roosevelt):—*continued*

African-American to become a major league baseball broadcaster, *1675*

Major league baseball player to be named Rookie of the Year, and the first African-American to win the award, *1556*

Team to race the men's 4 x 100-meter relay in under 40 seconds, *5042*

Robinson, Jem: Jockey who won six Derbys at Epsom Downs, *4269*

Robinson, Mack (Matthew): Team to race the men's 4 x 100-meter relay in under 40 seconds, *5042*

Robustelli, Andrew: National Football League player to win the *Pro Football Weekly* Most Valuable Player Award, *3265*

Roche, Tony: Wimbledon Open men's doubles tennis title, *6129*

Wimbledon Open men's singles tennis title, *6130*

Rockne, Knute: Use of the forward pass in American-style football, *3135*

Röderer, Conrad Karl: Military revolver and military rifle team shooting events held in the Olympic Games, *5280*

Rodgers, Bill: New York Marathon to traverse New York City's five boroughs, *4499*

Runner to win four consecutive New York Marathons, *4504*

Runner to win the men's title in both the Boston Marathon and the New York Marathon in the same year, *4503*

Rodman, Charmayne James: Rider to win ten consecutive women's barrel racing titles, *4900*

Rodman, Dennis: Basketball player to lead the National Basketball Association (NBA) in rebounds for seven consecutive seasons, *2405*

Detroit Pistons player to be named National Basketball Association (NBA) Defensive Player of the Year, *2292*

Rodnina, Irina: Figure skater to win 10 consecutive pairs titles in the world championships, *3080*

Figure skater to win a pairs title in the Olympic Winter Games with two different partners, *3075*

Figure skater to win three consecutive medals in pairs competition at the Olympic Winter Games, *3084*

Rodriguez, Francisco: Athlete from Venezuela to win a gold medal in the Olympic Games, *4729*

Light flyweight boxing event held in the Olympic Games, *2570*

Rodriquez, Evelyn: Women's national championships in boxing, *2594*

Roehm, Otto: Lightweight freestyle wrestling event held in the Olympic Games, *6366*

Roelants, Gaston: Runner to race the men's 5000-meter steeplechase in under 8:30.0 minutes, *5075*

Roetsch, Frank-Peter: Athlete to win two biathlon gold medals at a single Olympic Winter Games, *2438*

Rogers, A. Douglas: Men's heavyweight judo event in the Olympic Games, *4535*

Rogers, Annette: Runner to win two gold medals in the women's 4 x 100-meter relay in the Olympic Games, *5041*

Team from the United States to win the women's 4 x 100-meter relay running event in the Olympic Games, *5030*

Rogov, Aleksandr: Men's Canadian singles 500-meter canoeing event held in the Olympic Games, *2616*

Rojcewicz, Sue: College women's basketball All-America team, *2110*

Rolinska, Eulalia: Women to compete in shooting events in the Olympic Games, *5311*

Rollard, Douglas: Golf match to charge fees for spectators, *3601*

Rollay, Heinz: Woman equestrian to win a team dressage medal in the Olympic Games, *2863*

Rom, Dagmar: Women's events to be included in the Alpine skiing world championships, *5392*

Roman, Pavel: Figure skaters from Czechoslovakia to win the ice dancing title in the world championships, *3061*

Romankov, Aleksandr: Fencer to win five men's foil titles in the world championships, *2939*

Romanova, Eva: Figure skaters from Czechoslovakia to win the ice dancing title in the world championships, *3061*

Romaschkova, Nina *See* Ponomaryeva, Nina Romaschkova

Romig, John: National collegiate track and field (athletics) championships sponsored by the National Collegiate Athletic Association (NCAA), *6206*

Romme, Gianni: Speed skater to skate the 10,000 meters in under 13:30 minutes, *5729*

Speed skater to skate the 5000 meters in under 6:30 minutes, *5728*

Rono, Henry: Record in the men's 5000-meter steeplechase to last for more than 10 years, *5108*

Roosevelt, Ellen: Sisters to win the women's doubles title at the United States national tennis championships, *6028*

Tennis player to win two consecutive mixed doubles titles at the United States national tennis championships, *6034*

Roosevelt, Franklin D.: Major league baseball night game, *1517*

Roosevelt, Grace: Sisters to win the women's doubles title at the United States national tennis championships, *6028*

Root, Jack: Boxer to hold the undisputed world light heavyweight title, *2525*

Roper, Jim: National Association for Stock Car Auto Racing (NASCAR) Winston Cup (Grand National) Series, *1073*

Roper, Marion: National team to sweep the top medals in the women's platform diving event in the Olympic Games, *2800*

Rosani, Danuta: Woman athlete to be disqualified from the Olympic Games because of a positive drug test, *4743*

Rosberg, Keke: Australian Grand Prix automobile race, *1132*

Rose, Erica: Women's 5-kilometer river/sea swim event held in the world championships, *5977*

Rose, I. Murray: Swimmer to win two consecutive men's 400-meter freestyle titles in the Olympic Games, *5837*

Rose, Pete: Major league baseball player to reach 4,192 career hits, *1783*

Rose, Ralph: Discus throw event in the Olympic Games to be decided by a throw-off, *2755*

Men's shot put event for both hands held in the Olympic Games, *5332*

Shot-putter to hold the officially accepted world record in the men's event, *5331*

Rosell, Ernst: Running deer (single shot) team shooting event held in the Olympic Games, *5286*

Rosen, Hans von: Equestrian to win two consecutive medals in the team jumping (Prix des Nations) event in the Olympic Games, *2851*

Team jumping (Prix des Nations) equestrian event held in the Olympic Games, *2847*

Rosenfeld, Fanny: Women's 4 x 100-meter relay running event held in the Olympic Games, *5023*

Rosewall, Ken: Australian Open men's doubles tennis title, *6136*

Davis Cup to be a full open tournament for professionals and amateurs, *6151*

French Open men's doubles tennis match, *6117*

French Open men's singles tennis match, *6118*

Tennis player to win four consecutive United States mixed doubles national championships, and nine overall, *6105*

Wimbledon Open men's doubles tennis title, *6129*

Roshin, Anatoliy: Super heavyweight event held in the world Greco-Roman wrestling championships, *6396*

Ross, Barney: Boxer to win three different world boxing titles within one year, *2550*

Ross, J. K. L.: Horse to win America's Triple Crown, *4289*

Ross, Norman: Swimmer from the United States to win the men's 1500-meter freestyle title in the Olympic Games, *5811*

Rossi, Paolo: Soccer (international football) player to be named World Footballer of the Year, *5564*

Rossner, Petra: Women's 3000-meter individual pursuit cycling event in the Olympic Games, *2719*

Rósza, Norbert: Swimmer to win two consecutive men's 100-meter breaststroke titles at the world championships, *5970*

Roth, Richard: Men's 400-meter individual medley swimming event held in the Olympic Games, *5848*

Rothenberger, Sven: Male rider to win the world cup in dressage, *2891*

Rothenburger, Christa *See* Luding-Rothenburger, Christa

Rotherham, Hugh: Bogey as a score in golf, *3598*

Rothhammer, Keena: Women's 200-meter freestyle swimming event held in the world championships, *5901*

Rothrock, Arthur: Shooters from the United States to win the small-bore rifle team title in the Olympic Games, *5300*

Rotter, Emilie: Figure skaters from Hungary to win the pairs title in the world championships, *3009*

Figure skaters to win two, and then three, consecutive pairs titles in the world championships, *3018*

Roubanis, Georgios: Fiberglass pole to be used in the men's pole vault event in the Olympic Games, *4842*

Rougier, Henri: Monte Carlo Rally, *1053*

Round, Dorothy: Tennis player to win three consecutive Wimbledon mixed doubles championships, *6096*

Rousseau, Florian: Men's Keirin cycling event held in the Olympic Games, *2731*

Men's Olympic sprint cycling event held in the Olympic Games, *2729*

Rowan, Chad (Akebono): Sumo wrestler born outside Japan to be named grand champion (yokozuna), *6415*

Rozelle, Pete: Sports commissioner to be named *Sports Illustrated* Sportsman of the Year, *1154*

Rozier, Clifford: Basketball player to have a perfect field goal percentage in a Division I National Collegiate Athletic Association (NCAA) game, *2331*

Rozier, Jean-François Pilâtre de *See* Pilâtre de Rozier, Jean-François

Rozsnyói, Sándor: Runner to hold the officially accepted world record in the men's 5000-meter steeplechase, *5062*

Rubin, Barbara Jo: Woman jockey to win a professional horse race in the United States, *4306*

Rubinstein, Louis: National ice skating organization in North America, *2957*

Ruby, Karine: Giant slalom and snowboard cross events held in the snowboarding world championships, *5523*

Women's giant slalom snow-boarding event held at the Olympic Winter Games, *5525*

Rudd, Bevil: Runner from Africa to win the men's 400-meters title in the Olympic Games, *5010*

Ruddy, Joseph: Water polo team from the United States to win the title at the Olympic Games, *6302*

Rudi, Joe: Seattle Mariners regular season baseball game played at the Seattle Kingdome, *1744*

Rudolph, Marco: Mexican-American boxer to win the lightweight title in the Olympic Games, *2589*

Rudolph, Wilma: African-American runner to win the women's 100- and 200-meter titles in the Olympic Games, *5069*

African-American woman to win the Sullivan Award, *1153*

Ruffo, Bruno: World championships in motorcycle racing, *4578*

Ruiz-Conforto, Tracie: Duet synchronized swimming event held in the Olympic Games, *5941*

Solo synchronized swimming event held in the Olympic Games, *5942*

Rüle, Frank: Rowers to win two consecutive titles in the men's four-oared shell without coxswain event in the Olympic Games, *4943*

Runyan, Joe: Sled dog racer to win both the Iditarod and the Yukon Quest sled dog races, *5514*

Rupert, Frances: National track and field (athletics) championships for women in the United States, *6207*

Ruska, Willem: Judo artist to win two gold medals in a single Olympic Games, *4540*

Russell, Bill: African-American basketball players to be named to an All–National Basketball Association (NBA) first team, *1981*

African-American National Basketball Association (NBA) head coach, *2036*

Basketball player to average 29.5 rebounds per game in an National Basketball Association (NBA) Finals series, *1982*

Basketball player to collect 189 rebounds in a National Basketball Association (NBA) Finals series, *2011*

Basketball player to collect 40 rebounds in a single National Basketball Association (NBA) Finals game, *1996*

Basketball player to grab 32 rebounds in a single half of a National Basketball Association (NBA) game, *1973*

Basketball player to have 27 rebounds in a single Division I National Collegiate Athletic Association (NCAA) Final Four championship series game, *1960*

Basketball player to win the National Basketball Association (NBA) Most Valuable Player Award five times, *2032*

Basketball player to win three consecutive National Basketball Association (NBA) Most Valuable Player Awards, *2021*

Professional basketball player to be named *Sports Illustrated* Sportsman of the Year, *2058*

Russell, Douglas: Men's 100-meter butterfly swimming event held in the Olympic Games, *5856*

Ruth, Babe (George Herman): Baseball player in the American League to hit four grand slam home runs in a single season, *1434*

Baseball player to have 100 extra-base hits in a single American League season, *1450*

Baseball player to hit a home run in major league baseball's All-Star Game, *1508*

Baseball player to lead the American League in bases on balls for three consecutive years, *1483*

Baseball player to lead the American League in bases on balls for two consecutive years, *1451*

Baseball player to lead the American League in home runs for six consecutive years, *1496*

Baseball player to lead the American League in slugging average for seven consecutive years, *1469*

Grand slam home run in major league baseball, *1256*

Home run hit by Babe Ruth as a New York Yankees player, *1442*

Major league baseball player of the 20th century to score 177 runs in a single season, *1453*

Major league baseball player to earn $80,000 per year, *1491*

Major league baseball player to have 170 walks in a single season, *1464*

Major league baseball player to hit 27 home runs in a single season, *1275*

Major league baseball player to hit 500 home runs, *1487*

Major league baseball player to hit 59 home runs in a single season, *1459*

Major league baseball player to hit 60 home runs in a single season, *1481*

Major league baseball player to hit 61 home runs in a single season, *1649*

Major league baseball player to hit 700 home runs, *1513*

Major league baseball player to hit 715 career home runs, *1738*

Major league baseball player to hit for a World Series average of .625, *1484*

Major league baseball player to reach a career total of 600 home runs, *1501*

Major league baseball player to reach a total of 2,000 bases on balls, *1514*

Major league baseball player to score four runs in a single World Series game, *1477*

Major league baseball players to be named to the Baseball Hall of Fame, *1520*

New York Yankees baseball player to be named Most Valuable Player, *1479*

New York Yankees regular season baseball game played at Yankee Stadium, *1467*

Woman to pitch against a major league baseball team, *1500*

Ruthaly, Janos *See* Root, Jack

Ruud, Birger: National team to sweep the medals in the men's 90-meter ski jump at the Olympic Winter Games, *5379*

Skier to win two consecutive men's individual ski jump titles in the Olympic Winter Games, *5385*

Ryan, Elizabeth: Tennis player to win nine Wimbledon women's doubles titles, *6088*

Tennis player to win seven Wimbledon mixed doubles championships, *6091*

Tennis player to win six French national women's doubles championships after the event became international, and four times consecutively, *6101*

Tennis player to win two consecutive Wimbledon mixed doubles championships, *6083*

Tennis players to win five consecutive Wimbledon women's doubles championships, *6068*

Ryan, Joseph: Men's pair-oared shell without coxswain rowing event held in the Olympic Games, *4931*

Ryan, Nolan: Major league baseball player to earn $1 million a year, *1753*

Major league pitcher to reach 4,000 career strikeouts, *1782*

Major league pitcher to reach 5,000 career strikeouts, *1808*

Ryan, Paddy: Boxer to be undisputed world heavyweight champion, *2515*

Boxer to be world heavyweight champion under the Queensberry rules, *2517*

Ryan, Patrick: Hammer-thrower to hold the officially accepted world record in the men's event, *3982*

Ryskal, Inna: Volleyball players to win two consecutive women's gold medals in the Olympic Games, *6283*

Ryun, Jim: Runner to complete the men's mile race in under 3:53 minutes, *5080*

Runner to race the men's 1500 meters in less than 3:35 minutes, *5083*

Rzhishchin, Semyon: Runner to race the men's 5000-meter steeplechase in under 8:39 minutes, *5064*

S

Saaristo, Juho Julius: Men's javelin event for both hands held in the Olympic Games, *4383*

Saberhagen, Brett: Kansas City Royals pitcher to win the Cy Young Award, *1780*

Sachs, Hans: Written reference to tobogganing, *4445*

Sailer, Toni (Anton): National team to sweep the medals in the men's giant slalom in the Olympic Winter Games, *5403*

Skier to sweep the men's individual Alpine events at the Olympic Winter Games, *5406*

Saint Cyr, Henri: Equestrian to be stripped of his dressage title because he was not a commissioned officer, *2860*

Equestrian to win two consecutive individual and team dressage titles in the Olympic Games, *2866*

Saito, Hitoshi: Judo artist to win two consecutive gold medals in the men's heavyweight title in the Olympic Games, *4551*

Judo artist to win two consecutive men's middleweight gold medals in the Olympic Games, *4550*

Sakata, Harold: Weightlifter from the United States to win the light heavyweight title in the Olympic Games, *6336*

Sakorafa, Sofia: Javelin-thrower to break the 240-foot barrier in the women's event, *4406*

Salah, Ahmed: World Cup Marathon, *4514*

Salamone, Melissa: Women's national championships in boxing, *2594*

Salchow, Ulrich: Figure skater to perform the salchow jump in competition, *2970*

Salchow, Ulrich:—*continued*

Figure skater to win 10 men's singles titles at the world championships, *2983*

Figure skater to win five consecutive men's singles titles at the world championships, *2967*

Figure skater to win seven consecutive men's singles titles in the world championships, *3020*

Figure skater to win the men's singles title in the Olympic Games, *2975*

National team to sweep the men's singles figure skating medals at the Olympic Winter Games, *2979*

Salikhova, Roza: Volleyball players to win two consecutive women's gold medals in the Olympic Games, *6283*

Salisbury, Sylvester: Silver trophy known to be awarded at a sporting event in North America, *1146*

Sallay, Andras: Figure skaters from Hungary to win the ice dancing title in the world championships, *3083*

Salmon, Tim: California Angels baseball player to be named Rookie of the Year, *1821*

Salnikov, Vladimir: National team to sweep the medals in the men's 400-meter freestyle event in the Olympic Games, *5934*

Swimmer to win two consecutive men's 1500-meter freestyle titles at the world championships, *5937*

Swimmer to win two consecutive men's 400-meter freestyle titles at the world championships, *5938*

Saltza, S. Christine Von *See* Von Saltza, S. Christine

Salumäe, Erika: Cyclist to win two consecutive women's titles in the 1000-meter match sprint in the Olympic Games, *2718*

Women's 1000-meter match sprint cycling event held in the Olympic Games, *2713*

Salvesen, Anton: World championships in luge (toboggan), *4453*

Salvi, Paolo: Gymnasts to win two consecutive gold medals in the men's team combined exercises in the Olympic Games, *3922*

Sampras, Pete: Grand Slam Cup, *6182*

Tennis player to win 13 men's singles grand slam titles, *6193*

Tennis player to win six Wimbledon men's singles championships in the Open era, *6190*

Sampson, Charles: African-American cowboy to hold a world rodeo title, *4899*

Sampson, Ralph: Basketball player to be named Division I National Collegiate Athletic Association (NCAA) Associated Press (AP) Player of the Year in three consecutive years, *2183*

Samuelson, Frank: Athletes to row across the Atlantic Ocean, *4923*

Samuelson, Joan Benoit: Runner to win both the women's title in the Boston Marathon and the women's marathon in the Olympic Games, *4513*

Runner to win two official women's championships in the Boston Marathon, *4511*

Women's marathon held in the Olympic Games, *4512*

Samuelson, Ralph: Water-ski jump, *6310*

Water-skiing, *6309*

Samusenko, Tatyana Petrenko: Fencers to win three gold medals in the women's team foil competition in the Olympic Games, *2938*

Fencers to win two gold medals in the women's team foil competition in the Olympic Games, *2937*

Women's team foil fencing competition held in the Olympic Games, *2935*

Sand, Todd: Figure skaters to receive six perfect scores (6.0) for artistic impression in the U.S. national pairs competition, *3111*

Sanders, Barry: College football player to score 30 points in a major bowl game, *3423*

National Collegiate Athletic Association major college football player to gain 2,628 yards in a single season, *3418*

National Football League player to gain 1,000 or more yards rushing in ten consecutive years, *3493*

National Football League player to rush for 100 or more yards in ten consecutive games, *3483*

Sandras, Gustave: Men's all-around gymnastics competition held in the Olympic Games, *3909*

Sands, Charles: Men's golf event in the Olympic Games, *3629*

Sandström, Thure: World championships in bowling, *2489*

Saneyev, Viktor: Triple-jumper to win three consecutive men's titles in the Olympic Games, *6259*

Sanford, Jack: Philadelphia Phillies baseball player to be named Rookie of the Year, *1626*

Sang Xue: Women's synchronized platform diving event held in the Olympic Games, *2829*

Santana, Manuel: Tennis player to win six consecutive French national men's doubles championships after the event became international, *6113*

Saportas, F. C.: National championships in track and field (athletics) in the United States, *6201*

Sarazen, Gene: Golfer to win all four of golf's major tournaments, *3700*

Golfer to win the U.S. Open and the Professional Golfers' Association (PGA) Championship in the same year, *3674*

Sarbu, Iosif: Athlete from Romania to win a gold medal in the Olympic Games, *4702*

Sargent, Nellie: U.S. Women's Amateur golf tournament, *3615*

Sarron, Petey: Boxer to win three different world boxing titles within one year, *2550*

Sarycheva, Tatyana: Volleyball players to win two consecutive women's gold medals in the Olympic Games, *6283*

Sasahara, Fumio: Men's half-heavyweight judo event in the Olympic Games, *4538*

"Saskatoon Lily" *See* Catherwood, Ethel

Sauldsberry, Woody: Philadelphia Warriors player to be named National Basketball Association (NBA) Rookie of the Year, *1978*

Saunders, David: Volleyball team from the United States to win the men's title in the Olympic Games, *6285*

Saunders, Nell: Boxing match between women on record in the United States, *2513*

Sautin, Dmitri: Men's synchronized platform diving event held in the Olympic Games, *2826*

Savage, Joseph: Figure skaters to win the ice dancing title at the U.S. national championships, *3021*

Saville, Eleanor Garatti: Swimmer to win two women's 4 x 100-meter freestyle relay titles in the Olympic Games, *5824*

Savinkova, Balina: Discus-thrower to break the 240-foot barrier, *2783*

Savinkova, Lyudmila: World championships in rhythmic sportive gymnastics, *3949*

Sawchuk, Terry: National Hockey League goaltender to reach 400 career wins, *4148*

National Hockey League goaltender to reach a career total of 103 shutouts, *4154*

Sawicki, Michal: World championships in target archery, *1030*

Schabel, Richard: World championships for freestyle skiing, *5451*

Schaefer, Louis J.: Horse to be named Horse of the Year twice consecutively, *4296*

Schafer, Karl: Figure skater from Austria to win the men's singles titles in the Olympic Winter Games, *3012*

Figure skater to win seven consecutive men's singles titles in the world championships, *3020*

Figure skaters to complete a grand slam, winning the European, world, and Olympic titles in the same year, *3010*

Schalkwyk, Theunis van *See* van Schalkwyk, Theunis

Scheiblich, Christine: Women's single sculls event held in the Olympic Games, *4947*

World championships in rowing to include women's competitions, *4945*

Scheidel, Wolfgang: National team to sweep the medals in the men's singles luge (toboggan) event at the Olympic Winter Games, *4459*

Scheidt, Robert: Laser-class sailing event held in the Olympic Games, *5256*

Schemansky, Norbert: Middle heavyweight weightlifting event held in the Olympic Games, *6338*

Schenk, Ard (Adrianus): Speed skater to skate the 10,000 meters in under 15 minutes, *5685*

Speed skater to skate the 1500 meters in under 2 minutes, *5684*

Speed skater to skate the 3000 meters in under 4:10 minutes, *5689*

Speed skater to skate the 3000 meters in under 4:20 minutes, *5679*

Scherbo, Vitaly: Gymnast to win six gold medals in a single Olympic Games, *3976*

Scherrer, Eduard: Bobsled event held at the Olympic Winter Games, *2467*

Schinegger, Eric: Olympic Games to institute sex tests for women athletes, *4723*

Schinegger, Erica: Olympic Games to institute sex tests for women athletes, *4723*

Schlaak, Evelin *See* Jahl, Evelin Schlaak

Schläppi, Alfred: Bobsled event held at the Olympic Winter Games, *2467*

Schläppi, Heinrich: Bobsled event held at the Olympic Winter Games, *2467*

Schlunegger, Hedy: Women's downhill skiing event held at the Olympic Winter Games, *5387*

Schmal, Adolf: Cyclist to win the men's 12-hour cycling race in the Olympic Games, *2687*

Schmidt, Birgit Fischer: Canoe racer to win five gold medals, and eight medals overall, in women's events in the Olympic Games, *2628*

Schmidt, Józef: Triple-jumper to break both the 55-foot and 17-meter barriers, *6257*

Schmidt, Walter: Hammer-thrower to break the 250-foot and 260-foot barriers, *3993*

Schmitz, Frank: World championships in trampolining to include individual tumbling and synchronized pairs competitions, *6229*

Schneider, Vreni: Skier to win 14 women's Alpine World Cup races in a single season, *5461*

Skier to win five women's giant slalom titles in skiing's world cup, *5494*

Skier to win six women's slalom titles in skiing's world cup, *5495*

Schneider, Vreni:—*continued*

Woman skier to win three gold medals, and to win five medals overall, in Alpine skiing at the Olympic Winter Games, *5492*

Schnelldorfer, Manfred: Figure skater from Germany to win the men's singles title at the Olympic Winter Games, *3063*

Schockenmöhle, Alwin: Equestrians to win two consecutive titles in team jumping in the Olympic Games, *2867*

Schoettle, Michael: 5.5-meter-class sailing event in the Olympic Games, *5218*

Schofield, Dick: New York Mets regular season baseball game played at Shea Stadium, *1671*

Schollander, Donald: Men's 4 x 100-meter freestyle relay swimming event held in the Olympic Games, *5847*

Swimmer to win four gold medals in a single Olympic Games, *5850*

Scholz, Jackson: Runner to hold the officially accepted world record in the men's 100-meter dash, *5001*

Team from the United States to win the men's 4 x 100-meter relay track event in the Olympic Games, *5011*

Scholz, Rudolph: Rugby players to win two Olympic gold medals in rugby, *4968*

Schön, Emil: Men's team sabre fencing competition held in the Olympic Games, *2911*

Schönbächler, Sonny (Andreas): Men's aerials freestyle skiing event at the Olympic Winter Games, *5488*

Schonbrunn, Gabi: Woman speed skater to skate the 3000 meters in under 4:30 minutes, *5698*

Schöne, Andrea Mitscherlich: National team to sweep the medals in the women's 3000-meter speed-skating event at the Olympic Winter Games, *5702*

Woman speed skater to skate the 5000 meters in under 8 minutes, *5699*

School, Joe: National Collegiate Athletic Association (NCAA) consensus Division I All-American college basketball team, *1890*

Schöpfer, Ida: Women's Alpine combination event held in the Alpine skiing world championships, *5391*

Schramm, Beate: Women's quadruple sculls event held in the Olympic Games, *4955*

Schreck, Gerald: Sailors from the United States to win the Dragon-class event in the Olympic Games, *5225*

Schridde, Hermann: Equestrian to win three consecutive titles in team jumping in the Olympic Games, *2869*

Schriver, Ollie: Shooters from the United States to win the small-bore rifle team title in the Olympic Games, *5300*

Schroth, Frances: National team to sweep the medals in the women's 100-meter freestyle swimming event in the Olympic Games, *5810*

Swimmers from the United States to win the women's 4 x 100-meter freestyle relay title in the Olympic Games, *5814*

Schubert, Dieter: Rowers to win two consecutive titles in the men's four-oared shell without coxswain event in the Olympic Games, *4943*

Schuhmann, Carl: Men's long horse vault gymnastics competition held in the Olympic Games, *3903*

Unlimited weight (super heavyweight) Greco-Roman wrestling event held in the Olympic Games, *6358*

Schul, Robert: Runner from the United States to win the men's 5000-meter title at the Olympic Games, *5078*

Schuler, Carolyn: Women's 4 x 100-meter medley relay swimming event held in the Olympic Games, *5840*

Schuler, Casandra: World championships in endurance riding, *2887*

Schult, Jurgen: Discus-thrower to break the 240-foot barrier in the men's event, *2784*

Schulte, Frank: Major league baseball players to be named Most Valuable Players of their leagues, *1405*

Schulz, Christel: Long-jumper to break the 20-foot and 6-meter barriers in the women's event, *4435*

Schumacher, Günther: Cyclist to win two consecutive titles in the men's 4000-meter team pursuit in the Olympic Games, *2704*

Schwarz, Hubert: Men's Nordic combined team event held in the Olympic Winter Games, *5456*

Schweitzer, Henry Hoyle: Sailboard, *5189*

Schwomeyer, Judy: Figure skaters to win five consecutive ice dancing titles with the same partner at the U.S. national championships, *3068*

Score, Herb: Cleveland Indians baseball player to be named Rookie of the Year, *1613*

Scott, Barbara Ann: Figure skater from Canada and from the Americas to win the women's singles title in the world championships, *3028*

Figure skater from Canada or from the Americas to win the women's singles title at the Olympic Winter Games, *3032*

Scott, Dave: Athlete to win the men's Hawaii Ironman triathlon two, three, four, five, and six times, *6237*

Scott, Dennis: Basketball player to make 11 3-point field goals in a single National Basketball Association (NBA) game, *2373*

Basketball player to make 267 3-point field goals in a single National Basketball Association (NBA) season, *2366*

Basketball player to score 28 3-point goals in a single set of National Basketball Association (NBA) playoffs, *2346*

Scott, Jake: Miami Dolphins win in professional football's Super Bowl, *3331*

Scott, Lady Margaret: British Ladies' Open Amateur golf championship, *3604*

Scott, Mike: Houston Astros pitcher to win the Cy Young Award, *1787*

Scott, Norman: Figure skater to win the men's singles title in the U.S. national championships, *2987*

Figure skaters to win the pairs title in the U.S. national championships, *2990*

Sears, Fred: Tennis tournament on record in the United States, *6007*

Sears, Richard: Men's singles competition at the United States national tennis championships, *6013*

Tennis player to win seven consecutive men's singles titles at the United States national championships, *6020*

Tennis player to win six consecutive men's doubles titles at the United States national championships, *6021*

Seaver, Tom: New York Mets baseball player to be named Rookie of the Year, *1693*

New York Mets pitcher to win the Cy Young Award, *1706*

Sebring, Jimmy: World Series home run, *1357*

Sedykh, Yuriy: Hammer-thrower to break the 280-foot barrier, *3996*

Seguso, Robert: Tennis players to win the men's doubles title in the Olympic Games after tennis competition resumed in 1988, *6181*

Seidler, Helga: Women's 4 x 400-meter relay track event held in the Olympic Games, *5095*

Seignious, Hope: Organization for women golf professionals in the United States, *3712*

Seisenbacher, Peter: Judo artist to win two consecutive men's middleweight gold medals in the Olympic Games, *4550*

Seizinger, Katja: Skier to win five women's super giant slalom titles in skiing's world cup, *5496*

Skier to win two consecutive Olympic titles in the women's downhill, and the first to win both the downhill and Alpine combination events in the same Olympic Winter Games, *5503*

Sekaric, Jasna: Women's air pistol individual shooting event held in the Olympic Games, *5322*

Selby, Vera: Women's world open championships in snooker, *2460*

Seletti, Jean-Maria: Person to swim the English Channel, *5783*

Selnikov, Vladimir: Swimmer to race the men's 1500-meter freestyle in under 15 minutes, *5933*

Seltzer, Leo: Roller derby, *4905*

Roller derby to be televised, *4908*

Selvy, Frank: Basketball player to score 100 points in a single Division I National Collegiate Athletic Association (NCAA) game, *1949*

Basketball player to shoot 355 free throws during a single Division I National Collegiate Athletic Association (NCAA) season, *1945*

Seminario, Gladys de: Women to compete in shooting events in the Olympic Games, *5311*

Senna, Ayrton: Automobile racer to have eight wins in a single season on the Formula One Grand Prix circuit, *1136*

Automobile racer to win five Belgian Grand Prix races, *1140*

Serbina, Svilana: Women's synchronized platform diving event held at the world championships, *2824*

Seredina, Antonina: Women's 500-meter pairs kayaking event held in the Olympic Games, *2610*

Shablis, Helen: World championships in bowling to include women, *2498*

Shack, Eddie: National Hockey League player to be named Most Valuable Player of the NHL All-Star Game, *4143*

Shain, Eva: Woman boxing judge to officiate at a world championship bout, *2576*

Shakrai, Sergei: Figure skaters to perform a quadruple twist lift in competition, *3078*

Figure skaters to perform simultaneous triple jumps in competition, *3082*

Shalamanov, Naum: Weightlifter to win three gold medals in the Olympic Games, *6352*

Shapiro, Fred: Perfect game in the Little League World Series, *1578*

Sharman, Bill: Basketball player to lead the National Basketball Association (NBA) in free throw percentage for five consecutive years, *1964*

Basketball player to lead the National Basketball Association (NBA) in free throw percentage for seven years, *2004*

Sharp, Graham: Figure skater from Great Britain to win the men's singles title at the world championships, *3024*

Shavers, Earnie: Woman boxing judge to officiate at a world championship bout, *2576*

Shaw, Tim: Swimmer to hold world titles in the men's 200-, 400-, and 1500-meter freestyle at the same time, *5913*

Shaw, Wilbur: Automobile racer to win the Indianapolis 500 three times, and to win it twice in a row, *1068*

Automobile racer to win the Indianapolis 500 with an average speed of more than 110 miles per hour, *1066*

Shea, Frank J.: National collegiate track and field (athletics) championships sponsored by the National Collegiate Athletic Association (NCAA), *6206*

Shea, John: Olympic speed skating events to be held as races, rather than in pairs, *5648*

Speed skater from the United States to win the men's 1500-meter title at the Olympic Winter Games, *5649*

Sheard, Alison: Women's Professional Golfers' Association (WPGA) European Tour, *3822*

Sheckard, Jimmy: Baseball player to lead the National League in bases on balls for two consecutive years, *1408*

Sheehan, Patty: Three-Tour Challenge, *3874*

Sheetz, Shelley: College women's basketball Associated Press (AP) All-American first team, *2348*

Sheldon, George: Men's platform diving event held in the Olympic Games, *2791*

Sheldon, Richard: National team to sweep the top spots in the men's shot put in the Olympic Games, *5330*

Shepard, Alan: Golf shot taken on the moon, *3795*

Sheppard, Melvin: Men's 4 x 400-meter relay track event held in the Olympic Games, *4997*

Runner to win two consecutive gold medals in the men's 4 x 400-meter relay in the Olympic Games, *5007*

Sherer, John F.: Development of modern polo, *4853*

Sheridan, Martin: Discus throw event in the Olympic Games to be decided by a throw-off, *2755*

Discus-thrower from the United States to win the men's Greek-style title in the Olympic Games, *2759*

Discus-thrower to win two, and then three, consecutive men's titles in the Olympic Games, *2757*

National team to sweep the top spots in the men's discus throw in the Olympic Games, *2758*

Shermer, Michael: Race Across America (RAAM) bicycle marathon, *2705*

Shero, Fred: National Hockey League coach to be named Coach of the Year, *4164*

Shevtsova, Lyudmyla: Women's 800-meter race held in the Olympic Games after a 32-year ban, *5073*

Shiley, Jean: High-jumpers to hold the officially accepted world record in the women's event, and the first from the United States to win the women's event in the Olympic Games, *4023*

Shilkov, Boris: Speed skater to skate the 5000 meters in under 8 minutes, *5665*

Shimizu, Hiroyasu: Speed skater to skate the 500 meters in under 35 seconds, *5734*

Shishkova, Yevgeniya: Champions Series in figure skating, *3112*

Shishova, Lyudmila: Women's team foil fencing competition held in the Olympic Games, *2935*

Shoemaker, Bill: Jockey to win 8,834 horse races, *4319*

Shore, Eddie: All-Star National Hockey League Team selected by the Professional Hockey Writers' Association, *4102*

Shouaa, Ghada: Athlete from Syria to win a gold medal in the Olympic Games, *4796*

Shoulders, Jim: Cowboy to be named All-Around Cowboy four consecutive times, and five overall, *4894*

Shriver, Eunice Kennedy: Special Olympics, *2752*

Shriver, Pam: Tennis player to win the French Open women's doubles title five consecutive times, *6176*

Tennis players to win the women's doubles title in the Olympic Games after tennis competition resumed in 1988, *6179*

Shrubb, Alfred: International Cross-Country Championships, *4984*

Shugarova, Galina: Gymnast to win the all-around title two, and then three, times in the world championships of rhythmic sportive gymnastics, *3957*

Shula, Don: Professional football coach to take his team to six Super Bowl, *3362*

Professional football coach to win 328 games, *3468*

Shuttleworth, Pamela: Women to be caddies at the U.S. Open golf tournament, *3831*

Siegl, Siegrun: National team to sweep the medals in the women's pentathlon in the Olympic Games, *4831*

Sievers, Roy: Baltimore Orioles baseball player to be named Rookie of the Year, *1571*

Sifford, Charles: African-American golfer to be classified as an "approved player" on the Professional Golfers' Association (PGA) Tour, *3755*

African-American golfer to play in a Professional Golfers' Association (PGA) Tour tournament in the South, *3763*

African-American golfer to win a featured event on the Professional Golfers' Association (PGA) Tour, *3790*

African-American golfer to win a Senior Professional Golfers' Association (PGA) Tour event, *3834*

African-American golfer to win a title in a significant predominantly white tournament, *3750*

Sijbesma, Thea: World championships in duathlon, *2835*

Sikes, Dan: Senior Professional Golfers' Association (PGA) Tour, *3830*

Sikma, Jack: Basketball player to make 35 consecutive field goals in the National Basketball Association (NBA) playoffs, *2248*

Silivas, Daniela: Gymnast to win two women's balance beam titles in the world championships, *3975*

Silk, Dave: World Cup series of competitions for speed skating, *5703*

Silva, Jackie: Beach volleyball event held in the Olympic Games, *6286*

Silvester, Jay: Discus-thrower to break the 220-foot barrier, *2776*

Discus-thrower to break the 60-meter barrier, *2771*

Simanainen, Matti: World championships in Greco-Roman wrestling held on a regular basis, *6388*

Simion, Mircea: Boxer to win two, and then three, consecutive heavyweight titles, and three boxing titles in a single class, in the Olympic Games, *2575*

Simionov, Toma: Canoer to win three titles in the men's Canadian pairs 1000-meter event in the Olympic Games, *2622*

Simmen, Gian: Men's halfpipe snowboarding event held at the Olympic Winter Games, *5526*

Simms, Phil: New York Giants win in professional football's Super Bowl, *3414*

Simms, Veronica: Women's national championships in boxing, *2594*

Simon, Hugo: World Cup in show jumping, *2882*

Simon, Johann Friedrich: Gymnastics school to teach the modern sport, *3900*

Simon, "Monkey": African-American jockey known by name, *4265*

Simonsen, Inge: London Marathon, *4507*

Simpson, George: Golfer born in the United States to win the U.S. Open, *3650*

Simpson O. J. (Orenthal James): African-American college football player to receive the Maxwell Award, *3286*

National Football League player to rush for 200 or more yards in six different games during his career, *3360*

Singh, Vijay: Golfer to win more than $2.5 million in official prize money in a single season, *3889*

Sipatova, Yelena: Runner to hold the officially accepted world record in the women's 10,000-meter race, *5123*

Sirch, Cornelia: Swimmer to win two consecutive women's 200-meter backstroke world titles, *5947*

Sites, Sharon: Woman to sail across the Pacific alone, *5226*

Sjödelius, Sven-Olov: Canoe racer to win six gold medals, and eight medals overall, in the Olympic Games, *2609*

Skarlatos, Konstantinos: Dueling pistol shooting events held in the Olympic Games, *5282*

Skatteboe, Gudbrand: Athletes from Norway to win official gold medals at the Olympic Games, *4637*

Skiles, Scott: Basketball player to have 30 assists in a single National Basketball Association (NBA) game, *2299*

Skoblikova, Lydia: Athlete to win four gold medals at a single Olympic Winter Games, and six Olympic gold medals overall, *4715*

National team to sweep the medals in the women's 500-meter speed-skating event at the Olympic Winter Games, *5675*

Speed skater to win four gold medals in speed skating in a single Olympic Winter Games, *5678*

Speed skater to win two consecutive women's 1500-meter and 3000-meter titles at the Olympic Winter Games, *5677*

Women's 1500-meter speed skating event held at the Olympic Winter Games, *5670*

Women's 3000-meter speed skating event held at the Olympic Winter Games, *5668*

Skolimowska, Kamila: Women's hammer-throw event held in the Olympic Games, *3998*

Skutnabb, Julius: Men's 10,000-meter speed skating event held in the Olympic Winter Games, *5641*

Slack, Charlie: Basketball player to have an average of 25.6 rebounds per game during a single Division I National Collegiate Athletic Association (NCAA) season, *1954*

Sladky, James: Figure skaters to win five consecutive ice dancing titles with the same partner at the U.S. national championships, *3068*

Slaney, Mary Decker: International Amateur Athletic Federation (IAAF) Grand Prix, *6223*

Runner from the United States to hold the world record in the women's 5000- and 10,000-meter races, *5124*

Runner to win the women's 1500-meter race in the World Championships in Athletics, *5134*

Smith, Sid: Boxer to be undisputed world fly-weight champion, *2536*

Smith, Spencer: Athlete to win two consecutive men's titles in the world triathlon championships, *6244*

Smith, Stan: U.S. Open men's doubles tennis title, *6124*

Smith, Susan: College women's basketball player to score nine consecutive 3-point goals in a single Division I National Collegiate Athletic Association (NCAA) game, *2273*

Smith, Sydney: All-England Championships in badminton to include individual competitions, *1167*

Smith, Timmy: Professional football player to rush for 204 yards in a single Super Bowl game, *3420*

Smith, Tommie: Runner to complete the men's 200-meter race in under 20 seconds, *5088*

Smithson, Forrest: Hurdler to hold the officially accepted world record in the men's 110-meter hurdles, and to set a 110-meter hurdle record that would stand for more than 10 years, *4327*

Smoleyeva, Nina: Volleyball players to win two consecutive women's gold medals in the Olympic Games, *6283*

Smyers, Karen: World cup in the triathlon, *6241*

Snead, Sam: Golf tournament to be shown on television, *3716*

Golfer to win more than 80 tournaments on the Professional Golfers' Association (PGA) Tour, and to win the same PGA event eight times, *3780*

Golfer to win the Masters tournament three times, *3742*

Legends of Golf tournament, *3817*

National golf team that won the Canada Cup twice, *3748*

National golf team to win five consecutive Canada Cup tournaments, *3776*

Senior Professional Golfers' Association (PGA) Tour, *3830*

Snell, Peter: Runner from New Zealand to win the men's 800-meter title in the Olympic Games, *5071*

Runner to complete the men's 800-meter race in under 1:45 minutes, *5074*

Snook, James: Rapid-fire pistol and free pistol team events held in the Olympic Games, *5299*

Snow, Neil: College football player to score five rushing touchdowns in a major bowl game, *3130*

Sobek, Joe: Racquetball game, *4873*

Sockalexis, Louis: Native American major league baseball player, *1317*

Sohn Kee Chung: Olympic Games attended by athletes of independent Korea, *4690*

Record in the men's marathon to stand for more than 10 years, *4480*

Runner officially representing South Korea to hold the world record in the men's marathon, and to win the Boston Marathon, *4482*

Solberg, Magnar: Athlete to win two consecutive gold medals in the biathlon in the Olympic Winter Games, *2433*

Solodukhin, Nikolai: Men's half-lightweight judo event held in the Olympic Games, *4548*

Soltani, Hocine: Athlete from Algeria to win a gold medal in the Olympic Games, *4799*

Sólyomnári, János: World cup in weightlifting, *6348*

Son, Kitei: Olympic Games attended by athletes of independent Korea, *4690*

Record in the men's marathon to stand for more than 10 years, *4480*

Son Tae-whan: World championships in taekwondo to include additional weight classes for men, *4543*

Song Hur: World championships in taekwondo to include additional weight classes for men, *4543*

Song Jae-kun: Men's 5000-meter relay short track speed skating event held at the Olympic Winter Games, *5716*

Sorenstam, Annika: Woman golfer to have a season scoring average of under 70, *3891*

Sorgers, Jana: Women's quadruple sculls event held in the Olympic Games, *4955*

Soria, Sixto: Brothers to win Olympic boxing titles on the same day, *2574*

Sörsdal, Sverre: Light heavyweight boxing event held in the Olympic Games, *2538*

Sosa, Sammy: Major league baseball player to hit 70 home runs in a single season, *1853*

Major league baseball player to hit at least 60 home runs in two consecutive seasons, *1857*

Season in which both major league baseball Most Valuable Player Awards went to Hispanic players, *1849*

Sotomayor Sanabria, Javier: High-jumper to reach, and then break, the 8-foot barrier, *4032*

Souchak, Mike: Golfer to score 257 for 72 holes in a Professional Golfers' Association (PGA) recognized event, *3745*

Golfer to score under 260 for 72 holes in a Professional Golfers' Association (PGA)–recognized event, *3713*

Souza, Ken: World championships in duathlon, *2835*

Spahn, Warren: Milwaukee Braves pitcher to win the Cy Young Award, *1625*

Spalding, Albert: Baseball teams from the United States to tour England and Ireland, *1214*

Major sporting goods business, *5740*

National League championship, *1232*

Pitcher to pitch a shutout in baseball's National League, *1223*

Professional baseball pitcher to win 200 games, *1216*

United States baseball team to tour the world, and to visit Australia, *1294*

Spångberg, Arvid: National team to sweep the top medals in men's platform diving in the Olympic Games, *2793*

Spanger, Harry: Lightweight boxing event held in the Olympic Games, *2530*

Welterweight boxing event held in the Olympic Games, *2532*

Spanks, Carole: Softball player to win three consecutive Erv Lind Awards, *5606*

Speaker, Tris: Baseball player to lead the American League in doubles in four consecutive years, *1463*

Specht, Bobby: Season for the Ice Capades, *3026*

Speedie, Mac: Cleveland Browns regular season football game played at Municipal Stadium, *3205*

Speirs, Annie: Women's 4 x 100-meter freestyle relay swimming event in the Olympic Games, *5808*

Spellman, Frank: Weightlifter from the United States to win the middleweight title in the Olympic Games, *6335*

Spence, B.: Australian national tennis championships, *6045*

Spence, Pat: Tennis player to win two consecutive Wimbledon mixed doubles championships, *6083*

Spencer, Galen: Team archery event held in the Olympic Games, *1028*

Spencer, John: Masters Tournament in snooker, *2459*

Spezio, Ed: San Diego Padres regular season baseball game played at San Diego Stadium, *1709*

Spiller, Bill: African-American golfers to play in a Professional Golfers' Association (PGA)–recognized event, *3720*

Lifting of the "no blacks allowed" clause from the constitution of the Professional Golfers' Association (PGA), *3759*

Spinks, Leon: Boxer to win the world heavyweight championship three times, *2566*

Brothers to win Olympic boxing titles on the same day, *2574*

Spinks, Michael: Brothers to win Olympic boxing titles on the same day, *2574*

Spirin, Leonid: Men's 20,000-meter walk event held in the Olympic Games, *6292*

Spitz, Mark: Athlete to win seven gold medals in a single Olympic Games, *4740*

Men's 100-meter butterfly swimming event held in the Olympic Games, *5856*

National team to sweep the medals in the men's 200-meter butterfly swimming event in the Olympic Games, *5864*

Swimmer to win two consecutive gold medals in the men's 4 x 100-meter freestyle relay in the Olympic Games, *5865*

Spotts, Ralph: Shooters from the United States to win the trap (clay pigeon) team shooting event in the Olympic Games, *5294*

Spradley, Benjamin: Middleweight boxing event held in the Olympic Games, *2531*

Spurgin, Pat: Women's air rifle individual shooting event in the Olympic Games, *5318*

St. George, Floris: Australian women's doubles national tennis championships, *6062*

St. John, Miss (first name unknown): All-England Championships in badminton, *1166*

Stadelhofen, Marcel Meyer de: Free rifle team shooting event held in the Olympic Games, *5281*

Stagg, Alonzo: All-America college football team named by Walter Camp, *3121*

Stagg, Amos Alonso: Basketball Hall of Fame, *1975*

Stäheli, Konrad: Free rifle team shooting event held in the Olympic Games, *5281*

Military revolver and military rifle team shooting events held in the Olympic Games, *5280*

Military rifle individual shooting event held in the Olympic Games, *5279*

Staksrud, Michael: Speed skater to skate the 3000 meters in under 5 minutes, *5652*

Stanchev, Nikola: Athlete from Bulgaria to win a gold medal in the Olympic Games, *4707*

Stanczyk, Stanley: Weightlifter from the United States to win the light heavyweight title in the Olympic Games, *6336*

Stanfield, Andy: Runner to hold an officially accepted world record in the men's 200-meter race run on a curved track, *5053*

Stanley, Frederick Arthur (Baron Stanley of Preston): Ice hockey team to win the Stanley Cup, *4045*

Staples, Curtis: Basketball player to shoot 413 field goals during a single Division I National Collegiate Athletic Association (NCAA) season, *2251*

Stargell, Willie: New York Mets regular season baseball game played at Shea Stadium, *1671*

Starr, Bart: Professional football player to be named Most Valuable Player in the Super Bowl twice in a row, *3295*

Professional football team to win two consecutive Super Bowl games, *3290*

Super Bowl, *3282*

Staubach, Roger: Dallas Cowboys win in professional football's Super Bowl, *3324*

Stearns, Sally: Woman to serve as coxswain on a men's varsity rowing team in the United States, *4938*

Stecher, Renate Meissner: Runner to race the women's 100 meters in under 11.0 seconds, *5097*

Steedman, Charles: International swimming competition on record, *5779*

Steen, James: Water polo team from the United States to win the title at the Olympic Games, *6302*

Steer, Irene: Women's 4 x 100-meter freestyle relay swimming event in the Olympic Games, *5808*

Stefan, Maria Mihoreanu: Women's 500-meter fours kayaking event held in the Olympic Games, *2623*

Steffers, Kent: Beach volleyball event held in the Olympic Games, *6286*

Steinbach, Christian: World championships in hang gliding, *3533*

Steiner, Roswitha: Skier to win five women's slalom world cup titles, *5449*

Steiner, Walter: World ski flying championships, *5419*

Steinkraus, William: Equestrian from the United States to win the individual jumping title in the Olympic Games, *2873*

Steinseifer, Carrie: Swimmers to win gold medals in the same event at the same Olympic Games, *5939*

Stengl, Manfred: Two-seater luge (toboggan) event at the Olympic Winter Games, *4456*

Stenmark, Ingemar: Skier to win 13 men's Alpine world cup races, and to win 10 in one category, in a single season, *5425*

Skier to win eight men's slalom world cup titles, *5439*

Skier to win seven men's giant slalom world cup titles, *5441*

Stenshjemmet, Kav A.: Speed skater to skate the 5000 meters in under 7 minutes, *5693*

Stephens, Helen: Runner to win two gold medals in the women's 4 x 100-meter relay in the Olympic Games, *5041*

Stephens, Sandy: African-American quarterback to appear in the Rose Bowl college football game, *3260*

Sterkel, Jill: Woman swimmer to win Olympic medals 12 years apart, *5956*

Stern, Bill: Baseball game to be televised, *1537*

College football game to be televised, *3187*

Sterry, Charlotte: Women's doubles championships at Wimbledon, *6054*

Stevens, Curtis: Two-man bobsled competition held in the Olympic Games, *2471*

Stevens, J. Hubert: Two-man bobsled competition held in the Olympic Games, *2471*

Stewart, J. C.: Championship Meeting in golf, *3572*

Stewart, Jackie: Automobile racer to be named *Sports Illustrated* Sportsman of the Year, *1118*

Stewart, Kordell: Cleveland Browns regular season game played in the Cleveland Browns Stadium, *3510*

Stewart, Philip Batelle: Batting and fielding cage in baseball, *1280*

Stewart, Raymond: Runner to reach three consecutive finals in the men's 100-meter dash at the Olympic Games, *5157*

Stewart, Robert: Introduction of *chole* to the British Isles, *2630*

Stichweh, Rollie: Instant replay, *3269*

Stillwagon, Jim: College football player to win the Lombardi Award, *3299*

Stinchcomb, Gaylord: National collegiate track and field (athletics) championships sponsored by the National Collegiate Athletic Association (NCAA), *6206*

Stives, Karen: Woman to win a medal in the three-day event team equestrian competition in the Olympic Games, and to lead her team to a gold medal, *2884*

Women to win medals in the three-day individual equestrian event in the Olympic Games, *2885*

Stockhoff, Arthur: Men's four-oared shell without coxswain rowing event held in the Olympic Games, *4930*

Stockton, John: Basketball player to have 115 assists in the National Basketball Association (NBA) playoffs, *2263*

Basketball player to have 1,164 assists in a single National Basketball Association (NBA) season, *2300*

Basketball player to have an average of 14.5 assists per game in a single National Basketball Association (NBA) season, *2289*

Basketball player to have more than 2,700 steals in his National Basketball Association (NBA) career, *2413*

Basketball player to lead the National Basketball Association (NBA) in assists for nine consecutive years, *2365*

Basketball player to make more than 13,000 assists in his National Basketball Association (NBA) career, *2414*

Stofflet, Ty: Softball player to win five Most Valuable Player Awards in the Amateur Softball Association Major Fast Pitch National Tournament, *5614*

Stokes, Dudley: Caribbean Cup, *2476*

Stokes, Maurice: African-American to be elected to an All–National Basketball Association (NBA) team, *1959*

Rochester Royals player to be named National Basketball Association (NBA) Rookie of the Year, *1963*

Stolle, Fred: Australian Open men's doubles tennis title, *6136*

French Open men's doubles tennis match, *6117*

Tennis player to win six consecutive French national men's doubles championships after the event became international, *6113*

Wimbledon Open men's doubles tennis title, *6129*

Stone, Nikki: Skier from the United States to win the women's aerials freestyle skiing event in the Olympic Winter Games, *5501*

Stone, Toni: Woman to play as a fully recognized regular on a men's major league baseball team, *1596*

Stotz, Carl: Little League baseball league, *1533*

Stoudamire, Damon: Toronto Raptors player to be named National Basketball Association (NBA) Rookie of the Year, *2371*

Stovgarrd, Steen: World championships in badminton, *1171*

Straka, Martin: Florida Panthers regular season hockey game played at Miami Arena, *4209*

Strandli, Sverre: Hammer-thrower to break the 200-foot barrier, *3988*

Strange, Curtis: Golfer to earn more than $1 million in a single season in official prize money, *3858*

Golfer to win the Tour Championship in a playoff, *3860*

Strath, David: Golfer to win the British Open after a default in a playoff, *3590*

Straub, Anja: Women's épée competition held in the world championships of fencing, *2941*

Street, Picabo: Skier from the United States to win the women's super giant slalom at the Olympic Winter Games, *5498*

Strickland, Earl: World championships for nine-ball pool, *2464*

Strief, George: Major league baseball player to get four triples, and five extra-base hits, in a single game, *1283*

Strode, Woody (Woodrow Wilson): African-American professional football players to play in the National Football League in the modern period, and the first to play with the Los Angeles Rams, *3198*

Strug, Kerri: Gymnasts from the United States to win the women's team title in the Olympic Games, *3978*

Stuart family: Iron skates in England, *2948*

Stubrick, Christa: Runners to finish first and second in both the women's 100- and 200-meter races in the Olympic Games, *5065*

Stückelberger, Christine: Individual dressage equestrian competition in the Olympic Games in which women riders swept the top medals, *2890*

Stukelj, Leon: Athlete from Yugoslavia to win a gold medal in the Olympic Games, *4661*

Gymnast to win two consecutive men's rings titles in the world championships, *3925*

Styles, William: Small-bore rifle moving and disappearing target individual shooting events held in the Olympic Games, *5289*

Suggs, Louise: Ladies Professional Golf Association (LPGA) Championship, *3746*

President of the Ladies Professional Golf Association (LPGA), *3722*

Sukniewicz, Teresa: Hurdler to hold the officially accepted world record in the women's 100-meter hurdles, *4342*

Suleimanov, Naim: Weightlifter to win three gold medals in the Olympic Games, *6352*

Suleymanoglü, Naim: Weightlifter to win three gold medals in the Olympic Games, *6352*

Sullivan, John L.: Boxer to be undisputed world heavyweight champion, *2515*

Boxer to be world heavyweight champion under the Queensberry rules, *2517*

Sumi, Peter: Gymnast to win two consecutive men's all-around titles in the world championships, *3923*

Summitt, Pat: College women's basketball coach to receive the Naismith Coach of the Year Award four times, *2408*

College women's basketball Naismith Coach of the Year Award, *2252*

Sun Caiyun: Pole-vaulter to hold the officially accepted world record in the women's event, *4850*

World cup in weightlifting to include women, *6351*

Sundstrom, Patrick: National Hockey League player to score eight points in a single Stanley Cup playoffs game, *4199*

Supcik, Bedrich: Athlete from Czechoslovakia to win a gold medal in the Olympic Games, *4660*

Surkont, Max: Major league baseball pitcher to strike out eight consecutive opposing batters, *1599*

Susanti, Susi: Athlete from Indonesia to win a gold medal in the Olympic Games, *4777*

Badminton events held in the Olympic Games as medal sports, *1174*

Sutherland, Murray: Boxer to hold the world super middleweight title, *2580*

Sutter, Brian: Detroit Red Wings regular season hockey game played at Joe Louis Arena, *4177*

Sutton, Henry: 8-meter-class sailing event in the Olympic Games, *5206*

Svan, Bunde: Skier to win two consecutive titles in the men's 4 x 10-kilometer relay Nordic (cross-country) at the Olympic Winter Games, *5455*

Svanberg, Olavi: Ski orienteering world championships, *4809*

Swahn, Alfred: Running deer (single shot) individual shooting event held in the Olympic Games, *5285*

Running deer (single shot) team shooting event held in the Olympic Games, *5286*

Swahn, Oscar: Running deer (single shot) individual shooting event held in the Olympic Games, *5285*

Running deer (single shot) team shooting event held in the Olympic Games, *5286*

Sweeney, Charlie: Major league pitcher to strike out 19 batters in a single 9-inning game, *1278*

Sweeney, Dennis J.: Bowling league for women in the United States, *2484*

National bowling organization for women in the United States, *2487*

Sweetser, Jesse: Golfer born in the United States to win the British Amateur Championship, *3681*

Swenson, Rick: Sled dog racer to win the Iditarod sled dog race five times, and the first to win across three decades, *5518*

Sled dog racer to win the Iditarod sled dog race four times, and the first to win it twice in a row, *5511*

Swingley, Doug: Sled dog racer to complete the Iditarod sled dog race in less than 10 days, *5520*

Switzer, Katherine: Woman to run in the Boston Marathon wearing an official number, *4491*

Syers, Edgar: Figure skater to win the women's singles title at the Olympic Games, *2977*

Syers, Madge (Florence): Figure skater to win the women's singles title at the Olympic Games, *2977*

Figure skater to win the women's singles title in the world championships, *2968*

Figure skater to win two consecutive women's singles titles in the world championships, *2971*

Woman figure skater to compete in a world championship, and to win a world figure skating medal, *2966*

Syrovatka, Vladimir: Canoer to win two men's Canadian pairs 1000-meter titles in the Olympic Games, *2602*

Men's Canadian pairs 1000-meter canoeing event held in the Olympic Games, *2596*

Szalai, György: World cup in weightlifting, *6348*

Szewinska, Irena Kirszenstein: Runner to race the women's 400 meters in under 50 seconds, *5100*

Szollas, Laszlo: Figure skaters from Hungary to win the pairs title in the world championships, *3009*

Figure skaters to win two, and then three, consecutive pairs titles in the world championships, *3018*

Szondy, István: Men's modern pentathlon team event held in the Olympic Games, *4823*

Sztantics, György: Men's 3000-meter walk event held in the Olympic Games, *6288*

T

Ta, Jacqueline: Women's amateur boxing match sponsored by USA Boxing, *2590*

Tabarly, Éric: Sailor to win the Single-Handed Transatlantic Race (STAR) twice, *5234*

Taber, Norman: Men's 3000-meter team running event held in the Olympic Games, *5004*

Tachell, Tom: Australian national tennis championships, *6045*

Tafelmeier, Klaus: Javelin-throw world record set using the new javelin in the men's event, *4409*

Taft, William Howard: United States President to throw out the first ball in a major league baseball opening day game, *1399*

Taggart, Michelle: Snowboarding world championships, *5521*

Taipale, Armas: Men's discus throw event for both hands held in the Olympic Games, *2761*

Tajima, Naoto: Triple-jumper to reach a distance of 16 meters in the men's event, *6254*

Takács, Károly: Shooter to win two consecutive men's rapid-fire pistol titles in the Olympic Games, *5307*

Takemoto, Masao: Gymnast to win two consecutive men's floor exercise titles in the world championships, *3942*

Talts, Jaan: Heavyweight weightlifting event held in the Olympic Games, *6346*

Taormina, Sheila: Women's 4 x 200-meter freestyle relay swimming event held in the Olympic Games, *5973*

Tarkenton, Fran (Francis): National Football League player to be named Most Valuable Player by the Professional Football Writers Association, *3340*

Taub, Sam: Boxing match to be broadcast on television in the United States, *2552*

Tauber, Ulrike: Women's 400-meter individual medley event in the Olympic Games in which all the medalists had times under five minutes, *5925*

Taylor, Branda: Women's four-oared shell without coxswain event held in the Olympic Games, *4957*

Taylor, Fred: Men's doubles competition at the United States national tennis championships, *6012*

Taylor, Henry: Swimmer to win two consecutive men's 1500-meter freestyle titles in the Olympic Games, *5803*

Taylor, Howard: United States intercollegiate tennis championships, *6015*

Taylor, John: Athlete of Black African descent to win an Olympic gold medal, *4639*
Men's 4 x 400-meter relay track event held in the Olympic Games, *4997*

Taylor, John Henry: Association of professional golfers, *3631*
British Open golf tournament held in England, *3605*

Taylor, Tony: Houston Astros regular season baseball game played at the Houston Astrodome, *1680*

Taylor, Vern: Figure skater to perform a triple axel in competition, *3079*

Taylor, William: Patent for dimple-patterned golf balls, *3642*

Taylor, William H.: Sportswriter to win a Pulitzer Prize, *5748*

Taylor-Smith, Shelley: Women's 25-kilometer river/sea swim event held in the world championships, *5961*

Tcherkasova, Marina: Figure skaters to perform a quadruple twist lift in competition, *3078*
Figure skaters to perform simultaneous triple jumps in competition, *3082*

Teague, Charles: College baseball player to win the Outstanding Player Award, *1573*

Tegart, Judy *See* Dalton, Judy Tegart

Temesvari, Andrea: Tennis player to win the French Open women's doubles title five consecutive times, *6176*

Temme, Edward: Swimmer to swim the English Channel in both directions, *5827*

Temple, Deborah: College women's basketball player to have 40 rebounds in a single Division I National Collegiate Athletic Association (NCAA) game, *2188*

Templeton, Gary: Baseball player to lead the National League in triples in three consecutive years, *1750*

Temu, Naftali: Athlete from Kenya to win a gold medal in the Olympic Games, *4732*
Runner from Africa to win the men's 10,000-meter title at the Olympic Games, *5085*

Ten Eyck, Ned: Rower from the United States to win the Diamond Sculls at the Henley Regatta, *4924*

Terentyev, Fedor: Skiers from the Soviet Union to win the men's 4 x 10-kilometer relay Nordic (cross-country) title at the Olympic Winter Games, *5405*

Teuscher, Cristina: Women's 4 x 200-meter freestyle relay swimming event held in the Olympic Games, *5973*

Tewksbury, John Walter: Men's 200-meter race held in the Olympic Games, *4981*
Men's 400-meter hurdles event held in the Olympic Games, *4324*

Thaden, Louise: Woman to win the Bendix Trophy airplane race, *1012*
Women's Air Derby, *1007*

Thaler, Herbert: World championships in luge (toboggan), *4453*

Thall, Thelma: Heydusek Prize, *5991*

Thams, Jacob Tullin: Men's individual ski jump event held at the Olympic Winter Games, *5368*

Thayer, Frederick: Catcher's mask used in a National League game, *1237*

Thayer, George: College football All-America team named by Grantland Rice, *3153*

Theodosius, Roman Emperor: Ban on the Olympic Games, *4601*
Olympic Games, *4599*

Thible, Elisabeth: Woman to fly in a hot-air balloon, *1177*

Thiedemann, Fritz: Equestrians to win two consecutive titles in team jumping in the Olympic Games, *2867*
Woman equestrian to win a team dressage medal in the Olympic Games, *2863*

Thigpen, Bobby: Major league baseball player of the 20th century to pitch 57 saves in a single season, *1811*

Thode, Earl: Cowboy to be named All-Around Cowboy, *4885*

Thom, Linda: Women's sport pistol individual shooting event held in the Olympic Games, *5316*

Thomas, Debi: African-American athlete to win a medal in the Olympic Winter Games, *4763*

African-American figure skater to win the women's singles title at the U.S. national championships, *3089*

African-American figure skater to win the women's singles title in the world championships, *3090*

Thomas, Derrick: African-American college football player to win the Butkus Award, *3417*

National Football League player to make seven sacks in a single game, *3442*

Thomas, Duane: Dallas Cowboys regular season football game played at Texas Stadium, *3319*

Thomas, George: World team Thomas Cup badminton championships for men, *1169*

Thomas, Herb: Automobile racer to win more than 10 races in a single season in the National Association for Stock Car Auto Racing (NASCAR) Winston Cup series, *1090*

Thomas, John: High-jumper to set or equal four world records in the men's event in a single year, *4027*

Thomas, Lucille: Woman baseball team owner, *1499*

Thomas, Vera: Pope Trophy, *5992*

Thompson, David: Basketball player to score 13 field goals in a single quarter of a National Basketball Association (NBA) game, *2141*

Thompson, Frank: African-American professional baseball team, *1279*

Thompson, Hank (Henry): African-American baseball player to play for the New York Giants, *1570*

African-American baseball player to play for the St. Louis Browns, *1559*

Two African-American major league baseball players to play for the same club in the same game, *1561*

Thompson, Jenny: Women's 4 x 200-meter freestyle relay swimming event held in the Olympic Games, *5973*

Thompson, John: National Collegiate Athletic Association (NCAA) consensus Division I All-American college basketball team, *1890*

Thompson, Marie: National golf organization founded by African-Americans, *3683*

Thompson, Tina: Women's National Basketball Association (WNBA) All-WNBA First Team, *2387*

Thompson, Will: National archery tournament in the United States, *1024*

Thompson, William: Team archery event held in the Olympic Games, *1028*

Thompson, William "Bendigo": Boxing title fight under the London Prize Ring Rules, *2511*

Thomson, Earl: Hurdler to hold the officially accepted world record in the men's 110-meter hurdles, and to set a 110-meter hurdle record that would stand for more than 10 years, *4327*

Thomson, Earl J.: National collegiate track and field (athletics) championships sponsored by the National Collegiate Athletic Association (NCAA), *6206*

Thomson, Peter: Presidents Cup Match won by the international team, *3893*

Thomson (later Larcombe), Ethel: All-England Championships in badminton to include individual competitions, *1167*

Thon, Øyvin: World cup in orienteering, *4811*

Thorne, Ross: World cup in squash, *5765*

Thornycroft, Thomas: Motorboat-racing event held in the Olympic Games, *4565*

Thorpe, Jim (James): Athlete to win both the men's decathlon and pentathlon in the Olympic Games, and the first Native American to win an Olympic gold medal, *2738*

Jim Thorpe Award, *3401*

Native-American athlete to win a gold medal at the Olympic Games, *4645*

Pro Football Hall of Fame, *3268*

Use of the double-wing formation in football, *3138*

Thorvaldsen, Thor: Dragon-class sailing event held in the Olympic Games, *5216*

Thost, Nicola: Women's halfpipe snowboarding event held at the Olympic Winter Games, *5527*

Thrower, Willie: African-American quarterback to play regularly on a professional football team, *3287*

Thubron, Émile: Motorboat-racing event held in the Olympic Games, *4565*

Thugwane, Josia: Black African athlete from South Africa to win a gold medal in the Olympic Games, *4802*

Thunberg, A. Clas: Athlete to win five individual gold medals, and seven medals overall, in the Olympic Winter Games, *4665*

Men's 1500-meter speed skating event held at the Olympic Winter Games, *5642*

Men's 5000-meter speed skating event held at the Olympic Winter Games, *5640*

Men's four races combined speed skating title offered at the Olympic Winter Games, *5643*

Olympic speed skating events to be held as races, rather than in pairs, *5648*

Speed skater to skate the 1000 meters in under 1:30 minutes, *5646*

Speed skater to win two consecutive men's 1500-meter speed skating titles at the Olympic Winter Games, *5645*

Thurmond, Nate: Basketball player to average 23.3 rebounds in a Division I National Collegiate Athletic Association (NCAA) championship series, *2020*

Basketball player to have 18 rebounds in a single quarter of a National Basketball Association (NBA) game, *2035*

Thys, Philippe: Cyclist to win the Tour de France three times, *2694*

Thysen, N.: World championships in gymnastics, *3910*

Tiampo, Mary Jo: World championships for freestyle skiing, *5451*

Tickey, Bertha: Softball player to be named the top pitcher, *5603*

Tikhonov, Aleksandr: Men's 4 x 7.5-kilometer relay biathlon team event held at the Olympic Winter Games, *2432*

Tikhonova, Tamara: National team to sweep the medals in the women's individual 20-kilometer Nordic (cross-country) event at the Olympic Winter Games, *5459*

Tilden, Bill: Tennis player to win 98 straight men's singles matches, *6075*

Tennis player to win four consecutive United States mixed doubles national championships, and nine overall, *6105*

United States men's singles national tennis championship matches played at the new West Side Tennis Club stadium, *6069*

Tillman, Henry: Heavyweight boxing event with a limited weight held in the Olympic Games, *2581*

Timmermann, Ulf: Shot-putter to break the 23-meter barrier, *5350*

Timmons, Stephen: Volleyball team from the United States to win the men's title in the Olympic Games, *6285*

Tiraboschi, Enrique: Swimmer to swim across the English Channel from France to England, *5816*

Titova, Lyudmila: Spring world championships in speed skating, *5682*

Woman speed skater to skate the 1000 meters in under 1:30 minutes, *5683*

Titus, Constance: National team to sweep the medals in the men's single sculls rowing event in the Olympic Games, *4932*

Tjun, Tjun: World championships in badminton, *1171*

Todorova, Antoaneta: Javelin-thrower to break the 230-foot barrier in the women's event, *4405*

Tolan, Eddie (Thomas): African-American runner to hold the record in the men's 100-meter dash, *5024*

African-American runner to win the men's 100- and 200-meter titles in the Olympic Games, *5032*

Tomba, Alberto: Skier to win two consecutive individual titles in an Alpine event in the Olympic Winter Games, *5479*

Tootel, Frederick: Hammer-thrower born in the United States to win the men's event in the Olympic Games, *3983*

Torrance, Jack: Shot-putter to break the 17-meter barrier, *5335*

Torres, José: Boxer to win three gold medals, and two consecutive light middleweight titles, in the Olympic Games, *2560*

Torriani, Richard: Athlete to win medals in the Olympic Winter Games 20 years apart, *4691*

Torvill, Jayne: Figure skaters from the Soviet Union to win the ice dancing title in the world championships, *3066*

Figure skaters to win unanimous top scores for artistic impression, and the first from Great Britain to win the ice dancing title, at the Olympic Winter Games, *3087*

Tourischeva, Lyudmila: Gymnast to win two consecutive women's floor exercise titles in the world championships, *3958*

World cup in gymnastics, *3959*

Tournant, Arnaud: Men's Olympic sprint cycling event held in the Olympic Games, *2729*

Towns, Forrest: Hurdler to race the men's 110-meter hurdles in under 14 seconds, *4335*

Townsend, Bertha: Sisters to win the women's doubles title at the United States national tennis championships, *6028*

Tennis player to win two consecutive women's singles titles at the United States national championships, *6025*

United States women's doubles national tennis championships, *6027*

Townsend, Ron: African-American golfer to become a member of the Augusta National Golf Club, *3862*

Train, Andrew: Canoe marathon world championships, *2624*

Train, Stephen: Canoe marathon world championships, *2624*

Trammell, Alan: Chicago White Sox regular season baseball game played at New Comiskey Park, *1816*

Traun, Fredrich "Fritz": Men's doubles tennis event held in the Olympic Games, *6035*

Travers, Jerome: Golfer to win four U.S. Amateur titles, *3654*

Travis, Walter J.: Golfer from the United States to win the British Amateur Championship, *3638*

Golfer to win a major tournament with a rubber-cored golf ball, *3633*

Golfer to win three men's U.S. Amateur titles, *3636*

Rubber-cored golf ball, and the first golf ball manufactured in the United States, *3623*

Treiber, Birgit: National team to sweep the medals in the women's 100-meter backstroke, and the women's 200-meter backstroke, in the Olympic Games, *5935*

Trevino, Lee: Golfer to be named Rookie of the Year and Player of the Year on the Senior Professional Golfers' Association (PGA) Tour, *3864*

Golfer to win more than $1 million in a single season on the Senior Professional Golfers' Association (PGA) Tour, *3865*

Golfer to win the U.S., Canadian, and British Opens in the same year, *3793*

Trice, Bob: African-American baseball player to play for the Philadelphia Athletics, *1601*

Tsai Wen-Yee: Athletes from China and Taiwan to share the medal platform in the Olympic Games, *4757*

Tsuruta, Yoshiyuki: Olympic men's 200-meter breaststroke event in which the medalists all had times under three minutes, *5821*

Swimmer to win two consecutive men's 200-meter breaststroke titles, *5826*

Tsybulenko, Viktor: Javelin-thrower to break the 280-foot barrier and to hold the world record in the men's event, *4397*

Tucker, Michael: Atlanta Braves regular season baseball game played at Turner Field, *1844*

Tucker, Nion: Bobsledders from the United States to win the five-man bobsled title at the Olympic Winter Games, *2468*

Tuckey, Agnes Daniell: Mixed doubles championships at Wimbledon, *6053*

Tuero, Linda: Tennis player to win the United States interscholastic girls' singles national championship, *6123*

Tuganoo, Etsuko: World championships in badminton, *1171*

Tulu, Derartu: Black African woman to win an Olympic medal, *4780*

Runner from Africa to win the women's 10,000-meter title, and the first Black African woman to win a medal, at the Olympic Games, *5159*

Tunnel, Emlen: African-American professional football player to be named to the Pro Football Hall of Fame, *3278*

African-American professional football player to join the New York Giants in the modern period, *3209*

Tunney, Gene (James Joseph): Boxer named Fighter of the Year by *Ring* magazine, *2548*

Turchyna, Zinaida: Handball players to win two consecutive gold medals in women's team handball in the Olympic Games, *4008*

Turco, John: College baseball player to score 11 runs in a College World Series, *1590*

Turley, Bob: New York Yankees pitcher to win the Cy Young Award, *1630*

Turnbull, Don: Tennis player to win 10 consecutive Australian national men's doubles championships, *6102*

Turner, Cathy: Speed skater to win two consecutive women's 500-meter short track titles at the Olympic Winter Games, *5724*

Women's 500-meter short track speed skating event held at the Olympic Winter Games, *5717*

Turner, Roger: Figure skater to win six, and then seven, consecutive men's singles titles in the U.S. national championships, *3015*

Turner, Roscoe: Pilot to win both the Thompson Trophy and Bendix Trophy airplane races, *1010*

Pilot to win the Thompson Trophy airplane race twice, and then three times, *1013*

Turnesa, Jim: JCPenney Classic golf tournament, *3761*

Turnesa, Joe: Golfer to win the Professional Golfers' Association (PGA) Championship four times in a row, and five times overall, *3686*

Tymoshkina, Natalya Sherstyuk: Handball players to win two consecutive gold medals in women's team handball in the Olympic Games, *4008*

Tyng, Louis: Catcher's mask used in a National League game, *1237*

Tyranski, Ed: Softball player to be batting champion of the Amateur Softball Association Major Fast Pitch league, *5590*

Tysoe, Alfred: Runner from Europe to win the men's 800-meter title in the Olympic Games, *4980*

Tyson, Mike: Boxer to hold the undisputed world heavyweight title after 1980, *2586*

Tyus, Wyomia: Runner to win two consecutive women's 200-meter titles in the Olympic Games, *5086*

U

Ubartas, Romas: Athlete from newly independent Lithuania to win a gold medal in the Olympic Games, *4778*

Uber, Betty: World team Uber Cup badminton championships for women, *1170*

Udella, Franco: Boxer to be world junior flyweight (light-flyweight) champion, *2572*

Uelses, John: Pole-vaulter to clear 16 feet, *4844*

Ueshiba, Morihei: School for aikido, *4530*

Ulanov, Alexsei: Figure skater to win 10 consecutive pairs titles in the world championships, *3080*

Figure skater to win a pairs title in the Olympic Winter Games with two different partners, *3075*

Figure skater to win three consecutive medals in pairs competition at the Olympic Winter Games, *3084*

Uller: Literary reference to skating, *2945*

Ullrich, Frank: Men's 10-kilometer biathlon competition at the Olympic Winter Games, *2435*

Ulvang, Vegard: Men's 10-kilometer Nordic (cross-country) skiing event held at the Olympic Winter Games, *5472*

National team to sweep the medals in the men's 30-kilometer Nordic (cross-country) skiing event at the Olympic Winter Games, *5471*

Unitas, Johnny: Johnny Unitas Golden Arm Award, *3407*

National Football League player to be named Most Valuable Player in the Pro Bowl for two consecutive years, *3258*

National Football League player to lead the league in passing touchdowns for four consecutive years, *3253*

Unseld, Wes: Baltimore Bullets player to be named National Basketball Association (NBA) Most Valuable Player of the Year, *2060*

Professional basketball player to win the Pro Basketball Writers Association J. Walter Kennedy Citizenship Award, *2112*

Uphoff, Nicole: Individual dressage equestrian competition in the Olympic Games in which women riders swept the top medals, *2890*

Woman rider, and the first horse, to win two consecutive gold medals in the individual dressage competition, and in team dressage, in the Olympic Games, *2893*

Uriza, Rubén: Athletes from Mexico to win gold medals in the Olympic Games, *4697*

Urmanov, Aleksei: Champions Series in figure skating, *3112*

Figure skater from Russia to win the men's singles title at the Olympic Winter Games, *3107*

Urrutia, Maria Isabel: Women's weightlifting events held in the Olympic Games, *6353*

Usova, Maia: Figure skaters to win two consecutive ice dancing titles at the Olympic Winter Games, *3114*

Utz, H. S.: Australian mixed doubles national tennis championships, *6061*

Utz, Lorna: Australian mixed doubles national tennis championships, *6061*

Australian women's doubles national tennis championships, *6062*

V

Vails, Maxwell: Intercollegiate golf tournament for African-American players, *3708*

Välbe, Yelena: Skier to win four medals in the same Nordic skiing event in the Olympic Winter Games, *5478*

Women's 30-kilometer cross-country event held in the world championships of Nordic skiing, *5463*

Valdes, Alberto: Athletes from Mexico to win gold medals in the Olympic Games, *4697*

Valentine, Ellis: Montreal Expos regular season baseball game played at Olympic Stadium, *1746*

Valenzuela, Fernando: Major league baseball rookie to win the Cy Young Award, *1759*

Van Brocklin, Norm: National Football League player to pass for 554 yards in a single game, *3230*

Van Cleef, George: Water polo team from the United States to win the title at the Olympic Games, *6302*

Van de Velde, Jean: Golfer to come from 10 strokes behind to win a Professional Golfers' Association (PGA) recognized tournament, *3897*

Van den Berg, Stephan *See* Berg, Stephan Van den

Van Dyken, Amy: Woman athlete from the United States to win four gold medals at a single Olympic Games, *4793*

Van Ert, Sandra: Giant slalom and snowboard cross events held in the snowboarding world championships, *5523*

van Gennip, Yvonne *See* Gennip, Yvonne van

van Innis, Hubert *See* Innis, Hubert van

Van Praag, Lionel: World championships in dirt-track (speedway) motorcycle racing, *4576*

van Ranst *See* Ranst, (first name unknown) van

Van Rensselaer, Alexander: Men's doubles competition at the United States national tennis championships, *6012*

van Rietschoten, Cornelis *See* Rietschoten, Cornelis van

van Schalkwyk, Theunis: Light middleweight boxing event held in the Olympic Games, *2558*

van Ziip, Adolph van der Voort *See* Ziip, Adolph van der Voort van

Van Zo Post, Albertson: Men's team foil fencing competition held in the Olympic Games, *2906*

Vána, Bohumil: Iran Cup, *5990*

Vance, Dazzy: Baseball pitcher to lead the National League in strikeouts for seven consecutive years, *1482*

Vander Meer, Johnny: Major league baseball player to pitch two successive no-hitters, *1530*

Vanderstock, Geoffrey: Hurdler to race the men's 400-meter hurdles in under 49 seconds, *4341*

Varayev, Adlan: Wrestler of Black African descent to win a gold medal in wrestling in the Olympic Games, *6409*

Vardon, Harry: Amateur golfer to win the U.S. Open, *3653*

Golfer to win both the U.S. Open and British Open, *3628*

Golfer to win British Open titles in three decades, *3651*

Golfer to win six British Open golf championships, *3656*

Golfer to win the Vardon Trophy, *3704*

Vare, Glenna Collett: Golfer to win four, and then five and six, U.S. Women's Amateur Championships, *3688*

Golfer to win six U.S. Women's Amateur championships, *3701*

Golfer to win the Vare Trophy for the lowest average score on the Ladies Professional Golf Association (LPGA) Tour, *3736*

Varley, William: Men's double sculls rowing event held in the Olympic Games, *4929*

Varona, Donna *See* De Varona, Donna

Vasa, Gustaf *See* Gustaf I, King of Sweden (Gustaf Vasa)

Vasquez Cam, Edwin: Athlete from Peru to win a gold medal in the Olympic Games, *4693*

Velde, Jean Van de *See* Van de Velde, Jean

Veldkamp, Bart: Speed skater to skate the 3000 meters in under 3:50 minutes, *5733*

Vendeville, Charles de: Men's underwater swimming race held in the Olympic Games, *5791*

Veney, Keith: Basketball player to shoot 15 3-point field goals in a single Division I National Collegiate Athletic Association (NCAA) game, *2377*

Ventura, Frantisek: Equestrian to win the individual jumping event in the Olympic Games without a single fault, *2856*

Venturi, Ken: Golfer on the Professional Golfers' Association (PGA) Tour to be named Rookie of the Year, *3751*

U.S. Junior Amateur golf championship, *3719*

Verbrugge, Cyril: Fencer to win both the men's masters épée and masters sabre competitions in the Olympic Games, *2907*

Verner, William Frank: Runner from the United States to win the men's 1500-meter race in the Olympic Games, *4989*

Vero, Emiko: World championships in badminton, *1171*

Versalles, Xoilo: Minnesota Twins baseball player to be named Most Valuable Player, *1679*

Vezina, Georges: National Hockey League shutout, *4068*

Vicenzo, Roberto *See* de Vicenzo, Roberto

Vidmar, Peter: Gymnasts from the United States to win the men's combined exercises title in the Olympic Games, *3972*

Vigneron, Thierry: Pole-vaulter to clear 19 feet, *4847*

Vilagos, Penny: Pairs of twins to take the top two spots in the synchronized swimming duet competition in the Olympic Games, *5968*

Vilagos, Vicky: Pairs of twins to take the top two spots in the synchronized swimming duet competition in the Olympic Games, *5968*

Vilas, Guillermo: Tennis player to win 145 men's singles matches in a single season, *6163*

Vinci, Charles: Weightlifter to win two consecutive bantamweight titles in the Olympic Games, *6341*

Vinent Charon, Héctor: Boxer to win two consecutive light welterweight titles in the Olympic Games, *2591*

Vinogradov, Aleksandr: Men's Canadian pairs 500-meter canoeing event held in the Olympic Games, *2618*

Vinson, Maribel *See* Owen, Maribel Vinson

Viren, Lasse: Runner to win two consecutive men's 5000- and 10,000-meter titles at the Olympic Games, *5107*

Virgil, Ozzie (Osvaldo): Dominican major league baseball player, *1620*

Major league baseball player widely recognized as black to play for the Detroit Tigers, *1634*

Visser, Leo: Speed skater to skate the 3000 meters in under 4 minutes, *5706*

Vlasto, Didi: Tennis players to win a French national mixed doubles championship after the event became international, *6078*

Tennis players to win the French national women's doubles championship after the event became international, *6080*

Vogel, Renate: Swimmer to hold both the women's 100- and 200-meter breaststroke world titles at the same time, *5889*

Vogel, Renate:—*continued*

Women's 100-meter breaststroke event held in the world championships, *5895*

Women's 200-meter breaststroke event held in the world championships, *5899*

Voigt, Emil: National team to sweep the top honors in the men's horizontal bar, long horse vault, side (pommel) horse, and rings gymnastics competitions in the Olympic Games, *3913*

Volkov, Sergei: Figure skater from the Soviet Union to win the men's singles title at the world championships, *3071*

von Barnekow, Marten *See* Barnekow, Marten von

Von Bremen, Wilhelmina: Team from the United States to win the women's 4 x 100-meter relay running event in the Olympic Games, *5030*

Von Elm, George: Golfer to win a major tournament using steel-shafted golf clubs, *3694*

von Langen-Parow, Carl Friedrich Freiherr *See* Langen-Parow, Carl Friedrich Freiherr von

von Lotzbeck, Eugen Freiherr *See* Lotzbeck, Eugen Freiherr von

von nagel, Ida *See* Nagel, Ida von

von Rosen, Hans *See* Rosen, Hans von

Von Saltza, S. Christine: Olympic women's 400-meter freestyle event in which the medalists all had times under five minutes, *5839*

Women's 4 x 100-meter medley relay swimming event held in the Olympic Games, *5840*

Vorobyov, Arkady: Weightlifter to win two consecutive middle heavyweight titles in the Olympic Games, *6342*

Voss, Carl: National Hockey League player to be named Rookie of the Year, *4108*

Vrzanova, Alena: Figure skater from Czechoslovakia to win the women's singles title in the world championships, *3037*

Vuckovich, Pete: Milwaukee Brewers American League pennant, *1765*

Vukovich, Bill: Automobile racer to win the Indianapolis 500 with an average speed of more than 130 miles per hour, *1093*

W

Waddell, Rube: Baseball pitcher to lead the American League in strikeouts for six consecutive years, *1373*

Wade, Mark: Basketball player to have 406 assists during a single Division I National Collegiate Athletic Association (NCAA) season, *2247*

Wade, Virginia: Player to be named Women's Tennis Association (WTA) Player of the Year, *6162*

U.S. Open women's singles tennis title, *6128*

Wadkins, Lanny: Sudden-death playoff in one of golf's major tournaments, *3814*

Wadlow, Marie: Softball Hall of Fame opened, *5588*

Wagner, Barbara: Figure skaters from Canada to win the pairs title at the Olympic Winter Games, *3055*

Wagner, Honus: Baseball player to lead the National League in batting average for four consecutive years, *1385*

Baseball player to lead the National League in doubles in four consecutive years, *1386*

Baseball player to lead the National League in runs batted in for four consecutive years, *1387*

Baseball player to lead the National League in slugging average for three consecutive years, *1388*

Baseball player to lead the National League in total bases for four consecutive years, *1389*

Major league baseball players to be named to the Baseball Hall of Fame, *1520*

Wagner, Leon: San Francisco Giants regular season baseball game played at Candlestick Park (later 3Com Park), *1643*

Wahjudi, Johan: World championships in badminton, *1171*

Waite, Charles: Baseball glove on record, *1215*

Waitz, Grete Andersen: Runner to race the women's marathon in under 2:30 hours, *4505*

Wakelam, Teddy: Cricket game to be broadcast on television, *2658*

Walasiewicz, Stanislawa: Runner to hold the officially accepted world record in the women's 100-meter dash, *5033*

Runner to hold the officially accepted world record in the women's 200 meters, *5035*

Walcott, Jersey Joe: Heavyweight boxing match to be broadcast nationally on television, *2556*

Waldorf, Lynn: College football coach to be named Coach of the Year, *3168*

Waldrop, Rob: Bronko Nagurski Award, *3456*

Walker, Chet: All–National Basketball Association (NBA) Rookie Team, *2019*

Walker, Doak: Doak Walker National Running Back Award, *3436*

Walker, George Herbert: Walker Cup golf match, *3673*

Walker, John: Runner to complete the men's mile race in under 3:50 minutes, *5103*

Walker, Larry: Colorado Rockies baseball player to be named Most Valuable Player, *1838*

Major league baseball player from Canada to be named Most Valuable Player in either league, *1840*

Walker, Moses Fleetwood: African-American major league baseball player, *1274*

Walker, Reginald: Athlete from Africa, and from South Africa, to win a gold medal in the Olympic Games, *4638*

Runner from Africa to win the men's 100-meter race in the Olympic Games, *4995*

Walker, Steffi Martin: Slider to win two consecutive women's singles luge (toboggan) titles at the Olympic Winter Games, *4463*

Walker, Weldy: African-American major league baseball player, *1274*

Wallace, Felix: African-American All-Star Team in professional baseball, *1402*

Wallace, Nunc: Boxer of African descent to win a national boxing title, *2519*

Wallach, Tim: Florida Marlins regular season baseball game played at Joe Robbie Stadium, *1823*

Waller, Frank: National team to sweep the top three medals in the men's 400-meter running event in the Olympic Games, *4985*

Walliser, Maria: Super giant slalom events held in the Alpine skiing world championships, *5452*

Walsh, Stella *See* Walasiewicz, Stanislawa

Walton, Bill: Basketball player to be named Division I National Collegiate Athletic Association (NCAA) United States Basketball Writers Association Player of the Year in three consecutive years, *2101*

Basketball player to have 8 blocked shots in a National Basketball Association (NBA) Finals game, *2134*

Basketball player to have 91 defensive rebounds in a National Basketball Association (NBA) Finals series, *2128*

Basketball player to have a field goal average of 95.5 percent in a single Division I National Collegiate Athletic Association (NCAA) Final Four championship series game, *2092*

Portland Trail Blazers player to be named National Basketball Association (NBA) Most Valuable Player of the Year, *2140*

Waltrip, Darrell: Automobile racer to win more than $1 million in a single season in the National Association for Stock Car Auto Racing (NASCAR) Winston Cup series, *1129*

Walz, Allen "Skip": Professional football game to be televised, *3188*

Wambsganss, Bill: Unassisted triple play in the World Series, *1440*

Wang Junxia: Runner to race the women's 10,000 meters in under 30 minutes, *5169*

Women's 5000-meter race held in the Olympic Games, *5181*

Wang Liping: Women's 20-kilometer walk event held in the Olympic Games, *6297*

Wangila, Robert: Black African-born boxer to win a boxing title in the Olympic Games, *2585*

Ward, Aaron: Mighty Ducks of Anaheim regular season hockey game played at The Pond of Anaheim, *4208*

Ward, Jem: Boxer to be barred by a boxing authority for throwing a fight, *2509*

Ward, John Montgomery: Major league baseball players' union, *1284*

Major league pitcher to hit two home runs in a single game, *1270*

Ward, Rodger: Automobile racer to win the Indianapolis 500 with an average speed of more than 140 miles per hour, *1104*

Ware, Andre: National Collegiate Athletic Association major college football player to gain 510 yards in a single half of a game, *3424*

Wäre, Eemil: Wrestler to win two consecutive lightweight Greco-Roman titles in the Olympic Games, *6376*

Warmerdam, Dutch (Cornelius): Pole-vaulter to clear 15 feet, *4841*

Warner, Karl: Team to race the men's 4 x 400-meter relay in under 3:10 minutes, *5031*

Warner, Kurt: St. Louis Rams Super Bowl win, *3513*

Warner, Pop: Use of the double-wing formation in football, *3138*

Washington, Claudell: Major league baseball club to hit a total of 10,000 home runs, *1801*

Washington, Kenny: African-American professional football players to play in the National Football League in the modern period, and the first to play with the Los Angeles Rams, *3198*

Washington, Ora: African-American women's basketball team, *1891*

Wasmeier, Markus: Men's super giant slalom to be included in the world cup for Alpine skiing, *5448*

Wassberg, Thomas: Skier to win two consecutive titles in the men's 4 x 10-kilometer relay Nordic (cross-country) at the Olympic Winter Games, *5455*

Waterbury, Larry: Polo team from the United States to win the Westchester Cup, *4866*

Waterbury, Monty: Polo team from the United States to win the Westchester Cup, *4866*

Watson, Lillian: Women's singles tennis championships at Wimbledon, *6017*

Watson, Maud: Tennis player to win two consecutive women's singles championships at Wimbledon, *6018*

Women's singles tennis championships at Wimbledon, *6017*

Watson, Pokey (Lillian): Women's 200-meter backstroke event held in the Olympic Games, *5861*

Watson, Ray: National collegiate track and field (athletics) championships sponsored by the National Collegiate Athletic Association (NCAA), *6206*

Watson, Tom: British Open golf championship in which the top ten golfers were all from the United States, *3811*

Golfer to earn more than $500,000 in official prize money in a single season, *3825*

Golfer to win the British Open in 267 for 72 holes, *3875*

Professional Golfers' Association (PGA) Tour event with a purse of $2 million, *3853*

Tour Championship, *3855*

Watt, Lionel: Radio broadcast of a cricket game, *2655*

Watzl, Rudolf: Lightweight Greco-Roman wrestling event held in the Olympic Games, *6370*

Weatherby, James: *Racing Calendar, 4258*

Stud book for horse racing, *4263*

Weatherspoon, Teresa: Basketball team from the United States to win the women's title in a non-boycotted Olympic Games, *2275*

Women's National Basketball Association (WNBA) Defensive Player of the Year, *2389*

Weaver, Jeff: College baseball player to pitch 21 strikeouts in a single game, *1845*

Webb, Karrie: Golfer to win more than $1 million in her rookie year on the Ladies Professional Golf Association (LPGA) Tour, *3884*

Woman golfer to have a season scoring average of under 70, *3891*

Webb, Matthew: Person to swim the English Channel, *5783*

Webster, Erika Puetz: United States intercollegiate women's singles and women's doubles national championships, *6111*

Weckman, Verner: Athlete from Finland to win an official gold medal in the Olympic Games, *4641*

Light heavyweight Greco-Roman wrestling event held in the Olympic Games, *6373*

Wedderburn, David: Golf book, *3543*

Weder, Gustav: Bobsledders to win two consecutive two-man bobsled titles at the Olympic Winter Games, *2477*

Wedman, Scott: Basketball player to make all his field goal attempts in a National Basketball Association (NBA) Finals game, *2225*

Weekes, James: Sailors from the United States to win the 6-meter-class event in the Olympic Games, *5217*

Wegner, Gudrun: Women's 400-meter individual medley swimming event held in the world championships, *5906*

Wehling, Ulrich: Skier to win three consecutive men's individual Nordic combined titles in the Olympic Winter Games, *5443*

Wehrli, Ursula: World figure skating championships for roller skating, *4909*

Wei, Yang *See* Yang Wei

Wei Qingguang: Men's doubles table tennis event held in the Olympic Games, *5994*

Weigang, Birte: Women's 100-meter butterfly event in the Olympic Games in which all the medalists had times under one minute, *5953*

Weinbrecht, Donna: Women's moguls freestyle skiing event held at the Olympic Winter Games, *5474*

Weingärtner, Hermann: Men's horizontal bar gymnastics competitions held in the Olympic Games, *3902*

Weir, Ed: College football All-America team named by Grantland Rice, *3153*

Weiss, Walt: Colorado Rockies regular season baseball game played at Coors Field, *1831*

Weissmuller, Johnny: National team to sweep the medals in the men's 100-meter freestyle in the Olympic Games, *5809*

Swimmer to race the men's 100-meter freestyle in under one minute, *5815*

Swimmer to win Olympic gold medals 8 years apart, and to win Olympic medals 12 years apart, *5813*

Swimmer to win two consecutive gold medals in the men's 4 x 200-meter freestyle relay swimming event in the Olympic Games, *5822*

Wekman, Verner: Middleweight Greco-Roman wrestling event held in the Olympic Games, *6371*

Weld, Phil: Sailor from the United States to win the Single-Handed Transatlantic Race (STAR), and the first to make the crossing in under 20 hours, *5238*

Weld, Theresa *See* Blanchard, Theresa Weld

Wellborn, Nancy: Softball player to win three consecutive Bertha Tickey Awards, *5608*

Wells, Willie: Batting helmet in professional baseball, *1544*

Wenzel, Hanni: Athlete from Liechtenstein to win an Olympic gold medal, *4750*

Werth, Isabell: Freestyle dressage equestrian event held in the Olympic Games, *2894*

West, Jerry: Basketball player to be named Most Valuable Player of the National Basketball Association (NBA) Finals, *2062*

Basketball player to make 840 free throws in a single National Basketball Association (NBA) season, *2038*

Basketball player to make 86 free throws in one set of National Basketball Association (NBA) playoffs, *2029*

Basketball player to score an average of 46.5 points in one set of National Basketball Association (NBA) playoffs, *2031*

Westergren, Carl: Wrestler to win gold medals in three different divisions in the Olympic Games, *6378*

Westermann, Liesel: Discus-thrower to break the 60-meter and 200-foot barriers in the women's event, *2775*

Weston, Edward Payson: Walker to be considered a professional, *6287*

Westwood, Jean: Figure skaters to win the ice dancing title in the world championships, and the first to win it two, three, and four times, *3046*

Whang Soo-yong: World championships in taekwondo to include additional weight classes for men, *4543*

Whigham, H. J.: Golfer to win the U.S. Amateur Championship twice in a row, *3617*

Whitbread, Fatima: Javelin-thrower to break the 250-foot barrier in the women's event, *4408*

White, Albert: Diver to win both the men's springboard and platform diving titles in the same Olympic Games, *2799*

White, Bill: African-American to become president of a major baseball league, *1803*

White, Byron "Whizzer": College football player to rush for 1,000 yards or more in a single season, *3179*

White, Cheryl: African-American woman to win a Thoroughbred horse race in the United States, *4309*

White, Edgar: 5.5-meter-class sailing event in the Olympic Games, *5218*

White, J. Andrew: Boxing match to have a $1 million gate, and the first heavyweight bout to be broadcast on radio, *2541*

White, Jack: Golf match to charge fees for spectators, *3601*

Golfer to win the British Open golf championship in under 300 for 72 holes, *3639*

White, Jerry: College baseball player to score five runs in a single game, *1638*

White, Jim: Hit in an all-professional baseball game, *1208*

White, Natalie: College women's basketball player to have 191 steals, and an average of 6.4 steals per game, in a single Division I National Collegiate Athletic Association (NCAA) season, *2351*

White, Nera: College softball player to win the Erv Lind Award, *5599*

White, Reggie: National Football League defensive player to reach 192.5 career sacks, *3490*

White, Reginald: Tornado-class sailing event held in the Olympic Games, *5236*

White, Rod: Archers from the United States to win a gold medal in the team event in the Olympic Games, *1040*

White, Stanford: Golf clubhouse in the United States, *3600*

White, Sumner: 5.5-meter-class sailing event in the Olympic Games, *5218*

Whitfield, Malvin G.: African-American athlete to win the Sullivan Award, *1150*

Whitfield, Simon: Men's modern triathlon event held in the Olympic Games, *6248*

Whitmore, Walter James: Open championship in croquet, *2665*

Whitney, Harry Payne: Polo team from the United States to win the Westchester Cup, *4866*

Whitney, Jim: Baseball player to score 6 runs in a 9-inning National League game, *1271*

Pitcher to lead the National League in wins and in losses in the same season, *1254*

Whiton, Herman: Sailors from the United States to win the 6-meter-class event in the Olympic Games, *5217*

Whitten, Erin: Woman goaltender to be credited with a win in a professional hockey game, *4211*

Women's college hockey Player of the Year Award, *4214*

Whitworth, Kathy: Golfer to be named Ladies Professional Golf Association (LPGA) Player of the Year, *3782*

Golfer to be named Ladies Professional Golf Association (LPGA) Player of the Year seven times, *3800*

Woman golfer to earn more than $1 million in official prize money during her career, *3835*

Wichman, Sharon: Swimmer from the United States to win the women's 200-meter breaststroke title in the Olympic Games, *5858*

Wickersham, Ned: Softball player to win two consecutive batting titles in the Amateur Softball Association Major Fast Pitch National League, *5600*

Wickham, Tracey: Swimmer to hold both the women's 400- and 800-meter freestyle world titles at the same time, *5930*

Wicks, Sue: College women's basketball United States Basketball Writers Association All-American first team, *2271*

Wideman, Lydia: National team to sweep the medals in the women's 10-kilometer Nordic (cross-country) skiing event in the Olympic Winter Games, *5395*

Women's individual 10-kilometer Nordic (cross-country) event held at the Olympic Winter Games, *5396*

Wigg, Simon: Motorcycle racer to win five individual long-track world titles, *4594*

Wigger, Lones: Shooter from the United States to win the men's small-bore rifle (three positions) title in the Olympic Games, *5310*

Wightman, Hazel Hotchkiss: Tennis player to win six United States mixed doubles titles, *6059*

Tennis player to win three consecutive women's singles titles at the United States national championships, *6051*

Tennis players from the United States to win the mixed doubles event in the Olympic Games, *6072*

Tennis players from the United States to win the women's doubles title in the Olympic Games, *6070*

Wilber, Doreen: Women's individual archery event in the modern format held in the Olympic Games, *1036*

Wilding, Tony: Tennis player to win two Australian national men's doubles championships, *6052*

Wilke, Marina: Women's eight-oared shell with coxswain event held in the Olympic Games, *4949*

Wilkie, David: Men's 200-meter breaststroke event held in the world championships, *5880*

Swimmer to hold world titles in both the men's 100- and 200-meter breaststroke at the same time, *5912*

Swimmer to win two consecutive men's 200-meter breaststroke titles in the world championships, *5915*

Wilkins, Mac: Discus-thrower to break the 230-feet and 70-meter barriers in the men's event, *2781*

Wilkinson, Colleen: World championships in barefoot water-skiing, *6319*

Wilkinson, George: Water polo event held in the Olympic Games, *6301*

Water polo player to win two, and then three, gold medals in the Olympic Games, *6303*

Willard, John: Tennis player to win four Australian national mixed doubles titles, *6085*

William IV, King of England: Golf club to be awarded the title "Royal", *3566*

Williams, Archie: African-American runner to win the men's 400-meter title in the Olympic Games, *5039*

Williams, Billy: Chicago Cubs baseball player to be named Rookie of the Year, *1645*

Williams, Buck: New Jersey Nets player to be named National Basketball Association (NBA) Rookie of the Year, *2177*

Williams, Dean: World cup in squash, *5765*

Williams, Doug: African-American quarterback to play in and to win football's Super Bowl, *3419*

Williams, Edward: Men's doubles tennis championship at Wimbledon, *6016*

Williams, (first name unknown): Monaco Grand Prix automobile race, *1064*

Williams, Jimmy: Baseball player to lead the American League in triples in two consecutive years, *1343*

Williams, John: Men's individual archery event in the modern format held in the Olympic Games, *1035*

Williams, Kenny: Baseball player to steal more than 30 bases and hit more than 30 home runs in a single season in the American League, *1461*

Williams, Michael: Basketball player to make 97 consecutive free throws in the National Basketball Association (NBA), *2330*

Williams, Percy: Runner from Asia to hold the officially accepted world record in the men's 100-meter dash, *5034*

Runner from Canada to win the men's 100-meter race in the Olympic Games, *5018*

Williams, Richard Norris: Tennis players from the United States to win the mixed doubles event in the Olympic Games, *6072*

Williams, Ricky: National Collegiate Athletic Association major college football player to rush for 6,279 college career yards, *3489*

Williams, Robert: Team archery event held in the Olympic Games, *1028*

Williams, Serena: Sisters to each win a women's singles grand slam title in tennis, *6192*

Sisters to face each other in the finals of a professional tennis tournament, *6191*

Sisters to win the women's doubles title at the U.S. Open, *6189*

Williams, Sherman: College football player to gain 359 all-purpose yards in a major bowl game, *3469*

Williams, Ted: Baseball player to lead the American League in bases on balls for four consecutive years, *1572*

Kansas City Royals baseball player to be named Most Valuable Player, *1755*

Triple Crown hitter in 2 seasons in the American League, *1557*

Williams, Venus: Sisters to each win a women's singles grand slam title in tennis, *6192*

Sisters to face each other in the finals of a professional tennis tournament, *6191*

Sisters to win the women's doubles tennis title at the U.S. Open, *6189*

Williams, Willie: Runner to race the men's 100-meter dash in 10.1 seconds, *5063*

Williamson, Ned: Major league baseball player to hit 27 home runs in a single season, *1275*

Wills, Helen: Tennis player from the United States to win the women's singles tennis title in the Olympic Games, *6071*

Tennis player to win 158 straight women's singles matches, *6093*

Tennis player to win nine Wimbledon women's doubles titles, *6088*

Tennis player to win the Wimbledon women's singles championship eight times, *6099*

Tennis player to win three consecutive French national women's singles championships, and then four overall, after the event became international, *6092*

Tennis players from the United States to win the women's doubles title in the Olympic Games, *6070*

Wills, Judy: World championships in trampolining, *6228*

World championships in trampolining to include individual tumbling and synchronized pairs competitions, *6229*

Wills, Maury: Baseball player to lead the National League in stolen bases for six consecutive years, *1677*

Major league baseball player to have 104 steals in one season, *1662*

Wills, Thomas: Australian rules football, *3515*

Wilmarth, Dick: Iditarod sled dog race, *5509*

Wilson, Eric C.: National collegiate track and field (athletics) championships sponsored by the National Collegiate Athletic Association (NCAA), *6206*

Wilson, George: College football All-America team named by Grantland Rice, *3153*

Wilson, Hack: Major league baseball player to bat in 190 runs in a single season, *1490*

Wilson, Larry: National Football League player to be named Defensive Player of the Year, *3276*

Wilson, Michelle: College women's basketball player to have 151 blocked shots, and 5.6 rebounds per game, in a single Division I National Collegiate Athletic Association (NCAA) season, *2284*

Wilson, Tracy: Figure skaters from Canada to win a medal in ice dancing at the Olympic Winter Games, *3093*

Wiltse, Hooks: Major league pitcher of the 20th century to strike out four batters in a single inning, *1370*

Winans, Walter: Running deer (double shot) individual shooting event held in the Olympic Games, *5284*

Winder, Charles: Shooters from the United States to win the military rifle team shooting title in the Olympic Games, *5288*

Wing, Brett: World championships in barefoot water-skiing, *6319*

Wing, John Ian: Olympic Games to have a formal closing ceremony, *4708*

Wingate, George W.: International rifle tournament held in the United States, *5267*

Wingfield, Walter: Tennis game in its modern form, *6005*

Winkler, Anton: World cup in luge (toboggan), *4461*

Winkler, Hans-Günter: Equestrian to win four titles in team jumping in the Olympic Games, *2880*

Equestrian to win three consecutive titles in team jumping in the Olympic Games, *2869*

Equestrians to win two consecutive titles in team jumping in the Olympic Games, *2867*

Wint, Arthur: Athlete from Jamaica to win a gold medal in the Olympic Games, *4695*

Runner from the Caribbean to win the men's 400-meter title in the Olympic Games, *5050*

Winter, Martin: Men's quadruple sculls rowing event held in the Olympic Games, *4948*

Wiranata, Andy B.: World cup/grand prix competition in badminton, *1173*

Wires, Kurt: Canoe racers to win both the men's 1000- and 10,000-meter pairs kayak events in the Olympic Games, *2606*

Witt, Katarina: African-American athlete to win a medal in the Olympic Winter Games, *4763*

African-American figure skater to win the women's singles title in the world championships, *3090*

Figure skaters to win Emmy awards for a television special, *3095*

Wöckel, Bärbel Eckert: Runner to win two consecutive gold medals in the women's 4 x 100-meter relay in the Olympic Games, *5117*

Runner to win two consecutive women's 200-meter titles at the Olympic Games, *5116*

Wolbert, Babe: National track and field (athletics) championships for women in the United States, *6207*

Wolf, Sigrid: Women's super giant slalom event held at the Olympic Winter Games, *5453*

Wolfe, Jack "Kid": Boxer to be undisputed world super-bantamweight (junior featherweight) champion, *2543*

Wolfe, Rowland: Men's tumbling gymnastics competition held in the Olympic Games, *3929*

Wolfgramm, Michael: Men's quadruple sculls rowing event held in the Olympic Games, *4948*

Wood, Arthur: 8-meter-class sailing event in the Olympic Games, *5206*

Wood, Sidney: United States national women's and men's singles tennis championships to both be played at the West Side Tennis Club stadium, *6095*

Woodard, Lynette: Basketball team from the United States to win the women's title in the Olympic Games, *2208*

Major college women's basketball player to score more than 3,500 points during her college career, *2168*

Woman basketball player to sign with the Harlem Globetrotters, *2223*

Woodbridge, Margaret: Swimmers from the United States to win the women's 4 x 100-meter freestyle relay title in the Olympic Games, *5814*

Woodbridge, Todd: Tennis players to win five Wimbledon men's doubles titles in the Open era, *6188*

Wooden, John: Basketball team to win seven consecutive Division I National Collegiate Athletic Association (NCAA) championships, *2096*

College basketball coach to be named *Sports Illustrated* Sportsman of the Year, *2084*

Sports Illustrated Sportsman of the Year award to be given to a woman and to be shared, *1155*

Woodforde, Mark: Tennis players to win five Wimbledon men's doubles titles in the Open era, *6188*

Woodruff, John: African-American runner to win the men's 800-meter title in the Olympic Games, *5037*

Woods, Tiger (Eldrick): African-American golfer to win the U.S. Junior Amateur title, *3871*

Athlete of Asian or Native American descent to be named *Sports Illustrated* Sportsman of the Year, *1161*

Golf event to be broadcast live on network television in prime time, *3898*

Golfer of African-American or Asian-American descent to win one of golf's major tournaments, *3888*

Golfer of African-American or Asian-American descent to win the U.S. Amateur Championship, *3879*

Golfer to hold the record low (under-par) scores in all four Professional Golfers Association (PGA) major tournaments, *3899*

Golfer to win more than $2.5 million in official prize money in a single season, *3889*

Golfer to win more than $2 million in official prize money in a single season, *3886*

Golfer to win more than $7 million in official prize money in a single season, *3894*

Woodward, Vivian: Soccer (international football) player to win two gold medals in the Olympic Games, *5548*

Worley, Al: National Collegiate Athletic Association major college football player to intercept 14 passes in a single season, *3288*

Worsham, Lew: Golf tournament to be shown on television, *3716*

Golf tournament to be televised nationally, *3733*

Worthington, Jackie: Agreement to encourage women's events in rodeos, *4893*

Worthington, Kay: Women's four-oared shell without coxswain event held in the Olympic Games, *4957*

Worthington, Willa *See* McGuire, Willa Worthington

Wrede, Ludwig: Figure skater to win both the singles and pairs title at the same world championships, *3003*

Figure skater to win five consecutive women's singles championships, *3004*

Wrenn, Robert: United States national interscholastic boys singles tennis championships, *6030*

Wright, Beals: National team to sweep the medals in the men's doubles tennis event in the Olympic Games, *6043*

Tennis player from the United States to win the men's singles title in the Olympic Games, *6044*

Wright, Bill: African-American golfer to win a national championship, *3756*

Wright, Bronwyn: World championships in water-ski-racing, *6320*

Wright, Catherine: National track and field (athletics) championships for women in the United States, *6207*

Wright, Ian: Introduction of racquetball to England, *4875*

Wright, Irving: Tennis player to win six United States mixed doubles titles, *6059*

Wright, Marc: Pole-vaulter to hold the officially accepted world record in the men's event, *4839*

X

Y

Yaw, Susan: College women's basketball All-America team, *2110*

Yegorova, Lyubov: Skier to win four medals in the same Nordic skiing event in the Olympic Winter Games, *5478*

Skier to win two consecutive women's combined pursuit Nordic (cross-country) skiing titles at the Olympic Winter Games, *5486*

Women's combined pursuit Nordic (cross-country) skiing event in the Olympic Winter Games, *5477*

Women's individual 15-kilometer Nordic (cross-country) skiing event at the Olympic Winter Games, *5470*

Yerlhsu, Tennur: World championships in taekwondo to include women, *4549*

Yermoleyeva, Galina: World championships in rowing to include women's competitions, *4945*

Yipulli, Tuomo: Men's team ski-jumping event held in the Olympic Winter Games, *5457*

Yoo Nam-kyu: Men's and women's doubles events to be included in the world cup in table tennis, *5998*

Men's singles table tennis event held in the Olympic Games, *5996*

Yordanova, Zdravka: Women's double sculls event held in the Olympic Games, *4946*

Yorgova, Diana: Wedding between Olympic athletes held at the Olympic Games, *4717*

York, Duke of *See* James II, King of England (Duke of York)

Yorke, Billie (Adeline): Tennis player to win six French national women's doubles championships after the event became international, and four times consecutively, *6101*

Yorzyk, William: Men's 200-meter butterfly swimming event held in the Olympic Games, *5834*

Yoshioka, Takayoshi: Runner from Asia to hold the officially accepted world record in the men's 100-meter dash, *5034*

Young, Albert: Welterweight boxing event held in the Olympic Games, *2532*

Young, Buddy: African-American college football player to score a touchdown in the Rose Bowl, *3212*

African-American professional football player to join the New York Yankees, *3210*

Young, Cy: Baseball pitcher to lead the American League in shutouts for two consecutive years, *1358*

Baseball pitcher to lead the American League in strikeouts, *1320*

Pitcher to win a World Series game, *1354*

Young, Cyrus: Javelin-thrower from the United States to win the men's event in the Olympic Games, *4393*

Young, Gerald: Honduran major league baseball player, *1792*

Young, Kevin: Hurdler to race the men's 400-meter hurdles in under 47 seconds, *4353*

Young, Robert: World professional championships in surfing, *5774*

Young, Sheila: Speed skater to win three consecutive women's titles at the world speed skating championships, *5691*

"Young Griffo" *See* Griffiths, Albert

Younger, Paul: African-American football player from an African-American college to join a major professional football team, *3222*

Yount, Robin: Milwaukee Brewers American League pennant, *1765*

Yücel, Ali: World championships in freestyle wrestling, *6389*

Yun Bok Suh: Record in the men's marathon to stand for more than 10 years, *4480*

Runner officially representing South Korea to hold the world record in the men's marathon, and to win the Boston Marathon, *4482*

Yun Chi Choi: Runners from a single country outside the United States to take the top three spots in the Boston Marathon, *4483*

Z

Zabelina, Aleksandra: Fencers to win three gold medals in the women's team foil competition in the Olympic Games, *2938*

Fencers to win two gold medals in the women's team foil competition in the Olympic Games, *2937*

Women's team foil fencing competition held in the Olympic Games, *2935*

Zabirova, Zulfiya: Women's road time trial cycling event held in the Olympic Games, *2726*

Zacharias, Georg: Men's 440-yard (later 400-meter) breaststroke event held in the Olympic Games, *5796*

Zafer, Haydar: World championships in freestyle wrestling, *6389*

World championships in freestyle wrestling, *6389*

Zaharias, Babe Didrikson: Golfer from the United States to win the British Women's Amateur Championship, *3717*

Golfer to win the U.S. Women's Open three times, *3744*

Golfer to win three major tournaments, and six titles overall, on the Ladies Professional Golf Association (LPGA) Tour in a single season, *3725*

Golfer to win two U.S. Women's Open championships, *3726*

High-jumpers to hold the officially accepted world record in the women's event, and the first from the United States to win the women's event in the Olympic Games, *4023*

Women's 80-meter hurdles event held in the Olympic Games, *4332*

Women's javelin-throw event held in the Olympic Games, *4390*

Zaitsev, Aleksandr: Figure skater to win 10 consecutive pairs titles in the world championships, *3080*

Figure skater to win a pairs title in the Olympic Winter Games with two different partners, *3075*

Figure skater to win three consecutive medals in pairs competition at the Olympic Winter Games, *3084*

Zamba, Frieda: Surfer to win four women's professional world titles, *5777*

Zamboni, Frank J.: Zamboni ice-resurfacing machine sold commercially, *5749*

Zampori, Giorgio: Floor exercise competition held at the world championships in gymnastics, *3919*

Gymnast to win three consecutive gold medals in the men's team combined exercises in the Olympic Games, *3924*

Gymnasts to win two consecutive gold medals in the men's team combined exercises in the Olympic Games, *3922*

Zaremba, Ota: First Heavyweight weightlifting event held in the Olympic Games, *6349*

Zaslofsky, Max: All–National Basketball Association (NBA) First Team, *1914*

Zátopek, Emil: Runner to race the men's 10,000 meters in under 29:00 minutes, *5061*

Runner to win two consecutive men's 10,000-meter titles in the Olympic Games, *5056*

Zaychuk, Boris: Hammer-thrower to break the 80-meter barrier, *3994*

Zayev, Pyotr: Boxer to win two, and then three, consecutive heavyweight titles, and three boxing titles in a single class, in the Olympic Games, *2575*

Zehrt, Monika: Women's 4 x 400-meter relay track event held in the Olympic Games, *5095*

Zelezny, Ján: Javelin-thrower to break the 310- and 320-foot barriers with the new javelin, *4413*

Zendejas, Luis: Phoenix Cardinals regular season football game played at Sun Devil Stadium, *3421*

Zeng Xinling: World championships for women's weightlifting, *6350*

Zhelezovski, Igor: Speed skater to win six men's world speed skating sprint championships, *5718*

Zheng Lihui: Gymnasts from China to win the men's team title at the Olympic Games, *3980*

Zhong, Chen *See* Chen Zhong

Zhuang Xiaoyan: Women's heavyweight judo event held in the Olympic Games, *4553*

Zhulin, Aleksandr: Figure skaters to win two consecutive ice dancing titles at the Olympic Winter Games, *3114*

Zhupyna, Olena: Women's synchronized platform diving event held at the world championships, *2824*

Ziip, Adolph van der Voort van: Equestrians to win two consecutive three-day event team titles, *2854*

Zimmerman, Arthur: World championships in cycling, *2684*

Zimmerman, Heinie: Triple Crown hitter in the National League, *1411*

Zimmermann, Annemarie: Canoe racers to win two consecutive women's 500-meter kayak pairs event in the Olympic Games, *2613*

Zimyatov, Nikolai: Skier to win two consecutive men's 30-kilometer Nordic (cross-country) titles in the Olympic Winter Games, *5442*

Zinn, Guy: Boston Red Sox regular season baseball game played at Fenway Park, *1413*

Zogg, David: World championships in Alpine skiing, *5377*

Zorzi, Angelo: Gymnasts to win two consecutive gold medals in the men's team combined exercises in the Olympic Games, *3922*

Zsivótsky, Gyula: Hammer-thrower to break the 240-foot barrier, *3992*

Zuend, Stefan: Ski flying event held in the world cup for Nordic skiing, *5467*

Zumkeller, Günther: World championships in rowing, *4940*

Zurbriggen, Pirmin: Skier to win four men's super giant slalom world cup titles, *5465*

Skier to win seven men's giant slalom world cup titles, *5441*

Super giant slalom events held in the Alpine skiing world championships, *5452*

Zürner, Albert: Men's springboard diving event held in the Olympic Games, *2792*

National team to sweep the top medals in men's springboard diving in the Olympic Games, *2794*

Zutter, Louis: Athlete from Switzerland to win a gold medal in the Olympic Games, *4612*

Men's side (pommel) horse gymnastics competition held in the Olympic Games, *3905*

Zybina, Galina: Shot-putter to break the 16-meter barrier in the women's event, *5339*
Shot-putter to break the 50-foot barrier in the women's event, *5338*

Geographical Index

The Geographical Index is a listing of key locations in the main text of the book, arranged alphabetically by nation, state or province, and city. Each index entry includes key information about the "first" and a 4-digit number in italics. That number directs you to the full entry in the main text, where entries are numbered in order, starting with 1001.

To find the full entry, look in the main text for the entry tagged with that 4-digit number. For example, to find the entry on the first athlete from Algeria to win a gold medal in the Olympic Games, look for the entry numbered 4799 in the main text.

Under each country's name, entries that contain only the country's name are listed first. Following those are entries listed by state or province, and then by city, alphabetically. For example, under Australia, entries with only country references are listed first. Following those are index references under the city names Adelaide, Brisbane, Canberra, and so on. As an example of states and provinces, the index entry on the Yukon Quest sled dog race is found under Canada, subhead Yukon Territory, subhead Whitehorse.

Note that locations are generally identified by their modern names. In some cases, entries are listed under the name of the country at the time of the event. For example, during the time of the Soviet Union, entries will be listed under that name. However, before and after that time, entries will be listed under the names of individual countries, such as Russia, Belarus, or Uzbekistan. Similarly, East Germany and West Germany and the cities within those countries are, for some years during the 20th century, broken out separately under the overall heading Germany.

For historical reasons, England, Scotland, and Wales are (except for very early times) grouped under the heading Great Britain. However, Ireland is listed separately.

For more information, see "How to Use This Book," on page ix.

787

ARGENTINA—*continued*

Belgian Grand Prix automobile race to be part of the Formula One Grand Prix circuit, *1081*

Canada Cup golf tournament, *3732*

Cup of the Americas (Copa de las Americas) polo competition, *4867*

French Grand Prix automobile race to be part of the Formula One Grand Prix circuit, *1082*

Monaco Grand Prix automobile race to be part of the Formula One Grand Prix circuit, *1078*

Pan-American Games, *4370*

Sailor to complete a solo circumnavigation of the world in under a year, *5213*

Spanish Grand Prix automobile race to be part of the Formula One Grand Prix circuit, *1085*

Swimmer to swim across the English Channel and back consecutively, *5843*

Team from Africa to win the men's soccer event in the Olympic Games, *5570*

Tennis player to win 145 men's singles matches in a single season, *6163*

U.S. Senior Open golf tournament, *3833*

World championships in three-day event equestrian competition, *2872*

World cup in soccer (international football), *5553*

Buenos Aires

Argentine Grand Prix automobile race, *1091*

Soccer (international football) team from Argentina to win the world cup, *5563*

ARMENIA

Athlete from Armenia to win a gold medal in the Olympic Games, *4791*

AUSTRALIA

Athlete to win two consecutive women's titles in the world triathlon championships, *6243*

Australian mixed doubles national tennis championships, *6061*

Australian mixed doubles national tennis championships, *6061*

Australian national tennis championships, *6045*

Australian Open men's doubles tennis title, *6136*

Australian Open men's singles tennis title, *6137*

Australian Open tennis tournament, *6138*

Australian Open women's doubles tennis title, *6139*

Australian Open women's singles tennis title, *6140*

Australian rules football, *3515*

Australian women's doubles national tennis championships, *6062*

Australian women's singles national tennis championships, *6063*

Automobile racer to have five consecutive wins in a single season on the Formula One Grand Prix circuit, *1100*

Automobile racer to win two Austrian Grand Prix races, *1127*

Boston Marathon to offer prize money, *4515*

British Empire Games (later the British Commonwealth Games), *4369*

Canadian Grand Prix automobile race, *1112*

Canoe marathon world championships, *2624*

Canoe polo world championships, *2627*

Cricket game to be broadcast on television, *2658*

Cricket team from outside the British Isles to tour England, *2649*

Federation Cup championships, *6112*

French Open men's doubles tennis match, *6117*

French Open men's singles tennis match, *6118*

Golfer to win more than $1 million in her rookie year on the Ladies Professional Golf Association (LPGA) Tour, *3884*

Golfer to win more than $10 million in official prize money during a career, *3885*

Gymnast to win two consecutive women's floor exercise titles in the Olympic Games, *3941*

Inter-Empire Sports tournament, *4366*

Inter-state carnival in Australian rules football, *3519*

Inter-state game in Australian rules football, *3517*

International Championships in rugby, *4970*

International cricket organization, *2654*

International cricket organization for women, *2659*

International organization for surfing, *5772*

Men's 1500-meter freestyle event held at the world championships, *5878*

Men's 200-meter freestyle swimming event held in the Olympic Games, *5789*

Men's 20,000-meter walk event held in the Olympic Games, *6292*

Men's 5000-meter team running event held in the Olympic Games, *4982*

Men's 800-meter and 1500-meter running events held in the Olympic Games, *4974*

Men's double trap (clay pigeon) individual shooting event held in the Olympic Games, *5326*

Men's Madison cycling event held in the Olympic Games, *2732*

Men's obstacle swimming race held in the Olympic Games, *5790*

National team to sweep the medals in the men's 100-meter freestyle in the Olympic Games, *5809*

Olympic Games to be boycotted by member countries, *4703*

Olympic men's 1500-meter freestyle event in which the medalists all had times under 18 minutes, *5841*

Rower to win both the single and double sculls events at the Henley Regatta, *4939*

Runner from Australia to win the women's 100- and 200-meter titles in the Olympic Games, *5059*

Runner to complete the men's mile race in under 3:55 minutes, *5068*

Runner to race the men's marathon in under 2:12 hours, and the first representing Australia to hold the world record in the event, *4492*

Runner to win the men's marathon in the World Championships in Athletics, *4508*

Skier to be killed during the Olympic Winter Games, *5409*

State organization for Australian rules football, *3516*

Surfer not born in Hawaii to win the International Surfing Championships, *5771*

Surfer to win five men's professional world titles, *5776*

Swimmer to hold both the women's 400- and 800-meter freestyle world titles at the same time, *5930*

Swimmer to race 100 yards in one minute, *5793*

Swimmer to race the women's 100-meter freestyle in under 1:20 minutes, *5804*

Swimmer to race the women's 100-meter freestyle in under one minute, *5844*

Swimmer to race the women's 400-meter freestyle event in under five minutes, *5833*

Swimmer to win three consecutive titles in the same event in the Olympic Games, *5845*

Swimmer to win two and then three consecutive women's 100-meter freestyle titles in the Olympic Games, *5842*

Tennis player of the modern era to win the United States women's singles title five times, *6154*

Tennis player to win 10 consecutive Australian national men's doubles championships, *6102*

Tennis player to win 17 men's singles tournaments in one season, *6141*

Tennis player to win 21 women's singles tournaments in a single season, *6144*

Tennis player to win five Australian national women's singles championships, and the first to win three in a row, *6087*

Tennis player to win five consecutive Australian national men's singles championships, and six overall, *6116*

Tennis player to win four Australian national mixed doubles titles, *6085*

Tennis player to win four consecutive Australian national women's singles championships, *6103*

Tennis player to win seven consecutive Australian national women's singles championships, and 11 overall, *6114*

Tennis player to win six consecutive French national men's doubles championships after the event became international, *6113*

Tennis player to win three consecutive Australian national men's singles championships, and four overall, *6094*

Tennis player to win two Australian national men's doubles championships, *6052*

Tennis player to win two Australian national men's singles championships, *6050*

Tennis player to win two consecutive Australian national women's doubles championships, *6066*

Tennis player to win two consecutive Australian national women's singles tennis championships, *6067*

Tennis player to win two Grand Slams, *6142*

Tennis players to win five consecutive Australian national women's doubles championships, *6104*

Tennis players to win five Wimbledon men's doubles titles in the Open era, *6188*

Tennis players to win three Australian national mixed doubles championships, *6082*

U.S. Open women's doubles tennis title, *6127*

Wimbledon Open men's singles tennis title, *6130*

Women's 100-meter freestyle swimming event held in the Olympic Games, *5805*

Women's 25-kilometer river/sea swim event held in the world championships, *5961*

Women's 4 x 100-meter freestyle relay swimming event in the Olympic Games, *5808*

Women's 400-meter race held in the Olympic Games, *5076*

Women's heptathlon event held in the Olympic Games, *4013*

World amateur championships in squash, *5761*

World championships for water polo to include women, *6307*

World championships in barefoot water-skiing, *6319*

World championships in dirt-track (speedway) motorcycle racing, *4576*

World championships in hang gliding, *3533*

World championships in netball, *4598*

World championships in short track speed skating, *5694*

World championships in water-ski-racing, *6320*

World cup in men's cricket, *2661*

World cup in squash, *5765*

World open championships in squash, *5763*

World outdoor championships in bowls, *2499*

World professional championships in surfing, *5774*

World Surfing Championships, *5773*

World team championships in squash, *5762*

Written reference to tennis, *6002*

AUSTRALIA—*continued*
Adelaide

Australian Grand Prix automobile race, *1132*
Automobile racer to win two Australian Grand Prix races, *1137*
Golf club in Australia, *3583*

Brisbane

Women's test match in cricket, *2657*

Canberra

Runner to set seven world records in the women's 400 meters, *5145*

Essendon

Grand final for Australian rules football, *3518*

Hobart

Sydney-Hobart Race, *5214*

Melbourne

African-American decathlete to win the men's title in the Olympic Games, *2743*
Athlete from Bulgaria to win a gold medal in the Olympic Games, *4707*
Australian rules football, *3515*
Boxer to win three gold medals, and two consecutive light middleweight titles, in the Olympic Games, *2560*
Canoe racer to win two, and then three, consecutive titles in the men's singles 1000-meter kayak event in the Olympic Games, *2607*
Diver to win two consecutive titles in both springboard and platform diving events, and the first to win four gold medals in diving, in the Olympic Games, *2804*
Fencer to win two consecutive men's individual foil titles in the Olympic Games, *2933*
Fencer to win two, three, and four men's team épée titles in the Olympic Games, *2931*
Fiberglass pole to be used in the men's pole vault event in the Olympic Games, *4842*
Grand final for Australian rules football, *3518*
Hurdler to win two consecutive titles in the women's 80-meter hurdles in the Olympic Games, *4338*
Ice hockey game played in Australia, *4056*
Javelin-thrower to break the 280-foot barrier and to hold the world record in the men's event, *4397*
Melbourne Cup horse race, *4274*
Men's 200-meter butterfly swimming event held in the Olympic Games, *5834*
Olympic Games held in the Southern Hemisphere, and in Australia, *4706*

Olympic Games to have a formal closing ceremony, *4708*
Pentathlete to win two consecutive titles in the men's modern pentathlon in the Olympic Games, *4825*
Pole-vaulter to break the 14-foot barrier in the women's event, *4851*
Pole-vaulter to win two consecutive titles in the men's event in the Olympic Games, *4843*
Presidents Cup Match won by the international team, *3893*
Runners to finish first and second in both the women's 100- and 200-meter races in the Olympic Games, *5065*
Sailor to win the men's Finn-class event two, three, and four times in the Olympic Games, *5219*
Shot-putter to win two consecutive men's titles in the Olympic Games, *5341*
Swimmer to win two and then three consecutive women's 100-meter freestyle titles in the Olympic Games, *5842*
Test match in cricket, *2650*
Triple-jumper to win two consecutive men's titles in the Olympic Games, *6256*
Weightlifter from the United States to win the featherweight title in the Olympic Games, *6340*
Woman athlete to win seven track and field medals in the Olympic Games, *6214*
Women's 100-meter butterfly event held in the Olympic Games, *5835*
World championships in fast-pitch softball, *5601*

Perth

Diver to hold the women's world titles in both the one- and three-meter springboard diving at the same time, *2820*
Men's 25-kilometer river/sea swim event held in the world championships, *5957*
Men's 5-kilometer river/sea swim event held in the world championships, *5975*
Men's one-meter springboard diving event held at the world championships, *2821*
Swimmer to hold world titles in both the 5- and 25-kilometer river/sea swim at the same time, *5976*
Swimmer to win two consecutive men's 100-meter freestyle titles at the world championships, *5958*
Swimmer to win two consecutive men's 200-meter individual medley titles at the world championships, *5959*
Swimmer to win two consecutive men's 50-meter freestyle titles at the world championships, *5960*
Women's 25-kilometer river/sea swim event held in the world championships, *5961*

AUSTRIA—*continued*

Figure skater from Austria to win the women's singles title in the world championships, *2992*

Figure skater to win both the singles and pairs title at the same world championships, *3003*

Figure skater to win five consecutive women's singles championships, *3004*

Figure skater to win seven consecutive men's singles titles in the world championships, *3020*

Figure skater to win two, and then three, men's singles titles at the world championships, *2965*

Figure skaters from Austria to win the pairs title at the Olympic Winter Games, *3002*

Figure skaters from Austria to win the pairs title in the world championships, *2986*

Figure skaters to complete a grand slam, winning the European, world, and Olympic titles in the same year, *3010*

Giant slalom and snowboard cross events held in the snowboarding world championships, *5523*

International figure skating competition, *2960*

International governing body for ice skating, *2962*

International team handball match, *4002*

Judo artist to win two consecutive men's middleweight gold medals in the Olympic Games, *4550*

Lightweight Greco-Roman wrestling event held in the Olympic Games, *6370*

Men's 500-meter freestyle event held in the Olympic Games, *5787*

Men's pairs 1000-meter kayaking event held in the Olympic Games, *2598*

Men's singles 100-meter kayak event held in the Olympic Games, *2599*

Modern Olympic Games at which member countries were barred from competing, *4649*

Nations' Cup for skiing, *5418*

Olympic Games to institute sex tests for women athletes, *4723*

Ski jumping event held in the world cup for Nordic skiing, *5430*

Ski jumping Nations' Cup in the world cup for Nordic skiing, *5434*

Skier to sweep the men's individual Alpine events at the Olympic Winter Games, *5406*

Skier to win both the women's slalom and the women's Alpine combination in the same Olympic Winter Games, and the first from Austria to win the Olympic women's slalom title, *5480*

Skier to win five men's downhill world cup titles, *5440*

Skier to win five women's slalom world cup titles, *5449*

Skier to win seven women's downhill world cup titles, *5426*

Skier to win six women's overall world cup titles, *5427*

Uneven (asymmetrical) bars competition held in the world championships for gymnastics, *3933*

Woman figure skater to perform the sit spin, *2969*

Woman speed skater to skate the 500 meters in under 1 minute, *5647*

Women's events to be included in the Alpine skiing world championships, *5392*

Women's super giant slalom event held at the Olympic Winter Games, *5453*

World Biathlon Championships, *2430*

World championships in luge (toboggan), *4453*

World Cup in show jumping, *2882*

World Cup series of competitions for speed skating, *5703*

Innsbruck

Athlete to win four gold medals at a single Olympic Winter Games, and six Olympic gold medals overall, *4715*

Athlete to win nine medals in the Olympic Winter Games, *4716*

Figure skater from Germany to win the men's singles title at the Olympic Winter Games, *3063*

Figure skater from Great Britain to win the men's singles title at the Olympic Winter Games, *3077*

Figure skater from the Netherlands to win the women's singles title at the Olympic Winter Games, *3065*

Figure skater to win a pairs title in the Olympic Winter Games with two different partners, *3075*

Figure skaters from the Soviet Union to win the pairs title at the Olympic Winter Games, *3064*

Figure skaters from the United States to win an Olympic medal in ice dancing, *3074*

Figure skaters to win the ice dancing title in the Olympic Winter Games, *3076*

Men's 1000-meter speed skating event held in the Olympic Winter Games, *5692*

Men's individual 70-meter ski jump event held at the Olympic Winter Games, *5410*

Men's singles luge (toboggan) event held in the Olympic Winter Games, *4455*

National team to sweep the medals in the men's 5000-meter speed-skating event at the Olympic Winter Games, *5676*

National team to sweep the medals in the women's 500-meter speed-skating event at the Olympic Winter Games, *5675*

National team to sweep the medals in the women's downhill event in the Olympic Winter Games, *5413*

Olympic Games to be voted down by the selected host region, *4742*

Olympic Winter Games at which an athlete was killed, *4713*

Olympic Winter Games held in Austria, *4714*

Olympic Winter Games in which more than 1000 athletes competed, *4712*

Skier to be killed during the Olympic Winter Games, *5409*

Skier to win both the men's individual 70- and 90-meter ski jumps in the same Olympic Winter Games, *5414*

Skier to win two consecutive women's Nordic (cross-country) skiing titles in the Olympic Winter Games, *5423*

Skier to win two titles in the men's 50-kilometer freestyle Nordic (cross-country) skiing at the Olympic Winter Games, *5411*

Speed skater to win four gold medals in speed skating in a single Olympic Winter Games, *5678*

Speed skater to win two consecutive women's 1500-meter and 3000-meter titles at the Olympic Winter Games, *5677*

Two-seater luge (toboggan) event at the Olympic Winter Games, *4456*

Women's individual 5-kilometer Nordic (cross-country) event in the Olympic Winter Games, *5412*

Women's singles luge (toboggan) event held in the Olympic Winter Games, *4457*

Kossen

World championships in hang gliding, *3533*

Vienna

Figure skater to perform a triple jump in competition, *3047*

Figure skater to win both the singles and pairs title at the same world championships, *3003*

Figure skater to win three and then four consecutive women's singles titles in the world championships, *2982*

Figure skater to win two consecutive women's singles titles in the world championships, *2971*

Figure skaters from Finland to win the pairs title in the world championships, *2984*

Ice skating club in mainland Europe, *2953*

Open-air rink featuring artificial ice, *2981*

World championships in Greco-Roman wrestling, *6361*

AZERBAIJAN

Women's skeet shooting event held in the Olympic Games, *5328*

BARBADOS

Record of cricket being played in the West Indies, *2641*

BELARUS

Athlete from newly independent Belarus to win a gold medal in the Olympic Games, *4794*

Gymnast to win six gold medals in a single Olympic Games, *3976*

BELGIUM

Archer to win four Olympic gold medals in a single Olympic Games, and six overall, *1026*

Archery events held in the Olympic Games, *1025*

Belgian Grand Prix automobile race, *1061*

Cyclist to win the Tour de France three times, *2694*

Fencer to win both the men's masters épée and masters sabre competitions in the Olympic Games, *2907*

Figure skaters from Belgium to win the pairs title in the world championships, *3031*

Ice hockey event to be held in the Olympic Games, *4073*

Individual jumping equestrian event held in the Olympic Games, *2841*

International rowing competition, *4920*

Major international ice hockey organization, *4057*

Men's points cycling race held in the Olympic Games, *2711*

Olympic Games in which animals were deliberately killed, *4619*

Roller skates, *4901*

Speed skater to skate the 3000 meters in under 3:50 minutes, *5733*

Tour of Spain (Vuelta a España) cycling race, *2697*

World championship in moto-cross racing to include the 125 cc class, *4587*

World championships for judo to include women, *4546*

World championships in water-skiing, *6316*

World figure skating championships for roller skating, *4909*

Written reference to *chole*, *2629*

Antwerp

Archer to win four Olympic gold medals in a single Olympic Games, and six overall, *1026*

Athlete from Brazil to win a gold medal in the Olympic Games, *4650*

Athlete from Estonia to win a gold medal in the Olympic Games, *4651*

Athlete to win gold medals in both the Summer and Winter Olympics, *4674*

BELGIUM—Antwerp—*continued*

Diver from the United States to win the men's springboard diving event in the Olympic Games, *2796*

Equestrian to win two consecutive medals in the team jumping (Prix des Nations) event in the Olympic Games, *2851*

Featherweight weightlifting event held in the Olympic Games, *6328*

Fencer to win five gold medals in a single Olympic Games, and to win two consecutive men's individual foil titles in the Olympic Games, *2916*

Figure riding individual and team events held in the Olympic Games, *2850*

Figure skater from Sweden to win the women's singles title in the Olympic Games, *2997*

Figure skaters from Finland to win the pairs title in the Olympic Games, *2999*

Flag showing five interlocking rings to symbolize the Olympic Games, *4647*

Gymnasts to win two consecutive gold medals in the men's team combined exercises in the Olympic Games, *3922*

International figure skating competition at which recorded music was standard, *2996*

Light heavyweight boxing event held in the Olympic Games, *2538*

Light heavyweight freestyle wrestling event held in the Olympic Games, *6377*

Light heavyweight weightlifting event held in the Olympic Games, *6331*

Lightweight weightlifting event held in the Olympic Games, *6329*

Men's Finn-class sailing event in the Olympic Games, *5208*

Middleweight weightlifting event held in the Olympic Games, *6330*

Modern Olympic Games at which member countries were barred from competing, *4649*

National team to sweep the medals in the men's 100-meter freestyle in the Olympic Games, *5809*

National team to sweep the medals in the women's 100-meter freestyle swimming event in the Olympic Games, *5810*

National team to win two Olympic gold medals in the tug-of-war competition, *6268*

Olympic Games held in Belgium, *4648*

Rapid-fire pistol and free pistol team events held in the Olympic Games, *5299*

Runner from Africa to win the men's 400-meters title in the Olympic Games, *5010*

Running deer (double shot) team shooting event held in the Olympic Games, *5297*

Shooters from the United States to win the small-bore rifle team title in the Olympic Games, *5300*

Swimmer from the United States to win the men's 1500-meter freestyle title in the Olympic Games, *5811*

Swimmer to win Olympic gold medals 8 years apart, and to win Olympic medals 12 years apart, *5813*

Swimmers from the United States to win the women's 4 x 100-meter freestyle relay title in the Olympic Games, *5814*

Team from the United States to win the men's 4 x 100-meter relay track event in the Olympic Games, *5011*

Team from the United States to win the rugby event in the Olympic Games, *4967*

Thrower from the United States to win the men's 56-pound weight throw in the Olympic Games, *6324*

Woman figure skater to perform a full-revolution jump, the salchow, in competition, *2998*

Women's 300-meter (later 400-meter) freestyle event held in the Olympic Games, *5812*

Women's doubles tennis event held in the Olympic Games, *6060*

Women's springboard diving event held in the Olympic Games, *2797*

World championships in gymnastics, *3910*

Wrestler to win gold medals in three different divisions in the Olympic Games, *6378*

Wrestler to win two consecutive lightweight Greco-Roman titles in the Olympic Games, *6376*

Spa-Francorchamps

Automobile racer to win five Belgian Grand Prix races, *1140*

Automobile racer to win two Austrian Grand Prix races, *1127*

Belgian Grand Prix automobile race to be part of the Formula One Grand Prix circuit, *1081*

Woman automobile racer to compete in a Grand Prix race eligible for world-championship points, *1097*

Zoute

Reigning monarch to play in a national golf championship, *3710*

BERMUDA

Bermuda Race, *5204*

British Empire Games (later the British Commonwealth Games), *4369*

BRAZIL

Athlete from Brazil to win a gold medal in the Olympic Games, *4650*

CANADA—*continued*

Hockey player to be named *Sports Illustrated* Sportsman of the Year, *4153*

Ice hockey competition in the Olympic Winter Games to be boycotted, *4161*

Ice hockey event to be held in the Olympic Games, *4073*

Ice hockey team to win the Stanley Cup three times, *4052*

Inter-Empire Sports tournament, *4366*

International Cricket Conference (ICC) competition, *2662*

International cricket match outside Great Britain, *2647*

International curling competition between Canada and the United States, *2675*

International soccer (international football) match involving the United States, *5537*

Lacrosse event held in the Olympic Games, *4420*

Men's 100-meter butterfly event held in the world championships, *5876*

Men's 10,000-meter walk held in the Olympic Games, *6290*

Men's 56-pound weight throw event held in the Olympic Games, *6323*

Men's Canadian singles 1000-meter canoeing event held in the Olympic Games, *2597*

Men's giant slalom snowboarding event held at the Olympic Winter Games, *5524*

Men's heavyweight judo event in the Olympic Games, *4535*

Men's steeplechase event held at the Olympic Games, *4977*

Men's world championships in ice hockey, *4070*

National ice skating organization in North America, *2957*

National organization for lacrosse, *4417*

National team to win five ice hockey titles at the Olympic Winter Games, *4122*

National team to win six ice hockey titles at the Olympic Winter Games, *4128*

Pairs of twins to take the top two spots in the synchronized swimming duet competition in the Olympic Games, *5968*

Rhythmic gymnastics all-around individual competition held in the Olympic Games, *3974*

Runner from Asia to hold the officially accepted world record in the men's 100-meter dash, *5034*

Runner to win two consecutive Boston Marathons, *4470*

Runner to win two consecutive officially accepted men's 100-meter titles at the Olympic Games, *5150*

Sailor to complete a solo circumnavigation of the world, *5202*

Strathcona Cup curling competition, *2676*

Stud book for horse racing published in North America, *4287*

Woman to swim across the English Channel and back consecutively, *5928*

Woman to win gold medals in two biathlon events in the same Olympic Winter Games, *2442*

Women's 3000-meter short track relay speed skating event held at the Olympic Winter Games, *5715*

Women's 4 x 100-meter relay running event held in the Olympic Games, *5023*

Women's four-oared shell without coxswain event held in the Olympic Games, *4957*

Women's high jump event held in the Olympic Games, *4022*

Women's sport pistol individual shooting event held in the Olympic Games, *5316*

Women's world championships in ice hockey, *4200*

Women's world championships in roller hockey (rink hockey), *4241*

World championships for freestyle skiing, *5451*

World championships in curling, *2677*

World championships in mountain biking, *2716*

World championships in short track speed skating to be officially recognized, *5697*

World cup circuit for freestyle skiing, *5431*

World cup series of competitions in Alpine skiing, *5416*

World four-wall handball championships, *4010*

Alberta

Calgary

African-American athlete to win a medal in the Olympic Winter Games, *4763*

Athlete to win eight medals in individual events in the Olympic Winter Games, *4764*

Athlete to win two biathlon gold medals at a single Olympic Winter Games, *2438*

Calgary Flames regular season hockey game played at the Olympic Saddledome, *4186*

Calgary Stampede rodeo, *4883*

Figure skaters from Canada to win a medal in ice dancing at the Olympic Winter Games, *3093*

Men's Nordic combined team event held in the Olympic Winter Games, *5456*

Men's super giant slalom event held at the Olympic Winter Games, *5454*

Men's team ski-jumping event held in the Olympic Winter Games, *5457*

National team to sweep the medals in the women's individual 20-kilometer Nordic (cross-country) event at the Olympic Winter Games, *5459*

Olympic Winter Games held in Canada, *4761*

Olympic Winter Games held on artificial snow, *4762*

Skier of African ancestry to compete in the Olympic Winter Games, *5458*

Skier to win two consecutive titles in the men's 4 x 10-kilometer relay Nordic (cross-country) at the Olympic Winter Games, *5455*

Skier to win two individual ski-jumping gold medals in the same Olympic Winter Games, *5460*

Slider to win two consecutive women's singles luge (toboggan) titles at the Olympic Winter Games, *4463*

Speed skater to skate the 1000 meters in under 1:10 minutes, *5735*

Speed skater to skate the 10,000 meters in under 14 minutes, *5707*

Speed skater to skate the 3000 meters in under 3:50 minutes, *5733*

Speed skater to skate the 500 meters in under 35 seconds, *5734*

Speed skater to win two consecutive men's 5000-meter titles at the Olympic Winter Games, *5710*

Women's 5000-meter speed skating event held in the Olympic Winter Games, *5709*

Women's super giant slalom event held at the Olympic Winter Games, *5453*

Edmonton

Edmonton Oilers regular season hockey game played at the Northlands Coliseum, *4175*

British Columbia

Little League in Canada, and the first outside the United States, *1585*

Vancouver

Figure skater to win the women's singles U.S., world, and Olympic championships in the same year, *3056*

National Hockey League team to win the Stanley Cup, *4067*

Professional ice hockey league on North America's West Coast, *4059*

Vancouver Canucks regular season hockey game played at General Motors Place, *4220*

Vancouver Canucks regular season hockey game played at the Pacific Coliseum, *4156*

Manitoba

Winnipeg

National team to win four consecutive ice hockey titles at the Olympic Winter Games, *4107*

Winnipeg Jets regular season hockey game played at the Winnipeg Arena, *4176*

New Brunswick

St. John

Major league baseball player born in Canada, *1244*

Newfoundland

British Empire Games (later the British Commonwealth Games), *4369*

Nova Scotia

Ice hockey game, *4041*

Ontario

Bowmanville

Canadian Grand Prix automobile race, *1112*

Dunnville

Professional ice hockey player of Black African ancestry on record, *4051*

Fort Erie

African-American boxer born in the United States to win a world boxing title, *2524*

Hamilton

British Empire Games (later the British Commonwealth Games), *4369*

Kanata

Ottawa Senators regular season hockey game played at the Palladium, *4223*

Ottawa

Canadian ice hockey league, *4043*

Figure skater from Canada or from the Americas to win the women's singles title at the Olympic Winter Games, *3032*

Figure skater to perform a triple axel in competition, *3079*

Figure skater to win 10 consecutive pairs titles in the world championships, *3080*

Ice hockey team to win the Stanley Cup three times in a row, *4055*

Ottawa Senators regular season hockey game played at the Ottawa Civic Center, *4205*

Women's world championships in ice hockey, *4200*

Toronto

Football game on record in Canada, *3520*

CANADA—Ontario—Toronto—*continued*

Golfer to win more than 10 straight titles, and to win 18 titles overall during a single year, on the Professional Golfers' Association (PGA) Tour, *3714*

Golfer to win two of golf's major tournaments in her rookie year on the Ladies Professional Golf Association (LPGA) Tour, *3844*

Grey Cup awarded to the rugby football champion in Canada, *4966*

National Hockey League All-Star Game, *4111*

National Hockey League Amateur Draft, *4145*

National team to win three consecutive ice hockey titles at the Olympic Winter Games, *4096*

Olympics for the Physically Disabled to include athletes other than those with spinal injuries, *2753*

Toronto Blue Jays regular season baseball game played at Exhibition Stadium, *1745*

Toronto Blue Jays regular season baseball game played at the Skydome, *1807*

Toronto Maple Leafs regular season hockey game played at Air Canada Centre, *4234*

Toronto Maple Leafs regular season hockey game played at Maple Leaf Gardens, *4104*

Toronto Raptors regular season basketball game played at the Air Canada Centre, *2419*

Vancouver Grizzlies regular season basketball game played at Bear Country at General Motors Place, *2362*

World championships for men's lacrosse, *4424*

Quebec

Montreal

470-class sailing event held at the Olympic Games, *5235*

African-American hurdler to win the men's 400-meter title in the Olympic Games, *4345*

Athlete from South Korea to win a gold medal in the Olympic Games, *4746*

Athlete from Trinidad and Tobago to win an Olympic gold medal, *4745*

Canada Cup golf tournament, *3732*

Canadian ice hockey league, *4043*

Collegiate sporting event at which admission was charged, *5739*

Cyclist to win two consecutive titles in the men's 4000-meter team pursuit in the Olympic Games, *2704*

Decathlete to score more than 8500 points in the men's decathlon, *2744*

Diver to win three consecutive men's platform diving titles in the Olympic Games, *2811*

Du Maurier Classic, *3823*

Equestrians from the United States to win the three-day event individual competition, and team competition, in the Olympic Games, *2881*

Father and son to both win gold medals in track and field in the Olympic Games, *6213*

Figure skaters to win four pairs titles in the world championships, *3011*

Golf club in Canada, *3587*

Ice hockey game, *4041*

Ice hockey team to win the Stanley Cup, *4045*

Ice hockey team to win the Stanley Cup three times, *4052*

Ice hockey team to win the Stanley Cup twice in a row, *4046*

International ice hockey tournament, *4044*

Javelin-thrower to break the 310-foot barrier, *4403*

Lacrosse organization, *4416*

Major league baseball team situated in Canada, *1705*

Men's Canadian pairs 500-meter canoeing event held in the Olympic Games, *2618*

Men's Canadian singles 500-meter canoeing event held in the Olympic Games, *2616*

Men's pairs 500-meter kayaking event held in the Olympic Games, *2617*

Men's quadruple sculls rowing event held in the Olympic Games, *4948*

Men's singles 500-meter kayak event held in the Olympic Games, *2619*

Montreal Canadiens regular season hockey game played at the Molson Center (La Centre Molson), *4224*

Montreal Expos regular season baseball game played at Jarry Park, *1710*

Montreal Expos regular season baseball game played at Olympic Stadium, *1746*

National Hockey League Amateur Draft, *4145*

National Team to sweep the medals in the men's 200-meter freestyle in the Olympic Games, *5921*

Olympic Games held in Canada, *4744*

Olympic men's 1500-meter freestyle event in which the medalists all had times under 16 minutes, *5922*

Olympic men's 400-meter freestyle event at which all the medalists had times under four minutes, *5923*

Rower to win gold medals in both the women's single and double sculls events in the Olympic Games, *4953*

Runner from the Caribbean to win the men's 200-meter title at the Olympic Games, *5106*

Swimmer to break the two-minute barrier in the men's 200-meter backstroke event, *5924*

Swimmer to race the men's 100-meter freestyle in under 50 seconds, *5926*

Tornado-class sailing event held in the Olympic Games, *5236*

Weightlifter to compete in five Olympic Games, *6347*

Woman athlete to be disqualified from the Olympic Games because of a positive drug test, *4743*

Woman swimmer to win four gold medals at a single Olympic Games, *5927*

Woman swimmer to win Olympic medals 12 years apart, *5956*

Woman to win a medal in shooting at the Olympic Games, *5313*

Women's 400-meter individual medley event in the Olympic Games in which all the medalists had times under five minutes, *5925*

Women's basketball event held in the Olympic Games, *2125*

Women's double sculls event held in the Olympic Games, *4946*

Women's eight-oared shell with coxswain event held in the Olympic Games, *4949*

Women's single sculls event held in the Olympic Games, *4947*

Women's team handball event held in the Olympic Games, *4007*

Wrestler to win two consecutive heavyweight freestyle wrestling titles in the Olympic Games, *6403*

Quebec

Curling games in the Americas, *2672*

Quebec Nordiques regular season hockey game played at the Colisée de Québec, *4163*

Woman to play in a professional hockey game, *4204*

Sainte Foy

Speed skater to win six women's titles in the world speed skating sprint championships, *5705*

Yukon Territory

Whitehorse

Yukon Quest sled dog race, *5513*

CANARY ISLANDS

Las Palmas

Woman to sail around the world alone, *5237*

CHINA

Athlete from China to win a gold medal in the Olympic Games, *4756*

Athletes from China and Taiwan to share the medal platform in the Olympic Games, *4757*

Diver to hold the women's world titles in both the one- and three-meter springboard diving at the same time, *2820*

Diver to win two consecutive women's highboard platform diving titles at the world championships, *2823*

Far Eastern Games, *4367*

Gymnasts from China to win the men's team title at the Olympic Games, *3980*

Men's doubles table tennis event held in the Olympic Games, *5994*

Men's synchronized springboard diving event held in the Olympic Games, *2828*

Olympic Winter Games to be boycotted by a member country, *4749*

Runner to race the women's 10,000 meters in under 30 minutes, *5169*

Swimmer to race the women's 50-meter freestyle in under 25 seconds, *5950*

Table tennis player to win both singles and doubles titles in the Olympic Games, *6000*

Triple-jumper to hold the officially accepted world record in the women's event, *6261*

Women's 100-meter butterfly event in the Olympic Games in which all the medalists had times under one minute, *5953*

Women's 10,000-meter walk held in the Olympic Games, *6296*

Women's 5000-meter race held in the Olympic Games, *5181*

Women's heavyweight judo event held in the Olympic Games, *4553*

Women's one-meter springboard diving event held at the world championships, *2822*

Women's singles event to be included in the world cup in table tennis, *6001*

Women's singles table tennis event held in the Olympic Games, *5997*

Women's small-bore rifle (three positions) individual shooting event held in the Olympic Games, *5319*

Women's soccer event held in the Olympic Games, *5569*

Women's synchronized platform diving event held in the Olympic Games, *2829*

Women's World Cup in soccer (international football), *5566*

World cup/grand prix competition in badminton, *1173*

World cup in table tennis, *5993*

World cup in weightlifting to include women, *6351*

World team cup in table tennis, *5999*

Beijing (earlier Peking)

International and transcontinental automobile race, *1050*

Runner to race the women's 10,000 meters in under 30 minutes, *5169*

Hong Kong

Happy Valley horse race track, *4272*

CHINA—*continued*

Macau

Happy Valley horse race track, *4272*

Nanjing

Pole-vaulter to hold the officially accepted world record in the women's event, *4850*

Peking (now Beijing)

International and transcontinental automobile race, *1050*

COLOMBIA

Cali

Diver to win two, and then three, consecutive men's springboard diving titles in the world championships, *2809*

Diver to win two consecutive men's highboard platform diving titles at the world championships, *2810*

Swimmer to hold both the women's 200- and 400-meter freestyle world titles at the same time, *5910*

Swimmer to hold the world titles in both the men's 200- and 400-meter individual medleys at the same time, *5911*

Swimmer to hold world titles in both the men's 100- and 200-meter breaststroke at the same time, *5912*

Swimmer to hold world titles in the men's 200-, 400-, and 1500-meter freestyle at the same time, *5913*

Swimmer to win two consecutive men's 100-meter backstroke titles in the world championships, *5914*

Swimmer to win two consecutive men's 200-meter breaststroke titles in the world championships, *5915*

Swimmer to win two consecutive men's 400-meter individual medley titles at the world championships, *5916*

Swimmer to win two consecutive women's 100-meter backstroke world titles, *5917*

Swimmer to win two consecutive women's 100-meter butterfly world titles, *5918*

Swimmer to win two consecutive women's 100-meter freestyle world titles, *5919*

Swimmer to win two consecutive women's 200-meter butterfly world titles, *5920*

CONGO

All-African Games, *4376*

COSTA RICA

Athlete from Costa Rica to win a gold medal in the Olympic Games, *4790*

CUBA

Athlete from Cuba to win a gold medal in the Olympic Games, *4617*

Baseball event held in the Olympic Games, *1820*

Boxer to win two, and then three, consecutive heavyweight titles, and three boxing titles in a single class, in the Olympic Games, *2575*

High-jumper to reach, and then break, the 8-foot barrier, *4032*

Men's amateurs and masters épée fencing competition held in the Olympic Games, *2904*

Men's individual épée fencing competition held in the Olympic Games, *2902*

Men's team foil fencing competition held in the Olympic Games, *2906*

Runner to win two consecutive titles in the women's 800-meter event in the World Championships in Athletics, *5185*

Women's middleweight judo event held in the Olympic Games, *4556*

World amateur boxing championships, *2571*

World championships for freestyle skiing, *5451*

CZECH REPUBLIC

Adler

Hammer-thrower to hold the officially accepted world record in the women's event, *3997*

CZECHOSLOVAKIA

Canoe racer to win two consecutive men's Canadian singles 1000-meter titles in the Olympic Games, *2605*

Canoer to win two men's Canadian pairs 1000-meter titles in the Olympic Games, *2602*

Equestrian to win the individual jumping event in the Olympic Games without a single fault, *2856*

Figure skater from Czechoslovakia to win the men's singles title at the Olympic Winter Games, *3070*

Figure skater from Czechoslovakia to win the men's singles title at the world championships, *3067*

Figure skater from Czechoslovakia to win the women's singles title in the world championships, *3037*

Figure skater to perform a quadruple jump in the Olympic Games, *3101*

Floor exercise competition held at the world championships in gymnastics, *3919*

Gymnast to win three consecutive men's horizontal bar titles in the world championships, *3920*

Gymnast to win two consecutive men's all-around titles in the world championships, *3923*

Gymnast to win two consecutive women's all-around titles in the world championships, *3931*

Gymnast to win two consecutive women's horse vault titles in the world championships, *3953*

Gymnast to win two consecutive women's side horse vault titles in the Olympic Games, *3954*

Iran Cup, *5990*

Javelin-thrower to break the 310- and 320-foot barriers with the new javelin, *4413*

Men's 18-kilometer cross-country event held in the world championships of Nordic skiing, *5371*

Men's 4000-meter individual pursuit cycling event held in the Olympic Games, *2702*

Men's 50-kilometer cross-country event held in the world championships of Nordic skiing, *5372*

Men's Canadian pairs 1000-meter canoeing event held in the Olympic Games, *2596*

Men's ski jumping (normal hill) event held in the world championships of Nordic skiing, *5373*

Nordic combined event held in the world championships of Nordic skiing, *5374*

Runner to race the men's 10,000 meters in under 29:00 minutes, *5061*

Runner to race the women's 400 meters in under 48 seconds, *5137*

Runner to win the women's 400- and 800-meter events in the World Championships in Athletics, *5136*

Runner to win two consecutive men's 10,000-meter titles in the Olympic Games, *5056*

Soccer (international football) team from Italy to win the world cup, *5554*

Tennis player to win the men's singles title in the Olympic Games after tennis competition resumed in 1988, *6178*

Women's 400-meter race in which the top three runners had times of under 50 seconds, *5115*

World championships in gymnastics to award women's titles in specific events, *3932*

World championships in gymnastics to include women, *3930*

World championships in orienteering to include short events, *4812*

World Sculls Cup series of rowing races, *4956*

Ostrava

Runner to race the women's 100 meters in under 11.0 seconds, *5097*

Prague

Runner to race the women's 400 meters in under 49 seconds, *5109*

Stara Boleslav

Runner to complete the 1500-meter race in under 3:40 minutes, *5067*

Troppau

Figure skater from Hungary to win the women's singles title in the world championships, *2972*

Turnov

Discus-thrower to break the 210-foot barrier, *2774*

DENMARK

All-around wrestling title awarded in the Olympic Games, *6369*

Athlete to compete in eight Olympic Games, *4733*

Athlete to compete in seven Olympic Games, *4687*

Athletes from Sweden to win a gold medal in the Olympic Games, *4622*

Athletes to compete in the Olympic Games over a period of 40 years, *4688*

Canoe marathon world championships, *2624*

Decathlon championship on record, *2736*

Men's 1000-meter time trial cycling event held in the Olympic Games, *2696*

Men's lightweight four-oared shells without coxswain rowing event held in the Olympic Games, *4960*

Military rifle individual shooting event held in the Olympic Games, *5279*

Pentathlete to win three, and then four, titles in the women's world championships, *4834*

Sailor to win the men's Finn-class event two, three, and four times in the Olympic Games, *5219*

Tug-of-war event held in the Olympic Games, *6267*

Woman equestrian to win an individual dressage medal in the Olympic Games, *2864*

Women's 500-meter singles kayaking event held in the Olympic Games, *2603*

Women's individual foil fencing competition held in the Olympic Games, *2920*

World championships in badminton, *1171*

World cup in dressage, *2889*

DJIBOUTI

World Cup Marathon, *4514*

ECUADOR

Athlete from Ecuador to win a gold medal in the Olympic Games, *4792*

Guayaquil

Diver to hold the men's world titles in both springboard diving and highboard platform diving at the same time, *2815*
Diver to win three consecutive men's highboard platform diving titles in the world championships, *2816*
Swimmer to hold world titles in both the men's 200-meter freestyle and butterfly at the same time, and to hold both twice consecutively, *5936*
Swimmer to win two consecutive men's 1500-meter freestyle titles at the world championships, *5937*
Swimmer to win two consecutive men's 400-meter freestyle titles at the world championships, *5938*

EGYPT

Depictions of wrestling matches, *6354*
Evidence of organized running events, *4971*
Olympic Games to be boycotted by member countries, *4703*
United States baseball team to tour the world, and to visit Australia, *1294*
World championships in Greco-Roman wrestling held on a regular basis, *6388*

ESTONIA

Athlete from Estonia to win a gold medal in the Olympic Games, *4651*
Bantamweight Greco-Roman wrestling event held in the Olympic Games, *6380*
Cyclist to win two consecutive women's titles in the 1000-meter match sprint in the Olympic Games, *2718*
Decathlete to hold the officially accepted world record in the men's decathlon, *2739*
Lightweight weightlifting event held in the Olympic Games, *6329*
World championships in weightlifting, *6332*
Wrestler to win heavyweight titles in both freestyle and Greco-Roman wrestling in the Olympic Games, *6385*

ETHIOPIA

Black African runner to win the men's marathon title at the Olympic Games, and to hold the world record in the event, *4487*
Black African woman to win an Olympic medal, *4780*

Runner from Africa, and from Ethiopia, to win the women's marathon at the Olympic Games, *4526*
Runner from Africa to win the women's 10,000-meter title, and the first Black African woman to win a medal, at the Olympic Games, *5159*
Runner from Africa to win the women's 10,000-meter title, and the first Black African woman to win a medal, at the Olympic Games, *5159*
Runner from Africa to win the women's title in the Boston Marathon, *4527*
Runner from Africa to win the women's title in the Boston Marathon, *4527*
Runner to race the men's 5000 meters in under 12:55 minutes, *5179*
Runner to race the men's marathon in under 2:7 hours, *4517*
Runner to win two consecutive marathon titles in the Olympic Games, *4489*
Runner to win two, three, and then four consecutive titles in the men's 10,000-meter event in the World Championships in Athletics, *5174*

FIJI

Golfer to win more than $2.5 million in official prize money in a single season, *3889*

FINLAND

Athlete from Finland to win an official gold medal in the Olympic Games, *4641*
Athlete to win 12 medals in the Olympic Games, *4669*
Athlete to win five gold medals in a single Olympic Games, *4658*
Athlete to win five individual gold medals, and seven medals overall, in the Olympic Winter Games, *4665*
Athlete to win six medals overall in a single Olympic Games, *4652*
Australian Grand Prix automobile race, *1132*
Javelin-thrower to break the 210-foot barrier, *4385*
Javelin-thrower to win two consecutive men's titles in the Olympic Games, *4386*
Light heavyweight Greco-Roman wrestling event held in the Olympic Games, *6373*
Men's 10,000-meter speed skating event held in the Olympic Winter Games, *5641*
Men's 15-kilometer cross-country event held in the world championships of Nordic skiing, *5398*
Men's 1500-meter speed skating event held at the Olympic Winter Games, *5642*
Men's 30-kilometer cross-country event held in the world championships of Nordic skiing, *5375*

Men's 30-kilometer Nordic (cross-country) ski event held at the Olympic Winter Games, *5402*

Men's 4 x 10-kilometer relay Nordic (cross-country) event held in the Olympic Winter Games, *5384*

Men's 5000- and 10,000-meter events held in the Olympic Games, *5008*

Men's 5000-meter speed skating event held at the Olympic Winter Games, *5640*

Men's discus throw event for both hands held in the Olympic Games, *2761*

Men's four races combined speed skating title offered at the Olympic Winter Games, *5643*

Men's Greek-style discus throw event held in the Olympic Games, *2756*

Men's individual 70-meter ski jump event held at the Olympic Winter Games, *5410*

Men's individual cross-country event held in the Olympic Games, *5006*

Men's javelin event for both hands held in the Olympic Games, *4383*

Men's team ski-jumping event held in the Olympic Winter Games, *5457*

Middleweight Greco-Roman wrestling event held in the Olympic Games, *6371*

National team to sweep the medals in the women's 10-kilometer Nordic (cross-country) skiing event in the Olympic Winter Games, *5395*

Open 49er-class sailing event held in the Olympic Games, *5258*

Rower to win three consecutive men's single sculls rowing titles in the Olympic Games, *4941*

Runner to hold the world record in both the men's 5000- and 10,000-meter events, *5013*

Runner to win two consecutive men's 5000- and 10,000-meter titles at the Olympic Games, *5107*

Runner to win two consecutive titles in the men's individual cross-country in the Olympic Games, *5015*

Ski orienteering world championships, *4809*

Ski orienteering world championships to include sprint competitions, *4810*

Skier to win two individual ski-jumping gold medals in the same Olympic Winter Games, *5460*

Skier to win two medals in the men's 90-meter team ski-jumping event in the Olympic Winter Games, *5475*

Speed skater to skate the 1000 meters in under 1:30 minutes, *5646*

Speed skater to win two consecutive men's 1500-meter speed skating titles at the Olympic Winter Games, *5645*

Speed skaters to become world champions in speed skating sprints, *5686*

Women's 15-kilometer cross-country event held in the world championships of Nordic skiing, *5462*

Women's 3 x 5-kilometer relay Nordic (cross-country) skiing event held at the Olympic Winter Games, *5401*

Women's individual 10-kilometer Nordic (cross-country) event held at the Olympic Winter Games, *5396*

Women's individual 20-kilometer Nordic (cross-country) event held at the Olympic Winter Games, *5445*

World championships in Greco-Roman wrestling held on a regular basis, *6388*

World Cross-Country Championships, *5096*

Wrestler to win two consecutive lightweight Greco-Roman titles in the Olympic Games, *6376*

Wrestler to win two consecutive middleweight Greco-Roman titles in the Olympic Games, *6384*

Wrestling event in the Olympic Games to have no gold-medalist, *6375*

Helsinki

5.5-meter-class sailing event in the Olympic Games, *5218*

African-American boxers to win gold medals in the Olympic Games, *2557*

African-American hurdler to win the men's 110-meter titles in the Olympic Games, *4336*

African-American women to win gold medals in a track relay event in the Olympic Games, *5058*

Athlete from Romania to win a gold medal in the Olympic Games, *4702*

Canoe racer to win two, and then three, consecutive titles in the men's singles 1000-meter kayak event in the Olympic Games, *2607*

Canoe racer to win two consecutive men's Canadian singles 1000-meter titles in the Olympic Games, *2605*

Canoe racers to win both the men's 1000- and 10,000-meter pairs kayak events in the Olympic Games, *2606*

Decathlete to hold the officially accepted world record in the men's decathlon, *2739*

Decathlete to win two consecutive titles in the men's decathlon in the Olympic Games, *2742*

Discus-thrower to break the 210-foot barrier in the women's event, *2778*

Diver to win two consecutive men's platform diving titles in the Olympic Games, *2803*

Fencer to win two, three, and four men's team épée titles in the Olympic Games, *2931*

Figure skaters to perform a quadruple twist lift in competition, *3078*

FINLAND—Helsinki—*continued*

Figure skaters to win two, and then three, consecutive pairs titles in the world championships, *3018*

Hammer-thrower to break the 60-meter barrier, *3987*

Hurdler to win the men's 110-meter event in the World Championships in Athletics, *4347*

Hurdler to win the men's 400-meter hurdles held in the World Championships in Athletics, *4348*

Individual and team dressage equestrian competitions open to women, and to men other than commissioned military officers, in the Olympic Games, *2862*

International hockey game between Sweden and Finland, *4094*

Javelin-thrower from the United States to win the men's event in the Olympic Games, *4393*

Light middleweight boxing event held in the Olympic Games, *2558*

Light welterweight boxing event, and the first match between a Soviet and a United States boxer, in the Olympic Games, *2559*

Men's modern pentathlon team event held in the Olympic Games, *4823*

Middle heavyweight weightlifting event held in the Olympic Games, *6338*

Olympic Games held in Finland, *4701*

Olympic Games in which athletes from the Soviet Union participated, *4698*

Olympic men's 1500-meter freestyle event in which the medalists all had times under 19 minutes, *5832*

Pentathlete from a non-military background to win the men's modern pentathlon in the Olympic Games, *4824*

Runner from Australia to win the women's 100- and 200-meter titles in the Olympic Games, *5059*

Runner from the United States to win the men's 3000-meter steeplechase title in the Olympic Games, *5057*

Runner to qualify for the finals men's of the 100-, 200-, and 400-meter races in the Olympic Games, *5054*

Runner to race the men's 10,000 meters in under 30:00 minutes, *5045*

Runner to race the men's 5000-meter steeplechase in under 8:20 minutes, *5098*

Runner to race the men's 5000 meters in under 14:10 minutes, *5043*

Runner to race the men's 5000 meters in under 14:28.0 minutes, *5028*

Runner to race the women's 400 meters in under 48 seconds, *5137*

Runner to win the men's 100-meter race held in the World Championships in Athletics, *5125*

Runner to win the men's 10,000-meter race held in the World Championships in Athletics, *5126*

Runner to win the men's 1500-meter race held in the World Championships in Athletics, *5127*

Runner to win the men's 200-meter race held in the World Championships in Athletics, *5128*

Runner to win the men's 3000-meter steeplechase held in the World Championships in Athletics, *5129*

Runner to win the men's 400-meter race held in the World Championships in Athletics, *5130*

Runner to win the men's 5000-meter race held in the World Championships in Athletics, *5131*

Runner to win the men's 800-meter race held in the World Championships in Athletics, *5132*

Runner to win the men's marathon in the World Championships in Athletics, *4508*

Runner to win the women's 100-meter race in the World Championships in Athletics, *5133*

Runner to win the women's 1500-meter race in the World Championships in Athletics, *5134*

Runner to win the women's 200-meter title in the World Championships in Athletics, *5135*

Runner to win the women's 400- and 800-meter events in the World Championships in Athletics, *5136*

Runner to win two consecutive men's 10,000-meter titles in the Olympic Games, *5056*

Running deer (single and double shot) individual shooting event held in the Olympic Games, *5308*

Sailor to win the men's Finn-class event two, three, and four times in the Olympic Games, *5219*

Separate world championships for track and field events, *6222*

Shooter to win two consecutive men's rapid-fire pistol titles in the Olympic Games, *5307*

Shot-putter to break the 50-foot barrier in the women's event, *5338*

Small-bore rifle (three positions) individual shooting event held in the Olympic Games, *5309*

Triple-jumper of Black African ancestry to win the men's title in the Olympic Games, *6255*

Weightlifter from the United States to win the lightweight weightlifting title in the Olympic Games, *6337*

Weightlifter to win two consecutive titles in the unlimited weight (super heavyweight) competition in the Olympic Games, *6339*

Woman equestrian to win a team dressage medal in the Olympic Games, *2863*

Woman equestrian to win an individual dressage medal in the Olympic Games, *2864*

Woman speed skater to skate the 1500 meters in under 3 minutes, *5653*

Women's all-around gymnastics competition held in the Olympic Games, *3934*

Women's balance beam gymnastics competition held in the Olympic Games, *3935*

Women's floor exercises gymnastics competition held in the Olympic Games, *3936*

Women's side horse vault gymnastics competition held in the Olympic Games, *3937*

Women's uneven (asymmetrical) bars gymnastics competition held in the Olympic Games, *3938*

World championships in freestyle wrestling, *6389*

World championships in Greco-Roman wrestling regarded as official, *6379*

Kuhmoinen

Javelin-thrower to break the 270-foot barrier, *4396*

Turku

Javelin-thrower to break the 240- and 250-foot barriers, *4391*

Viipuri

Javelin-thrower to break the 220-foot barrier, *4387*

FRANCE

Air rifle shooting individual event held in the Olympic Games, *5320*

Archery events held in the Olympic Games, *1025*

Athlete from France to win a gold medal in the Olympic Games, *4609*

Automobile racer to have more than 50 wins on the Formula One Grand Prix circuit, *1143*

Automobile racer to win the Brazilian Grand Prix three, four, five, and six times, *1130*

Automobile racer to win three Austrian Grand Prix races, *1134*

Automobile racer to win two Australian Grand Prix races, *1137*

Boxing match to have a $1 million gate, and the first heavyweight bout to be broadcast on radio, *2541*

Canoe slalom world championships, *2604*

Cyclist from the United States to win the Tour de France, *2712*

Cyclist to win the Tour de France five consecutive times, *2721*

Cyclist to win the Tour de France five times, and four times consecutively, *2701*

Cyclist to win the Tour de France three consecutive times, *2699*

Cyclist to win the Tour de France three times, *2694*

Cyclist to win the Tour de France twice consecutively, *2691*

Cyclist to win two, and then three, cycling gold medals in the Olympic Games, *2688*

Cyclist to win two consecutive men's titles in the 1000-meter match sprint in the Olympic Games, *2703*

Cyclo-cross races, *2695*

Diver to win both the men's springboard and platform diving titles in the same Olympic Games, *2799*

Documented horse race, *4249*

Dueling pistol shooting events held in the Olympic Games, *5282*

Equestrian to win two consecutive titles in team dressage in the Olympic Games, *2858*

Fencer to win both the men's individual sabre and épée titles in the Olympic Games, *2912*

Fencer to win men's individual and team épée titles in the same Olympic Games, *2908*

Fencer to win three, and then four, men's foil titles in the world championships, *2932*

Fencer to win three men's épée titles in the world championships, *2927*

Fencer to win two consecutive men's épée titles in the world championships, *2924*

Fencer to win two consecutive men's individual foil titles in the Olympic Games, *2933*

Fencer to win two men's team foil titles in the Olympic Games, *2926*

Figure skaters for France to win the ice dancing title in the world championships, *3096*

Figure skaters from France to win the pairs title in the Olympic Winter Games, *3008*

Figure skaters from France to win the pairs title in the world championships, *3005*

Figure skaters to win four pairs titles in the world championships, *3011*

Figure skaters to win two consecutive pairs titles at the Olympic Winter Games, *3013*

French national tennis championships, *6029*

French national tennis championships open to those who were not citizens or residents of France, *6074*

Giant slalom and snowboard cross events held in the snowboarding world championships, *5523*

Golfer from outside Great Britain to win the British Open, *3645*

Gymnast to win two consecutive men's horse vault titles in the world championships, *3914*

Gymnast to win two consecutive men's parallel bar titles in the world championships, *3915*

Gymnast to win two men's horizontal bar titles in the world championships, *3916*

FRANCE—*continued*

Individual dressage equestrian competition in the Olympic Games in which women riders swept the top medals, *2890*

International balloon race, *1182*

International championships in tennis, *6004*

International governing body for tennis, *6055*

International sailing championships for women, *5233*

International soccer (international football) match played by women, *5550*

Introduction of *chole* to the British Isles, *2630*

Jai alai game in the United States, *4380*

Light heavyweight weightlifting event held in the Olympic Games, *6331*

Major international ice hockey organization, *4057*

Men's 1000-meter match sprint cycling race held in the Olympic Games, *2685*

Men's downhill skiing event held at the Olympic Winter Games, *5386*

Men's extra-lightweight judo event held in the Olympic Games, *4545*

Men's individual foil fencing competition held in the Olympic Games, *2897*

Men's Keirin cycling event held in the Olympic Games, *2731*

Men's masters épée fencing competition held in the Olympic Games, *2903*

Men's Olympic sprint cycling event held in the Olympic Games, *2729*

Men's super giant slalom event held at the Olympic Winter Games, *5454*

Men's team épée fencing competition held in the Olympic Games, *2910*

Men's underwater swimming race held in the Olympic Games, *5791*

Middleweight weightlifting event held in the Olympic Games, *6330*

Monte Carlo Rally, *1053*

Motorboat-racing event held in the Olympic Games, *4565*

Olympic Games at which Beethoven's "Ode to Joy" was sung, *4603*

People to fly in a balloon, *1176*

Prix du Jockey Club horse race, *4270*

Proposal to revive the Olympic Games in modern times, *4602*

Runner from the Caribbean to win the women's 400-meter title in the Olympic Games, *5158*

Runner to win two titles in the women's 400-meter event in the World Championships in Athletics, *5177*

Sailor in the Single-Handed Transatlantic Race (STAR) to cross the Atlantic in under 11 days, *5248*

Sailor to complete a solo circumnavigation of the world in under 130 days, *5246*

Sailor to complete a solo circumnavigation of the world in under 170 days, *5231*

Sailor to win the Single-Handed Transatlantic Race (STAR) twice, *5234*

Sailor to win the Single-Handed Transatlantic Race (STAR) twice consecutively, *5255*

Sailor to win two consecutive Tornado-class sailing titles in the Olympic Games, *5251*

Schneider Cup international seaplane (hydro-aeroplane) race, *1004*

Skier to win four women's super giant slalom world cup titles, *5468*

Snowboarding world championships, *5521*

Swimmer to swim the English Channel in both directions, *5827*

Tennis player to win a French national men's singles championship after the event became international, *6076*

Tennis player to win five consecutive Wimbledon women's singles championships, *6065*

Tennis player to win four French national men's singles championships after the event became international, *6090*

Tennis player to win six French national women's doubles championships after the event became international, and four times consecutively, *6101*

Tennis player to win the French national women's singles championship after the event became international, *6077*

Tennis player to win three, four, and then five French national men's doubles championships after the event became international, *6089*

Tennis player to win three French national men's singles championships after the event became international, *6086*

Tennis player to win three gold medals in tennis in the same Olympic Games, *6048*

Tennis players to win a French national mixed doubles championship after the event became international, *6078*

Tennis players to win five consecutive Wimbledon women's doubles championships, *6068*

Tennis players to win the French national men's doubles championship after the event became international, *6079*

Tennis players to win the French national women's doubles championship after the event became international, *6080*

Tennis star to turn professional, *6081*

Tour de France cycling race, *2689*

United States baseball team to tour the world, and to visit Australia, *1294*

Vendée Globe round-the-world challenge race, *5250*

Water-skier to win five consecutive men's overall titles at the world championships, *6322*

Weightlifter to win two consecutive light heavyweight titles in the Olympic Games, *6333*

Woman to fly in a hot-air balloon, *1177*

Woman to swim the English Channel from England to France, and to swim it in both directions, *5831*

Woman to win an Olympic gold medal in sailing, *5210*

Women's 500-meter time trial cycling event held in the Olympic Games, *2728*

Women's extra-lightweight judo event held in the Olympic Games, *4559*

Women's giant slalom snow-boarding event held at the Olympic Winter Games, *5525*

Women's half-middleweight judo event held in the Olympic Games, *4557*

Women's individual and team épée competitions held in the Olympic Games, *2944*

Women's points race cycling event held in the Olympic Games, *2722*

Women's shot put event held in the Olympic Games, *5336*

Women's World Amateur Team Championship, *3777*

World championships for freestyle skiing, *5451*

World championships in cyclo-cross, *2698*

World championships in fencing, *2917*

World championships in gymnastics, *3910*

World championships in rowing, *4940*

World championships in shooting, *5274*

World championships in target archery, *1030*

World cup in rugby, *4969*

World cup series of competitions in Alpine skiing, *5416*

World Endurance Championship in motorcycle racing, *4592*

World long-distance triathlon championships, *6245*

World sky diving championships, *5504*

Written reference to billiards, *2443*

Written reference to *chole*, *2629*

Written reference to tennis, *6002*

Albertville

Athlete from the Southern Hemisphere to win a gold medal in the Olympic Winter Games, *4774*

Athlete to win ten medals in the Olympic Winter Games, *4772*

Bobsledders to win two consecutive two-man bobsled titles at the Olympic Winter Games, *2477*

Female athlete from the United States to win three gold medals in the Olympic Winter Games, *4770*

Female athlete to win gold medals in two different sports in the Olympic Winter Games, *4771*

Figure skater from Ukraine to win the men's singles title at the Olympic Winter Games, *3100*

Figure skater to perform a quadruple jump in the Olympic Games, *3101*

Japanese-American figure skater to win the women's singles title at the Olympic Winter Games, *3102*

Male figure skater to win the pairs title at the Olympic Winter Games with two different partners, *3115*

Men's 10-kilometer Nordic (cross-country) skiing event held at the Olympic Winter Games, *5472*

Men's 1000-meter short track speed skating event held in the Olympic Winter Games, *5714*

Men's 5000-meter relay short track speed skating event held at the Olympic Winter Games, *5716*

Men's combined pursuit Nordic (cross-country) skiing event held at the Olympic Winter Games, *5476*

Men's moguls freestyle skiing event at the Olympic Winter Games, *5473*

National team to sweep the medals in the men's 30-kilometer Nordic (cross-country) skiing event at the Olympic Winter Games, *5471*

National team to sweep the medals in the women's 5000-meter speed-skating event at the Olympic Winter Games, *5713*

Skier to win both the women's slalom and the women's Alpine combination in the same Olympic Winter Games, and the first from Austria to win the Olympic women's slalom title, *5480*

Skier to win four medals in the same Nordic skiing event in the Olympic Winter Games, *5478*

Skier to win two consecutive individual titles in an Alpine event in the Olympic Winter Games, *5479*

Skier to win two medals in the men's 90-meter team ski-jumping event in the Olympic Winter Games, *5475*

Speed skater from the United States to win the women's 1000-meter title at the Olympic Winter Games, *5712*

Speed skater to win two consecutive women's 1000-meter speed skating titles at the Olympic Winter Games, *5723*

Speed skater to win two consecutive women's 500-meter titles in the Olympic Winter Games, *5711*

Women's 15-kilometer biathlon competition held in the Olympic Winter Games, *2441*

Women's 30-kilometer Nordic (cross-country) skiing event held at the Olympic Winter Games, *5469*

Women's 3000-meter short track relay speed skating event held at the Olympic Winter Games, *5715*

FRANCE—Albertville—*continued*

Women's 4 x 7.5-kilometer biathlon relay competition held in the Olympic Winter Games, *2440*

Women's 500-meter short track speed skating event held at the Olympic Winter Games, *5717*

Women's 7.5-kilometer biathlon competition held in the Olympic Winter Games, *2439*

Women's combined pursuit Nordic (cross-country) skiing event in the Olympic Winter Games, *5477*

Women's individual 15-kilometer Nordic (cross-country) skiing event at the Olympic Winter Games, *5470*

Women's moguls freestyle skiing event held at the Olympic Winter Games, *5474*

Avignon

World championships in the triathlon, *6240*

Bordeaux

Organized long-distance automobile race, *1045*

Calais

Flyers to cross the English Channel in a balloon, *1178*

Cap Gris-Nez

Person to swim the English Channel, *5783*
Woman to swim the English Channel, *5820*

Chamonix

Athlete to receive an Olympic medal 50 years after the competition, *4741*

Athlete to win a gold medal at the Olympic Winter Games, *4654*

Bobsled event held at the Olympic Winter Games, *2467*

Figure skater from Austria to win the women's singles title at the Olympic Games, *3000*

Figure skater to win two, and then three, consecutive men's singles titles in the Olympic Games, *3001*

Figure skaters from Austria to win the pairs title at the Olympic Winter Games, *3002*

Men's 10,000-meter speed skating event held in the Olympic Winter Games, *5641*

Men's 1500-meter speed skating event held at the Olympic Winter Games, *5642*

Men's 50-kilometer freestyle Nordic (cross-country) skiing event held at the Olympic Winter Games, *5365*

Men's 500-meter speed skating event held at the Olympic Winter Games, *5639*

Men's 5000-meter speed skating event held at the Olympic Winter Games, *5640*

Men's four races combined speed skating title offered at the Olympic Winter Games, *5643*

Men's individual 18-kilometer Nordic (cross-country) event held at the Olympic Winter Games, *5366*

Men's individual Nordic combined (cross-country and ski jump) event held in the Olympic Winter Games, *5367*

Men's individual ski jump event held at the Olympic Winter Games, *5368*

National team to sweep the medals in the men's combined individual Nordic (cross-country) skiing event at the Olympic Winter Games, *5369*

Olympic Winter Games, *4653*

Skier for the United States to win a ski-jumping medal at the Olympic Winter Games, *5370*

World Biathlon Championships to include women's competitions, *2436*

Grenoble

Men's 4 x 7.5-kilometer relay biathlon team event held at the Olympic Winter Games, *2432*

Men's giant slalom to have two runs on separate days, rather than a single run, at the Olympic Winter Games, *5417*

Olympic Games to institute sex tests for women athletes, *4723*

Juan Les Pins

World championships in water-skiing, *6316*

Le Havre

Athletes to row across the Atlantic Ocean, *4923*

Le Mans

Grand Prix automobile race, *1049*
Le Mans 24-hours sports car race, *1057*

Lyons

Woman to fly in a hot-air balloon, *1177*

Macon

Pole-vaulter to clear 19 feet, *4847*

Nantes

Motorcycle race on record, *4569*

Nice

Runner to complete the men's 1500-meter race in under 3:30 minutes, *5144*

FRANCE—Paris—*continued*

Men's 400-meter hurdles event held in the Olympic Games, *4324*

Men's 4000-meter freestyle swimming event held in the Olympic Games, *5792*

Men's 4000-meter steeplechase event held in the Olympic Games, *4979*

Men's 5000-meter team running event held in the Olympic Games, *4982*

Men's 60-meter running event held in the Olympic Games, *4976*

Men's all-around gymnastics competition held in the Olympic Games, *3909*

Men's amateurs and masters épée fencing competition held in the Olympic Games, *2904*

Men's eight-oared shell with coxswain rowing event held in the Olympic Games, *4925*

Men's four-oared shell with coxswain rowing event held in the Olympic Games, *4928*

Men's golf event in the Olympic Games, *3629*

Men's individual épée fencing competition held in the Olympic Games, *2902*

Men's masters épée fencing competition held in the Olympic Games, *2903*

Men's obstacle swimming race held in the Olympic Games, *5790*

Men's pair-oared shell with coxswain rowing event held in the Olympic Games, *4926*

Men's single sculls rowing event held in the Olympic Games, *4927*

Men's standing high jump event held in the Olympic Games, *4020*

Men's standing long jump event held in the Olympic Games, *4427*

Men's standing triple jump event held in the Olympic Games, *6250*

Men's steeplechase event held at the Olympic Games, *4977*

Military revolver and military rifle team shooting events held in the Olympic Games, *5280*

Military rifle individual shooting event held in the Olympic Games, *5279*

Mixed doubles tennis event held in the Olympic Games, *6039*

Motorcycle race on record, *4569*

Moving target individual shooting event held in the Olympic Games, *5277*

National team to sweep the medals in the men's 110-meter hurdles in the Olympic Games, *4323*

National team to sweep the medals in the men's individual foil fencing competition in the Olympic Games, *2900*

National team to sweep the medals in the men's singles tennis event in the Olympic Games, *6040*

National team to sweep the rapid-fire pistol individual shooting event in the Olympic Games, *5278*

National team to sweep the top spots in the men's shot put in the Olympic Games, *5330*

National team to sweep the top spots in the men's triple jump in the Olympic Games, *6251*

Olympic Games held in France, and outside Greece, *4626*

Olympic Games in which animals were deliberately killed, *4619*

Olympic Games in which more than 100 women participated, *4655*

Olympic Games to include women athletes, *4615*

Organized long-distance automobile race, *1045*

Pole-vaulter to clear 6 meters, *4848*

Polo event held in the Olympic Games, *4865*

Proposal to revive the Olympic Games in modern times, *4602*

Rowers to win two consecutive medals in the men's double sculls event in the Olympic Games, *4935*

Rugby event held in the Olympic Games, *4965*

Rugby players to win two Olympic gold medals in rugby, *4968*

Runner from Europe to win the men's 100-meter title in the Olympic Games, *5014*

Runner from Europe to win the men's 1500-meter title in the Olympic Games, *4978*

Runner from Europe to win the men's 800-meter title in the Olympic Games, *4980*

Runner to complete the men's 1500-meter race in under 3:50 minutes, *5025*

Runner to complete the men's mile race in under 4:10 minutes, *5026*

Runner to hold the officially accepted world record in the men's 10,000-meter event, *4999*

Runner to win two consecutive gold medals in the men's 4 x 100-meter relay in the Olympic Games, *5016*

Runner to win two consecutive titles in the men's individual cross-country in the Olympic Games, *5015*

Shooter to win two consecutive titles in the men's free rifle (three positions) individual shooting event, and in the free rifle team event, in the Olympic Games, *5302*

Shooter to win two consecutive titles in the running deer (double shot) individual shooting event in the Olympic Games, *5303*

Shot-putter to break the 22-meter barrier, *5349*

Soccer (international football) event held in the Olympic Games, *5544*

Soccer (international football) team to win the world cup twice in a row, *5555*

Swimmer to win two consecutive men's 100-meter backstroke titles in the Olympic Games, *5817*

Tennis player from the United States to win the women's singles tennis title in the Olympic Games, *6071*

Tennis players from the United States to win the mixed doubles event in the Olympic Games, *6072*

Tennis players from the United States to win the women's doubles title in the Olympic Games, *6070*

Trap (clay pigeon) shooting individual event held in the Olympic Games, *5276*

Tug-of-war event held in the Olympic Games, *6267*

Water polo event held in the Olympic Games, *6301*

Woman from the United States to win a gold medal in the Olympic Games, *4625*

Woman to win a gold medal in the Olympic Games, *4620*

Women's 100-meter backstroke event held in the Olympic Games, *5819*

Women's 200-meter breaststroke event held in the Olympic Games, *5818*

Women's golf event in the Olympic Games, *3630*

Women's individual foil fencing competition held in the Olympic Games, *2920*

Women's singles tennis event held in the Olympic Games, *6041*

World cup in rowing, *4962*

World indoor track and field (athletics) championships, *6224*

Wrestler to win gold medals in three different divisions in the Olympic Games, *6378*

Pau

Golf club on the European mainland, *3570*

Rheims

French Grand Prix automobile race to be part of the Formula One Grand Prix circuit, *1082*

International airplane races, *1001*

Saint Cloud

Reigning monarch to play in a national golf championship, *3710*

Saint-Denis

Soccer (international football) team from France to win the world cup, *5571*

Strasbourg

Figure skaters to perform simultaneous triple jumps in competition, *3082*

Talence

Decathlete to score 8,891 points in the men's decathlon, *2745*

GERMANY

Book on diving, *2786*

Cycling team to break the 4-minute mark in the men's 4000-meter team pursuit race in the Olympic Games, *2730*

Equestrian to win both an individual and a team medal in dressage in the Olympic Games, *2853*

Equestrian to win four titles in team jumping in the Olympic Games, *2880*

Equestrian to win three consecutive titles in team jumping in the Olympic Games, *2869*

Equestrians to win two consecutive titles in team jumping in the Olympic Games, *2867*

Fencer to win two, and then three, women's foil titles in the world championships, *2925*

Figure skater to win the men's singles title at the world championships, *2963*

Figure skater to win three and then four consecutive women's singles titles in the world championships, *2982*

Figure skaters to win four consecutive pairs titles in the world championships, *3025*

Figure skaters to win the pairs title at the Olympic Games, *2978*

Figure skaters to win the pairs title in the world championships, and the first to win two titles, *2973*

Freestyle dressage equestrian event held in the Olympic Games, *2894*

Gymnastics school to teach the modern sport, *3900*

Hammer-thrower to break the 190-foot barrier, *3986*

Hammer-thrower to break the 190-foot barrier, *3986*

Hurdler to hold the officially accepted world record in the women's 80-meter event, *4333*

Ice hockey team from Great Britain to win the gold medal at the Olympic Winter Games, *4115*

Individual dressage equestrian competition in the Olympic Games in which women riders swept the top medals, *2890*

International governing body for gliding (soaring) competitions, *3530*

International governing body for ice skating, *2962*

Marcel Corbillon Cup, *5988*

Men's 200-meter backstroke swimming event held in the Olympic Games, *5788*

Men's 440-yard (later 400-meter) breaststroke event held in the Olympic Games, *5796*

Men's 880-yard freestyle swimming event held in the Olympic Games, *5797*

Men's doubles tennis event held in the Olympic Games, *6035*

Men's horizontal bar gymnastics competitions held in the Olympic Games, *3902*

GERMANY—*continued*

Men's long horse vault gymnastics competition held in the Olympic Games, *3903*

Men's parallel bars gymnastics competitions held in the Olympic Games, *3906*

Men's singles luge (toboggan) event held in the Olympic Winter Games, *4455*

Men's springboard diving event held in the Olympic Games, *2792*

Modern handball, *4000*

Modern Olympic Games at which member countries were barred from competing, *4649*

National soccer (international football) league in Germany, *5543*

National team to sweep the medals in the men's 200-meter breaststroke event in the Olympic Games, *5806*

National team to sweep the medals in the women's individual foil fencing competition in the Olympic Games, *2940*

National team to sweep the top medals in men's springboard diving in the Olympic Games, *2794*

Olympic Games at which athletes from more than 50 countries participated, *4692*

Pentathlete to hold the officially accepted world record in the women's pentathlon, *4816*

Pole vault stand, *4836*

Runner to hold the officially accepted world record in the women's 800-meter event, *5021*

Runner to race the men's 800 meters in under 1:48 minutes, *5044*

Runner to win three consecutive women's titles in the Boston Marathon, *4525*

Runner to win two consecutive gold medals in the women's 4 x 100-meter relay in the Olympic Games, *5117*

Shot-putter to hold the officially accepted world record in the women's event, *5334*

Skier to win five women's super giant slalom titles in skiing's world cup, *5496*

Skier to win two consecutive Olympic titles in the women's downhill, and the first to win both the downhill and Alpine combination events in the same Olympic Winter Games, *5503*

Slider to win two, and then three, consecutive men's singles luge (toboggan) titles in the Olympic Winter Games, *4465*

Speed skater to be women's world champion in long-distance speed skating eight times, *5736*

Speed skater to skate the women's 5000-meter event in under 7 minutes, *5730*

Team dressage equestrian event held in the Olympic Games, *2855*

Tennis player (man or woman) to be ranked number one in the world for 186 consecutive weeks, *6183*

Tennis player to win at least four women's singles titles at each of the four Grand Slam tournaments, *6186*

Tennis player to win the women's singles title in the Olympic Games after tennis competition resumed in 1988, *6180*

Unlimited weight (super heavyweight) Greco-Roman wrestling event held in the Olympic Games, *6358*

Unseeded tennis player to win the men's singles title at Wimbledon, *6172*

Woman equestrian to win a gold medal in team dressage in the Olympic Games, *2875*

Woman equestrian to win a team dressage medal in the Olympic Games, *2863*

Woman rider, and the first horse, to win two consecutive gold medals in the individual dressage competition, and in team dressage, in the Olympic Games, *2893*

Women's 15-kilometer biathlon competition held in the Olympic Winter Games, *2441*

Women's 3000-meter individual pursuit cycling event in the Olympic Games, *2719*

Women's 800-meter running event held in the Olympic Games, *5022*

Women's halfpipe snowboarding event held at the Olympic Winter Games, *5527*

World championships in fencing to include women, *2923*

World championships in figure skating, *2964*

World championships in handball, *4005*

Berlin

African-American high-jumper to win the men's title in the Olympic Games, *4024*

African-American runner to win the men's 400-meter title in the Olympic Games, *5039*

African-American runner to win the men's 800-meter title in the Olympic Games, *5037*

Athlete from Turkey to win a gold medal in the Olympic Games, *4685*

Basketball event held in the Olympic Games, *1894*

Boxer to be awarded the Val Barker Cup, *2549*

Discus-thrower to hold the officially accepted world record in the women's event, *2766*

Diver to win two consecutive women's platform diving titles in the Olympic Games, *2801*

Equestrian to win gold medals in both individual and team jumping in the same Olympic Games, *2859*

Equestrian to win two consecutive titles in team dressage in the Olympic Games, *2858*

Field hockey players to win three gold medals in the Olympic Games, *4039*

Figure skaters from France to win the pairs title in the world championships, *3005*

Figure skaters from Hungary to win the pairs title in the world championships, *3009*

International hockey game played in Sweden, *4075*

Javelin-thrower to break the 330- and 340-foot and 100-meter barriers in the men's event, *4407*

Long-jumper to break the 20-foot and 6-meter barriers in the women's event, *4435*

Men's Canadian pairs 1000-meter canoeing event held in the Olympic Games, *2596*

Men's Canadian singles 1000-meter canoeing event held in the Olympic Games, *2597*

Men's pairs 1000-meter kayaking event held in the Olympic Games, *2598*

Men's singles 100-meter kayak event held in the Olympic Games, *2599*

Men's team handball event held in the Olympic Games, *4004*

Modern Olympic Games to be canceled because of war, *4646*

Olympic Games at which more than 4000 athletes participated, *4684*

Olympic Games to be televised, *4680*

Olympic Games to have a torch relay, *4681*

Pentathlete to achieve a perfect score in the shooting portion of the men's modern pentathlon in the Olympic Games, *4817*

Runner from New Zealand to win the men's 1500-meter title at the Olympic Games and to hold the world record in the event, *5038*

Runner to race the men's 100-meter dash in 10.1 seconds, *5063*

Runner to win three gold medals in the men's 4 x 100-meter relay in the Olympic Games, *5040*

Runner to win two gold medals in the women's 4 x 100-meter relay in the Olympic Games, *5041*

Shot-putter to break the 70-foot barrier in the women's event, *5348*

Speed skater to skate the 1500 meters in under 1:50 minutes, *5727*

Speed skater to win three consecutive women's titles at the world speed skating championships, *5691*

Team to race the men's 4 x 100-meter relay in under 40 seconds, *5042*

Triple-jumper to reach a distance of 16 meters in the men's event, *6254*

World Youth Games, *4371*

Wrestler to win heavyweight titles in both freestyle and Greco-Roman wrestling in the Olympic Games, *6385*

Bochum

Shot-putter to break the 16-meter barrier, *5333*

Garmisch-Partenkirchen

Female athlete to win three consecutive titles in the same event in the Olympic Winter Games, *4683*

Figure skater to win two, and then three, consecutive women's singles titles at the Olympic Winter Games, *3014*

Figure skaters to take all three medals in the same order in the U.S., world, and Olympic men's singles competitions, *3051*

Jewish athlete to represent Germany in the 1936 Olympic Winter Games, *4679*

Men's 4 x 10-kilometer relay Nordic (cross-country) event held in the Olympic Winter Games, *5384*

Men's Alpine combined event held at the Olympic Winter Games, *5383*

Olympic Winter Games held in Germany, *4682*

Olympic Winter Games when ski instructors were barred from competition as professionals, *5381*

Skier to win two consecutive men's individual ski jump titles in the Olympic Winter Games, *5385*

Speed skater to win three gold medals in speed skating at a single Olympic Winter Games, *5658*

Speed skater to win two Olympic gold medals in men's 5000-meter speed skating, *5657*

Women's Alpine combined event held at the Olympic Winter Games, *5382*

Hamburg

International speed skating competition, *5629*

Men's four-oared shell with coxswain rowing event held in the Olympic Games, *4928*

Inzell

Speed skater to skate the 1000 meters in under 1:20 minutes, *5681*

Speed skater to skate the 10,000 meters in under 15 minutes, *5685*

Speed skater to skate the 3000 meters in under 4:10 minutes, *5689*

Speed skater to skate the 3000 meters in under 4:20 minutes, *5679*

Woman speed skater to skate the 3000 meters in under 5 minutes, *5680*

Jena

Javelin-thrower to break the 310- and 320-foot barriers with the new javelin, *4413*

Munich

Figure skaters for France to win the ice dancing title in the world championships, *3096*

Figure skaters from the United States to sweep the women's singles medals in the world championships, *3097*

World cup in rowing, *4962*

GERMANY—*continued*
Stuttgart

Hurdler from Great Britain to win the men's title in the 110-meter hurdles in the World Championships in Athletics, *4354*

Runner from the United States to win the men's marathon in the World Championships in Athletics, *4523*

Runner from the United States to win the women's 100-meter dash in the World Championships in Athletics, *5164*

Runner from the United States to win the women's 400-meter race in the World Championships in Athletics, *5165*

Runner to win two, and then three, consecutive titles in the men's 1500-meter event in the World Championships in Athletics, *5166*

Runner to win two, and then three, consecutive titles in the men's 3000-meter steeplechase in the World Championships in Athletics, *5167*

Triple-jumper to break the 15-meter barrier in the women's event, *6262*

World championships in roller hockey (rink hockey), *4240*

Wasserkuppe

World championships in gliding (soaring), *3531*

East Germany

African-American figure skater to win the women's singles title in the world championships, *3090*

Athlete to win eight medals in individual events in the Olympic Winter Games, *4764*

Athlete to win two biathlon gold medals at a single Olympic Winter Games, *2438*

Canoe racer to win five gold medals, and eight medals overall, in women's events in the Olympic Games, *2628*

Figure skaters to win Emmy awards for a television special, *3095*

Gymnast to win two, and then three, consecutive women's uneven (asymmetrical) bars titles in the world championships, *3968*

Heptathlete to hold the world record in the women's heptathlon, *4012*

Hurdler to hold the officially accepted world record in the women's 100-meter hurdles, *4342*

Javelin-thrower to break the 330- and 340-foot and 100-meter barriers in the men's event, *4407*

Javelin-thrower to win two consecutive women's titles in the Olympic Games, *4402*

Men's kayak slalom white-water canoeing events held in the Olympic Games, *2615*

Men's quadruple sculls competition held in the world championships in rowing, *4944*

Men's quadruple sculls rowing event held in the Olympic Games, *4948*

Men's ski jumping (large hill) event held in the world championships of Nordic skiing, *5407*

Men's team Nordic combined event held in the world championships of Nordic skiing, *5435*

National team to sweep the medals in the men's singles luge (toboggan) event at the Olympic Winter Games, *4459*

National team to sweep the medals in the women's 3000-meter speed-skating event at the Olympic Winter Games, *5702*

National team to sweep the medals in the women's pentathlon in the Olympic Games, *4831*

National team to sweep the medals in the women's singles luge (toboggan) event at the Olympic Winter Games, *4460*

Rowers to win two consecutive titles in the men's four-oared shell without coxswain event in the Olympic Games, *4943*

Rowers to win two consecutive titles in the pair-oared shell without coxswain event in the Olympic Games, *4950*

Rowers to win two consecutive titles in the women's quadruple sculls in the Olympic Games, *4958*

Runner to race the women's 100 meters in under 11.0 seconds, *5097*

Runner to race the women's 400 meters in under 49 seconds, *5109*

Runner to win both the women's 100- and 200-meter titles in the World Championships in Athletics, *5146*

Runner to win the women's 100-meter race in the World Championships in Athletics, *5133*

Runner to win the women's 200-meter title in the World Championships in Athletics, *5135*

Runners to finish first and second in both the women's 100- and 200-meter races in the Olympic Games, *5065*

Shot-putter to break the 23-meter barrier, *5350*

Shot-putter to break the 70-foot barrier in the women's event, *5348*

Skier to win three consecutive men's individual Nordic combined titles in the Olympic Winter Games, *5443*

Speed skater to win five women's long-distance speed skating titles in the world championships, *5708*

Speed skater to win six women's titles in the world speed skating sprint championships, *5705*

Super giant slalom events held in the Alpine skiing world championships, *5452*

Swimmer to hold both the women's 100-meter freestyle and 100-meter butterfly world titles at the same time, *5890*

Swimmer to hold world titles in both the 100- and 200-meter backstroke at the same time, *5892*

Two-seater luge (toboggan) event to have two pairs of gold medalists in a single Olympic Winter Games, *4458*

Woman speed skater to skate the 1500 meters in under 2 minutes, *5704*

Woman speed skater to skate the 3000 meters in under 4:30 minutes, *5698*

Woman speed skater to skate the 500 meters in under 40 seconds, *5700*

Woman speed skater to skate the 5000 meters in under 8 minutes, *5699*

Women's 4 x 400-meter relay track event held in the Olympic Games, *5095*

Women's 400-meter race in which the top three runners had times of under 50 seconds, *5115*

Women's slalom singles kayaking event held in the Olympic Games, *2614*

Women's super giant slalom to be included in the world cup for Alpine skiing, *5450*

World championships in rowing to include women's competitions, *4945*

World Cup Marathon, *4514*

World Cup series of competitions for speed skating, *5703*

World Sculls Cup series of rowing races, *4956*

Karl-Marx-Stadt

Runner to race the women's 200 meters in under 22 seconds, *5110*

Leipzig

Shot-putter to break the 17- and 18-meter, and 60-foot, barriers in the women's event, *5342*

Neubrandenburg

Discus-thrower to break the 240-foot barrier in the men's event, *2784*

Discus-thrower to break the 250-foot barrier, *2785*

Potsdam

Javelin-thrower to break the 210- and 220-foot barriers in the women's event, *4401*

Javelin-thrower to break the 260-foot barrier, and to reach the 80-meter barrier, in the women's event, *4410*

West Germany

Cyclist to win two consecutive titles in the men's 4000-meter team pursuit in the Olympic Games, *2704*

Discus-thrower to break the 60-meter and 200-foot barriers in the women's event, *2775*

European Formula 3000 automobile racing circuit, *1131*

Figure skater from Germany to win the women's singles title in the world championships, *3049*

International Handball Federation (IHF) Cup team competition, *4009*

Javelin-throw world record set using the new javelin in the men's event, *4409*

Male rider to win the world cup in dressage, *2891*

Men's super giant slalom to be included in the world cup for Alpine skiing, *5448*

Runner to win the men's 3000-meter steeplechase held in the World Championships in Athletics, *5129*

Runner to win the men's 800-meter race held in the World Championships in Athletics, *5132*

Runners to complete the men's 400-meter race in under 45 seconds, *5072*

Soccer (international football) player to be named World Footballer of the Year by the Fédération Internationale de Football Association (FIFA), *5565*

Soccer (international football) team from Germany to win the world cup, *5556*

Speed skaters to become world champions in speed skating sprints, *5686*

World championship in moto-cross racing to include the sidecar class, *4591*

World championships for freestyle skiing, *5451*

World championships in dressage, *2871*

World championships in taekwondo to include light-middleweight and light-heavyweight classes for men, *4544*

World championships in vaulting, *2888*

World cup in bobsledding, *2475*

World cup in luge (toboggan), *4461*

Augsburg

Hurdler to hold the officially accepted world record in the women's 400-meter hurdles, *4344*

Dortmund

Figure skaters from Hungary to win the ice dancing title in the world championships, *3083*

Düsseldorf

World Cup in track and field (athletics), *6220*

Frankfurt am Main

Discus-thrower to break the 60-meter barrier, *2771*

Hammer-thrower to break the 250-foot and 260-foot barriers, *3993*

Koblenz

Hurdler to set four new world records in the men's 400-meter hurdles, *4349*

GERMANY—West Germany—Koblenz—*continued*

Runner to race the men's 1500 meters in under 3:32 minutes, *5119*

Lahr

Hammer-thrower to break the 250-foot and 260-foot barriers, *3993*

Munich

Athlete from North Korea to win a gold medal in the Olympic Games, *4737*

Athlete from Uganda to win a gold medal in the Olympic Games, *4738*

Athlete to compete in eight Olympic Games, *4733*

Athlete to win seven gold medals in a single Olympic Games, *4740*

Basketball team from the Soviet Union to win the men's title in the Olympic Games, *2088*

Cyclist to win two consecutive men's titles in the 1000-meter match sprint in the Olympic Games, *2703*

Electronically timed world record in the men's 110-meter hurdles, *4343*

Equestrian to win four titles in team jumping in the Olympic Games, *2880*

Fencers to win three gold medals in the women's team foil competition in the Olympic Games, *2938*

Flyweight weightlifting event held in the Olympic Games, *6345*

Heavyweight freestyle wrestling event held in the Olympic Games, *6397*

Heavyweight Greco-Roman wrestling event held in the Olympic Games, *6400*

Heavyweight weightlifting event held in the Olympic Games, *6346*

Judo artist to win two gold medals in a single Olympic Games, *4540*

Light flyweight Greco-Roman wrestling event held in the Olympic Games, *6401*

Men's 200-meter individual medley event in which the top four swimmers broke the world record, *5870*

Men's half-heavyweight judo event in the Olympic Games, *4538*

Men's half-middleweight judo event in the Olympic Games, *4539*

Men's individual archery event in the modern format held in the Olympic Games, *1035*

Men's kayak slalom white-water canoeing events held in the Olympic Games, *2615*

National team to sweep the medals in the men's 200-meter butterfly swimming event in the Olympic Games, *5864*

National team to sweep the medals in the women's 200-meter butterfly in the Olympic Games, *5872*

Olympic Games at which athletes were killed by terrorists, *4739*

Olympic Games at which more than 1000 women athletes participated, *4736*

Olympic Games at which organized drug testing was performed, *4734*

Olympic men's 100-meter backstroke event in which the medalists all had times under one minute, *5866*

Olympic men's 1500-meter freestyle event in which the medalists all had times under 17 minutes, *5871*

Olympic women's 100-meter freestyle event in which the medalists all had times under one minute, *5867*

Rowers to win two consecutive titles in the men's four-oared shell without coxswain event in the Olympic Games, *4943*

Sailor to win both the America's Cup and an Olympic gold medal in sailing, *5253*

Sailor to win gold medals in three different sailing events in the Olympic Games, *5239*

Sailor to win two consecutive gold medals in the Flying Dutchman–class event in the Olympic Games, *5228*

Shot-putter to break the 20- and 21-meter barriers in the women's event, *5347*

Soling-class sailing event held in the Olympic Games, *5229*

Soling-class sailing event held in the Olympic Games, *5229*

Swimmer from the United States to win the women's 100-meter breaststroke in the Olympic Games, *5868*

Swimmer to win two consecutive gold medals in the men's 4 x 100-meter freestyle relay in the Olympic Games, *5865*

Swimmer to win two consecutive men's 1500-meter freestyle titles in the Olympic Games, *5863*

Swimmer to win two consecutive men's 200-meter backstroke titles in the Olympic Games, *5869*

Tempest-class sailing event in the Olympic Games, *5230*

Volleyball players to win two consecutive women's gold medals in the Olympic Games, *6283*

Woman equestrian to win an individual jumping medal in the Olympic Games, *2874*

Woman equestrian to win the individual dressage title in the Olympic Games, *2879*

Women's 1500-meter event held in the Olympic Games, *5094*

Women's 4 x 400-meter relay track event held in the Olympic Games, *5095*

Women's individual archery event in the modern format held in the Olympic Games, *1036*

Women's slalom singles kayaking event held in the Olympic Games, *2614*

Wrestler to win the light flyweight freestyle competition in the Olympic Games when it resumed in 1972, *6398*

Wrestler to win two consecutive flyweight Greco-Roman wrestling titles in the Olympic Games, *6402*

Wrestler to win two consecutive super heavyweight freestyle titles in the Olympic Games, and wrestling gold medals in three consecutive Olympic Games, *6399*

Stuttgart

Javelin-thrower to break the 250-foot barrier in the women's event, *4408*

Runner to race the women's 800 meters in under 2:00 minutes, *5093*

West Berlin

Diver to hold women's world titles in both springboard and highboard platform diving at the same time, *2812*

Diver to win three consecutive men's highboard platform diving titles in the world championships, *2816*

Diver to win two, and then three, consecutive men's springboard diving titles in the world championships, *2809*

Diver to win two consecutive women's world titles in springboard diving, *2813*

Swimmer to hold both the women's 100- and 200-meter backstroke world titles at the same time, *5929*

Swimmer to hold both the women's 400- and 800-meter freestyle world titles at the same time, *5930*

Swimmer to hold the women's 200-meter butterfly and both the 200- and 400-meter individual medley world titles at the same time, *5931*

GREAT BRITAIN

Admiral's Cup race, *5221*

Association of professional golfers, *3631*

Athlete from Great Britain to win a gold medal in the Olympic Games, *4610*

Athlete to be named *Sports Illustrated* Sportsman of the Year, *1151*

Athlete to win three men's titles in the world triathlon championships, *6246*

Athlete to win two consecutive men's titles in the world triathlon championships, *6244*

Automobile racer to be named *Sports Illustrated* Sportsman of the Year, *1118*

Automobile racer to have nine wins in a single season on the Formula One Grand Prix circuit, *1141*

Book on ice skating techniques, *2950*

Boxer to be undisputed world flyweight champion, *2536*

Boxer to hold world titles in three different weight classes, *2526*

Boxer to win two consecutive middleweight titles in the Olympic Games, *2545*

Canoe marathon world championships, *2624*

Cricket event at the Olympic Games, *2653*

Davis Cup match, *6038*

Development of water polo, *6298*

Diving tournament on record, *2787*

Field hockey players to win three gold medals in the Olympic Games, *4039*

Field hockey players to win two gold medals in the Olympic Games, *4038*

Figure skater from Great Britain to win the men's singles title at the Olympic Winter Games, *3077*

Figure skater from Great Britain to win the men's singles title at the world championships, *3024*

Figure skater to win the women's singles title at the Olympic Games, *2977*

Figure skater to win the women's singles title in the world championships, *2968*

Figure skater to win two consecutive women's singles titles in the world championships, *2971*

Figure skaters from Great Britain, and the first married couple, to win the pairs title in the world championships, *2980*

Figure skaters from the Soviet Union to win the ice dancing title in the world championships, *3066*

Figure skaters to win the ice dancing title in the world championships, and the first to win it two, three, and four times, *3046*

Figure skaters to win unanimous top scores for artistic impression, and the first from Great Britain to win the ice dancing title, at the Olympic Winter Games, *3087*

Football Association (FA) Challenge Cup for soccer (international football), *5534*

French Open women's doubles tennis match, *6121*

Hurdler from Great Britain to win the men's title in the 110-meter hurdles in the World Championships in Athletics, *4354*

Ice hockey exhibition game in Great Britain, *4047*

Ice hockey team from Great Britain to win the gold medal at the Olympic Winter Games, *4115*

Importation of North American hickory to Britain for golf clubs, *3563*

Intercollegiate ice hockey game, *4042*

International air race in the United States, *1002*

International governing body for ice skating, *2962*

International moto-cross competition, *4577*

International moto-cross competition for 250 cc motorcycles, *4581*

GREAT BRITAIN—*continued*

International polo competition, *4862*

Introduction of field hockey into the United States, *4035*

Javelin-thrower to break the 250-foot barrier in the women's event, *4408*

Javelin-thrower to break the 300-foot and 90-meter barriers with the new javelin, *4412*

Major international ice hockey organization, *4057*

Men's 200-meter breaststroke event held in the Olympic Games, *5801*

Men's 200-meter breaststroke event held in the world championships, *5880*

Men's 4 x 100-meter relay track event held in the Olympic Games, *5003*

Men's 4000-meter freestyle swimming event held in the Olympic Games, *5792*

Men's 5-mile event held in the Olympic Games, *4992*

Men's 5000-meter team running event held in the Olympic Games, *4982*

Men's 50,000-meter walk held in the Olympic Games, *6291*

Men's doubles tennis event held in the Olympic Games, *6035*

Men's singles tennis event held in the Olympic Games, *6036*

Mixed doubles tennis event held in the Olympic Games, *6039*

Modern slalom course, *5363*

National governing body in motorcycle racing, *4571*

National organization for roller hockey (rink hockey), *4239*

National team to sweep the medals in the men's singles tennis event in the Olympic Games, *6040*

National team to win two Olympic gold medals in the tug-of-war competition, *6268*

Official code of rules for billiards, *2449*

Olympic Winter Games at which an athlete was killed, *4713*

Organization for croquet in Britain, *2669*

Organized downhill ski race, *5362*

Player to be named Women's Tennis Association (WTA) Player of the Year, *6162*

Polo event held in the Olympic Games, *4865*

Rackets event held in the Olympic Games, *4872*

Result of an Olympic event to be changed after viewing of the film of the race, *4678*

Rotterdam Marathon, *4506*

Runner from Europe to win the men's 100-meter title in the Olympic Games, *5014*

Runner from Europe to win the men's 1500-meter title in the Olympic Games, *4978*

Runner from Europe to win the men's 800-meter title in the Olympic Games, *4980*

Runner to complete the men's 1500-meter race in under 3:30 minutes, *5144*

Runner to complete the men's 800-meter race in under 1:43 minutes, *5111*

Runner to complete the men's 800-meter race in under 1:50 minutes, *5029*

Runner to complete the men's mile race in under 3:48 minutes, *5121*

Runner to complete the men's mile race in under 3:49 minutes, *5113*

Runner to hold the officially accepted world record in the women's 5000-meter race, *5122*

Runner to race the men's 1500 meters in under 3:32 minutes, *5119*

Runner to win the Jesse Owens International Award, *5120*

Runner to win the men's 1500-meter race held in the World Championships in Athletics, *5127*

Runner to win two consecutive men's 800-meter titles in the Olympic Games, *5019*

Runner to win two consecutive officially accepted titles in the men's 1500-meters at the Olympic Games, *5141*

Ryder Cup golf match, *3687*

Ryder Cup to include players from the European mainland, *3821*

Sailor to win two consecutive gold medals in the Flying Dutchman–class event in the Olympic Games, *5228*

Scottish Highland Gathering, *4364*

Season for the Ice Capades, *3026*

Shooter to win two consecutive titles in the small-bore rifle (three positions) individual event in the Olympic Games, *5323*

Small-bore rifle (prone) individual shooting event held in the Olympic Games, *5290*

Soccer (international football) event held in the Olympic Games, *5544*

Soccer (international football) player to win two gold medals in the Olympic Games, *5548*

Swimmer to hold world titles in both the men's 100- and 200-meter breaststroke at the same time, *5912*

Swimmer to win two consecutive men's 1500-meter freestyle titles in the Olympic Games, *5803*

Swimmer to win two consecutive men's 200-meter breaststroke titles in the world championships, *5915*

Tennis player to win two men's doubles titles in the Olympic Games, *6042*

Tornado-class sailing event held in the Olympic Games, *5236*

Triple-jumper to break the 18-meter and 60-foot barriers, *6264*

U.S. Open mixed doubles tennis title, *6125*

U.S. Open women's singles tennis title, *6128*

England

GREAT BRITAIN—England—*continued*

Single-handed, non-stop, round-the-world sailing race, *5224*

Skipper to win the America's Cup sailing race twice in a row, *5203*

Standardized rules for badminton, *1164*

Stud book for horse racing, *4263*

Substitute for live birds in shooting competitions, *5264*

Swimmer to swim across the English Channel and back consecutively, *5843*

Swimmer to swim across the English Channel from France to England, *5816*

Swimmer to swim the English Channel in both directions, *5827*

Table tennis equipment, *5980*

Team to win the championship in England's Football League, *5540*

Waterloo Cup, *2831*

Woman to swim across the English Channel and back consecutively, *5928*

Woman to swim the English Channel from England to France, and to swim it in both directions, *5831*

Women's lacrosse organization, *4421*

Women's soccer (international football) game, *5541*

Women's world open championships in snooker, *2460*

World amateur championships in billiards, *2452*

World amateur snooker championships, *2457*

World championships in tug-of-war, *6270*

World cup in women's cricket, *2660*

World indoor championships in bowls, *2502*

World matchplay championships in snooker, *2463*

World outdoor championships in bowls, *2499*

World professional championships in billiards, *2444*

World professional championships in snooker, *2453*

World team Thomas Cup badminton championships for men, *1169*

World team Uber Cup badminton championships for women, *1170*

Yacht club in England, *5195*

Aylesbury

Wheelchair sports tournaments, *2748*

Birmingham

Figure skater from China to win the women's singles title in the world championships, *3109*

Figure skaters from the Czech Republic to win the pairs title in the world championships, *3110*

Brackley

British Grand Prix automobile race to be part of the Formula One Grand Prix circuit, *1077*

Bury

Rules for modern darts, *2734*

Camberley

Moto-cross race, *4575*

Cambridge

Code of rules for soccer (international football), *5530*

Golf match to charge fees for spectators, *3601*

National ice skating organization in Great Britain, *2959*

University golf clubs, *3589*

Cheltenham

Champion Hurdle horse race, *4293*

Cheltenham Gold Cup horse race, *4291*

International governing body for badminton, *1168*

Copthall Common

African-American boxer to fight in a title bout, *2507*

Cowes

Fastnet Race, *5209*

Transatlantic sailing race, *5199*

Woman driver to win an automobile race, *1047*

Cromer

International match between female golfers, *3641*

Deal

British Open golf championship to be administered by the Royal and Ancient Golf Club of St. Andrews, *3664*

Doncaster

St. Leger horse race, *4259*

Dover

Flyers to cross the English Channel in a balloon, *1178*

Person to swim the English Channel, *5783*

Epsom

Derby horse race, *4261*

Horse bred and trained in the United States to win England's Derby, *4281*

Jockey who won five Derbys at Epsom Downs, *4266*

Jockey who won seven, eight, and nine Derbys at Epsom Downs, *4311*

Jockey who won six Derbys at Epsom Downs, *4269*

Jockey who won three Derbys at Epsom Downs, *4262*

Oaks horse race, *4260*

Esher

Whitbread Gold Cup horse race, *4302*

Gravesend

Sailing challenge race on record, *5193*

Greenwich

Sailing challenge race on record, *5193*

Guildford

Cricket reference, *2631*
Women's cricket match, *2637*

Hambledon Lock

University Boat Race, *4913*

Heather

Boxing title fight under the London Prize Ring Rules, *2511*

Henley

Diamond Challenge Sculls rowing race, *4919*
Henley Regatta rowing races, *4914*
Rower from the United States to win the Diamond Sculls at the Henley Regatta, *4924*
Rower to win both the single and double sculls events at the Henley Regatta, *4939*
Rower to win two consecutive men's single sculls rowing titles in the Olympic Games, *4937*
University Boat Race, *4913*

Hoylake

Amateur golfer to win three British Open championships, *3691*
Amateur golfer to win two British Open championships, *3616*
British Amateur Championship, *3594*
Golfer from outside Great Britain to win the British Open, *3645*
Golfer to win the British Open golf championship in under 290 for 72 holes, *3685*

Huddersfield

Rugby League, *4964*

Hurlingham

Champion Cup polo competition, *4859*
Governing body for polo, *4857*
Polo team from the United States to win the Westchester Cup, *4866*

Jersey, Island of

Golfer to win both the U.S. Open and British Open, *3628*

Kennington Common

Cricket ground set aside for play, *2634*

Kingsdown

Woman to swim the English Channel, *5820*

Leeds

Ryder Cup golf match played in Britain, *3690*

Liverpool

Cricket team from outside England to play in England, *2646*
Cycling club, *2681*
Grand National Steeplechase horse race, *4271*
Women's touring cricket team, *2652*

London

6-meter-class sailing event held in the Olympic Games, *5205*
8-meter-class sailing event in the Olympic Games, *5206*
African-American basketball player to win an Olympic gold medal, *1921*
Asian-American athlete to win a gold medal in the Olympic Games, *4694*
Athlete from Africa, and from South Africa, to win a gold medal in the Olympic Games, *4638*
Athlete from Belgium to win a gold medal in the Olympic Games, *4616*
Athlete from Finland to win an official gold medal in the Olympic Games, *4641*
Athlete from Jamaica to win a gold medal in the Olympic Games, *4695*
Athlete from Peru to win a gold medal in the Olympic Games, *4693*
Athlete from Russia to win a gold medal in the Olympic Games, *4640*
Athlete of Black African descent to win an Olympic gold medal, *4639*

GREAT BRITAIN—England—London—*continued*

Athletes from Mexico to win gold medals in the Olympic Games, *4697*

Athletes from Norway to win official gold medals at the Olympic Games, *4637*

Bantamweight weightlifting event held in the Olympic Games, *6334*

Baseball teams from the United States to tour England and Ireland, *1214*

Boxer of African descent to win a national boxing title, *2519*

Boxing school, *2505*

Canoer to win two men's Canadian pairs 1000-meter titles in the Olympic Games, *2602*

Cricket game to be broadcast on television, *2658*

Cricket ground set aside for play, *2634*

Cricket match at which admission was charged, and the first cricket game to be fully documented, *2636*

Cricket match on record at Lord's Cricket Ground, *2639*

Cricket match on record at the current location of Lord's Cricket Ground, *2642*

Cricket match on record between teams from Oxford and Cambridge universities, *2645*

Discus-thrower from the United States to win the men's Greek-style title in the Olympic Games, *2759*

Discus-thrower to win two, and then three, consecutive men's titles in the Olympic Games, *2757*

Diver to win both the women's springboard and platform diving titles in the same Olympic Games, *2802*

Dragon-class sailing event held in the Olympic Games, *5216*

Equestrian show jumping competition held in England, *2839*

Equestrian to be stripped of his dressage title because he was not a commissioned officer, *2860*

Father-and-son team to win the Star-class sailing event in the Olympic Games, *5215*

Father and son to both win gold medals in track and field in the Olympic Games, *6213*

Federation Cup championships, *6112*

Fencer to win two consecutive men's individual sabre titles, and men's team sabre titles, in the Olympic Games, *2914*

Fencer to win two consecutive women's individual foil titles in the Olympic Games, *2929*

Figure skater to win the men's singles title in the Olympic Games, *2975*

Figure skater to win the title for special figures in the Olympic Games, *2976*

Figure skater to win the women's singles title at the Olympic Games, *2977*

Figure skaters from the United States to win the pairs title in the world championships, *3040*

Figure skaters to win the pairs title at the Olympic Games, *2978*

Figure skating competition at the Olympic Games, *2974*

Flyweight Greco-Roman wrestling event held in the Olympic Games, *6387*

Football Association Challenge Cup tournament, *5551*

Golf club outside Scotland, *3557*

Governing body for diving, *2790*

Governing body in cricket, *2638*

Hurdler to hold the officially accepted world record in the men's 110-meter hurdles, and to set a 110-meter hurdle record that would stand for more than 10 years, *4327*

Hurdler to hold the officially accepted world record in the men's 400-meter hurdles, and to set a 400-meter hurdle record that would stand for more than 10 years, *4326*

Hurdler to hold the officially accepted world record in the women's 80-meter event, *4333*

Ice skating rink in Great Britain to use artificial ice, *2955*

Individual jumping equestrian event held in the Olympic Games, *2841*

Inter-Empire Sports tournament, *4366*

International pairs figure skating competition in which all the medalists were brother-and-sister pairs, *3041*

International society of Olympics researchers, *4769*

Jeu de paume (court tennis or real tennis) event in the Olympic Games, *6049*

Light heavyweight Greco-Roman wrestling event held in the Olympic Games, *6373*

London Marathon, *4507*

London Prize Ring Rules for boxing, *2510*

Men's 200-meter breaststroke event held in the Olympic Games, *5801*

Men's 3-mile team race held in the Olympic Games, *4994*

Men's 3500-meter and 10-mile walks held in the Olympic Games, *6289*

Men's 4 x 400-meter relay track event held in the Olympic Games, *4997*

Men's 4000-meter team pursuit cycling event held in the Olympic Games, *2692*

Men's field hockey event held in the Olympic Games, *4036*

Men's freestyle javelin event held in the Olympic Games, *4381*

Men's javelin-throw event held at the Olympic Games, *4382*

Men's springboard diving event held in the Olympic Games, *2792*

Middleweight freestyle wrestling event held in the Olympic Games, *6372*

GREAT BRITAIN—England—London—*continued*

Wrestler from the United States to win the middleweight freestyle wrestling title in the Olympic Games, *6386*

Written reference to football, *5528*

Manchester

Soccer (international football) league, *5539*

Water polo event held in the Olympic Games, *6301*

Water polo player to win two, and then three, gold medals in the Olympic Games, *6303*

Midhurst

British Open Championship polo tournament, *4869*

Moreton-on-Marsh

Open championship in croquet, *2665*

Mortlake

Dead heat on record in the University Boat Race, *4918*

University Boat Race, *4913*

Netherby

Horse race in Britain, *4245*

Newmarket

1000 Guineas horse race, *4268*

2000 Guineas horse race, *4267*

Jockey Club in England, *4255*

Newmarket Town Four Mile Race, *4251*

Organized record of match race performances, *4253*

Rules for horse racing, *4250*

Wearing of racing colors by jockeys, *4257*

Nottingham

Canoe marathon world championships, *2624*

World professional darts championships, *2735*

Nun Appleton

Women's cricket club, *2651*

Oxford

High-jumper to clear six feet, *4017*

Runner to race the mile in under 4:00 minutes, *5060*

University golf clubs, *3589*

Pimlico

Tennis game in its modern form, *6005*

Plymouth

Fastnet Race, *5209*

Single-Handed Transatlantic Race (STAR), *5222*

Woman to sail across the Atlantic alone, *5220*

Portsmouth

Whitbread Round-the-World Race, *5232*

Putney

Dead heat on record in the University Boat Race, *4918*

National swimming championship, *5781*

Organized regatta, or series of boat races, on record, *4912*

University Boat Race, *4913*

Richmond

Motorcycle race for two-wheeled vehicles, *4570*

Sandwich

British Open golf tournament held in England, *3605*

Golfer born in the United States to win the British Open, *3670*

Golfer from the British Commonwealth to win the British Open, *3721*

Golfer from the United States to win the British Amateur Championship, *3638*

Golfer to win the British Open golf championship in under 300 for 72 holes, *3639*

Golfer to win the British Open in 267 for 72 holes, *3875*

Sevenoaks

Cricket ground set aside for play, *2634*

Sheffield

Professional touring cricket team, *2648*

Soccer (international football) club, *5531*

Smithfield

Public track for horse racing in Britain, *4246*

Sunningdale

Golf course developed on cleared land, with grass grown entirely from seed, *3632*

Ullswater

Motorboat (powerboat) racer to go faster than 200 miles per hour, *4568*

British Open golf championship open to amateurs, *3578*

British Open golf tournament, *3576*

Course specifically designed for golf, *3568*

Golfer to win four British Open championships, *3581*

Golfer to win six British Open golf championships, *3656*

Golfer to win the British Open, *3577*

Golfer to win the British Open championship four times in a row, *3585*

Golfer to win the British Open championship three times in a row, *3584*

Golfer to win the British Open championship twice in a row, *3579*

Golfer under the age of 20 to win the British Open championship, *3582*

St. Andrews

British Open golf championship held at Musselburgh, Scotland, *3588*

British Open golf championship held at the Old Course at St. Andrews, Scotland, *3586*

British Open golf championship to be administered by the Royal and Ancient Golf Club of St. Andrews, *3664*

British win of the Walker Cup golf tournament, *3707*

Championship Meeting in golf, *3572*

Championship Meeting in golf employing the individual match play format, *3573*

Confirmation of the public's right to play golf, *3538*

Golf ball made of gutta-percha, *3567*

Golf club for women, *3580*

Golf course to host the British Open championship 25 times, *3881*

Golf course with 18 holes, *3555*

Golf rules to be published, *3552*

Golfer from the United States to become captain of the Royal and Ancient Golf Club of St. Andrews, *3727*

Golfer to complete a grand slam, *3693*

Golfer to hold the record low (under-par) scores in all four Professional Golfers Association (PGA) major tournaments, *3899*

Golfer to score under 80 at the Old Course at St. Andrews, Scotland, *3574*

Golfer to win five British Open championships, *3649*

Golfer to win the British Open after a default in a playoff, *3590*

Golfer to win the British Open golf championship in under 290 for 72 holes, *3685*

Open golf competition at St. Andrews, Scotland, *3553*

Rules of Golf committee, *3619*

Ruling limiting the size and weight of a golf ball, *3668*

Stroke play game recorded in golf, *3554*

Walker Cup golf match played in Britain, *3676*

Troon

Golfer to win the British Open golf championship in under 280 for 72 holes, *3724*

Turnberry

British Open golf championship in which the top ten golfers were all from the United States, *3811*

Golfer to win the British Open golf championship in under 270 for 72 holes, *3813*

Wales

British Empire Games (later the British Commonwealth Games), *4369*

Grand Prix in snooker, *2462*

International championship in soccer (international football), *5535*

World professional darts championships, *2735*

World rankings for snooker, *2461*

Nantclwyd

Tennis game in its modern form, *6005*

GREECE

Boxing event in the Olympic Games, *2504*

Fiberglass pole to be used in the men's pole vault event in the Olympic Games, *4842*

Horse races held in the Olympic Games, *4243*

Olympic Games, *4599*

Olympic Games to have a torch relay, *4681*

Pentathlon, *4813*

Races for horses and riders held in the Olympic Games, *4244*

Track event in the Olympic Games, *6197*

Woman recorded as participating in the original Olympic Games, *4600*

Wrestling event in the Olympic Games, *6355*

Athens

All-around wrestling title awarded in the Olympic Games, *6369*

Athlete, and the first from the United States, to win a gold medal in the modern Olympic Games, *4604*

Athlete from Australia to win a gold medal in the modern Olympic Games, *4607*

Athlete from Denmark to win a gold medal in the Olympic Games, *4608*

Athlete from France to win a gold medal in the Olympic Games, *4609*

Athlete from Great Britain to win a gold medal in the Olympic Games, *4610*

Athlete from Greece to win a gold medal in the modern Olympic Games, *4611*

GREECE—Athens—*continued*

Athlete from Hungary to win a gold medal in the modern Olympic Games, *4614*

Athlete from Switzerland to win a gold medal in the Olympic Games, *4612*

Brothers to win gold and silver medals in the same event in the Olympic Games, *4613*

Cyclist to win the men's 12-hour cycling race in the Olympic Games, *2687*

Cyclist to win two, and then three, cycling gold medals in the Olympic Games, *2688*

Discus-thrower to win two, and then three, consecutive men's titles in the Olympic Games, *2757*

Dueling pistol shooting events held in the Olympic Games, *5282*

Event held in the modern Olympic Games, *4605*

Fencer to win both the men's individual sabre and épée titles in the Olympic Games, *2912*

Fencer to win both the men's masters épée and masters sabre competitions in the Olympic Games, *2907*

Fencer to win men's individual and team épée titles in the same Olympic Games, *2908*

Fencer to win two men's individual sabre titles in the Olympic Games, *2909*

Free pistol shooting individual event held in the Olympic Games, *5271*

Free rifle individual shooting event held in the Olympic Games, *5269*

Free rifle team shooting event held in the Olympic Games, *5281*

Free rifle (three position) individual shooting event held in the Olympic Games, *5273*

Lightweight Greco-Roman wrestling event held in the Olympic Games, *6370*

Long-jumper to win two consecutive men's titles in the Olympic Games, *4429*

Marathon runner to be stripped of his medal, *4467*

Men's 100- and 400-meter running events held in the Olympic Games, *4975*

Men's 100-meter freestyle swimming event held in the Olympic Games, *5785*

Men's 1000-meter match sprint cycling race held in the Olympic Games, *2685*

Men's 110-meter hurdles event held in the Olympic Games, *4322*

Men's 1200-meter freestyle swimming event held in the Olympic Games, *5786*

Men's 3000-meter walk event held in the Olympic Games, *6288*

Men's 4 x 250-meter (later 4 x 200-meter) freestyle relay swimming event held in the Olympic Games, *5799*

Men's 5-mile event held in the Olympic Games, *4992*

Men's 500-meter freestyle event held in the Olympic Games, *5787*

Men's 800-meter and 1500-meter running events held in the Olympic Games, *4974*

Men's discus throw event held in the Olympic Games, *2754*

Men's doubles tennis event held in the Olympic Games, *6035*

Men's freestyle javelin event held in the Olympic Games, *4381*

Men's Greek-style discus throw event held in the Olympic Games, *2756*

Men's high jump event held in the Olympic Games, *4019*

Men's horizontal bar gymnastics competitions held in the Olympic Games, *3902*

Men's individual foil fencing competition held in the Olympic Games, *2897*

Men's individual sabre fencing competition held in the Olympic Games, *2899*

Men's long horse vault gymnastics competition held in the Olympic Games, *3903*

Men's long jump event held in the Olympic Games, *4426*

Men's marathon race held in the Olympic Games, *4468*

Men's masters foil fencing competition held in the Olympic Games, *2898*

Men's parallel bars gymnastics competitions held in the Olympic Games, *3906*

Men's pentathlon held in the modern Olympic Games, *4814*

Men's pole vault event held in the Olympic Games, *4837*

Men's rings gymnastics competition held in the Olympic Games, *3904*

Men's road race cycling event held in the Olympic Games, *2686*

Men's rope climbing gymnastics competition held in the Olympic Games, *3907*

Men's shot put event held in the Olympic Games, *5329*

Men's side (pommel) horse gymnastics competition held in the Olympic Games, *3905*

Men's singles tennis event held in the Olympic Games, *6036*

Men's stone throw event held in the Olympic Games, *5769*

Men's team épée fencing competition held in the Olympic Games, *2910*

Men's team sabre fencing competition held in the Olympic Games, *2911*

Men's triple jump event held in the Olympic Games, *6249*

Middleweight Greco-Roman wrestling event held in the Olympic Games, *6371*

Military revolver individual shooting event held in the Olympic Games, *5270*

Modern Olympic Games, *4606*

National team sent from the United States to the Olympic Games, *4631*

Olympic Games held after two years, instead of four, *4632*

Pole-vaulter to clear 18 feet, *4846*

Rapid-fire pistol shooting individual event held in the Olympic Games, *5272*

Rowers to win two gold medals in pair-oared shell with coxswain rowing events in the same Olympic Games, *4934*

Runner to win both the men's 400- and 800-meter events in the same Olympic Games, *4993*

Runner to win two consecutive titles in the women's 800-meter event in the World Championships in Athletics, *5185*

Runner to win two, three, and then four consecutive titles in the men's 10,000-meter event in the World Championships in Athletics, *5174*

Runner to win two, three, and then four consecutive titles in the men's 400-meter event in the World Championships in Athletics, *5175*

Tennis player to win three gold medals in tennis in the same Olympic Games, *6048*

Unlimited weight (super heavyweight) Greco-Roman wrestling event held in the Olympic Games, *6358*

Unlimited weight weightlifting events held in the Olympic Games, *6325*

Khania

Javelin-thrower to break the 240-foot barrier in the women's event, *4406*

Shot-putter to break the 23-meter barrier, *5350*

Marathon

Men's road race cycling event held in the Olympic Games, *2686*

Sparta

Woman recorded as participating in the original Olympic Games, *4600*

GUADELOUPE

Runner from the Caribbean to win the women's 400-meter title in the Olympic Games, *5158*

Runner to win two consecutive titles in the women's 400-meter race in the Olympic Games, *5182*

Runner to win two titles in the women's 400-meter event in the World Championships in Athletics, *5177*

GUYANA (BRITISH GUINEA)

British Empire Games (later the British Commonwealth Games), *4369*

HAITI

Long-jumper to break the 26-foot barrier, *4432*

HUNGARY

Boxer from a Communist country to turn professional, *2561*

Boxer to compete in four Olympic Games, *2579*

Boxer to win three gold medals, and two consecutive light middleweight titles, in the Olympic Games, *2560*

Canoe marathon world championships, *2624*

Father and son to both win gold medals in track and field in the Olympic Games, *6213*

Fencer to win two consecutive men's individual sabre titles, and men's team sabre titles, in the Olympic Games, *2914*

Fencer to win two consecutive women's épée titles in the world championships, *2942*

Fencer to win two consecutive women's foil titles in the world championships, *2928*

Fencer to win two consecutive women's individual foil titles in the Olympic Games, *2929*

Figure skater to win three and then four consecutive women's singles titles in the world championships, *2982*

Figure skaters from Hungary to win the ice dancing title in the world championships, *3083*

Figure skaters from Hungary to win the pairs title in the world championships, *3009*

Gymnast to win two consecutive women's floor exercise titles in the Olympic Games, *3941*

Hammer-thrower to break the 60-meter barrier, *3987*

International championships in table tennis, *5984*

International governing body for ice skating, *2962*

International pairs figure skating competition in which all the medalists were brother-and-sister pairs, *3041*

Javelin-thrower to break the 310-foot barrier, *4403*

Light middleweight boxing event held in the Olympic Games, *2558*

Men's 100-meter freestyle swimming event held in the Olympic Games, *5785*

Men's 1200-meter freestyle swimming event held in the Olympic Games, *5786*

Men's 3000-meter walk event held in the Olympic Games, *6288*

Men's 400-meter individual medley event held at the world championships, *5888*

Men's 50-yard (later 50-meter) freestyle swimming event held in the Olympic Games, *5795*

Men's floor exercises gymnastics competition held in the Olympic Games, *3928*

HUNGARY—*continued*

Men's modern pentathlon team event held in the Olympic Games, *4823*

Modern Olympic Games at which member countries were barred from competing, *4649*

Olympic Games to be boycotted by member countries, *4703*

Pentathlete to win five consecutive men's titles in the world pentathlon championships, *4830*

Pentathlete to win two pentathlon gold medals in the same Olympic Games, *4827*

Runner to hold the officially accepted world record in the men's 5000-meter steeplechase, *5062*

Soccer (international football) team from Germany to win the world cup, *5556*

Soccer (international football) team to win the world cup twice in a row, *5555*

Swaythling Cup, *5983*

Swimmer to hold the world titles in both the men's 200- and 400-meter individual medleys at the same time, *5911*

Swimmer to win five individual gold medals, and three consecutive medals in the women's 200-meter backstroke, in the Olympic Games, *5972*

Swimmer to win two consecutive gold medals in the women's 200-meter backstroke in the Olympic Games, *5966*

Swimmer to win two consecutive men's 100-meter breaststroke titles at the world championships, *5970*

Swimmer to win two consecutive men's 200-meter individual medley titles at the world championships, *5959*

Swimmer to win two consecutive men's 200-meter individual medley titles in the Olympic Games, *5967*

Swimmer to win two consecutive men's 400-meter individual medley titles at the world championships, *5916*

Swimmer to win two consecutive men's 400-meter individual medley titles in the Olympic Games, *5962*

Table tennis player to win five men's singles titles in the world championships, *5989*

Water polo player to win medals in five different Olympic Games, *6304*

Weightlifter to compete in five Olympic Games, *6347*

Woman gymnast to win 10 medals in the Olympic Games, *3940*

Women's floor exercises gymnastics competition held in the Olympic Games, *3936*

Women's long jump event held in the Olympic Games, *4436*

Women's uneven (asymmetrical) bars gymnastics competition held in the Olympic Games, *3938*

World championships for water polo, *6305*

World championships in Greco-Roman wrestling held on a regular basis, *6388*

World championships in handball to include women, *4006*

World cup for water polo, *6306*

World cup in weightlifting, *6348*

Wrestler to win two consecutive super heavyweight Greco-Roman titles in the Olympic Games, *6392*

Budapest

Figure skater from Great Britain to win the men's singles title at the world championships, *3024*

Figure skater to perform a quadruple jump in competition, *3091*

Figure skaters to win four consecutive pairs titles in the world championships, *3025*

Figure skaters to win two, and then three, consecutive pairs titles in the world championships, *3018*

International governing body for canoeing, *2595*

Debrecen

Hammer-thrower to break the 240-foot barrier, *3992*

INDIA

Asian Games, *4372*

Cricket club in India, *2640*

Development of modern polo, *4853*

Field hockey club established in India, *4034*

Field hockey players to win three gold medals in the Olympic Games, *4039*

Field hockey players to win two gold medals in the Olympic Games, *4038*

Golf club in Asia, *3564*

Introduction of polo in Europe, *4855*

Polo club, *4854*

Snooker game on record, *2445*

Standardized rules for badminton, *1164*

World amateur snooker championships, *2457*

INDONESIA

Athlete from Indonesia to win a gold medal in the Olympic Games, *4777*

Badminton events held in the Olympic Games as medal sports, *1174*

Sudirman Trophy awarded at the badminton world championships, *1172*

World championships in badminton, *1171*

World cup/grand prix competition in badminton, *1173*

IRAN

Light flyweight freestyle wrestling event held in the world wrestling championships, *6395*

IRAQ

Olympic Games to be boycotted by member countries, *4703*

IRELAND

Boxer to be undisputed world lightweight champion, *2518*
Boxer to hold the undisputed world light heavyweight title, *2525*
British Empire Games (later the British Commonwealth Games), *4369*
Code of rules for Gaelic football, *3523*
Discus-thrower to win two, and then three, consecutive men's titles in the Olympic Games, *2757*
Establishment of the Tailteann Games, *4363*
Hammer-thrower born in the United States to win the men's event in the Olympic Games, *3983*
International court (four-wall) handball competition, *3999*
National organization for hurling, *4356*
Queen Elizabeth II Cup, *2861*
Runner from Canada to win the men's 200-meter race in the Olympic Games, *4996*
Runner to win the men's 5000-meter race held in the World Championships in Athletics, *5131*
Steeplechase horse race, *4256*
Women's world indoor championships in bowls, *2503*
World cup in cycling, *2715*

Cóbh

International motorboat (powerboat) race, *4563*

Cork

Hammer-thrower to break the 280-foot barrier, *3996*
Yacht club, *5194*

Dublin

All-Ireland championships in Gaelic football, *3524*
All-Ireland Championships in hurling, *4358*
Cricket team from outside England to play in England, *2646*
Equestrian show jumping competition, *2837*
Long-jumper to hold the officially accepted world record in the men's event, *4428*

National tennis championships in Ireland, *6010*
Runner to complete the men's mile race in under 3:55 minutes, *5068*

Kildare

Golf club in Ireland, *3569*

Kilkenny

Ban on hurling, *4355*

Louth

Gaelic football match, *3522*

Meath

Gaelic football match, *3522*

Slane

Gaelic football match, *3522*

Thurles

Standardization of the rules of hurling, *4357*

Tipperary

All-Ireland Championships in hurling, *4358*

ISRAEL

Olympic Games at which athletes were killed by terrorists, *4739*

ITALY

Argentine Grand Prix automobile race, *1091*
Athlete to qualify for the finals of the same event in four Olympic Games, *4759*
Athlete to win 13 medals in the Olympic Games, *4709*
Austrian Grand Prix automobile race to be part of the Formula One Grand Prix circuit, *1107*
Automobile race at the Circuit Pescara, *1058*
Automobile racer to have nine consecutive wins over two seasons on the Formula One Grand Prix circuit, *1089*
Automobile racer to have six wins in a single season on the Formula One Grand Prix circuit, *1087*
Basketball team from Yugoslavia to win the men's title in the Olympic Games, *2163*
Boxer to be world junior flyweight (light-flyweight) champion, *2572*
Boxer to hold the super-featherweight (junior lightweight) title, *2542*
British Grand Prix automobile race to be part of the Formula One Grand Prix circuit, *1077*

ITALY—*continued*

Diver to win three consecutive men's platform diving titles in the Olympic Games, *2811*

Diver to win two consecutive men's highboard platform diving titles at the world championships, *2810*

Dutch Grand Prix automobile race to be part of the Formula One Grand Prix circuit, *1088*

Fencer to win 13 medals in the Olympic Games, *2934*

Fencer to win five gold medals in a single Olympic Games, and to win two consecutive men's individual foil titles in the Olympic Games, *2916*

Fencer to win two consecutive men's foil titles in the world championships, *2922*

Fencer to win two, three, and four men's team épée titles in the Olympic Games, *2931*

Figure skater to land a triple lutz jump in competition, *3060*

Floor exercise competition held at the world championships in gymnastics, *3919*

Flyweight Greco-Roman wrestling event held in the Olympic Games, *6387*

French Grand Prix automobile race to be part of the Formula One Grand Prix circuit, *1082*

German Grand Prix automobile race to be part of the Formula One Grand Prix circuit, *1084*

Giant slalom and snowboard cross events held in the snowboarding world championships, *5523*

Gymnast to win three, and then four, men's rings titles in the world championships, *3977*

Gymnast to win three consecutive gold medals in the men's team combined exercises in the Olympic Games, *3924*

Gymnast to win two consecutive men's all-around titles in the Olympic Games, *3918*

Gymnast to win two consecutive men's pommel horse titles in the world championships, *3921*

Gymnasts to win two consecutive gold medals in the men's team combined exercises in the Olympic Games, *3922*

International and transcontinental automobile race, *1050*

International moto-cross competition for 125 cc cycles, *4593*

Italian Grand Prix automobile race to be part of the Formula One Grand Prix circuit, *1083*

Masters sabre fencing competition held in the Olympic Games, *2905*

Men's foil competition held in the world championships of fencing, *2921*

Men's giant slalom event held in the Alpine skiing world championships, *5390*

Men's highboard platform diving event held at the world championships, *2805*

Pescara Grand Prix automobile race, *1059*

Pommel horse competition held at the world championships in gymnastics, *3917*

Runner to complete the men's 200-meter race in under 19.8 seconds, *5112*

Runner to hold the officially accepted world record in the men's marathon, and the first United States runner to win the Olympic marathon, *4472*

Runner to win the men's 10,000-meter race held in the World Championships in Athletics, *5126*

Shooter to win two consecutive individual trap (clay pigeon) shooting titles in the Olympic Games, *5317*

Skier to win two consecutive individual titles in an Alpine event in the Olympic Winter Games, *5479*

Skier to win two consecutive titles in the women's giant slalom in the Olympic Winter Games, *5502*

Soccer (international football) team to win the world cup twice in a row, *5555*

Swimmer to swim across the English Channel from France to England, *5816*

Swiss Grand Prix automobile race to be part of the Formula One Grand Prix circuit, *1080*

Tour of Italy (Giro d'Italia) cycling race, *2693*

Two-seater luge (toboggan) event to have two pairs of gold medalists in a single Olympic Winter Games, *4458*

United States baseball team to tour the world, and to visit Australia, *1294*

Woman automobile racer to compete in a Grand Prix race eligible for world-championship points, *1097*

Woman automobile racer to win world-championship points in a Grand Prix race, *1119*

Women's 30-kilometer Nordic (cross-country) skiing event held at the Olympic Winter Games, *5469*

Women's 800-meter freestyle swimming event held in the world championships, *5907*

Women's cross-country cycling race held in the Olympic Games, *2724*

Women's pursuit (5 kilometers classical and 10 kilometers freestyle) event held in the world championships of Nordic skiing, *5483*

World championship for automobile racers, *1076*

World championships in bobsledding, *2469*

World championships in motorcycle racing, *4578*

World Cross-Country Championships, *5096*

World Cup Marathon, *4514*

World rally championship for drivers, *1125*

World speed skating championships for roller skating, *4907*

Wrestler to win two consecutive light flyweight Greco-Roman wrestling titles in the Olympic Games, *6408*

Como

Javelin-throw world record set using the new javelin in the men's event, *4409*

Cortina d'Ampezzo

Figure skater from the United States to win the women's singles title at the Olympic Winter Games, *3053*

Figure skaters to take all three medals in the same order in the U.S., world, and Olympic men's singles competitions, *3051*

Ice hockey team from the Soviet Union to win the gold medal at the Olympic Winter Games, *4135*

Men's 30-kilometer Nordic (cross-country) ski event held at the Olympic Winter Games, *5402*

Men's individual 15-kilometer Nordic (cross-country) event at the Olympic Winter Games, *5404*

National team to sweep the medals in the men's giant slalom in the Olympic Winter Games, *5403*

Olympic Winter Games at which athletes from the Soviet Union participated, *4705*

Olympic Winter Games to be held in Italy, and the first to be televised, *4704*

Skier to sweep the men's individual Alpine events at the Olympic Winter Games, *5406*

Skiers from the Soviet Union to win the men's 4 x 10-kilometer relay Nordic (cross-country) title at the Olympic Winter Games, *5405*

Women's 3 x 5-kilometer relay Nordic (cross-country) skiing event held at the Olympic Winter Games, *5401*

Genoa

National soccer (international football) league in Italy, *5542*

Milan

Figure skater to perform a double axel in competition, *3042*

Figure skater to perform a triple loop–triple loop combination jump in competition, *3044*

Primavera cycling race, *2690*

Runner to complete the men's 800-meter race in under 1:44 minutes, *5099*

Runner to race the men's 800 meters in under 1:48 minutes, *5044*

Rieti

Runner to complete the men's mile race in under 3:45 minutes, *5170*

Runner to race the men's 1500 meters in less than 3:29 minutes, *5163*

Rome

African-American runner to win the women's 100- and 200-meter titles in the Olympic Games, *5069*

African-American woman to win the Sullivan Award, *1153*

Athlete from Ethiopia, and Black athlete from Africa, to win a gold medal at the Olympic Games, *4710*

Black African runner to win the men's marathon title at the Olympic Games, and to hold the world record in the event, *4487*

Boxer from the United States to win the light middleweight title in the Olympic Games, *2563*

Discus-thrower to win two titles in the women's event in the Olympic Games, *2770*

Diver to win two consecutive women's highboard platform diving titles at the world championships, *2823*

Equestrians to win two consecutive titles in team jumping in the Olympic Games, *2867*

Fencer to win two, three, and four men's team épée titles in the Olympic Games, *2931*

Flying Dutchman–class sailing event held in the Olympic Games, *5223*

Gymnast to win two consecutive men's horizontal bar titles in the Olympic Games, *3947*

Gymnast to win two consecutive titles in the men's rings competition in the Olympic Games, *3948*

Gymnast to win two consecutive women's all-around titles in the Olympic Games, *3944*

Gymnasts to win two consecutive gold medals in the women's team combined exercises, *3945*

Hurdler to win two, and then three, consecutive titles in the men's 110-meter hurdles in the World Championships in Athletics, *4351*

Hurdler to win two consecutive titles in the men's 110-meter hurdles in the Olympic Games, *4340*

Hurdler to win two consecutive titles in the men's 400-meter hurdles in the Olympic Games, *4339*

Hurdler to win two consecutive titles in the men's 400-meter hurdles in the World Championships in Athletics, *4352*

Javelin-thrower to break the 210- and 220-foot barriers in the women's event, *4401*

Men's 4 x 100-meter medley relay swimming event held in the Olympic Games, *5838*

Men's long jump event in which the top four contestants jumped more than 26 feet, *4437*

National team to sweep the top medals in the women's all-around gymnastics competition in the Olympic Games, *3946*

ITALY—Rome—*continued*

Olympic light heavyweight boxing champion to become world heavyweight champion, *2565*

Olympic men's 1500-meter freestyle event in which the medalists all had times under 18 minutes, *5841*

Olympic women's 400-meter freestyle event in which the medalists all had times under five minutes, *5839*

Olympics-like tournament for athletes with disabilities, *2751*

Pentathlete to win two pentathlon gold medals in the same Olympic Games, *4827*

Pole-vaulter to clear 19 feet, *4847*

Runner from New Zealand to win the men's 5000-meter title in the Olympic Games, *5070*

Runner from New Zealand to win the men's 800-meter title in the Olympic Games, *5071*

Runner to race the men's 1500 meters in 3:26 minutes, *5186*

Runner to race the men's 5000 meters in under 13:00 minutes, *5149*

Runner to win both the women's 100- and 200-meter titles in the World Championships in Athletics, *5146*

Runner to win two, and then three, consecutive titles in the men's 100-meter event in the World Championships in Athletics, *5147*

Runner to win two consecutive titles in the men's 200-meter event in the World Championships in Athletics, *5148*

Runners to complete the men's 400-meter race in under 45 seconds, *5072*

Sailor to win the men's Finn-class event two, three, and four times in the Olympic Games, *5219*

Soccer (international football) team from Italy to win the world cup, *5554*

Swimmer to win two and then three consecutive women's 100-meter freestyle titles in the Olympic Games, *5842*

Swimmer to win two consecutive men's 100-meter breaststroke titles at the world championships, *5970*

Swimmer to win two consecutive men's 400-meter freestyle titles in the Olympic Games, *5837*

Swimmer to win two consecutive women's 800-meter freestyle world titles, *5971*

Weightlifter to win two consecutive bantamweight titles in the Olympic Games, *6341*

Weightlifter to win two consecutive middle heavyweight titles in the Olympic Games, *6342*

Women's 4 x 100-meter medley relay swimming event held in the Olympic Games, *5840*

Women's 500-meter pairs kayaking event held in the Olympic Games, *2610*

Women's 800-meter race held in the Olympic Games after a 32-year ban, *5073*

Women's team foil fencing competition held in the Olympic Games, *2935*

Wrestler to win two consecutive welterweight Greco-Roman titles in the Olympic Games, *6390*

San Remo

Primavera cycling race, *2690*

Siena

Palio horse race, *4248*

Turin

Javelin-thrower to break the 240- and 250-foot barriers, *4391*

Venice

Rowers to win two gold medals in pair-oared shell with coxswain rowing events in the same Olympic Games, *4934*

JAMAICA

Boxer to win two, and then three, consecutive heavyweight titles, and three boxing titles in a single class, in the Olympic Games, *2575*

Runner from the Caribbean to win the men's 200-meter title at the Olympic Games, *5106*

Runner from the Caribbean to win the men's 400-meter title in the Olympic Games, *5050*

Runner to qualify for the finals men's of the 100-, 200-, and 400-meter races in the Olympic Games, *5054*

Runner to reach three consecutive finals in the men's 100-meter dash at the Olympic Games, *5157*

Runner to win the men's 400-meter race held in the World Championships in Athletics, *5130*

Runner to win two consecutive titles in the women's 200-meter event in the World Championships in Athletics, *5173*

Sweep of the medals in an event by athletes of Black African ancestry at the Olympic Games, *4726*

JAPAN

Development of judo, *4528*

Far Eastern Games, *4367*

Figure skater from Japan to win the women's singles title in the world championships, *3094*

Golf club in Japan, *3655*

Gymnast to win two consecutive men's floor exercise titles in the world championships, *3942*

Gymnast to win two consecutive men's horizontal bar titles in the Olympic Games, *3947*

Gymnast to win two consecutive men's parallel bars titles in the Olympic Games, *3963*

Ice hockey competition in the Olympic Winter Games to be boycotted, *4161*

Japanese Grand Prix automobile race, *1122*

Male gymnast to win 8 gold medals, and 12 medals overall, in the Olympics Games, *3961*

Men's half-heavyweight judo event in the Olympic Games, *4538*

Men's half-middleweight judo event in the Olympic Games, *4539*

Olympic Games at which athletes from more than 50 countries participated, *4692*

Olympic men's 1500-meter freestyle event in which the medalists all had times under 20 minutes, *5825*

Olympic men's 200-meter breaststroke event in which the medalists all had times under three minutes, *5821*

Oyakazu archery contest, *1018*

Runner from Asia to hold the officially accepted world record in the men's 100-meter dash, *5034*

Runner officially representing South Korea to hold the world record in the men's marathon, and to win the Boston Marathon, *4482*

Skiers to win two consecutive men's Nordic combined team titles at the Olympic Winter Games, *5489*

Speed skater to skate the 500 meters in under 35 seconds, *5734*

Speed skater to win six men's world speed skating sprint championships, *5718*

Sumo wrestling matches, *6356*

Swimmer to win two consecutive men's 200-meter breaststroke titles, *5826*

Swimming races on record, *5778*

Triple-jumper to reach a distance of 16 meters in the men's event, *6254*

Weightlifter to win two consecutive featherweight titles in the Olympic Games, *6343*

Woman to sail across the Pacific alone, *5226*

World championships for judo, *4532*

World championships in badminton, *1171*

World championships in karate, *4537*

World championships in short track speed skating to be officially recognized, *5697*

World Half Marathon Championship, *4521*

Fukuoka

Asahi Marathon, *4481*

Fukuoka Marathon, *4484*

Runner to race the men's marathon in under 2:12 hours, and the first representing Australia to hold the world record in the event, *4492*

Hiroshima

World Cup Marathon, *4514*

Kumamoto

Asahi Marathon, *4481*

Nagano

Curling event held in the Olympic Games, *2680*

Figure skaters to win two consecutive ice dancing titles at the Olympic Winter Games, *3114*

Male athlete to win six individual gold medals in the Olympic Winter Games, *4804*

Male figure skater to win the pairs title at the Olympic Winter Games with two different partners, *3115*

Men's giant slalom snowboarding event held at the Olympic Winter Games, *5524*

Men's halfpipe snowboarding event held at the Olympic Winter Games, *5526*

Olympic Winter Games in which more than 2000 athletes competed, and more than 55 percent were women, *4803*

Skier from the United States to win the men's aerials freestyle skiing event in the Olympic Winter Games, *5500*

Skier from the United States to win the men's moguls freestyle skiing event in the Olympic Winter Games, *5497*

Skier from the United States to win the women's aerials freestyle skiing event in the Olympic Winter Games, *5501*

Skier from the United States to win the women's super giant slalom at the Olympic Winter Games, *5498*

Skier to win two consecutive men's 10-kilometer Nordic (cross-country) skiing titles, and the first male athlete to win six gold medals overall, at the Olympic Winter Games, *5499*

Skier to win two consecutive Olympic titles in the women's downhill, and the first to win both the downhill and Alpine combination events in the same Olympic Winter Games, *5503*

Skier to win two consecutive titles in the women's giant slalom in the Olympic Winter Games, *5502*

Slider to win two, and then three, consecutive men's singles luge (toboggan) titles in the Olympic Winter Games, *4465*

Speed skater to skate the 10,000 meters in under 13:30 minutes, *5729*

Speed skater to skate the 5000 meters in under 6:30 minutes, *5728*

Speed skater to skate the women's 5000-meter event in under 7 minutes, *5730*

JAPAN—Nagano—*continued*

Speed skater to win two consecutive women's 1000-meter short track titles in the Olympic Winter Games, *5732*

Speed skater to win two consecutive women's 5000-meter titles in the Olympic Winter Games, *5731*

Women's giant slalom snow-boarding event held at the Olympic Winter Games, *5525*

Women's halfpipe snowboarding event held at the Olympic Winter Games, *5527*

Women's ice hockey event held in the Olympic Games, *4230*

Okinawa

Formal instruction in karate, *4529*

Osaka

Long-jumper to hold the officially accepted world record in the women's event, and the first female athlete from Asia to set a world track and field record, *4431*

Women's volleyball event held in the Olympic Games, *6280*

Sapporo

Athlete to win two consecutive gold medals in the biathlon in the Olympic Winter Games, *2433*

Figure skater from Czechoslovakia to win the men's singles title at the Olympic Winter Games, *3070*

Figure skater to win a pairs title in the Olympic Winter Games with two different partners, *3075*

National team to sweep the medals in the men's 70-meter ski jump at the Olympic Winter Games, *5420*

National team to sweep the medals in the men's singles luge (toboggan) event at the Olympic Winter Games, *4459*

National team to sweep the medals in the women's singles luge (toboggan) event at the Olympic Winter Games, *4460*

Olympic Winter Games held in Asia, *4735*

Olympic Winter Games to be canceled because of war, *4686*

Skier to win both the women's downhill and giant slalom titles in the same Olympic Winter Games, *5421*

Speed skater from the United States to win the women's 1500-meter title at the Olympic Winter Games, *5687*

Speed skater from the United States to win the women's 500-meter title at the Olympic Winter Games, *5688*

Speed skater to skate the 1500 meters in under 2 minutes, *5684*

Triple-jumper to hold the officially accepted world record in the women's event, *6261*

Two-seater luge (toboggan) event to have two pairs of gold medalists in a single Olympic Winter Games, *4458*

Tokyo

Athletes from the Bahamas to win gold medals in the Olympic Games, *4719*

Boxer to hold the undisputed world heavyweight title after 1980, *2586*

Equestrian to win three consecutive titles in team jumping in the Olympic Games, *2869*

Gymnast to win three consecutive gold medals in the team combined exercises in the Olympic Games, *3951*

Gymnast to win two consecutive titles in the women's uneven (asymmetrical) bars in the Olympic Games, *3952*

High-jumper to win two consecutive women's titles in the Olympic Games, *4030*

Hurdler to win two, and then three, consecutive titles in the men's 110-meter hurdles in the World Championships in Athletics, *4351*

Javelin-thrower to break the 200-foot and 60-meter barriers in the women's event, *4400*

Men's 4 x 100-meter freestyle relay swimming event held in the Olympic Games, *5847*

Men's 400-meter individual medley swimming event held in the Olympic Games, *5848*

Men's 4000-meter individual pursuit cycling event held in the Olympic Games, *2702*

Men's fours 1000-meter kayaking event held in the Olympic Games, *2611*

Men's heavyweight judo event in the Olympic Games, *4535*

Men's lightweight judo event in the Olympic Games, *4534*

Men's open judo event in the Olympic Games, *4536*

Men's volleyball event held in the Olympic Games, *6279*

National team to sweep the medals in the men's 200-meter backstroke event in the Olympic Games, *5846*

Olympic Games held in Asia, or in Japan, *4718*

Pentathlete to win two gold medals in the men's modern pentathlon team competition in the Olympic Games, *4828*

Professional baseball team in Japan, *1488*

Record in the men's marathon to stand for more than 10 years, *4480*

Rower to win three consecutive men's single sculls rowing titles in the Olympic Games, *4941*

Runner from Asia to hold the officially accepted world record in the men's 100-meter dash, *5034*

Runner from the United States to win the men's 10,000-meter title at the Olympic Games, *5077*

Runner from the United States to win the men's 5000-meter title at the Olympic Games, *5078*

Runner to race the men's 100 meters in under 9.9 seconds, *5156*

Runner to win two, and then three, consecutive titles in the men's 100-meter event in the World Championships in Athletics, *5147*

Runner to win two consecutive marathon titles in the Olympic Games, *4489*

Runner to win two consecutive titles in the men's 800-meter event in the World Championships in Athletics, *5155*

Shooter from the United States to win the men's small-bore rifle (three positions) title in the Olympic Games, *5310*

Shot-putter to win two consecutive titles in the women's event in the Olympic Games, *5344*

Swimmer to win four gold medals in a single Olympic Games, *5850*

Swimmer to win two and then three consecutive women's 100-meter freestyle titles in the Olympic Games, *5842*

Water polo player to win medals in five different Olympic Games, *6304*

Wedding between Olympic athletes held at the Olympic Games, *4717*

Weightlifter to win two consecutive lightweight titles in the Olympic Games, *6344*

Woman to compete in the three-day event individual equestrian competition in the Olympic Games, *2868*

Women's 400-meter individual medley swimming event held in the Olympic Games, *5849*

Women's 400-meter race held in the Olympic Games, *5076*

Women's pentathlon held in the Olympic Games, *4829*

Women's volleyball event held in the Olympic Games, *6280*

West Tokyo

Little League World Series won by an East Asian team, *1692*

KAZAKHSTAN

Athlete from newly independent Kazakhstan to win a gold medal at the Olympic Games, *4787*

Skier to win the 50-kilometer Nordic (cross-country) title in the Olympic Winter Games after it was converted from freestyle to classical style, *5493*

KENYA

Black African-born boxer to win a boxing title in the Olympic Games, *2585*

Record in the men's 5000-meter steeplechase to last for more than 10 years, *5108*

Runner from Africa to hold the world record in the men's 5000 meters, *5079*

Runner from Africa to win the men's 10,000-meter title at the Olympic Games, *5085*

Runner from Africa to win the men's 1500-meter title at the Olympic Games, *5092*

Runner from Africa to win the men's 3000-meter steeplechase title in the Olympic Games, *5087*

Runner from Africa to win the men's 800-meter title at the Olympic Games, *5151*

Runner from Africa to win the men's title in the Boston Marathon, *4518*

Runner from Africa to win the men's title in the New York Marathon, *4516*

Runner from Africa to win the women's title in the New York Marathon, *4524*

Runner to race the men's 10,000 meters in under 27:00 minutes, *5168*

Runner to race the men's 10,000 meters in under 27:00 minutes, *5168*

Runner to race the men's 5000-meter steeplechase in under 8:00 minutes, *5178*

Runner to race the men's 5000-meter steeplechase in under 8:20 minutes, *5098*

Runner to race the men's 5000-meter steeplechase in under 8:20 minutes, *5098*

Runner to win two, and then three, consecutive titles in the men's 3000-meter steeplechase in the World Championships in Athletics, *5167*

Runner to win two consecutive titles in the men's 5000-meter event in the World Championships in Athletics, *5172*

World Half Marathon Championship, *4521*

World Road Relay Championship, *4522*

LEBANON

Olympic Games to be boycotted by member countries, *4703*

LIECHTENSTEIN

Athlete from Liechtenstein to win an Olympic gold medal, *4750*

LITHUANIA

Athlete from newly independent Lithuania to win a gold medal in the Olympic Games, *4778*

Women's trap shooting event held in the Olympic Games, *5327*

LUXEMBOURG

Skier to win five men's overall titles in skiing's world cup, *5482*

World championships in gymnastics, *3910*

MALAYSIA

Golf ball made of gutta-percha, *3567*

World team Thomas Cup badminton championships for men, *1169*

MEXICO

Avila Camacho Cup polo competition, *4868*

Stud book for horse racing published in North America, *4287*

Whitbread Round-the-World Race, *5232*

World Race Walking Cup, *6294*

Mexico City

Athlete from Iran to win a gold medal in the Olympic Games, *4731*

Athlete from Kenya to win a gold medal in the Olympic Games, *4732*

Athlete from Tunisia to win a gold medal in the Olympic Games, *4728*

Athlete from Venezuela to win a gold medal in the Olympic Games, *4729*

Athlete to win the gold medal in the same event in four consecutive Olympic Games, *4727*

Athletes from Pakistan to win gold medals in the Olympic Games, *4730*

Boxer to win two consecutive light middleweight titles in the Olympic Games, *2568*

Boxer to win two consecutive light welterweight titles in the Olympic Games, *2569*

Canoe racer to win two consecutive titles in the women's 500-meter singles kayak event, *2612*

Canoe racers to win two consecutive women's 500-meter kayak pairs event in the Olympic Games, *2613*

Discus-thrower to win four consecutive men's titles in the Olympic Games, and the first to win any Olympic event four consecutive times, *2777*

Equestrian from the United States to win the individual jumping title in the Olympic Games, *2873*

Fencers to win two gold medals in the women's team foil competition in the Olympic Games, *2937*

Gymnast to win three consecutive men's side (pommel) horse titles in the world championships, *3956*

Gymnast to win two consecutive men's side (pommel) horse titles in the Olympic Games, *3955*

Gymnast to win two consecutive women's side horse vault titles in the Olympic Games, *3954*

Hammer-thrower to break the 240-foot barrier, *3992*

High-jumper to use the "Fosbury flop" jumping method, *4031*

Light flyweight boxing event held in the Olympic Games, *2570*

Long-jumper to break the 28- and 29-foot barriers, *4439*

Men's 100-meter breaststroke event held in the Olympic Games, *5851*

Men's 100-meter butterfly swimming event held in the Olympic Games, *5856*

Men's 200-meter individual medley swimming event held in the Olympic Games, *5853*

Mexican Grand Prix automobile race to be part of the Formula One Grand Prix circuit, *1106*

Olympic Games held in Mexico, *4724*

Olympic Games to include athletes from more than 100 countries, *4722*

Runner from Africa to win the men's 10,000-meter title at the Olympic Games, *5085*

Runner from Africa to win the men's 1500-meter title at the Olympic Games, *5092*

Runner from Africa to win the men's 3000-meter steeplechase title in the Olympic Games, *5087*

Runner from Africa to win the men's 5000-meter title in the Olympic Games, *5089*

Runner from the United States to win the women's 800-meter title at the Olympic Games, *5091*

Runner to complete the men's 200-meter race in under 19.8 seconds, *5112*

Runner to complete the men's 200-meter race in under 20 seconds, *5088*

Runner to complete the men's 400-meter race in under 44 seconds, *5090*

Runner to win two consecutive women's 200-meter titles in the Olympic Games, *5086*

Sailor to win gold medals in three different sailing events in the Olympic Games, *5239*

Sailors from the United States to win the Dragon-class event in the Olympic Games, *5225*

Shot-putter to break the 19-meter barrier in the women's event, *5346*

Skeet shooting individual event held in the Olympic Games, *5312*

Soccer (international football) team to win the world cup three times, *5562*

Sweep of the medals in an event by athletes of Black African ancestry at the Olympic Games, *4726*

Swimmer from the United States to win the women's 200-meter breaststroke title in the Olympic Games, *5858*

Swimmer to win three individual gold medals in a single Olympic Games, *5862*

Swimmer to win two consecutive gold medals in the men's 4 x 100-meter freestyle relay in the Olympic Games, *5865*

Triple-jumper to break the 58-foot barrier, *6258*

Volleyball players to win two consecutive men's gold medals in the Olympic Games, *6282*

Walker to win two titles in the men's 20,000-meter walk in the Olympic Games, *6293*

Weightlifter to win two consecutive lightweight titles in the Olympic Games, *6344*

Woman equestrian to win a gold medal in team dressage in the Olympic Games, *2875*

Women to compete in shooting events in the Olympic Games, *5311*

Women's 100-meter breaststroke event held in the Olympic Games, *5852*

Women's 200-meter backstroke event held in the Olympic Games, *5861*

Women's 200-meter butterfly event held in the Olympic Games, *5859*

Women's 200-meter freestyle event held in the Olympic Games, *5857*

Women's 200-meter individual medley swimming event held in the Olympic Games, *5855*

Women's 800-meter freestyle swimming event held in the Olympic Games, *5860*

World championships in fast-pitch softball to include men's teams, *5602*

Wrestler to win two consecutive light heavyweight Greco-Roman titles in the Olympic Games, *6391*

Wrestler to win two consecutive super heavyweight Greco-Roman titles in the Olympic Games, *6392*

Monterrey

Little League World Series won by a team from outside the United States, *1624*

MONACO

Schneider Cup international seaplane (hydroaeroplane) race, *1004*

MOROCCO

Athlete from Morocco to win a gold medal at the Olympic Games, and the first female athlete from an Islamic country to win an Olympic medal, *4758*

Runner to race the men's 1500 meters in 3:26 minutes, *5186*

Runner to race the men's 5000 meters in under 13:00 minutes, *5149*

Runner to race the men's mile race in under 3:44.00 minutes, *5154*

Swimmer to swim across the Strait of Gibraltar, *5830*

Women's 400-meter hurdles event held in the Olympic Games, *4350*

MOZAMBIQUE

Runner to race the women's 1000 meters in under 2:30 minutes, *5180*

NETHERLANDS

Athlete 10 years old or under to earn a gold medal in the Olympic Games, *4623*

Automobile racer to win the Indianapolis 500 with an average speed of more than 180 miles per hour, *1139*

Dutch Grand Prix automobile race to be part of the Formula One Grand Prix circuit, *1088*

Equestrian to win two consecutive three-day event individual titles, *2857*

Equestrians to win two consecutive three-day event team titles, *2854*

Fencer to win two consecutive men's sabre titles in the world championships, *2919*

Figure skater from the Netherlands to win the women's singles title at the Olympic Winter Games, *3065*

Figure skater from the Netherlands to win the women's singles title in the world championships, *3059*

Ice boating club in the United States, *4359*

International governing body for ice skating, *2962*

International governing body for ice skating, *2962*

Iron skates in England, *2948*

Judo artist to win two gold medals in a single Olympic Games, *4540*

Men's cross-country (mountain bike) race held in the Olympic Games, *2723*

Men's Finn-class sailing event in the Olympic Games, *5208*

Men's one-meter springboard diving event held at the world championships, *2821*

Men's open judo event in the Olympic Games, *4536*

Men's sabre competition held in the world championships of fencing, *2918*

Men's sailboarding event held in the Olympic Games, *5191*

Olympic Games to be boycotted by member countries, *4703*

Runner to win both the women's 100- and 200-meter titles in the same Olympic Games, *5052*

Sailor to win the Whitbread Round-the-World Race twice consecutively, *5241*

Soccer (international football) team from Argentina to win the world cup, *5563*

Speed skater to be world champion in men's long-distance speed skating twice, and then three times, in a row, *5635*

NETHERLANDS—*continued*

Speed skater to skate the 10,000 meters in under 13:30 minutes, *5729*

Speed skater to skate the 10,000 meters in under 15 minutes, *5685*

Speed skater to skate the 10,000 meters in under 18 minutes, *5636*

Speed skater to skate the 1500 meters in under 1:50 minutes, *5727*

Speed skater to skate the 1500 meters in under 2 minutes, *5684*

Speed skater to skate the 3000 meters in under 4 minutes, *5706*

Speed skater to skate the 3000 meters in under 4:10 minutes, *5689*

Speed skater to skate the 3000 meters in under 4:20 minutes, *5679*

Speed skater to skate the 5000 meters in under 6:30 minutes, *5728*

Speed skater to skate the 5000 meters in under 9 minutes, *5634*

Speed skater to win four women's titles at the long-distance speed skating championships, *5690*

Woman athlete to win four gold medals in track and field in a single Olympic Games, *6212*

Woman speed skater to skate the 5000 meters in under 8 minutes, *5699*

Women's 200-meter butterfly event held in the Olympic Games, *5859*

Women's 200-meter race held in the Olympic Games, *5051*

Women's 5000-meter speed skating event held in the Olympic Winter Games, *5709*

Women's team combined exercises gymnastics competition held in the Olympic Games, *3926*

World championships in duathlon, *2835*

World championships in gymnastics, *3910*

World championships in taekwondo to include women, *4549*

World long-distance triathlon championships, *6245*

Written reference to *kolven*, *4414*

Written reference to *kolven* in North America, *4415*

Amsterdam

Athlete from Egypt to win an Olympic gold medal, *4662*

Athlete from independent Ireland to win a gold medal in the Olympic Games, *3984*

Athlete from Japan to win a gold medal in the Olympic Games, *4671*

Athlete from New Zealand to win an Olympic gold medal, *4672*

Athlete from Poland to win a gold medal in the Olympic Games, *4670*

Athlete to win 12 medals in the Olympic Games, *4669*

Athletes from Asia, and from India, to win gold medals in the Olympic Games, *4668*

Athletes from Spain to win gold medals in the Olympic Games, *4673*

Athletes from the Netherlands to win gold medals in the Olympic Games, *4624*

Equestrian to win the individual jumping event in the Olympic Games without a single fault, *2856*

Equestrians to win two consecutive three-day event team titles, *2854*

Hammer-thrower representing Ireland to win the men's event in the Olympic Games, *3985*

Men's 1000-meter time trial cycling event held in the Olympic Games, *2696*

Men's pair-oared shell with coxswain rowing event held in the Olympic Games, *4926*

Olympic Games to include track and field events for women, *4667*

Olympic men's 200-meter breaststroke event in which the medalists all had times under three minutes, *5821*

Olympic Winter Games held in a different country from the Summer Games, *4663*

Pentathlete to hold the officially accepted world record in the women's pentathlon (type B), *4822*

Rower to win three consecutive medals in the men's double sculls event in the Olympic Games, *4936*

Runner from Canada to win the men's 100-meter race in the Olympic Games, *5018*

Runner to hold the officially accepted world record in the women's 800-meter event, *5021*

Runner to win two consecutive men's 800-meter titles in the Olympic Games, *5019*

Swimmer to win two consecutive gold medals in the men's 4 x 200-meter freestyle relay swimming event in the Olympic Games, *5822*

Team dressage equestrian event held in the Olympic Games, *2855*

Woman to win an Olympic gold medal in sailing, *5210*

Women's 100-meter running event, and the first women's track event, held in the Olympic Games, *5020*

Women's 4 x 100-meter relay running event held in the Olympic Games, *5023*

Women's 800-meter running event held in the Olympic Games, *5022*

Women's discus throw event, and the first women's field event, held in the Olympic Games, *2762*

Women's high jump event held in the Olympic Games, *4022*

World championship in speed skating, *5630*

NORWAY—*continued*

Formally measured ski jump, *5355*

Ice hockey team from Sweden to win the title at the Olympic Winter Games, *4215*

Individual skiing-and-shooting competition, *2429*

Javelin-thrower to break the 280-foot barrier and to hold the world record in the men's event, *4397*

London Marathon, *4507*

Male athlete to win six individual gold medals in the Olympic Winter Games, *4804*

Men's 10-kilometer cross-country (classical) event held in the world championships of Nordic skiing, *5466*

Men's 10-kilometer Nordic (cross-country) skiing event held at the Olympic Winter Games, *5472*

Men's combined pursuit Nordic (cross-country) skiing event held at the Olympic Winter Games, *5476*

Men's individual 15-kilometer Nordic (cross-country) event at the Olympic Winter Games, *5404*

Men's individual Nordic combined (cross-country and ski jump) event held in the Olympic Winter Games, *5367*

Men's individual ski jump event held at the Olympic Winter Games, *5368*

Men's pursuit (10 kilometers classical and 15 kilometers freestyle) event held in the world championships of Nordic skiing, *5481*

Men's team ski jumping event held in the world championships of Nordic skiing, *5436*

National organization for skiing, *5358*

National team to sweep the medals in the men's 15-kilometer Nordic (cross-country) skiing event in the Olympic Winter Games, *5376*

National team to sweep the medals in the men's 30-kilometer Nordic (cross-country) skiing event at the Olympic Winter Games, *5471*

National team to sweep the medals in the men's 5000-meter speed-skating event at the Olympic Winter Games, *5676*

National team to sweep the medals in the men's 90-meter ski jump at the Olympic Winter Games, *5379*

National team to sweep the medals in the men's combined individual Nordic (cross-country) skiing event at the Olympic Winter Games, *5369*

Nordic combination event held in the world cup for Nordic skiing, *5438*

Organized Nordic (cross-country) ski races, *5354*

Runner to race the women's 5000 meters in under 15 minutes, *5138*

Running deer (double shot) team shooting event held in the Olympic Games, *5297*

Ski and shooting club, *2428*

Ski-jumping contest focusing on jumping alone, *5356*

Ski orienteering world championships to include sprint competitions, *4810*

Skier to win both the men's individual 70- and 90-meter ski jumps in the same Olympic Winter Games, *5414*

Skier to win two consecutive men's 10-kilometer Nordic (cross-country) skiing titles, and the first male athlete to win six gold medals overall, at the Olympic Winter Games, *5499*

Skier to win two consecutive men's individual Nordic combined titles in the Olympic Winter Games, *5378*

Skier to win two consecutive men's individual ski jump titles in the Olympic Winter Games, *5385*

Skiing and shooting competition (later known as biathlon), *2427*

Skiing manual, *5353*

Small-bore rifle (three positions) individual shooting event held in the Olympic Games, *5309*

Snowboarder to win two consecutive titles in a world championship event, *5522*

Snowboarding world championships, *5521*

Speed skater to be women's world champion in speed skating twice in a row, *5661*

Speed skater to be world champion in men's long-distance speed skating five times, *5637*

Speed skater to skate the 1000 meters in under 1:20 minutes, *5681*

Speed skater to skate the 10,000 meters in under 14 minutes, *5707*

Speed skater to skate the 10,000 meters in under 16 minutes, *5672*

Speed skater to skate the 10,000 meters in under 17 minutes, *5662*

Speed skater to skate the 10,000 meters in under 20 minutes, *5632*

Speed skater to skate the 3000 meters in under 4:30 minutes, *5674*

Speed skater to skate the 5000 meters in under 7 minutes, *5693*

Speed skater to win three gold medals in speed skating at a single Olympic Winter Games, *5658*

Speed skater to win two Olympic gold medals in men's 5000-meter speed skating, *5657*

Speed skaters to be named *Sports Illustrated* Sportsmen of the Year, *5719*

Woman speed skater to skate the 3000 meters in under 5 minutes, *5680*

Woman speed skater to skate the 3000 meters in under 6 minutes, *5659*

Woman speed skater to skate the 5000 meters in under 10 minutes, *5660*

Women's Europe-class sailing event held in the Olympic Games, *5252*

Women's World Cup in soccer (international football), *5566*

World championships in luge (toboggan), *4453*

World championships in orienteering, *4808*

World cup for Nordic skiing, *5428*

World cup in orienteering, *4811*

Brandbu

Woman speed skater to skate the 1000 meters in under 2 minutes, *5651*

Hamar

Speed skater to skate the 10,000 meters in under 18 minutes, *5636*

Speed skater to skate the 1500 meters in under 2:30 minutes, *5633*

Speed skater to skate the 3000 meters in under 5 minutes, *5652*

Speed skater to skate the 500 meters in under 50 seconds, *5631*

Speed skater to skate the 5000 meters in under 9 minutes, *5634*

Lillehammer

Athlete from newly independent Kazakhstan to win a gold medal at the Olympic Games, *4787*

Athlete from newly independent Ukraine to win a gold medal at the Olympic Games, *4786*

Athlete from newly independent Uzbekistan to win a gold medal at the Olympic Games, *4785*

Athlete from the United States to win six medals at the Olympic Winter Games, and the first female U.S. athlete to win five gold medals at the winter or summer Games, *4784*

Athlete under the age of 14 to win a gold medal in the Olympic Winter Games, *4783*

Bobsledders to win two consecutive two-man bobsled titles at the Olympic Winter Games, *2477*

Coed luge (toboggan) event in the Olympic Winter Games, *4464*

Figure skater from Russia to win the men's singles title at the Olympic Winter Games, *3107*

Figure skater from Ukraine to win the women's singles title at the Olympic Winter Games, *3108*

Male skier to win five gold medals in Nordic (cross-country) skiing in the Olympic Winter Games, and the first to win two consecutive men's combined pursuit titles, *5487*

Men's 500-meter short track speed skating event held in the Olympic Winter Games, *5725*

Men's aerials freestyle skiing event at the Olympic Winter Games, *5488*

National team to sweep the medals in the men's Alpine combined skiing event at the Olympic Winter Games, *5490*

Olympic Winter Games at which professional athletes were allowed to compete, *4781*

Olympic Winter Games not held in the same year as the Summer Games, *4782*

Professional figure skaters to win a gold medal in the Olympic Winter Games after being reinstated to amateur competition, *3106*

Skier to win five medals in Alpine events at the Olympic Winter Games, *5491*

Skier to win the 30-kilometer Nordic (cross-country) title in the Olympic Winter Games after it was converted from classical style to freestyle, *5485*

Skier to win the 50-kilometer Nordic (cross-country) title in the Olympic Winter Games after it was converted from freestyle to classical style, *5493*

Skier to win two consecutive women's combined pursuit Nordic (cross-country) skiing titles at the Olympic Winter Games, *5486*

Skiers to win two consecutive men's Nordic combined team titles at the Olympic Winter Games, *5489*

Slider to win two, and then three, consecutive men's singles luge (toboggan) titles in the Olympic Winter Games, *4465*

Speed skater to win three consecutive women's 500-meter titles at the Olympic Winter Games, *5721*

Speed skater to win two consecutive men's 1000-meter short track titles at the Olympic Winter Games, *5722*

Speed skater to win two consecutive titles in the men's 1500-meters at the Olympic Winter Games, *5720*

Speed skater to win two consecutive women's 1000-meter speed skating titles at the Olympic Winter Games, *5723*

Speed skater to win two consecutive women's 500-meter short track titles at the Olympic Winter Games, *5724*

Speed skaters to be named *Sports Illustrated* Sportsmen of the Year, *5719*

Woman skier to win three gold medals, and to win five medals overall, in Alpine skiing at the Olympic Winter Games, *5492*

Woman to win gold medals in two biathlon events in the same Olympic Winter Games, *2442*

Women's aerials freestyle skiing event held at the Olympic Winter Games, *5484*

Women's short track 1000-meter speed skating event held at the Olympic Winter Games, *5726*

NORWAY—*continued*

Narvik

Runner to hold the officially accepted world record in the women's 5000-meter race, *5122*

Oslo

Discus-thrower to break the 170-foot barrier, *2765*

Figure skater from Germany to win the women's singles title in the world championships, *3049*

Figure skater from Norway to win the women's singles title in the world championships, *3006*

Figure skater to perform a triple jump in competition, *3047*

Figure skater to win 10 consecutive women's singles titles in the world championships, *3019*

Figure skater to win the men's singles U.S., world, and Olympic championships in the same year, and then twice in a row, *3034*

Figure skaters from Canada to win the pairs title in the world championships, *3050*

Figure skaters to win three pairs titles in the world championships, *2995*

Hammer-thrower to break the 200-foot barrier, *3988*

Hurdler to race the men's 110-meter hurdles in under 14 seconds, *4335*

International governing body for competitive skiing, *5361*

Javelin-thrower to break the 300-foot and 90-meter barriers in the men's event, *4399*

Men's giant slalom event held at the Olympic Winter Games, *5394*

National team to sweep the medals in the women's 10-kilometer Nordic (cross-country) skiing event in the Olympic Winter Games, *5395*

National team to win six ice hockey titles at the Olympic Winter Games, *4128*

Olympic event to be attended by 150,000 people, *4700*

Olympic Winter Games held in Norway, *4699*

Runner to complete the men's 800-meter race in under 1:43 minutes, *5111*

Runner to complete the men's mile race in under 3:49 minutes, *5113*

Runner to race the men's 10,000 meters in under 27:00 minutes, *5168*

Runner to race the women's 5000 meters in under 15 minutes, *5138*

Shot-putter to break the 17-meter barrier, *5335*

Skier from the United States to win two Olympic gold medals, *5397*

Speed skater to skate the 1500 meters in under 2:20 minutes, *5638*

Woman speed skater to skate the 500 meters in under 50 seconds, *5654*

Women's giant slalom event held at the Olympic Winter Games, *5393*

Women's individual 10-kilometer Nordic (cross-country) event held at the Olympic Winter Games, *5396*

World championships in luge (toboggan), *4453*

Tolga

Speed skater to skate the 3000 meters in under 4:30 minutes, *5674*

PAKISTAN

Athletes from Pakistan to win gold medals in the Olympic Games, *4730*

Squash player to win eight men's singles world open titles, *5768*

Squash player to win six men's singles world open titles, *5766*

World cup in squash, *5765*

PANAMA

Runner from Central or South America to set or equal a world track and field record, *5049*

PAPUA NEW GUINEA

World outdoor championships in bowls to include women players, *2501*

PERU

Swimmer to swim across the Strait of Gibraltar, *5830*

Women to compete in shooting events in the Olympic Games, *5311*

PHILIPPINES

International competition in volleyball, *6273*

Manila

Far Eastern Games, *4367*

POLAND

Archer to win two, and then up to seven, women's individual world championships, *1031*

Boxer to win two consecutive light welterweight titles in the Olympic Games, *2569*

Fencer to win three men's sabre titles in the world championships, *2936*

Flyweight weightlifting event held in the Olympic Games, *6345*

Hurdler to hold the officially accepted world record in the women's 400-meter hurdles, *4344*

International Universities Games, *4368*

Judo artist to win gold medals in two different weight classes in the Olympic Games, *4555*

Weightlifter to win two consecutive lightweight titles in the Olympic Games, *6344*

Woman athlete to be disqualified from the Olympic Games because of a positive drug test, *4743*

Woman to sail around the world alone, *5237*

Women to compete in shooting events in the Olympic Games, *5311*

Women's discus throw event, and the first women's field event, held in the Olympic Games, *2762*

Women's hammer-throw event held in the Olympic Games, *3998*

World championships in gymnastics to award women's titles in specific events, *3932*

Chorzow

Shot-putter to break the 20- and 21-meter barriers in the women's event, *5347*

Lvov

World championships in target archery, *1030*

Olsztyn

Triple-jumper to break both the 55-foot and 17-meter barriers, *6257*

Warsaw

Hurdler to hold the officially accepted world record in the women's 100-meter hurdles, *4342*

Runner to hold the officially accepted world record in the women's 100-meter dash, *5033*

Runner to hold the officially accepted world record in the women's 200 meters, *5035*

Runner to race the women's 400 meters in under 50 seconds, *5100*

Shot-putter to hold the officially accepted world record in the women's event, *5334*

PORTUGAL

Athlete to die while participating in the modern Olympic Games, *4644*

Runner to win the women's championship in the Rotterdam Marathon, *4509*

Runner to win two consecutive women's titles in the Boston Marathon, and three overall, *4519*

PUERTO RICO

Stud book for horse racing published in North America, *4287*

San Juan

High-jumper to reach, and then break, the 8-foot barrier, *4032*

ROMANIA

Athlete to compete in track and field events in six Olympic Games, *6217*

Canoer to win three titles in the men's Canadian pairs 1000-meter event in the Olympic Games, *2622*

Discus-thrower to break the 220-foot barrier in the women's event, *2779*

Gymnast to receive a perfect score of 10 in the Olympic Games, *3960*

Gymnast to win two consecutive titles in the women's balance beam competition in the Olympic Games, *3966*

Gymnast to win two women's balance beam titles in the world championships, *3975*

Heavyweight Greco-Roman wrestling event held in the Olympic Games, *6400*

High-jumper to set more than 10 world records in the women's event, *4028*

High-jumper to win two consecutive women's titles in the Olympic Games, *4030*

Light flyweight event held in the world Greco-Roman wrestling championships, *6394*

Light flyweight Greco-Roman wrestling event held in the Olympic Games, *6401*

Men's singles 500-meter kayak event held in the Olympic Games, *2619*

Rower to win gold medals in both the women's single and double sculls events in the Olympic Games, *4953*

Tennis player to be ranked number one in the Association of Tennis Professionals (ATP) rankings, *6157*

Women's 3000-meter race held at the Olympic Games, *5140*

Women's 50-meter freestyle swimming event held in the world championships, *5949*

Women's 500-meter fours kayaking event held in the Olympic Games, *2623*

Women's lightweight double sculls rowing event held in the Olympic Games, *4961*

World championships in rowing to include women's competitions, *4945*

Bucharest

High-jumper to clear six feet in the women's event, *4026*

ROMANIA—*continued*
Ploesti

Shot-putter to break the 15-meter barrier in the women's event, *5337*

RUSSIA

Athlete from Russia to win a gold medal in the Olympic Games, *4640*

Champions Series in figure skating, *3112*

Fencer to win four men's sabre titles in the world championships, *2943*

Figure skater from Russia to win the men's singles title at the Olympic Winter Games, *3107*

Figure skater to win the title for special figures in the Olympic Games, *2976*

Figure skaters to win two consecutive ice dancing titles at the Olympic Winter Games, *3114*

Hammer-thrower to hold the officially accepted world record in the women's event, *3997*

Male figure skater to win the pairs title at the Olympic Winter Games with two different partners, *3115*

Men's 5-kilometer river/sea swim event held in the world championships, *5975*

Men's synchronized platform diving event held in the Olympic Games, *2826*

Professional figure skaters to win a gold medal in the Olympic Winter Games after being reinstated to amateur competition, *3106*

Skier to win two consecutive women's combined pursuit Nordic (cross-country) skiing titles at the Olympic Winter Games, *5486*

Swimmer to hold world titles in both the 5- and 25-kilometer river/sea swim at the same time, *5976*

Triple-jumper to break the 15-meter barrier in the women's event, *6262*

Women's road time trial cycling event held in the Olympic Games, *2726*

Women's synchronized springboard diving event held in the Olympic Games, *2827*

Women's synchronized three-meter springboard diving event held at the world championships, *2825*

Wrestler to win two consecutive light heavyweight freestyle wrestling titles in the Olympic Games, *6414*

Wrestler to win two consecutive lightweight freestyle wrestling titles in the Olympic Games, *6411*

St. Petersburg

Figure skater to win the men's singles title at the world championships, *2963*

Figure skaters to win the pairs title in the world championships, and the first to win two titles, *2973*

Ice hockey game on record in Russia, *4050*

World championships in figure skating, *2964*

SLOVAKIA

Athlete from the newly independent Slovak Republic to win a gold medal in the Olympic Games, *4795*

SOUTH AFRICA

Athletes from South Africa to win medals in the Olympic Games, after the lifting of the ban on their country because of its racist policies, *4779*

Black African woman to win an Olympic medal, *4780*

Black athletes from Africa to participate in the Olympic Games, *4630*

British Empire Games (later the British Commonwealth Games), *4369*

Golf club in Africa, *3595*

Golfer from the British Commonwealth to win the British Open, *3721*

Golfer to win the British Open golf championship in under 280 for 72 holes, *3724*

International cricket organization, *2654*

Olympic Games held in Canada, *4744*

Runner from Africa to win the men's 100-meter race in the Olympic Games, *4995*

Runner from Africa to win the men's 400-meters title in the Olympic Games, *5010*

Runner from Africa to win the women's 10,000-meter title, and the first Black African woman to win a medal, at the Olympic Games, *5159*

Skins Game, *3841*

Tennis player classified as "non-white" by South Africa's then-racist government to win a South African tennis tournament, *6153*

World outdoor championships in bowls to include women players, *2501*

World outdoor championships in bowls to include women players, *2501*

Pietersburg

Javelin-thrower to break the 310- and 320-foot barriers with the new javelin, *4413*

SOUTH KOREA

Athlete to win medals in both the Summer and Winter Olympic Games in the same year, *4768*

Athlete under the age of 14 to win a gold medal in the Olympic Winter Games, *4783*

Badminton event for mixed doubles in the Olympic Games, *1175*

Badminton events held in the Olympic Games as medal sports, *1174*

Men's 1000-meter short track speed skating event held in the Olympic Winter Games, *5714*

Men's 500-meter short track speed skating event held in the Olympic Winter Games, *5725*

Men's 5000-meter relay short track speed skating event held at the Olympic Winter Games, *5716*

Men's and women's doubles events to be included in the world cup in table tennis, *5998*

Record in the men's marathon to stand for more than 10 years, *4480*

Runner officially representing South Korea to hold the world record in the men's marathon, and to win the Boston Marathon, *4482*

Runners from a single country outside the United States to take the top three spots in the Boston Marathon, *4483*

Speed skater to win two consecutive men's 1000-meter short track titles at the Olympic Winter Games, *5722*

Speed skater to win two consecutive women's 1000-meter short track titles in the Olympic Winter Games, *5732*

U.S. Women's Open to be won in a sudden-death playoff, *3892*

Women's half-heavyweight judo event held in the Olympic Games, *4554*

Women's short track 1000-meter speed skating event held at the Olympic Winter Games, *5726*

World championships in taekwondo to include light-middleweight and light-heavyweight classes for men, *4544*

World championships in taekwondo to include women, *4549*

Seoul

Archer to win two titles in women's events in a single Olympic Games, *1038*

Athlete from Suriname to win a gold medal in the Olympic Games, *4767*

Basketball team from the United States to win the women's title in a non-boycotted Olympic Games, *2275*

Black African-born boxer to win a boxing title in the Olympic Games, *2585*

Canoe racer from the United States to win the men's singles 1000-meter kayak event, and to win a gold medal in any kayaking event, in the Olympic Games, *2626*

Canoe racers to win two consecutive titles in the men's pairs 500-meter kayak event in the Olympic Games, *2625*

Diver to win both the men's platform and springboard diving titles in two consecutive Olympic Games, *2818*

Heptathlete from the United States, and the first African-American, to win the women's heptathlon in the Olympic Games, *4015*

Individual dressage equestrian competition in the Olympic Games in which women riders swept the top medals, *2890*

Javelin-thrower to break the 260-foot barrier, and to reach the 80-meter barrier, in the women's event, *4410*

Judo artist to win gold medals in two different weight classes in the Olympic Games, *4555*

Judo artist to win two consecutive gold medals in the men's heavyweight title in the Olympic Games, *4551*

Judo artist to win two consecutive men's middleweight gold medals in the Olympic Games, *4550*

Little League World Series won by a Korean team, *1774*

Long-jumper from the United States to win the women's event in the Olympic Games, *4442*

Men's 50-meter freestyle swimming event held in the Olympic Games, *5954*

Men's doubles table tennis event held in the Olympic Games, *5994*

Men's singles table tennis event held in the Olympic Games, *5996*

Men's team archery event held in the Olympic Games, *1037*

National team to sweep the medals in the women's individual foil fencing competition in the Olympic Games, *2940*

Olympic Games at which athletes from more than 150 countries participated, *4765*

Olympic Games held in South Korea, *4766*

Olympic Games held in Spain, *4776*

Olympic men's 100-meter freestyle swimming event in which all the medalists had times under 50 seconds, *5952*

Runner from Africa to win the men's 800-meter title at the Olympic Games, *5151*

Runner to race the women's 100 meters in under 10:50 seconds, and the 200 meters in under 21.50 seconds, *5153*

Runner to reach three consecutive finals in the men's 100-meter dash at the Olympic Games, *5157*

Runner to win two consecutive officially accepted men's 100-meter titles at the Olympic Games, *5150*

Shooter to win two consecutive titles in the small-bore rifle (three positions) individual event in the Olympic Games, *5323*

Tennis player to win the men's singles title in the Olympic Games after tennis competition resumed in 1988, *6178*

Tennis player to win the women's singles title in the Olympic Games after tennis competition resumed in 1988, *6180*

SOUTH KOREA—Seoul—*continued*

Tennis players to win the men's doubles title in the Olympic Games after tennis competition resumed in 1988, *6181*

Tennis players to win the women's doubles title in the Olympic Games after tennis competition resumed in 1988, *6179*

Woman swimmer to win Olympic medals 12 years apart, *5956*

Women's 100-meter butterfly event in the Olympic Games in which all the medalists had times under one minute, *5953*

Women's 1000-meter match sprint cycling event held in the Olympic Games, *2713*

Women's 10,000-meter running event held in the Olympic Games, *5152*

Women's 470-class sailing event held in the Olympic Games, *5249*

Women's 50-meter freestyle swimming event held in the Olympic Games, *5955*

Women's air pistol individual shooting event held in the Olympic Games, *5322*

Women's doubles table tennis event held in the Olympic Games, *5995*

Women's quadruple sculls event held in the Olympic Games, *4955*

Women's singles table tennis event held in the Olympic Games, *5997*

World championships in taekwondo, *4541*

Wrestler of Black African descent to win a gold medal in wrestling in the Olympic Games, *6409*

Wrestler to win two bantamweight freestyle wrestling titles in the Olympic Games, *6410*

Wrestler to win two consecutive light flyweight Greco-Roman wrestling titles in the Olympic Games, *6408*

SOVIET UNION

Athlete to win 18 medals in the Olympic Games, *4711*

Athlete to win eight medals in a single Olympic Games, *3967*

Athlete to win four gold medals at a single Olympic Winter Games, and six Olympic gold medals overall, *4715*

Athlete to win ten medals in the Olympic Winter Games, *4772*

Basketball team from the Soviet Union to win the men's title in the Olympic Games, *2088*

Boxer to win two consecutive light middleweight titles in the Olympic Games, *2568*

Canoe racer to win three gold medals in a single Olympic Games, *2621*

Canoe racer to win two consecutive titles in the women's 500-meter singles kayak event, *2612*

Cross-country Nations' Cup in the world cup for Nordic skiing, *5432*

Cyclist to win two consecutive women's titles in the 1000-meter match sprint in the Olympic Games, *2718*

Discus-thrower to break the 190-foot barrier in the women's event, *2772*

Discus-thrower to break the 210-foot barrier in the women's event, *2778*

Discus-thrower to break the 230-foot and 70-meter barriers, *2780*

Discus-thrower to win two titles in the women's event in the Olympic Games, *2770*

Diver to hold women's world titles in both springboard and highboard platform diving at the same time, *2812*

Diver to win two consecutive women's world titles in springboard diving, *2813*

European Cup, *6215*

European Cup, *6215*

Female athlete to win gold medals in two different sports in the Olympic Winter Games, *4771*

Female athlete to win medals in the Olympic Winter Games 16 years apart, *4773*

Fencer to win five men's foil titles in the world championships, *2939*

Fencer to win four men's sabre titles in the world championships, *2943*

Fencers to win three gold medals in the women's team foil competition in the Olympic Games, *2938*

Fencers to win two gold medals in the women's team foil competition in the Olympic Games, *2937*

Figure skater from the Soviet Union to win the men's singles title at the world championships, *3071*

Figure skater from Ukraine to win the men's singles title at the Olympic Winter Games, *3100*

Figure skater to win 10 consecutive pairs titles in the world championships, *3080*

Figure skater to win a pairs title in the Olympic Winter Games with two different partners, *3075*

Figure skater to win three consecutive medals in pairs competition at the Olympic Winter Games, *3084*

Figure skaters from the Soviet Union to win the ice dancing title in the world championships, *3066*

Figure skaters from the Soviet Union to win the pairs title at the Olympic Winter Games, *3064*

Figure skaters from the Soviet Union to win the pairs title in the world championships, *3062*

Figure skaters to perform a quadruple twist lift in competition, *3078*

Figure skaters to perform simultaneous triple jumps in competition, *3082*

SOVIET UNION—*continued*

Runner to race the men's 5000-meter steeple-chase in under 8:39 minutes, *5064*

Runner to race the women's 1500 meters in under 4 minutes, *5104*

Runner to race the women's 800 meters in under 2:10 minutes, *5055*

Sailor to win gold medals in three different sailing events in the Olympic Games, *5239*

Shot-putter to break the 15-meter barrier in the women's event, *5337*

Shot-putter to break the 16-meter barrier in the women's event, *5339*

Shot-putter to break the 17- and 18-meter, and 60-foot, barriers in the women's event, *5342*

Shot-putter to break the 20- and 21-meter barriers in the women's event, *5347*

Shot-putter to break the 22-meter barrier, *5349*

Shot-putter to break the 22-meter barrier, *5349*

Shot-putter to break the 50-foot barrier in the women's event, *5338*

Shot-putter to win two consecutive titles in the women's event in the Olympic Games, *5344*

Skeet shooting individual event held in the Olympic Games, *5312*

Skier to win four medals in the same Nordic skiing event in the Olympic Winter Games, *5478*

Skier to win two consecutive men's 30-kilometer Nordic (cross-country) titles in the Olympic Winter Games, *5442*

Skier to win two consecutive women's Nordic (cross-country) skiing titles in the Olympic Winter Games, *5423*

Skiers from the Soviet Union to win the men's 4 x 10-kilometer relay Nordic (cross-country) title at the Olympic Winter Games, *5405*

Speed skater to skate the 1500 meters in under 2:10 minutes, *5666*

Speed skater to skate the 500 meters in under 40 seconds, *5673*

Speed skater to skate the 5000 meters in under 8 minutes, *5665*

Speed skater to win four gold medals in speed skating in a single Olympic Winter Games, *5678*

Speed skater to win six men's world speed skating sprint championships, *5718*

Speed skater to win three consecutive women's titles in the world championships, *5663*

Speed skater to win two consecutive titles in the men's 500 meters at the Olympic Winter Games, *5671*

Speed skater to win two consecutive women's 1500-meter and 3000-meter titles at the Olympic Winter Games, *5677*

Spring world championships in speed skating, *5682*

Super heavyweight event held in the world Greco-Roman wrestling championships, *6396*

Swimmer to win two consecutive men's 1500-meter freestyle titles at the world championships, *5937*

Swimmer to win two consecutive men's 400-meter freestyle titles at the world championships, *5938*

Team event held in the ice speedway motorcycle racing world championships, *4590*

Tempest-class sailing event in the Olympic Games, *5230*

Triple-jumper to break the 50-foot barrier in the women's event, *6263*

Triple-jumper to win three consecutive men's titles in the Olympic Games, *6259*

Volleyball players to win two consecutive women's gold medals in the Olympic Games, *6283*

Walker to win two titles in the men's 20,000-meter walk in the Olympic Games, *6293*

Weightlifter to win two consecutive middle heavyweight titles in the Olympic Games, *6342*

Woman rider to win the world championships in dressage, *2876*

Woman speed skater to skate the 1000 meters in under 1:20 minutes, *5701*

Woman speed skater to skate the 1000 meters in under 1:30 minutes, *5683*

Woman speed skater to skate the 1500 meters in under 2:30 minutes, *5664*

Women's 10-kilometer cross-country event held in the world championships of Nordic skiing, *5399*

Women's 1000-meter match sprint cycling event held in the Olympic Games, *2713*

Women's 1000-meter speed skating event held at the Olympic Winter Games, *5667*

Women's 10,000-meter running event held in the Olympic Games, *5152*

Women's 1500-meter event held in the Olympic Games, *5094*

Women's 1500-meter speed skating event held at the Olympic Winter Games, *5670*

Women's 20-kilometer cross-country event held in the world championships of Nordic skiing, *5424*

Women's 30-kilometer cross-country event held in the world championships of Nordic skiing, *5463*

Women's 3000-meter speed skating event held at the Olympic Winter Games, *5668*

Women's 5-kilometer cross-country event held in the world championships of Nordic skiing, *5408*

Women's 500-meter pairs kayaking event held in the Olympic Games, *2610*

Women's 7.5-kilometer biathlon competition held in the Olympic Winter Games, *2439*

Women's 800-meter race held in the Olympic Games after a 32-year ban, *5073*

Women's all-around gymnastics competition held in the Olympic Games, *3934*

Women's balance beam gymnastics competition held in the Olympic Games, *3935*

Women's cross-country relay event held in the world championships of Nordic skiing, *5400*

Women's individual 15-kilometer Nordic (cross-country) skiing event at the Olympic Winter Games, *5470*

Women's individual 5-kilometer Nordic (cross-country) event in the Olympic Winter Games, *5412*

Women's pentathlon held in the Olympic Games, *4829*

Women's side horse vault gymnastics competition held in the Olympic Games, *3937*

Women's team foil fencing competition held in the Olympic Games, *2935*

Women's team handball event held in the Olympic Games, *4007*

World Biathlon Championships to include women's competitions, *2436*

World championships in ice speedway motorcycle racing, *4583*

World championships in rhythmic sportive gymnastics, *3949*

World championships in rowing, *4940*

World championships in rowing to include women's competitions, *4945*

World championships in volleyball, *6277*

World championships in volleyball to include women, *6278*

World cup for Nordic skiing, *5428*

World cup in gymnastics, *3959*

World cup in rhythmic sportive gymnastics, *3970*

World cup in volleyball, *6281*

World cup in volleyball to include women, *6284*

Wrestler of Black African descent to win a gold medal in wrestling in the Olympic Games, *6409*

Wrestler to win the light flyweight freestyle competition in the Olympic Games when it resumed in 1972, *6398*

Wrestler to win two bantamweight freestyle wrestling titles in the Olympic Games, *6410*

Wrestler to win two consecutive heavyweight freestyle wrestling titles in the Olympic Games, *6403*

Wrestler to win two consecutive light heavyweight freestyle wrestling titles in the Olympic Games, *6414*

Wrestler to win two consecutive lightweight freestyle wrestling titles in the Olympic Games, *6411*

Wrestler to win two consecutive super heavyweight freestyle titles in the Olympic Games, and wrestling gold medals in three consecutive Olympic Games, *6399*

Baku

Hammer-thrower to break the 210-foot barrier, *3989*

Kiev

Heptathlete to hold the world record in the women's heptathlon, *4012*

Javelin-thrower to break the 180-foot barrier in the women's event, *4395*

Runner to race the women's 800 meters in under 2:10 minutes, *5055*

Kishinev

Long-jumper to break the 7-meter barrier in the women's event, *4440*

Leselidze

Javelin-thrower to reach the 190-foot barrier in the women's event, *4398*

Medeo

Speed skater to skate the 1500 meters in under 2:10 minutes, *5666*

Speed skater to skate the 500 meters in under 40 seconds, *5673*

Speed skater to skate the 5000 meters in under 7 minutes, *5693*

Speed skater to skate the 5000 meters in under 8 minutes, *5665*

Woman speed skater to skate the 1000 meters in under 1:20 minutes, *5701*

Woman speed skater to skate the 1000 meters in under 1:30 minutes, *5683*

Woman speed skater to skate the 1500 meters in under 2 minutes, *5704*

Woman speed skater to skate the 1500 meters in under 2:30 minutes, *5664*

Woman speed skater to skate the 3000 meters in under 4:30 minutes, *5698*

Woman speed skater to skate the 500 meters in under 40 seconds, *5700*

Moscow

Athletes from Zimbabwe to win gold medals in the Olympic Games, *4752*

Canoe racer to win a gold medal in both the singles and pairs in the women's 500 meters in the Olympic Games, *2620*

Canoe racer to win three gold medals in a single Olympic Games, *2621*

First Heavyweight weightlifting event held in the Olympic Games, *6349*

National team to sweep the medals in the men's 400-meter freestyle event in the Olympic Games, *5934*

SOVIET UNION—Moscow—*continued*

National team to sweep the medals in the women's 100-meter backstroke, and the women's 200-meter backstroke, in the Olympic Games, *5935*

Swimmer to race the men's 1500-meter freestyle in under 15 minutes, *5933*

Swimmer to race the women's 100-meter freestyle in under 55 seconds, *5932*

Twin brothers to win gold medals in wrestling in the same Olympic Games, *6404*

Women's 400-meter race in which the top three runners had times of under 50 seconds, *5115*

Women's eight-oared shell with coxswain event held in the Olympic Games, *4949*

Nalchik

Shot-putter to break the 17- and 18-meter, and 60-foot, barriers in the women's event, *5342*

Podolsk

Javelin-thrower to break the 70-meter barrier in the women's event, *4404*

Runner to race the women's 1500 meters in under 4 minutes, *5104*

Tashkent

Hammer-thrower to break the 220-foot barrier, *3990*

SPAIN

Cyclist to win the Tour de France five consecutive times, *2721*

Golfer to win more than $7 million in official prize money in a single season, *3894*

Jai alai game in the United States, *4380*

Olympic Games to be boycotted by member countries, *4703*

Rhythmic gymnastics team competition held in the Olympic Games, *3979*

Rower to win gold medals in both the women's single and double sculls events in the Olympic Games, *4953*

Rowers to win two consecutive titles in the women's quadruple sculls in the Olympic Games, *4958*

Swimmer to swim across the Strait of Gibraltar, *5830*

Tour of Spain (Vuelta a España) cycling race, *2697*

World championships in show jumping, *2865*

World championships in taekwondo to include women, *4549*

Barcelona

Athlete from Indonesia to win a gold medal in the Olympic Games, *4777*

Athlete from newly independent Lithuania to win a gold medal in the Olympic Games, *4778*

Athletes from South Africa to win medals in the Olympic Games, after the lifting of the ban on their country because of its racist policies, *4779*

Badminton events held in the Olympic Games as medal sports, *1174*

Baseball event held in the Olympic Games, *1820*

Black African woman to win an Olympic medal, *4780*

Boxing competitions in the Olympic Games to use computer scoring, *2588*

Cyclist to win two consecutive women's titles in the 1000-meter match sprint in the Olympic Games, *2718*

Gymnast to win six gold medals in a single Olympic Games, *3976*

Handball player to win two consecutive gold medals in men's team handball in the Olympic Games, *4011*

Heptathlete to win two consecutive women's heptathlon titles in the Olympic Games, *4016*

Hurdler to race the men's 400-meter hurdles in under 47 seconds, *4353*

International organization for roller skating and roller hockey, *4904*

Jewish athlete to represent Germany in the 1936 Olympic Winter Games, *4679*

Judo artist to win gold medals in two different weight classes in the Olympic Games, *4555*

Long-jumper to win three, and then four, consecutive men's titles in the Olympic Games, *4443*

Mexican-American boxer to win the lightweight title in the Olympic Games, *2589*

Olympic basketball competition to include openly professional athletes, *2316*

Olympic Games at which the number of female athletes was more than 40 percent of the number of male athletes, *4775*

Olympic men's 200-meter backstroke event in which the medalists all had times under two minutes, *5963*

Pairs of twins to take the top two spots in the synchronized swimming duet competition in the Olympic Games, *5968*

Runner from Africa to win the women's 10,000-meter title, and the first Black African woman to win a medal, at the Olympic Games, *5159*

Runner from Africa to win the women's 1500-meter title at the Olympic Games, *5160*

Runner from the Caribbean to win the women's 400-meter title in the Olympic Games, *5158*

Runner to reach three consecutive finals in the men's 100-meter dash at the Olympic Games, *5157*

Runner to win three consecutive gold medals in the women's 4 x 100-meter relay at the Olympic Games, *5161*

Sailor to win two consecutive Tornado-class sailing titles in the Olympic Games, *5251*

Shooter from the United States to win the women's small-bore rifle (three positions) event at the Olympic Games, *5324*

Swimmer to race the women's 50-meter freestyle in under 25 seconds, *5950*

Swimmer to win three consecutive gold medals in the men's 4 x 100-meter freestyle relay in the Olympic Games, *5964*

Swimmer to win two consecutive gold medals in the women's 200-meter backstroke in the Olympic Games, *5966*

Swimmer to win two consecutive men's 200-meter individual medley titles in the Olympic Games, *5967*

Swimmer to win two consecutive men's 400-meter individual medley titles in the Olympic Games, *5962*

Swimmer to win two consecutive women's 800-meter freestyle titles in the Olympic Games, *5965*

Table tennis player to win both singles and doubles titles in the Olympic Games, *6000*

Woman automobile racer to win world-championship points in a Grand Prix race, *1119*

Woman rider, and the first horse, to win two consecutive gold medals in the individual dressage competition, and in team dressage, in the Olympic Games, *2893*

Women's 10,000-meter walk held in the Olympic Games, *6296*

Women's 1500-meter race in which the top four finishers all had times under 4 minutes, *5162*

Women's 3000-meter individual pursuit cycling event in the Olympic Games, *2719*

Women's Europe-class sailing event held in the Olympic Games, *5252*

Women's extra-lightweight judo event held in the Olympic Games, *4559*

Women's four-oared shell without coxswain event held in the Olympic Games, *4957*

Women's half-heavyweight judo event held in the Olympic Games, *4554*

Women's half-lightweight judo event held in the Olympic Games, *4558*

Women's half-middleweight judo event held in the Olympic Games, *4557*

Women's heavyweight judo event held in the Olympic Games, *4553*

Women's lightweight judo event held in the Olympic Games, *4552*

Women's middleweight judo event held in the Olympic Games, *4556*

Women's sailboarding event held in the Olympic Games, *5192*

Wrestler from the United States to win two super heavyweight freestyle titles in the Olympic Games, *6412*

Wrestler to win two consecutive featherweight freestyle wrestling titles in the Olympic Games, *6413*

Wrestler to win two consecutive light heavyweight freestyle wrestling titles in the Olympic Games, *6414*

Wrestler to win two consecutive lightweight freestyle wrestling titles in the Olympic Games, *6411*

Madrid

Diver to hold the men's world titles in both springboard diving and highboard platform diving at the same time, *2815*

Diver to win three consecutive men's highboard platform diving titles in the world championships, *2816*

Men's 50-meter freestyle event held at the world championships, *5944*

Soccer (international football) player to be named World Footballer of the Year, *5564*

Swimmer to hold world titles in both the men's 200-meter freestyle and butterfly at the same time, and to hold both twice consecutively, *5936*

Swimmer to win two consecutive men's 200-meter butterfly titles at the world championships, *5945*

Swimmer to win two consecutive men's 200-meter freestyle titles at the world championships, *5946*

Swimmer to win two consecutive women's 200-meter backstroke world titles, *5947*

Women's 4 x 200-meter freestyle swimming event held in the world championships, *5948*

Women's 50-meter freestyle swimming event held in the world championships, *5949*

Pedralbes

Spanish Grand Prix automobile race to be part of the Formula One Grand Prix circuit, *1085*

Salamanca

High-jumper to reach, and then break, the 8-foot barrier, *4032*

Triple-jumper to break the 18-meter and 60-foot barriers, *6264*

Seville

Runner to win both the men's 100- and 200-meter titles in the same World Championships in Athletics, *5187*

Runner to race the men's 5000-meter steeple-chase in under 8:10 minutes, *5102*

Ski-jumper to spread the skis in a V formation in the air, *5447*

Skier to win 13 men's Alpine world cup races, and to win 10 in one category, in a single season, *5425*

Skier to win eight men's slalom world cup titles, *5439*

Skier to win seven men's giant slalom world cup titles, *5441*

Skier to win two consecutive titles in the men's 4 x 10-kilometer relay Nordic (cross-country) at the Olympic Winter Games, *5455*

Skier to win two titles in the men's 50-kilometer freestyle Nordic (cross-country) skiing at the Olympic Winter Games, *5411*

Skiing and shooting competition (later known as biathlon), *2427*

Speed skater to skate the 3000 meters in under 4:30 minutes, *5674*

Speed skater to win two consecutive men's 5000-meter titles at the Olympic Winter Games, *5710*

Team event in the dirt-track (speedway) motorcycle racing world championships, *4580*

Tennis player of the Open era to win the Wimbledon men's singles title five consecutive times, *6168*

Tennis player to win the French Open men's singles title six times, *6169*

Three-day event individual equestrian competition held in the Olympic Games, *2848*

Tug-of-war event held in the Olympic Games, *6267*

Uneven (asymmetrical) bars competition held in the world championships for gymnastics, *3933*

Welterweight Greco-Roman wrestling event held in the Olympic Games, *6383*

Woman golfer to have a season scoring average of under 70, *3891*

Women's highboard platform diving event held in the world championships, *2807*

World championship in moto-cross racing, *4579*

World championship in moto-cross racing to include the 250 cc class, *4582*

World championships in bowling, *2489*

World championships in freestyle wrestling, *6389*

World championships in Greco-Roman wrestling held on a regular basis, *6388*

World championships in orienteering, *4808*

World championships in the pentathlon, *4820*

World championships in tug-of-war to include women, *6271*

World Cup series of competitions for speed skating, *5703*

World Flying Disc Conference, *3529*

World pentathlon championships for women, *4832*

World team cup in table tennis, *5999*

Worldloppet Cup, *5429*

Wrestler to win gold medals in three different divisions in the Olympic Games, *6378*

Wrestler to win two super heavyweight freestyle titles in the Olympic Games, *6382*

Wrestling event in the Olympic Games to have no gold-medalist, *6375*

Eskilstuna

Speed skaters to become world champions in speed skating sprints, *5686*

Gothenberg

Figure skater to perform a back flip in competition, *3073*

Runner to complete the men's 1500 meters in under 3:45.0 minutes, *5048*

Runner to complete the men's mile race in under 3:50 minutes, *5103*

Runner to race the men's 5000 meters in under 14:00 minutes, *5047*

Runner to win both the men's 200- and 400-meter titles in the same World Championships in Athletics, *5171*

Runner to win two, and then three, consecutive titles in the men's 1500-meter event in the World Championships in Athletics, *5166*

Runner to win two, and then three, consecutive titles in the men's 3000-meter steeplechase in the World Championships in Athletics, *5167*

Runner to win two consecutive titles in the men's 5000-meter event in the World Championships in Athletics, *5172*

Runner to win two consecutive titles in the women's 200-meter event in the World Championships in Athletics, *5173*

Runner to win two, three, and then four consecutive titles in the men's 10,000-meter event in the World Championships in Athletics, *5174*

Runner to win two, three, and then four consecutive titles in the men's 400-meter event in the World Championships in Athletics, *5175*

Runner to win two titles in the women's 1500-meter event in the World Championships in Athletics, *5176*

Runner to win two titles in the women's 400-meter event in the World Championships in Athletics, *5177*

Triple-jumper to break the 18-meter and 60-foot barriers, *6264*

Triple-jumper to break the 50-foot barrier in the women's event, *6263*

SWEDEN—continued
Malmö

Pole-vaulter to clear 20 feet, *4849*
Shot-putter to break the 16-meter barrier in the women's event, *5339*

Mora

Vasalopp long-distance ski race, *5364*

Sälen

Vasalopp long-distance ski race, *5364*

Stockholm

African-American runner to hold the record in the men's 100-meter dash, *5024*
Athlete to die while participating in the modern Olympic Games, *4644*
Athlete to win both the men's decathlon and pentathlon in the Olympic Games, and the first Native American to win an Olympic gold medal, *2738*
Equestrian to win two consecutive individual and team dressage titles in the Olympic Games, *2866*
Fencer to win two consecutive men's individual sabre titles, and men's team sabre titles, in the Olympic Games, *2914*
Figure skater from Austria to win the women's singles title in the world championships, *2992*
Figure skater from Canada and from the Americas to win the women's singles title in the world championships, *3028*
Figure skater from Switzerland to win the men's singles title at the world championships, *3029*
Figure skater to perform the flying camel spin, *3030*
Figure skater to win five consecutive men's singles titles at the world championships, *2967*
Figure skater to win five consecutive women's singles championships, *3004*
Figure skaters from Austria to win the pairs title in the world championships, *2986*
Figure skaters from Belgium to win the pairs title in the world championships, *3031*
Figure skaters from Great Britain, and the first married couple, to win the pairs title in the world championships, *2980*
Gymnast to win two consecutive men's all-around titles in the Olympic Games, *3918*
Hammer-thrower to break the 190-foot barrier, *3986*
Hurdler to hold the world record in both the men's 110- and 400-meter events, *4331*
Hurdler to race the men's 400-meter hurdles in under 52 seconds, *4334*

Ice skate sailing competition, *4360*
Icewing sail for ice skate sailing, *4361*
Individual dressage equestrian competition held in the Olympic Games, *2845*
International governing organization for track and field (athletics), *6204*
Javelin-thrower to break the 210-foot barrier, *4385*
Javelin-thrower to break the 230-foot and 70-meter barriers, *4388*
Javelin-thrower to hold the officially accepted world record in the men's event, *4384*
Men's 10,000-meter walk held in the Olympic Games, *6290*
Men's 3000-meter team running event held in the Olympic Games, *5004*
Men's 4 x 100-meter relay track event held in the Olympic Games, *5003*
Men's 5000- and 10,000-meter events held in the Olympic Games, *5008*
Men's cross-country team track race held in the Olympic Games, *5005*
Men's discus throw event for both hands held in the Olympic Games, *2761*
Men's individual cross-country event held in the Olympic Games, *5006*
Men's javelin event for both hands held in the Olympic Games, *4383*
Men's modern pentathlon held in the Olympic Games, *4815*
Men's plain high dive event held in the Olympic Games, *2795*
Men's shot put event for both hands held in the Olympic Games, *5332*
National team to sweep the medals in the men's 200-meter breaststroke event in the Olympic Games, *5806*
National team to sweep the top medals in men's springboard diving in the Olympic Games, *2794*
Native-American athlete to win a gold medal at the Olympic Games, *4645*
Olympic Games held in Sweden, or in Scandinavia, *4642*
Olympic Games held in the Southern Hemisphere, and in Australia, *4706*
Olympic Games to use electronic timing devices and a public address system, *4643*
Runner to complete the men's mile race in under 4:05 minutes, *5046*
Runner to hold the officially accepted world record in the men's 800-meter event, *5002*
Runner to race the men's 5000-meter steeplechase in under 8:10 minutes, *5102*
Runner to win two consecutive gold medals in the men's 4 x 400-meter relay in the Olympic Games, *5007*
Shooter from the United States to win the men's trap (clay pigeon) individual shooting title in the Olympic Games, *5295*

Shooter to win both the rapid-fire pistol and the free pistol individual events, and the first from the United States to win either event, in the Olympic Games, *5296*

Shooters from the United States to win the trap (clay pigeon) team shooting event in the Olympic Games, *5294*

Soccer (international football) player to win two gold medals in the Olympic Games, *5548*

Soccer (international football) team from Brazil to win the world cup, *5557*

Speed skater to skate the 10,000 meters in under 20 minutes, *5632*

Swimmer from the United States to win the men's 100-meter backstroke title in the Olympic Games, *5807*

Swimmer to race the women's 100-meter freestyle in under 1:20 minutes, *5804*

Team jumping (Prix des Nations) equestrian event held in the Olympic Games, *2847*

Three-day event individual equestrian competition held in the Olympic Games, *2848*

Three-day event team equestrian competition held in the Olympic Games, *2849*

Water polo player to win two, and then three, gold medals in the Olympic Games, *6303*

Women's 100-meter freestyle swimming event held in the Olympic Games, *5805*

Women's 4 x 100-meter freestyle relay swimming event in the Olympic Games, *5808*

World Equestrian Games, *2892*

Wrestling event in the Olympic Games to have no gold-medalist, *6375*

Uppsala

International hockey game played in Sweden, *4075*

SWITZERLAND

Bobsled event held at the Olympic Winter Games, *2467*

Bobsledders to win two consecutive two-man bobsled titles at the Olympic Winter Games, *2477*

Curling event held in the Olympic Games, *2680*

Figure skater from Switzerland to win the men's singles title at the world championships, *3029*

Figure skater from Switzerland to win the women's singles title in the world championships, *3086*

Individual dressage equestrian competition in the Olympic Games in which women riders swept the top medals, *2890*

Major international ice hockey organization, *4057*

Men's aerials freestyle skiing event at the Olympic Winter Games, *5488*

Men's halfpipe snowboarding event held at the Olympic Winter Games, *5526*

Men's lightweight double sculls rowing event held in the Olympic Games, *4959*

Men's side (pommel) horse gymnastics competition held in the Olympic Games, *3905*

Military revolver and military rifle team shooting events held in the Olympic Games, *5280*

Military rifle individual shooting event held in the Olympic Games, *5279*

Olympic Games to be boycotted by member countries, *4703*

Ski flying event held in the world cup for Nordic skiing, *5467*

Skier to win 14 women's Alpine World Cup races in a single season, *5461*

Skier to win both the women's downhill and giant slalom titles in the same Olympic Winter Games, *5421*

Skier to win five women's giant slalom titles in skiing's world cup, *5494*

Skier to win five women's slalom world cup titles, *5449*

Skier to win four men's super giant slalom world cup titles, *5465*

Skier to win seven men's giant slalom world cup titles, *5441*

Skier to win six women's slalom titles in skiing's world cup, *5495*

Snowboarding world championships, *5521*

Super giant slalom events held in the Alpine skiing world championships, *5452*

Woman figure skater to perform a triple lutz in competition, *3081*

Woman figure skater to perform an axel in competition, *2985*

Woman skier to win three gold medals, and to win five medals overall, in Alpine skiing at the Olympic Winter Games, *5492*

Women's Alpine combination event held in the Alpine skiing world championships, *5391*

Women's épée competition held in the world championships of fencing, *2941*

Women's world championships in curling, *2679*

World championships for freestyle skiing, *5451*

World championships in carriage driving, *2878*

World championships in long-distance duathlon, *2836*

World figure skating championships for roller skating, *4909*

World ski flying championships, *5419*

Ascona

Reigning monarch to play in a national golf championship, *3710*

SWITZERLAND—*continued*
Bern

Runner to hold the officially accepted world record in the men's 5000-meter steeplechase, *5062*

Soccer (international football) team from Germany to win the world cup, *5556*

Château-d'Oex

People to circle the globe in a balloon, *1183*

Crans-Montana

Organized downhill ski race, *5362*

Davos

Figure skater from the United States to win the men's singles title at the world championships, *3033*

Figure skater from the United States to win the women's singles title in the world championships, *3048*

Figure skater to win the men's singles U.S., world, and Olympic championships in the same year, and then twice in a row, *3034*

Figure skater to win the women's singles title in the world championships, *2968*

Figure skater to win two, and then three, men's singles titles at the world championships, *2965*

Grand National luge (toboggan) race, *4449*

Ice skating rink in Switzerland, *2956*

International luge (toboggan) competition, *4447*

Specially built luge (toboggan) runs, *4446*

Speed skater to skate the 1000 meters in under 1:30 minutes, *5646*

Speed skater to skate the 10,000 meters in under 17 minutes, *5662*

Speed skater to skate the 1500 meters in under 2 minutes, *5684*

Woman figure skater to perform the sit spin, *2969*

Woman speed skater to skate the 3000 meters in under 6 minutes, *5659*

Woman speed skater to skate the 500 meters in under 1 minute, *5647*

Woman speed skater to skate the 5000 meters in under 10 minutes, *5660*

Geneva

African-American figure skater to win the women's singles title in the world championships, *3090*

International governing body in water-skiing, *6314*

People to circle the globe in a balloon, *1183*

Soccer (international football) club outside Britain, *5533'*

Lucerne

Shooting club, *5261*

World championships in rowing, *4940*

World cup in rowing, *4962*

Mürren

World championships in Alpine skiing, *5377*

St. Moritz

Athlete to win five individual gold medals, and seven medals overall, in the Olympic Winter Games, *4665*

Athlete to win medals in the Olympic Winter Games 20 years apart, *4691*

Athlete to win three consecutive gold medals in the same event in the Olympic Winter Games, *4666*

Bobsledders from the United States to win the five-man bobsled title at the Olympic Winter Games, *2468*

Figure skater from Canada or from the Americas to win the women's singles title at the Olympic Winter Games, *3032*

Figure skater from Norway to win the women's singles title at the Olympic Winter Games, *3007*

Figure skater from the United States to win the men's singles titles in the Olympic Games, *3035*

Figure skater to win the men's singles U.S., world, and Olympic championships in the same year, and then twice in a row, *3034*

Figure skater to win two, and then three, consecutive men's singles titles in the Olympic Games, *3001*

Figure skaters from Belgium to win the pairs title at the Olympic Winter Games, *3036*

Figure skaters from France to win the pairs title in the Olympic Winter Games, *3008*

Grand National luge (toboggan) race, *4449*

Intercollegiate ice hockey game, *4042*

Men's 10,000-meter Olympic speed skating race to be voided, *5644*

Men's downhill skiing event held at the Olympic Winter Games, *5386*

Men's skeleton luge event at the Olympic Winter Games, *4452*

Men's slalom event held at the Olympic Winter Games, *5388*

National team to sweep the medals in the men's 15-kilometer Nordic (cross-country) skiing event in the Olympic Winter Games, *5376*

National team to win five ice hockey titles at the Olympic Winter Games, *4122*

National team to win three consecutive ice hockey titles at the Olympic Winter Games, *4096*

Olympic Winter Games held in a different country from the Summer Games, *4663*

Olympic Winter Games held in Switzerland, *4664*

Runs specially built for bobsleds, *2465*

Skeleton luge (toboggan), *4448*

Slider to ride the skeleton (Cresta Run) luge (toboggan) face forward, *4450*

Sliding seat developed for the luge (toboggan), *4451*

Speed skater to win two consecutive men's 1500-meter speed skating titles at the Olympic Winter Games, *5645*

Women's downhill skiing event held at the Olympic Winter Games, *5387*

Women's slalom event held at the Olympic Winter Games, *5389*

Zürich

Discus-thrower to break the 230-foot and 70-meter barriers, *2780*

Hurdler to race the men's 110-meter hurdles in under 13 seconds, *4346*

International governing body in shooting, *5283*

Runner to race the men's 5000-meter steeplechase in under 8:00 minutes, *5178*

Runner to race the men's 5000 meters in under 12:55 minutes, *5179*

Shooting tournament on record, *5262*

SYRIA

Athlete from Syria to win a gold medal in the Olympic Games, *4796*

Aleppo

Cricket game on record played outside the British Isles, *2632*

TAIWAN

Athletes from China and Taiwan to share the medal platform in the Olympic Games, *4757*

Olympic Winter Games to be boycotted by a member country, *4749*

World championships in taekwondo to include women, *4549*

Taipei

Baseball team to win the Little League World Series in five consecutive years, *1757*

TANZANIA

Olympic Games held in Canada, *4744*

Runner from Africa to win the men's title in the Boston Marathon, *4518*

THAILAND

Athlete from Thailand to win a gold medal in the Olympic Games, *4801*

South-East Asia Games, *4374*

TRINIDAD AND TOBAGO

Runner from the Caribbean to win the men's 100-meter dash at the Olympic Games, *5105*

TUNISIA

Runner from Africa to win the men's 5000-meter title in the Olympic Games, *5089*

TURKEY

Modern Olympic Games at which member countries were barred from competing, *4649*

Weightlifter to win three gold medals in the Olympic Games, *6352*

World championships in freestyle wrestling, *6389*

World championships in Greco-Roman wrestling held on a regular basis, *6388*

World championships in taekwondo to include women, *4549*

Wrestler to win two consecutive welterweight Greco-Roman titles in the Olympic Games, *6390*

UGANDA

Athlete from Uganda to win a gold medal in the Olympic Games, *4738*

UKRAINE

Athlete from newly independent Ukraine to win a gold medal at the Olympic Games, *4786*

Cycling team to break the 4-minute mark in the men's 4000-meter team pursuit race in the Olympic Games, *2730*

Figure skater from Ukraine to win the men's singles title at the Olympic Winter Games, *3100*

Figure skater from Ukraine to win the men's singles title at the world championships, *3098*

Figure skater from Ukraine to win the women's singles title at the Olympic Winter Games, *3108*

Figure skater from Ukraine to win the women's singles title in the world championships, *3103*

Triple-jumper to break the 50-foot barrier in the women's event, *6263*

Women's 10,000-meter walk held in the Olympic Games, *6296*

UKRAINE—*continued*

Women's triple jump event held in the Olympic Games, *6265*

UNITED STATES

5.5-meter-class sailing event in the Olympic Games, *5218*

African-American athlete to be named *Sports Illustrated* Sportsman of the Year, *1152*

African-American basketball player to win an Olympic gold medal, *1921*

African-American high-jumper to win the men's title in the Olympic Games, *4024*

African-American runner to hold the record in the men's 100-meter dash, *5024*

African-American runner to win the men's 100- and 200-meter titles in the Olympic Games, *5032*

African-American tennis player to win the men's singles championship at Wimbledon, *6158*

African-American tennis player to win the men's singles title at the Australian Open, *6143*

African-American to win a world title in billiards, *2458*

African-American to win the Jesse Owens International Award, *1159*

African-American woman college basketball player to be named an All-American, *1951*

African-American woman to win the Jesse Owens International Award, *1160*

African-American women to win gold medals in a track relay event in the Olympic Games, *5058*

Amateur golfer to win three British Open championships, *3691*

America's Cup sailing race won by New Zealand, *5254*

Athlete of Asian or Native American descent to be named *Sports Illustrated* Sportsman of the Year, *1161*

Athlete of Black African ancestry to compete in the Olympic Games, *4629*

Athlete of Black African ancestry to win an individual gold medal in the Olympic Games, *4657*

Athlete of Black African descent to win an Olympic gold medal, *4639*

Athlete to receive an Olympic medal 50 years after the competition, *4741*

Athlete to win 10 gold medals in the Olympic Games, *4633*

Athlete to win a gold medal at the Olympic Winter Games, *4654*

Athlete to win an Olympic gold medal, or to hold the world record, in both the men's decathlon and an individual track and field event, *2741*

Athlete to win an Olympic gold medal, or to hold the world record, in both the men's decathlon and an individual track and field event, *2741*

Athlete to win both the men's decathlon and pentathlon in the Olympic Games, and the first Native American to win an Olympic gold medal, *2738*

Athlete to win five individual gold medals in a single Olympic Games, *4748*

Athlete to win four gold medals in a single Olympic Games, *4627*

Athlete to win gold medals in both the Summer and Winter Olympics, *4674*

Athlete to win medals in the Olympic Winter Games 20 years apart, *4691*

Athlete to win Olympic medals in both diving and swimming, *2798*

Athlete to win seven gold medals in a single Olympic Games, *4740*

Athlete to win the Jesse Owens International Award, *1157*

Athlete to win the men's Hawaii Ironman triathlon competition four, and then five, times consecutively, and six times overall, *6242*

Athlete to win the men's Hawaii Ironman triathlon two, three, four, five, and six times, *6237*

Athlete to win two Jesse Owens International Awards, *1162*

Automobile racer to earn more than $100,000 in a single season in the National Association for Stock Car Auto Racing (NASCAR) Winston Cup series, *1110*

Automobile racer to earn more than $4 million in a single season in the National Association for Stock Car Auto Racing (NASCAR) Winston Cup series, *1144*

Automobile racer to win more than 20 races in a single season in the National Association for Stock Car Auto Racing (NASCAR) Winston Cup series, *1111*

Automobile racer to win the Indianapolis 500 with an average speed of more than 160 miles per hour, *1117*

Automobile racer to win the Indianapolis 500 with an average speed of more than 170 miles per hour, *1133*

Automobile racer to win three, four, five, six, and seven championships on the National Association for Stock Car Auto Racing (NASCAR) Winston Cup circuit, *1116*

Avila Camacho Cup polo competition, *4868*

Bantamweight weightlifting event held in the Olympic Games, *6334*

Basketball event held in the Olympic Games, *1894*

Basketball team from the Soviet Union to win the men's title in the Olympic Games, *2088*

UNITED STATES—*continued*

Diver to win two consecutive women's platform diving titles in the Olympic Games, *2801*

Dubai World Cup horse race, *4318*

Duet synchronized swimming event held in the Olympic Games, *5941*

Electronically timed world record in the men's 110-meter hurdles, *4343*

Event held in the modern Olympic Games, *4605*

Federation Cup championships, *6112*

Figure skater, and the first female athlete, to sign a contract for $1 million a year, *3072*

Figure skater from the United States to win the men's singles title at the world championships, *3033*

Figure skater from the United States to win the men's singles titles in the Olympic Games, *3035*

Figure skater from the United States to win the women's singles title at the Olympic Winter Games, *3053*

Figure skater from the United States to win the women's singles title in the world championships, *3048*

Figure skater from Ukraine to win the women's singles title at the Olympic Winter Games, *3108*

Figure skater to perform a back flip in competition, *3073*

Figure skater to perform a double axel in competition, *3042*

Figure skater to perform a triple jump in competition, *3047*

Figure skater to perform a triple loop–triple loop combination jump in competition, *3044*

Figure skater to perform the double loop–double loop combination jump in competition, *3038*

Figure skater to perform the flying camel spin, *3030*

Figure skater to win the James E. Sullivan Award, *3039*

Figure skaters from the United States to sweep the men's singles medals in the world championships, *3045*

Figure skaters from the United States to sweep the women's singles medals in the world championships, *3097*

Figure skaters from the United States to win an Olympic medal in ice dancing, *3074*

Figure skaters from the United States to win the pairs title in the world championships, *3040*

Figure skaters to win Emmy awards for a television special, *3095*

Free pistol shooting individual event held in the Olympic Games, *5271*

French Open women's singles tennis match, *6122*

Frisbee, *3525*

Giant slalom and snowboard cross events held in the snowboarding world championships, *5523*

Golf book published in the United States, *3611*

Golf clubs made in the United States, *3606*

Golf course to host the British Open championship 25 times, *3881*

Golf shot taken on the moon, *3795*

Golfer to be named *Sports Illustrated* Sportsman of the Year, *3760*

Golfer to complete a grand slam, *3693*

Golfer to earn more than $500,000 in official prize money in a single season, *3825*

Golfer to win both the U.S. Open and the British Open in the same year, *3682*

Golfer to win five U.S. Amateur titles, *3692*

Golfer to win more than $2.5 million in official prize money in a single season, *3889*

Golfer to win more than $200,000 in official prize money in a single season, *3792*

Golfer to win more than $300,000 in official prize money in a single season, *3798*

Golfer to win the British Open golf championship in under 270 for 72 holes, *3813*

Golfer to win the British Open golf championship in under 290 for 72 holes, *3685*

Golfer to win the U.S. Amateur Championship twice in a row, *3617*

Goodwill Games, *4379*

Governing body for croquet in the United States, *2667*

Governing body for drag racing, *1074*

Grand Slam Cup, *6182*

Gymnast to be named *Sports Illustrated* Sportsman of the Year, *3971*

Hammer-throw event held at the Olympic Games, *3981*

Hammer-thrower born in the United States to win the men's event in the Olympic Games, *3983*

Hammer-thrower to break the 70-meter and 230-foot barriers, *3991*

Hammer-thrower to hold the officially accepted world record in the men's event, *3982*

Hawaii Ironman triathlon to include women, *6236*

Heptathlete from the United States, and the first African-American, to win the women's heptathlon in the Olympic Games, *4015*

Heptathlete to win two consecutive women's heptathlon titles in the Olympic Games, *4016*

Heydusek Prize, *5991*

High-jumper to clear seven feet, *4025*

High-jumper to hold the officially accepted world record in the men's event, *4021*

High-jumper to set or equal four world records in the men's event in a single year, *4027*

UNITED STATES—*continued*

Men's 200-meter hurdles event held in the Olympic Games, *4325*

Men's 200-meter individual medley swimming event held in the Olympic Games, *5853*

Men's 200-meter race held in the Olympic Games, *4981*

Men's 25-kilometer river/sea swim event held in the world championships, *5957*

Men's 3000-meter team running event held in the Olympic Games, *5004*

Men's 4 x 100-meter freestyle relay swimming event held in the Olympic Games, *5847*

Men's 4 x 100-meter freestyle swimming event held at the world championships, *5884*

Men's 4 x 100-meter medley relay event held at the world championships, *5885*

Men's 4 x 200-meter freestyle swimming event held at the world championships, *5886*

Men's 4 x 400-meter relay track event held in the Olympic Games, *4997*

Men's 400-meter freestyle event held at the world championships, *5887*

Men's 400-meter hurdles event held in the Olympic Games, *4324*

Men's 400-meter individual medley swimming event held in the Olympic Games, *5848*

Men's 440-yard (later 400-meter) breaststroke event held in the Olympic Games, *5796*

Men's 50-meter freestyle event held at the world championships, *5944*

Men's 50-meter freestyle swimming event held in the Olympic Games, *5954*

Men's 500-meter speed skating event held at the Olympic Winter Games, *5639*

Men's 60-meter running event held in the Olympic Games, *4976*

Men's discus throw event held in the Olympic Games, *2754*

Men's golf event in the Olympic Games, *3629*

Men's high jump event held in the Olympic Games, *4019*

Men's individual archery event in the modern format held in the Olympic Games, *1035*

Men's long jump event held in the Olympic Games, *4426*

Men's long jump event in which the top four contestants jumped more than 26 feet, *4437*

Men's modern pentathlon held in the Olympic Games, *4815*

Men's pole vault event held in the Olympic Games, *4837*

Men's shot put event for both hands held in the Olympic Games, *5332*

Men's shot put event held in the Olympic Games, *5329*

Men's skeleton luge event at the Olympic Winter Games, *4452*

Men's springboard diving event held at the world championships, *2806*

Men's standing high jump event held in the Olympic Games, *4020*

Men's standing long jump event held in the Olympic Games, *4427*

Men's standing triple jump event held in the Olympic Games, *6250*

Men's triple jump event held in the Olympic Games, *6249*

Middle heavyweight weightlifting event held in the Olympic Games, *6338*

Military revolver individual shooting event held in the Olympic Games, *5270*

National championship in Indy Car racing, *1051*

National governing body for motorboat (power-boat) racing, *4564*

National governing body for taekwondo in the United States, *4542*

National governing body for water-skiing, *6312*

National organization for harness (trotting) horse owners in the United States, *4280*

National polo organization in the United States, *4863*

National team to sweep the medals in the men's 110-meter hurdles in the Olympic Games, *4323*

National team to sweep the medals in the men's 200-meter backstroke event in the Olympic Games, *5846*

National team to sweep the medals in the men's 200-meter butterfly swimming event in the Olympic Games, *5864*

National Team to sweep the medals in the men's 200-meter freestyle in the Olympic Games, *5921*

National team to sweep the medals in the women's 100-meter freestyle swimming event in the Olympic Games, *5810*

National team to sweep the medals in the women's 200-meter butterfly in the Olympic Games, *5872*

National team to sweep the top spots in the men's discus throw in the Olympic Games, *2758*

National team to sweep the top spots in the men's pole vault in the Olympic Games, *4838*

National team to sweep the top spots in the men's shot put in the Olympic Games, *5330*

National team to sweep the top spots in the men's triple jump in the Olympic Games, *6251*

Native-American athlete to win a gold medal at the Olympic Games, *4645*

Netball, *4595*

Olympic Games held in the Soviet Union, and the first in a Communist country, *4751*

Olympic heavyweight boxing champion to become world heavyweight champion, *2567*

Olympic light heavyweight boxing champion to become world heavyweight champion, *2565*

Olympic men's 100-meter freestyle swimming event in which all the medalists had times under 50 seconds, *5952*

Olympic men's 1500-meter freestyle event in which the medalists all had times under 16 minutes, *5922*

Olympic men's 1500-meter freestyle event in which the medalists all had times under 17 minutes, *5871*

Olympic men's 1500-meter freestyle event in which the medalists all had times under 19 minutes, *5832*

Olympic men's 400-meter freestyle event at which all the medalists had times under five minutes, *5823*

Olympic men's 400-meter freestyle event at which all the medalists had times under four minutes, *5923*

Olympic women's 100-meter freestyle event in which the medalists all had times under one minute, *5867*

Olympic women's 400-meter freestyle event in which the medalists all had times under five minutes, *5839*

Pairs of twins to take the top two spots in the synchronized swimming duet competition in the Olympic Games, *5968*

Pentathlete to achieve a perfect score in the shooting portion of the men's modern pentathlon in the Olympic Games, *4817*

Playing of darts on record in North America, *2733*

Pole-vaulter to clear 14 feet, *4840*

Pole-vaulter to clear 17 feet, *4845*

Pole-vaulter to win two consecutive titles in the men's event in the Olympic Games, *4843*

Polo competitions in the United States, *4860*

Polo event held in the Olympic Games, *4865*

Professional baseball team in Japan, *1488*

Rider to win ten consecutive women's barrel racing titles, *4900*

Rower to win three consecutive medals in the men's double sculls event in the Olympic Games, *4936*

Rowers to win two consecutive medals in the men's double sculls event in the Olympic Games, *4935*

Rugby players to win two Olympic gold medals in rugby, *4968*

Runner from the United States to win the men's 10,000-meter title at the Olympic Games, *5077*

Runner from the United States to win the men's 5000-meter title at the Olympic Games, *5078*

Runner from the United States to win the men's steeplechase event at the Olympic Games, *4986*

Runner from the United States to win the women's 100-meter dash in the World Championships in Athletics, *5164*

Runner from the United States to win the women's 400-meter race in the World Championships in Athletics, *5165*

Runner from the United States to win the women's 800-meter title at the Olympic Games, *5091*

Runner to complete the men's 200-meter race in under 19.7 seconds, *5183*

Runner to complete the men's 200-meter race in under 20 seconds, *5088*

Runner to complete the men's 400-meter race in under 44 seconds, *5090*

Runner to complete the men's marathon in under 2:30 hours, *4477*

Runner to complete the men's marathon in under 2:55 hours, *4473*

Runner to hold an officially accepted world record in the men's 200-meter race run on a curved track, *5053*

Runner to hold the officially accepted world record in the men's 100-meter dash, *5001*

Runner to hold the officially accepted world record in the men's 400-meter event, *4983*

Runner to hold the officially accepted world record in the men's 800-meter event, *5002*

Runner to hold the officially accepted world record in the women's 100-meter dash, *5033*

Runner to hold the officially accepted world record in the women's 200 meters, *5035*

Runner to race the 100-yard dash in under 10 seconds, *4973*

Runner to race the men's 100-meter dash in 10.1 seconds, *5063*

Runner to race the men's 100-meter dash in under 10 seconds, *5084*

Runner to race the men's 100 meters in under 9.9 seconds, *5156*

Runner to race the men's 1500 meters in less than 3:35 minutes, *5083*

Runner to race the women's 100 meters in under 10:50 seconds, and the 200 meters in under 21.50 seconds, *5153*

Runner to win both the men's 100- and 200-meter races in the same Olympic Games, *4991*

Runner to win both the men's 100- and 200-meter titles in the same World Championships in Athletics, *5187*

Runner to win both the men's 200- and 400-meter titles in the same World Championships in Athletics, *5171*

Runner to win both the men's 400- and 800-meter events in the same Olympic Games, *4993*

UNITED STATES—*continued*

Runner to win both the women's 200-and 400-meter titles at a single Olympic Games, and the first runner from the United States, or African-American, to win the 400-meter event, *5143*

Runner to win four consecutive New York Marathons, *4504*

Runner to win seven Boston Marathons, *4479*

Runner to win the men's 100-meter race held in the World Championships in Athletics, *5125*

Runner to win the men's 200- and 400-meter titles in the same Olympic Games, *5184*

Runner to win the men's 200-meter race held in the World Championships in Athletics, *5128*

Runner to win the men's title in both the Boston Marathon and the New York Marathon in the same year, *4503*

Runner to win the women's 1500-meter race in the World Championships in Athletics, *5134*

Runner to win three consecutive Boston Marathons, *4476*

Runner to win three consecutive gold medals in the women's 4 x 100-meter relay at the Olympic Games, *5161*

Runner to win three gold medals in the men's 4 x 100-meter relay in the Olympic Games, *5040*

Runner to win two, and then three, consecutive titles in the men's 100-meter event in the World Championships in Athletics, *5147*

Runner to win two consecutive gold medals in the men's 4 x 100-meter relay in the Olympic Games, *5016*

Runner to win two consecutive men's 400-meter titles in the Olympic Games, *5188*

Runner to win two consecutive officially accepted men's 100-meter titles at the Olympic Games, *5150*

Runner to win two consecutive titles in the men's 200-meter event in the World Championships in Athletics, *5148*

Runner to win two consecutive women's 200-meter titles in the Olympic Games, *5086*

Runner to win two gold medals in the women's 4 x 100-meter relay in the Olympic Games, *5041*

Runner to win two, three, and then four consecutive titles in the men's 400-meter event in the World Championships in Athletics, *5175*

Runners to complete the men's 400-meter race in under 45 seconds, *5072*

Running deer (double shot) individual shooting event held in the Olympic Games, *5284*

Ryder Cup to include players from the European mainland, *3821*

Sailor to complete a solo circumnavigation of the world in 150 days, *5245*

Sailors from the United States to win the 6-meter-class event in the Olympic Games, *5217*

Season for the Ice Capades, *3026*

Shooter from the United States to win the women's small-bore rifle (three positions) event at the Olympic Games, *5324*

Shooter to win both the rapid-fire pistol and the free pistol individual events, and the first from the United States to win either event, in the Olympic Games, *5296*

Shooter to win five gold medals in shooting in the Olympic Games, *5298*

Shooter to win two consecutive titles in the men's free rifle (three positions) individual shooting event, and in the free rifle team event, in the Olympic Games, *5302*

Shooters from the United States to win the trap (clay pigeon) team shooting event in the Olympic Games, *5294*

Shot-putter to break the 17-meter barrier, *5335*

Shot-putter to win two consecutive men's titles in the Olympic Games, *5341*

Single-handed sailing across the Atlantic, *5200*

Single-handed transatlantic race, *5201*

Sisters to win the women's doubles tennis title at the U.S. Open, *6189*

Sisters to win the women's doubles title at the United States national tennis championships, *6028*

Skier for the United States to win a ski-jumping medal at the Olympic Winter Games, *5370*

Skier from the United States to win the men's aerials freestyle skiing event in the Olympic Winter Games, *5500*

Skier from the United States to win the men's downhill title at the Olympic Winter Games, *5444*

Skier from the United States to win the men's moguls freestyle skiing event in the Olympic Winter Games, *5497*

Skier from the United States to win the men's slalom title at the Olympic Winter Games, *5446*

Skier from the United States to win the women's aerials freestyle skiing event in the Olympic Winter Games, *5501*

Skier from the United States to win the women's super giant slalom at the Olympic Winter Games, *5498*

Skier from the United States to win two Olympic gold medals, *5397*

Skier to introduce skating techniques into Nordic (cross-country) skiing in international competition, *5437*

Skipper to win the America's Cup sailing race twice in a row, *5203*

Sky diver from the United States to win the men's title in the world sky diving championships, *5505*

Snowboarding world championships, *5521*

Soccer (international football) team from Britain to play in the United States, *5547*

Softball event held at the Pan-American Games, *5616*

Softball player to be batting champion of the Amateur Softball Association Major Fast Pitch league, *5590*

Soling-class sailing event held in the Olympic Games, *5229*

Solo synchronized swimming event held in the Olympic Games, *5942*

Speed skater from the United States to win the women's 1000-meter title at the Olympic Winter Games, *5712*

Speed skater from the United States to win the women's 1500-meter title at the Olympic Winter Games, *5687*

Speed skater from the United States to win the women's 500-meter title at the Olympic Winter Games, *5688*

Speed skater to sweep all five men's speed skating events in a single Olympic Winter Games, *5696*

Speed skater to win the men's 10,000-meter title at the Olympic Winter Games, *5650*

Speed skater to win the women's title in the world championships, *5655*

Speed skater to win three consecutive women's 500-meter titles at the Olympic Winter Games, *5721*

Speed skater to win three consecutive women's titles at the world speed skating championships, *5691*

Speed skater to win two consecutive women's 1000-meter speed skating titles at the Olympic Winter Games, *5723*

Speed skater to win two consecutive women's 500-meter short track titles at the Olympic Winter Games, *5724*

Speed skater to win two consecutive women's 500-meter titles in the Olympic Winter Games, *5711*

Speed skaters to be named *Sports Illustrated* Sportsmen of the Year, *5719*

Sports commissioner to be named *Sports Illustrated* Sportsman of the Year, *1154*

Star-class sailing event held in the Olympic Games, *5212*

Steel tennis rackets came into widespread use, *6115*

Stud book for horse racing published in North America, *4287*

Sumo wrestler born outside Japan to be named grand champion (yokozuna), *6415*

Surfer to win four women's professional world titles, *5777*

Sweep of the medals in an event by athletes of Black African ancestry at the Olympic Games, *4726*

Swimmer from the United States to win the men's 100-meter backstroke title in the Olympic Games, *5807*

Swimmer to break the two-minute barrier in the men's 200-meter backstroke event, *5924*

Swimmer to hold both the women's 100- and 200-meter backstroke world titles at the same time, *5929*

Swimmer to hold both the women's 200- and 400-meter freestyle world titles at the same time, *5910*

Swimmer to hold the women's 200-meter butterfly and both the 200- and 400-meter individual medley world titles at the same time, *5931*

Swimmer to hold the world titles in both the men's 100-meter and 200-meter freestyle events at the same time, *5891*

Swimmer to hold world titles in the men's 200-, 400-, and 1500-meter freestyle at the same time, *5913*

Swimmer to race the men's 100-meter backstroke event in under 55 seconds, *5951*

Swimmer to race the men's 100-meter freestyle in under 50 seconds, *5926*

Swimmer to race the men's 100-meter freestyle in under one minute, *5815*

Swimmer to win both the men's 220-yard (later 200-meter) and 440-yard (later 400-meter) freestyle events in a single Olympic Games, *5798*

Swimmer to win four gold medals in a single Olympic Games, *5850*

Swimmer to win the women's 100-meter butterfly title in the Olympic Games with a time of under one minute, *5940*

Swimmer to win three consecutive gold medals in the men's 4 x 100-meter freestyle relay in the Olympic Games, *5964*

Swimmer to win three individual gold medals in a single Olympic Games, *5862*

Swimmer to win two consecutive gold medals in the men's 4 x 100-meter freestyle relay in the Olympic Games, *5865*

Swimmer to win two consecutive men's 100-meter backstroke titles in the Olympic Games, *5817*

Swimmer to win two consecutive men's 100-meter freestyle titles at the world championships, *5958*

Swimmer to win two consecutive men's 100-meter freestyle titles in the Olympic Games, *5802*

Swimmer to win two consecutive men's 1500-meter freestyle titles in the Olympic Games, *5863*

UNITED STATES—*continued*

Swimmer to win two consecutive men's 50-meter freestyle titles at the world championships, *5960*

Swimmer to win two consecutive women's 800-meter freestyle titles in the Olympic Games, *5965*

Swimmer to win two consecutive women's 800-meter freestyle world titles, *5971*

Swimmers to win gold medals in the same event at the same Olympic Games, *5939*

Synchronized swimming team event held in the world championships, *5893*

Team from the United States to win the men's 4 x 100-meter relay track event in the Olympic Games, *5011*

Team from the United States to win the rugby event in the Olympic Games, *4967*

Team to race the men's 4 x 100-meter relay in under 40 seconds, *5042*

Team to race the men's 4 x 400-meter relay in under 3:10 minutes, *5031*

Tennis player classified as "non-white" by South Africa's then-racist government to win a South African tennis tournament, *6153*

Tennis player to achieve a Grand Slam, *6098*

Tennis player to be named Association of Tennis Professionals (ATP) Player of the Year, *6160*

Tennis player to be ranked number one in the Association of Tennis Professionals (ATP) rankings for 160 consecutive weeks, *6165*

Tennis player to be ranked number one in the Women's Tennis Association (WTA) rankings, *6161*

Tennis player to be ranked number one in the Women's Tennis Association (WTA) rankings for 156 consecutive weeks, *6173*

Tennis player to win 10 consecutive women's doubles titles at the United States national championships, and 13 overall, *6106*

Tennis player to win 10 consecutive women's doubles titles at the United States national championships, and 13 overall, *6106*

Tennis player to win 109 men's singles tournaments during his career, *6187*

Tennis player to win 112 women's singles matches in a single season, *6147*

Tennis player to win 1,438 women's singles matches during her career, *6184*

Tennis player to win 158 straight women's singles matches, *6093*

Tennis player to win 98 straight men's singles matches, *6075*

Tennis player to win eight women's singles titles at the United States national championships, *6084*

Tennis player to win five consecutive women's doubles titles at the United States national championships, *6037*

Tennis player to win four consecutive United States mixed doubles national championships, and nine overall, *6105*

Tennis player to win four straight women's singles titles at the United States national championships, *6058*

Tennis player to win four women's singles titles at the United States national championships, *6046*

Tennis player to win seven consecutive men's singles titles at the United States national championships, *6020*

Tennis player to win seven Wimbledon mixed doubles championships, *6091*

Tennis player to win six consecutive men's doubles titles at the United States national championships, *6021*

Tennis player to win six United States mixed doubles titles, *6059*

Tennis player to win six Wimbledon men's singles championships in the Open era, *6190*

Tennis player to win the French Open women's doubles title five consecutive times, *6176*

Tennis player to win the French Open women's singles title seven times, *6174*

Tennis player to win the U.S. Open men's singles title five times, *6171*

Tennis player to win the U.S. Open men's singles title three consecutive times, *6170*

Tennis player to win the U.S. Open women's singles title four consecutive times, *6166*

Tennis player to win the Wimbledon women's singles championship eight times, *6099*

Tennis player to win the Wimbledon women's singles title six consecutive times, *6175*

Tennis player to win the Women's Tennis Association (WTA) championship eight times, *6177*

Tennis player to win the Women's Tennis Association (WTA) championship four times, *6164*

Tennis player to win three consecutive French national women's singles championships, and then four overall, after the event became international, *6092*

Tennis player to win three consecutive women's singles titles at the United States national championships, *6051*

Tennis player to win two consecutive mixed doubles titles at the United States national tennis championships, *6034*

Tennis player to win two consecutive Wimbledon mixed doubles championships, *6083*

Tennis player to win two consecutive women's doubles titles at the United States national championships, *6031*

Tennis player to win two consecutive women's singles titles at the United States national championships, *6025*

UNITED STATES—*continued*

Women's 470-class sailing event held in the Olympic Games, *5249*

Women's 5-kilometer river/sea swim event held in the world championships, *5977*

Women's 500-meter short track speed skating event held at the Olympic Winter Games, *5717*

Women's 80-meter hurdles event held in the Olympic Games, *4332*

Women's 800-meter freestyle swimming event held in the Olympic Games, *5860*

Women's amateur boxing match sponsored by USA Boxing, *2590*

Women's basketball small college National Invitation Tournament, *2113*

Women's boxing match to be watched by more than 1 million television viewers, *2593*

Women's coxless fours event held in the world championships in rowing, *4954*

Women's giant slalom event held at the Olympic Winter Games, *5393*

Women's golf event in the Olympic Games, *3630*

Women's ice hockey event held in the Olympic Games, *4230*

Women's individual archery event in the modern format held in the Olympic Games, *1036*

Women's javelin-throw event held in the Olympic Games, *4390*

Women's moguls freestyle skiing event held at the Olympic Winter Games, *5474*

Women's pole vault event held in the Olympic Games, *4852*

Women's professional baseball league, *1546*

Women's road race cycling event held in the Olympic Games, *2708*

Women's road time trial cycling event held in the Olympic Games, *2726*

Women's slalom event held at the Olympic Winter Games, *5389*

Women's soccer event held in the Olympic Games, *5569*

Women's solo and duet synchronized swimming events held in the world championships, *5908*

Women's springboard diving event held in the Olympic Games, *2797*

Women's Tennis Association (WTA) championships, *6156*

Women's Tour de France cycling race, *2706*

Women's World Cup in soccer (international football), *5566*

Women's World Road Race Championship, *4510*

World championship in billiards, *2447*

World championships for freestyle skiing, *5451*

World championships for men's lacrosse, *4424*

World championships for nine-ball pool, *2464*

World championships for roller hockey (rink hockey) played with in-line skates, *4242*

World championships for women's weightlifting, *6350*

World championships in 18.1 balkline billiards, *2450*

World championships in bowling to include women, *2498*

World championships in duathlon, *2835*

World championships in endurance riding, *2887*

World championships in mountain biking, *2716*

World championships in racquetball, *4877*

World championships in short track speed skating, *5694*

World championships in slow pitch softball, *5619*

World championships in taekwondo to include women, *4549*

World championships in the triathlon, *6240*

World championships in trampolining, *6228*

World championships in trampolining to include double mini trampoline competitions, *6230*

World championships in trampolining to include individual tumbling and synchronized pairs competitions, *6229*

World championships in water-skiing, *6316*

World cup for water polo, *6306*

World cup in bobsledding, *2475*

World Cup in ice hockey, *4222*

World cup in the triathlon, *6241*

World Cup in track and field (athletics), *6220*

World Cup series of competitions for speed skating, *5703*

World figure skating championship to be canceled other than because of war, *3057*

World figure skating championships for roller skating, *4909*

World team Uber Cup badminton championships for women, *1170*

Worldloppet Cup to include women Nordic skiers, *5464*

Wrestler from the United States to win two super heavyweight freestyle titles in the Olympic Games, *6412*

Wrestler of Black African descent to win a gold medal in wrestling in the Olympic Games, *6409*

Wrestler to win two consecutive featherweight freestyle wrestling titles in the Olympic Games, *6413*

Written reference to tennis, *6002*

Alabama

Birmingham

Little League World Series to be televised, *1594*

World Football League championship, *3337*

UNITED STATES—California—*continued*

Berkeley

Runner to complete the men's mile race in under 3:53 minutes, *5080*

Beverly Hills

Golfer to win four, and then five and six, U.S. Women's Amateur Championships, *3688*

Burbank

Woman to fly in the Bendix Trophy airplane race, *1011*

Carlsbad

African-American golfer to win the Tournament of Champions, *3848*
Golfer to win the Tournament of Champions four and five times, *3802*

Chula Vista

Golfer to win the U.S. Women's Open four times, *3778*

Compton

Shot-putter to break the 18- and 19-meter, and 60-foot, barriers, *5340*

Culver City

Runner to break the 1926 record in the women's marathon, and the first from the United States to hold the world record in the event, *4488*
Woman to race the marathon in under 3:00 hours, *4495*

Echo Summit

Hurdler to race the men's 400-meter hurdles in under 49 seconds, *4341*

Emeryville

Mechanical rabbit used in dog racing, *2834*

Fresno

Pole-vaulter to clear 15 feet, *4841*
Runner from Central or South America to set or equal a world track and field record, *5049*

Inglewood

Jockey to win 8,834 horse races, *4319*

Los Angeles Lakers regular season basketball game played at the Forum, *2054*

La Quinta

Golfer to win more than $400,000 in the Skins Game, *3890*

Long Beach

African-American golfer to win a title in a significant predominantly white tournament, *3750*
College women's basketball player to score 60 points in a single Division I National Collegiate Athletic Association (NCAA) game, *2259*
College women's basketball player to score 974 points in a single Division I National Collegiate Athletic Association (NCAA) season, *2254*
College women's basketball team to score 149 points in a single Division I National Collegiate Athletic Association (NCAA) game, *2260*
Figure skaters to win five consecutive ice dancing titles with the same partner at the U.S. national championships, *3068*
Pilot to win the Bendix Trophy race three times in a row, *1016*
Softball team to win six consecutive titles in the International Softball Congress World Championships, *5596*
Woman figure skater to perform a triple salchow in competition, *3069*

Los Angeles

African-American golfers to play in a Professional Golfers' Association (PGA)–recognized event, *3720*
African-American runner to win the men's 100- and 200-meter titles in the Olympic Games, *5032*
Air rifle shooting individual event held in the Olympic Games, *5320*
Athlete from China to win a gold medal in the Olympic Games, *4756*
Athlete from Morocco to win a gold medal at the Olympic Games, and the first female athlete from an Islamic country to win an Olympic medal, *4758*
Athlete from Portugal to win a gold medal in the Olympic Games, *4760*
Athlete to hold the world record in both the men's long jump and triple jump, *4433*
Athlete to qualify for the finals of the same event in four Olympic Games, *4759*
Athlete who was paraplegic to compete in the Olympic Games, *4753*
Athletes from China and Taiwan to share the medal platform in the Olympic Games, *4757*

Basketball team from the United States to win the women's title in the Olympic Games, *2208*

Basketball team to score 25 points in a single overtime period of a National Basketball Association (NBA) game, *2376*

Bendix Trophy airplane race, *1009*

Canoer to win three titles in the men's Canadian pairs 1000-meter event in the Olympic Games, *2622*

Cyclist from the United States to win the men's 1000-meter match sprint in the Olympic Games, *2710*

Cyclist from the United States to win the men's 4000-meter individual pursuit in the Olympic Games, *2709*

Cyclist from the United States to win the men's road race in the Olympic Games, *2707*

Discus-thrower from the United States to win the women's event in the Olympic Games, *2764*

Discus-thrower to break the 200-foot barrier, *2773*

Duet synchronized swimming event held in the Olympic Games, *5941*

Equestrian to win two consecutive three-day event individual titles, *2857*

Fencer to win two men's team foil titles in the Olympic Games, *2926*

Field hockey players to win two gold medals in the Olympic Games, *4038*

Golf tournament to offer a $10,000 purse, *3680*

Golfer to win the U.S. Open in under 280 for 72 holes, *3718*

Gymnast from the United States to win the all-around women's title in the Olympic Games, *3973*

Gymnasts from the United States to win the men's combined exercises title in the Olympic Games, *3972*

Heavyweight boxing event with a limited weight held in the Olympic Games, *2581*

High-jumper to clear seven feet, *4025*

High-jumpers to hold the officially accepted world record in the women's event, and the first from the United States to win the women's event in the Olympic Games, *4023*

Hurdler to race the men's 400-meter hurdles in under 50 seconds, *4337*

Hurdler to race the men's 400-meter hurdles in under 52 seconds, *4334*

Los Angeles Angels regular season baseball game played at Dodger Stadium, *1658*

Los Angeles Clippers regular season basketball game played at the Memorial Sports Arena, *2209*

Los Angeles Clippers regular season game played in the Staples Center, *2423*

Los Angeles Dodgers regular season baseball game played at Dodger Stadium, *1655*

Los Angeles Dodgers regular season baseball game played at Los Angeles Memorial Coliseum, *1633*

Los Angeles Kings regular season game played in the Staples Center, *4236*

Los Angeles Lakers regular season game played in the Staples Center, *2424*

Los Angeles Raiders American Football Conference championship, *3393*

Los Angeles Raiders regular season football game played at the Los Angeles Memorial Coliseum, *3375*

Los Angeles Rams National Football League championship, *3231*

Men's 50,000-meter walk held in the Olympic Games, *6291*

Men's floor exercises gymnastics competition held in the Olympic Games, *3928*

Men's points cycling race held in the Olympic Games, *2711*

Men's sailboarding event held in the Olympic Games, *5191*

Men's tumbling gymnastics competition held in the Olympic Games, *3929*

Miami Dolphins win in professional football's Super Bowl, *3331*

National Football League Pro Bowl, *3186*

National team to sweep the top medals in the women's platform diving event in the Olympic Games, *2800*

Olympic Games held in the Soviet Union, and the first in a Communist country, *4751*

Olympic Games to be privately financed, rather than government funded, *4755*

Olympic Games to have medalists stand on a platform, and to play the gold medalist's national anthem, *4675*

Olympic Games to use automatic timing and photofinish cameras, *4677*

Olympic men's 1500-meter freestyle event in which the medalists all had times under 20 minutes, *5825*

Olympic men's 400-meter freestyle event at which all the medalists had times under five minutes, *5823*

Result of an Olympic event to be changed after viewing of the film of the race, *4678*

Rhythmic gymnastics all-around individual competition held in the Olympic Games, *3974*

Rower to win two consecutive men's single sculls rowing titles in the Olympic Games, *4937*

Run across the United States, *5017*

Runner from South America to win the men's 800-meter title at the Olympic Games, *5139*

Runner to complete the men's 800-meter race in under 1:50 minutes, *5029*

Runner to race the men's 1500 meters in less than 3:35 minutes, *5083*

Modesto

Long-jumper to break the 27-foot barrier, *4438*

Oakland

Figure skater from Ukraine to win the men's singles title at the world championships, *3098*

Kansas City Chiefs American Football League championship, *3304*

Oakland Athletics regular season baseball game played at the Oakland Alameda County Coliseum, *1700*

Oakland Raiders American Football Conference championship, *3352*

Oakland Raiders American Football League championship, *3285*

Pittsburgh Steelers American Football Conference championship, *3338*

San Francisco Warriors regular season basketball game played at the Oakland Coliseum, *2044*

Orange

Softball player to win three consecutive Bertha Tickey Awards, *5608*

Softball player to win three consecutive Erv Lind Awards, *5606*

Palo Alto

Discus-thrower to break the 160-foot and 50-meter barriers, *2763*

High-jumper to hold the officially accepted world record in the men's event, *4021*

High-jumper to set or equal four world records in the men's event in a single year, *4027*

Professional football player to score 18 points in a single Super Bowl game, *3400*

Pasadena

African-American college football player to play in the Rose Bowl, *3140*

African-American college football player to score a touchdown in the Rose Bowl, *3212*

African-American quarterback to appear in the Rose Bowl college football game, *3260*

College football player to score five rushing touchdowns in a major bowl game, *3130*

Columbia University win in college football's Rose Bowl, *3166*

Discus-thrower to break the 190-foot barrier, *2769*

Georgia Tech win in college football's Rose Bowl, *3159*

Harvard University win in college football's Rose Bowl, *3145*

Hurdler to race the 400-meter hurdles in under 55 seconds, *4328*

Javelin-thrower to break the 260-foot and 80-meter barriers, and the first from the United States to hold the world record in the men's event, *4394*

New York Giants win in professional football's Super Bowl, *3414*

Northwestern University win in college football's Rose Bowl, *3223*

Notre Dame University win in college football's Rose Bowl, *3154*

Oakland Raiders win in professional football's Super Bowl, *3355*

Oregon State University win in college football's Rose Bowl, and the only Rose Bowl not played in Pasadena, California, *3191*

Purdue University win in college football's Rose Bowl, *3281*

Rose Bowl football game, *3133*

Soccer (international football) team to win the world cup four times, *5567*

Soccer (international football) team to win the world cup three times, *5562*

Stanford University win in college football's Rose Bowl, *3157*

University of Alabama win in college football's Rose Bowl, *3156*

University of California at Los Angeles win in college football's Rose Bowl, *3275*

University of California win in college football's Rose Bowl, *3149*

University of Georgia win in college football's Rose Bowl, *3192*

University of Illinois win in college football's Rose Bowl, *3214*

University of Iowa win in college football's Rose Bowl, *3244*

University of Michigan win in college football's Rose Bowl, *3220*

University of Minnesota win in college football's Rose Bowl, *3266*

University of Oregon win in college football's Rose Bowl, *3142*

University of Pittsburgh win in college football's Rose Bowl, *3181*

University of Southern California win in college football's Rose Bowl, *3152*

Washington Redskins win in professional football's Super Bowl, *3383*

Washington State University win in college football's Rose Bowl, *3141*

Zamboni ice-resurfacing machine sold commercially, *5749*

Pebble Beach

Golfer to hold the record low (under-par) scores in all four Professional Golfers Association (PGA) major tournaments, *3899*

Golfer to win the Tour Championship in a playoff, *3860*

UNITED STATES—California—Pebble Beach—*continued*

Sudden-death playoff in one of golf's major tournaments, *3814*

Pomona

Drag racer to reach a speed over 290 miles per hour, *1138*

Rancho Mirage

Dinah Shore golf tournament, *3799*

Golfer to win two of golf's major tournaments in her rookie year on the Ladies Professional Golf Association (LPGA) Tour, *3844*

Ladies Professional Golf Association (LPGA) Tour tournament to be nationally televised for all four rounds, *3839*

Redlands

Runner to race the men's 100-meter event in less than 10.5 seconds, *5012*

Sacramento

Runner to race the men's 100-meter dash in under 10 seconds, *5084*

Sacramento Kings regular season basketball game played at the ARCO Arena, *2280*

San Bernardino

Woman to be licensed as a boxing referee, *2553*

San Diego

African-American quarterback to play in and to win football's Super Bowl, *3419*

American Football League team to win two consecutive conference championships, *3262*

Denver Broncos win in professional football's Super Bowl, *3496*

Professional-amateur golf tournament, *3705*

Professional football player to rush for 204 yards in a single Super Bowl game, *3420*

San Diego Chargers American Football League championship, *3271*

San Diego Chargers regular season football game played at San Diego Stadium, *3283*

San Diego Padres regular season baseball game played at San Diego Stadium, *1709*

Team to win the championship of the North American Soccer League, *5561*

Woman to sail across the Pacific alone, *5226*

San Francisco

Dallas Cowboys National Football Conference championship, *3313*

Gay Games, *4378*

San Francisco 49ers National Football Conference championship, *3372*

San Francisco 49ers regular season football game played at Candlestick Park, *3318*

San Francisco Giants regular season baseball game played at Pacific Bell Park, *1860*

San Francisco Giants regular season baseball game played at Seals Stadium, *1632*

Shot-putter to hold the officially accepted world record in the men's event, *5331*

San Jose

Discus-thrower to break the 230-feet and 70-meter barriers in the men's event, *2781*

San Jose Sharks regular season hockey game played at San Jose Arena, *4210*

San Pedro

Girl from the United States to appear in a Little League baseball World Series, *1806*

Santa Barbara

Pole-vaulter to clear 16 feet, *4844*

Santa Clara

World Games, *4377*

Santa Monica

Beach volleyball, *6275*

Race Across America (RAAM) bicycle marathon, *2705*

Women's Air Derby, *1007*

Squaw Valley

Figure skater to win the women's singles U.S., world, and Olympic championships in the same year, *3056*

Figure skaters from Canada to win the pairs title at the Olympic Winter Games, *3055*

Ice hockey team from the United States to win the title at the Olympic Winter Games, *4141*

Men's 20-kilometer biathlon competition at the Olympic Winter Games, *2431*

Olympic Winter Games host city to refuse to build a bobsled run, *2474*

Speed skater to skate the 10,000 meters in under 16 minutes, *5672*

Speed skater to win two consecutive titles in the men's 500 meters at the Olympic Winter Games, *5671*

Women's 1000-meter speed skating event held at the Olympic Winter Games, *5667*

Women's 1500-meter speed skating event held at the Olympic Winter Games, *5670*

Women's 3000-meter speed skating event held at the Olympic Winter Games, *5668*

Women's 500-meter speed skating event held at the Olympic Winter Games, *5669*

Stanford

Runner to complete the men's 400-meter race in under 47 seconds, *5027*

Track world record for which there was an official wind-speed reading, *6209*

State Beach

Organized tournament in beach volleyball, *6276*

Thousand Oaks

Golf event to be broadcast live on network television in prime time, *3898*

Van Nuys

Pilot to win the Bendix Trophy–Jet Division airplane race, *1014*

Walnut

Hammer-thrower to break the 70-meter and 230-foot barriers, *3991*

Shot-putter to break the 20-meter barrier, *5343*

Colorado

Colorado Springs

Figure skater from the Soviet Union to win the men's singles title at the world championships, *3071*

Figure skater to land three quadruple jumps, and two different ones, in a single international competition, *3116*

Figure skater to win the men's singles U.S., world, and Olympic championships in the same year, and then twice in a row, *3034*

National Collegiate Athletic Association college hockey championship, *4121*

National Collegiate Athletic Association college hockey championship, *4121*

Deer Trail

Bronco-riding contest for cash prizes, *4878*

Denver

Basketball player to have 14 assists in a single quarter of a National Basketball Association (NBA) game, *2206*

Basketball player to have 30 assists in a single National Basketball Association (NBA) game, *2299*

Basketball team to score 186 points, and 74 field goals, in a single National Basketball Association (NBA) game, *2193*

Colorado Avalanche regular season hockey game played at the Pepsi Center, *4235*

Colorado Rockies regular season baseball game played at Coors Field, *1831*

Colorado Rockies regular season baseball game played at Mile High Stadium, *1824*

Denver Broncos American Football Conference championship, *3358*

Denver Broncos regular season football game played at Mile High Stadium, *3255*

Denver Nuggets regular season game played at McNichols Sports Arena, *2117*

Golfer to win three major tournaments, and six titles overall, on the Ladies Professional Golf Association (LPGA) Tour in a single season, *3725*

Introduction of the name "softball", *5578*

National Basketball Association (NBA) game in which a total of 370 points was scored, *2194*

Olympic Games to be voted down by the selected host region, *4742*

Softball team to win the Amateur Softball Association Super Slow Pitch National Championships, *5617*

United States Football League championship, *3381*

Connecticut

Bristol

All-sports television network, *5752*

Greenwich

Racquetball game, *4873*

Hartford

African-American golfer to be classified as an "approved player" on the Professional Golfers' Association (PGA) Tour, *3755*

Baseball chest protector, *1233*

Figure skater from Switzerland to win the women's singles title in the world championships, *3086*

New England Whalers regular season hockey game played at the Hartford Civic Center Coliseum, *4169*

New Haven

Batting and fielding cage in baseball, *1280*

Figure skater to win six, and then seven, consecutive men's singles titles in the U.S. national championships, *3015*

Figure skater to win six consecutive women's singles titles, and nine overall, at the U.S. national championships, *3016*

UNITED STATES—Connecticut—New Haven—*continued*

Figure skater to win the men's singles title in the U.S. national championships, *2987*

Figure skater to win the women's singles title at the U.S. national championships, *2988*

Figure skaters to win a gold medal in ice dancing in the U.S. national championships, *2989*

Figure skaters to win the pairs title in the U.S. national championships, *2990*

National figure skating championships in the United States, *2991*

Sandy Hook

Transatlantic sailing race, *5199*

Stratford

Softball player to be named the top pitcher, *5603*

Softball team to win eight consecutive titles in the Amateur Softball Association Women's Major Fast Pitch National Championships, *5615*

District of Columbia

Washington

African-American basketball team at Howard University, *1882*

African-American to work as an umpire in major league baseball, *1686*

Brooklyn Dodgers regular season baseball game played at Washington Park, *1277*

Golf club for African-American women, *3684*

National Football League team to win two consecutive league championships, *3189*

National golf organization founded by African-Americans, *3683*

President's Cup motorboat (powerboat) race, *4567*

Professional basketball major league, *1888*

Rule establishing that no baseball game can be completed until five innings have been played by both teams, *1202*

Runner to race the 100-yard dash in under 10 seconds, *4973*

Team archery event held in the Olympic Games, *1028*

United States President to throw out the first ball in a major league baseball opening day game, *1399*

Walker to be considered a professional, *6287*

Washington Capitals regular season hockey game played at the MCI Center, *4229*

Washington Redskins National Football Conference championship, *3327*

Washington Redskins regular season football game played at DC Stadium, *3261*

Washington Senators regular season baseball game played at DC Stadium, *1654*

Washington Senators regular season baseball game played at Griffith Stadium, *1352*

Washington Senators regular season baseball game played at Griffith Stadium, *1646*

Washington Senators regular season baseball game played in American League Park, *1337*

Washington Wizards regular season basketball game played at the MCI Center, *2398*

World figure skating championships for roller skating, *4909*

Florida

Avon Park

JCPenney Classic golf tournament, *3761*

Boca Raton

Women's Tennis Association (WTA) championships, *6156*

Clearwater

Softball player to win the Most Valuable Player Award, *5593*

Daytona Beach

24 Hours of Daytona automobile race, *1103*

Automobile race sponsored by the National Association for Stock Car Auto Racing (NASCAR), *1070*

Automobile racer to win the Winston $1 million bonus for winning three of the top four National Association for Stock Car Auto Racing (NASCAR) races in a single season, *1114*

Daytona 500 automobile race, *1098*

National Association for Stock Car Auto Racing (NASCAR), *1071*

National Association for Stock Car Auto Racing (NASCAR) automobile race of 500 miles to be televised live from start to finish, *1128*

National Association for Stock Car Auto Racing (NASCAR) race to be televised, *1102*

World championships for women's weightlifting, *6350*

Gainesville

Drag racer to reach a speed over 300 miles per hour, *1142*

Gator Bowl football game, *3204*

Hialeah

Use of an electric-eye photo finish camera in horse racing, *4294*

Woman jockey to race at a pari-mutuel track in the United States, *4305*

Jacksonville

Jacksonville Jaguars regular season football game played at the ALLTEL Stadium, *3470*

Orange Blossom Classic, *3163*

Lake Eloise

Water-skier known to have skied barefoot, *6315*

Melbourne

African-American golfer to win a Senior Professional Golfers' Association (PGA) Tour event, *3834*

Miami

African-American football players to appear in the Orange Bowl, *3239*

Baltimore Colts win in professional football's Super Bowl, *3314*

Basketball player to make 20 free throws in a single half of a National Basketball Association (NBA) game, *2320*

Boxer to win the world heavyweight championship three times, *2566*

Florida Marlins regular season baseball game played at Joe Robbie Stadium, *1823*

Florida Panthers regular season hockey game played at Miami Arena, *4209*

Golfer to win more than 10 straight titles, and to win 18 titles overall during a single year, on the Professional Golfers' Association (PGA) Tour, *3714*

Miami Dolphins regular season football game played at Joe Robbie Stadium, *3415*

Miami Heat regular season basketball game played at the Miami Arena, *2278*

New England Patriots American Football Conference championship, *3404*

New York Jets win in the National Football League's Super Bowl, *3296*

Olympic light heavyweight boxing champion to become world heavyweight champion, *2565*

Orange Bowl football game, *3169*

Pole-vaulter to clear 17 feet, *4845*

Professional football player to be named Most Valuable Player in the Super Bowl twice in a row, *3295*

Professional football player to gain 215 yards receiving in a single Super Bowl game, *3428*

Professional football player to gain 357 yards passing in a single Super Bowl game, *3429*

Professional football player to kick four field goals in a single Super Bowl game, *3289*

Professional football team to win two consecutive Super Bowl games, *3290*

Woman to sail across the Atlantic alone, *5220*

Milton

Father and son to win golf tournaments on the same day, *3896*

Naples

Golfer to win the World Championship of Women's Golf twice in a row, *3836*

Orlando

Japanese-American figure skater to win the women's singles title at the U.S. national championships, *3099*

Orlando Magic regular season basketball game played at the Orlando Arena, *2288*

Solheim Cup golf competition, *3869*

Tangerine Bowl football game, *3213*

Palm Beach Gardens

Golfer to win two Professional Golfers' Association (PGA) Championships, after the tournament was converted to a stroke play format, *3794*

Ponte Vedra Beach

African-American golfer to win the Tournament Players Championship, *3845*

Father and son to win golf tournaments on the same day, *3896*

Golfer of African-American or Asian-American descent to win the U.S. Amateur Championship, *3879*

Sebring

JCPenney Classic golf tournament, *3761*

United States Grand Prix automobile race to be part of the Formula One Grand Prix circuit, *1099*

St. Petersburg

Golfer to score eight consecutive birdies in a Professional Golfers' Association (PGA) recognized event, *3764*

Sunrise

Florida Panthers regular season hockey game played at the National Car Rental Center, *4231*

Tampa

Girl from the United States to appear in a Little League baseball World Series, *1806*

UNITED STATES—Florida—Tampa—*continued*

Hall of Fame Bowl football game, *3406*

Los Angeles Raiders win in professional football's Super Bowl, *3394*

Los Angeles Rams National Football Conference championship, *3365*

Tampa Bay Buccaneers regular season football game played at Tampa Stadium, *3349*

Tampa Bay Devil Rays regular season baseball game played at Tropicana Field, *1851*

Tampa Bay Lightning regular season hockey game played at the Ice Palace, *4228*

Tampa Bay Lightning regular season hockey game played at the Thunderdome, *4206*

Tampa Bay

Tampa Bay Buccaneers regular season football game played at Raymond James Stadium, *3499*

Georgia

Atlanta

African-American college baseball league, *1315*

Archer from the United States to win the men's individual gold medal in the Olympic Games, *1039*

Archers from the United States to win a gold medal in the team event in the Olympic Games, *1040*

Athlete from Africa to win the long jump, or any field event, in the Olympic Games, *4444*

Athlete from Algeria to win a gold medal in the Olympic Games, *4799*

Athlete from Armenia to win a gold medal in the Olympic Games, *4791*

Athlete from Burundi to win a gold medal in the Olympic Games, *4800*

Athlete from Costa Rica to win a gold medal in the Olympic Games, *4790*

Athlete from Ecuador to win a gold medal in the Olympic Games, *4792*

Athlete from Hong Kong to win a gold medal in the Olympic Games, *4797*

Athlete from newly independent Belarus to win a gold medal in the Olympic Games, *4794*

Athlete from Nigeria to win a gold medal in the Olympic Games, *4798*

Athlete from Syria to win a gold medal in the Olympic Games, *4796*

Athlete from Thailand to win a gold medal in the Olympic Games, *4801*

Athlete from the newly independent Slovak Republic to win a gold medal in the Olympic Games, *4795*

Atlanta Braves regular season baseball game played at Atlanta–Fulton County Stadium, *1687*

Atlanta Braves regular season baseball game played at Turner Field, *1844*

Atlanta Falcons regular season football game played at the Georgia Dome, *3454*

Atlanta Hawks regular season basketball game played at The Omni, *2089*

Atlanta Hawks regular season basketball game played at the Philips Arena, *2425*

Atlanta Thrashers regular season hockey game played at the Philips Arena, *4233*

Badminton event for mixed doubles in the Olympic Games, *1175*

Basketball player to win three, and then four, gold medals in the Olympic Games, *2380*

Beach volleyball event held in the Olympic Games, *6286*

Black African athlete from South Africa to win a gold medal in the Olympic Games, *4802*

Boxer to win two consecutive light welterweight titles in the Olympic Games, *2591*

Gymnasts from the United States to win the women's team title in the Olympic Games, *3978*

Heritage Bowl African-American college football game, *3446*

Laser-class sailing event held in the Olympic Games, *5256*

Long-jumper to win three, and then four, consecutive men's titles in the Olympic Games, *4443*

Men's cross-country (mountain bike) race held in the Olympic Games, *2723*

Men's double trap (clay pigeon) individual shooting event held in the Olympic Games, *5326*

Men's lightweight double sculls rowing event held in the Olympic Games, *4959*

Men's lightweight four-oared shells without coxswain rowing event held in the Olympic Games, *4960*

Men's road time trial cycling event held in the Olympic Games, *2725*

Olympic Games in which more than 10,000 athletes competed, and more than 50 percent were women, *4789*

Peach Bowl football game, *3294*

Professional football player to complete 31 passes in a single Super Bowl game, *3460*

Rhythmic gymnastics team competition held in the Olympic Games, *3979*

Runner from Africa, and from Ethiopia, to win the women's marathon at the Olympic Games, *4526*

Runner to complete the men's 200-meter race in under 19.7 seconds, *5183*

Runner to win both the women's 100- and 200-meter titles in the same Olympic Games, *5052*

Runner to win the men's 200- and 400-meter titles in the same Olympic Games, *5184*

Runner to win two consecutive titles in the women's 400-meter race in the Olympic Games, *5182*

St. Louis Rams Super Bowl win, *3513*

Swimmer to win five individual gold medals, and three consecutive medals in the women's 200-meter backstroke, in the Olympic Games, *5972*

Synchronized swimming event held in the Olympic Games, *5974*

Team from Africa to win the men's soccer event in the Olympic Games, *5570*

Tournament Players Championship, *3806*

Woman athlete from the United States to win four gold medals at a single Olympic Games, *4793*

Women's 4 x 200-meter freestyle relay swimming event held in the Olympic Games, *5973*

Women's 5000-meter race held in the Olympic Games, *5181*

Women's cross-country cycling race held in the Olympic Games, *2724*

Women's double trap (clay pigeon) individual shooting event held in the Olympic Games, *5325*

Women's fast pitch softball event held in the Olympic Games, *5626*

Women's lightweight double sculls rowing event held in the Olympic Games, *4961*

Women's points race cycling event held in the Olympic Games, *2722*

Women's triple jump event held in the Olympic Games, *6265*

Augusta

African-American golfer to become a member of the Augusta National Golf Club, *3862*

African-American golfer to play in the Masters tournament, *3808*

Golfer of African-American or Asian-American descent to win one of golf's major tournaments, *3888*

Golfer to hold the record low (under-par) scores in all four Professional Golfers Association (PGA) major tournaments, *3899*

Golfer to win 18 titles in golf's four major tournaments, and six Masters championships, *3850*

Golfer to win five Masters tournaments, *3807*

Golfer to win the Masters in under 280 for 72 holes, *3709*

Golfer to win the Masters three times, *3728*

Golfer to win the Masters tournament four times, *3775*

Golfer to win the Masters tournament three times, *3742*

Golfer to win the Masters tournament twice in a row, *3783*

Golfer to win the U.S. Open, the Masters, and the British Open in the same year, and the first to score under 275 for 72 holes, *3735*

Golfer to win three major tournaments, and six titles overall, on the Ladies Professional Golf Association (LPGA) Tour in a single season, *3725*

Golfer to win two Masters championships, *3702*

Masters golf tournament, *3698*

Professional Golfers' Association (PGA) Seniors' Championship, *3706*

Women's national championships in boxing, *2594*

Hawaii

National team to sweep the medals in the men's 100-meter freestyle in the Olympic Games, *5809*

Person to introduce baseball as played under Cartwright's Rules to Hawaii, *1189*

Sumo wrestler born outside Japan to be named grand champion (yokozuna), *6415*

Women's competition to be included in the world professional championships in surfing, *5775*

Honolulu

Aloha Bowl football game, *3376*

National Football League Pro Bowl played at Aloha Stadium, *3366*

Kona

Athlete to win the men's Hawaii Ironman triathlon competition four, and then five, times consecutively, and six times overall, *6242*

Athlete to win the men's Hawaii Ironman triathlon two, three, four, five, and six times, *6237*

Athlete to win the women's Hawaii Ironman triathlon three and up to eight times, *6239*

Athlete to win two consecutive women's Hawaii Ironman triathlons, *6238*

Makaha

International Surfing Championships, *5770*

Surfer not born in Hawaii to win the International Surfing Championships, *5771*

Oahu

Hawaii Ironman triathlon, *6235*

Hawaii Ironman triathlon to include women, *6236*

Idaho

Boise

Humanitarian Bowl football game, *3485*

Illinois

Aurora

Softball player to win two consecutive batting titles in the Amateur Softball Association Major Fast Pitch National League, *5600*

World championships in fast-pitch softball to include men's teams, *5602*

Chicago

African-American bowler to bowl a 300 game in an American Bowling Congress (ABC) tournament, *2494*

Amateur Softball Association of America (ASA) national championships, *5579*

Baseball player to hit a home run in major league baseball's All-Star Game, *1508*

Boxer to hold a world boxing title for more than 10 years, and to defend a world boxing title 25 times, *2555*

Chicago Bears National Football Conference championship, *3403*

Chicago Bears regular season football game played at Soldier Field, *3315*

Chicago Blackhawks regular season game played in the United Center, *4218*

Chicago Bulls regular season game played in the United Center, *2341*

Chicago Cardinals National Football League championship, *3215*

Chicago Marathon, *4500*

Chicago White Sox regular season baseball game played at Comiskey Park, *1401*

Chicago White Sox regular season baseball game played at New Comiskey Park, *1816*

Chicago White Sox World Series victory, *1371*

Chicago White Stockings regular season baseball game played at Lakefront Park, *1243*

Chicago White Stockings regular season baseball game played at the State Street Grounds, *1226*

Chicago White Stockings regular season baseball game played at the West Side Grounds, *1309*

Chicago White Stockings regular season baseball game played at West Side Park, *1282*

College football All-Star Game, *3165*

Father and son to play at the same time in major league baseball, *1805*

Golf tournament to be televised nationally, *3733*

Golf tournament to offer a $100,000 purse, *3740*

Javelin-thrower to hold the officially accepted world record in the women's event, *4389*

Major league baseball All-Star Game, *1509*

Major league baseball player to steal seven bases in a single game, *1255*

Major sporting goods business, *5740*

National archery tournament in the United States, *1024*

National bowling championships in the United States, *2482*

National collegiate track and field (athletics) championships sponsored by the National Collegiate Athletic Association (NCAA), *6206*

National Football League championship, *3164*

National Football League team to win two consecutive league championships, *3189*

National golf organization founded by African-Americans, *3683*

National governing body in softball, *5580*

Negro League East-West All-Star Game, *1510*

Organized automobile race in the United States, *1043*

Organized softball game, following George Hancock's rules, and with the diamond, ball, and bat he introduced, *5573*

Playground softball organization, *5577*

Roller derby, *4905*

Roller derby to be televised, *4908*

Runner from the United States to win the men's 1500-meter race in the Olympic Games, *4989*

Runner to race the men's 100-meter dash in 10.2 seconds, *5036*

Softball game, *5572*

Sporting event at which the United States national anthem was played, *5746*

Thompson Trophy airplane race, *1008*

Washington Redskins National Football League championship, *3182*

Women's softball team, *5576*

World championships in cycling, *2684*

World Tournament of professional basketball, *1896*

Evanston

National Collegiate Athletic Association (NCAA) Division I tournament basketball championship game, *1898*

Organized automobile race in the United States, *1043*

Glencoe

Golfer to win the U.S. Open and the Professional Golfers' Association (PGA) Championship in the same year, *3674*

U.S. Open golf tournament to charge admission to spectators, *3672*

Golf

Golfer to win the U.S. Open championship four times, and two and three times consecutively, *3640*

Western Open, *3626*

Hinckley

Harlem Globetrotters professional basketball game, *1887*

Lake Forest

Golfer born in the United States to win a U.S. national championship, *3627*

Golfer to win the U.S. Open with a 72-hole score under 300, *3644*

Wheaton

Eighteen-hole golf course in the United States, *3610*

Golfer born in the United States to win the U.S. Open, *3650*

Golfer to win both the U.S. Open and British Open, *3628*

National governing body for golf in the United States, *3609*

Indiana

Crawfordsville

National organization for archery in the United States, *1023*

Elkhart

Use of glass ball targets in United States shooting competitions, *5265*

Fort Wayne

All-professional baseball game on record, *1207*

Hit in an all-professional baseball game, *1208*

Ladies Professional Golf Association (LPGA) Championship, *3746*

French Lick

Golfer to win two, and then three, Ladies Professional Golf Association (LPGA) Championships, *3762*

Indianapolis

Automobile racer to be named Rookie of the Year in the Indianapolis 500, *1086*

Automobile racer to win the Indianapolis 500 four times, *1123*

Automobile racer to win the Indianapolis 500 three times, and to win it twice in a row, *1068*

Automobile racer to win the Indianapolis 500 twice, *1056*

Automobile racer to win the Indianapolis 500 with an average speed of more than 100 miles per hour, *1060*

Automobile racer to win the Indianapolis 500 with an average speed of more than 110 miles per hour, *1066*

Automobile racer to win the Indianapolis 500 with an average speed of more than 120 miles per hour, *1072*

Automobile racer to win the Indianapolis 500 with an average speed of more than 130 miles per hour, *1093*

Automobile racer to win the Indianapolis 500 with an average speed of more than 140 miles per hour, *1104*

Automobile racer to win the Indianapolis 500 with an average speed of more than 160 miles per hour, *1117*

Automobile racer to win the Indianapolis 500 with an average speed of more than 170 miles per hour, *1133*

Automobile racer to win the Indianapolis 500 with an average speed of more than 180 miles per hour, *1139*

Automobile racer to win the Indianapolis 500 with an average speed of over 150 miles per hour, *1109*

Circle City Classic African-American college football game, *3386*

Indiana Pacers regular season basketball game played at the Conseco Fieldhouse, *2426*

Indiana Pacers regular season game played at Market Square Arena, *2107*

Indianapolis 500, *1054*

Indianapolis 500 automobile race to be part of the Formula One Grand Prix circuit, *1079*

Indianapolis Colts regular season football game played at the RCA Dome, *3395*

Long-jumper from the United States to set or equal the world record in the women's event, *4441*

Paved automobile racing track, *1052*

Runner to race the women's 100 meters in under 10:50 seconds, and the 200 meters in under 21.50 seconds, *5153*

Woman automobile racer to race in the Indianapolis 500, *1124*

Iowa

Cedar Rapids

Trampoline, *6226*

UNITED STATES—*continued*
Kansas

Bronson

International horseshoe tournament, *4321*

Topeka

Woman baseball team owner, *1499*

Wichita

Golfer to win three major tournaments, and six titles overall, on the Ladies Professional Golf Association (LPGA) Tour in a single season, *3725*

Golfer to win two U.S. Women's Open championships, *3726*

Kentucky

Louisville

Golfer to hold the record low (under-par) scores in all four Professional Golfers Association (PGA) major tournaments, *3899*

Jockey to win the Kentucky Derby five times, *4301*

Jockey to win three Kentucky Derbys, and the first to win two in a row, *4283*

Kentucky Derby horse race, *4279*

Pitcher to pitch a shutout in baseball's National League, *1223*

Woman jockey to ride in the Kentucky Derby, *4307*

Newport

Softball team to win the Amateur Softball Association Men's Slow Pitch National Championships, *5592*

Louisiana

New Orleans

Basketball player to score 33 points in a single quarter of a National Basketball Association (NBA) game, *2142*

Bayou Classic African-American college football game, *3335*

Chicago Bears win in professional football's Super Bowl, *3405*

Dallas Cowboys win in professional football's Super Bowl, *3324*

Kansas City Chiefs win in professional football's Super Bowl, *3306*

National Football League player to gain 99 yards with a single Super Bowl punt return, *3481*

New Orleans Saints regular season football game played at the Louisiana Superdome, *3345*

Pittsburgh Steelers win in professional football's Super Bowl, *3344*

Professional football player to complete 13 consecutive passes in a single Super Bowl game, *3440*

Professional football player to kick seven points after touchdown in a single Super Bowl game, *3439*

Softball team to win the Amateur Softball Association Women's Major Fast Pitch National Championships in three consecutive years, *5585*

Sugar Bowl football game, *3170*

Tennis club formed in the United States, *6006*

Women's basketball game in the South that was open to the public, *1871*

Women's basketball published set of rules, *1872*

Women's college basketball team in the South, *1870*

Shreveport

Independence Bowl football game, *3351*

Maine

Lewiston

Boxer to win the world heavyweight championship three times, *2566*

Maryland

Baltimore

Baltimore Colts American Football Conference championship, *3312*

Baltimore Orioles regular season baseball game played at Camden Yards, *1819*

Baltimore Orioles regular season baseball game played at Memorial Stadium in Baltimore, *1607*

Baltimore Orioles regular season baseball game played at Oriole Park, *1330*

Baltimore Ravens regular season game played in the PSINet Stadium, *3498*

Basketball player to have 18 rebounds in a single quarter of a National Basketball Association (NBA) game, *2035*

Miami Dolphins American Football Conference championship, *3323*

National Award tournament in duck pin bowling, *2492*

Preakness Stakes horse race, *4278*

St. Louis Browns regular season baseball game played at Sportsman's Park, *1347*

UNITED STATES—Massachusetts—Boston—
continued

Runner to win the women's title in both the Boston Marathon and the New York Marathon in the same year, *4501*

Runner to win three consecutive Boston Marathons, *4476*

Runner to win three consecutive women's titles in the Boston Marathon, *4525*

Runner to win two consecutive Boston Marathons, *4470*

Runner to win two consecutive women's titles in the Boston Marathon, and three overall, *4519*

Runner to win two official women's championships in the Boston Marathon, *4511*

Runners from a single country outside the United States to take the top three spots in the Boston Marathon, *4483*

Sailor to complete a solo circumnavigation of the world, *5202*

Three-point goal scored in a National Basketball Association (NBA) game, *2153*

Walker to be considered a professional, *6287*

Wheelchair entrant in the Boston Marathon, *4498*

Woman to complete the Boston Marathon in under 3:00 hours, *4497*

Woman to race in the Boston Marathon, *4490*

Woman to run in the Boston Marathon wearing an official number, *4491*

World Series, *1355*

World Series game, *1356*

World Series home run, *1357*

Brookline

Amateur golfer to win the U.S. Open, *3653*

National governing body for golf in the United States, *3609*

World Championship of Women's Golf, *3829*

Cambridge

Collegiate sporting event at which admission was charged, *5739*

High-jumper to set or equal four world records in the men's event in a single year, *4027*

Long-jumper to break the 25-foot barrier, *4430*

Pole-vaulter to hold the officially accepted world record in the men's event, *4839*

Runner to hold the officially accepted world record in the men's 1500-meter event, *5000*

Runner to hold the officially accepted world record in the men's mile race, *5009*

United States national interscholastic boys singles tennis championships, *6030*

Foxboro

New England Patriots regular season football game played at Foxboro Stadium, *3316*

Hamilton

Golfer to win a major tournament with a rubber-cored golf ball, *3633*

Golfer to win the U.S. Open championship four times, and two and three times consecutively, *3640*

Golfer to win the U.S. Open in a playoff, *3634*

Golfer to win two U.S. Open championships, *3637*

U.S. Open to use a 72-hole format, *3624*

Holyoke

Volleyball, *6272*

Lynn

Catcher's mask used in a National League game, *1237*

Manchester

Golfer to win the U.S. Women's Amateur Championship twice, and then three times, in a row, *3622*

Medford

Practical four-wheeled roller skates, *4902*

Nahant

Tennis tournament on record in the United States, *6007*

Nantasket Beach

Night baseball game on record, *1251*

Northampton

Women's basketball program, *1866*

Peabody

Golfer to win the U.S. Women's Open three times, *3744*

Pittsfield

Intercollegiate baseball game, *1193*

Springfield

Basketball game, *1864*

Basketball Hall of Fame, *1975*

Basketball team, *1865*

Grand Circuit series of harness horse races, *4277*

Stowe

National golf organization founded by African-Americans, *3683*

Wellesley

Collegiate rowing program for women, *4917*

Worcester

Ryder Cup golf match, *3687*

Michigan

Curling organization in the United States, *2673*
Invention of paddle tennis, *6194*

Ann Arbor

Long-jump record to stand for more than 25 years, *4434*
Precision team figure skating event, *3052*
Track-and-field star to set five new world records and equal a sixth in less than an hour, *6210*

Auburn Hills

Detroit Pistons regular season game played at The Palace of Auburn Hills, *2277*

Birmingham

Golfer to win four, and then five and six, U.S. Women's Amateur Championships, *3688*

Detroit

Basketball player to score 13 field goals in a single quarter of a National Basketball Association (NBA) game, *2141*
Detroit Lions National Football League championship, *3172*
Detroit Red Wings regular season hockey game played at Joe Louis Arena, *4177*
Detroit Tigers regular season baseball game played at Bennett Park, *1333*
Detroit Tigers regular season baseball game played at Comerica Park, *1858*
Detroit Tigers regular season baseball game played at Tiger Stadium, *1414*
Figure skater to be stripped of the U.S. national women's singles title, *3104*
Golfer to win the Ladies Professional Golf Association (LPGA) Championship in a sudden-death playoff, *3749*
Major league baseball player to hit 700 home runs, *1513*
Major league baseball player to hit a home run on the season's first pitch, *1788*
National Hockey League All-Star Game to be televised, *4126*
National speed skating championships in roller skating in the United States, *4906*
Shooter to achieve a perfect score in international competition, *5305*

Softball championship to be broadcast nationally on radio, *5581*
Use of underwater photography to determine the winner of a swimming event, *5829*

Escanaba

International Frisbee Tournament, *3526*

Pontiac

Detroit Lions regular season football game played at the Pontiac Silverdome, *3346*
Motor City Bowl football game, *3484*
San Francisco 49ers win in professional football's Super Bowl, *3373*

Portage Lakes

Professional ice hockey club in the United States, *4053*

Minnesota

State to recognize women's high school ice hockey as a varsity sport, *4213*

Lake City

Water-skiing, *6309*

Lake Pepin

Water-ski jump, *6310*

Minneapolis

Atlanta Falcons National Football Conference championship, *3508*
Basketball player to have 19 assists in a single half of a National Basketball Association (NBA) game, *1986*
Basketball player to miss on 17 consecutive field goal attempts in a single National Basketball Association (NBA) game, *2312*
Discus-thrower to break the 180-foot barrier, *2767*
Golfer to complete a grand slam, *3693*
Golfer to win both the U.S. Amateur and U.S. Open championships in the same year, and to win the U.S. Open in under 290 for 72 holes, *3659*
Golfer to win six U.S. Women's Amateur championships, *3701*
Married figure skaters to win the pairs title at the U.S. national championships, *3054*
Minnesota Timberwolves regular season basketball game played at the Target Center, *2298*
Minnesota Twins regular season baseball game played at Metropolitan Stadium, *1647*
Minnesota Twins regular season baseball game played at the Hubert H. Humphrey Metrodome, *1766*

UNITED STATES—Minnesota—Minneapolis—*continued*

Minnesota Vikings National Football League championship, *3305*

Minnesota Vikings regular season football game played at the Hubert H. Humphrey Metrodome, *3374*

National Basketball Association (NBA) game in which a total of only 37 points was scored, *1929*

World Series game to be played indoors, *1796*

Red Wing

Organized ski-jumping competition in the United States, *5359*

Mississippi

Mississippi City

Boxer to be undisputed world heavyweight champion, *2515*

Missouri

Clayton

Golf tournament to be shown on television, *3716*

Kansas City

African-American college basketball team to win a national title, *1941*

Asian-American figure skater to win the women's singles title at the U.S. national championships, *3088*

Basketball player to have 11 steals in a single National Basketball Association (NBA) game, *2119*

Convention of the Negro National League, *1441*

Kansas City Athletics regular season baseball game played at Muncipal Stadium, *1614*

Kansas City Chiefs regular season football game played at Arrowhead Stadium, *3325*

Kansas City Royals regular season baseball game at Kauffman Stadium, *1732*

Kansas City Royals regular season baseball game played at Municipal Stadium, *1708*

Women's National Basketball Championship, *2172*

St. Louis

Archery events for women held in the Olympic Games, *1027*

Athlete of Black African ancestry to compete in the Olympic Games, *4629*

Bantamweight and featherweight boxing events held in the Olympic Games, and the first boxer to win two gold medals in a single Olympic Games, *2527*

Bantamweight freestyle wrestling event held in the Olympic Games, *6362*

Black athletes from Africa to participate in the Olympic Games, *4630*

Bowling league for women in the United States, *2484*

Discus throw event in the Olympic Games to be decided by a throw-off, *2755*

Featherweight freestyle wrestling event held in the Olympic Games, *6363*

Flyweight boxing event in the Olympic Games, *2528*

Flyweight freestyle wrestling event held in the Olympic Games, *6364*

Gymnast with a wooden leg to win a medal in the Olympic Games, *3912*

Heavyweight boxing event held in the Olympic Games, *2529*

Jai alai game in the United States, *4380*

Jewish major league baseball player, *1218*

Lacrosse event held in the Olympic Games, *4420*

Light flyweight freestyle wrestling event held in the Olympic Games, *6365*

Lightweight boxing event held in the Olympic Games, *2530*

Lightweight freestyle wrestling event held in the Olympic Games, *6366*

Major league baseball player to hit 70 home runs in a single season, *1853*

Major league baseball player to hit five home runs in a doubleheader, *1609*

Men's 100-yard (later 100-meter) backstroke swimming event held in the Olympic Games, *5794*

Men's 4-mile team race held in the Olympic Games, *4988*

Men's 440-yard (later 400-meter) breaststroke event held in the Olympic Games, *5796*

Men's 50-yard (later 50-meter) freestyle swimming event held in the Olympic Games, *5795*

Men's 56-pound weight throw event held in the Olympic Games, *6323*

Men's 880-yard freestyle swimming event held in the Olympic Games, *5797*

Men's decathlon event held in the Olympic Games, *2737*

Men's double sculls rowing event held in the Olympic Games, *4929*

Men's four-oared shell without coxswain rowing event held in the Olympic Games, *4930*

Men's pair-oared shell without coxswain rowing event held in the Olympic Games, *4931*

Men's platform diving event held in the Olympic Games, *2791*

Men's team combined exercises gymnastics competition in the Olympic Games, *3911*

Men's team foil fencing competition held in the Olympic Games, *2906*

Men's triathlon event held in the Olympic Games, *6234*

Middleweight boxing event held in the Olympic Games, *2531*

Milwaukee Brewers regular season baseball game played at Lloyd Street Park, *1339*

National bowling championships for women in the United States, *2486*

National bowling organization for women in the United States, *2487*

National Senior Olympics, *5754*

National team to sweep the medals in the men's doubles tennis event in the Olympic Games, *6043*

National team to sweep the medals in the men's single sculls rowing event in the Olympic Games, *4932*

National team to sweep the top honors in the men's horizontal bar, long horse vault, side (pommel) horse, and rings gymnastics competitions in the Olympic Games, *3913*

National team to sweep the top spots in the men's pole vault in the Olympic Games, *4838*

National team to sweep the top spots in the men's triple jump in the Olympic Games, *6251*

National team to sweep the top three medals in the men's 100- and 200-meter running events in the Olympic Games, *4990*

National team to sweep the top three medals in the men's 400-meter running event in the Olympic Games, *4985*

Olympic Games held in the United States, *4628*

Roque event (a type of croquet) at the Olympic Games, *2671*

Rowers to win two consecutive gold medals in the men's eight-oared shell with coxswain competition in the Olympic Games, *4933*

Runner for the United States to win the men's marathon at the Olympic Games, *4471*

Runner from the United States to win the men's 1500-meter race in the Olympic Games, *4989*

Runner from the United States to win the men's 800-meter race in the Olympic Games, *4987*

Runner from the United States to win the men's steeplechase event at the Olympic Games, *4986*

Runner to win both the men's 100- and 200-meter races in the same Olympic Games, *4991*

St. Louis Blues regular season hockey game played at the Kiel Center, *4238*

St. Louis Browns regular season baseball game played at a field called Sportsman's Park, *1261*

St. Louis Browns regular season baseball game played at Sportsman's Park, *1347*

St. Louis Cardinals regular season baseball game played at Busch Memorial Stadium, *1689*

St. Louis Cardinals regular season baseball game played at Sportsman's Park II, *1445*

St. Louis Rams regular season football game played at the Trans World Dome, *3472*

Super heavyweight freestyle wrestling event held in the Olympic Games, *6367*

Swimmer to win both the men's 220-yard (later 200-meter) and 440-yard (later 400-meter) freestyle events in a single Olympic Games, *5798*

Team archery event held in the Olympic Games, *1028*

Tennis player from the United States to win the men's singles title in the Olympic Games, *6044*

Triple-jumper to win two consecutive men's titles in the Olympic Games, *6252*

Water polo team from the United States to win the title at the Olympic Games, *6302*

Weightlifter to win two medals in the same Olympic Games, and the first from the United States to win a weightlifting Olympic gold medal, *6326*

Welterweight boxing event held in the Olympic Games, *2532*

Welterweight freestyle wrestling event held in the Olympic Games, *6368*

Nebraska

Lincoln

African-American professional baseball team west of the Mississippi, *1299*

Hurdler to race the men's 400-meter hurdles in under 53 seconds, *4330*

North Platte

Professional rodeo, *4879*

Omaha

College women's softball team to win the National Collegiate Athletic Association (NCAA) Division I College World Series, *5618*

Nevada

Las Vegas

Golfer to win the Ladies Professional Golf Association (LPGA) Championship with a score under 280, *3774*

UNITED STATES—Nevada—Las Vegas—
continued
Golfer to win the Tournament of Champions, *3734*
Golfer to win the Tournament of Champions four and five times, *3802*
Golfer to win the Tournament of Champions in a playoff, *3784*
Golfer to win the Tournament of Champions twice, and then three times, in a row, *3747*
Golfer to win two, and then three, Ladies Professional Golf Association (LPGA) Championships, *3762*
Las Vegas Bowl football game, *3455*
World Series of the United States Slo-Pitch Association, *5609*

Reno

Discus-thrower to break the 220-foot barrier, *2776*

New Hampshire

Organized competition for freestyle skiing, *5422*

Attitash

Freestyle skiing competition on record, *5415*

Berlin

Ski club in the United States, *5357*

Lake Winnepesaukee

Collegiate rowing competition, and the first intercollegiate athletic competition, on record in the United States, *4915*

Peterborough

Non-collegiate women's baseball team, *1201*

New Jersey

Camden

Professional basketball league, *1877*

Delaware

Perfect game in the Little League World Series, *1578*

East Rutherford

Jockey to win nine races in a single day, *4316*
New Jersey Devils regular season hockey game played at Brendan Byrne Arena, *4185*

New Jersey Nets regular season basketball game played at the Brendan Byrne Arena, *2173*
New York Giants regular season football game played at Giants Stadium, *3350*
New York Jets regular season football game played at Giants Stadium, *3396*

Englishtown

Drag racer to reach a speed over 320 miles per hour, *1145*

Great Meadows

Drag racer to reach a speed of over 200, and then 250, miles per hour, *1108*

Hoboken

Inter-club baseball game on record under Cartwright's Rules, *1187*

Jersey City

African-American baseball player in the International League in the 20th century, *1550*
Boxing match to have a $1 million gate, and the first heavyweight bout to be broadcast on radio, *2541*

Maplewood

Ultimate, *3527*

Millville

Professional basketball league, *1877*

Morristown

Separate golf course for women in the United States, *3607*

New Brunswick

Intercollegiate Ultimate match, *3528*

Northfield

Tournament on the Senior Professional Golfers' Association (PGA) Tour, *3832*

Oceanport

Sporting event to be televised in color in the United States, *5750*

Short Hills

Golfer to win the U.S. Open championship four times, and two and three times consecutively, *3640*

Golfer to win two U.S. Open championships, *3637*

Springfield

Golfer to win the U.S. Open in under 275, and to win the U.S. Open twice on the same course, *3827*

U.S. Open golf tournament to be televised nationally, *3743*

Women to be caddies at the U.S. Open golf tournament, *3831*

Trenton

Professional basketball game, *1874*
Professional basketball league, *1877*
Professional basketball team, *1873*

West Orange

Film of a sporting event, *5743*

New Mexico

Albuquerque

Golfer on the Ladies Professional Golf Association (LPGA) Tour to win four consecutively scheduled tournaments, *3768*

New York

Gold Cup motorboat (powerboat) race, *4562*
Golfer over 50 to win a Professional Golfers' Association (PGA) recognized tournament, *3703*
Governing body for boxing in the United States, *2537*
Pulitzer Trophy airplane race, *1005*

Albany

Baseball club tour, *1194*
Grand slam home run in major league baseball, *1256*
Written reference to *kolven* in North America, *4415*

Ardsley

Golfer to win the U.S. Women's Amateur Championship twice, and then three times, in a row, *3622*
Intercollegiate golf tournament in the United States, *3621*

Babylon

African-American professional baseball team, *1279*

Belmont Park

Belmont Stakes horse race, *4276*
International air race in the United States, *1002*
Woman jockey to win one of America's Triple Crown horse races, *4317*

Bronxville

Professional Golfers' Association (PGA) Championship, *3658*

Buffalo

Baseball club tour, *1194*
Bowler to bowl two consecutive 300 games, *2490*
Buffalo Bills American Football Conference championship, *3452*
Buffalo Bills American Football League championship, *3272*
Buffalo Bills regular season football game played at Rich Stadium, *3332*
Buffalo Sabres regular season hockey game played at Marine Midland Arena, *4227*
Buffalo Sabres regular season hockey game played at Memorial Auditorium, *4157*
Grand Circuit series of harness horse races, *4277*
Kansas City Chiefs American Football League championship, *3280*

Cooperstown

Baseball team on record, *1184*

Creedmor

International rifle tournament held in the United States, *5267*

Elmont

Woman jockey to win one of America's Triple Crown horse races, *4317*

Garden City

Golfer to shoot under 80 in all four rounds of the U.S. Open, *3635*
Golfer to win four U.S. Amateur titles, *3654*

Glen Cove

Golfer to win three men's U.S. Amateur titles, *3636*

Great Kills

Boxer to be world middleweight champion, *2516*

Hempstead (Hansted Plains)

Organized horse races in colonial North America, *4252*

Silver trophy known to be awarded at a sporting event in North America, *1146*

Hicksville

African-American figure skater to win the women's singles title at the U.S. national championships, *3089*

Jones Beach

National water-skiing championships, *6313*

Lake Placid

African-American athletes to compete in the Olympic Winter Games, *4747*

Athlete from Liechtenstein to win an Olympic gold medal, *4750*

Athlete to win five individual gold medals in a single Olympic Games, *4748*

Athlete to win gold medals in both the Summer and Winter Olympics, *4674*

Bobsled run in the United States, *2470*

Bobsledders to win two straight titles in the four-man bobsled at the Olympic Winter Games, *2472*

Figure skater from Austria to win the men's singles titles in the Olympic Winter Games, *3012*

Figure skater from Germany to win the women's singles title at the Olympic Winter Games, *3085*

Figure skater to win three consecutive medals in pairs competition at the Olympic Winter Games, *3084*

Figure skater to win two, and then three, consecutive women's singles titles at the Olympic Winter Games, *3014*

Figure skaters to win two consecutive pairs titles at the Olympic Winter Games, *3013*

Men's 10-kilometer biathlon competition at the Olympic Winter Games, *2435*

National team to sweep the medals in the men's 90-meter ski jump at the Olympic Winter Games, *5379*

National team to win four consecutive ice hockey titles at the Olympic Winter Games, *4107*

Olympic speed skating events to be held as races, rather than in pairs, *5648*

Olympic Winter Games held in the United States, *4676*

Olympic Winter Games to be boycotted by a member country, *4749*

Skier to win two consecutive men's individual Nordic combined titles in the Olympic Winter Games, *5378*

Sliders to win two consecutive luge (toboggan) titles at the Olympic Winter Games, *4462*

Speed skater from the United States to win the men's 1500-meter title at the Olympic Winter Games, *5649*

Speed skater to sweep all five men's speed skating events in a single Olympic Winter Games, *5696*

Speed skater to win the men's 10,000-meter title at the Olympic Winter Games, *5650*

Two-man bobsled competition held in the Olympic Games, *2471*

Mamaroneck

U.S. Senior Open golf tournament, *3833*

Massapequa

Water-skiing tournament, *6311*

New York

African-American basketball club in the New York City area, *1878*

African-American professional basketball team, *1886*

African-American professional basketball team to win a world championship, *1892*

African-American tennis player to win the women's singles championship at Wimbledon, *6110*

African-American to become a member of the Collegiate Basketball Officials Association, *1974*

American Amateur Hockey League championship, *4049*

America's Cup, *5198*

Athletes to row across the Atlantic Ocean, *4923*

Automatic pin-setter to be used in a bowling alley, *2495*

Baltimore Colts National Football League championship, *3246*

Baltimore Orioles regular season baseball game played at Oriole Park, *1330*

Baseball box score, *1199*

Baseball club tour, *1194*

Baseball game on record at which admission was charged, *1192*

Baseball game on record played under Cartwright's Rules, *1185*

Baseball game on record to go into extra innings, *1190*

Baseball game to be televised, *1537*

Baseball player in the American League to hit four grand slam home runs in a single season, *1434*

Baseball player to die of injuries suffered during a major league baseball game, *1446*

UNITED STATES—North Carolina—Durham—*continued*

Runner to hold the officially accepted world record in the women's 3000-meter event, *5101*

Greensboro

African-American golfer to play in a Professional Golfers' Association (PGA) Tour tournament in the South, *3763*

All-Star Classic (All-American Classic) in women's college basketball, *2135*

Golfer to win more than 80 tournaments on the Professional Golfers' Association (PGA) Tour, and to win the same PGA event eight times, *3780*

High Point

Woman golfer to score 20 below par in 72 holes, *3847*

Pinehurst

Golf practice range, *3665*

Golfer to win $100,000 in a single tournament, *3805*

Miniature golf course, *3657*

Raleigh

Carolina Hurricanes regular season hockey game played at the Raleigh Entertainment and Sports Arena, *4237*

Ohio

Akron

Golfer to win the World Series of Golf in its new 72-hole format, *3809*

Golfer to win the World Series of Golf twice in a row, *3770*

World Series of Golf, *3767*

World Series of Golf won in a playoff, *3819*

Canton

Pro Football Hall of Fame, *3268*

Cincinnati

Baseball player to hit a home run in the National League, *1225*

Cincinnati Bengals American Football Conference championship, *3371*

Cincinnati Bengals regular season football game played at Paul Brown Stadium, *3514*

Cincinnati Bengals regular season football game played at Riverfront Stadium, *3308*

Cincinnati Red Stockings regular season baseball game played at the Avenue Grounds, *1224*

Cincinnati Reds regular season baseball game played at Crosley Field, *1412*

Cincinnati Reds regular season baseball game played at Riverfront Stadium (later Cinergy Field), *1716*

Cincinnati Reds regular season baseball game played at the Bank Street Grounds, *1246*

Cincinnati Reds regular season baseball game played at The Palace of the Fans, *1346*

Clay pigeons for target shooting, *5268*

Indoor track meet, *6198*

Major league baseball night game, *1517*

Scheduled Sunday game in the National League, *1307*

Softball team to win the Amateur Softball Association Men's Slow Pitch National Championships, *5592*

Softball team to win three consecutive titles at the Amateur Softball Association Major Slow Pitch National Championships, *5598*

Sudden death rule to end games in major league baseball, *1247*

Cleveland

All America Football Conference (AAFC) championship, *3199*

American League baseball game, *1331*

Bendix Trophy airplane race, *1009*

Cleveland Browns National Football League championship, *3226*

Cleveland Browns regular season football game played at Municipal Stadium, *3205*

Cleveland Browns regular season game played in the Cleveland Browns Stadium, *3510*

Cleveland Cavaliers regular season game played in the Gund Arena, *2342*

Cleveland Indians regular season baseball game played at Jacobs Field, *1827*

Cleveland Indians regular season baseball game played at League Park I, *1336*

Cleveland Indians regular season baseball game played at League Park II, *1400*

Cleveland Rams National Football League championship, *3196*

Davis Cup to be a full open tournament for professionals and amateurs, *6151*

Detroit Lions National Football League championship in the modern era, *3233*

Grand Circuit series of harness horse races, *4277*

Grand slam home run in World Series history, *1448*

Home run by a pitcher in a World Series, *1449*

Major league baseball player to reach a total of 2,000 bases on balls, *1514*

"Mixed" female-male softball team league, *5595*

Pilot to win both the Thompson Trophy and Bendix Trophy airplane races, *1010*

Pilot to win the Bendix Trophy–Jet Division airplane race, *1014*

Pilot to win the Bendix Trophy race three times in a row, *1016*

Pilot to win the Thompson Trophy airplane race twice, and then three times, *1013*

Pilot to win the Thompson Trophy–Jet Division airplane race, *1015*

Softball team to win two consecutive titles in the Amateur Softball Association Women's Major Fast Pitch National Championships, *5582*

Unassisted triple play in the World Series, *1440*

Woman to fly in the Bendix Trophy airplane race, *1011*

Women's Air Derby, *1007*

Dayton

Balloon race in the United States, *1181*

Delaware

Little Brown Jug harness race, *4299*

Fostoria

Harness race held at night, *4282*

Shaker Heights

Golfer to win the World Championship of Women's Golf twice in a row, *3836*

Toledo

Golfer to win a major tournament using steel-shafted golf clubs, *3694*

Vandalia

Woman to win the Grand American Trapshoot, *5306*

Oklahoma

Oklahoma City

Softball Hall of Fame opened, *5588*

Tulsa

Golfer to win the Professional Golfers' Association (PGA) Championship in under 270, *3877*

Oregon

Eugene

Runner from the United States to hold the world record in the women's 5000- and 10,000-meter races, *5124*

Shot-putter to break the 18- and 19-meter, and 60-foot, barriers, *5340*

Pendleton

Pendleton Round-Up rodeo, *4882*

Portland

Basketball team to make 39 consecutive free throws in a single National Basketball Association (NBA) game, *2182*

Little League World Series won by a team from outside the United States, *1624*

Portland Trail Blazers regular season basketball game played at the Memorial Coliseum, *2076*

Portland Trail Blazers regular season basketball game played at The Rose Garden, *2360*

Pennsylvania

Ardmore

Golfer to win both the U.S. Amateur and U.S. Open championships in the same year, and to win the U.S. Open in under 290 for 72 holes, *3659*

Golfer to win five U.S. Amateur titles, *3692*

Beaver Falls

Intercollegiate men's basketball game, *1869*

Bethlehem

Basketball player to score 58 points in a single National Basketball Association (NBA) game, *1994*

Hershey

Basketball player to score 100 points in a single National Basketball Association (NBA) game, *2017*

Llanerch

Golfer to win the Professional Golfers' Association (PGA) Championship after it was converted into a stroke play tournament, *3753*

Lock Haven

Little League World Series, *1555*

Meadville

Horseshoe club on record, *4320*

New Castle

African-American baseball player known to have played professionally with a previously all-white team, *1238*

UNITED STATES—Pennsylvania—continued

Oakmont

Golfer to win the U.S. Open and the Professional Golfers' Association (PGA) Championship in the same year, *3674*

Golfer to win the U.S. Open in a sudden-death playoff, *3878*

Golfer to win the U.S. Open, the Masters, and the British Open in the same year, and the first to score under 275 for 72 holes, *3735*

Philadelphia

African-American women's basketball team, *1891*

Archery club in the United States, *1022*

Balloon flight in the United States, *1179*

Brooklyn Dodgers regular season baseball game played at Washington Park II, *1318*

Brother-and-sister figure skaters to win the pairs title at the U.S. national championships, *3017*

College football player to receive the Maxwell Award, *3178*

Figure skater to win six, and then seven, consecutive men's singles titles in the U.S. national championships, *3015*

Figure skater to win two consecutive men's singles titles in the U.S. national championships, *2993*

Figure skater to win two straight women's singles titles at the U.S. national championships, *2994*

Figure skaters to take all three medals in the same order in the U.S., world, and Olympic men's singles competitions, *3051*

Figure skaters to win two consecutive ice dancing titles at the U.S. national championships, *3023*

Golfer to complete a grand slam, *3693*

Heavyweight boxing match to be broadcast nationally on television, *2556*

High-jumper to set or equal four world records in the men's event in a single year, *4027*

Ice skating club in the United States, *2951*

Liberty Bowl football game, *3250*

Men's eight-oared shell with coxswain rowing event held in the Olympic Games, *4925*

Men's team combined exercises gymnastics competition in the Olympic Games, *3911*

National Air Races, *1006*

National Collegiate Athletic Association (NCAA) Division I tournament basketball game, *1897*

National Football League college draft, *3176*

National League baseball game, *1222*

Negro Leagues World Series, *1472*

Philadelphia 76ers regular season basketball game played at the First Union Center, *2375*

Philadelphia 76ers regular season basketball game played at The Spectrum, *2052*

Philadelphia Athletics regular season baseball game played at Columbia Park, *1335*

Philadelphia Athletics regular season baseball game played at Shibe Park, *1393*

Philadelphia Eagles National Football Conference championship, *3369*

Philadelphia Eagles National Football League championship, *3221*

Philadelphia Eagles regular season football game played at Veterans Stadium, *3317*

Philadelphia Flyers regular season hockey game played at the First Union Center, *4225*

Philadelphia Flyers regular season hockey game played at The Spectrum, *4150*

Philadelphia Phillies regular season baseball game played at Huntington Street Grounds, *1289*

Philadelphia Phillies regular season baseball game played at Recreation Park, *1269*

Philadelphia Phillies regular season baseball game played at Veterans Stadium, *1721*

Pole-vaulter to clear 14 feet, *4840*

Professional basketball league, *1877*

Rowers to win two consecutive gold medals in the men's eight-oared shell with coxswain competition in the Olympic Games, *4933*

Runner to hold an officially accepted world record in the men's 200-meter race run on a curved track, *5053*

Tennis player to win the women's singles title at the United States national championships, *6022*

United States men's singles national tennis championship matches played at the new West Side Tennis Club stadium, *6069*

United States national tennis championships to include mixed doubles competition, *6032*

United States national tennis championships to include women, *6023*

United States women's doubles national tennis championships, *6027*

Pittsburgh

Basketball player to make 18 consecutive field goals in a single National Basketball Association (NBA) game, *2048*

Boxing match to be broadcast on radio, *2540*

Golfer to win two consecutive U.S. Women's Open titles, *3757*

Leondi Big Five, *1883*

Major league baseball game to be broadcast on radio, *1458*

Major league baseball player to hit 714 home runs, *1518*

National championships in volleyball in the United States, *6274*

National Colored League baseball game, *1290*

National Hockey League player to be named Most Valuable Player of the NHL All-Star Game three times, *4201*

Pittsburgh Penguins regular season hockey game played at the Pittsburgh Civic Arena, *4149*

Pittsburgh Pirates regular season baseball game played at Forbes Field, *1394*

Pittsburgh Pirates regular season baseball game played at Three Rivers Stadium, *1717*

Pittsburgh Steelers regular season football game played at Three Rivers Stadium, *3307*

Union Association in baseball, *1273*

United States Slo-Pitch Softball Association meeting, *5604*

World Series, *1355*

World Series game to be broadcast by radio, *1460*

Reading

Golfer to win her first tournament on the Ladies Professional Golf Association (LPGA) Tour, *3729*

Softball player to win five Most Valuable Player Awards in the Amateur Softball Association Major Fast Pitch National Tournament, *5614*

Waynesburg

Boys' baseball league, *1380*

Williamsport

Little League baseball league, *1533*

Little League World Series, *1555*

Rhode Island

Newport

Bermuda Race, *5204*

Extreme Games, *2896*

International polo competition, *4862*

Men's doubles competition at the United States national tennis championships, *6012*

Men's singles competition at the United States national tennis championships, *6013*

National golf championship in the United States, *3608*

National governing body for golf in the United States, *3609*

Polo club in the United States, *4861*

Roller-skating rink, *4903*

Sailor to complete a solo circumnavigation of the world, *5202*

Single-Handed Transatlantic Race (STAR), *5222*

U.S. Amateur golf tournament, *3613*

U.S. Open golf tournament, *3614*

United States men's singles tennis national championship matches played at the West Side Tennis Club, *6057*

United States national tennis championships, *6014*

United States National Tennis Hall of Fame, *6108*

Providence

Figure skaters to receive six perfect scores (6.0) for artistic impression in the U.S. national pairs competition, *3111*

Westbury

U.S. Women's Amateur golf tournament, *3615*

South Carolina

Charleston

Golf club in the Americas, and the first outside Great Britain, *3561*

Darlington

Automobile racer to win the Winston $1 million bonus for winning three of the top four National Association for Stock Car Auto Racing (NASCAR) races in a single season, *1114*

Southern 500 automobile race, *1075*

Myrtle Beach

Golf package, *3765*

Tennessee

Chattanooga

Woman to pitch against a major league baseball team, *1500*

Memphis

Golfer to score under 60 in an 18-hole round in a Professional Golfers' Association (PGA) recognized event, *3815*

Nashville

College softball player to win the Erv Lind Award, *5599*

Iroquois Steeplechase horse race, *4298*

Music City Bowl football game, *3502*

Nashville Predators regular season hockey game played at the Nashville Arena, *4232*

Sport of Kings Challenge steeplechase horse race, *4315*

UNITED STATES—Tennessee—Nashville—
continued

Tennessee Titans regular season football game played at the Adelphia Coliseum, *3511*

Texas

Girls' Rodeo Association, *4892*

Golfer to win three straight individual titles at the U.S. intercollegiate golf championships, *3803*

Texas Open golf tournament, *3675*

Arlington

Texas Rangers regular season baseball game played at Arlington Stadium, *1725*

Texas Rangers regular season baseball game played at The Ballpark, *1828*

Austin

Javelin-thrower to break the 290-foot barrier with the new javelin, *4411*

Legends of Golf tournament, *3817*

Bonham

Women-only rodeo, *4889*

College Station

Shot-putter to break the 70-foot and 21-meter barriers, *5345*

Dallas

Basketball player to play more than 900 consecutive games in the National Basketball Association (NBA), *2397*

Basketball team to have 19 3-point goals in a single National Basketball Association (NBA) game, *2378*

Basketball team to have a .707 field goal percentage in a single National Basketball Association (NBA) game, *2191*

Cotton Bowl football game, *3180*

Dallas Mavericks regular season game played at Reunion Arena, *2164*

Dallas Stars regular season hockey game played at the Reunion Arena, *4207*

Golfer to win the Professional Golfers' Association (PGA) Championship four times in a row, and five times overall, *3686*

Irrigation system for fairways on a golf course, *3679*

Minnesota Vikings National Football Conference championship, *3334*

National Finals Rodeo (NFR), *4895*

El Paso

Sun Bowl football game, *3175*

Houston

African-American college football bowl game, *3158*

American Football Conference championship, *3259*

Basketball team to win the Women's National Basketball Association (WNBA) championship twice in a row, *2411*

Dallas Texans American Football League championship, *3267*

Houston Astros regular season baseball game played at Enron Field, *1859*

Houston Astros regular season baseball game played at the Houston Astrodome, *1680*

Houston Oilers regular season football game played at the Houston Astrodome, *3291*

Houston Rockets regular season game played at The Summit, *2118*

Women's National Basketball Association (WNBA) championship, *2396*

Women's National Basketball Association (WNBA) team to win the league championship three times, and in three consecutive years, *2422*

Irving

Dallas Cowboys regular season football game played at Texas Stadium, *3319*

Pecos

Documented rodeo competition, *4880*

San Antonio

Alamo Bowl football game, *3458*

Golfer to score 257 for 72 holes in a Professional Golfers' Association (PGA) recognized event, *3745*

Golfer to score under 190 for three consecutive 18-hole rounds in a Professional Golfers' Association (PGA) recognized event, *3741*

San Antonio Spurs regular season basketball game played at the Alamodome, *2329*

Tour Championship, *3855*

Utah

Salt Lake City

Golfer on the Ladies Professional Golf Association (LPGA) Tour to win four consecutively scheduled tournaments, *3768*

Utah Jazz regular season basketball game played at the Delta Center, *2309*

Vermont

Burlington

International ice hockey tournament, *4044*

Virginia

Alexandria

African-American college football player, *3120*

Hot Springs

Amateur golfer to win the U.S. Women's Open, *3787*

Jamestown

Written reference to sports in Britain's American colonies, *5738*

Lake Manassas

Presidents Cup Match in golf, *3880*

Richmond

Amateur Softball Association Women's Major Slow Pitch National Championships, *5594*

Virginia Beach

Batting title of the Amateur Softball Association Major Slow Pitch National Championship batting crown, *5605*
Women's Basketball Coaches Association convention, *2178*

Westover

Cricket reference in North America, *2633*

Washington

Seattle

Figure skater to win the women's singles U.S., world, and Olympic championships in the same year, *3056*
Golfer to score under 260 for 72 holes in a Professional Golfers' Association (PGA)–recognized event, *3713*
Hockey team from outside Canada to win the Stanley Cup, *4063*
Record in the men's 5000-meter steeplechase to last for more than 10 years, *5108*
Seattle Mariners regular season baseball game played at SAFECO Field, *1855*
Seattle Mariners regular season baseball game played at the Seattle Kingdome, *1744*
Seattle Seahawks regular season football game played at the Seattle Kingdome, *3348*
Seattle SuperSonics regular season game played in the Key Arena, *2361*

Spokane

U.S. Women's Open golf championship, *3715*

Tacoma

Golf club on the West Coast of North America, *3612*

West Virginia

African-American woman to win a Thoroughbred horse race in the United States, *4309*

Charleston

Jockey club in North America, *4254*
Woman jockey to win a professional horse race in the United States, *4306*

White Sulphur Springs

African-American golfer to represent the United States in the Ryder Cup tournament, *3824*

Wisconsin

Green Bay

Automobile race on record, *1041*
Green Bay Packers National Football Conference championship, *3480*
Green Bay Packers regular season football game played at Lambeau Field, *3245*

Kohler

U.S. Women's Open to be won in a sudden-death playoff, *3892*

Madison

Automobile race on record, *1041*

Milwaukee

Milwaukee Braves regular season baseball game played at County Stadium, *1597*
Milwaukee Brewers regular season baseball game played at County Stadium, *1715*
Milwaukee Brewers regular season baseball game played at Lloyd Street Park, *1339*
Milwaukee Bucks regular season basketball game played at the Bradley Center, *2279*
National League team to top 2 million paying customers at home in a single season, *1604*
Softball player to be named Most Valuable Player of the United States Slo-Pitch Association World Series, *5607*
Women's Professional Basketball League game, *2144*
World Series of the United States Slo-Pitch Association, *5609*

West Allis

Speed skater to win four consecutive men's titles at the world speed skating sprint championships, *5695*

UNITED STATES—*continued*

Wyoming

Cheyenne

Cheyenne Frontier Days rodeo, *4881*

URUGUAY

Montevideo

World cup in soccer (international football), *5553*

UZBEKISTAN

Athlete from newly independent Uzbekistan to win a gold medal at the Olympic Games, *4785*

Women's aerials freestyle skiing event held at the Olympic Winter Games, *5484*

VENEZUELA

Boxer to be world super-flyweight (junior bantamweight) champion, *2578*

Hispanic-American major league baseball player to play in the All-Star Game, *1584*

Light flyweight boxing event held in the Olympic Games, *2570*

VIRGIN ISLANDS

Skier of African ancestry to compete in the Olympic Winter Games, *5458*

WEST INDIES

World cup in men's cricket, *2661*

YUGOSLAVIA

Basketball team from Yugoslavia to win the men's title in the Olympic Games, *2163*

Gymnast to win three consecutive men's side (pommel) horse titles in the world championships, *3956*

Gymnast to win two consecutive men's all-around titles in the world championships, *3923*

Gymnast to win two consecutive men's rings titles in the world championships, *3925*

Gymnast to win two consecutive men's side (pommel) horse titles in the Olympic Games, *3955*

Skier to win three consecutive men's individual Nordic combined titles in the Olympic Winter Games, *5443*

Women's 100-meter breaststroke event held in the Olympic Games, *5852*

Women's air pistol individual shooting event held in the Olympic Games, *5322*

World sky diving championships, *5504*

Belgrade

Diver to win two, and then three, consecutive men's springboard diving titles in the world championships, *2809*

Introduction of skin-tight Lycra bathing suits into women's international swimming competition, *5873*

Men's 100-meter backstroke event held in the world championships, *5874*

Men's 100-meter breaststroke event held in the world championships, *5875*

Men's 100-meter butterfly event held in the world championships, *5876*

Men's 100-meter freestyle event held at the world championships, *5877*

Men's 1500-meter freestyle event held at the world championships, *5878*

Men's 200-meter backstroke event held in the world championships, *5879*

Men's 200-meter breaststroke event held in the world championships, *5880*

Men's 200-meter butterfly event held in the world championships, *5881*

Men's 200-meter freestyle event held at the world championships, *5882*

Men's 200-meter individual medley event held at the world championships, *5883*

Men's 4 x 100-meter freestyle swimming event held at the world championships, *5884*

Men's 4 x 100-meter medley relay event held at the world championships, *5885*

Men's 4 x 200-meter freestyle swimming event held at the world championships, *5886*

Men's 400-meter freestyle event held at the world championships, *5887*

Men's 400-meter individual medley event held at the world championships, *5888*

Men's highboard platform diving event held at the world championships, *2805*

Men's springboard diving event held at the world championships, *2806*

Swimmer to hold both the women's 100- and 200-meter breaststroke world titles at the same time, *5889*

Swimmer to hold the world titles in both the men's 100-meter and 200-meter freestyle events at the same time, *5891*

Swimmer to hold world titles in both the 100- and 200-meter backstroke at the same time, *5892*

Synchronized swimming team event held in the world championships, *5893*

Women's 100-meter backstroke event held in the world championships, *5894*

Women's 100-meter breaststroke event held in the world championships, *5895*

Women's 100-meter butterfly event held in the world championships, *5896*

Women's 100-meter freestyle swimming event held in the world championships, *5897*

Women's 200-meter backstroke event held in the world championships, *5898*

Women's 200-meter breaststroke event held in the world championships, *5899*

Women's 200-meter butterfly event held in the world championships, *5900*

Women's 200-meter freestyle swimming event held in the world championships, *5901*

Women's 200-meter individual medley swimming event held in the world championships, *5902*

Women's 4 x 100-meter freestyle swimming event held in the world championships, *5903*

Women's 4 x 100-meter medley relay swimming event held in the world championships, *5904*

Women's 400-meter freestyle swimming event held in the world championships, *5905*

Women's 400-meter individual medley swimming event held in the world championships, *5906*

Women's 800-meter freestyle swimming event held in the world championships, *5907*

Women's highboard platform diving event held in the world championships, *2807*

Women's solo and duet synchronized swimming events held in the world championships, *5908*

Women's springboard diving event held at the world championships, *2808*

World championships in swimming and diving, *5909*

Sarajevo

Figure skaters to win unanimous top scores for artistic impression, and the first from Great Britain to win the ice dancing title, at the Olympic Winter Games, *3087*

National team to sweep the medals in the women's 3000-meter speed-skating event at the Olympic Winter Games, *5702*

Olympic Winter Games held in Yugoslavia, *4754*

Skier from the United States to win the men's downhill title at the Olympic Winter Games, *5444*

Skier from the United States to win the men's slalom title at the Olympic Winter Games, *5446*

Skier to win two consecutive men's 30-kilometer Nordic (cross-country) titles in the Olympic Winter Games, *5442*

Women's individual 20-kilometer Nordic (cross-country) event held at the Olympic Winter Games, *5445*

Zagreb

International Handball Federation (IHF) Cup team competition, *4009*

Javelin-thrower to break the 230-foot barrier in the women's event, *4405*

ZAIRE

Kinshasa

Boxer to win the world heavyweight championship three times, *2566*

ZIMBABWE

Athlete to win the women's Hawaii Ironman triathlon three and up to eight times, *6239*

Athletes from Zimbabwe to win gold medals in the Olympic Games, *4752*

Women's field hockey event held in the Olympic Games, *4040*